S0-ABY-072

Katie.

Zhang Ziying

2020.5.8.

PRINCIPLES OF FINANCIAL ACCOUNTING

CANADIAN EDITION

Jerry J. Weygandt *Ph.D., CPA*
University of Wisconsin–Madison

Donald E. Kieso *Ph.D., CPA*
Northern Illinois University

Paul D. Kimmel *Ph.D., CPA*
University of Wisconsin—Milwaukee

Barbara Trenholm *MBA, FCA*
University of New Brunswick—Fredericton

Valerie A. Kinnear *M.Sc. (Bus. Admin.), CA*
Mount Royal University

Joan E. Barlow *B.Comm., CA*
Mount Royal University

Michael J. Atkins *B.Comm., B.Ed.*
Stouffville District Secondary School
York Region District School Board

Copyright © 2014 John Wiley & Sons Canada, Ltd.

Accounting Principles, Sixth Canadian Edition Copyright © 2013 John W & Sons Inc.

All rights reserved. No part of this work covered by the copyrigherein may be reproduced or used in any form or by any means—graphic, electronic, or ıhanical—without the prior written permission of the publisher.

Any request for photocopying, recording, taping, or inclusion information storage and retrieval systems of any part of this book shall be directed in ting to The Canadian Copyright Licensing Agency (Access Copyright). For an Access›pyright Licence, call toll-free, 1-800-893-5777.

Care has been taken to trace ownership of copyright material ctained in this text. The publishers will gladly receive any information that will enable thero rectify any erroneous reference or credit line in subsequent editions.

Library and Archives Canada Cataloguing in Publication

Weygandt, Jerry J.
[Accounting principles]

Principles of financial accounting / Jerry J. Weygandt, Ph.D., CP, University of Wisconsin—Madison, Donald E. Kieso, Ph.D., CPA, Northern Illinois University,aul D. Kimmel, Ph.D., CPA, University of Wisconsin—Milwaukee, Barbara Trenholm, MBA, FCA, ıiversity of New Brunswick—Fredericton, Valerie A. Kinnear, M.Sc. (Bus. Admin.), CA, Mount Rol University, Joan E. Barlow, BComm, CA, Mount Royal University, Michael J. Atkins, B.Ed, BCommStouffville District Secondary School, York Region District School Board.—Canadian edition.

Revision of: Accounting principles / Jerry J. Weygandt . . . [et al.].—3rdanadian ed.
Mississauga, Ont. : J. Wiley & Sons Canada, c2009.
Includes bibliographical references and indexes.
ISBN 978-1-118-75714-7 (bound)

1. Accounting–Textbooks. I. Kieso, Donald E., author] Kinnear, Valerie Ann, 1954- author, III. Kimmel, Paul D., author IV. Trenholm, Barbara, authc V. Atkins, Michael J., 1967-, author VI. Barlow, Joan E., 1956-, author VII. Title.

HF5636 A33 2014 657'.042 C2014-900202-5

Production Credits

Acquisitions Editor: Zoë Craig
Vice President and Publisher: Veronica Visentin
Director of Marketing: Joan Lewis-Milne
Marketing Manager: Anita Osborne
Editorial Manager: Karen Staudinger
Developmental Editor: Daleara Jamasji Hirjikaka
Media Editor: Luisa Begani
Interior Design and Cover: Adrian So
Production and Typesetting: Aptara
Cover Photo: iStockphoto/jpbcpa
Printing and Binding: Friesens Corporation

Printed and bound in Canada
1 2 3 4 5 FP 18 17 16 15 14

John Wiley & Sons Canada, Ltd.
5353 Dundas Street West, Suite 400
Toronto, ON, M9B 6H8 Canada

AUTHOR TEAM

Canadian Edition

Barbara Trenholm, MBA, FCA, is a professor emerita at the University of New Brunswick, for which she continues to teach locally and internationally. Her teaching and educational leadership has been widely recognized. She is a recipient of the Leaders in Management Education Award, the Global Teaching Excellence Award, and the University of New Brunswick's Merit Award and Dr. Allan P. Stuart Award for Excellence in Teaching.

Professor Trenholm is a member of the boards of several public and private companies, including Plaza Retail REIT. She is a past board member of Atomic Energy of Canada Limited, the Canadian Institute of Chartered Accountants, and the Atlantic School of Chartered Accountancy and past president of the New Brunswick Institute of Chartered Accountants. She has also served as a chair of the Canadian Institute of Chartered Accountants Academic Research Committee, Interprovincial Education Committee, and Canadian Institute of Chartered Accountants/Canadian Academic Accounting Association Liaison Committee. She has served as a member of the Canadian Institute of Chartered Accountants Qualification Committee, International Qualifications Appraisal Board, and Education Reengineering Task Force and the American Accounting Association's Globalization Initiatives Task Force, in addition to numerous other committees at the international, national, and provincial levels of the profession.

She has presented at many conferences and published widely in the field of accounting education and standard setting in journals, including *Accounting Horizons, Journal of the Academy of Business Education, CAmagazine, CGA Magazine,* and *CMA Magazine.*

Valerie Kinnear, M.Sc. (Bus. Admin.), CA, is an associate professor of accounting and a Nexen Scholar of teaching and learning at Mount Royal University in Calgary, Alberta. She has a wide range of teaching experience and is a recipient of the Chartered Accountants Education Foundation Teaching Award for her work on team-based learning in accounting. Professor Kinnear has held a variety of administrative positions at Mount Royal, including acting dean of the School of Business and acting director of Business Education in the Faculty of Continuing Education and academic chair of a variety of business programs, including Accounting, Financial Services, Supply Chain Management, Marketing, Human Resources, and Insurance. She has been nominated for both the Distinguished Faculty Award and the Distinguished Managers Award at Mount Royal.

She has also been active in the accounting profession. She participated in the Institute of Chartered Accountants of Alberta student education program in a variety of roles, including as an instructor, marker, author, and member of the Alberta Institute's Examinations Committee. She has also served as a member of the Professional Services Policy Board of the Canadian Institute of Chartered Accountants, as a board member of the Canadian Accounting Academic Association, and as treasurer for many volunteer community organizations in Calgary.

Professor Kinnear has a Bachelor of Social Work from the University of Calgary, a Master of Science in Business Administration from the University of British Columbia, and professional accounting experience with PricewaterhouseCoopers, Farvolden and Company Chartered Accountants, and Kinnear & Smistad Chartered Accountants.

Joan Barlow, B.Comm., CA, is an associate professor of accounting at Mount Royal University, in Calgary, Alberta. She has a wide range of teaching experience in financial and management accounting as well as auditing and is a recipient of the Chartered Accountants Education Foundation Teaching Award for her work on team-based learning in accounting.

Professor Barlow has a Bachelor of Commerce from the University of Calgary and professional accounting experience from Deloitte and Stephen Johnson Chartered Accountants. She was the recipient of the Alberta Silver Medal the year she wrote the uniform final examination for her CA designation. She has also served as treasurer on a number of not-for-profit organizations.

Michael Atkins, B.Comm., B.Ed., is the Head of Business Studies at Stouffville District Secondary School in Stouffville, Ontario. During his career with the York Region District School Board, he has taught a range of business courses and previously taught at King City Secondary School, Markville Secondary School, and Middlefield Collegiate Institute. He serves on the executive of the Ontario Business Educators' Association (OBEA) and has chaired the OBEA Accounting Contest. Mr. Atkins has Bachelor of Commerce and Bachelor of Education degrees from the University of Windsor and has worked with CGA-Ontario to develop classroom resources for high school accounting students.

U.S. Edition

Jerry J. Weygandt, Ph.D., CPA, is the Arthur Andersen Alumni Professor of Accounting at the University of Wisconsin—Madison. He holds a Ph.D. in accounting from the University of Illinois. His articles have appeared in *Accounting Review, Journal of Accounting Research, Accounting Horizons, Journal of Accountancy*, and other academic and professional journals. Professor Weygandt is the author of other accounting and financial reporting books and is a member of the American Accounting Association, the American Institute of Certified Public Accountants, and the Wisconsin Society of Certified Public Accountants. He has been actively involved with the American Institute of Certified Public Accountants and has been a member of the Accounting Standards Executive Committee of that organization. He served on the FASB task force that examined the reporting issues related to accounting for income taxes and as a trustee of the Financial Accounting Foundation. Professor Weygandt has received the Chancellor's Award for Excellence in Teaching and the Beta Gamma Sigma Dean's Teaching Award. He is the recipient of the Wisconsin Institute of CPAs' Outstanding Educator's Award and the Lifetime Achievement Award. In 2001 he received the American Accounting Association's Outstanding Accounting Educator Award.

Donald E. Kieso, Ph.D., CPA, received his bachelor's degree from Aurora University and his doctorate in accounting from the University of Illinois. He has served as chairman of the Department of Accountancy and is currently the KPMG Emeritus Professor of Accounting at Northern Illinois University. He has public accounting experience with PricewaterhouseCoopers (San Francisco and Chicago) and Arthur Andersen & Co. (Chicago) and research experience with the Research Division of the American Institute of Certified Public Accountants (New York). He has done post-doctoral work as a Visiting Scholar at the University of California at Berkeley and is a recipient of NIU's Teaching Excellence Award and four Golden Apple Teaching Awards. Professor Kieso is the author of other accounting and business books and is a member of the American Accounting Association, the American Institute of Certified Public Accountants, and the Illinois CPA Society. He has served as a member of the board of directors of the Illinois CPA Society, the AACSB's Accounting Accreditation Committees, and the State of Illinois Comptroller's Commission; as secretary-treasurer of the Federation of Schools of Accountancy; and as secretary-treasurer of the American Accounting Association. He is the recipient of the Outstanding Accounting Educator Award from the Illinois CPA Society, the FSA's Joseph A. Silvoso Award of Merit, the NIU Foundation's Humanitarian Award for Service to Higher Education, the Distinguished Service Award from the Illinois CPA Society, and in 2003 an honorary doctorate from Aurora University.

Paul D. Kimmel, Ph.D., CPA, received his bachelor's degree from the University of Minnesota and his doctorate in accounting from the University of Wisconsin. He is an Associate Professor at the University of Wisconsin—Milwaukee, and has public accounting experience with Deloitte & Touche (Minneapolis). He was the recipient of the UWM School of Business Advisory Council Teaching Award and the Reggie Taite Excellence in Teaching Award, and is a three-time winner of the Outstanding Teaching Assistant Award at the University of Wisconsin. He is also a recipient of the Elijah Watts Sells Award for Honorary Distinction for his results on the CPA exam. Professor Kimmel is the author of other accounting and business books and is a member of the American Accounting Association and the Institute of Management Accountants and has published articles in *Accounting Review, Accounting Horizons, Advances in Management Accounting, Managerial Finance, Issues in Accounting Education*, and *Journal of Accounting Education*, as well as other journals. His research interests include accounting for financial instruments and innovation in accounting education. He has published papers and given numerous talks on incorporating critical thinking into accounting education, and helped prepare a catalogue of critical thinking resources for the Federated Schools of Accountancy.

How to Use the Study Aids in This Book

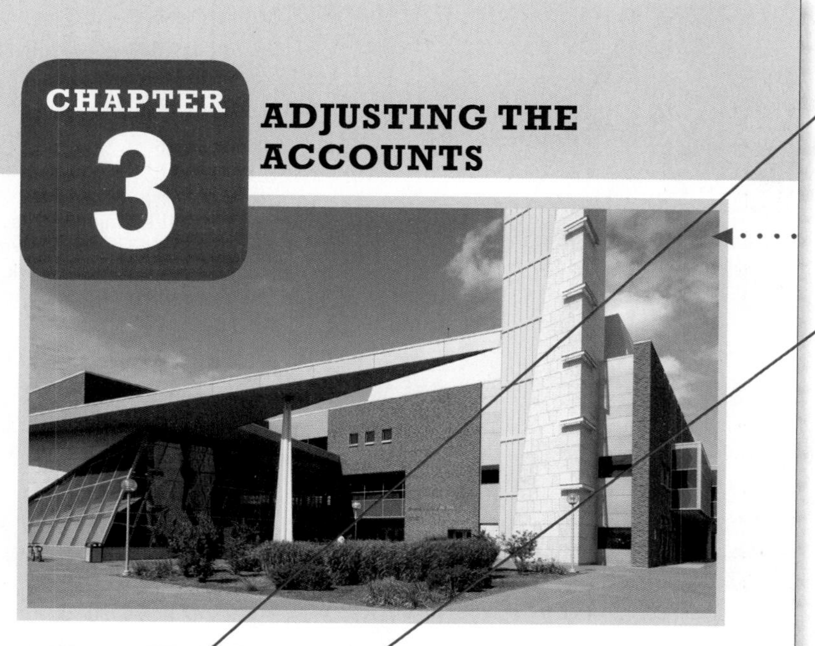

THE NAVIGATOR

- Understand *Concepts for Review*
- Read *Feature Story*
- Scan *Study Objectives*
- Read *Chapter Preview*
- Read text and answer *Before You Go On*
- Review *Comparing IFRS and ASPE*
- Work *Demonstration Problem*
- Review *Summary of Study Objectives*
- Answer *Self-Study Questions*
- Complete assignments

CONCEPTS FOR REVIEW

Before studying this chapter, you should understand or, if necess

A. The double-entry accounting system. (Ch. 2, p. 53)

B. How to increase and decrease assets, liabilities, and owner's and credit procedures. (Ch. 2, pp. 50–53)

C. How to journalize transactions. (Ch. 2, pp. 55–57)

D. How to post transactions to the general ledger. (Ch. 2, pp. 5

E. How to prepare a trial balance. (Ch. 2, pp. 67–68)

The Navigator is a learning system designed to guide you through each chapter and help you succeed in learning the material. It consists of (1) a checklist at the beginning of each chapter, which outlines text features and study skills you will need, and (2) a series of check boxes that prompts you to use the learning aids in the chapter and set priorities as you study.

Concepts for Review, listed at the beginning of each chapter, are the accounting concepts you learned in the previous chapters that you will need to know in order to understand the topics you are about to cover. Page references are provided for your review before reading the chapter.

ADJUSTING THE BOOKS AFTER HITTING THE BOOKS

TORONTO, ON—Once you begin your post-secondary education, you will probably pay your tuition just before classes start in September, but how will your college or university account for your money after that?

In Ontario, all colleges have a fiscal year that ends on March 31, which is also the provincial government's fiscal year end. "All the colleges' financial information is fully consolidated onto the province's books," explains Jeanette Dias D'Souza, former Vice President of Finance and Administration at Seneca College of Applied Arts & Technology, with 10 locations in the Greater Toronto area.

Many academic years end in late April, however. According to what's called accrual accounting, any revenues for services performed after March 31 have to be recognized in the following fiscal year, even though the money was collected earlier. So if a study term ends in late April, a small portion of the tuition for that semester will be recognized as revenue by the college in the next fiscal year.

The same revenue recognition criteria applies for students who study in the summer term: if they pay tuition before March 31, it can't be recognized as revenue until the teaching services are performed in the summer. That term is important for Seneca. "We have a very large summer program," says Ms. Dias D'Souza.

Seneca's main sources of operating funding are provincial grants and student tuition fees. It also receives revenue from private and corporate training. As with tuition fees, revenue from this training is recognized in the period in which the training is provided.

The college also receives revenue from renting space for private functions, including Eaton Hall, a former estate of the famed Eaton retailing family that is located on one of Seneca's campuses. If an engaged couple puts down a deposit in February for their July wedding, that revenue is not recognized until the wedding takes place in the next fiscal year, Ms. Dias D'Souza says.

Expenses, too, must be recorded in the year when they are incurred. For example, Seneca's invoices for utilities and legal fees for the last month of the fiscal year tend to come in after the year end, so the college uses estimates to accrue for these expenses at the year end.

Recording revenues and expenses in the correct period is a challenge, but one that must be met to properly reflect the school's activity in each period.

THE NAVIGATOR

The **Feature Story** helps you picture how the chapter topic relates to the real world of accounting and business. Throughout the chapter, references to the Feature Story will help you put new ideas in context, organize them, and remember them.

STUDY OBJECTIVES

After studying this chapter, you should be able to:

1. Explain accrual basis accounting, and when to recognize revenues and expenses.
2. Prepare adjusting entries for prepayments.
3. Prepare adjusting entries for accruals.
4. Describe the nature and purpose of an adjusted trial balance, and prepare one.
5. Prepare adjusting entries for the alternative treatment of prepayments (Appendix 3A).

THE NAVIGATOR

Study Objectives at the beginning of each chapter provide you with a framework for learning the specific concepts and procedures covered in the chapter. Each study objective reappears at the point within the chapter where the concept is discussed. You can review all the study objectives in the **Summary of Study Objectives** at the end of the chapter. End-of-chapter material is keyed to study objectives.

PREVIEW OF CHAPTER THREE

In Chapter 2, we learned the accounting cycle up to and including the preparation of the trial balance. In this chapter, we will learn that additional steps are usually needed before preparing the financial statements. These steps adjust accounts for timing mismatches, like the ones Seneca College has with the tuition it receives for its summer classes and the costs it incurs to offer these classes. In this chapter, we introduce the accrual accounting concepts that guide the adjustment process.

The chapter is organized as follows:

Adjusting the Accounts

- **Timing Issues**
  - Accrual versus cash basis accounting
  - Revenue and expense recognition
- **The Basics of Adjusting Entries**
  - Adjusting entries for prepayments
  - Adjusting entries for accruals
- **The Adjusted Trial Balance and Financial Statements**
  - Preparing the adjusted trial balance
  - Preparing financial statements

The **Preview** graphically outlines the major topics and subtopics that will be discussed. This narrative and visual preview gives you a mental framework upon which to arrange the new information you are about to learn.

TIMING ISSUES

STUDY OBJECTIVE 1
Explain accrual basis accounting, and when to recognize revenues and expenses.

Accounting would be simple if we could wait until a company ended its operations before preparing its financial statements. As the following anecdote shows, if we waited until then we could easily determine the amount of lifetime profit earned:

> A grocery store owner from the old country kept his accounts payable on a wire memo spike, accounts receivable on a notepad, and cash in a shoebox. His daughter, a CGA, chided her father: "I don't understand how you can run your business this way. How do you know what you've earned?"
>
> "Well," her father replied, "when I arrived in Canada 40 years ago, I had nothing but the pants I was wearing. Today, your brother is a doctor, your sister is a teacher, and you are a CGA. Your mother and I have a nice car, a well-furnished house, and a home by the lake. We have a good business and everything is paid for. So, you add all that together, subtract the pants, and there's your profit."

Although the grocer may be correct in his evaluation about how to calculate his profit over his lifetime, most companies need more immediate feedback on how they are doing. For example, management usually wants monthly financial statements. Investors want to view the results of publicly traded companies at least quarterly. The Canada Revenue Agency requires financial statements to be filed with annual income tax returns.

Helpful hint Time periods are consistent in length and are used to measure profits and losses as governed by the time period concept.

Consequently, accountants divide the life of a business into specific time periods, such as a month, a three-month quarter, or a year. This practice follows the concept under GAAP known as the time period concept. An accounting time period that is one year long is called a **fiscal year**. Time periods of less than one year are called **interim periods**.

Alternative terminology The fiscal year may also be referred to as the *financial year*.

The fiscal year used by many businesses is the same as the calendar year However, it can be different. Seneca College's fiscal year is April 1 through many colleges, universities, and governments. Some retail companies use exactly one year, for their fiscal year. Reitmans (Canada) Limited does t Saturday in January as the end of its fiscal year. But because 52 weeks isn't e years Reitmans has to use a 53-week period with the first Saturday in Febru

Because the life of a business is divided into accounting time periods, transactions is important. Many business transactions affect more than one example, equipment is used over several years. We also saw in the feature College collects tuition fees in one fiscal year and then teaches the course in lowing section, we will see that deciding when to recognize revenues and e impact on the usefulness of financial statements.

recorded, both assets and revenues are understated. Accordingly, as shown below, an adjusting entry for accrued revenues results in an increase (debit) to an asset account and an increase (credit) to a revenue account.

Accrued Revenue

Asset		Revenue	
Debit Adjusting Entry (+)			Credit Adjusting Entry (+)

In October, Pioneer Advertising Agency earned $200 in fees for advertising services that were not billed to clients until November. Because these services have not been billed, they have not been recorded. An adjusting entry on October 31 is required as follows:

ADJUSTMENT 5
Accrued Revenue—Accounts Receivable

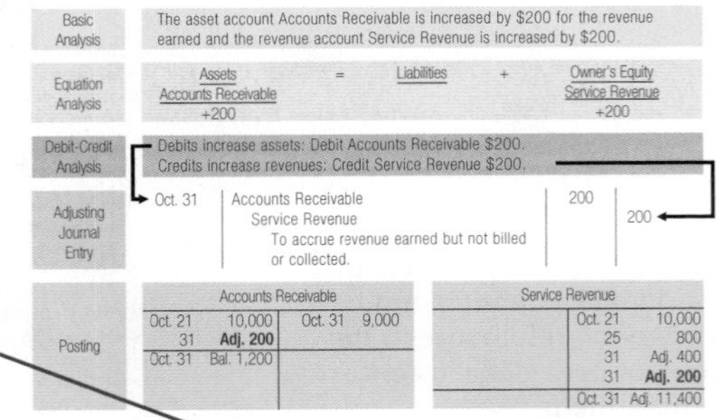

Basic Analysis	The asset account Accounts Receivable is increased by $200 for the revenue earned and the revenue account Service Revenue is increased by $200.
Equation Analysis	Assets: Accounts Receivable +200 = Liabilities + Owner's Equity: Service Revenue +200
Debit-Credit Analysis	Debits increase assets: Debit Accounts Receivable $200. Credits increase revenues: Credit Service Revenue $200.
Adjusting Journal Entry	Oct. 31 Accounts Receivable 200; Service Revenue 200; To accrue revenue earned but not billed or collected.

Posting:

Accounts Receivable			Service Revenue	
Oct. 21	10,000	Oct. 31 9,000	Oct. 21	10,000
31	**Adj. 200**		25	800
Oct. 31 Bal.	1,200		31	Adj. 400
			31	**Adj. 200**
			Oct. 31 Adj.	11,400

The asset Accounts Receivable shows that $1,200 is owed by clients at the balance sheet date. The balance of $11,400 in Service Revenue represents the total revenue earned during the month. If the adjusting entry is not made, assets and owner's equity on the balance sheet, and revenues and profit on the income statement, will all be understated.

On November 10, Pioneer receives $200 cash for the services performed in October. The following entry is made:

Nov. 10	Cash	200	
	Accounts Receivable		200
	To record cash collected on account.		

A = L + OE
+200
−200
Cash flows: +200

The **Accounting Equation** has been inserted in the margin next to journal entries throughout the text. This feature helps you understand the impact of each accounting transaction on the financial position and cash flows.

Alternative Terminology familiarizes you with other commonly used terms.

Accrued Expenses

Expenses incurred but not yet paid or recorded at the statement date are called **accrued expenses**. Interest, rent, property taxes, and salaries can be accrued expenses. As we saw in our feature story, Seneca College uses estimates to accrue for legal and utility expenses because the actual invoices are received after its year end. Accrued expenses result from the same causes as accrued revenues. In fact, an accrued expense on the books of one company is an accrued revenue for another company. For example, the $200 accrual of revenue by Pioneer is an accrued expense for the client that received the service.

Alternative terminology Accrued expenses are also called *accrued liabilities*.

ACCOUNTING IN ACTION
ALL ABOUT YOU INSIGHT

We all know the importance of literacy. But what about *financial literacy*—the ability to understand and manage your finances? It seems Canadians don't place the same importance on financial literacy—but with rising household debt levels, falling savings levels, increasing personal bankruptcies, and continuing economic uncertainty, they should. According to Statistics Canada research, in 2009 only half of Canadians had a household budget and one in three were struggling to pay their bills. On a scale of 1 to 100, Canadians scored an average of 66 in terms of their ability to keep track of their finances and 61 out of 100 in terms of planning for life goals such as buying a house or retiring. To improve the situation the federal government launched a Task Force on Financial Literacy. The task force recommended that financial literacy be taught at a young age and that Canadians continue learning about finances throughout their lives. Making the right financial decisions can have a major impact on an individual's financial well-being, health, and happiness.

Learning the basics of accounting will help you make the right financial decisions. Accounting will help you make investment decisions, determine how much interest you are paying on your student loan or credit cards, and prepare your personal budget. To demonstrate the value of accounting to you, included in each chapter is an "All About You" feature and a related personal financial literacy activity (BYP–4) that links accounting to your life as a student or to a situation you are likely to face.

Sources: Task Force on Financial Literacy, *Canadians and Their Money: Building a Brighter Financial Future*, December 2010; Financial Consumer Agency of Canada, *The Future of Financial Education: Report on the 2011 FCAC-OECD Conference on Financial Literacy*, 2011; Robin Taub and Mary Teresa Bitt, "It Pays to Know," *CA Magazine*, October 2011.

How might learning accounting help you make sure that your employer or bank hasn't made an error with your paycheque or bank account?

Accounting in Action insight boxes give you glimpses into how companies make decisions using accounting information. These high-interest boxes are classified by three different points of view—Across the Organization, Business Insight, Ethics Insight, and All About You Insight. Each ends with a question to show the relevance of the box. Suggested answers appear at the end of the chapter.

USING ACCOUNTING INFORMATION

There are two broad groups of users of accounting information: internal users and external users.

Accounting in Action insights give examples of accounting situations from different perspectives: all about you, across the organization, and in terms of business and ethics. At the end of the chapter, you will find answers to the questions that are asked after each insight.

Internal Users

Internal users of accounting information plan, organize, and run companies. They work for the company. This includes finance directors, marketing managers, human resources personnel, production supervisors, and company officers. In running a business, internal users must answer many important questions, as shown in Illustration 1-1.

Colour illustrations, such as this infographic, help you visualize and apply the information as you study. They summarize and reinforce important concepts.

ILLUSTRATION 1-1
Questions asked by internal users

Finance
Is there enough cash to pay the bills?

Marketing
What price should we sell smart phones for to maximize profits?

Human Resources
How many employees can we afford to hire this year?

Production
Which product line is the most profitable?

To answer these and other questions, users need detailed information on a timely basis; that is, it must be available when needed. Some examples of information that internal users need include forecasts of cash flows for the next year, projections of profit from new sales campaigns, financial comparisons of operating alternatives, analyses of salary costs, and budgeted financial statements. Internal users generally have direct access to the business's accounting information and are able to request a wide variety of custom reports designed for their specific needs.

External Users

There are several types of *external users* of accounting information. **Investors**, who are owners—or potential owners—of the business, use accounting information to make decisions to buy, hold, or sell their ownership interest. **Creditors**—persons or other businesses that are owed money by the business such as suppliers and bankers—use accounting information to evaluate the risks of granting credit or lending money. Investors and creditors are the main external users of accounting information, but there are also many other external users with a large variety of information needs and questions.

Cash Flow Statement

Alternative terminology The cash flow statement is sometimes called the *statement of cash flows*.

Investors and creditors need information on the business's ability to generate cash from its business activities and how the business uses cash. The **cash flow statement** gives information about the cash receipts and cash payments for a specific period of time. The cash flow statement gives answers to the following simple but important questions:

1. Where did the cash come from during the period?
2. What was the cash used for during the period?
3. What was the change in the cash balance during the period?

To help investors, creditors, and others analyze a company's cash, the cash flow statement reports the following: (1) the cash effects of the company's operating activities during a period; (2) the cash inflows and outflows from investing transactions (for example, the purchase and sale of land, buildings, and equipment); (3) the cash inflows and outflows from financing transactions (for example, borrowing and repayments of debt, and investments and withdrawals by the owner); (4) the net increase or decrease in cash during the period; and (5) the cash amount at the end of the period.

Accounting Differences by Type of Business Organization

Previously, you were introduced to different forms of business organizations: the proprietorship, partnership, and corporation. Basically, accounting for assets, liabilities, revenues, expenses, and cash flows is the same, regardless of the form of business organization. The main distinction between the forms of organizations is found in (1) the terminology that is used to name the equity section, (2) the accounting for the owner's investments and withdrawals, and (3) the name of the statement showing the changes in owner's equity. In Illustration 1-7, we summarize these differences.

Key Terms that represent essential concepts are printed in blue where they are first explained in the text. They are defined again in the end-of-chapter **Glossary**.

ILLUSTRATION 1-7
Accounting differences by type of business organization

	Proprietorship	Partnership	Corporation
Equity section called:	Owner's equity	Partners' equity	Shareholders' equity
Investments by owners added to:	Owner's capital	Partners' capital	Share capital
Profits added to:	Owner's capital	Partners' capital	Retained earnings
Withdrawals by owners called:	Drawings	Drawings	Dividends
Withdrawals deducted from:	Owner's capital	Partners' capital	Retained earnings
Name of statement:	Statement of Owner's Equity	Statement of Partners' Equity	Statement of Retained Earnings (ASPE)
Statement of Comprehensive Income	Not allowed	Not allowed	Statement of Shareholders' Equity (IFRS): Not allowed under ASPE; required under IFRS

Helpful Hints in the margins help clarify concepts being discussed.

ASPE icons in the margin highlight differences between International Financial Reporting Standards (IFRS) and Accounting Standards for Private Enterprises (ASPE).

Helpful hint When using a capital or drawings account, it is good practice to include the owner's name as part of the account name. This is particularly important for partnerships, as each partner will have his or her own individual capital and drawings account.

In a proprietorship, equity is summarized and reported in a one-line capital account. In a partnership, equity is summarized and reported in separate one-line capital accounts for each partner. In a corporation, investments by all of the shareholders are grouped together and called "share capital." In a corporation, regardless of the number of shareholders, one account called Retained Earnings is used to record the accumulated profit (or earnings) of the company that has been retained (that is, not paid out to shareholders) in the company.

ASPE

A close examination of Reitmans' financial statements in Appendix A shows that, in addition to these statements, it has also prepared a Statement of Comprehensive Income. That is because Reitmans follows IFRS, not simply because it is a corporation. You will learn more about that statement in Chapter 14. For companies following ASPE, there is no such thing as a statement of comprehensive income.

THE EXPANDED ACCOUNTING EQUATION

The basic accounting equation in Illustration 1-5 simply shows that assets are equal to liabilities plus owner's equity. Recall that the basic equation is a summary of the information shown on the balance sheet. But we also know that it is necessary to report on revenues, expenses, and other changes in owner's equity. In Illustration 1-8, we have expanded the basic accounting equation to show the

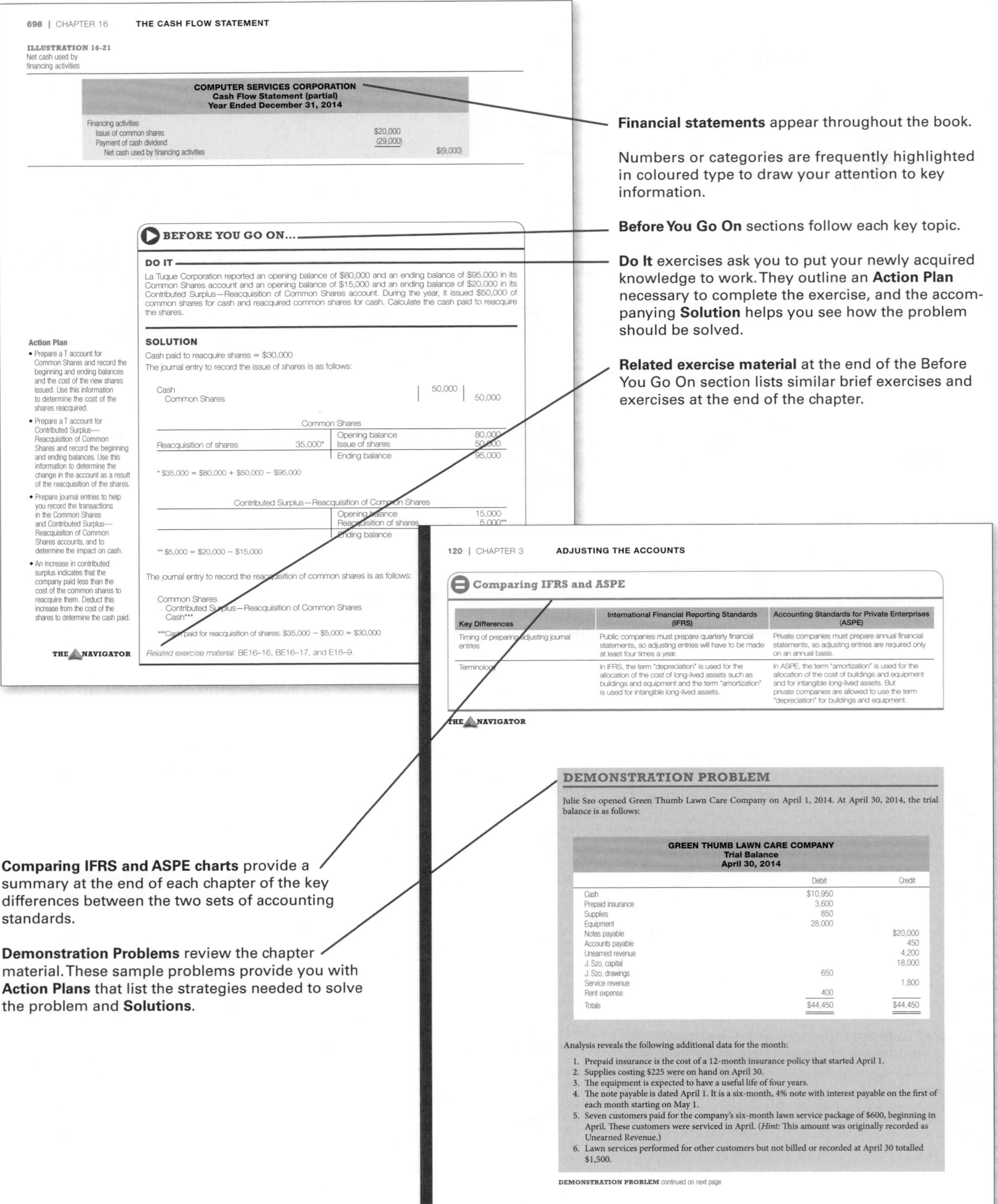

698 | CHAPTER 16 THE CASH FLOW STATEMENT

ILLUSTRATION 16-21
Net cash used by financing activities

COMPUTER SERVICES CORPORATION
Cash Flow Statement (partial)
Year Ended December 31, 2014

Financing activities		
Issue of common shares	$20,000	
Payment of cash dividend	(29,000)	
Net cash used by financing activities		$(9,000)

BEFORE YOU GO ON...

DO IT

La Tuque Corporation reported an opening balance of $80,000 and an ending balance of $95,000 in its Common Shares account and an opening balance of $15,000 and an ending balance of $20,000 in its Contributed Surplus—Reacquisition of Common Shares account. During the year, it issued $50,000 of common shares for cash and reacquired common shares for cash. Calculate the cash paid to reacquire the shares.

Action Plan

- Prepare a T account for Common Shares and record the beginning and ending balances and the cost of the new shares issued. Use this information to determine the cost of the shares reacquired.
- Prepare a T account for Contributed Surplus—Reacquisition of Common Shares and record the beginning and ending balances. Use this information to determine the change in the account as a result of the reacquisition of the shares.
- Prepare journal entries to help you record the transactions in the Common Shares and Contributed Surplus—Reacquisition of Common Shares accounts, and to determine the impact on cash.
- An increase in contributed surplus indicates that the company paid less than the cost of the common shares to reacquire them. Deduct this increase from the cost of the shares to determine the cash paid.

SOLUTION

Cash paid to reacquire shares = $30,000
The journal entry to record the issue of shares is as follows:

Cash	50,000	
Common Shares		50,000

Common Shares

		Opening balance	80,000
Reacquisition of shares	35,000*	Issue of shares	50,000
		Ending balance	95,000

* $35,000 = $80,000 + $50,000 − $95,000

Contributed Surplus—Reacquisition of Common Shares

		Opening balance	15,000
		Reacquisition of shares	5,000**
		Ending balance	

** $5,000 = $20,000 − $15,000

The journal entry to record the reacquisition of common shares is as follows:

Common Shares
Contributed Surplus—Reacquisition of Common Shares
Cash***

***Cash paid for reacquisition of shares: $35,000 − $5,000 = $30,000

Related exercise material: BE16–16, BE16–17, and E16–9.

THE NAVIGATOR

120 | CHAPTER 3 ADJUSTING THE ACCOUNTS

Comparing IFRS and ASPE

Key Differences	International Financial Reporting Standards (IFRS)	Accounting Standards for Private Enterprises (ASPE)
Timing of preparing adjusting journal entries	Public companies must prepare quarterly financial statements, so adjusting entries will have to be made at least four times a year.	Private companies must prepare annual financial statements, so adjusting entries are required only on an annual basis.
Terminology	In IFRS, the term "depreciation" is used for the allocation of the cost of long-lived assets such as buildings and equipment and the term "amortization" is used for intangible long-lived assets.	In ASPE, the term "amortization" is used for the allocation of the cost of buildings and equipment and for intangible long-lived assets. But private companies are allowed to use the term "depreciation" for buildings and equipment.

THE NAVIGATOR

DEMONSTRATION PROBLEM

Julie Szo opened Green Thumb Lawn Care Company on April 1, 2014. At April 30, 2014, the trial balance is as follows:

GREEN THUMB LAWN CARE COMPANY
Trial Balance
April 30, 2014

	Debit	Credit
Cash	$10,950	
Prepaid insurance	3,600	
Supplies	850	
Equipment	28,000	
Notes payable		$20,000
Accounts payable		450
Unearned revenue		4,200
J. Szo, capital		18,000
J. Szo, drawings	650	
Service revenue		1,800
Rent expense	400	
Totals	$44,450	$44,450

Analysis reveals the following additional data for the month:

1. Prepaid insurance is the cost of a 12-month insurance policy that started April 1.
2. Supplies costing $225 were on hand on April 30.
3. The equipment is expected to have a useful life of four years.
4. The note payable is dated April 1. It is a six-month, 4% note with interest payable on the first of each month starting on May 1.
5. Seven customers paid for the company's six-month lawn service package of $600, beginning in April. These customers were serviced in April. (*Hint:* This amount was originally recorded as Unearned Revenue.)
6. Lawn services performed for other customers but not billed or recorded at April 30 totalled $1,500.

DEMONSTRATION PROBLEM continued on next page

Financial statements appear throughout the book.

Numbers or categories are frequently highlighted in coloured type to draw your attention to key information.

Before You Go On sections follow each key topic.

Do It exercises ask you to put your newly acquired knowledge to work. They outline an **Action Plan** necessary to complete the exercise, and the accompanying **Solution** helps you see how the problem should be solved.

Related exercise material at the end of the Before You Go On section lists similar brief exercises and exercises at the end of the chapter.

Comparing IFRS and ASPE charts provide a summary at the end of each chapter of the key differences between the two sets of accounting standards.

Demonstration Problems review the chapter material. These sample problems provide you with **Action Plans** that list the strategies needed to solve the problem and **Solutions**.

124 | CHAPTER 3 ADJUSTING THE ACCOUNTS

Summary of Study Objectives

1. ***Explain accrual basis accounting, and when to recognize revenues and expenses.*** In order to provide timely information, accountants divide the life of a business into specific time periods. Therefore it is important to record transactions in the correct time period. Under accrual basis accounting, events that change a company's financial statements are recorded in the periods in which the events occur, rather than in the periods in which the company receives or pays cash. Revenue and expense recognition criteria provide guidance about when to recognize revenues and expenses. Revenue is recognized when the service has been performed or the goods have been sold and delivered, as long as the revenue can be reliably measured and collection is reasonably certain based on the Revenue Recognition Principle. Expenses are recorded in the same period as revenue is recognized, if there is a direct association between the revenues and expenses to ensure that they are matched. If there is no association between revenues and expenses, expenses are recorded in the period they are incurred.

2. ***Prepare adjusting entries for prepayments.*** Prepayments are either prepaid expenses or unearned revenues. Adjusting entries for prepayments record the portion of the prepayment that applies to the expense or revenue of the current accounting period. The adjusting entry for prepaid expenses debits (increases) an expense account and credits (decreases) an asset account. For a long-lived asset, the contra asset account Accumulated Depreciation is used instead of crediting the asset account directly. The adjusting entry for unearned revenues debits (decreases) a liability account and credits (increases) a revenue account.

3. ***Prepare adjusting entries for accruals.*** Accruals are either accrued revenues or accrued expenses. Adjusting entries for accruals record revenues and expenses that apply to the current accounting period and that have not yet been recognized through daily journal entries. The adjusting entry for accrued revenue debits (increases) a receivable account and credits (increases) a revenue account. The adjusting entry for an accrued expense debits (increases) an expense account and credits (increases) a liability account.

4. ***Describe the nature and purpose of an adjusted trial balance, and prepare one.*** An adjusted trial balance shows the balances of *all* accounts, including those that have been adjusted, at the end of an accounting period. It proves that the total of the accounts with debit balances is still equal to the total of the accounts with credit balances after the adjustments have been posted. Financial statements are prepared from an adjusted trial balance in the following order: (1) income statement, (2) statement of owner's equity, and (3) balance sheet.

5. ***Prepare adjusting entries for the alternative treatment of prepayments (Appendix 3A).*** Under certain circumstances, prepayments may initially be debited (increased) to an expense account. Unearned revenues may initially be credited (increased) to a revenue account. At the end of the period, these revenue or expense accounts may be overstated. The adjusting entries for prepaid expenses are a debit (increase) to an asset account and a credit (decrease) to an expense account. Adjusting entries for unearned revenues are a debit (decrease) to a revenue account and a credit (increase) to a liability account. It does not matter which alternative is used to record and adjust prepayments, as the ending account balances will be the same with both methods, assuming that the entries are prepared correctly.

THE NAVIGATOR

Glossary

Accrual basis accounting A basis for accounting in which revenues are recorded when earned and expenses are recorded when incurred. (p. 97)

Accrued expenses Expenses incurred but not yet paid in cash or recorded. (p. 107)

Accrued revenues Revenues earned but not yet received in cash or recorded. (p. 106)

Accumulated depreciation The cumulative sum of the depreciation expense since the asset was purchased. As a contra asset, its normal balance is on the credit side. (p. 103)

Adjusted trial balance A list of accounts and their balances after all adjustments have been posted. (p. 113)

Adjusting entries Entries made at the end of an accounting period to ensure that the revenue and expense recognition criteria are followed. (p. 99)

Carrying amount The difference between the cost of a depreciable asset and its accumulated depreciation; in other words, it is the unallocated or unexpired portion of the depreciable asset's cost. (p. 104)

Cash basis accounting A basis for accounting in which revenue is recorded when cash is received and an expense is recorded when cash is paid. (p. 97)

Contra asset account An account with the opposite balance (credit) compared with its relate... debit balance. A contra asset is de... on the balance sheet. (p. 103)

Depreciation The allocation of the cost... over its useful life in a rational and s...

Expense recognition criteria Crit... about when to record expenses. ... when there is a direct associatio... the earning of revenue (matching...

Fiscal year An accounting period that is... to start and end on the same days...

The **Summary of Study Objectives** relates the study objectives to the key points in the chapter. It gives you another opportunity to review, as well as to see how all the key topics within the chapter are related.

The **Glossary** defines all the terms and concepts introduced in the chapter. Page references help you find any terms you need to study further.

446 | CHAPTER 10 CURRENT LIABILITIES

Notes payable Obligations in the form of written promissory notes. (p. 435)

Operating line of credit Pre-authorized approval to borrow money at a bank when it is needed, up to a pre-set limit. (p. 435)

Prime rate The interest rate banks charge their best customers. (p. 435)

Product warranties Promises made by the seller to a buyer to repair or replace a product if it is defective or does not perform as intended. (p. 437)

Provisions Liabilities of uncertain timing or amount. (p. 440)

Trade payables Accounts and notes payable that result from purchase transactions with suppliers. (p. 435)

Self-Study Questions

Answers are at the end of the chapter.

(SO 1) C 1. Which of the following statements is the best description of a liability?
(a) A liability is a commitment to pay an amount in the future.
(b) A liability arises when an expense is incurred.
(c) A liability is an amount that should have been paid in the past.
(d) A liability is a present obligation, arising from past events, to make future payments of assets or services.

(SO 1) AP 2. Gibraltar Company borrows $55,200 on July 31, 2014, from the East Coast Bank by signing a seven-month, 5% note. Interest is payable at maturity. Assuming Gibraltar has a December 31 fiscal year end, how much interest expense will Gibraltar record in 2014 and in 2015?

	2014	2015
(a)	$ 0	$1,610
(b)	$1,150	$ 460
(c)	$1,380	$ 230
(d)	$1,971	$ 789

(SO 2) AP 3. Big Al's Appliance Store offers a two-year warranty on all appliances sold. The company estimates that 5% of all appliances sold need to be serviced at an average cost of $100 each. At December 31, 2013, the Warranty Liability account had a balance of $20,000. During 2014, the store spends $14,500 repairing 145 appliances. An additional 4,500 appliances are sold in 2014. On the 2014 income statement, warranty expense will be:
(a) $28,000.
(b) $22,500.
(c) $14,500.
(d) $20,000.

(SO 2) K 4. Friendly Department Store has a customer loyalty program in which customers receive points when they make a purchase. The points can be redeemed on future purchases. The value of the points issued should be recorded as:
(a) a contra revenue when the points are issued.
(b) an expense when the points are issued.
(c) a contra revenue when the points are redeemed.
(d) an expense when the points are redeemed.

(SO 3) K 5. Under IFRS, a contingent loss and the related liability should be recorded in the accounts when:
(a) it is probable the contingency will happen, but the amount cannot be reasonably estimated.
(b) it is probable the contingency will happen, and the amount can be reasonably estimated.
(c) it is highly unlikely the contingency will happen, but the amount can be reasonably estimated.
(d) it is unlikely that the users of the financial statements will read the notes.

(SO 5) K 6. On November 1, 2014, SSNL Company borrows $120,000 cash from the bank and issues a two-year, 4% note payable. SSNL must make payments of $5,000 plus interest at the end of each month. On December 31, 2014, what amount will be included in current and in non-current liabilities on the balance sheet?

	Current Liabilities	Non-Current Liabilities
(a)	$60,000	$ 50,000
(b)	$60,000	$ 60,000
(c)	$10,000	$100,000
(d)	$50,000	$ 70,000

THE NAVIGATOR

Questions

(SO 1) K 1. What is a determinable liability? List some examples.

(SO 1) K 2. Why is a present commitment to purchase an asset in the future not recorded as a liability?

(SO 1) K 3. How is interest calculated on a note payable? How is the amount of interest payable at the fiscal year end calculated?

(SO 1) K 4. What is the difference between an operating line of credit and a bank overdraft?

(SO 1) C 5. Laurel Hyatt believes that if a company has a long-term liability, the entire amount should be classified as non-current liabilities. Is Laurel correct? Explain.

Self-Study Questions form a practice test that gives you an opportunity to check your knowledge of important topics. Answers appear on the last page of the chapter.

Self-study questions are keyed to study objectives. In addition, the level of cognitive skill required to solve the question has been classified with a letter code following Bloom's Taxonomy. You will find more information about Bloom's Taxonomy and this coding system on page xiii of this Preface.

Questions allow you to explain your understanding of concepts and relationships covered in the chapter. (These are keyed to study objectives and Bloom's Taxonomy.)

(SO 6) C 21. Under IFRS and ASPE, what are the differences between the treatment of impairment losses for (a) finite life intangible assets, (b) indefinite life intangible assets, and (c) goodwill?

(SO 6) C 22. What is goodwill? Why can it not be sold to raise cash if a company is planning to expand?

(SO 7) K 23. How should long-lived assets be reported on the balance sheet and income statement? What information should be disclosed in the notes to the financial statements?

(SO 7) C 24. Harpreet understands that inventory turnover refers to the number of times that a company can sell and replace its inventory over the course of the year, but doesn't understand the meaning of asset turnover. Explain the difference between the two ratios to Harpreet.

Brief Exercises

BE9–1 The following costs were incurred by Shumway Company in purchasing land: cash price, $85,000; legal fees, $1,500; removal of old building, $5,000; clearing and grading, $3,500; installation of a parking lot, $5,000. (a) What is the cost of the land? (b) What is the cost of the land improvements?

Determine cost of land and land improvements. (SO 1) AP

BE9–2 Vroom Company incurs the following costs in purchasing equipment: invoice price, $40,375; transportation-in, $625; installation and testing, $1,000; one-year insurance policy, $1,750. What is the cost of the equipment?

Determine cost of equipment. (SO 1) AP

BE9–3 In the space provided, indicate whether each of the following items is an operating expenditure (O) or a capital expenditure (C):

Identify operating and capital expenditures. (SO 1) K

(a) ______ Repaired building roof, $1,500
(b) ______ Replaced building roof, $27,500
(c) ______ Purchased building, $480,000
(d) ______ Paid insurance on equipment in transit, $550
(e) ______ Purchased supplies, $350
(f) ______ Purchased truck, $55,000
(g) ______ Purchased oil and gas for truck, $125
(h) ______ Rebuilt engine on truck, $5,000
(i) ______ Replaced tires on truck, $600
(j) ______ Estimated retirement cost of plant, $1,000,000
(k) ______ Added new wing to building, $250,000
(l) ______ Painted interior of building, $1,500
(m) ______ Replaced an elevator, $17,500

BE9–4 Rainbow Company purchased land, a building, and equipment on January 2, 2014, for $850,000. The company paid $170,000 cash and signed a mortgage note payable for the remainder. Management's best estimate of the value of the land was $352,000; of the building, $396,000; and of the equipment, $132,000. Record the purchase.

Record basket purchase. (SO 1) AP

BE9–5 Butters Company acquires equipment at a cost of $42,000 on January 3, 2014. Management estimates the equipment will have a residual value of $6,000 at the end of its four-year useful life. Assume the company uses the straight-line method of depreciation. Calculate the depreciation expense (a) for each year of the equipment's life, and (b) in total over the equipment's life. Butters has a December 31 fiscal year end

Calculate straight-line depreciation. (SO 2) AP

BE9–6 Refer to the data given for Butters Company in BE9–5. Assume instead that the company uses th diminishing-balance method and that the diminishing-balance depreciation rate is double the straigh line rate. Calculate the depreciation expense (a) for each year of the equipment's life, and (b) in total ov the equipment's life.

BE9–7 Speedy Taxi Service uses the units-of-production method in calculating depreciation on its taxicab Each cab is expected to be driven 550,000 km. Taxi 10 cost $38,950 and is expected to have a residual valu of $4,300. Taxi 10 is driven 90,000 km in 2013, and 135,000 km in 2014. Calculate (a) the depreciable co per kilometre (use three decimals), and (b) the depreciation expense for 2013 and 2014.

BE9–8 Refer to the data given for Butters Company in BE9–5. Assume the equipment was purchased o April 6, 2014, and that the company pro-rates depreciation to the nearest month. Using the straight-li method, calculate the depreciation expense (a) for each year of the equipment's life, and (b) in total ov the equipment's life.

Brief Exercises generally focus on one study objective at a time. They help you build confidence in your basic skills and knowledge. (These are keyed to study objectives and Bloom's Taxonomy.)

Determine missing amounts for cost of goods sold section—periodic system. (SO 7) AP

*E5–15 Below are the cost of goods sold sections for the two most recent years for two companies using a periodic inventory system:

	St. Pierre Co.		Silva Co.	
	Year 1	Year 2	Year 1	Year 2
Beginning inventory	$ 250	$ (e)	$1,000	$ (n)
Purchases	1,500	(f)	(j)	9,550
Purchase returns and allowances	50	100	300	400
Purchase discounts	30	50	150	100
Net purchases	(a)	1,850	7,210	(o)
Freight in	110	(g)	(k)	550
Cost of goods purchased	(b)	(h)	7,900	(p)
Cost of goods available for sale	(c)	2,300	(l)	(q)
Ending inventory	(d)	400	1,450	1,250
Cost of goods sold	1,480	(i)	(m)	(r)

Instructions
Fill in the missing amounts to complete the cost of goods sold sections.

Prepare multiple-step income statement and closing entries—periodic system. (SO 7) AP

*E5–16 The following selected information is for Okanagan Company for the year ended January 31, 2014:

Freight in	$ 6,500	Purchase discounts	$ 12,000
Freight out	7,000	Purchase returns and allowances	16,000
Insurance expense	12,000	Rent expense	20,000
Interest expense	6,000	Salaries expense	61,000
Merchandise inventory, beginning	61,000	Salaries payable	2,500
Merchandise inventory, ending	42,000	Sales	325,000
O. G. Pogo, capital	105,000	Sales discounts	14,000
O. G. Pogo, drawings	42,000	Sales returns and allowances	20,000
Purchases	210,000	Unearned sales revenue	4,500

Instructions
(a) Prepare a multiple-step income statement.
(b) Prepare closing entries.

Exercises that gradually increase in difficulty help you to build your confidence in your ability to use the material learned in the chapter. (These are keyed to study objectives and Bloom's Taxonomy.)

Problems: Set A

Each **Problem** helps you pull together and apply several concepts of the chapter.

Identify problems and recommend inventory system. (SO 1) C

P5–1A AAA Dog 'n Cat Shop sells a variety of merchandise to pet owners, including pet food, grooming supplies, toys, and kennels. Most customers use the option to purchase on account and take 60 days, on average, to pay their accounts. The owner of AAA Dog 'n Cat Shop, Adam Fleming, has decided the company needs a bank loan because the accounts payable need to be paid in 30 days. Adam estimates that it takes 45 days, on average, to sell merchandise from the time it arrives at his store. Since the company earns a good profit every year, the bank manager is willing to give AAA Dog 'n Cat Shop a loan but wants monthly financial statements.

Adam has also noticed that, while some of the merchandise sells very quickly, other items do not. Sometimes he wonders just how long he has had some of those older items. He has also noticed that he regularly seems to run out of some merchandise items. Adam is also concerned about preparing monthly financial statements. The company uses a periodic inventory system and Adam counts inventory once a year. He is wondering how he is going to calculate the cost of goods sold for the month without counting the inventory at the end of every month. He has come to you for help.

Instructions
(a) Explain to Adam what an operating cycle is and why he is having problems paying the bills.
(b) Explain to Adam how the periodic inventory system is contributing to his problems.

Taking It Further is an extra question at the end of each problem designed to challenge you to think beyond the basic concepts covered in the problem, and to provide written explanations. Your teacher may assign problems with or without this extra element.

TAKING IT FURTHER Make a recommendation about what inventory system the company should use and why.

Record and post inventory transactions—perpetual system. Calculate net sales and gross profit. (SO 1, 2, 3) AP

P5–2A At the beginning of the current tennis season, on April 1, 2014, Kicked-Back Tennis Shop's inventory consisted of 50 tennis racquets at a cost of $40 each. Kicked-Back uses a perpetual inventory system. The following transactions occurred in April:

194 | CHAPTER 4 **COMPLETION OF THE ACCOUNTING CYCLE**

CONTINUING COOKIE CHRONICLE

(*Note:* This is a continuation of the Cookie Chronicle from Chapters 1 through 3.)

Natalie had a very busy December. At the end of the month, after Natalie has journalized and posted her adjusting entries, her company has the following adjusted trial balance:

COOKIE CREATIONS
Adjusted Trial Balance
December 31, 2013

	Debit	Credit
Cash	$2,929	
Accounts receivable	675	
Supplies	95	
Equipment	1,550	
Accumulated depreciation—equipment		$ 78
Accounts payable		76
Salaries payable		48
Unearned revenue		100
Interest payable		8
Notes payable, 3%, principal and interest due November 28, 2014		3,000
N. Koebel, capital		1,450
Revenue		1,225
Advertising expense	325	
Salaries expense	48	
Telephone expense	174	
Supplies expense	103	
Depreciation expense	78	
Interest expense	8	
	$5,985	$5,985

Instructions

Using the information in the adjusted trial balance, do the following:

(a) Prepare an income statement for the two months ended December 31, 2013, if you have not already done so in Chapter 3.
(b) Prepare a statement of owner's equity for the two months ended December 31, 2013, and a classified balance sheet at December 31, 2013.
(c) Calculate Cookie Creations' working capital, current ratio, and acid-test ratio. Comment on Cookie Creations' liquidity.
(d) Natalie has decided that her year end will be December 31, 2013. Prep
(e) Prepare a post-closing trial balance.
(f) Natalie has reviewed the financial statements that you have prepar purchase of equipment in December, she thought the equipment sh expense." After reviewing her accounting text, she remembered tha should be recorded as an asset and made an entry to correct her error ing entry, what impact would that journal entry have had on the fina 2013?

Cumulative Coverage—Chapters 2

Alou Equipment Repair has a September 30 year end. The company adj on an annual basis. On August 31, 2014, the account balances of Alou follows:

The **Continuing Cookie Chronicle** is a serial problem found in each chapter. It follows the operations of a hypothetical small company, Cookie Creations, throughout the text. The company is owned by a student and the purpose of the serial problem is to reinforce the application of accounting to the type of business a student could operate.

In selected chapters, a **Cumulative Coverage Problem** follows the Problems. The cumulative coverage problem pulls together and uses topics you have learned over several chapters.

142 | CHAPTER 3 **ADJUSTING THE ACCOUNTS**

The company adjusts its accounts on a monthly basis. Adjustment data consist of the following:

1. Supplies on hand at September 30 cost $1,280.
2. Accrued salaries payable at September 30 total $775.
3. Equipment has an expected useful life of five years.
4. Unearned service revenue of $450 is still not earned at September 30.
5. Interest is payable on the first of each month.

Instructions

(a) Enter the August 31 balances in general ledger accounts.
(b) Journalize the September transactions.
(c) Post to the ledger accounts.
(d) Prepare a trial balance at September 30.
(e) Journalize and post adjusting entries.
(f) Prepare an adjusted trial balance.
(g) Prepare an income statement and a statement of owner's equity for September, and a balance sheet.

CHAPTER 3 BROADENING YOUR PERSPECTIVE

Collaborative Learning Activity

Note to instructor: Additional instructions and material for this group activity can be found on the Instructor Resource Site and in *WileyPLUS.*

BYP3–1 In this group activity, you will work in two different groups to improve your understanding of adjusting entries. First you will work in "expert" groups in which you will ensure that each group member thoroughly understands one type of adjusting journal entry. Then you will move to a second group consisting of one student from each of the different expert groups, and take turns teaching the different types of adjusting entries (that is, prepaid expenses, unearned revenues, accrued expenses, accrued revenues, and depreciation).

Communication Activity

BYP3–2 Some people believe that cash basis accounting is better than accrual basis accounting in predicting a company's future success. This idea became more popular after many reports of corporate financial scandals where management manipulated the timing of recognizing expenses and revenues in accrual accounting to influence profit. Others argue it is easier to manipulate profit using cash basis accounting.

Instructions

Write a memo discussing the following issues:

(a) What is the difference in calculating profit using accrual basis accounting versus cash basis accounting?
(b) Identify one way that management might be able to increase profit by manipulating the timing of revenue or expense recognition under accrual accounting.
(c) Identify one way that management might be able to increase profit using cash basis accounting.
(d) Which basis do you believe is more reliable for measuring performance and why?

Ethics Case

BYP3–3 Die Hard Company is a pesticide manufacturer. Its sales dropped a lot this year because of new legislation that outlawed the sale of many of Die Hard's chemical pesticides. In the coming year, Die Hard will have new, environmentally safe chemicals to replace these discontinued products. Sales in the next year are expected to be much higher than sales of any previous year. The drop in sales and profits appears to be a one-year exception.

Still, the company president is afraid that a large drop in the current year's profits could cause a significant drop in the market price of Die Hard's shares, and could make the company a takeover target. To avoid this possibility, the company president urges Carole Chiasson, the controller, to accrue all possible revenues and to defer as many expenses as possible when preparing this period's December 31 year-end adjusting entries. He says to Carole, "We need the revenues this year, and next year we can easily absorb expenses deferred from this year." Carole did not record the adjusting entries until January 17, but she dated the entries December 31 as if they were recorded then. Carole also did everything possible to follow the president's request.

The **Broadening Your Perspective** section helps you pull together various concepts covered in the chapter and apply them to real-life business decisions.

Dec. 13 Natalie pays the amount outstanding on her cell phone bill.
16 Natalie receives and deposits the amount outstanding from the November 26 transaction.
17 Natalie receives an unexpected invitation to teach a cookie-making class at a children's Christmas party. At the end of the class, she prepares an invoice for $500 and leaves it with the organization's corporate controller. The controller indicates that the invoice will likely be paid in the next 30 days.
30 A $76 invoice is received for the use of Natalie's cell phone. The invoice is for services provided in December and is due on January 15, 2014.

Instructions
(a) Prepare journal entries to record the transactions.
(b) Post the journal entries to ledger accounts. Use T accounts.
(c) Prepare a trial balance as at December 31, 2013.

BROADENING YOUR PERSPECTIVE CHAPTER 2

Collaborative Learning Activity

Note to instructor: Additional instructions and material for this group activity can be found on the Instructor Resource Site and in *WileyPLUS*.

BYP2–1 In this group activity, students will be given a trial balance and will be asked to work backwards to create a set of journal entries that would result in the trial balance.

Communication Activity

BYP2–2 White Glove Company offers home cleaning services. Three common transactions for the company are signing contracts with new customers, billing customers for services performed, and paying employee salaries. For example, on March 15 the company did the following:

1. Signed a contract with a new customer for $125 per week starting the first week in April.
2. Sent bills that totalled $6,000 to customers.
3. Paid $2,000 in salaries to employees.

Instructions
Write an e-mail to your instructor that explains if and how these transactions are recorded in the double-entry system. Include in your e-mail (a) whether, and why, the transaction should or should not be recorded, and (b) how the debit and credit rules are applied if the transaction is recorded.

Ethics Case

BYP2–3 Vu Hung is the assistant chief accountant at Lim Company, a manufacturer of computer chips and cellular phones. The company currently has total sales of $20 million. It is the end of the first quarter. Vu is hurriedly trying to prepare a general ledger trial balance so that quarterly financial statements can be prepared and released to management and regulatory agencies. The credits on the trial balance add up to $1,000 more than the debits.

In order to meet the 4:00 p.m. deadline, Vu decides to force the debits and credits into balance by adding the amount of the difference to the Equipment account. She chose Equipment because it is one the larger account balances. Proportionally, it will be the least misstated. She believes that the differen will not affect anyone's decisions. She wishes that she had more time to find the error, but realizes that t financial statements are already late.

Instructions
(a) Who are the stakeholders in this situation?
(b) What are the ethical issues involved?
(c) What are Vu's alternatives?

All About You: Personal Financial Literacy Activity

BYP2–4 The "All About You" feature indicates that Luca Pacioli, who described the double-entr accounting system used over 500 years ago, wrote "a person should not go to sleep at night until the debi equalled the credits."

Collaborative Learning Activities prepare you for the business world, where you will be working with many people, by giving you practice in solving problems with colleagues. They also allow you to learn from fellow students.

Communication Activities ask you to engage in real-life business situations using your writing, speaking, or presentation skills.

Through **Ethics Cases,** you will reflect on ethical situations an accountant typically confronts.

All About You: Personal Financial Literacy Activities ask you questions about the All About You feature in the chapter, helping you apply accounting principles to your personal finances.

Instructions
(a) Who are the stakeholders in this situation?
(b) What are the ethical considerations of (1) the president's request, and (2) Carole's decision to date the adjusting entries December 31?
(c) Can Carole aggressively accrue revenues and defer expenses and still be ethical?

All About You: Personal Financial Literacy Activity

BYP3–4 A critical issue for accountants is the decision as to whether an expenditure should be recorded as an asset or an expense. The distinction between asset and expense is not always clear. In certain instances, businesses have been forced to restate their financial statements because management has recorded an asset when an expense should be recorded. The "All About You" feature indicates that post-secondary education results in higher earnings over an adult's working life and thus the money you are spending on your education today should be of significant future benefit. The question then is whether your future post-secondary education would meet the accounting definition of an asset or an expense.

Instructions
(a) Consider the nature of the cost of your plans for your post-secondary education. What factors suggest that it should be considered an asset? What factors suggest that it should be considered an expense?
(b) Do you think the nature of the program you're planning to take should affect whether the cost of your education should be considered an asset or an expense? Recall that both assets and expenses increase on the debit side. Explain.
(c) Economic theory suggests that people are rational decision-makers and will always consider the benefit and cost of any expenditure and only incur the cost if the expected benefit is greater. Wouldn't this mean that every expenditure would meet the definition of an asset? Would you consider the cost of a vacation to Hawaii to be as valuable as a year of college? Would you record them both as assets on a personal balance sheet? Why or why not?
(d) If you were applying for a loan, what might the potential effect be on the success of your application if you understated your assets? What might be the potential effect on the bank if your assets are overstated and expenses understated?

ANSWERS TO CHAPTER QUESTIONS

ANSWERS TO ACCOUNTING IN ACTION INSIGHT QUESTIONS

All About You Insight, p. 99

Q: How should you account for the cost of your post-secondary education in the future? Should you be recognizing the cost as an expense each year or should you recognize it as an asset?

A: Expenses are recognized when there has been a decrease in an asset or an increase in a liability. Paying for an education will reduce assets such as cash and may also increase liabilities if you have to take out student loans. Therefore, most accountants would tell you that you should record the cost of your education as an expense as you incur those costs. On the other hand, it could be argued that your education is creating an asset—your increased future earning power. But then you would have to estimate the value of this asset. As with many situations in accounting, it is not easy to determine the correct answer.

Business Insight, p. 105

Q: If a business collects cash when the gift card is sold, how can gift card sales in December result in revenues in January?

A: Gift cards sales are simply another example of unearned revenues. At the time the gift card is sold, the business must record unearned revenue, which is a liability. When a customer redeems the gift card by making a purchase, then the company will reduce the liability and record revenue.

ANSWERS TO SELF-STUDY QUESTIONS

1. b 2. d 3. d 4. b 5. c 6. d 7. a 8. a 9. b 10. a 11. a *12. a *13. c

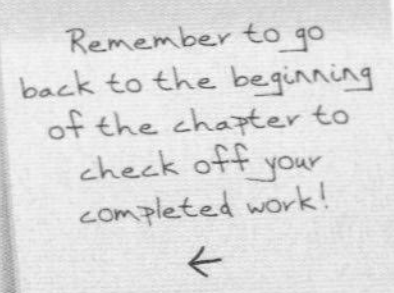
Remember to go
back to the beginning
of the chapter to
check off your
completed work!

Answers to Chapter Questions offer suggested answers for questions that appear in the chapter's **Accounting in Action** insight boxes and the **Self-Study Questions**.

After you complete your assignments, it's a good idea to go back to **The Navigator** checklist at the start of the chapter to see if you have used all the study aids of the chapter.

The Use of Bloom's Taxonomy

Bloom's Taxonomy is a classification framework that you can use to develop your skills from the most basic to the most advanced competence levels: knowledge, comprehension, application, analysis, synthesis, and evaluation. These levels are in a hierarchy. In order to perform at each level, you must have mastered all prior levels.

Questions, exercises, and problems at the end of each chapter of this text have been classified by the knowledge level required in answering each one. Below you will learn what your role is in each of the six skill levels and how you can demonstrate mastery at each level. Key word clues will help you recognize the skill level required for a particular question.

(K) Knowledge (Remembering)

Student's role: "I read, listen, watch, or observe; I take notes and am able to recall information; ask and respond to questions."
Student demonstrates knowledge by stating who, what, when, why, and how in the same form in which they learned it.
Key word clues: define, identify, label, name, etc.

(C) Comprehension (Understanding)

Student's role: "I understand the information or skill. I can recognize it in other forms and I can explain it to others and make use of it."
Student demonstrates comprehension by giving an example of how the information would be used.
Key word clues: describe, distinguish, give example, compare, differentiate, explain, etc.

(AP) Application (Solving the Problem)

Student's role: "I can apply my prior knowledge and understanding to new situations."
Student demonstrates knowledge by solving problems independently, recognizing when the information or skill is needed and using it to solve new problems or complete tasks.
Key word clues: calculate, illustrate, prepare, complete, use, produce, etc.

(AN) Analysis (Detecting)

Student's role: "I can break down the information into simpler parts and understand how these parts are related."
Student demonstrates knowledge by recognizing patterns and hidden meanings, filling in missing information, correcting errors, and identifying components and effects.
Key word clues: analyze, break down, compare, contrast, deduce, differentiate, etc.

(S) Synthesis (Creating)

Student's role: "I use all knowledge, understanding, and skills to create alternatives. I can convey this information to others effectively."
Student demonstrates knowledge by acting as a guide to others, designing, and creating.
Key word clues: relate, tell, write, categorize, devise, formulate, generalize, create, design, etc.

(E) Evaluation (Appraisal)

Student's role: "I am open to and appreciative of the value of ideas, procedures, and methods and can make well-supported judgements, backed up by knowledge, understanding, and skills."
Student demonstrates knowledge by formulating and presenting well-supported judgement, displaying consideration of others, examining personal options, and making wise choices.
Key word clues: appraise, assess, criticize, critique, decide, evaluate, judge, justify, recommend, etc.

Learning Styles Chart

Everybody has a preferred learning style. One part of that learning style is your preference for the intake and the output of ideas and information. This textbook contains features to help you learn best, whatever your learning style. Look at this page for how you can apply an understanding of your learning style to this course. Then read the Study Aids section to view the features of this textbook and to understand their purpose.

	What to do in class	What to do when studying	Text features that may help you	What to do prior to exams
VISUAL	• Pay close attention to charts, drawings, and handouts your teacher uses. • Underline and highlight. • Use different colours. • Use symbols, flow charts, graphs, different arrangements on the page, white space.	Convert your class notes into "page pictures." To do this: • Use the "What to do in class" strategies. • Reconstruct images in different ways. • Redraw pages from memory. • Replace words with symbols and initials. • Look at your pages.	• The Navigator • Feature Story • Preview • Infographics/Illustrations • Photos • Accounting in Action insight boxes • Accounting Equation Analyses in margins • Key Terms in blue • Words in bold or italics • Demonstration Problem/Action Plan • Questions/Exercises/Problems	• Recall your "page pictures." • Draw diagrams where appropriate. • Practise turning your visuals back into words.
AURAL	• Attend classes and tutorials. • Discuss topics with students and teachers. • Explain new ideas to other people. • Leave spaces in your class notes for later recall. • Describe overheads, pictures, and visuals to somebody who was not in class.	You may take poor notes because you prefer to listen. Therefore: • Expand your notes by talking with others and with information from your textbook. • Record summarized notes and listen. • Read summarized notes out loud. • Explain your notes to another "aural" person.	• Preview • Infographics/Illustrations • Accounting in Action insight boxes • Do It/Action Plan • Summary of Study Objectives • Glossary • Demonstration Problem/Action Plan • Self-Study Questions • Questions/Exercises/Problems • Broadening Your Perspective, particularly the Collaborative Learning Activities	• Talk with the teacher. • Spend time in quiet places recalling the ideas. • Practise writing answers to old exam questions. • Say your answers out loud.
READING/ WRITING	• Use lists and headings. • Use dictionaries, glossaries, and definitions. • Read handouts, textbooks, and supplemental library readings. • Use class notes.	• Write out words again and again. • Reread notes silently. • Rewrite ideas and principles into other words. • Turn charts, diagrams, and other illustrations into statements.	• The Navigator • Feature Story • Study Objectives • Preview • Accounting Equation Analysis in margins • Do It/Action Plan • Summary of Study Objectives • Glossary • Self-Study Questions • Questions/Exercises/Problems/ Taking It Further • Writing Problems • Broadening Your Perspective, particularly the Communication activities and the Collaborative Learning activities	• Write exam answers. • Practise with multiple-choice questions. • Write paragraphs, beginnings, and endings. • Write your lists in outline form. • Arrange your words into hierarchies and points.
KINESTHETIC	• Use all your senses. • Listen to real-life examples. • Pay attention to applications. • Use hands-on approaches. • Use trial-and-error methods.	You may take poor notes because topics do not seem concrete or relevant. Therefore: • Put examples in your summaries. • Use case studies and applications to help with principles and abstract concepts. • Talk about your notes with another "kinesthetic" person. • Use pictures and photographs that illustrate an idea.	• The Navigator • Feature Story • Preview • Infographics/Illustrations • Do It/Action Plan • Summary of Study Objectives • Demonstration Problem/Action Plan • Self-Study Questions • Questions/Exercises/Problems • Broadening Your Perspective, particularly the All About You activities and the Collaborative Learning activities	• Write practice answers. • Role-play the exam situation.

For all learning styles: Be sure to use the learning aids on the companion website and in *WileyPLUS* to enhance your understanding of the text's concepts and procedures. In particular, use the tutorials, study aids (including the searchable glossary, PowerPoint® presentations, and problem-solving techniques), and practice tools (including additional demonstration problems, key term matching activities, and quizzes).

To the Teacher

Student-Focused and Teacher-Friendly—*The* Solution for Your Accounting Principles Class!

In previous editions of this text, we tried to create a book about accounting that made the subject clear and fascinating to students. And that is still our passion: to empower students to succeed by giving them the tools and the motivation they need to excel in their accounting courses and their future careers. We are confident that you will enjoy teaching from this textbook, with its strong pedagogical foundations, continuing currency and accuracy of material, and exciting features.

Preparing *Principles of Financial Accounting*, Canadian Edition

In this text we have incorporated International Financial Reporting Standards (IFRS) and Accounting Standards for Private Enterprises (ASPE) into the text material. Differences between IFRS and ASPE are highlighted throughout each chapter with an ASPE logo ASPE where applicable. Each chapter concludes with a *Comparing IFRS and ASPE* table to provide a quick summary of key differences between the two sets of standards.

While the implementation of these new accounting standards represents a significant change, from an introductory accounting point of view, much is still the same. The basic accounting cycle remains unchanged and the focus for introductory students continues to be the fundamental principles. We have undertaken to reduce unnecessary complexities where possible and have decreased the number of account titles used in the textbook. Our goal is to keep students focused on the concepts that really matter.

Pedagogical Effectiveness

Our Navigator learning system empowers students to succeed by teaching them how to study, what to study, and why they should study. The textbook places increased emphasis, throughout the text, on the processes students go through as they learn.

Our Learning Styles model is used throughout the text to help students with different learning approaches better understand the material. The text has also been thoroughly vetted to ensure that it offers unprecedented clarity and readability.

Stepped-out pedagogy was used to break down complex topics, making the material more manageable for students. Bloom's Taxonomy, which underlies the structure of the textbook, continues to facilitate progressive learning by categorizing material in building block fashion. Summaries throughout the chapter help students stop and digest the material they have just learned. Before You Go On feedback sections include a Do It feature, a brief demonstration problem illustrating concepts that students have just been exposed to. A list of related exercises within the Before You Go On feedback section encourages self-study and practice. End-of-chapter demonstration problems were augmented in number coverage and level of difficulty to ease student understanding.

WileyPLUS

WileyPLUS is an innovative, research-based online environment for effective teaching and learning.

WileyPLUS builds students' confidence because it takes the guesswork out of studying by providing students with a clear roadmap: what to do, how to do it, if they did it right. Students will take more initiative so you'll have greater impact on their achievement in the classroom and beyond.

Relevance for Users

In order to illustrate the importance of financial accounting, we started Chapter 1 with a section about why accounting is important to everyone, not just accountants. We consistently emphasize this point throughout the text and have an Accounting in Action insight box in each chapter called All About You Insight. These boxes demonstrate how learning accounting is useful for students in managing their own financial affairs. We also have many Across the Organization, Business Insight and Ethics Insight boxes. These clearly demonstrate how accounting is used to address issues in marketing, finance, management, and other functions and have questions to engage critical thinking skills.

Our focus company for the text is Reitmans (Canada) Limited—Canada's largest women's specialty retailer. Reitmans was chosen because its stores have high name recognition with students, it operates in a single industry, and it has relatively simple financial statements. References to Reitmans have been included throughout the textbook, including ratio analysis and in Reitmans' financial statements in Appendix A at the end of the textbook.

The textbook provides current real-world examples, including the chapter-opening feature stories, the Accounting in Action insight boxes, and references to real-world examples in the chapters and end-of-chapter material. Our textbook includes references to over 170 real companies.

We continue to feature problem material that allows students to tie the concepts they are learning together and place them in context. Central to this is the Continuing Cookie Chronicle. This serial problem allows students to apply chapter topics in an ongoing scenario where a young entrepreneur builds her small business.

Topical Coverage and Chapter Changes

Changes were made to ensure that the content of the book meets the learning outcomes of BAT4M1. To this effect some material was streamlined and other material was deleted. The particulars of these changes are as follows:

- In Chapter 3, new tables were added to help students understand common revenue transactions and the differences between expenses and drawings.
- Additional T accounts were included in Chapters 8 (receivables), 9 (long-lived assets), and 12 (partnerships) to facilitate step-by-step understanding of preparing entries to reverse write offs, making adjusting entries for depreciation, and recording partnership capital under varying scenarios.
- Pie charts were added in the margins to encourage comprehension of other core concepts like showing shareholders' equity before and after issuing stock dividends (Chapter 14: Corporations).

We also listened to instructors and students when they told us that they wanted the textbook to be more portable and handy. Topics covered by earlier iterations of this text that are no longer included in the curriculum were deleted. As such, the textbook no longer deals with topics such as bank reconciliation, petty cash, sales tax, leases, payroll, and special journals. Instead the text includes appendices on investments and the present value concepts. The deletion of extraneous topics makes this textbook more compact and student friendly.

Helping Teachers Teach

The best way to empower students is to empower teachers. All material previously available on the Navigator CD has been made available on the web. Tutorials have been prepared on topics that students have trouble dealing with, including cash flow, bonds, inventory cost flow assumptions, and depreciation. The accounting cycle has been broken down into bite-sized animated tutorials for ease of understanding. An interactive and animated Annual Report Walkthrough tutorial demonstrates all the features of an annual report. The companion site does not contain a traditional Teacher's Manual divided into chapters but provides an easily searchable database of resources for teachers with all levels of experience in teaching. Similar in structure to our student resource sites, the database lists the types of resources available and allows teachers to access them directly or search by chapter. Resources include quizzes, games, lecture notes, an additional problem set (Problem Set B), and more. A **student workbook** is available with journals, ledgers, T accounts, and other required working papers for the end-of-chapter brief exercises, exercises, and problems.

Teacher's Resource Binder

The Teacher's Resource Binder includes:

- a sample syllabus
- a curriculum correlation
- a problem correlation
- an introduction to Simply Accounting
- culminating tasks, followed by solutions
- an introduction to *WileyPLUS*

The Teacher's Resource Binder also includes a Teacher's Manual. Each chapter of the book has a corresponding chapter in the manual.

Unparalleled End-of-Chapter Material

The textbook has a complete range of end-of-chapter material to satisfy all courses. This material guides students through the basic levels of cognitive understanding—knowledge, comprehension, application, analysis, synthesis, and evaluation—in a step-by-step process, starting first with questions, followed by brief exercises, exercises, problems, and finally, integrative cases to broaden a student's perspective.

Teachers told us they wanted more breadth and depth within each of these groupings to give them more flexibility in assigning end-of-chapter material. Using Bloom's Taxonomy of Learning, all of the end-of-chapter material was carefully reviewed. Topical gaps were identified and material added as required to facilitate progressive learning. Complexities were added to the Before You Go On, Self-Study Questions, and selected end-of-chapter material to increase the range and difficulty level of material available to test critical problem-solving skills.

A Taking It Further question is included at the end of every problem. These questions are designed to help you determine how far your students have taken their understanding of the material. To ensure maximum flexibility, problems can also be assigned with or without the Taking It Further question. They also make excellent classroom discussion questions.

The Continuing Cookie Chronicle, a serial problem in each chapter, follows the life of a simulated student-owned company. This edition has been revised to include moving the business into a family-owned corporation. The conceptual material in each problem attempts to integrate real-life experience and examples with the changing demands of financial accounting and reporting requirements.

The Collaborative Learning Activities address several major concerns related to improving student learning. They provide an effective method of actively engaging students that cannot be accomplished through traditional classes and large group discussion. Students benefit from the opportunity to hear multiple perspectives from their group members and enhance their learning through explaining ideas to other students. Teacher resource material includes information on how to use these in class as well as suggestions for modifying them depending on the amount of time available for the activity.

Additional financial reporting problems and problems that involve interpreting financial statements are available for each chapter and are included in the Teacher's Resource Binder.

The All About You boxes mentioned earlier are mirrored in the Broadening Your Perspective section. The All About You activities have been designed to help students appreciate that learning accounting is helpful for everyone, regardless of their current and future career plans.

In total, we have over 1,700 end-of-chapter items for students to test their understanding of accounting. We have added several new questions, brief exercises, exercises, and problems to the end-of-chapter material.

Acknowledgements

During the course of developing *Principles of Financial Accounting*, Canadian Edition, the authors benefited from the feedback from several teachers of accounting principles courses. The constructive suggestions and innovative ideas helped focus this revision on motivating students to want to learn accounting. In addition, the input and advice of the ancillary authors, contributors, and proofreaders provided valuable feedback throughout the development of this edition.

Reviewers

Patrick Dertinger, ***Waterloo-Oxford District Secondary School, Baden, Waterloo Region District School Board***

Brett Dugan, ***Adult High School, Ottawa, Ottawa-Carleton District School Board***

Jahanara Kamath, ***Thistletown Collegiate Institute, Toronto, Toronto District School Board***

Ingrid Montarras, ***Oakwood Collegiate Institute, Toronto, Toronto District School Board***

Edward Ponikvar, ***Our Lady of Mount Carmel Secondary School, Mississauga, Dufferin-Peel Catholic District School Board***

John Truong, ***Louise Arbour Secondary School, Brampton, Peel District School Board***

Wilma VanSegbrook, ***Forest Heights Collegiate, Kitchener, Waterloo Region District School Board***

Textbook Contributors

Sally Anderson, *Mount Royal University*
Dal Pirot, *Grant MacEwan University*

Supplement Contributors

Vida Barker, *Centennial College*
Maria Belanger, *Algonquin College*
Angela Davis, *Booth University College*
Robert Ducharme, *University of Waterloo*
Ilene Gilborn, *Mount Royal University*
Rosalie Harms, *University of Winnipeg*
Amy Hoggard, *Camosun College*
Cécile Laurin, *Algonquin College*
Kayla Levesque, *Cambrian College*
Richard Michalski, *McMaster University*
Debbie Musil, *Kwantlen Polytechnic University*
Marie Sinnott, *College of New Caledonia*
Traven Reed, *Canadore College*
Ruth Ann Strickland, *Western University*
Brian Trenholm
Jerry P. Zdril, *Grant MacEwan University*
Patricia Zima, *Mohawk College*

Through their editorial contributions, Laurel Hyatt and Denise Showers added to the real-world flavour of the text and its clarity.

Accuracy

We have made every effort to ensure that this text is error-free. *Principles of Financial Accounting* has been extensively reviewed and proofed at various production stages prior to publication. In addition, the end-of-chapter material has been independently solved and then checked by at least three individuals, in addition to the authors, prior to publication of the text. We would like to express our sincere gratitude to everyone who spent countless hours ensuring the accuracy of this text and the solutions to the end-of-chapter material.

A Final Note of Thanks

We appreciate the exemplary support and professional commitment given us by the talented team in the Wiley Canada higher education division, including Luisa Begani, Editorial Assistant; Zoë Craig, Acquisitions Editor; Deanna Durnford, Supplements Coordinator; Daleara Hirjikaka, Developmental Editor; Anita Osborne, Marketing Manager; Karen Staudinger, Editorial Manager; Maureen Talty, General Manager, Higher Education; Veronica Visentin, Vice-President and Publisher; and Carolyn Wells, Vice-President, Digital Solutions. We wish to also thank Wiley's dedicated sales representatives who work tirelessly to serve your needs.

It would not have been possible to write this text without the understanding of our employers, colleagues, students, family, and friends. Together, they provided a creative and supportive environment for our work.

We have tried our best to produce a text and supplement package that is error-free and meets your specific needs. Suggestions and comments from all users—instructors and students alike—are encouraged and appreciated.

Valerie Kinnear
Calgary, Alberta

Joan Barlow
Calgary, Alberta

Michael Atkins
Markham, Ontario

March 2014

BRIEF CONTENTS

CONTENTS

PRINCIPLES OF FINANCIAL ACCOUNTING

CANADIAN EDITION

CHAPTER 1 ACCOUNTING IN ACTION

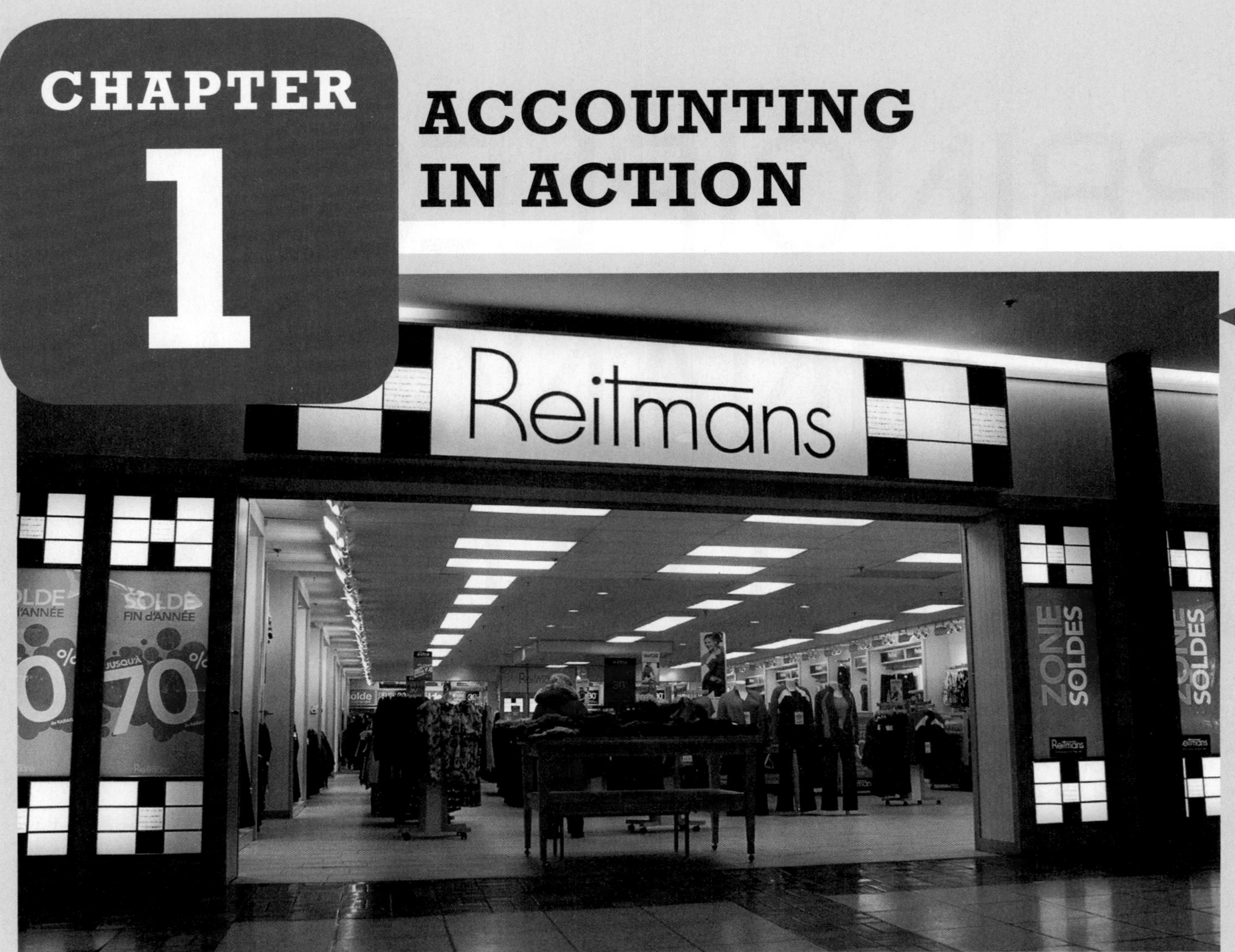

The **Navigator** learning system encourages you to use the learning aids in the chapter and set priorities as you study.

Concepts for Review highlight concepts from your earlier reading that you need to understand before starting the new chapter.

THE NAVIGATOR

- ☐ Understand *Concepts for Review*
- ☐ Read *Feature Story*
- ☐ Scan *Study Objectives*
- ☐ Read *Chapter Preview*
- ☐ Read text and answer *Before You Go On*
- ☐ Review *Comparing IFRS and ASPE*
- ☐ Work *Demonstration Problem*
- ☐ Review *Summary of Study Objectives*
- ☐ Answer *Self-Study Questions*
- ☐ Complete assignments

CONCEPTS FOR REVIEW

Before studying this chapter, you should understand or, if necessary, review:

A. How to use the study aids in this book. (pp. v–xii)

B. What the Bloom's Taxonomy classifications (K, C, AP, AN, S, and E) mean. (p. xiii)

C. The learning styles chart. (p. xiv)

The **Feature Story** helps you see how the chapter topic fits with the real world of accounting and business. The story will be mentioned frequently throughout the chapter.

DRESSED FOR SUCCESS

MONTREAL, Que.—When Herman and Sarah Reitman opened a small department store in Montreal in the early 1900s, they likely would never have predicted that it would grow into Canada's largest women's specialty clothing retailer. The couple's department store was so popular, they opened a second store in 1926, selling only women's clothing. That remains the company's focus as the Reitmans' children and grandchildren carry on the family tradition.

Today, Reitmans (Canada) Limited operates more than 950 stores in every province and territory, under several names (or "banners"): Reitmans, Smart Set, RW&CO., Penningtons, Addition-Elle, and Thyme Maternity. Each banner focuses on affordable women's clothing, catering to a particular niche, such as age or size. And in 2010, Reitmans joined the e-commerce trend by selling Reitmans, Penningtons, and Addition-Elle merchandise on-line. In total, the company brings in more than $1 billion in sales every year.

How did Reitmans go from one store to a billion-dollar company? By using accounting to keep a close eye on all its numbers. Reitmans, like all successful companies, makes decisions by analyzing the costs and rewards of each move to determine if they make financial sense. The company partially credits its solid performance in a tough retail environment to keeping costs low, such as the cost of merchandise, foreign exchange, and distribution—something only possible by maintaining reliable cost information.

The company says it "continues to grow all areas of its business by investing in stores, technology and people." On an ongoing basis, Reitmans assesses the viability of each store by constantly monitoring its profitability. These strategic decisions require good accounting information to decide on where to make those investments.

Not only do Reitmans' managers rely on accounting information, but external users want to know how the company is faring as well. As a company whose shares trade on the Toronto Stock Exchange (under the ticker symbol RET), Reitmans makes its financial information available to the public through its annual report. Reitmans has thousands of owners in the form of shareholders. Potential and existing shareholders are interested in the company's consistent issuing of dividends and its continuing ability to grow and be profitable. Other external users are banks and other lenders that provide loans to Reitmans, which want to know about the company's cash flow and whether it can pay its obligations. In its most recent annual report, for the year ended January 28, 2012, Reitmans' revenues were $1.02 billion, with profits of $47.5 million.

Equipped with solid accounting numbers, Reitmans is dressed for success.

Sources: "Announcing Reitmans(dot)com: The Canadian Company That Dresses Everybody and Every Body Has Taken Its Unique Proposition Online," company news release, December 16, 2010; Reitmans Annual Report 2012; Simon Avery, "Reitmans' Dominance Helps it Take on Retail Sector's Hurdles," *Globe and Mail*, March 29, 2011; John Heinzl, "Why Investors Should Try Reitmans on for Size," *Globe and Mail*, June 9, 2011.

Study Objectives show what you should be able to do after learning the specific concepts presented in the chapter.

THE NAVIGATOR

STUDY OBJECTIVES

After studying this chapter, you should be able to:

1. Identify the use and users of accounting and the objective of financial reporting.
2. Compare different forms of business organizations and explain how Canadian accounting standards apply to these organizations.
3. Describe the components of the financial statements and explain the accounting equation.
4. Determine what events are recognized in the financial statements and how the events are measured.
5. Analyze the effects of business transactions on the accounting equation.
6. Prepare financial statements.

THE NAVIGATOR

PREVIEW OF CHAPTER ONE

The **Chapter Preview** outlines the major topics and subtopics you will see in the chapter.

The feature story about Reitmans highlights the importance of having good financial information to make good business decisions. This applies not just to companies but also to individuals. You cannot earn a living, spend money, buy on credit, make an investment, or pay taxes without receiving, using, or giving financial information. Good decision-making for companies and individuals depends on good information.

This chapter shows you that accounting is the system that produces useful financial information for decision-making. The chapter is organized as follows:

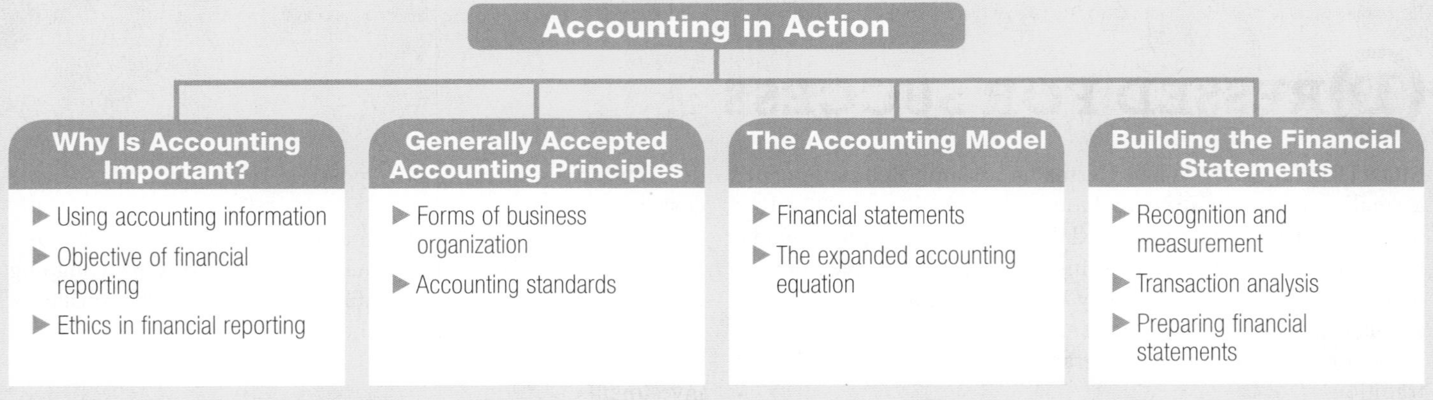

Accounting in Action
Why Is Accounting Important?
▶ Using accounting information
▶ Objective of financial reporting
▶ Ethics in financial reporting
Generally Accepted Accounting Principles
▶ Forms of business organization
▶ Accounting standards
The Accounting Model
▶ Financial statements
▶ The expanded accounting equation
Building the Financial Statements
▶ Recognition and measurement
▶ Transaction analysis
▶ Preparing financial statements

WHY IS ACCOUNTING IMPORTANT?

STUDY OBJECTIVE 1

Identify the use and users of accounting and the objective of financial reporting.

Essential (key) terms are printed in blue when they first appear, and are defined in the end-of-chapter glossary.

Accounting is the information system that identifies, records, and communicates the economic events of an organization to a wide variety of interested users. The world's economic systems depend on highly transparent and relevant financial reporting that provides a true representation of the economic events. When that does not happen, it can have disastrous results. Lehman Brothers, a major United States bank, used misleading accounting practices to reduce its debt and make its financial position appear healthier than it was. Not only were Lehman Brothers' investors and lenders unaware of the bank's financial difficulties when the company went into bankruptcy, but economists believe the bankruptcy was a major contributor to the worldwide economic crisis that began in 2008.

A vital part of communicating economic events is the accountant's ability and responsibility to analyze and interpret the reported information. In analysis, accountants use ratios, percentages, graphs, and charts to highlight significant financial trends and relationships. In interpretation, they explain the uses, meaning, and limitations of the reported data. Accounting has long been labelled the "language of business" and has consistently ranked as one of the top career opportunities in business.

You might think this is all well and good for students who want to become accountants, but what about someone who has plans to be anything *but* an accountant?

Understanding the basics of accounting is helpful for almost every endeavour you can think of. By studying accounting, you will learn how the world of business—large and small—actually works. Whether you plan to own your own business in the future, work for someone else in their business, or invest in a business, learning how to read and interpret financial information is a valuable set of skills.

When you study accounting, you will also learn a lot about management, finance, and marketing, which will give you a solid foundation for your future studies. For example, you will learn how making a sale is meaningless unless it is a profitable sale and the money can eventually be collected from the customer. Marketing managers must also be able to plan and implement pricing strategies based on costs. Accounting is what quantifies these costs and explains why a product or service costs what it does. So think of this textbook as your introduction to accounting across the organization.

It doesn't matter if you plan to become a doctor, lawyer, social worker, teacher, engineer, architect, or entrepreneur—whatever you choose, a working knowledge of accounting will be relevant and useful. Accounting is all about you. Make the most of this course—it will serve you for a lifetime in ways you cannot now imagine.

ACCOUNTING IN ACTION
ALL ABOUT YOU INSIGHT

We all know the importance of literacy. But what about *financial literacy*—the ability to understand and manage your finances? It seems Canadians don't place the same importance on financial literacy—but with rising household debt levels, falling savings levels, increasing personal bankruptcies, and continuing economic uncertainty, they should. According to Statistics Canada research, in 2009 only half of Canadians had a household budget and one in three were struggling to pay their bills. On a scale of 1 to 100, Canadians scored an average of 66 in terms of their ability to keep track of their finances and 61 out of 100 in terms of planning for life goals such as buying a house or retiring. To improve the situation the federal government launched a Task Force on Financial Literacy. The task force recommended that financial literacy be taught at a young age and that Canadians continue learning about finances throughout their lives. Making the right financial decisions can have a major impact on an individual's financial well-being, health, and happiness.

Learning the basics of accounting will help you make the right financial decisions. Accounting will help you make investment decisions, determine how much interest you are paying on your student loan or credit cards, and prepare your personal budget. To demonstrate the value of accounting to you, included in each chapter is an "All About You" feature and a related personal financial literacy activity (BYP–4) that links accounting to your life as a student or to a situation you are likely to face.

Sources: Task Force on Financial Literacy, *Canadians and Their Money: Building a Brighter Financial Future*, December 2010; Financial Consumer Agency of Canada, *The Future of Financial Education: Report on the 2011 FCAC-OECD Conference on Financial Literacy*, 2011; Robin Taub and Mary Teresa Bitt, "It Pays to Know," *CA Magazine*, October 2011.

How might learning accounting help you make sure that your employer or bank hasn't made an error with your paycheque or bank account?

USING ACCOUNTING INFORMATION

Accounting in Action insights give examples of accounting situations from different perspectives: all about you, across the organization, and in terms of business and ethics. At the end of the chapter, you will find answers to the questions that are asked after each insight.

There are two broad groups of users of accounting information: internal users and external users.

Internal Users

Internal users of accounting information plan, organize, and run companies. They work for the company. This includes finance directors, marketing managers, human resources personnel, production supervisors, and company officers. In running a business, internal users must answer many important questions, as shown in Illustration 1-1.

ILLUSTRATION 1-1
Questions asked by internal users

Finance
Is there enough cash to pay the bills?

Marketing
What price should we sell smart phones for to maximize profits?

Human Resources
How many employees can we afford to hire this year?

Production
Which product line is the most profitable?

To answer these and other questions, users need detailed information on a timely basis; that is, it must be available when needed. Some examples of information that internal users need include forecasts of cash flows for the next year, projections of profit from new sales campaigns, financial comparisons of operating alternatives, analyses of salary costs, and budgeted financial statements. Internal users generally have direct access to the business's accounting information and are able to request a wide variety of custom reports designed for their specific needs.

External Users

There are several types of *external users* of accounting information. **Investors**, who are owners—or potential owners—of the business, use accounting information to make decisions to buy, hold, or sell their ownership interest. **Creditors**—persons or other businesses that are owed money by the business, such as suppliers and bankers—use accounting information to evaluate the risks of granting credit or lending money. Investors and creditors are the main external users of accounting information, but there are also many other external users with a large variety of information needs and questions.

For example, labour unions want to know whether the owners can afford to pay increased salaries and benefits. Customers are interested in whether a company will continue to honour its product warranties and support its product lines. Taxing authorities, such as Canada Revenue Agency, want to know whether the company respects the tax laws. Regulatory agencies, such as provincial securities commissions that regulate companies that sell shares to the public, want to know whether the company is respecting established rules. And economic planners use accounting information to forecast economic activity.

Some questions that external users may ask about a company are shown in Illustration 1-2.

ILLUSTRATION 1-2
Questions asked by external users

Investors
Is the company earning enough to give me a return on my investment?

Creditors
Will the company be able to pay its debts as they come due?

Labour Unions
Can the company afford the pay raise we are asking for?

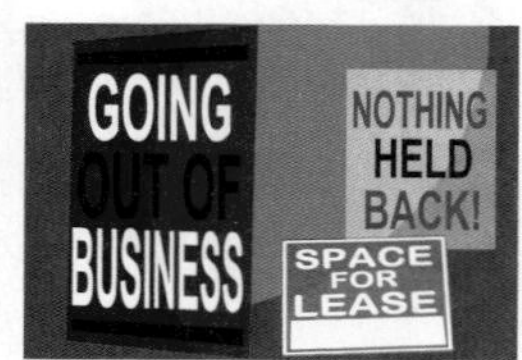

Customers
Will the company stay in business long enough to service the products I buy from it?

Unlike internal users, external users have access to only the accounting information provided to them by the business. Because external users are not able to request specific information, there are many rules about what information must be provided. Determining what information should be provided to external users, and how, is the focus of financial accounting.

OBJECTIVE OF FINANCIAL REPORTING

Accounting information is communicated in financial reports, and the most common reports are financial statements. The main objective of financial statements is to provide useful information to investors and creditors (external users) to make decisions about a business. To make the decision to invest in a business or to lend to a business, users need information about the business's ability to earn a profit and generate cash. Consequently, financial statements must give information about the following:

1. The business's economic resources. What resources does the business have that it can use to carry out its business activities?
2. The claims to the business's economic resources. What are the amounts owed by the business and the owner's rights to the business's resources?
3. Economic performance. Is the business generating a profit and sufficient cash to pay its debts, and provide a return to its owners?

We will learn more about financial statements in the following sections.

ETHICS IN FINANCIAL REPORTING

In order for financial information to have value for its users, whether internal or external, it must be prepared by individuals with high standards of ethical behaviour. Ethics in accounting is of the utmost importance to accountants and decision makers who rely on the financial information they produce.

Fortunately, most individuals in business are ethical. Their actions are both legal and responsible. They consider the organization's and the public's interests when they make decisions. Accountants and other professionals have extensive rules of conduct to guide their behaviour with each other and the public. In addition, many companies today have codes of conduct, or statements of corporate values, that outline their commitment to ethical behaviour in their internal and external relationships. The behaviour of management is critical for creating the appropriate tone from the top of the organization.

Throughout this textbook, ethical considerations will be presented to highlight the importance of ethics in financial reporting. Every chapter includes an Ethics Case in the end-of-chapter material that simulates a business situation and asks you to put yourself in the position of a key decision maker. When you analyze these ethical situations, you should follow the steps outlined in Illustration 1-3.

ILLUSTRATION 1-3
Steps used to analyze ethics cases and situations

1. Recognize an ethical situation and the ethical issues involved.
Use your personal ethics or an organization's code of ethics to identify ethical situations and issues. Some business and professional organizations provide written codes of ethics for guidance in common business situations.

2. Identify and analyze the main elements in the situation.
Identify the *stakeholders*—persons or groups who may be harmed or benefited. Ask the question: What are the responsibilities and obligations of the parties involved?

3. Identify the alternatives, and weigh the impact of each alternative on various stakeholders.
Select the most ethical alternative, considering all the consequences. Sometimes there will be one right answer. Other situations involve more than one possible solution. These situations require an evaluation of each alternative and the selection of the best one.

The companion website to this text includes a discussion of ethics and ethical issues that involve accounting and financial reporting.

Before You Go On Do It exercises like the one here ask you to put your new knowledge to work. They also outline an Action Plan you need to follow to do the exercise. *Related exercise material* tells you which Brief Exercises (BE) and Exercises (E) at the end of the chapter have similar study objectives.

BEFORE YOU GO ON...

DO IT

The following is a list of some users of accounting information. For each user, indicate:

(a) whether they are an internal or external user and
(b) an example of a question that might be asked by that user.

1. Creditor
2. Canada Revenue Agency
3. Investor
4. Production department
5. Human resources department

Action Plan

- Understand that internal users work for the company and have direct access to the business's accounting information.
- Understand that external users are users that do not work for the company and have access to only the accounting information provided to them by the company.
- Understand that users require information to make decisions.

SOLUTION

User	(a) Internal or External	(b) Question
1. Creditor	External	Will the business be able to pay back the loan?
2. Canada Revenue Agency	External	Is the company following the tax laws?
3. Investor	External	Should I invest money in the company?
4. Production department	Internal	How much will it cost to produce the product?
5. Human resources department	Internal	Can the company afford to give the employees raises?

Related exercise material: BE1–1, BE1–2, and E1–1.

THE NAVIGATOR

STUDY OBJECTIVE 2
Compare different forms of business organizations and explain how Canadian accounting standards apply to these organizations.

GENERALLY ACCEPTED ACCOUNTING PRINCIPLES

Businesses can be organized in different ways. The specific financial statements prepared, and the accounting standards followed, differ depending on the form and nature of the business organization.

FORMS OF BUSINESS ORGANIZATION

The most common forms of business organizations are the proprietorship, partnership, and corporation. Illustration 1-4 compares some of the characteristics of these forms.

ILLUSTRATION 1-4
Characteristics of business organizations

	Proprietorship	Partnership	Corporation
Owners	Proprietor: one	Partners: two or more	Shareholders: one or more
Owner's liability	Unlimited	Unlimited	Limited
Private or public	Private	Usually private	Private or public
Taxation of profits	Paid by the owner	Paid by the partners	Paid by the corporation
Life of organization	Limited	Limited	Indefinite

Proprietorship

A business owned by one person is a **proprietorship**. The owner is usually the operator of the business. Small service businesses (hair stylists, plumbers, and mechanics), farms, and small retail stores (antique shops, corner grocery stores, and independent bookstores) are often proprietorships.

Often only a relatively small amount of money (capital) is needed to start in business as a proprietorship. The owner (the proprietor) receives any profits, suffers any losses, and is personally liable (responsible) for all debts of the business. This is known as **unlimited liability**.

Although the business and its owner represent two separate and distinct economic entities, there is no distinction between the two from a legal standpoint. Thus the life of a proprietorship is limited to the life of the owner. This also means that the profits of the business are reported and taxed on the owner's personal income tax return. However, for accounting purposes, the records of the proprietorship's business activities are kept separate from the personal records and activities of the owner. This is consistent with the economic entity concept, which will be introduced later in this chapter.

Many businesses in Canada are proprietorships, but they earn only a small percentage of the revenue earned by Canadian businesses as a whole. In this textbook, we start with proprietorships because many students organize their first business this way.

Partnership

A business owned by two or more persons who are associated as partners is a **partnership**. In most aspects, a partnership is similar to a proprietorship, except that there is more than one owner. Partnerships are often used to organize service-type businesses, including professional practices (lawyers, doctors, architects, and accountants) who are not allowed to incorporate.

Typically, a **partnership agreement** (written or oral) defines the initial investments of each partner, the duties of each partner, how profit (or loss) will be divided, and what the settlement will be if a partner dies or withdraws. As in a proprietorship, for accounting purposes a partnership's business activities must be kept separate from the personal activities of each partner. The partners' share of the profit must be reported and taxed on the partners' income tax returns.

Each partner generally has unlimited liability for all debts of the partnership, even if one of the other partners created the debt. This means that any of the partners can be forced to give up his or her personal assets in order to repay the partnership debt, just as can happen to an owner in a proprietorship. We will learn more about partnerships in Chapter 12.

Corporation

Helpful hints help clarify concepts or items that are being discussed.

Helpful hint You can usually tell if a company is a corporation by looking at its name. The words *Limited (Ltd.)*, *Incorporated (Inc.)*, or *Corporation (Corp.)* usually follow its name.

A business that is organized (incorporated) as a separate legal entity under federal or provincial corporate law is a **corporation**. A corporation is responsible for its debts and paying taxes on its profit. A corporation's ownership is divided into transferable shares. The corporation's separate legal status provides the owners of the shares (shareholders) with **limited liability** as they risk losing only the amount that they have invested in the company's shares. They are not personally liable for the debts of the corporate entity. Shareholders may sell all or part of their shares to other investors at any time. Easy changes of ownership are part of what makes it attractive to invest in a corporation. Because ownership can be transferred through the sale of shares and without dissolving the corporation, the corporation enjoys an unlimited life.

Although there are many more proprietorships and partnerships than corporations in Canada, the revenue produced by corporations is far greater. Most of the largest companies in Canada—for example, Royal Bank of Canada, Suncor Energy, BlackBerry, and Barrick Gold—are corporations.

Corporations such as these are publicly traded. That is, their shares are listed on Canadian stock exchanges. Public corporations commonly distribute their financial statements to shareholders, creditors, other interested parties, and the general public upon request. Reitmans is a public corporation, whose shares are traded on the Toronto Stock Exchange. You can review its financial statements in Appendix A at the back of this textbook.

Other companies are private corporations, as they do not issue publicly traded shares. Some of the largest private companies in Canada include Bombardier Aerospace, McCain Foods, and EllisDon Inc. Like proprietorships and partnerships, these companies almost never distribute their financial statements publicly. We will discuss the corporate form of organization in Chapters 13 and 14.

ACCOUNTING STANDARDS

To make the information in financial statements meaningful, accountants have to prepare the reports in a standardized way. Every profession develops a body of theory based on principles and assumptions. Accounting is no exception.

The accounting profession has developed a set of standards that are generally accepted and universally practised. This common set of standards, called **generally accepted accounting principles (GAAP)**, includes broad principles and practices, as well as rules and procedures. These standards indicate how to report economic events.

Alternative terminology notes give synonyms that you may hear or see in the workplace, in companies' financial statements, and occasionally in this textbook.

In Canada, the Accounting Standards Board (AcSB), an independent standard-setting body created by the Chartered Professional Accountants of Canada (CPA Canada), has the main responsibility for developing GAAP. The AcSB's most important criterion for accounting standards is this: the standard should lead to external users having the most useful financial information possible when they are making business decisions.

Alternative terminology The terms *standard* and *principle* mean the same thing in accounting.

International Financial Reporting Standards and Accounting Standards for Private Enterprises

The AcSB recognizes that "one size does not necessarily fit all" and has developed and adopted separate standards for publicly accountable enterprises and for private enterprises. Canadian public enterprises must follow **International Financial Reporting Standards (IFRS)**, a set of global standards developed by the International Accounting Standards Board (IASB). **Publicly accountable enterprises** include publicly traded corporations, as well as securities brokers and dealers, banks, and credit unions whose role is to hold assets for the public as part of their primary business. Reitmans is a public company and therefore is required to follow IFRS.

Helpful hint Accounting standards use the word "enterprise" as it is a broader term than "company" or "business." The word "enterprise" means that the accounting standard applies to the different forms of business organizations, as well as specific projects. Throughout this text, instead of using the word "enterprise," we will frequently use the words "company" or "business," as they are more common terms.

Traditionally, accounting standards differed from country to country, making it difficult for investors, creditors, and others to make informed decisions about companies doing business in today's increasingly global environment. The IASB has worked, and continues to do so, with accounting standard setters across the globe to harmonize accounting standards where possible. IFRS are used as the main basis of financial reporting in more than 100 countries, including Australia, Brazil, Russia, members of the European Union, China, India, Japan, Mexico, and Canada. Although the United States does not use IFRS, its standard setters are working on a joint project with the IASB to develop and revise accounting standards so that they are consistent between U.S. GAAP and IFRS.

Following IFRS enhances Canadian public companies' ability to compete in an increasingly global marketplace. When IFRS are used, the financial statements of Canadian public companies are understood by investors and creditors throughout the world. Using IFRS also helps Canadian companies that operate in multiple countries, by allowing them to produce one set of financial statements rather than multiple sets with different accounting principles.

On the other hand, the users of a private company's financial statements generally have the ability to obtain additional information from the company if required. Because these users typically require less information in the financial statements, the AcSB developed **Accounting Standards for Private Enterprises (ASPE)**. ASPE requires considerably less information in financial statements than is required by IFRS. While public companies have to follow IFRS, Canadian private companies, including private corporations such as McCain Foods and EllisDon Inc., have the choice to report under ASPE or IFRS. As proprietorships and partnerships are private companies, these companies will generally follow ASPE for financial reporting.

ASPE

The **ASPE Icon** indicates where differences between IFRS and ASPE are explained. These differences are also summarized at the end of each chapter.

Given the differences between IFRS and ASPE, and the fact that private companies have a choice, financial statement users will need to know which standards the company is following. Companies are required to report this in their financial statements. In this textbook, as we proceed through the material, we will point out where there are differences in the two sets of standards. However, the two sets of standards have a great deal in common in the type of material covered in an introductory accounting textbook.

Both IFRS and ASPE are considered "principles-based" as opposed to "rules-based" standards. Principles-based standards are designed to encourage the use of professional judgement in applying basic accounting principles. As you learn more about accounting, you will see that we will frequently refer to basic principles, as opposed to detailed rules, when deciding how to account for specific events. In this chapter, we introduce a few of these basic principles and concepts.

It is important to understand that GAAP is not static and that it changes over time. The AcSB and IASB continue to create new standards and modify GAAP. AcSB and IASB use a process that involves consultation with organizations and individuals that are interested in, or affected by, the standards. This process can take a long time but it ensures that the main purpose of financial statements—providing information that is relevant to decision-making—continues to be met.

The length of time involved in adding new or changing existing accounting standards can make it difficult to determine what information we should include in this textbook—should it be the currently approved standard or the proposed new standard? Sometimes the proposals are modified or dropped altogether before being approved. Normally the textbook will cover only the currently approved standards. But where we believe it is important to do so, we will introduce new standards that were proposed at the time the textbook was written.

Economic Entity Concept

Alternative terminology The economic entity concept is also known as the *business entity concept.*

Financial statements are prepared for a business or economic unit. This is referred to as the **economic entity concept**. The concept requires that the accounting for an economic entity's activities be kept separate and distinct from the accounting for the activities of its owner and all other economic entities. An economic entity can be any organization or unit in society. You will recall that proprietorships' and partnerships' records of their business activities are kept separate from the personal records of their owners. That is because proprietorships and partnerships are considered economic entities for financial reporting purposes. Similarly, a corporation (such as Reitmans) is considered an economic entity for financial reporting purposes. If one corporation owns another corporation, the two corporations combined may be considered an economic entity for financial reporting purposes. Other examples of economic entities are a governmental unit (such as the Province of Manitoba), a municipality (such as the Ville de Montréal), a native band council (such as the Kingsclear Indian Band), a school board (such as the Burnaby School Board), and a club (such as the Melfort Rotary Club).

It is important to understand that an economic entity may not necessarily be a separate legal entity. For example, proprietorships and partnerships are not a separate legal entity from their owners. Regardless, the economic entity concept requires separate financial reporting.

Going Concern Assumption

Alternative terminology The going concern assumption is also known as the *continuing concern assumption.*

The **going concern assumption** is the assumption that the economic entity will continue to operate in the foreseeable future. Although some businesses fail, most companies continue operating for a long time. The going concern assumption presumes that the company will operate long enough to use its resources for their intended purpose and to complete the company's commitments.

This assumption is one of the most important assumptions in GAAP as it has implications regarding what information is useful for decision makers and affects many of the accounting standards you will learn. If a company is a going concern, then financial statement users will find it useful for the company to report certain resources, such as land, at their cost. Land is acquired so a company can use it, not so it can be resold. Therefore, what matters is the amount the company gave up to acquire the land, not an estimate of its current worth. If a company is not a going concern, and the land is going to be sold, then financial statement users will be more interested in the land's current value.

If a company is not regarded as a going concern, or if there are significant doubts about its ability to continue as a going concern, then this must be stated in the financial statements, along with the reason why the company is not regarded as a going concern. Otherwise, you can assume that the company is a going concern—even though this is not explicitly stated. Since it is not necessary to include in the financial statements that the company is a going concern, this assumption is considered an underlying assumption.

BEFORE YOU GO ON...

DO IT

For each type of organization (proprietorship, partnership, and corporation) indicate:

1. Number and type of owners.
2. If it has limited or unlimited liability.
3. If it is a separate legal entity from its owners.

Action Plan

- Understand the characteristics of the most common forms of business organizations.

SOLUTION

	Proprietorship	Partnership	Corporation
1.	Proprietor: one	Partners: two or more	Shareholders: one or more
2.	Unlimited	Unlimited	Limited
3.	Not a separate legal entity from its owners	Not a separate legal entity from its owners	Separate legal entity from the shareholders

Related exercise material: BE1–3, BE1–4, and E1–2.

THE ACCOUNTING MODEL

FINANCIAL STATEMENTS

STUDY OBJECTIVE 3

Describe the components of the financial statements and explain the accounting equation.

You will recall that the main objective of the financial statements is to provide information about the business's resources, claims to its resources, and its ability to earn a profit and generate cash to allow investors and creditors (external users) to make decisions about a business. Here we will introduce four basic financial statements and show how this information is included in these statements. Later in the chapter, we will illustrate how to prepare these statements.

The specific financial statements prepared differ depending on the nature of the business organization; however, all businesses prepare a balance sheet and income statement. As you go through this section, we recommend you refer to Reitmans' financial statements for the year ended January 28, 2012, in Appendix A of this textbook, for an example. We will refer to these statements often throughout the textbook.

Balance Sheet

Users need information on the economic resources that the business can use to carry out its business activities to earn a profit and the claims to these economic resources. In accounting, economic resources that are owned or controlled by a business are called "assets." Claims on the economic resources are the amounts owed by the business and the owner's rights to the resources. In accounting, amounts owed by the business are called "liabilities" and the owner's right to these resources is called "owner's equity." **Assets, liabilities, and owner's equity are reported in the balance sheet.**

Alternative terminology The balance sheet is sometimes called the *statement of financial position.*

The balance sheet is like a snapshot of the company's financial condition at a specific moment in time (usually the end of a month, quarter, or year). The heading of a balance sheet must identify the company, statement, and date. To indicate that the balance sheet is at a specific point in time, the date only mentions the point in time (there is no indication of a time period). Let's look at the categories in the balance sheet in more detail.

Assets.

Assets are the resources owned or controlled by a business that are expected to provide future services or economic benefits. In a company, that future service potential or economic benefit eventually results in cash inflows (receipts).

Assets are used to carry out activities such as the production and distribution of merchandise. For example, imagine that a local pizza parlour, called Campus Pizza, owns a delivery truck. The truck provides economic benefits and helps the business generate revenue because it is used to deliver pizzas. Campus Pizza also owns other assets, such as tables, chairs, a sound system, a cash register, an oven, dishes, supplies, and, of course, cash.

Other common assets include merchandise held for resale (inventory), investments, land, buildings, patents, and copyrights. **Accounts receivable** is the asset created when a company sells services or products to customers who promise to pay cash for the service or product in the future. **Prepaid expenses**, another category of assets, are created when a business pays cash for costs incurred in advance of being used or consumed. Common prepaid expenses are insurance, rent, and supplies.

Liabilities.

Liabilities are current obligations, arising from past events, to make a future payment of assets or services. That is, liabilities are present debts and obligations. For example, businesses of all sizes usually borrow money and purchase merchandise inventory on credit. If a business borrows money to do such things as purchase equipment, it usually has a note payable for the amount borrowed. A **note payable** is supported by a written promise to pay a specific amount, generally principal plus interest, at a specific time, in the future. Obligations to pay cash to suppliers in the future are called **accounts payable**.

Sometimes customers might pay a business in advance of being provided a service or product. This advance by the customer is a liability, **unearned revenue**, as the business has an obligation to provide the service or product in the future. Unearned revenue arises when a professional sports team or musical act sells tickets in advance. Businesses may also have salaries payable to employees, Goods and Services Tax (GST/HST) payable and Provincial Sales Tax (PST) payable to the federal and provincial governments, and property taxes payable to the municipality.

Recall that persons or other businesses that are owed money by the business, such as suppliers and bankers, are called "creditors." A creditor who is not paid after a certain length of time has the legal right to force the liquidation of a business. In that case, the law requires that creditor claims be paid before ownership claims are paid.

Owner's Equity.

The owner's claim on the assets of the company is known as **owner's equity**. It is equal to total assets minus total liabilities. Since the claims of creditors must be paid before ownership claims, the owner's equity is often called "residual equity." If the equity is negative—that is, if total liabilities are more than total assets—the term "owner's deficiency" (or deficit) describes the shortage. Owner's equity is a general accounting term that could be used for any type of organization. It is used most frequently for proprietorships. Partnerships use the term "partners' equity"; corporations, such as Reitmans, use "shareholders' equity."

The Accounting Equation.

Alternative terminology The accounting equation is sometimes referred to as the *balance sheet equation* or the *fundamental accounting equation.*

The relationship between assets, liabilities, and owner's equity is expressed as an equation, called the **accounting equation**. Assets must equal the sum of liabilities and owner's equity. Liabilities are shown before owner's equity in the accounting equation because creditors' claims are paid before ownership claims if a business is liquidated. Illustration 1-5 shows the accounting equation for Reitmans at January 28, 2012.

ILLUSTRATION 1-5
Accounting equation

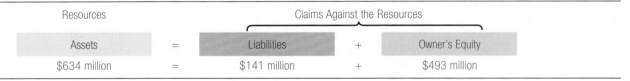

Resources		Claims Against the Resources		
Assets	=	Liabilities	+	Owner's Equity
$634 million	=	$141 million	+	$493 million

The accounting equation is the same for all economic entities regardless of their size, nature of business, or form of business organization. It applies to a small proprietorship such as a corner grocery store as much as it does to a large corporation such as Reitmans. Not only is the balance sheet based on the equation, but as we will see, the equation is the basis for recording and summarizing the economic events of a company.

Because the balance sheet is based on the accounting equation, you should never see a balance sheet where assets are not equal to liabilities plus owner's equity. If you do, it contains one or more errors. In that situation, we would say that the balance sheet is not balanced.

The accounting equation also shows that a business's assets are financed by a combination of debts owed to creditors (that is, liabilities) and the owner's investment (that is, equity).

Income Statement

Alternative terminology The income statement is sometimes called the *statement of earnings* or *statement of operations.*

Investors and creditors want to know if the business is generating a profit from its business activities. The main purpose of the **income statement** is to report the profitability of the business's operations over a specified period of time (a month, quarter, or year). **Profit** is measured by the difference between revenues and expenses. Profit results when revenues are greater than expenses and conversely a **loss** results when expenses are greater than revenues.

Revenues.

Revenues result from business activities that are done to earn profit, such as performing services, selling merchandise inventory, renting property out to tenants, and lending money. Revenues result in an increase in an asset (or a decrease in a liability when a customer has paid in advance) and an increase in owner's equity. They come from different sources and are given different names, depending on the type of business. Campus Pizza, for instance, has two categories of revenue: food sales and beverage sales. Common sources of revenue include sales, fees, services, commissions, interest, and rent.

Alternative terminology Profit is sometimes called *net income* or *earnings* or *net earnings*.

Expenses.

Expenses are the costs of assets that are consumed and services that are used in a company's business activities. Essentially, they can be thought of as the "costs of doing business" in the sense that they help a business generate revenue. Expenses are decreases in assets or increases in liabilities, excluding withdrawals made by the owners, and result in a decrease to owner's equity. Like revenues, there are many kinds of expenses and they are identified by various names, depending on the type of asset consumed or service used. For example, Campus Pizza recognizes (records) the following expenses: cost of ingredients (such as meat, flour, cheese, tomato paste, and mushrooms), cost of beverages, salaries expense, utilities expense (electric, gas, and water expense), telephone expense, delivery expense (such as gasoline, repairs, and licences), supplies expense (such as napkins, detergents, and aprons), rent expense, insurance expense, and interest expense.

Statement of Owner's Equity

The **statement of owner's equity** shows the changes in owner's equity for the same period of time as the income statement. In a proprietorship, owner's equity is increased by investments made by the owner and decreased by withdrawals made by the owner. Owner's equity is also increased when a business generates a profit from business activities or decreased if the business has a loss. Let's look at each of these equity components in more detail.

Investments.

Investments by the owner are contributions of cash or other assets (such as a vehicle or computer) made by the owners from their personal resources to the business. In a proprietorship, investments are recorded as increases to what is known as the owner's capital account. Accordingly, investments by owners result in an increase in an asset and an increase in owner's equity.

Drawings.

An owner may withdraw cash (or other assets) for personal use. In a proprietorship, these withdrawals could be recorded as a direct decrease to the owner's capital account. However, it is generally considered better to use a separate account classification called **drawings** so that the total withdrawals for the accounting period can be determined. Drawings result in a decrease in an asset and a decrease in owner's equity.

Helpful hint The owner of a business is not an employee. When the owner pays an employee it is recorded as an expense. When the owner pays herself, it is recorded as drawings. Since drawings do not represent a cost associated with generating revenue, they do not appear on the income statement.

Profit.

As previously explained, revenues increase owner's equity and expenses decrease owner's equity. We also learned that profit results from revenues being greater than expenses and a loss results if expenses are greater than revenues. Therefore, profit increases owner's equity and losses decrease owner's equity.

Illustration 1-6 summarizes the transactions that change owner's equity.

ILLUSTRATION 1-6
Transactions that increase and decrease owner's equity

Increases in owner's equity	Decreases in owner's equity
Investments by the owner	Drawings by the owner
Revenues	Expenses

We will see later in the chapter how this information is shown in the statement of owner's equity.

Cash Flow Statement

Alternative terminology The cash flow statement is sometimes called the *statement of cash flows.*

Investors and creditors need information on the business's ability to generate cash from its business activities and how the business uses cash. The **cash flow statement** gives information about the cash receipts and cash payments for a specific period of time. The cash flow statement gives answers to the following simple but important questions:

1. Where did the cash come from during the period?
2. What was the cash used for during the period?
3. What was the change in the cash balance during the period?

To help investors, creditors, and others analyze a company's cash, the cash flow statement reports the following: (1) the cash effects of the company's operating activities during a period; (2) the cash inflows and outflows from investing transactions (for example, the purchase and sale of land, buildings, and equipment); (3) the cash inflows and outflows from financing transactions (for example, borrowing and repayments of debt, and investments and withdrawals by the owner); (4) the net increase or decrease in cash during the period; and (5) the cash amount at the end of the period.

Accounting Differences by Type of Business Organization

Previously, you were introduced to different forms of business organizations: the proprietorship, partnership, and corporation. Basically, accounting for assets, liabilities, revenues, expenses, and cash flows is the same, regardless of the form of business organization. The main distinction between the forms of organizations is found in (1) the terminology that is used to name the equity section, (2) the accounting for the owner's investments and withdrawals, and (3) the name of the statement showing the changes in owner's equity. In Illustration 1-7, we summarize these differences.

ILLUSTRATION 1-7
Accounting differences by type of business organization

	Proprietorship	Partnership	Corporation
Equity section called:	Owner's equity	Partners' equity	Shareholders' equity
Investments by owners added to:	Owner's capital	Partners' capital	Share capital
Profits added to:	Owner's capital	Partners' capital	Retained earnings
Withdrawals by owners called:	Drawings	Drawings	Dividends
Withdrawals deducted from:	Owner's capital	Partners' capital	Retained earnings
Name of statement:	Statement of Owner's Equity	Statement of Partners' Equity	Statement of Retained Earnings (ASPE)
Statement of Comprehensive Income	Not allowed	Not allowed	Statement of Shareholders' Equity (IFRS): Not allowed under ASPE; required under IFRS

Helpful hint When using a capital or drawings account, it is good practice to include the owner's name as part of the account name. This is particularly important for partnerships, as each partner will have his or her own individual capital and drawings account.

In a proprietorship, equity is summarized and reported in a one-line capital account. In a partnership, equity is summarized and reported in separate one-line capital accounts for each partner. In a corporation, investments by all of the shareholders are grouped together and called "share capital." In a corporation, regardless of the number of shareholders, one account called Retained Earnings is used to record the accumulated profit (or earnings) of the company that has been retained (that is, not paid out to shareholders) in the company.

ASPE

A close examination of Reitmans' financial statements in Appendix A shows that, in addition to these statements, it has also prepared a Statement of Comprehensive Income. That is because Reitmans follows IFRS, not simply because it is a corporation. You will learn more about that statement in Chapter 14. For companies following ASPE, there is no such thing as a statement of comprehensive income.

THE EXPANDED ACCOUNTING EQUATION

The basic accounting equation in Illustration 1-5 simply shows that assets are equal to liabilities plus owner's equity. Recall that the basic equation is a summary of the information shown on the balance sheet. But we also know that it is necessary to report on revenues, expenses, and other changes in owner's equity. In Illustration 1-8, we have expanded the basic accounting equation to show the different parts of owner's equity and the relationship between revenues, expenses, profit (or loss), and owner's equity.

ILLUSTRATION 1-8
Expanded accounting equation

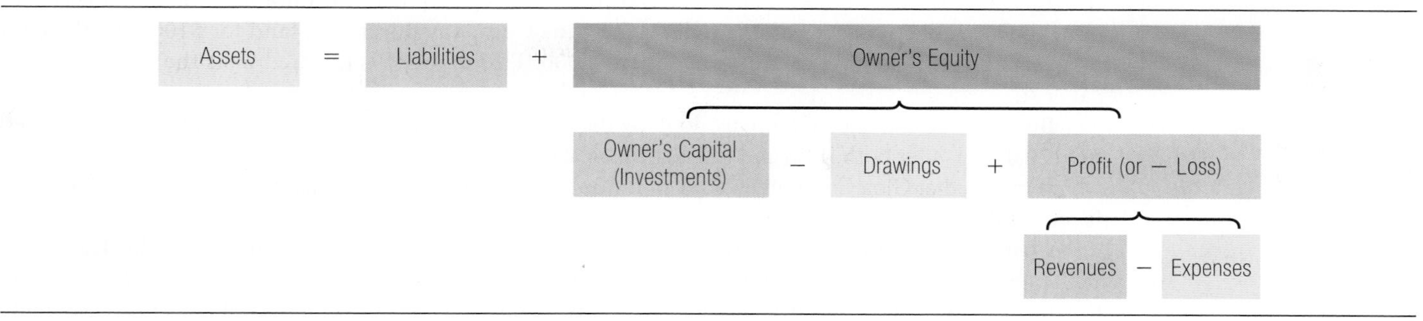

By expanding the equation, we have created a framework that can be used to report the information required in the income statement and the statement of owner's equity, as well as the balance sheet. The components in the expanded accounting equation are known as the **elements of the financial statements.**

Remember that the equation must always balance. Assets must equal liabilities plus owner's equity. From the expanded equation we can see that if revenue increases, owner's equity increases and therefore either assets increase or liabilities decrease to keep the equation balanced. Conversely, if expenses increase, owner's equity decreases and therefore either assets decrease or liabilities increase to keep the equation balanced.

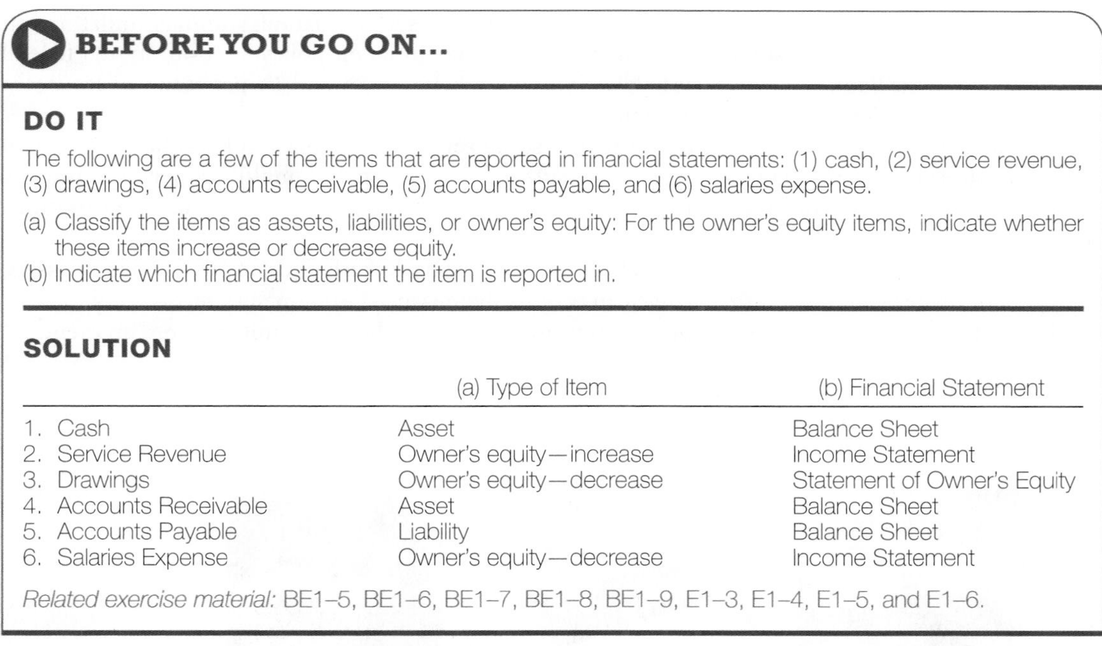

BEFORE YOU GO ON...

DO IT

The following are a few of the items that are reported in financial statements: (1) cash, (2) service revenue, (3) drawings, (4) accounts receivable, (5) accounts payable, and (6) salaries expense.

(a) Classify the items as assets, liabilities, or owner's equity: For the owner's equity items, indicate whether these items increase or decrease equity.
(b) Indicate which financial statement the item is reported in.

SOLUTION

	(a) Type of Item	(b) Financial Statement
1. Cash	Asset	Balance Sheet
2. Service Revenue	Owner's equity—increase	Income Statement
3. Drawings	Owner's equity—decrease	Statement of Owner's Equity
4. Accounts Receivable	Asset	Balance Sheet
5. Accounts Payable	Liability	Balance Sheet
6. Salaries Expense	Owner's equity—decrease	Income Statement

Related exercise material: BE1–5, BE1–6, BE1–7, BE1–8, BE1–9, E1–3, E1–4, E1–5, and E1–6.

Action Plan

- Understand that assets are resources that are capable of providing future service or benefit that are owned or controlled by a business.
- Understand that liabilities are amounts owed by a business.
- Review which transactions affect owner's equity.
- Recall what information is included in each of the financial statements.

THE NAVIGATOR

BUILDING THE FINANCIAL STATEMENTS

RECOGNITION AND MEASUREMENT

STUDY OBJECTIVE 4
Determine what events are recognized in the financial statements and how the events are measured.

The first step in preparing financial statements is to determine what the company should record. Not all events are recorded and reported in the financial statements. For example, suppose a new employee is hired. Should this event be recorded in the company's accounting records? The answer is no. Why? Only events that cause changes in assets, liabilities, or owner's equity should be recorded. These events are called **accounting transactions.** While the hiring of an employee will lead to future accounting transactions (for example, the payment of a salary after the work has been completed), an accounting transaction has not occurred at the time of hiring.

Recognition is the process of recording an asset, liability, revenue, or expense in the accounting records. Once a transaction has been recognized or recorded, it will be included in the financial statements. **Measurement** is the process of determining the amount that should be recognized. At the time something is acquired, the transaction is first measured at the amount of cash that was paid or at the value exchanged. For example, if the Gjoa Company purchased land for $100,000, the land is recorded in Gjoa's records at its cost of $100,000. This amount is referred to as the asset's historical cost.

Alternative terminology The cost principle is also known as the *historical cost principle.*

But what should Gjoa Company do if, by the end of the next year, the land's fair value has increased to $120,000? Under both IFRS and ASPE, historical cost is the primary basis used in financial statements, which means that Gjoa Company would continue to report the land at its historical cost of $100,000. This is often called the **cost principle**.

Cost has an important advantage over other valuations. Cost is definite and verifiable. The values exchanged at the time something is acquired can be objectively measured. Users can therefore rely on the information that is supplied, as they know it is based on fact. Cost is relevant if a business is a going concern and the asset is going to continue to be used in the business. What is relevant is, what did the business give up to acquire the asset to use in the business?

However, cost may not always be the most relevant measure of certain types of assets. Fair values may provide more useful information. For example, with an investment purchased for the purpose of trading to make a gain, the fair value of the investment provides more relevant information to the user. **Fair value** generally would be the amount the asset could be sold for in the market.

Fundamental to this discussion is that only transactions that can be reliably expressed as an amount of money can be included in the accounting records. This has been known as the **monetary unit assumption**. This assumption makes it possible for accounting to quantify (measure) economic events. In Canada, we mainly use the Canadian dollar to record these transactions. However, some companies report their results in U.S. dollars. In Europe, the euro (€) is used; in China, the yuan (CNY) is used; and so on.

The monetary unit assumption allows us to ignore the impact of inflation. Although inflation can be a significant accounting issue in some countries, Canada's inflation policy—set out by the federal government and the Bank of Canada—is to keep inflation at between 1% and 3% per year. Consequently, inflation is not considered an issue for accounting in Canada.

The monetary unit assumption does prevent some relevant information from being included in the accounting records. For example, the health of the owner, the quality of service, and the morale of employees would not be included, because they cannot be reliably quantified in monetary amounts.

In summary, a transaction is recognized in the accounting records if there is a change in assets, liabilities, or owner's equity and the change can be reliably measured in monetary terms.

Illustration 1-9 summarizes the process that is used to decide whether or not to record an event.

ILLUSTRATION 1-9
Transaction identification process

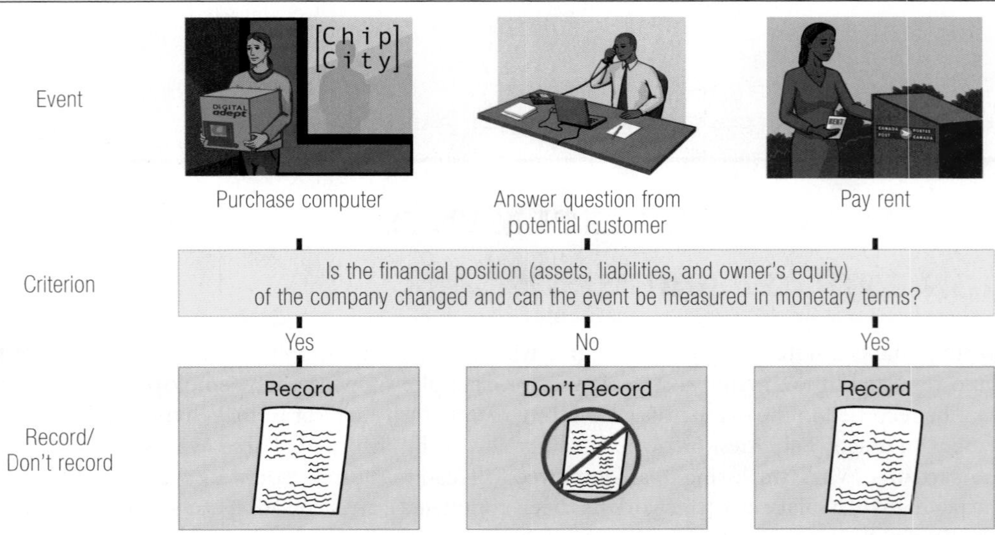

BEFORE YOU GO ON...

DO IT

For each of the following events, indicate if it should be recognized (recorded) in the accounting records. Explain your reason.

1. An auto repair shop received $10,000 cash from the bank, to be repaid in a year.
2. A consulting company paid $20,000 cash to purchase equipment.
3. A hockey team recruits a talented new player.

SOLUTION

1. The transaction will be recorded. There is a change in assets and liabilities and the amount can be reliably measured. The asset cash increased by $10,000. A liability increased because $10,000 is owed to the bank.
2. The transaction will be recorded. There is a change in two assets and the amount can be reliably measured. The asset cash decreased by $20,000 and the asset equipment increased by $20,000.
3. The event will not be recorded. The financial position of the business may have improved as the result of hiring this new hockey player; however, the team does not control the player and the change cannot be reliably measured.

Related exercise material: BE1–10, E1–7, and E1–8.

Action Plan

- Recall that only events that change an asset, liability, or owner's equity are recorded as accounting transactions.
- Determine if the event can be reliably quantified in monetary terms before recognizing it in the accounting records.

THE NAVIGATOR

TRANSACTION ANALYSIS

STUDY OBJECTIVE 5
Analyze the effects of business transactions on the accounting equation.

Once it has been determined that an event or transaction should be recognized, it must be analyzed for its effect on the components of the accounting equation before it can be recorded. This analysis must identify the specific items that are affected and the amount of change in each item.

Each transaction must have a dual effect on the equation for the two sides of the accounting equation to remain equal. For example, if an asset is increased, there must be a corresponding

1. decrease in another asset, or
2. increase in a liability, or
3. increase in owner's equity.

Two or more items could be affected by a transaction. For example, an asset (equipment) could increase by $10,000, a different asset (cash) could decrease by $6,000, and a liability (notes payable) could increase by $4,000.

As a general example, we will now look at transactions incurred by Softbyte, a computer programming business, during its first month of operations. You should study these transactions until you are sure you understand them. They are not difficult, but they are important to your success in this course. Being able to analyze how transactions affect the accounting equation is essential for understanding accounting.

To keep it simple, we will not include cents in the dollar amounts we record in the following analysis of Softbyte's transaction. In reality, it is important to understand that cents should be, and are, used when transactions are recorded in a company's internal accounting records.

Transaction (1): Investment by Owner.

Marc Doucet decides to open a computer programming business, which he names Softbyte. On September 1, 2014, he invests $15,000 cash in the business, which he deposits in a bank account opened under the name of Softbyte. This transaction results in an equal increase in both assets and owner's equity for Softbyte.

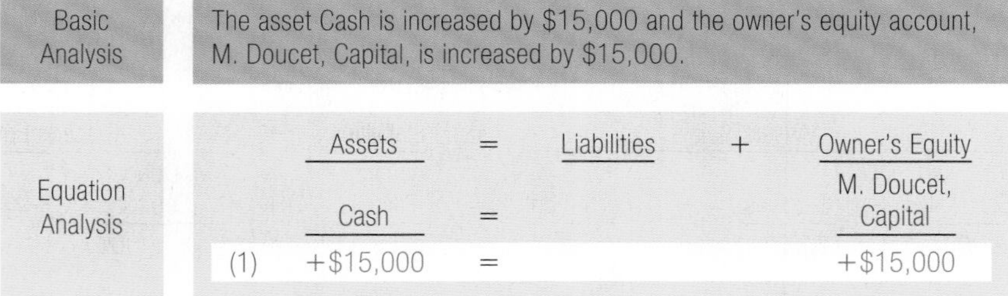

Basic Analysis	The asset Cash is increased by $15,000 and the owner's equity account, M. Doucet, Capital, is increased by $15,000.				
Equation Analysis		**Assets**	=	**Liabilities** +	**Owner's Equity**
		Cash	=		M. Doucet, Capital
	(1)	+$15,000	=		+$15,000

Notice that the two sides of the basic equation remain equal. Note also that investments by an owner are **not** revenues and are not included in calculating profit. The increase therefore has to be recorded as an investment in the owner's capital account rather than as revenue from operations.

Helpful hint Recall the economic entity concept: Marc's assets and equity *in the business* have increased as a result of his investment.

Transaction (2): Purchase of Equipment for Cash.

Softbyte purchases computer equipment for $7,000 cash. This transaction results in an increase in one asset with an equal decrease in another asset. Therefore, the total assets will not change. The specific effect of this transaction and the cumulative effect of the first two transactions are:

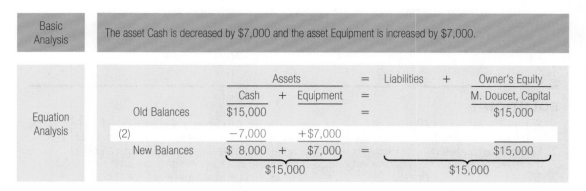

Basic Analysis: The asset Cash is decreased by $7,000 and the asset Equipment is increased by $7,000.

Equation Analysis:

		Assets			=	Liabilities	+	Owner's Equity
		Cash	+	Equipment	=			M. Doucet, Capital
	Old Balances	$15,000			=			$15,000
(2)		−7,000		+$7,000				
	New Balances	$ 8,000	+	$7,000	=			$15,000
		$15,000				$15,000		

Notice that total assets are still $15,000, and that Doucet's equity also remains at $15,000, the amount of his original investment.

Transaction (3): Purchase of Supplies on Credit.

Softbyte purchases $1,600 of computer paper and other supplies that are expected to last several months from the Chuah Supply Company. Chuah Supply agrees to allow Softbyte to pay this bill next month (in October). This transaction is referred to as a purchase on account, or a credit purchase. Assets are increased because of the expected future benefits of using the paper and supplies. Liabilities are increased by the amount that is due to Chuah Supply Company.

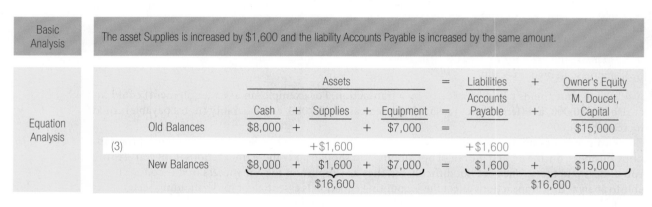

Basic Analysis: The asset Supplies is increased by $1,600 and the liability Accounts Payable is increased by the same amount.

Equation Analysis:

		Assets					=	Liabilities	+	Owner's Equity
		Cash	+	Supplies	+	Equipment	=	Accounts Payable	+	M. Doucet, Capital
	Old Balances	$8,000	+		+	$7,000	=			$15,000
(3)				+$1,600				+$1,600		
	New Balances	$8,000	+	$1,600	+	$7,000	=	$1,600	+	$15,000
		$16,600						$16,600		

Helpful hint A purchase on account will always result in an increase to a liability account (either Accounts Payable or Notes Payable).

Total assets are now $16,600. This total is matched by a $1,600 creditor's claim and a $15,000 ownership claim.

Transaction (4): Services Provided for Cash.

Softbyte receives $1,200 cash from customers for programing services it has provided. This transaction is Softbyte's main revenue-producing activity. Remember that revenue increases profit, which then increases owner's equity.

Basic Analysis: The asset Cash is increased by $1,200 and the owner's equity account Service Revenue is increased by $1,200.

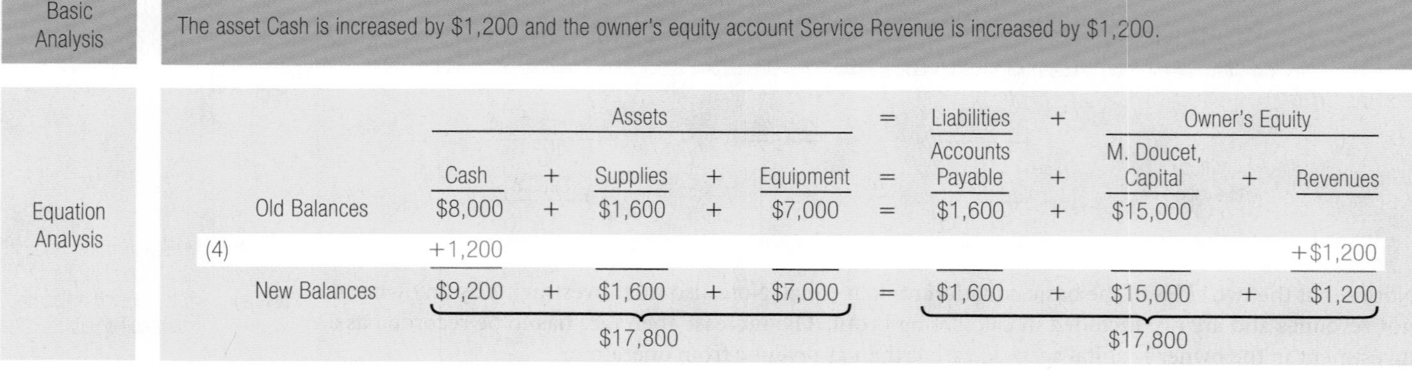

Equation Analysis:

		Assets					=	Liabilities	+	Owner's Equity		
		Cash	+	Supplies	+	Equipment	=	Accounts Payable	+	M. Doucet, Capital	+	Revenues
	Old Balances	$8,000	+	$1,600	+	$7,000	=	$1,600	+	$15,000		
(4)		+1,200										+$1,200
	New Balances	$9,200	+	$1,600	+	$7,000	=	$1,600	+	$15,000	+	$1,200
		$17,800						$17,800				

The two sides of the equation still balance at $17,800.

We don't have room to give details for each revenue and expense account in this illustration, so revenues (and expenses when we get to them) will be summarized under one column heading for Revenues and one for Expenses. However, it is important to keep track of the account titles that are affected (such as Service Revenue), as they will be needed when the income statement is prepared in the next section.

Transaction (5): Purchase of Advertising on Credit.

Softbyte receives a bill for $250 from the local newspaper for advertising the opening of its business. It postpones payment of the bill until a later date. The cost of advertising is an expense, and not an asset, because the benefits have already been used. Owner's equity decreases because an expense is incurred. Expenses reduce profit and owner's equity.

Basic Analysis: The liability Accounts Payable is increased by $250 and the owner's equity account Advertising Expense is increased by $250.

Equation Analysis:

	Assets			=	Liabilities +	Owner's Equity		
	Cash	+ Supplies	+ Equipment	=	Accounts Payable	+ M. Doucet, Capital	+ Revenues	− Expenses
Old Balances	$9,200	+ $1,600	+ $7,000	=	$1,600	+ $15,000	+ $1,200	
(5)					+$250			−$250
New Balances	$9,200	+ $1,600	+ $7,000	=	$1,850	+ $15,000	+ $1,200	− $250
	$17,800				$17,800			

The two sides of the equation still balance at $17,800. Note that, although the expense increases, this is shown as a negative number because expenses reduce owner's equity.

Not all expenses have to be paid in cash at the time they are incurred. When payment is made on the later date, the liability Accounts Payable will be decreased and the asset Cash will also be decreased [see transaction (8)].

Transaction (6): Services Provided for Cash and Credit.

Softbyte provides $3,500 of programming services for customers. Cash of $1,500 is received from customers, and the balance of $2,000 is billed to customers on account. This transaction results in an equal increase in assets and owner's equity.

Basic Analysis: Three specific items are affected: the asset Cash is increased by $1,500; the asset Accounts Receivable is increased by $2,000; and the owner's equity account Service Revenue is increased by $3,500.

Equation Analysis:

	Assets				=	Liabilities +	Owner's Equity		
	Cash	+ Accounts Receivable	+ Supplies	+ Equipment	=	Accounts Payable	+ M. Doucet, Capital	+ Revenues	− Expenses
Old Balances	$ 9,200		+ $1,600	+ $7,000	=	$1,850	+ $15,000	+ $1,200	− $250
(6)	+1,500	+$2,000						+3,500	
New Balances	$10,700	+ $2,000	+ $1,600	+ $7,000	=	$1,850	+ $15,000	+ $4,700	− $250
	$21,300					$21,300			

You might wonder why owner's equity is increased by $3,500 when only $1,500 has been collected. The reason is that the assets from earning revenues do not have to be in cash. Owner's equity is increased when revenues are earned. In Softbyte's case, revenues are earned when the service is provided. When collections on account are received at a later date, Cash will be increased and Accounts Receivable will be decreased [see transaction (9)].

Helpful hint When a company provides goods or services for a customer, it will record an increase to an asset (either Cash or a Receivable) and an increase to a revenue account.

Transaction (7): Payment of Expenses.

The expenses paid in cash for September are store rent, $600; salaries of employees, $900; and utilities, $200. These payments result in an equal decrease in assets and owner's equity.

Basic Analysis The asset Cash is decreased by $1,700 in total ($600 + $900 + $200) and owner's equity expense accounts are increased by the same amount, which then decreases owner's equity.

Equation Analysis

	Assets				=	Liabilities +	Owner's Equity		
	Cash	+ Accounts Receivable	+ Supplies	+ Equipment	=	Accounts Payable	+ M. Doucet, Capital	+ Revenues	− Expenses
Old Balances	$10,700	+ $2,000	+ $1,600	+ $7,000	=	$1,850	+ $15,000	+ $4,700	− $ 250
(7)	−600 −900 −200								−600 −900 −200
New Balances	$ 9,000	+ $2,000	+ $1,600	+ $7,000	=	$1,850	+ $15,000	+ $4,700	− $ 1,950
	$19,600					$19,600			

The two sides of the equation now balance at $19,600. Three lines are needed in the analysis in order to show the different types of expenses that have been paid. Note that total expenses increase but, as explained in transaction (5), it is shown as a negative number because expenses decrease owner's equity.

Transaction (8): Payment of Accounts Payable.

Softbyte pays its $250 advertising bill in cash. Remember that the bill was previously recorded in transaction (5) as an increase in Accounts Payable and a decrease in owner's equity.

Basic Analysis The asset Cash is decreased by $250 and the liability Accounts Payable is decreased by $250.

Equation Analysis

	Assets				=	Liabilities +	Owner's Equity		
	Cash	+ Accounts Receivable	+ Supplies	+ Equipment	=	Accounts Payable	+ M. Doucet, Capital	+ Revenues	− Expenses
Old Balances	$9,000	+ $2,000	+ $1,600	+ $7,000	=	$1,850	+ $15,000	+ $4,700	− $1,950
(8)	−250					−250			
New Balances	$8,750	+ $2,000	+ $1,600	+ $7,000	=	$1,600	+ $15,000	+ $4,700	− $1,950
	$19,350					$19,350			

Notice that the payment of a liability for an expense that has previously been recorded does not affect owner's equity. The expense was recorded in transaction (5) and should not be recorded again.

Transaction (9): Receipt of Cash on Account.

The sum of $600 in cash is received from some customers who were billed for services in transaction (6). This transaction does not change total assets, but it does change the composition of those assets.

Basic Analysis The asset Cash is increased by $600 and the asset Accounts Receivable is decreased by $600.

Equation Analysis

	Assets				=	Liabilities +	Owner's Equity		
	Cash	+ Accounts Receivable	+ Supplies	+ Equipment	=	Accounts Payable	+ M. Doucet, Capital	+ Revenues	− Expenses
Old Balances	$8,750	+ $2,000	+ $1,600	+ $7,000	=	$1,600	+ $15,000	+ $4,700	− $1,950
(9)	+600	−600							
New Balances	$9,350	+ $1,400	+ $1,600	+ $7,000	=	$1,600	+ $15,000	+ $4,700	− $1,950
	$19,350					$19,350			

Note that a collection of an account receivable for services that were billed and recorded earlier does not affect owner's equity. Revenue was already recorded in transaction (6) and should not be recorded again.

Transaction (10): Signed Contract to Rent Equipment in October.

Marc Doucet and an equipment supplier sign a contract for Softbyte to rent equipment for the months of October and November at the rate of $250 per month. Softbyte is to pay each month's rent at the start of the month. There is no effect on the accounting equation because the assets, liabilities, and owner's equity have not been changed by the signing of the contract. An accounting transaction has not occurred. At this point, Softbyte has not paid for anything, nor has it used the equipment, and therefore it has not incurred any expenses.

	Assets				=	Liabilities +	Owner's Equity		
	Cash	+ Accounts Receivable	+ Supplies	+ Equipment	=	Accounts Payable	+ M. Doucet, Capital	+ Revenues	− Expenses
Old Balances	$9,350 +	$1,400	+ $1,600	+ $7,000	=	$1,600	+ $15,000	+ $4,700	− $1,950
(10) No entry									
New Balances	$9,350 +	$1,400	+ $1,600	+ $7,000	=	$1,600	+ $15,000	+ $4,700	− $1,950
	$19,350					$19,350			

Note that the new balances are all identical to the old balances as nothing has changed.

Transaction (11): Withdrawal of Cash by Owner.

Marc Doucet withdraws $1,300 in cash from the business for his personal use. This transaction results in an equal decrease in assets and owner's equity.

Basic Analysis The asset Cash is decreased by $1,300, and the owner's equity account Drawings is increased by $1,300, which then decreases owner's equity, as follows:

Equation Analysis

	Assets				=	Liabilities +	Owner's Equity			
	Cash	+ Accounts Receivable	+ Supplies	+ Equipment	=	Accounts Payable	+ M. Doucet, Capital	− M. Doucet, Drawings	+ Revenues	− Expenses
Old Balances	$9,350 +	$1,400	+ $1,600	+ $7,000	=	$1,600	+ $15,000		+ $4,700	− $1,950
(11)	−1,300							−$1,300		
New Balances	$8,050 +	$1,400	+ $1,600	+ $7,000	=	$1,600	+ $15,000	− $1,300	+ $4,700	− $1,950
	$18,050					$18,050				

Note that both drawings and expenses reduce owner's equity, as shown in the accounting equation above. However, **owner's drawings are not expenses.** Expenses are incurred for the purpose of earning revenue and are reported in the income statement. Drawings do not generate revenue. They are a *disinvestment*; that is, the effect of an owner's cash withdrawal is the opposite of the effect of an owner's investment. Like owner's investments, drawings are not included in the determination of profit and are shown on the statement of owner's equity rather than the income statement.

Summary of Transactions

Softbyte's transactions are summarized in Illustration 1-10 to show their cumulative effect on the accounting equation. The transaction number and the specific effects of each transaction are indicated.

ILLUSTRATION 1-10
Tabular summary of Softbyte transactions

	Assets				=	Liabilities +	Owner's Equity			
	Cash	+ Accounts Receivable	+ Supplies	+ Equipment	=	Accounts Payable	+ M. Doucet, Capital	− M. Doucet, Drawings	+ Revenues	− Expenses
(1)	+$15,000						+$15,000			
(2)	−7,000			+$7,000						
(3)			+$1,600			+$1,600				
(4)	+1,200								+$1,200	
(5)						+250				−$ 250
(6)	+1,500	+$2,000							+3,500	
(7)	−600									−600
	−900									−900
	−200									−200
(8)	−250					−250				
(9)	+600	−600								
(10)	No entry									
(11)	−1,300							−$1,300		
	$ 8,050 +	$1,400	+ $1,600	+ $7,000	=	$1,600	+ $15,000	− $1,300	+ $4,700	− $1,950
	$18,050					$18,050				

The illustration demonstrates some significant facts.

1. Each transaction must be analyzed for its effects on:
   (a) the three components (assets, liabilities, and owner's equity) of the accounting equation, and
   (b) specific items within each component.
2. The two sides of the equation must always be equal.

This section on transaction analysis does not show the formal method of recording transactions. We will start illustrating that in Chapter 2. But understanding how transactions change assets, liabilities, and owner's equity is fundamental to understanding accounting and also business in general.

BEFORE YOU GO ON...

DO IT

Transactions for the month of August by Verma & Co., a public accounting firm, are shown below. Make a table that shows the effects of these transactions on the accounting equation, like the tabular analysis shown in Illustration 1-10.

1. The owner, Anil Verma, invested $25,000 of cash in the business.
2. Equipment was purchased on credit, $7,000.
3. Services were performed for customers for $8,000. Of this amount, $2,000 was received in cash and $6,000 is due on account.
4. Rent of $850 was paid for the month.
5. Customers on account paid $4,000 (see transaction 3).
6. The owner withdrew $1,000 of cash for personal use.

Action Plan

- Analyze the effects of each transaction on the accounting equation.
- Use appropriate account names for the account titles (not descriptions).
- Keep the accounting equation in balance.

SOLUTION

	Assets			=	Liabilities	+	Owner's Equity						
	Cash	+	Accounts Receivable	+	Office Equipment	=	Accounts Payable	+	A. Verma, Capital	−	A. Verma, Drawings	+	Revenues	−	Expenses
1.	+$25,000								+$25,000						
2.					+$7,000		+$7,000								
3.	+2,000		+$6,000										+$8,000		
4.	−850														−$850
5.	+4,000		−4,000												
6.	−1,000										−$1,000				
	$29,150	+	$2,000	+	$7,000	=	$7,000	+	$25,000	−	$1,000	+	$8,000	−	$850
	$38,150						$38,150								

Related exercise material: BE1–11, BE1–12, BE1–13, E1–9, E1–10, E1–11, and E1–12.

THE NAVIGATOR

PREPARING FINANCIAL STATEMENTS

STUDY OBJECTIVE 6
Prepare financial statements.

The next step in accounting is to prepare the financial statements. You will recall that these include the balance sheet, income statement, statement of owner's equity, and cash flow statement.

Illustration 1-11 shows Softbyte's statements prepared from the transaction analysis in Illustration 1-10 and how the statements are interrelated. It is important to note that because of the interrelationships of the financial statements, they are always prepared in the following order: (1) income statement, (2) statement of owner's equity, (3) balance sheet, and (4) cash flow statement.

The essential features of Softbyte's four financial statements, and their interrelationships, are briefly described in the following sections.

Helpful hint The income statement, statement of owner's equity, and cash flow statement all report information for a period of time. The balance sheet reports information at a point in time.

Income Statement

The income statement is prepared from the data in the owner's equity columns (specifically the Revenues and Expenses columns) of Illustration 1-10. The statement's heading names the company and type of statement, and to indicate that it applies to a period of time, the income statement date names the time period. For Softbyte, this appears as Month Ended September 30, 2014, which means the statement is for a one-month period—September 1 to 30, 2014.

ILLUSTRATION 1-11
Financial statements and their interrelationships

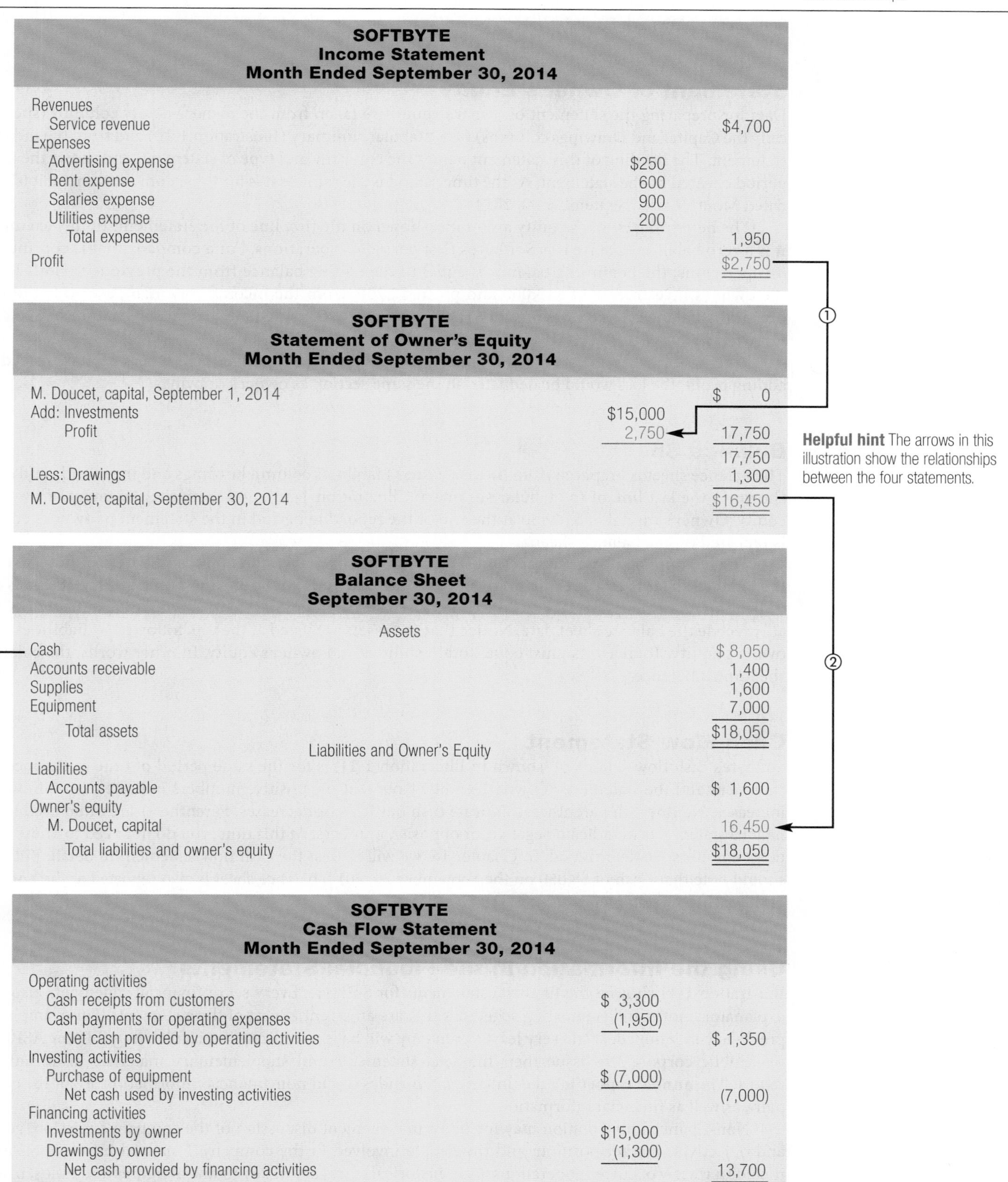

SOFTBYTE
Income Statement
Month Ended September 30, 2014

Revenues		
Service revenue		$4,700
Expenses		
Advertising expense	$250	
Rent expense	600	
Salaries expense	900	
Utilities expense	200	
Total expenses		1,950
Profit		$2,750

SOFTBYTE
Statement of Owner's Equity
Month Ended September 30, 2014

M. Doucet, capital, September 1, 2014		$ 0
Add: Investments	$15,000	
Profit	2,750	17,750
		17,750
Less: Drawings		1,300
M. Doucet, capital, September 30, 2014		$16,450

SOFTBYTE
Balance Sheet
September 30, 2014

Assets	
Cash	$ 8,050
Accounts receivable	1,400
Supplies	1,600
Equipment	7,000
Total assets	$18,050
Liabilities and Owner's Equity	
Liabilities	
Accounts payable	$ 1,600
Owner's equity	
M. Doucet, capital	16,450
Total liabilities and owner's equity	$18,050

SOFTBYTE
Cash Flow Statement
Month Ended September 30, 2014

Operating activities		
Cash receipts from customers	$ 3,300	
Cash payments for operating expenses	(1,950)	
Net cash provided by operating activities		$ 1,350
Investing activities		
Purchase of equipment	$ (7,000)	
Net cash used by investing activities		(7,000)
Financing activities		
Investments by owner	$15,000	
Drawings by owner	(1,300)	
Net cash provided by financing activities		13,700
Net increase in cash		8,050
Cash, September 1, 2014		0
Cash, September 30, 2014		$ 8,050

Helpful hint The arrows in this illustration show the relationships between the four statements.

On the income statement, revenues of $4,700 appear first, followed by a list of the expenses totalling $1,950. Finally, profit of $2,750 is determined. The income statement is always prepared first in order to determine the amount of profit (to be added to capital) or loss (to be subtracted from capital) in the Statement of Owner's Equity.

Statement of Owner's Equity

Data for preparing the statement of owner's equity are taken from the owner's equity columns (specifically the Capital and Drawings columns) of the tabular summary (Illustration 1-10) and from the income statement. The heading of this statement names the company and type of statement, and shows the time period covered by the statement. As the time period is the same as it is for the income statement, it is also dated Month Ended September 30, 2014.

The beginning owner's equity amount is shown on the first line of the statement. In this example, it is a zero balance because it is Softbyte's first period of operations. For a company that is continuing its operations, the beginning balance is equal to the ending balance from the previous period. Then the owner's investments of $15,000 and profit $2,750, from the income statement, are added to the beginning balance. Then drawings of $1,300 are deducted to calculate the ending balance of $16,450 in owner's equity.

What if Softbyte reported a loss in its first month? The loss would reduce owner's capital. Instead of adding profit, the loss would be deducted in the same section as owner's drawings.

Balance Sheet

The balance sheet is prepared from the Assets and Liabilities column headings and the month-end data shown in the last line of the tabular summary (Illustration 1-10), and from the statement of owner's equity. Owner's capital of $16,450 at the end of the reporting period in the statement of owner's equity is reported on the balance sheet.

The heading of a balance sheet must identify the company, statement, and date. To indicate that the balance sheet is at a specific point in time, the date only mentions the point in time (there is no indication of a time period). For Softbyte, the date is September 30, 2014. Sometimes, the words "as at" precede the balance sheet date. Notice that the assets are listed at the top, followed by liabilities and owner's equity. Total assets must equal total liabilities and owner's equity. In other words, the balance sheet must balance.

Cash Flow Statement

Softbyte's cash flow statement, shown in Illustration 1-11, is for the same period of time as the income statement and the statement of owner's equity. Note that the positive numbers indicate cash inflows or increases. Numbers in parentheses indicate cash outflows or decreases. Parentheses are often used in financial statements to indicate negative, or opposite, numbers. At this time, you do not need to know how these amounts are determined. In Chapter 16, we will look at the cash flow statement in detail. But you should note that Cash of $8,050 on the September 30, 2014, balance sheet is also reported at the bottom of the cash flow statement.

Using the Information in the Financial Statements

Illustration 1-11 showed the financial statements for Softbyte. Every set of financial statements also has explanatory notes and supporting schedules that are an essential part of the statements. For example, as previously mentioned, at the very least a company will have to indicate if it is following IFRS or ASPE.

Public corporations issue their financial statements and supplementary materials in an annual report. The **annual report** is a document that includes useful non-financial information about the company, as well as financial information.

Non-financial information may include a management discussion of the company's mission, goals, and objectives; market position; and the people involved in the company. Financial information may include a review of current operations and a historical summary of key financial figures and ratios, in addition to comparative financial statements. Public company financial statements are audited by a public accounting firm and include the auditors' report. There is also a statement of management responsibility for the statements.

Now is a good time to look again at Reitmans' financial statements in Appendix A. Carefully examine the format and content of each financial statement and compare them with Softbyte's financial statements in Illustration 1-11. What similarities can you find between Softbyte's financial statements and the more complicated financial statements for Reitmans?

You will see that Reitmans' transactions have been accumulated for the year ended January 28, 2012, and grouped together in categories. When similar transactions are grouped together, they are being reported in aggregate (in other words, summarized). By presenting recorded data in aggregate, the accounting information system simplifies a large number of transactions. As a result, the company's activities are easier to understand and are more meaningful. This simplification does mean less detail, however. Reitmans' financial statements are highly condensed and some critics might argue that the statements are too simple. Still, Reitmans is not the only organization that reports in this way. Most companies report condensed information for two reasons: it's simpler, and it also avoids revealing significant details to competitors.

You should note that financial statement amounts are normally rounded to the nearest dollar, thousand dollars, or million dollars, depending on the size of the company. Reitmans rounds its numbers to the nearest thousand dollars. This is done to remove unimportant detail and make the information easier for the reader to understand.

ACCOUNTING IN ACTION
ETHICS INSIGHT

What would you do if you suspected a co-worker was stealing? Would you confront them or tell your employer or the authorities? Would you keep quiet if you feared losing your job? What to do about suspected fraud is an ethical question facing not just those working in the accounting field, but employees in any role. Workplace fraud can take many forms. It could be an employee forging a cheque or stealing inventory. But it could also be an executive who "cooks the books" to make their department's sales figure look better, to meet company targets and collect a bonus, or to keep their job. Organizations need to send a strong message that they won't tolerate fraud. One way of doing that is to protect and encourage "whistleblowers"—employees who suspect fraud and report it to their employers. As an example, in 2007, the federal government passed the *Public Servants Disclosure Protection Act* to protect whistleblowers working in federal departments and agencies. The Ontario Securities Commission has proposed legislation to protect employees of public companies who blow the whistle to the regulator. Another way to discourage fraud is to set up an internal crime hotline for employees to report suspected wrongdoing. Alerting an employer to a possible fraud is not tattling—it could save employers millions of dollars and assure shareholders and the public that a company's financial statements are accurate.

Sources: Marjo Johne, "Don't Fall Victim to an Inside Job," *Globe and Mail*, December 14, 2011; David Malamed, "Whistle Where You Work?", *CA Magazine*, January/February 2012; Michael McKiernan, "Regulator at a Crossroads," *Canadian Lawyer*, April 2012.

What risks might you face as an employee and individual if you don't blow the whistle on fraud?

BEFORE YOU GO ON...

DO IT

Listed below, in alphabetical order, are the financial statement items for Park Accounting Services. Prepare an income statement, statement of owner's equity, and balance sheet for the month ended January 31, 2014.

Accounts payable	$ 5,000	M. Park, capital, January 1, 2014	$10,350
Accounts receivable	2,500	M. Park, drawings	3,000
Advertising expense	500	Prepaid rent	1,300
Cash	8,200	Rent expense	850
Equipment	10,000	Service revenue	11,000

BEFORE YOU GO ON... continued on next page

BEFORE YOU GO ON...
continued from previous page

Action Plan

- Understand what components are reported in the income statement, statement of owner's equity, and balance sheet.
- Each statement's heading includes the company name, the name of the statement, and a date line. The date line for the income statement and statement of owner's equity covers a specified period of time and the date line for the balance sheet is at a specific point in time.
- Understand that the profit reported in the income statement is added to the owner's capital in the statement of owner's equity.
- Understand that the owner's capital at the end of the period reported in the statement of owner's equity is reported in the owner's equity section of the balance sheet.

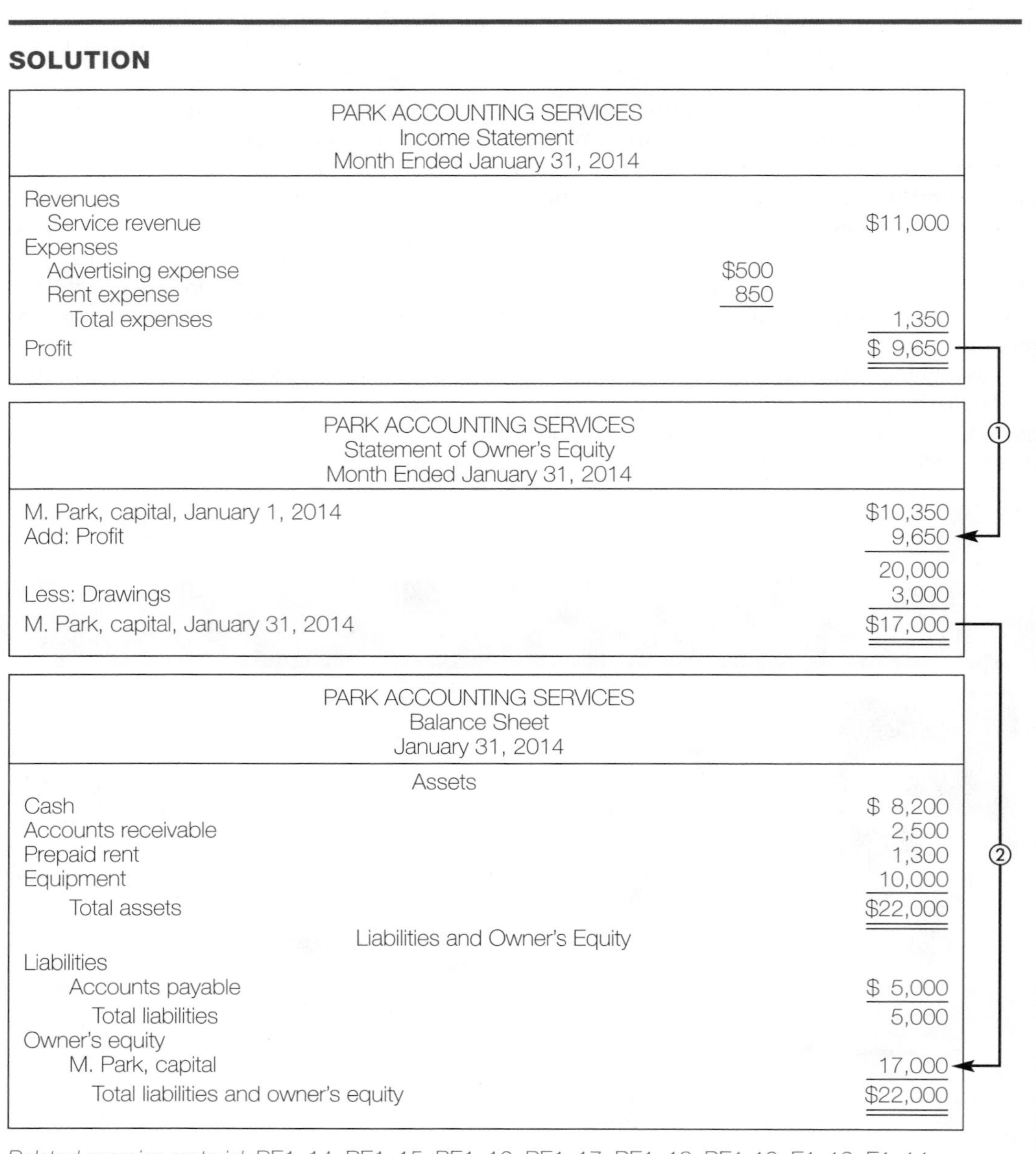

SOLUTION

PARK ACCOUNTING SERVICES
Income Statement
Month Ended January 31, 2014

Revenues		
Service revenue		$11,000
Expenses		
Advertising expense	$500	
Rent expense	850	
Total expenses		1,350
Profit		$ 9,650

PARK ACCOUNTING SERVICES
Statement of Owner's Equity
Month Ended January 31, 2014

M. Park, capital, January 1, 2014	$10,350
Add: Profit	9,650
	20,000
Less: Drawings	3,000
M. Park, capital, January 31, 2014	$17,000

PARK ACCOUNTING SERVICES
Balance Sheet
January 31, 2014

Assets	
Cash	$ 8,200
Accounts receivable	2,500
Prepaid rent	1,300
Equipment	10,000
Total assets	$22,000
Liabilities and Owner's Equity	
Liabilities	
Accounts payable	$ 5,000
Total liabilities	5,000
Owner's equity	
M. Park, capital	17,000
Total liabilities and owner's equity	$22,000

Related exercise material: BE1–14, BE1–15, BE1–16, BE1–17, BE1–18, BE1-19, E1–13, E1–14, E1–15, and E1–16.

THE NAVIGATOR

Comparing IFRS and ASPE

Key Differences	International Financial Reporting Standards (IFRS)	Accounting Standards for Private Enterprises (ASPE)
Accounting standards	Required for publicly accountable enterprises and optional for private enterprises	Private enterprises only
Level of accounting information required	Users require extensive detailed information	Users require less information
Equity reporting	Statement of Shareholders' Equity	• Proprietorships: Statement of Owner's Equity • Partnerships: Statement of Partners' Equity • Corporation: Statement of Retained Earnings
Income reporting	Income Statement and Statement of Comprehensive Income	Income Statement

DEMONSTRATION PROBLEM

Raman Balakra opens his own law office on July 1, 2014. During the first month of operations, the following transactions occurred:

1. Invested $11,000 of his personal savings in cash in the law practice.
2. Hired a legal assistant to work part-time for $500 per month.
3. Paid $800 for July rent on office space.
4. Purchased equipment on account, $3,000.
5. Provided legal services to clients for cash, $1,500.
6. Borrowed $700 cash from a bank on a note payable.
7. Provided legal services to a client on account, $2,000.
8. Collected $500 of the amount owed by a client on account (see transaction 7).
9. Paid monthly expenses: salaries, $500; telephone, $100; and utilities, $300.
10. Withdrew $1,000 cash for personal use.

Instructions

(a) Complete the chart showing the change resulting from these transactions.
(b) Prepare the income statement, statement of owner's equity, and balance sheet for Raman Balakra, Barrister & Solicitor.

The **Demonstration Problem** is a final review before you work on the assignment material. The problem-solving strategies in the margins give you tips about how to approach the problem. The solutions show both the form and the content of complete answers.

Action Plan

- Make sure that assets equal liabilities plus owner's equity in each transaction.
- Investments and revenues increase owner's equity. Withdrawals and expenses decrease owner's equity.
- Prepare the financial statements in the order listed.
- The income statement shows revenues and expenses for a period of time.

SOLUTION TO DEMONSTRATION PROBLEM

(a)

	Assets					=	Liabilities				Owner's Equity						
Transaction	Cash	+	Accounts Receivable	+	Equipment	=	Notes Payable	+	Accounts Payable	+	R. Balakra Capital	−	R. Balakra, Drawing	+	Revenues	−	Expenses
(1)	+$11,000										+$11,000						
(2) No Entry																	
(3)	−800																−$800
(4)					+$3,000				+$3,000								
(5)	+1,500														+$1,500		
(6)	+700						+$700										
(7)			+$2,000												+2,000		
(8)	+500		−500														
(9)	−500																−500
	−100																−100
	−300																−300
	−1,000												−$1,000				
	$11,000	+	$1,500	+	$3,000	=	$700	+	$3,000	+	$11,000	−	$1,000	+	$3,500	−	$1,700
			$15,500								$15,500						

SOLUTION TO DEMONSTRATION PROBLEM continued on next page

- Profit (or loss) is calculated on the income statement and carried forward to the statement of owner's equity.
- The statement of owner's equity shows the changes in owner's equity for the same period of time as the income statement.
- The owner's capital at the end of the period is carried forward from the statement of owner's equity to the balance sheet.
- The balance sheet reports assets, liabilities, and owner's equity at a specific date.

SOLUTION TO DEMONSTRATION PROBLEM continued from previous page

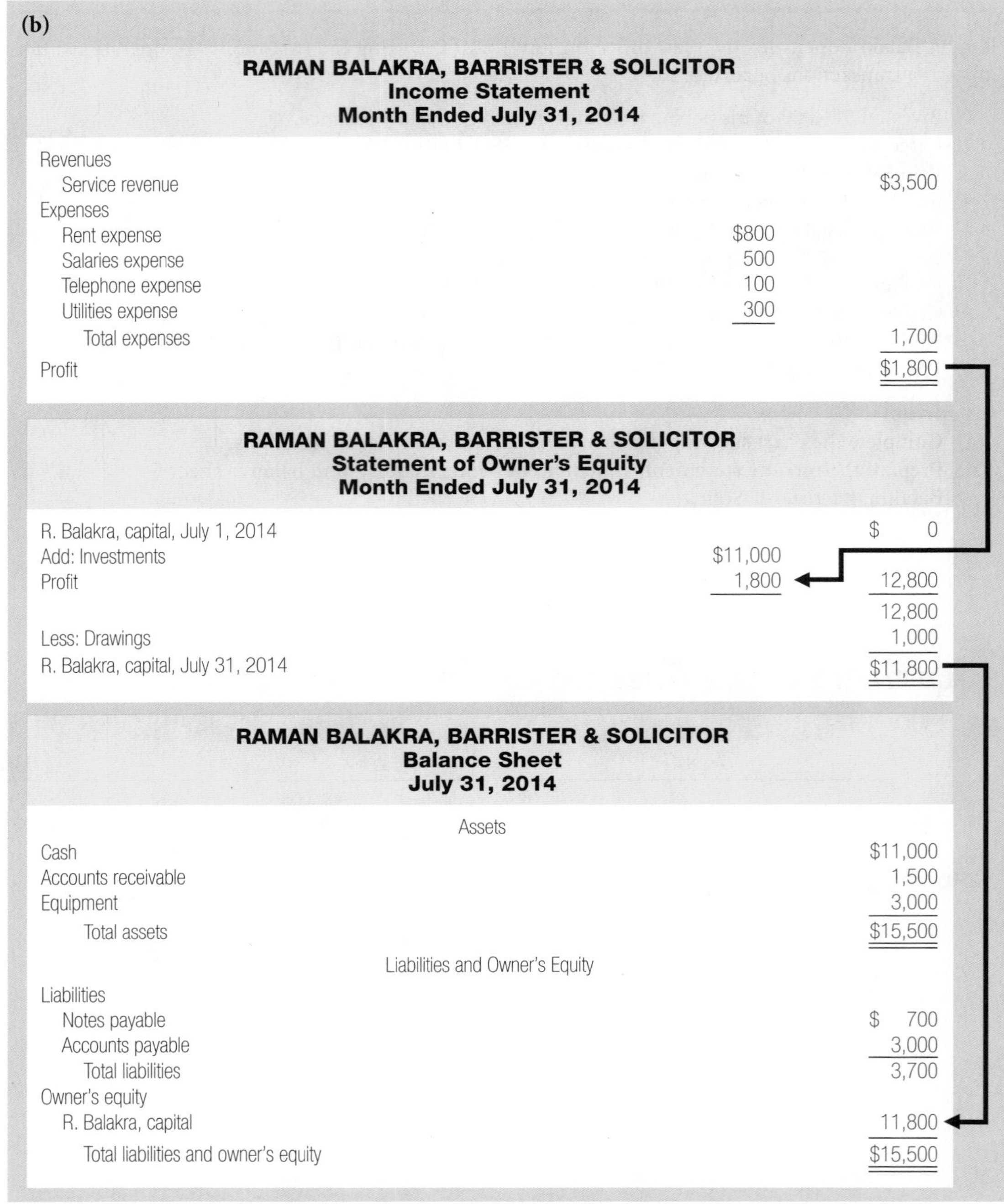

(b)

RAMAN BALAKRA, BARRISTER & SOLICITOR
Income Statement
Month Ended July 31, 2014

Revenues		
Service revenue		$3,500
Expenses		
Rent expense	$800	
Salaries expense	500	
Telephone expense	100	
Utilities expense	300	
Total expenses		1,700
Profit		$1,800

RAMAN BALAKRA, BARRISTER & SOLICITOR
Statement of Owner's Equity
Month Ended July 31, 2014

R. Balakra, capital, July 1, 2014		$ 0
Add: Investments	$11,000	
Profit	1,800	12,800
		12,800
Less: Drawings		1,000
R. Balakra, capital, July 31, 2014		$11,800

RAMAN BALAKRA, BARRISTER & SOLICITOR
Balance Sheet
July 31, 2014

Assets	
Cash	$11,000
Accounts receivable	1,500
Equipment	3,000
Total assets	$15,500
Liabilities and Owner's Equity	
Liabilities	
Notes payable	$ 700
Accounts payable	3,000
Total liabilities	3,700
Owner's equity	
R. Balakra, capital	11,800
Total liabilities and owner's equity	$15,500

THE NAVIGATOR

Summary of Study Objectives

1. ***Identify the use and users of accounting and the objective of financial reporting.*** Accounting is the information system that identifies, records, and communicates the economic events of an organization to a wide variety of interested users. Good accounting is important to people both inside and outside the organization. Internal users, such as management, use accounting information to plan, control, and evaluate business operations. External users include investors and creditors, among others. Accounting data are used by investors (owners or potential owners) to decide whether to buy, hold, or sell their financial interests. Creditors (suppliers and bankers) evaluate the risks of granting credit or lending money based on the accounting information. The objective of financial reporting is to provide useful information to investors and creditors to make these decisions. Users need information about the business's ability to earn a profit and generate cash. For our economic system to function smoothly, reliable and ethical accounting and financial reporting are critical.

2. ***Compare different forms of business organizations and explain how Canadian accounting standards apply to these organizations.*** The most common examples of business organizations

are proprietorships, partnerships, and corporations. Generally accepted accounting principles are a common set of guidelines that are used to prepare and report accounting information. In Canada, there are two sets of standards for profit-oriented businesses. Publicly accountable enterprises follow International Financial Reporting Standards (IFRS) and private enterprises have the choice of following IFRS or Accounting Standards for Private Enterprises (ASPE).

The economic entity concept requires the business activities of each economic entity to be kept separate from the activities of its owner and other economic entities. The going concern assumption presumes that a business will continue operations for enough time to use its assets for their intended purpose and to fulfill its commitments.

3. ***Describe the components of the financial statements and explain the accounting equation.*** Assets, liabilities, and owner's equity are reported in the balance sheet. Assets are resources owned or controlled by a business that are expected to provide future services or benefits. Liabilities are current obligations arising from past events to make future payments of assets or services. Owner's equity is the owner's claim on the company's assets and is equal to total assets minus total liabilities. The balance sheet is based on the accounting equation: Assets = Liabilities + Owner's Equity.

   The income statement reports the profit or loss for a specified period of time. Profit is equal to revenues minus expenses. Revenues are the increase in assets, or decrease in liabilities, that result from business activities that are done to earn profit. Expenses are the cost of assets consumed or services used in a company's ordinary business activities. They are decreases in assets or increases in liabilities, excluding withdrawals made by the owners, and result in a decrease to owner's equity.

   The statement of owner's equity summarizes the changes in owner's equity during the period. Owner's equity is increased by investments by the owner and profits. It is decreased by drawings and losses. Investments are contributions of cash or other assets by owners. Drawings are withdrawals of cash or other assets from the business for the owner's personal use. Owner's equity in a partnership is referred to as partners' equity and in a corporation as shareholders' equity.

   A cash flow statement summarizes information about the cash inflows (receipts) and outflows (payments) for a specific period of time.

4. ***Determine what events are recognized in the financial statements and how the events are measured.*** Only events that cause changes in assets, liabilities, or owner's equity are recorded. Recognition is the process of recording items and measurement is the process of determining the amount that should be recognized. The cost principle states that assets should be recorded at their historical (original) cost. Fair value may be a more appropriate measure for certain types of assets. Generally fair value is the amount the asset could be sold for in the market. The monetary unit assumption requires that only transaction data that can be expressed as an amount of money be included in the accounting records, and it assumes that the monetary unit is stable.

5. ***Analyze the effects of business transactions on the accounting equation.*** Each business transaction must have a dual effect on the accounting equation. For example, if an individual asset is increased, there must be a corresponding (1) decrease in another asset, (2) increase in a liability, and/or (3) increase in owner's equity.

6. ***Prepare financial statements.*** The income statement is prepared first. Expenses are deducted from revenues to calculate the profit or loss for a specific period of time. Then the statement of owner's equity is prepared using the profit or loss reported in the income statement. The profit is added to (losses are deducted from) the owner's equity at the beginning of the period. Drawings are then deducted to calculate owner's equity at the end of the period. A balance sheet reports the assets, liabilities, and owner's equity of a business as at the end of the accounting period. The owner's equity at the end of period, as calculated in the statement of owner's equity, is reported in the balance sheet in the owner's equity section.

THE NAVIGATOR

Glossary

Accounting The information system that identifies, records, and communicates the economic events of an organization to a wide variety of interested users. (p. 4)

Accounting equation Assets = Liabilities + Owner's Equity. (p. 12)

Accounting Standards for Private Enterprises (ASPE) A set of standards developed by the Accounting Standards Board (AcSB) that may be used for financial reporting by private enterprises in Canada. (p. 9)

Accounting transaction An economic event that is recorded in the accounting records because it changes the assets, liabilities, or owner's equity items of the organization. (p. 15)

Accounts payable A liability created by buying services or products on credit. It is an obligation to pay cash to a supplier in the future. (p. 12)

Accounts receivable An asset created when selling services or products to customers who promise to pay cash in the future. (p. 11)

Annual report Information that a corporation gives each year to its shareholders and other interested parties about its operations and financial position. It includes the financial statements and auditors' report, in addition to information and reports by management. (p. 24)

Assets Resources owned or controlled by a business that are expected to provide future services or benefits. (p. 11)

Balance sheet A financial statement that reports the assets, liabilities, and owner's equity at a specific date. (p. 11)

Cash flow statement A financial statement that provides information about the cash receipts and cash payments for a specific period of time. (p. 14)

Corporation A business organized as a separate legal entity under corporation law, with ownership divided into transferable shares. (p. 8)

Cost principle An accounting principle that states that assets should be recorded at their historical (original) cost. (p. 16)

Creditors All of the persons or entities that a company owes money to. (p. 5)

Drawings Withdrawals of cash or other assets from an unincorporated business for the owner's personal use. Drawings result in a decrease in an asset and a decrease in owner's equity. (p. 13)

Economic entity concept The concept that the accounting for an economic entity's activities be kept separate and distinct from the accounting for the activities of its owner and all other economic entities. (p. 10)

Elements of the financial statements The components in the financial statements. Assets, liabilities, owner's equity, revenues, and expenses. (p. 15)

Expenses The cost of assets consumed or services used in a company's ordinary business activities. Expenses are decreases in assets or increases in liabilities, excluding withdrawals made by the owners, and result in a decrease to owner's equity. (p. 13)

Fair value Generally the amount the asset could be sold for in the market assuming the company is a going concern, not the amount that a company would receive in an involuntary liquidation or distress sale. (p. 16)

Generally accepted accounting principles (GAAP) An accepted set of accounting standards that includes broad principles and practices, as well as rules and procedures. These standards indicate how to report economic events. (p. 9)

Going concern assumption An assumption that a company will continue to operate in the foreseeable future. (p. 10)

Income statement A financial statement that presents the revenues and expenses and resulting profit (or loss) for a specific period of time. (p. 12)

International Financial Reporting Standards (IFRS) A set of global standards developed by the International Accounting Standards Board (IASB) used for financial reporting by publicly accountable enterprises. (p. 9)

Investments by the owner The increase in owner's equity that results from assets put into the business by the owner. (p. 13)

Investors Owners or potential owners of a business. (p. 5)

Liabilities Current obligations, arising from past events, to make future payments of assets or services. (p. 12)

Limited liability The legal principle that the owners' liability for the debts of the business is limited to the amount they invested in the business. (p. 8)

Loss The amount by which expenses are greater than revenues. A loss decreases owner's equity. (p. 13)

Measurement The process of determining the amount that should be recognized. (p. 16)

Monetary unit assumption An assumption that states that only transaction data that can be expressed as an amount of money may be included in the accounting records. It is also assumed that the monetary unit is stable. (p. 16)

Note payable A liability supported by a written promise to pay a specific amount, with interest, at a specific time, in the future. (p. 12)

Owner's equity The owner's claim on the assets of the company, which is equal to total assets minus total liabilities. (p. 12)

Partnership An association of two or more persons to carry on as co-owners of a business for profit. (p. 8)

Prepaid expense The asset created when a business pays cash for costs incurred in advance of being used or consumed. (p. 12)

Profit The amount by which revenues are greater than expenses. Profit increases owner's equity. (p. 13)

Proprietorship A small business owned by one person. (p. 8)

Publicly accountable enterprises Publicly traded companies, as well as securities brokers and dealers, banks, and credit unions whose role is to hold assets for the public as part of their primary business. (p. 9)

Recognition The process of recording a transaction in the accounting records. (p. 16)

Revenues The increase in assets, or decrease in liabilities, that result from business activities that are done to earn profit; result in an increase in owner's equity. (p. 13)

Statement of owner's equity A financial statement that summarizes the changes in owner's equity for a specific period of time. (p. 13)

Unearned revenue The liability created when a customer pays in advance of being provided a service or product. (p. 12)

Unlimited liability The principle that the owners of a business are personally liable (responsible) for all debts of the business. (p. 8)

Self-Study Questions

Answers are at the end of the chapter.

Notes in the margin beside end-of-chapter questions tell you what **study objectives** the question relates to and which **learning style** in Bloom's taxonomy the question uses.

(SO 1) K 1. The main objective of the financial statements is to provide useful information to
   (a) government in deciding if the company is respecting tax laws.
   (b) increase the value of the company.
   (c) investors and creditors that is useful when they are making decisions about the business.
   (d) management that is useful when they are making decisions about the business.

(SO 2) K 2. Which of the following characteristics are related to corporations as opposed to partnerships and proprietorships?
   (a) Simple to form, unlimited legal liability, limited life
   (b) Limited legal liability, limited life, income taxes on profit paid by the organization
   (c) More than one owner, income taxes on profit paid by the owners, unlimited legal liability
   (d) Income taxes paid by the organization, limited legal liability, indefinite life

(SO 2) K 3. Which of the following statements about International Financial Reporting Standards (IFRS) is correct?
   (a) All Canadian enterprises must follow IFRS.
   (b) Under IFRS, companies that operate in more than one country must produce separate financial statements for each of those countries.

(c) All Canadian publicly accountable enterprises must use IFRS.
(d) Canadian private enterprises are not allowed to use IFRS. They must use ASPE.

(SO 2) C 4. Which of the following statements about the going concern assumption is correct?
(a) The going concern assumption is the assumption that the economic entity will continue to operate in the future.
(b) Under the going concern assumption, all of the business's assets must be reported at their fair value.
(c) The financial statements must report whether or not a company is a going concern.
(d) The going concern assumption is not followed under ASPE.

(SO 3) C 5. Which of the following items is not reported on the statement of owner's equity?
(a) Investments by the owner
(b) Drawings
(c) Profit
(d) Revenues

(SO 3) AP 6. As at December 31, after its first year of operations, Stoneland Company has assets of $8,500; revenues of $6,000; expenses of $3,500; owner's capital of $5,000; and drawings of $500. What are the liabilities for Stoneland Company as at December 31?
(a) $1,500
(b) $2,500
(c) $500
(d) $3,500

(SO 4) K 7. Which of the following best describes when an event should be recognized in the accounting records?
(a) An event should be recognized in the accounting records if there is a change in assets, liabilities, or owner's equity and the change can be measured in monetary terms.
(b) An event should be recognized in the accounting records if it involves an interaction between the company and another external entity.
(c) Where there is uncertainty about a future event occurring or not, it should not be recognized.
(d) Accountants use tradition to determine which events to recognize.

(SO 5) AP 8. Genesis Company buys a $10,000 machine on credit. Initially, this transaction will only affect the:
(a) income statement.
(b) balance sheet.
(c) income statement and statement of owner's equity.
(d) income statement, statement of owner's equity, and balance sheet.

(SO 5) AP 9. Bing Company pays $700 for store rent for the month. The basic analysis of this transaction on the accounting records is:
(a) the asset Cash is increased by $700 and the expense Rent Expense is increased by $700.
(b) the asset Cash is decreased by $700 and the expense Rent Expense is increased by $700.
(c) the asset Cash is decreased by $700 and the liability Rent Payable is increased by $700.
(d) the asset Cash is increased by $700 and the liability Rent Payable is decreased by $700.

(SO 6) C 10. Which of the following statements about the income statement and balance sheet is correct?
(a) The income statement and the balance sheet both show information as at a specific point in time.
(b) The income statement shows information as at a specific point in time; the balance sheet shows information for a specified time period.
(c) The income statement and the balance sheet both show information for a specified time period.
(d) The income statement shows information for a specified time period; the balance sheet shows information as at a specific point in time.

THE NAVIGATOR

Questions

(SO 1) C 1. "Accounting is ingrained in our society and it is vital to our economic system." How is this statement true?

(SO 1) C 2. Why should everyone study accounting whether they are going to be an accountant or not?

(SO 1) C 3. Distinguish between internal and external users of accounting data. Include in your answer what kinds of questions both internal and external users might want answered.

(SO 1) K 4. What is the main objective of financial reporting?

(SO 1) C 5. Why is ethics important to the accounting profession? To statement users?

(SO 2) C 6. Explain the differences between the following forms of business organization: (a) proprietorship, (b) partnership, (c) public corporation, and (d) private corporation.

(SO 2) C 7. Veronica argues that all Canadian companies should follow the same set of generally accepted accounting principles. Explain to Veronica why there are two sets of standards for profit-oriented enterprises in Canada and how she can tell what standards the company is using.

(SO 2) K 8. What is the economic entity concept?

(SO 3) K 9. What is the accounting equation and what is its purpose?

(SO 3) K 10. (a) Define assets, liabilities, and owner's equity. (b) Of the following items—revenues, expenses, drawings and investments—which ones increase owner's equity? Which ones decrease owner's equity?

(SO 3) K 11. What is the difference between Accounts Payable and Accounts Receivable?

(SO 3) K 12. What are revenues and expenses and how do they affect profit?

(SO 3) K 13. Amal can never remember which accounts belong on the balance sheet and which accounts belong on the income statement. Provide Amal with an explanation that will help her remember what to do.

(SO 4) C 14. Wayne thinks that all events must be recognized in the accounting records. He argues that, if they aren't recognized, the records will be incomplete. Explain to Wayne why he is incorrect and provide him with two examples of events that are not recorded.

(SO 4) C 15. What is the monetary unit assumption? What type of information is not included in the financial statements because of this assumption?

(SO 5) C 16. Can a business have a transaction in which only the left (assets) side of the accounting equation is affected? If yes, give an example.

(SO 5) AP 17. Paul Dumas withdrew $10,000 from his business, Dumas Pharmacy, which is organized as a proprietorship. Dumas' accountant recorded this withdrawal as an increase in an expense and a decrease in cash. Is this treatment correct? Why or why not?

(SO 6) C 18. A company's profit appears directly on the income statement and the statement of owner's equity. It is also included indirectly in the company's balance sheet. Do you agree or disagree? Explain.

(SO 6) C 19. André is puzzled as he reads **Reitmans'** financial statements. He notices that the numbers have all been rounded to the nearest thousand. He thought financial statements were supposed to be accurate and he is now wondering what happened to the rest of the money. Respond to André's concern.

When the financial results of **real companies** are used in the end-of-chapter material, the company's name is shown in red.

Brief Exercises

Activity statements in the margin beside Brief Exercises, Exercises, and Problems describe what the question asks you to do.

Identify users of accounting information. **(SO 1) K**

BE1–1 A list of decisions made by different users of accounting information follows:

1. Decide whether the company pays fair salaries.
2. Decide whether the company can pay its obligations.
3. Decide whether a marketing proposal will be cost-effective.
4. Decide whether the company's profit will permit an increase in drawings.
5. Decide how the company should finance its operations.

The different users are identified in the table that follows. (a) Insert the number (1–5) of the kind of decision described above that each user would likely make. (b) Indicate whether the user is internal or external.

User	(a) Kind of Decision	(b) Internal or External User
Owner		
Marketing manager		
Creditor		
Chief financial officer		
Labour union		

Discuss ethical issues. **(SO 1) AN**

BE1–2 Describe an ethical dilemma that each of the following individuals might encounter:

(a) A student in an introductory accounting course
(b) A production supervisor
(c) A salesperson
(d) A banker
(e) The prime minister of Canada

Identify forms of business organization. **(SO 2) C**

BE1–3 Match each of the following forms of business organization with the correct set of characteristics: proprietorship (PP), partnership (P), and corporation (C).

(a) ________ Shared control; combined skills and resources
(b) ________ Easier to transfer ownership and raise funds; no personal liability; entity pays income tax
(c) ________ Simple to set up; founder keeps control

BE1–4 For each of the following statements, indicate whether the statement is true or false by placing a T or an F in the blank at the start of each statement.

Identify application of IFRS and ASPE. **(SO 2) C**

(a) ________ Canadian publicly accountable enterprises have the choice to report under IFRS or ASPE.
(b) ________ All private enterprises must follow ASPE.
(c) ________ There are more requirements to provide information in the financial statements under ASPE than under IFRS.
(d) ________ Companies are required to include a note in their financial statements stating if they are using IFRS or ASPE.
(e) ________ Using IFRS may help Canadian public companies attract investors from around the globe.

BE1–5 Match the following components with the best description below and indicate if the component is reported on the balance sheet (BS) or income statement (IS).

Identify the components of the financial statements. **(SO 3) (C)**

1. Assets
2. Liabilities
3. Owner's Equity
4. Revenues
5. Expenses
6. Profit

Description	Component	Balance Sheet or Income Statement
(a) The increase in assets, or decrease in liabilities, resulting from business activities done to earn profit.		
(b) Resources owned or controlled by a business that are expected to provide future benefits.		
(c) The owner's claim on the resources of the company.		
(d) Current obligations to make future payments of assets or services.		
(e) The cost of resources consumed or services used in the company's business activities.		

BE1–6 Presented below is the accounting equation. Determine the missing amounts:

Solve accounting equation. **(SO 3) AP**

Assets	=	Liabilities	+	Owner's Equity
$75,000		$24,000		(a)
(b)		$150,000		$91,000
$89,000		(c)		$52,000

BE1–7 Use the accounting equation to answer each of the following questions:

Solve accounting equation. **(SO 3) AP**

(a) Greenway Co. has total assets of $600,000 and its owner's equity is equal to one third of its total assets. What is the amount of Greenway Co.'s liabilities?
(b) May Company has liabilities of $280,000. The balance in C. May, Capital, is $130,000; in C. May, Drawings, $40,000; revenues, $440,000; and expenses, $330,000. What is the amount of May Company's total assets?
(c) Fereira Company has total assets of $90,000. The balance in Sharon Fereira's Capital is $35,000; in drawings, $7,000; revenues, $55,000; and expenses, $45,000. What is the amount of the company's total liabilities?

BE1–8 Butler Company is owned by Rachel Butler. The company had total assets of $850,000 and total liabilities of $550,000 at the beginning of the year. Answer each of the following independent questions:

Solve accounting equation. **(SO 3) AP**

(a) During the year, total assets increased by $130,000 and total liabilities decreased by $80,000. What is the amount of owner's equity at the end of the year?
(b) Total liabilities decreased by $95,000 during the year. The company incurred a loss of $40,000. R. Butler made an additional investment of $100,000 and made no withdrawals. What is the amount of total assets at the end of the year?
(c) During the year, total assets increased by $100,000. Profit was $185,000. There were no additional owner's investments, but R. Butler withdrew $50,000. What is the amount of total liabilities at the end of the year?
(d) Total assets increased by $45,000, and total liabilities decreased by $50,000. There were no additional owner's investments, and R. Butler withdrew $40,000. What is the amount of profit or loss for the year?

Identify assets, liabilities, and owner's equity. **(SO 3) AP**

BE1–9 Below are some items found in the financial statements of Stefan Knoler, MD. Indicate (a) whether each of the following items is an asset (A), liability (L), or part of owner's equity (OE); and (b) which financial statement—income statement (IS), statement of owner's equity (SOE), or balance sheet (BS)—it would be reported on. The first one has been done for you as an example.

	(a)	(b)
1. Accounts receivable	A	BS
2. Salaries payable	______	______
3. Salaries expense	______	______
4. Supplies	______	______
5. Supplies expense	______	______
6. S. Knoler, capital	______	______
7. Service revenue	______	______
8. Equipment	______	______
9. Notes payable	______	______
10. Cash	______	______
11. Prepaid expense	______	______
12. S. Knoler, drawings	______	______

Identify GAAP concepts. **(SO 2, 4) C**

BE1–10 Match each of the following terms with the best description below:

1. Cost principle
2. Generally accepted accounting principles
3. Going concern assumption
4. Economic entity concept
5. Monetary unit assumption

(a) ______ Transactions are recorded in terms of units of money.
(b) ______ Transactions are recorded based on the actual amount received or paid.
(c) ______ Accounting for a business excludes any personal transactions of the owner and the transactions of any other entity.
(d) ______ The broad principles and practices, as well as rules and procedures, that indicate how to report economic events.
(e) ______ Businesses are expected to continue operating indefinitely.

Determine effects of transactions on accounting equation. **(SO 5) AP**

BE1–11 Presented below are eight business transactions. Indicate whether the transactions increased (+), decreased (−), or had no effect (NE) on each element of the accounting equation.

(a) Purchased $250 of supplies on account.
(b) Performed $500 of services on account.
(c) Paid $300 of operating expenses.
(d) Paid $250 cash on account for the supplies purchased in item 1 above.
(e) Invested $1,000 cash in the business.
(f) Owner withdrew $400 cash.
(g) Hired an employee to start working the following month.
(h) Received $500 from a customer who had been billed previously in item (b) above.
(i) Purchased $450 of equipment in exchange for a note payable.

Use the following format, in which the first one has been done for you as an example:

			Owner's Equity			
Transaction	Assets	Liabilities	Capital	Drawings	Revenues	Expenses
1	+$250	+$250	NE	NE	NE	NE

Compare and contrast the characteristics of expenses and drawings. **(SO 3, 5) AN**

BE1–12 Place the number corresponding to each of the following characteristics in the appropriate section of the diagram. If a characteristic applies to both expenses and drawings, place that number in the intersection or overlapping section of the diagram.

1. Appears on the income statement.
2. Appears on the statement of owner's equity.
3. Represents a decrease in owner's equity.
4. Is part of the equation for calculating profit.
5. Increases on the debit side.

BE1–13 Match the following basic transaction analysis with the best description of the economic event.

Match basic transaction analysis with transaction description. **(SO 5) AP**

1. Cash increased by $10,000 and the owner's equity account, D. Morris, Capital, is increased by $10,000.
2. Cash is decreased by $2,500 and the asset account Prepaid Insurance is increased.
3. Supplies is increased by $1,000 and the liability account Accounts Payable is increased by $1,000.
4. Accounts receivable is increased by $500 and the revenue account Service Revenue is increased by $500.
5. Cash is decreased by $1,000 and the liability account Accounts Payable is decreased by $1,000.
6. Cash is increased by $500 and the account Accounts Receivable is decreased by $500.

Description	Transaction Analysis
(a) Cash collected on account.	______
(b) Owner invests cash in the business.	______
(c) Supplies are purchased on account.	______
(d) Company provides service on account.	______
(e) Payment on account made to supplier.	______
(f) Company purchases an insurance policy.	______

BE1–14 Classify each of the following items as owner's investments (I), drawings (D), revenue (R), expenses (E), or as having no effect on owner's equity (NE):

Determine effects of transactions on owner's equity. **(SO 3, 5) AP**

(a) ______ Costs incurred for advertising
(b) ______ Commission earnings
(c) ______ Equipment received from the company owner
(d) ______ Amounts paid to employees
(e) ______ Cash paid to purchase equipment
(f) ______ Services performed on account
(g) ______ Rent received
(h) ______ Utilities incurred
(i) ______ Cash withdrawn by company owner
(j) ______ Collection of an account receivable
(k) ______ Cash collected in advance of providing service

BE1–15 Presented below is information from the statements of owner's equity for Kerkan Consulting for the first three years of operation. Determine the missing amounts.

Determine missing items in owner's equity. **(SO 3, 6) AP**

	2013	2014	2015
J. Kerkan, capital, January 1	$0	$68,000	(c)
Investment in the year	50,000	0	20,000
Profit (loss) for the year	25,000	(b)	17,000
Drawings in the year	(a)	33,000	12,000
J. Kerkan, capital, December 31	68,000	65,000	(d)

BE1–16 Clinton Enterprises' statement of owner's equity showed the following balances for the owner's capital account:

Calculate profit from information on the statement of owner's equity. **(SO 6) AP**

1. Beginning of the year: $225,000
2. End of the year: $260,000
   (a) If the owner made no additional investments or withdrawals, what is the profit for the year?
   (b) Assume instead the owner made an additional investment of $10,000 but no withdrawals during the year. What is the profit for the year?
   (c) Assume instead the owner made an additional investment of $5,000 and a withdrawal of $7,000. What is the profit for the year?

BE1–17 Prairie Company is owned and operated by Natasha Woods. In alphabetical order below are the financial statement items for Prairie Company. Using the appropriate items, prepare an income statement for the month ended October 31, 2014.

Prepare an income statement. **(SO 6) AP**

Accounts payable	$90,000	N. Woods, capital, October 1, 2014	$36,000
Accounts receivable	77,500	N. Woods, drawings	6,000
Advertising expense	3,600	Rent expense	2,600
Cash	59,300	Service revenue	23,000

Prepare a statement of owner's equity. **(SO 6) AP**

BE1–18 Refer to the data in BE1–17. Using these data and the information from Prairie's income statement, prepare a statement of owner's equity.

Prepare a balance sheet. **(SO 6) AP**

BE1–19 Refer to the data in BE1–17. Using these data and the information from Prairie's statement of owner's equity prepared in BE1–18, prepare a balance sheet for Prairie Company.

Exercises

Identify users and uses of accounting information. **(SO 1) C**

E1–1 Roots Canada Ltd., a private company, is known around the world for its clothing and accessories. It has more than 120 stores in Canada and the United States, and more than 40 locations in Asia.

Instructions

(a) Identify two internal users of Roots' accounting information. Write a question that each user might try to answer by using accounting information.
(b) Identify two external users of Roots' accounting information. Write a question that each user might try to answer by using accounting information.

Relate concepts to forms of business organization. **(SO 2) C**

E1–2 Listed below are several statements regarding different forms of business organization.

Instructions

For each statement, indicate if that statement is true or false for each of the forms of business organizations by placing a T or an F in each column.

	Proprietorship	Partnership	Publicly Traded Corporation
(a) Owners have limited liability.	_______	_______	_______
(b) Records of the business are combined with the personal records of the owner or owners.	_______	_______	_______
(c) Required to follow IFRS.	_______	_______	_______
(d) Entity pays income taxes on its profits.	_______	_______	_______
(e) Owners are called "shareholders."	_______	_______	_______
(f) Will have more than one owner.	_______	_______	_______
(g) Entity has a limited life.	_______	_______	_______
(h) The entity has a separate legal existence from its owners.	_______	_______	_______

Match words with descriptions. **(SO 1, 2, 3) K**

E1–3 Here are some terms from the chapter:

1. Accounts payable
2. Expenses
3. Creditor
4. International Financial Reporting Standards (IFRS)
5. Prepaid expense
6. Profit
7. Assets
8. Corporation
9. Unearned revenue
10. Generally accepted accounting principles
11. Accounts receivable
12. Owner's equity

Instructions

Match each term with the best description that follows:

(a) _______ A company that raises money by issuing shares
(b) _______ An accepted set of accounting standards that includes broad principles, practices, rules, and procedures
(c) _______ Obligations to suppliers of goods
(d) _______ Amounts due from customers
(e) _______ Owner's claims against the company's resources
(f) _______ Payment of cash for costs incurred in advance of being used
(g) _______ A business that a company owes money to
(h) _______ Resources owned by a business that have the ability to provide a future benefit
(i) _______ The set of accounting standards that all publicly accountable enterprises in Canada have to follow
(j) _______ Results when revenues exceed expenses
(k) _______ The cost of assets consumed or services used in a company's ordinary business activities
(l) _______ A liability arising when a customer pays in advance of receiving service

E1–4 Summaries of selected data for three companies follow. Three items are missing from each summary.

Determine missing items. **(SO 3) AP**

	Midway Company	Ferris Company	Wheel Company
Beginning of year:			
Total assets	$ 95,000	$162,000	(g)
Total liabilities	72,000	(d)	30,000
Total owner's equity	(a)	85,000	33,000
End of year:			
Total assets	110,000	(e)	79,000
Total liabilities	(b)	61,000	42,000
Total owner's equity	37,000	98,000	(h)
Changes during year in owner's equity:			
Investments by owner	(c)	0	5,000
Drawings	22,000	(f)	25,000
Total revenues	179,000	99,000	85,000
Total expenses	$150,000	48,000	(i)

Instructions

Determine the missing amounts.

E1–5 Shane Cooke began a business, Cooke Company, on January 1, 2012, with an investment of $100,000. The company had the following assets and liabilities on the dates indicated:

Calculate profit (or loss). **(SO 3) AP**

December 31	Total Assets	Total Liabilities
2012	$370,000	$210,000
2013	440,000	290,000
2014	525,000	355,000

Instructions

Use the accounting equation and the change in owner's equity during the year to calculate the profit (or loss) for:

(a) 2012, assuming Shane Cooke's drawings were $50,000 for the year.
(b) 2013, assuming Shane Cooke made an additional investment of $40,000 and had no drawings in 2013.
(c) 2014, assuming Shane Cooke made an additional investment of $10,000 and his drawings were $60,000 for the year.

E1–6 Below are some items found in the financial statements of Peter Zizler, Orthodontist.

Classify accounts. **(SO 3) C**

	(a)	(b)
1. Accounts payable	L	BS
2. Accounts receivable		
3. Cash		
4. Equipment		
5. Interest payable		
6. Interest revenue		
7. Interest expense		
8. Investment by the owner		
9. Service revenue		
10. Prepaid rent		
11. P. Zizler, capital (opening balance)		
12. P. Zizler, drawings		
13. Salaries expense		
14. Supplies		
15. Supplies expense		
16. Unearned revenue		

Instructions

Indicate (a) whether each of the above items is an asset (A), liability (L), or part of owner's equity (OE); and (b) which financial statement—income statement (IS), statement of owner's equity (SOE), or balance sheet (BS)—it would be reported on. The first one has been done for you as an example.

Identify GAAP. **(SO 2, 4) C**

E1–7 Stanley Company, a proprietorship owned by Dave Stanley, had the following selected business transactions during the year:

1. Land with a cost of $208,000 was reported at its fair value of $260,000.
2. A lease agreement to rent equipment from an equipment supplier starting next year was signed. The rent is $500 per month and the lease is for two years. Payments are due at the start of each month. Nothing was recorded in Stanley Company's accounting records when the lease was signed.
3. Stanley paid the rent for an apartment for Dave's personal use and charged it to Rent Expense.
4. Stanley wanted to make its profit look worse than it really was, so it adjusted its expenses upward to include the effects of inflation.
5. Stanley included a note in its financial statements stating the company is a going concern and is following ASPE.

Instructions

(a) In each situation, identify whether the accounting treatment is correct or not, and why.
(b) If it is incorrect, state what should have been done.

Determine events to be recognized. **(SO 4) C**

E1–8 The following is a list of independent events:

1. A company pays $10,000 cash to purchase equipment at a bankruptcy sale. The equipment's fair value is $15,000.
2. A Canadian company purchases equipment from a company in the United States and pays US $5,000 cash. When the Canadian company went to its bank to buy a bank draft for US $5,000 to pay for the equipment, it cost them $5,200 Canadian.
3. A company provides $4,000 of services to a new customer on account.
4. A company hires a new chief executive officer, who will bring significant economic benefit to the company. The company agrees to pay the new executive officer $500,000 per year.
5. A company signs a contract to provide $10,000 of services to a customer. The customer pays the company $4,000 cash at the time the contract is signed.

Instructions

(a) Should the transaction be recorded in the accounting records? Explain why or why not.
(b) If the transaction should be recorded, indicate the amount. Explain.

Give examples of transactions. **(SO 5) C**

E1–9 A list of effects on the accounting equation follows.

1. Increases an asset and increases a liability.
2. Increases an asset and increases owner's equity.
3. Decreases an asset and decreases a liability.
4. Decreases owner's equity and decreases an asset.
5. Increases a liability and decreases owner's equity.
6. Increases one asset and decreases another asset.

Instructions

For each effect, give an example of a transaction that would cause it.

Analyze effects of transactions for new company. **(SO 5) AP**

E1–10 Here are the transactions for Great Gardens during August, its first month of operations:

1. Holly Sevigny, the owner, made a $25,000 cash investment to start business.
2. Purchased equipment for $7,000. Paid $2,000 cash and signed a note for the balance.
3. Incurred $250 of advertising expense on account.
4. Billed customers for services performed, $3,200.
5. Holly Sevigny withdrew cash for her personal use, $2,000.
6. Received $2,100 from customers billed in transaction 4.
7. Received $3,000 cash from customers for work to be performed in September.
8. Received $1,000 cash from customers for services performed.
9. Paid $250 for advertising expense incurred in transaction 3.
10. Paid $700 for a 12-month insurance policy starting September 1.

Instructions

Prepare a tabular analysis of the above transactions, as shown in Illustration 1-10 in the text.

Analyze effects of transactions for existing company. **(SO 5) AP**

E1–11 At the beginning of March, Brister Software Company had Cash of $12,000, Accounts Receivable of $18,000, Accounts Payable of $4,000, and G. Brister, Capital of $26,000. During the month of March, the following transactions occurred:

1. Purchased equipment for $23,000 from Digital Equipment. Paid $3,000 cash and signed a note payable for the balance.
2. Received $12,000 from customers for contracts billed in February.
3. Paid $3,000 for March rent of office space.
4. Paid $2,500 of the amounts owing to suppliers at the beginning of March.
5. Provided software services to Brie Construction Company for $7,000 cash.
6. Paid BC Hydro $1,000 for energy used in March.
7. G. Brister withdrew $5,000 cash from the business.
8. Paid Digital Equipment $2,100 on account of the note payable issued for the equipment purchased in transaction 1. Of this, $100 was for interest expense.
9. Hired an employee to start working in April.
10. Incurred advertising expense on account for March, $1,500.

Instructions

Prepare a tabular analysis of the above transactions, as shown in Illustration 1-10 in the text. The first row contains the amounts the company had at the beginning of March.

Analyze transactions. Calculate profit and increase in owner's equity. **(SO 5) AP**

E1–12 A tabular summary of the transactions for Star & Co., an accounting firm, for its first month of operations, July 2014, follows:

	Cash	+ Accounts Receivable	+ Prepaid Insurance	+ Equipment	= Accounts Payable	+ B. Star, Capital	− B. Star, Drawings	+ Revenues	− Expenses
1	$18,000			$6,000		$24,000			
2	−4,000			8,000	$4,000				
3	−750		$750						
4	3,500	$4,800						$8,300	
5	−2,000				−2,000				
6	−3,300						−$3,300		
7	−800								−800 Rent
8	1,350	−1,350							
9	−2,700								−2,700 Salaries
10					420				−420 Utilities

Instructions

(a) Describe each transaction that occurred in the month.
(b) Calculate the amount of profit for the month.
(c) Calculate the increase in owner's equity for the month.

Prepare financial statements. **(SO 6) AP**

E1–13 An analysis of transactions for Star & Co. for July 2014 was presented in E1–12.

Instructions

Prepare an income statement and statement of owner's equity for July and a balance sheet at July 31.

Prepare income statement and statement of owner's equity. **(SO 6) AP**

E1–14 Atlantic Cruise Co. is owned by Irina Temelkova. The following information is an alphabetical listing of financial statement items for the company for the year ended May 31, 2014:

Accounts payable	$ 49,000	Interest expense	$ 20,000
Accounts receivable	42,000	Investments by owner	6,000
Advertising expense	3,500	Maintenance expense	83,000
Cash	19,400	Notes payable	400,000
Equipment	120,000	Prepaid insurance	1,200
Food, fuel, and other expenses	65,500	Salaries expense	128,000
I. Temelkova, capital, June 1, 2013	275,000	Ships	550,000
I. Temelkova, drawings	35,000	Supplies	15,000
Insurance expense	2,400	Ticket revenue	355,000

Instructions

Prepare an income statement and a statement of owner's equity for the year.

Prepare balance sheet. **(SO 6) AP**

E1–15 Refer to the financial information in E1–14 for the Atlantic Cruise Co. at May 31, 2014.

Instructions

Prepare the balance sheet.

Calculate profit and owner's equity and prepare balance sheet. (SO 6) AP

E1–16 Judy Cumby is the sole owner of Deer Park, a public camping ground near Gros Morne National Park. Judy has gathered the following financial information for the year ended March 31, 2014:

Revenues—camping fees	$150,000	Revenues—general store	$ 40,000
Operating expenses	150,000	Cash on hand	9,400
Supplies on hand	2,500	Original cost of equipment	110,000
Fair value of equipment	125,000	Notes payable	70,000
Accounts payable	11,500	J. Cumby, capital, April 1, 2013	17,000
Accounts receivable	21,000	J. Cumby, drawings	5,000
Camping fees collected for April	10,000	Insurance paid for in advance for April to June, 2014	600

Instructions

(a) Calculate Deer Park's profit for the year.
(b) Calculate Judy's owner's equity at March 31.
(c) Prepare a balance sheet at March 31.

Problems: Set A

Identify users and uses of accounting information. (SO 1) S

P1–1A Specific financial decisions often depend more on one type of accounting information than another. Consider the following independent, hypothetical situations:

1. Pierson Industries is thinking about extending credit to a new customer. The terms of credit would require the customer to pay within 45 days of receipt of the goods.
2. An investor is considering purchasing a company called Organic Food Solutions Ltd. The investor plans on owning the company for at least five years.
3. The president of Hi-tech Adventure Limited is trying to determine whether the company is generating enough cash to increase the amount of dividends paid to shareholders and still have enough cash to buy additional equipment when needed.
4. Standen Bank is thinking about extending a loan to a small company. The company would be required to make interest payments at the end of each year for five years, and to repay the loan at the end of the fifth year.

Taking It Further is an extra question at the end of each problem designed to challenge you to think beyond the basic concepts covered in the problem, and to provide written explanations. Your teacher may assign problems with or without this extra element.

Instructions

(a) Identify types of user(s) of accounting information in each situation and indicate if they are external or internal.
(b) For each situation, state whether the user making the decision would depend mostly on information about (1) the business's economic resources and claims to the resources, or (2) the economic performance of the business. Justify your choice.

TAKING IT FURTHER Why is it important to users of financial statements to know that the statements have been prepared by individuals who have high standards of ethical behaviour?

Determine forms of business organization and type of accounting standards. (SO 2) AP

P1–2A Five independent situations follow:

1. Tom Courtney, a student looking for summer employment, started a dog-walking business. He picks up the dog while its owner is at work and returns it after a walk.
2. Joseph Counsell and Sabra Surkis each own a bike shop. They have decided to combine their businesses and try to expand their operations to include snowboards. They expect that in the coming year they will need funds to expand their operations.
3. Three chemistry professors have formed a business that uses bacteria to clean up toxic waste sites. Each has contributed an equal amount of cash and knowledge to the venture. The use of bacteria in this situation is experimental, and legal obligations could result.
4. Abdur Rahim has run a successful but small organic food store for over five years. The increased sales at his store have made him believe the time is right to open a chain of organic food stores across the country. Of course, this will require a substantial investment for inventory and equipment, as well as for employees and other resources. Abdur has minimal personal savings.
5. Evelyn Church, Amaan Abu, and Brenda Gorny have recently passed their professional accounting exams. They have decided to start an accounting practice in their hometown.

Instructions

(a) In each case, explain what form of organization the business is likely to take: proprietorship, partnership, or corporation. Give reasons for your choice.

(b) In each case indicate what accounting standards, IFRS or ASPE, the business is likely to use in its financial statements. Give reasons for your choice.

TAKING IT FURTHER Frequently, individuals start a business as a proprietorship and later incorporate the business. What are some of the advantages of doing this?

P1–3A The following selected data are for Perron Importers Limited for its first three years of operations:

Determine missing items. **(SO 3) AP**

	2013	2014	2015
January 1:			
Total assets	$ 40,000	$ (f)	(j)
Total liabilities	0	50,000	(k)
Total owner's equity	(a)	75,000	(l)
December 31:			
Total assets	(b)	140,000	172,000
Total liabilities	50,000	(g)	65,000
Total owner's equity	(c)	97,000	(m)
Changes during year in owner's equity:			
Investments by owner during the year	7,000	0	(n)
Drawings by owner during the year	15,000	(h)	36,000
Profit or loss for the year	(d)	40,000	(o)
Total revenues for the year	132,000	(i)	157,000
Total expenses for the year	(e)	95,000	126,000

Instructions

Determine the missing amounts.

TAKING IT FURTHER What information does the owner of a company need in order to decide whether he or she is able to withdraw cash from the business?

P1–4A Listed in alphabetical order, the following selected items (in thousands) were taken from Sunrise Cruise Ltd.'s December 31 financial statements:

Classify accounts and prepare accounting equation. **(SO 3) AP**

1.	L	BS	Accounts payable	$ 2,598	12.	______	______	Other assets	$ 905
2.	______	______	Accounts receivable	869	13.	______	______	Other expenses	4,650
3.	______	______	Cash	1,700	14.	______	______	Other liabilities	1,735
4.	______	______	Equipment	26,785	15.	______	______	Other revenue	230
5.	______	______	Food service revenues	5,500	16.	______	______	Passenger revenues	19,765
6.	______	______	Fuel expense	1,750	17.	______	______	Port fee expense	429
7.	______	______	G. Hirsch, capital, Jan. 1	2,738	18.	______	______	Salaries expense	5,675
8.	______	______	G. Hirsch, drawings	2,500	19.	______	______	Supplies	550
9.	______	______	Interest expense	675	20.	______	______	Unearned passenger revenues	2,000
10.	______	______	Maintenance expense	1,578					
11.	______	______	Notes payable	13,500					

Instructions

(a) In each case, identify on the blank line in the first column whether the item is an asset (A), liability (L), capital (C), drawings (D), revenue (R), or expense (E) item. The first one has been done for you as an example.

(b) Indicate on the blank line in the second column which financial statement—income statement (IS), statement of owner's equity (SOE), or balance sheet (BS)—each item would be reported on. The first one has been done for you as an example.

(c) Show the amounts in Sunset Cruise's accounting equation by calculating the value of total assets, total liabilities, and total owner's equity at December 31.

TAKING IT FURTHER Is it important for Sunset Cruise to keep track of its different types of revenues as separate items? Explain.

P1–5A Four independent situations follow:

Assess accounting treatment. **(SO 2, 4) C**

1. Human Solutions Incorporated believes its people are its most significant asset. It estimates and records their value on its balance sheet.

2. Sharon Barton, president and owner of Barton Industries, has instructed the accountant to report the company's land and buildings at its current value of $500,000 instead of its cost of $350,000. "Reporting the land and buildings at $500,000 will make it easier to get a loan from the bank next month," Sharon states.
3. Will Viceira, owner of the Music To You Company, bought an electric guitar for his personal use. He paid for the guitar with company funds and debited the equipment account.
4. Colour Photo Company is potentially on the verge of bankruptcy and the accountant is preparing its financial statements. The accountant advises the owner that it will be necessary to include a note to this effect in the financial statements.

Instructions

(a) For each of the above situations, determine if the accounting treatment of the situation is correct or incorrect. Explain why.
(b) If the accounting treatment is incorrect, explain what should be done.

TAKING IT FURTHER Why is it important for companies to follow generally accepted accounting principles when preparing their financial statements?

Analyze transactions and calculate owner's equity.
(SO 3, 5) AP

P1–6A On June 1, Leanne Aiken established Leanne's Travel Agency. The following transactions are for her first month of operations:

June 1 Deposited $23,000 in the agency's bank account at the Scotiabank.
2 Purchased equipment for $6,800, paying $3,000 cash and signing a note payable for the balance.
3 Paid rent for the month, $2,500.
7 Paid $675 for supplies.
8 Incurred $300 of advertising expense, on account.
15 Earned $11,000 for services provided, with $3,500 paid in cash and the remainder on account.
22 Withdrew $1,500 for personal use.
25 Paid the amount due in the June 8 transaction.
30 Paid employee salaries, $5,750.
30 Received a bill for utilities for the month, $300.
30 Received $6,000 from customers who were billed in the June 15 transaction.
30 Paid $2,400 for a one-year insurance policy, starting July 1.

Instructions

(a) Prepare a tabular analysis of the effects of the above transactions on the accounting equation.
(b) From an analysis of the owner's equity, calculate the account balance in L. Aiken, Capital, at June 30.

TAKING IT FURTHER Assume on June 30 there is $300 of supplies on hand and that $375 of supplies had been used during June. What amount should be reported as an asset, Supplies, on the June 30 balance sheet? What amount should be reported as an expense?

Analyze transactions and prepare balance sheet.
(SO 3, 4, 5, 6) AP

P1–7A The following events concern Anita LeTourneau, a Manitoba law school graduate, for March 2014:

1. On March 4, she spent $20 on a lottery ticket.
2. On March 7, she won $250,000 in the lottery and immediately quit her job as a junior lawyer.
3. On March 10, she decided to open her own law practice, and deposited $50,000 of her winnings in a business chequing account, LeTourneau Legal Services.
4. On March 14, she purchased a new luxury condominium with a down payment of $150,000 from her personal funds plus a home mortgage of $200,000.
5. On March 15, Anita signed a rental agreement for her law office space for $2,500 a month, starting March 15. She paid the first month's rent, as it is due on the 15th of each month.
6. On March 19, she hired a receptionist. He will be paid $500 a week and will begin working on March 24.
7. On March 20, she purchased equipment for her law practice from a company that had just declared bankruptcy. The equipment was worth at least $15,000 but Anita was able to buy it for only $10,000.
8. On March 21, she purchased $400 of supplies on account.
9. On March 24, she purchased an additional $6,500 of equipment for her law practice for $3,000 plus a $3,500 note payable due in six months.

10. On March 31, she performed $3,500 of legal services on account.
11. On March 31, she received $2,500 cash for legal services to be provided in April.
12. On March 31, she paid her receptionist $500 for the week.
13. On March 31, she paid $400 for the supplies purchased on account on March 21.

Instructions

(a) Prepare a tabular analysis of the effects of the above transactions on the accounting equation.
(b) Calculate profit and owner's equity for the month ended March 31.
(c) Prepare a balance sheet at March 31.

TAKING IT FURTHER How should Anita determine which transactions should be recorded and which ones should not be recorded?

P1–8A Lise Anderson opened a medical office under the name Lise Anderson, MD, on August 1, 2014. On August 31, the balance sheet showed Cash $3,000; Accounts Receivable $1,500; Supplies $600; Equipment $7,500; Accounts Payable $5,500; Note Payable $3,000; and L. Anderson, Capital, $4,100. During September, the following transactions occurred:

Analyze transactions and prepare financial statements. **(SO 4, 5, 6) AP**

Sept. 4 Collected $800 of accounts receivable.
5 Provided services of $10,500, of which $7,700 was collected from patients and the remainder was on account.
7 Paid $2,900 of the accounts payable.
12 Purchased additional equipment for $2,300, paying $800 cash and leaving the balance on account.
15 Paid salaries, $2,800; rent for August, $1,900; and advertising expenses, $275.
18 Collected the balance of the accounts receivable from August 31.
20 Withdrew $1,000 for personal use.
26 Borrowed $3,000 from the Bank of Montreal on a note payable.
28 Signed a contract to provide medical services, not covered under the government health plan, to employees of CRS Corp. in October for $5,700. CRS Corp. will pay the amount owing after the medical services have been provided.
29 Received the telephone bill for September, $325.
30 Billed the government $10,000 for services provided to patients in September.

Instructions

(a) Beginning with the August 31 balances, prepare a tabular analysis of the effects of the September transactions on the accounting equation.
(b) Prepare an income statement and statement of owner's equity for September, and a balance sheet at September 30.

TAKING IT FURTHER What are the differences between purchasing an item on account and signing a note payable for the amount owing?

P1–9A Bennett's Home Renovations was started in 2008 by Jim Bennett. Jim operates the business from an office in his home. Listed below, in alphabetical order, are the company's assets and liabilities as at December 31, 2014, and the revenues, expenses, and drawings for the year ended December 31, 2014:

Prepare financial statements. **(SO 6) AP**

Accounts payable	$ 7,850	Prepaid insurance	$ 1,685
Accounts receivable	10,080	Service revenue	153,750
Cash	8,250	Supplies	595
Equipment	29,400	Supplies expense	20,095
Insurance expense	3,375	Salaries expense	88,230
Interest expense	1,195	Unearned revenue	15,000
J. Bennett, drawings	44,800	Vehicles	42,000
Notes payable	30,800	Vehicle operating expenses	3,545

Jim's capital at the beginning of 2014 was $45,850. He made no investments during the year.

Instructions

Prepare an income statement, statement of owner's equity, and balance sheet.

TAKING IT FURTHER Why is it necessary to prepare the income statement first, then the statement of owner's equity, and the balance sheet last?

Determine missing amounts, and comment. **(SO 6) AN**

P1–10A Here are incomplete financial statements for Lee Company:

LEE COMPANY
Balance Sheet
February 28, 2014

Assets		Liabilities and Owner's Equity	
Cash	$ 9,500	Liabilities	
Accounts receivable	5,300	Notes payable	$26,000
Land	(i)	Accounts payable	(iii)
Building and equipment	41,500	Total liabilities	43,800
Total assets	$ (ii)	M. Lee, Capital	(iv)
		Total liabilities and owner's equity	$91,300

LEE COMPANY
Income Statement
Year Ended February 28, 2014

Revenues		
Service revenues		$95,000
Expenses		
Salaries expense	$32,000	
Other expenses	(v)	
Supplies expense	1,500	
Total expenses		59,500
Profit		(vi)

LEE COMPANY
Statement of Owner's Equity
Year Ended February 28, 2014

M. Lee, capital, March 1, 2013	$22,000
Add: Investments	(vii)
Profit	(viii)
	62,500
Less: M. Lee, drawings	(ix)
M. Lee, capital, February 28, 2014	(x)

Instructions

(a) Calculate the missing amounts (i) to (x).

(b) Write a memo explaining (1) the sequence for preparing the financial statements, and (2) the interrelationships between the income statement, statement of owner's equity, and balance sheet.

TAKING IT FURTHER Why isn't the balance sheet dated the same way as the income statement and statement of owner's equity: "Year Ended February 28, 2014"?

CONTINUING COOKIE CHRONICLE

The **Continuing Cookie Chronicle** starts in this chapter and continues in every chapter throughout the book. This feature chronicles the growth of a hypothetical small business to show how the concepts you learn in each chapter can be applied in the real world.

Natalie Koebel spent much of her childhood learning the art of cookie-making from her grandmother. They passed many happy hours mastering every type of cookie imaginable and later creating new recipes that were both healthy and delicious. Now at the start of her second year in college, Natalie is investigating various possibilities for starting her own business as part of the requirements of the Entrepreneurship program she is taking. A long-time friend insists that Natalie has to somehow include cookies in her business plan and, after a series of brainstorming sessions, Natalie settles on the idea of operating a cookie-making school. She will start on a part-time basis and offer her services in peoples' homes. Now that she has started thinking about it, the possibilities seem endless. During the fall, she will concentrate on Christmas cookies. She will offer group sessions (which will probably be more entertainment than education for the participants) and individual lessons. Natalie also decides to include children in her target market. The first difficult decision is coming up with the perfect name for her business. In the end, she settles on "Cookie Creations" and then moves on to more important issues.

Instructions

(a) What form of business organization—proprietorship, partnership, or corporation—do you recommend that Natalie use for her business? Discuss the benefits and weaknesses of each form and give the reasons for your choice.
(b) What types of information will Natalie need? Why will she require this information? How often will she need this information?
(c) In addition to Natalie, who do you anticipate to be the users of Natalie's accounting information? What information will these identified users need and why?
(d) Which set of accounting standards will Natalie likely adopt when compiling her accounting information? Why?
(e) Identify specific asset, liability, and equity accounts that Cookie Creations will likely use to record its business transactions.
(f) Should Natalie open a separate bank account for the business? Why or why not?

BROADENING YOUR PERSPECTIVE — CHAPTER 1

Collaborative Learning Activity

Note to instructor: Additional instructions and material for this group activity can be found on the Instructor Resource Site and in *WileyPLUS*.

BYP1–1 In this group activity, students will be asked to identify (or determine) the information they would require if they were making a decision whether or not to lend money or to invest in a company.

Communication Activity

BYP1–2 Robert Joote is the owner of Peak Company. Robert has prepared the following balance sheet:

PEAK COMPANY Balance Sheet Month Ended December 31, 2014	
Assets	
Equipment	$20,500
Cash	10,500
Supplies	2,000
Accounts payable	(5,000)
Total assets	$28,000
Liabilities and Owner's Equity	
R. Joote, capital	$23,500
Accounts receivable	(3,000)
R. Joote, drawings	(2,000)
Prepaid insurance	(2,500)
Notes payable	12,000
Total liabilities and owner's equity	$28,000

Robert didn't know how to determine the balance for his capital account so he just "plugged" the number. (He made up a number that would give him the result that he wanted.) He had heard somewhere that assets had to equal the total of liabilities and owner's equity so he made up a number for capital so that these would be equal.

Instructions

In a memo, explain to Robert (a) how to determine the balance for his capital account, (b) why his balance sheet is incorrect, and (c) what he should do to correct it. Include in your explanation how the financial statements are interrelated, and why the order of preparation is important.

Ethics Case

BYP1–3 Chief executive officers (CEOs) and chief financial officers (CFOs) of publicly traded companies must personally certify that their companies' financial statements and other financial information contain no untrue statements and do not leave out any important facts. After many corporate scandals, the certification requirement was introduced as a way to hold top executives personally responsible for the integrity of their company's financial information.

Khan Corporation just hired a new management team, and its members say they are too new to the company to know whether the most recent financial reports are accurate or not. They refuse to sign the certification.

Instructions

(a) Who are the stakeholders in this situation?
(b) Should the CEO and CFO sign the certification? Explain why or why not.
(c) What are the CEO's and CFO's alternatives?

All About You: Personal Financial Literacy Activity

BYP1–4 In the All About You feature, we introduced the idea that being financially literate has a major impact on our ability to meet our financial goals and even on our health and happiness. We all face financial decisions each day. Some of these decisions are small and others are critical. Making the right financial decisions is important to your well-being. Following are three financial decisions that you as a student will likely have to make.

1. You will have to pay for your tuition, books, and spending money during college or university. You will try to decide what kind of summer job you should apply for and whether or not you need to work part-time during the school year.
2. You will need to have transportation to get back and forth to college or university each day. You will try to decide if you can afford to buy a second-hand car and pay for parking or whether you should use public transit. You will have to borrow money to purchase the car.
3. When you graduate, you might receive job offers from two different companies. You will decide which company you should work for, and you want to accept a position in a company that is financially stable and has growth potential.

Instructions

(a) For each decision, indicate what financial information you would want to have in order to make an optimal decision.
(b) Based on what you have learned in Chapter 1, how will learning about accounting help you with the above decisions?

ANSWERS TO CHAPTER QUESTIONS

ANSWERS TO ACCOUNTING IN ACTION INSIGHT QUESTIONS

All About You Insight, p. 5

Q: How might learning accounting help you make sure that your employer or bank hasn't made an error with your paycheque or bank account?

A: Learning accounting will provide you with tools that will help you track your transactions and ensure that the bank balance is correct. You will learn how to calculate how much your paycheque should be. You will learn how to calculate interest on loans and the total cost of borrowing. Examining your potential employer's financial statements will help you predict if the company will have enough cash to pay you now and if the company has growth potential. Stay tuned to the "All About You" features and related activities for more!

Ethics Insight, p. 25

Q: What risks might you face as an employee and individual if you don't blow the whistle on fraud?

A: If you do not blow the whistle on fraud, you risk your personal reputation. For example, if you are working for a company whose management purposely misstates the financial statements and shareholders and other stakeholders are hurt, will you want that company's name on your resumé when the misstatement is discovered and made public?

What if you are aware that another employee is stealing from the company and you do not report it? Your boss may question your integrity when it is later discovered that you were aware of the theft.

ANSWERS TO SELF-STUDY QUESTIONS

1. c 2. b 3. c 4. a 5. d 6. a 7. a 8. b 9. b 10. d

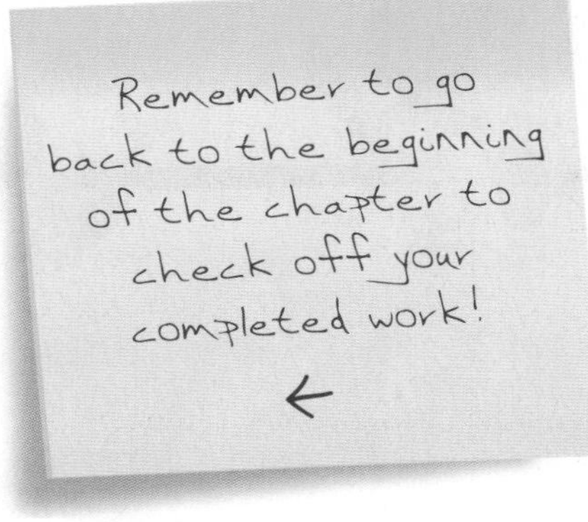
Remember to go
back to the beginning
of the chapter to
check off your
completed work!
←

CHAPTER 2

THE RECORDING PROCESS

THE NAVIGATOR

- ☐ Understand *Concepts for Review*
- ☐ Read *Feature Story*
- ☐ Scan *Study Objectives*
- ☐ Read *Chapter Preview*
- ☐ Read text and answer *Before You Go On*
- ☐ Review *Comparing IFRS and ASPE*
- ☐ Work *Demonstration Problem*
- ☐ Review *Summary of Study Objectives*
- ☐ Answer *Self-Study Questions*
- ☐ Complete assignments

CONCEPTS FOR REVIEW

Before studying this chapter, you should understand or, if necessary, review:

A. Why assets equal liabilities plus owner's equity. (Ch. 1, p. 12).

B. What assets, liabilities, owner's capital, drawings, revenues, and expenses are. (Ch. 1, pp. 11–12).

C. What transactions are, and how they affect the basic accounting equation. (Ch. 1, pp. 17–22).

DANCING TO HER OWN BUSINESS TUNE

CALGARY, AB—At the Prestige Dance Academy, tiny pink ballerinas admire themselves before the mirrors. Their energetic teacher, Amanda Hunsley, dances along with them, encouraging them to express themselves through music.

Even when she was a young child taking dance lessons, Ms. Hunsley knew she wanted to run her own business. At just 19, while in her second year of studies at Mount Royal College (now Mount Royal University), she opened her own dance school. Ten years later, the Prestige Dance Academy has a part-time staff of 11 teaching some 850 students tap, jazz, ballet, creative performing arts, lyrical, preschool, mom and me, hip-hop, and competitive dance.

"I combined my love for kids and for business," Ms. Hunsley says. She takes care of hiring and scheduling the staff, registrations and any other administrative work, and advertising and marketing.

While the dance academy provides birthday parties and summer camps, the bulk of the business is weekly dance lessons that run from September to June. Parents register their children in the fall, providing postdated cheques or a lump-sum payment for the entire year.

Ms. Hunsley uses QuickBooks accounting software. As the business has grown, so has the number of items in her chart of accounts—the list of account names for revenues and expenses, and assets and liabilities. Under revenues, she has accounts for student fees for regular classes and birthday parties, as well as sales of promotional dancewear bearing the Prestige logo. Her expense accounts include dance studio expenses, advertising and promotion, lease payments, bank service charges, business taxes and permits, insurance, meals and entertainment, and mileage. Other expense accounts are salaries, employer deductions, professional fees such as legal fees, and repairs and maintenance.

Prestige's asset accounts include long-lived assets such as computers, video camera (to record recitals), and leasehold improvements. "Even though I lease the building, we expanded a couple of years ago and we had to do all the renovations inside," Ms. Hunsley explains. The cost of those renovations, called leasehold improvements, is considered an asset and is included in the other assets account.

In terms of liabilities, Prestige's accounts include GST payable, and federal and provincial income tax payable for the business. Finally, the owner's equity account shows the amount that Ms. Hunsley, as Prestige's single owner, has invested and retained in the business.

It may seem like a lot of accounts, but Ms. Hunsley doesn't require as many as a larger business does. "I try to keep things as simple as possible" to easily keep track of the business, she says.

She also has an additional priority in her life: a baby boy, her second child. While her family responsibilities have reduced her teaching to three hours a week, she still keeps an eye on the accounting. "I don't think you could run a business properly without being so on top of the finances."

THE NAVIGATOR

STUDY OBJECTIVES

After studying this chapter, you should be able to:

1. Define debits and credits and illustrate how they are used to record transactions.
2. Explain the recording process and analyze, journalize, and post transactions.
3. Explain the purpose of a trial balance, and prepare one.

THE NAVIGATOR

PREVIEW OF CHAPTER TWO

In Chapter 1, we used the accounting equation to analyze transactions. The combined effects of these transactions were presented in a tabular form. This method could work for small companies like Softbyte (the fictitious company discussed in Chapter 1) because they have relatively few transactions. But imagine Prestige Dance in the feature story using the same tabular format as Softbyte. With 850 students, the dance academy has too many transactions to record each one this way. Instead, a set of procedures and records are used to keep track of transaction data more easily.

This chapter introduces and illustrates the basic procedures and records. It is organized as follows:

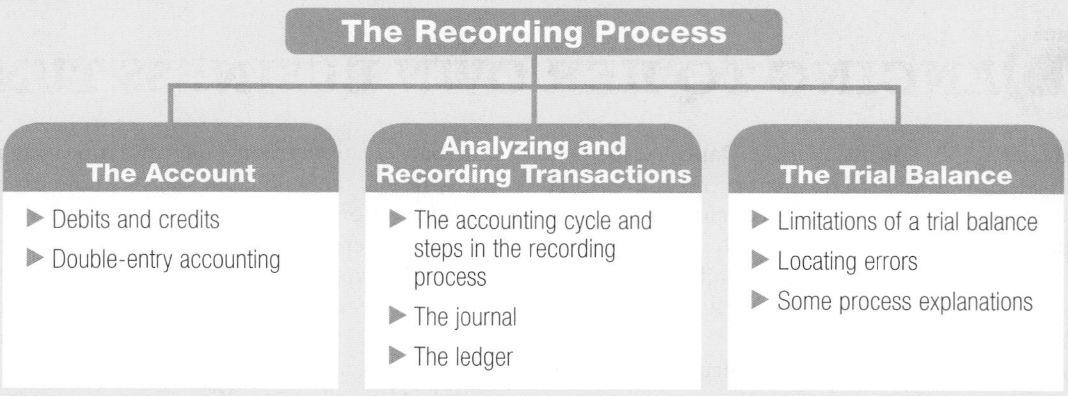

THE ACCOUNT

STUDY OBJECTIVE 1
Define debits and credits and illustrate how they are used to record transactions.

An **account** is an individual accounting record of increases and decreases in a specific asset, liability, or owner's equity item. For example, Softbyte has separate accounts called Cash, Accounts Receivable, Accounts Payable, Service Revenue, Salaries Expense, and so on.

In its simplest form, an account has three parts: (1) the title of the account, (2) a left or a debit side, and (3) a right or a credit side. Because these parts of an account are positioned like the letter T, it is called a **T account**. The basic form of an account is shown in Illustration 2-1.

ILLUSTRATION 2-1
Basic form of T account

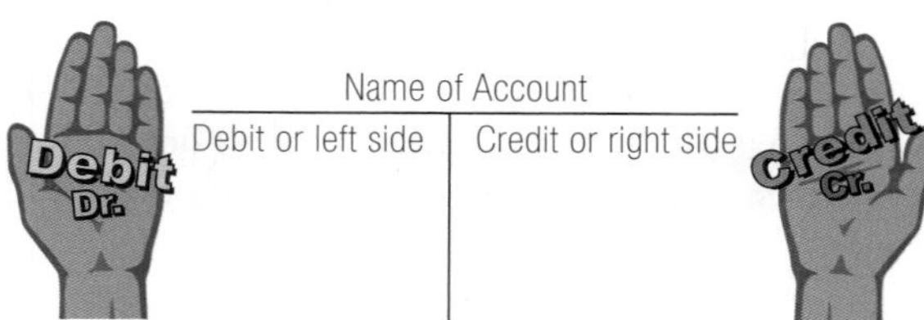

The actual format that is used in real life is more complex than the above T, and will be explained later in the chapter. The T account format is a learning tool that will be used throughout the book to explain basic accounting relationships. It is also a format used by professional accountants for analytical purposes.

DEBITS AND CREDITS

The term **debit** means left. The term **credit** means right. These terms are often abbreviated Dr. for debit and Cr. for credit. Debit and credit are simply directional signals that describe where entries are made in the accounts. Entering an amount on the left side of an account is called debiting the account. Entering an amount on the right side is called crediting the account.

When the totals of the two sides are compared, an account will have a debit balance if the total of the debit amounts exceeds the credits. On the other hand, an account will have a credit balance if the credit amounts are more than the debits.

The recording of debits and credits in an account is shown in Illustration 2-2 for Softbyte's cash transactions. The data are taken from the Cash column of the tabular summary in Illustration 1-10.

ILLUSTRATION 2-2
Tabular summary and account form comparison

Tabular Summary Cash
+$15,000
−7,000
+1,200
+1,500
−600
−900
−200
−250
+600
−1,300
$ 8,050

Account Form Cash	(Debits)	(Credits)
	15,000	7,000
	1,200	600
	1,500	900
	600	200
		250
		1,300
Balance	8,050	

In the tabular summary, every positive item is a receipt of cash. Every negative amount is a payment of cash. Notice that in the account format the increases in cash are recorded as debits, and the decreases in cash are recorded as credits. The account balance, a debit of $8,050, indicates that Softbyte had $8,050 more increases than decreases in cash. We will learn in the next section why debits and credits are used in this way.

Debit and Credit Procedure

It is very important to understand that debit does not mean increase nor does it mean decrease. Sometimes we use a debit to increase an account and sometimes we use a debit to decrease an account. Credits are the same—sometimes a credit is used to increase an account and sometimes a credit is used to decrease an account. The system of using debits and credits is based on the accounting equation, introduced in Chapter 1, and the definitions of debit and credit, as shown in the following diagram:

Assets	=	Liabilities	+	Owner's Equity
Debit or left side	=	Credit or right side		

We will use this diagram to apply debit and credit procedures to each part of the accounting equation—assets, liabilities, and owner's equity—in the following sections.

Assets and Liabilities.

As assets are on the left or debit side of the accounting equation, the normal balance of an asset is also on the left or debit side of the account. Logically, then, for the balance in an asset account to be on the debit side, increases also need to be recorded on the debit side and decreases in assets must be entered on the right or credit side. This is why in Illustration 2-2, the Softbyte illustration, increases in Cash—an asset account—were entered on the debit side, and decreases in Cash were entered on the credit side.

Similarly, because liabilities are on the right or credit side of the accounting equation, liability accounts normally show credit balances. That means increases in liabilities must be entered on the right or credit side, and decreases in liabilities must be entered on the left or debit side.

To summarize, because assets are on the opposite side of the accounting equation from liabilities, increases and decreases in assets are recorded opposite from increases and decreases in liabilities. The effects that debits and credits have on assets and liabilities and the normal balances are as follows:

Assets	
Debit for increase	Credit for decrease
Normal balance	

Liabilities	
Debit for decrease	Credit for increase
	Normal balance

Helpful hint Increases in accounts are always on the same side as the normal balance for that account.

Knowing the normal balance in an account may also help you find errors. In automated systems, the software is programmed to find these normal balance exceptions and to print out error or exception reports. In manual systems, a careful inspection of the accounts has to be done to find balances that are not normal. For example, a credit balance in an asset account such as Land or a debit balance in a liability account such as Wages Payable probably means there was a recording error. Occasionally, an abnormal balance may be correct. The Cash account, for example, will have a credit balance when a company has overdrawn its bank balance.

Owner's Equity.

As liabilities and owner's equity are on the same side of the accounting equation, the rules of debit and credit are the same for these two types of accounts. Credits increase owner's equity and debits decrease owner's equity. And as explained in Chapter 1, owner's equity is increased by owner's investments and revenues. It is decreased by owner's drawings and expenses. Separate accounts are kept for each of these types of transactions.

Owner's Capital. Investments by owners are credited to the owner's capital account because they increase owner's equity. For example, when cash is invested in the business, the Cash account is debited and Owner's Capital is credited.

The rules of debit and credit for the Owner's Capital account and the normal balance are as follows:

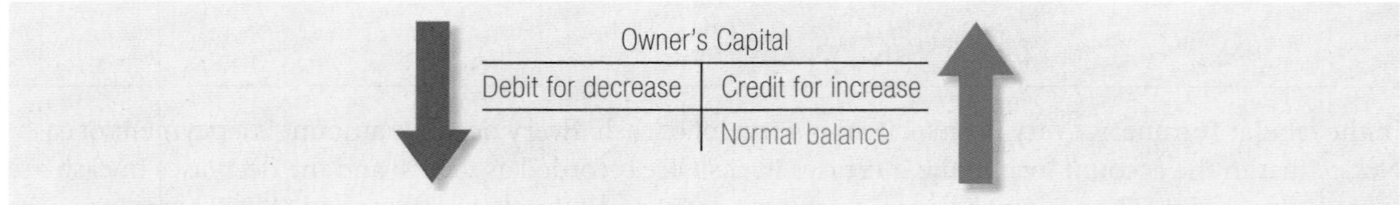

Owner's Drawings. An owner may withdraw cash or other assets for personal use. Withdrawals are recorded as debits because withdrawals decrease owner's equity. Withdrawals could be debited directly to Owner's Capital. However, it is better to have a separate account, called Drawings, as we did in Chapter 1. The separate account makes it easier to add up the total withdrawals for the accounting period and to prepare the statement of owner's equity.

Because withdrawals decrease owner's equity, the drawings account has a normal debit balance. Credits to an owner's drawings account are unusual, but might be used, for example, to correct a withdrawal recorded in error.

The rules of debit and credit for the Drawings account and the normal balance are as follows:

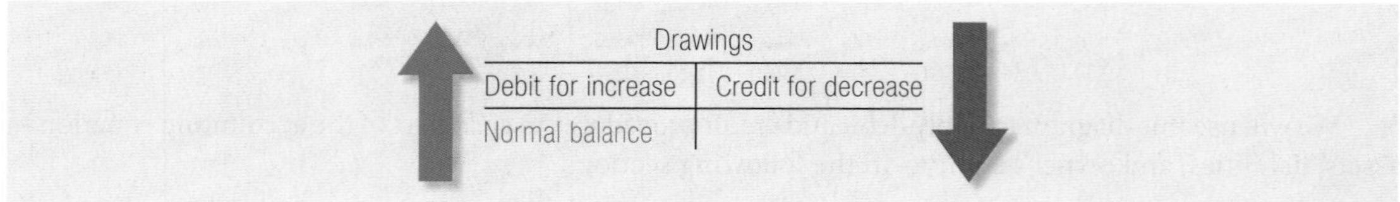

Note that increases and decreases to the drawings account are recorded opposite to increases and decreases in Owner's Capital. That is because investments, which increase owner's equity, are recorded in Owner's Capital, and withdrawals, which decrease owner's equity, are recorded in Drawings.

Revenues and Expenses. When revenues are earned, owner's equity is increased. As credits increase owner's equity, revenues are recorded as credits. Thus, Revenue accounts normally show credit balances. Similar to the Owner's Capital account, Revenue accounts are increased by credits and decreased by debits. Credits to revenue accounts should exceed the debits.

Expenses have the opposite effect: expenses decrease owner's equity. As a result, expenses are recorded as debits because debits decrease owner's equity. Thus, Expense accounts normally show debit balances. Similar to the Owner's Drawings account, expense accounts are increased by debits and decreased by credits. Debits to expense accounts should exceed the credits.

Since revenues are the positive factor in calculating profit, and expenses are the negative factor, it is logical that the increase and decrease sides of revenue accounts should be the reverse of expense accounts.

The effect of debits and credits on revenues and expenses and the normal balances are as follows:

Revenues	
Debit for decrease	Credit for increase
	Normal balance

Expenses	
Debit for increase	Credit for decrease
Normal balance	

Summary of Debit and Credit Effects

Illustration 2-3 shows the expanded accounting equation and a summary of the debit/credit rules on each type of account.

ILLUSTRATION 2-3
Summary of debit/credit rules and effects for the expanded accounting equation

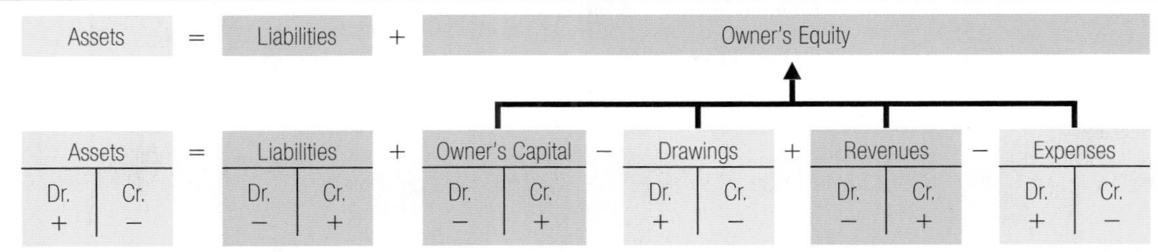

Remember, the normal balance of each account is on its increase side. So assets, drawings, and expense accounts have a normal debit balance, while liabilities, owner's capital, and revenue accounts have a normal credit balance.

DOUBLE-ENTRY ACCOUNTING

In Chapter 1, you learned that each transaction must affect two or more accounts to keep the basic accounting equation in balance. This is known as the **double-entry accounting system** in which the dual (two-sided) effect of each transaction is recorded in the appropriate accounts. This system provides a logical method for recording transactions and ensuring the amounts are recorded accurately.

Helpful hint Debits must equal credits for each transaction.

Now that you have learned the debit and credit procedure of recording transactions, you should also see that, for each transaction, debits must equal credits. The equality of debits and credits is the basis for the double-entry accounting system of recording transactions.

If every transaction is recorded with equal debits and credits, then the sum of all the debits to the accounts must equal the sum of all the credits. And, if the debit and credit procedures are correctly applied, the total amount of debits will always equal the total amount of credits and the accounting equation stays in balance.

Carefully reviewing Illustration 2-3, previously shown, will also help you to understand the basics of the double-entry accounting system.

BEFORE YOU GO ON...

DO IT

Eszter Schwenke has just rented space in a shopping mall where she will open a beauty salon called Hair It Is. Eszter has determined that the company will need the following accounts:

1. Accounts Payable
2. Cash
3. E. Schwenke, Capital
4. E. Schwenke, Drawings
5. Rent Expense
6. Equipment
7. Service Revenue
8. Supplies
   (a) Indicate whether each of these accounts is an asset, liability, or owner's equity account. If it is an owner's equity account, indicate what type it is (for example, owner's capital, drawings, revenue, or expense).
   (b) What is the normal balance of these accounts?
   (c) Will a debit increase or decrease these accounts?

BEFORE YOU GO ON... continued on next page

BEFORE YOU GO ON...
continued from previous page

Action Plan

- Use the expanded accounting equation to determine the type of account.
- Remember that the normal balance of an account is on its increase side.
- Remember that assets are increased by debits, and that liabilities and owner's equity are increased by credits.

THE NAVIGATOR

SOLUTION

Account	(a) Type of Account	(b) Normal Balance	(c) Debit Effect
1. Accounts Payable	Liability	Credit	Decrease
2. Cash	Asset	Debit	Increase
3. E. Schwenke, Capital	Owner's Equity	Credit	Decrease
4. E. Schwenke, Drawings	Owner's Equity (drawing)	Debit	Increase
5. Rent Expense	Owner's Equity (expense)	Debit	Increase
6. Equipment	Asset	Debit	Increase
7. Service Revenue	Owner's Equity (revenue)	Credit	Decrease
8. Supplies	Asset	Debit	Increase

Related exercise material: BE2–1, BE2–2, BE2–3, BE2–4, BE2–5, BE2–6, E2–2, and E2–3.

STUDY OBJECTIVE 2
Explain the recording process and analyze, journalize, and post transactions.

ANALYZING AND RECORDING TRANSACTIONS

THE ACCOUNTING CYCLE AND STEPS IN THE RECORDING PROCESS

The **accounting cycle** is a series of steps followed by accountants in preparing financial statements. We will learn about the first four steps of the accounting cycle in this chapter and the remaining steps in Chapters 3 and 4. The procedures used in analyzing and recording transaction information are the first three steps, shown in Illustration 2-4. These three steps are also known as the **recording process**.

ILLUSTRATION 2-4
The accounting cycle—Steps 1 to 3

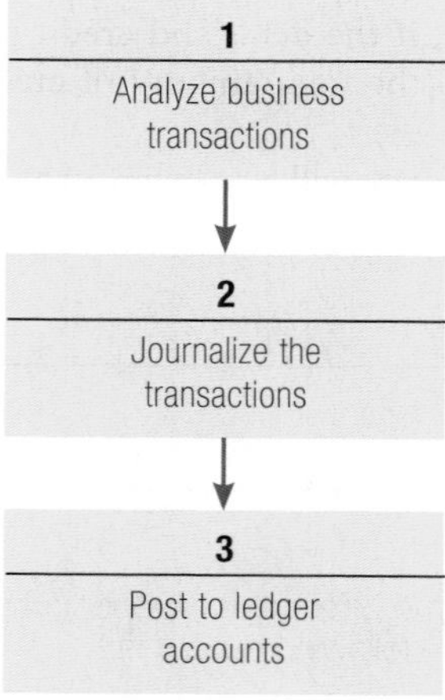

Analyzing Business Transactions

As shown in Illustration 2-4, the recording process begins with analyzing the transaction. Evidence of a transaction comes from a **source document**, such as a sales slip, cheque, bill, cash register tape, or bank statement.

We started to learn how to analyze transactions in Chapter 1. Deciding what to record is the most critical point in the accounting cycle. Recall from Chapter 1 that a transaction is recorded only if it causes the company's financial position (assets, liabilities, and owner's equity) to change.

Recall also from Chapter 1 that, once it had been determined that a transaction should be recorded, it was analyzed for its specific effect on the elements of the accounting equation. We saw in the transaction analysis process that it is necessary to identify the accounts that were changed and to determine if these accounts had increased or decreased and by how much. Remember that if the amount cannot be measured, it cannot be recorded. This is often referred to as the **basic analysis** of the transaction.

After the basic analysis is complete, then the debit and credit procedures you learned in the previous section of this chapter are applied to determine which account or accounts should be debited and which account or accounts should be credited. This is often referred to as the **debit/credit analysis** of the transaction.

Analyzing transactions is the most difficult part of the accounting cycle because there are so many different types of transactions. Throughout this textbook, and in later accounting courses, you will continue to be introduced to different transactions. As you learn about new transactions, remember to first do your basic analysis and then the debit/credit analysis. If you follow this system, your ability to correctly analyze and record transactions will improve.

After the transaction has been analyzed, then it can be entered in the accounting records—steps 2 and 3 of the accounting cycle. We will explain how this is done in the following sections on the journal and the ledger.

The Recording Process in Computerized and Manual Accounting Systems

The first two steps in the recording process—analyzing and journalizing transactions—must be done by a person even when a computerized system is used. The major difference between a computerized and a manual accounting system is in Step 3—transferring information from the journal to the ledger. In computerized systems, this is done automatically by the computer, which substantially reduces the possibility of making mistakes.

ACCOUNTING IN ACTION
BUSINESS INSIGHT

Does hiring a great employee add value for a company? In the case of sports teams, owners, players, and fans all agree that having the most talented players makes a huge difference. But how does a team attract and keep those players? Is simply offering the player a contract sufficient to attract talent? Not these days. And accountants would agree that simply having a player sign a contract doesn't change the team's assets, liabilities, or owner's equity. This isn't a transaction that would get recorded in the team's accounting records even if it does bring value to the team.

Signing bonuses are different because they affect cash. And they are used partly to deal with the league's salary caps, which restrict how much can be included in individual players' and the whole team's salaries in each year. A signing bonus can be paid in one year but be included in the team's salary cap in a year that's financially advantageous to the team. To make matters even more interesting, there was a new twist in defenceman Andrej Sekera's four-year, $11-million deal signed with the Buffalo Sabres in July 2011. The contract wasn't just front-loaded: it was heavily so, with $6 million, or 55% of the contract, due in the first 11.5 months. Then the Sabres traded Sekera to the Carolina Hurricanes in 2013. The accounting question as to whether these bonuses should be considered assets or expenses may become more complicated than ever.

Sources: James Mirtle, "Big Signing Bonuses Becoming NHL's New Norm," *Globe and Mail* blog, July 20, Michael Smith, "Canes Acquire Sekera in Second-Round Trade," June 30, 2013, Carolina Hurricanes website. Collective Bargaining Agreement FAQs, NHL website.

What are the issues involved in determining if a signing bonus is an asset or an expense?

THE JOURNAL

Transactions are first recorded in chronological (date) order in a **journal**. For this reason, the journal is referred to as the book of original entry. For each transaction, the journal shows the debit and credit effects on specific accounts. Companies can use various kinds of specialized journals, but every company has the most basic form of journal, a **general journal**. Whenever we use the term "journal" in this textbook without a description of it, we mean the general journal.

The journal makes some important contributions to the recording process:

- It discloses the complete effect of a transaction in one place.
- It provides a chronological record of transactions.
- It helps to prevent and locate errors, because the debit and credit amounts for each entry can be easily compared.
- It gives an explanation of the transaction and, if there is one, identifies the source document.

Journalizing

The second step in the accounting cycle, entering transaction data in the journal, is known as **journalizing**. A separate journal entry is made for each transaction. A complete entry consists of the following: (1) the date of the transaction, (2) the accounts and amounts to be debited and credited, and (3) a brief explanation of the transaction.

To illustrate the technique of journalizing, let's look at the first two transactions of Softbyte from Chapter 1. These transactions were (1) September 1, Marc Doucet invested $15,000 cash in the business, and (2) computer equipment was purchased for $7,000 cash. (We will assume that this transaction also occurred on September 1.) In tabular form, as shown in Chapter 1, these transactions appeared as follows:

	Assets		=	Liabilities	+	Owner's Equity
	Cash	+ Equipment				M. Doucet, Capital
(1)	+$15,000					+$15,000
(2)	−7,000	+$7,000				

In journal form, these transactions would appear as follows:

A	=	L	+	OE
+15,000				+15,000

Cash flows: +15,000

A	=	L	+	OE
+7,000				
−7,000				

Cash flows: −7,000

GENERAL JOURNAL **J1**

Date	Account Titles and Explanation	Ref	Debit	Credit
2014				
Sept. 1	Cash		15,000	
	M. Doucet, Capital			15,000
	Invested cash in business.			
1	Equipment		7,000	
	Cash			7,000
	Purchased equipment for cash.			

In the margins next to journal entries are **equation analyses** that show the effect of the transaction on the accounting equation (A = L + OE) and on cash flows. You should think of these as part of Step 1 of the accounting cycle.

Since this is the first page of Softbyte's general journal, it is numbered J1. You should note the following features of journal entries:

1. The date of the transaction is entered in the Date column.
2. The account to be debited is entered first at the left margin of the column headed Account Titles and Explanation. The account to be credited is then entered on the next line and indented from the left margin. The indentation visually separates the accounts to be debited and credited, so there is less chance of switching the debits and credits.
3. The amounts for the debits are recorded in the Debit (left) column and the amounts for the credits are recorded in the Credit (right) column.
4. A brief explanation of the transaction is given on the line below the credit account title. To simplify the illustrations in this textbook, journal entry explanations are often left out. Remember, however, that in real life, explanations are essential for every journal entry.

5. The column titled Ref. (which stands for "reference") is left blank when the journal entry is made. This column is used later, when the journal entries are transferred to the ledger accounts.

It is important to use correct and specific account titles in journal entries. While there is some flexibility in creating accounting names, **each title has to accurately describe the account's content**. For example, the account title used for the computer equipment purchased by Softbyte may be Equipment, Computer Equipment, Computers, or Office Equipment. However, once a company chooses the specific title to use, all transactions for the account should be recorded with the same title.

When you complete the assignments in this text, if specific account titles are given, you should use those. If account titles are not given, you should create account titles that identify the nature and content of each account. **Account titles used in journalizing should not contain explanations (such as Cash Paid or Cash Received).**

If an entry affects only two accounts, it will have one debit and one credit. This is considered a simple journal entry. Some transactions, however, involve more than two accounts. When three or more accounts are required in one journal entry, the entry is called a **compound entry**. To illustrate, recall from Chapter 1 that Softbyte provided $3,500 of programming services to customers. (Assume this was on September 9.) It received $1,500 cash from the customers for these services. The balance, $2,000, was owed on account. The compound entry to record this transaction is as follows:

GENERAL JOURNAL				J1
Date	Account Titles and Explanation	Ref	Debit	Credit
2014				
Sept. 9	Cash		1,500	
	Accounts Receivable		2,000	
	Service Revenue			3,500
	Performed services for cash and credit.			

A	=	L	+	OE
+1,500				+3,500
+2,000				

↑Cash flows: +1,500

In a compound entry, just as in a simple entry, the total debit and credit amounts must be equal. Also, all of the debits are listed before the credits are listed.

THE LEDGER

The entire group of accounts maintained by a company is called the ledger. The **ledger** keeps all the information about changes in each account in one place.

Companies can use different kinds of ledgers, but every company has a general ledger. A **general ledger** contains accounts for all the assets, liabilities, equities, revenues, and expenses. Whenever we use the term "ledger" on its own in this textbook, we mean the general ledger.

A business can use a loose-leaf binder or card file for the ledger, with each account kept on a separate sheet or card. However, most companies use a computerized accounting system that keeps each account in a separate file. In a computerized system, such as the QuickBooks accounting software used by Prestige Dance Academy in the feature story, each account is numbered so that it is easier to identify.

The accounts in the ledger should be arranged in the same order that is used to present the accounts in the financial statements, beginning with the balance sheet accounts. The asset accounts come first, followed by liability accounts, owner's capital, drawings, revenues, and expenses. The ledger gives the balance in each account. The ledger will also show all of the increases and decreases that have been made to each account.

Standard Form of Account

The simple T account form used in accounting textbooks is often very useful for analyzing illustrations, and for learning accounting. However, in practice, the account forms that are used in ledgers are designed to include additional information. A very popular form in both manual and computerized systems, using the data (and assumed dates) from Softbyte's Cash account in Illustration 2-2, follows:

GENERAL LEDGER					
CASH					
Date	Explanation	Ref	Debit	Credit	Balance
2014					
Sept. 1			15,000		15,000
1				7,000	8,000
3			1,200		9,200
9			1,500		10,700
17				600	10,100
17				900	9,200
20				200	9,000
25				250	8,750
30			600		9,350
30				1,300	8,050

This form is often called the **three-column form of account** because it has three money columns: debit, credit, and balance. The balance in the account is determined after each transaction. The explanation and reference columns make it possible to give more information about the transaction than can be included in the T account form. In manual accounting systems, the explanation column is usually left blank because it is too time-consuming to copy explanations from the general journal. Computerized accounting systems will automatically copy the explanation that was originally recorded in the journal entry into the ledger.

Posting

The procedure of transferring journal entries to the ledger accounts is called **posting**. It is the third step in the accounting cycle. Posting has the following steps:

1. General Ledger. In the ledger, enter the date, journal page, and debit or credit amount shown in the journal in the correct columns of each affected account.
2. General Journal. In the reference column of the journal, write the account numbers to which the debit and credit amounts were posted in the ledger.

These steps are shown in Illustration 2-5 using Softbyte's first journal entry.

ILLUSTRATION 2-5
Posting a journal entry

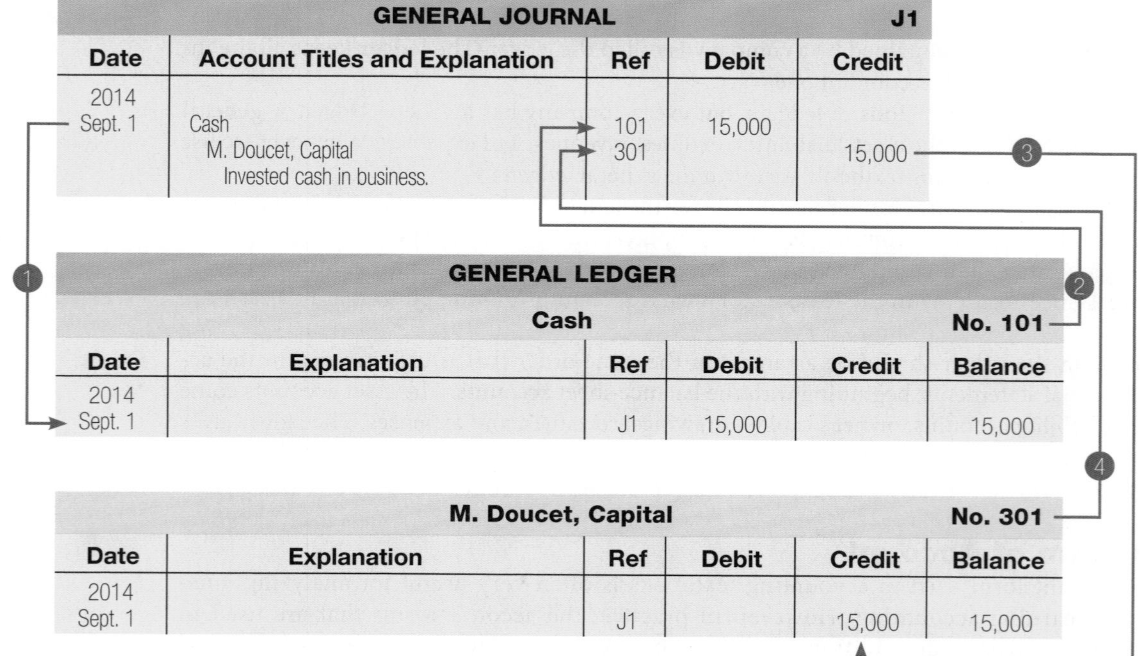

1. Post to debit account: enter date, journal page number, and amount.
2. Enter debit account number in journal reference column.
3. Post to credit account: enter date, journal page number, and amount.
4. Enter credit account number in journal reference column.

The reference column in the journal shows the entries that have been posted. The references also show the account numbers to which the amounts have been posted. The reference column of a ledger account indicates the journal page where the transaction was posted from.

Posting should be done in chronological order. That is, all the debits and credits of one journal entry should be posted before going to the next journal entry. Postings should be made on a timely basis to keep the ledger up to date. In a computerized accounting system, posting is done automatically, usually right after each journal entry is prepared.

Chart of Accounts

The first step in designing an accounting system—whether computerized or manual—is to create a chart of accounts. The **chart of accounts** is a list of the accounts and account numbers that identify where the accounts are in the ledger. It is the framework for the entire database of accounting information. The numbering system that is used to identify the accounts usually starts with the balance sheet accounts. The income statement accounts come next.

Because each company is different, the types of accounts they have and how many they have are also different. The number of accounts depends on the amount of detail that management wants. The management of one company may want one account for all types of utility expense. Another company may keep separate expense accounts for each type of utility expense, such as gas, electricity, and water. Many companies, such as Prestige Dance Academy, in our feature story, use different revenue accounts for different sources of revenue.

The chart of accounts for Pioneer Advertising Agency, a proprietorship owned by Chris Bedard, is shown in Illustration 2-6. Accounts 100–199 indicate asset accounts; 200–299 indicate liabilities; 300–399 indicate owner's equity accounts; 400–499, revenues; and 500–999, expenses. There are gaps in the numbering system to permit the insertion of new accounts as needed during the life of the business.

ILLUSTRATION 2-6
Chart of accounts

PIONEER ADVERTISING AGENCY
Chart of Accounts

Assets		Owner's Equity	
101	Cash	301	C. Bedard, Capital
112	Accounts Receivable	306	C. Bedard, Drawings
129	Supplies	350	Income Summary
130	Prepaid Insurance		
151	Equipment		**Revenues**
152	Accumulated Depreciation—Equipment	400	Service Revenue
			Expenses
	Liabilities	711	Depreciation Expense
200	Notes Payable	722	Insurance Expense
201	Accounts Payable	726	Rent Expense
209	Unearned Revenue	729	Salaries Expense
212	Salaries Payable	740	Supplies Expense
230	Interest Payable	905	Interest Expense

In this and the next two chapters, we will show the accounting cycle for Pioneer Advertising Agency—a service company. Accounts shown in red are used in this chapter; accounts shown in black are explained in later chapters.

The Recording Process Illustrated

In the following section, we show the three steps in the recording process—analyze, journalize, and post—using the October 2014 transactions of Pioneer Advertising Agency. The agency's accounting period is one month. As Pioneer Advertising Agency is started on October 1, 2014, there are no balances in its accounts from prior transactions.

Study these transactions carefully. Remember that in Step 1 of the recording process the transaction is analyzed to identify (1) the type of accounts involved, (2) whether the accounts are increased or decreased, and (3) whether the accounts need to be debited or credited. This is shown in the basic analysis and the debit/credit analysis for each transaction in the illustrations before journalizing and posting. For simplicity, the illustrations use the T account form to show posting instead of the standard account form.

TRANSACTION 1
Investment of cash by owner

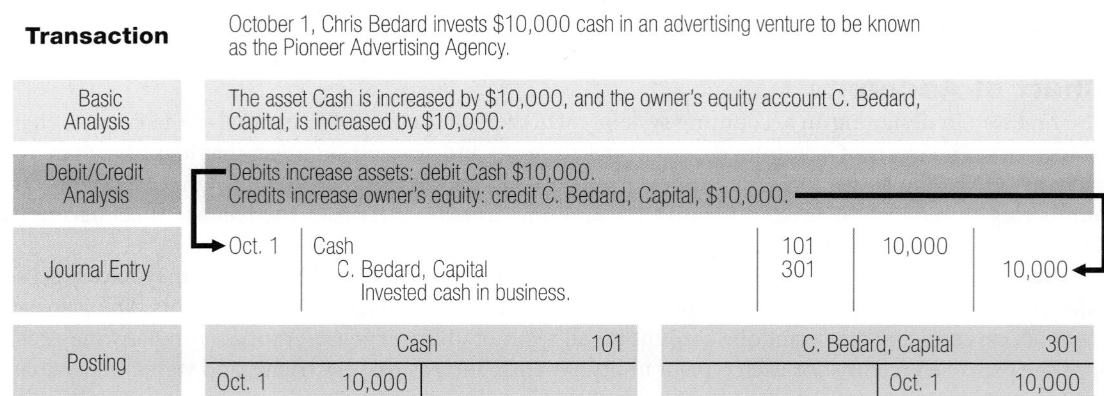

TRANSACTION 2
Purchase of office equipment

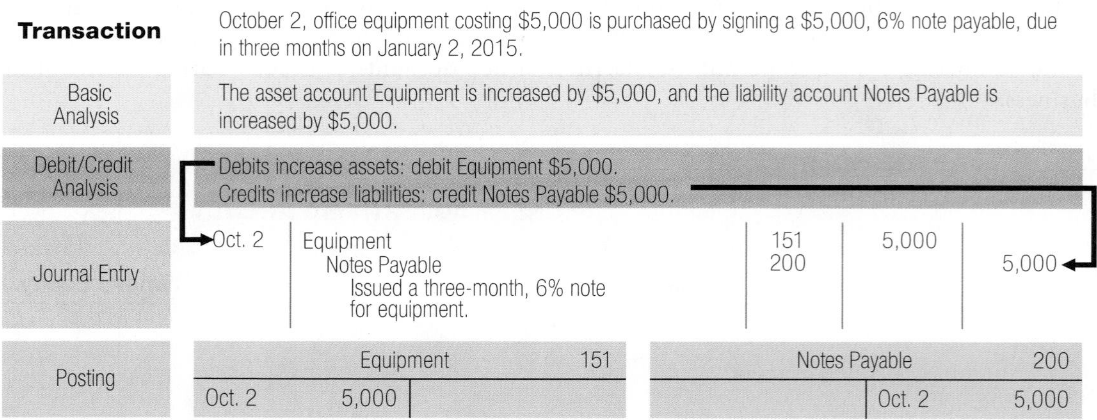

TRANSACTION 3
Receipt of cash in advance from customer

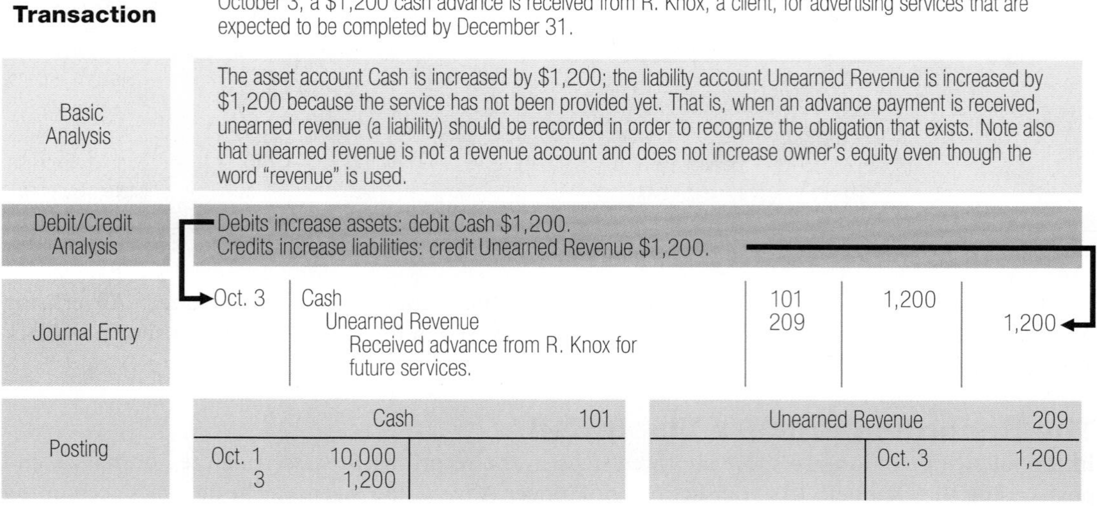

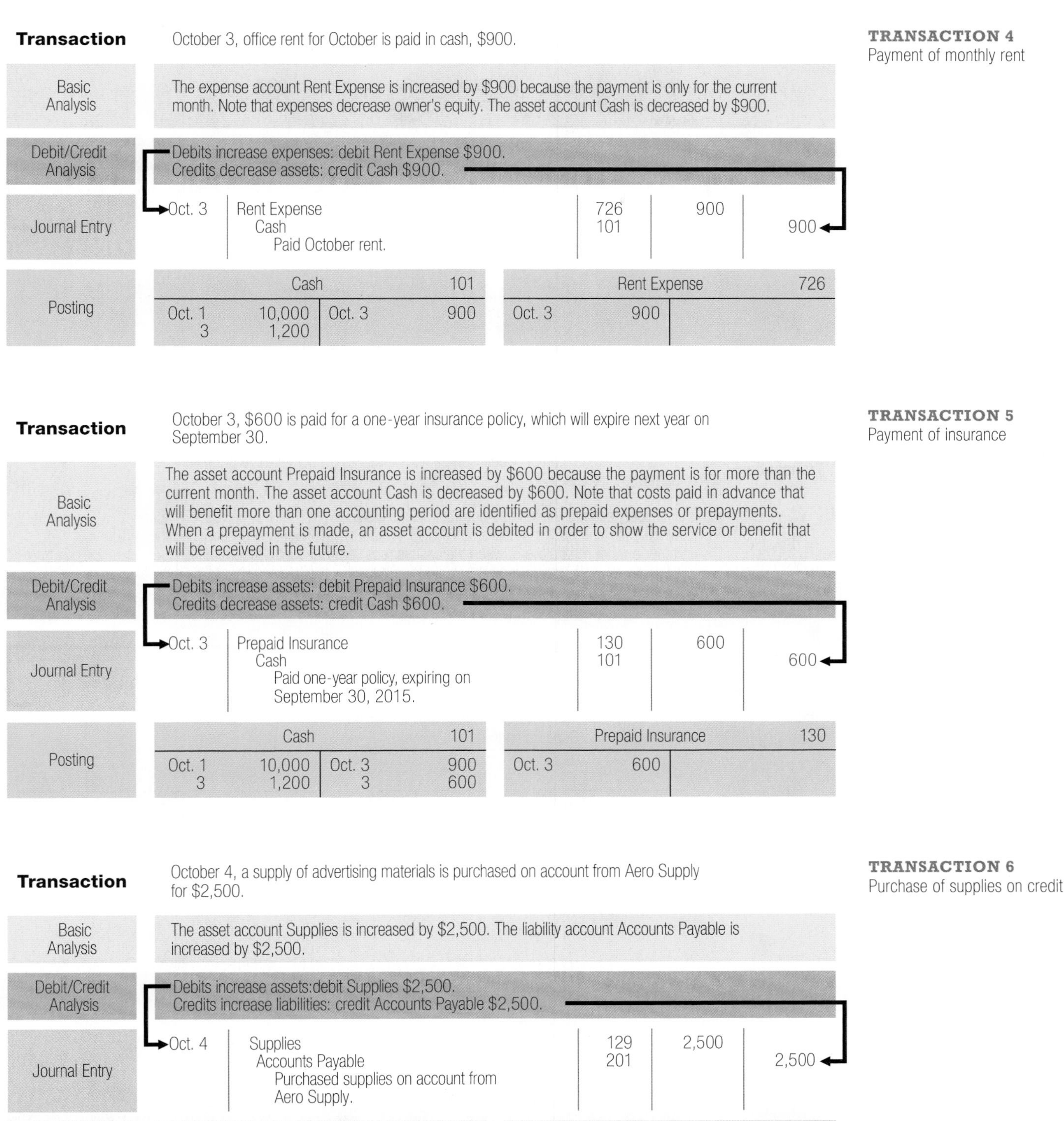

TRANSACTION 4
Payment of monthly rent

Transaction October 3, office rent for October is paid in cash, $900.

Basic Analysis The expense account Rent Expense is increased by $900 because the payment is only for the current month. Note that expenses decrease owner's equity. The asset account Cash is decreased by $900.

Debit/Credit Analysis Debits increase expenses: debit Rent Expense $900.
Credits decrease assets: credit Cash $900.

Journal Entry

Oct. 3	Rent Expense	726	900	
	Cash	101		900
	Paid October rent.			

Posting

Cash			101
Oct. 1	10,000	Oct. 3	900
3	1,200		

Rent Expense			726
Oct. 3	900		

TRANSACTION 5
Payment of insurance

Transaction October 3, $600 is paid for a one-year insurance policy, which will expire next year on September 30.

Basic Analysis The asset account Prepaid Insurance is increased by $600 because the payment is for more than the current month. The asset account Cash is decreased by $600. Note that costs paid in advance that will benefit more than one accounting period are identified as prepaid expenses or prepayments. When a prepayment is made, an asset account is debited in order to show the service or benefit that will be received in the future.

Debit/Credit Analysis Debits increase assets: debit Prepaid Insurance $600.
Credits decrease assets: credit Cash $600.

Journal Entry

Oct. 3	Prepaid Insurance	130	600	
	Cash	101		600
	Paid one-year policy, expiring on September 30, 2015.			

Posting

Cash			101
Oct. 1	10,000	Oct. 3	900
3	1,200	3	600

Prepaid Insurance			130
Oct. 3	600		

TRANSACTION 6
Purchase of supplies on credit

Transaction October 4, a supply of advertising materials is purchased on account from Aero Supply for $2,500.

Basic Analysis The asset account Supplies is increased by $2,500. The liability account Accounts Payable is increased by $2,500.

Debit/Credit Analysis Debits increase assets:debit Supplies $2,500.
Credits increase liabilities: credit Accounts Payable $2,500.

Journal Entry

Oct. 4	Supplies	129	2,500	
	Accounts Payable	201		2,500
	Purchased supplies on account from Aero Supply.			

Posting

Supplies			129
Oct. 4	2,500		

Accounts Payable			201
		Oct. 4	2,500

TRANSACTION 7
Hiring of employees

Transaction October 9, four employees are hired to begin work on October 13. Each employee is to receive a weekly salary of $500 for a five-day workweek (Monday–Friday), payable every two weeks. The first payment will be on October 24.

Basic Analysis An accounting transaction has not occurred. There is only an agreement between the employer and the employees to enter into a business transaction beginning on October 13. Thus, a debit/credit analysis is not needed because there is no accounting entry. (See October 24 transaction for first entry.)

TRANSACTION 8
Withdrawal of cash by owner

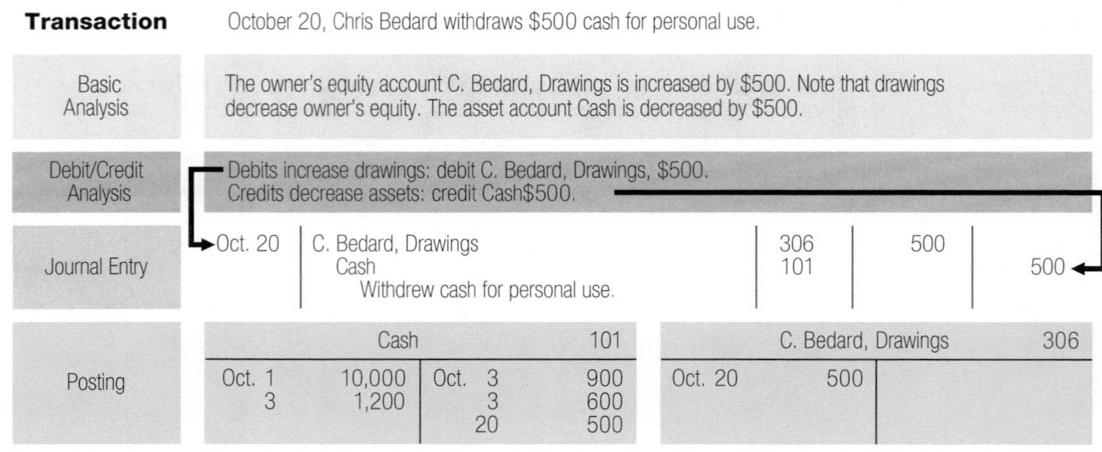

Transaction October 20, Chris Bedard withdraws $500 cash for personal use.

Basic Analysis The owner's equity account C. Bedard, Drawings is increased by $500. Note that drawings decrease owner's equity. The asset account Cash is decreased by $500.

Debit/Credit Analysis Debits increase drawings: debit C. Bedard, Drawings, $500. Credits decrease assets: credit Cash$500.

Journal Entry

Date	Account Titles and Explanation	Ref.	Debit	Credit
Oct. 20	C. Bedard, Drawings	306	500	
	Cash	101		500
	Withdrew cash for personal use.			

Posting

Cash			101
Oct. 1	10,000	Oct. 3	900
3	1,200	3	600
		20	500

C. Bedard, Drawings			306
Oct. 20	500		

TRANSACTION 9
Service performed on account

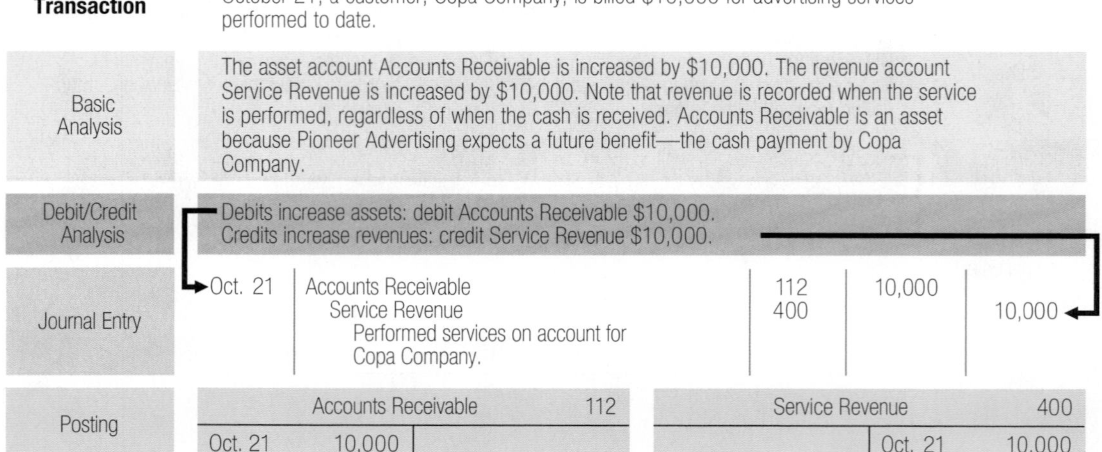

Transaction October 21, a customer, Copa Company, is billed $10,000 for advertising services performed to date.

Basic Analysis The asset account Accounts Receivable is increased by $10,000. The revenue account Service Revenue is increased by $10,000. Note that revenue is recorded when the service is performed, regardless of when the cash is received. Accounts Receivable is an asset because Pioneer Advertising expects a future benefit—the cash payment by Copa Company.

Debit/Credit Analysis Debits increase assets: debit Accounts Receivable $10,000. Credits increase revenues: credit Service Revenue $10,000.

Journal Entry

Date	Account Titles and Explanation	Ref.	Debit	Credit
Oct. 21	Accounts Receivable	112	10,000	
	Service Revenue	400		10,000
	Performed services on account for Copa Company.			

Posting

Accounts Receivable			112
Oct. 21	10,000		

Service Revenue			400
		Oct. 21	10,000

TRANSACTION 10
Payment of salaries

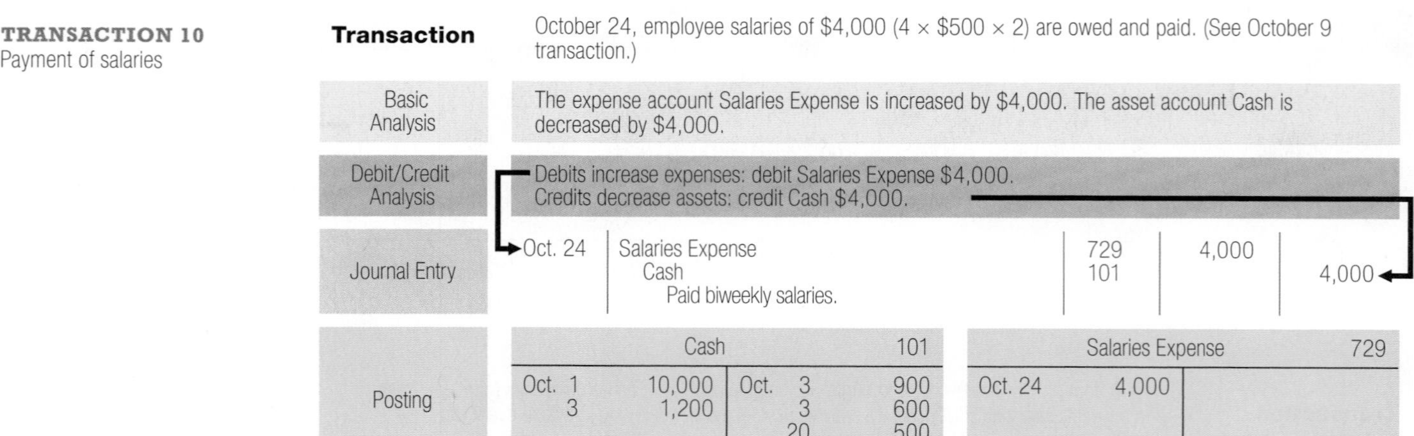

Transaction October 24, employee salaries of $4,000 (4 × $500 × 2) are owed and paid. (See October 9 transaction.)

Basic Analysis The expense account Salaries Expense is increased by $4,000. The asset account Cash is decreased by $4,000.

Debit/Credit Analysis Debits increase expenses: debit Salaries Expense $4,000. Credits decrease assets: credit Cash $4,000.

Journal Entry

Date	Account Titles and Explanation	Ref.	Debit	Credit
Oct. 24	Salaries Expense	729	4,000	
	Cash	101		4,000
	Paid biweekly salaries.			

Posting

Cash			101
Oct. 1	10,000	Oct. 3	900
3	1,200	3	600
		20	500
		24	4,000

Salaries Expense			729
Oct. 24	4,000		

TRANSACTION 11
Receipt of cash for services provided

Transaction October 25, services were provided to a customer and $800 cash was received immediately.

Basic Analysis The asset account Cash is increased by $800. The revenue account Service Revenue is increased by $800.

Debit/Credit Analysis
Debits increase assets: debit Cash $800.
Credits increase revenues: credit Service Revenue $800

Journal Entry

Date	Account Titles and Explanation	Ref.	Debit	Credit
Oct. 25	Cash	101	800	
	Service Revenue	400		800
	Received cash for services provided.			

Posting

Cash			101
Oct. 1	10,000	Oct. 3	900
3	1,200	3	600
25	800	20	500
		24	4,000

Service Revenue			400
		Oct. 21	10,000
		25	800

TRANSACTION 12
Receipt of cash from collecting part of an account receivable

Transaction October 31, received $9,000 cash from Copa Company in payment of part of its account. (See October 21 transaction.)

Basic Analysis The asset account Cash is increased by $9,000. The asset account Accounts Receivable is decreased by $9,000. Note that service revenue is not recorded here; it was recorded on October 21 when the service was performed.

Debit/Credit Analysis
Debits increase assets: debit Cash $9,000.
Credits decrease assets: credit Accounts Receivable $9,000.

Journal Entry

Date	Account Titles and Explanation	Ref.	Debit	Credit
Oct. 31	Cash	101	9,000	
	Accounts Receivable	112		9,000
	Received cash on account from Copa Company.			

Posting

Cash			101
Oct. 1	10,000	Oct. 3	900
3	1,200	3	600
25	800	20	500
31	9,000	24	4,000

Accounts Receivable			112
Oct. 21	10,000	Oct. 31	9,000

TRANSACTION 13
Partial payment of account payable

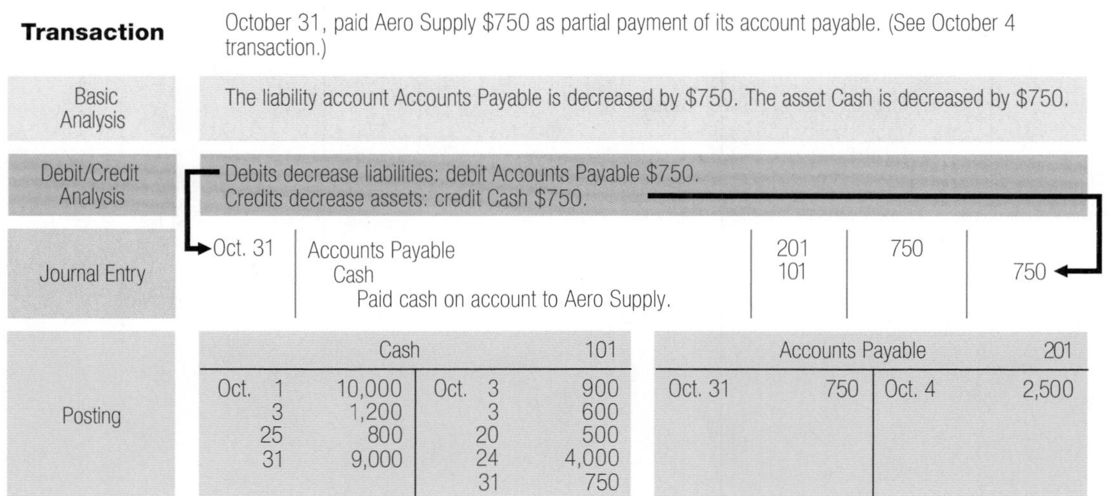

Transaction October 31, paid Aero Supply $750 as partial payment of its account payable. (See October 4 transaction.)

Basic Analysis The liability account Accounts Payable is decreased by $750. The asset Cash is decreased by $750.

Debit/Credit Analysis
Debits decrease liabilities: debit Accounts Payable $750.
Credits decrease assets: credit Cash $750.

Journal Entry

Date	Account Titles and Explanation	Ref.	Debit	Credit
Oct. 31	Accounts Payable	201	750	
	Cash	101		750
	Paid cash on account to Aero Supply.			

Posting

Cash			101
Oct. 1	10,000	Oct. 3	900
3	1,200	3	600
25	800	20	500
31	9,000	24	4,000
		31	750

Accounts Payable			201
Oct. 31	750	Oct. 4	2,500

Summary Illustration of Journalizing and Posting

You should always think through the basic analysis and debit/credit analysis before journalizing a transaction. The analysis will help you understand the journal entries discussed in this chapter, as well as more complex journal entries in later chapters.

However, the actual accounting records will not show this analysis for each transaction. Instead the accounting records will show a chronological list of the transactions in the journal, and a ledger showing the effect on each account of posting all of the transactions.

The general journal for Pioneer Advertising Agency for October 2014 is summarized as follows:

GENERAL JOURNAL				J1
Date	**Account Titles and Explanation**	**Ref**	**Debit**	**Credit**
2014				
Oct. 1	Cash	101	10,000	
	C. Bedard, Capital	301		10,000
	Invested cash in business.			
2	Equipment	151	5,000	
	Notes Payable	200		5,000
	Issued three-month, 6% note for equipment.			
3	Cash	101	1,200	
	Unearned Revenue	209		1,200
	Received advance from R. Knox for future services.			
3	Rent Expense	726	900	
	Cash	101		900
	Paid October rent.			
3	Prepaid Insurance	130	600	
	Cash	101		600
	Paid one-year policy, expiring on September 30, 2015.			
4	Supplies	129	2,500	
	Accounts Payable	201		2,500
	Purchased supplies on account from Aero Supply.			
20	C. Bedard, Drawings	306	500	
	Cash	101		500
	Withdrew cash for personal use.			
21	Accounts Receivable	112	10,000	
	Service Revenue	400		10,000
	Performed services on account for Copa Company.			
24	Salaries Expense	729	4,000	
	Cash	101		4,000
	Paid biweekly salaries.			
25	Cash	101	800	
	Service Revenue	400		800
	Received cash for services provided.			
31	Cash	101	9,000	
	Accounts Receivable	112		9,000
	Received cash on account from Copa Company.			
31	Accounts Payable	201	750	
	Cash	101		750
	Paid cash on account to Aero Supply.			

The general ledger, with all account balances highlighted in red, for Pioneer Advertising Agency follows:

GENERAL LEDGER

Cash 101

Oct. 1	10,000	Oct. 3	900
3	1,200	3	600
25	800	20	500
31	9,000	24	4,000
		31	750
Bal.	14,250		

Accounts Receivable 112

Oct. 21	10,000	Oct. 31	9,000
Bal.	1,000		

Supplies 129

Oct. 4	2,500		
Bal.	2,500		

Prepaid Insurance 130

Oct. 3	600		
Bal.	600		

Equipment 151

Oct. 2	5,000		
Bal.	5,000		

Notes Payable 200

		Oct. 2	5,000
		Bal.	5,000

Accounts Payable 201

Oct. 31	750	Oct. 4	2,500
		Bal.	1,750

Unearned Revenue 209

		Oct. 3	1,200
		Bal.	1,200

C. Bedard, Capital 301

		Oct. 1	10,000
		Bal.	10,000

C. Bedard, Drawings 306

Oct. 20	500		
Bal.	500		

Service Revenue 400

		Oct. 21	10,000
		25	800
		Bal.	10,800

Rent Expense 726

Oct. 23	900		
Bal.	900		

Salaries Expense 729

Oct. 24	4,000		
Bal.	4,000		

BEFORE YOU GO ON...

DO IT

Selected transactions from the first two weeks of business for Hair It Is, a hair salon owned by Eszter Schwenke, follow:

1. On May 1, Eszter Schwenke opened a bank account in the name of Hair It Is and deposited $20,000 of her own money in this account as her initial investment.
2. On May 3, Hair It Is purchased equipment on account (to be paid in 30 days), for a total cost of $4,800.
3. Hired a stylist who started working on May 7 and agreed to pay her $500 per week.
4. During the first two weeks, performed $1,280 of hairstyling services, all collected in cash. (Note: Date this May 14.)
5. On May 15, paid the employee, hired on May 7, her $500 weekly salary.

(a) For each of the transactions, prepare a basic analysis, a debit/credit analysis, and a journal entry.
(b) Post the journal entries to the general ledger.

BEFORE YOU GO ON... continued on next page

BEFORE YOU GO ON...
continued from previous page

Action Plan

- Understand which activities need to be recorded and which do not.
- Analyze the transactions. Determine the accounts affected and whether the transaction increases or decreases the account.
- Apply the debit and credit rules.
- Record the transactions in the general journal following the formatting rules. Remember that the name of the account to be credited is indented and the amount is recorded in the right-hand column.
- Posting involves transferring the journalized debits and credits to specific accounts in the ledger.
- Determine the ending balances by netting (calculating the difference between) the total debits and credits.

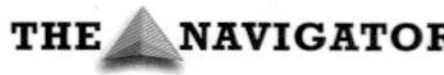

SOLUTION

(a)

Transaction1:

Basic Analysis	The asset account Cash is increased by $20,000. The owner's equity account E. Schwenke, Capital is increased by $20,000.
Debit/Credit Analysis	Debits increase assets: debit Cash $20,000. Credits increase owner's equity: credit E. Schwenke, Capital $20,000.
Journal Entry	May 1 Cash 20,000 E. Schwenke, Capital 20,000 Invested cash in business.

Transaction 2:

Basic Analysis	The asset account Equipment is increased by $4,800. The liability account Accounts Payable is increased by $4,800.
Debit/Credit Analysis	Debits increase assets: debit Equipment $4,800. Credits increase liabilities: credit Accounts Payable $4,800.
Journal Entry	May 3 Equipment 4,800 Accounts Payable 4,800 Purchased equipment on account.

Transaction 3:

Basic Analysis	An accounting transaction has not occurred.

Transaction 4:

Basic Analysis	The asset account Cash is increased by $1,280. The revenue account Service Revenue is increased by $1,280.
Debit/Credit Analysis	Debits increase assets: debit Cash $1,280. Credits increase revenues: credit Service Revenue $1,280.
Journal Entry	May 14 Cash 1,280 Service Revenue 1,280 Performed services for cash.

Transaction 5:

Basic Analysis	The expense account Salaries Expense is increased by $500. The asset account Cash is decreased by $500.
Debit/Credit Analysis	Debits increase expenses: debit Salaries Expense $500. Credits decrease assets: credit Cash $500.
Journal Entry	May 14 Salaries Expense 500 Cash 500 Paid salary for a week.

(b)

Cash	
20,000	
1,280	500
20,780	

Equipment	
4,800	

Accounts Payable	
	4,800

E. Schwenke, Capital	
	20,000

Service Revenue	
	1,280

Salaries Expense	
500	

Related exercise material: BE2-7, BE2-8, BE2-9, BE2-10, BE2-11, BE2-12, E2-4, E2-5, E2-6, E2-7, and E2-8.

THE TRIAL BALANCE

STUDY OBJECTIVE 3

Explain the purpose of a trial balance, and prepare one.

As discussed earlier in the chapter, the steps in the recording process are the first three steps in the accounting cycle. The fourth step in the accounting cycle, as shown in Illustration 2-7, is to prepare a trial balance.

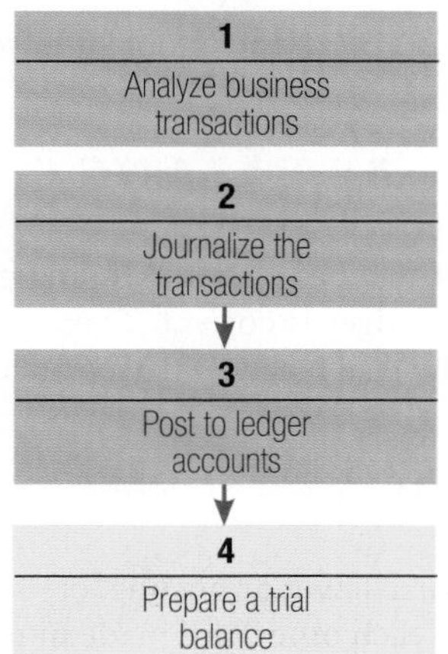

ILLUSTRATION 2-7
The accounting cycle—Steps 1 to 4

A **trial balance** is a list of the accounts in the ledger and the account balances at a specific time. If any accounts have a zero balance, they can be omitted from the trial balance. It is prepared at the end of an accounting period. In the trial balance, the accounts are listed in the same order as they are in the ledger, with debit balances in the left column and credit balances in the right column.

The main purpose of a trial balance is to prove (check) that the debits equal the credits after posting. That is, the sum of the debit account balances must equal the sum of the credit account balances. If the totals are not the same, this means an error was made in journalizing or posting the transactions, or in preparing the trial balance. For example, the trial balance will not balance if an incorrect amount is posted in the ledger. If the trial balance does not balance, then the error must be located and corrected before proceeding.

Helpful hint When the totals of the two columns are equal, the trial balance is considered "balanced."

A trial balance is also useful in preparing financial statements, as will be explained in the next two chapters. The procedure for preparing a trial balance is as follows:

1. List the account titles and their balances in the same order as in the chart of accounts. Debit balances are entered in the debit column and credit balances are entered in the credit column.
2. Total the debit and credit columns.
3. Ensure that the totals of the two columns are equal.

To illustrate how a trial balance is prepared, we will continue with the Pioneer Travel Agency illustration in the previous section of this chapter. We use the information in Pioneer Travel Agency's general ledger to prepare its trial balance shown in Illustration 2-8.

ILLUSTRATION 2-8
Pioneer Advertising Agency's trial balance

PIONEER ADVERTISING AGENCY
Trial Balance
October 31, 2014

	Debit	Credit
Cash	$14,250	
Accounts receivable	1,000	
Supplies	2,500	
Prepaid insurance	600	
Equipment	5,000	
Notes payable		$ 5,000
Accounts payable		1,750
Unearned revenue		1,200
C. Bedard, capital		10,000
C. Bedard, drawings	500	
Service revenue		10,800
Rent expense	900	
Salaries expense	4,000	
Totals	$28,750	$28,750

You should note the following:

1. The accounts are listed in the same order they were in the general ledger (and chart of accounts in Illustration 2-6).
2. The balance at October 31, 2014, of each account in the general ledger is included in the correct debit or credit column.
3. The total of the debit accounts, $28,750, is equal to the total of the credit accounts, $28,750.

LIMITATIONS OF A TRIAL BALANCE

ETHICS NOTE
An error is the result of an unintentional mistake; it is neither ethical nor unethical. An irregularity is an intentional mistake, which is generally viewed as unethical.

Although a trial balance can reveal many types of bookkeeping errors, it does not prove that all transactions have been recorded or that the ledger is correct. There can be many errors even when the trial balance columns agree. For example, the trial balance may balance even when:

1. a transaction is not journalized,
2. a correct journal entry is not posted,
3. a journal entry is posted twice,
4. incorrect accounts are used in journalizing or posting, or
5. offsetting errors (errors that hide each other) are made in recording the amount of a transaction.

As long as equal debits and credits are posted, even to the wrong account or in the wrong amount, the total debits will equal the total credits when the trial balance is prepared.

LOCATING ERRORS

Errors generally result from mathematical mistakes, incorrect postings, or simply recopying data incorrectly. (Note that an error is the result of an unintentional mistake; it is neither ethical nor unethical. An irregularity is an intentional mistake, which is generally viewed as unethical.) In a computerized system, the trial balance is usually balanced because most computerized systems will not let you enter an unbalanced journal entry, and because there are rarely software errors in posting or in the preparation of the trial balance.

What do you do if you have a manual trial balance that does not balance? First determine the amount of the difference between the two columns of the trial balance. After you know this amount, try the following steps:

1. If the error is an amount such as $1, $100, or $1,000, re-add the trial balance columns and recalculate the account balances.

ACCOUNTING IN ACTION
ALL ABOUT YOU INSIGHT

The double-entry accounting system used by many businesses today is in fact more than 500 years old. An Italian friar, Luca Pacioli, is considered to be the "Father of Accounting." His book, *Summa de Arithmetica, Geometria, Proportioniet Proportionalita* (Everything about Arithmetic, Geometry, and Proportions), published in 1494, included a section on accounting. However, Pacioli didn't invent double-entry accounting; he simply described a method that Venetian merchants used during the Italian Renaissance. Pacioli's chapters on accounting, entitled "De Computis et Scripturis" (Of Reckonings and Writings), included most of the accounting cycle known today. They described journals and ledgers, assets (including receivables and inventories), liabilities, capital, revenue, and expense accounts. The book demonstrated year-end closing entries and proposed using a trial balance to prove a balanced ledger. The details of the bookkeeping method Pacioli presented have been followed in accounting texts and the profession for centuries and are just as appropriate for individuals to use as for businesses.

Sources: L. Murphy Smith, "Luca Pacioli: The Father of Accounting" (revised 2011), from the website of the American Accounting Association.

Pacioli also wrote "a person should not go to sleep at night until the debits equalled the credits." Is this still good advice over 500 years later?

2. If the error can be evenly divided by two, scan the trial balance to see if a balance equal to half the error has been entered in the wrong column.
3. If the error can be evenly divided by nine, retrace the account balances on the trial balance to see whether they are incorrectly copied from the ledger. For example, if a balance was $12 but was listed as $21, a $9 error has been made. Reversing the order of numbers is called a transposition error.
4. If the error cannot be evenly divided by two or nine, scan the ledger to see whether an account balance in the amount of the error has been omitted from the trial balance. Scan the journal to see whether a posting in the amount of the error has been omitted.

SOME PROCESS EXPLANATIONS

Use of Dollars and Cents

In this textbook, in order to simplify the process, we have not included cents in the amounts we record in journal entries, general ledger accounts, and trial balances. In reality, cents are used in the formal accounting records. When a transaction is recorded in the journal and then posted to the ledger, cents are always used. But when the financial statements are prepared, the account balances are normally rounded to the nearest dollar, and in larger companies, they may be rounded to the nearest thousand or even million. Even though the Canadian government eliminated the penny for cash transactions, cheques can still be written to the nearest cent.

Use of Dollar Signs and Underlining

Both in practice and in accounting textbooks, dollar signs are not used in the journals or ledgers. Dollar signs are used only in the trial balance and the financial statements. Generally, a dollar sign is shown only for the first item in the column, and for the total of that column.

A single line is placed under a column of figures to be added or subtracted. Total amounts are double-underlined to indicate they are the final sum. In other words, a double underline under a number means that no further amounts will be added to, or subtracted from, that amount.

Account Numbers

As previously mentioned, in practice companies use both account names and account numbers. In this textbook, we have included account numbers in some of our examples and in some of the end-of-chapter exercises and problems. But in most of the examples throughout the textbook, we will use only account names, not account numbers, to simplify the process.

BEFORE YOU GO ON...

DO IT

Koizumi Kollections has the following alphabetical list of accounts and balances at July 31, 2014:

Account	Amount	Account	Amount
Accounts payable	$33,700	Land	$ 51,000
Accounts receivable	71,200	Notes payable	49,500
Building	86,500	Operating expenses	102,000
Cash	3,200	Prepaid insurance	3,100
Equipment	35,700	Service revenue	171,100
J. Koizumi, capital	99,400	Unearned revenue	3,000
J. Koizumi, drawings	4,000		

Each of the above accounts has a normal balance. Prepare a trial balance with the accounts in the same order as they would be in the ledger (in other words, in financial statement order).

BEFORE YOU GO ON... continued on next page

BEFORE YOU GO ON...
continued from previous page

Action Plan

- Reorder the accounts as they would normally be in the general ledger: balance sheet accounts are listed first (assets, liabilities, and equity) followed by income statement accounts (revenues and expenses).
- Determine whether each account has a normal debit or credit balance.
- List the amounts in the appropriate debit or credit column.
- Total the trial balance columns. Total debits must equal total credits or a mistake has been made.

SOLUTION

KOIZUMI KOLLECTIONS
Trial Balance
July 31, 2014

	Debit	Credit
Cash	$ 3,200	
Accounts receivable	71,200	
Prepaid insurance	3,100	
Land	51,000	
Building	86,500	
Equipment	35,700	
Accounts payable		$ 33,700
Unearned revenue		3,000
Notes payable		49,500
J. Koizumi, capital		99,400
J. Koizumi, drawings	4,000	
Service revenue		171,100
Operating expenses	102,000	
Totals	$356,700	$356,700

THE  NAVIGATOR

Related exercise material: BE2–13, BE2–14, E2–1, E2–9, E2–10, E2–11, E2–12, E2–13, and E2–14.

Comparing IFRS and ASPE

Key Differences	International Financial Reporting Standards (IFRS)	Accounting Standards for Private Enterprises (ASPE)
No significant differences		

THE NAVIGATOR

DEMONSTRATION PROBLEM

Nge Aung opened the Campus Laundromat on September 1, 2014. During the first month of operations, the following transactions occurred:

Sept.	1	Invested $15,000 cash and laundry equipment worth $5,000 in the business.
	2	Paid $1,000 cash for store rent for the month of September.
	3	Borrowed $15,000 cash from the bank and signed a $15,000, 6-month, 5% note payable.
	3	Purchased washers and dryers for $20,000 cash.
	6	Paid $1,200 for a one-year insurance policy.
	10	Received a bill from *The Daily News* for advertising the opening of the laundromat, $300.
	15	Billed a nearby restaurant $500 for laundry services performed on account.
	20	Withdrew $700 cash for personal use.
	25	Received $300 cash from the restaurant billed on September 15. The balance of the account will be collected in October.
	29	Received $400 cash advance from the college residence for services to be performed in October.
	30	Cash receipts for laundry services performed for the month were $6,200.
	30	Paid employee salaries of $1,600.
	30	Paid *The Daily News* $200 of the amount owed from the bill received September 10.

DEMONSTRATION PROBLEM continued on next page

DEMONSTRATION PROBLEM continued from previous page

The chart of accounts for the company is the same as the one for Pioneer Advertising Agency in Illustration 2-6 except for the following: No. 610 Advertising Expense.

Instructions

(a) Journalize the September transactions.
(b) Open ledger accounts and post the September transactions.
(c) Prepare a trial balance at September 30, 2014.
(d) Prepare an income statement, statement of owner's equity, and balance sheet for Campus Laundromat.

SOLUTION TO DEMONSTRATION PROBLEM

(a)

GENERAL JOURNAL **J1**

Date	Account Titles and Explanation	Ref	Debit	Credit
2014				
Sept. 1	Cash	101	15,000	
	Equipment	151	5,000	
	N. Aung, Capital			20,000
	Invested cash and equipment in business.	301		
2	Rent Expense	726	1,000	
	Cash	101		1,000
	Paid September rent.			
3	Cash	101	15,000	
	Notes Payable	200		15,000
	Borrowed from bank and signed a 6-month, 5% note payable.			
3	Equipment	151	20,000	
	Cash	101		20,000
	Purchased laundry equipment for cash.			
6	Prepaid Insurance	130	1,200	
	Cash	101		1,200
	Paid for a one-year insurance policy.			
10	Advertising Expense	610	300	
	Accounts Payable	201		300
	Received bill from *The Daily News* for advertising.			
15	Accounts Receivable	112	500	
	Service Revenue	400		500
	Performed laundry services on account.			
20	N. Aung, Drawings	306	700	
	Cash	101		700
	Withdrew cash for personal use.			
25	Cash	101	300	
	Accounts Receivable	112		300
	Received cash on account.			
29	Cash	101	400	
	Unearned Revenue	209		400
	Received cash in advance from customer.			
30	Cash	101	6,200	
	Service Revenue	400		6,200
	Received cash for laundry services.			
30	Salaries Expense	729	1,600	
	Cash	101		1,600
	Paid employee salaries.			
30	Accounts Payable	201	200	
	Cash	101		200
	Made a partial payment to *The Daily News.*			

Action Plan

- Determine if the transaction should be recorded or not.
- Do a basic analysis of the transaction. Identify the accounts that were changed and determine if these accounts increased or decreased and by how much.
- Do a debit/credit analysis of the transaction. Determine which account or accounts should be debited and which account or accounts should be credited and make sure debits equal credits.
- In the journal entry, use specific account titles taken from the chart of accounts.
- Include an appropriate description of each journal entry.
- Arrange the ledger in statement order, beginning with the balance sheet accounts.
- Post in chronological order.
- Put account numbers in the reference column of the journal to indicate the amount has been posted.
- In the trial balance, list the accounts in the same order as in the ledger (financial statement order).
- List debit balances in the left column of the trial balance and credit balances in the right column.
- Prepare the income statement first, then the statement of owner's equity, then the balance sheet.
- Use the profit from the income statement when preparing the statement of owner's equity.
- Use the owner's capital balance at September 30, 2014, in the statement of owner's capital when preparing the balance sheet.
- Remember that an income statement and a statement of owner's equity are for a period of time. A balance sheet is at a point in time.

SOLUTION TO DEMONSTRATION PROBLEM continued on next page

SOLUTION TO DEMONSTRATION PROBLEM continued from previous page

(b)

GENERAL LEDGER

Cash 101

Sept. 1	15,000	Sept. 2	1,000
3	15,000	3	20,000
25	300	6	1,200
29	400	20	700
30	6,200	30	1,600
		30	200
Bal.	12,200		

Accounts Receivable 112

Sept. 15	500	Sept. 25	300
Bal.	200		

Prepaid Insurance 130

Sept. 6	1,200		
Bal.	1,200		

Equipment 151

Sept. 1	5,000		
3	20,000		
Bal.	25,000		

Notes Payable 200

		Sept. 3	15,000
		Bal.	15,000

Accounts Payable 201

Sept. 30	200	Sept. 10	300
		Bal.	100

Unearned Revenue 209

		Sept. 29	400
		Bal.	400

N. Aung, Capital 301

		Sept. 1	20,000
		Bal.	20,000

N. Aung, Drawings 306

Sept. 20	700		
Bal.	700		

Service Revenue 400

		Sept. 15	500
		30	6,200
		Bal.	6,700

Advertising Expense 610

Sept. 10	300		
Bal.	300		

Rent Expense 726

Sept. 2	1,000		
Bal.	1,000		

Salaries Expense 729

Sept. 30	1,600		
Bal.	1,600		

(c)

CAMPUS LAUNDROMAT
Trial Balance
September 30, 2014

	Debit	Credit
Cash	$12,200	
Accounts receivable	200	
Prepaid insurance	1,200	
Equipment	25,000	
Notes payable		$15,000
Accounts payable		100
Unearned revenue		400
N. Aung, capital		20,000
N. Aung, drawings	700	
Service revenue		6,700
Advertising expense	300	
Rent expense	1,000	
Salaries expense	1,600	
Totals	$42,200	$42,200

SOLUTION TO DEMONSTRATION PROBLEM continued on next page

SOLUTION TO DEMONSTRATION PROBLEM continued from previous page

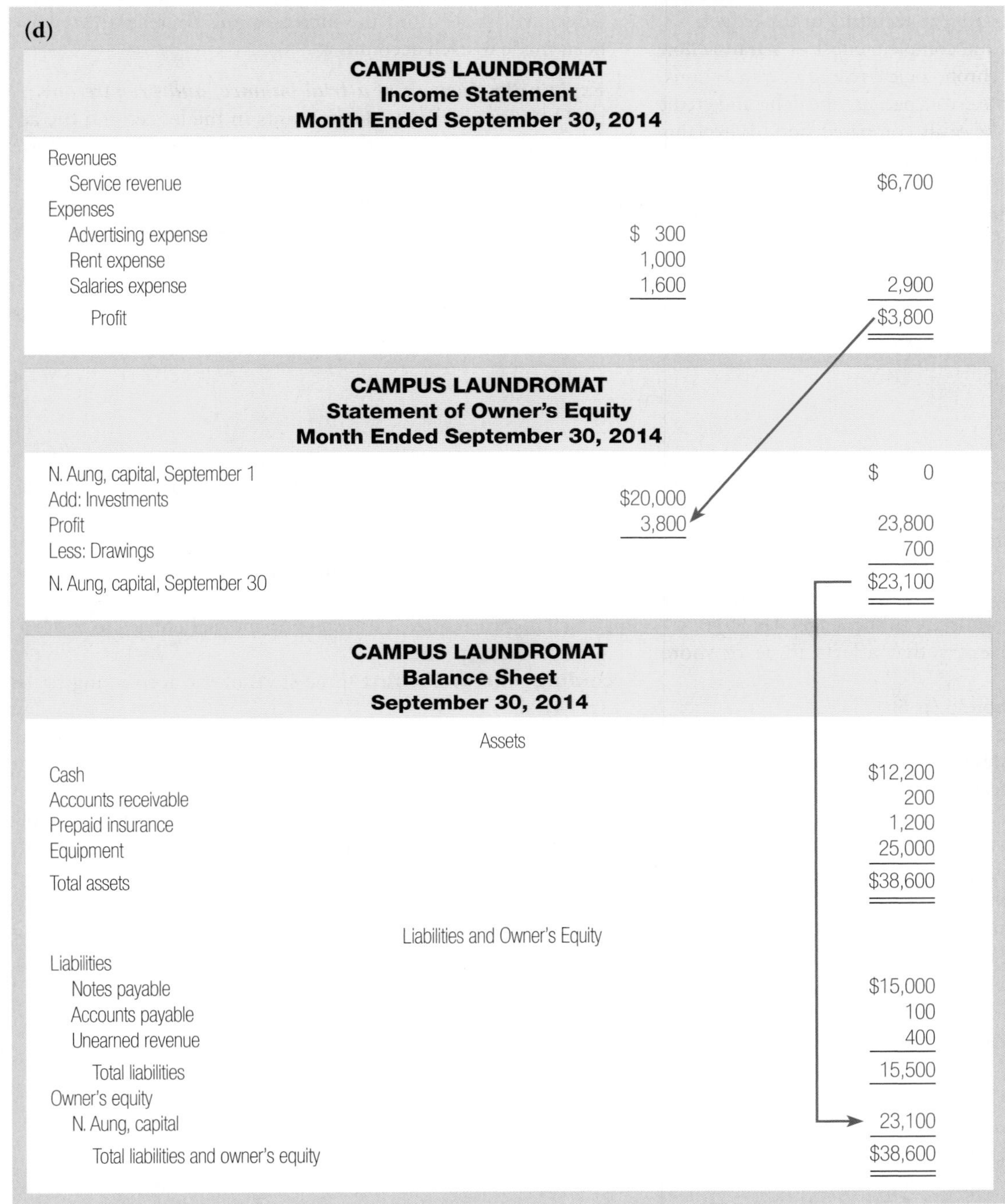

(d)

CAMPUS LAUNDROMAT
Income Statement
Month Ended September 30, 2014

Revenues		
Service revenue		$6,700
Expenses		
Advertising expense	$ 300	
Rent expense	1,000	
Salaries expense	1,600	2,900
Profit		$3,800

CAMPUS LAUNDROMAT
Statement of Owner's Equity
Month Ended September 30, 2014

N. Aung, capital, September 1		$ 0
Add: Investments	$20,000	
Profit	3,800	23,800
Less: Drawings		700
N. Aung, capital, September 30		$23,100

CAMPUS LAUNDROMAT
Balance Sheet
September 30, 2014

Assets	
Cash	$12,200
Accounts receivable	200
Prepaid insurance	1,200
Equipment	25,000
Total assets	$38,600
Liabilities and Owner's Equity	
Liabilities	
Notes payable	$15,000
Accounts payable	100
Unearned revenue	400
Total liabilities	15,500
Owner's equity	
N. Aung, capital	23,100
Total liabilities and owner's equity	$38,600

THE NAVIGATOR

Summary of Study Objectives

1. ***Define debits and credits and illustrate how they are used to record transactions.*** Debit means left and credit means right. The normal balance of an asset is a debit because assets are on the left side of the accounting equation. Assets are increased by debits and decreased by credits. The normal balance of liabilities and owner's capital is a credit because they are on the right side of the accounting equation. Liabilities and owner's capital are increased by credits and decreased by debits. Revenues increase owner's equity and therefore are recorded as credits because credits increase owner's equity. Credits increase revenues and debits decrease revenues. Expenses and drawings decrease owner's equity and therefore are recorded as debits because debits decrease owner's equity. Expenses and drawings are increased by debits and decreased by credits.

2. ***Explain the recording process and analyze, journalize, and post transactions.*** The steps in the recording process are the first three steps in the accounting cycle. These steps

are: (a) analyze each transaction for its effect on the accounts, (b) record the transaction in a journal, and (c) transfer the journal information to the correct accounts in the ledger.

A journal (a) discloses the complete effect of a transaction in one place, (b) provides a chronological record of transactions, (c) helps to prevent and locate errors because the debit and credit amounts for each entry can be easily compared, and (d) explains the transaction and, if there is one, identifies the source document.

The entire group of accounts maintained by a company is called the ledger. The ledger keeps in one place all the information about changes in each of the specific account balances.

Posting is the procedure of transferring journal entries to the ledger accounts. After the journal entries have been posted, the ledger will show all of the increases and decreases that have been made to each account.

3. ***Explain the purpose of a trial balance, and prepare one.*** A trial balance is a list of the accounts in the ledger and the account balances at a specific time. Its main purpose is to prove that debits and credits are equal after posting. A trial balance uncovers certain types of errors in journalizing and posting, and is useful in preparing financial statements. Preparing a trial balance is the fourth step in the accounting cycle.

THE NAVIGATOR

Glossary

Account A record of increases and decreases in a specific asset, liability, or owner's equity item. (p. 50)

Accounting cycle A series of steps followed by accountants in preparing financial statements. (p. 54)

Chart of accounts A list of accounts and the account numbers that identify where the accounts are in the ledger. (p. 59)

Compound entry A journal entry that affects three or more accounts. (p. 57)

Credit The right side of an account. (p. 50)

Debit The left side of an account. (p. 50)

Double-entry accounting system A system that records the dual (two-sided) effect of each transaction in appropriate accounts. (p. 53)

General journal The most basic form of journal in which transactions are recorded when they are not recorded in other specialized journals. (p. 56)

General ledger A ledger that contains accounts for all assets, liabilities, equities, revenues, and expenses. (p. 57)

Journal An accounting record where transactions are recorded in chronological (date) order. It shows the debit and credit effect of each transaction on specific accounts. (p. 55)

Journalizing The entering of transaction data in the journal. (p. 56)

Ledger A record that contains all of a company's accounts. It keeps all the information about changes in each account in one place. (p. 57)

Posting The procedure of transferring journal entries to the ledger accounts. (p. 58)

Recording process The first three steps of the accounting cycle. (p. 54)

T account A form of account that looks like the letter T. It has the title above the horizontal line. Debits are shown to the left of the vertical line, credits to the right. (p. 50)

Three-column form of account An account form with columns for debit, credit, and balance amounts in an account. (p. 58)

Trial balance A list of the accounts in the ledger and the account balances at a specific time, usually at the end of the accounting period. (p. 67)

Self-Study Questions

Answers are at the end of the chapter.

(SO 1) K 1. Which of the following statements about an account is true?
(a) The left side of an account is the credit or decrease side.
(b) An account is an individual accounting record of increases and decreases in specific asset, liability, and owner's equity items.
(c) There are separate accounts for specific assets and liabilities but only one account for owner's equity items.
(d) The right side of an account is the debit or increase side.

(SO 1) K 2. Credits:
(a) increase both assets and liabilities.
(b) decrease both assets and liabilities.
(c) increase assets and decrease liabilities.
(d) decrease assets and increase liabilities.

(SO 1) K 3. An expense account:
(a) is increased by debits.
(b) has a normal balance of a credit.
(c) is decreased by debits.
(d) is increased by credits.

(SO 1) K 4. Accounts that normally have debit balances are:
(a) assets, expenses, and revenues.
(b) assets, expenses, and owner's capital.
(c) assets, liabilities, and drawings.
(d) assets, expenses, and drawings.

(SO 2) K 5. What is the correct sequence of steps in the recording process?
(a) Analyzing transactions; preparing a trial balance
(b) Analyzing transactions; entering transactions in a journal; posting transactions
(c) Entering transactions in a journal; posting transactions; preparing a trial balance
(d) Entering transactions in a journal; posting transactions; analyzing transactions

(SO 2) AP 6. Performing services for a customer on account should result in:
(a) a decrease in the liability account Accounts Payable and an increase in the revenue account Service Revenue.
(b) an increase in the asset account Cash and a decrease in the asset account Accounts Receivable.
(c) an increase to the asset account Accounts Receivable and an increase to the liability account Unearned Revenue.
(d) an increase to the asset account Accounts Receivable and an increase to the revenue account Service Revenue.

(SO 2) AP 7. The purchase of equipment on account should result in:
(a) a debit to Equipment and a credit to Accounts Payable.
(b) a debit to Equipment Expense and a credit to Accounts Payable.
(c) a debit to Equipment and a credit to Cash.
(d) a debit to Accounts Receivable and a credit to Equipment.

(SO 2) K 8. Which of these statements about a journal is false?
(a) It is not a book of original entry.
(b) It provides a chronological record of transactions.
(c) It helps to locate errors because the debit and credit amounts for each entry can be easily compared.
(d) It shows in one place the complete effect of a transaction.

(SO 2) K 9. A ledger:
(a) contains only asset and liability accounts.
(b) should show accounts in alphabetical order.
(c) is a collection of the entire group of accounts maintained by a company.
(d) is a book of original entry.

(SO 2) K 10. Posting:
(a) is normally done before journalizing.
(b) transfers ledger transaction data to the journal.
(c) is an optional step in the recording process.
(d) transfers journal entries to ledger accounts.

(SO 3) K 11. A trial balance:
(a) is a list of accounts with their balances at a specific time.
(b) proves that journalized transactions are accurate.
(c) will not balance if a correct journal entry is posted twice.
(d) proves that all transactions have been recorded.

(SO 3) AP 12. A trial balance will not balance if:
(a) the collection of an account receivable is posted twice.
(b) the purchase of supplies on account is debited to Supplies and credited to Cash.
(c) a $100 cash drawing by the owner is debited to Drawings for $1,000 and credited to Cash for $100.
(d) a $450 payment on account is debited to Accounts Payable for $45 and credited to Cash for $45.

THE NAVIGATOR

Questions

(SO 1) C 1. What is an account? Will a company need more than one account? Explain.

(SO 1) K 2. What is debiting an account? What is crediting an account?

(SO 1) K 3. Explain the relationship between the normal balance in each type of account and the accounting equation.

(SO 1) C 4. Kim Nguyen, a beginning accounting student, believes credit balances are favourable and debit balances are unfavourable. Is Kim correct? Discuss.

(SO 1) C 5. Dmitri Karpov doesn't understand how a debit increases Equipment and a credit increases Accounts Payable. He believes that debits and credits cannot both increase account balances. Explain to Dmitri why he is wrong.

(SO 1) C 6. Why are increases to drawings and expenses recorded as debits?

(SO 1) C 7. Jermyn Orsen, an introductory accounting student, thinks that a double-entry accounting system means that each transaction is recorded twice. Is Jermyn correct? Explain.

(SO 2) C 8. Jennifer Halford doesn't understand why some events are recorded as accounting transactions but others are not. Explain.

(SO 2) C 9. What is involved in analyzing a business transaction?

(SO 2) K 10. What is the difference between a simple and a compound journal entry? What rule must be followed when recording a compound entry so the accounting equation remains balanced?

(SO 2) K 11. Hiroshi Benoit, a fellow student, is unclear about similarities and differences between using a manual system or a computerized system in the recording process. Briefly explain, including the benefit of a computerized system.

(SO 2) C 12. A company receives cash from a customer. List three different accounts that could be credited and the circumstances under which each of these accounts would be credited.

(SO 2) C 13. Amber Rose believes that accounting would be more efficient if transactions were recorded directly in the ledger accounts. Explain to Amber the advantages of first recording transactions in the journal, and then posting them to the ledger.

(SO 2) C 14. Explain the differences between the format of a T account and the standard form of accounts. In your explanation, include the benefits of each format, and when each format is typically used.

(SO 2) C 15. What are the differences between a ledger and a chart of accounts?

(SO 3) K 16. What is a trial balance? What are its purposes?

(SO 3) C 17. Does it matter in what order the accounts are listed on a trial balance? Explain.

(SO 3) C 18. Yue Shin thinks it doesn't matter in what order the first four steps in the accounting cycle are completed, as long as they are all done before moving on to remaining steps. Do you agree or disagree with Yue? Explain.

(SO 3) C 19. Jamal Nazari is doing the accounting for a company that has a December 31 year end. He is wondering if the heading on its trial balance should read "Year Ended December 31" or just "December 31." Which one is correct? Explain why.

(SO 3) AN 20. Two students are discussing the use of a trial balance. They wonder if the following errors in different companies would prevent a trial balance from balancing. For each error, what would you tell the students?

(a) The bookkeeper debited Supplies for $750 and debited Accounts Payable for $750 for the purchase of supplies on account.

(b) Cash collected on account was debited to Cash for $1,000 and credited to Service Revenue for $1,000.

(c) A journal entry recording the payment of rent expense was posted to the general ledger as a $650 debit to Rent Expense and a $560 credit to Cash.

(SO 3) AP 21. Maureen Melnyk has just prepared a trial balance for a company and found that the total debits were $450 higher than the total credits. Assuming that the account balances in the ledger are correct, give Maureen three examples of things that she might have done incorrectly when preparing the trial balance.

Brief Exercises

Calculate missing amounts and account balances.
(SO 1) AP

BE2–1 For the three accounts that follow, fill in the missing amounts (a) through (f):

Accounts Receivable	
7,500	
16,700	
	15,400
Bal. (a)	
13,100	
	(b)
Bal. 4,700	

Supplies	
6,400	
(c)	
	6,800
Bal. 3,800	
7,700	
	5,900
Bal. (d)	

Notes Payable	
	100,000
24,000	
	45,000
	Bal. (e)
	(f)
27,000	
	Bal. 149,000

Indicate type of account and normal balance.
(SO 1) K

BE2–2 For each the following accounts, indicate (a) if the account is an asset, liability, or owner's equity account; and (b) whether the account would have a normal debit or credit balance.

1. Accounts Receivable
2. Accounts Payable
3. Equipment
4. Rent Expense
5. B. Damji, Drawings
6. Supplies
7. Unearned Revenue
8. Cash
9. Service Revenue
10. Prepaid Insurance
11. Utilities Expense
12. Notes Payable

BE2–3 For each of the following accounts, indicate (a) the normal balance, (b) the effect of a debit on the account, and (c) the effect of a credit on the account:

Indicate normal balance and debit and credit effects. **(SO 1) K**

1. Accounts Payable
2. Accounts Receivable
3. Cash
4. Supplies
5. J. Takamoto, Capital
6. J. Takamoto, Drawings
7. Prepaid Rent
8. Rent Expense
9. Service Revenue
10. Unearned Revenue

BE2–4 For each of the following, indicate (a) if the account is an asset, liability, or owner's equity account; and (b) whether you would use a debit or credit to record the change:

Indicate type of account and when to use debits and credits. **(SO 1) K**

1. Increase in D. Parmelee, Capital
2. Decrease in Cash
3. Decrease in Notes Payable
4. Increase in Rent Expense
5. Increase in D. Parmelee, Drawings
6. Increase in Equipment
7. Increase in Accounts Payable
8. Increase in Service Revenue

BE2–5 Levine Legal Services had the following transactions:

Prepare basic analysis and debit/credit analysis for transactions. **(SO 1) C**

1. Cash is paid for the purchase of $445 of office supplies.
2. Customer is billed $1,500 for services provided that day.
3. Equipment with a cost of $2,500 is purchased on account.
4. The current month's utility bill of $225 is paid in cash.
5. Cash of $500 is received for services provided that day.
6. Ruben Levine, the company's owner, withdraws $800 cash from the company's bank account for personal use.
7. Cash of $2,200 is paid to employees for the current month's wages.
8. Cash of $750 is received for services to be provided in the next month.

For each transaction, prepare a basic analysis and a debit/credit analysis. Use the following format, in which the first one has been done for you as an example:

Transaction 1:

Basic Analysis	The asset Cash is decreased by $445. The asset Supplies is increased by $445.
Debit/Credit Analysis	Debits increase assets: debit Supplies $445. Credits decrease assets: credit Cash $445.

BE2–6 Fleming's Logistics Consulting has the following transactions during August:

Identify accounts and debit/credit analysis. **(SO 1) C**

Aug.	1	Received $16,750 cash from the company's owner, Barbara Fleming.
	4	Paid rent in advance for three months, $3,900.
	5	Purchased $645 of office supplies on account.
	6	Received $950 from clients for services provided.
	17	Billed clients $1,500 for services provided.
	27	Paid secretary $875 salary.
	29	Paid the company's owner, Barbara Fleming, $700 cash for personal use.

For each transaction, indicate (a) the basic type of account to be debited and credited (asset, liability, owner's equity); (b) the specific accounts to debit and credit (for example, Cash, Service Revenue, Accounts Payable); and (c) whether each account is increased (+) or decreased (−), and by what amount. Use the following format, in which the first one has been done for you as an example:

	Account Debited			Account Credited		
Transaction	(a) Basic Type	(b) Specific Account	(c) Effect	(a) Basic Type	(b) Specific Account	(c) Effect
Aug. 1	Asset	Cash	+$16,750	Owner's Equity	B. Fleming, Capital	+$16,750

BE2–7 Princess Printing Company had the following transactions with a customer during January: (1) performed services, such as printing flyers, and billed the customer; (2) collected cash on account from the customer; and (3) sent a statement at the end of the month, showing the balance owing, to the customer. Analyze each of these transactions and determine if they should be recorded or not. Explain why or why not for each transaction.

Analyze transactions. **(SO 2) AP**

Prepare basic analysis, debit/credit analysis, and journal entry. **(SO 1, 2) AP**

BE2–8 Pridham Welding Company had the following transactions for June.

June	1	Tyler Pridham invested $9,500 cash in a small welding business.
	2	Bought used welding equipment on account for $3,000.
	5	Hired an employee to start work on July 15. Agreed on a salary of $3,600 per month.
	17	Billed R. Windl $1,975 for welding work done.
	27	Received $1,000 cash from R. Windl for work billed on June 17.
	29	Paid for equipment purchased on June 2.
	30	Paid employee $1,800 for one-half of a month's work.

For each transaction, prepare a basic analysis, a debit/credit analysis, and journalize the transaction. Use the following format, in which the first one has been done for you as an example:

June 1 transaction:

Basic Analysis	The asset account Cash is increased by $9,500. The owner's equity account T. Pridham, Capital is increased by $9,500.
Debit/Credit Analysis	Debits increase assets: debit Cash $9,500. Credits increase owner's equity: credit T. Pridham, Capital $9,500.
Journal Entry	June 1 Cash 9,500 T. Pridham, Capital 9,500 Invested cash in business.

Record transactions. **(SO 2) AP**

BE2–9 Using the data in BE2–5 for Levine Legal Services, journalize the transactions. Assume all of the transactions occurred on August 31.

Record transactions. **(SO 2) AP**

BE2–10 Using the data in BE2–6 for Fleming's Logistics Consulting, journalize the transactions.

Post journal entries. **(SO 2) AP**

BE2–11 Using T accounts, post the journal entries from BE2–10 to the general ledger.

Post journal entries. **(SO 2) AP**

BE2–12 Using T accounts, post the following journal entries to the general ledger.

GENERAL JOURNAL

Date	Account title and explanation	Debit	Credit
Sept. 2	Accounts Receivable	2,275	
	Service Revenue		2,275
4	Supplies	750	
	Accounts Payable		750
10	Cash	1,050	
	Service Revenue		1,050
14	Utilities Expense	95	
	Cash		95
15	Salaries Expense	850	
	Cash		850
28	Cash	1,325	
	Accounts Receivable		1,325
30	Accounts Payable	450	
	Cash		450

Prepare trial balance. **(SO 3) AP**

BE2–13 Use the ledger balances that follow to prepare a trial balance for the Pettipas Company at April 30, 2014. All account balances are normal.

Accounts payable	$ 3,300	Prepaid rent	$ 800
Accounts receivable	5,000	Rent expense	4,500
C. Pettipas, capital	22,500	Salaries expense	1,000
C. Pettipas, drawings	1,100	Service revenue	8,000
Cash	6,400	Supplies	650
Equipment	14,600	Unearned revenue	250

BE2–14 There are two errors in the following trial balance: (1) one account has been placed in the wrong column, and (2) there is a transposition error in the balance of the L. Bourque, Capital account. Explain the two errors.

Explain errors in trial balance. **(SO 3) AP**

BOURQUE COMPANY
Trial Balance
December 31, 2014

	Debit	Credit
Cash	$15,000	
Accounts receivable	1,800	
Prepaid insurance		$ 3,500
Accounts payable		2,000
Unearned revenue		2,200
L. Bourque, capital		15,400
L. Bourque, drawings	4,900	
Service revenue		27,500
Rent	2,400	
Salaries	18,600	
Totals	$42,700	$50,600

Exercises

E2–1 Here are some of the concepts discussed in the chapter:

Match concepts with descriptions. **(SO 1, 2, 3) K**

1. Account
2. Analyzing transactions
3. Chart of accounts
4. Credit
5. Debit
6. Journal
7. Journalizing
8. Ledger
9. Posting
10. Trial balance

Instructions

Match each concept with the best description below. Each concept may be used more than once, or may not be used at all.

(a) ________ The normal balance for liabilities
(b) ________ The first step in the recording process
(c) ________ The procedure of transferring journal entries to the ledger accounts
(d) ________ A record of increases and decreases in a specific asset, liability, or owner's equity item
(e) ________ The left side of an account
(f) ________ The entering of transaction data in the journal
(g) ________ A list of accounts and their balances at a specific time
(h) ________ Used to decrease the balance in an asset account
(i) ________ A list of all of a company's accounts
(j) ________ An accounting record where transactions are recorded in chronological (date) order

E2–2 Kobayashi Company has the following accounts:

Identify type of account, financial statement, and normal balance. Explain normal balances. **(SO 1) C**

Account	(1) Type of Account	(2) Financial Statement	(3) Normal Balance
Cash	Asset	Balance Sheet	Debit
M. Kobayashi, Capital			
Accounts Payable			
Building			
Fees Earned			
Insurance Expense			
Interest Revenue			
M. Kobayashi, Drawings			
Notes Receivable			
Prepaid Insurance			
Rent Expense			
Supplies			

Instructions

(a) Complete the table. Identify (1) the type of account as asset, liability, or owner's equity (for owner's equity accounts, also identify if it is a capital, drawings, revenue, or expense account); (2) what financial statement it is presented on; and (3) the normal balance of the account. The first one has been done for you as an example.

(b) Explain why the normal balance for each of the different types of accounts is either a debit or credit. Refer to the accounting equation in your explanation.

Identify accounts and determine debits and credits. **(SO 1) C**

E2–3 In the first month of business, Jakmak Interior Design Company had the following transactions:

Mar. 3 The owner, Jackie MacKenzie, invested $10,000 cash in the business.
4 Borrowed $10,000 from the bank and signed a note payable.
6 Purchased a used car for $9,500 cash, for use in the business.
7 Purchased supplies on account for $1,500.
12 Billed customers $2,100 for services performed.
21 Paid $525 cash for advertising the launch of the business.
25 Received $1,200 cash from customers billed on March 12.
28 Paid for the supplies purchased on March 7.
30 Received $750 cash from a customer for services to be performed in April.
31 Paid Jackie MacKenzie $1,400 cash for her personal use.

Instructions

For each transaction, indicate:

(a) the basic type of account debited and credited (asset, liability, owner's equity).
(b) the specific account debited and credited (Cash, Rent Expense, Service Revenue, and so on).
(c) whether each account is increased (+) or decreased (−), and by what amount.

Use the following format, in which the first transaction is given as an example:

	Account Debited			Account Credited		
	(a)	(b)	(c)	(a)	(b)	(c)
Transaction	Basic Type	Specific Account	Effect	Basic Type	Specific Account	Effect
Mar. 3	Asset	Cash	+$10,000	Owner's Equity	J. MacKenzie, Capital	+$10,000

Prepare basic analysis, debit/credit analysis, and journal entry. **(SO 1, 2) AP**

E2–4 Bratt Plumbing Company had the following transactions for June:

June 1 Paid $550 for rent for the month of June.
2 Paid $175 for one month of insurance.
5 Collected an account of $1,255 for plumbing services provided in May. This account was billed and correctly recorded in May.
9 Provided Jeff Dupuis, a potential customer, with an estimate of $5,000 for plumbing work that will be performed in July if the customer hires Bratt Plumbing.
14 Paid $675 for supplies purchased on account in May. The purchase in May had been correctly recorded.
17 Billed Rudy Holland $1,420 for plumbing work done.
19 Jeff Dupuis agreed to hire Bratt Plumbing (see the June 9 transaction) and gave Bratt Plumbing a down payment of $1,000.
29 Purchased $1,575 of equipment on account.
30 Paid an employee $850.
30 Paid D. Bratt, the company owner, $1,250.

Instructions

For each transaction, prepare a basic analysis and a debit/credit analysis, and journalize the transaction. Use the format shown in BE2–8.

Record transactions. **(SO 2) AP**

E2–5 Data for Jakmak Interior Design Company are presented in E2–3.

Instructions

Journalize the transactions.

Record transactions and identify impact on owner's equity. **(SO 2) AP**

E2–6 At the end of March 2014, total owner's equity for Beaulieu Group Company was $8,050. During April, the following transactions occurred:

Apr. 1 Provided services to a client and received $1,785 cash.
1 Paid $965 for April's rent.

Apr. 4	Purchased $480 of supplies on account.
6	Provided services to a client and billed the client $2,160.
9	Collected $1,000 from the client billed on April 6.
13	Received $5,000 cash from the bank and signed a one-year, 5% note payable.
18	Used the cash received on April 12 to purchase equipment.
21	Received $800 cash from a client for services to be provided in May.
24	Paid $850 cash for radio advertising that will be aired in May.
27	Paid for the supplies purchased on account on April 4.
28	Shehla Beaulieu, the owner, withdrew $1,565 cash for personal use.

Instructions

(a) Journalize the transactions.
(b) For each transaction, identify if it increased, decreased, or had no effect on owner's equity and explain why.
(c) Calculate total owner's equity as at April 30.

E2–7 Selected transactions for Polland Real Estate Agency during its first month of business follow:

Record transactions.
(SO 2) AP

Oct. 1	Samantha Polland opened Polland Real Estate Agency with an investment of $14,000 cash and $3,000 of equipment.
2	Paid $1,200 for a one-year insurance policy.
3	Purchased additional equipment for $4,450, paying $850 cash and signing a note payable for the balance.
10	Received $350 cash as a fee for renting an apartment.
16	Sold a house and lot to B. Rollins. The commission due from Rollins is $7,500. (It is not paid by Rollins at this time.)
27	Paid $700 for advertising costs during October.
29	Received a $95 bill for telephone service during the month of October. (The bill is paid in November.)
30	Paid an administrative assistant $2,000 in salary for October.
31	Received $7,500 cash from B. Rollins for the October 16 transaction.

Instructions

Journalize the transactions.

E2–8 Journal entries for Polland Real Estate Agency's transactions were prepared in E2–7.

Post journal entries.
(SO 2) AP

Instructions

Post the journal entries to the general ledger, using T accounts.

E2–9 Fortin Co.'s ledger is as follows:

Record transactions and prepare trial balance.
(SO 2, 3) AP

Cash

Oct. 1	1,200	Oct. 3	400
10	650	12	500
15	3,000	30	600
20	800	31	250
25	2,000	31	500

Accounts Receivable

Oct. 6	1,000	Oct. 20	800
20	940		

Supplies

Oct. 4	800		

Equipment

Oct. 3	5,400		

Notes Payable

		Oct. 3	5,000

Accounts Payable

Oct. 12	500	Oct. 4	800
		28	400

A. Fortin, Capital

		Oct. 1	1,200
		25	2,000

A. Fortin, Drawings

Oct. 30	600		

Service Revenue

		Oct. 6	1,000
		10	650
		15	3,000
		20	940

Advertising Expense

Oct. 28	400		

Rent Expense

Oct. 31	250		

Salaries Expense

Oct. 31	500		

Instructions

(a) Journalize the October transactions, and give explanations for each entry.
(b) Determine the October 31, 2014, balance for each account. Prepare a trial balance at October 31, 2014.

Post journal entries and prepare trial balance. **(SO 2, 3) AP**

E2–10 On July 31, 2014, Lee Meche, MD, had the following balances in the ledger for his medical practice: Cash $8,800; Accounts Receivable $2,750; Supplies $585; Equipment $15,550; Notes Payable $10,000; Accounts Payable $850; L. Meche, Capital $15,000; L. Meche, Drawings $5,125; Fees Earned $10,410; Rent Expense $1,200; and Salaries Expense $2,250. Selected transactions during August 2014 follow:

GENERAL JOURNAL

Date	Account title and explanation	Ref	Debit	Credit
2014				
Aug. 1	Rent Expense		1,200	
	Cash			1,200
10	Accounts Payable		420	
	Cash			420
12	Cash		2,400	
	Accounts Receivable			2,400
25	Salaries Expense		2,250	
	Cash			2,250
30	Notes Payable		500	
	Interest Expense		40	
	Cash			540
31	Cash		5,910	
	Accounts Receivable		2,550	
	Fees Earned			8,460
31	L. Meche, Drawings		4,770	
	Cash			4,770

Instructions

(a) Create T accounts and enter the July 31 balances.
(b) Post the transactions to the T accounts. Create new T accounts if needed.
(c) Prepare a trial balance at August 31.

Prepare and post journal entries. Prepare trial balance and financial statements. **(SO 2, 3) AP**

E2–11 Ahuja Dental Services' general ledger at April 30, 2014, included the following: Cash, $6,000; Supplies, $1,000; Equipment, $65,000; Notes Payable, $50,000; Accounts Payable, $800; and S. Ahuja, Capital, $21,200. During May 2014, the following transactions occurred:

May 2 Paid May's rent of $1,200.
4 Purchased $700 supplies on account.
15 Paid the accounts payable owing from April 30, 2014.
31 Paid the dental assistant's salary of $1,800.
31 Earned revenue of $10,000 for dental services during May. Collected $9,500 of this in cash.

Instructions

(a) Journalize May's transactions.
(b) Using T accounts, enter the balances as at April 30, 2014, then post May's journal entries.
(c) Prepare a trial balance.
(d) Prepare financial statements for May.

Prepare trial balance and financial statements. **(SO 3) AP**

E2–12 A list of accounts and their balances of O'Neill's Psychological Services, at its year end July 31, 2014, is presented below.

Supplies	$ 790	Notes Payable	$22,960
Unearned Revenue	1,350	Salaries Expense	45,540
Supplies Expense	5,960	T. O'Neill, Drawings	57,980
Cash	6,470	Equipment	58,900
Accounts Receivable	7,340	T. O'Neill, Capital	64,340
Accounts Payable	9,030	Service Revenue	96,180
Rent Expense	10,880		

Instructions

(a) Prepare a trial balance in financial statement order.
(b) Prepare an income statement, statement of owner's equity, and balance sheet.

E2–13 The accountant for Smistad Guitar Repair Company made a number of errors in journalizing and posting, as described below:

Analyze errors and their effect on the trial balance. **(SO 3) AN**

1. A credit posting of $400 to Accounts Payable was omitted.
2. A debit posting of $750 for Rent Expense was debited to Prepaid Rent.
3. A collection on account of $100 was journalized and posted as a $100 debit to Cash and a $100 credit to Service Revenue.
4. A credit posting of $500 to Accounts Payable was made twice.
5. A cash purchase of supplies for $250 was journalized and posted as a $25 debit to Supplies and a $25 credit to cash.
6. A debit of $475 to Advertising Expense was posted as $457.
7. A journal entry for the payment of $1,200 of salaries expense was posted twice.

Instructions

Considering each error separately, indicate the following using the format below, where error number 1 is given as an example.

(a) Will the trial balance be in balance?
(b) What is the amount of the error if the trial balance will not balance?
(c) Which trial balance column will have the larger total?
(d) Which account or accounts have an incorrect balance? If the balance in all of the accounts is correct, write "all correct."

	(a)	(b)	(c)	(d)
Error	In Balance	Difference	Larger Column	Incorrect Accounts
1	No	$400	Debit	Accounts Payable

E2–14 Terry Zelinski, the owner of Royal Mountain Tours, prepared the following trial balance at March 31, 2014.

Prepare corrected trial balance. **(SO 3) AP**

Cash	$12,800	
Accounts receivable	4,090	
Supplies	840	
Equipment	7,350	
Accounts payable		$ 2,500
T. Zelinski, capital		24,000
T. Zelinski, drawings		3,650
Service revenue	6,750	
Advertising expense	3,700	
Salaries expense	400	
Totals	$35,930	$30,150

A review shows that Terry made the following errors in the accounting records:

1. A purchase of $400 of supplies on account was recorded as a credit to cash. The debit entry was correct.
2. A $100 credit to accounts receivable was posted as $1,000.
3. A journal entry to record service revenue of $770 earned on account was not prepared or posted.
4. A journal entry to record the payment of $240 for an advertising expense was correctly prepared but the credit to cash was posted as a debit. The debit to advertising expense was properly posted.

Instructions

Prepare the correct trial balance at March 31, 2014, using the format shown in the chapter. (*Hint*: You should also make sure that the account balances are recorded in the correct columns on the trial balance.)

Problems: Set A

Identify type of account, financial statement, normal balances, and debits and credits. **(SO 1) K**

P2–1A Miranda Brock, Lawyer, has the following accounts:

Accounts Payable	Land	Rent Revenue
Accounts Receivable	Fees Earned	Salaries Expense
Building	M. Brock, Capital	Salaries Payable
Cash	M. Brock, Drawings	Supplies
Equipment	Notes Receivable	Supplies Expense
Insurance Expense	Prepaid Insurance	Unearned Revenue
Interest Revenue	Rent Expense	

Instructions

For each of these accounts, identify (a) the type of account (such as asset, liability, owner's capital, drawings, revenue, expense); (b) what financial statement it is presented on; (c) the normal balance of the account; (d) whether the account is increased by a debit or credit; and (e) whether the account is decreased by a debit or credit. Use the following format, in which the first one has been done as an example.

Account	(a) Type of Account	(b) Financial Statement	(c) Normal Balance	(d) Increase	(e) Decrease
Accounts Payable	Liability	Balance sheet	Credit	Credit	Debit

TAKING IT FURTHER Explain the relationship between the normal balance in each type of account and the basic accounting equation.

Perform transaction analysis and journalize transactions. **(SO 1, 2) AP**

P2–2A JB Paint Designs began operations on April 1, 2014. The company completed the following transactions in its first month:

Apr.	1	The owner, Jay Barr, invested $13,500 cash in the company.
	2	Purchased a one-year insurance policy effective April 1, and paid the first month's premium of $115.
	2	Purchased equipment for $5,000 on account.
	3	Paid for $435 of supplies.
	7	Paid cash for $870 of advertising expenses.
	8	Finished a painting project for Maya Angelina and collected $750 cash.
	10	Received a $1,500 contract from a customer, SUB Terrain Inc., to paint its new office space. SUB Terrain will pay when the project is complete.
	25	Completed the contract with SUB Terrain Inc. from April 10 and collected the amount owing.
	28	The owner, Jay Barr, withdrew $975 cash for his personal use.
	29	Received $1,250 cash from Memphis Shek for a painting project that JB Paint Designs will start on May 5.
	30	Paid for the equipment purchased on account on April 2.

Instructions

(a) For each transaction, indicate: (1) the basic type of account debited and credited (asset, liability, or owner's equity); (2) the specific account debited and credited (Cash, Rent Expense, Service Revenue, and so on); and (3) whether each account is increased (+) or decreased (−), and by what amount. Use the following format, in which the first transaction is given as an example:

	Account Debited			Account Credited		
Transaction	(1) Basic Type	(2) Specific Account	(3) Effect	(1) Basic Type	(2) Specific Account	(3) Effect
Apr. 1	Asset	Cash	+$13,500	Owner's Equity	J. Barr, Capital	+$13,500

(b) Prepare a journal entry for each transaction.

TAKING IT FURTHER Jay doesn't understand why a debit increases the cash account and yet a credit to J. Barr, Capital increases that account. He reasons that debits and credits cannot both increase account balances. Explain to Jay why he is wrong.

P2–3A Bucket Club Miniature Golf and Driving Range was opened on May 1. The following events and transactions are for May:

Journalize transactions. **(SO 2) AP**

May 1 Amin Mawani, the owner, invested $75,000 cash in the business.
2 Purchased Lee's Golf Land for $250,000. The price consists of land, $120,000; building, $80,000; and equipment, $50,000. Paid $60,000 cash and signed a note payable for the balance.
4 Purchased golf clubs and other equipment for $16,000 from Woods Company on account.
5 Hired a golf pro to teach lessons at the golf range at a rate of $40 per hour.
6 Paid $2,760 cash for a one-year insurance policy.
15 Collected $2,000 golf fees earned in cash from customers.
19 Paid Woods Company $5,000 for the items purchased on May 4.
20 Billed a customer, Deer Fern Inc., $1,500 for golf fees earned. Deer Fern Inc. paid $500 and agreed to pay the remaining amount owing in 10 days.
30 Received $1,000 from Deer Fern Inc. for the May 20 transaction.
31 Collected $4,000 cash from customers for golf fees earned.
31 Paid salaries of $2,480.
31 Paid $715 of interest on the note payable.
31 Paid Amin Mawani $1,750 for his personal use.

The company's chart of accounts includes the following accounts: Cash; Accounts Receivable; Prepaid Insurance; Land; Buildings; Equipment; Accounts Payable; Notes Payable; A. Mawani, Capital; A. Mawani, Drawings; Fees Earned; Salaries Expense; and Interest Expense.

Instructions
Journalize the May transactions.

TAKING IT FURTHER After Amin has reviewed the journal entries, he complains that they don't seem to be very useful. Explain to Amin the purpose of the journal entries and the next step in the accounting cycle. Include in your answer whether or not Amin will find any useful information after the next step is completed.

P2–4A Grete Rodewald formed a dog grooming and training business called Grete Kanines on September 1, 2014. After consulting with a friend who had taken introductory accounting, Grete created a chart of accounts for the business as follows: No. 101 Cash; No. 112 Accounts Receivable; No. 130 Prepaid Insurance; No. 151 Equipment; No. 201 Accounts Payable; No. 209 Unearned Revenue; No. 301 G. Rodewald, Capital; No. 306 G. Rodewald, Drawings; No. 400 Service Revenue; No. 610 Advertising Expense; No. 726 Rent Expense; and No. 737 Utilities Expense. During September, the following events and transactions occurred:

Journalize transactions, post, and prepare trial balance. **(SO 2, 3) AP**

Sept. 1 Grete transferred $9,000 from her personal bank account to a bank account under the company name, Grete Kanines.
1 Signed a one-year rental agreement for $650 per month. Paid the first month's rent.
2 Paid $720 for a one-year insurance policy effective September 1, 2014.
3 Purchased $2,500 of equipment on credit.
6 Paid $450 for advertising in several community newsletters in September.
15 Collected $500 cash for providing dog grooming services.
19 Attended a dog show and provided $700 of dog grooming services for one of the major kennel owners. The kennel owner will pay the amount owing within two weeks.
24 Collected $500 from the kennel owner for the services provided on September 19. The kennel owner promised to pay the rest on October 2.
25 Paid $175 for utilities for the month of September.
26 Paid $1,500 of the amount owed from the September 3 equipment purchase.
29 Received $850 cash for dog training lessons that will start on October 7.
30 Collected $975 cash for providing dog grooming services.
30 Paid the owner, Grete Rodewald, $1,350 for her personal use.

Instructions
(a) Journalize the transactions.
(b) Post to the ledger accounts. Use the standard form of account.
(c) Prepare a trial balance as at September 30, 2014.

TAKING IT FURTHER Grete thinks she needs only one account for investments, drawings, revenues, and expense because these are all owners' equity accounts. Explain to her why she needs separate accounts.

Journalize transactions, post, and prepare trial balance. (SO 2, 3) AP

P2–5A Abramson Financial Services was formed on May 1, 2014. The following events and transactions are from its first month:

May 1	Jacob Abramson invested $40,000 cash and equipment worth $10,000 in the company.
1	Hired one employee to work in the office for a salary of $2,475 per month.
2	Paid $3,300 cash for a one-year insurance policy.
5	Signed a two-year rental agreement on an office and paid $4,800 cash. Half was for the May 2014 rent and the other half was for the final month's rent. (*Hint:* The portion for the final month is considered prepaid rent.)
8	Purchased additional equipment costing $17,000. A cash payment of $7,000 was made immediately. Signed a note payable for the balance.
9	Purchased supplies for $500 cash.
15	Purchased more supplies for $750 on account.
17	Completed a contract for a client for $3,000 on account.
22	Paid $250 for May's telephone bill.
25	Completed services for a client and immediately collected $1,100.
26	Paid Jacob Abramson $1,600 cash for his personal use.
28	Collected $2,500 from the client billed on May 17.
30	Paid for the supplies purchased on account on May 15.
30	Paid $50 interest expense on the note payable.
31	Received a cash advance of $500 for services to be completed in June.
31	Paid the employee's monthly salary, $2,475.

Instructions

(a) Prepare journal entries to record the transactions.
(b) Post the journal entries to ledger accounts. Use T accounts.
(c) Prepare a trial balance as at May 31, 2014.

TAKING IT FURTHER Jacob asks if the change in his cash account balance, from the beginning to the end of the month, is equal to his profit or loss for the month. Explain to Jacob whether or not this is true and why.

Journalize transactions, post, and prepare trial balance. (SO 2, 3) AP

P2–6A Sequel Theatre, owned by Nadia Fedkovych, is unique as it shows only movies that are part of a theme with sequels. As at June 30, 2014, the ledger of Sequel Theatre showed the following: Cash, $17,000; Land, $80,000; Buildings, $70,000; Equipment, $20,000; Accounts Payable, $5,000; Mortgage Payable, $118,000; and N. Fedkovych, Capital, $64,000. In July, the following events and transactions occurred:

July 1	Rented the first four *Harry Potter* movies, to be shown in the first two weeks of July. The film rental was $25,000. Of that amount, $10,000 was paid in cash and the balance will be paid on July 15.
2	Hired M. Brewer to operate the concession stand. Brewer agreed to pay Sequel Theatre 15% of gross concession receipts, on the last day of each month, for the right to operate the concession stand.
3	Paid advertising expenses, $1,150.
14	Received $35,600 cash from customers for admissions.
15	Paid the balance due from the July 1 movie rental transaction.
16	Received the final four *Harry Potter* movies to be shown in the last two weeks of July. The film rental cost was $30,000. Paid $15,000 cash and the balance will be paid on August 1.
27	Paid the accounts payable owing at the end of June.
30	Paid salaries of $6,200.
31	Received statement from Brewer showing gross receipts from concessions of $27,300 and the balance due to Sequel Theatre of $4,095 ($27,300 × 15%) for July. Brewer paid $2,500 of the balance due and will pay the rest on August 5.
31	Received $42,400 cash from admissions.
31	Made a $1,725 mortgage payment. Of this amount, $1,250 is a principal payment, and $475 is interest on the mortgage.

In addition to the accounts identified above, Sequel Theatre's ledger includes the following: Accounts Receivable; Admission Revenue; Concession Revenue; Advertising Expense; Film Rental Expense; Interest Expense; and Salaries Expense.

Instructions

(a) Journalize the July transactions.
(b) Enter the beginning balances in the ledger as at July 1. Use the standard form of account.

(c) Post the July journal entries to the ledger.
(d) Prepare a trial balance at the end of July.

TAKING IT FURTHER A friend of yours is considering buying Sequel Theatre from the current owner. Using the information in the trial balance, comment on whether or not this may be a sound company for your friend to purchase.

P2–7A Aduke Zhawaki is a talented musician who runs a business teaching music and playing in gigs with a variety of other musicians. Her business is operated as a proprietorship, under the name A to Z Music, which has a December 31 year end. On November 30, 2014, the company's general ledger included the following accounts (all accounts have normal balances):

Journalize transactions, post, and prepare trial balance. (SO 2, 3) AP

Cash	$ 2,965	A. Zhawaki, drawings	$31,350
Accounts receivable	2,200	Fees earned	47,075
Supplies	1,450	Insurance expense	3,410
Equipment	17,500	Rent expense	5,225
Accounts payable	4,235	Telephone expense	1,485
Unearned revenue	825	Travel expense	6,050
A. Zhawaki, capital	19,500		

December transactions were as follows:

Dec.	1	Paid December rent on her studio space, $475.
	1	Purchased additional sound equipment for $3,500 from a friend who was going back to school to study accounting. The equipment was probably worth $5,000, but the friend needed the cash for tuition and was anxious to sell it. Paid $1,500 cash and promised to pay the remaining amount by December 5.
	3	Borrowed $2,500 cash from her parents and signed a note payable.
	4	Paid her friend the remaining amount owing on the December 1 transaction.
	4	Collected $1,800 from customers in payment of their accounts.
	7	Paid the $310 monthly insurance premium.
	8	Paid for $150 of supplies.
	10	Paid $2,130 of the accounts payable from November.
	15	Gave musical performances at two recitals and earned $825. The customers had paid her in November. (*Hint:* In November Aduke had recorded the $825 received in advance as a liability, Unearned Revenue. By performing at the recitals, she has "paid" this obligation.)
	20	Received $3,300 cash from students for music lessons provided in December.
	21	Paid her monthly telephone bill of $135.
	22	Billed customers $2,250 for providing music at several holiday parties.
	24	Withdrew $3,000 for personal use.
	29	Received $525 cash advance from a customer for a performance in January.
	30	Paid travel expenses of $695 for December in cash.
	31	Paid her parents $210. Of this amount, $10 is interest and the remainder is a principal payment on the note payable.

Instructions

(a) Enter the November 30 balances in ledger accounts. Use T accounts.
(b) Journalize the December transactions.
(c) Post the December journal entries to the T accounts. Add new accounts if needed.
(d) Prepare a trial balance at December 31, 2014.

TAKING IT FURTHER Comment on A to Z Music's cash balance at December 31, 2014. What concerns or suggestions do you have for Aduke to consider in January?

P2–8A Refer to the trial balance for Abramson Financial Services prepared in P2–5A, part (c).

Prepare financial statements. (SO 3) AP

Instructions

(a) Prepare an income statement for May.
(b) Prepare a statement of owner's equity for May.
(c) Prepare a balance sheet at the end of May 2014.

TAKING IT FURTHER Discuss how well the company performed in its first month of operations.

Journalize transactions, post, and prepare trial balance. (SO 2, 3) AP

P2–9A Derek Scoffin owns and operates YH Curling School on evenings and weekends. The company had the following balances in its general ledger at January 31, 2014: Cash, $2,100; Accounts Receivable, $720; Equipment, $12,400; Accounts Payable, $1,470; and D. Scoffin, Capital, $13,750. The following events and transactions occurred during February 2014.

Feb. 1	Received and paid a $430 advertising bill.
2	Paid the YH Curling Club $1,050 rent for use of the ice for lessons during the first two weeks of February.
3	Collected $4,240 cash for February's curling lessons.
4	Collected all of the accounts receivable at January 31 in cash.
6	Paid $970 of the accounts payable at January 31.
14	Paid his part-time assistant $400.
15	Paid the YH Curling Club $1,050 rent for use of the ice for lessons during the last two weeks of February.
23	Provided $1,475 of coaching services to curlers preparing for a tournament. The curlers will pay him on March 2.
26	Paid $185 cash for his Internet bill for February. This is a business, not a personal, expense.
27	Received $2,830 cash for curling lessons in March.
27	Withdrew $575 cash. Used the cash to pay his Visa bill.
28	Paid his part-time assistant $400.
28	Paid the YH Curling Club $1,050 rent for use of the ice for lessons during the first two weeks of March.

Instructions

(a) Prepare journal entries to record each of YH Curling School's February transactions. (*Hint*: use the revenue account Fees Earned, for all revenue earned in February.)
(b) Open ledger accounts for each of the accounts listed in the trial balance, and enter the January 31, 2014, balances. Use T accounts.
(c) Post the journal entries to the accounts in the ledger.
(d) Prepare a trial balance as at February 28, 2014.

TAKING IT FURTHER Are the February payments to YH Curling Club for ice rental an asset, a reduction of a liability, or an expense? Explain.

Prepare financial statements. (SO 3) AP

P2–10A Refer to the trial balance prepared in part (d) of P2–9A for YH Curling School.

Instructions

Use the trial balance to do the following:

(a) Prepare an income statement for YH Curling School.
(b) Prepare a statement of owner's equity.
(c) Prepare a balance sheet.

TAKING IT FURTHER Derek has reviewed the financial statements. He does not understand why the company's revenue is not equal to the cash he collected from customers. Explain.

Prepare trial balance and financial statements. (SO 3) AP

P2–11A The ledger of Super Delivery Service has the following account balances at the company's year end, August 31, 2014:

Accounts Payable	$ 3,235	Repairs Expense	$ 1,580
Accounts Receivable	4,275	Salaries Expense	5,665
Cash	?	Salaries Payable	925
Equipment	49,720	Service Revenue	37,780
Fuel Expense	12,145	Supplies	265
Insurance Expense	2,020	Supplies Expense	2,650
Interest Expense	975	T. Rowe, Capital	48,750
Notes Payable	19,500	T. Rowe, Drawings	24,400
Prepaid Insurance	405	Unearned Revenue	675

Instructions

(a) Prepare a trial balance, with the accounts arranged in ledger (financial statement) order, as illustrated in the chapter, and determine the missing amount for Cash.
(b) Prepare an income statement, statement of owner's equity, and balance sheet.

TAKING IT FURTHER The owner, Tom Rowe, is not sure how much cash he can withdraw from the company each year. After reviewing the financial statements, comment on the amount he withdrew this year.

P2–12A A co-op student, working for Insidz Co., recorded the company's transactions for the month. At the end of the month, the owner of Insidz Co. reviewed the student's work and had some questions about the following transactions:

Analyze errors and effects on trial balance.
(SO 3) AN

1. Insidz Co. received $425 cash from a customer on account, which was recorded as a debit to Cash of $425 and a credit to Accounts Receivable of $425.
2. A service provided for cash was posted as a debit to Cash of $2,000 and a credit to Service Revenue of $2,000.
3. A credit of $750 for interest earned was neither recorded nor posted. The debit was recorded and posted correctly.
4. The debit to record $1,000 of drawings was posted to the Salary Expense account. The credit was posted correctly.
5. Services of $325 were provided to a customer on account. The co-op student debited Accounts Receivable $325 and credited Unearned Revenue $325.
6. A purchase of supplies for $770 on account was recorded as a credit to Supplies and a credit to Accounts Payable.
7. Insidz Co. received a cash advance of $500 from a customer for work to be done next month. Cash was debited $500 but there was no credit because the co-op student was not sure what to credit.
8. A cash payment of $495 for salaries was recorded as a debit to Salaries Expense and a credit to Salaries Payable.
9. Insidz Co. purchased $2,600 of equipment on account and made a $6,200 debit to Equipment and a $2,600 credit to Accounts Payable.
10. A $650 utility bill for the month was received at the end of the month. It was not recorded because it had not been paid.

Instructions

(a) Indicate which transactions are correct and which are incorrect.
(b) For each error identified in (a), answer the following:
   1. Will the trial balance be in balance?
   2. Which account(s) will be incorrectly stated because of the error?
   3. For each account you identified in (2) as being incorrect, is the account overstated or understated? By how much?
   4. Is the debit column total of the trial balance stated correctly? If not, does correcting the errors increase or decrease the total and by how much?
   5. Is the credit column total of the trial balance stated correctly? If not, does correcting the errors increase or decrease the total and by how much?

TAKING IT FURTHER Your best friend thinks it is a waste of time to correct all of the above errors. Your friend reasons that as long as the trial balance is balanced, then there is no need to correct an error. Do you agree or disagree with your friend? Explain, using at least two of the above errors to make your points.

P2–13A The trial balance of Winter Co. does not balance:

Prepare correct trial balance. **(SO 3) AN**

WINTER CO.
Trial Balance
June 30, 2014

	Debit	Credit
Cash	$ 2,835	
Accounts receivable	1,861	
Supplies	500	
Equipment		$ 7,900
Accounts payable		2,695
Unearned revenue	1,855	
F. Winter, capital		11,231
F. Winter, drawings	800	
Service revenue		3,460
Office expense	1,010	
Salaries expense	3,000	
	$11,861	$25,286

Your review of the ledger reveals that each account has a normal balance. You also discover the following errors:

1. Cash received from a customer on account was debited to Cash for $750 and Accounts Receivable was credited for the same amount. The actual collection was $570.
2. The purchase of supplies on account for $360 was recorded as a debit to Equipment for $360 and a credit to Accounts Payable for $360.
3. Services of $980 were performed on account for a client. Accounts Receivable was debited for $98 and Fees Earned was credited for $980.
4. A debit posting to Office Expense of $500 was not done.
5. A payment on account for $806 was credited to Cash for $806 and debited to Accounts Payable for $608.
6. The withdrawal of $400 cash for Françoise Winter's personal use was debited to Salaries Expense for $400 and credited to Cash for $400.
7. A transposition error (reversal of digits) was made when copying the balance in Service Revenue to the trial balance. The correct balance recorded in the account was $4,360.
8. The general ledger contained a Prepaid Insurance account with a debit balance of $655.

Instructions
Prepare a correct trial balance.

TAKING IT FURTHER After the trial balance is corrected for the above errors, could there still be errors in any of the account balances? Explain why or why not.

CONTINUING COOKIE CHRONICLE

(*Note:* The Continuing Cookie Chronicle began in Chapter 1 and will continue in each chapter.)

After researching the different forms of business organization, Natalie Koebel decides to operate Cookie Creations as a proprietorship. She then starts the process of getting the business running. During the months of November and December 2013, the following activities take place:

Nov. 12 Natalie cashes her Canada Savings Bonds and receives $980, which she deposits in her personal bank account.

12 She opens a bank account under the name "Cookie Creations" and transfers $900 from her personal account to the new account.

18 Natalie pays $325 to advertise in the November 29 issue of her community newspaper. Natalie hopes that this ad will generate revenue during the months of November and December.

20 She buys supplies, such as flour, sugar, butter, and chocolate chips, for $198 cash.

25 Natalie starts to gather some equipment to take with her when teaching the cookie classes. She has an excellent top-of-the-line food processor and mixer that originally cost her $825. Natalie decides to start using it only in her new business. She estimates that the equipment is currently worth $550.

26 Natalie teaches her first class, a group of Grade 2 students, how to make sugar cookies. At the end of the class, Natalie leaves an invoice for $300 with the school principal. The principal says that she will pass the invoice along to the school board and the invoice will be paid sometime in December.

27 A $98 invoice is received for the use of Natalie's cell phone. The cell phone is used exclusively for Cookie Creations' business. The invoice is for services provided in November and is due on December 13.

29 Natalie realizes that her initial cash investment is not enough. Her grandmother lends her $3,000 cash, for which Natalie signs a one-year, 3% note payable in the name of the business. Natalie deposits the money in the business bank account.

Dec. 2 Natalie teaches a class and collects $250 cash.

3 Natalie buys more equipment for $1,000 cash.

9 The school where Natalie taught her first class is in touch and wishes for Natalie to teach all of the Grade 3 and 4 students how to make sugar cookies. Natalie is thrilled! She anticipates teaching at least five classes at the school. She receives $125 in advance as a down payment.

Dec. 13 Natalie pays the amount outstanding on her cell phone bill.

16 Natalie receives and deposits the amount outstanding from the November 26 transaction.

17 Natalie receives an unexpected invitation to teach a cookie-making class at a children's Christmas party. At the end of the class, she prepares an invoice for $500 and leaves it with the organization's corporate controller. The controller indicates that the invoice will likely be paid in the next 30 days.

30 A $76 invoice is received for the use of Natalie's cell phone. The invoice is for services provided in December and is due on January 15, 2014.

Instructions

(a) Prepare journal entries to record the transactions.
(b) Post the journal entries to ledger accounts. Use T accounts.
(c) Prepare a trial balance as at December 31, 2013.

BROADENING YOUR PERSPECTIVE — CHAPTER 2

Collaborative Learning Activity

Note to instructor: Additional instructions and material for this group activity can be found on the Instructor Resource Site and in *WileyPLUS*.

BYP2–1 In this group activity, students will be given a trial balance and will be asked to work backwards to create a set of journal entries that would result in the trial balance.

Communication Activity

BYP2–2 White Glove Company offers home cleaning services. Three common transactions for the company are signing contracts with new customers, billing customers for services performed, and paying employee salaries. For example, on March 15 the company did the following:

1. Signed a contract with a new customer for $125 per week starting the first week in April.
2. Sent bills that totalled $6,000 to customers.
3. Paid $2,000 in salaries to employees.

Instructions

Write an e-mail to your instructor that explains if and how these transactions are recorded in the double-entry system. Include in your e-mail (a) whether, and why, the transaction should or should not be recorded, and (b) how the debit and credit rules are applied if the transaction is recorded.

Ethics Case

BYP2–3 Vu Hung is the assistant chief accountant at Lim Company, a manufacturer of computer chips and cellular phones. The company currently has total sales of $20 million. It is the end of the first quarter. Vu is hurriedly trying to prepare a general ledger trial balance so that quarterly financial statements can be prepared and released to management and regulatory agencies. The credits on the trial balance add up to $1,000 more than the debits.

In order to meet the 4:00 p.m. deadline, Vu decides to force the debits and credits into balance by adding the amount of the difference to the Equipment account. She chose Equipment because it is one of the larger account balances. Proportionally, it will be the least misstated. She believes that the difference will not affect anyone's decisions. She wishes that she had more time to find the error, but realizes that the financial statements are already late.

Instructions

(a) Who are the stakeholders in this situation?
(b) What are the ethical issues involved?
(c) What are Vu's alternatives?

All About You: Personal Financial Literacy Activity

BYP2–4 The "All About You" feature indicates that Luca Pacioli, who described the double-entry accounting system used over 500 years ago, wrote "a person should not go to sleep at night until the debits equalled the credits."

In the double-entry system, debits and credits are used to record the dual effect of each transaction in the appropriate accounts and to keep the basic accounting equation in balance. For each transaction, the debits must equal the credits; therefore, the total debits and credits for all of the accounts should be equal. If the total debits do not equal the credits, there is an error in the accounting records.

You are a first-year university student and very excited about moving away from home to go to university. Your parents have given you $4,000 and you have a $14,000 student loan. Your parents have told you that $4,000 is all you get for the school year and you are not to phone home for more money.

At September 1, you had $18,000 cash ($4,000 + $14,000), $1,000 worth of clothes, and a cell phone that cost $200. You have kept all of the receipts for all of your expenditures between September 1 and December 15. The following is a complete list of your receipts.

Receipts	Amount
Rent on room in furnished apartment ($400 per month)	$1,600
Damage deposit on apartment room	400
Groceries	1,200
Tuition for September to December	2,800
Textbooks	600
Entertainment (movies, beverages, restaurants)	1,500
New clothes	1,500
Cell phone charges	250
Cable TV and Internet bill	200
Computer	1,000
Eight-month bus pass (September to April)	500
Airfare to go home at Christmas	450

PERSONAL TRIAL BALANCE
December 15, 2014

Account	Debit	Credit
Cash	$ 6,500	
Clothes	2,500	
Cell phone	200	
Computer	100	
Student loan		$14,000
Personal equity		5,200
Rent expense	2,000	
Groceries		1,200
Tuition for September to December	2,800	
Textbooks for September to December	600	
Entertainment expense	1,500	
Cell phone expense	250	
Cable TV and Internet expense	200	
Bus pass expense	500	
Airfare	540	
	$17,690	$20,400

On December 15, you checked the balance in your bank account and you only have $6,000 cash. You can't sleep, because you know there are some errors in your accounting records and that you will probably have to ask your parents for more money for the next semester.

Instructions

(a) Calculate your personal equity (deficit) at September 1, 2014.
(b) Prepare a corrected trial balance at December 15, 2014. For each error identified, describe the error.
(c) Calculate your total expenses for the semester and your personal equity (deficit) at December 15, 2014.
(d) Prepare a personal balance sheet at December 15, 2014.
(e) Assuming you will have the same expenses in the second semester, will you have enough cash to pay for them?
(f) Are there any expenses you might be able to avoid in the second semester to save cash?
(g) Are there any additional cash expenditures that will need to be made in the second semester?
(h) Will it be necessary for you to ask your parents for more money for the next semester? Explain.

ANSWERS TO CHAPTER QUESTIONS

ANSWERS TO ACCOUNTING IN ACTION INSIGHT QUESTIONS

Business Insight, p. 55

Q: What are the issues involved in determining if a signing bonus is an asset or an expense?

A: Signing bonuses are paid because a company expects to benefit in the future from hiring the individual. Bonuses could be recorded as an asset at the time they are paid. A decision would be made by the team's management to treat the bonus as an expense once the benefit represented by this asset was used up. In the NHL, they would have to consider such things as the length of the contract, how well the player is performing, and whether or not the player is injured in order to decide when to record the bonus as an expense.

All About You Insight, p. 68

Q: Pacioli also wrote "a person should not go to sleep at night until the debits equalled the credits." Is this still good advice over 500 years later?

A: Perseverance can be a very useful attribute for an accounting student. Sometimes it can be difficult and time-consuming to find an error and correct it. Many students find this very frustrating and give up too soon and thus miss the opportunity to learn and increase their confidence. On the other hand, sleep is very important and can provide you with a fresh perspective the next day.

ANSWERS TO SELF-STUDY QUESTIONS

1. b 2. d 3. a 4. d 5. b 6. d 7. a 8. a 9. c 10. d 11. a 12. c

Remember to go back to the beginning of the chapter to check off your completed work!

←

CHAPTER 3

ADJUSTING THE ACCOUNTS

THE NAVIGATOR

- ☐ Understand *Concepts for Review*
- ☐ Read *Feature Story*
- ☐ Scan *Study Objectives*
- ☐ Read *Chapter Preview*
- ☐ Read text and answer *Before You Go On*
- ☐ Review *Comparing IFRS and ASPE*
- ☐ Work *Demonstration Problem*
- ☐ Review *Summary of Study Objectives*
- ☐ Answer *Self-Study Questions*
- ☐ Complete assignments

CONCEPTS FOR REVIEW

Before studying this chapter, you should understand or, if necessary, review:

A. The double-entry accounting system. (Ch. 2, p. 53)

B. How to increase and decrease assets, liabilities, and owner's equity accounts using debit and credit procedures. (Ch. 2, pp. 50–53)

C. How to journalize transactions. (Ch. 2, pp. 55–57)

D. How to post transactions to the general ledger. (Ch. 2, pp. 57–59)

E. How to prepare a trial balance. (Ch. 2, pp. 67–68)

ADJUSTING THE BOOKS AFTER HITTING THE BOOKS

TORONTO, ON—Once you begin your post-secondary education, you will probably pay your tuition just before classes start in September, but how will your college or university account for your money after that?

In Ontario, all colleges have a fiscal year that ends on March 31, which is also the provincial government's fiscal year end. "All the colleges' financial information is fully consolidated onto the province's books," explains Jeanette Dias D'Souza, former Vice President of Finance and Administration at Seneca College of Applied Arts & Technology, with 10 locations in the Greater Toronto area.

Many academic years end in late April, however. According to what's called accrual accounting, any revenues for services performed after March 31 have to be recognized in the following fiscal year, even though the money was collected earlier. So if a study term ends in late April, a small portion of the tuition for that semester will be recognized as revenue by the college in the next fiscal year.

The same revenue recognition criteria applies for students who study in the summer term: if they pay tuition before March 31, it can't be recognized as revenue until the teaching services are performed in the summer. That term is important for Seneca. "We have a very large summer program," says Ms. Dias D'Souza.

Seneca's main sources of operating funding are provincial grants and student tuition fees. It also receives revenue from private and corporate training. As with tuition fees, revenue from this training is recognized in the period in which the training is provided.

The college also receives revenue from renting space for private functions, including Eaton Hall, a former estate of the famed Eaton retailing family that is located on one of Seneca's campuses. If an engaged couple puts down a deposit in February for their July wedding, that revenue is not recognized until the wedding takes place in the next fiscal year, Ms. Dias D'Souza says.

Expenses, too, must be recorded in the year when they are incurred. For example, Seneca's invoices for utilities and legal fees for the last month of the fiscal year tend to come in after the year end, so the college uses estimates to accrue for these expenses at the year end.

Recording revenues and expenses in the correct period is a challenge, but one that must be met to properly reflect the school's activity in each period.

THE NAVIGATOR

STUDY OBJECTIVES

After studying this chapter, you should be able to:

1. Explain accrual basis accounting, and when to recognize revenues and expenses.
2. Prepare adjusting entries for prepayments.
3. Prepare adjusting entries for accruals.
4. Describe the nature and purpose of an adjusted trial balance, and prepare one.
5. Prepare adjusting entries for the alternative treatment of prepayments (Appendix 3A).

THE NAVIGATOR

PREVIEW OF CHAPTER THREE

In Chapter 2, we learned the accounting cycle up to and including the preparation of the trial balance. In this chapter, we will learn that additional steps are usually needed before preparing the financial statements. These steps adjust accounts for timing mismatches, like the ones Seneca College has with the tuition it receives for its summer classes and the costs it incurs to offer these classes. In this chapter, we introduce the accrual accounting concepts that guide the adjustment process.

The chapter is organized as follows:

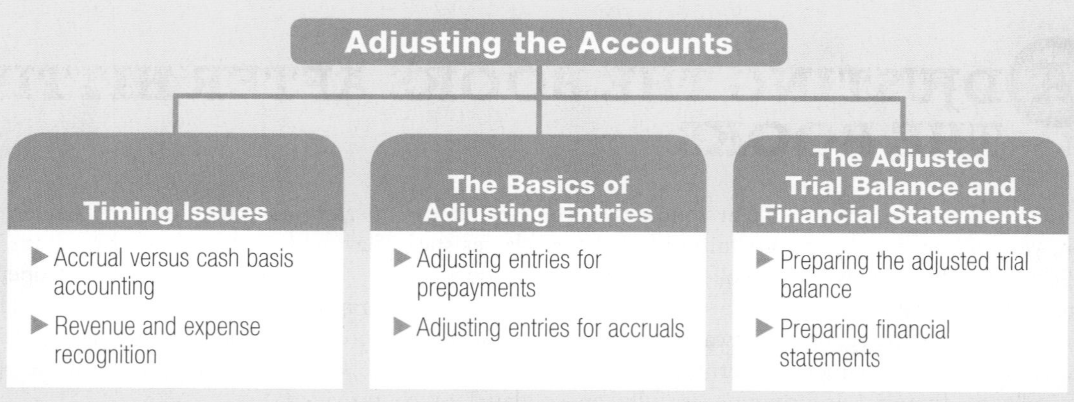

TIMING ISSUES

STUDY OBJECTIVE 1

Explain accrual basis accounting, and when to recognize revenues and expenses.

Accounting would be simple if we could wait until a company ended its operations before preparing its financial statements. As the following anecdote shows, if we waited until then we could easily determine the amount of lifetime profit earned:

> A grocery store owner from the old country kept his accounts payable on a wire memo spike, accounts receivable on a notepad, and cash in a shoebox. His daughter, a CGA, chided her father: "I don't understand how you can run your business this way. How do you know what you've earned?"
>
> "Well," her father replied, "when I arrived in Canada 40 years ago, I had nothing but the pants I was wearing. Today, your brother is a doctor, your sister is a teacher, and you are a CGA. Your mother and I have a nice car, a well-furnished house, and a home by the lake. We have a good business and everything is paid for. So, you add all that together, subtract the pants, and there's your profit."

Although the grocer may be correct in his evaluation about how to calculate his profit over his lifetime, most companies need more immediate feedback on how they are doing. For example, management usually wants monthly financial statements. Investors want to view the results of publicly traded companies at least quarterly. The Canada Revenue Agency requires financial statements to be filed with annual income tax returns.

Helpful hint Time periods are consistent in length and are used to measure profits and losses as governed by the time period concept.

Consequently, accountants divide the life of a business into specific time periods, such as a month, a three-month quarter, or a year. This practice follows the concept under GAAP known as the time period concept. An accounting time period that is one year long is called a **fiscal year**. Time periods of less than one year are called **interim periods**.

Alternative terminology The fiscal year may also be referred to as the *financial year*.

The fiscal year used by many businesses is the same as the calendar year (January 1 to December 31). However, it can be different. Seneca College's fiscal year is April 1 through March 31, which is typical of many colleges, universities, and governments. Some retail companies use a 52-week period, instead of exactly one year, for their fiscal year. Reitmans (Canada) Limited does this, and has chosen the last Saturday in January as the end of its fiscal year. But because 52 weeks isn't exactly equal to one year, some years Reitmans has to use a 53-week period with the first Saturday in February as its fiscal year end.

Because the life of a business is divided into accounting time periods, determining when to record transactions is important. Many business transactions affect more than one accounting time period. For example, equipment is used over several years. We also saw in the feature story that sometimes Seneca College collects tuition fees in one fiscal year and then teaches the course in the next fiscal year. In the following section, we will see that deciding when to recognize revenues and expenses will have a significant impact on the usefulness of financial statements.

ACCRUAL VERSUS CASH BASIS ACCOUNTING

There are two ways of deciding when to recognize or record revenues and expenses:

1. **Accrual basis accounting** means that transactions and other **events are recorded in the period when they occur, and not when the cash is paid or received.** For example, service revenue is recognized when it is earned, rather than when the cash is received. Expenses are recognized when services (such as salaries) or goods (such as supplies) are used or consumed, rather than when the cash is paid.
2. Under **cash basis accounting**, revenue is recorded when cash is received, and expenses are recorded when cash is paid.

Which one provides better information for users when they make decisions about companies? To answer that question, consider this simple example. Suppose you own a painting company and you paint a large building during year 1. In year 1, you pay $50,000 cash for the cost of the paint and your employees' salaries. Assume that you bill your customer $80,000 at the end of year 1, and that you receive the cash from your customer in year 2.

On an accrual basis, the revenue is reported during the period when the service is performed—year 1. Expenses, such as employees' salaries and the paint used, are recorded in the period in which the employees provide their services and the paint is used—year 1. Thus, your profit for year 1 is $30,000. No revenue or expense from this project is reported in year 2.

If, instead, you were reporting on a cash basis, you would report expenses of $50,000 in year 1 because you paid for them in year 1. Revenues of $80,000 would be recorded in year 2 because you received cash from the customer in year 2. For year 1, you would report a loss of $50,000. For year 2, you would report a profit of $80,000.

Illustration 3-1 summarizes this information and shows the differences between the accrual-based numbers and cash-based numbers.

ILLUSTRATION 3-1
Accrual versus cash basis accounting

	Year 1		Year 2	
Activity	Purchased paint, painted building, paid employees		Received payment for work done in year 1	
Accrual basis	Revenue	$80,000	Revenue	$ 0
	Expenses	50,000	Expenses	0
	Profit	$30,000	Profit	$ 0
Cash basis	Revenue	$ 0	Revenue	$80,000
	Expenses	50,000	Expenses	0
	Loss	$(50,000)	Profit	$80,000

Note that the total profit for years 1 and 2 is $30,000 for both the accrual and cash bases. However, the difference in when the revenue and expense are recognized causes a difference in the amount of profit or loss each year. Which basis provides better information about how profitable your efforts were each year? It's the accrual basis, because it shows the profit earned on the job in the same year as when the work was performed.

Helpful hint In accounting, a negative number (a loss) is indicated by placing brackets around it.

Thus, accrual basis accounting is widely recognized as being significantly more useful for decision-making than cash basis accounting. In fact, it is assumed that all financial statements are prepared using accrual basis accounting. This means there is no need to report that the accrual basis has been used.

While accrual basis accounting provides better information, it is more complex than cash basis accounting. It is easy to determine when to recognize revenues or expenses if the only determining factor is when the cash is received or paid. But when using the accrual basis, it is necessary to have standards about when to record revenues and expenses.

REVENUE AND EXPENSE RECOGNITION

Recall that revenue results in an increase in owner's equity as the result of the company's business activities (the sale of goods and services) with its customers and an increase in owner's equity occurs as a result of the credit entry to a revenue account. Under GAAP's revenue recognition principle, **revenue recognition criteria** provide guidance about when this increase in assets (or decrease in liabilities) has happened and thus when revenue is to be recognized. In general, revenue is recognized when the service has been performed or the goods have been sold and delivered. We also need to ensure that revenue can be reliably measured, and collection is reasonably certain, when recognizing revenue. Bad debts, which result from revenue that has been earned but is unlikely to be received, are addressed in Chapter 8.

The following table analyzes some common revenue transactions and how to record them:

Type of Transaction	Entry	When the Cash Is Received from the Customer
Cash sale	Dr. Cash Cr. Revenue	At the time that the goods or services are provided
Credit sale	Dr. Accounts Receivable Cr. Revenue	After the goods or services are provided
Earning revenue that was received in advance	Dr. Unearned Revenue Cr. Revenue	Before the goods or services are provided

Note that in each case, under accrual basis accounting, Revenue is credited when it is earned, regardless of when the cash is received.

Revenue recognition criteria follow accrual basis accounting—revenue is recognized in the period when it is earned. Recall that in the painting example shown in Illustration 3-1, revenue was recorded in year 1 when the service was performed. At that point, there was an increase in the painting business's assets—specifically Accounts Receivable—as the result of doing the work. At the end of year 1, the painting business would report the receivable on its balance sheet and revenue on its income statement for the service performed. In year 2, when the cash is received, the painting business records a reduction of its receivables, not revenue.

Expense recognition criteria provide guidance about when to record expenses. Recall that expenses represent a decrease in owner's equity excluding transactions with the owner (that is, drawings). Expenses are the costs of assets that are consumed and services that are used in a company's business activities. Expense recognition is tied to revenue recognition when there is a direct association between costs incurred and the earning of revenue. For example, as we saw with the painting business, under accrual basis accounting the salaries and cost of the paint for the painting in year 1 are reported in the income statement for the same period in which the service revenue is recognized. This process is commonly referred to as matching.

Sometimes, however, there is no *direct* relationship between expenses and revenue. For example, we will see in the next section that long-lived assets may be used to help generate revenue over many years, but the use of the asset is not directly related to earning specific revenue. In these cases, we will see that expenses are recognized in the income statement over the life of the asset.

In other cases, the benefit from the expenditure is fully used in the current period, or there is a great deal of uncertainty about whether or not there is a future benefit. In these situations, the costs are reported as expenses in the period in which they occur.

The following table shows the differences between expenses and drawings.

	Expenses	Drawings
What they represent	"The costs of doing business" in the sense that they support a company's efforts to generate revenue.	Cash or other assets that the owner(s) withdraw(s) from the business for their own personal use.
Effect on owner's equity	Reduction	Reduction
Normal balance/Side on which increases are recorded	Debit	Debit
Financial statement upon which it appears	Income statement	Statement of owner's equity

ACCOUNTING IN ACTION
ALL ABOUT YOU INSIGHT

Over the coming years, you and your parents will probably be paying a lot for your education. According to Statistics Canada, in 2013–14, the average undergraduate tuition fee for Canadian full-time university students was $5,772. If the cost of books, supplies, student fees, transportation, housing, and other expenses is factored in, that amount can rise substantially. In 2009, it was estimated that the average four-year undergraduate degree in Canada costs about $55,000 for those living at home and $84,000 for students living away from home.

That is the cost, but what is the future value of your education? According to the TD Bank, "Investment in post-secondary education remains the single best investment that one can make." Post-secondary graduates are more likely to be employed, and typically earn more money over their lifetimes. The 2006 Census found that university graduates in Canada earned an average of $35,168 a year after taxes, compared with $27,741 for college graduates, $19,744 for high school graduates, and $15,523 for those who did not graduate from high school.

There are also indirect benefits of post-secondary education. Graduates tend to have higher literacy and financial management skills, manage their health better, are more active in their community, and are more likely to pursue continuing education and therefore adapt better to the information economy.

When you consider all these benefits, the money you're saving now for your education should be a significant advantage to you in the future.

Sources: CanLearn website; TD Economics, "Post-Secondary Education Is the Best Investment You Can Make," Special Report, September 12, 2011; Statistics Canada, "University Tuition Fees 2013/2014," *The Daily*, September 13, 2013.

How should you account for the cost of your post-secondary education in the future? Should you be recognizing the cost as an expense each year or should you recognize it as an asset? Be prepared to justify your opinion.

BEFORE YOU GO ON...

DO IT

On January 1, 2014, customers owed Jomerans Co. $30,000 for services provided in 2013. During 2014, Jomerans received $125,000 cash from customers. On December 31, 2014, customers owed Jomerans $19,500 for services provided in 2014. Calculate revenue for 2014 using (a) cash basis accounting, and (b) accrual basis accounting.

SOLUTION

(a) Revenue for 2014, using cash basis accounting	$125,000
(b) Cash received from customers in 2014	$125,000
Deduct: Collection of 2013 receivables	(30,000)
Add: Amounts receivable at December 31, 2014	19,500
Revenue for 2014, using accrual basis accounting	$114,500

Related exercise material: BE3–1 and E3–1.

Action Plan

- For cash basis accounting, revenue is equal to the cash received during the fiscal year.
- For accrual basis accounting, revenue is recognized in the period in which it is earned, not when it is collected.
- Under accrual basis accounting, cash collected in 2014 for revenue earned in 2013 should not be included in the 2014 revenue. It would have already been recorded as revenue in 2013.
- Under accrual basis accounting, amounts receivable at the end of 2014 for services provided in 2014 should be included in the 2014 revenue.

THE NAVIGATOR

THE BASICS OF ADJUSTING ENTRIES

For revenues and expenses to be recorded in the correct period, adjusting entries are made at the end of the accounting period. **Adjusting entries** are needed to ensure that revenue and expense recognition criteria are followed, resulting in an accurate income statement, and that the correct amounts for assets, liabilities, and owner's equity are reported on the balance sheet.

Adjusting entries are needed every time financial statements are prepared. Companies reporting under IFRS must prepare quarterly financial statements and thus adjusting entries are required every quarter. Companies following ASPE must prepare annual financial statements and thus need only annual adjusting entries. For both public and private companies, if management wants monthly statements, then adjustments are prepared every month end.

You will recall that we learned the first four steps of the accounting cycle in Chapter 2. Adjusting entries are Step 5 of the accounting cycle, as shown in Illustration 3-2.

ILLUSTRATION 3-2
The accounting cycle—Steps 1 to 5

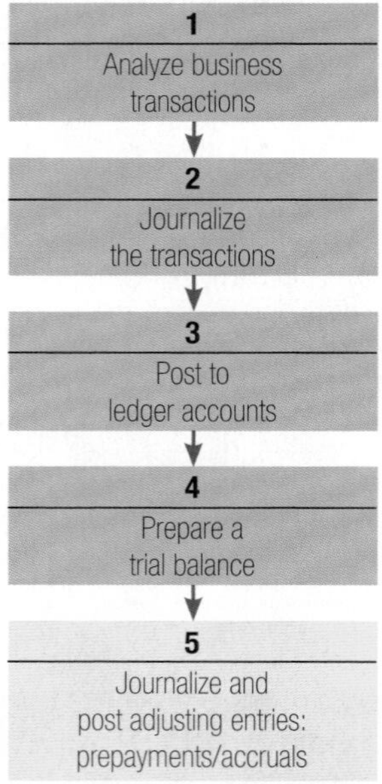

There are some common reasons why the trial balance—from Step 4 in the accounting cycle—may not contain complete and up-to-date data.

1. Some events are not recorded daily because it would not be efficient to do so. For example, companies do not record the daily use of supplies or the earning of wages by employees.
2. Some costs are not recorded during the accounting period because they expire with the passage of time rather than through daily transactions. Examples are rent and insurance.
3. Some items may be unrecorded at the end of the fiscal year. An example is a utility bill for services in the current accounting period that will not be received until the next accounting period.

Therefore, we must analyze each account in the trial balance to see if it is complete and up to date. The analysis requires a full understanding of the company's operations and the interrelationship of accounts. Preparing adjusting entries is often a long process. For example, to accumulate the adjustment data, a company may need to count its remaining supplies. It may also need to prepare supporting schedules of insurance policies, rental agreements, and other contractual commitments.

Adjustment data are often not available until after the end of the period; for example, telephone and other bills received after the month end or year end. In such cases, the data are gathered as soon as possible after the end of the period and adjusting entries are made but they are still dated as at the balance sheet date.

Adjusting entries can be classified as prepayments or accruals, as follows:

PREPAYMENTS	ACCRUALS
1. Prepaid Expenses Expenses paid in cash and recorded as assets before they are used or consumed. 2. Unearned Revenues Cash received and recorded as a liability before revenue is earned.	1. Accrued Expenses Expenses incurred but not yet paid in cash or recorded. 2. Accrued Revenues Revenues earned but not yet received in cash or recorded.

Examples and explanations of each type of adjustment are given on the following pages. Each example is based on the October 31 trial balance of Pioneer Advertising Agency from Chapter 2, reproduced here in Illustration 3-3.

ILLUSTRATION 3-3
Trial balance

PIONEER ADVERTISING AGENCY
Trial Balance
October 31, 2014

	Debit	Credit
Cash	$14,250	
Accounts receivable	1,000	
Supplies	2,500	
Prepaid insurance	600	
Equipment	5,000	
Notes payable		$ 5,000
Accounts payable		1,750
Unearned revenue		1,200
C. Bedard, capital		10,000
C. Bedard, drawings	500	
Service revenue		10,800
Rent expense	900	
Salaries expense	4,000	
Totals	$28,750	$28,750

For illustration purposes, we assume that Pioneer Advertising uses an accounting period of one month. Thus, monthly adjusting entries will be made and they will be dated October 31.

ADJUSTING ENTRIES FOR PREPAYMENTS

STUDY OBJECTIVE 2
Prepare adjusting entries for prepayments.

Prepayments are either prepaid expenses or unearned revenues. Adjusting entries are used to record the portion of the prepayment consumed in the current accounting period and to reduce the asset account where the prepaid expense was originally recorded. This type of adjustment is necessary because the prepayment no longer has future benefit and consequently is no longer an asset—it has been used.

For unearned revenues, the adjusting entry records the revenue earned in the current period and reduces the liability account where the unearned revenue was originally recorded. This type of adjustment is necessary because the unearned revenue is no longer owed and so is no longer a liability—the service has been provided and the revenue earned.

Prepaid Expenses

Recall from Chapter 1 that costs paid in cash *before* they are used are called **prepaid expenses**. When such a cost is incurred, an asset (prepaid) account is debited to show the service or benefit that will be received in the future and cash is credited.

Helpful hint A cost can be an asset or an expense. If it has future benefits, it is an asset. If the benefits have expired or been used, it is an expense.

Prepaid expenses are assets that expire either with the passage of time (such as rent and insurance) or as the asset is used up (such as supplies). It is not practical to record the expiration of these assets daily. Instead, they are recorded when financial statements are prepared. At each statement date, companies make adjusting entries: (1) to record an expense for the cost of the asset that has been used up that period, and (2) to show an accurate, up-to-date value of the asset for the remaining amount (unexpired costs).

Before the prepaid expenses are adjusted, assets are overstated and expenses are understated. Therefore, as shown below, **an adjusting entry for prepaid expenses results in an increase (debit) to an expense account and a decrease (credit) to an asset account.**

Prepaid Expenses

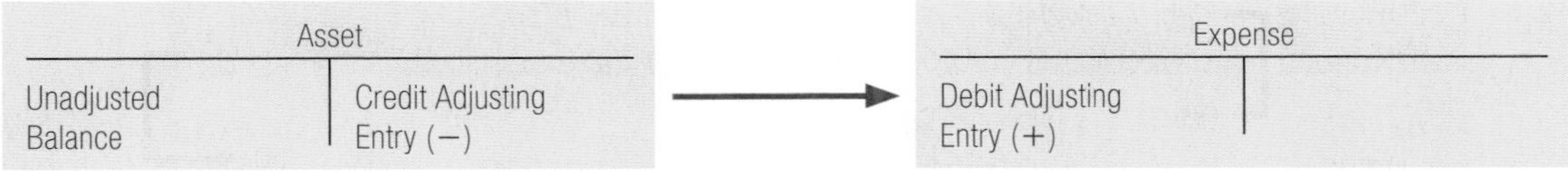

In the following section, we will look at three examples of adjusting prepaid expenses: supplies, insurance, and depreciation.

Supplies.

The purchase of supplies, such as pens and paper, generally results in an increase (debit) to an asset account. During daily operations, supplies are used up. Rather than recording journal entries as the supplies are used, **supplies expense** is recorded at the end of the accounting period as an adjustment. At that point, the remaining supplies are counted (a physical inventory of supplies is taken). The difference between the balance in the supplies (asset) account and the cost of supplies actually remaining gives the supplies used (the expense) for the period.

Recall from Chapter 2 that Pioneer Advertising Agency purchased supplies costing $2,500 on October 4. A debit (increase) was made to the asset account Supplies. This account shows a balance of $2,500 in the October 31 trial balance. An inventory count at the close of business on October 31 reveals that only $1,000 of supplies remains. That means $1,500 ($2,500 − $1,000) of the supplies have been used.

The following illustration outlines the analysis used to determine the adjusting journal entry to record and post. Note that the debit-credit rules you learned in Chapter 2 are also used for adjusting journal entries.

ADJUSTMENT 1
Prepaid Expenses—Supplies

Basic Analysis	The use of the supplies decreases the asset account Supplies by $1,500 and increases the expense account Supplies Expense by $1,500.
Equation Analysis	Assets: Supplies −1,500 = Liabilities + Owner's Equity: Supplies Expense −1,500
Debit-Credit Analysis	Debits increase expenses: Debit Supplies Expense $1,500. Credits decrease assets: Credit Supplies $1,500.
Adjusting Journal Entry	Oct. 31 Supplies Expense 1,500; Supplies 1,500; To record supplies used.

Oct. 31			
Oct. 31	Supplies Expense	1,500	
	Supplies		1,500
	To record supplies used.		

Posting:

Supplies			
Oct. 4	2,500	Oct. 31 **Adj.**	**1,500**
Oct. 31 Bal.	1,000		

Supplies Expense	
Oct. 31 **Adj. 1,500**	

After the adjustment, the asset account Supplies now shows a balance of $1,000, which is equal to the cost of supplies remaining at the statement date. Supplies Expense shows a balance of $1,500, which is the cost of supplies used in October. If the adjusting entry is not made, October expenses will be understated and profit overstated by $1,500. Also, both assets and owner's equity will be overstated by $1,500 on the October 31 balance sheet.

Insurance.

Companies purchase insurance to protect themselves from losses caused by fire, theft, and unforeseen accidents. Insurance must be paid in advance and the term of coverage is usually one year. Insurance payments (premiums) made in advance are normally charged to the asset account **Prepaid Insurance** when they are paid. At the financial statement date, it is necessary to make an adjustment to debit (increase) Insurance Expense and credit (decrease) Prepaid Insurance for the cost that has expired during the period.

On October 3, Pioneer Advertising Agency paid $600 for a one-year fire insurance policy. The starting date for the coverage was October 1. The premium was charged to Prepaid Insurance when it was paid. This account shows a balance of $600 in the October 31 trial balance. An analysis of the policy reveals that $50 ($600 ÷ 12 months) of insurance expires each month. The adjusting entry for prepaid insurance is made as follows:

ADJUSTMENT 2
Prepaid Expenses—Insurance

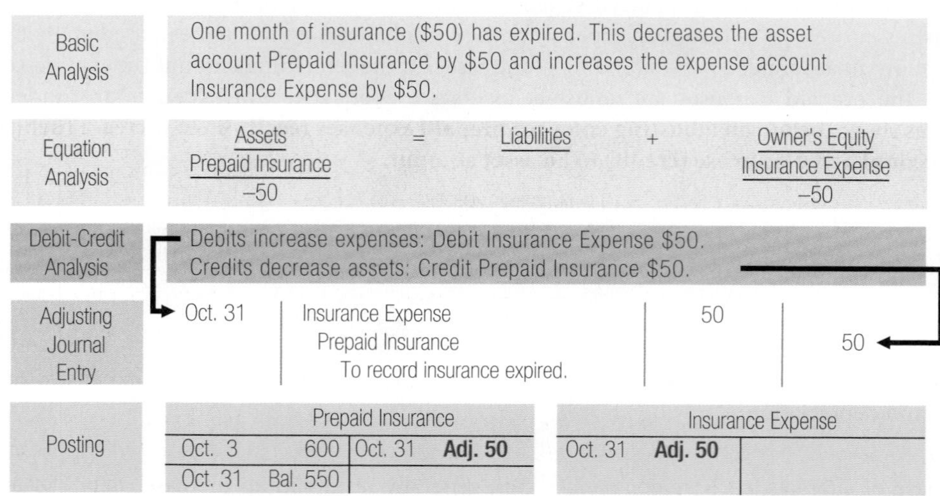

Basic Analysis
One month of insurance ($50) has expired. This decreases the asset account Prepaid Insurance by $50 and increases the expense account Insurance Expense by $50.
Equation Analysis
Assets = Liabilities + Owner's Equity
Prepaid Insurance −50
Insurance Expense −50
Debit-Credit Analysis
Debits increase expenses: Debit Insurance Expense $50.
Credits decrease assets: Credit Prepaid Insurance $50.
Adjusting Journal Entry
Oct. 31 Insurance Expense 50
Prepaid Insurance 50
To record insurance expired.
Posting
Prepaid Insurance
Oct. 3 600 Oct. 31 Adj. 50
Oct. 31 Bal. 550
Insurance Expense
Oct. 31 Adj. 50

After the adjustment, the asset Prepaid Insurance shows a balance of \$550. This amount represents the unexpired cost for the remaining 11 months of coverage (11 × \$50). The \$50 balance in Insurance Expense is equal to the insurance cost that has expired in October. If this adjustment is not made, October expenses will be understated by \$50 and profit overstated by \$50. Also, both assets and owner's equity will be overstated by \$50 on the October 31 balance sheet.

Depreciation.

A business usually owns a variety of assets that have long lives such as land, buildings, and equipment. These long-lived assets provide service for a number of years. The length of service is called the **useful life**.

From an accounting perspective, the purchase of a long-lived asset is basically a long-term prepayment for services. Similar to other prepaid expenses, it is necessary to recognize the cost that has been used up (the expense) during the period, and report the unused cost (the asset) at the end of the period. **Depreciation** is the process of allocating the cost of long-lived assets to expense over their expected useful lives in a systematic and rational manner. Only assets with limited useful lives are depreciated. We call them depreciable assets. When an asset, such as land, has an unlimited useful life, it is not depreciated.

It is important to note that depreciation is an allocation concept. The portion of the long-lived asset that is used up in each period is reported as depreciation expense. Depreciation is not an attempt to recognize the change in the value of the long-lived asset.

Some companies use the term "amortization" instead of "depreciation," especially private companies following ASPE. The two terms mean the same thing—allocation of the cost of a long-lived asset to expense over its useful life. In Chapter 9, we will learn that the term "amortization" is also used under both ASPE and IFRS for the allocation of cost to expense for certain intangible long-lived assets.

Calculation of Depreciation. A common method of calculating depreciation expense is to divide the cost of the asset by its useful life. This is called the **straight-line depreciation method**. The useful life must be estimated because, at the time an asset is acquired, the company does not know exactly how long the asset will be used. Thus, depreciation is an estimate rather than a factual measurement of the expired cost.

Pioneer Advertising purchased equipment that cost \$5,000 on October 2. If its useful life is expected to be five years, annual depreciation is \$1,000 (\$5,000 ÷ 5). Illustration 3-4 shows the formula to calculate annual depreciation expense in its simplest form.

ILLUSTRATION 3-4
Formula for straight-line depreciation

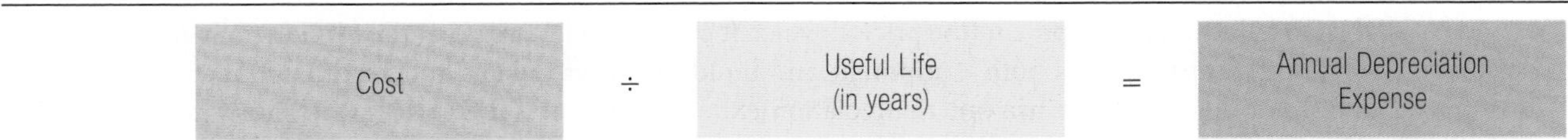

Of course, if you are calculating depreciation for partial periods, the annual expense amount must be adjusted for the relevant portion of the year. For example, if we want to determine the depreciation for one month, we would multiply the annual expense by $\frac{1}{12}$ as there are 12 months in a year.

Helpful hint To make the depreciation calculation easier to understand, we have assumed the asset has no value at the end of its useful life. In Chapter 9, we will show how to calculate depreciation when there is an estimated value at the end of the asset's useful life.

Adjustments of prepayments involve decreasing (or crediting) an asset by the amount that has been used or consumed. Therefore, it would be logical to expect we should credit Equipment when recording depreciation. But in the financial statements we must report both the original cost of long-lived assets and the total cost that has been used. We therefore use an account called **Accumulated Depreciation** to show the cumulative sum of the depreciation expense since the asset was purchased. This account is a **contra asset account** because it has the opposite (credit) balance to its related asset Equipment, which has a debit balance.

For Pioneer Advertising, depreciation on the equipment is estimated to be \$83 per month (\$1,000 × $\frac{1}{12}$). Because depreciation is an estimate, we can ignore the fact that Pioneer Advertising bought the equipment on October 2, not October 1. The adjusting entry to record the depreciation on the equipment for the month of October is made as follows:

ADJUSTMENT 3
Prepaid Expenses—Depreciation

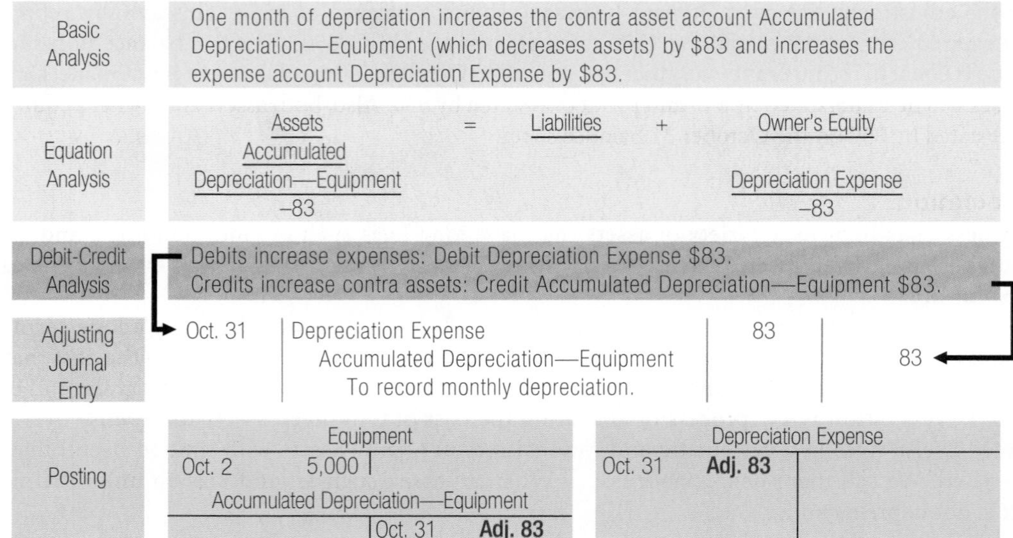

Basic Analysis
One month of depreciation increases the contra asset account Accumulated Depreciation—Equipment (which decreases assets) by $83 and increases the expense account Depreciation Expense by $83.
Equation Analysis
Assets = Liabilities + Owner's Equity
Accumulated Depreciation—Equipment −83
Depreciation Expense −83
Debit-Credit Analysis
Debits increase expenses: Debit Depreciation Expense $83.
Credits increase contra assets: Credit Accumulated Depreciation—Equipment $83.
Adjusting Journal Entry
Oct. 31 Depreciation Expense 83
Accumulated Depreciation—Equipment 83
To record monthly depreciation.
Posting
Equipment
Oct. 2 5,000
Accumulated Depreciation—Equipment
Oct. 31 Adj. 83
Depreciation Expense
Oct. 31 Adj. 83

Helpful hint Increases, decreases, and normal balances of contra accounts are the opposite of the accounts they relate to.

Helpful hint A contra asset cannot exist on its own; since it represents the running total of the depreciation that has been recorded on an asset, it must be "attached to" a depreciable asset.

The balance in the Accumulated Depreciation account will increase by $83 each month and the balance in the Equipment account will remain unchanged until the asset is sold. We will learn in Chapter 9 that both the accumulated depreciation and the equipment accounts are reduced when the asset is sold.

As in the case of other prepaid expenses, if this adjusting entry is not made, total assets, owner's equity, and profit will be overstated and expenses will be understated.

Statement Presentation. Accumulated Depreciation—Equipment, a contra asset account, has the opposite balance from its related asset account Equipment. In the financial statements, **a contra account is always offset against (deducted from) its related account.** Thus, on the balance sheet, Accumulated Depreciation—Equipment is deducted from Equipment, as follows:

Equipment	$5,000
Less: Accumulated depreciation—equipment	83
Carrying amount	$4,917

Alternative terminology An asset's carrying amount is also called its *carrying value, net book value*, or *book value.*

Helpful hint Depreciation expense is closed to zero at the end of the fiscal year, whereas accumulated depreciation balances carry over from year to year.

Alternative terminology Unearned revenues are sometimes referred to as *deferred revenues* or *future revenues.*

The difference between the cost of any depreciable asset and its accumulated depreciation is called the **carrying amount** of that asset. In the above diagram, the carrying amount of the equipment at October 31, 2014, is $4,917. Remember, depreciation does not attempt to show what an asset is worth. The carrying amount and the fair value of the equipment (the price at which it could be sold) are generally two different amounts.

If a company owns both equipment and buildings, it calculates and records depreciation expense on each category. It can use one depreciation expense account but it must create separate accumulated depreciation accounts for each category.

Unearned Revenues

Cash received before revenue is earned is recorded by increasing (crediting) a liability account for unearned revenues. Examples are rent, magazine subscriptions, tickets for sporting and entertainment events, and customer deposits for future services. Airlines such as Air Canada treat receipts from the sale of tickets as unearned revenue until the flight service is provided. Similarly, tuition fees that are received prior to the start of an academic session, as in the feature story about the summer session at Seneca College, are considered unearned revenue.

Unearned revenues are the opposite of prepaid expenses. Indeed, unearned revenue on the books of one company is likely to be a prepayment on the books of the company that has made the advance payment. For example, a landlord will have unearned rent revenue when the tenant has prepaid rent.

Recall that, when a payment is received for services that will be provided in a future accounting period, Cash is debited (increased) and an unearned revenue account (a liability) should be credited (increased) to recognize the obligation that exists. Unearned revenues become earned when the service is provided to the customer.

It may not be practical to make daily journal entries as the revenue is earned. Instead, recognition of earned revenue is normally delayed until the end of the accounting period. Then an adjusting entry is made to record the revenue that has been earned and to show the liability that remains at the end of the accounting period. Before adjustment, liabilities are overstated and revenues are understated. If revenues are understated, then profit and owner's equity will also be understated. As shown below, the adjusting entry for unearned revenues results in a decrease (debit) to a liability account and an increase (credit) to a revenue account.

Unearned Revenue

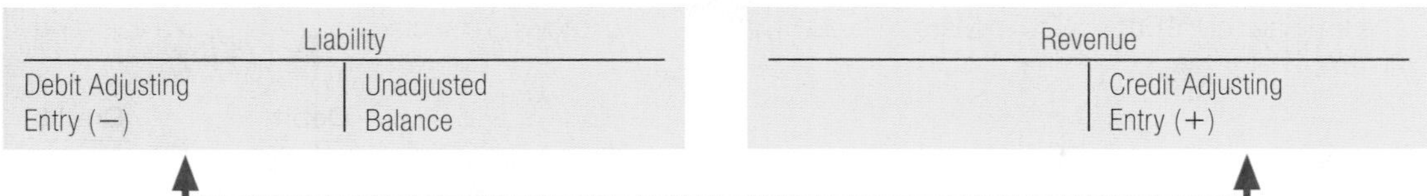

In our Pioneer Advertising Agency example, the company received $1,200 on October 3 from R. Knox for advertising services that will be completed by December 31. The payment was originally credited to Unearned Revenue, and this account shows a balance of $1,200 in the October 31 trial balance. An evaluation of work performed by Pioneer for Knox during October shows that $400 of work was done. The following adjusting entry is used to record earning this revenue:

ADJUSTMENT 4
Unearned Revenues

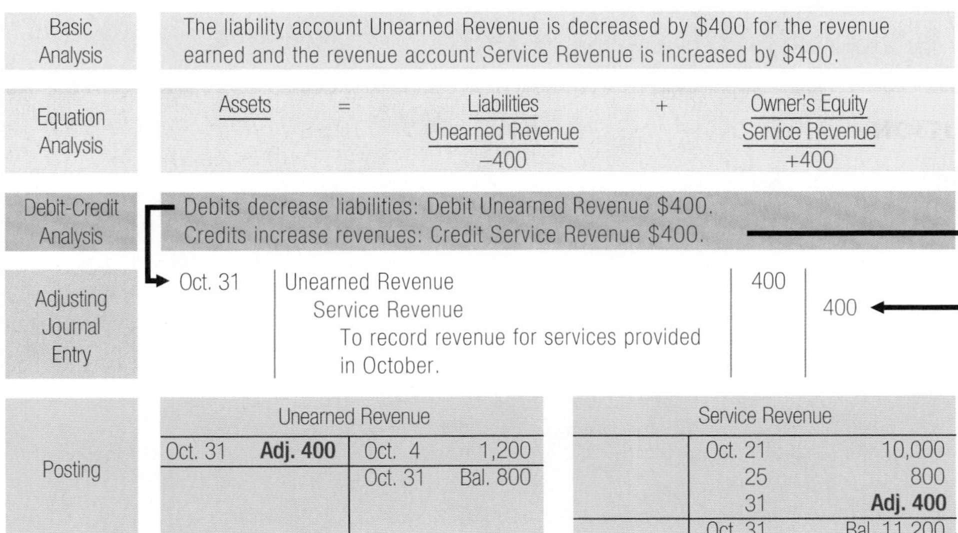

Basic Analysis	The liability account Unearned Revenue is decreased by $400 for the revenue earned and the revenue account Service Revenue is increased by $400.
Equation Analysis	Assets = Liabilities (Unearned Revenue −400) + Owner's Equity (Service Revenue +400)
Debit-Credit Analysis	Debits decrease liabilities: Debit Unearned Revenue $400. Credits increase revenues: Credit Service Revenue $400.

Adjusting Journal Entry:

Date	Account	Debit	Credit
Oct. 31	Unearned Revenue	400	
	Service Revenue		400
	To record revenue for services provided in October.		

Posting:

Unearned Revenue			
Oct. 31	**Adj. 400**	Oct. 4	1,200
		Oct. 31	Bal. 800

Service Revenue			
		Oct. 21	10,000
		25	800
		31	**Adj. 400**
		Oct. 31	Bal. 11,200

The liability Unearned Revenue now shows a balance of $800. This amount represents the remaining advertising services that will be performed in the future. At the same time, Service Revenue shows additional revenue of $400 earned in October. If this adjustment is not made, revenues and profit will be understated by $400 in the income statement. As well, liabilities will be overstated by $400 and owner's equity understated by that amount on the October 31 balance sheet.

ACCOUNTING IN ACTION
BUSINESS INSIGHT

Gift cards have become more popular in Canada. And with recent legislation in Ontario, Alberta, British Columbia, Nova Scotia, and other provinces eliminating the use of expiry dates on the cards, their benefits to the consumer have increased. But what is the benefit to businesses? Many have discovered that gift card sales in December give their revenues in the new year a boost. Many gift cards sold in December are used in January or February. In fact, Statistics Canada has found that the usual drop in sales from December to January has started to moderate, which it attributes in part to the redemption of gift cards early in the new year. Businesses must recognize revenue from gift cards when they're redeemed, which boosts revenues in traditionally slower times.

Sources: "Nova Scotia to Ban Gift Card Expiry Dates," CBC News online, December 3, 2009; "B.C. Government Bans Gift Cards with Fees or Expiry Dates," CanWest MediaWorks, October 18, 2008; Daniel Bahta, Rhoda Tsang, and Monica Weise, "Gift Cards: The Gift of Choice," Statistics Canada analytical paper, 2006.

If a business collects cash when the gift card is sold, how can gift card sales in December result in revenues in January?

BEFORE YOU GO ON...

Action Plan

- Make sure you prepare adjustments for the correct time period.
- Adjusting entries for prepaid expenses require a debit to an expense account and a credit to an asset or contra asset account.
- Adjusting entries for unearned revenues require a debit to a liability account and a credit to a revenue account.

DO IT

The trial balance of Panos Co. on March 31, 2014, includes the following selected accounts before adjusting entries:

	Debit	Credit
Prepaid insurance	$ 1,200	
Supplies	2,800	
Equipment	24,000	
Accumulated depreciation—equipment		$2,200
Unearned revenue		9,300

An analysis of the accounts shows the following:

1. A one-year insurance policy for $1,200 was purchased on March 1, 2014.
2. Supplies on hand at March 31, 2014, total $800.
3. Equipment was purchased on April 1, 2013, and has an estimated useful life of 10 years.
4. One third of the unearned revenue was earned in March 2014.

Prepare the adjusting entries for the month of March.

SOLUTION

1.	Mar. 31	Insurance Expense	100	
		Prepaid Insurance		100
		To record insurance expired: $1,200 ÷ 12.		
2.	31	Supplies Expense	2,000	
		Supplies		2,000
		To record supplies used: $2,800 previously on hand − $800 currently on hand = $2,000 used.		
3.	31	Depreciation Expense	200	
		Accumulated Depreciation—Equipment		200
		To record monthly depreciation: $24,000 ÷ 10 × $\frac{1}{12}$.		
4.	31	Unearned Revenue	3,100	
		Service Revenue		3,100
		To record revenue earned: $9,300 × $\frac{1}{3}$ = $3,100 earned.		

Related exercise material: BE3–2, BE3–3, BE3–4, BE3–5, and E3–4.

THE NAVIGATOR

ADJUSTING ENTRIES FOR ACCRUALS

STUDY OBJECTIVE 3

Prepare adjusting entries for accruals.

The second category of adjusting entries is accruals. Unlike prepayments, which have already been recorded in the accounts, accruals are not recognized through transaction journal entries and thus are not included in the accounts. Accruals are required in situations where cash will be paid or received after the end of the accounting period.

Until an accrual adjustment is made, the revenue account (and the related asset account) is understated for accrued revenues. Similarly, the expense account (and the related liability account) is understated for accrued expenses. Thus, adjusting entries for accruals increase both a balance sheet account and an income statement account. We now look at each type of adjusting entry for accruals—accrued revenues and accrued expenses—in more detail.

Accrued Revenues

Alternative terminology

Accrued revenues are also called *accrued receivables.*

Revenues earned but not yet received in cash or recorded at the statement date are **accrued revenues.** Accrued revenues may accumulate (accrue) with the passage of time, as happens with interest revenue and rent revenue. Or they may result when services have been performed but the payment has not been billed or received, as can happen with commissions and fees. The former are unrecorded because the earning of interest and rent does not involve daily transactions. The latter may be unrecorded because only a portion of the total service has been provided or the bill has not been prepared.

An adjusting entry is required for two purposes: (1) to show the receivable that exists at the balance sheet date, and (2) to record the revenue that has been earned during the period. Before the adjustment is recorded, both assets and revenues are understated. Accordingly, as shown below, an adjusting entry for accrued revenues results in an increase (debit) to an asset account and an increase (credit) to a revenue account.

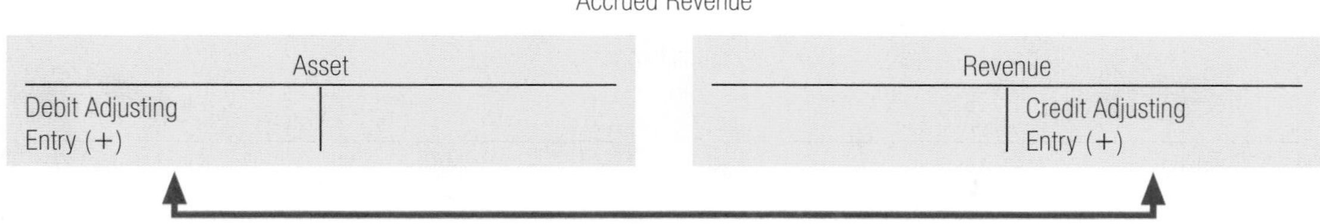

In October, Pioneer Advertising Agency earned $200 in fees for advertising services that were not billed to clients until November. Because these services have not been billed, they have not been recorded. An adjusting entry on October 31 is required as follows:

ADJUSTMENT 5
Accrued Revenue—Accounts Receivable

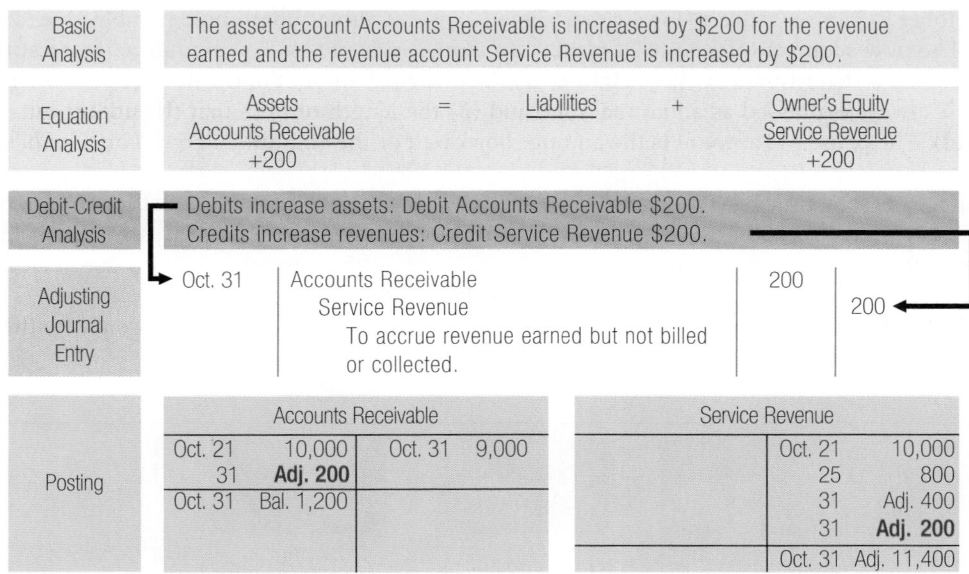

The asset Accounts Receivable shows that $1,200 is owed by clients at the balance sheet date. The balance of $11,400 in Service Revenue represents the total revenue earned during the month. If the adjusting entry is not made, assets and owner's equity on the balance sheet, and revenues and profit on the income statement, will all be understated.

On November 10, Pioneer receives $200 cash for the services performed in October. The following entry is made:

Nov. 10	Cash	200	
	Accounts Receivable		200
	To record cash collected on account.		

A	=	L	+	OE
+200				
−200				

↑ Cash flows: +200

Accrued Expenses

Expenses incurred but not yet paid or recorded at the statement date are called **accrued expenses**. Interest, rent, property taxes, and salaries can be accrued expenses. As we saw in our feature story, Seneca College uses estimates to accrue for legal and utility expenses because the actual invoices are received after its year end. Accrued expenses result from the same causes as accrued revenues. In fact, an accrued expense on the books of one company is an accrued revenue for another company. For example, the $200 accrual of revenue by Pioneer is an accrued expense for the client that received the service.

Alternative terminology
Accrued expenses are also called *accrued liabilities.*

Adjustments for accrued expenses are needed for two purposes: (1) to record the obligations that exist at the balance sheet date, and (2) to recognize the expenses that apply to the current accounting period. Before adjustment, both liabilities and expenses are understated. Profit and owner's equity are overstated. An adjusting entry for accrued expenses results in an increase (debit) to an expense account and an increase (credit) to a liability account, as follows.

Accrued Expenses

Expense	
Debit Adjusting Entry (+)	

Liability	
	Credit Adjusting Entry (+)

There are many types of expenses that might need to be accrued at the end of an accounting period. Two of the most common are interest and salaries.

Interest.

On October 2, Pioneer Advertising Agency signed a $5,000, three-month note payable, due January 2, 2015. The note requires interest to be paid at an annual rate of 6%. The amount of interest that has accumulated is determined by three factors: (1) the principal amount of the note; (2) the interest rate, which is always expressed as an annual rate; and (3) the length of time that the note is outstanding (unpaid). The **principal** amount is the amount borrowed or the amount still owed on a loan, separate from interest.

Helpful hint To make the illustration easier to understand, a simplified method for calculating interest is used. In reality, interest is calculated using the exact number of days in the interest period and year.

Interest is sometimes due monthly, and sometimes when the principal is due. For Pioneer, the total interest due on the $5,000 note at its due date three months later is $75 ($5,000 × 6% × $^3/_{12}$ months). *Interest rates are always expressed as an annual rate.* Because the interest rate is for one year, the time period must be adjusted for the fraction of the year that the note is outstanding.

The formula for calculating interest and how it applies to Pioneer Advertising Agency for the month of October are shown in Illustration 3-5.

ILLUSTRATION 3-5
Formula for calculating interest

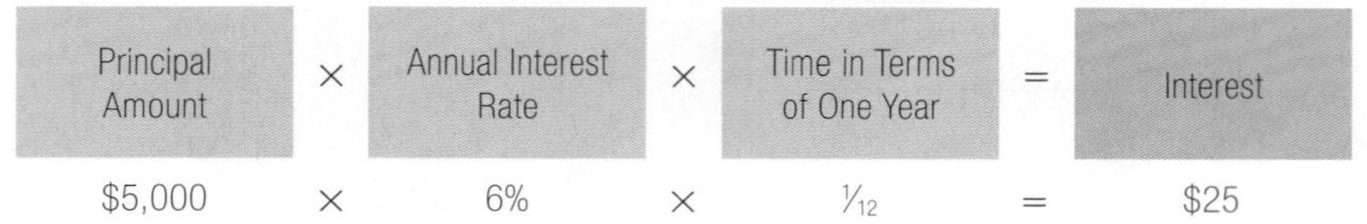

Principal Amount × Annual Interest Rate × Time in Terms of One Year = Interest
$5,000 × 6% × 1⁄12 = $25

The accrued interest expense adjusting entry at October 31 follows:

ADJUSTMENT 6
Accrued Expenses—Interest

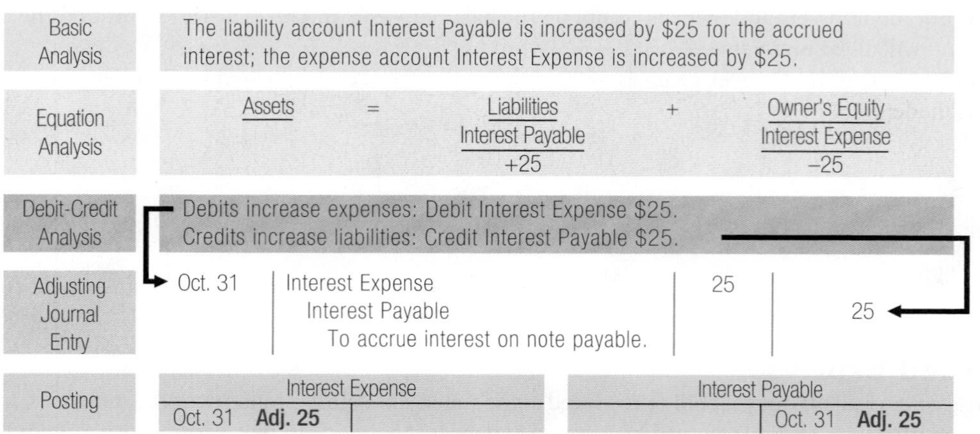

Interest Expense shows the interest charges for the month of October. The amount of interest owed at the statement date is shown in Interest Payable. It will not be paid until the note comes due, on January 2, 2015. The Interest Payable account is used instead of crediting Notes Payable in order to show the two types of obligations (interest and principal) in the accounts and statements. If this adjusting entry is not made, liabilities and expenses will be understated, and profit and owner's equity will be overstated.

Since this is a three-month note, Pioneer Advertising will also need to make identical adjustments at the end of November and at the end of December to accrue for interest expense incurred in each of these months. After the three adjusting entries have been posted, the balance in Interest Payable is \$75 (\$25 × 3). The following entry is made on January 2, 2015, when the note and interest are paid:

Helpful hint The credit balance in Notes Payable shows the principal amount of the note.

Jan. 2	Interest Payable	75	
	Note Payable	5,000	
	Cash		5,075
	To record payment of note and interest.		

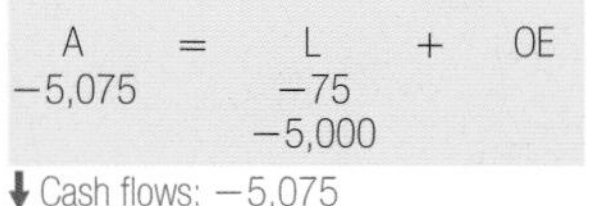

Cash flows: −5,075

This entry does two things: (1) it eliminates the liability for Interest Payable that was recorded in the October 31, November 30, and December 31 adjusting entries; and (2) it eliminates the note payable. Notice also that the Interest Expense account is not included in this entry, because the full amount of interest incurred was accrued and recorded in previous months.

Salaries.

Some types of expenses, such as employee salaries and commissions, are paid *after* the work has been performed. At Pioneer Advertising, employees began work on October 13. They are paid every two weeks and were last paid on October 24. The next payment of salaries will not occur until November 7. As shown on the calendar, in Illustration 3-6, there are five working days that remain unpaid at October 31 (October 27–31).

ILLUSTRATION 3-6
Calendar showing Pioneer Advertising's pay periods

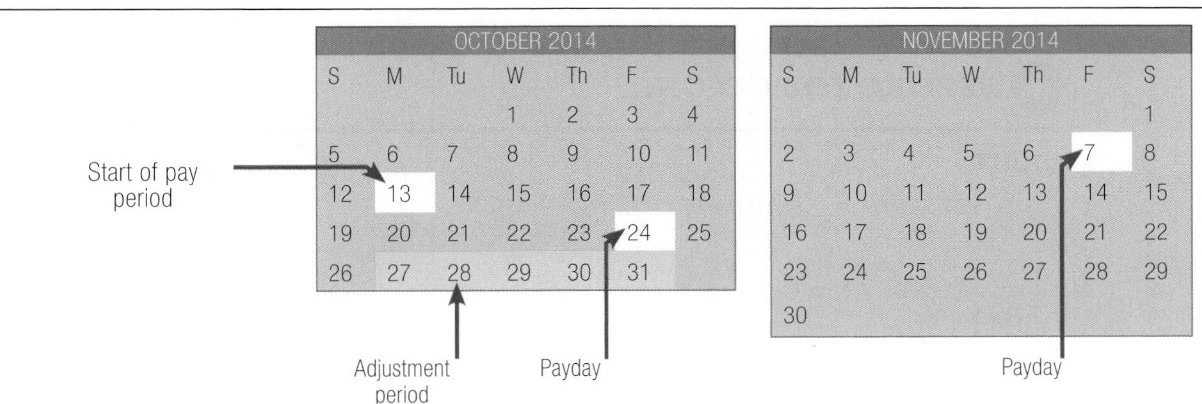

At October 31, the salaries for the last five working days (Monday, October 27, to Friday, October 31) represent an accrued expense and a related liability for Pioneer Advertising because the employees have worked but have not been paid for this work as at October 31. Recall from Chapter 2 that each of the four employees earns a salary of \$500 for a five-day workweek, which is \$100 per day. Thus, at October 31 the accrued salaries are \$2,000 (4 employees × \$100/day × 5 days). Pioneer's accrued salaries expense adjusting entry follows:

Helpful hint Recognition of an accrued expense does not mean that a company is slow or bad at paying its debts. The accrued liability may not be payable until after the balance sheet date.

ADJUSTMENT 7
Accrued Expenses—Salaries

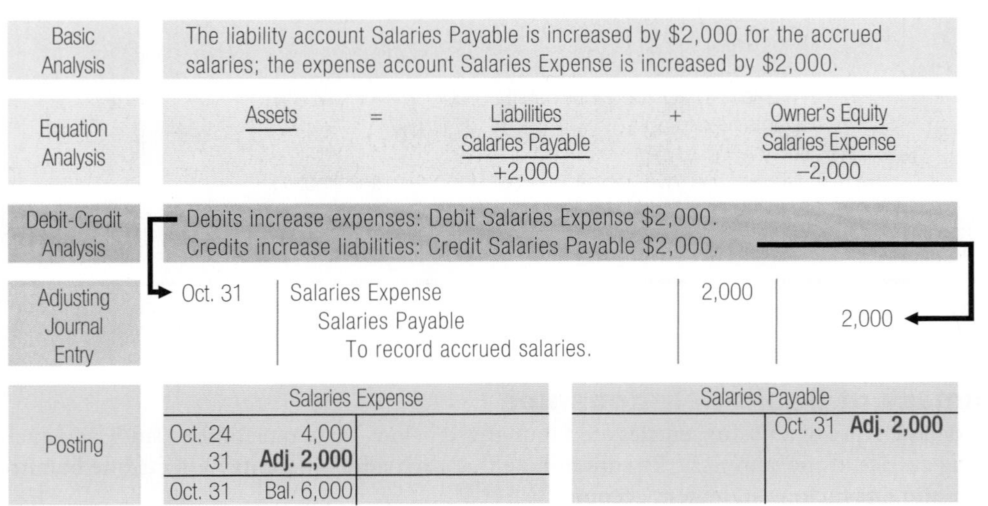

After this adjustment, the balance in Salaries Expense of $6,000 (4 employees × $100/day × 15 days) is the actual salary expense for October. (The employees have worked 15 days in October.) The balance in Salaries Payable of $2,000 is the amount of the liability for salaries owed as at October 31. If the $2,000 adjustment for salaries is not recorded, Pioneer's expenses and liabilities will be *understated* by $2,000. Profit and owner's equity will be overstated by $2,000.

At Pioneer Advertising, salaries are payable every two weeks. The next payday is November 7, when total salaries of $4,000 will again be paid. The November 7 payment consists of $2,000 of salaries payable at October 31 plus $2,000 of salaries expense for November (4 employees × $100/day × 5 working days [for the period November 3–7]). The following entry is therefore made on November 7:

A	=	L	+	OE
−4,000		−2,000		−2,000

↓Cash flows: −4,000

Date	Account	Debit	Credit
Nov. 7	Salaries Payable	2,000	
	Salaries Expense	2,000	
	Cash		4,000
	To record November 7 payroll.		

This entry does two things: (1) it eliminates the liability for salaries payable that was recorded in the October 31 adjusting entry, and (2) it records the proper amount of salaries expense for the five-day period from Monday, November 3, to Friday, November 7.

BEFORE YOU GO ON...

Action Plan

- Remember that accruals are adjusting entries for revenues earned or expenses incurred that have not been recorded. The cash is received or paid after the end of the accounting period.
- Adjusting entries for accrued revenues increase a receivable account (an asset) and increase a revenue account.
- Remember that debits increase assets and credits increase revenues.
- Adjusting entries for accrued expenses increase a payable account (a liability) and increase an expense account.
- Remember that debits increase expenses and credits increase liabilities.

DO IT

Alvin Tsui is the owner of the new company Micro Computer Services. At the end of August 2014, the first month of business, Alvin is trying to prepare monthly financial statements. The following information is for August:

1. At August 31, Micro Computer Services owed its employees $800 in salaries that will be paid on September 2.
2. On August 1, Micro Computer Services borrowed $30,000 from a local bank on a five-year term loan. The annual interest rate is 5% and interest is paid monthly on the first of each month.
3. Service revenue earned in August but not yet billed or recorded at August 31 totalled $1,100.

Prepare the adjusting entries needed at August 31, 2014.

SOLUTION

	Date	Account	Debit	Credit
1.	Aug. 31	Salaries Expense	800	
		Salaries Payable		800
		To record accrued salaries.		
2.	31	Interest Expense	125	
		Interest Payable		125
		To record accrued interest: $30,000 × 5% × 1/12.		
3.	31	Accounts Receivable	1,100	
		Service Revenue		1,100
		To accrue revenue earned but not billed or collected.		

Related exercise material: BE3–7, BE3–8, BE3–9, BE3–10, BE3–11, BE3–12, E3–5, E3–6, E3–7, and E3–8.

Summary of Basic Relationships

The two basic types of adjusting entries are summarized below. Take some time to study and analyze the adjusting entries in the summary. Be sure to note that **each adjusting entry affects one balance sheet account and one income statement account.**

	Type of Adjustment	Reason for Adjustment	Accounts before Adjustment	Adjusting Entry
Prepayments	Prepaid expenses	Prepaid expenses, originally recorded in asset accounts, have been used.	Assets overstated; expenses understated	Dr. Expense Cr. Asset
	Unearned revenues	Unearned revenues, originally recorded in liability accounts, have been earned.	Liabilities overstated; revenues understated	Dr. Liability Cr. Revenue
Accruals	Accrued revenues	Revenues have been earned but not yet received in cash or recorded.	Assets understated; revenues understated	Dr. Asset Cr. Revenue
	Accrued expenses	Expenses have been incurred but not yet paid in cash or recorded.	Expenses understated; liabilities understated	Dr. Expense Cr. Liability

Note that adjusting entries never involve the Cash account. In the case of prepayments, cash has already been received or paid, and was already recorded in the original journal entry. The adjusting entry reallocates or adjusts amounts between a balance sheet account (such as prepaid assets or unearned revenues) and an income statement account (such as expenses or revenues). In the case of accruals, cash will be received or paid in the future and recorded then. The adjusting entry records the receivable or payable and the related revenue or expense.

Pioneer Advertising Agency Illustration

The journalizing and posting of adjusting entries for Pioneer Advertising Agency on October 31 are shown below and on the following page. The title "Adjusting Entries" may be inserted in the general journal between the last transaction entry from Chapter 2 and the first adjusting entry so that the adjusting entries are clearly identified. As you review the general ledger, note that the adjustments are highlighted in colour.

GENERAL JOURNAL **J2**

Date	Account Titles and Explanation	Ref	Debit	Credit
2014	Adjusting Entries			
Oct. 31	Supplies Expense	740	1,500	
	Supplies	129		1,500
	To record supplies used.			
31	Insurance Expense	722	50	
	Prepaid Insurance	130		50
	To record insurance expired.			
31	Depreciation Expense	711	83	
	Accumulated Depreciation—Equipment	152		83
	To record monthly depreciation.			
31	Unearned Revenue	209	400	
	Service Revenue	400		400
	To record revenue for services provided in October.			
31	Accounts Receivable	112	200	
	Service Revenue	400		200
	To accrue revenue earned but not billed or collected.			
31	Interest Expense	905	25	
	Interest Payable	230		25
	To accrue interest on note payable.			
31	Salaries Expense	729	2,000	
	Salaries Payable	212		2,000
	To record accrued salaries.			

GENERAL LEDGER

Cash			101
Oct. 1	10,000	Oct. 3	900
3	1,200	3	600
25	800	20	500
31	9,000	24	4,000
		31	750
Bal.	14,250		

Accounts Receivable			112
Oct. 21	10,000	Oct. 31	9,000
31 Adj.	200		
Bal.	1,200		

Supplies			129
Oct. 4	2,500	Oct. 31 Adj.	1,500
Bal.	1,000		

Prepaid Insurance			130
Oct. 3	600	Oct. 31 Adj.	50
Bal.	550		

Equipment			151
Oct. 2	5,000		
Bal.	5,000		

Accumulated Depreciation—Equipment			152
		Oct. 31 Adj.	83
		Bal.	83

Notes Payable			200
		Oct. 2	5,000
		Bal.	5,000

Accounts Payable			201
Oct. 31	750	Oct. 4	2,500
		Bal.	1,750

Unearned Revenue			209
Oct. 31 Adj.	400	Oct. 3	1,200
		Bal.	800

Salaries Payable			212
		Oct. 31 Adj.	2,000
		Bal.	2,000

Interest Payable			230
		Oct. 31 Adj.	25
		Bal.	25

C. Bedard, Capital			301
		Oct. 1	10,000
		Bal.	10,000

C. Bedard, Drawings			306
Oct. 20	500		
Bal.	500		

Service Revenue			400
		Oct. 21	10,000
		25	800
		31 Adj.	400
		31 Adj.	200
		Bal.	11,400

Depreciation Expense			711
Oct. 31 Adj.	83		
Bal.	83		

Insurance Expense			722
Oct. 31 Adj.	50		
Bal.	50		

Rent Expense			726
Oct. 3	900		
Bal.	900		

Salaries Expense			729
Oct. 24	4,000		
31 Adj.	2,000		
Bal.	6,000		

Supplies Expense			740
Oct. 31 Adj.	1,500		
Bal.	1,500		

Interest Expense			905
Oct. 31 Adj.	25		
Bal.	25		

THE ADJUSTED TRIAL BALANCE AND FINANCIAL STATEMENTS

STUDY OBJECTIVE 4

Describe the nature and purpose of an adjusted trial balance, and prepare one.

After all adjusting entries have been journalized and posted, another trial balance is prepared from the general ledger accounts. This is called an **adjusted trial balance**. Financial statements are then prepared from the adjusted trial balance. Preparation of the adjusted trial balance and the financial statements are steps 6 and 7 of the accounting cycle, as shown in Illustration 3-7.

ILLUSTRATION 3-7
The accounting cycle—Steps 1 to 7

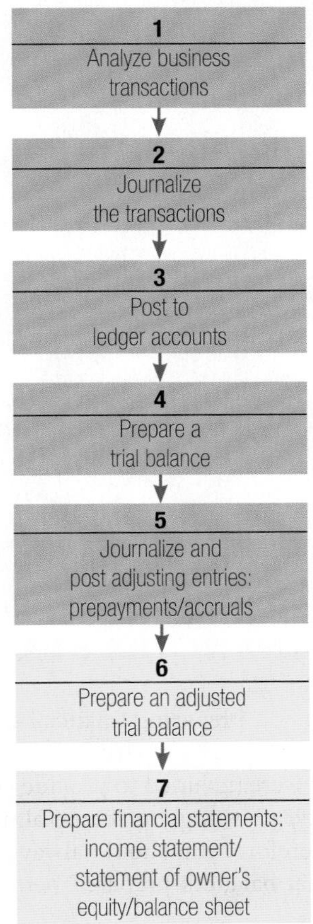

PREPARING THE ADJUSTED TRIAL BALANCE

The procedures for preparing an adjusted trial balance are the same as those described in Chapter 2 for preparing a trial balance. An adjusted trial balance, like a trial balance, only proves that the ledger is mathematically accurate. As discussed in Chapter 2, it *does not* prove that there are no mistakes in the ledger.

An adjusted trial balance proves that the total of the debit and credit balances in the ledger are equal after all adjustments have been posted. The adjusted trial balance gives all data that are needed for preparing financial statements.

The adjusted trial balance for Pioneer Advertising Agency is presented in Illustration 3-8. It has been prepared from the ledger accounts shown in the previous section. The amounts affected by the adjusting entries are highlighted in colour in the adjusted trial balance columns. Compare these amounts with those in the trial balance in Illustration 3-3.

ILLUSTRATION 3-8
Adjusted trial balance

PIONEER ADVERTISING AGENCY Adjusted Trial Balance October 31, 2014		
	Debit	**Credit**
Cash	$14,250	
Accounts receivable	1,200	
Supplies	1,000	
Prepaid insurance	550	
Equipment	5,000	
Accumulated depreciation—equipment		$ 83
Notes payable		5,000
Accounts payable		1,750
Unearned revenue		800
Salaries payable		2,000
Interest payable		25
C. Bedard, capital		10,000
C. Bedard, drawings	500	
Service revenue		11,400
Depreciation expense	83	
Insurance expense	50	
Rent expense	900	
Salaries expense	6,000	
Supplies expense	1,500	
Interest expense	25	
	$31,058	$31,058

PREPARING FINANCIAL STATEMENTS

As shown in Illustration 3-7, preparing financial statements is the seventh step in the accounting cycle. In Chapter 2, you saw examples of preparing financial statements from a trial balance, without adjusting entries. Those examples were included to provide you with opportunities to practise preparing financial statements. But in reality, adjusting entries are almost always necessary to prepare financial statements on an accrual basis. Therefore, you should always prepare financial statements from an **adjusted trial balance**, never from trial balances prepared before adjusting entries (also known as unadjusted trial balances).

The preparation of financial statements from the adjusted trial balance of Pioneer Advertising Agency and the interrelationships of the data are shown in Illustrations 3-9 and 3-10. As Illustration 3-9 shows, companies first prepare the income statement from the revenue and expense accounts. Next, the statement of owner's equity is prepared from the owner's capital and drawings accounts, and from the profit (or loss) shown in the income statement. As Illustration 3-10 shows, companies then prepare the balance sheet from the asset and liability accounts and the ending owner's capital balance that is reported in the statement of owner's equity.

ILLUSTRATION 3-9
Preparation of the income statement and statement of owner's equity from the adjusted trial balance

PIONEER ADVERTISING AGENCY
Adjusted Trial Balance
October 31, 2014

	Debit	Credit
Cash	$14,250	
Accounts receivable	1,200	
Supplies	1,000	
Prepaid insurance	550	
Equipment	5,000	
Accumulated depreciation—equipment		$ 83
Notes payable		5,000
Accounts payable		1,750
Unearned revenue		800
Salaries payable		2,000
Interest payable		25
C. Bedard, Capital		10,000
C. Bedard, drawings	500	
Service revenue		11,400
Depreciation expense	83	
Insurance expense	50	
Rent expense	900	
Salaries expense	6,000	
Supplies expense	1,500	
Interest expense	25	
	$31,058	$31,058

PIONEER ADVERTISING AGENCY
Income Statement
Month Ended October 31, 2014

Revenues		
Service revenue		$11,400
Expenses		
Depreciation expense	$ 83	
Insurance expense	50	
Rent expense	900	
Salaries expense	6,000	
Supplies expense	1,500	
Interest expense	25	
Total expenses		8,558
Profit		$ 2,842

PIONEER ADVERTISING AGENCY
Statement of Owner's Equity
Month Ended October 31, 2014

C. Bedard, capital, October 1	$ 0
Add: Investments	10,000
Profit	2,842
	12,842
Less: Drawings	500
C. Bedard, capital, October 31	$12,342

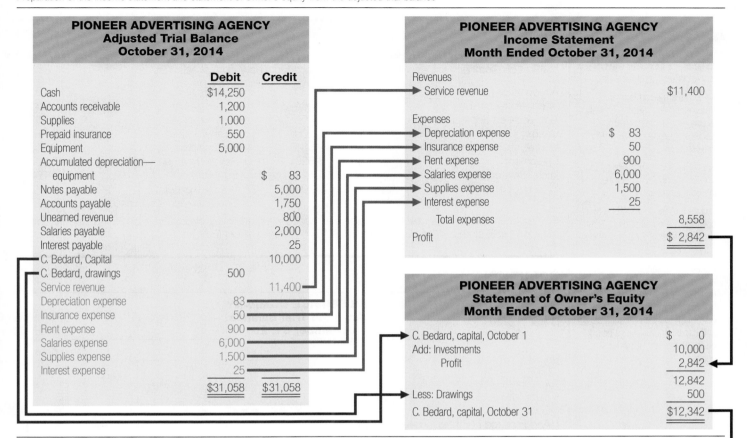

ILLUSTRATION 3-10
Preparation of the balance sheet from the adjusted trial balance

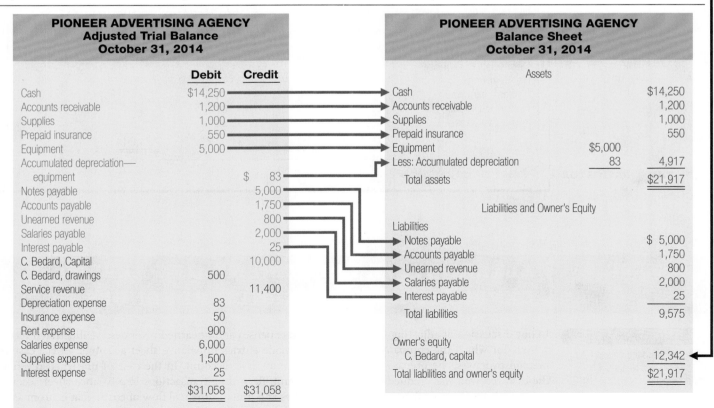

PIONEER ADVERTISING AGENCY
Adjusted Trial Balance
October 31, 2014

	Debit	Credit
Cash	$14,250	
Accounts receivable	1,200	
Supplies	1,000	
Prepaid insurance	550	
Equipment	5,000	
Accumulated depreciation—equipment		$ 83
Notes payable		5,000
Accounts payable		1,750
Unearned revenue		800
Salaries payable		2,000
Interest payable		25
C. Bedard, Capital		10,000
C. Bedard, drawings	500	
Service revenue		11,400
Depreciation expense	83	
Insurance expense	50	
Rent expense	900	
Salaries expense	6,000	
Supplies expense	1,500	
Interest expense	25	
	$31,058	$31,058

PIONEER ADVERTISING AGENCY
Balance Sheet
October 31, 2014

Assets		
Cash		$14,250
Accounts receivable		1,200
Supplies		1,000
Prepaid insurance		550
Equipment	$5,000	
Less: Accumulated depreciation	83	4,917
Total assets		$21,917
Liabilities and Owner's Equity		
Liabilities		
Notes payable		$ 5,000
Accounts payable		1,750
Unearned revenue		800
Salaries payable		2,000
Interest payable		25
Total liabilities		9,575
Owner's equity		
C. Bedard, capital		12,342
Total liabilities and owner's equity		$21,917

BEFORE YOU GO ON...

Action Plan

- The trial balance title includes the name of the company, the type of trial balance, and the date.
- Accounts are listed in financial statement order: assets (as well as any contra assets), liabilities, owner's equity, revenues, and expenses.
- Apply the normal balance rules and list the account balances in the correct columns.
- Ensure that the totals of the two columns are equal and apply the short-cut tests for locating errors if they aren't.
- Recall that assets and their contra assets, liabilities, and capital belong on the balance sheet; revenues and expenses belong on the income statement; and capital and drawings belong on the statement of owner's equity.

DO IT

Listed below, in alphabetical order, are the account balances (after adjustments) from the general ledger of KS Service Company at December 31, 2014. All accounts have normal balances.

Accounts payable	$4,660	K. Samji, drawings	$11,700
Accounts receivable	9,584	Note payable	1,000
Accumulated depreciation—equipment	1,764	Rent expense	20,762
Cash	1,100	Salaries expense	30,714
Depreciation expense	588	Salaries payable	310
Equipment	8,820	Service revenue	67,200
Interest expense	524	Supplies	180
K. Samji, capital	8,700	Supplies expense	672
		Unearned service revenue	1,010

Prepare the adjusted trial balance. Beside each account, identify if it should be included on the income statement (IS), statement of owner's equity (SOE), or balance sheet (BS).

SOLUTION

KS SERVICE COMPANY
Adjusted Trial Balance
December 31, 2014

	Debit	Credit	Statement
Cash	$ 1,100		BS
Accounts receivable	9,584		BS
Supplies	180		BS
Equipment	8,820		BS
Accumulated depreciation—equipment		$ 1,764	BS
Note payable		1,000	BS
Accounts payable		4,660	BS
Salaries payable		310	BS
Unearned service revenue		1,010	BS
K. Samji, capital		8,700	SOE & BS
K. Samji, drawings	11,700		SOE
Service revenue		67,200	IS
Depreciation expense	588		IS
Rent expense	20,762		IS
Salaries expense	30,714		IS
Supplies expense	672		IS
Interest expense	524		IS
	$84,644	$84,644	

THE NAVIGATOR

Related exercise material: BE3–13, E3–9, and E3–10.

APPENDIX 3A ALTERNATIVE TREATMENT OF PREPAID EXPENSES AND UNEARNED REVENUES

STUDY OBJECTIVE 5
Prepare adjusting entries for the alternative treatment of prepayments.

In our discussion of adjusting entries for prepaid expenses and unearned revenues, we illustrated transactions for which the company had previously made entries in balance sheet accounts. In the case of prepaid expenses, the prepayment was debited to an asset account. In the case of unearned revenue, the cash received was credited to a liability account. Recording transactions in a balance sheet account improves internal control over assets and liabilities and imitates the real flow of costs (that is, from asset to expense).

Some businesses use an alternative treatment: (1) When a company prepays an expense, it debits that amount to an expense account instead of an asset. (2) When it receives cash for future services, it credits a revenue account instead of a liability account. The following sections describe the circumstances that justify such entries and the different adjusting entries that may be needed.

PREPAID EXPENSES

Prepaid expenses become expired costs either as time passes, as with insurance, or as they are used up, as with supplies. If, when it makes a purchase, the company expects to consume the supplies before the next financial statement date, it may be more convenient to first debit (increase) an expense account rather than an asset account.

Assume that Pioneer Advertising expects that all of the supplies purchased on October 4 will be used before the end of the month. A debit of $2,500 to Supplies Expense on October 4, rather than to the asset account Supplies, will eliminate the need for an adjusting entry on October 31, if all the supplies are used. At October 31, the Supplies Expense account will show a balance of $2,500, which is the cost of supplies purchased between October 4 and October 31.

But what if the company does not use all the supplies? What if an inventory of $1,000 of supplies remains on October 31? Obviously, an adjusting entry is needed. Pioneer will need to decrease its Supplies Expense account because it didn't use all of the supplies purchased. And it will need to increase an asset account, Supplies, to show it has supplies on hand. The following adjusting entry is then made:

Date	Account	Debit	Credit
Oct. 31	Supplies	1,000	
	Supplies Expense		1,000
	To record supply inventory.		

A	=	L	+	OE
+1,000				+1,000

Cash flows: no effect

After posting of the adjusting entry, the accounts show the following:

Helpful hint Note that under this method, the adjustment involves a debit to Supplies and a credit to Supplies Expense; this is the opposite to what would take place under the traditional method.

Supplies				Supplies Expense			
Oct. 31	**Adj.**	**1,000**		Oct. 4	2,500	Oct. 31 **Adj.**	**1,000**
				Bal.	1,500		

After adjustment, the asset account Supplies shows a balance of $1,000, which is equal to the cost of supplies on hand at October 31. In addition, Supplies Expense shows a balance of $1,500, which is equal to the cost of supplies used between October 4 and October 31 ($2,500 − $1,000). If the adjusting entry is not made, expenses will be overstated and profit will be understated by $1,000 in the October income statement. Also, both assets and owner's equity will be understated by $1,000 on the October 31 balance sheet.

A comparison of the entries and accounts for supplies in the chapter and here in the appendix follows:

Prepayment Debited to Asset Account (as in chapter)

Date	Account	Debit	Credit
Oct. 4	Supplies	2,500	
	Accounts Payable		2,500
31	Supplies Expense	1,500	
	Supplies		1,500

Prepayment Debited to Expense Account (as in appendix)

Date	Account	Debit	Credit
Oct. 4	Supplies Expense	2,500	
	Accounts Payable		2,500
31	Supplies	1,000	
	Supplies Expense		1,000

After posting of the entries, the accounts appear as follows:

Prepayment Debited to Asset Account (as in chapter)

Supplies

Oct. 4		2,500	Oct. 31	**Adj.**	**1,500**
	Bal.	**1,000**			

Supplies Expense

Oct. 31	**Adj.**	**1,500**			

Prepayment Debited to Expense Account (as in appendix)

Supplies

Oct. 31	**Adj.**	**1,000**			

Supplies Expense

Oct. 4		2,500	Oct. 31	**Adj.**	**1,000**
	Bal.	**1,500**			

Note that the account balances under each alternative are the same at October 31 (Supplies $1,000, and Supplies Expense $1,500).

UNEARNED REVENUES

Unearned revenues are earned either as time passes, as with unearned rent, or by providing the service, as with unearned fees. Rather than first crediting (increasing) an unearned revenue (liability) account, a revenue account may be credited (increased) when cash is received for future services. Then a different adjusting entry may be necessary.

To illustrate, assume that when Pioneer Advertising received $1,200 for future services on October 3, the services were expected to be performed before October 31. In such a case, Service Revenue would be credited. If all the revenue is in fact earned before October 31, no adjustment is needed. However, if at the statement date $800 of the services have not been provided, an adjusting entry is needed to reduce revenue and increase liabilities by $800. The following adjusting entry is made:

A	=	L	+	OE
		+800		−800

Cash flows: no effect

Oct. 31	Service Revenue	800	
	Unearned Revenue		800
	To record unearned revenue.		

After posting of the adjusting entry, the accounts show:

Unearned Revenue

			Oct. 31	**Adj.**	**800**

Service Revenue

Oct. 31	**Adj.**	**800**	Oct. 3		1,200
				Bal.	400

Helpful hint Note that under this method, the adjustment involves a debit to Service Revenue and a credit to Unearned Revenue; this is the opposite to what would take place under the traditional method.

The liability account Unearned Revenue shows a balance of $800, which is equal to the services that are still owed and will be provided in the future. In addition, the $400 balance in Service Revenue is equal to the services provided in October ($1,200 − $800). If the adjusting entry is not made, both revenues and profit will be overstated by $800 in the October income statement. On the October 31 balance sheet, liabilities will also be *understated* by $800, and owner's equity will be *overstated* by $800.

A comparison of the entries and accounts for service revenue and unearned revenue in the chapter and here in the appendix follows:

Unearned Revenue Credited to Liability Account (as in chapter)

Oct. 3	Cash	1,200	
	Unearned Revenue		1,200
31	Unearned Revenue	400	
	Service Revenue		400

Unearned Revenue Credited to Revenue Account (as in appendix)

Oct. 3	Cash	1,200	
	Service Revenue		1,200
31	Service Revenue	800	
	Unearned Revenue		800

After posting the entries, the accounts will show:

Unearned Revenue Credited to Liability Account (as in chapter)

Unearned Revenue

Oct. 31	Adj.	400	Oct. 3		1,200
			Oct. 31	Bal.	800

Service Revenue

			Oct. 31	Adj.	400

Unearned Revenue Credited to Revenue Account (as in appendix)

Unearned Revenue

			Oct. 31	Adj.	800

Service Revenue

Oct. 31	Adj.	800	Oct. 3		1,200
			Oct. 31	Bal.	400

Note that the month-end balances in the accounts are the same under the two alternatives (Unearned Revenue $800, and Service Revenue $400).

As companies always record long-lived assets as assets, there isn't an alternative method of making an adjusting entry for depreciation. And there isn't an alternative method of making adjusting entries for accruals, because no entries occur before accrual adjusting entries are made. Remember, with an accrual, cash is paid or received after the end of the accounting period.

BEFORE YOU GO ON...

DO IT

Mansell Consulting records prepayments as expenses and cash received in advance of providing services as revenue. During February, the following transactions occurred:

Feb. 4 Paid $950 for supplies.
10 Received $2,350 from a client for services to be performed in the future.

On February 28, Mansell determined that $1,750 of the service revenue had been earned and that there was $750 of supplies on hand.

1. Journalize the February transactions.
2. Journalize the adjusting entries at February 28.

Action Plan

- Expenses are recorded as debits and revenues as credits.
- If a prepayment is recorded as an expense, an adjustment will be required at the end of the period if an asset exists.
- If cash received in advance of providing services is recorded as revenue, an adjustment will be required at the end of the period if part of the revenue is still unearned.

SOLUTION

1.	Feb. 4	Supplies Expense	950	
		Cash		950
		To record purchase of supplies.		
	10	Cash	2,350	
		Service Revenue		2,350
		To record cash received for services to be provided.		
2.	28	Supplies	750	
		Supplies Expense		750
		To record supplies on hand as an asset.		
	28	Service Revenue	600	
		Unearned Revenue		600
		To record the obligation to provide services in the future ($2,350 − $1,750).		

Related exercise material: *BE3–14, *BE3–15, *E3–11, and *E3–12.

THE NAVIGATOR

Comparing IFRS and ASPE

Key Differences	International Financial Reporting Standards (IFRS)	Accounting Standards for Private Enterprises (ASPE)
Timing of preparing adjusting journal entries	Public companies must prepare quarterly financial statements, so adjusting entries will have to be made at least four times a year.	Private companies must prepare annual financial statements, so adjusting entries are required only on an annual basis.
Terminology	In IFRS, the term "depreciation" is used for the allocation of the cost of long-lived assets such as buildings and equipment and the term "amortization" is used for intangible long-lived assets.	In ASPE, the term "amortization" is used for the allocation of the cost of buildings and equipment and for intangible long-lived assets. But private companies are allowed to use the term "depreciation" for buildings and equipment.

THE NAVIGATOR

DEMONSTRATION PROBLEM

Julie Szo opened Green Thumb Lawn Care Company on April 1, 2014. At April 30, 2014, the trial balance is as follows:

GREEN THUMB LAWN CARE COMPANY
Trial Balance
April 30, 2014

	Debit	Credit
Cash	$10,950	
Prepaid insurance	3,600	
Supplies	850	
Equipment	28,000	
Notes payable		$20,000
Accounts payable		450
Unearned revenue		4,200
J. Szo, capital		18,000
J. Szo, drawings	650	
Service revenue		1,800
Rent expense	400	
Totals	$44,450	$44,450

Analysis reveals the following additional data for the month:

1. Prepaid insurance is the cost of a 12-month insurance policy that started April 1.
2. Supplies costing $225 were on hand on April 30.
3. The equipment is expected to have a useful life of four years.
4. The note payable is dated April 1. It is a six-month, 4% note with interest payable on the first of each month starting on May 1.
5. Seven customers paid for the company's six-month lawn service package of $600, beginning in April. These customers were serviced in April. (*Hint:* This amount was originally recorded as Unearned Revenue.)
6. Lawn services performed for other customers but not billed or recorded at April 30 totalled $1,500.

DEMONSTRATION PROBLEM continued on next page

DEMONSTRATION PROBLEM continued from previous page

Instructions

(a) Prepare the adjusting entries for the month of April. Show calculations.
(b) Prepare T accounts for the accounts affected by the adjusting entries by entering the opening account balances. Post the adjusting entries to the T accounts.
(c) Prepare an adjusted trial balance at April 30, 2014.
(d) Prepare an income statement, statement of owner's equity, and balance sheet.

SOLUTION TO DEMONSTRATION PROBLEM

(a)

GENERAL JOURNAL

Date	Account Titles and Explanation	Debit	Credit
	Adjusting Entries		
Apr. 30	Insurance Expense	300	
	Prepaid Insurance		300
	To record insurance expired:		
	$3,600 ÷ 12 = $300 per month.		
30	Supplies Expense	625	
	Supplies		625
	To record supplies used: $850 − $225 = $625.		
30	Depreciation Expense	583	
	Accumulated Depreciation—Equipment		583
	To record monthly depreciation:		
	$28,000 ÷ 4 = $7,000 × 1/12 = $583 per month.		
30	Interest Expense	67	
	Interest Payable		67
	To accrue interest on note payable:		
	$20,000 × 4% × 1/12 = $67.		
30	Unearned Revenue	700	
	Service Revenue		700
	To record service revenue:		
	$600 ÷ 6 months = $100 per month;		
	$100 per month × 7 customers = $700.		
30	Accounts Receivable	1,500	
	Service Revenue		1,500
	To accrue revenue earned but not billed or collected.		

(b)

GENERAL LEDGER

Accounts Receivable

Date		Debit	Date		Credit
Apr. 30	Adj.	1,500			
	Bal.	1,500			

Prepaid Insurance

Date		Debit	Date		Credit
Apr. 30	Bal.	3,600	Apr. 30	Adj.	300
	Bal.	3,300			

Supplies

Date		Debit	Date		Credit
Apr. 30	Bal.	850	Apr. 30	Adj.	625
	Bal.	225			

Accumulated Depreciation—Equipment

Date		Debit	Date		Credit
			Apr. 30	Adj.	583
				Bal.	583

Interest Payable

Date		Debit	Date		Credit
			Apr. 30	Adj.	67
				Bal.	67

Unearned Revenue

Date		Debit	Date		Credit
Apr. 30	Adj.	700	Apr. 30	Bal.	4,200
				Bal.	3,500

SOLUTION TO DEMONSTRATION PROBLEM continued on next page

Action Plan

- Note that adjustments are being made for one month.
- Before trying to determine what adjustments are necessary, look at how the amounts are currently recorded in the accounts.
- Select account titles carefully. Use existing titles whenever possible.
- Determine what the balances in the ledger accounts should be after the adjusting entries are posted.
- Do a basic and a debit-credit analysis to ensure the adjustment will result in the desired balance in the accounts.
- The adjusted trial balance is prepared the same way as the trial balance, but it will include more accounts.
- Prepare the financial statements in the order listed.
- Revenues and expenses belong on the income statement; assets, contra assets, and liabilities on the balance sheet.
- Remember that an income statement and a statement of owner's equity are for a period of time; the balance sheet is at the end of the accounting period. This is reflected in the final (date) line of the heading.

SOLUTION TO DEMONSTRATION PROBLEM continued from previous page

Service Revenue

Debit			Credit		
			Apr. 30	Bal.	1,800
			30	Adj.	700
			30	Adj.	1,500
				Bal.	4,000

Supplies Expense

Debit			Credit
Apr. 30	Adj.	625	
	Bal.	625	

Interest Expense

Debit			Credit
Apr. 30	Adj.	67	
	Bal.	67	

Depreciation Expense

Debit			Credit
Apr. 30	Adj.	583	
	Bal.	583	

Insurance Expense

Debit			Credit
Apr. 30	Adj.	300	
	Bal.	300	

(c)

GREEN THUMB LAWN CARE COMPANY
Adjusted Trial Balance
April 30, 2014

	Debit	Credit
Cash	$10,950	
Accounts receivable	1,500	
Prepaid insurance	3,300	
Supplies	225	
Equipment	28,000	
Accumulated depreciation—equipment		$ 583
Notes payable		20,000
Accounts payable		450
Interest payable		67
Unearned revenue		3,500
J. Szo, capital		18,000
J. Szo, drawings	650	
Service revenue		4,000
Depreciation expense	583	
Insurance expense	300	
Interest expense	67	
Rent expense	400	
Supplies expense	625	
Totals	$46,600	$46,600

SOLUTION TO DEMONSTRATION PROBLEM continued on next page

SOLUTION TO DEMONSTRATION PROBLEM continued from previous page

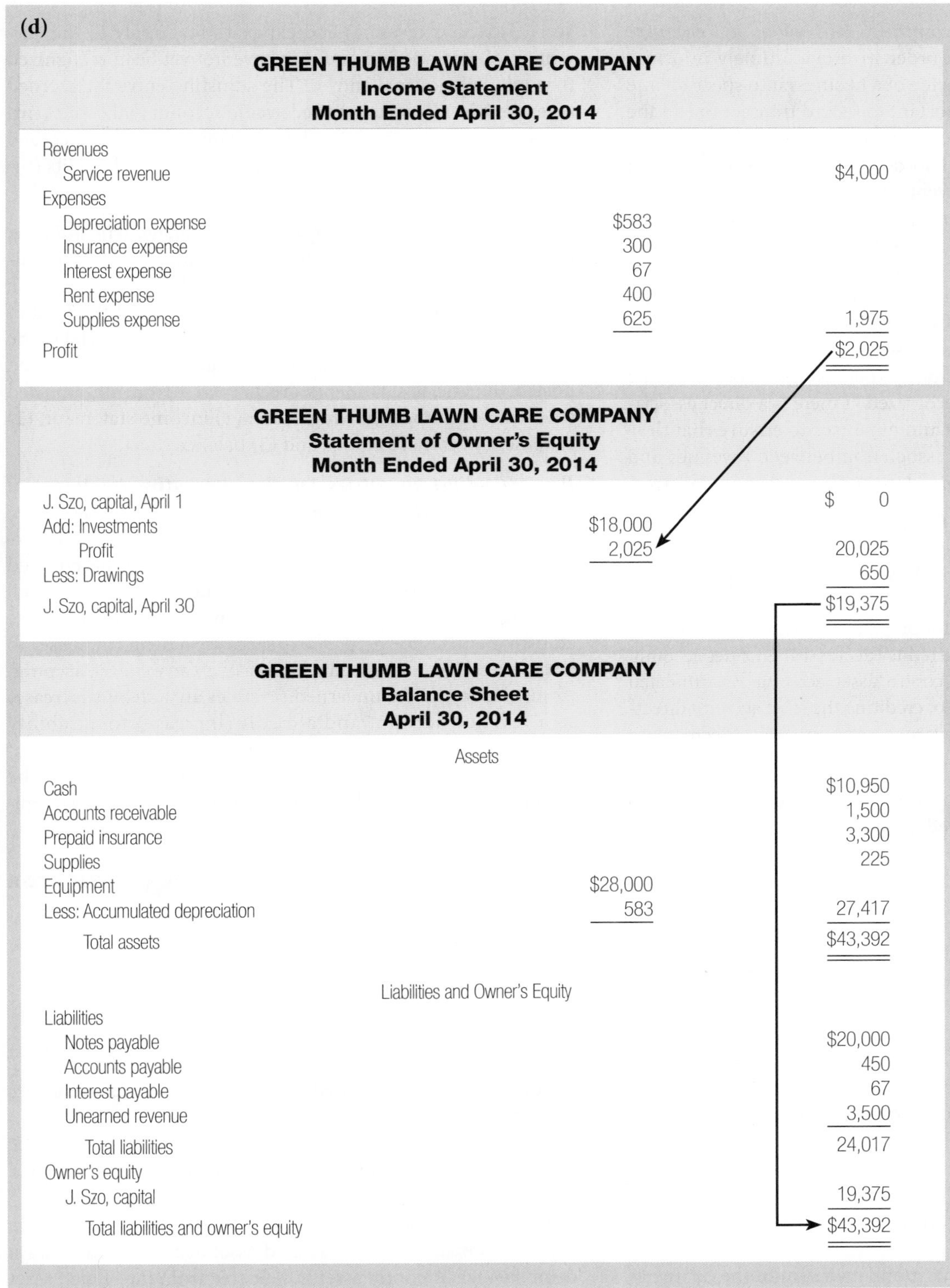

(d)

GREEN THUMB LAWN CARE COMPANY
Income Statement
Month Ended April 30, 2014

Revenues		
Service revenue		$4,000
Expenses		
Depreciation expense	$583	
Insurance expense	300	
Interest expense	67	
Rent expense	400	
Supplies expense	625	1,975
Profit		$2,025

GREEN THUMB LAWN CARE COMPANY
Statement of Owner's Equity
Month Ended April 30, 2014

J. Szo, capital, April 1		$ 0
Add: Investments	$18,000	
Profit	2,025	20,025
Less: Drawings		650
J. Szo, capital, April 30		$19,375

GREEN THUMB LAWN CARE COMPANY
Balance Sheet
April 30, 2014

Assets		
Cash		$10,950
Accounts receivable		1,500
Prepaid insurance		3,300
Supplies		225
Equipment	$28,000	
Less: Accumulated depreciation	583	27,417
Total assets		$43,392
Liabilities and Owner's Equity		
Liabilities		
Notes payable		$20,000
Accounts payable		450
Interest payable		67
Unearned revenue		3,500
Total liabilities		24,017
Owner's equity		
J. Szo, capital		19,375
Total liabilities and owner's equity		$43,392

THE NAVIGATOR

Summary of Study Objectives

1. ***Explain accrual basis accounting, and when to recognize revenues and expenses.*** In order to provide timely information, accountants divide the life of a business into specific time periods. Therefore it is important to record transactions in the correct time period. Under accrual basis accounting, events that change a company's financial statements are recorded in the periods in which the events occur, rather than in the periods in which the company receives or pays cash. Revenue and expense recognition criteria provide guidance about when to recognize revenues and expenses. Revenue is recognized when the service has been performed or the goods have been sold and delivered, as long as the revenue can be reliably measured and collection is reasonably certain based on the Revenue Recognition Principle. Expenses are recorded in the same period as revenue is recognized, if there is a direct association between the revenues and expenses to ensure that they are matched. If there is no association between revenues and expenses, expenses are recorded in the period they are incurred.

2. ***Prepare adjusting entries for prepayments.*** Prepayments are either prepaid expenses or unearned revenues. Adjusting entries for prepayments record the portion of the prepayment that applies to the expense or revenue of the current accounting period. The adjusting entry for prepaid expenses debits (increases) an expense account and credits (decreases) an asset account. For a long-lived asset, the contra asset account Accumulated Depreciation is used instead of crediting the asset account directly. The adjusting entry for unearned revenues debits (decreases) a liability account and credits (increases) a revenue account.

3. ***Prepare adjusting entries for accruals.*** Accruals are either accrued revenues or accrued expenses. Adjusting entries for accruals record revenues and expenses that apply to the current accounting period and that have not yet been recognized through daily journal entries. The adjusting entry for accrued revenue debits (increases) a receivable account and credits (increases) a revenue account. The adjusting entry for an accrued expense debits (increases) an expense account and credits (increases) a liability account.

4. ***Describe the nature and purpose of an adjusted trial balance, and prepare one.*** An adjusted trial balance shows the balances of *all* accounts, including those that have been adjusted, at the end of an accounting period. It proves that the total of the accounts with debit balances is still equal to the total of the accounts with credit balances after the adjustments have been posted. Financial statements are prepared from an adjusted trial balance in the following order: (1) income statement, (2) statement of owner's equity, and (3) balance sheet.

5. ***Prepare adjusting entries for the alternative treatment of prepayments (Appendix 3A).*** Under certain circumstances, prepayments may initially be debited (increased) to an expense account. Unearned revenues may initially be credited (increased) to a revenue account. At the end of the period, these revenue or expense accounts may be overstated. The adjusting entries for prepaid expenses are a debit (increase) to an asset account and a credit (decrease) to an expense account. Adjusting entries for unearned revenues are a debit (decrease) to a revenue account and a credit (increase) to a liability account. It does not matter which alternative is used to record and adjust prepayments, as the ending account balances will be the same with both methods, assuming that the entries are prepared correctly.

THE NAVIGATOR

Glossary

Accrual basis accounting A basis for accounting in which revenues are recorded when earned and expenses are recorded when incurred. (p. 97)

Accrued expenses Expenses incurred but not yet paid in cash or recorded. (p. 107)

Accrued revenues Revenues earned but not yet received in cash or recorded. (p. 106)

Accumulated depreciation The cumulative sum of the depreciation expense since the asset was purchased. As a contra asset, its normal balance is on the credit side. (p. 103)

Adjusted trial balance A list of accounts and their balances after all adjustments have been posted. (p. 113)

Adjusting entries Entries made at the end of an accounting period to ensure that the revenue and expense recognition criteria are followed. (p. 99)

Carrying amount The difference between the cost of a depreciable asset and its accumulated depreciation; in other words, it is the unallocated or unexpired portion of the depreciable asset's cost. (p. 104)

Cash basis accounting A basis for accounting in which revenue is recorded when cash is received and an expense is recorded when cash is paid. (p. 97)

Contra asset account An account with the opposite balance (credit) compared with its related asset account, which has a debit balance. A contra asset is deducted from the related asset on the balance sheet. (p. 103)

Depreciation The allocation of the cost of a long-lived asset to expense over its useful life in a rational and systematic manner. (p. 103)

Expense recognition criteria Criteria that provide guidance about when to record expenses. Tied to revenue recognition when there is a direct association between costs incurred and the earning of revenue (matching). (p. 98)

Fiscal year An accounting period that is one year long. It does not need to start and end on the same days as the calendar year. (p. 96)

Interim periods Accounting time periods that are less than one year long such as a month or a quarter of a year. (p. 96)

Principal The amount borrowed or the amount still owed on a loan, separate from interest. (p. 108)

Revenue recognition criteria Criteria that provide guidance about when to record revenue. In general, it is recorded when the service has been performed or the goods sold and delivered, as long as the revenue can be reliably measured and collection is reasonably certain. (p. 98)

Straight-line depreciation method A depreciation method in which depreciation expense is calculated as the cost divided by the useful life. For each full year of the asset's life, the depreciation expense amount will be the same. (p. 103)

Useful life The length of service of a depreciable asset. (p. 103)

Note: All questions, exercises, and problems below with an asterisk (*) relate to material in Appendix 3A.

Self-Study Questions

Answers are at the end of the chapter.

(SO 1) C 1. The accrual basis of accounting is considered superior to the cash basis of accounting because it:
(a) is easier to use.
(b) provides better information about the activities of the business.
(c) records events in the period in which the cash is paid.
(d) is used by most businesses.

(SO 1) K 2. Revenue should be recognized when:
(a) it is earned.
(b) there is an increase in assets or decrease in liabilities as the result of the company's business activities with its customers.
(c) the service is provided or the goods are sold and delivered.
(d) All of the above.

(SO 1) K 3. Adjusting entries are made to ensure that:
(a) revenues and expenses are recorded in the correct accounting period.
(b) the accrual basis of accounting is used.
(c) assets and liabilities have up-to-date balances at the end of an accounting period.
(d) All of the above.

(SO 2) AP 4. A company pays $1,140 for a one-year insurance policy effective April 1, 2014. The payment is recorded as a debit to Prepaid Insurance. On April 30, 2014, an adjusting entry is required to:
(a) increase (debit) the asset Prepaid Insurance by $95 and increase (debit) the expense Insurance Expense by $95.
(b) decrease (credit) the asset Prepaid Insurance by $95 and increase (debit) the expense Insurance Expense by $95.
(c) decrease (credit) the asset Prepaid Insurance by $1,045 and increase (debit) the expense Insurance Expense by $1,045.
(d) increase (debit) the asset Prepaid Insurance by $1,045 and increase (debit) the expense Insurance Expense by $1,045.

(SO 2) AP 5. The trial balance shows Supplies $1,350 and Supplies Expense $0. If $600 of supplies are on hand at the end of the period, the adjusting entry is:

(a) Supplies	600	
Supplies Expense		600
(b) Supplies	750	
Supplies Expense		750
(c) Supplies Expense	750	
Supplies		750
(d) Supplies Expense	600	
Supplies		600

(SO 2) K 6. Accumulated Depreciation is:
(a) an expense account.
(b) an owner's equity account.
(c) a liability account.
(d) a contra asset account.

(SO 2) AP 7. Queenan Company calculates $1,000 as depreciation on its equipment for the month of June. The adjusting journal entry to record this depreciation expense is:

(a) Depreciation Expense	1,000	
Accumulated Depreciation—Equipment		1,000
(b) Depreciation Expense	1,000	
Equipment		1,000
(c) Equipment Expense	1,000	
Equipment		1,000
(d) Accumulated Depreciation—Equipment	1,000	
Equipment		1,000

(SO 2) K 8. A company records all cash received in advance of providing a service as a liability. At the end of the accounting period, an adjustment for unearned revenues is required to:
(a) decrease liabilities and increase revenues.
(b) increase assets and increase revenues.
(c) decrease revenues and increase liabilities.
(d) decrease revenues and decrease assets.

(SO 3) AP 9. A bank has a three-month, 4%, $6,000 note receivable, issued on November 1. Interest is due at maturity. What adjusting entry should the bank record on November 30?

(a) Cash	20	
Interest Revenue		20
(b) Interest Receivable	20	
Interest Revenue		20
(c) Interest Receivable	60	
Unearned Interest Revenue		60
(d) Interest Receivable	60	
Interest Revenue		60

(SO 3) AP 10. Kathy Kiska earned a salary of $400 in the last week of September. She will be paid for this in October. The adjusting entry for Kathy's employer at September 30 is:

(a) Salaries Expense	400	
Salaries Payable		400
(b) Salaries Expense	400	
Cash		400
(c) Salaries Payable	400	
Cash		400
(d) No entry is required		

(SO 4) C 11. Which of the following statements about the adjusted trial balance is *correct*?
(a) An adjusted trial balance proves that the total debit balances and the total credit balances in the ledger are equal after all adjustments are made.
(b) The adjusted trial balance is prepared after preparing financial statements.
(c) The adjusted trial balance lists the account balances divided into assets and liabilities.
(d) The adjusted trial balance proves that the total debits in the adjusting journal entries are equal to the total credits in the adjusting journal entries.

(SO 5) AP *12. The trial balance shows Supplies $0 and Supplies Expense $1,350. If $600 of supplies are on hand at the end of the period, the adjusting entry is:

(a) Supplies	600	
Supplies Expense		600
(b) Supplies Expense	750	
Supplies		750
(c) Supplies	750	
Supplies Expense		750
(d) Supplies Expense	600	
Supplies		600

(SO 5) AP *13. On February 1, Mag City received $6,000 for services to be provided in the future and credited the Service Revenue account. As at February 28, $3,200 of the services have been provided. How should this be reported in the February 28 financial statements?

	Balance Sheet	Income Statement
(a)	Unearned revenue $3,200	Service revenue $2,800
(b)	Service revenue $2,800	Unearned revenue $3,200
(c)	Unearned revenue $2,800	Service revenue $3,200
(d)	Service revenue $3,200	Unearned revenue $2,800

THE NAVIGATOR

Questions

(SO 1) K 1. (a) Why do accountants divide the life of a business into specific time periods? (b) What is the difference between a fiscal year and a calendar year?

(SO 1) C 2. Why is an accrual basis income statement more useful than a cash basis income statement?

(SO 1) C 3. Pierce Dussault, a lawyer, accepts a legal engagement in March, does the work in April, and is paid in May. If Dussault's law firm prepares monthly financial statements, when should it recognize revenue from this engagement? Why?

(SO 1) C 4. In completing the engagement in question 3, Dussault incurred $500 of salary expenses in March that are specifically related to this engagement, $2,500 in April, and none in May. How much expense should be deducted from revenue in the month(s) when the revenue is recognized? Why?

(SO 1) C 5. Balsam College collects tuition for the fall term in August. The fall term runs from September to December. In what month(s) should the college recognize the revenue earned from tuition fees? Explain your reasoning.

(SO 2) C 6. The name Prepaid Expense suggests that this account is an expense and belongs on an income statement. Instead the account appears on the balance sheet as an asset. Explain why this is appropriate and why prepaid expenses may need to be adjusted at the end of each period.

(SO 2) C 7. Roger is a college business student. He forgot to keep track of how much school supplies he used during the semester. Explain to Roger how he can still determine his supply expense even though he didn't keep detailed records of what he used.

(SO 2) C 8. "Depreciation is a process of valuation that results in the reporting of the fair value of the asset." How is this incorrect? Explain.

(SO 2) K 9. Explain the difference between (a) depreciation expense and accumulated depreciation, and (b) cost and carrying amount.

(SO 2) C 10. Why do we credit the contra asset account Accumulated Depreciation—Equipment when recording depreciation instead of crediting Equipment? How is it presented in the financial statements?

(SO 2) C 11. The name Unearned Revenue suggests that this type of account is a revenue account and belongs on the income statement. Instead the account appears on the balance sheet as a liability. Explain why this is appropriate and why unearned revenues may need to be adjusted at the end of the period.

(SO 3) C 12. Waiparous General Store has a note receivable from a customer. The customer pays the interest for the previous month on the first day of each month. Assuming Waiparous prepares monthly financial statements, will it need to accrue for interest revenue on the note at the end of each month? Why or why not? When the interest payment is received each month, what accounts will Waiparous debit and/or credit?

(SO 3) C 13. On February 4, ARU Company receives and pays a utility bill for the month of January. If ARU prepares monthly statements, is it necessary to make an adjusting entry for January? Why or why not? If yes, specify the name and type of accounts that need to be adjusted and whether the accounts should be increased or decreased.

(SO 3) AP 14. Sophie has been reading about a recent accounting scandal where the company overstated its revenue on purpose. She then argues that it is never appropriate to make adjusting entries to accrue for revenue. Do you agree or disagree? Why?

(SO 2, 3) K 15. Adjusting entries for accruals always involve the Cash account, and adjusting entries for prepayments never include the Cash account. Do you agree or disagree? Why?

(SO 2, 3) C 16. "An adjusting entry may affect two balance sheet or two income statement accounts." Do you agree? Why or why not?

(SO 4) C 17. Identify the similarities and differences between a trial balance and an adjusted trial balance. What is the purpose of each one?

(SO 4) C 18. On Silver Company's trial balance, Accounts Payable is $4,250. After the adjusting entries have been posted, the balance in this account is still $4,250. Since there is no change, it is not necessary to include Accounts Payable on the adjusted trial balance. Do you agree or disagree? Why?

(SO 4) C 19. Jeremiah is preparing a balance sheet. He includes the amount shown in the adjusted trial balance for the owner's capital account on the balance sheet. Will the balance sheet balance? Why or why not? (*Hint:* Think of the Statement of Owner's Equity)

(SO 5) C *20. Some companies debit an expense account at the time an expense is prepaid instead of debiting an asset account. The problem with this approach is that expenses will always be overstated, and assets understated at the end of the fiscal year. Do you agree or disagree? Why?

(SO 5) C *21. If a company credits a revenue account when cash is received in advance of providing a service, then the adjusting entry is the same as if the company had debited a liability account when it received the cash. Is this correct? Why or why not?

Brief Exercises

BE3–1 AA Lawn Care had the following transactions in May, its first month of business:

Determine profit using cash and accrual bases. **(SO 1) AP**

1. Collected $500 cash from customers for services provided in May.
2. Billed customers $600 for services provided in May.
3. Received $100 from customers for services to be provided in June.
4. Purchased $250 of supplies on account. All of the supplies were used in May but were paid for in June.
   (a) Calculate profit for May using cash basis accounting.
   (b) Calculate profit for May using accrual basis accounting.

BE3–2 Calculate the missing information in each of the following independent situations:

Calculate missing data for supplies. **(SO 2) AP**

	Red Co.	Blue Co.
Supplies on hand, May 31, 2013	$ 795	$ 985
Supplies purchased during the year	3,830	3,070
Supplies on hand, May 31, 2014	665	?
Supplies used during the year	?	2,750

BE3–3 Hahn Consulting Company's general ledger showed $825 in the Supplies account on January 1, 2014. On May 31, 2014, the company paid $3,165 for additional supplies. A count on December 31, 2014, showed $1,015 of supplies on hand. Hahn treats supplies as an asset at the time of purchase.

Prepare and post transaction and adjusting entries for supplies. **(SO 2) AP**

(a) Using T accounts, enter the January 1, 2014, balance in the Supplies and Supplies Expense accounts.
(b) Prepare the journal entry to record the purchase of supplies on May 31, 2014. Post the part of the journal entry that affects only the Supplies or Supplies Expense accounts.

(c) Calculate the amount of supplies used in 2014.
(d) Determine what amounts should appear on the 2014 financial statements for Supplies and Supplies Expense.
(e) Prepare and post the adjusting entry required at December 31, 2014.

Prepare and post transaction and adjusting entries for insurance.
(SO 2) AP

BE3–4 On March 1, 2014, Eire Co. paid $4,800 to Big North Insurance for a one-year insurance policy. Eire Co. has a December 31 fiscal year end and adjusts accounts annually. Eire treats insurance as an asset at the time of purchase. Complete the following for Eire Co.

(a) Prepare the March 1, 2014, journal entry.
(b) Calculate the amount of insurance that expired during 2014 and the unexpired cost at December 31, 2014.
(c) Prepare the adjusting entry required at December 31, 2014.
(d) Using T accounts, post the journal entries in parts (a) and (c) above, and indicate the adjusted balance in each account.

Prepare transaction and adjusting entries for depreciation; show statement presentation.
(SO 2) AP

BE3–5 Reed Company paid $18,000 to purchase equipment on January 1, 2013. Reed Company has a December 31 fiscal year end and uses straight-line depreciation. The company estimates the equipment will have a six-year useful life.

(a) Prepare the journal entry to record the purchase of the equipment on January 1, 2013.
(b) Prepare the adjusting entries required on December 31, 2013 and 2014.
(c) Show the balance sheet presentation of the equipment at December 31, 2013 and 2014.
(d) What amount of depreciation expense will be included in the 2013 and 2014 income statements?

Prepare adjusting and transaction entries for accrued revenue.
(SO 3) AP

BE3–6 Refer to BE3–4. On March 1, 2014, Big North Insurance received $4,800 cash from Eire Co. for a one-year insurance policy. Big North Insurance has an October 31 fiscal year end and adjusts accounts annually. Complete the following for Big North Insurance.

(a) Prepare the March 1, 2014, journal entry.
(b) Calculate the amount of revenue earned during 2014 and the amount unearned at October 31, 2014.
(c) Prepare the adjusting entry required on October 31, 2014.
(d) Using T accounts, post the entries for parts (a) and (c) above and indicate the adjusted balance in each account.

Prepare adjusting and transaction entries for accrued revenue.
(SO 3) AP

BE3–7 Ullmann Maintenance Co. has a $455 monthly contract with the sports store Rackets Plus for general maintenance services. Ullmann invoices Rackets Plus on the first of the month for the previous month's services provided. Rackets Plus must then pay for the previous month's services by the 10th of the following month.

(a) Ullmann has a November 30 fiscal year end. Why will it need to prepare an adjusting entry on November 30?
(b) Prepare Ullmann's November 30 adjusting entry.
(c) Will Ullmann need to record a journal entry on December 1 when it invoices Rackets Plus? Why or why not?
(d) Ullmann receives $455 from Rackets Plus on December 9 for services provided in November. Prepare Ullmann's journal entry.

Prepare adjusting and transaction entries for accrued expenses.
(SO 3) AP

BE3–8 Refer to BE3–7. Assume that Rackets Plus adjusts its accounts on a monthly basis.

(a) Will Rackets Plus need to prepare an adjusting entry on November 30? If so, prepare the entry.
(b) Prepare Racket Plus's journal entry on December 9 when it pays Ullmann $455.

Prepare transaction and adjusting entries for salaries.
(SO 3) AP

BE3–9 Vintage Clothing Co. is open for business six days a week. Weekly total salaries of $6,000 are paid every Monday morning to employees for salary earned during the previous six-day workweek (Monday through Saturday). The company has a July 31 fiscal year end, which falls on Thursday this year. Salaries were last paid on Monday, July 28 (for July 21 to 26). The next payday is Monday, August 4 (for July 28 to August 2). Prepare the journal entries to record the following:

(a) The payment of salaries on July 28
(b) The adjusting journal entry to accrue salaries at July 31
(c) The payment of salaries on August 4

BE3–10 Butternut Squash Company has the following two notes receivable at May 31, 2014, its fiscal year end:

Calculate and record accrued interest. **(SO 3) AP**

1. $40,000 six-month, 5% note issued January 1, 2014
2. $10,000 three-month, 6% note issued April 30, 2014

Interest is payable at maturity for both notes. Assume that they do not make adjusting entries on a monthly basis.

(a) Calculate the accrued interest on both notes at May 31, 2014.
(b) Prepare one adjusting journal entry to record the accrued interest on both notes.

BE3–11 On July 31, 2013, a company purchased equipment for use in the business for $50,000, paying $14,000 cash and signing a 4.5% note payable for the remainder. The interest and principal of the note are due on January 31, 2014. Prepare the journal entry to record the following:

Prepare adjusting and transaction entries for interest. **(SO 3) AP**

(a) The purchase of the equipment on July 31, 2013
(b) The accrual of the interest at year end, November 30, 2013, assuming interest has not previously been accrued
(c) The repayment of the interest and note on January 31, 2014

BE3–12 In Chapter 3, you learned about four types of adjustments: (1) prepaid expenses; (2) unearned revenues; (3) accrued revenues; and (4) accrued expenses. For each type of adjustment, indicate the following:

Identify effect of adjustment on elements of financial statements. **(SO 2, 3) C**

(a) The reason the adjustment is required.
(b) The effect of the balance sheet and income statement if the adjustment is not recorded.

BE3–13 The account balances (after adjustments) from the general ledger of Winterholt Company at September 30, 2014, follow in alphabetical order. All accounts have normal balances.

Prepare adjusted trial balance and identify financial statement. **(SO 4) AP**

Accounts payable	$ 2,890	Rent expense	$ 1,560
Accounts receivable	6,050	Salaries expense	12,215
Accumulated depreciation—equipment	6,400	Salaries payable	875
Cash	1,100	Service revenue	48,450
Depreciation expense	3,100	Unearned service revenue	840
Equipment	29,800	W. Winterholt, capital	16,150
Prepaid rent	780	W. Winterholt, drawings	21,000

(a) Prepare an adjusted trial balance.
(b) Beside each account, identify whether it is an asset (A), liability (L), capital (C), drawing (D), revenue (R), or expense (E).
(c) Beside each account, identify whether it should be included on the income statement (IS), statement of owner's equity (SOE), or balance sheet (BS).

***BE3–14** Refer to BE3–3. Assume that instead of debiting an asset account for the purchases of supplies, Hahn Consulting Company debits an expense account. Recall that (1) on January 1, 2014, the company had supplies of $825 on hand; (2) the company purchased $3,165 of supplies on May 31, 2014; and that (3) on December 31, 2014, a count showed there was $1,015 of supplies on hand.

Prepare and post adjusting entry for supplies. **(SO 5) AP**

(a) Using T accounts, enter the January 1, 2014, balance in the Supplies and Supplies Expense accounts.
(b) Prepare the journal entry to record the purchase of supplies on May 31, 2014. Post the part of the journal entry that affects only the Supplies or Supplies Expense accounts.
(c) Determine what amounts should appear on the 2014 financial statements for Supplies and Supplies Expense.
(d) Prepare and post the adjusting entry required at December 31, 2014.
(e) Compare part (c) above with part (c) in BE3–3. Does it matter whether an original entry is recorded to an asset account or an expense account? Explain.

***BE3–15** Refer to BE3–6. Assume that instead of crediting a liability account for the $4,800, one-year insurance policy, Big North Insurance credits a revenue account on March 1, 2014.

Prepare and post adjusting entry for unearned revenue. **(SO 5) AP**

(a) Prepare the adjusting entry at October 31, 2014. Using T accounts, enter the balances in the accounts, post the adjusting entry, and indicate the adjusted balance in each account.
(b) Compare the adjusted balances in BE3–6, where a liability account was originally credited, with the adjusted balances you determined here in part (a), where a revenue account was originally credited. Does it matter whether an original entry is recorded to a liability account or a revenue account? Explain.

Exercises

Identify when revenue is recognized. **(SO 1) AP**

E3–1 For the following independent situations, use professional judgement to determine when the company should recognize revenue from the transactions:

(a) **WestJet Airlines** sells you a nonrefundable airline ticket in September for a flight at Christmas.
(b) **Leon's Furniture** sells you a home theatre in January on a "no money down, no interest, and no payments for one year" promotional deal.
(c) The **Toronto Blue Jays** sell season tickets to games at the Rogers Centre on-line. Fans can purchase the tickets at any time, although the season does not officially begin until April. It runs from April through October.
(d) The **RBC Financial Group** lends you money at the beginning of August. The loan and the interest are repayable in full at the end of November.
(e) In August, you order a sweater from **Sears** using its on-line catalogue. Sears ships the sweater to you in September and you charge it to your Sears credit card. In October, you receive your Sears bill and pay it.
(f) You pay for a one-year subscription to ***Canadian Business*** magazine in May.
(g) You purchase a gift card in December from **iTunes** to give to your friend for her birthday. Your friend uses the gift card in January.

Instructions
Identify when revenue should be recognized in each of the above situations.

Prepare basic analysis, debit/credit analysis, and adjusting journal entry. **(SO 2, 3) AP**

E3–2 Havanese Services Company records adjusting entries on an annual basis. The following information is available to be used in recording adjusting entries for the year ended December 31, 2014.

1. Prepaid insurance totalling $350 has expired.
2. Supplies of $300 have been used.
3. Annual depreciation on equipment is $1,140.
4. Unearned service revenue of $260 has been earned.
5. Salaries of $800 are unpaid.
6. Utility expenses for 2014 of $225 are unrecorded and unpaid.
7. Services provided but not collected in cash or recorded total $1,000.
8. Interest of $125 on a note payable has accrued.

Instructions
For each adjustment, prepare a basic analysis, a debit/credit analysis, and the adjusting journal entry. Use the following format, in which the first one has been done for you as an example:

Adjustment 1:

Basic Analysis	The asset Prepaid Insurance is decreased by $350. The expense Insurance Expense is increased by $350.			
Debit/Credit Analysis	Debits increase expenses: debit Insurance Expense $350. Credits decrease assets: credit Prepaid Insurance $350.			
Adjusting Journal Entry	Dec. 31	Insurance Expense Prepaid Insurance To record insurance expired.	350	 350

Prepare and post transaction and adjusting entries for prepayments. **(SO 2) AP**

E3–3 Action Quest Games adjusts its accounts annually. Assume that any prepaid expenses are initially recorded in asset accounts. Assume that any revenue collected in advance is initially recorded as liabilities. The following information is available for the year ended December 31, 2014:

1. A $4,020 one-year insurance policy was purchased on April 1, 2014.
2. Paid $6,500 on August 31, 2014, for five months' rent in advance.
3. On September 27, 2014, received $3,600 cash from a corporation that sponsors games for the most improved students attending a nearby school. The $3,600 was for 10 games, worth $360 each, that are played on the first Friday of each month starting in October. (Use the Unearned Revenue account.)
4. Signed a contract for cleaning services starting December 1, 2014, for $500 per month. Paid for the first three months on November 30, 2014.
5. On December 15, 2014, sold $935 of gift certificates to a local game club. On December 31, 2014, determined that $545 of these gift certificates had not yet been redeemed. (Use the account Unearned Gift Certificate Revenue.)

Instructions

(a) For each transaction: (1) prepare the journal entry to record the initial transaction, then (2) prepare the adjusting journal entry required on December 31, 2014. Do both for each transaction before doing the next transaction.
(b) Post each of these entries to T accounts and calculate the final balance in each account. (*Note:* Posting to the Cash account is not necessary.)

E3–4 Action Quest Games owns the following long-lived assets:

Prepare adjusting entries for depreciation; calculate accumulated depreciation and carrying amount.
(SO 2) AP

Asset	Date Purchased	Cost	Estimated Useful Life
Building	January 1, 2010	$68,000	25 years
Vehicles	December 31, 2013	28,000	7 years
Equipment	July 1, 2012	12,600	4 years

Instructions

(a) Prepare adjusting entries to record depreciation for Action Quest Games for the year ended December 31, 2014.
(b) For each asset, calculate its accumulated depreciation and carrying amount at December 31, 2014.

E3–5 Action Quest Games records adjusting entries on an annual basis. The company has the following information available on accruals that must be recorded for the year ended December 31, 2014:

Prepare adjusting and related transaction entries for accruals.
(SO 3) AP

1. Action Quest has a 4% note payable with its bank for $48,000. Interest is payable on a monthly basis on the first of the month.
2. Action Quest is open seven days a week and employees are paid a total of $3,500 every Monday for a seven-day (Monday–Sunday) workweek. December 31, 2014, is a Wednesday, so employees will have worked three days (Monday–Wednesday) in 2014 that they have not been paid for as at December 31. Employees will be paid next on Monday, January 5, 2015.
3. Action Quest receives a commission from Pizza Shop next door for all pizzas sold to customers using Action Quest's facility. The amount owing for December is $520, which Pizza Shop will pay on January 7, 2015.
4. The December utility bill for $425 didn't arrive until January 7, 2015. Action Quest paid the bill on January 9.
5. Action Quest sold some equipment on October 1, 2014, in exchange for a $6,000, 6% note receivable. The principal and interest are due on February 1, 2015.

Instructions

(a) For each of the above items, prepare the adjusting entry required at December 31, 2014.
(b) For each of the above items, prepare the journal entry to record the related cash transaction in 2015. Assume all payments and receipts are made as indicated.

E3–6 Nile Company had the following trial balance at June 30, 2014 (its year end):

Prepare transaction and adjusting entries.
(SO 2, 3) AP

	Debit	Credit
Cash	$ 5,840	
Accounts receivable	850	
Supplies	1,100	
Equipment	9,360	
Accumulated depreciation—equipment		$ 3,900
Unearned service revenue		1,500
R. Nile, capital		11,750
Totals	$17,150	$17,150

During the month of July, the following selected transactions took place:

July 2	Paid $750 cash (in total) for rent for July, August, and September.
10	Purchased $200 of supplies for cash.
14	Collected the full balance of accounts receivable.
20	Received $700 cash from a customer for services to be provided in August.
25	Provided $1,300 of services for a customer and immediately collected cash.

Additional information:

1. At July 31, the company had provided $800 of services for a client that it had not billed or recorded.
2. Supplies on hand at July 31 were $800.
3. The equipment has a six-year useful life.
4. As at July 31, the company had earned $900 of revenue that it had received in advance.

Instructions

(a) Record the July transactions.
(b) Prepare monthly adjusting entries at July 31.

Prepare transaction and adjusting entries for notes and interest.
(SO 3) AP

E3–7 During 2014, Aubergine Co. borrowed cash from Chartreuse Company by issuing notes payable as follows:

1. July 1, 2014, issued an eight-month, 4% note for $75,000. Interest and principal are payable at maturity.
2. November 1, 2014, issued a three-month, 5% note for $42,000. Interest is payable monthly on the first day of the month. Principal is payable at maturity.

Aubergine has a December 31 fiscal year end and prepares adjusting entries on an annual basis.

Instructions

Prepare all necessary journal entries for Aubergine in 2014 and 2015 regarding the notes and interest including year-end adjusting entries. Prepare separate adjusting entries for each note.

Prepare transaction and adjusting entries for notes and interest.
(SO 3) AP

E3–8 Refer to the information provided in E3–7 for Aubergine Co. and Chartreuse Company. Chartreuse has a November 30 fiscal year end and prepares adjusting entries on an annual basis.

Instructions

Prepare all necessary journal entries for Chartreuse in 2014 and 2015 regarding the notes and interest, including adjusting entries. Prepare separate adjusting entries for each note.

Prepare adjusting entries from analysis of trial balances. **(SO 2, 3, 4) AP**

E3–9 The trial balances before and after adjustment for Lane Company at October 31, 2014, which is the end of its fiscal year are as follows:

	Before Adjustment		After Adjustment	
	Debit	Credit	Debit	Credit
Cash	$ 9,100		$ 9,100	
Accounts receivable	8,700		9,230	
Supplies	2,450		710	
Prepaid insurance	3,775		2,525	
Equipment	34,100		34,100	
Accumulated depreciation—equipment		$ 3,525		$ 5,800
Accounts payable		5,900		5,900
Notes payable		40,000		40,000
Salaries payable		0		1,125
Interest payable		0		500
Unearned service revenue		1,600		900
E. Lane, capital		5,600		5,600
E. Lane, drawings	10,000		10,000	
Service revenue		45,000		46,230
Depreciation expense	0		2,275	
Insurance expense	0		1,250	
Interest expense	1,500		2,000	
Rent expense	15,000		15,000	
Salaries expense	17,000		18,125	
Supplies expense	0		1,740	
Totals	$101,625	$101,625	$106,055	$106,055

Instructions

Prepare the adjusting entries that were made.

E3–10 The adjusted trial balance for Lane Company is given in E3–9.

Prepare financial statements from adjusted trial balance.
(SO 4) AP

Instructions

Prepare Lane Company's income statement, statement of owner's equity, and balance sheet.

***E3–11** Refer to the transaction information provided in E3–3 for Action Quest Games. Assume that prepaid expenses are initially recorded as expenses (not as assets as in E3–3). Assume that revenues collected in advance of the work are initially recorded as revenue (not as liabilities as in E3–3).

Prepare and post transaction and adjusting entries for prepayments.
(SO 5) AP

Instructions

(a) For each transaction: (1) prepare the journal entry to record the initial transaction, and (2) prepare the adjusting journal entry required on December 31, 2014.
(b) Post each of these entries to T accounts and calculate the final balance in each account. (*Note:* Posting to the Cash account is not necessary.)
(c) Compare your balances in part (b) above with those obtained in E3–3, part (b). Comment on your findings.

***E3–12** At Richmond Company, the following select transactions occurred in January, the company's first month of operations:

Prepare and post transaction and adjusting entries for prepayments.
(SO 2, 5) AP

Jan.	1	Paid rent of $1,000 for January.
	2	Paid $1,920 for a one-year insurance policy.
	5	Paid $1,700 for supplies.
	19	Received $6,100 cash for services to be performed in the future.
	31	Paid rent of $1,000 for February.

Additional information:

1. On January 31, it is determined that $2,500 of the service revenue has been earned.
2. On January 31, a count of supplies shows that there is $650 of supplies on hand.

Instructions

(a) Assume Richmond records all prepaid costs as expenses, and all revenue collected in advance as revenue. Journalize the January transactions and post to T accounts. (*Note:* Posting to the Cash account is not necessary.)
(b) Journalize and post the January 31 adjustments.
(c) Determine the ending balances in each of the accounts.

Problems: Set A

P3–1A Ouellette & Associates began operations on January 1, 2014. Its fiscal year end is December 31 and it prepares financial statements and adjusts its accounts annually. Selected transactions for 2014 follow:

Prepare and post prepayment transaction entries. Prepare basic analysis, debit/credit analysis, and journal entry, and post adjustments for the prepayments.
(SO 2) AP

1. On January 10, bought office supplies for $3,400 cash. A physical count at December 31, 2014, revealed $925 of supplies still on hand.
2. Paid cash for a $3,780, one-year insurance policy on February 1, 2014. The policy came into effect on this date.
3. On March 31, purchased equipment for $21,240 cash. The equipment has an estimated six-year useful life.
4. Leased a truck on September 1 for a one-year period for $500 per month. Paid the full lease cost of $6,000 in cash.
5. On October 15, received a $1,800 advance cash payment from a client for accounting services expected to be provided in the future. As at December 31, one third of these services had not been performed.
6. On November 1, rented out unneeded office space for a six-month period starting on this date, and received a $1,725 cheque for the first three months' rent.

Instructions

(a) Prepare individual journal entries to record transactions 1 to 6. All prepaid costs should be recorded in asset accounts. All revenue collected in advance of providing services should be recorded as liabilities.
(b) An adjusting entry at December 31, 2014, is required for each of these transactions. Using the format shown in E3–2, prepare the following:
   1. A basic analysis and a debit-credit analysis of the required adjustment.
   2. The adjusting journal entry.

(c) Post the transactions and adjusting entries to T accounts and calculate the final balance in each account. (*Note:* Posting to the Cash account is not necessary.)

TAKING IT FURTHER Could Ouellette & Associates avoid the need to record adjusting entries by originally recording items 1 through 4 as expenses, and items 5 and 6 as revenues? Explain.

Prepare entries for accrual adjustments and subsequent cash transactions. **(SO 3) AP**

P3–2A Ouellette & Associates records adjusting entries on an annual basis. The company has the following information available on accruals that must be recorded for the year ended December 31, 2014:

1. Ouellette has a $10,000, 8% note receivable with a customer. The customer pays the interest on a monthly basis on the first of the month. Assume the customer pays the correct amount each month.
2. Ouellette pays its employees a total of $6,500 every second Tuesday. Employees work a five-day week, Monday to Friday, and are paid for all statutory holidays. December 31, 2014, is a Wednesday. Employees were paid on Tuesday, December 23, 2014 (for the pay period starting Wednesday, December 10, and ending Tuesday, December 23) and will be paid again on Tuesday, January 6, 2015 (for the pay period starting on Wednesday, December 24, and ending on Tuesday, January 6).
3. Ouellette has a contract with a customer where it provides services prior to billing the customer. On December 31, 2014, this customer owed Ouellette $3,375. Ouellette billed the customer on January 7, 2015, and collected the full amount on January 18, 2015.
4. Ouellette received the $485 December utility bill on January 10, 2015. The bill was paid on its due date, January 22, 2015.
5. Ouellette has a $25,000, 5% note payable. Interest is paid every six months, on October 31 and April 30. Assume that Ouellette made the correct interest payment on October 31, 2014, and April 30, 2015.

Instructions

For each of the above items, do the following:

(a) Prepare the adjusting journal entries required on December 31, 2014.

(b) Prepare the journal entry to record the related cash transaction in 2015. Assume all payments and receipts are made as indicated.

TAKING IT FURTHER Indicate which elements in the financial statements (assets, liabilities, owner's equity, revenue, expenses, and profit) would be either understated or overstated at December 31, 2014, if the accounts were not adjusted.

Prepare transaction and adjusting entries. **(SO 2, 3) AP**

P3–3A The following independent items for Last Planet Theatre during the year ended December 31, 2014, may require a transaction journal entry, an adjusting entry, or both. The company records all prepaid costs as assets and all unearned revenues as liabilities and adjusts accounts annually.

1. Supplies on hand amounted to $535 on December 31, 2013. On February 10, 2014, additional supplies were purchased for $1,085 cash. On December 31, 2014, a physical count showed that supplies on hand amounted to $370.
2. Purchased equipment on September 2, 2014, for $23,500 cash. The equipment was estimated to have a useful life of 10 years.
3. Last Planet Theatre puts on seven plays each season. Season tickets sell for $200 each and 250 sold in October for the upcoming 2014–2015 season, which begins in November 2014 and ends in May 2015 (one play per month). Last Planet Theatre credited Unearned Revenue for the full amount received.
4. Every Tuesday, the total payroll is $4,200 for wages earned during the previous six-day workweek (Tuesday to Sunday). Wages were last paid on Tuesday, December 30. This year, December 31 falls on a Wednesday.
5. Last Planet Theatre rents the theatre to a local children's choir, which uses the space for rehearsals twice a week at a rate of $500 per month. The choir was short of cash at the beginning of December and sent Last Planet Theatre a cheque for $350 on December 5, and a promise to pay the balance

in January. On January 7, 2015, Last Planet Theatre received a cheque for the balance owing from December plus all of January's rent.

6. On June 1, 2014, the theatre borrowed $25,100 from its bank at an annual interest rate of 4.25%. The principal and interest are to be repaid on March 1, 2015.
7. Upon reviewing its accounting records on December 31, 2014, the theatre noted that the telephone bill for the month of December had not yet been received. A call to the phone company determined that the December telephone bill was $325. The bill was paid on January 10, 2015.

Instructions

(a) Prepare the journal entries to record the 2014 transactions for items 1 though 6.
(b) Prepare the year-end adjusting entry for items 1 through 7.
(c) Prepare the journal entries to record:
   1. the payment of wages on Tuesday, January 6 (item 4)
   2. the receipt of the cheque from the children's choir on January 7 (item 5)
   3. the payment of the telephone bill on January 10 (item 7)
   4. the payment of the note and interest on March 1, 2015 (item 6)

TAKING IT FURTHER There are three basic reasons why an unadjusted trial balance may not contain complete or up-to-date data. List these reasons and provide examples of each one using items 1 to 7 to illustrate your explanation.

P3–4A A review of the ledger of Greenberg Company at December 31, 2014, produces the following important data for the preparation of annual adjusting entries:

Prepare adjusting entries. **(SO 2, 3) AP**

1. Prepaid Advertising, December 31, 2014, unadjusted balance, $15,600. This balance consists of payments on two advertising contracts for monthly advertising in two trade magazines. The terms of the contracts are as follows:

Contract	First Month	Amount	Number of Magazine Issues
A650	May 2014	$ 6,000	12
B974	October 2014	9,600	24
		$15,600	

2. Vehicles, December 31, 2014, unadjusted balance, $70,000. The company owns two vehicles used for delivery purposes. The first, purchased for $30,000 on January 2, 2012, has an estimated five-year useful life. The second, purchased for $40,000 on June 1, 2014, has an estimated six-year useful life.
3. Prepaid Insurance, December 31, 2014, unadjusted balance, $17,250. This balance consists of two insurance policies: a two-year policy effective July 1, 2013, to June 30, 2015, that cost $12,360 and a one-year policy effective May 1, 2014, to April 30, 2015, that cost $7,980. (*Hint:* Appropriate adjusting entries were made at December 31, 2013.)
4. Notes Payable, December 31, 2014, unadjusted balance, $85,000. This consists of an eight-month, 6.5% note, dated August 1. Interest is payable at maturity.
5. Salaries Payable, December 31, 2014, unadjusted balance, $0. There are nine salaried employees. Salaries are paid every Saturday for a six-day workweek (Monday–Saturday). Six employees receive a salary of $750 per week, and three employees earn $600 per week. December 31, 2014, is a Wednesday.
6. Unearned Revenue, December 31, 2014, unadjusted balance, $270,000. Greenberg began renting office space to tenants in its new building on November 1. At December 31, Greenberg had the following rental contracts that were paid in full for the entire term of the lease:

Rental Term	Monthly Rent	Number of Tenants	Total Rent Paid
Nov. 1, 2014, to Apr. 30, 2015	$4,000	6	$144,000
Dec. 1, 2014, to May 31, 2015	7,000	3	126,000
			$270,000

Instructions

(a) Prepare the adjusting entries at December 31, 2014. Show all your calculations.
(b) For item 2, calculate the accumulated depreciation and carrying amount of each vehicle on December 31, 2014.

TAKING IT FURTHER What is the purpose of recording depreciation? Why is land not depreciated?

Prepare transaction and adjusting entries for notes and interest. **(SO 3) AP**

P3–5A During 2014, Cobalt Co. borrowed cash from Azores Enterprises by issuing notes payable as follows:

1. March 31, 2014, issued a one-year, 4% note for $100,000. Interest is payable quarterly, on June 30, September 30, and December 31, 2014, and March 31, 2015. Principal is payable at maturity.
2. June 1, 2014, issued a nine-month, 4.5% note for $60,000. Interest and principal are payable at maturity.
3. September 1, 2014, issued a three-month, 5% note for $25,000. Interest is payable monthly on the first day of the month. Principal is payable at maturity.

Both Cobalt and Azores prepare adjusting entries on an annual basis. Cobalt has a September 30 fiscal year end. Azores' fiscal year end is October 31.

Instructions

(a) Prepare all necessary journal entries for Cobalt in 2014 and 2015 regarding the notes and interest including adjusting entries. Prepare separate adjusting entries for each note if an adjustment is required.
(b) Prepare all necessary journal entries for Azores in 2014 and 2015 regarding the notes and interest including adjusting entries. Prepare separate adjusting entries for each note if an adjustment is required.

TAKING IT FURTHER Is it appropriate for Cobalt to have interest payable on its September 30, 2014, balance sheet if the interest isn't payable until some point after the year end? Explain.

Prepare and post adjusting entries, and prepare adjusted trial balance. **(SO 2, 3, 4) AP**

P3–6A Reyes Rides is owned by Jason Reyes. The company has an August 31 fiscal year end and prepares adjustments on an annual basis. The following is an alphabetical list of its accounts at August 31, 2014, before adjustments. All accounts have normal balances.

Accounts payable	$ 5,700	J. Reyes, drawings	$141,000
Accounts receivable	7,080	Notes payable	162,000
Accumulated depreciation—equipment	25,200	Prepaid insurance	12,660
Accumulated depreciation—vehicles	175,500	Rent expense	22,810
Cash	9,000	Salaries expense	140,625
Equipment	40,320	Service revenue	334,300
Fuel expense	23,972	Supplies	4,455
Interest expense	9,653	Unearned revenue	25,000
J. Reyes, capital	105,075	Vehicles	421,200

Additional information:

1. On August 31, a physical count shows $630 of supplies on hand.
2. The insurance policy has a one-year term that began on November 1, 2013.
3. The equipment has an estimated useful life of eight years. The vehicles have an estimated useful life of 10 years.
4. The company collects cash in advance for any special services requested by customers. As at August 31, the company has provided all but $4,500 of these services.
5. The note payable has an annual interest rate of 6.5%. Interest is paid on the first day of each month.
6. Employees are paid a combined total of $545 per day. At August 31, 2014, three days of salaries are unpaid.
7. On August 31, the company provided $1,350 of services for a senior citizens' group. The group was not billed for the services until September 2. They paid on September 3.
8. Additional fuel costs of $620 have been incurred but not recorded. (Use the Accounts Payable account.)

Instructions

(a) Journalize the annual adjusting entries at August 31, 2014.
(b) Prepare a ledger. Enter the trial balance amounts and post the adjusting entries.
(c) Prepare an adjusted trial balance at August 31, 2014.

TAKING IT FURTHER As at August 31, 2014, approximately how old are the equipment and vehicles?

P3–7A The Highland Cove Resort has an August 31 fiscal year end and prepares adjusting entries on a monthly basis. The following trial balance was prepared before recording the August 31 month-end adjustments:

Prepare and post adjusting entries, and prepare adjusted trial balance and financial statements. **(SO 2, 3, 4) AP**

HIGHLAND COVE RESORT
Trial Balance
August 31, 2014

	Debit	Credit
Cash	$ 17,520	
Prepaid insurance	4,240	
Supplies	995	
Land	35,000	
Buildings	150,000	
Accumulated depreciation—buildings		$ 47,750
Furniture	33,000	
Accumulated depreciation—furniture		12,925
Accounts payable		8,500
Unearned revenue		15,000
Mortgage payable		96,000
K. MacPhail, capital		85,000
K. MacPhail, drawings	42,735	
Rent revenue		246,150
Depreciation expense	5,775	
Insurance expense	6,890	
Interest expense	5,720	
Repairs expense	14,400	
Salaries expense	153,000	
Supplies expense	4,450	
Utilities expense	37,600	
	$511,325	$511,325

Additional information:

1. The company pays $6,360 for its annual insurance policy on March 31 of each year.
2. A count shows $560 of supplies on hand on August 31, 2014.
3. The buildings have an estimated useful life of 50 years.
4. The furniture has an estimated useful life of 10 years.
5. Customers must pay a $100 deposit if they want to book a room during peak times. An analysis of these bookings indicates that 150 deposits were received (all credited to Unearned Revenue) and only 40 of the deposits have not yet been earned by August 31, 2014.
6. The mortgage interest rate is 6.5% per year. Interest has been paid to August 1, 2014.
7. Salaries accrued to the end of August were $1,450.
8. The August utility bill of $3,420 is unrecorded and unpaid.
9. On August 31, Highland Cove has earned $1,350 of rent revenue from customers who are currently renting rooms but will not pay the amount owing until they check out in September. This amount is in addition to any deposits earned in item (5) above.

Instructions

(a) Prepare the monthly adjusting journal entries on August 31.
(b) Prepare a ledger, enter the trial balance amounts, and post the adjusting entries.
(c) Prepare an adjusted trial balance at August 31.
(d) Prepare an income statement and a statement of owner's equity for the year ended August 31, and a balance sheet as at August 31, 2014.

TAKING IT FURTHER Is the owner's capital account on the August 31, 2014, adjusted trial balance the same amount as shown in the August 31, 2014, balance sheet? Why or why not?

Prepare adjusting entries and financial statements. **(SO 2, 3, 4) AP**

P3–8A The unadjusted and adjusted trial balances of the Queen Street Advertising Agency as at November 30, 2014, follow:

QUEEN STREET ADVERTISING AGENCY
Trial Balance
November 30, 2014

	Unadjusted		Adjusted	
	Debit	Credit	Debit	Credit
Accounts payable		$ 4,200		$ 4,800
Accounts receivable	$ 13,650		$ 14,750	
Accumulated depreciation—equipment		28,500		34,000
Cash	9,000		9,000	
Depreciation expense	0		5,500	
Equipment	66,000		66,000	
Insurance expense	0		1,600	
Interest expense	875		1,000	
Interest payable		0		125
Note payable		30,000		30,000
Prepaid insurance	2,400		800	
Rent expense	7,150		7,750	
S. Dufferin, capital		17,800		17,800
S. Dufferin, drawings	27,200		27,200	
Salaries expense	12,875		14,350	
Salaries payable		0		1,475
Service revenue		58,750		60,750
Supplies	7,200		1,265	
Supplies expense	0		5,935	
Unearned revenue		7,100		6,200
	$146,350	$146,350	$155,150	$155,150

Instructions

(a) Prepare the adjusting entries that were made.
(b) Prepare an income statement and a statement of owner's equity for the year ended November 30, 2014, and a balance sheet at November 30, 2014.
(c) Calculate the annual interest rate on the note. The note payable has been outstanding for eight months. Interest is paid on a monthly basis at the beginning of each month.
(d) Determine the balance in Salaries Payable on November 30, 2013. The company paid $15,250 in salaries in 2014.

TAKING IT FURTHER A friend of yours is considering purchasing the company from Sally Dufferin and asks you to comment on the company's results of operations and its financial position. Is the company performing well or not? Does the financial position appear healthy or weak? Use specific information from the financial statements to support your answer.

Prepare adjusting entries, adjusted trial balance, and financial statements. **(SO 2, 3, 4) AP**

P3–9A Agopian Enterprises is owned by Edmund Agopian and has a January 31 fiscal year end. The company prepares adjusting entries on an annual basis. The following trial balance was prepared before adjustments:

AGOPIAN ENTERPRISES
Trial Balance
January 31, 2014

	Debit	Credit
Cash	$ 4,970	
Accounts receivable	14,540	
Prepaid insurance	3,960	
Supplies	6,580	
Equipment	32,350	
Accumulated depreciation—equipment		$ 12,940
Accounts payable		7,760
Note payable		11,000
Unearned revenue		7,480
E. Agopian, capital		18,320
E. Agopian, drawings	119,000	
Service revenue		214,500
Rent expense	20,750	
Salaries expense	66,950	
Telephone expense	2,900	
	$272,000	$272,000

Additional information:

1. A one-year insurance policy was purchased on July 1, 2013.
2. A count of supplies on January 31, 2014, shows $920 of supplies on hand.
3. The equipment has an estimated useful life of five years.
4. An analysis of the Unearned Revenue account shows that $5,230 has been earned by January 31, 2014.
5. The eight-month, 6% note was issued on November 1, 2013. Interest and principal are due on the maturity date.
6. Salaries accrued to January 31, 2014, were $1,315.
7. On January 31, 2014, the company had earned but not billed or recorded consulting revenue of $2,675.
8. The telephone bill for January 2014 was $170. It has not been recorded or paid. (Use the Accounts Payable account.)

Instructions

(a) Prepare adjusting journal entries for the year ended January 31, 2014, as required.
(b) Prepare an adjusted trial balance at January 31, 2014.
(c) Prepare an income statement and statement of owner's equity for the year ended January 31, 2014, and a balance sheet at January 31, 2014.

TAKING IT FURTHER Comment on the company's results of operations and its financial position. In your analysis, refer to specific items in the financial statements.

***P3–10A** Horowitz Piano Co. began operations on January 1, 2014. Its fiscal year end is December 31. It prepares financial statements and adjusts its accounts annually. Selected transactions for 2014 follow:

Prepare and post transaction and adjusting entries for prepayments. **(SO 2, 5) AP**

1. On January 15, 2014, bought supplies for $960 cash. A physical count on December 31, 2014, revealed $245 of supplies still on hand.
2. Bought a $3,090, one-year insurance policy for cash on April 1, 2014. The policy came into effect on this date.
3. On November 1, 2014, received a $1,750 advance cash payment from five clients ($350 each) for services expected to be provided in the future. As at December 31, 2014, services had still not been performed for two of the clients.

Instructions

(a) Assume that Horowitz Piano Co. records all prepaid costs as assets and all revenues collected in advance as liabilities.
   1. Prepare the journal entries for the original transactions.
   2. Prepare the adjusting journal entries at December 31, 2014.
   3. Post these journal entries to T accounts and calculate the balance in each account after adjustments. You do not need to post to the Cash account.

(b) Assume instead that Horowitz Piano Co. records all prepaid costs as expenses and all revenues collected in advance as revenues.
1. Prepare the journal entries for the original transactions.
2. Prepare the adjusting journal entries at December 31, 2014.
3. Post these journal entries to T accounts and calculate the balance in each account after adjustments. You do not need to post to the Cash account.

TAKING IT FURTHER Compare the balance in each account calculated under part (a) above with the balances calculated in part (b). Comment on your findings.

Prepare adjusting entries and adjusted trial balance using the alternative treatment of prepayments. **(SO 3, 4, 5) AP**

***P3–11A** Winter Designs was organized on January 1, 2014, by Katie Brownsey. Winter Designs records all prepaid costs as expenses and revenue received in advance as revenue. At the end of the first year of operations, the trial balance had the following accounts:

WINTER DESIGNS
Trial Balance
December 31, 2014

	Debit	Credit
Cash	$ 16,600	
Accounts receivable	26,000	
Equipment	80,000	
Accounts payable		$ 14,820
Note payable		44,000
K. Brownsey, capital		60,000
K. Brownsey, drawings	40,000	
Service revenue		121,400
Insurance expense	4,020	
Rent expense	7,800	
Salaries expense	59,900	
Supplies expense	5,900	
	$240,220	$240,220

Analysis reveals the following additional data:

1. On February 1, 2014, the company purchased a one-year insurance policy.
2. The one-year, 5% note payable was issued on March 1, 2014. Interest and principal are payable on the maturity date.
3. The equipment was purchased on March 2, 2014, and has an estimated useful life of eight years.
4. At December 31, 2014, there was $785 of supplies on hand.
5. At December 31, 2014, service revenue of $2,550 was unearned.
6. Service revenue earned but unbilled and unrecorded at December 31, 2014, totalled $1,275.
7. January 2015 rent of $600 was paid on December 31, 2014, and is included in Rent Expense.

Instructions

(a) Journalize the adjusting entries at December 31, 2014. (Adjustments are recorded annually.)
(b) Prepare an adjusted trial balance.

TAKING IT FURTHER If Winter Designs initially recorded all prepaid costs as assets and all revenue received in advance as a liability, would this result in different numbers in the adjusted trial balance than in part (b)? Explain.

CONTINUING COOKIE CHRONICLE

(*Note:* This is a continuation of the Cookie Chronicle from Chapters 1 and 2. Use the information from the previous chapters and follow the instructions below using the ledger accounts you have already prepared.)

It is the end of December and Natalie has been in touch with her grandmother. Her grandmother is curious to know if Natalie has been profitable and if Natalie requires another loan to help finance her business. Natalie too would like to know if she has been profitable during her first two months of operation.

Natalie realizes that, in order to accurately determine Cookie Creations' income, she must first make adjustments. Natalie puts together the following additional information:

1. A count reveals that $95 of supplies remain at the end of December.
2. Natalie was invited to teach a cookie-making class at a children's New Year's Eve function at her local community centre. At the end of the class, she left an invoice for $175 with the program director. Natalie had not had time to record this invoice in her accounting records. Because there were so many children expected to attend, she asked a friend to help with the class and promised to pay her $12 an hour. The payment to her friend was made on January 4, 2014, for four hours of work.
3. Natalie estimates that all of her equipment will have a useful life of three years or 36 months. (Assume Natalie decides to record a full month's worth of depreciation, regardless of when the equipment was acquired by the business.)
4. Recall that Natalie's grandmother is charging 3% interest on the note payable extended on November 29. The loan plus interest is to be repaid in 12 months. (Calculate interest to the nearest month.)

Instructions

Using the information that you have gathered through Chapter 2, and based on the new information above, do and answer the following:

(a) Prepare and post the adjusting journal entries. Round all amounts to the nearest dollar.
(b) Prepare an adjusted trial balance.
(c) Prepare an income statement for the two-month period ended December 31, 2013.
(d) Was Cookie Creations profitable during these first two months of operation? Why is it better for Cookie Creations to measure profitability after adjusting journal entries have been prepared and posted instead of before?
(e) How much cash is available to Natalie to operate her business? Why is the amount of cash different than the amount of profit that Cookie Creations has earned? What is the most likely reason that Natalie may need to borrow additional money from her grandmother?

Cumulative Coverage—Chapters 1 to 3

On August 31, 2014, the account balances of Pitre Equipment Repair were as follows:

PITRE EQUIPMENT REPAIR
Trial Balance
August 31, 2014

	Debit	Credit
Cash	$ 1,880	
Accounts receivable	3,720	
Supplies	800	
Equipment	15,000	
Accumulated depreciation—equipment		$ 1,500
Accounts payable		3,100
Unearned revenue		400
Salaries payable		700
R. Pitre, capital		15,700
	$21,400	$21,400

During September, the following transactions were completed:

Sept.	1	Borrowed $10,000 from the bank and signed a two-year, 5% note payable.
	8	Paid $1,100 for employees' salaries, of which $400 is for September and $700 for August.
	10	Received $1,200 cash from customers on account.
	12	Received $3,400 cash for services performed in September.
	17	Purchased additional supplies on account, $1,500.
	20	Paid creditors $4,500 on account.
	22	Paid September and October rent, $1,000 ($500 per month).
	25	Paid salaries, $1,200.
	27	Performed services on account and billed customers for services provided, $900.
	29	Received $700 from customers for future services.
	30	Purchased additional equipment on account, $3,000.

The company adjusts its accounts on a monthly basis. Adjustment data consist of the following:

1. Supplies on hand at September 30 cost $1,280.
2. Accrued salaries payable at September 30 total $775.
3. Equipment has an expected useful life of five years.
4. Unearned service revenue of $450 is still not earned at September 30.
5. Interest is payable on the first of each month.

Instructions

(a) Enter the August 31 balances in general ledger accounts.
(b) Journalize the September transactions.
(c) Post to the ledger accounts.
(d) Prepare a trial balance at September 30.
(e) Journalize and post adjusting entries.
(f) Prepare an adjusted trial balance.
(g) Prepare an income statement and a statement of owner's equity for September, and a balance sheet.

CHAPTER 3 BROADENING YOUR PERSPECTIVE

Collaborative Learning Activity

Note to instructor: Additional instructions and material for this group activity can be found on the Instructor Resource Site and in *WileyPLUS*.

BYP3–1 In this group activity, you will work in two different groups to improve your understanding of adjusting entries. First you will work in "expert" groups in which you will ensure that each group member thoroughly understands one type of adjusting journal entry. Then you will move to a second group consisting of one student from each of the different expert groups, and take turns teaching the different types of adjusting entries (that is, prepaid expenses, unearned revenues, accrued expenses, accrued revenues, and depreciation).

Communication Activity

BYP3–2 Some people believe that cash basis accounting is better than accrual basis accounting in predicting a company's future success. This idea became more popular after many reports of corporate financial scandals where management manipulated the timing of recognizing expenses and revenues in accrual accounting to influence profit. Others argue it is easier to manipulate profit using cash basis accounting.

Instructions

Write a memo discussing the following issues:

(a) What is the difference in calculating profit using accrual basis accounting versus cash basis accounting?
(b) Identify one way that management might be able to increase profit by manipulating the timing of revenue or expense recognition under accrual accounting.
(c) Identify one way that management might be able to increase profit using cash basis accounting.
(d) Which basis do you believe is more reliable for measuring performance and why?

Ethics Case

BYP3–3 Die Hard Company is a pesticide manufacturer. Its sales dropped a lot this year because of new legislation that outlawed the sale of many of Die Hard's chemical pesticides. In the coming year, Die Hard will have new, environmentally safe chemicals to replace these discontinued products. Sales in the next year are expected to be much higher than sales of any previous year. The drop in sales and profits appears to be a one-year exception.

Still, the company president is afraid that a large drop in the current year's profits could cause a significant drop in the market price of Die Hard's shares, and could make the company a takeover target. To avoid this possibility, the company president urges Carole Chiasson, the controller, to accrue all possible revenues and to defer as many expenses as possible when preparing this period's December 31 year-end adjusting entries. He says to Carole, "We need the revenues this year, and next year we can easily absorb expenses deferred from this year." Carole did not record the adjusting entries until January 17, but she dated the entries December 31 as if they were recorded then. Carole also did everything possible to follow the president's request.

Instructions

(a) Who are the stakeholders in this situation?
(b) What are the ethical considerations of (1) the president's request, and (2) Carole's decision to date the adjusting entries December 31?
(c) Can Carole aggressively accrue revenues and defer expenses and still be ethical?

All About You: Personal Financial Literacy Activity

BYP3–4 A critical issue for accountants is the decision as to whether an expenditure should be recorded as an asset or an expense. The distinction between asset and expense is not always clear. In certain instances, businesses have been forced to restate their financial statements because management has recorded an asset when an expense should be recorded. The "All About You" feature indicates that post-secondary education results in higher earnings over an adult's working life and thus the money you are spending on your education today should be of significant future benefit. The question then is whether your future post-secondary education would meet the accounting definition of an asset or an expense.

Instructions

(a) Consider the nature of the cost of your plans for your post-secondary education. What factors suggest that it should be considered an asset? What factors suggest that it should be considered an expense?
(b) Do you think the nature of the program you're planning to take should affect whether the cost of your education should be considered an asset or an expense? Recall that both assets and expenses increase on the debit side. Explain.
(c) Economic theory suggests that people are rational decision-makers and will always consider the benefit and cost of any expenditure and only incur the cost if the expected benefit is greater. Wouldn't this mean that every expenditure would meet the definition of an asset? Would you consider the cost of a vacation to Hawaii to be as valuable as a year of college? Would you record them both as assets on a personal balance sheet? Why or why not?
(d) If you were applying for a loan, what might the potential effect be on the success of your application if you understated your assets? What might be the potential effect on the bank if your assets are overstated and expenses understated?

ANSWERS TO CHAPTER QUESTIONS

ANSWERS TO ACCOUNTING IN ACTION INSIGHT QUESTIONS

All About You Insight, p. 99

Q: How should you account for the cost of your post-secondary education in the future? Should you be recognizing the cost as an expense each year or should you recognize it as an asset?

A: Expenses are recognized when there has been a decrease in an asset or an increase in a liability. Paying for an education will reduce assets such as cash and may also increase liabilities if you have to take out student loans. Therefore, most accountants would tell you that you should record the cost of your education as an expense as you incur those costs. On the other hand, it could be argued that your education is creating an asset—your increased future earning power. But then you would have to estimate the value of this asset. As with many situations in accounting, it is not easy to determine the correct answer.

Business Insight, p. 105

Q: If a business collects cash when the gift card is sold, how can gift card sales in December result in revenues in January?

A: Gift cards sales are simply another example of unearned revenues. At the time the gift card is sold, the business must record unearned revenue, which is a liability. When a customer redeems the gift card by making a purchase, then the company will reduce the liability and record revenue.

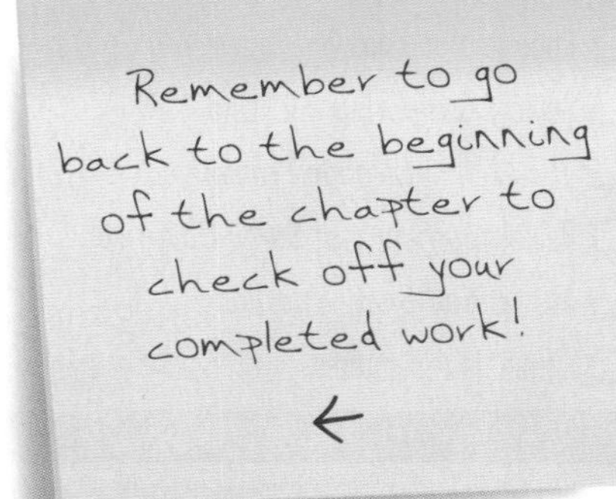
Remember to go
back to the beginning
of the chapter to
check off your
completed work!

ANSWERS TO SELF-STUDY QUESTIONS

1. b 2. d 3. d 4. b 5. c 6. d 7. a 8. a 9. b 10. a 11. a *12. a *13. c

CHAPTER 4

COMPLETION OF THE ACCOUNTING CYCLE

THE NAVIGATOR

- ☐ Understand *Concepts for Review*
- ☐ Read *Feature Story*
- ☐ Scan *Study Objectives*
- ☐ Read *Chapter Preview*
- ☐ Read text and answer *Before You Go On*
- ☐ Review *Comparing IFRS and ASPE*
- ☐ Work *Demonstration Problem*
- ☐ Review *Summary of Study Objectives*
- ☐ Answer *Self-Study Questions*
- ☐ Complete assignments

CONCEPTS FOR REVIEW

Before studying this chapter, you should understand or, if necessary, review:

A. How to increase and decrease assets, liabilities, and owner's equity accounts using debit and credit procedures. (Ch. 2, pp. 50–54)

B. When to recognize revenues and expenses. (Ch. 3, p. 98)

C. How to make adjusting entries. (Ch. 3, p. 106)

D. How to prepare an adjusted trial balance. (Ch. 3, pp. 113–116)

E. How the balance sheet, income statement, and statement of owner's equity are connected. (Ch. 3, p. 115)

NO "SHORT CUTS" IN ACCOUNTING

OTTAWA, ON.—Before launching a career as a hair stylist, Nelson Hickey studied accounting in high school and university. That's why he's so involved in the bookkeeping of Character Salon, which he opened in 2004 in a trendy Ottawa neighbourhood.

Mr. Hickey closes his books at year end. "We all know that everything has to balance—left and right, debit and credit—at the end of the year. If you are out by pennies, it's going to cause problems," he says.

If he does find any discrepancies at year end, he looks for the error. "That's one of the hardest things at the end of the year, if I'm out $4," Mr. Hickey says. Often, he will uncover a transposition error, where numbers were reversed when entered, such as $94 instead of $49. He still appreciates the tip he learned in school that if the discrepancy is divisible by 9 (in this case, $45), it can indicate a transposition error. When he finds the error, he makes a correcting entry in his Simply Accounting software. Mr. Hickey also makes adjusting entries to estimate final expenses for the year, such as an electricity bill that he hasn't received yet for the last month of the year.

Closing the books at year end became easier when Mr. Hickey recently installed another software program, Salonware, to track his revenues, which he used to compile manually at the end of every day in a spreadsheet program. Salonware is also his point-of-sale system when customers pay for their hair services and products. By tracking the sales of his five stylists, the software makes it easier to pay their salaries and commissions. All of this means he now can make general journal entries for sales weekly instead of daily, with far fewer errors that need to be corrected at year end. "It's definitely simplified the amount of data entry," he says.

When all the correcting and adjusting entries are made, Mr. Hickey makes closing entries and then Simply Accounting automatically generates an income statement and balance sheet that he gives to his accountant to prepare his annual income tax return. While today's technology makes bookkeeping much easier, he's glad he learned accounting principles on paper. "That's basically the only way to understand bookkeeping," he says.

In other words, there are no "short cuts" in accounting.

THE NAVIGATOR

STUDY OBJECTIVES

After studying this chapter, you should be able to:

1. Prepare closing entries and a post-closing trial balance.
2. Explain the steps in the accounting cycle including optional steps.
3. Prepare correcting entries.
4. Prepare a classified balance sheet.
5. Illustrate measures used to evaluate liquidity.
6. Prepare a work sheet (Appendix 4A).
7. Prepare reversing entries (Appendix 4B).

THE NAVIGATOR

PREVIEW OF CHAPTER FOUR

In Chapter 3, we learned about the adjusting process and how to prepare financial statements from the adjusted trial balance. In this chapter, we will explain the remaining steps in the accounting cycle—the closing process. Once again, we will use the Pioneer Advertising Agency as an example.

After that, we will look at correcting entries. As Nelson Hickey of Character Salon notes in the feature story, locating and correcting errors is very important. We end by discussing the classification and use of balance sheets. The chapter is organized as follows:

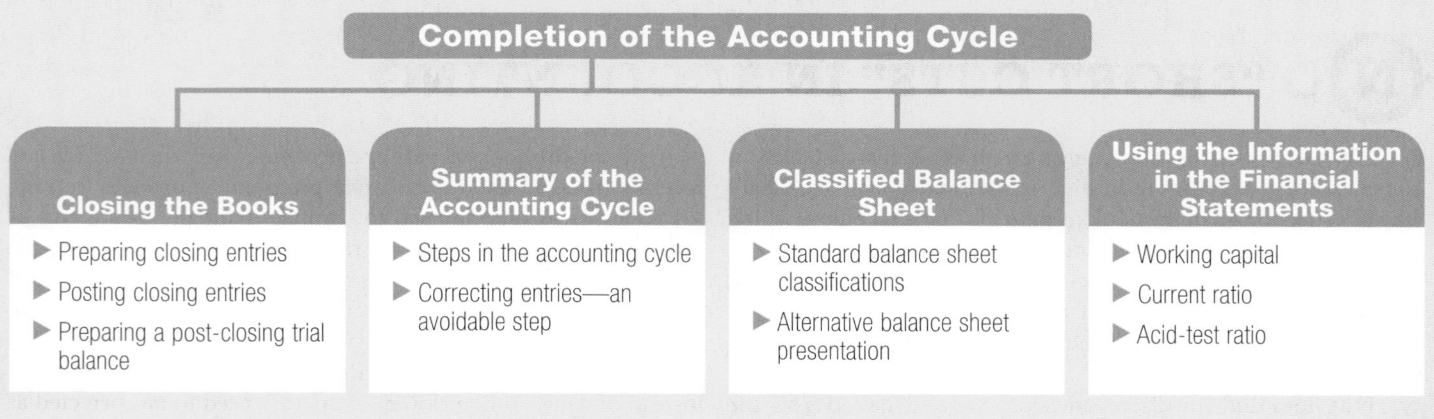

CLOSING THE BOOKS

STUDY OBJECTIVE 1
Prepare closing entries and a post-closing trial balance.

At the end of the accounting period, after the adjusting entries have been posted and the financial statements prepared, it is necessary to get the accounts in the general ledger ready for the next period. This is the next step in the accounting cycle and is called **closing the books**. This step involves bringing the balances in all revenue, expense, and drawings accounts to zero, and updating the balance in the owner's capital account.

Why is this necessary? Recall from Illustration 1-6 in Chapter 1 that revenues and investments by the owner increase owner's equity, and expenses and drawings decrease owner's equity. Also recall from Chapters 1 and 2 that investments by the owner are directly recorded in the owner's capital account, but that revenues, expenses, and drawings are all recorded in separate accounts. We use separate accounts for revenues, expenses, and drawings in order to create the information needed to prepare an income statement and a statement of owner's equity for the accounting period.

Helpful hint Temporary accounts will have zero balances at the beginning of the fiscal year.

At the start of the next accounting period, we need to begin that period with zero in the revenue, expense, and drawings accounts. This will allow us to create the information to prepare the income statement and statement of owner's equity for the next accounting period. Thus all revenue, expense, and drawings accounts are considered **temporary accounts** because they contain data for only a single accounting period and are closed at the end of the period. The journal entries to close the temporary accounts also update the balance in the owner's capital account.

Alternative terminology Temporary accounts are also called *nominal accounts*. Permanent accounts are also called *real accounts*.

In contrast, balance sheet accounts are considered **permanent accounts** because their balances are carried forward into the next accounting period. It is important to know the difference between temporary and permanent accounts. Temporary accounts are closed; permanent accounts are not closed. Illustration 4-1 summarizes temporary versus permanent accounts.

ILLUSTRATION 4-1
Temporary versus permanent accounts

TEMPORARY These accounts are closed.	PERMANENT These accounts are not closed.
All revenue accounts	All asset accounts All contra-asset accounts
All expense accounts	All liability accounts
Owner's drawings account	Owner's capital account

PREPARING CLOSING ENTRIES

The journal entries used to close the temporary accounts are called **closing entries.** Closing entries reduce the balance in the temporary accounts (revenues, expenses, and drawings) to zero and transfer the balances of these accounts to the permanent owner's capital account. The temporary accounts are then ready to collect data in the next accounting period.

After the closing entries are prepared and posted, the balance in the owner's capital account is equal to the end-of-period balance shown on the statement of owner's equity and the balance sheet. The **statement of owner's equity shows users of financial statements** the effect of that period's profit (or loss)—revenues minus expenses—and drawings on the owner's capital account. **Closing entries update the ledger to show the effect of that period's profit (or loss) and the owner's drawings on the owner's capital account.**

When closing entries are prepared, each income statement account could be closed directly to the owner's capital account. However, to do so would result in an excessive amount of detail in the owner's capital account. Instead, companies first close the revenue and expense accounts to another temporary account, **Income Summary**. The balance in the income summary account after closing revenues and expenses is equal to that period's profit or loss. Then the profit or loss is transferred from the income summary account to owner's capital.

The closing entry process is based on the expanded accounting equation shown in Illustration 1-8. Recall that the expanded accounting equation shows the relationship between revenues, expenses, profit (or loss), and owner's equity. Similarly, Illustration 4-2 shows the impact of the steps in the closing process on the owner's capital account. It also shows that the closing process does not affect the asset and liability accounts.

Helpful hint The acronym "RED" is a useful reminder of the key accounts that are closed to zero: revenue, expenses, and drawings.

Helpful hint Before closing entries are prepared and posted, the balance in the owner's capital account is equal to the balance from the beginning of the year plus any additional investments by the owner during the period. Recall that other changes to owner's equity are shown in the revenue, expense, and owner's drawings accounts.

Helpful hint After the revenue and expense accounts have been closed, the balance in the Income Summary account must equal the profit or loss for the period. If it doesn't, this means there is an error in the closing entries (or in the income statement) that needs to be found and corrected.

ILLUSTRATION 4-2
Closing process

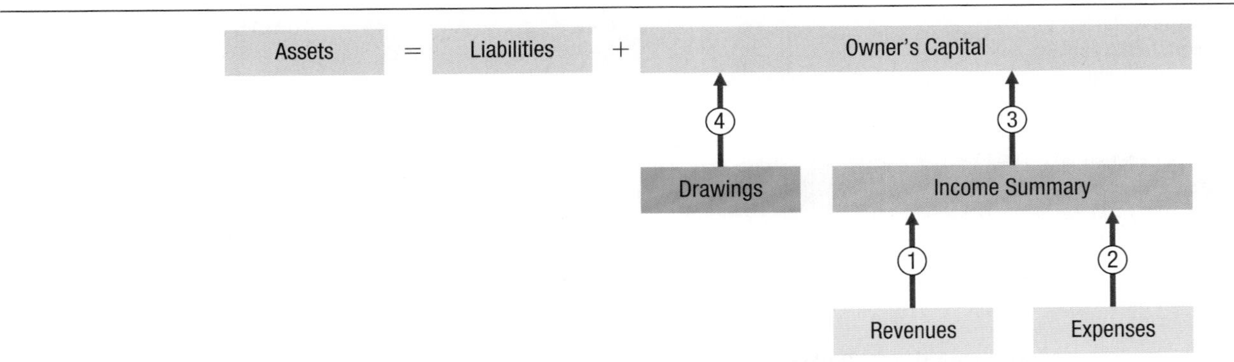

The four steps in Illustration 4-2 represent four closing entries:

1. **Close revenue accounts.** *Debit* each individual revenue account for the same amount as its balance to "zero it," and credit Income Summary for total revenues.
2. **Close expense accounts.** Debit Income Summary for total expenses, and *credit* each individual expense account for its balance to "zero" their balances.
3. **Close Income Summary account.** Debit Income Summary for its balance (or credit it if there is a loss) and credit (debit) the owner's capital account.
4. **Close drawings.** Debit the owner's capital account and *credit* the owner's drawings account for the balance in drawings. This will reduce the balance in drawings to zero.

Companies record closing entries in the general journal. The heading "Closing Entries," inserted in the journal between the last adjusting entry and the first closing entry, identifies these entries. Then the company posts the closing entries to the ledger accounts.

Helpful hint Preparing closing entries can be tricky in the sense that we will be making entries that are the *opposite* of what we would typically do (that is, debiting revenue and crediting expenses and drawings). This is done to reduce these account balances to zero. T accounts can be an important visual aid in the process of preparing closing entries.

Closing Entries Illustrated

To illustrate the journalizing and posting of closing entries, we will continue using the example of Pioneer Advertising Agency introduced in Chapters 2 and 3. In practice, companies generally prepare closing entries only at the end of the fiscal year. Most companies, including Character Salon, introduced in the

Helpful hint As with regular "day-to-day" and adjusting entries, closing entries are first recorded in the journal and then posted to the ledger.

feature story, close their books once a year. However, to illustrate the process, we will assume that Pioneer Advertising Agency closes its books monthly.

Pioneer Advertising's adjusted trial balance on October 31, 2014, first shown in Chapter 3 (Illustration 3-8), is shown again here in Illustration 4-3. The temporary accounts have been highlighted in red. C. Bedard, Capital is a permanent account. It is highlighted in blue because it is used in the closing process, but it is not a temporary account. While C. Bedard, Capital will not be closed to zero, its balance will be updated during the process of closing the temporary accounts.

ILLUSTRATION 4-3
Adjusted trial balance

PIONEER ADVERTISING AGENCY
Adjusted Trial Balance
October 31, 2014

	Debit	Credit
Cash	$14,250	
Accounts receivable	1,200	
Supplies	1,000	
Prepaid insurance	550	
Equipment	5,000	
Accumulated depreciation—equipment		$ 83
Notes payable		5,000
Accounts payable		1,750
Unearned revenue		800
Salaries payable		2,000
Interest payable		25
C. Bedard, capital		**10,000**
C. Bedard, drawings	**500**	
Service revenue		**11,400**
Depreciation expense	**83**	
Insurance expense	**50**	
Rent expense	**900**	
Salaries expense	**6,000**	
Supplies expense	**1,500**	
Interest expense	**25**	
	$31,058	$31,058

Notice that the C. Bedard, Capital account balance of $10,000 in the adjusted trial balance is the opening balance of $0 plus the $10,000 investment made by C. Bedard during the period—it is not the ending balance of $12,342 that appears in the statement of owner's equity and balance sheet in Illustrations 3-9 and 3-10. This permanent account is updated to its ending balance by the closing entries as follows:

CLOSING ENTRY 1
Revenues to income summary

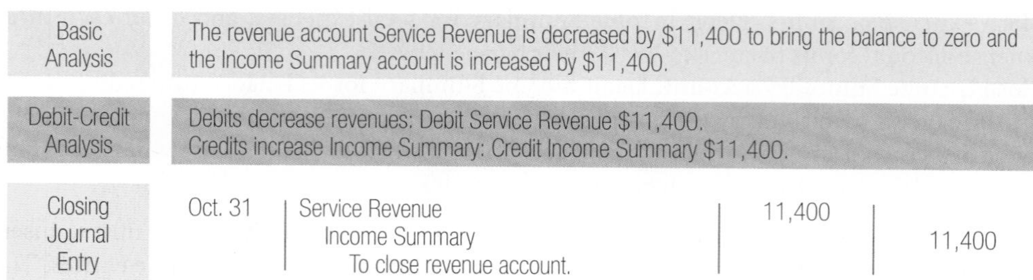

Basic Analysis	The revenue account Service Revenue is decreased by $11,400 to bring the balance to zero and the Income Summary account is increased by $11,400.
Debit-Credit Analysis	Debits decrease revenues: Debit Service Revenue $11,400. Credits increase Income Summary: Credit Income Summary $11,400.

Closing Journal Entry				
	Oct. 31	Service Revenue	11,400	
		Income Summary		11,400
		To close revenue account.		

This closing entry transfers revenue to the Income Summary account. If there are two or more revenue accounts, they are all closed in one entry with a separate debit to each revenue account and one credit to Income Summary for the total amount.

CLOSING ENTRY 2
Expenses to income summary

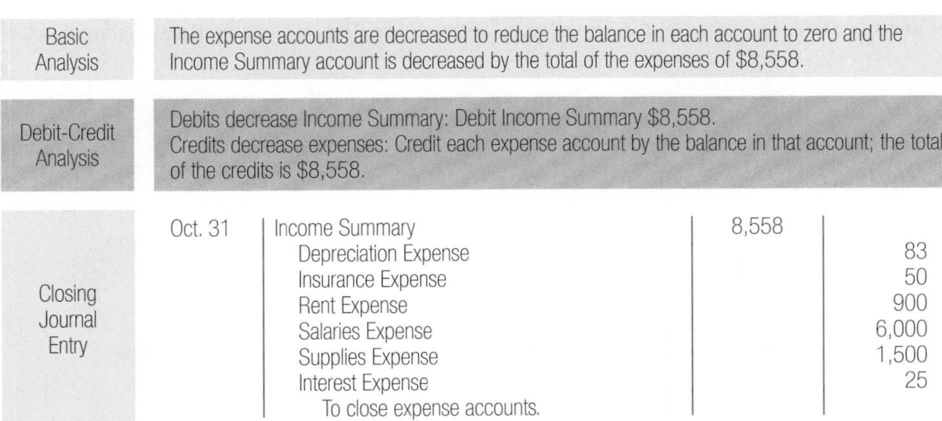

Basic Analysis	The expense accounts are decreased to reduce the balance in each account to zero and the Income Summary account is decreased by the total of the expenses of $8,558.
Debit-Credit Analysis	Debits decrease Income Summary: Debit Income Summary $8,558. Credits decrease expenses: Credit each expense account by the balance in that account; the total of the credits is $8,558.

Closing Journal Entry				
	Oct. 31	Income Summary	8,558	
		Depreciation Expense		83
		Insurance Expense		50
		Rent Expense		900
		Salaries Expense		6,000
		Supplies Expense		1,500
		Interest Expense		25
		To close expense accounts.		

This closing entry transfers the expenses to the Income Summary account. Notice that the closing entry includes **a separate credit to each of the expense accounts** but only one debit for the total amount to Income Summary.

As a result of these two closing entries, there is a credit balance of $2,842 ($11,400 − $8,558) in the Income Summary account. There is a credit balance because revenues were greater than expenses. The credit balance is equal to Pioneer's profit for October as shown in Illustration 3-9. If expenses were greater than revenues, Pioneer would have a loss and this would result in a debit balance in the Income Summary account after closing revenues and expenses.

Helpful hint While journalizing the second closing entry, the order in which the expenses are listed doesn't matter as long as they are listed after the debits. The expenses, however, should be listed in alphabetical order on the income statement and trial balance.

CLOSING ENTRY 3
Income summary to owner's capital

Basic Analysis	The Income Summary account is decreased by the balance in the account of $2,842 to bring it to zero and the owner's equity account C. Bedard, Capital is increased by $2,842 because profit increases owner's equity.
Debit-Credit Analysis	Debits decrease Income Summary: Debit Income Summary $2,842. Credits increase owner's equity: Credit C. Bedard, Capital $2,842.

Closing Journal Entry				
	Oct. 31	Income Summary	2,842	
		C. Bedard, Capital		2,842
		To close profit to capital.		

This closing entry adds the profit to the capital account. If Pioneer had a loss then it would have been necessary to credit the Income Summary account to bring it to zero and debit the owner's capital account. Since losses decrease owner's equity, it makes sense to debit the capital account when there is a loss.

CLOSING ENTRY 4
Drawings to owner's capital

Basic Analysis	The drawings account C. Bedard, Drawings is decreased by $500 to bring the balance to zero and the owner's equity account C. Bedard, Capital is decreased by $500 because drawings decrease owner's equity.
Debit-Credit Analysis	Debits decrease owner's equity: Debit C. Bedard, Capital $500. Credits decrease drawings: Credit C. Bedard, Drawings $500.

Closing Journal Entry				
	Oct. 31	C. Bedard, Capital	500	
		C. Bedard, Drawings		500
		To close drawings account.		

This closing entry transfers the drawings to the capital account. Always close drawings separately from revenues and expenses. Drawings are not used to determine profit. Remember, drawings are shown on the statement of owner's equity as a separate item and thus are also closed in a separate entry.

The closing entries are recorded in the general journal for Pioneer Advertising Agency as follows:

GENERAL JOURNAL J3

Date	Account Titles and Explanation	Ref.	Debit	Credit
	Closing Entries			
2014	(1)			
Oct. 31	Service Revenue	400	11,400	
	Income Summary	350		11,400
	To close revenue account.			
	(2)			
31	Income Summary	350	8,558	
	Depreciation Expense	711		83
	Insurance Expense	722		50
	Rent Expense	726		900
	Salaries Expense	729		6,000
	Supplies Expense	740		1,500
	Interest Expense	905		25
	To close expense accounts.			
	(3)			
31	Income Summary	350	2,842	
	C. Bedard, Capital	301		2,842
	To close profit to capital.			
	(4)			
31	C. Bedard, Capital	301	500	
	C. Bedard, Drawings	306		500
	To close drawings account.			

Be careful when you prepare closing entries. Remember that the reason for making closing entries is to bring the temporary accounts to zero balances. Do not make the mistake of doubling the revenue, expense, drawings, and income summary account balances, rather than bringing them to zero. Using T accounts can be particularly helpful in ensuring that closing entries are done correctly.

POSTING CLOSING ENTRIES

The asset and liability accounts are never affected by the closing process. Thus we have not included them in the following diagram. The only accounts that will change are the temporary accounts and the owner's capital account.

After the closing entries have been posted, all of the increases and decreases to owner's equity during the period are recorded in the owner's capital account. The posting of the closing entries ("Clos.") and the updated balances ("Bal.") are as follows:

GENERAL LEDGER

C. Bedard, Capital 301

Debit			Credit		
			Oct. 1		10,000
Oct. 31	Clos.	500	31	Clos.	2,842
			Oct. 31	Bal.	12,342

C. Bedard, Drawings 306

Debit			Credit		
Oct. 20		500	Oct. 31	Clos.	500
Oct. 31	Bal.	0			

Income Summary 350

Debit			Credit		
			Oct. 31	Clos.	11,400
Oct. 31	Clos.	8,558			
			Oct. 31	Bal.	2,842
Oct. 31	Clos.	2,842			
			Oct. 31	Bal.	0

Service Revenue 400

Debit			Credit		
			Oct. 21		10,000
			25		800
			31	Adj.	400
Oct. 31	Clos.	11,400	31	Adj.	200
			Oct. 31	Bal.	0

Depreciation Expense 711

Debit			Credit		
Oct. 31	Adj.	83	Oct. 31	Clos.	83
Oct. 31	Bal.	0			

Insurance Expense 722

Debit			Credit		
Oct. 31	Adj.	50	Oct. 31	Clos.	50
Oct. 31	Bal.	0			

Rent Expense					726
Oct. 3		900	Oct. 31	Clos.	900
Oct. 31	Bal.	0			

Supplies Expense					740
Oct. 31	Adj.	1,500	Oct. 31	Clos.	1,500
Oct. 31	Bal.	0			

Salaries Expense					729
Oct. 24		4,000			
31	Adj.	2,000	Oct. 31	Clos.	6,000
Oct. 31	Bal.	0			

Interest Expense					905
Oct. 31	Adj.	25	Oct. 31	Clos.	25
Oct. 31	Bal.	0			

Stop and check your work after the closing entries are posted:

1. The balance in Income Summary, immediately before the final closing entry to transfer the balance to the owner's capital account, should equal the profit (or loss) reported in the income statement (see Illustration 3-9 in Chapter 3).
2. All temporary accounts (revenues, expenses, owner's drawings, and Income Summary) should have zero balances.
3. The balance in the capital account should equal the ending balance reported in the statement of owner's equity and balance sheet (see Illustrations 3-9 and 3-10 in Chapter 3).

PREPARING A POST-CLOSING TRIAL BALANCE

After all four closing entries have been journalized and posted, another trial balance is prepared from the ledger. It is called a **post-closing trial balance** and it represents the final step in the accounting cycle. The post- (or after-) closing trial balance lists permanent accounts and their balances after closing entries have been journalized and posted. The purpose of this trial balance is to prove the equality of the permanent account balances that are carried forward into the next accounting period. Since all temporary accounts have zero balances after closing, the post-closing trial balance contains only permanent—balance sheet—accounts.

Helpful hint Total debits in a post-closing trial balance will not equal total assets on the balance sheet if contra accounts, such as accumulated depreciation, are present. Accumulated depreciation is deducted from assets on the balance sheet but added to the credit column in a trial balance.

The post-closing trial balance for Pioneer Advertising Agency is shown in Illustration 4-4. Note that the account balances are the same as the ones in the company's balance sheet. (Pioneer Advertising's balance sheet is shown in Chapter 3, Illustration 3-10.)

ILLUSTRATION 4-4
Post-closing trial balance

PIONEER ADVERTISING AGENCY
Post-Closing Trial Balance
October 31, 2014

	Debit	Credit
Cash	$14,250	
Accounts receivable	1,200	
Supplies	1,000	
Prepaid insurance	550	
Equipment	5,000	
Accumulated depreciation—equipment		$ 83
Notes payable		5,000
Accounts payable		1,750
Unearned revenue		800
Salaries payable		2,000
Interest payable		25
C. Bedard, capital		**12,342**
	$22,000	$22,000

A post-closing trial balance provides evidence that the journalizing and posting of closing entries has been completed properly. It also shows that the accounting equation is in balance at the end of the accounting period and the beginning of the next accounting period.

As in the case of the trial balance, the post-closing trial balance does not prove that all transactions have been recorded or that the ledger is correct. For example, the post-closing trial balance will still balance if a transaction is not journalized and posted, or if a transaction is journalized and posted twice.

Accounting software, such as Simply Accounting, used by Character Salon in our feature story, will automatically record and post closing entries when given instructions to prepare the accounting records for the next fiscal year. But it is still very important to understand what is happening in the closing process. You will find your understanding of adjusting entries is enhanced once you have mastered closing entries.

BEFORE YOU GO ON...

Action Plan

- Debit each individual revenue account for its balance and credit the total to Income Summary.
- Credit each individual expense account for its balance and debit the total to Income Summary.
- Stop and check your work: Does the balance in Income Summary equal the reported profit?
- Debit the balance in Income Summary and credit the amount to the owner's capital account. (Do the opposite if the company had a loss.)
- Credit the balance in the drawings account and debit the amount to the owner's capital account. Do not close drawings with the expenses.
- Stop and check your work: Will your closing entries result in the temporary accounts having zero balances? Does the ending balance in the owner's capital account equal the closing owner's capital reported on the statement of owner's equity?

DO IT

The adjusted trial balance for the Nguyen Company shows the following:

	Debit	Credit
Cash	$20,000	
Equipment	35,000	
Accounts payable		$10,000
H. Nguyen, capital		42,000
H. Nguyen, drawings	5,000	
Service revenue		18,000
Rent expense	2,000	
Salaries expense	7,500	
Supplies expense	500	
	$70,000	$70,000

Nguyen Company's statement of owner's equity for the year showed a profit of $8,000 and closing owner's capital of $45,000.

(a) Prepare the closing entries at December 31.
(b) Create T accounts for Income Summary and H. Nguyen, Capital, and post the closing entries to these accounts.

SOLUTION

		Debit	Credit
Dec. 31	Service Revenue	18,000	
	Income Summary		18,000
	To close revenue account.		
31	Income Summary	10,000	
	Rent Expense		2,000
	Salaries Expense		7,500
	Supplies Expense		500
	To close expense accounts.		
31	Income Summary	8,000	
	H. Nguyen, Capital		8,000
	To close Income Summary.		
31	H. Nguyen, Capital	5,000	
	H. Nguyen, Drawings		5,000
	To close drawings.		

Income Summary

Clos.	10,000	Clos.	18,000
		Bal.	8,000*
Clos.	8,000		
		Bal.	0

*Check if this equals profit.

H. Nguyen, Capital

		Bal.	42,000
Clos.	5,000	Clos.	8,000
		Bal.	45,000**

**Check if this equals closing owner's capital.

Related exercise material: BE4–1, BE4–2, BE4–3, BE4–4, E4–1, E4–2, and E4–3.

THE NAVIGATOR

SUMMARY OF THE ACCOUNTING CYCLE

In Chapter 2, we introduced the accounting cycle as series of steps that accountants take to prepare financial statements. You have now learned all of the steps. In the following section, we review the cycle and discuss optional steps.

STEPS IN THE ACCOUNTING CYCLE

STUDY OBJECTIVE 2
Explain the steps in the accounting cycle including optional steps.

As introduced in Chapter 2, the cycle begins with the analysis and recording of business transactions (Steps 1, 2, and 3). This is followed by the preparation of a trial balance (Step 4), as also shown in Chapter 2. Chapter 3 covered the adjustment process and the preparation of financial statements (Steps 5, 6, and 7). In the first part of Chapter 4, the final steps of the accounting cycle—the closing process (Steps 8 and 9)—were covered. The full accounting cycle is reproduced here in Illustration 4-5.

ILLUSTRATION 4-5
Steps in the accounting cycle

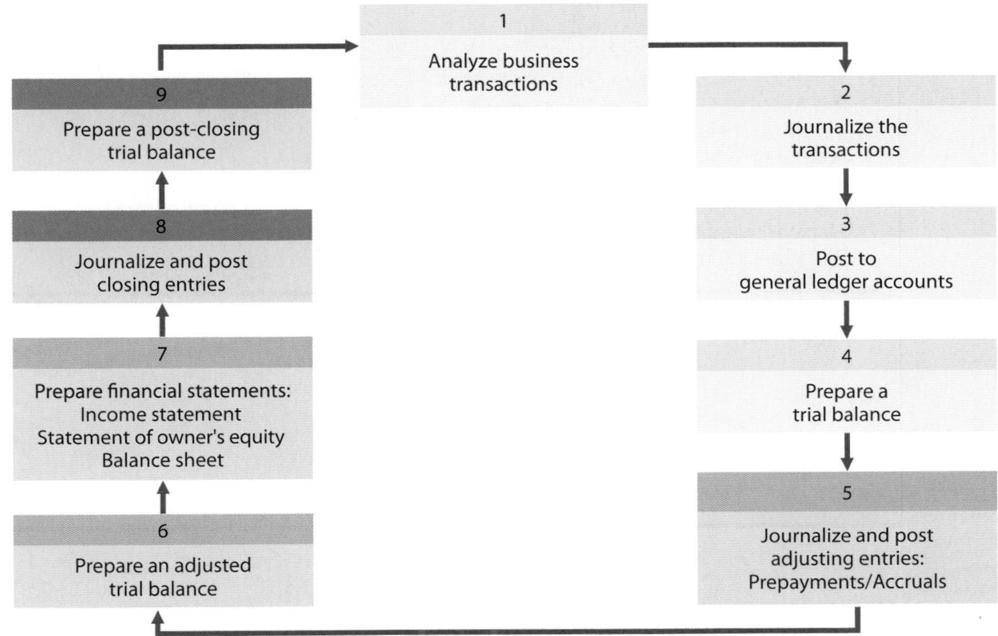

Optional steps: If a work sheet is prepared, Steps 4, 5, and 6 are done in the work sheet, and adjusting entries are journalized and posted after Step 7. If reversing entries are prepared, they occur between Steps 9 and 1.

The steps in the cycle are completed in sequence (Steps 1 to 9). Once Step 9 is completed for an accounting period, the company can begin again with Step 1 in the next accounting period and repeat the steps for that accounting period and so on. Because the steps are repeated each accounting period, we show the full accounting cycle as a circle. Steps 1, 2, and 3 can occur every day during the accounting period, as explained in Chapter 2. Steps 4 through 7 are done periodically, such as monthly, quarterly, or annually. Steps 8 and 9, closing entries and a post-closing trial balance, are usually done only at the end of a company's fiscal year. There are also two optional steps in the accounting cycle: work sheets and reversing entries. These optional steps are explained in the following two sections.

Work Sheets—An Optional Step

Some accountants like to use an optional multiple-column form known as a **work sheet** to help them prepare adjusting entries and the financial statements. As its name suggests, the work sheet is a working tool. It is not a permanent accounting record; it is neither a journal nor a part of the general ledger. Companies generally computerize work sheets using an electronic spreadsheet program such as Excel.

Although using a work sheet is optional, it is useful. For example, a work sheet makes it easier to prepare interim (such as monthly or quarterly) financial information. The monthly or quarterly adjusting entries can be entered in the work sheet, and interim financial statements can then be easily developed.

As the preparation of a work sheet is optional, its basic form and the procedure for preparing it are explained in Appendix 4A at the end of the chapter.

Reversing Entries—An Optional Step

Some accountants prefer to reverse certain adjusting entries by making a reversing entry at the beginning of the next accounting period. A **reversing entry** is the exact opposite of the adjusting entry made in the previous period. Use of reversing entries is an optional bookkeeping procedure; it is not a required step in the accounting cycle. We have therefore chosen to explain this topic in Appendix 4B at the end of the chapter.

BEFORE YOU GO ON...

Action Plan

- Review the accounting cycle.

DO IT

Indicate which of the following statements are true and which are false with a T or F.

1. Reversing entries are an optional step in the accounting cycle.
2. The first step in the accounting cycle is journalizing transactions.
3. A work sheet is an optional step in the accounting cycle.
4. Reversing entries are used to reverse closing entries.
5. Closing entries must be prepared on a monthly basis if financial statements are prepared monthly.
6. There are three different types of trial balances used in the accounting cycle.
7. If a work sheet is used, it is not necessary to prepare adjusting entries.
8. Financial statements are prepared after the adjustment process.

SOLUTION

1. T
2. F
3. T
4. F
5. F
6. T
7. F
8. T

Related exercise material: BE4–5, BE4–6, E4–4, and E4–6.

THE NAVIGATOR

CORRECTING ENTRIES—AN AVOIDABLE STEP

STUDY OBJECTIVE 3

Prepare correcting entries.

Unfortunately, errors may happen in the recording process. The accounting cycle does not include a specific step for correcting errors because this step is not needed if the accounting records have no errors. But if errors exist, they should be corrected as soon as they are discovered, regardless of when they occur in the accounting cycle, by journalizing and posting **correcting entries**. If the accounting records have no errors, no correcting entries are needed.

You should understand several differences between correcting entries and adjusting entries. First, adjusting entries are an integral part of the accounting cycle. Correcting entries, on the other hand, are unnecessary if the records have no errors. Second, adjustments are journalized and posted only at the end of an accounting period. In contrast, correcting entries are made whenever an error is discovered. Finally, adjusting entries always affect at least one balance sheet account (not Cash) and one income statement account. In contrast, correcting entries can involve any combination of accounts that need to be corrected. Adjusting and correcting entries do have one thing in common, however: in both cases, they must be journalized and posted before closing entries.

Correcting Entries Illustrated

To determine the correcting entry, it is useful to compare the incorrect entry with the entry that should have been made. Doing this helps identify the accounts and amounts that should—and should not—be corrected. After comparison, a correcting entry is made to correct the accounts. This approach is shown in the following two cases.

Case 1.

On May 10, a $50 cash collection on account from a customer is journalized and posted as a debit to Cash $50 and as a credit to Service Revenue $50. The error is discovered on May 20 when the customer pays the remaining balance in full.

Incorrect Entry (May 10)		
Cash	50	
Service Revenue		50

Correct Entry (May 10)		
Cash	50	
Accounts Receivable		50

Comparison of the incorrect entry with the correct entry that should have been made (but was not) reveals that the debit to Cash of $50 is correct. However, the $50 credit to Service Revenue should have been credited to Accounts Receivable. As a result, both Service Revenue and Accounts Receivable are overstated in the ledger. The following correcting entry is needed:

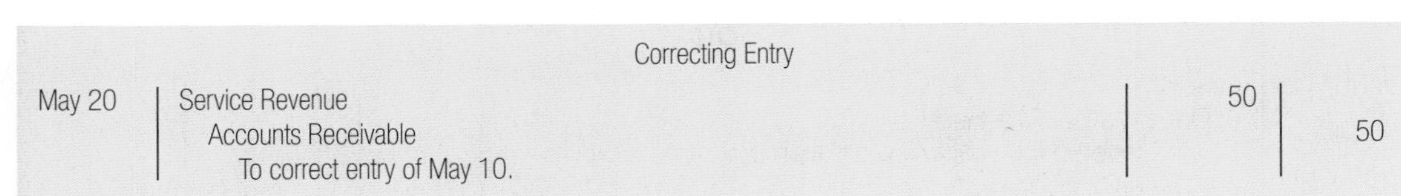

Correcting Entry			
May 20	Service Revenue	50	
	Accounts Receivable		50
	To correct entry of May 10.		

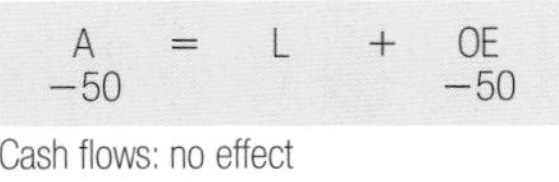

A	=	L	+	OE
−50				−50

Cash flows: no effect

Case 2.

On May 18, equipment that costs $450 is purchased on account. The transaction is journalized and posted as a debit to Supplies $45 and as a credit to Accounts Payable $45. The error is discovered on June 3 when the monthly statement for May is received from the creditor.

Incorrect Entry (May 18)		
Supplies	45	
Accounts Payable		45

Correct Entry (May 18)		
Equipment	450	
Accounts Payable		450

A comparison of the two entries shows that three accounts are incorrect. Supplies is overstated by $45; Equipment is understated by $450; and Accounts Payable is understated by $405 ($450 − $45). The correcting entry is as follows:

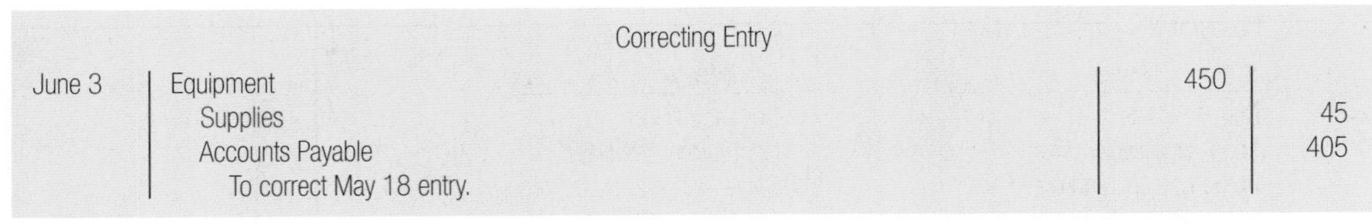

Correcting Entry			
June 3	Equipment	450	
	Supplies		45
	Accounts Payable		405
	To correct May 18 entry.		

A	=	L	+	OE
+450				+450
−45				

Cash flows: no effect

Alternative Approach

Instead of preparing a correcting entry, many accountants simply reverse the incorrect entry and then record the correct entry. This approach will result in more entries and postings, but it is often easier and more logical.

Sometimes errors are not found until after the temporary accounts have been closed. A correcting entry that fixes an error from a previous accounting year is called a prior period adjustment. These correcting entries can be very complex, and will be covered in a later chapter.

Helpful hint T-accounts can provide a useful visual aid in preparing correcting entries.

BEFORE YOU GO ON...

Action Plan

- Determine the correct entry that should have been made.
- Compare it with the incorrect entry made and make the required corrections. Note that three accounts must be corrected.
- You could instead use the alternative approach of reversing the incorrect journal entry and recording the correct journal entry.

DO IT

The Chip 'N Dough Company made the following adjusting journal entry to record $5,200 of depreciation expense on a vehicle at year end:

Feb. 28	Depreciation Expense	520	
	Cash		520
	To record depreciation on a vehicle.		

Prepare the required correcting entry.

SOLUTION

Feb. 28	Cash	520	
	Depreciation Expense ($5,200 − $520)	4,680	
	Accumulated Depreciation—Vehicles		5,200
	To correct depreciation adjustment.		

OR

Feb. 28	Cash	520	
	Depreciation Expense		520
	To reverse incorrect depreciation adjustment.		
28	Depreciation Expense	5,200	
	Accumulated Depreciation—Vehicles		5,200
	To record the correct depreciation entry.		

Related exercise material: BE4–7, BE4–8, E4–6, E4–7, and E4–8.

CLASSIFIED BALANCE SHEET

STUDY OBJECTIVE 4
Prepare a classified balance sheet.

The balance sheet presents a snapshot of a company's financial position at a point in time. The balance sheets that we have seen so far have all been very basic, with items classified simply as assets, liabilities, or owner's equity. To improve users' understanding of a company's financial position, companies often group similar assets and similar liabilities together.

Alternative terminology The balance sheet is also known as the *statement of financial position.*

STANDARD BALANCE SHEET CLASSIFICATIONS

A **classified balance sheet** generally has the standard classifications listed in Illustration 4-6.

ILLUSTRATION 4-6
Standard balance sheet classifications

Assets	Liabilities and Owner's Equity
Current assets	Current liabilities
Long-term investments	Non-current liabilities
Property, plant, and equipment	Owner's (shareholders') equity
Intangible assets	
Goodwill	

These groupings help readers determine such things as (1) whether the company has enough assets to pay its debts as they come due, and (2) the claims of short- and long-term creditors on total assets. These classifications are shown in the balance sheet of MacDonald Company in Illustration 4-7. In the sections that follow, we explain each of these groupings.

ILLUSTRATION 4-7
Classified balance sheet

MACDONALD COMPANY Balance Sheet November 30, 2014			
Assets			
Current assets			
Cash		$ 6,600	
Short-term investments		2,000	
Accounts receivable		7,000	
Inventories		4,000	
Supplies		2,100	
Prepaid insurance		400	
Total current assets			$ 22,100
Long-term investments			
Equity investment		$ 5,200	
Debt investment		2,000	
Total long-term investments			7,200
Property, plant, and equipment			
Land		$35,000	
Building	$75,000		
Less: Accumulated depreciation	15,000	60,000	
Equipment	$24,000		
Less: Accumulated depreciation	5,000	19,000	
Total property, plant, and equipment			114,000
Licences			5,000
Goodwill			3,100
Total assets			$151,400
Liabilities and Owner's Equity			
Current liabilities			
Short-term notes payable		$11,000	
Accounts payable		2,100	
Unearned revenue		900	
Salaries payable		1,600	
Interest payable		450	
Current portion of long-term notes payable		1,000	
Total current liabilities			$ 17,050
Non-current liabilities			
Mortgage payable		$ 9,000	
Long-term notes payable		1,300	
Total non-current liabilities			10,300
Total liabilities			27,350
Owner's equity			
J. MacDonald, capital			124,050
Total liabilities and owner's equity			$151,400

Current Assets

Current assets are normally cash and other assets that will be converted to cash, sold, or used up within one year from the balance sheet date. Some companies use a period longer than one year to classify assets as current because they have an operating cycle that is longer than one year.

The **operating cycle** of a company is the time it takes to go from starting with cash to ending with cash in producing revenues. Illustration 4-8 shows the basic steps involved in an operating cycle.

ILLUSTRATION 4-8
Steps in the operating cycle

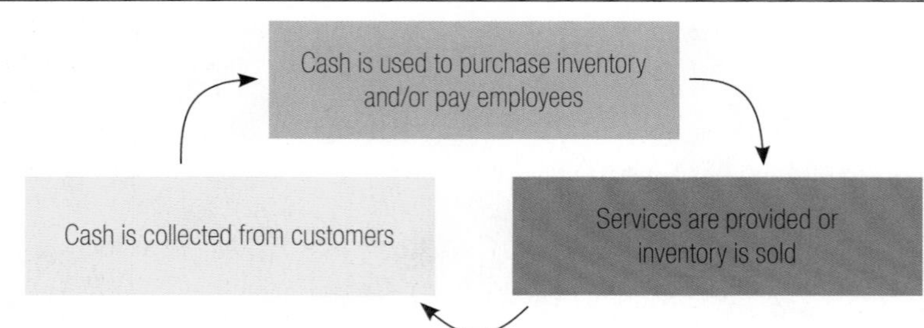

For most businesses, this cycle is less than one year, so they use the one-year cutoff. But for some businesses, such as vineyards or airplane manufacturers, this period may be longer than one year. Except where noted, we will assume companies use one year as a threshold to determine whether an asset is current or non-current.

Common types of current assets are: (1) cash; (2) short-term investments, such as equity and long-term debt securities that are held for trading, or short-term debt securities; (3) receivables, such as notes receivable, accounts receivable, and interest receivable; (4) inventories or merchandise available for sale; (5) supplies; and (6) prepaid expenses, such as rent and insurance. Accounts receivable are current assets because they will be collected and converted to cash within one year. Inventory is a current asset because a company expects to sell it within one year. Supplies are a current asset because a company expects to use or consume supplies within one year. In Illustration 4-7, MacDonald Company had current assets of $22,100.

In Canada, companies generally list current assets in the order of their liquidity; that is, in the order in which they are expected to be converted into cash. Some international companies list current assets in reverse order of liquidity.

Current assets for Canada Post Corporation, one of the largest Crown corporations owned by the federal government, are shown in Illustration 4-9. Note that Canada Post lists its current assets in order of liquidity and that it calls its balance sheet "statement of financial position," as do many companies.

ILLUSTRATION 4-9
Current assets section

CANADA POST CORPORATION
Statement of Financial Position (partial)
December 31, 2011
(in millions)

Current assets	
Cash and cash equivalents	$ 271
Marketable securities	842
Trade and other receivables	662
Income taxes receivable	56
Other assets	115
Total current assets	1,946

Alternative terminology Short-term investments are sometimes called *marketable securities, trading investments,* or *trading securities.*

We have already learned about most of these accounts in previous chapters except for "cash equivalents." Cash equivalents are investments in very liquid debt securities that can easily be converted into cash. Canada Post uses the term "marketable securities," which is another name for short-term investments used in the MacDonald Company example in Illustration 4-7.

The assets described in the next three sections are **non-current assets**. These are assets that will not be converted to cash, sold, or used by the business within one year of the balance sheet date or its operating cycle. Basically that means that non-current assets are everything that is not classified as a current asset.

Long-Term Investments

Long-term investments include (1) investments in long-term debt (for example, loans, notes, bonds, or mortgages) that management intends to hold to earn interest, and (2) equity securities (for example, shares) of other corporations that management plans to hold for many years for strategic reasons. These assets are classified as long-term because they are not readily marketable or expected to be converted into cash within one year. In Illustration 4-7, MacDonald Company reported long-term investments of $7,200 on its balance sheet.

Some companies have only one line on the balance sheet showing total long-term investments, and provide all of the details in the notes to the financial statements. If an item is simply called an "investment," without specifying if it is a short- or long-term investment, it is assumed to be a long-term investment.

Empire Company Limited (shown in the partial balance sheet in Illustration 4-10) has three lines for long-term investments on its balance sheet. Additional information on these investments is included in note 6. A total for long-term investments is not included in Illustration 4-10, as Empire does not show a subtotal for all of its long-term investments on the balance sheet.

ILLUSTRATION 4-10
Long-term investments section

EMPIRE COMPANY LIMITED
Balance Sheet (partial)
November 5, 2011
(in millions)

Loans and other receivables	$ 71.9
Investments	13.6
Investments, at equity (Note 6)	261.6

Investments that are accounted for using the equity method must be shown separately, as Empire has done. Equity accounting is used when a company owns enough of another company to have a significant influence over its operations.

Property, Plant, and Equipment

Property, plant, and equipment are long-lived, tangible assets that are used in the production of goods or services and are not intended for sale. This category includes land, buildings, equipment, vehicles, and furniture. In Illustration 4-7, MacDonald Company reported property, plant, and equipment of $114,000.

Alternative terminology
Property, plant, and equipment are sometimes called *capital assets* or *fixed assets.*

Although the order of property, plant, and equipment on the balance sheet can vary among companies, in Canada these assets have traditionally been listed in their order of permanency. That is, land is usually listed first, because it has an indefinite life, and is followed by the asset with the next longest useful life (normally buildings), and so on.

Since property, plant, and equipment benefit future periods, their cost is allocated to expense over their useful lives through depreciation, as we learned in Chapter 3. Assets that are depreciated are reported at their carrying amount (cost minus accumulated depreciation).

Danier Leather Inc. reported the total carrying amount (or "net carrying value" as Danier calls it) of $15,315 thousand for its property, plant, and equipment on its balance sheet. Danier reports the cost, accumulated depreciation (or "accumulated amortization" as Danier calls it), and net carrying value of each category of property, plant, and equipment in a note to the financial statements, as shown in Illustration 4-11. This practice is very common for public companies to keep the balance sheet from looking too cluttered.

ILLUSTRATION 4-11
Property, plant, and equipment section

DANIER LEATHER INC.
Notes to the Financial Statements
December 24, 2011
(in thousands)

Note 7. Property and Equipment

	Cost	Accumulated Amortization	Net Carrying Value
Land	$ 1,000	$ –	$ 1,000
Building	6,063	2,275	3,788
Roof	308	193	115
Heating, ventilation, and air conditioning	793	554	239
Leasehold improvements	23,745	17,364	6,381
Furniture & equipment	9,277	6,369	2,908
Computer hardware	3,277	2,393	884
	$44,463	$29,148	$15,315

Note that, except for land (which has an unlimited useful life), all other property, plant, and equipment items are depreciated. This includes leasehold improvements, which are long-lived additions or renovations made to leased property.

Intangible Assets and Goodwill

Intangible assets are long-lived assets that do not have physical substance. They give a company rights and privileges and include such things as patents, copyrights, franchises, trademarks, trade names, and licences.

Intangible assets are normally divided into two groups for accounting purposes: those with definite lives and those with indefinite lives. Similar to buildings and equipment, the cost of intangible assets with definite useful lives is allocated to expense over their useful lives. Similar to land, the cost of intangible assets with indefinite lives is not allocated over future periods.

As we learned in Chapter 3, the term "depreciation" is normally used for the allocation of cost over the useful lives of property, plant, and equipment; the term "amortization" is used for the allocation of the cost of intangible assets. We will learn more about intangible assets in Chapter 9.

An asset that is similar to intangible assets is goodwill. Goodwill results from the acquisition of another company when the price paid for the company is higher than the fair value of the purchased company's net assets. In Illustration 4-7, MacDonald Company reported $5,000 of an intangible asset, licences, and $3,100 of goodwill.

Illustration 4-12 shows how Research In Motion Limited (now called BlackBerry Limited) reported intangible assets and goodwill in its balance sheet. The word "net" indicates accumulated amortization has been deducted from the cost of the intangible assets. The notes to the financial statements explain that the intangible assets are composed of patents, licences, and acquired technology. As required by IFRS, Research In Motion's balance sheet reports goodwill separately from intangible assets.

ILLUSTRATION 4-12
Intangible assets and goodwill section

RESEARCH IN MOTION LIMITED
Balance Sheet (partial)
November 26, 2011
(in USD millions)

Intangible assets, net	$2,472
Goodwill	659

Current Liabilities

Current liabilities are obligations that are expected to be settled within one year from the balance sheet date or in the company's operating cycle. As with current assets, companies use a period longer than one year if their operating cycle is longer than one year. In this textbook, we will always assume an operating cycle equal to, or shorter than, one year.

Common examples of current liabilities are notes payable, accounts payable, salaries payable, interest payable, sales taxes payable, unearned revenues, and current maturities of non-current liabilities (payments to be made within the next year on long-term debt). Corporations may also have income taxes payable included in the current liabilities section of the balance sheet. In Illustration 4-7, MacDonald Company reported six different types of current liabilities, for a total of $17,050.

Similar to current assets, North American companies often list current liabilities in order of liquidity. That is, the liabilities that will be due first are listed first. However, many companies simply list the items in their current liabilities section according to a company tradition. Some international companies list current liabilities in reverse order of liquidity, similar to current assets.

The current liabilities section from Tim Hortons Inc.'s balance sheet is shown in Illustration 4-13.

Users of financial statements look closely at the relationship between current assets and current liabilities. This relationship is important in evaluating a company's ability to pay its current liabilities. We will talk more about this later in the chapter when we learn how to use the information in the financial statements.

ILLUSTRATION 4-13
Current liabilities section

TIM HORTONS INC. Balance Sheet (partial) January 1, 2012 (in thousands)	
Current liabilities	
Accounts payable (note 13)	$177,918
Accrued liabilities	
Salaries and wages	23,531
Taxes	26,465
Other (note 13)	179,315
Advertising fund restricted liabilities (note 21)	59,420
Current portion of long-term obligations	10,001
	476,650

Non-Current Liabilities

Obligations that are expected to be paid after one year or longer are classified as **non-current liabilities.** Liabilities in this category can include bonds payable, mortgages payable, notes payable, lease liabilities, and deferred income taxes (income taxes payable after more than one year), among others. In Illustration 4-7, MacDonald Company reported non-current liabilities of $10,300.

Alternative terminology
Non-current liabilities are sometimes called *long-term liabilities, long-term obligations,* or *long-term debt.*

Illustration 4-14 shows the non-current liabilities that Sears Canada Inc. reported on a recent balance sheet, or statement of financial position as Sears calls it.

ILLUSTRATION 4-14
Non-current liabilities section

SEARS CANADA INC. Statement of Financial Position (partial) January 28, 2012 (in millions)	
Non-current liabilities	
Long-term obligations (notes 14, 17, 19, and 24)	$117.6
Deferred revenue (note 13)	89.2
Retirement benefit liability (note 20.1)	144.1
Deferred tax liabilities (note 22)	48.9
Other long-term liabilities (notes 16 and 18)	75.8
	475.6

The notes contain additional details about the liabilities, including how much must be paid during each of the next five years. The notes also contain information about restrictions placed on Sears Canada as a result of these obligations.

Equity

As introduced in Chapter 1, the name and specific accounts of the equity section vary with the form of business organization. In a proprietorship, there is one capital account under the heading "Owner's equity." In a partnership, there is a capital account for each partner under the heading "Partners' equity."

For a corporation, shareholders' equity always includes two parts: share capital and retained earnings. Amounts that are invested in the business by the shareholders are recorded as share capital. Profit that is kept for use in the business is recorded in the retained earnings account. We will learn more about corporation equity accounts in later chapters.

ALTERNATIVE BALANCE SHEET PRESENTATION

It is important to note that, when it comes to balance sheet presentation, both IFRS and ASPE allow for some choices. It is also interesting to note that, as different countries have adopted IFRS, where choices exist, companies have continued to follow the practices they used prior to adopting IFRS. Thus, the differences

in balance sheet presentation when following IFRS, as compared with ASPE, are not necessarily that significant.

We will look at three differences that could arise.

Statement Name

IFRS uses "statement of financial position" and ASPE uses "balance sheet" in the written standards. But both sets of standards allow companies to use either of these titles. While "statement of financial position" more accurately describes the content of the statement, "balance sheet" has been much more widely used in Canada. As many Canadian companies, both public and private, continue to use "balance sheet," we also use that term in this textbook.

Classification of Assets

Both IFRS and ASPE require companies to separately present current assets; property, plant, and equipment; intangible assets; goodwill; and long-term investments in the same way as in Illustration 4-7. The standards are designed to ensure separate presentation on the face of the balance sheet for items that are different in nature or function.

In practice, companies following IFRS typically include the heading "non-current assets" on the balance sheet, and group property, plant, and equipment; intangible assets; goodwill; and long-term investments under this heading. You will note that this method is used in Reitmans' balance sheet in Appendix A at the end of this book.

We did not use the heading "non-current assets" in the MacDonald Company example in Illustration 4-7 because it has not been used by many Canadian companies. It has always been assumed that if an asset is not included with current assets, then it must be a non-current asset. Because of this assumption, it is not necessary to use the "non-current asset" heading under IFRS and ASPE. Therefore, we do not use it in illustrations in this textbook.

Order of Items

Illustration 4-7 uses the common Canadian practice of ordering items on the balance sheet in order of liquidity (from the most to the least liquid). Accounting standards do not lay down the order in which items are to be presented in the balance sheet. Companies are allowed to choose how to order items, depending on the nature of the company and its transactions, to provide information that is relevant to understanding the company's financial position.

As mentioned earlier, international companies often present the balance sheet in reverse order of liquidity. Some Canadian companies, particularly financial institutions and real estate companies, use the reverse-liquidity order format as well.

Statements prepared using reverse-liquidity order usually show assets first, followed by shareholders' equity, then liabilities. Non-current assets are shown before current assets and non-current liabilities before current liabilities.

Alternative Presentation Illustrated

In order to help you understand some of the potential differences in balance sheet presentation, we have created a balance sheet for a hypothetical company, International MacDonald Limited, shown in Illustration 4-15. The information is based on the balance sheet for MacDonald Company, shown earlier in Illustration 4-7.

In Illustration 4-15, we have assumed the business is an incorporated company, not a proprietorship as in Illustration 4-7, in order to show the differences in the equity section. Notice the different statement name, the different classifications, and the different order of items in the statement. But total assets, and total liabilities and equity, are still the same amounts.

ILLUSTRATION 4-15
Classified statement of financial position in reverse order of liquidity

INTERNATIONAL MACDONALD LIMITED
Statement of Financial Position
November 30, 2014

Assets			
Non-current assets			
Goodwill			$ 3,100
Licences			5,000
Property, plant, and equipment			
Land		$35,000	
Building	$75,000		
Less: Accumulated depreciation	15,000	60,000	
Equipment	$24,000		
Less: Accumulated depreciation	5,000	19,000	
Total property, plant, and equipment			114,000
Long-term investments			
Equity investment		$ 5,200	
Debt investment		2,000	
Total long-term investments			7,200
Total non-current assets			129,300
Current assets			
Prepaid insurance		$ 400	
Supplies		2,100	
Inventories		4,000	
Accounts receivable		7,000	
Short-term investments		2,000	
Cash		6,600	
Total current assets			22,100
Total assets			$151,400
Equity and Liabilities			
Shareholders' equity			
Share capital		$74,000	
Retained earnings		50,050	
Total shareholders' equity			$124,050
Non-current liabilities			
Mortgage payable		$ 9,000	
Long-term notes payable		1,300	
Total non-current liabilities			$ 10,300
Current liabilities			
Current portion of long-term notes payable		$ 1,000	
Interest payable		450	
Salaries payable		1,600	
Unearned revenue		900	
Accounts payable		2,100	
Short-term notes payable		11,000	
Total current liabilities			17,050
Total liabilities			27,350
Total equity and liabilities			$151,400

ACCOUNTING IN ACTION
ALL ABOUT YOU INSIGHT

Similar to a company's balance sheet, a personal balance sheet reports what you own and what you owe. What are the items of value that you own—your personal assets? Some assets are liquid—such as cash or short-term savings. Others, such as vehicles, real estate, and some types of investments, are less liquid. Some assets, such as real estate and investments, tend to increase in value, thereby increasing your personal equity. Other assets, such as vehicles and electronics, tend to decline in value, thereby decreasing your personal equity.

What are the amounts that you owe—your personal liabilities? Loans, credit cards? Your equity is the difference between your total assets and total liabilities. Financial planners call this your *net worth* or *personal equity*.

Each quarter, Statistics Canada reports on the national balance sheet accounts and net worth of households in Canada. Household debt continued to rise in 2011, from $44,500 per capita to $46,700. At the same time, Canadian stock prices fell significantly, resulting in a drop in household net worth from $183,300 per capita to $182,200. You could use this information to create the average household's balance sheet at December 31, 2011, as follows:

Assets	=	Liabilities (Debt)	+	Equity (Net Worth)
$228,900	=	$46,700	+	$182,200

In more general terms this also means that the average household had 26 cents of debt for every $1 of net worth as at December 31, 2011. While this might not be a problem, it is the trend that concerns the government. At December 31, 2010, the average household had only 24 cents of debt for every $1 of net worth.

How can you increase your net worth? As a student, you may not have a lot of assets now, but by learning to control your spending and using debt wisely, you will be better able to increase your net worth when you start working full-time.

Source: Statistics Canada, "National balance sheet accounts," *The Daily*, Thursday, March 15, 2012.

How can preparing a personal balance sheet help you manage your net worth?

BEFORE YOU GO ON...

Action Plan

- Current assets include all assets that will be realized within one year.
- Current liabilities are obligations that are expected to be paid within one year.
- Non-current assets are all assets that will be realized in more than one year.
- Obligations that are due after more than one year are classified as non-current liabilities.

DO IT

The following selected accounts were taken from a company's balance sheet:

Accounts payable	Merchandise inventories
Accounts receivable	Mortgage payable (due in 10 years)
Accumulated depreciation—buildings	Notes receivable (due in 5 years)
Current portion of notes payable	Other investments
Goodwill	Short-term investments
Intangibles	Unearned revenue
Interest payable	Vehicles

Classify each of the above accounts as current assets, non-current assets, current liabilities, or non-current liabilities.

SOLUTION

Account	Balance Sheet Classification
Accounts payable	Current liabilities
Accounts receivable	Current assets
Accumulated depreciation—buildings	Non-current assets
Current portion of notes payable	Current liabilities
Goodwill	Non-current assets
Intangibles	Non-current assets
Interest payable	Current liabilities
Merchandise inventories	Current assets
Mortgage payable (due in 10 years)	Non-current liabilities
Notes receivable (due in 5 years)	Non-current assets

BEFORE YOU GO ON... continued on next page

BEFORE YOU GO ON...
continued from previous page

Account	Balance Sheet Classification
Other investments	Non-current assets
Short-term investments	Current assets
Unearned revenue	Current liabilities
Vehicles	Non-current assets

Related exercise material: BE4–9, BE4–10, and E4–9.

THE NAVIGATOR

USING THE INFORMATION IN THE FINANCIAL STATEMENTS

STUDY OBJECTIVE 5
Illustrate measures used to evaluate liquidity.

In Chapter 1, we briefly discussed how the financial statements give information about a company's performance and financial position. In this chapter, we will begin to learn about a tool, called ratio analysis, that can be used to analyze financial statements in order to make a more meaningful evaluation of a company. Ratio analysis expresses the relationships between selected items in the financial statements to help management identify areas for improvement.

As you study the chapters of this book, you will learn about three general types of ratios that are used to analyze financial statements: liquidity, profitability, and solvency ratios. **Liquidity ratios** measure a company's **liquidity**—the company's ability to pay its obligations as they come due within the next year and to meet unexpected needs for cash. As the name suggests, **profitability ratios** measure a company's profit or operating success for a specific period of time. **Solvency ratios** measure a company's ability to pay its total liabilities and survive over a long period of time. In this chapter, we introduce three liquidity ratios: working capital, the current ratio, and the acid-test ratio.

Helpful hint Liquidity ratios focus on the short term, whereas solvency ratios focus on the long term.

WORKING CAPITAL

When liquidity is being evaluated, an important relationship is the one between current assets and current liabilities. The difference between current assets and current liabilities is called **working capital**. Working capital is important because it shows a company's ability to pay its short-term debts. When current assets are more than current liabilities at the balance sheet date, the company will likely be able to pay its liabilities. When the reverse is true, short-term creditors may not be paid.

Reitmans' working capital is $277,851 thousand, as shown in Illustration 4-16, where amounts are in thousands.

ILLUSTRATION 4-16
Working capital

CURRENT RATIO

A second measure of short-term debt-paying ability is the **current ratio**, which is calculated by dividing current assets by current liabilities. The current ratio is a more dependable indicator of liquidity measures than working capital. Two companies with the same amount of working capital may have very different current ratios.

Illustration 4-17 (in thousands of dollars) shows the current ratio for Reitmans at January 28, 2012:

ILLUSTRATION 4-17
Current ratio

This ratio tells us that on January 28, 2012, Reitmans had $4.12 of current assets for every dollar of current liabilities. As a general rule, a higher current ratio indicates better liquidity.

The current ratio is useful, but it does not take into account the composition of the current assets. For example, a satisfactory current ratio does not disclose the fact that a portion of current assets may be tied up in slow-moving inventory or overdue receivables.

ACCOUNTING IN ACTION

BUSINESS INSIGHT

Generally, a higher current ratio is better as it indicates more liquidity—a company's ability to pay its short-term debts. But how high is too high? Some analysts argue that a current ratio of more than 3 or 4 is not good because it might mean that accounts receivable or inventory is building up. It could also mean that the company has too much cash and short-term investments that are not earning a greater rate of return or are not being put back into the business. But sometimes a high current ratio can be good, such as when a company is building up cash for strategic moves. For example, after Microsoft Corporation's current ratio reached 4, it paid shareholders its first dividend ever, made more acquisitions, and repurchased billions of dollars worth of shares. Afterwards, Microsoft's current ratio returned to a more moderate range of between 2 and 3. What is considered a desirable current ratio also varies by industry. For example, restaurants tend to have low current ratios because they usually have little or no accounts receivable.

Sources: "Current Ratio," Reuters Financial Glossary; Joshua Kennon, "The Current Ratio," the About website; Bloomberg Businessweek, "Microsoft Corp."

Does a current ratio of less than 1 indicate the company will have problems paying its obligations?

ACID-TEST RATIO

Alternative terminology
The acid-test ratio is also known as the *quick ratio.*

The **acid-test ratio** is a measure of the company's immediate short-term liquidity. The ratio is calculated by dividing the sum of cash, short-term investments, and receivables by current liabilities. These assets are highly liquid compared with inventory and prepaid expenses. The inventory may not be readily saleable, and the prepaid expenses may not be transferable to others.

Illustration 4-18 (in thousands of dollars) shows the acid-test ratio for Reitmans at January 28, 2012.

ILLUSTRATION 4-18
Acid-test ratio

(Cash + Short-Term Investments + Receivables)	÷	Current Liabilities	=	Acid-Test Ratio
$271,310	÷	$89,132	=	3.04

This ratio tells us that on January 28, 2012, Reitmans had $3.04 of highly liquid assets for every dollar of current liabilities. As with the current ratio, a higher acid-test ratio generally indicates better liquidity.

Ratios should never be interpreted without considering certain factors: (1) general economic and industry conditions, (2) other specific financial information about the company over time, and (3) comparison with ratios for other companies in the same or related industries. We will have a longer discussion about how to interpret ratios in Chapter 17.

BEFORE YOU GO ON...

DO IT

Selected financial information is available at December 31 for Dominic Co.

	2014	2013
Cash	$ 5,460	$ 6,645
Accounts receivable	3,505	3,470
Current assets	18,475	19,035
Current liabilities	18,860	17,305

(a) Calculate (1) working capital, (2) the current ratio, and (3) the acid-test ratio for 2013 and 2014.
(b) Indicate whether there was an improvement or deterioration in liquidity for Dominic in 2014.

Action Plan

- Subtract current liabilities from current assets to calculate working capital.
- Divide current assets by current liabilities to calculate current ratio.

BEFORE YOU GO ON...
continued on next page

SOLUTION

(a)

	2014	2013
(1) Working capital	= $18,475 − $18,860	= $19,035 − $17,305
	= $(385)	= $1,730
(2) Current ratio	= $18,475 ÷ $18,860	= $19,035 ÷ $17,305
	= 0.98 to 1	= 1.1 to 1
(3) Acid-test ratio	= ($5,460 + $3,505) / $18,860	= ($6,645 + $3,470) / $17,305
	= 0.48 to 1	= 0.58 to 1

(b) Working capital, the current ratio, and the acid-test ratio have all decreased in 2014 from 2013. This means that the company's liquidity has deteriorated during 2014.

Related exercise material: BE4–11, BE4–12, and E4–11.

BEFORE YOU GO ON...
continued from previous page

- Divide cash plus accounts receivable by current liabilities to calculate acid-test ratio.
- Recall if higher or lower ratios indicate if liquidity has improved or deteriorated.

THE NAVIGATOR

WORK SHEETS

APPENDIX 4A

STUDY OBJECTIVE 6
Prepare a work sheet.

As discussed in the chapter, a work sheet is a multiple-column form that may be used in the adjustment process and in preparing financial statements. The five steps for preparing a work sheet are described in the next section. They must be done in the order they are presented in.

STEPS IN PREPARING A WORK SHEET

We will use the October 31 trial balance and adjustment data for Pioneer Advertising Agency from Chapter 3 to show how to prepare a work sheet. Each step of the process is described below and is shown in Illustration 4A-1.

Step 1. Prepare a Trial Balance on the Work Sheet.

Enter all ledger accounts with balances in the account title space. Debit and credit balances from the ledger are entered in the trial balance columns.

Step 2. Enter the Adjustments in the Adjustment Columns.

When a work sheet is used, all adjustments are entered in the adjustment columns. In entering the adjustments, relevant trial balance accounts should be used. If additional accounts are needed, they should be inserted on the lines immediately below the trial balance totals. A different letter identifies the corresponding debit and credit for each adjusting entry.

Helpful hint Additional accounts, such as supplies expense and depreciation expense, are only used at year end.

Year-end adjustments must still be recorded in the journal, but not until after the work sheet is completed and the financial statements have been prepared.

The adjustments on Pioneer Advertising Agency's work sheet in Illustration 4A-1 are the adjustments from the Pioneer Advertising Agency example in Chapter 3. They are recorded in the adjustment columns of the work sheet (and noted by letter in the Item column) as follows:

(a) Debit Supplies Expense (an additional account) $1,500 for the cost of supplies used, and credit Supplies $1,500.
(b) Debit Insurance Expense (an additional account) $50 for the insurance that has expired, and credit Prepaid Insurance $50.
(c) Debit Unearned Revenue $400 for fees previously collected and now earned, and credit Service Revenue $400.
(d) Debit Accounts Receivable $200 for fees earned but not billed, and credit Service Revenue $200.
(e) Two additional accounts relating to interest are needed. Debit Interest Expense $25 for accrued interest, and credit Interest Payable $25.
(f) Debit Salaries Expense $2,000 for accrued salaries, and credit Salaries Payable (an additional account) $2,000.
(g) Two additional accounts are needed. Debit Depreciation Expense $83 for the month's depreciation, and credit Accumulated Depreciation—Equipment $83.

ILLUSTRATION 4A-1
Preparing a work sheet—Steps 1 to 5

Pioneer Advertising Agency
Work Sheet
Month Ended October 31, 2014

Account Titles	Unadjusted Trial Balance Dr.	Unadjusted Trial Balance Cr.	Adjustments Dr.	Item	Adjustments Cr.	Adjusted Trial Balance Dr.	Adjusted Trial Balance Cr.	Income Statement Dr.	Income Statement Cr.	Balance Sheet Dr.	Balance Sheet Cr.
Cash	14,250					14,250				14,250	
Accounts receivable	1,000		200	(d)		1,200				1,200	
Supplies	2,500			(a)	1,500	1,000				1,000	
Prepaid insurance	600			(b)	50	550				550	
Equipment	5,000					5,000				5,000	
Notes payable		5,000					5,000				5,000
Accounts payable		1,750					1,750				1,750
Unearned revenue		1,200	400	(c)			800				800
C. Bedard, capital		10,000					10,000				10,000
C. Bedard, drawings	500					500				500	
Service revenue		10,800		(c)	400		11,400		11,400		
				(d)	200						
Rent expense	900					900		900			
Salaries expense	4,000		2,000	(f)		6,000		6,000			
Supplies expense			1,500	(a)		1,500		1,500			
Insurance expense			50	(b)		50		50			
Interest expense			25	(e)		25		25			
Interest payable				(e)	25		25				25
Salaries payable				(f)	2,000		2,000				2,000
Depreciation expense			83	(g)		83		83			
Accumulated depreciation–equipment				(g)	83		83				83
Totals	28,750	28,750	4,258		4,258	31,058	31,058	8,558	11,400	22,500	19,658
Profit						-		2,842			2,842
								11,400	11,400	22,500	22,500

1. Prepare a trial balance on the work sheet

2. Enter adjustment data

3. Enter adjusted balances

4. Enter adjusted balances in appropriate statement columns

5. Total the statement columns, calculate profit (or loss), and complete the work sheet

Note in the illustration that, after all the adjustments have been entered, the adjustment columns are totalled to prove the equality of the two adjustment column totals.

Step 3. Enter the Adjusted Balances in the Adjusted Trial Balance Columns.

The adjusted balance of an account is calculated by combining the amounts entered in the first four columns of the work sheet for each account. For example, the Prepaid Insurance account in the trial balance columns in Illustration 4A-1 has a $600 debit balance and a $50 credit in the adjustment columns. These two amounts combine to result in a $550 debit balance in the adjusted trial balance columns. For each account on the work sheet, the amount in the adjusted trial balance columns is equal to the account balance that will appear in the ledger after the adjusting entries have been journalized and posted. The balances in these columns are the same as those in the adjusted trial balance in Illustration 4-3.

After all account balances have been entered in the adjusted trial balance columns, the columns are totalled to prove the equality of the two columns. If these columns do not agree, the financial statement columns will not balance and the financial statements will be incorrect. The total of each of these two columns in Illustration 4A-1 is $31,058.

Step 4. Enter the Adjusted Trial Balance Amounts in the Correct Financial Statement Columns.

The fourth step is to enter adjusted trial balance amounts in the income statement or balance sheet columns of the work sheet. Balance sheet accounts are entered in the correct balance sheet debit and credit columns. For instance, Cash is entered in the balance sheet debit column and Notes Payable is entered in the credit column. Accumulated Depreciation is entered in the credit column because it has a credit balance.

Helpful hint Every adjusted trial balance amount must appear in *exactly* one of the four statement columns.

Because the work sheet does not have columns for the statement of owner's equity, the balance in owner's capital is entered in the balance sheet credit column. In addition, the balance in the owner's drawings account is entered in the balance sheet debit column because it is an owner's equity account with a debit balance.

The amounts in revenue and expense accounts such as Service Revenue and Salaries Expense are entered in the correct income statement columns. The last four columns of Illustration 4A-1 show where each account is entered.

Step 5. Total the Statement Columns, Calculate the Profit (or Loss), and Complete the Work Sheet.

Each of the financial statement columns must be totalled. The profit or loss for the period is then found by calculating the difference between the totals of the two income statement columns. If total credits are more than total debits, profit has resulted. In such a case, as shown in Illustration 4A-1, the word "Profit" is inserted in the account title space. The amount is then entered in the income statement debit column so that the totals of the two income statement columns are equal.

The profit or loss must also be entered in the balance sheet columns. If there is a profit, as is the case for Pioneer Advertising Agency, the amount is entered in the balance sheet credit column. The credit column is used because profit increases owner's equity. It is also necessary to enter the *exact* same amount in the credit column of the balance sheet as was entered in the debit column of the income statement so the financial statement columns will balance.

Conversely, if total debits in the income statement columns are more than total credits, a loss has occurred. In such a case, the amount of the loss is entered in the income statement credit column (to balance the income statement columns) and the balance sheet debit column (because a loss decreases owner's equity).

Helpful hint If total credits (revenues) in the income statement section of the work sheet are greater than total debits (expenses), the balancing figure represents a profit.

After the profit or loss has been entered, new column totals are determined. The totals shown in the debit and credit income statement columns will now match. The totals shown in the debit and credit balance sheet columns will also match. If either the income statement columns or the balance sheet columns are not equal after the profit or loss has been entered, there is an error in the work sheet.

PREPARING FINANCIAL STATEMENTS FROM A WORK SHEET

After a work sheet has been completed, all the data required to prepare the financial statements are at hand. The income statement is prepared from the income statement columns. The balance sheet and statement of owner's equity are prepared from the balance sheet columns.

Note that the amount shown for owner's capital in the work sheet is the account balance before considering drawings and profit (loss). When there have been no additional investments of capital by the owner during the period, this amount is the balance at the beginning of the period.

Helpful hint The work sheet can be thought of as the "rough copy" while the financial statements can be thought of as the "good copy."

Using a work sheet, accountants can prepare financial statements before adjusting entries have been journalized and posted. However, the completed work sheet is not a substitute for formal financial statements. Data in the financial statement columns of the work sheet are not properly arranged for statement purposes. Also, as noted earlier, the financial statement presentation for some accounts differs from their statement columns on the work sheet. A work sheet is basically an accountant's working tool. It is not given to management or other parties.

BEFORE YOU GO ON...

DO IT

Susan Elbe is preparing a work sheet. Explain to Susan how she should extend the following adjusted trial balance accounts to the financial statement columns of the work sheet.

Accumulated Depreciation—Equipment
B. Sykes, Drawings
Cash
Equipment
Salaries Expense
Salaries Payable
Service Revenue

Action Plan

- Assets and drawings belong in the balance sheet debit column.
- Liabilities, capital, and contra assets belong in the balance sheet credit column.
- Revenues belong in the income statement credit column.
- Expenses belong in the income statement debit column.

SOLUTION

Account	Work Sheet Column
Accumulated Depreciation—Equipment	Balance sheet credit column
B. Sykes, Drawings	Balance sheet debit column
Cash	Balance sheet debit column
Equipment	Balance sheet debit column
Salaries Expense	Income statement debit column
Salaries Payable	Balance sheet credit column
Service Revenue	Income statement credit column

Related exercise material: *BE4–13, *BE4–14, and *E4–11.

THE  NAVIGATOR

APPENDIX 4B REVERSING ENTRIES

STUDY OBJECTIVE 7
Prepare reversing entries.

After the financial statements are prepared and the books are closed, it can be helpful to reverse some of the adjusting entries before recording the regular transactions of the next period. Such entries are called reversing entries. A reversing entry is made at the beginning of the next accounting period and is the exact opposite of the adjusting entry that was made in the previous period. The recording of reversing entries is an optional step in the accounting cycle.

The purpose of reversing entries is to simplify the recording of future transactions that are related to an adjusting entry. As you may recall from Chapter 3, Pioneer Advertising Agency's payment of salaries on November 7 after an adjusting entry resulted in two debits: one to Salaries Payable and the other to Salaries Expense. With reversing entries, the entire later payment can be debited to Salaries Expense.

You do not have to remember what has gone on before. The use of reversing entries does not change the amounts reported in the financial statements. It simply makes it easier to record transactions in the next accounting period.

ACCOUNTING WITH AND WITHOUT REVERSING ENTRIES

Reversing entries are used to reverse two types of adjusting entries: accrued revenues and accrued expenses. To illustrate the optional use of reversing entries for accrued expenses, we will use the salaries expense transactions for Pioneer Advertising Agency shown in Chapters 2, 3, and 4. The transaction and adjustment data were as follows:

1. October 24 (initial salary entry): Salaries of $4,000 earned between October 13 and October 24 are paid.
2. October 31 (adjusting entry): Salaries earned between October 24 and October 31 are $2,000. The company will pay the employees this amount in the November 7 payroll.
3. November 7 (subsequent salary entry): Salaries paid are $4,000. Of this amount, $2,000 applies to accrued salaries payable and $2,000 was earned between November 1 and November 7.

The comparative entries with and without reversing entries are as follows.

When Reversing Entries Are Not Used (as in the chapter)

Date	Account	Debit	Credit
	Initial Salary Entry		
Oct. 24	Salaries Expense	4,000	
	Cash		4,000
	Adjusting Entry		
31	Salaries Expense	2,000	
	Salaries Payable		2,000
	Closing Entry		
31	Income Summary	6,000	
	Salaries Expense		6,000
	Reversing Entry		
Nov. 1	**No reversing entry is made.**		
	Subsequent Salary Entry		
7	**Salaries Payable**	2,000	
	Salaries Expense	2,000	
	Cash		4,000

When Reversing Entries Are Used (as in the appendix)

Date	Account	Debit	Credit
	Initial Salary Entry		
Oct. 24	(Same Entry)		
	Adjusting Entry		
31	(Same Entry)		
	Closing Entry		
31	(Same Entry)		
	Reversing Entry		
Nov. 1	**Salaries Payable**	**2,000**	
	Salaries Expense		**2,000**
	Subsequent Salary Entry		
7	**Salaries Expense**	**4,000**	
	Cash		**4,000**

The first three entries are the same whether or not reversing entries are used. The last two entries are different. The November 1 reversing entry eliminates the $2,000 balance in Salaries Payable that was created by the October 31 adjusting entry. The reversing entry also creates a $2,000 credit balance in the Salaries Expense account. As you know, it is unusual for an expense account to have a credit balance. The balance is correct in this instance, though, because it anticipates that the entire amount of the first salary payment in the new accounting period will be debited to Salaries Expense. This debit will eliminate the credit balance, and the resulting debit balance in the expense account will equal the actual salaries expense in the new accounting period ($2,000 in this example).

When reversing entries are made, all cash payments of expenses can be debited to the expense account. This means that on November 7 (and every payday) Salaries Expense can be debited for the amount paid without regard to any accrued salaries payable. Being able to make the same entry each time simplifies the recording process: future transactions can be recorded as if the related adjusting entry had never been made.

The posting of the entries with reversing entries is as follows, using T accounts.

Salaries Expense

Debit		Credit	
Oct. 24 Paid	4,000		
31 Adj.	2,000		
Oct. 31 Bal.	6,000	Oct. 31 Clos.	6,000
Oct. 31 Bal.	0	**Nov. 1 Rev.**	**2,000**
Nov. 7 Paid	**4,000**		
Nov. 7 Bal.	2,000		

Salaries Payable

Debit		Credit	
Nov. 1 Rev.	**2,000**	Oct. 31 Adj.	2,000
		Nov. 1 Bal.	0

Pioneer Advertising Agency could also have used reversing entries for accrued revenues. Recall that Pioneer had accrued revenues of $200, which were recorded by a debit to Accounts Receivable and credit to Service Revenue. Thus, the reversing entry on November 1 is:

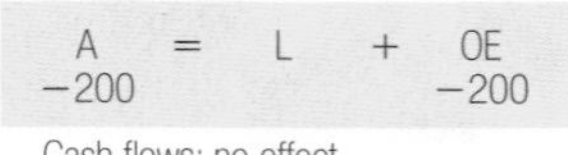

Cash flows: no effect

Date	Account	Debit	Credit
Nov. 1	Service Revenue	200	
	Accounts Receivable		200
	To reverse Oct. 31 accrued revenue adjusting entry.		

Later in November, when Pioneer collects the accrued revenue, it debits Cash and credits Service Revenue for the full amount collected. There would be no need to refer back to the October 31 adjusting entries to see how much relates to the prior month. Thus, as shown in the previous example with accrued expenses, the recording process is simplified.

BEFORE YOU GO ON...

DO IT

Pelican Company has a note receivable with a customer. On March 31, Pelican recorded an adjusting entry to accrue $300 of interest earned on the note. On April 30, Pelican collected $400 cash from the customer for interest earned from January 1 to April 30. Record Pelican's (a) March 31 adjusting entry, (b) April 1 reversing entry, and (c) April 30 entry.

Action Plan

- Adjusting entries for accrued revenues are required when revenue has been earned but not yet received in cash or recorded.
- A reversing entry is the exact opposite of the adjusting entry.
- When a reversing entry has been recorded, it is not necessary to refer to the previous adjustment when recording the subsequent receipt of cash.

SOLUTION

Date	Account	Debit	Credit
(a) Mar. 31	Interest Receivable	300	
	Interest Revenue		300
	To record accrued interest.		
(b) Apr. 1	Interest Revenue	300	
	Interest Receivable		300
	To reverse Mar. 31 adjusting entry.		
(c) Apr. 3	Cash	400	
	Interest Revenue		400
	To record interest collected.		

Related exercise material: *BE4–15, *BE4–16, *E4–12, and *E4–13.

THE NAVIGATOR

Comparing IFRS and ASPE

Key Differences	International Financial Reporting Standards (IFRS)	Accounting Standards for Private Enterprises (ASPE)
Statement name	Use "statement of financial position" but "balance sheet" is allowed.	Use "balance sheet" but "statement of financial position" is allowed.
Classification of assets	May group together property, plant, and equipment; intangibles; goodwill; and long-term investments under "non-current assets."	Typically do not use the subheading "non-current assets."
Order of presentation	May present assets, liabilities, and shareholders' equity in reverse order of liquidity.	Typically present assets and liabilities in order of liquidity.

THE NAVIGATOR

DEMONSTRATION PROBLEM

At the end of its first month of operations, Paquet Answering Service has the following unadjusted trial balance, with the accounts presented in alphabetical order rather than in financial statement order:

PAQUET ANSWERING SERVICE
Trial Balance
August 31, 2014

	Debit	Credit
Accounts payable		$ 2,400
Accounts receivable	$ 2,800	
Accumulated depreciation—building		500
Accumulated depreciation—equipment		1,000
Advertising expense	400	
Cash	5,400	
Building	150,000	
Depreciation expense	1,500	
Equipment	60,000	
Insurance expense	200	
Interest expense	350	
Interest payable		1,350
Land	50,000	
Long-term debt investments	15,000	
Long-term equity investments	7,000	
Mortgage payable		140,000
Prepaid insurance	2,200	
R. Paquet, capital		155,000
R. Paquet, drawings	1,000	
Rent revenue		700
Salaries expense	3,200	
Service revenue		5,000
Short-term investments	4,800	
Supplies	1,000	
Supplies expense	300	
Utilities expense	800	
Totals	$305,950	$305,950

DEMONSTRATION PROBLEM continued on next page

DEMONSTRATION PROBLEM continued from previous page

Instructions

(a) Calculate the profit or loss for the month.
(b) Calculate owner's equity at August 31, 2014.
(c) Prepare a classified balance sheet for Paquet Answering Service at August 31, 2014. Assume that $5,000 of the mortgage payable is due over the next year.
(d) Journalize the closing entries.
(e) Create T accounts for Income Summary and R. Paquet, Capital, and post the closing entries.
(f) Prepare a post-closing trial balance.
(g) Calculate working capital, current ratio, and acid-test ratio.

Action Plan

- Identify which accounts are balance sheet accounts and which are income statement accounts.
- If revenues are more than expenses, this results in a profit; if expenses are more than revenues, this results in a loss.
- In preparing a classified balance sheet, know the contents of each section.
- In journalizing closing entries, remember that there are four entries. Revenues and expenses are closed to the Income Summary account; the Income Summary account and the drawings account are closed to owner's capital.
- Always check your work. Make sure the balance in Income Summary equals profit before closing the Income Summary account. Make sure that the balance in the owner's capital account after posting the closing entries equals the amount reported on the balance sheet.
- In preparing a post-closing trial balance, put the accounts in financial statement order. Remember that all temporary accounts will have a zero balance and do not need to be included.
- Use the formulae to calculate ratios.

SOLUTION TO DEMONSTRATION PROBLEM

(a) Profit (loss) = Revenue − expenses
= $700 + $5,000 − $400 − $1,500 − $200 − $350 − $3,200 − $300 − $800
= $(1,050)

(b) Owner's equity at August 31, 2014 = Opening capital − loss − drawings
= $155,000 − $1,050 − $1,000
= $152,950

(c)

PAQUET ANSWERING SERVICE
Balance Sheet
August 31, 2014

Assets			
Current assets			
Cash			$ 5,400
Short-term investments			4,800
Accounts receivable			2,800
Prepaid insurance			2,200
Supplies			1,000
Total current assets			16,200
Long-term investments			
Equity investments		$ 7,000	
Debt investments		15,000	
Total long-term investments			22,000
Property, plant, and equipment			
Land		$ 50,000	
Building	$150,000		
Less: Accumulated depreciation	500	149,500	
Equipment	$ 60,000		
Less: Accumulated depreciation	1,000	59,000	258,500
Total assets			$296,700
Liabilities and Owner's Equity			
Current liabilities			
Accounts payable			$ 2,400
Interest payable			1,350
Current portion of mortgage payable			5,000
Total current liabilities			8,750
Non-current liabilities			
Mortgage payable			135,000
Total liabilities			143,750
Owner's equity			
R. Paquet, capital			152,950
Total liabilities and owner's equity			$296,700

SOLUTION TO DEMONSTRATION PROBLEM continued on next page

SOLUTION TO DEMONSTRATION PROBLEM continued from previous page

(d)

Aug. 31	Service Revenue	5,000	
	Rent Revenue	700	
	Income Summary		5,700
	To close revenue account.		
	Income Summary	6,750	
	Advertising Expense		400
	Depreciation Expense		1,500
	Insurance Expense		200
	Interest Expense		350
	Salaries Expense		3,200
	Supplies Expense		300
	Utilities Expense		800
	To close expense accounts.		
31	R. Paquet, Capital	1,050	
	Income Summary		1,050
	To close Income Summary.		
31	R. Paquet, Capital	1,000	
	R. Paquet, Drawings		1,000
	To close drawings.		

(e)

Income Summary

Clos.	6,750	Clos.	5,700
Bal.	1,050		
		Clos.	1,050
		Bal.	0

R. Paquet, Capital

		Bal.	155,000
Clos.	1,050		
Clos.	1,000		
		Bal.	152,950

(f)

PAQUET ANSWERING SERVICE
Post-Closing Trial Balance
August 31, 2014

	Debit	Credit
Cash	$ 5,400	
Short-term investments	4,800	
Accounts receivable	2,800	
Prepaid insurance	2,200	
Supplies	1,000	
Long-term equity investments	7,000	
Long-term debt investments	15,000	
Land	50,000	
Building	150,000	
Accumulated depreciation—building		$ 500
Equipment	60,000	
Accumulated depreciation—equipment		1,000
Accounts payable		2,400
Interest payable		1,350
Mortgage payable		140,000
R. Paquet, capital		152,950
Totals	$298,200	$298,200

SOLUTION TO DEMONSTRATION PROBLEM continued on next page

SOLUTION TO DEMONSTRATION PROBLEM continued from previous page

(g)

(1)	Working capital = Current assets − Current liabilities	= \$16,200 − \$8,750 = \$7,450
(2)	Current ratio = Current assets ÷ Current liabilities	= \$16,200 ÷ \$8,750 = 1.85 to 1
(3)	Acid-test ratio = (Cash + Short-term investments + Accounts receivable) / Current liabilities	= (\$5,400 + \$4,800 + \$2,800) / \$8,750 = 1.49 to 1

THE NAVIGATOR

Summary of Study Objectives

1. ***Prepare closing entries and a post-closing trial balance.*** At the end of an accounting period, the temporary account balances (revenues, expenses, income summary, and owner's drawings) are transferred to the owner's capital account by journalizing and posting closing entries. Separate entries are made to close revenues and expenses to Income Summary; then Income Summary to owner's capital; and, finally, owner's drawings to owner's capital. The temporary accounts begin the new period with zero balances and the owner's capital account is updated to show its end-of-period balance. A post-closing trial balance has the balances in permanent accounts (that is, balance sheet accounts) that are carried forward to the next accounting period. The purpose of this balance, as with other trial balances, is to prove the equality of these account balances.

2. ***Explain the steps in the accounting cycle including optional steps.*** The steps in the accounting cycle are (1) analyze business transactions, (2) journalize the transactions, (3) post to ledger accounts, (4) prepare a trial balance, (5) journalize and post adjusting entries, (6) prepare an adjusted trial balance, (7) prepare financial statements, (8) journalize and post closing entries, and (9) prepare a post-closing trial balance. A work sheet may be used to help prepare adjusting entries and financial statements. Reversing entries are an optional step that may be used at the beginning of the next accounting period.

3. ***Prepare correcting entries.*** Correcting entries are recorded whenever an error (an incorrect journal entry) is found. A correcting entry can be determined by comparing the incorrect entry with the journal entry that should have been recorded (the correct entry). The comparison will show which accounts need to be corrected and by how much. The correcting entry will correct the accounts. An equally acceptable alternative is to reverse the incorrect entry and then record the correct entry.

4. ***Prepare a classified balance sheet.*** In a classified balance sheet, assets are classified as current assets; long-term investments; property, plant, and equipment; intangible assets; and goodwill. Liabilities are classified as either current or non-current. Current assets are assets that will be consumed or converted into cash within one year of the balance sheet date. Current liabilities are liabilities that must be paid from current assets within one year of the balance sheet date. The classified balance also includes an equity section, which varies with the form of business organization.

5. ***Illustrate measures used to evaluate liquidity.*** One of the measures used to evaluate a company's short-term liquidity is its working capital, which is the excess of current assets over current liabilities. This can also be expressed as the current ratio (current assets ÷ current liabilities). The acid-test ratio is a measure of the company's immediate short-term liquidity and is calculated by dividing the sum of cash, short-term investments, and receivables by current liabilities.

6. ***Prepare a work sheet (Appendix 4A).*** A work sheet is an optional multi-column form, used to assist in preparing adjusting entries and financial statements. The steps in preparing a work sheet are (1) prepare a trial balance on the work sheet; (2) enter the adjustments in the adjustment columns; (3) enter adjusted balances in the adjusted trial balance columns; (4) enter adjusted trial balance amounts in the correct financial statement columns; and (5) total the statement columns, calculate profit (or loss), and complete the work sheet.

7. ***Prepare reversing entries (Appendix 4B).*** Reversing entries are optional entries used to simplify bookkeeping. They are made at the beginning of the new accounting period and are the direct opposite of the adjusting entry made in the preceding period. Only accrual adjusting entries are reversed. If reversing entries are used, then subsequent cash transactions can be recorded without referring to the adjusting entries prepared at the end of the previous period.

THE NAVIGATOR

Glossary

Acid-test ratio A measure of the company's immediate short-term liquidity. (p. 166)

Classified balance sheet A balance sheet that has several classifications or sections. (p. 156)

Closing entries Entries made at the end of an accounting period to transfer the balances of temporary accounts (revenues, expenses, income summary, and drawings) to the permanent owner's equity account, owner's capital. (p. 147)

Closing the books The process of journalizing and posting closing entries to update the capital account and prepare the temporary accounts for the next period's postings by reducing their balances to zero. (p. 146)

Correcting entries Entries to correct errors that were made when transactions were recorded. (p. 154)

Current assets Cash and other assets that will be converted to cash, sold, or used up within one year from the balance sheet date or in the company's normal operating cycle. (p. 157)

Current liabilities Obligations that are expected to be settled within one year from the balance sheet date or in the company's normal operating cycle. (p. 160)

Current ratio A measure of short-term debt-paying ability that is determined by dividing current assets by current liabilities. (p. 165)

Income Summary A temporary account that is used in closing revenue and expense accounts. (p. 147)

Intangible assets Long-lived assets that do not have physical substance and are rights and privileges that result from ownership. They include patents, copyrights, trademarks, trade names, and licences. (p. 160)

Liquidity The ability of a company to pay obligations as they come due within the next year and to meet unexpected needs for cash. (p. 165)

Long-term investments Investments in long-term debts that management intends to hold to earn interest or in equity of other companies that management plans to hold for many years as a strategic investment. (p. 158)

Non-current assets Assets that will not be converted to cash, sold, or used by the business within one year of the balance sheet date or its operating cycle. (p. 158)

Non-current liabilities Obligations that are expected to be paid after one year or longer. (p. 161)

Operating cycle The time it takes to go from starting with cash to ending with cash in producing revenues. (p. 157)

Permanent accounts Balance sheet accounts, whose balances are carried forward to the next accounting period. (p. 146)

Post-closing trial balance A list of debit and credit balances of the permanent (balance sheet) accounts after closing entries have been journalized and posted. (p. 151)

Property, plant, and equipment Long-lived tangible assets that are used in the operations of the business and are not intended for sale. They include land, buildings, equipment, and furniture. (p. 159)

Reversing entry An entry made at the beginning of the next accounting period that is the exact opposite of the adjusting entry made in the previous period. (p. 154)

Temporary accounts Revenue, expense, income summary, and drawings accounts, whose balances are transferred to owner's capital at the end of an accounting period. (p. 146)

Working capital The difference between current assets and current liabilities. (p. 165)

Work sheet A multiple-column form that may be used in the adjustment process and in preparing financial statements. (p. 153)

Note: All questions, exercises, and problems below with an asterisk (*) relate to material in Appendices 4A and 4B.

Self-Study Questions

Answers are at the end of the chapter.

(SO 1) K 1. When a loss has occurred, the journal entry to close the Income Summary account is:
(a) debit Income Summary; credit owner's capital.
(b) debit owner's capital; credit Income Summary.
(c) debit Income Summary; credit owner's drawings.
(d) debit owner's drawings; credit Income Summary.

(SO 1) K 2. After the closing entries have been posted, the balance in the owner's capital account should equal:
(a) the profit or loss reported on the income statement.
(b) the opening capital balance reported on the statement of owner's equity.
(c) the ending capital balance reported on the statement of owner's equity and balance sheet.
(d) the opening capital balance plus any investments made by the owner during the period.

(SO 1) K 3. Which accounts will appear in the post-closing trial balance?
(a) Assets, liabilities, and owner's capital
(b) Revenues, expenses, owner's drawings, and owner's capital
(c) Assets, liabilities, revenues, and expenses
(d) All accounts

(SO 2) K 4. The proper order of the following steps in the accounting cycle is:
(a) prepare unadjusted trial balance, journalize transactions, post to ledger accounts, journalize and post adjusting entries.
(b) journalize transactions, prepare unadjusted trial balance, post to ledger accounts, journalize and post adjusting entries.

(c) journalize transactions, post to ledger accounts, prepare unadjusted trial balance, journalize and post adjusting entries.
(d) prepare unadjusted trial balance, journalize and post adjusting entries, journalize transactions, post to ledger accounts.

(SO 2) C 5. Which of the following is an optional step in the accounting cycle?
(a) Journalizing and posting closing entries
(b) Journalizing and posting adjusting entries
(c) Analyzing transactions
(d) Journalizing and posting reversing entries

(SO 3) K 6. When Zander Company purchased supplies worth $500, it incorrectly recorded a credit to Supplies for $5,000 and a debit to Cash for $5,000. Before correcting this error:
(a) Cash is overstated and Supplies is overstated.
(b) Cash is understated and Supplies is understated.
(c) Cash is understated and Supplies is overstated.
(d) Cash is overstated and Supplies is understated.

(SO 3) AP 7. Cash of $550 is received at the time a service is provided. The transaction is journalized and posted as a debit to Accounts Receivable of $550 and a credit to Service Revenue of $550. The correcting entry is:

(a) Accounts Receivable	550	
Service Revenue		550
(b) Service Revenue	550	
Accounts Receivable		550
(c) Cash	550	
Service Revenue		550
(d) Cash	550	
Accounts Receivable		550

(SO 4) K 8. Which of the following statements about classifying assets is *correct*?
(a) Supplies are not current assets and should be included as part of property, plant, and equipment on the balance sheet.
(b) Current assets normally are cash and other assets that will be converted to cash, sold, or used up within one year from the balance sheet date.
(c) Some companies use a period shorter than one year to classify assets as current because they have an operating cycle that is shorter than one year.
(d) Prepaid expenses are considered non-current assets because they are intangible assets.

(SO 4) K 9. Non-current liabilities:
(a) are obligations that are expected to be paid before one year from the balance sheet date.
(b) cannot be called long-term liabilities.
(c) are sometimes listed on the balance sheet before current liabilities, if the company is following International Financial Reporting Standards.
(d) include accounts payable, salaries payable, and interest payable.

(SO 5) AP 10. A company reports current assets of $10,000 and current liabilities of $8,000. Its current ratio is:
(a) $2,000.
(b) 80%.
(c) 1.25:1.
(d) unknown without information about the amount of cash, short-term investments, and receivables, which is needed to calculate the ratio.

(SO 6) K *11. In a work sheet, profit is entered in the following columns:
(a) income statement (Dr.) and balance sheet (Dr.).
(b) income statement (Cr.) and balance sheet (Dr.).
(c) income statement (Dr.) and balance sheet (Cr.).
(d) income statement (Cr.) and balance sheet (Cr.).

(SO 7) AP *12. On December 31, 2014, Mott Company correctly made an adjusting entry to recognize $2,000 of accrued salaries payable. On January 8, 2015, total salaries of $3,400 were paid. Assuming the correct reversing entry was made on January 1, 2015, the entry on January 8, 2015, will result in a credit to Cash of $3,400, and the following debit(s):
(a) Salaries Expense $3,400.
(b) Salaries Payable $1,400, and Salaries Expense $2,000.
(c) Salaries Payable $2,000, and Salaries Expense $1,400.
(d) Salaries Payable $3,400.

THE NAVIGATOR

Questions

(SO 1) C 1. What are permanent and temporary accounts? What are the key differences between them?

(SO 1) C 2. What are the two reasons for recording closing entries?

(SO 1) C 3. What is the purpose of using an income summary account? If an income summary account was not used, how would the closing entries change?

(SO 1) C 4. Why is the owner's drawings account not closed with the expense accounts? Why is a separate entry required to close this account?

(SO 1) C 5. Brenda has been told that, after the closing entries have been posted, she should stop and check her work. Explain to Brenda what she should be checking for.

(SO 2) C 6. Balpreet thinks that analyzing business transactions is an optional step in the accounting cycle. Explain if this is correct or not.

(SO 2) C 7. Explain the differences between the three trial balances (i.e., trial balance, adjusted trial balance and post-closing trial balance) used in the accounting cycle and why is it important to prepare all three.

(SO 2) K 8. Which steps in the accounting cycle may be done daily? Which steps are done on a periodic basis (monthly, quarterly, or annually)? Which steps are usually done only at the company's fiscal year end?

(SO 2, 3) C 9. Eduardo argues that correcting entries and reversing entries are the same thing. Is Eduardo correct? Explain why or why not.

(SO 3) K 10. Complete the following table:

	Adjusting Entries	Correcting Entries
Are they a specific step in the accounting cycle? (Yes, no)		
When are they journalized?		
What types of accounts do they affect?		

(SO 3) C 11. Christobal thinks that correcting entries are unnecessary. He suggests that, if an incorrect journal entry is found, it should be erased or removed and then the correct entry can be recorded in its place. Explain to Christobal why this is not the correct thing to do.

(SO 3) C 12. Describe how to determine which accounts, and what amounts, to include in a correcting entry.

(SO 4) C 13. What are current assets and current liabilities? How are they different from non-current assets and non-current liabilities?

(SO 4) C 14. What is meant by the term "operating cycle"?

(SO 4) C 15. A Canadian company has the following current assets listed in alphabetical order: accounts receivable, cash, inventory, prepaid insurance, short-term investments, and supplies. In what order will they appear on the company's balance sheet and why?

(SO 4) C 16. What are the differences between the four categories of non-current assets: long-term investments; property, plant, and equipment; intangible assets; and goodwill?

(SO 4) K 17. What alternative methods of presentation can a company follow when preparing its balance sheet? Are these choices affected by whether or not the company is using IFRS or ASPE?

(SO 5) C 18. What is liquidity? Identify one measure of liquidity.

(SO 5) C 19. What comparisons should be made when interpreting ratios?

(SO 5) C 20. What are the differences between the current ratio and the acid-test ratio?

(SO 6) C *21. How is profit or loss calculated on a work sheet? How is this number entered on the work sheet if the company has profit? How is it entered if the company has a loss?

(SO 6) C *22. Why is it necessary to journalize and post adjusting entries if they have already been entered on the work sheet?

(SO 6) C *23. Although using a work sheet is optional, it is useful. Explain why this statement is true.

(SO 7) C *24. What are reversing entries and how are they related to adjusting entries? When are they prepared?

(SO 7) C *25. How is it helpful to use reversing entries? Explain if the use of reversing entries changes the amounts reported in the financial statements or not.

Brief Exercises

Identify accounts to be closed. **(SO 1) K**

BE4–1 The following accounts were included on a company's adjusted trial balance. In the blank space, identify which accounts should be closed (C) or not closed (NC) at the year end.

________ Accounts payable	________ Notes payable
________ Accounts receivable	________ Rent revenue
________ Depreciation expense	________ Prepaid expenses
________ Operating expenses	________ Equipment
________ Unearned revenue	________ S. Young, drawings
________ Interest expense	________ Accumulated depreciation
________ S. Young, capital	________ Supplies

Calculate profit, prepare closing entries, and calculate capital account balance. **(SO 1) AP**

BE4–2 Rizzo Company has the following year-end account balances on November 30, 2014: Service Revenue $38,500; Insurance Expense $2,750; Rent Expense $8,000; Supplies Expense $1,500; L. Wilfrid, Capital $42,000; and L. Wilfrid, Drawings $29,000.

(a) Calculate profit or loss for the year.
(b) Prepare the closing entries.
(c) Calculate the balance in L. Wilfrid, Capital after the closing entries are posted.

Prepare and post closing entries. (SO 1) AP

BE4–3 The adjusted trial balance for Mosquera Golf Club at its October 31, 2014, year end included the following:

	Debit	Credit
Cash	$ 7,500	
Prepaid expenses	3,000	
Equipment	65,000	
Accumulated depreciation—equipment		$ 15,000
Accounts payable		14,000
Unearned revenue		1,500
N. Mosquera, capital		65,000
N. Mosquera, drawings	45,000	
Service revenue		130,000
Maintenance expense	23,000	
Rent expense	10,000	
Salaries expense	72,000	

(a) Prepare closing entries.
(b) Using T accounts, post the closing entries and calculate the balance in each account.

Prepare post-closing trial balance. (SO 1) AP

BE4–4 Refer to the information in BE4–3 for Mosquera Golf Club. Prepare a post-closing trial balance.

List steps in accounting cycle. (SO 2) K

BE4–5 The required steps in the accounting cycle are listed below in random order. List the steps in the correct order by writing the numbers 1 to 9 in the blank spaces.

(a) ______ Prepare a post-closing trial balance.
(b) ______ Prepare an adjusted trial balance.
(c) ______ Analyze business transactions.
(d) ______ Prepare a trial balance.
(e) ______ Journalize the transactions.
(f) ______ Journalize and post the closing entries.
(g) ______ Prepare the financial statements.
(h) ______ Journalize and post the adjusting entries.
(i) ______ Post to the ledger accounts.

Apply the steps in the accounting cycle to the purchase and use of supplies. (SO 1, 2) AP

BE4–6 Flamingo Company opened for business on April 1, 2013, and purchased supplies on April 15, 2013, for $1,850 cash. On March 31, 2014, the company's year end, it had $400 of supplies on hand. Complete the following steps in the accounting cycle with regard to the supplies:

(a) Journalize the April 15, 2013, transaction.
(b) Post to the ledger accounts. (Use T accounts; ignore the Cash account.)
(c) Journalize and post any required adjusting entries at March 31, 2014.
(d) Journalize and post required closing entries.

Identify impact of error. (SO 3) AP

BE4–7 At Hébert Company, the following errors were discovered after the transactions had been journalized and posted:

1. A collection of cash on account from a customer for $750 was recorded as a debit to Cash of $750 and a credit to Service Revenue of $750.
2. An invoice to a customer for $600 of services that were performed on account was recorded as a $600 debit to Accounts Receivable and a $600 credit to Unearned Revenue.
3. A $500 cash payment to the owner, Roch Hébert, was recorded as a debit to Salary Expense of $500 and a credit to Cash of $500.
4. The payment of cash to a creditor of $280 was recorded as a $280 credit to Accounts Payable and a $280 debit to Cash.

Indicate the impact of each error on the balance sheet and income statement by stating whether assets, liabilities, owner's equity, revenues, expenses, and profit are understated (U), overstated (O), or if there is no effect (NE). Use the following format, in which the answer for the first error is given as an example:

	Balance Sheet			Income Statement		
Error	Assets	Liabilities	Owner's Equity	Revenues	Expenses	Profit
1	O	NE	O	O	NE	O

Prepare correcting entries. (SO 3) AP

BE4–8 Refer to the information in BE4–7 for Hébert Company. Prepare the correcting journal entries.

BE4–9 The December 31, 2014, adjusted trial balance of Darius Company includes the following accounts:

Prepare current assets section of balance sheet and classify other accounts. (SO 4) AP

Accounts receivable	$14,500	Patents	$ 3,900
Prepaid insurance	1,600	Unearned revenue	2,900
Goodwill	9,250	Cash	16,400
Supplies	4,200	Short-term investments	8,200
Vehicles	22,500	Merchandise inventory	9,000
Notes receivable (due February 1, 2016)	5,500		

(a) Determine which accounts are current assets and prepare the current assets section of the balance sheet as at December 31, 2014, with the accounts in order of decreasing liquidity.
(b) For each account that is not classified as a current asset, indicate how it would be classified on the balance sheet.

BE4–10 The December 31, 2014, adjusted trial balance of Odom Company includes the following accounts:

Classify balance sheet accounts. (SO 4) AP

Supplies	$ 2,900	Land	$ 85,000
Notes payable (due March 1, 2017)	28,000	Buildings	125,000
Accumulated depreciation—equipment	25,800	Patents	12,300
Equipment	43,000	Goodwill	5,520
Accumulated depreciation—building	37,400	Merchandise inventory	14,000
Notes receivable (due April 1, 2015)	7,800		

(a) Determine which accounts are non-current assets and prepare the non-current assets section of the balance sheet as at December 31, 2014.
(b) For each item that is not classified as a non-current asset, indicate how it would be classified on the balance sheet.

BE4–11 On December 31, 2014, Big River Company had $1 million of current assets and $900,000 of current liabilities. On the same day, Small Fry Company had $200,000 of current assets and $100,000 of current liabilities. Calculate the working capital and current ratio for both companies and compare the results. Which liquidity measure is more relevant?

Calculate working capital and current ratio and compare liquidity ratio measures. (SO 5) K

BE4–12 Selected financial information is available at July 31 for Drew Co.

Calculate working capital, current ratio, and acid-test ratio, and comment on liquidity. (SO 5) AP

	2014	2013
Cash and accounts receivable	$22,680	$20,430
Current assets	35,100	33,510
Current liabilities	24,460	24,800

(a) Calculate (1) working capital, (2) the current ratio, and (3) the acid-test ratio for 2013 and 2014.
(b) Indicate whether there was an improvement or deterioration in liquidity for Drew in 2014.

***BE4–13** The accountant for Coulombe Company is almost finished preparing the work sheet for the year ended July 31, 2014. The totals of the accounts in the income statement and balance sheet columns are presented below. Calculate the profit or loss, write this number in the proper columns, and calculate the final totals for these columns. Clearly indicate whether the company had a profit or a loss.

Complete work sheet. (SO 6) AP

	Income Statement		Balance Sheet	
	Dr.	Cr.	Dr.	Cr.
Totals	75,000	95,500	191,000	170,500
Profit or loss				
Totals				

***BE4–14** The accountant for Orange Line Company is almost finished preparing the work sheet for the year ended August 31, 2014. The totals of the accounts in the income statement and balance sheet columns are presented below. Calculate the profit or loss, write this in the proper columns, and calculate the final totals for these columns. Clearly indicate whether the company had a profit or loss.

Complete work sheet. (SO 6) AP

	Income Statement		Balance Sheet	
	Dr.	Cr.	Dr.	Cr.
Totals	53,875	43,425	55,550	66,000
Profit or loss				
Totals				

Prepare and post adjusting, closing, reversing, and subsequent entries. **(SO 7) AP**

***BE4–15** At December 31, 2014, Giselle Company made an accrued expense adjusting entry of $1,700 for salaries. On January 4, 2015, it paid salaries of $3,000: $1,700 for December salaries and $1,300 for January salaries. (a) Prepare the December 31 adjusting entry. (b) Prepare the December 31 closing entry for salaries. (c) Prepare the January 1 reversing entry and the January 4 journal entry to record the payment of salaries. (d) Indicate the balances in Salaries Payable and Salaries Expense after posting these entries.

Prepare adjusting, reversing, and subsequent entries. **(SO 7) AP**

***BE4–16** At December 31, 2014, Giselle Company had a five-month, 5%, $90,000 note receivable that was issued on October 1, 2014. Interest and principal are payable at maturity on March 1, 2015. (a) Prepare the December 31, 2014, adjusting entry for accrued interest. (b) Prepare the January 1, 2015, reversing entry. (c) Prepare the March 1, 2015, entry to record the receipt of cash at maturity for the note.

Exercises

Prepare closing entries. **(SO 1) AP**

E4–1 Selected T accounts for Welker Training Services follow. The May 31 postings include both adjusting and closing entries.

L. Welker, Capital

		May 1 Bal.	11,000
May 31	2,500	31	3,700
		May 31 Bal.	12,200

Advertising Expense

May 1	600		
31	700	May 31	1,300
May 31 Bal.	0		

L. Welker, Drawings

May 13	1,000	May 31	2,500
25	1,500		
May 31 Bal.	0		

Rent Expense

May 1	3,000	May 31	3,000
May 31 Bal.	0		

Service Revenue

		May 15	14,500
May 31	16,800	31	2,300
		May 31 Bal.	0

Salaries Expense

May 1	7,200		
31	1,600	May 31	8,800
May 31 Bal.	0		

Instructions

(a) Using the above information, and without doing any calculations, what was the company's profit or loss for May? Indicate how you determined this amount.
(b) What is total owner's equity at May 31?
(c) Prepare the closing entries that were made.
(d) Post the closing entries to the Income Summary.

Prepare a statement of owner's equity and closing entries. **(SO 1) AP**

E4–2 Selected T accounts for Victoire Esthetics to August 31, 2014, follow.

B. Victoire, Capital

		Aug. 1 Bal.	9,000
		10	2,000
		Aug. 31 Bal.	11,000

B. Victoire, Drawings

Aug. 15	2,200		
25	2,500		
Aug. 31 Bal.	4,700		

Income Summary

Aug. 31	8,000	Aug. 31	15,000
		Aug. 31 Bal.	7,000

Instructions

(a) Prepare a statement of owner's equity for August 2014.
(b) Prepare entries to close the income summary and drawings accounts. Post these entries.

E4–3 An alphabetical list of the adjusted account balances (all accounts have normal balances) at August 31, 2014, for Alpine Bowling Lanes is as follows:

Prepare and post closing entries and prepare post-closing trial balance.
(SO 1) AP

Accounts payable	$ 8,200	Interest revenue	$ 400
Accounts receivable	10,980	Notes payable	25,000
Accumulated depreciation—equipment	18,600	Prepaid insurance	820
Cash	17,940	Service revenue	35,900
Debt investments	10,000	Supplies	740
Depreciation expense	9,300	Supplies expense	7,845
Equipment	93,000	T. Williams, capital	85,500
Insurance expense	4,100	T. Williams, drawings	18,500
Interest expense	1,500	Unearned revenue	980
Interest payable	145		

Instructions

(a) Prepare the closing entries at August 31.
(b) Prepare T accounts for the accounts affected by the closing entries. Post the closing entries.
(c) Prepare a post-closing trial balance at August 31, 2014.

E4–4 Tim Sasse started Sasse Roof Repairs on April 2, 2014, by investing $4,000 cash in the business. During April, the following transactions occurred:

Apply the steps in the accounting cycle.
(SO 1, 2) AP

Apr.	6	Purchased supplies for $1,500 cash.
	15	Repaired a roof for a customer and collected $600 cash.
	25	Received $2,200 cash in advance from a customer for roof repairs to his house and garage.

On April 30, 2014, the following information was available:

1. Earned but unbilled revenue at April 30 was $600.
2. There is $800 of supplies on hand.
3. Of the $2,200 received on April 25, the company has earned $800 by completing repairs to the garage roof.

Instructions

(a) Journalize the transactions.
(b) Post to the ledger accounts. (Use T accounts.)
(c) Journalize and post any required adjusting entries.
(d) Prepare an adjusted trial balance.
(e) Assuming the company closes its books on a monthly basis, journalize and post closing entries.

E4–5 The unadjusted trial balance for Swift Creek Engineering at its year end, December 31, 2014, is as follows:

Prepare adjusting and closing entries.
(SO 1, 2) AP

SWIFT CREEK ENGINEERING
Trial Balance
December 31, 2014

	Debit	Credit
Cash	$ 8,450	
Accounts receivable	6,250	
Supplies	5,260	
Prepaid insurance	7,440	
Notes receivable	12,000	
Equipment	27,800	
Accumulated depreciation—equipment		$ 8,340
Accounts payable		4,560
H. Duguay, capital		34,900
H. Duguay, drawings	53,500	
Service revenue		112,300
Salaries expense	39,400	
	$160,100	$160,100

Additional information:

1. Revenue of $1,440 was earned but unrecorded as at December 31, 2014.
2. On June 1, the company purchased a one-year insurance policy.
3. Depreciation on the equipment for 2014 is $2,780.
4. A count on December 31, 2014, showed $750 of supplies on hand.
5. The four-month, 4% note receivable was issued on October 1, 2014. Interest and principal are payable on the maturity date.

Instructions

(a) Prepare adjusting entries for the year ended December 31, 2014.
(b) Prepare closing entries.

Prepare correcting entries and analyze impact of error. (SO 3) AP

E4–6 Choi Company has an inexperienced accountant. During the first two weeks on the job, the accountant made the following errors in journalizing transactions. All incorrect entries were posted.

1. A payment on account of $1,750 to a creditor was debited $750 to Accounts Payable and credited $750 to Cash.
2. The purchase of supplies on account for $860 was not recorded.
3. A $400 withdrawal of cash for L. Choi's personal use was debited $400 to Salaries Expense and credited $400 to Cash.
4. Received $700 cash from a customer on account. Cash was debited $700 and Service Revenue was credited $700.
5. A customer was billed $350 for services provided. Accounts Receivable was debited $350 and Unearned Revenue was credited $350.

Instructions

(a) Prepare the correcting entries.
(b) Indicate the impact of each error on the balance sheet and income statement by stating whether total assets, liabilities, owner's equity, revenues, expenses, and profit are understated (U), overstated (O), or if there is no effect (NE). Use the following format, in which the answer for the first error is given as an example:

	Balance Sheet			Income Statement		
Error	Assets	Liabilities	Owner's Equity	Revenues	Expenses	Profit
1	O	O	NE	NE	NE	NE

Prepare correcting entries. (SO 3) AP

E4–7 The owner of D'Addario Company has been doing all of the company's bookkeeping. When the accountant arrived to do the year-end adjusting entries, she found the following errors:

1. A payment of salaries of $625 was debited to Supplies and credited to Cash, both for $625.
2. The investment of cash of $2,000 by the owner, Toni D'Addario, was debited to Short-Term Investments and credited to Cash, both for $2,000.
3. The collection of an account receivable of $780 was debited to Cash and credited to Accounts Receivable, both for $870.
4. The company had purchased $440 of supplies on account. This entry was correctly recorded. When the account was paid, Supplies was debited $440 and Cash was credited $440.
5. Equipment costing $3,500 was purchased by signing a six-month note payable. Equipment Expense was debited and Accounts Payable was credited, both for $3,500.

Instructions

(a) Correct the errors by reversing the incorrect entry and preparing the correct entry.
(b) Correct the errors without reversing the incorrect entry.

E4–8 At the end of its fiscal year, the adjusted trial balance of Donatello Company is as follows:

Prepare financial statements. **(SO 4) AP**

DONATELLO COMPANY
Adjusted Trial Balance
July 31, 2014

	Debit	Credit
Cash	$ 4,650	
Accounts receivable	11,400	
Prepaid rent	500	
Supplies	750	
Debt investments	8,000	
Equipment	19,950	
Accumulated depreciation—equipment		$ 5,700
Patents	18,300	
Accounts payable		4,245
Interest payable		750
Unearned revenue		2,050
Notes payable (due on July 1, 2016)		45,000
B. Donatello, capital		28,285
B. Donatello, drawings	16,500	
Service revenue		75,000
Interest revenue		320
Depreciation expense	2,850	
Interest expense	3,000	
Rent expense	18,550	
Salaries expense	36,050	
Supplies expense	20,850	
	$161,350	$161,350

Instructions

(a) Prepare an income statement and statement of owner's equity for the year. Mr. Donatello invested $5,000 cash in the business during the year.
(b) Prepare a classified balance sheet at July 31, 2014.

E4–9 Selected financial information for JPC Enterprises as of December 31, 2014, follows:

Prepare classified balance sheet and comment on liquidity. **(SO 4, 5) AN**

Accounts payable	$210,100	Land	$105,600
Accounts receivable	197,000	Licences	58,300
Accumulated depreciation—building	79,900	Merchandise inventory	173,200
Accumulated depreciation—equipment	71,100	Mortgage payable	230,000
Building	256,300	Notes payable	55,000
Cash	16,500	Notes receivable (due in 2016)	34,700
Debt investments	62,600	Prepaid expenses	6,900
Equipment	92,100	Salaries payable	28,700
Equity investments	45,800	Supplies	10,100
Goodwill	36,000	Unearned revenue	27,400
Interest payable	16,500		
J. Chrowder, capital	376,400		

Additional information:

1. All accounts have normal balances.
2. $17,250 of the mortgage payable will be paid before December 31, 2015.
3. The company intends to keep its investment in bonds (a debt instrument) until the bonds mature in 2020.
4. The notes payable are payable on May 17, 2015.

Instructions

(a) Prepare a classified balance sheet.
(b) Calculate working capital, the current ratio, and the acid-test ratio.
(c) Based on the ratio calculations, do you feel that the company's liquidity is satisfactory?

Calculate working capital, current ratio, and acid-test ratio, and comment on liquidity. (SO 5) AN

E4–10 Shoppers Drug Mart Corporation is Canada's largest retail pharmacy, with stores in each province (including Pharmaprix in Quebec) and two territories. The following data (in thousands) were taken from Shoppers' financial statements (before Shoppers merged with Loblaw Companies Limited):

	Dec. 31, 2011	Jan. 1, 2011	Jan. 2, 2010
Cash	$ 118,566	$ 64,354	$ 44,391
Accounts receivable	493,338	432,089	470,935
Inventory	2,042,302	1,957,525	1,852,441
Current assets	2,695,647	2,542,820	2,441,973
Current liabilities	1,776,238	1,527,567	1,706,541

Instructions

(a) Calculate the working capital, current ratio, and acid-test ratio for each year.
(b) Discuss Shoppers Drug Mart's liquidity on December 31, 2011, compared with the two previous years.

Prepare work sheet. (SO 6) AP

***E4–11** The unadjusted trial balance at December 31, 2014, and the year-end adjustment data for Swift Creek Engineering is presented in E4–5.

Instructions

Prepare the work sheet for the year ended December 31, 2014.

Prepare and post adjusting, closing, reversing, and subsequent entries. (SO 1, 7) AP

***E4–12** On December 31, the unadjusted trial balance of Masterson Employment Agency shows the following selected data:

Accounts receivable	$24,000	Cash	$ 7,600
Interest expense	7,800	Service revenue	92,000
I. Masterson, capital	48,000	Interest payable	0

Analysis shows that adjusting entries are required to (1) accrue $4,400 of service revenue, and (2) accrue $1,500 of interest expense.

Instructions

(a) Prepare and post (1) the adjusting entries and (2) the closing entries for the temporary accounts at December 31.
(b) Prepare and post reversing entries on January 1.
(c) Prepare and post the entries to record (1) the collection of $6,200 of service revenue (including the accrued service revenue from December 31) on January 10, and (2) the payment of $2,235 interest on January 31 (consisting of the accrued interest from December 31 plus January's interest).

Prepare adjusting, reversing, and subsequent entries. (SO 7) AP

***E4–13** Rosborough Company provides property management services to a variety of companies. At its fiscal year end on April 30, 2014, adjustments were required for the following items:

1. Service revenue of $600 was earned but not recorded.
2. Of the balance in the Unearned Revenue account, $250 had been earned.
3. Depreciation expense for the year ended April 30, 2014, was $4,850.
4. Interest of $545 on a note payable had accrued.
5. Prepaid insurance of $385 had expired.
6. Property taxes for the calendar year are payable every year on June 30. The company estimated property taxes for 2014 to be $3,912.

Instructions

(a) Identify the adjustments for which it could be useful to prepare reversing entries.
(b) Prepare these reversing entries on May 1, 2014.
(c) Explain why and how the reversing entries are useful for these adjustments but not for the other adjustments.

Problems: Set A

P4–1A The adjusted trial balance for Marine Fishing Centre is as follows:

Prepare financial statements, closing entries, and post-closing trial balance. **(SO 1, 4) AP**

MARINE FISHING CENTRE Adjusted Trial Balance March 31, 2014		
	Debit	Credit
Cash	$ 7,720	
Interest receivable	750	
Supplies	1,425	
Debt investments	30,000	
Land	46,800	
Building	186,900	
Accumulated depreciation—building		$ 31,150
Equipment	36,200	
Accumulated depreciation—equipment		18,100
Accounts payable		5,875
Interest payable		990
Unearned revenue		2,190
Notes payable ($6,000 must be paid in 2015)		66,000
R. Falkner, capital		165,300
R. Falkner, drawings	46,200	
Service revenue		124,300
Interest revenue		1,500
Depreciation expense	9,850	
Interest expense	3,960	
Insurance expense	4,500	
Salaries expense	30,000	
Supplies expense	5,700	
Utilities expense	5,400	
	$415,405	$415,405

Instructions

(a) Calculate profit or loss for the year. (*Note:* It is not necessary to prepare an income statement.)
(b) Prepare a statement of owner's equity. The owner, Rachael Falkner, invested $2,300 cash in the business during the year. (*Note:* This transaction has been correctly recorded.)
(c) Prepare a classified balance sheet.
(d) Prepare closing entries in general journal form.
(e) Use T accounts to post the closing entries and calculate the balance in each account. (Ignore the accounts not affected by the closing entries.)
(f) Prepare a post-closing trial balance and compare the balance in the R. Falkner, Capital account with the information in the statement of owner's equity.

TAKING IT FURTHER What alternatives should be considered when deciding on the presentation of information in the classified balance sheet?

Prepare adjusting entries, adjusted trial balance, financial statements, and closing entries. **(SO 1, 4) AP**

P4–2A The following is Spartan Cycle Repair Shop's trial balance at January 31, 2014, the company's fiscal year end:

SPARTAN CYCLE REPAIR SHOP
Trial Balance
January 31, 2014

	Debit	Credit
Cash	$ 3,200	
Accounts receivable	6,630	
Prepaid insurance	6,420	
Supplies	5,240	
Land	50,000	
Building	90,000	
Accumulated depreciation—building		$ 11,000
Equipment	27,000	
Accumulated depreciation—equipment		4,500
Accounts payable		6,400
Unearned revenue		1,950
Mortgage payable		102,000
H. Dude, capital		61,000
H. Dude, drawings	101,100	
Service revenue		235,550
Salaries expense	115,200	
Utilities expense	12,000	
Interest expense	5,610	
	$422,400	$422,400

Additional information:

1. Service revenue earned but not recorded at January 31, 2014, was $1,550.
2. The 12-month insurance policy was purchased on March 1, 2013.
3. A physical count of supplies shows $580 on hand on January 31, 2014.
4. The building has an estimated useful life of 45 years. The equipment has an estimated useful life of 15 years.
5. Salaries of $1,520 are accrued and unpaid at January 31, 2014.
6. The mortgage payable has a 6% interest rate. Interest is paid on the first day of each month for the previous month's interest.
7. By January 31, 2014, $850 of the unearned revenue has been earned.
8. During the next fiscal year, $4,500 of the mortgage payable is to be paid.

Instructions

(a) Prepare the adjusting entries.
(b) Prepare an adjusted trial balance.
(c) Prepare an income statement, statement of owner's equity, and classified balance sheet. The owner, Henry Dude, invested $5,000 cash in the business on November 17, 2013.
(d) Prepare the closing entries.

TAKING IT FURTHER Henry Dude is concerned that he had to invest cash in the business this year. Based on the information in the financial statements, what do you suggest to Henry?

Complete all steps in the accounting cycle. **(SO 1, 2, 4) AP**

P4–3A Lee Chang opened Lee's Window Washing on July 1, 2014. In July, the following transactions were completed:

July	1	Lee invested $20,000 cash in the business.
	1	Purchased a used truck for $25,000, paying $5,000 cash and signing a note payable for the balance.
	3	Purchased supplies for $2,100 on account.

5 Paid $1,800 on a one-year insurance policy, effective July 1.
12 Billed customers $4,500 for cleaning services.
18 Paid $1,400 of amount owed on supplies.
20 Paid $2,000 for employee salaries.
21 Collected $3,400 from customers billed on July 12.
25 Billed customers $9,000 for cleaning services.
31 Paid $550 for fuel for the month on the truck.
31 Withdrew $1,600 cash for personal use.

Instructions

(a) Journalize and post the July transactions.
(b) Prepare a trial balance at July 31.
(c) Journalize and post the following adjustments:
1. Earned but unbilled fees at July 31 were $1,500.
2. The truck is to be depreciated over its estimated useful life of four years.
3. One-twelfth of the insurance expired.
4. An inventory count shows $700 of supplies on hand at July 31.
5. Accrued but unpaid employee salaries were $800.
6. The note payable has a 5.5% annual interest rate.
(d) Prepare an adjusted trial balance.
(e) Prepare the income statement and statement of owner's equity for July, and a classified balance sheet at July 31, 2014. Of the note payable, $5,000 must be paid by July 1, 2015.
(f) Journalize and post the closing entries.
(g) Prepare a post-closing trial balance at July 31.

TAKING IT FURTHER Do companies need to make adjusting and closing entries at the end of every month?

P4–4A Silver Ridge Plumbing's year end is October 31. The company's trial balance prior to adjustments follows:

Prepare adjusting entries, adjusted trial balance, financial statements, and closing entries.
(SO 1, 2, 4) AP

SILVER RIDGE PLUMBING
Trial Balance
October 31, 2014

	Debit	Credit
Cash	$ 15,420	
Supplies	26,000	
Debt investments	20,000	
Equipment	120,000	
Accumulated depreciation—equipment		$ 42,000
Vehicles	110,000	
Accumulated depreciation—vehicles		48,125
Accounts payable		7,950
Unearned revenue		5,000
Notes payable		55,000
H. Burke, capital		75,750
H. Burke, drawings	36,000	
Service revenue		200,125
Interest revenue		400
Fuel expense	28,038	
Insurance expense	9,500	
Interest expense	3,392	
Rent expense	21,000	
Salaries expense	45,000	
	$434,350	$434,350

Additional information:

1. The equipment has an expected useful life of 10 years. The vehicles' expected useful life is eight years.
2. A physical count showed $2,000 of supplies on hand at October 31, 2014.
3. As at October 31, 2014, there was $1,000 of revenue received in advance that was still unearned.
4. Silver Ridge has a debt investment (in bonds) that it intends to hold to earn interest until the bonds mature in 15 years. The bonds have an interest rate of 4% and pay interest on May 1 and November 1 each year.
5. Accrued salaries payable at October 31, 2014, were $2,550.
6. Interest on the 5.5% note payable is payable at the end of each month and $10,000 of the principal must be paid on December 31 each year. Interest payments are up to date as at October 31, 2014.
7. The owner, H. Burke, invested $2,000 cash in the business on December 28, 2013. (*Note:* This has been correctly recorded.)

Instructions

(a) Prepare the adjusting entries and an adjusted trial balance.
(b) Calculate profit or loss for the year.
(c) Prepare a statement of owner's equity and a classified balance sheet.
(d) Prepare the closing entries. Using T accounts, post to the income summary, and owner's drawings and capital accounts. Compare the ending balance in the owner's capital account with the information in the statement of owner's equity.

TAKING IT FURTHER Why do you need to know the amount the owner invested in the business this year if it has been correctly recorded?

Analyze errors and prepare corrections. **(SO 3) AP**

P4–5A Bob Chen, CGA, was hired by Edgemont Entertainment Installations to prepare its financial statements for April 2014. Using all the ledger balances in the owner's records, Bob put together the following trial balance:

EDGEMONT ENTERTAINMENT INSTALLATIONS
Trial Balance
April 30, 2014

	Debit	Credit
Cash	$ 4,010	
Accounts receivable	3,225	
Supplies	3,800	
Equipment	11,460	
Accumulated depreciation—equipment		$ 2,200
Accounts payable		2,275
Salaries payable		650
Rent payable	950	
Unearned revenue		1,250
S. Morris, capital		17,700
Service revenue		7,950
Salaries expense	7,400	
Advertising expense	585	
Miscellaneous expense	595	
Totals	$32,025	$32,025

Bob reviewed the records and found the following errors:

1. The first salary payment made in April was for $1,900, which included $650 of salaries payable on March 31. The payment was recorded as a debit to Salaries Expense of $2,100 and a credit to Cash of $2,100. (No reversing entries were made on April 1.)
2. The owner, Stuart Morris, paid himself $2,400 and recorded this as salary expense.
3. April rent of $950 was paid on April 26. It was recorded as a debit to rent payable and a credit to cash, both for $950.

4. Cash paid on account was recorded as $740 instead of $470.
5. A payment of $195 for an advertising expense was entered as a debit to Miscellaneous Expense of $95 and a credit to Cash of $95.
6. A cash payment for a repair expense on equipment of $460 was recorded as a debit to Equipment of $460 and a credit to Accounts Payable of $460.
7. Services of $1,250 were provided to a customer on account. Accounts receivable was debited $1,250 and Unearned Revenue was credited the same amount.
8. The depreciation expense for the month of April has not been recorded. All of the company's equipment is expected to have a five-year useful life.

Instructions

(a) Prepare an analysis of each error that shows (1) the incorrect entry, (2) the correct entry, and (3) the correcting entry.
(b) Prepare a correct trial balance.

TAKING IT FURTHER Explain how the company's financial statements would be incorrect if error 2 was not corrected and why it is important to correct this error.

Calculate capital account balance; prepare classified balance sheet and liquidity ratios. **(SO 1, 4, 5) AP**

P4–6A Below is an alphabetical list of the adjusted accounts of Dunder Tour Company at its year end, December 31, 2014. All accounts have normal balances.

Accounts payable	$ 7,300	Interest receivable	$ 100
Accounts receivable	3,500	Interest revenue	1,100
Accumulated depreciation—equipment	15,000	Notes payable	40,000
Cash	4,500	Notes receivable	18,400
Depreciation expense	10,000	Patents	15,000
Equipment	50,000	Prepaid insurance	2,900
F. Dunder, capital	17,300	Service revenue	65,000
F. Dunder, drawings	33,000	Short-term investments	2,700
Insurance expense	1,500	Supplies	3,100
Interest expense	2,800	Supplies expense	2,400
Interest payable	700	Unearned revenue	3,500

Additional information:

1. In 2015, $3,000 of the notes payable becomes due.
2. The note receivable is due in 2016.
3. On July 18, 2014, Fred Dunder invested $3,200 cash in the business.

Instructions

(a) Calculate the post-closing balance in F. Dunder, Capital on December 31, 2014.
(b) Prepare a classified balance sheet.
(c) On December 31, 2013, Dunder Tour Company had current assets of $17,400 and current liabilities of $22,300. Calculate the company's working capital and current ratio on December 31, 2013, and December 31, 2014.
(d) On December 31, 2013, the total of Dunder Tour Company's cash, short-term investments, and current receivables was $15,600. Calculate the company's acid-test ratio on December 31, 2013, and December 31, 2014.

TAKING IT FURTHER Has the company's ability to pay its debts improved or weakened over the year?

Calculate current assets and liabilities, working capital, current ratio, and acid-test ratio; comment on liquidity. **(SO 5) AN**

P4–7A Danier Leather Inc. is one of the largest publicly traded specialty apparel leather retailers in the world. The following information (all amounts in thousands) can be found on its recent balance sheets (or statements of financial position, as Danier Leather calls them):

	Dec. 24, 2011	June 25, 2011	Dec. 25, 2010
Cash and cash equivalents	$31,803	$28,698	$25,406
Accounts receivable	1,686	391	385
Inventories	36,789	28,964	41,163
Prepaid expenses	426	901	381

	Dec. 24, 2011	June 25, 2011	Dec. 25, 2010
Property and equipment	15,315	14,404	15,808
Other long-term assets	2,677	2,732	2,943
Payables and accruals	16,010	11,024	19,650
Income taxes payable	583	278	1,097
Other current liabilities	3,586	1,536	3,659
Non-current liabilities	1,392	1,318	1,414
Shareholders' equity	67,125	60,272	61,928

Instructions

(a) Calculate Danier Leather's current assets and current liabilities for each period.
(b) Calculate Danier Leather's working capital, current ratio, and acid-test ratio for each period.
(c) What does each of the measures calculated in part (b) show? Comment on Danier's liquidity.

TAKING IT FURTHER The three balance sheet dates given in the problem are at two different points in the year (December and June). How, if at all, might that affect the comparability of the ratios?

Prepare work sheet.
(SO 6) AP

***P4–8A** The unadjusted trial balance and adjustment data for Spartan Cycle Repair Shop are presented in P4–2A.

Instructions

Prepare a work sheet for the year ended January 31, 2014.

TAKING IT FURTHER Is it still necessary to record the adjusting entries in the journal and post them to the ledger accounts when using a work sheet?

Prepare work sheet.
(SO 6) AP

***P4–9A** The unadjusted trial balance and adjustment data for Silver Ridge Plumbing are presented in P4–4A.

Instructions

Prepare a work sheet for the year ended October 31, 2014.

TAKING IT FURTHER Explain why preparing a work sheet is an optional step in the accounting cycle.

Prepare and post adjusting, closing, reversing, and cash transaction entries.
(SO 1, 7) AP

***P4–10A** Bugatti Company has a September 30 fiscal year end and prepares adjusting entries on an annual basis. The trial balance included the following selected accounts:

Accumulated depreciation	$ 4,250
Depreciation expense	0
Interest expense	3,333
Interest payable	0
Interest receivable	0
Interest revenue	0
Salaries expense	153,000
Salaries payable	0

Additional information for its September 30, 2014, year-end adjustments:

1. Bugatti has a two-year, 3.5% note receivable for $50,000 that was issued on April 1, 2014. Interest is payable every six months, on October 1 and April 1. Principal is payable at maturity. Bugatti collected the correct amount on October 1, 2014.
2. Accrued salaries as at September 30, 2014, were $2,400. Payroll totalling $3,000 was paid on October 2, 2014.
3. Bugatti has a five-year, 5% note payable for $80,000 issued in 2012. Interest is payable quarterly on January 31, April 30, July 31, and October 31 each year. Bugatti paid the correct amounts in 2014.
4. Depreciation expense for the year ended September 30, 2014, was $4,250.

Instructions

(a) Prepare T accounts and record the September 30, 2014, balances.
(b) Prepare and post adjusting journal entries for items 1 to 4 above.
(c) Prepare entries to close these revenue and expense accounts. Post to the T accounts. *Note:* Do not post to the income summary account.
(d) Prepare and post reversing journal entries on October 1, 2014, as appropriate.
(e) Prepare and post the journal entry to record the cash transactions that occurred in October 2014.

TAKING IT FURTHER Comment on the usefulness of reversing entries.

***P4–11A** The unadjusted trial balance for Veda's Video Arcade at its fiscal year end of May 31, 2014, is as follows:

Prepare adjusting, reversing, and subsequent cash entries. **(SO 7) AP**

VEDA'S VIDEO ARCADE
Trial Balance
May 31, 2014

	Debit	Credit
Cash	$ 5,940	
Supplies	2,910	
Equipment	115,000	
Accumulated depreciation—equipment		$ 46,000
Notes payable		60,000
Unearned revenue		1,500
V. Gupta, capital		32,200
V. Gupta, drawings	35,400	
Service revenue		81,250
Rent expense	12,600	
Salaries expense	45,800	
Interest expense	3,300	
	$220,950	$220,950

Additional information:

1. On May 31, 2014, Veda's Video Arcade had earned but not collected or recorded $750 of revenue. On June 19, it collected this amount plus an additional $1,150 for revenue earned in June.
2. There was $765 of supplies on hand on May 31, 2014.
3. The equipment has an estimated useful life of 10 years.
4. Accrued salaries to May 31 were $1,390. The next payday is June 3 and the employees will be paid a total of $1,980 that day.
5. The note payable has a 6% annual interest rate. Interest is paid monthly on the first day of the month.
6. As at May 31, 2014, there was $700 of unearned revenue.

Instructions

(a) Prepare adjusting journal entries for the year ended May 31, 2014, as required.
(b) Prepare reversing entries where appropriate.
(c) Prepare journal entries to record the June 2014 cash transactions.
(d) Now assume reversing entries were not prepared as in part (b) above. Prepare journal entries to record the June 2014 cash transactions.

TAKING IT FURTHER Why is it not appropriate to use reversing entries for all of the adjusting entries?

CONTINUING COOKIE CHRONICLE

(*Note:* This is a continuation of the Cookie Chronicle from Chapters 1 through 3.)

Natalie had a very busy December. At the end of the month, after Natalie has journalized and posted her adjusting entries, her company has the following adjusted trial balance:

COOKIE CREATIONS
Adjusted Trial Balance
December 31, 2013

	Debit	Credit
Cash	$2,929	
Accounts receivable	675	
Supplies	95	
Equipment	1,550	
Accumulated depreciation—equipment		$ 78
Accounts payable		76
Salaries payable		48
Unearned revenue		100
Interest payable		8
Notes payable, 3%, principal and interest due November 28, 2014		3,000
N. Koebel, capital		1,450
Revenue		1,225
Advertising expense	325	
Salaries expense	48	
Telephone expense	174	
Supplies expense	103	
Depreciation expense	78	
Interest expense	8	
	$5,985	$5,985

Instructions

Using the information in the adjusted trial balance, do the following:

(a) Prepare an income statement for the two months ended December 31, 2013, if you have not already done so in Chapter 3.

(b) Prepare a statement of owner's equity for the two months ended December 31, 2013, and a classified balance sheet at December 31, 2013.

(c) Calculate Cookie Creations' working capital, current ratio, and acid-test ratio. Comment on Cookie Creations' liquidity.

(d) Natalie has decided that her year end will be December 31, 2013. Prepare closing entries.

(e) Prepare a post-closing trial balance.

(f) Natalie has reviewed the financial statements that you have prepared. When she recorded the purchase of equipment in December, she thought the equipment should be recorded as "supplies expense." After reviewing her accounting text, she remembered that the purchase of equipment should be recorded as an asset and made an entry to correct her error. Had she not done a correcting entry, what impact would that journal entry have had on the financial statements at the end of 2013?

Cumulative Coverage—Chapters 2 to 4

Alou Equipment Repair has a September 30 year end. The company adjusts and closes its accounts on an annual basis. On August 31, 2014, the account balances of Alou Equipment Repair were as follows:

ALOU EQUIPMENT REPAIR
Trial Balance
August 31, 2014

	Debit	Credit
Cash	$ 2,790	
Accounts receivable	7,910	
Supplies	8,500	
Equipment	9,000	
Accumulated depreciation—equipment		$ 1,800
Accounts payable		3,100
Unearned revenue		400
J. Alou, capital		21,200
J. Alou, drawings	15,600	
Service revenue		49,600
Rent expense	5,500	
Salaries expense	24,570	
Telephone expense	2,230	
	$76,100	$76,100

During September, the following transactions were completed:

Sept. 1 Borrowed $10,000 from the bank and signed a two-year, 5% note payable.
2 Paid September rent, $500.
8 Paid employee salaries, $1,050.
12 Received $1,500 cash from customers on account.
15 Received $5,700 cash for services performed in September.
17 Purchased additional supplies on account, $1,300.
20 Paid creditors $2,300 on account.
21 Paid September telephone bill, $200.
22 Paid employee salaries, $1,050.
27 Performed services on account and billed customers for services provided, $900.
29 Received $550 from customers for services to be provided in the future.
30 Paid J. Alou $800 cash for personal use.

Adjustment data consist of the following:

1. Supplies on hand at September 30 cost $1,000.
2. Accrued salaries payable at September 30 total $630.
3. The equipment has an expected useful life of five years.
4. Unearned revenue of $450 is still not earned at September 30.
5. Interest is payable on the first of each month.

Instructions

(a) Prepare T accounts and enter the August 31 balances.
(b) Journalize the September transactions.
(c) Post to T accounts.
(d) Prepare a trial balance at September 30.
(e) Journalize and post adjusting entries.
(f) Prepare an adjusted trial balance at September 30.
(g) Prepare an income statement and a statement of owner's equity, and a classified balance sheet.
(h) Prepare and post closing entries.
(i) Prepare post-closing trial balance at September 30.

CHAPTER 4 BROADENING YOUR PERSPECTIVE

Collaborative Learning Activity

Note to instructor: Additional instructions and material for this group activity can be found on the Instructor Resource Site and in *WileyPLUS*.

BYP4–1 In this group activity, you will create a classified balance sheet by piecing together the information, and using the clues, given to you by your teacher.

Communication Activity

BYP4–2 Your best friend is thinking about opening a business. He has never studied accounting and has no idea about the steps that must be followed in order to produce financial statements for his business.

Instructions

Write a memo to your friend that lists and explains each of the steps in the accounting cycle in the order in which they should be completed. Include information on when each of these steps should be done and explain the purpose of the different types of journal entries and trial balances. Your memo should also discuss the optional steps in the accounting cycle.

Ethics Case

BYP4–3 As the controller of Select Cleaning Services, you discover a significant error in the previous year's financial statements. Two journal entries for services provided on account were recognized in the previous fiscal year but should have been recognized this fiscal year. The incorrect financial statements were issued to banks and other creditors less than a month ago.

After much thought about the consequences of telling the president, Eddy Lieman, about this misstatement, you gather your courage to inform him. Eddy says, "Hey! What they don't know won't hurt them. We have earned that revenue by now so it doesn't really matter when it was recorded. We can afford to have lower revenues this year than last year anyway! Just don't make that kind of mistake again."

Instructions

(a) Assuming the error is not corrected, how, if at all, does this error affect last year-end's balance sheet and current ratio? This year-end's balance sheet and current ratio?
(b) Who are the stakeholders in this situation and what are the ethical issues?
(c) As the controller, what would you do in this situation?

All About You: Personal Financial Literacy

BYP4–4 As discussed in the "All About You" feature, in order to evaluate your personal financial position, you need to prepare a personal balance sheet. Assume that you will have gathered the following information about your current personal finances when you are at university or college.

Amount owed on student loan (long-term)	$10,000
Balance in chequing account	1,200
Automobile	8,000
Balance on automobile loan (short-term)	2,400
Balance on automobile loan (long-term)	3,600
Computer and accessories	1,200
Clothes and furniture	4,000
Balance owed on credit cards	1,000

Instructions

(a) Prepare a personal balance sheet using the format you have learned for a balance sheet for a proprietorship. For the Capital account, use Personal Equity (Deficit).
(b) Assume that you borrow an additional $5,000 in student loans to cover the cost of tuition for the upcoming school year. What is the impact on your Personal Equity (Deficit) if the cost of tuition is considered an expense? What is the impact on your Personal Equity (Deficit) if the cost of tuition is considered an asset?

(c) Assume that, instead of borrowing to cover the cost of tuition, you earn $8,000 working during the summer and that after paying for your tuition you have $2,000 in your chequing account. What is the impact on your Personal Equity (Deficit) if the cost of the tuition is considered an expense?

(d) Assume that you make a $600 payment from your chequing account on your automobile loan. What is the impact on your Personal Equity (Deficit)?

ANSWERS TO CHAPTER QUESTIONS

ANSWERS TO ACCOUNTING IN ACTION INSIGHT QUESTIONS

All About You Insight, p. 164

Q: How can preparing a personal balance sheet help you manage your net worth?

A: In order to attain your financial objectives, you need to set goals early. A personal balance sheet provides a benchmark that allows you to measure your progress toward your financial goals.

Business Insight, p. 166

Q: Does a current ratio of less than 1 indicate that the company will have problems paying its obligations?

A: Not necessarily. A current ratio of less than 1 only indicates that at the balance sheet date the company would not have been able to pay off all of its current liabilities. But current liabilities don't have to be paid on the balance sheet date; a current liability is an obligation to pay an amount at some point over the following year. Therefore, as long as a company is able to generate cash quickly enough through its sales, it will have the cash available to pay the obligations as they come due.

ANSWERS TO SELF-STUDY QUESTIONS

1. b 2. c 3. a 4. c 5. d 6. d 7. d 8. b 9. c 10. c *11. c *12. a

Remember to go back to the beginning of the chapter to check off your completed work!

←

CHAPTER 5 ACCOUNTING FOR MERCHANDISING OPERATIONS

THE NAVIGATOR

- ☐ Understand *Concepts for Review*
- ☐ Read *Feature Story*
- ☐ Scan *Study Objectives*
- ☐ Read *Chapter Preview*
- ☐ Read text and answer *Before You Go On*
- ☐ Review *Comparing IFRS and ASPE*
- ☐ Work *Demonstration Problems*
- ☐ Review *Summary of Study Objectives*
- ☐ Answer *Self-Study Questions*
- ☐ Complete assignments

CONCEPTS FOR REVIEW

Before studying this chapter, you should understand or, if necessary, review:

A. How to increase and decrease assets, liabilities, and owner's equity accounts using debit and credit procedures. (Ch. 2, pp. 50–54)

B. When to recognize revenues and expenses. (Ch. 3, p. 98)

C. How to close revenue, expense, and drawings accounts. (Ch. 4, pp. 146–152)

D. The steps in the accounting cycle. (Ch. 4, p. 153)

E. How to prepare an income statement. (Ch. 3, p. 115)

F. How to prepare a classified balance sheet. (Ch. 4, pp. 156–165)

TRACKING FASHION AND INVENTORY TRENDS

WINNIPEG, MB—Style knows no borders, but an international retailer does.

Moulé operates four boutiques in Winnipeg, Vancouver, and Portland, Oregon, selling women's and men's fashions and gifts. Its buying office is in Vancouver, where buyers issue purchase orders to various distributors. Goods from American distributors destined for the Portland store are shipped directly there, while U.S. goods bound for the Canadian stores are sent to the central warehouse in Winnipeg. "We try to minimize shipping costs," says Chief Operations Officer Laurie Gorenstein, whose family owns Moulé.

In both cases, staff receiving the goods ensure they got what they ordered and are billed for. "Our purchase orders are always checked against invoices," Mr. Gorenstein says. If there's any discrepancy in price, colour, style, or quantity, he will phone the distributor to rectify it. The items are coded with a barcode and entered into Moulé's point-of-sale (POS) computerized inventory system. In Winnipeg, goods are then packed into smaller shipments and sent to the two Vancouver stores, where the managers scan the barcodes and enter the items into their stores' own inventory as they stock the shelves and racks.

Even though the stores are boutiques, they still carry a total of 24,000 stock-keeping units, or individual items. In addition to clothes, these items range from rock memorabilia to a $1,500 table, Mr. Gorenstein says. The Winnipeg warehouse receives at least one shipment a day, getting up to five a day in the pre-holiday rush in October and November. The POS system allows Moulé to use a perpetual inventory system, so it constantly knows what it has in stock and its value.

Moulé recently opened an online store with selected merchandise. The items come from whichever store has an item in stock, so when filling an online order, the company checks its POS system to see where an item will be shipped from.

Retailers that carry the same items year-round worry about stockouts—running out of a particular item. But because Moulé sells seasonal trendy fashions, it constantly has to rejuvenate its inventory, ordering six months in advance. When quantities get low, "sometimes we can reorder an item, but most of the time we can't. With fashion, it comes in for the season and it goes out," Mr. Gorenstein says. Although it can't keep a particular item in stock, the retailer still wants to maintain a certain inventory level in a particular category, such as women's jeans. It does this by tracking past sales to determine how much to order. For example, "We know how much denim we've sold in the last 10 years."

While Moulé uses the QuickBooks software for its accounting, its POS system is used to generate inventory-related reports such as the stores' gross profit margin and profit margin so managers can keep an eye on trends of the financial kind.

THE NAVIGATOR

STUDY OBJECTIVES

After studying this chapter, you should be able to:

1. Describe the differences between service and merchandising companies.
2. Prepare entries for purchases under a perpetual inventory system.
3. Prepare entries for sales under a perpetual inventory system.
4. Perform the steps in the accounting cycle for a merchandising company.
5. Prepare single-step and multiple-step income statements.
6. Calculate the gross profit margin and profit margin.
7. Prepare the entries for purchases and sales under a periodic inventory system and calculate cost of goods sold (Appendix 5A).

THE NAVIGATOR

PREVIEW OF CHAPTER FIVE

The first four chapters of this text focused mostly on service companies, like the fictional Pioneer Advertising Agency. Other examples of service companies include Air Canada, Canada Post, College Pro Painters, and Scotiabank. Moulé, as indicated in the feature story, buys and sells goods instead of performing services to earn a profit. Merchandising companies that purchase and sell directly to consumers—such as Moulé, Reitmans, Canadian Tire, Mountain Equipment Co-op, and Toys "R" Us—are called retailers.

The chapter is organized as follows:

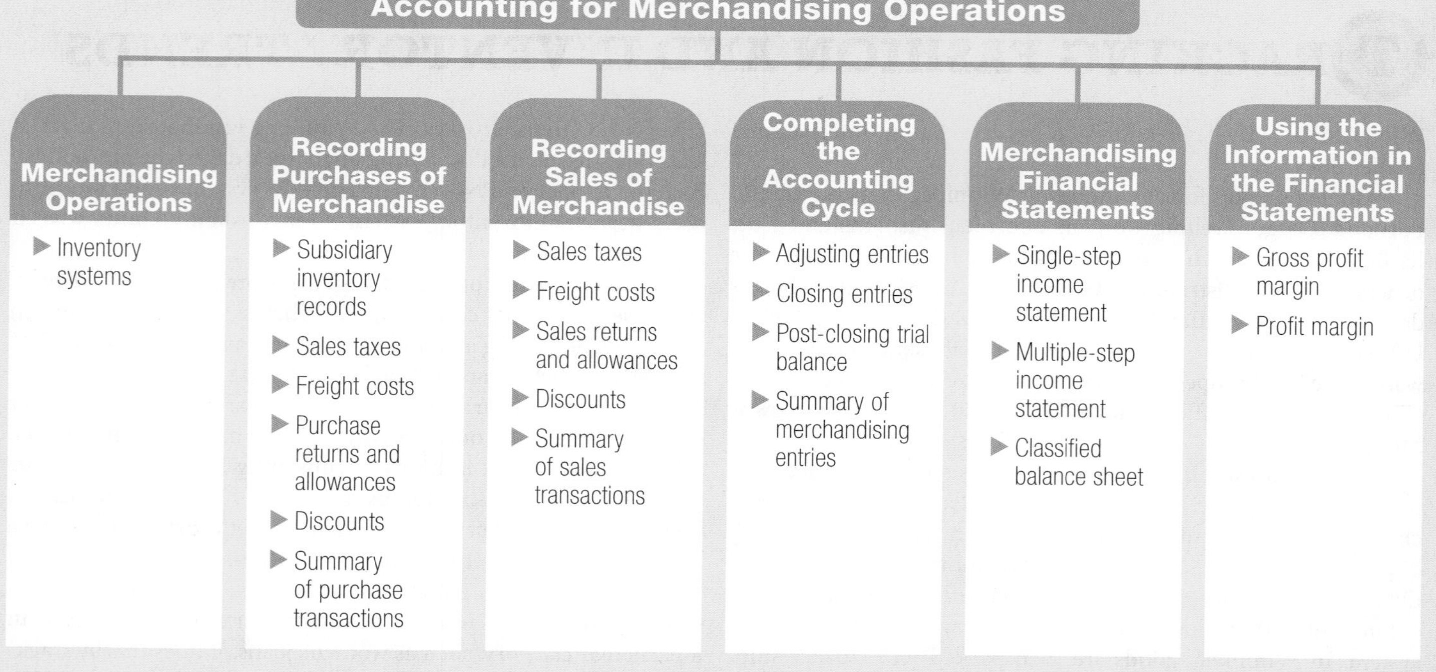

Accounting for Merchandising Operations
Merchandising Operations
▶ Inventory systems
Recording Purchases of Merchandise
▶ Subsidiary inventory records
▶ Sales taxes
▶ Freight costs
▶ Purchase returns and allowances
▶ Discounts
▶ Summary of purchase transactions
Recording Sales of Merchandise
▶ Sales taxes
▶ Freight costs
▶ Sales returns and allowances
▶ Discounts
▶ Summary of sales transactions
Completing the Accounting Cycle
▶ Adjusting entries
▶ Closing entries
▶ Post-closing trial balance
▶ Summary of merchandising entries
Merchandising Financial Statements
▶ Single-step income statement
▶ Multiple-step income statement
▶ Classified balance sheet
Using the Information in the Financial Statements
▶ Gross profit margin
▶ Profit margin

MERCHANDISING OPERATIONS

STUDY OBJECTIVE 1

Describe the differences between service and merchandising companies.

Merchandising involves purchasing products—also called merchandise inventory or just inventory—to resell to customers. The steps in the accounting cycle for a merchandising company are the same as the steps for a service company. However, merchandising companies need additional accounts and entries in order to record merchandising transactions.

Measuring profit for a merchandising company is basically the same as for a service company. That is, profit (or loss) is equal to revenues less expenses. In a merchandising company, the main source of revenues is the sale of merchandise. These revenues are called **sales revenue**, or simply **sales**. Expenses for a merchandising company are divided into two categories: (1) cost of goods sold, and (2) operating expenses. A service company does not have a cost of goods sold because it provides services, not goods.

The **cost of goods sold** is the total cost of merchandise sold during the period. This expense is directly related to the revenue earned from the sale of the goods, as a merchandiser must purchase the goods to be able to sell them to its customers. Sales revenue less cost of goods sold is called **gross profit**. For example, when a calculator that costs $15 is sold for $25, the gross profit is $10. Merchandisers report gross profit earned on sales in the income statement.

After gross profit is calculated, operating expenses are deducted to determine profit (or loss). **Operating expenses** are expenses that are incurred in the process of earning sales revenue or service revenue. The operating expenses of a merchandising company include the same basic expenses found in a service company, such as salaries, advertising, insurance, rent, and depreciation.

The calculations of profit for both a service and a merchandising company are shown in Illustration 5-1. As you can see, the items in the two blue boxes are used only by a merchandising company because service companies do not sell goods.

ILLUSTRATION 5-1
Earnings measurement process for a service and a merchandising company

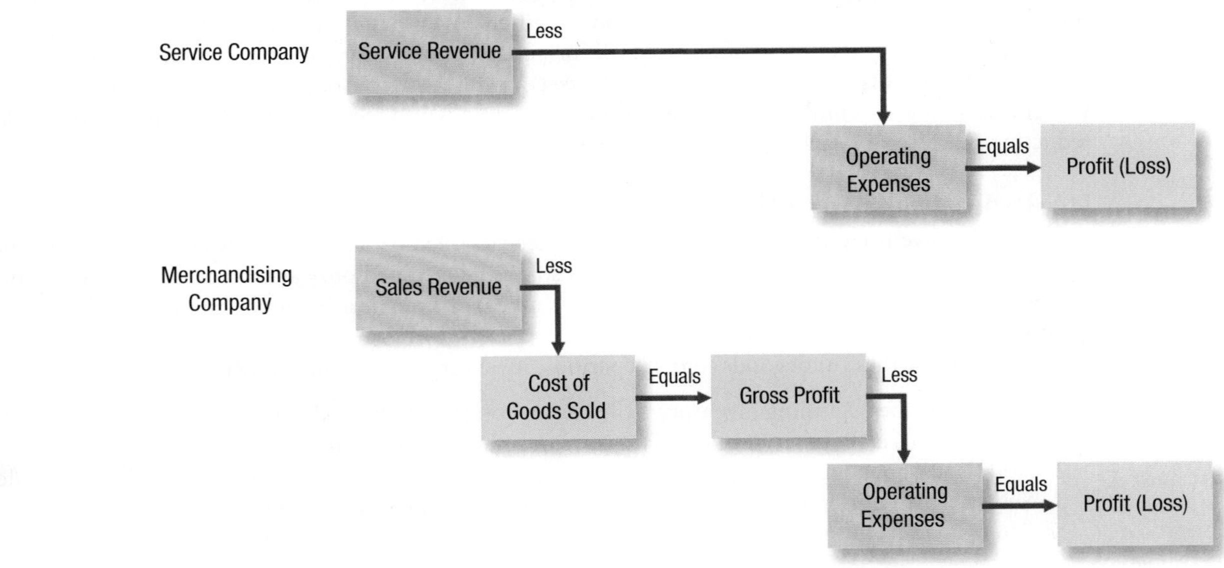

In addition, you will recall from Chapter 4 that the operating cycle—the time it takes to go from cash to cash in producing revenues—is usually longer in a merchandising company than in a service company. The purchase of merchandise inventory and the lapse of time until it is sold lengthen the cycle. We will learn more about measuring the length of the operating cycle in later chapters.

INVENTORY SYSTEMS

A merchandising company must keep track of its inventory to determine what is available for sale (inventory) and what has been sold (cost of goods sold). The flow of costs for a merchandising company is as follows: Beginning inventory (inventory on hand at the beginning of the period) plus the cost of goods purchased is the cost of goods available for sale. As goods are sold, the cost of these goods becomes an expense (cost of goods sold). Those goods not sold by the end of the accounting period represent ending inventory. The ending inventory is reported as a current asset on the balance sheet. The cost of goods sold is an expense on the income statement. Illustration 5-2 describes these relationships.

Helpful hint The ending inventory from one fiscal year becomes the beginning inventory for the next fiscal year.

ILLUSTRATION 5-2
Flow of inventory costs for a merchandising company

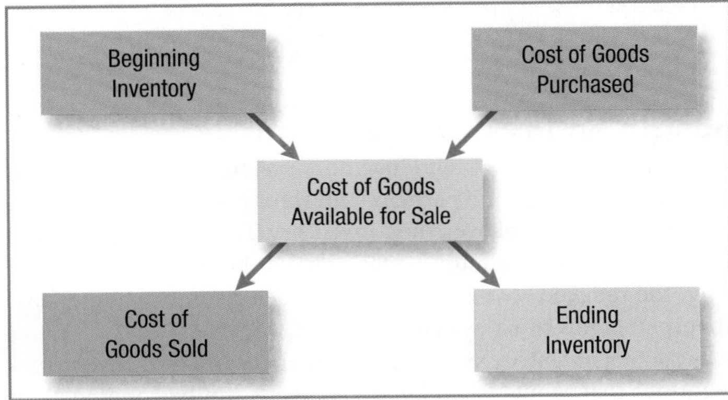

Companies use one of two kinds of systems to account for inventory: a *perpetual inventory system* or a *periodic inventory system.*

Perpetual Inventory System

In a **perpetual inventory system**, the company keeps detailed records of each inventory purchase and sale. This system continuously—perpetually—shows the quantity and cost of the inventory that should be on hand for every item. With the use of bar codes, optical scanners, and point-of-sale software, a store can keep a running record of every item that it buys and sells. Moulé in our feature story uses its perpetual inventory system so it constantly knows how much inventory it has in stock and its value based on its cost price.

When inventory is purchased under a perpetual system, the purchase is recorded by increasing (debiting) the Merchandise Inventory account. When inventory items are sold under a perpetual inventory system, the cost of the goods sold (the original purchase cost of the merchandise) is transferred from the Merchandise Inventory account (an asset) to the Cost of Goods Sold account (an expense). Under a perpetual inventory system, the company determines and records the cost of goods sold and the reduction in inventory **each time a sale occurs**.

Periodic Inventory System

In a **periodic inventory system**, companies do not keep detailed inventory records of the goods on hand throughout the period. Instead, the cost of goods sold is determined **only at the end of the accounting period**; that is, *periodically*. At that point, the company takes a *physical inventory count* to determine the quantity and cost of the goods on hand.

To determine the cost of goods sold in a periodic inventory system, the following steps are necessary:

Helpful hint Cost of Goods Sold does not represent a ledger account. Rather, it shows the total value of the merchandise that a merchandiser had in its possession during the fiscal year (that is, what it started the year with plus goods that it purchased during the year).

1. Determine the beginning inventory—the cost of goods on hand at the beginning of the accounting period. (This is the same amount as the previous period's ending inventory.)
2. Add the cost of goods purchased during the period to determine the cost of goods available for sale.
3. Subtract the ending inventory—the cost of goods on hand at the end of the accounting period as determined from the physical inventory count—from the cost of goods available for sale.

Illustration 5-3 compares when each activity is done and the timing of the cost of goods sold calculation under the two inventory systems.

ILLUSTRATION 5-3
Comparing perpetual and periodic inventory systems

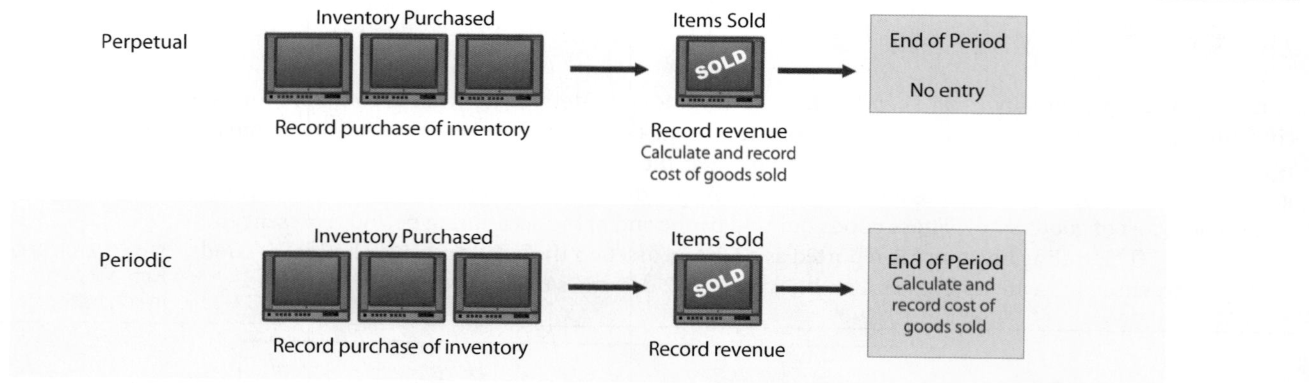

Choosing an Inventory System

How do companies decide which inventory system to use? They compare the cost of the detailed record keeping that is required for a perpetual inventory system with the benefits of having the additional information about, and control over, their inventory. Traditionally, only companies that sold merchandise with high unit values—such as automobiles or major home appliances—used the perpetual inventory system. However, the reduced cost of computers and electronic scanners has enabled many more companies to install perpetual inventory systems.

Helpful hint Note that under the perpetual inventory system, the inventory records indicate how much inventory the merchandiser *is supposed to have.* The actual quantity will generally be lower, as inventory lost due to shoplifting, employee theft, and so on would not have been tracked.

A perpetual inventory system gives better control over inventories. Since the inventory records show the quantities that *should be on hand*, the goods can be counted at any time to see whether the amount of goods actually on hand agrees with the inventory records. Any shortages that are uncovered can be immediately investigated.

A perpetual inventory system also makes it easier to answer questions from customers about merchandise availability. Management can also maintain optimum inventory levels and avoid running out of stock. As discussed in the feature story, Moulé likes to keep a certain inventory level in particular categories and uses its perpetual inventory system to track past sales. This helps the buyers to determine how much to buy and stock at each store.

Some businesses find it unnecessary or uneconomical to invest in a computerized perpetual inventory system. Many small businesses, in particular, find that a perpetual inventory system costs more than it is worth. Managers of these businesses can control merchandise and manage day-to-day operations using a periodic inventory system.

A complete physical inventory count is always taken at least once a year under both the perpetual and periodic inventory systems. Companies using a periodic inventory system must count their merchandise to determine quantities on hand and establish the cost of the goods sold and the ending inventory for accounting purposes. In a perpetual inventory system, they must count their merchandise to verify that the accounting records are correct. We will learn more about how to determine the quantity and cost of inventory later in this chapter and in the next chapter.

Because the perpetual inventory system is widely used, we illustrate it in this chapter. The periodic system is described in Appendix 5A.

BEFORE YOU GO ON...

DO IT

Darubra Company began the year with $15,000 of inventory. During the year, it purchased an additional $75,000 of inventory and earned $120,000 in sales revenue. At its year end, Darubra had to count its inventory to determine that it had $20,000 of inventory on hand.

(a) What kind of an inventory system does the company appear to be using?
(b) Determine the following: (1) cost of good available for sale; (2) cost of goods sold.
(c) With regard to its inventory, what will appear on Darubra's income statement and the balance sheet?

SOLUTION

(a) It appears the company is using the periodic system because it had to count its inventory in order to know how much was on hand. And there was no specific information given about the cost of goods sold during the year. From the information provided, cost of goods sold can only be calculated after counting the ending inventory.

(b) (1) Cost of Goods Available for Sale = $15,000 + $75,000 = $90,000
(2) Cost of Goods Sold = $90,000 − $20,000 = $70,000

(c)

Income statement:		Balance Sheet:	
Sales	$120,000	Current assets	
Cost of goods sold	70,000	Merchandise Inventory	$20,000

Related exercise material: BE5–1.

Action Plan

- Recall that in a perpetual system the cost of goods sold is calculated and recorded with each sale, and in the periodic system it is determined at the end of the year.
- Remember that beginning inventory + cost of goods purchased = cost of goods available for sale.
- Cost of goods available for sale − cost of inventory on hand = cost of goods sold.
- Expenses (including cost of goods sold) appear on an income statement; assets on the balance sheet.

THE NAVIGATOR

RECORDING PURCHASES OF MERCHANDISE

STUDY OBJECTIVE 2

Prepare entries for purchases under a perpetual inventory system.

Companies purchase inventory using either cash or credit (on account). They normally record purchases when the goods are received from the seller. Every purchase should be supported by a document, either a hard copy or an electronic copy, that provides written evidence of the transaction.

For example, there should be a cash receipt that indicates the items purchased and the amounts paid for each cash purchase. Cash purchases are recorded by an increase in Merchandise Inventory and a decrease in Cash.

Credit purchases should be supported by a purchase invoice showing the total purchase price and other relevant information. The purchaser uses a copy of the sales invoice sent by the seller as a purchase invoice. For example, in Illustration 5-4, Chelsea Electronics (the buyer) uses as a purchase invoice the sales invoice prepared by Highpoint Audio & TV Supply (the seller).

The buyer, Chelsea Electronics, makes the following entry to record the purchase of merchandise from Highpoint Audio & TV Supply. The entry increases (debits) Merchandise Inventory and increases (credits) Accounts Payable.

May 4	Merchandise Inventory	3,800	
	Accounts Payable		3,800
	To record goods purchased on account per invoice #731, terms 2/10, n/30.		

A	=	L	+	OE
+3,800		+3,800		

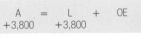

Cash flows: no effect

ILLUSTRATION 5-4
Sales/purchase invoice

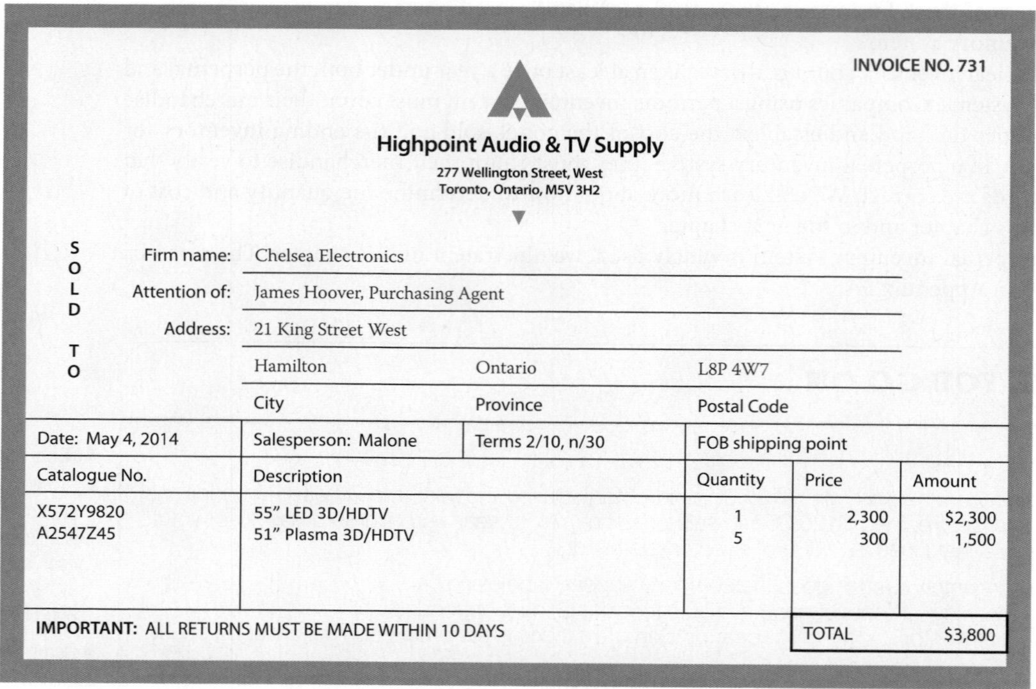
INVOICE NO. 731

Highpoint Audio & TV Supply
277 Wellington Street, West
Toronto, Ontario, M5V 3H2

SOLD TO

Firm name: Chelsea Electronics
Attention of: James Hoover, Purchasing Agent
Address: 21 King Street West
Hamilton (City) Ontario (Province) L8P 4W7 (Postal Code)

Date: May 4, 2014	Salesperson: Malone	Terms 2/10, n/30	FOB shipping point		
Catalogue No.	Description		Quantity	Price	Amount
X572Y9820	55" LED 3D/HDTV		1	2,300	$2,300
A2547Z45	51" Plasma 3D/HDTV		5	300	1,500
IMPORTANT: ALL RETURNS MUST BE MADE WITHIN 10 DAYS				TOTAL	$3,800

Helpful hint When deciding which asset to debit, it is important to consider *why* the company is buying it. A furniture store that purchased a desk for *resale* would debit Merchandise Inventory, but if it purchased a similar desk for *its own use* in its office, it would debit Office Equipment.

Only the goods purchased to sell to customers are recorded in the Merchandise Inventory account. As we learned in Chapter 2, purchases of assets to use in the business—such as supplies or equipment—should be debited to the specific asset accounts.

SUBSIDIARY INVENTORY RECORDS

Imagine an organization like Moulé recording purchases and sales of its 24,000 inventory items in only one general ledger account—Merchandise Inventory. It would be almost impossible to determine the balance remaining of any particular inventory item at any specific time.

Instead, under a perpetual inventory system, a subsidiary ledger is used to organize and track individual inventory items. A **subsidiary ledger** is a group of accounts that share a common characteristic (for example, all inventory accounts). The subsidiary ledger frees the general ledger from the details of individual balances. In addition to having one for inventory, it is very common to have subsidiary ledgers for accounts receivable (to track individual customer balances), accounts payable (to track individual creditor balances), and payroll (to track individual employee pay records).

A subsidiary ledger is an addition to, and an expansion of, the general ledger, as Illustration 5-5 shows.

ILLUSTRATION 5-5
Relationship of general ledger and subsidiary ledgers

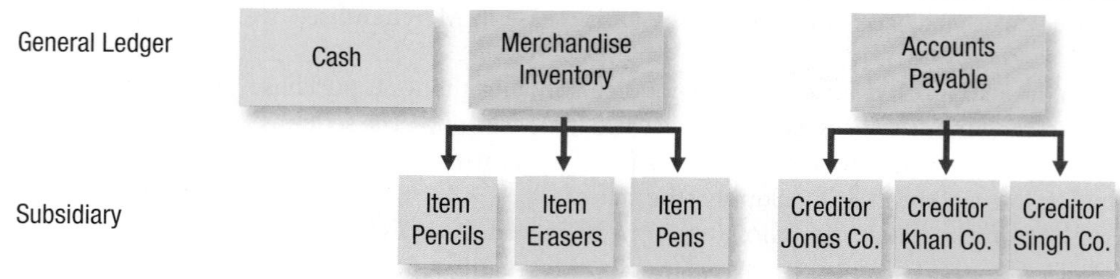

The general ledger account that summarizes the subsidiary ledger data is called a **control account**. In this illustration, the general ledger accounts Merchandise Inventory and Accounts Payable are control accounts with subsidiary ledgers. Cash is not a control account because there is no subsidiary ledger for this account.

Purchases and sales of each item of merchandise are recorded and posted to the individual inventory subsidiary ledger account. At any point in time, the inventory subsidiary ledger shows detailed information about the quantity and cost of each inventory item.

The detailed individual data from the inventory subsidiary ledger are summarized in the Merchandise Inventory control account in the general ledger. At all times, the control account balance must equal the total of all the individual inventory account balances.

Helpful hint Merchandise inventory, as with other assets, is valued at its cost price (the price that the merchandiser paid for it) as opposed to the price that it hopes to charge when it sells the goods. This follows the cost principle under GAAP.

SALES TAXES

Sales taxes include the federal Goods and Services Tax (GST), the Provincial Sales Tax (PST), and in several provinces, the Harmonized Sales Tax (HST), which is a combination of GST and PST. GST or HST are paid by merchandising companies on the goods they purchase for resale. However, this cost is rarely part of the cost of the merchandise, because in most businesses companies can get back any GST or HST they pay on purchases by offsetting it against the GST or HST they collect from customers or by filing a claim with the government.

PST is not paid by a merchandiser—it is paid only by the final consumer. Therefore, retail businesses do not have to pay PST on any merchandise they purchase for resale.

The accounting transactions described in this textbook are presented without the added complexity of sales taxes. That is why Invoice No. 731 shown in Illustration 5-4 did not include HST, which would normally be added to the invoice price for a business operating in Ontario.

FREIGHT COSTS

The sales/purchase invoice should indicate when ownership of the goods transfers from the seller to the buyer. The company that owns the goods while they are being transported to the buyer's place of business pays the transportation charges and is responsible for any damage to the merchandise during transit. The point where ownership is transferred is called the FOB point and may be expressed as either "FOB destination" or "FOB shipping point." The letters FOB mean "free on board."

Alternative terminology Other common shipping terms include *FCA* (free carrier), *CIF* (cost, insurance, freight), *FAS* (free alongside), and *CPT* (carriage paid to).

FOB shipping point means:

1. Ownership changes from the seller to the buyer when the goods are placed on the carrier by the seller—the "shipping point."
2. The buyer pays the freight costs and is responsible for damages.

FOB destination means:

1. Ownership changes from the seller to the buyer when the goods are delivered by the carrier to the buyer's place of business—the "destination."
2. The seller pays the freight and is responsible for damages.

For example, the purchase invoice in Illustration 5-4 indicates that freight is FOB shipping point. The buyer (Chelsea Electronics) therefore pays the freight charges. Illustration 5-6 demonstrates these shipping terms.

ILLUSTRATION 5-6
Terms of shipping

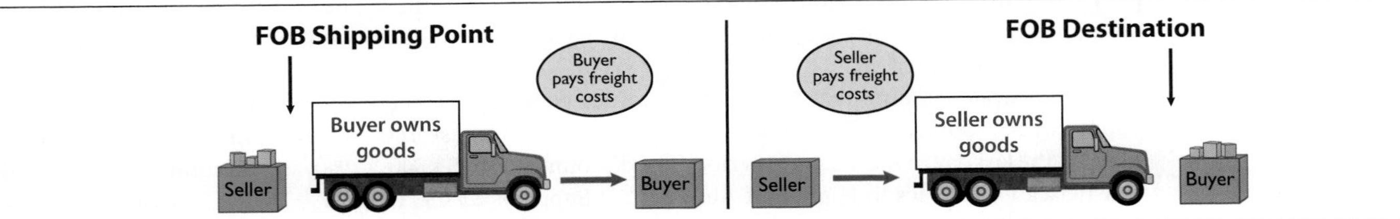

When the buyer pays for the freight costs, Merchandise Inventory is debited for the cost of the transportation. Why? Freight is just another part of the cost of purchasing the goods.

For example, if upon delivery of the goods to Chelsea Electronics on May 4, Chelsea pays Public Carrier Co. $150 for freight charges, the entry on Chelsea Electronics' books is:

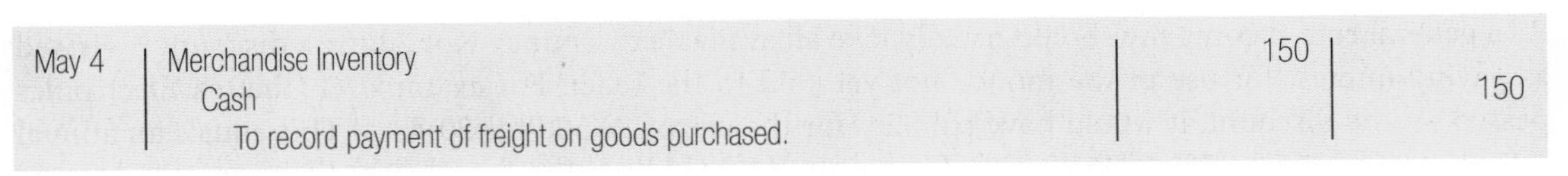

May 4	Merchandise Inventory	150	
	Cash		150
	To record payment of freight on goods purchased.		

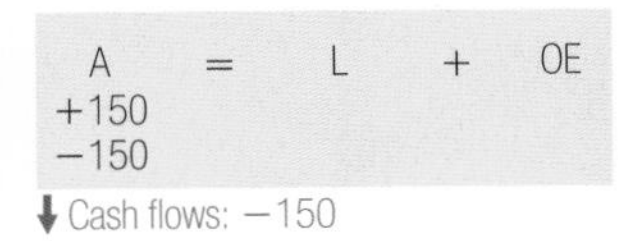

A	=	L	+	OE
+150				
−150				

Cash flows: −150

Thus, any freight costs incurred by the buyer are included in the cost of the merchandise.

PURCHASE RETURNS AND ALLOWANCES

A purchaser may be dissatisfied with the merchandise received if the goods are damaged or defective or of inferior quality, or if the goods do not meet the purchaser's specifications. In such cases, the purchaser may return the goods to the seller. This transaction is known as a **purchase return**. Alternatively, the purchaser may choose to keep the merchandise if the seller is willing to grant an allowance (deduction) from the purchase price. This transaction is known as a **purchase allowance**.

Assume that Chelsea Electronics returned goods costing $300 to Highpoint Audio & TV Supply on May 9. Highpoint will issue Chelsea a credit, which allows Chelsea to reduce its accounts payable. The entry by Chelsea Electronics for the returned merchandise is as follows:

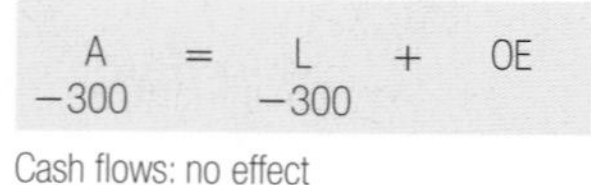

Cash flows: no effect

May 9	Accounts Payable	300	
	Merchandise Inventory		300
	To record return of goods to Highpoint Audio & TV Supply.		

Because Chelsea Electronics increased Merchandise Inventory when the goods were purchased, Merchandise Inventory is decreased when Chelsea Electronics returns the goods (or when it is granted an allowance).

DISCOUNTS

Some events do not require a separate journal entry. For example, the terms of a credit purchase may include an offer of a **quantity discount** for a bulk purchase. A quantity discount gives a reduction in price according to the volume of the purchase—in other words, the larger the number of items purchased, the better the discount. Quantity discounts are not recorded or accounted for separately.

Quantity discounts are not the same as **purchase discounts**, which are offered to customers for early payment of the balance due. This incentive offers advantages to both parties: the purchaser saves money and the seller shortens its operating cycle by more quickly converting accounts receivable to cash.

Purchase discounts are noted on the invoice by the use of credit terms that specify the amount and time period for the purchase discount. They also indicate the length of time the buyer has to pay the full invoice price. In the sales invoice in Illustration 5-4, credit terms are 2/10, n/30 (read "two ten, net thirty"). This means that a 2% cash discount may be taken on the invoice price (less any returns or allowances) if payment is made within 10 days of the invoice date (the discount period). Otherwise, the invoice price, less any returns or allowances, is due 30 days from the invoice date.

Although purchase discounts are common in certain industries, not every seller offers them. When the seller chooses not to offer a discount for early payment, credit terms will specify only the maximum time period for paying the balance due. For example, the time period may be stated as n/30, meaning that the net amount must be paid in 30 days.

In contrast to quantity discounts, purchase discounts are recorded separately. When an invoice is paid within the discount period, the Merchandise Inventory account will be reduced by the amount of the discount because inventory is recorded at cost. By paying within the discount period, a company reduces the cost of its inventory.

To illustrate, assume that Chelsea Electronics pays the balance owing to Highpoint Audio & TV Supply of $3,500 (gross invoice price of $3,800 less purchase returns and allowances of $300) on May 14, the last day of the discount period. The discount is $70 ($3,500 × 2%), and the amount of cash paid by Chelsea Electronics to Highpoint Audio & TV Supply is $3,430 ($3,500 − $70). Chelsea Electronics' entry to record its May 14 payment to Highpoint Audio & TV Supply is:

A = L + OE
−70 −3,500
−3,430

Cash flows: −3,430

May 14	Accounts Payable	3,500	
	Merchandise Inventory		70
	Cash		3,430
	To record payment of invoice #731 within discount period.		

As a general rule, a company should usually take all available discounts. Not taking a discount is viewed as paying interest for use of the money not yet paid to the seller. For example, if Chelsea Electronics passed up the discount, it would have paid 2% for the use of $3,500 for 20 days. This equals an annual interest rate of 36.5% (2% × 365 ÷ 20). Obviously, it would be better for Chelsea Electronics to borrow at bank interest rates than to lose the purchase discount.

If, contrary to best practices, Chelsea Electronics did not take advantage of the purchase discount and instead made full payment of $3,500 on June 3, the journal entry to record this payment would be:

June 3	Accounts Payable	3,500	
	Cash		3,500
	To record payment of invoice #731 with no discount taken.		

A	=	L	+	OE
−3,500		−3,500		

↓ Cash flows: −3,500

SUMMARY OF PURCHASE TRANSACTIONS

The following T account (with transaction descriptions in parentheses) gives a summary of the effects of the transactions on Merchandise Inventory. Chelsea Electronics originally purchased $3,800 worth of inventory for resale. It paid $150 in freight charges. It then returned $300 worth of goods. And Chelsea Electronics received a discount of $70 by paying Highpoint Audio & TV Supply in the discount period. This results in a balance in Merchandise Inventory of $3,580.

	Merchandise Inventory				
Purchase	May 4	3,800	May 9	300	**Purchase return**
Freight	4	150	14	70	**Purchase discount**
	Bal.	3,580			

BEFORE YOU GO ON...

DO IT

New Idea Company had the following transactions in September:

Sept. 4	Bought merchandise on account from Juno Company for $1,500, terms 2/10, n/30, FOB destination.
5	The correct company paid freight charges of $75.
8	Returned $200 of the merchandise to Juno Company.
14	Paid the total amount owing.

(a) Record the transactions on New Idea Company's books and (b) post the transactions to the inventory account.

SOLUTION

(a)

New Idea Company (buyer)

Sept. 4	Merchandise Inventory	1,500	
	Accounts Payable		1,500
	To record goods purchased on account.		
5	No journal entry. Terms FOB destination, therefore seller pays the freight.		
8	Accounts Payable	200	
	Merchandise Inventory		200
	To record return of goods.		
14	Accounts Payable ($1,500 − $200)	1,300	
	Merchandise Inventory ($1,300 × 2%)		26
	Cash ($1,300 − $26)		1,274
	To record cash payment within the discount period.		

Action Plan

- Purchases of goods for resale are debited to the asset account Merchandise Inventory.
- Freight costs are paid by the seller when the freight terms are FOB destination.
- Freight charges paid by the purchaser increase the cost of the merchandise inventory.
- The Merchandise Inventory account is reduced by the cost of merchandise returned.
- Calculate purchase discounts using the net amount owing.
- The Merchandise Inventory account should be reduced by the amount of the purchase discount.

BEFORE YOU GO ON... continued on next page

BEFORE YOU GO ON...
continued from previous page

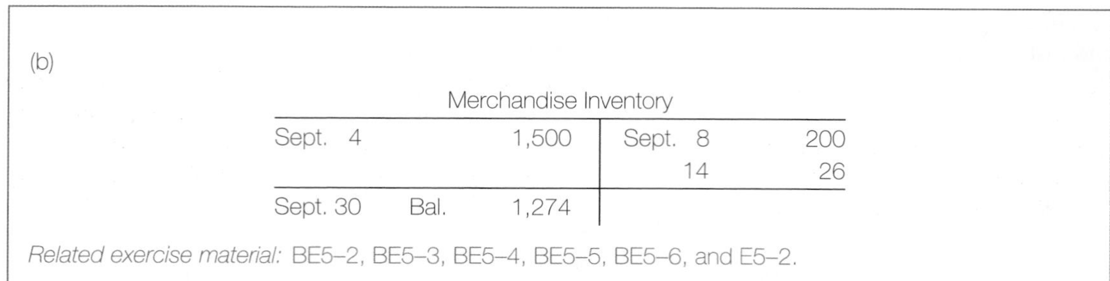

(b)

Merchandise Inventory				
Sept. 4		1,500	Sept. 8	200
			14	26
Sept. 30	Bal.	1,274		

Related exercise material: BE5–2, BE5–3, BE5–4, BE5–5, BE5–6, and E5–2.

RECORDING SALES OF MERCHANDISE

STUDY OBJECTIVE 3
Prepare entries for sales under a perpetual inventory system.

Sales revenue, like service revenue, is recorded when there is an increase in assets (typically cash or accounts receivable) resulting from the company's business activities with its customers. For merchandising companies, this means that sales revenue is recorded (recognized) when the ownership of the goods is transferred from the seller to the buyer. This is typically when the goods have been sold and delivered. At this point, the sales transaction is completed and the sale price has been established. Alternatively, if the customer has paid in advance, a merchandiser may decrease a liability (unearned sales revenue) when the sales transaction is completed.

Helpful hint Recall that under the revenue recognition principle, revenue is recognized (that is, credited) when it is earned. This is not necessarily when the cash is received.

Sales of merchandise may be made on credit or for cash. Every sales transaction should be supported by a business document that gives written evidence of the sale. Cash register tapes provide evidence of cash sales. A sales invoice, like the one shown in Illustration 5-4, provides support for a credit or cash sale. The seller prepares the invoice and gives a copy to the buyer.

Two entries are made for each sale in a perpetual inventory system:

1. The first entry records the sales revenue: Cash (or Accounts Receivable, if it is a credit sale) is increased by a debit, and the revenue account Sales is increased by a credit for the selling (invoice) price of the goods.
2. The second entry records the cost of the merchandise sold: the expense account Cost of Goods Sold is increased by a debit, and the asset account Merchandise Inventory is decreased by a credit for the cost of the goods. This entry ensures that the Merchandise Inventory account will always show the amount of inventory that should be on hand.

To illustrate a credit sales transaction, we will use the sales invoice shown in Illustration 5-4. Assuming that the merchandise cost Highpoint $2,400 when purchased, Highpoint Audio & TV Supply's $3,800 sale to Chelsea Electronics on May 4 is recorded as follows:

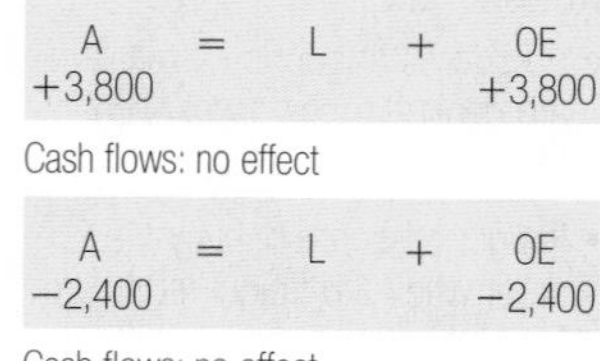

Date	Account Titles and Explanation	Debit	Credit
May 4	Accounts Receivable	3,800	
	Sales		3,800
	To record credit sale to Chelsea Electronics per invoice #731.		
4	Cost of Goods Sold	2,400	
	Merchandise Inventory		2,400
	To record cost of merchandise sold to Chelsea Electronics per invoice #731.		

For internal decision-making purposes, merchandisers may use more than one sales account, just as they use more than one inventory account. For example, Highpoint Audio & TV Supply may keep separate sales accounts for its televisions, DVD players/recorders, and home theatre systems. By using separate sales accounts for major product lines, company management can monitor sales trends more closely and respond more strategically to changes in sales patterns. For example, if home theatre system sales are increasing while DVD player/recorder sales are decreasing, the company can re-evaluate its advertising and pricing policies on each of these items.

On the income statement shown to outside investors, a merchandiser would normally give only a single sales figure—the sum of all of its individual sales accounts. This is done for two reasons. First, giving details on individual sales accounts would add too much length to the income statement and possibly make it less understandable. Second, companies do not want their competitors to know the details of their operating results.

SALES TAXES

Sales taxes are collected by merchandising companies on the goods that they sell. When a company collects sales taxes on the sale of a good or service, these sales taxes are recorded as a liability rather than as revenue. The sales taxes are collected for the federal and provincial governments, and are owed to these collecting authorities. Sales taxes that are collected on the sale of a good or service are shown as a liability until they are paid to the governments.

FREIGHT COSTS

As discussed earlier in the chapter, freight terms—FOB destination and FOB shipping point—on the sales invoice indicate when ownership is transferred, and they therefore indicate who is responsible for shipping costs. As explained earlier, if the term is FOB destination, the seller is responsible for getting the goods to their intended destination.

In Highpoint Audio & TV Supply's sale of electronic equipment to Chelsea Electronics, the freight terms (FOB shipping point) indicate that the purchaser, Chelsea Electronics, must pay the cost of shipping the goods from Highpoint Audio & TV Supply's location in Toronto to Chelsea Electronics' location in Hamilton. **Highpoint Audio & TV Supply, the seller, makes no journal entry to record the cost of shipping, since this is Chelsea's cost and therefore will not cause Highpoint's financial position to change.**

If the freight terms on the invoice in Illustration 5-4 had been FOB destination, then Highpoint Audio & TV Supply would have paid the delivery charge. Freight costs paid by the seller on merchandise sold are an operating expense to the seller and are debited to the Freight Out account. Costs incurred to earn revenue are recorded as expenses. **The following journal entry shows how Highpoint would have recorded the freight transaction if the terms had been FOB destination:**

Alternative terminology The *Freight Out* account is also called *Delivery Expense* by some companies.

May 4	Freight Out	150	
	Cash		150
	To record payment of freight on goods sold.		

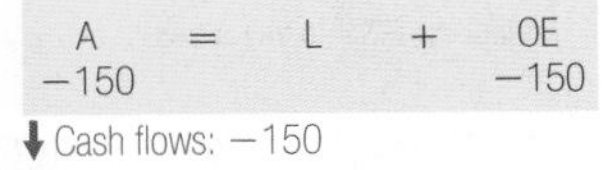

A	=	L	+	OE
−150				−150

⬇ Cash flows: −150

When the seller pays the freight charges, it will usually establish a higher invoice price for the goods to cover the shipping expense.

SALES RETURNS AND ALLOWANCES

We now look at the "flip side" of purchase returns and allowances, which the seller records as **sales returns and allowances.** When customers (purchasers) return goods, or are given price reductions, the seller will either return cash to the buyer, or reduce the buyer's account receivable if the goods were originally purchased on credit.

The seller will need to record the reduction in cash or accounts receivable as well as the reduction in sales. But it is important for management to know about the amount of sales returns and allowances. If there is a large amount of returns and allowances, this suggests that there is inferior merchandise, inefficiencies in filling orders, errors in billing customers, and/or mistakes in the delivery or shipment of goods. In order to provide information on sales returns and allowances to management, a **contra revenue account** called Sales Returns and Allowances is used. Recall that a contra account is deducted from its related account in the financial statements. By using a contra account, management can keep track of both the original sales and the amount of sales returns and allowances. To illustrate, Highpoint Audio & TV Supply will make the following entry to record the goods returned on May 9 by Chelsea Electronics for a credit of $300:

Helpful hint Remember that the increases, decreases, and normal balances (that is, debits and credits) of contra accounts are the opposite of the accounts they correspond to.

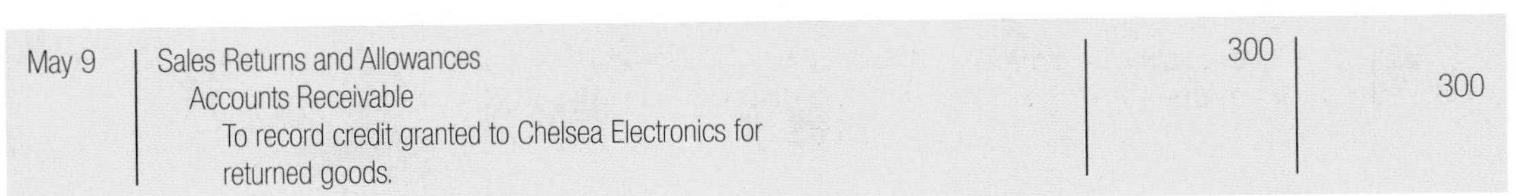

May 9	Sales Returns and Allowances	300	
	Accounts Receivable		300
	To record credit granted to Chelsea Electronics for returned goods.		

A	=	L	+	OE
−300				−300

Cash flows: no effect

If the merchandise is not damaged and can be sold again, the seller will also need to record a second entry when goods are returned. Assuming this is the case with the goods returned by Chelsea, and assuming that the goods originally cost Highpoint $140, Highpoint Audio & TV Supply will record a second entry as follows:

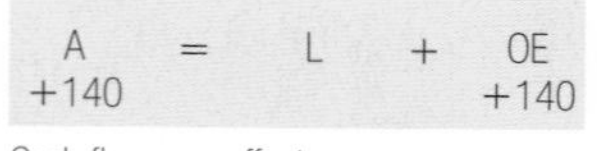

Cash flows: no effect

May 9	Merchandise Inventory	140	
	Cost of Goods Sold		140
	To record cost of returned goods.		

Notice that these two entries are basically the reverse of the entries recorded when the sale was originally made. Since the customer is reversing the original sale, it should make sense that the journal entries reflect this reversal.

If the goods are damaged or defective and can no longer be sold, the second entry is not prepared. The second entry is also not required when the seller gives the buyer an allowance. If the goods have not been returned, or are defective and cannot be resold, the seller cannot increase its Merchandise Inventory and the original cost of goods sold recorded is still the correct amount. Giving a customer a sales allowance, or letting it return defective goods, does not change the original cost of the goods sold.

ACCOUNTING IN ACTION

BUSINESS INSIGHT

Returned goods can put a dent in a business's profits. When a customer returns a product, the business has to decide whether to scrap, liquidate, refurbish, return to seller, or return to stock. Mississauga-based XS Cargo, one of the largest close-out retailers in Canada, has made a successful venture out of offering companies an opportunity to get some value out of unwanted products by liquidating them. It buys returned, refurbished, and excess merchandise from retailers, wholesalers, and manufacturers and sells it in outlets across Canada at deep discounts. It's essentially a win-win situation for businesses and consumers: consumers get good value on a variety of quality goods, while manufacturers, wholesalers, and retailers have a place to dispose of unwanted merchandise.

Source: "Duncan Reith Named President and CEO of XS Cargo," company news release, January 11, 2012; "Glitches Hurt XS Cargo," *Edmonton Journal*, May 10, 2007; XS Cargo website.

What accounting information would help a manager decide what to do with returned goods?

DISCOUNTS

Sales are recorded at invoice price—whether it is the full retail price, a sales price, or a volume discount price. No separate entry is made to record a quantity discount, or to show that the goods were sold at a special sales price.

Another type of discount, as discussed earlier in the chapter, is a cash discount for the early payment of the balance due. A seller may offer this to a customer to provide an incentive to pay early. From the seller's point of view, this is called a **sales discount**.

Basically, a sales discount is a reduction in the selling price that a customer may or may not take advantage of. At the point of sale, it is not known if the customer will use the discount, so the revenue recorded at the point of sale is the full invoice price. If the customer subsequently decides to take advantage of the discount, then the seller must record the fact that revenue has been reduced.

As with sales returns and allowances, management will want to monitor whether customers are taking advantage of the sales discounts. Thus, a second contra revenue account, **Sales Discounts**, is used instead of directly reducing the Sales account. The entry by Highpoint Audio & TV Supply to record the cash receipt from Chelsea Electronics on May 14 (within the discount period) is:

A	=	L	+	OE
+3,430				−70
−3,500				

↑Cash flows: +3,430

May 14	Cash	3,430	
	Sales Discounts	70	
	Accounts Receivable		3,500
	To record collection of invoice #731 within discount period.		

Helpful hint Note that increases to Sales Returns and Allowances and Sales Discounts are recorded on the debit side.

If the discount is not taken, and Chelsea Electronics instead pays the full amount on June 3, Highpoint Audio & TV Supply increases Cash and decreases Accounts Receivable by $3,500 at the date of collection, as shown on the next page:

June 3	Cash	3,500	
	Accounts Receivable		3,500
	To record collection of invoice #731 with no discount taken.		

A	=	L	+	OE
+3,500				
−3,500				

Cash flows: +3,500

SUMMARY OF SALES TRANSACTIONS

Highpoint Audio & TV Supply sold merchandise for $3,800, with $300 of it later returned. A sales discount of $70 was given because the invoice was paid within the discount period. In contrast to the purchase transactions shown earlier in the chapter, which affected only one account, Merchandise Inventory, sales transactions are recorded in different accounts. A summary of these transactions is provided in the following T accounts:

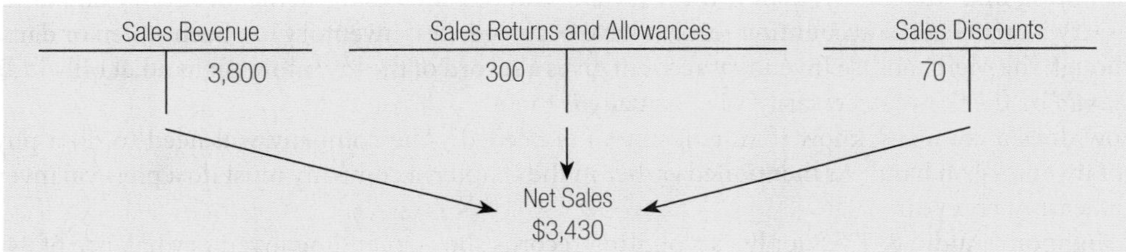

Helpful hint There is no ledger account called Net Sales. It is a calculation that shows the difference between Gross Sales and the combined total of Sales Returns and Allowances and Sales Discounts.

These three accounts are combined to determine net sales. **Net sales** is the balance in the Sales account (a credit) minus the balances in Sales Discounts and in Sales Returns and Allowances (both debits). Total sales, before deducting the contra revenue accounts, is also known as **gross sales**.

Net Sales = Gross Sales − Sales Returns and Allowances − Sales Discounts

BEFORE YOU GO ON...

DO IT

Record the following transactions for Juno Company:

Sept. 4	Sold merchandise for $1,500 on account to New Idea Company, terms 2/10, n/30, FOB destination. The original cost of the merchandise to Juno Company was $800.
5	The correct company pays freight charges of $75.
8	New Idea Company returned goods with a selling price of $200 and a cost of $80. The goods are restored to inventory.
14	Received the correct payment from New Idea Company.

SOLUTION

Juno Company (seller)

Sept. 4	Accounts Receivable	1,500	
	Sales		1,500
	To record credit sale.		
4	Cost of Goods Sold	800	
	Merchandise Inventory		800
	To record cost of goods sold.		
5	Freight Out	75	
	Cash		75
	To record freight paid on goods sold.		
8	Sales Returns and Allowances	200	
	Accounts Receivable		200
	To record credit given for receipt of returned goods.		
8	Merchandise Inventory	80	
	Cost of Goods Sold		80
	To record cost of goods returned.		
14	Cash ($1,300 − $26)	1,274	
	Sales Discounts ($1,300 × 2%)	26	
	Accounts Receivable ($1,500 − $200)		1,300
	To record cash receipt within the discount period.		

Related exercise material: BE5–7, BE5–8, BE5–9, E5–3, E5–4, and E5–5.

Action Plan

- Record both the sale and the cost of goods sold at the time of the sale.
- Freight costs are paid by the seller when the freight terms are FOB destination.
- Record sales returns in the contra account Sales Returns and Allowances and reduce Cost of Goods Sold when merchandise is returned to inventory.
- Calculate sales discounts using the net amount owing.
- Record sales discounts in the contra account Sales Discounts.

THE NAVIGATOR

COMPLETING THE ACCOUNTING CYCLE

STUDY OBJECTIVE 4

Perform the steps in the accounting cycle for a merchandising company.

Up to this point, we have shown the basic entries for recording transactions for purchases and sales in a perpetual inventory system. Now, it is time to consider the remaining steps in the accounting cycle for a merchandising company. All of the steps in the accounting cycle for a service company are also used for a merchandising company.

ADJUSTING ENTRIES

A merchandising company generally has the same types of adjusting entries as a service company. But a merchandiser that uses a perpetual inventory system may need one additional adjustment to ensure that the accounting inventory records show the same amount of goods as the actual inventory on hand. This is necessary if errors in the accounting records have occurred, or if inventory has been stolen or damaged. Even though the Merchandise Inventory account gives a record of the inventory on hand, it only indicates what *should* be there, not necessarily what actually *is* there.

How does a company know if an adjustment is needed? The company will need to do a physical count of inventory on hand. As mentioned earlier in the chapter, a company must do a physical inventory count at least once a year.

If Highpoint Audio & TV Supply's accounting records show an ending inventory balance of $40,500 at the end of May and a physical inventory count indicates only $40,000 on hand, the following adjusting journal entry should be prepared.

A	=	L	+	OE
−500				−500

Cash flows: no effect

Date	Account	Debit	Credit
May 31	Cost of Goods Sold	500	
	Merchandise Inventory		500
	To record difference between inventory records and physical units on hand.		

The procedures involved in doing a physical count, and arriving at the total cost of the items counted, are covered in Chapter 6.

ACCOUNTING IN ACTION
ALL ABOUT YOU INSIGHT

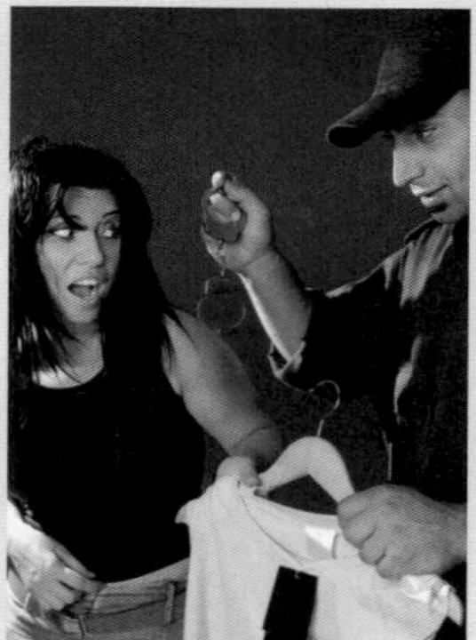

Retailers around the world lost an estimated US$119 billion in 2011 to shrinkage—inventory loss due to theft and other reasons. In Canada, shrinkage amounted to US$3.6 billion, or 1.49% of total sales. Globally, the causes of shrinkage were shoplifters (thought to be responsible for about 43% of inventory loss), employee theft (35%), internal errors including mispricing (16%), and dishonest suppliers/vendors (6%). Retailers are fighting back, spending more than US$28.3 billion on loss prevention measures in 2011. In Canada, for example, women's clothing chain Le Château became the first retailer to implement technology called Fitting Room Central, which allows staff to scan and keep track of items as they go in and out of the fitting rooms—one of the most popular places for shoplifting to occur. Within eight months, Le Château's largest Montreal store, with 20 change rooms, reduced shrinkage by $30,000. Other loss prevention technology measures used by stores are radio frequency identification tags, magnetic tags, and surveillance cameras. Retailers also use low-tech methods to protect inventory, such as employing security guards; counting the number of items customers bring in and out of fitting rooms; publicizing anti-theft policies to customers, employees, and suppliers; and prosecuting those caught in the act of stealing to send a strong signal that theft will not be tolerated.

Sources: Centre for Retail Research, "Global Retail Theft Barometer 2011"; PricewaterhouseCoopers Canada, "Q&A: Canadian Retail Security Survey 2008"; Denise Deveau, "Out of Fitting Rooms, into the Profits," *Canadian Retailer*, September/October 2007.

Are there advantages to you as a customer when retailers increase theft prevention measures?

CLOSING ENTRIES

Using assumed data, an adjusted trial balance follows in Illustration 5-7 for Highpoint Audio & TV Supply at May 31, the company's year end. The accounts that are used only by a merchandising company are highlighted in red.

ILLUSTRATION 5-7
Adjusted trial balance

HIGHPOINT AUDIO & TV SUPPLY
Adjusted Trial Balance
May 31, 2014

	Debit	Credit
Cash	$ 9,500	
Notes receivable	20,000	
Accounts receivable	7,900	
Merchandise inventory	**40,000**	
Equipment	70,000	
Accumulated depreciation—equipment		$ 24,000
Accounts payable		25,800
Notes payable		36,000
R. Lamb, capital		45,000
R. Lamb, drawings	15,000	
Sales		**480,000**
Sales returns and allowances	**16,700**	
Sales discounts	**4,300**	
Cost of goods sold	**315,000**	
Salaries expense	45,000	
Rent expense	19,000	
Utilities expense	17,000	
Advertising expense	16,000	
Depreciation expense	8,000	
Freight out	**7,000**	
Insurance expense	2,000	
Interest revenue		1,000
Rent revenue		2,400
Interest expense	1,800	
Totals	$614,200	$614,200

A merchandising company, just like a service company, closes all accounts that affect profit to Income Summary. In journalizing, the company credits all temporary accounts with debit balances, and debits all temporary accounts with credit balances, as shown below for Highpoint Audio & TV Supply.

Date	Account	Debit	Credit
May 31	**Sales**	**480,000**	
	Interest Revenue	1,000	
	Rent Revenue	2,400	
	Income Summary		483,400
	To close income statement accounts with credit balances.		
31	Income Summary	451,800	
	Sales Returns and Allowances		**16,700**
	Sales Discounts		**4,300**
	Cost of Goods Sold		**315,000**
	Salaries Expense		45,000
	Rent Expense		19,000
	Utilities Expense		17,000
	Advertising Expense		16,000
	Depreciation Expense		8,000
	Freight Out		**7,000**
	Insurance Expense		2,000
	Interest Expense		1,800
	To close income statement accounts with debit balances.		
31	Income Summary	31,600	
	R. Lamb, Capital		31,600
	To close income summary to capital.		
	R. Lamb, Capital	15,000	
	R. Lamb, Drawings		15,000
	To close drawings to capital.		

Helpful hint A merchandising company has more temporary accounts than a service company. Remember that Sales Returns and Allowances, Sales Discounts, Cost of Goods Sold, and Freight Out are temporary accounts with debit balances and must be closed to Income Summary.

POST-CLOSING TRIAL BALANCE

After the closing entries are posted, all temporary accounts have zero balances. The R. Lamb, Capital account will have the same balance as is reported on the statement of owner's equity and balance sheet, and will be carried over to the next period. As with a service company, the final step in the accounting cycle is to prepare a post-closing trial balance. You will recall that the purpose of this trial balance is to ensure that debits equal credits in the permanent (balance sheet) accounts after all temporary accounts have been closed.

The only new account in the post-closing trial balance of a merchandising company is the current asset account Merchandise Inventory. The post-closing trial balance is prepared in the same way as described in Chapter 4 and is not shown again here.

SUMMARY OF MERCHANDISING ENTRIES

Illustration 5-8 summarizes the entries for the merchandising accounts using a perpetual inventory system.

ILLUSTRATION 5-8
Daily recurring, adjusting, and closing entries

	Transactions	Daily Recurring Entries	Debit	Credit
Purchases	Purchasing merchandise for resale.	Merchandise Inventory	XX	
		Cash or Accounts Payable		XX
	Paying freight costs on merchandise purchases, FOB shipping point.	Merchandise Inventory	XX	
		Cash		XX
	Receiving purchase returns or allowances from suppliers.	Cash or Accounts Payable	XX	
		Merchandise Inventory		XX
	Paying creditors on account within discount period.	Accounts Payable	XX	
		Merchandise Inventory		XX
		Cash		XX
	Paying creditors on account after the discount period.	Accounts Payable	XX	
		Cash		XX
Sales	Selling merchandise to customers.	Cash or Accounts Receivable	XX	
		Sales		XX
		Cost of Goods Sold	XX	
		Merchandise Inventory		XX
	Giving sales returns or allowances to customers.	Sales Returns and Allowances	XX	
		Cash or Accounts Receivable		XX
		Merchandise Inventory	XX	
		Cost of Goods Sold		XX
	Paying freight costs on sales, FOB destination.	Freight Out	XX	
		Cash		XX
	Receiving payment on account from customers within discount period.	Cash	XX	
		Sales Discounts	XX	
		Accounts Receivable		XX
	Receiving payment on account from customers after discount period.	Cash	XX	
		Accounts Receivable		XX

ILLUSTRATION 5-8 *(continued)*

	Events	Adjusting and Closing Entries	Debit	Credit
Adjusting Entries	Determining, after a physical count, that inventory in general ledger is higher than inventory actually on hand.	Cost of Goods Sold	XX	
		Merchandise Inventory		XX
Closing Entries	Closing temporary accounts with credit balances.	Sales	XX	
		Other Revenues	XX	
		Income Summary		XX
	Closing temporary accounts with debit balances.	Income Summary	XX	
		Sales Returns and Allowances		XX
		Sales Discounts		XX
		Cost of Goods Sold		XX
		Freight Out		XX
		Other expenses		XX

BEFORE YOU GO ON...

DO IT

The trial balance of Yee Clothing Company at December 31 shows Merchandise Inventory $25,000; J. Yee, Capital $12,000; Sales $162,400; Sales Returns and Allowances $4,800; Sales Discounts $950; Cost of Goods Sold $110,000; Rental Revenue $6,000; Freight Out $1,800; Rent Expense $8,800; Salaries Expense $22,000; and J. Yee, Drawings $3,600. Yee Clothing Company's statement of owner's equity for the year showed profit of $20,050 and closing owner's capital of $28,450. (a) Prepare the closing entries for the above accounts. (b) Create T accounts for Income Summary and J. Yee, Capital, and post the closing entries to these accounts.

Action Plan

- Debit each temporary account with a credit balance for the same amount as its balance and credit the total to the Income Summary account.
- Credit each temporary account with a debit balance for the same amount as its balance and debit the total to the Income Summary account.
- Stop and check your work: Does the balance in the Income Summary account equal the reported profit?
- Debit the balance in the Income Summary account and credit the amount to the owner's capital account. (Do the opposite if the company had a loss.)
- Credit the balance in the drawings account and debit the amount to the owner's capital account. Do not close drawings with expenses.
- Stop and check your work: Do all the temporary accounts have zero balances? Does the balance in the owner's capital account equal the ending balance reported in the statement of owner's equity?

SOLUTION

Date	Account	Debit	Credit
Dec. 31	Sales	162,400	
	Rental Revenue	6,000	
	Income Summary		168,400
	To close income statement accounts with credit balances.		
31	Income Summary	148,350	
	Sales Returns and Allowances		4,800
	Sales Discounts		950
	Cost of Goods Sold		110,000
	Freight Out		1,800
	Rent Expense		8,800
	Salaries Expense		22,000
	To close income statement accounts with debit balances.		
31	Income Summary	20,050	
	J. Yee, Capital		20,050
	To close Income Summary account.		
31	J. Yee, Capital	3,600	
	J. Yee, Drawings		3,600
	To close drawings account.		

Income Summary

	Debit		Credit
Clos.	148,350	Clos.	168,400
		Bal.	20,050*
Clos.	20,050		
		Bal.	0

*Check = Profit

J. Yee, Capital

	Debit		Credit
		Bal.	12,000
Clos.	3,600	Clos.	20,050
		Bal.	28,450**

**Check = Closing owner's capital

Related exercise material: BE5–10, BE5–11, E5–6, and E5–7.

THE NAVIGATOR

MERCHANDISING FINANCIAL STATEMENTS

STUDY OBJECTIVE 5
Prepare single-step and multiple-step income statements.

Merchandisers widely use the classified balance sheet introduced in Chapter 4 and one of two forms of income statements. This section explains the use of these financial statements by merchandisers.

SINGLE-STEP INCOME STATEMENT

Helpful hint The single-step income statement is similar in appearance to the income statement of a service business.

The income statement form used in previous chapters of this textbook is the **single-step income statement**. The statement is so named because only one step—subtracting total expenses from total revenues—is required in determining profit.

In a single-step income statement, all data are classified under two categories: (1) revenues and (2) expenses. A single-step income statement for Highpoint Audio & TV Supply, using the data from the adjusted trial balance in Illustration 5-7, is shown in Illustration 5-9.

ILLUSTRATION 5-9
Single-step income statement

HIGHPOINT AUDIO & TV SUPPLY Income Statement Year Ended May 31, 2014		
Revenues		
Net sales		$459,000
Interest revenue		1,000
Rent revenue		2,400
Total revenues		462,400
Expenses		
Cost of goods sold	$315,000	
Salaries expense	45,000	
Rent expense	19,000	
Utilities expense	17,000	
Advertising expense	16,000	
Depreciation expense	8,000	
Freight out	7,000	
Insurance expense	2,000	
Interest expense	1,800	
Total expenses		430,800
Profit		**$ 31,600**

Note that net sales was calculated by deducting the contra revenue balances, sales returns and allowances, and sales discounts, from sales ($459,000 = $480,000 − $16,700 − $4,300). Revenue from investments, such as interest revenue, must be shown separately from other revenue. Cost of goods sold and interest expense (also income tax expense for corporations) must be reported separately on the income statement. Expenses that are not significant on their own can be included separately in the income statement as shown above, or grouped with other similar items, with additional details in the notes to the financial statements.

Under ASPE, companies do not have to list their expenses in any particular order. Under IFRS, companies must classify operating and other expenses based on either the **nature** of the expenses or their **function** within the company. Classifying expenses by nature means that expenses are reported based on what the resources were spent on (for example, depreciation, employee costs, transportation, and advertising). Classifying expenses by function means that expenses are reported based on which business function the resources were spent on (for example, costs of sales, administration, and selling).

Companies select the method, either nature or function, that provides the most relevant information. It should also be noted that if a company chooses to classify expenses according to function on the income statement, it has to report additional information about the nature of the expenses in the notes to the financial statements.

There are two main reasons for using the single-step format: (1) a company does not realize any profit until total revenues exceed total expenses, so it makes sense to divide the statement into these two categories; and (2) the single-step format is simple and easy to read.

MULTIPLE-STEP INCOME STATEMENT

The **multiple-step income statement** is so named because it shows several steps in determining profit (or loss). This form is often considered more useful than a single-step income statement because the steps give additional information about a company's profitability and distinguish between the company's operating and non-operating activities. The multiple-step income statement shows several steps, as explained below.

Net Sales

The multiple-step income statement for a merchandising company begins by presenting sales revenue. The contra revenue accounts Sales Returns and Allowances and Sales Discounts are deducted from Sales to arrive at **net sales**. The sales revenue section for Highpoint Audio & TV Supply (using data from the adjusted trial balance in Illustration 5-7) is as follows:

Sales revenue		
Sales		$480,000
Less: Sales returns and allowances	$16,700	
Sales discounts	4,300	21,000
Net sales		**459,000**

Many companies condense this information and report only the net sales figure in their income statement. This alternative was shown in the single-step income statement in Illustration 5-9.

Gross Profit

The next step is the calculation of gross profit. In Illustration 5-1, you learned that cost of goods sold is deducted from sales revenue to determine **gross profit**. For this calculation, companies use net sales as the amount of sales revenue. Based on the sales data above and the cost of goods sold in the adjusted trial balance in Illustration 5-7, the gross profit for Highpoint Audio & TV Supply is $144,000, calculated as follows:

Net sales	$459,000
Cost of goods sold	315,000
Gross profit	**144,000**

Operating Expenses

Operating expenses are the next component in measuring profit for a merchandising company. They are the recurring expenses associated with the central operations of the company—other than cost of goods sold—that are incurred in the process of earning sales revenue. These expenses are similar in service and merchandising companies.

Highpoint Audio & TV Supply would classify the following items in its adjusted trial balance (as shown in Illustration 5-7) as operating expenses: Salaries Expense, $45,000; Rent Expense, $19,000; Utilities Expense, $17,000; Advertising Expense, $16,000; Depreciation Expense, $8,000; Freight Out, $7,000; and Insurance Expense, $2,000. This results in total operating expenses of $114,000.

Recall our discussion in the single-step income statement section about classifying expenses by nature or function. Subdividing the operating expenses into selling expenses and administrative expenses is an example of classifying expenses by function. Selling expenses are associated with making sales. They include expenses for advertising and sales promotion, as well as the expenses of completing the sale (such as freight costs). Administrative expenses relate to general operating activities such as management, accounting, and legal costs. This classification method can be used in both multiple and single-step income statements.

Profit from Operations

Profit from operations, or the results of the company's normal operating activities, is determined by subtracting operating expenses from gross profit. Based on the gross profit and operating expenses data determined above, Highpoint Audio & TV Supply's profit from operations is $30,000, calculated as follows:

Gross profit	$144,000
Operating expenses	114,000
Profit from operations	**30,000**

The purpose of showing profit from operations as a separate number from overall profit is to assist users of financial statements in understanding the company's main operations. The additional information helps users in making projections of future financial performance.

Non-Operating Activities

Non-operating activities are other revenues and expenses not related to the company's main operations. Examples of other revenues include interest revenue, rental revenue (if earned from renting assets not needed for operations), and investment income. Examples of other expenses include interest expense.

Distinguishing between operating and non-operating activities is important to external users of financial statements. Non-operating activities are often short-term activities and are not expected to continue into the future as the company's main operating activities are. Separating the two in the income statement increases the predictive value of the statement.

Based on the data in Highpoint Audio & TV Supply's adjusted trial balance shown in Illustration 5-7, the company will show its non-operating activities as follows in its multiple-step income statement:

Other revenues	
Interest revenue	$1,000
Rent revenue	2,400
Total non-operating revenues	3,400
Other expenses	
Interest expense	1,800
Net non-operating revenues	**1,600**

It is also common for companies to combine the two non-operating sections—other revenues and other expenses—into a single "Other Revenues and Expenses" section.

Profit

Profit is the final outcome of all the company's operating and non-operating activities. Highpoint's profit is $31,600 after adding its net non-operating revenues of $1,600 to profit from operations as follows:

Profit from operations	$30,000
Net non-operating revenues	1,600
Profit	**$31,600**

If there are no non-operating activities, the company's profit from operations becomes its profit—or "bottom line."

Corporations, unlike proprietorships and partnerships, also have income tax expense. You will learn about how income tax expense is calculated and shown in an income statement in Chapter 13.

In Illustration 5-10, we bring together all of these steps in a comprehensive multiple-step income statement for Highpoint Audio & TV Supply.

Note that the profit amounts in Illustrations 5-9 (single-step) and 5-10 (multiple-step) are the same. The only differences between the two forms of income statements are the amount of detail shown and the order of presentation.

ILLUSTRATION 5-10
Multiple-step income statement

	HIGHPOINT AUDIO & TV SUPPLY Income Statement Year Ended May 31, 2014		
Calculation of net sales and gross profit	**Sales revenue**		
	Sales		$480,000
	Less: Sales returns and allowances	$16,700	
	Sales discounts	4,300	21,000
	Net sales		459,000
	Cost of goods sold		315,000
	Gross profit		144,000
Calculation of operating expenses and profit from operations	**Operating expenses**		
	Advertising expense	$16,000	
	Depreciation expense	8,000	
	Freight out	7,000	
	Insurance expense	2,000	
	Rent expense	19,000	
	Salaries expense	45,000	
	Utilities expense	17,000	
	Total operating expenses		114,000
	Profit from operations		30,000
Calculation of non-operating activities and profit	**Other revenues**		
	Interest revenue	$ 1,000	
	Rent revenue	2,400	
	Total non-operating revenues	3,400	
	Other expenses		
	Interest expense	1,800	
	Net non-operating revenues		1,600
	Profit		$ 31,600

CLASSIFIED BALANCE SHEET

Recall from Chapter 4 that merchandise inventory is a current asset because we expect to sell it within one year of the balance sheet date. Also recall from Chapter 4 that items are typically listed under current assets in their order of liquidity. Merchandise inventory is less liquid than accounts receivable and short-term notes receivable because the goods must first be sold before revenue can be collected from the customer. Thus, in the balance sheet, merchandise inventory is reported as a current asset immediately below accounts receivable. Illustration 5-11 presents the assets section of a classified balance sheet for Highpoint Audio & TV Supply.

Helpful hint Receivables can be thought of as being one step (their collection) away from being converted to cash. Merchandise inventory is two steps (the sale of the goods and the collection of the resulting receivable) from being converted to cash.

ILLUSTRATION 5-11
Assets section of a merchandising company's classified balance sheet

HIGHPOINT AUDIO & TV SUPPLY Balance Sheet (partial) May 31, 2014		
Assets		
Current assets		
Cash		$ 9,500
Notes receivable		20,000
Accounts receivable		7,900
Merchandise inventory		**40,000**
Total current assets		77,400
Property, plant, and equipment		
Equipment	$70,000	
Less: Accumulated depreciation	24,000	46,000
Total assets		$123,400

Helpful hint The $40,000 is the cost of the inventory on hand, not its expected selling price.

The remaining two financial statements, the statement of owner's equity and cash flow statement (to be discussed in Chapter 16), are the same as those of a service company. They are not shown in this chapter.

Action Plan

- Deduct Sales Returns and Allowances and Sales Discounts from Sales to arrive at net sales.
- Deduct Cost of Goods Sold from net sales to arrive at gross profit.
- Identify which expenses are operating expenses and which are non-operating expenses.
- Deduct operating expenses from gross profit to arrive at profit from operations.
- Deduct any non-operating expenses from (and add any non-operating revenues to) profit from operations to arrive at profit.

BEFORE YOU GO ON...

DO IT

Silver Store reported the following information: Sales $620,000; Sales Returns and Allowances $32,000; Sales Discounts $10,200; Cost of Goods Sold $422,000; Depreciation Expense $10,000; Freight Out $5,000; Interest Expense $1,700; Rent Expense $15,000; and Salaries Expense $80,000. Calculate the following amounts: (a) net sales, (b) gross profit, (c) total operating expenses, (d) profit from operations, and (e) profit.

SOLUTION

(a) Net sales: $620,000 − $32,000 − $10,200 = $577,800
(b) Gross profit: $577,800 − $422,000 = $155,800
(c) Total operating expenses: $10,000 + $5,000 + $15,000 + $80,000 = $110,000
(d) Profit from operations: $155,800 − $110,000 = $45,800
(e) Profit: $45,800 − $1,700 = $44,100

Related exercise material: BE5–12, BE5–13, E5–8, and E5–9.

USING THE INFORMATION IN THE FINANCIAL STATEMENTS

STUDY OBJECTIVE 6
Calculate the gross profit margin and profit margin.

In Chapter 4, we introduced a tool called ratio analysis that investors and creditors use to determine additional information about how a company is performing. In this chapter, we introduce two profitability ratios: **gross profit margin** and **profit margin**. **Profitability ratios** measure a company's operating success for a specific period of time.

GROSS PROFIT MARGIN

A company's gross profit may be expressed as a percentage, called the **gross profit margin**. This is calculated by dividing the amount of gross profit by net sales and converting the decimal to a percentage. Illustration 5-12 shows the gross profit margin for Reitmans for the year ended January 28, 2012 (expressed as thousands of dollars).

ILLUSTRATION 5-12
Gross profit margin

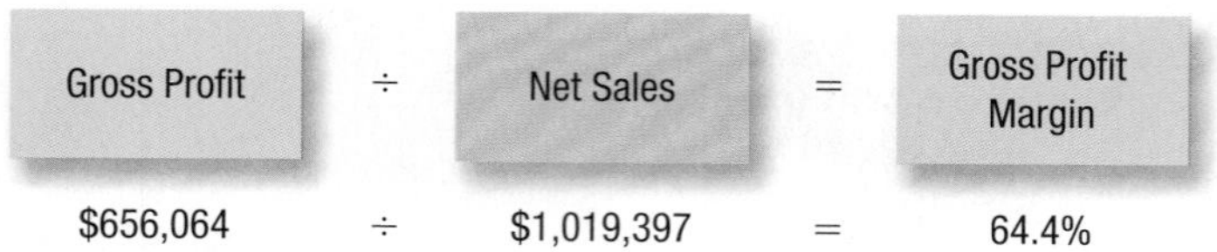

$656,064 ÷ $1,019,397 = 64.4%

The gross profit *margin* is generally considered to be more useful than the gross profit *amount* because the margin shows the relative relationship between net sales and gross profit. For example, a gross profit amount of $1 million may sound impressive. But, if it is the result of net sales of $50 million, then the gross profit margin is only 2%, which is not so impressive.

The amount and trend of gross profit are closely watched by management and other interested parties. They compare current gross profit margin with past periods' gross profit margin. They also compare the company's gross profit margin with the margin of competitors and with industry averages. Such comparisons give information about the effectiveness of a company's purchasing and the soundness of its pricing policies. In general, a higher gross profit margin is seen as being more favourable than a lower gross profit margin.

Gross profit is important because inventory has a significant effect on a company's profitability. Cost of goods sold is usually the largest expense on the income statement. Gross profit represents a company's merchandising profit. It is not a measure of the overall profitability, because operating expenses have not been deducted.

PROFIT MARGIN

Overall profitability is measured by examining profit. Profit is often expressed as a percentage of sales, similar to the gross profit margin. The **profit margin** measures the percentage of each dollar of sales that results in profit. It is calculated by dividing profit by net sales and expressing it as a percentage. Illustration 5-13 shows the profit margin for Reitmans for the year ended January 28, 2012 (dollars in thousands).

ILLUSTRATION 5-13
Profit margin

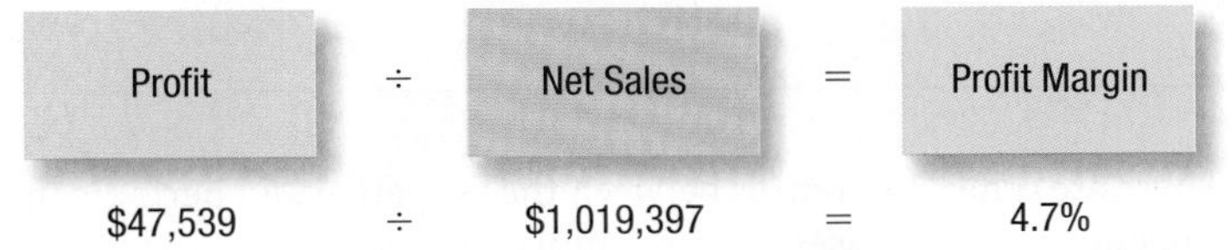

$47,539	÷	$1,019,397	=	4.7%

How do the gross profit margin and profit margin differ? The gross profit margin measures the difference between the amount that the merchandiser was able to sell its goods for, over and above the price they had to pay for the goods. The profit margin measures by how much the selling price covers all expenses (including the cost of goods sold). A company can improve its profit margin by increasing its gross profit margin, or by controlling its operating expenses (and non-operating activities), or by doing both.

Helpful hint For any business, the gross profit margin will always be greater than the profit margin.

BEFORE YOU GO ON...

DO IT

Selected financial information is available for two recent fiscal years for Antonia Co.

	2014	2013
Net sales	$550,000	$600,000
Cost of goods sold	300,000	350,000
Profit	50,000	25,000

(a) Calculate (1) gross profit, (2) gross profit margin, and (3) profit margin for 2013 and 2014.
(b) Comment on any changes in profitability.

SOLUTION

(a)

	2014	2013
(1) Gross profit	= $550,000 − $300,000 = $250,000	= $600,000 − $350,000 = $250,000
(2) Gross profit margin	= $250,000 ÷ $550,000 = 45.5%	= $250,000 ÷ $600,000 = 41.7%
(3) Profit margin	= $50,000 ÷ $550,000 = 9.1%	= $25,000 ÷ $600,000 = 4.2%

(b) The gross profit margin and profit margin have both increased in 2014 from 2013. In general, higher ratios indicate that the company's profitability has improved during 2014.

Related exercise material: BE5–14, E5–1, E5–10, and E5–11.

Action Plan

- Gross profit is net sales minus cost of goods sold.
- Divide gross profit by net sales and convert the decimal to a percentage to calculate gross profit margin.
- Divide profit by net sales and convert the decimal to a percentage to calculate profit margin.
- Recall whether higher or lower ratios indicate improvement or deterioration in profitability.

THE NAVIGATOR

APPENDIX 5A PERIODIC INVENTORY SYSTEM

STUDY OBJECTIVE 7
Prepare the entries for purchases and sales under a periodic inventory system and calculate cost of goods sold.

As described in this chapter, there are two basic systems of accounting for inventories: (1) the perpetual inventory system, and (2) the periodic inventory system. In the chapter, we focused on the characteristics of the more commonly used perpetual inventory system. In this appendix, we discuss and illustrate the periodic inventory system.

One key difference between the two inventory systems is the *timing* for calculating the cost of goods sold. In a periodic inventory system, the cost of the merchandise sold is not recorded on the date of sale. Instead, the cost of goods sold during the period is calculated by taking a physical inventory count at the end of the period and deducting the cost of this inventory from the cost of the merchandise available for sale during the period, as shown in Illustration 5A-1.

ILLUSTRATION 5A-1
Basic formula for cost of goods sold

There are other differences between the perpetual and periodic inventory systems. Under a periodic inventory system, purchases of merchandise are recorded in the **Purchases** expense account, rather than the Merchandise Inventory asset account. Also, under a periodic system, it is customary to record in separate accounts **purchase returns and allowances**, **purchase discounts**, and **freight in**. That way, accumulated amounts are known for each.

To illustrate the recording of merchandise transactions under a periodic inventory system, we will use the purchase/sale transactions between Highpoint Audio & TV Supply (the seller) and Chelsea Electronics (the buyer) from earlier in this chapter.

RECORDING PURCHASES OF MERCHANDISE

Based on the sales invoice (Illustration 5-4) and receipt of the merchandise ordered from Highpoint Audio & TV Supply, Chelsea Electronics records the $3,800 purchase as follows:

A	=	L	+	OE
		+3,800		−3,800

Cash flows: no effect

May 4	Purchases	3,800	
	Accounts Payable		3,800
	To record goods purchased on account per invoice #731, terms 2/10, n/30.		

Purchases is a temporary account whose normal balance is a debit.

Helpful hint Note that Purchases refers to purchases of goods for resale. This account is only used for goods that a merchandising business intends to sell to its customers and not to goods that it plans to use in the business.

Freight Costs

When the buyer pays for the freight costs, the account **Freight In** is debited. For example, Chelsea pays Public Carrier Co. $150 for freight charges on its purchase from Highpoint Audio & TV Supply. The entry on Chelsea's books is as follows:

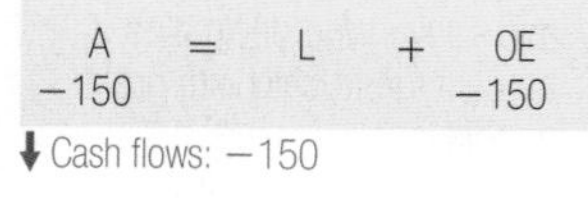

May 4	Freight In	150	
	Cash		150
	To record payment of freight on goods purchased and shipped FOB shipping point.		

Like Purchases, Freight In is a temporary (expense) account whose normal balance is a debit. Just as freight was a part of the cost of the merchandise inventory in a perpetual inventory system, freight in is part of the cost of goods purchased in a periodic inventory system. The cost of goods purchased should include any freight charges for transporting the goods to the buyer.

Purchase Returns and Allowances

Chelsea Electronics returns $300 worth of goods and prepares the following entry to recognize the return:

May 9	Accounts Payable	300	
	Purchase Returns and Allowances		300
	To record return of goods to Highpoint Audio & TV Supply.		

A	=	L	+	OE
		−300		+300

Cash flows: no effect

Purchase Returns and Allowances is a temporary account whose normal balance is a credit. It is a contra account that is subtracted from the Purchases account as part of the calculation to determine **Net Purchases**.

Purchase Discounts

Recall that the invoice terms were 2/10, n/30. On May 14, Chelsea Electronics pays the balance owing to Highpoint Audio & TV Supply of $3,500 ($3,800 less return of $300) less the 2% discount for payment within 10 days. Chelsea Electronics records the following entry:

May 14	Accounts Payable ($3,800 − $300)	3,500	
	Purchase Discounts ($3,500 × 2%)		70
	Cash ($3,500 − $70)		3,430
	To record payment of invoice #731 within discount period.		

A	=	L	+	OE
−3,430		−3,500		+70

↓ Cash flows: −3,430

Purchase Discounts is a temporary account whose normal balance is a credit. It is a contra account subtracted from the Purchases account.

In each of the above transactions, a temporary expense account was used to record the transactions related to purchases of merchandise rather than the Merchandise Inventory account that is used in a perpetual inventory system. A comparison of purchase transactions under the two inventory systems is shown later in the appendix.

RECORDING SALES OF MERCHANDISE

The seller, Highpoint Audio & TV Supply, records the sale of $3,800 of merchandise to Chelsea Electronics on May 4 (sales invoice in Illustration 5-4) as follows:

May 4	Accounts Receivable	3,800	
	Sales		3,800
	To record credit sale to Chelsea Electronics per invoice #731.		

A	=	L	+	OE
+3,800				+3,800

Cash flows: no effect

As previously explained, in a periodic inventory system, there is no entry to record the cost of goods sold and reduction of inventory at the point of sale.

Freight Costs

There is no difference between the accounting for freight costs by the seller in a perpetual and a periodic inventory system. In both systems, freight costs paid by the seller are debited to Freight Out, an operating expense account. Recall that in this example the freight terms were FOB shipping point, so Highpoint did not incur freight costs.

Sales Returns and Allowances

The $300 return of goods on May 9 is recorded by Highpoint Audio & TV Supply as follows:

May 9	Sales Returns and Allowances	300	
	Accounts Receivable		300
	To record credit given to Chelsea Electronics for returned goods.		

A	=	L	+	OE
−300				−300

Cash flows: no effect

Just as there is only one entry needed when sales are recorded in a periodic inventory system, one entry is also all that is needed to record a return. Unlike the perpetual system, it doesn't matter if the inventory is damaged and discarded, or returned to inventory; no entry is needed in the periodic inventory system.

Sales Discounts

On May 14, Highpoint Audio & TV Supply receives a payment of $3,430 on account from Chelsea Electronics. Highpoint records this payment as follows:

A	=	L	+	OE
+3,430				−70
−3,500				

↑Cash flows: +3,430

May 14	Cash ($3,500 − $70)	3,430	
	Sales Discounts ($3,500 × 2%)	70	
	Accounts Receivable ($3,800 − $300)		3,500
	To record collection of invoice #731 within discount period.		

COMPARISON OF ENTRIES—PERPETUAL VS. PERIODIC

Illustration 5A-2 summarizes the periodic inventory entries shown in this appendix and compares them with the perpetual inventory entries shown earlier in the chapter. Entries that are different in the two systems are shown in colour.

ILLUSTRATION 5A-2
Comparison of journal entries under perpetual and periodic inventory systems

ENTRIES ON CHELSEA ELECTRONICS' BOOKS (BUYER)

	Transaction	Perpetual Inventory System			Periodic Inventory System		
May 4	Purchase of merchandise on credit.	**Merchandise Inventory**	**3,800**		**Purchases**	**3,800**	
		Accounts Payable		3,800	Accounts Payable		3,800
4	Freight cost on purchases.	**Merchandise Inventory**	**150**		**Freight In**	**150**	
		Cash		150	Cash		150
9	Purchase returns and allowances.	Accounts Payable	300		Accounts Payable	300	
		Merchandise Inventory		**300**	**Purchase Returns and Allowances**		**300**
14	Payment on account with a discount.	Accounts Payable	3,500		Accounts Payable	3,500	
		Merchandise Inventory		**70**	**Purchase Discounts**		**70**
		Cash		3,430	Cash		3,430

ENTRIES ON HIGHPOINT AUDIO & TV SUPPLY'S BOOKS (SELLER)

	Transaction	Perpetual Inventory System			Periodic Inventory System		
May 4	Sale of merchandise on credit.	Accounts Receivable	3,800		Accounts Receivable	3,800	
		Sales		3,800	Sales		3,800
		Cost of Goods Sold	**2,400**		**No entry for cost of goods sold**		
		Merchandise Inventory		**2,400**			
9	Return of merchandise sold.	Sales Returns and Allowances	300		Sales Returns and Allowances	300	
		Accounts Receivable		300	Accounts Receivable		300
		Merchandise Inventory	**140**		**No entry for cost of goods sold**		
		Cost of Goods Sold		**140**			
14	Cash received on account with a discount.	Cash	3,430		Cash	3,430	
		Sales Discounts	70		Sales Discounts	70	
		Accounts Receivable		3,500	Accounts Receivable		3,500

CALCULATING COST OF GOODS SOLD

In a periodic inventory system, the Merchandise Inventory account is not continuously updated for each purchase and sale. As we saw in the entries above, temporary accounts are used instead to accumulate the cost of the goods purchased throughout the period, and no entries are made to accumulate the cost of goods sold. Thus, the dollar amount of merchandise on hand at the end of the period and the cost of goods sold for the period are not known by looking at the general ledger accounts.

Instead, these amounts will have to be determined at the end of the accounting period in a periodic inventory system. Recall from Illustration 5A-1 that the basic equation to calculate cost of goods sold is: Beginning Inventory + Cost of Goods Purchased = Cost of Goods Available for Sale − Ending Inventory = Cost of Goods Sold.

To illustrate the calculation of cost of goods sold, we will use assumed data for Highpoint Audio & TV Supply so we can compare the results with its cost of goods sold under the perpetual inventory system shown in the chapter. Assume that Highpoint Audio & TV Supply's general ledger, under the periodic inventory system, shows the following balances at its year end on May 31, 2014:

• Merchandise Inventory	$ 35,000
• Purchases	325,000
• Purchase Returns and Allowances	10,400
• Purchase Discounts	6,800
• Freight In	12,200

Beginning Inventory

If Highpoint Audio & TV Supply uses the periodic inventory system, it will not record any transactions in the Merchandise Inventory account during the period, and the balance in this account will not have changed since the beginning of the year. Thus **the $35,000 balance in the general ledger—as shown above—is equal to beginning inventory**.

Cost of Goods Purchased

In a periodic inventory system, four accounts—Purchases, Purchase Returns and Allowances, Purchase Discounts, and Freight In—are used to record the purchase of inventory. These four accounts are used to calculate the cost of goods purchased.

First, **net purchases** is calculated by subtracting purchase returns and allowances and purchase discounts (both credit balances) from purchases (a debit balance). This calculation for Highpoint for the year ended May 31, 2014, is $307,800 as shown in Illustration 5A-3.

ILLUSTRATION 5A-3
Formula for net purchases

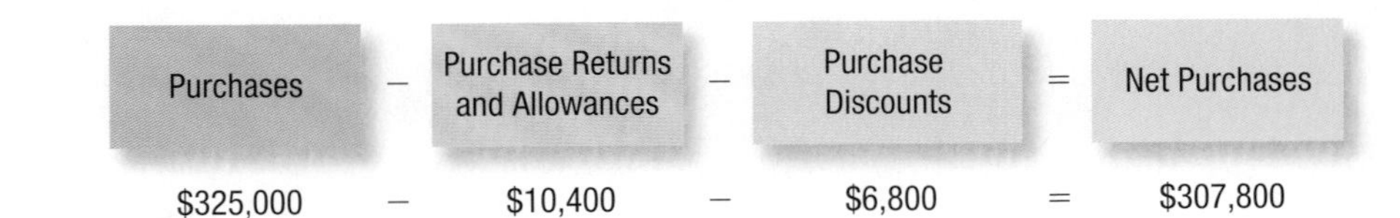

Then the **cost of goods purchased** is calculated by adding the balance in the Freight In account to net purchases. Highpoint's cost of goods purchased for the year ended May 31, 2104, is $320,000, as shown in Illustration 5A-4.

ILLUSTRATION 5A-4
Formula for cost of goods purchased

Net Purchases
+
Freight In
=
Cost of Goods Purchased
$307,800
+
$12,200
=
$320,000

Cost of Goods Available for Sale

As shown in Illustration 5A-1, the **cost of goods available for sale** is equal to the cost of the goods on hand at the beginning of the period (beginning inventory) plus the cost of goods purchased during the period. This is the total amount that the company could have sold during the period. Highpoint's cost of goods available for sale for the year ended May 31, 2014, is $355,000 ($35,000 + $320,000).

Cost of goods available for sale

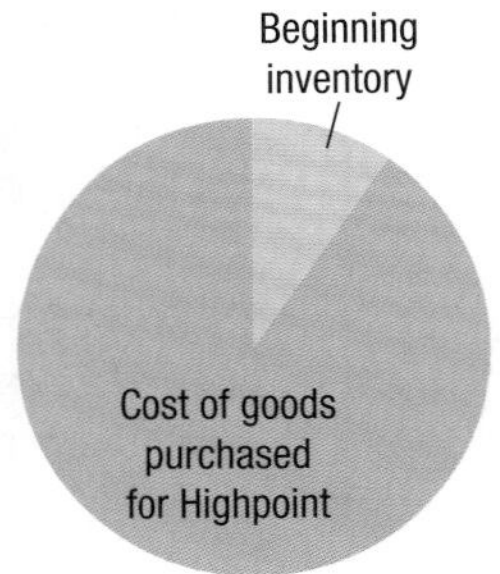

Ending Inventory

To determine the cost of the inventory on hand on May 31, 2014, Highpoint Audio & TV Supply must take a physical inventory. You will recall from earlier in this chapter that Highpoint determined that its cost of goods on hand on May 31, 2014 (ending inventory) is $40,000. The inventory on hand is the same

Helpful hint The cost of goods available for sale represents *all of the inventory* that a merchandiser held and *could have sold* during the year. However, merchandisers will almost always have some unsold inventory at the end of the year. The unsold goods still represent an asset and remain in Merchandise Inventory while the goods that were sold represent an expense and are included in Cost of Goods Sold.

regardless of the inventory system used. But with a periodic inventory system, Highpoint will have no way of knowing if there are inventory shortages or not.

You will learn later in this appendix that the balance in the Merchandise Inventory account is adjusted from the beginning balance of $35,000 to the ending balance of $40,000 as part of the closing process.

Cost of Goods Sold

As shown in Illustration 5A-1, once the ending inventory is determined, the cost of goods sold is calculated by subtracting the ending inventory from the cost of goods available for sale. Highpoint's cost of goods sold is $315,000 ($355,000 − $40,000).

MULTIPLE-STEP INCOME STATEMENT—PERIODIC

The only reporting difference in a multiple-step income statement is that the cost of goods sold section has more detail in a periodic inventory system—as shown in Illustration 5A-5—than in a perpetual inventory system, where only one line is reported for the cost of goods sold. Note that cost of goods sold, gross profit, and profit are the same amounts as shown in Illustration 5-10 in the chapter.

ILLUSTRATION 5A-5
Multiple-step income statement—periodic inventory system

HIGHPOINT AUDIO & TV SUPPLY
Income Statement
Year Ended May 31, 2014

Sales revenue				
Sales				$480,000
Less: Sales returns and allowances			$ 16,700	
Sales discounts			4,300	21,000
Net sales				459,000
Cost of goods sold				
Inventory, June 1, 2013			$ 35,000	
Purchases		$325,000		
Less: Purchase returns and allowances	$10,400			
Purchase discounts	6,800	17,200		
Net purchases		307,800		
Add: Freight in		12,200		
Cost of goods purchased			320,000	
Cost of goods available for sale			355,000	
Inventory, May 31, 2014			40,000	
Cost of goods sold				315,000
Gross profit				144,000
Operating expenses				
Advertising expense			$ 16,000	
Depreciation expense			8,000	
Freight out			7,000	
Insurance expense			2,000	
Rent expense			19,000	
Salaries expense			45,000	
Utilities expense			17,000	
Total operating expenses				114,000
Profit from operations				30,000
Other revenues				
Interest revenue			$ 1,000	
Rent revenue			2,400	
Total non-operating revenues			3,400	
Other expenses				
Interest expense			1,800	
Net non-operating revenues				1,600
Profit				$ 31,600

Using the periodic inventory system does not affect the content of the balance sheet. As in the perpetual system, merchandise inventory is reported in the current assets section, and at the same amount.

COMPLETING THE ACCOUNTING CYCLE

After preparing the financial statements, closing entries and a post-closing trial balance complete the accounting cycle. For a merchandising company, as for a service company, all accounts that affect the determination of profit as well as the owner's drawings are closed to the owner's capital account.

It is also necessary to update the balance of the Merchandise Inventory account as part of the closing process in a periodic inventory system. During the year, no entries are made to this account when inventory is purchased or sold. Therefore, the merchandise inventory balance in the adjusted trial balance is its beginning balance, not its ending balance.

Two closing journal entries are used to update the Merchandise Inventory account from the beginning balance of $35,000 to the ending balance of $40,000. These two entries for Highpoint Audio & TV Supply are as follows:

Date	Account	Debit	Credit
May 31	Income Summary	35,000	
	Merchandise Inventory		35,000
	To close beginning inventory.		
31	Merchandise Inventory	40,000	
	Income Summary		40,000
	To record ending inventory.		

A	=	L	+	OE
−35,000				−35,000

Cash flows: no effect

A	=	L	+	OE
+40,000				+40,000

Cash flows: no effect

The income summary account is used because beginning and ending inventory are used in the cost of goods sold calculation, which is then used to determine profit or loss for the period. After the closing entries are posted, the Merchandise Inventory account will show the following:

Merchandise Inventory

		Debit			Credit
June 1, 2013	Bal.	35,000	**May 31, 2014**	**Clos.**	**35,000**
May 31, 2014	**Clos.**	**40,000**			
May 31, 2014	Bal.	40,000			

The effect of the two closing journal entries on the Merchandise Inventory account is similar to the effect that the closing process has on the owner's capital account. The ending inventory and capital balances must be updated to agree with the balance sheet at the end of the period. The balance sheet reports these ending balances, not the amounts in the adjusted trial balance. The ending balance in Merchandise Inventory now becomes the beginning inventory amount for the next period.

The remaining closing entries are the same as those as we saw in prior chapters and are not shown here. The only difference between a merchandising company using the periodic inventory system and a service company is that there are several additional temporary accounts that must be closed.

Temporary accounts with credit balances include the Sales, Purchase Returns and Allowances, and Purchase Discounts accounts. These will need to be debited for their individual account balances and the total is credited to the Income Summary account. Temporary accounts with debit balances include the Sales Returns and Allowances, Sales Discounts, Purchases, and Freight In accounts. These will need to be credited for their individual account balances and the total is debited to the Income Summary account.

After the closing entries are posted, a post-closing trial balance is prepared. The post-closing trial balance is prepared in the same way as described in earlier chapters and is not explained again here.

BEFORE YOU GO ON...

DO IT

The following transactions occurred in August:

Aug. 1 White Company buys merchandise on account from Red Company for $1,000, terms 2/10, n/30, FOB destination.
1 The correct company pays freight charges of $70.
3 White Company returns $150 of the merchandise to Red Company. Red returns the goods to its inventory.
10 White Company pays the total amount owing.

Both companies use a periodic inventory system.

(a) Record White Company's transactions.
(b) Record Red Company's transactions.

Action Plan

- In a periodic system, purchases of inventory are recorded in the Purchases account.
- Examine freight terms to determine which company pays the freight charges.
- Calculate purchase discounts using the net amount owing and record in a Purchase Discounts account.
- In a periodic system, the cost of goods sold is not recorded at the time of the sale.
- In a periodic system, inventory is not adjusted for returned merchandise.
- Calculate purchase/sales discounts using the net amount owing and record in a Purchase/ Sales Discounts account.

SOLUTION

(a) White Company (buyer)

Aug. 1	Purchases	1,000	
	Accounts Payable		1,000
	Goods purchased on account.		
1	No entry; seller pays for freight		
3	Accounts Payable	150	
	Purchase Returns and Allowances		150
	Returned goods.		
10	Accounts Payable ($1,000 − $150)	850	
	Purchase Discounts ($850 × 2%)		17
	Cash ($850 − $17)		833
	Cash payment within discount period.		

(b) Red Company (seller)

Aug. 1	Accounts Receivable	1,000	
	Sales		1,000
	Credit sale of merchandise.		
1	Freight Out	70	
	Cash		70
	Payment of freight costs.		
3	Sales Returns and Allowances	150	
	Accounts Receivable		150
	Customer returned goods.		
10	Cash ($850 − $17)	833	
	Sales Discounts ($850 × 2%)	17	
	Accounts Receivable		850
	Cash receipt within discount period.		

Related exercise material: *BE5–15, *BE5–16, *BE5–17, *E5–12, *E5–13, *E5–14, *E5–15, and *E5–16.

THE NAVIGATOR

Comparing IFRS and ASPE

Key Differences	International Financial Reporting Standards (IFRS)	Accounting Standards for Private Enterprises (ASPE)
Classification of expense in the income statement	Expenses must be classified by either nature or function.	Expenses can be classified in any manner the company finds useful.

THE NAVIGATOR

DEMONSTRATION PROBLEM 1

Cappelio Retailers and AP Distributors had the following transactions in June. Both companies use a perpetual inventory system.

June 1 Cappelio Retailers purchased merchandise inventory for resale from AP Distributors for $7,000. Terms of purchase were 2/10, n/30, FOB shipping point.
2 The correct company paid $225 cash for freight charges.
3 Cappelio noted that some of the goods were not exactly as ordered and returned the goods to AP Distributors. AP Distributors granted Cappelio a $500 purchase return.
10 Cappelio paid AP Distributors the amount owing.

Additional information for AP Distributors:

1. The cost of the merchandise sold on June 1 was $4,200.
2. The cost of the merchandise returned on June 3 was $300. The goods were returned to inventory.

Instructions

(a) Journalize the June transactions for Cappelio Retailers.
(b) Journalize the June transactions for AP Distributors.

SOLUTION TO DEMONSTRATION PROBLEM 1

(a) Cappelio Retailers (buyer)

Date	Account Titles and Explanation	Debit	Credit
June 1	Merchandise Inventory	7,000	
	Accounts Payable		7,000
	Purchased merchandise on account.		
2	Merchandise Inventory	225	
	Cash		225
	Paid freight charges on goods purchased.		
3	Accounts Payable	500	
	Merchandise Inventory		500
	Returned merchandise		
10	Accounts Payable ($7,000 − $500)	6,500	
	Merchandise Inventory ($6,500 × 2%)		130
	Cash ($6,500 − $130)		6,370
	Paid for merchandise in discount period.		

(b) AP Distributors (seller)

Date	Account Titles and Explanation	Debit	Credit
June 1	Accounts Receivable	7,000	
	Sales		7,000
	Sold merchandise on account		
	Cost of goods sold	4,200	
	Merchandise Inventory		4,200
	Record cost of goods sold.		
2	No entry. Purchaser pays freight.		
3	Sales Returns and Allowances	500	
	Accounts Receivable		500
	Customer returned merchandise.		
	Merchandise Inventory	300	
	Cost of Goods Sold		300
	Cost of goods returned.		
10	Cash	6,370	
	Sales Discount	130	
	Accounts Receivable		6,500
	Received payment in discount period.		

Action Plan

- Merchandise Inventory account is used for all transactions that affect the cost of the goods purchased.
- Cost of goods sold must be calculated and recorded at point of sale in a perpetual inventory system.
- The contra revenue account, Sales Returns and Allowances, is used for sales allowances given to customers.
- The contra revenue account, Sales Discounts, is used for sales discounts taken by customers.

DEMONSTRATION PROBLEM 2

The adjusted trial balance data for the year ended December 31, 2014, for Dykstra Company are as follows:

DYKSTRA COMPANY
Adjusted Trial Balance
December 31, 2014

	Debit	Credit
Cash	$ 14,500	
Accounts receivable	15,100	
Merchandise inventory	29,000	
Prepaid insurance	2,500	
Land	150,000	
Building	500,000	
Accumulated depreciation—building		$ 40,000
Equipment	95,000	
Accumulated depreciation—equipment		18,000
Accounts payable		10,600
Property taxes payable		4,000
Mortgage payable—due before December 31, 2015		25,000
Mortgage payable—long-term		530,000
G. Dykstra, capital		81,000
G. Dykstra, drawings	12,000	
Sales		627,200
Sales returns and allowances	5,700	
Sales discounts	1,000	
Cost of goods sold	353,800	
Advertising expense	12,000	
Depreciation expense	29,000	
Freight out	7,600	
Insurance expense	4,500	
Property tax expense	24,000	
Salaries expense	61,000	
Utilities expense	18,000	
Interest revenue		2,500
Interest expense	3,600	
Totals	$1,338,300	$1,338,300

Instructions

(a) Prepare a single-step income statement for the year ended December 31, 2014.
(b) Prepare a multiple-step income statement for the year ended December 31, 2014.
(c) Prepare a statement of owner's equity for Dykstra Company for the year ended December 31, 2014. No additional investments were made by Mr. Dykstra during the year.
(d) Prepare a classified balance sheet as at December 31, 2014.
(e) Journalize and post closing entries.

SOLUTION TO DEMONSTRATION PROBLEM 2

(a)

DYKSTRA COMPANY
Income Statement
Year Ended December 31, 2014

Revenues		
Net sales		$620,500
Interest revenue		2,500
Total revenues		623,000
Expenses		
Cost of goods sold	$353,800	
Advertising expense	12,000	
Depreciation expense	29,000	
Freight out	7,600	
Insurance expense	4,500	
Interest expense	3,600	
Property tax expense	24,000	
Salaries expense	61,000	
Utilities expense	18,000	
Total expenses		513,500
Profit		$109,500

(b)

DYKSTRA COMPANY
Income Statement
Year Ended December 31, 2014

Sales revenue		
Sales		$627,200
Less: Sales returns and allowances	$ 5,700	
Sales discounts	1,000	6,700
Net sales		620,500
Cost of goods sold		353,800
Gross profit		266,700
Operating expenses		
Advertising expense	$12,000	
Depreciation expense	29,000	
Freight out	7,600	
Insurance expense	4,500	
Property tax expense	24,000	
Salaries expense	61,000	
Utilities expense	18,000	
Total operating expenses		156,100
Profit from operations		110,600
Other revenues and expenses		
Interest revenue	$ 2,500	
Interest expense	(3,600)	(1,100)
Profit		$109,500

SOLUTION TO DEMONSTRATION PROBLEM 2 continued on next page

Action Plan

- Recall that in a single-step income statement all revenues are together, then all of the expenses. Profit is the difference between the two subtotals.
- Remember that the major subtotal headings in the multiple-step income statement are net sales, gross profit, profit from operations, and profit (loss).
- Prepare the multiple-step income statement in steps:
  1. Sales less sales returns and allowances and sales discounts equals net sales.
  2. Net sales less cost of goods sold equals gross profit.
  3. Gross profit less operating expenses equals profit from operations.
  4. Profit from operations plus (minus) non-operating revenue (expense) items equals profit.
- Merchandise Inventory is a current asset in the classified balance sheet.
- Sales Returns and Allowances, Sales Discounts, and Cost of Goods Sold are temporary accounts with debit balances that must be closed.

SOLUTION TO DEMONSTRATION PROBLEM 2 continued from previous page

(c)

DYKSTRA COMPANY
Statement of Owner's Equity
Year Ended December 31, 2014

G. Dykstra, capital, January 1, 2014	$ 81,000
Add: Profit	109,500
	190,500
Deduct: Drawings	12,000
G. Dykstra, capital, December 31, 2014	$178,500

(d)

DYKSTRA COMPANY
Balance Sheet
December 31, 2014

Assets		
Current assets		
Cash		$ 14,500
Accounts receivable		15,100
Merchandise inventory		29,000
Prepaid insurance		2,500
Total current assets		61,100
Property, plant, and equipment		
Land		150,000
Building	$500,000	
Less: Accumulated depreciation	40,000	460,000
Equipment	$ 95,000	
Less: Accumulated depreciation	18,000	77,000
Total property, plant, and equipment		687,000
Total assets		$748,100
Liabilities and Owner's Equity		
Current liabilities		
Accounts payable		$ 10,600
Property taxes payable		4,000
Current portion of mortgage payable		25,000
Total current liabilities		39,600
Non-current liabilities		
Mortgage payable		530,000
Total liabilities		569,600
Owner's equity		
G. Dykstra, capital		178,500
Total liabilities and owner's equity		$748,100

SOLUTION TO DEMONSTRATION PROBLEM 2 continued on next page

SOLUTION TO DEMONSTRATION PROBLEM 2 continued from previous page

(e)

Dec. 31	Sales	627,200	
	Interest Revenue	2,500	
	Income Summary		629,700
	To close revenue accounts.		
31	Income Summary	520,200	
	Sales Returns and Allowances		5,700
	Sales Discounts		1,000
	Cost of Goods Sold		353,800
	Advertising Expense		12,000
	Depreciation Expense		29,000
	Freight Out		7,600
	Insurance Expense		4,500
	Property Tax Expense		24,000
	Salaries Expense		61,000
	Utilities Expense		18,000
	Interest Expense		3,600
	To close expense accounts.		
31	Income Summary (629,700 − 520,200)	109,500	
	G. Dykstra, Capital		109,500
	To close Income Summary.		
31	G. Dykstra, Capital	12,000	
	G. Dykstra, Drawings		12,000
	To close drawings.		

THE NAVIGATOR

Summary of Study Objectives

1. ***Describe the differences between service and merchandising companies.*** A service company performs services. It has service or fee revenue and operating expenses. A merchandising company sells goods. It has sales revenue, cost of goods sold, gross profit, and operating expenses. Merchandising companies must decide if they want to spend the extra resources to use a perpetual inventory system in which inventory records are updated with each purchase and sale. The benefit of the perpetual system is that it provides better information and control over inventory than a periodic system in which inventory records are updated only at the end of the accounting period.

2. ***Prepare entries for purchases under a perpetual inventory system.*** The Merchandise Inventory account is debited (increased) for all purchases of merchandise and freight, if freight is paid by the buyer. It is credited (decreased) for purchase returns and allowances and purchase discounts. Purchase discounts are cash reductions to the net invoice price for early payment.

3. ***Prepare entries for sales under a perpetual inventory system.*** When inventory is sold, two entries are required: (1) Accounts Receivable (or Cash) is debited and Sales is credited for the *selling price* of the merchandise. (2) Cost of Goods Sold (an expense) is debited (increased) and Merchandise Inventory (a current asset) is credited (decreased) for the *cost* of the inventory items sold. Contra revenue accounts are credited to record sales returns and allowances and sales discounts. Two entries are also required to record sales returns when the returned merchandise can be sold again in the future. Freight costs paid by the seller are recorded as an operating expense.

4. ***Perform the steps in the accounting cycle for a merchandising company.*** Each of the required steps in the accounting cycle for a service company is also completed for a merchandising company. An additional adjusting journal entry may be required under a perpetual inventory system. The Merchandise Inventory account must be adjusted to agree with the physical inventory count if there is a difference in the amounts. Merchandising companies have additional temporary accounts that must also be closed at the end of the accounting year.

5. ***Prepare single-step and multiple-step income statements.*** In a single-step income statement, all data are classified under two categories (revenues or expenses), and profit is determined by one step (that is, subtracting total expenses from total revenues). A multiple-step income statement shows several steps in determining profit. Net sales is calculated by deducting sales returns and allowances and sales discounts from sales. Next, gross profit is calculated by deducting the cost of goods sold from net sales. Profit (loss) from operations is then calculated by deducting operating expenses from gross profit. Total non-operating activities are added to (or deducted from) profit from operations to determine profit.

6. ***Calculate the gross profit margin and profit margin.*** The gross profit margin, calculated by dividing gross profit by net sales, measures the gross profit earned for each dollar of sales. The profit margin, calculated by dividing profit by net sales, measures the profit (total profit) earned for each dollar of sales. Both are measures of profitability that are closely watched by management and other interested parties.

7. ***Prepare the entries for purchases and sales under a periodic inventory system and calculate cost of goods sold (Appendix 5A).*** In a periodic inventory system, separate temporary accounts are used to record (a) purchases, (b) purchase returns and allowances, (c) purchase discounts, and (d) freight costs paid by the buyer. Purchases − purchase returns and allowances − purchase discounts = net purchases. Net purchases + freight in = cost of goods purchased.

In a periodic inventory system, only one journal entry is made to record a sale of merchandise. Cost of goods sold is not recorded at the time of the sale. Instead, it is calculated as follows at the end of the period after the ending inventory has been counted: Beginning inventory + cost of goods purchased = cost of goods available for sale. Cost of goods available for sale − ending inventory = cost of goods sold.

Glossary

Contra revenue account An account with the opposite balance (debit) compared with its related revenue account, which has a credit balance. The contra revenue account is deducted from the revenue account on the income statement. (p. 209)

Control account An account in the general ledger that summarizes the detail for a subsidiary ledger and controls it. (p. 204)

Cost of goods available for sale The cost of the goods on hand at the beginning of the period (beginning inventory) plus the cost of goods purchased during the period. (p. 225)

Cost of goods purchased Net purchases (purchases minus purchase returns and allowances and purchase discounts) plus freight in. (p. 225)

Cost of goods sold The total cost of merchandise sold during the period. In a perpetual inventory system, it is calculated and recorded for each sale. In a periodic inventory system, the total cost of goods sold for the period is calculated at the end of the accounting period by deducting ending inventory from the cost of goods available for sale. (p. 200)

FOB destination A freight term indicating that the buyer accepts ownership when the goods are delivered to the buyer's place of business. The seller pays the shipping costs and is responsible for damages to the goods during transit. (p. 205)

FOB shipping point A freight term indicating that the buyer accepts ownership when the goods are placed on the carrier by the seller. The buyer pays freight costs from the shipping point to the destination and is responsible for damages. (p. 205)

Function A method of classifying expenses on the income statement based on which business function the resources were spent on (such as, costs of sales, administration, and selling). (p. 216)

Gross profit Sales revenue (net sales) minus cost of goods sold. (p. 200)

Gross profit margin Gross profit expressed as a percentage of net sales. It is calculated by dividing gross profit by net sales. (p. 220)

Gross sales Total sales before deducting the contra revenue accounts. (p. 211)

Multiple-step income statement An income statement that shows several steps to determine profit or loss. (p. 217)

Nature A method of classifying expenses on the income statement based on what the resources were spent on (such as, depreciation, employee costs, transportation, and advertising). (p. 216)

Net purchases Purchases minus purchase returns and allowances and purchase discounts. (p. 225)

Net sales Sales minus sales returns and allowances and sales discounts. (p. 211)

Non-operating activities Other revenues and expenses that are unrelated to the company's main operations. (p. 218)

Operating expenses Expenses incurred in the process of earning sales revenues. They are deducted from gross profit in the income statement. (p. 200)

Periodic inventory system An inventory system where detailed inventory records are not updated whenever a transaction occurs. The cost of goods sold is determined only at the end of the accounting period. (p. 202)

Perpetual inventory system An inventory system where detailed records, showing the quantity and cost of each inventory item, are updated whenever a transaction occurs. The records continuously show the inventory that should be on hand. (p. 201)

Profit from operations Profit from a company's main operating activity, determined by subtracting operating expenses from gross profit. (p. 217)

Profit margin Profit expressed as a percentage of net sales. It is calculated by dividing profit by net sales. (p. 221)

Profitability ratios Measures of a company's profit or operating success (or shortcomings) for a specific period of time. (p. 220)

Purchase discount A discount, based on the invoice price less any returns and allowances, given to a buyer for early payment of a balance due. (p. 206)

Purchase returns (allowances) The return, or reduction in price, of unsatisfactory merchandise that was purchased. It results in a debit to Cash or Accounts Payable. (p. 206)

Quantity discount A cash discount that reduces the invoice price and is given to the buyer for volume purchases. (p. 206)

Sales discount A reduction, based on the sale price from the invoice price less any returns and allowances, given by a seller for early payment of a credit sale. (p. 210)

Sales returns (allowances) The return, or reduction in price, of unsatisfactory merchandise that was sold. It results in a credit to Cash or Accounts Receivable. (p. 209)

Sales revenue The main source of revenue in a merchandising company. (p. 200)

Single-step income statement An income statement that shows only one step (revenues less expenses) in determining profit (or loss). (p. 216)

Subsidiary ledger A group of accounts that give details for a control account in the general ledger. (p. 204)

Note: All questions, exercises, and problems below with an asterisk (*) relate to material in Appendix 5A.

Self-Study Questions

Answers are at the end of the chapter.

(SO 1) C 1. Which of the following statements is an advantage of a perpetual inventory system?
(a) It is not necessary to calculate and record the cost of goods sold with each sale with a perpetual inventory system.
(b) The perpetual inventory system provides better control over inventory because inventory shortages can be more easily identified.
(c) It is not necessary to do a physical count of the inventory in a perpetual inventory system.
(d) A perpetual inventory system results in less clerical work and is less costly than a periodic inventory system.

(SO 2) K 2. Which of the following statements is correct?
(a) If an inventory subsidiary ledger is used then it is not necessary to have a merchandise inventory account in the general ledger.
(b) An inventory subsidiary ledger is used to track the quantity of each inventory item; the merchandise inventory account in the general ledger is used to track the cost of each inventory item.
(c) It is common for companies to have a separate subsidiary ledger for each of their current assets.
(d) An inventory subsidiary ledger is used in a perpetual inventory system to organize and track the quantity and cost of individual inventory items.

(SO 2) AP 3. A $750 purchase of merchandise inventory is made on June 13, terms 2/10, n/30. On June 16, merchandise costing $50 is returned. What amount will be paid as payment in full on June 22?
(a) $686
(b) $700
(c) $735
(d) $750

(SO 2, 3) K 4. When goods are shipped with the freight terms FOB shipping point:
(a) the buyer pays the freight costs and debits Merchandise Inventory.
(b) the buyer pays the freight costs and debits Freight Expense.
(c) the seller pays the freight costs and debits Freight Out.
(d) the seller pays the freight costs and debits Cost of Goods Sold.

(SO 2, 3) C 5. Discounts offered to customers for early payment of the balance due:
(a) will reduce the cost of the merchandise for the purchaser and increase the cost of goods sold for the seller.
(b) reduce the cash paid by the purchaser, and the cash received by the seller, by the same amount.
(c) are required by provincial law.
(d) benefit the seller but generally do not benefit the purchaser.

(SO 3) K 6. To record the sale of goods for cash in a perpetual inventory system:
(a) only one journal entry is necessary to record the cost of goods sold and reduction of inventory.
(b) only one journal entry is necessary to record the receipt of cash and the sales revenue.
(c) two journal entries are necessary: one to record the receipt of cash and sales revenue, and one to record the cost of the goods sold and reduction of inventory.
(d) two journal entries are necessary: one to record the receipt of cash and reduction of inventory, and one to record the cost of the goods sold and sales revenue.

(SO 3) K 7. Which of the following is a contra revenue account that normally has a debit balance?
(a) Sales Returns and Allowances
(b) Sales
(c) Freight Out
(d) Cost of Goods Sold

(SO 4, 5) K 8. The steps in the accounting cycle for a merchandising company using the perpetual inventory system are the same as those for a service company *except*:
(a) closing journal entries are not required for a merchandising company.
(b) a post-closing trial balance is not required for a merchandising company.
(c) an additional adjusting journal entry for inventory may be needed in a merchandising company.
(d) a multiple-step income statement is required for a merchandising company.

(SO 5) K 9. Which of the following appears on both a single-step and a multiple-step income statement for a merchandising company?
(a) Merchandise inventory
(b) Gross profit
(c) Profit from operations
(d) Cost of goods sold

(SO 6) AP 10. Net sales are $400, cost of goods sold is $310, operating expenses are $60, and other revenues are $5. What are the gross profit margin and profit margin?
(a) 7.5% and 8.8%
(b) 22.5% and 7.4%
(c) 22.5% and 8.8%
(d) 77.5% and 8.8%

(SO 7) K *11. When goods are sold by a company using a periodic inventory system:
(a) the Sales account is credited with the selling price of the goods and the cost of the goods sold is not recorded.
(b) sales discounts are deducted from purchases on the income statement.
(c) sales returns are credited to Sales Returns and Allowances.
(d) freight costs are debited to cost of goods sold.

(SO 7) AP *12. If beginning inventory is $60, purchases are $400, purchase returns and allowances are $25, freight in is $5, and ending inventory is $50, what is the cost of goods sold?
(a) $385
(b) $390
(c) $410
(d) $430

Questions

(SO 1) C 1. In what way is determining profit for a merchandising company more complex than calculating profit for service company?

(SO 1) C 2. Explain the differences between a perpetual and a periodic inventory system. Include in your explanation why the words "perpetual" and "periodic" are used for the two systems.

(SO 1) C 3. Song Yee wonders why a physical inventory count is necessary in a perpetual inventory system. After all, the accounting records show how much inventory is on hand. Explain why a physical inventory count is required in a perpetual inventory system.

(SO 1) C 4. Describe the costs and the benefits of a perpetual inventory system compared with a periodic inventory system.

(SO 2) C 5. Jermyn argues that if the balance in the inventory subsidiary ledger must equal the balance in the Merchandise Inventory control account in the general ledger, then there is no reason for using a subsidiary ledger. Do you agree or disagree? Explain.

(SO 2) C 6. Rosalee tells a friend in her introductory accounting class that they don't have to worry about how to account for sales taxes on inventory purchases because merchandising companies don't pay sales tax. Do you agree or disagree? Explain.

(SO 2, 3) C 7. What are the differences between FOB shipping point and FOB destination? Explain the differences between how freight costs are recorded for inventory purchases as opposed to inventory sales.

(SO 2) C 8. Willow Ridge Company uses a perpetual inventory system. The company recently purchased merchandise for resale from one of its suppliers. Several of the items were not exactly what had been ordered. The supplier gave Willow Ridge a purchase allowance and it was agreed that Willow Ridge should keep the items. Willow Ridge's accountant does not want to credit the merchandise inventory account because the merchandise was not returned. Is this correct or not? Why?

(SO 2) C 9. Fukushima Company received an invoice for $16,000, terms 1/10, n/30. It will have to borrow from its bank in order to pay the invoice in 10 days. The interest rate Fukushima pays on its bank loans is 7.25%. Should Fukushima take advantage of the cash discount offered or not? Support your answer with calculations.

(SO 3) C 10. Shapiro Book Company sells a book that cost $50 for $75 cash. The accountant prepares a journal entry with a debit to Cash for $75, a credit to Merchandise Inventory for $50, and a credit to Gross Profit for $25. What part of this is incorrect and why is it important to use the correct accounts? The company uses a perpetual inventory system.

(SO 2, 3) C 11. Explain the difference between a quantity discount, a purchase discount, and a sales discount. Explain how each of them is recorded.

(SO 3) C 12. Chandler Retail has a December 31 fiscal year end and the company sells more merchandise in November and December than in any other month. The company has a "no questions asked" policy in terms of accepting sales returns up to six months after the initial sale. What uncertainties does the company face in terms of recognizing sales revenue? Should they consider adopting a different fiscal year end? Why?

(SO 3) C 13. Raymond is the accountant at an electronics retail store. He is friends with one of the sales people, Geoff. Geoff tells Raymond to simply debit sales whenever a customer returns an item that Geoff originally sold. Why might Geoff suggest this and what should Raymond do?

(SO 3) C 14. When the seller records a sales return or a sales allowance, sometimes they also adjust cost of goods sold and inventory, and sometimes they do not. Explain when it is necessary to also record an entry in the cost of goods sold and inventory accounts, what is debited and credited, and what amount is used.

(SO 4) C 15. "The steps in the accounting cycle for a merchandising company are different from those in the accounting cycle for a service company." Do you agree or disagree? Explain.

(SO 4) C 16. Neptune Stores uses a perpetual inventory system and has just completed its annual physical inventory count. The accountant determines that the physical inventory count is higher than the accounting records. How could this be possible and what adjustment should be recorded, if any?

(SO 4) K 17. Compared with a service company, what additional accounts must be closed for a merchandising company using a perpetual inventory system? Include in your answer whether the account should be debited or credited to close it.

(SO 5) K 18. Explain the differences between a single-step and a multiple-step income statement.

(SO 5) K 19. Explain the terms "net sales," "gross profit," "profit from operations," and "profit." Are these terms used only by merchandising companies or are they used by service companies also?

(SO 5) C 20. Why is interest expense reported as a non-operating expense instead of as an operating expense on a multiple-step income statement?

(SO 5) C 21. Is it possible for a company's profit from operations and its profit to be the same amount? If so, should any company bother to calculate both numbers?

(SO 6) C 22. What is the difference between gross profit and gross profit margin? Why is it useful to calculate a company's gross profit margin?

(SO 6) C 23. SnowCo monitors its gross profit margin on a regular basis. Is there any need for it to also monitor its profit margin?

(SO 7) K *24. Explain the differences between how inventory purchases are recorded in a periodic system and in a perpetual system. Also explain the differences in recording sales between a periodic system and a perpetual system.

(SO 7) K *25. Renata purchases merchandise at garage sales and later sells these goods at a flea market. Assuming Renata uses a periodic inventory system, how would she calculate her cost of goods sold and gross profit?

(SO 7) C *26. In a periodic inventory system, the closing entries include both a debit and a credit to the Merchandise Inventory account. What is the purpose of these entries?

Brief Exercises

BE5–1 The components in the income statements of companies A, B, C, and D follow. Determine the missing amounts.

Calculate missing amounts in determining profit or loss. **(SO 1) AP**

	Sales	Cost of Goods Sold	Gross Profit	Operating Expenses	Profit/(Loss)
Company A	$250,000	$170,000	$ (a)	$ 50,000	$ (b)
Company B	108,000	70,000	(c)	(d)	29,500
Company C	75,000	(e)	30,000	(f)	10,800
Company D	(g)	75,000	95,000	115,000	(h)

BE5–2 Old Fashioned Candy Company sells three types of candies. The company uses a perpetual inventory system and a subsidiary ledger to keep track of its inventory. Determine the balance in the inventory control account in the general ledger if the company had the following items on hand on March 31:

Calculate balance in inventory control account. **(SO 2) AP**

Inventory Item	Packages on Hand	Cost per Package
Bubble gum	600	$0.95
Jelly beans	400	1.25
Lollipops	350	1.60

BE5–3 Old Fashioned Candy Company (see BE5–2) has decided to expand its sales to include Canada Mints. It purchases 500 packages from its supplier at a cost of $5.50 per package, terms 2/10, n/30, FOB shipping point. The freight charges are $75. Old Fashioned Candy Company pays for the merchandise within the discount period. What are the total cost and cost per package of this inventory item, and the balance in the Merchandise Inventory control account in the general ledger after these transactions?

Calculate inventory balances. **(SO 2) AP**

BE5–4 Fresh Look Paint Store uses a perpetual inventory system. The company had the following transactions in March.

Record purchase transactions and indicate impact on assets, liabilities, and owner's equity. **(SO 2) C**

Mar. 16 Purchased $15,000 of merchandise from Central Paint Distributors, terms 2/10, n/30, FOB destination.
18 Fresh Look Paint Store received an allowance of $750 for the merchandise purchased on March 16 because of minor damage to the goods.
25 Paid the balance due to Central Paint Distributors.

For each transaction, (a) prepare a journal entry to record the transaction and (b) indicate the amount that the transaction increased or decreased total assets, total liabilities, and owner's equity. Indicate NE (no effect) if the transaction neither increased nor decreased any of these items.

Record purchase transactions—perpetual system. **(SO 2) AP**

BE5–5 Prepare the journal entries to record the following purchase transactions in Xiaoyan Company's books. Xiaoyan uses a perpetual inventory system.

Jan.	2	Xiaoyan purchased $20,000 of merchandise from Feng Company, terms n/30, FOB shipping point.
	4	The correct company paid freight costs of $215.
	6	Xiaoyan returned $1,500 of the merchandise purchased on January 2 because it was not needed.
Feb.	1	Xiaoyan paid the balance owing to Feng.

Record purchase transactions with a purchase discount—perpetual system. **(SO 2) AP**

BE5–6 Prepare the journal entries to record the following purchase transactions in Jarek Company's books. Jarek uses a perpetual inventory system.

Mar.	12	Jarek purchased $25,000 of merchandise from Dalibor Company, terms 2/10, n/30, FOB destination.
	13	The correct company paid freight costs of $265. (*Hint:* Check the shipping terms in the previous transaction.)
	14	Jarek returned $2,000 of the merchandise purchased on March 12 because it was damaged. (Ignore shipping charges on the return.)
	21	Jarek paid the balance owing to Dalibor.

Record sales transactions and indicate impact on assets, liabilities, and owner's equity. **(SO 3) C**

BE5–7 Central Paint Distributors uses a perpetual inventory system. The company had the following transactions in March.

Mar.	16	Sold $15,000 of merchandise to Fresh Look Paint Stores, terms 2/10, n/30, FOB destination. The merchandise had cost Central Paint Distributors $8,700.
	17	Paid freight costs of $170 for the March 16 sale.
	18	Gave Fresh Look Paint Stores an allowance of $750 for the March 16 sale. There was some minor damage to the goods.
	25	Collected the balance due from Fresh Paint Stores.

For each transaction, (a) prepare a journal entry to record the transaction and (b) indicate the amount that the transaction increased or decreased total assets, total liabilities, and owner's equity. Indicate NE (no effect) if the transaction neither increased nor decreased any of these items.

Record sales transactions with a sales discount—perpetual system. **(SO 3) AP**

BE5–8 Prepare journal entries to record the following sales transactions in Feng Company's books. Feng uses a perpetual inventory system.

Jan.	2	Feng sold $20,000 of merchandise to Xiaoyan Company, terms n/30, FOB shipping point. The cost of the merchandise sold was $7,900.
	4	The correct company paid freight costs of $215.
	6	Xiaoyan returned $1,500 of the merchandise purchased on January 2 because it was not needed. The cost of the merchandise returned was $590, and it was restored to inventory.
Feb.	1	Feng received the balance due from Xiaoyan.

Record sales transactions—perpetual system. **(SO 3) AP**

BE5–9 Prepare journal entries to record the following sales transactions in Dalibor Company's books. Dalibor uses a perpetual inventory system.

Mar.	12	Dalibor sold $25,000 of merchandise to Jarek Company, terms 2/10, n/30, FOB destination. The cost of the merchandise sold was $13,250.
	13	The correct company paid freight costs of $265.
	14	Jarek returned $2,000 of the merchandise purchased on March 12 because it was damaged. The cost of the merchandise returned was $1,060. Dalibor examined the merchandise, decided it was no longer saleable, and discarded it.
	22	Dalibor received the balance due from Jarek.

Prepare adjusting entry. **(SO 4) AP**

BE5–10 At its June 30 year end, the inventory records of Pajewski Company showed merchandise inventory of $89,000. Through a physical count, the company determined that its actual inventory on hand was $86,500. Record the necessary adjusting entry.

BE5–11 Home Goods Retail Company has the following merchandise account balances at its September 30 year end:

Prepare closing entries. **(SO 4) AP**

Cost of goods sold	$125,000	Sales	$218,750
Freight out	1,900	Sales discounts	950
Merchandise inventory	22,000	Sales returns and allowances	3,150
Salaries expense	40,000	Supplies	2,500

Prepare the entries to close the appropriate accounts to the Income Summary account.

BE5–12 Chocolate Treats has the following account balances:

Calculate net sales, gross profit, operating expenses, profit from operations, and profit. **(SO 5) AP**

Cost of goods sold	$385,000	Rent expense	$ 44,000
Depreciation expense	13,200	Salaries expense	55,000
Insurance expense	3,300	Sales	561,000
Interest expense	11,000	Sales discounts	5,500
Interest revenue	8,800	Sales returns and allowances	16,500

Assuming Chocolate Treats uses a multiple-step income statement, calculate the following: (a) net sales, (b) gross profit, (c) operating expenses, (d) profit from operations, and (e) profit.

BE5–13 Explain where each of the following items would appear on (a) a single-step income statement and (b) a multiple-step income statement: cost of goods sold, depreciation expense, freight out, insurance expense, interest expense, interest revenue, rent revenue, rent expense, sales revenue, and sales returns and allowances.

Identify placement of items on income statements. **(SO 5) AP**

BE5–14 Gabalon Retail reported the following for the past two fiscal years:

Calculate profitability ratios and comment. **(SO 6) AP**

	2014	2013
Net sales	$950,000	$800,000
Cost of goods sold	600,000	500,000
Profit	70,000	65,000

(a) Calculate the gross profit margin and profit margin for both years. (b) Comment on any changes in profitability.

***BE5–15** Prepare the journal entries to record these transactions on Allied Company's books. Allied Company uses a periodic inventory system.

Record purchase transactions—periodic system. **(SO 7) AP**

Feb. 5 Allied purchased $12,000 of merchandise from NW Wholesale Company, terms 2/10, n/30, FOB shipping point.
6 The correct company paid freight costs of $110.
8 Allied returned $1,000 of the merchandise purchased on February 5.
11 Allied paid the balance due to NW Wholesale.

***BE5–16** Prepare the journal entries to record these transactions on NW Wholesale Company's books. NW Wholesale Company uses a periodic inventory system.

Record sales transactions—periodic system. **(SO 7) AP**

Feb. 5 NW Wholesale sells $12,000 of merchandise to Allied, terms 2/10, n/30, FOB shipping point.
6 The correct company paid freight costs of $110.
8 Allied returned $1,000 of the merchandise purchased on February 5. The inventory is not damaged and can be resold. NW Wholesale restores it to inventory.
11 NW Wholesale collects the balance due from Allied.

***BE5–17** Clef Stores uses a periodic inventory system and reports the following information for 2014:

Calculate net purchases, cost of goods purchased, cost of goods sold, and gross profit. **(SO 7) AP**

Beginning inventory	$51,000	Net sales	$531,250
Ending inventory	68,000	Purchase discounts	6,800
Freight in	13,600	Purchase returns and allowances	9,350
Freight out	10,625	Purchases	340,000

Calculate (a) net purchases, (b) cost of goods purchased, (c) cost of goods available for sale, (d) cost of goods sold, and (e) gross profit.

Exercises

Match concepts with descriptions. **(SO 1, 2, 3, 4, 5, 6) K**

E5–1 The following are some of the terms discussed in the chapter:

1. Gross profit	9. Sales discounts
2. Perpetual inventory system	10. FOB destination
3. Cost of goods sold	11. Sales allowance
4. Purchase returns	12. Non-operating activities
5. Freight out	13. Profit margin
6. FOB shipping point	14. Contra revenue account
7. Periodic inventory system	15. Merchandise inventory
8. Subsidiary ledger	16. Purchase discounts

Instructions

Match each term with the best description below. Each term may be used more than once, or may not be used at all.

(a) ________ An expense account that shows the cost of merchandise sold

(b) ________ A group of accounts that share a common characteristic, such as all inventory accounts

(c) ________ An account, such as Sales Discounts, that is deducted from a revenue account on the income statement

(d) ________ The return of unsatisfactory purchased merchandise

(e) ________ Freight terms where the seller will pay for the cost of shipping the goods

(f) ________ An inventory system where the inventory records need to be updated at year end to show the inventory on hand

(g) ________ A reduction in price given for unsatisfactory inventory

(h) ________ Sales revenue less cost of goods sold

(i) ________ Revenues, expenses, gains, and losses that are not part of the company's main operations

(j) ________ Freight terms where the buyer will pay for the cost of shipping the goods

(k) ________ An inventory system where the cost of goods sold is calculated and recorded with every sales transaction

(l) ________ An asset that shows the cost of goods purchased for resale

(m) ________ Profit divided by net sales

(n) ________ A price reduction given by a seller for early payment on a credit sale

Record purchase transactions. **(SO 2) AP**

E5–2 Stellar Stores is a new company that started operations on March 1, 2014. The company has decided to use a perpetual inventory system. The following purchase transactions occurred in March:

Mar. 1 Stellar Stores purchases $9,000 of merchandise for resale from Octagon Wholesalers terms 2/10, n/30, FOB shipping point.

2 The correct company pays $155 for the shipping charges.

3 Stellar returns $1,000 of the merchandise purchased on March 1 because it was the wrong colour. Octagon gives Stellar a $1,000 credit on its account.

21 Stellar Stores purchases an additional $13,000 of merchandise for resale from Octagon Wholesalers terms 2/10, n/30, FOB destination.

22 The correct company pays $170 for freight charges.

23 Stellar returns $400 of the merchandise purchased on March 21 because it was damaged. Octagon gives Stellar a $400 credit on its account.

30 Stellar paid Octagon the amount owing for the merchandise purchased on March 1.

31 Stellar paid Octagon the amount owing for the merchandise purchased on March 21.

Instructions

(a) Prepare Stellar Stores' journal entries to record the above transactions.

(b) Post the transactions to the merchandise inventory account. Compare the total in this account with the total of the cash paid during March by Stellar for the purchase of inventory. (*Note:* assume there were no sales of inventory in March.)

Record sales transactions. **(SO 3) AP**

E5–3 Octagon Wholesalers uses a perpetual inventory system. Refer to the data in E5–2 regarding sales transactions with Stellar Stores and to the additional information below for Octagon.

Mar. 1 Octagon's cost of the merchandise sold to Stellar was $3,960.

3 Octagon's cost of the merchandise returned by Stellar was $440. As the merchandise was not damaged it was returned to Octagon's inventory.

21 Octagon's cost of the additional merchandise sold to Stellar Stores was $5,720.
23 Octagon's cost of the merchandise returned by Stellar was $176. As the merchandise was damaged, it was put in the recycling bin.

Instructions

(a) Prepare Octagon Wholesalers' journal entries to record the sale transactions with Stellar. Remember to record the freight and cash receipt transactions as appropriate.
(b) Calculate Octagon's net sales, cost of goods sold, and gross profit for these sales.

E5–4 The following transactions occurred in April and May. Both companies use a perpetual inventory system.

Record purchase and sales transactions—perpetual system. **(SO 1, 2, 3) AP**

Apr. 5 Olaf Company purchased merchandise from DeVito Company for $12,000, terms 2/10, n/30, FOB shipping point. DeVito had paid $8,500 for the merchandise.
6 The correct company paid freight costs of $300.
8 Olaf Company returned damaged merchandise to DeVito Company and was given a purchase allowance of $1,800. DeVito determined the merchandise could not be repaired and sent it to the recyclers. The merchandise had cost DeVito $1,275.
May 4 Olaf paid the amount due to DeVito Company in full.

Instructions

(a) Prepare the journal entries to record the above transactions for Olaf Company.
(b) Prepare the journal entries to record the above transactions for DeVito Company.
(c) Calculate the gross profit earned by DeVito on these transactions.

E5–5 The following merchandise transactions occurred in December. Both companies use a perpetual inventory system.

Record purchase and sales transactions—perpetual system. **(SO 1, 2, 3) AP**

Dec. 3 Pippen Company sold merchandise to Thomas Co. for $32,000, terms 2/10, n/30, FOB destination. This merchandise cost Pippen Company $18,000.
4 The correct company paid freight charges of $650.
8 Thomas Co. returned unwanted merchandise to Pippen. The returned merchandise had a sales price of $1,800 and a cost of $990. It was restored to inventory.
13 Pippen Company received the balance due from Thomas Co.

Instructions

(a) Prepare the journal entries to record these transactions on the books of Pippen Company.
(b) Prepare the journal entries to record these transactions on the books of Thomas Co.
(c) Calculate the gross profit earned by Pippen on the above transactions.

E5–6 The following transactions occurred in June and July. Pele Company uses a perpetual inventory system.

Record inventory transactions and closing entries—perpetual system. **(SO 2, 3, 4) AP**

June 10 Pele Company purchased $4,000 of merchandise from Duvall Company, terms 2/10, n/30, FOB shipping point.
11 The correct company paid $375 of freight costs to Hoyt Movers.
12 Damaged goods totalling $200 were returned to Duvall for credit.
20 Pele paid Duvall Company in full.
July 15 Pele sold all of the remaining merchandise purchased from Duvall for $9,275 cash.
15 Pele paid $350 of freight costs to AAA Transit to deliver the goods to the customer.
17 Pele gave its customer a $500 cash sales allowance for damaged goods. Pele uses a perpetual inventory system.

Instructions

(a) Record each of the above transactions on the books of Pele Company.
(b) Prepare closing entries on July 31 for the temporary accounts.

E5–7 Delta Furniture Supply sells various furniture items and uses a perpetual inventory system. On November 1 it had no tables in stock. The following transactions occurred during November:

Calculate cost of goods available for sale, ending inventory, cost of goods sold, net sales, and gross profit. Record adjusting entries—perpetual system. **(SO 1, 2, 3, 4) AP**

Nov. 3 Delta purchased 150 tables from Burnaby Manufacturing Ltd. for $13,500, terms n/30, FOB shipping point.
3 Delta paid $450 to Freight Forward Company for the delivery of the tables.
19 Delta sold 45 tables to Hobby Horse Inc. for $170 each on credit, terms 2/10, n/30, FOB destination.
19 Delta paid $135 cash to Freight Forward Company for the delivery of the tables to Hobby Horse Inc.
21 Hobby Horse Inc. returned five tables. Delta credited Hobby Horse's account and the tables were returned to inventory.

29 Delta received the amount owing from Hobby Horse Inc.
30 Paid Burnaby Manufacturing Ltd. for the tables purchased on November 3.

On November 30, Delta did an inventory count and found that there were 109 tables on hand.

Instructions

(a) Calculate the total cost of the tables purchased during the month and the average cost per table.
(b) Calculate the number of tables that the company should have on hand according to its subsidiary ledger and determine if an adjustment is required. If so, prepare the adjusting journal entry. Calculate the correct dollar amount for the tables in the subsidiary ledger after any required adjustments.
(c) Calculate cost of goods sold after recording any required adjustments.
(d) Calculate the net sales and gross profit that Delta earned on its tables during November.

Calculate missing amounts. **(SO 5) AP**

E5–8 Financial information follows for three different companies:

	Natural Cosmetics	Mattar Grocery	SE Footware
Sales	$215,000	$ (e)	$275,000
Sales returns and allowances	(a)	25,000	20,000
Net sales	201,000	335,000	(i)
Cost of goods sold	99,000	(f)	(j)
Gross profit	(b)	195,000	150,000
Operating expenses	45,000	(g)	95,000
Profit from operations	(c)	(h)	(k)
Other expenses	5,000	10,000	(l)
Profit	(d)	63,000	41,000

Instructions

Determine the missing amounts.

Prepare single-step and multiple-step income statements, closing entries, and post-closing trial balance—perpetual system. **(SO 4, 5) AP**

E5–9 The following is information from Lefebvre Company's adjusted trial balance at December 31, 2014:

	Debit	Credit
Cash	$ 75,700	
Notes receivable	100,000	
Merchandise inventory	70,000	
Equipment	450,000	
Accumulated depreciation—equipment		$ 135,000
Unearned revenue		8,000
Notes payable		175,000
C. Lefebvre, capital		235,000
C. Lefebvre, drawings	150,000	
Interest revenue		10,000
Rent revenue		24,000
Sales		1,980,000
Advertising expense	55,000	
Cost of goods sold	851,500	
Depreciation expense	45,000	
Freight out	25,000	
Insurance expense	15,000	
Interest expense	10,500	
Salaries expense	650,000	
Sales discounts	9,900	
Sales returns and allowances	59,400	
	$2,567,000	$2,567,000

Instructions

(a) Prepare a single-step income statement.
(b) Prepare a multiple-step income statement.
(c) Prepare closing entries and a post-closing trial balance.

Prepare financial statements and calculate ratios—perpetual system. **(SO 5, 6) AP**

E5–10 An alphabetical list of Rikard's adjusted accounts at its fiscal year end, August 31, 2014, follows. All accounts have normal balances.

Accounts payable	$ 15,500	Notes payable	$ 42,000
Accumulated depreciation—equipment	14,000	Prepaid insurance	575
Accumulated depreciation—furniture	17,500	R. Smistad, capital	65,750
Cash	15,450	R. Smistad, drawings	80,000
Cost of goods sold	271,500	Rent expense	24,000
Depreciation expense	7,000	Salaries expense	50,000
Equipment	35,000	Salaries payable	2,250
Furniture	42,000	Sales	465,000
Insurance expense	3,575	Sales returns and allowances	16,300
Interest expense	2,100	Supplies	950
Interest payable	525	Supplies expense	6,325
Merchandise inventory	70,350	Unearned sales revenue	2,600

Additional information:

1. Of the notes payable, $6,000 becomes due on February 17, 2015. The balance is due in 2016.
2. On July 18, 2014, Rikard invested $3,500 cash in the business.

Instructions

(a) Prepare a multiple-step income statement, statement of owner's equity, and classified balance sheet.
(b) Calculate the gross profit margin and profit margin.

E5–11 **Toys "R" Us, Inc.** reported the following information (in US$ millions) for the three fiscal years ended:

Calculate profitability ratios. **(SO 6) AN**

	Jan. 28, 2012	Jan. 29, 2011	Jan. 30, 2010
Net sales	$13,909	$13,864	$13,568
Cost of goods sold	8,939	8,939	8,790
Profit from operations	582	646	784
Profit	149	168	312

Instructions

(a) Calculate the gross profit margin and profit margin for Toys "R" Us for each of the three years.
(b) Recalculate profit margin using profit from operations as opposed to profit.
(c) Comment on whether the ratios improved or weakened over the three years.

***E5–12** Data for Olaf Company and DeVito Company are presented in E5–4.

Record purchase and sales transaction entries—periodic system. **(SO 7) AP**

Instructions

(a) Prepare the journal entries to record these transactions on the books of Olaf Company using a periodic inventory system instead of a perpetual system.
(b) Prepare the journal entries to record these transactions on the books of DeVito Company using a periodic inventory system instead of a perpetual system.

***E5–13** Data for Pippen Company and Thomas Co. are presented in E5–5.

Record purchase and sales transaction entries—periodic system. **(SO 7) AP**

Instructions

(a) Prepare the journal entries to record these transactions on the books of Pippen Company assuming a periodic inventory system is used instead of a perpetual system.
(b) Prepare the journal entries to record these transactions on the books of Thomas Co. assuming a periodic inventory system is used instead of a perpetual system.

***E5–14** Memories Company commenced operations on July 1. Memories Company uses a periodic inventory system. During July, Memories Company was involved in the following transactions and events:

Record inventory transactions and calculate gross profit—periodic system. **(SO 7) AP**

July	2	Purchased $15,000 of merchandise from Suppliers Inc. on account, terms 2/10, n/30, FOB shipping point.
	3	Returned $1,200 of merchandise to Suppliers Inc. as it was damaged. Received a credit on account from Suppliers.
	4	Paid $500 of freight costs on July 2 shipment.
	8	Sold merchandise for $2,000 cash.
	11	Paid Suppliers Inc. the full amount owing.
	15	Sold merchandise for $6,000 on account, 1/10, n/30, FOB shipping point.
	25	Received full payment for the merchandise sold on July 15.
	31	Memories did a physical count and determined there was $10,500 of inventory on hand.

Instructions

(a) Record the transactions in Memories Company's books.
(b) What was Memories' gross profit for July?

Determine missing amounts for cost of goods sold section—periodic system. (SO 7) AP

*E5–15 Below are the cost of goods sold sections for the two most recent years for two companies using a periodic inventory system:

	St. Pierre Co.		Silva Co.	
	Year 1	Year 2	Year 1	Year 2
Beginning inventory	$ 250	$ (e)	$1,000	$ (n)
Purchases	1,500	(f)	(j)	9,550
Purchase returns and allowances	50	100	300	400
Purchase discounts	30	50	150	100
Net purchases	(a)	1,850	7,210	(o)
Freight in	110	(g)	(k)	550
Cost of goods purchased	(b)	(h)	7,900	(p)
Cost of goods available for sale	(c)	2,300	(l)	(q)
Ending inventory	(d)	400	1,450	1,250
Cost of goods sold	1,480	(i)	(m)	(r)

Instructions

Fill in the missing amounts to complete the cost of goods sold sections.

Prepare multiple-step income statement and closing entries—periodic system. (SO 7) AP

*E5–16 The following selected information is for Okanagan Company for the year ended January 31, 2014:

Freight in	$ 6,500	Purchase discounts	$ 12,000
Freight out	7,000	Purchase returns and allowances	16,000
Insurance expense	12,000	Rent expense	20,000
Interest expense	6,000	Salaries expense	61,000
Merchandise inventory, beginning	61,000	Salaries payable	2,500
Merchandise inventory, ending	42,000	Sales	325,000
O. G. Pogo, capital	105,000	Sales discounts	14,000
O. G. Pogo, drawings	42,000	Sales returns and allowances	20,000
Purchases	210,000	Unearned sales revenue	4,500

Instructions

(a) Prepare a multiple-step income statement.
(b) Prepare closing entries.

Problems: Set A

Identify problems and recommend inventory system. (SO 1) C

P5–1A AAA Dog 'n Cat Shop sells a variety of merchandise to pet owners, including pet food, grooming supplies, toys, and kennels. Most customers use the option to purchase on account and take 60 days, on average, to pay their accounts. The owner of AAA Dog 'n Cat Shop, Adam Fleming, has decided the company needs a bank loan because the accounts payable need to be paid in 30 days. Adam estimates that it takes 45 days, on average, to sell merchandise from the time it arrives at his store. Since the company earns a good profit every year, the bank manager is willing to give AAA Dog 'n Cat Shop a loan but wants monthly financial statements.

Adam has also noticed that, while some of the merchandise sells very quickly, other items do not. Sometimes he wonders just how long he has had some of those older items. He has also noticed that he regularly seems to run out of some merchandise items. Adam is also concerned about preparing monthly financial statements. The company uses a periodic inventory system and Adam counts inventory once a year. He is wondering how he is going to calculate the cost of goods sold for the month without counting the inventory at the end of every month. He has come to you for help.

Instructions

(a) Explain to Adam what an operating cycle is and why he is having problems paying the bills.
(b) Explain to Adam how the periodic inventory system is contributing to his problems.

TAKING IT FURTHER Make a recommendation about what inventory system the company should use and why.

Record and post inventory transactions—perpetual system. Calculate net sales and gross profit. (SO 1, 2, 3) AP

P5–2A At the beginning of the current tennis season, on April 1, 2014, Kicked-Back Tennis Shop's inventory consisted of 50 tennis racquets at a cost of $40 each. Kicked-Back uses a perpetual inventory system. The following transactions occurred in April:

Apr. 2 Purchased 160 additional racquets from Roberts Inc. for $6,400, terms n/30.
4 Determined that five of the racquets purchased on April 2 were damaged and returned them to Roberts Inc. Roberts Inc. credited Kicked-Back's account.
5 Sold 45 racquets to Tennis Dome for $90 each, terms n/30.
6 Tennis Dome returned 15 of the racquets after determining it had purchased more racquets than it needed. Kicked-Back gave Tennis Dome a credit on its account and returned the racquets to inventory.
10 Sold 40 racquets at $90 each to cash customers.
12 Ten of these racquets were returned for cash. The customers claimed they never play tennis and had no idea how they had been talked into purchasing the racquets. Refunded cash to these customers and returned the racquets to inventory.
17 An additional 10 of the racquets sold on April 10 were returned because the racquets were damaged. The customers received cash refunds and the racquets were sent to a local children's club as a gift.
25 Sold 60 racquets to the Summer Club for $90 each, terms n/30.
29 Summer Club returned 25 of the racquets after the tennis pro had examined them and determined that these racquets were of inferior quality. Kicked-Back gave Summer Club a credit and decided to return the racquets to inventory with plans to sell them for the reduced price of $75 each.

Instructions

(a) Record the transactions for the month of April for Kicked-Back.
(b) Create T accounts for sales, sales returns, cost of goods sold, and merchandise inventory. Post the opening balance and April's transactions, and calculate the April 30 balances.
(c) Calculate net sales and gross profit.

TAKING IT FURTHER Assume that the owner of Kicked-Back hired an employee to run the store and is not involved in operating the business. The owner wants to know the amount of net sales and gross profit for the month. Will the owner be missing any important information by requesting only these two numbers? Explain.

P5–3A Presented below are selected transactions for Norlan Company during September and October of the current year. Norlan uses a perpetual inventory system.

Record inventory transactions—perpetual system. **(SO 2, 3) AP**

Sept. 1 Purchased merchandise on account from Hillary Company at a cost of $45,000, FOB destination, terms 1/15, n/30.
2 The correct company paid $2,000 of freight charges to Trucking Company on the September 1 merchandise purchase.
5 Returned for credit $3,000 of damaged goods purchased from Hillary Company on September 1.
15 Sold the remaining merchandise purchased from Hillary Company to Irvine Company for $70,000, terms 2/10, n/30, FOB destination.
16 The correct company paid $1,800 of freight charges on the September 15 sale of merchandise.
17 Issued Irvine Company a credit of $5,000 for returned goods. These goods had cost Norlan Company $3,000 and were returned to inventory.
25 Received the balance owing from Irvine Company for the September 15 sale.
30 Paid Hillary Company the balance owing for the September 1 purchase.
Oct. 1 Purchased merchandise on account from Kimmel Company at a cost of $52,000, terms 2/10, n/30, FOB shipping point.
2 The correct company paid freight costs of $1,100 on the October 1 purchase.
3 Obtained a purchase allowance of $2,000 from Kimmel Company to compensate for some minor damage to goods purchased on October 1.
10 Paid Kimmel Company the amount owing on the October 1 purchase.
11 Sold all of the merchandise purchased from Kimmel Company to Kieso Company for $83,500, terms 2/10, n/30, FOB shipping point.
12 The correct company paid $800 freight costs on the October 11 sale.
17 Issued Kieso Company a sales allowance of $1,500 because some of the goods did not meet Kieso's exact specifications.
31 Received a cheque from Kieso Company for the balance owing on the October 11 sale.

Instructions

Prepare journal entries to record the above transactions for Norlan Company.

TAKING IT FURTHER Explain why companies should always take advantage of purchase discounts even if they have to borrow from the bank. Refer to the two purchases made by Norlan Company in your answer.

Record inventory transactions and post to inventory account—perpetual system. **(SO 2, 3) AP**

P5–4A Travel Warehouse distributes suitcases to retail stores and extends credit terms of n/30 to all of its customers. Travel Warehouse uses a perpetual inventory system and at the end of June its inventory consisted of 25 suitcases purchased at $30 each. During the month of July, the following merchandising transactions occurred:

July 1 Purchased 50 suitcases on account for $30 each from Trunk Manufacturers, terms n/30, FOB destination.
2 The correct company paid $125 freight on the July 1 purchase.
4 Received $150 credit for five suitcases returned to Trunk Manufacturers because they were damaged.
10 Sold 45 suitcases on account to Satchel World for $55 each.
12 Issued a $275 credit for five suitcases returned by Satchel World because they were the wrong colour. The suitcases were returned to inventory.
15 Purchased 60 additional suitcases from Trunk Manufacturers for $27.50 each, terms n/30, FOB shipping point.
18 Paid $150 freight to AA Trucking Company for merchandise purchased from Trunk Manufacturers.
21 Sold 54 suitcases on account to Fly-By-Night for $55 each.
23 Gave Fly-By-Night a $110 credit for two returned suitcases. The suitcases had been damaged and were sent to the recyclers.
30 Paid Trunk Manufacturers for the July 1 purchase.
31 Received balance owing from Satchel World.

Instructions

(a) Record the transactions for the month of July for Travel Warehouse.
(b) Create a T account for Merchandise Inventory. Post the opening balance and July's transactions, and calculate the July 31 balance.
(c) Determine the number of suitcases on hand at the end of the month and calculate the average cost per suitcase of the inventory on hand.

TAKING IT FURTHER Explain how freight terms can affect the selling price, and the cost, of merchandise. Use the transactions on July 1 and 15 between Travel Warehouse and Trunk Manufacturers as part of your explanation.

Record and post inventory transactions—perpetual system. Prepare partial income statement.
(SO 2, 3, 5) AP

P5–5A At the beginning of June 2014, Willingham Distributing Company's ledger showed Cash $18,000, Merchandise Inventory $5,000, and D. Willingham, Capital, $23,000. During the month of June, the company had the following selected transactions:

June 1 Purchased $9,000 of merchandise inventory from Sun Supply Co., terms 1/15, n/30, FOB destination.
2 The correct company paid $225 cash for freight charges on the June 1 purchase.
5 Sold merchandise inventory to Moose Jaw Retailers for $12,000. The cost of the merchandise was $7,540 and the terms were 2/10, n/30, FOB destination.
6 Issued a $950 credit for merchandise returned by Moose Jaw Retailers. The merchandise originally cost $595 and was returned to inventory.
6 The correct company paid $290 freight on the June 5 sale.
7 Purchased $800 of supplies for cash.
10 Purchased $4,300 of merchandise inventory from Fey Wholesalers, terms 2/10, n/30, FOB shipping point.
10 The correct company paid $100 freight costs on the purchase from Fey Wholesalers.
12 Received a $300 credit from Fey Wholesalers for returned merchandise.
14 Paid Sun Supply Co. the amount due.
15 Collected the balance owing from Moose Jaw Retailers.
19 Sold merchandise for $7,250 cash. The cost of this merchandise was $4,570.
20 Paid Fey Wholesalers the balance owing from the June 10 purchase.
25 Made a $500 cash refund to a cash customer for merchandise returned. The returned merchandise had a cost of $315. The merchandise was damaged and could not be resold.
30 Sold merchandise to Bauer & Company for $4,280, terms n/30, FOB shipping point. Willingham's cost for this merchandise was $2,700.

Instructions

(a) Record the transactions assuming Willingham uses a perpetual inventory system.
(b) Set up general ledger accounts for Merchandise Inventory, Sales, Sales Returns and Allowances, Sales Discounts, and Cost of Goods Sold. Enter the beginning merchandise inventory balance, and post the transactions.
(c) Prepare a partial multiple-step income statement, up to gross profit, for the month of June 2014.

TAKING IT FURTHER Assume that Willingham has a "no questions asked" policy in terms of accepting sales returns up to six months after the initial sale. What uncertainties does the company face in terms of calculating its gross profit for June?

Prepare adjusting and closing entries, and single-step and multiple-step income statements—perpetual system. Calculate ratios. (SO 4, 5, 6) AP

P5–6A Wolcott Warehouse Store has an August 31 fiscal year end and uses a perpetual inventory system. An alphabetical list of its account balances at August 31, 2014, follows. All accounts have normal balances.

Accounts payable	$ 30,000	Interest revenue	$ 960
Accounts receivable	20,000	Merchandise inventory	57,440
Accumulated depreciation—equipment	26,720	Notes payable	36,000
		Notes receivable	32,000
Cash	12,525	Rent expense	16,000
Cost of goods sold	569,680	Sales	703,360
Depreciation expense	6,680	Sales discounts	3,700
Equipment	66,800	Sales returns and allowances	14,440
Freight out	4,720	Supplies expense	5,840
Insurance expense	2,895	Unearned revenue	6,040
Interest expense	2,160	V. Wolcott, capital	72,680
Interest receivable	240	V. Wolcott, drawings	60,640

Additional information:

1. All adjustments have been recorded and posted except for the inventory adjustment. According to the inventory count, the company has $55,000 of merchandise on hand.
2. Last year Wolcott Warehouse Store had a gross profit margin of 20% and a profit margin of 10%.

Instructions

(a) Prepare any additional required adjusting entries.
(b) Prepare a single-step income statement.
(c) Prepare a multiple-step income statement.
(d) Calculate gross profit margin and profit margin. Compare with last year's margins and comment on the results.
(e) Prepare the closing entries. Post to the Income Summary account. Before closing the Income Summary account, check that the balance is equal to profit.

TAKING IT FURTHER Compare the two income statements and comment on the usefulness of each one.

Prepare adjusting and closing entries and financial statements—perpetual system. Calculate ratios. (SO 4, 5, 6) AP

P5–7A The unadjusted trial balance of World Enterprises for the year ending December 31, 2014, follows:

WORLD ENTERPRISES
Trial Balance
December 31, 2014

	Debit	Credit
Cash	$ 15,000	
Accounts receivable	19,200	
Merchandise inventory	37,050	
Prepaid insurance	3,000	
Supplies	2,950	
Equipment	150,000	
Accumulated depreciation—equipment		$ 35,000
Furniture	45,000	
Accumulated depreciation—furniture		18,000
Accounts payable		33,200
Unearned revenue		4,000
Mortgage payable		125,000
S. Kim, capital		46,200
S. Kim, drawings	48,000	
Sales		265,000
Sales returns and allowances	2,500	
Sales discounts	3,275	
Cost of goods sold	153,000	
Interest expense	6,875	
Salaries expense	35,450	
Utilities expense	5,100	
	$526,400	$526,400

Additional information:

1. There is $750 of supplies on hand on December 31, 2014.
2. The one-year insurance policy was purchased on March 1, 2014.
3. Depreciation expense for the year is $10,000 for the equipment and $4,500 for the furniture.
4. Accrued interest expense at December 31, 2014, is $675.
5. Unearned revenue of $975 is still unearned at December 31, 2014. On the sales that were earned, cost of goods sold was $1,750.
6. A physical count of merchandise inventory indicates $32,750 on hand on December 31, 2014.
7. Of the mortgage payable, $8,500 is to be paid in 2015.
8. Seok Kim invested $5,000 cash in the business on July 19, 2014.
9. Last year, the company had a gross profit margin of 35%, and profit margin of 10%.

Instructions

(a) Prepare the adjusting journal entries assuming they are prepared annually.
(b) Prepare a multiple-step income statement, statement of owner's equity, and classified balance sheet.
(c) Prepare the closing entries.
(d) Calculate the gross profit margin and profit margin for 2014. Compare with the 2013 ratios and comment on any trends.

TAKING IT FURTHER Compare the presentation of information in a multiple-step income statement for a service company with one for merchandising company. How would they be similar and how would they be different?

Calculate ratios and comment. **(SO 6) AN**

P5–8A Magna International Inc. is a leading global supplier of technologically advanced automotive components, systems, and modules. Selected financial information (in US$ millions) follows:

	2011	2010	2009
Sales	$28,748	$23,465	$16,876
Cost of goods sold	25,401	20,456	15,387
Profit (loss)	1,018	1,003	(453)
Current assets	8,146	7,485	6,233
Current liabilities	5,724	4,968	4,232

Instructions

(a) Calculate the gross profit margin, profit margin, and current ratio for each year.
(b) Comment on whether the ratios have improved or deteriorated over the three years.

TAKING IT FURTHER Assume you are thinking about investing in Magna International Inc. What other information would be useful in assessing these ratios?

Record inventory transactions—periodic system. **(SO 7) AP**

***P5–9A** Data for Norlan Company are presented in P5–3A.

Instructions

Record the September and October transactions for Norlan Company, assuming a periodic inventory system is used instead of a perpetual inventory system.

TAKING IT FURTHER Why might a periodic system be better than a perpetual system for Norlan Company?

Record inventory transactions—periodic system. **(SO 7) AP**

***P5–10A** Data for Travel Warehouse are presented in P5–4A.

Instructions

Record the July transactions for Travel Warehouse, assuming a periodic inventory system is used instead of a perpetual inventory system.

TAKING IT FURTHER What are the costs and benefits for Travel Warehouse of using a perpetual, as opposed to a periodic, system?

***P5–11A** Data for Willingham Distributing Company are presented in P5–5A. A physical inventory count shows $3,715 of inventory on hand on June 30, 2014.

Record and post inventory transactions—periodic system. Prepare partial income statement. **(SO 7) AP**

Instructions

(a) Record the transactions assuming Willingham uses a periodic inventory system.
(b) Set up general ledger accounts for merchandise inventory and all of the temporary accounts used in the merchandising transactions. Enter beginning balances, and post the transactions.
(c) Prepare a partial multiple-step income statement, up to gross profit, for the month of June 2014.

TAKING IT FURTHER Will gross profit be higher, lower, or the same amount, if using a periodic inventory system instead of a perpetual inventory system? Explain.

***P5–12A** New West Company recently hired a new accountant whose first task was to prepare the financial statements for the year ended December 31, 2014. The following is what he produced:

Prepare correct multiple-step income statement, statement of owner's equity, and classified balance sheet—periodic system. **(SO 7) AP**

NEW WEST COMPANY
Income Statement
December 31, 2014

Sales			$395,000
Less: Unearned revenue		$ 5,500	
Purchase discounts		3,480	8,980
Total revenue			386,020
Cost of goods sold			
Purchases		$232,000	
Less: Purchase returns and allowances		4,000	
Net purchases		236,000	
Add: Sales returns and allowances		7,500	
Cost of goods available for sale		243,500	
Add: Freight out		9,500	
Cost of selling merchandise			253,000
Gross profit margin			133,020
Operating expenses			
Freight in		$ 4,500	
Insurance expense		10,500	
Interest expense		2,500	
Rent expense		18,000	
Salaries expense		42,000	
Total operating expenses			77,500
Profit margin			55,520
Other revenues			
Interest revenue	$ 1,500		
Investment by owner	3,500	5,000	
Other expenses			
Depreciation expense	7,000		
Drawings by owner	48,000	55,000	(50,000)
Profit from operations			$ 5,520

NEW WEST COMPANY Balance Sheet Year Ended December 31, 2014		
Assets		
Cash		$16,780
Accounts receivable		7,800
Merchandise inventory, January 1, 2014		30,000
Merchandise inventory, December 31, 2014		24,000
Equipment	$70,000	
Less: loan payable (for equipment purchase)	50,000	20,000
Total assets		$98,580
Liabilities and Owner's Equity		
Long-term debt investment		$50,000
Accumulated depreciation—equipment		21,000
Sales discounts		2,900
Total liabilities		73,900
Owner's equity		24,680
Total liabilities and owner's equity		$98,580

The owner of the company, Kylie Oliver, is confused by the statements and has asked you for your help. She doesn't understand how, if her owner's capital account was $75,000 at December 31, 2013, owner's equity is now only $24,680. The accountant tells you that $24,680 must be correct because the balance sheet is balanced. The accountant also tells you that he didn't prepare a statement of owner's equity because it is an optional statement. You are relieved to find out that, even though there are errors in the statements, the amounts used from the accounts in the general ledger are the correct amounts.

Instructions

Prepare the correct multiple-step income statement, statement of owner's equity, and classified balance sheet. You determine that $5,000 of the loan payable on the equipment must be paid during 2015.

TAKING IT FURTHER If a company uses a periodic inventory system, does it have to show on its income statement all of the details as to how cost of goods sold was calculated? Why or why not?

Prepare financial statements and closing entries—periodic system. **(SO 7) AP**

***P5–13A** The following is an alphabetical list of Bud's Bakery's adjusted account balances at the end of the company's fiscal year on November 30, 2014:

Accounts payable	$ 32,310	Merchandise inventory	$ 34,360
Accounts receivable	13,770	Mortgage payable	106,000
Accumulated depreciation—building	61,200	Prepaid insurance	4,500
Accumulated depreciation—equipment	19,880	Property tax expense	3,500
Building	175,000	Purchases	634,700
B. Hachey, capital	104,480	Purchase discounts	6,300
B. Hachey, drawings	12,000	Purchase returns and allowances	13,315
Cash	8,500	Rent revenue	2,800
Depreciation expense	14,000	Salaries expense	122,000
Equipment	57,000	Salaries payable	8,500
Freight in	5,060	Sales	872,000
Freight out	8,200	Sales discounts	8,250
Insurance expense	9,000	Sales returns and allowances	9,845
Interest expense	5,300	Unearned revenue	3,000
Land	85,000	Utilities expense	19,800

Additional facts:

1. Bud's Bakery uses a periodic inventory system.
2. Of the mortgage payable, $8,500 is due in the next year.
3. A physical count determined that merchandise inventory on hand at November 30, 2014, was $37,350.

Instructions

(a) Prepare a multiple-step income statement, statement of owner's equity, and classified balance sheet.
(b) Prepare the closing journal entries.
(c) Post closing entries to the merchandise inventory and capital accounts. Check that the balances in these accounts are the same as the amounts on the balance sheet.

TAKING IT FURTHER If you had not been told that Bud's Bakery uses a periodic inventory system, how could you have determined that? What information is available in a periodic inventory system that is not available in a perpetual inventory system?

CONTINUING COOKIE CHRONICLE

(*Note:* This is a continuation of the Cookie Chronicle from Chapters 1 through 4. From the information gathered in the previous chapters, follow the instructions below using the ledger account balances from Chapter 4.)

Because Natalie has had such a successful first few months, she is considering other opportunities to develop her business. One opportunity is the sale of fine European mixers. The owner of Kzinski Supply Co. has approached Natalie to become the exclusive Canadian distributor of these fine mixers. The current cost of a mixer is approximately $525 Canadian, and Natalie would sell each one for $1,050. Natalie comes to you for advice on how to account for these mixers. Each appliance has a serial number and can be easily identified.

Natalie asks you the following questions:

1. "Would you consider these mixers to be inventory? Or should they be classified as supplies or equipment?"
2. "I've learned a little about keeping track of inventory using both the perpetual and the periodic systems of accounting for inventory. Which system do you think is better? Which one would you recommend for the type of inventory that I want to sell?"
3. "How often do I need to count inventory if I maintain it using the perpetual system? Do I need to count inventory at all?"

In the end, Natalie decides to use the perpetual inventory system. The following transactions happen during the month of January 2014:

Jan.	6	Purchased and received three deluxe mixers on account from Kzinski Supply Co. for $1,575, FOB shipping point, terms n/30.
	7	Paid $60 freight on the January 6 purchase.
	8	Returned one of the mixers to Kzinski because it was damaged during shipping. Kzinski issued Cookie Creations a credit note for the cost of the mixer plus $20 for the cost of freight that was paid on January 6 for one mixer.
	9	Collected $500 of the accounts receivable from December 2013.
	13	Two deluxe mixers were sold on account for $2,100, FOB destination, terms n/30. The mixers were sold to Koebel's Family Bakery, the bakery that is owned and operated by Natalie's mom and dad. Natalie expects that the mixers will be paid for in early February.
	14	Paid the $75 of delivery charges for the two mixers that were sold on January 13.
	14	Purchased and received four deluxe mixers on account from Kzinski Supply Co. for $2,100, FOB shipping point, terms n/30.
	15	Received a deposit of $125 from another school in Natalie's area to teach a class during the month of February.
	20	Natalie was concerned that there was not enough cash available to pay for all of the mixers purchased. She invested an additional $1,000 cash in Cookie Creations.
	21	Paid $80 freight on the January 14 purchase.
	21	Sold two deluxe mixers for $2,100 cash.
	28	Natalie issued a cheque to her assistant for all the help the assistant has given her during the month. Her assistant worked 20 hours in January and was also paid the $48 owing at December 31, 2013. (Natalie's assistant earns $12 an hour.)
	29	Paid a $154 cell phone bill ($76 for the December 2013 account payable and $78 for the month of January). (Recall that the cell phone is only used for business purposes.)
	29	Paid Kzinski all amounts due.

As at January 31, the following adjusting entry data are available:

1. A count of baking supplies reveals that none were used in January.
2. Another month's worth of depreciation needs to be recorded on the baking equipment bought in November and December. (Recall that the equipment cost $1,550 and has a useful life of three years or 36 months.)
3. An additional month's worth of interest on her grandmother's loan needs to be accrued. (Recall that Cookie Creations borrowed $3,000 and the interest rate is 3%.)
4. An analysis of the unearned revenue account reveals that no lessons have been taught during the month of January. As a result, the opening balance in Unearned Revenue is still unearned. Natalie has been in contact with the schools that have provided deposits and lessons have been booked for early February.
5. An inventory count of mixers at the end of January reveals that Natalie has two mixers remaining.

Instructions

Using the information from previous chapters and the new information above, do the following:

(a) Answer Natalie's questions.
(b) Journalize and post the January 2014 transactions.
(c) Prepare a trial balance.
(d) Journalize and post the adjusting journal entries required.
(e) Prepare an adjusted trial balance.
(f) Prepare a multiple-step income statement for the month ended January 31, 2014.
(g) Calculate gross profit margin and profit margin.

Cumulative Coverage—Chapters 2 to 5

The Board Shop, owned by Andrew John, sells skateboards in the summer and snowboards in the winter. The shop has an August 31 fiscal year end and uses a perpetual inventory system. On August 1, 2014, the company had the following balances in its general ledger:

Cash	$21,385	A. John, drawings	$ 52,800
Merchandise inventory	64,125	Sales	485,500
Supplies	3,750	Rent revenue	1,200
Equipment	70,800	Sales returns and allowances	11,420
Accumulated depreciation—equipment	13,275	Cost of goods sold	301,010
Accounts payable	12,650	Salaries expense	68,200
Unearned revenue	4,680	Rent expense	18,150
Notes payable	42,000	Insurance expense	4,140
A. John, capital	58,400	Interest expense	1,925

During August, the last month of the fiscal year, the company had the following transactions:

Aug.	1	Paid $1,650 for August's rent.
	2	Paid $6,500 on account.
	4	Sold merchandise costing $7,900 for $12,260 cash.
	5	Purchased merchandise on account from Orange Line Co., FOB shipping point, for $24,500.
	5	Paid freight charges of $500 on merchandise purchased from Orange Line Co.
	8	Purchased supplies on account for $345.
	9	Refunded a customer $425 cash for returned merchandise. The merchandise had cost $265 and was returned to inventory.
	10	Sold merchandise on account to Spider Company for $15,750, terms 2/10, n/30, FOB shipping point. The merchandise had a cost of $9,765.
	11	Paid Orange Line Co. for half of the merchandise purchased on August 5.
	12	Spider Company returned $750 of the merchandise it purchased. Board Shop issued Spider a credit memo. The merchandise had a cost of $465 and was returned to inventory.
	15	Paid salaries, $3,100.
	19	Spider Company paid the amount owing.
	21	Purchased $9,900 of merchandise from Rainbow Option Co. on account, terms 2/10, n/30, FOB destination.
	23	Returned $800 of the merchandise to Rainbow Option Co. and received a credit memo.

24 Received $525 cash in advance from customers for merchandise to be delivered in September.
30 Paid salaries, $3,100.
30 Paid Rainbow Option Co. the amount owing.
31 Andrew John withdrew $4,800 cash.

Adjustment and additional data:

1. A count of supplies on August 31 shows $755 on hand.
2. The equipment has an estimated eight-year useful life.
3. Of the notes payable, $6,000 must be paid on September 1 each year.
4. An analysis of the Unearned Revenue account shows that $3,750 has been earned by August 31. A corresponding $2,325 for Cost of Goods Sold will also need to be recorded for these sales.
5. Interest accrued on the note payable to August 31 was $175.
6. A count of the merchandise inventory on August 31 shows $76,560 of inventory on hand.

Instructions

(a) Create a general ledger account for each of the above accounts and enter the August 1 balances.
(b) Record and post the August transactions.
(c) Prepare a trial balance at August 31, 2014.
(d) Record and post the adjustments required at August 31, 2014.
(e) Prepare an adjusted trial balance at August 31, 2014.
(f) Prepare a multiple-step income statement, statement of owner's equity, and classified balance sheet.
(g) Record and post closing entries.
(h) Prepare a post-closing trial balance at August 31, 2014.

BROADENING YOUR PERSPECTIVE — CHAPTER 5

Critical Thinking

Collaborative Learning Activity

Note to instructor: Additional instructions and material for this group activity can be found on the Instructor Resource Site and in *WileyPLUS*.

BYP5–1 The purpose of this group activity is to improve your understanding of merchandising journal entries. You will be given a merchandising company's general ledger in T account format with missing transaction data. With your group you will analyze these T accounts to determine the underlying journal entries and balance the general ledger.

Communication Activity

BYP5–2 Consider the following events listed in chronological order:

1. Dexter Maersk decides to buy a custom-made snowboard. He calls Great Canadian Snowboards and asks it to manufacture one for him.
2. The company e-mails Dexter a purchase order to fill out, which he immediately completes, signs, and sends back with the required 25% down payment.
3. Great Canadian Snowboards receives Dexter's purchase order and down payment, and begins working on the board.
4. Great Canadian Snowboards has its fiscal year end. At this time, Dexter's board is 75% completed.
5. The company completes the snowboard for Dexter and notifies him.
6. Dexter picks up his snowboard from the company and takes it home.
7. Dexter tries the snowboard out and likes it so much that he carves his initials in it.
8. Great Canadian Snowboards bills Dexter for the cost of the snowboard, less the 25% down payment.
9. The company receives partial payment (another 25%) from Dexter.
10. The company receives payment of the balance due from Dexter.

Instructions

In a memo to the president of Great Canadian Snowboards, answer these questions:

(a) When should Great Canadian Snowboards record the revenue and cost of goods sold related to the snowboard? Refer to the revenue and expense recognition criteria in your answer.

(b) Suppose that, with his purchase order, Dexter was required to pay for 100% of the board. Would that change your answer to part (a)?

Ethics Case

BYP5–3 Rita Pelzer was just hired as the assistant controller of Liu Stores. The company is a specialty chain store with nine retail stores concentrated in one metropolitan area. Among other things, the payment of all invoices is centralized in one of the departments Rita will manage. Her main responsibilities are to maintain the company's high credit rating by paying all bills when they are due and to take advantage of all cash discounts.

Jamie Caterino, the former assistant controller, who has now been promoted to controller, is training Rita in her new duties. He instructs Rita to continue the practice of preparing all cheques for the amount due less the discount and to date the cheques the last day of the discount period. "But," Jamie continues, "we always hold the cheques at least four days beyond the discount period before mailing them. That way we get another four days of interest on our money. Most of our creditors need our business and don't complain. And, if they scream about our missing the discount period, we blame it on Canada Post. I think everybody does it. By the way, welcome to our team!"

Instructions

(a) What are the ethical considerations in this case?
(b) Which stakeholders are harmed or benefited?
(c) Should Rita continue the practice started by Jamie? Does she have any choice?

All About You: Personal Financial Literacy Activity

BYP5–4 In the "All About You" feature, you learned about inventory theft and a relatively new technology to help prevent theft. You have recently accepted a part-time sales position at a clothing store called College Fashions. The owner-manager of the store knows that you are enrolled in a business program and seeks your advice on preventing inventory shrinkage due to theft. The owner-manager is aware that the industry average shrinkage rates are 1.49% of revenues but does not know College Fashions' shrinkage rate.

Instructions

(a) Assume the store uses a perpetual inventory system. Explain to the owner-manager how she can determine the amount of inventory shrinkage.
(b) The owner-manager wants to know if she should implement some type of technology to prevent theft. What would you advise her to consider before making an expenditure on technology to prevent theft?
(c) Assume that College Fashions' sales revenues are $400,000 and the shrinkage rate is 4%. What is the dollar amount that College Fashions loses due to shrinkage?
(d) Some believe that great customer service is the best defence against shoplifting. Discuss why great customer service may help prevent shoplifting.
(e) You also learned in the All About You feature that employee inventory theft is a significant problem. What procedures might management implement to prevent or reduce employee theft of inventory?
(f) In your part-time sales position, you have observed a fellow employee that you are friendly with provide unauthorized sales discounts to her friends when they purchase merchandise from the store. Is it appropriate for this employee to give her friend unauthorized sales discounts? Explain. What might be a consequence for you as an employee if you fail to inform management of these unauthorized sales discounts?

ANSWERS TO CHAPTER QUESTIONS

ANSWERS TO ACCOUNTING IN ACTION INSIGHT QUESTIONS

Business Insight, p. 210

Q: What accounting information would help a manager decide what to do with returned goods?

A: The manager would need to know the potential revenues and expenses for each alternative. For example, returning goods to stock and selling them again may provide the highest revenue but the cost of getting the goods ready for resale may also be high. The revenue earned from liquidating the returned goods may be much lower but the cost of doing this may also be very low. The manager should compare the estimated profit—not just the revenue earned—of each alternative when deciding what to do.

All About You Insight, p. 212

Q: Are there advantages to you as a customer when retailers increase theft prevention measures?

A: Many customers see theft prevention measures, such as locked fitting rooms, or having a store employee track the items they are taking into a fitting room, as a very annoying personal inconvenience. But there are benefits to the customers as well as the stores. Retailers have to be able to pass all of their costs on to customers in order to remain in business. When inventory theft increases, the selling price will also have to increase or the store will not be profitable. If customers are not willing to pay the increased prices, then the store may have to go out of business, resulting in less choice for consumers and fewer jobs. Inconveniences in using the fitting rooms may be a far smaller price to pay than the alternatives.

ANSWERS TO SELF-STUDY QUESTIONS

1. b 2. d 3. a 4. a 5. b 6. c 7. a 8. c 9. d 10. c *11. a *12. b

Remember to go back to the beginning of the chapter to check off your completed work!

←

CHAPTER 6

INVENTORY COSTING

THE NAVIGATOR

- ☐ Understand *Concepts for Review*
- ☐ Read *Feature Story*
- ☐ Scan *Study Objectives*
- ☐ Read *Chapter Preview*
- ☐ Read text and answer *Before You Go On*
- ☐ Review *Comparing IFRS and ASPE*
- ☐ Work *Demonstration Problems*
- ☐ Review *Summary of Study Objectives*
- ☐ Answer *Self-Study Questions*
- ☐ Complete assignments

CONCEPTS FOR REVIEW

Before studying this chapter, you should understand or, if necessary, review:

A. The cost principle (Ch. 1, p. 16) and expense recognition criteria (Ch. 3, p. 96).

B. The difference between calculating cost of goods sold in a perpetual inventory system and in a periodic inventory system. (Ch. 5, pp. 208–210 and 224–226)

C. How to journalize inventory transactions in perpetual and periodic inventory systems. (Ch. 5, pp. 208–215 and 222–224)

D. How to prepare financial statements for a merchandising company. (Ch. 5, pp. 216–220)

COUNTING INVENTORY IS NOT A "SHOE"-IN

EDMONTON, AB—With between 150 and 200 brands and more than 73,000 stock-keeping units (SKUs), counting inventory at gravitypope is an intensive process. The women's and men's footwear and clothing retailer does a physical count of all inventory once a year, close to its fiscal year end, with smaller counts throughout the year of pricier items.

"We have a lot of inventory to deal with," says CEO and founder Louise Dirks, who started with a shoe store in 1990 in Edmonton's trendy Whyte Avenue neighbourhood and now has shoe stores and gravitypope Tailored Goods clothing stores in Edmonton, Vancouver, Calgary, and Toronto. "If you see something on the shelf, we've got anywhere from 8 to 30 units of it in the back."

Over approximately a three-week period, inventory is counted in each of the stores, its two warehouses, and the third floor of the Edmonton shoe store that coordinates sales from its website. The counts are generally done after the stores close, and the inventory records are "frozen" before the count starts—no sales can take place during inventory counting so that the counts are accurate.

Each location is divided into batches of between 40 and 60 items. A team of three employees does the count of each batch. "I like to hold my people accountable and it's also much easier having employees do inventory because they know best where the product is located," Ms. Dirks says in explaining why she doesn't use a third party to count inventory. Employees use portable data transmitter (PDT) guns to scan the barcode of each item, while two other independent manual counts are done to ensure an unbiased count. When their counts all match, the team moves on to the next batch. If the counts don't match, they can quickly see where they went wrong. This is the reason that inventory is divided into small quantities. Sometimes it's a simple error of scanning a barcode incorrectly, Ms. Dirks says.

The data from the PDT guns are uploaded to and compared with the stores' point-of-sale (POS) system, which allows for a perpetual inventory system. Any discrepancies between the PDT and POS data are investigated. Sometimes a clerk may have sold an item under the wrong SKU or an inventory counter scanned the wrong barcode. If an item genuinely cannot be accounted for, it's written off with a journal entry as shrinkage due to loss or theft, says Ms. Dirks.

Gravitypope uses the first-in, first-out method to determine the cost of its inventory and calculate its cost of goods sold. For items that remain past a season, the company writes them down to their net realizable value. Because it imports more than half of its goods, the retailer's cost of goods sold includes the exchange rate for foreign currencies it uses to buy items, usually euros, British pounds, U.S. dollars, and Japanese yen—all part of selling fashions from around the globe.

THE NAVIGATOR

STUDY OBJECTIVES

After studying this chapter, you should be able to:

1. Describe the steps in determining inventory quantities.
2. Calculate cost of goods sold and ending inventory in a perpetual inventory system using the specific identification, FIFO, and average methods of cost determination.
3. Explain the financial statement effects of inventory cost determination methods.
4. Determine the financial statement effects of inventory errors.
5. Value inventory at the lower of cost and net realizable value.
6. Demonstrate the presentation and analysis of inventory.
7. Calculate ending inventory and cost of goods sold in a periodic inventory system using FIFO and average inventory cost formulas (Appendix 6A).
8. Estimate ending inventory using the gross profit and retail inventory methods (Appendix 6B).

THE NAVIGATOR

PREVIEW OF CHAPTER SIX

In the previous chapter, we discussed accounting for merchandise transactions. In this chapter, we first explain the procedures for determining inventory quantities. We then discuss the three methods for determining the cost of goods sold and the cost of inventory on hand: the specific identification method and the two cost formulas, FIFO and average. Next we see the effects of cost determination methods and inventory errors on a company's financial statements. We end by illustrating methods of reporting and analyzing inventory.

The chapter is organized as follows:

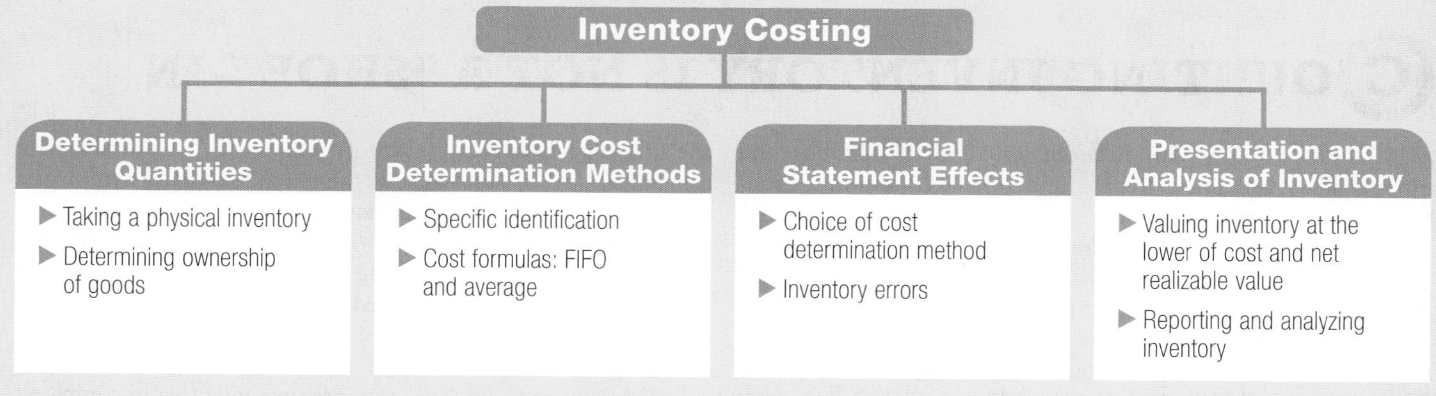

DETERMINING INVENTORY QUANTITIES

STUDY OBJECTIVE 1

Describe the steps in determining inventory quantities.

Companies count their entire inventory at least once a year, whether they are using a perpetual or a periodic inventory system. This is called taking a physical inventory. If they are using a perpetual system, like gravitypope in our feature story, they will use this information to check the accuracy of their perpetual inventory records. As we saw in Chapter 5, in a perpetual inventory system, the accounting records continuously—perpetually—show the amount of inventory that *should be on hand*, not necessarily the amount that *actually is on hand*. An adjusting entry is required if the physical inventory count does not match the balance that is shown in the Merchandise Inventory account in the general ledger.

In a periodic inventory system, inventory quantities are not continuously updated. Companies using a periodic inventory system must take a physical inventory to determine the amount on hand at the end of the accounting period. Once the ending inventory amount is known, this amount is then used to calculate the cost of goods sold for the period and to update the Merchandise Inventory account in the general ledger.

Inventory quantities are determined in two steps: (1) by taking a physical inventory of goods on hand, and (2) by determining the ownership of goods.

TAKING A PHYSICAL INVENTORY

Taking a physical inventory involves actually counting, weighing, or measuring each kind of inventory on hand. Taking a physical inventory can be an enormous task for many companies, especially for retail stores such as gravitypope, which has thousands of inventory items. An inventory count is generally more accurate when goods are not being sold or received during the counting. This is why companies often count their inventory when they are closed or when business is slow.

To make fewer errors in taking the inventory, a company should ensure that it has a good system of internal control. Internal control is the process designed and implemented by management to help the company achieve reliable financial reporting, effective and efficient operations, and compliance with relevant laws and regulations. Some of the internal control procedures for counting inventory are as follows:

1. The counting should be done by employees who are not responsible for either custody of the inventory or keeping inventory records.

2. Each counter should confirm that each inventory item actually exists, how many there are of it, and what condition each item is in. For example, does each box actually contain what it is supposed to contain?
3. There should be a second count by another employee or auditor. Counting should be done in teams of two.
4. Prenumbered inventory tags should be used to ensure that all inventory items are counted and that no items are counted more than once.

In our feature story, we saw how gravitypope incorporates many of these controls into its inventory count. We will learn more about internal controls in Chapter 7.

After the physical inventory is taken, the quantity of each kind of inventory item is listed on inventory summary sheets. The second count by another employee or auditor helps ensure the count is accurate. The quantity of each type of good is then multiplied by its unit cost to determine the total cost of the inventory; this will be explained later in the chapter, when we discuss inventory costing.

DETERMINING OWNERSHIP OF GOODS

When we take a physical inventory, we need to consider the ownership of goods. To determine ownership of the goods, two questions need to be answered: Do all of the goods included in the count belong to the company? Does the company own any goods that were not included in the count?

Goods in Transit

A complication in determining ownership is goods in transit (on board a public carrier such as a railway, airline, truck, or ship) at the end of the accounting period. The problem is determining which company should include the goods in its inventory: the purchaser or the seller.

Goods in transit should be included in the inventory of the company that has ownership (legal title) of the goods. We learned in Chapter 5 that the point in time when ownership changes hands is determined by the terms of sale, as shown in Illustration 6-1 and described below:

ILLUSTRATION 6-1
Terms of sale

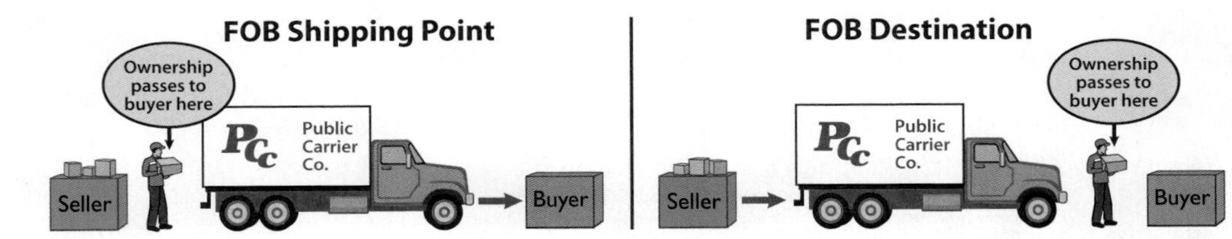

1. When the terms are *FOB (free on board) shipping point*, ownership (legal title) of the goods passes to the buyer *when the public carrier accepts the goods from the seller.*
2. When the terms are *FOB destination*, ownership (legal title) of the goods passes to the buyer when they actually *receive* the goods.

Inventory quantities may be seriously miscounted if goods in transit at the statement date are ignored. The company may have purchased goods that have not yet been received, or it may have sold goods that have not yet been delivered. For example, assume that Hill Company has 20,000 units of inventory in its warehouse on December 31. It also has the following goods in transit on December 31:

1. sales of 1,500 units shipped December 31, FOB destination, and,
2. purchases of 2,500 units shipped FOB shipping point by the seller on December 31.

Hill has legal title to both the units sold and the units purchased. If units in transit are ignored, inventory quantities would be understated by 4,000 units (1,500 + 2,500).

As we will see later in this chapter, inaccurate inventory quantities not only affect the inventory amount on the balance sheet, they also affect the cost of goods sold and, therefore, the net income or loss reported in the income statement.

Consigned Goods

For some businesses, it is customary to hold goods belonging to other parties and to sell them, for a fee, without ever taking ownership of the goods. These are called **consigned goods**.

Helpful hint Recall that merchandise inventory is an asset (an item of value that the company owns). Therefore, the goods should be included in the inventory of the business that has legal title to (ownership of) the goods.

For example, artists often display their paintings and other works of art on consignment at galleries. In such cases, the art gallery (the consignee) does not take ownership of the art—it still belongs to the artist (the consignor). Therefore, if an inventory count is taken, any art on consignment should not be included in the art gallery's inventory.

When a consigned good sells, the consignee then takes a commission and pays the consignor the remainder. Many craft stores, second-hand clothing and sporting goods stores, and antique dealers sell goods on consignment to keep their inventory costs down and to avoid the risk of purchasing an item they will not be able to sell.

Other Situations

Sometimes goods are not physically present at a company because they have been taken home *on approval* by a customer. Goods on approval *should be added* to the physical inventory count because they still belong to the seller. The customer will either return the item or decide to buy it.

In other cases, goods are sold but the seller is holding them for alteration, or until they are picked up or delivered to the customer. These goods should *not* be included in the physical count, because legal title to ownership has passed from the seller to the customer. Damaged or unsaleable goods should be separated from the physical count and any loss should be recorded as a debit to Cost of Goods Sold.

ACCOUNTING IN ACTION
ALL ABOUT YOU INSIGHT

Have you ever shopped in or sold some things at a consignment store? Many students buy and sell second-hand items such as clothing and furniture to save money and help the environment. That popularity has spread throughout the general Canadian population as the economy softened. In Vancouver, for example, consignment sales rose an estimated 25% in 2011. Shoppers are attracted to lower prices for higher-quality goods and making long-term investments in designer and classic items, while sellers want to earn some cash for things they don't use anymore. The Internet has exposed people to designer brands and unique looks that consumers are eager to try out on a budget. For consignment store owners, the business model is attractive, too, because they have virtually no inventory costs. The stores only pay for an item once it's sold. Typically, stores give a commission of about 40% of the sale price to the person who brought in the item. Often, the commission will drop as time passes and the sale price is reduced.

Source: "Consignment Sales Up as Fashionistas Get Frugal," CTV News British Columbia on-line, January 26, 2012; Colin McAllister and Justin Ryan, "Consignment Stores Hold Relics to Relish," *Vancouver Sun*, November 10, 2011; Ed Stoddard and Tim Gaynor, "Second-Hand Retailers Score During Recession," Reuters, *The Globe and Mail*, October 5, 2009.

What is one disadvantage of buying items on consignment?

Action Plan

Apply the rules of ownership to goods held on consignment:

- Goods held on consignment for another company are not included in inventory.
- Goods held on consignment by another company are included in inventory.

Apply the rules of ownership to goods in transit:

BEFORE YOU GO ON... continued on next page

BEFORE YOU GO ON...

DO IT

Too Good to Be Threw Company completed its inventory count on June 30. It arrived at a total inventory value of $200,000, counting everything currently on hand in its warehouse. You have been given the information listed below. How will the following information affect the inventory count and cost?

1. Goods costing $15,000 that are being held on consignment for another company were included in the inventory.
2. Goods purchased for $10,000 and in transit at June 30 (terms FOB shipping point) were not included in the count.
3. Inventory sold for $18,000 that cost $12,000 when purchased and was in transit at June 30 (terms FOB destination) was not included in the count.

SOLUTION

Original count	$200,000
1. Goods held on consignment from another company	(15,000)
2. Goods in transit purchased FOB shipping point	10,000
3. Goods in transit sold FOB destination	12,000
Adjusted count	$207,000

Related exercise material: BE6–1, BE6–2, E6–1, and E6–2.

BEFORE YOU GO ON...
continued from previous page

- FOB shipping point: Goods sold or purchased and shipped FOB shipping point belong to the buyer when in transit.
- FOB destination: Goods sold or purchased and shipped FOB destination belong to the seller until they reach their destination.

THE NAVIGATOR

INVENTORY COST DETERMINATION METHODS

STUDY OBJECTIVE 2
Calculate cost of goods sold and ending inventory in a perpetual inventory system using the specific identification, FIFO, and average methods of cost determination.

The physical inventory count we described in the last section determines the *quantities* on hand, but does not determine their *cost*. Before comparing the results of the physical inventory count with the perpetual inventory records, costs will need to be assigned to the inventory items. In a perpetual inventory system, costs must also be assigned to inventory items when calculating the cost of goods sold each time a sale is recorded.

When all identical inventory items have been purchased at the same unit cost, the calculations are simple. However, when identical items have been purchased at different costs during the period, it is difficult to decide which unit costs apply to the items that have been sold and which of the unit costs apply to the items that remain in inventory.

In Chapter 5, you did not have this problem because you were either told the cost of goods sold, or it was assumed for simplicity that all identical inventory items had the same unit cost. In Chapter 6, we build on what you learned in Chapter 5. In this chapter, identical items will be purchased at different per-unit prices and you will have to determine the cost of the goods sold and the cost of the ending inventory.

In the next section, we will examine three methods of determining cost of goods sold and the cost of the ending merchandise inventory. One method—specific identification—uses the actual physical flow of goods to determine cost. We will look at this method first.

SPECIFIC IDENTIFICATION

The **specific identification** method tracks the actual physical flow (movement) of the goods in a perpetual inventory system. Each item of inventory is marked, tagged, or coded with its specific unit cost so that, at any point in time, the cost of the goods sold and the cost of the ending inventory can be determined.

The specific identification method is used by companies that have unique or different products so that no two products are identical. For example, Demitre's Designs, a jewellery store that sells one-of-a-kind rings, would use specific identification. To illustrate, assume that Demitre's Designs had three rings available for sale in January with a total cost of $9,200 ($2,000 + $3,000 + $4,200).

As shown in Illustration 6-2, the cost of the two rings sold is $6,200 ($2,000 + $4,200), and the cost of the ring still on hand at the end of January is $3,000. Therefore, the cost of goods sold on the January income statement is $6,200 and the merchandise inventory on the January 31 balance sheet is $3,000. This determination is possible because it is easy to track the actual physical flow of the goods.

ILLUSTRATION 6-2
Specific identification

Specific identification **must be** used for goods that are not ordinarily interchangeable, or for goods that are produced for specific projects. In addition to the ring example, it would be used for any other customized products such as furniture and artistic work. Car manufacturers and dealerships also use specific identification for cars as each car has its own unique characteristics and vehicle identification number.

It may seem that specific identification is the ideal method for determining cost because it matches the actual cost of the good sold (expense) with the specific sale (revenue). But it can be time-consuming and expensive to apply. And if it is used for identical items, then management could manipulate profit by choosing which units to sell. Therefore, it can be used **only** for inventory that is not ordinarily interchangeable.

COST FORMULAS: FIFO AND AVERAGE

Because the specific identification method is only suitable for certain kinds of inventories, other methods of cost determination, known as cost formulas, are used. The two inventory cost formulas used in Canada and internationally are:

1. First-in, first-out (FIFO), where the cost of the first item purchased is considered to be the cost of the first item sold
2. Average, where the cost is determined using a weighted average of the cost of the items purchased

FIFO and average are known as "cost formulas" because they assume a flow of costs *that may not be the same as* the actual physical flow of goods, unlike the specific identification method.

While specific identification is normally used only in a perpetual inventory system, FIFO and average can be used in both the perpetual and periodic inventory systems. Recall from Chapter 5 that the two systems differ in determining when the cost of goods sold is calculated and recorded.

Under a perpetual inventory system, the cost of goods sold is calculated and updated as each item is sold. Under a periodic inventory system, the cost of goods available for sale (beginning inventory plus the cost of goods purchased) is allocated to ending inventory and to cost of goods sold at the end of the period. Recall that in a periodic system, the cost of goods sold is calculated by deducting the ending inventory from the cost of goods available for sale. The process of calculating cost of goods sold and ending inventory in a periodic system using the FIFO and average cost formulas is included in Appendix 6A.

To illustrate how the FIFO and average cost formulas are applied, we will assume that Bennett Lighting has the information shown in Illustration 6-3 for one of its products, the anti-bug lightbulb.

ILLUSTRATION 6-3
Inventory purchases, sales, and units on hand

BENNETT LIGHTING
Anti-Bug Lightbulb

Date	Explanation	Units	Unit Cost	Total Cost	Total Units in Inventory
Jan. 1	Beginning inventory	100	$10	$ 1,000	100
Apr. 15	Purchase	200	11	2,200	300
May 1	Sales	(150)			150
Aug. 24	Purchase	300	12	3,600	450
Sept. 1	Sales	(400)			50
Nov. 27	Purchase	400	13	5,200	450
				$12,000	

Perpetual Inventory System—First-In, First-Out (FIFO)

The **first-in, first-out (FIFO) cost formula** assumes that the earliest (oldest) goods purchased are the first ones to be sold. This does *not* necessarily mean that the oldest units are in fact sold first; only that the cost of the oldest units is used first to calculate cost of goods sold. It is used by a variety of companies including gravitypope in our feature story. Although the cost formula chosen by a company does not have to match the actual physical movement of the inventory, it should correspond as closely as possible. FIFO often *does* match the actual physical flow of merchandise, because it generally is good business practice to sell the oldest units first.

We will use the information for Bennett Lighting's anti-bug lightbulb in Illustration 6-3 to prepare a perpetual inventory schedule with the FIFO cost formula. Perpetual inventory schedules are organized to show how the cost of goods sold for each sale is calculated. They also show the cost and number of units of inventory on hand throughout the year.

A perpetual inventory schedule starts with the inventory on hand at the beginning of the year. Recall that this figure would have been determined through the physical inventory count that would have been conducted at the end of the previous fiscal year. Purchases are added and sales are deducted in the schedule in chronological order. Illustration 6-4 shows how to record the beginning inventory of 100 units costing $10 each and the April 15 purchase of 200 units costing $11 each. Notice that the $10 units are shown separately from the $11 units in the balance columns and that the total cost of $3,200 is equal to 100 units × $10/unit + 200 units × $11/unit.

ILLUSTRATION 6-4
Perpetual inventory schedule—FIFO (calculation as at April 15)

	PURCHASES			COST OF GOODS SOLD			BALANCE		
Date	Units	Cost	Total	Units	Cost	Total	Units	Cost	Total
Jan. 1							100	$10	$1,000
Apr. 15	200	$11	$2,200				100 200	10 11	} 3,200

Helpful hint Recall that under a perpetual inventory system, the seller of the goods must record two entries: the first entry debits Cash or a receivable and credits a revenue account for the goods' *sale price*, and the second entry debits Cost of Goods Sold and credits Merchandise Inventory for the goods' *cost price.*

The next transaction is the May 1 sale of 150 units. Remember that in a perpetual inventory system the cost of the goods sold is calculated every time a sale is made. Therefore, on May 1, we apply FIFO to determine if the 150 units that were sold cost $10, $11, or a mix of both amounts.

Under FIFO, the cost of the *oldest* goods on hand before the sale is allocated to the cost of goods sold. Accordingly, we start with the beginning inventory of 100 units costing $10 each. Since 150 units were sold on May 1, we are assuming that they sold the entire beginning inventory, and 50 of the $11 units. This leaves 150 (200 – 50) of the $11 units on hand after the sale is recorded. In Illustration 6-5, we have added this information to the perpetual inventory schedule started in Illustration 6-4.

ILLUSTRATION 6-5
Perpetual inventory schedule—FIFO (calculation as at May 1)

	PURCHASES			COST OF GOODS SOLD			BALANCE		
Date	Units	Cost	Total	Units	Cost	Total	Units	Cost	Total
Jan. 1							100	$10	$1,000
Apr. 15	200	$11	$2,200				100 200	10 11	} 3,200
May 1				100 50	$10 11	} $1,550	150	11	1,650

After additional purchases are made on August 24, the inventory on hand is assumed to consist of 150 units at $11 and 300 units at $12, which totals 450 units at $5,250, as shown in Illustration 6-6.

ILLUSTRATION 6-6
Perpetual inventory schedule—FIFO (calculation as at August 24)

	PURCHASES			COST OF GOODS SOLD			BALANCE		
Date	Units	Cost	Total	Units	Cost	Total	Units	Cost	Total
Jan. 1							100	$10	$1,000
Apr. 15	200	$11	$2,200				100 200	10 11	} 3,200
May 1				100 50	$10 11	} $1,550	150	11	1,650
Aug. 24	300	12	3,600				150 300	11 12	} 5,250

On September 1, when 400 units are sold, the cost of goods sold is assumed to consist of the remaining $11 units purchased on April 15 (150 units), and 250 of the $12 units purchased on August 24. This leaves 50 of the $12 units in inventory, or $600 in total.

After a purchase of 400 units on November 27, the inventory consists of 450 units, of which there are 50 of the $12 units from the August 24 purchase and 400 of the $13 units purchased on

November 27. These two transactions are shown in Illustration 6-7, to complete the perpetual inventory schedule started in Illustration 6-4.

ILLUSTRATION 6-7
Perpetual inventory schedule—FIFO (calculation as at November 27)

	PURCHASES			COST OF GOODS SOLD			BALANCE		
Date	Units	Cost	Total	Units	Cost	Total	Units	Cost	Total
Jan. 1							100	$10	$1,000
Apr. 15	200	$11	$2,200				100 200	10 11	} 3,200
May 1				100 50	$10 11	} $1,550	150	11	1,650
Aug. 24	300	12	3,600				150 300	11 12	} 5,250
Sept. 1				150 250	11 12	} 4,650	50	12	600
Nov. 27	400	13	5,200				50 400	12 13	} 5,800
	900		$11,000	550		$6,200			

Note that beginning inventory is $1,000, total purchases are $11,000, total cost of goods sold is $6,200, and ending inventory is $5,800. These numbers can be used to check the calculations in the perpetual inventory schedule. Remember that beginning inventory plus purchases (that is, the cost of goods available for sale) minus cost of goods sold equals ending inventory. In this case, we see that the schedule is balanced because $1,000 + $11,000 − $6,200 = $5,800.

Perpetual Inventory System—Average

The **average cost formula** recognizes that it is not practical to measure a specific physical flow of inventory when the goods available for sale are homogeneous and non-distinguishable. It is used by a variety of companies including gravitypope in our feature story to calculate the cost of goods sold for items that remain past a season. Under this cost formula, the allocation of the cost of goods available for sale is based on the *weighted* average unit cost. The formula of the **weighted average unit cost** is presented in Illustration 6-8.

ILLUSTRATION 6-8
Calculation of weighted average unit cost

Cost of Goods Available for Sale	÷	Total Units Available for Sale	=	Weighted Average Unit Cost

Note that the weighted average unit cost is **not** calculated by taking a simple average of the costs of each purchase. Rather, it is calculated by weighting the quantities purchased at each unit cost. This is done by dividing the cost of goods available for sale by the units available for sale at the date of each purchase.

We will again use the information for Bennett Lighting's anti-bug lightbulb, in Illustration 6-3, to prepare a perpetual inventory schedule with the average cost formula so you can compare the similarities and differences between the average and FIFO methods. In Illustration 6-9, notice that the beginning inventory of $1,000 and the April 15 purchase of $2,200 are combined to show a total cost of goods available for sale of $3,200 and that the 100 units in beginning inventory and the 200 units purchased on April 15 are combined to show a total of 300 units. Using the formula in Illustration 6-8, the weighted average unit cost on April 15 is $10.67 per unit ($3,200 ÷ 300). Note that we cannot simply take the average of the two unit prices of $10 and $11. Since Bennett Lighting has more $11 bulbs (200) than $10 bulbs (100), the weighted average cost of $10.67 per bulb is higher than the simple average cost of $10.50.

ILLUSTRATION 6-9
Perpetual inventory schedule—average (calculation as at April 15)

	PURCHASES			COST OF GOODS SOLD			BALANCE		
Date	Units	Cost	Total	Units	Cost	Total	Units	Cost	Total
Jan. 1							100	$10.00	$1,000.00
Apr. 15	200	$11.00	$2,200.00				300	**10.67**	3,200.00

On May 1, the cost of goods sold is calculated using the $10.67 weighted average unit cost. The cost of the remaining 150 units of inventory on hand is also calculated using the same unit cost.

On August 24, when 300 units costing $12 each are purchased, it is necessary to calculate a *new* weighted average unit cost. After adding the total cost of the August 24 purchase to the May 1 ending balance, the total cost of the goods available for sale is $5,200 ($3,600 + $1,600). There are 450 total units available for sale, calculated by adding the 300 units purchased on August 24 to the 150 units in inventory. The new weighted average unit cost is $11.56 ($5,200 ÷ 450). Note that the goods purchased on August 24 were added to the goods that Bennett still had in its inventory after it made the sale on May 1.

These two transactions have been added to the perpetual inventory schedule as shown in Illustration 6-10.

ILLUSTRATION 6-10
Perpetual inventory schedule—average (calculation as at August 24)

	PURCHASES			COST OF GOODS SOLD			BALANCE		
Date	Units	Cost	Total	Units	Cost	Total	Units	Cost	Total
Jan. 1							100	$10.00	$1,000.00
Apr. 15	200	$11.00	$2,200.00				300	10.67	3,200.00
May 1				150	$10.67	$1,600.00	150	10.67	1,600.00
Aug. 24	300	12.00	3,600.00				450	**11.56**	5,200.00

Helpful hint The weighted average cost per unit is a moving average that almost always changes when the company purchases more units. It never changes when the company sells units.

Notice that the May 1 sale *did not* change the average unit cost. But the August 24 purchase *did* change the average unit cost. This pattern is repeated with the September 1 sale and the November 27 purchase. The cost of goods sold and ending inventory on September 1 are calculated using the $11.56 average unit cost calculated on August 24. On November 27, after purchasing 400 units at $13 each, a new weighted average unit cost of $12.84 is determined ($5,777.88 ÷ 450). The August 24 and November 27 transactions are shown in Illustration 6-11, to complete the perpetual inventory schedule started in Illustration 6-9.

ILLUSTRATION 6-11
Perpetual inventory schedule—average (calculation as at November 27)

	PURCHASES			COST OF GOODS SOLD			BALANCE		
Date	Units	Cost	Total	Units	Cost	Total	Units	Cost	Total
Jan. 1							100	$10.00	$1,000.00
Apr. 15	200	$11.00	$ 2,200,00				300	10.67	3,200.00
May 1				150	$10.67	$1,600.00	150	10.67	1,600.00
Aug. 24	300	12.00	3,600.00				450	11.56	5,200.00
Sept. 1				400	11.56	4,622.22	50	11.56	577.78
Nov. 27	400	13.00	5,200.00				450	**12.84**	5,777.78
	900		$11,000.00	550		$6,222.22			

As with FIFO, it is important to check that beginning inventory + purchases − cost of goods sold = ending inventory. Once again we can see that the perpetual inventory schedule is balanced because $1,000.00 + $11,000.00 − $6,222.22 = $5,777.78.

In practice, these average unit costs may be rounded to the nearest cent, or even to the nearest dollar. In the calculations in Illustrations 6-9 to 6-11, the exact unit cost amounts were used, along with a computerized schedule. But for presentation purposes, the unit costs have been rounded to the nearest two digits. However, it is important to remember that this is a method of allocating costs and not a method to track actual costs. Using four digits, or even cents, may suggest a false level of accuracy but it will reduce rounding errors in the perpetual inventory schedules.

In summary, this cost formula uses the average unit cost of the goods that are available for sale to determine the cost of goods sold and ending inventory. When a perpetual inventory system is used, an updated average unit cost is determined after each purchase. This amount is then used to record the cost of goods sold on subsequent sales until another purchase is made and a new average unit cost is calculated. Because the average unit cost changes with each purchase, this cost formula is sometimes called the *moving average* cost formula.

BEFORE YOU GO ON...

DO IT

Wynneck Sports Company uses a perpetual inventory system. All inventory items are sold for $10 per unit and all sales and purchases are on account. The company's accounting records show the following:

Date	Explanation	Units	Unit Cost	Total Cost
Mar. 1	Beginning inventory	4,000	$3	$12,000
10	Purchase	6,000	4	24,000
19	Sales	(8,000)		
22	Purchase	5,000	5	25,000
28	Sales	(5,500)		
				$61,000

(a) Assume Wynneck uses FIFO. (1) Prepare a perpetual inventory schedule and determine the cost of goods sold and ending inventory. (2) Prepare journal entries to record the March 10 purchase and the March 19 sale.

(b) Assume Wynneck uses the average cost formula. (1) Prepare a perpetual inventory schedule and determine the cost of goods sold and ending inventory. (2) Prepare journal entries to record the March 10 purchase and the March 19 sale.

SOLUTION

Action Plan

- For FIFO, allocate the first costs (those of the oldest goods) to the cost of goods sold at the date of each sale. The latest costs (those of the newest goods) will be allocated to the goods on hand (ending inventory).
- For average, determine the weighted average unit cost (cost of goods available for sale ÷ number of units available for sale) after each purchase. Multiply this cost by the number of units sold to determine the cost of goods sold and by the number of units on hand to determine the cost of the ending inventory.
- Prove that beginning inventory + purchases − cost of goods sold = ending inventory.
- Use the information in the perpetual inventory schedules (purchases and costs of goods sold columns) when preparing the journal entries.

(a) FIFO—Perpetual

1. Perpetual Inventory Schedule

	PURCHASES			COST OF GOODS SOLD			BALANCE		
Date	Units	Cost	Total	Units	Cost	Total	Units	Cost	Total
Mar. 1							4,000	$3	$12,000
10	6,000	$4	$24,000				4,000 6,000	3 4	} 36,000
19				4,000 4,000	$3 4	} $28,000	2,000	4	8,000
22	5,000	5	25,000				2,000 5,000	4 5	} 33,000
28				2,000 3,500	4 5	} 25,500	1,500	5	7,500
	11,000		$49,000	13,500		$53,500			

Check: $12,000 + $49,000 − $53,500 = $7,500

2. Journal Entries

Mar. 10	Merchandise Inventory	24,000	
	Accounts Payable		24,000
	To record goods purchased on account.		
19	Accounts Receivable	80,000	
	Sales		80,000
	To record credit sale ($10 × 8,000).		
	Cost of Goods Sold	28,000	
	Merchandise Inventory		28,000
	To record cost of goods.		

(b) Average—Perpetual

1. Perpetual Inventory Schedule

	PURCHASES			COST OF GOODS SOLD			BALANCE		
Date	Units	Cost	Total	Units	Cost	Total	Units	Cost	Total
Mar. 1							4,000	$3.00	$12,000
10	6,000	$4	$24,000				10,000	3.60	36,000
19				8,000	$3.60	$28,800	2,000	3.60	7,200
22	5,000	5	25,000				7,000	4.60	32,200
28				5,500	4.60	25,300	1,500	4.60	6,900
	11,000		$49,000	13,500		$54,100			

BEFORE YOU GO ON... continued on next page

BEFORE YOU GO ON...
continued from previous page

Check: $12,000 + $49,000 − $54,100 = $6,900

2. Journal Entries:

Mar. 10	Merchandise Inventory	24,000	
	Accounts Payable		24,000
	To record goods purchased on account.		
19	Accounts Receivable	80,000	
	Sales		80,000
	To record credit sale ($10 × 8,000).		
	Cost of Goods Sold	28,800	
	Merchandise Inventory		28,800
	To record cost of goods.		

Related exercise material: BE6–3, BE6–4, BE6–5, BE6–6, BE6–7, BE6–8, E6–3, E6–4, and E6–5.

THE NAVIGATOR

FINANCIAL STATEMENT EFFECTS

Inventory affects both the income statement and the balance sheet. The ending inventory is included as a current asset on the balance sheet and cost of goods sold is an expense on the income statement. Cost of goods sold will affect profit, which in turn will affect owner's equity on the balance sheet. Thus, the choice of cost determination method can have a significant impact on the financial statements.

Errors can occur when a physical inventory is being taken or when the cost of the inventory is being determined. The effects of these errors on financial statements can be significant. We will address these topics in the next two sections.

CHOICE OF COST DETERMINATION METHOD

STUDY OBJECTIVE 3
Explain the financial statement effects of inventory cost determination methods.

If companies have goods that are not ordinarily interchangeable, or goods that have been produced for specific projects, they must use the specific identification method to determine the cost of their inventory. Otherwise, they must use either FIFO or average.

We learned in our feature story that gravitypope uses the FIFO cost formula. How should a company such as gravitypope choose between FIFO and average? It should consider the following objectives in determining the correct method:

1. Choose the method that corresponds as closely as possible to the physical flow of goods.
2. Report an inventory cost on the balance sheet that is close to the inventory's recent costs.
3. Use the same method for all inventories having a similar nature and use in the company. Note that a merchandiser may use different inventory costing methods for different classes of inventory.

After a company chooses a method of determining the cost of its inventory, this method should be used consistently from one period to the next. Consistency is what makes it possible to compare financial statements from one period to the next. This is in keeping with the consistency principle under GAAP, which requires a business to use the same accounting policies from period to period. Using FIFO in one year and average in the next year would make it difficult to compare the profits for the two years.

This is not to say that a company can never change from one method to another. However, a change in the method of cost determination can only occur if the physical flow of inventory changes and a different method would result in more relevant information in the financial statements. Such changes and their effect on profit should be disclosed in the notes to the financial statements. Where possible, companies must also go back and restate the prior years' financial statements using the new method. This respects the **full disclosure** requirement, in which all relevant information is to be disclosed. Full disclosure is discussed more in Chapter 11.

Income Statement Effects

To understand the impact of the FIFO and average cost formulas on the income statement, let's look at Bennett Lighting's sales, cost of goods sold, and operating expenses on the anti-bug lightbulb. The condensed income statements in Illustration 6-12 assume that Bennett Lighting sold 550 anti-bug lightbulbs for $11,500 and that operating expenses were $2,000. The cost of goods sold was previously calculated in Illustrations 6-7 and 6-11.

ILLUSTRATION 6-12
Comparative effects of inventory cost formulas

BENNETT LIGHTING
Condensed Income Statements

	FIFO	Average
Sales	$11,500	$11,500
Cost of goods sold	**6,200**	**6,222**
Gross profit	5,300	5,278
Operating expenses	2,000	2,000
Profit	**$ 3,300**	**$ 3,278**

The sales and the operating expenses are the same under both FIFO and average. But the cost of goods sold amounts are different. This difference is the result of how the unit costs are allocated under each cost formula. Each dollar of difference in cost of goods sold results in a corresponding dollar difference in gross profit and profit. For Bennett Lighting, there is a $22 difference in cost of goods sold and in profit between FIFO and average.

In periods of changing prices, the choice of inventory cost formula can have a significant impact on profit. In a period of rising prices, as is the case here, FIFO produces a higher profit. This happens because the expenses matched against revenues are the lower unit costs of the first units purchased. As shown in Illustration 6-12, FIFO reports the higher profit ($3,300) and average the lower profit ($3,278).

If prices are decreasing, the results from the use of FIFO and average are reversed. FIFO will report the lower profit and average the higher profit. If prices are stable, both cost formulas will report the same results.

Compared with FIFO, average will result in more recent costs being reflected in cost of goods sold. This will better match current costs with current revenues and provide a more accurate income statement valuation. But better matching is not critical in the choice of inventory cost determination methods. It is more important to use the cost formula that best approximates the physical flow of goods or represents recent costs on the balance sheet.

Balance Sheet Effects

The choice of inventory cost formula will also have an impact on the balance sheet; both merchandise inventory and owner's equity will be affected. In our Bennett Lighting example, profit is $22 higher under FIFO. Therefore, owner's equity is also $22 higher under FIFO. Bennett Lighting's inventory is also $22 higher under FIFO. As shown in Illustrations 6-7 and 6-11, it was $5,800 under FIFO and $5,778 under average.

In terms of the balance sheet, one advantage of FIFO is that the costs allocated to ending inventory will approximate the inventory item's current (replacement) cost. For example, for Bennett Lighting, 400 of the 450 units in the ending inventory are costed at the November 27 unit cost of $13. Since management needs to replace inventory after it is sold, a valuation that is closer to the replacement cost is helpful for decision-making.

By extension, a limitation of the average method is that in a period of inflation the costs allocated to inventory may be understated in terms of the current cost of the inventory. That is, the average cost formula results in older costs being included in inventory. The cost of the ending inventory includes the $10 unit cost of the beginning inventory. This understatement becomes even larger if the inventory includes goods that were purchased in one or more prior accounting periods.

Summary of Effects

When prices are constant, the cost of goods sold and ending inventory will be the same for all three cost determination methods. In specific identification, cost of goods sold and ending inventory depend on which specific units are sold and which are on hand. Thus we cannot make any general comments about how it will compare with FIFO and average.

We have seen that both inventory on the balance sheet and profit on the income statement are higher when FIFO is used in a period of rising prices. The reverse will happen in a period of falling prices. The key differences between the two cost formulas are summarized in Illustration 6-13.

ILLUSTRATION 6-13
A comparison of the FIFO and average methods when prices are rising or falling

	Rising Prices		Falling Prices	
Income statement	FIFO	Average	FIFO	Average
Cost of goods sold	Lower	Higher	Higher	Lower
Gross profit and profit	Higher	Lower	Lower	Higher
Balance sheet				
Cash flow	Same	Same	Same	Same
Ending inventory	Higher	Lower	Lower	Higher
Owner's equity	Higher	Lower	Lower	Higher

Notice in Illustration 6-13 that cash flow is the same with both cost formulas. In fact, all three methods of cost determination—specific identification, FIFO, and average—produce exactly the same cash flow. Sales and purchases are not affected by the methods of cost determination. The only thing that is affected is the allocation between ending inventory and cost of goods sold, which does not involve cash.

It is also worth remembering that all three cost determination methods will give exactly the same results over the life cycle of the business or its product. That is, the allocation between cost of goods sold and ending inventory may vary within a period, but will produce the same cumulative results over time.

BEFORE YOU GO ON...

DO IT

Hakim Paints reported sales of $10,000 and operating expenses of $2,000. If Hakim uses FIFO, cost of goods sold is $4,700. If the average method is used, cost of goods sold is $4,550.

(a) Prepare condensed income statements for each cost formula.
(b) Which method will result in higher owner's equity?
(c) Which method should Hakim Paints use?
(d) Are prices rising or falling? Explain.

SOLUTION

(a)

HAKIM PAINTS
Condensed Income Statements

	FIFO	Average
Sales	$10,000	$10,000
Cost of goods sold	4,700	4,550
Gross profit	5,300	5,450
Operating expenses	2,000	2,000
Profit	$ 3,300	$ 3,450

(b) Because profit is $150 ($3,450 – $3,300) higher using average, then owner's equity will also be $150 higher using average.
(c) The cost formula that should be used would be the one that best matches the physical flow of goods.
(d) Since FIFO has the higher costs of goods sold, then prices must be falling. FIFO has the oldest costs in its cost of goods sold; average will have a combination of older and more recent costs in its cost of goods sold.

Related exercise material: BE6–9, BE6–10, E6–6, and E6–7.

Action Plan

- In preparing comparative income statements, note that sales and operating expenses are the same for both cost formulas. Cost of goods sold, gross profit, and profit are different.
- Recall that profit is added to owner's equity.
- Review the objectives that should be considered in determining the correct method.
- Recall that FIFO uses the oldest costs in determining costs of goods sold while assigning the newest goods to Merchandise Inventory.

INVENTORY ERRORS

STUDY OBJECTIVE 4
Determine the financial statement effects of inventory errors.

Some inventory errors are caused by mistakes in counting or pricing the inventory. Other inventory errors result from mistakes in recognizing the timing of the transfer of legal title for goods in transit. These mistakes can result in errors in determining:

- beginning inventory
- cost of goods purchased
- ending inventory.

Any errors in determining these items can also cause an error in cost of goods sold. Recall that these items affect the Merchandise Inventory and Cost of Goods Sold accounts as follows:

Merchandise Inventory			Cost of Goods Sold	
Beginning inventory plus Cost of goods purchased	Cost of goods sold	→	Cost of goods sold	
Ending inventory				

Errors in cost of goods sold will affect the income statement. If there is an error in ending inventory it will affect the balance sheet, both in ending inventory and in owner's capital. In the following sections, we will illustrate these effects.

Income Statement Effects

Cost of goods sold will be incorrect if there is an error in any one of beginning inventory, cost of goods purchased, or ending inventory, while the other two are correct. This can more easily be seen if we arrange these components, as shown in the Merchandise Inventory account above, to: Beginning Inventory + Cost of Goods Purchased − Ending Inventory = Cost of Goods Sold.

A summary of the impact of errors in these components on cost of goods sold is shown in Illustration 6-14 by using the cost of goods sold formula.

ILLUSTRATION 6-14
Effects of inventory errors on cost of goods sold

Impact on Cost of Goods Sold	Error in Beginning Inventory		Error in Cost of Goods Purchased		Error in Ending Inventory	
Beginning Inventory	Overstated	Understated				
+ Cost of Goods Purchased			Overstated	Understated		
− Ending Inventory					Overstated	Understated
= Cost of Goods Sold	Overstated	Understated	Overstated	Understated	Understated	Overstated

Notice that errors in beginning inventory and cost of goods purchased have the same impact on cost of goods sold. That is, if beginning inventory or cost of goods purchased is overstated, in both cases, cost of goods sold will be overstated (assuming that there are no other offsetting errors). And if beginning inventory or cost of goods purchased is understated, in both cases, cost of goods sold is understated. This is because beginning inventory and cost of goods purchased are both *added* when determining cost of goods sold.

On the other hand, an overstatement of ending inventory has the opposite impact on cost of goods sold. If ending inventory is overstated, this results in an *understatement* of cost of goods sold; if ending inventory is understated, this results in an overstatement of costs of goods sold. This is because ending inventory is subtracted from cost of goods available for sale when determining cost of goods sold.

Once the impact of an error on cost of goods sold is determined, then we can determine the effect of this error on the income statement. These results are summarized in Illustration 6-15. U stands for understatement, O for overstatement, and NE for no effect.

ILLUSTRATION 6-15
Effects of inventory errors on income statement

Nature of Error	Net Sales	–	Cost of Goods Sold	=	Gross Profit	–	Operating Expenses	=	Profit
Overstate beginning inventory or cost of goods purchased	NE		O		U		NE		U
Understate beginning inventory or cost of goods purchased	NE		U		O		NE		O
Overstate ending inventory	NE		U		O		NE		O
Understate ending inventory	NE		O		U		NE		U

Notice that an error in cost of goods sold has the opposite impact on gross profit and profit. If cost of goods sold (an expense) is overstated, then gross profit and profit are understated. If cost of goods sold is understated, the gross profit and profit are overstated. This is because cost of goods sold is deducted from net sales when calculating gross profit.

Helpful hint Note that an inventory error will always have the same effect on both gross profit and profit.

Since the ending inventory of one period becomes the beginning inventory of the next period, **an error in ending inventory of the current period will have a reverse effect on the profit of the next period.** To illustrate, assume that on December 31, 2013, inventory is overstated by $3,000. The following T accounts show the impact of this error on the Merchandise Inventory account, and thus on cost of goods sold, over two years.

Merchandise Inventory (Incorrect Dec. 31, 2013, Inventory Amount)

Jan. 1/13		20,000		
Purchases		40,000	Cost of goods sold	**42,000**
Dec. 31/13	Bal.	**18,000**		
Purchases		40,000	Cost of goods sold	**48,000**
Dec. 31/14	Bal.	10,000		

Merchandise Inventory (Correct Dec. 31, 2013, Inventory Amount)

Jan. 1/13		20,000		
Purchases		40,000	Cost of goods sold	**45,000**
Dec. 31/13	Bal.	**15,000**		
Purchases		40,000	Cost of goods sold	**45,000**
Dec. 31/14	Bal.	10,000		

Because ending inventory in 2013 is overstated by $3,000 ($18,000 instead of $15,000), the 2013 costs of goods sold is understated by $3,000 ($42,000 instead of $45,000). This also means that beginning inventory for 2014 is overstated by $3,000 ($18,000 instead of $15,000), and cost of goods sold for 2014 is overstated by $3,000 ($48,000 instead of $45,000).

Assuming ending inventory in 2014 is correct, there is no further impact. But over the two-year period it will impact profit, as shown in Illustration 6-16.

ILLUSTRATION 6-16
Effects of inventory errors on income statements of two successive years

	2013		2014	
	Incorrect	Correct	Incorrect	Correct
Sales	$80,000	$80,000	$80,000	$80,000
Cost of goods sold	42,000	45,000	48,000	45,000
Gross profit	38,000	35,000	32,000	35,000
Operating expenses	10,000	10,000	10,000	10,000
Profit	$28,000	$25,000	$22,000	$25,000
	($3,000) Profit overstated		**$3,000** Profit understated	

The combined profit for two years is correct because the errors cancel each other out.

Note that in 2013, the $3,000 understatement of costs of goods sold results in a $3,000 overstatement of profit ($28,000 instead of $25,000). In 2014, the opposite occurs and profit is understated by $3,000 ($22,000 instead of $25,000).

Over the two years, total profit is correct. The errors offset one another. Notice that total profit using incorrect data is $50,000 ($28,000 + $22,000). This is the same as the total profit of $50,000 ($25,000 + $25,000) using correct data. Nevertheless, the distortion of the year-by-year results can have a serious impact on financial analysis and management decisions.

Note that an error in the beginning inventory does not result in a corresponding error in the ending inventory, since each fiscal year end's inventory is based on a physical count. The accuracy of the ending inventory depends entirely on correctly taking and costing the inventory at the balance sheet date.

Balance Sheet Effects

The effects of inventory errors on the balance sheet can be determined by using the basic accounting equation: assets = liabilities + owner's equity. These results are summarized in Illustration 6-17. U is for understatement, O is for overstatement, and NE is for no effect.

ILLUSTRATION 6-17
Effects of inventory errors on balance sheet

Nature of Error	Assets	=	Liabilities	+	Owner's Equity
Understate ending inventory	U		NE		U
Overstate ending inventory	O		NE		O

When ending inventory is understated, total assets are understated. Understating ending inventory (assuming there are no other offsetting errors) will also overstate cost of goods sold, which will understate profit. If profit is understated, then owner's equity will also be understated, because profit is part of owner's equity.

An error in ending inventory in one period will result in an error in beginning inventory in the next period. An example of this type of error was shown in Illustration 6-16. As previously noted, total profit for the two periods is correct. Thus, total assets and owner's equity reported on the balance sheet at the end of 2014 will also be correct. In other words, errors in beginning inventory have no impact on the balance sheet if ending inventory is correctly calculated at the end of that period.

Errors in the cost of goods purchased may also have an effect on the balance sheet. For example, if a company records a purchase of inventory on account in 2014 that should have been recorded in 2015, accounts payable will be overstated at December 31, 2014. And in this situation, owner's equity at December 31, 2014, will be understated because profit for 2014 is understated. Thus, the balance sheet will still balance even though it is incorrect.

You should also note that inventory errors can occur in either a perpetual or a periodic inventory system and that the errors have the same impact on the income statement and balance sheet regardless of which system is used. But one of the major benefits of a perpetual inventory system is that many inventory mistakes are much more likely to be caught, and corrected, when the accounting records are compared with the results of the inventory count.

BEFORE YOU GO ON...

DO IT

On December 31, Silas Company counted and recorded $600,000 of inventory. This count did not include $90,000 of goods in transit, shipped to Silas on December 29, FOB shipping point. Silas recorded the purchase on January 3 when the goods were received. (a) Determine the correct December 31 inventory balance. (b) Identify any accounts that are in error, and state the amount and direction (that is, overstatement or understatement) of the error.

SOLUTION

(a) The correct inventory count should have included the goods in transit. The correct December 31 inventory balance was $690,000 ($600,000 + $90,000).

(b) *Income statement accounts:* Because the purchase had not been recorded, the cost of goods purchased is understated (U) by $90,000. And because the inventory had not been included in the

BEFORE YOU GO ON...
continued on next page

inventory count, the ending inventory is also understated. Thus, as shown below, the two errors cancel each other out, and the cost of goods sold and profit will be correct.

Beginning inventory	No effect
Plus: Cost of goods purchased	U $90,000
Cost of goods available for sale	U $90,000
Less: Ending inventory	U $90,000
Cost of goods sold	No effect because the errors cancel each other out

Balance sheet accounts: Merchandise Inventory and Accounts Payable are both understated

Assets	=	Liabilities	+	Owner's equity
U $90,000	=	U $90,000	+	no effect

Related exercise material: BE6–11, BE6–12, E6–8, and E6–9.

BEFORE YOU GO ON...
continued from previous page

Action Plan

- Use the cost of goods sold and income statement relationships to determine the impact of an error on the income statement.
- Use the accounting equation to determine the impact of an error on the balance sheet.

THE NAVIGATOR

PRESENTATION AND ANALYSIS OF INVENTORY

Presenting inventory on the financial statements is important because inventory is usually the largest current asset (Merchandise Inventory) on the balance sheet and the largest expense (Cost of Goods Sold) on the income statement. In addition, these reported numbers are critical for analyzing how well a company manages its inventory. In the next sections, we will discuss the presentation and analysis of inventory.

VALUING INVENTORY AT THE LOWER OF COST AND NET REALIZABLE VALUE

STUDY OBJECTIVE 5
Value inventory at the lower of cost and net realizable value.

Before reporting inventory on the financial statements, we must first ensure that it is properly valued. The value of inventory items sometimes falls due to changes in technology or style. For example, suppose you manage a retail store that sells computers, and at the end of the year the computers' value has dropped almost 25%. Do you think inventory should be stated at cost, in accordance with the cost principle, or at its lower value?

As you probably reasoned, this situation requires an exception to following the cost basis of accounting. When the value of inventory is lower than its cost, the inventory is written down to its net realizable value at the end of the period. This is called the **lower of cost and net realizable value (LCNRV)** rule, which follows GAAP's **principle of conservatism**. This principle applies when accountants need to choose between two acceptable methods for reporting an item. The principle requires them to use the method that results in the lower, or more conservative, amount of net income or asset valuation. **Net realizable value (NRV)** is the selling price less any costs required to make the goods ready for sale.

The lower of cost or NRV rule is applied to the items in inventory at the end of the accounting period. To apply this rule, four steps are followed:

1. Determine the cost of the items in ending inventory using the appropriate cost determination method: specific identification, FIFO, or average.
2. Determine the net realizable value of the items in ending inventory.
3. Compare the values determined in steps 1 and 2.
4. Use the lower value to report inventory on the balance sheet.

Helpful hint The term "lower of cost and net realizable value (LCNRV)" uses the word "lower" rather than "lowest" because we are only comparing two numbers: the inventory's cost and the inventory's net realizable value. The LCNRV rule considers which of these two numbers is lower than the other. The word "lowest" would apply only if we were comparing three or more numbers.

To illustrate, assume that on March 31, 2014, Tony's Electronics Shop has the following lines of merchandise with costs and net realizable values as indicated. The lower of cost and NRV produces the following results:

	Cost	NRV	Lower of Cost and NRV
Television sets			
LCD	$ 60,000	$ 55,000	$ 55,000
Plasma	45,000	52,000	45,000
	105,000	107,000	100,000
Car video and audio equipment			
LCD media package	48,000	45,000	45,000
Global positioning system	15,000	14,000	14,000
	63,000	59,000	59,000
Total inventory	$168,000	$166,000	$159,000

This means Tony's Electronics Shop will report $159,000 for merchandise inventory on its balance sheet. The lower of cost and net realizable value rule is applied to *individual* inventory items, not *total* inventory. In some cases, it can be applied to *groups of similar items*. For instance, in the above example, all of the company's different types of LCD televisions were grouped together and we compared the cost of the LCD televisions with their total net realizable value.

If Tony's Electronics Shop uses a perpetual inventory system, the entry to adjust inventory from cost to net realizable value would be the following:

Cash flows: no effect

Mar. 31	Cost of Goods Sold	9,000	
	Merchandise Inventory		9,000
	To record decline in inventory value from original cost of $168,000 to net realizable value of $159,000.		

The Cost of Goods Sold account is debited directly for the loss because a decline in the value of inventory is considered to be part of the overall cost of buying and selling inventory. The amount of the loss must be separately reported and most companies do this in the notes to the financial statements. Thus, some companies may choose to debit a separate expense account to make it easier to keep track of the amount. Alternative methods of recording a decline in inventory value are covered in courses that are offered at the post-secondary level.

When there is clear evidence of an increase in net realizable value, because of changed economic circumstances, the amount of the writedown is reversed. The evidence required for this reversal would generally be an increase in selling prices. If the item of inventory that had been previously written down has been sold, there is no need to record a reversal. If the item of inventory that was previously written down to net realizable value is still on hand, and the selling price has increased, then the reversal is recorded. The reversing entry will consist of a debit to merchandise inventory and a credit to cost of goods sold.

It is not usual for reversals to happen. Most companies will sell their inventory at a reduced price, instead of waiting for the price to recover. Thus, it is not that often that a company will still have the inventory on hand a year later, and the selling price will have increased. While reversals are relatively rare, the amount of any such reversal must be reported in the notes to the financial statements.

If there is a recovery in the value of the inventory, the write-up can never be larger than the original writedown. (That is, it can never result in an overall increase in value.) The lower of cost or net realizable value rule will still be applied to the inventory. This ensures that the inventory is *never reported at an amount greater than its original cost.*

ACCOUNTING IN ACTION
BUSINESS INSIGHT

Blockbuster Canada was placed in receivership in the spring of 2011. Competition from on-line video services had increased and Blockbuster Canada could not find a buyer. That meant that all Canadian Blockbuster stores were to be liquidated by December 31, 2011. What happens when a company is liquidated? Well, it means that a company's assets, including inventory, are sold at discounted prices. As a customer, you benefit by paying a lower price to buy a movie or game than you would normally have paid. Any money that is collected from the sale of liquidated assets is held by the receiver (the firm Grant Thornton, in the case of Blockbuster). This money is then used to pay off the company's debt. Once a company is in receivership, it is not highly likely that money generated from selling the company's assets can pay off all of its debt.

Source: Jameson Berkow, "Blockbuster's Canadian Unit Seeks Bankruptcy Protection," *Financial Post*, May 5, 2011; The Canadian Press, "Blockbuster Canada to Close Remaining Stores," CBC News on-line, August 31, 2011; Marina Strauss and Iain Marlow, "Blockbuster to Pull Plug in Canada," *The Globe and Mail*, September 1, 2011.

When a company such as Blockbuster is placed in receivership, what would be the impact on how to account for its inventory?

BEFORE YOU GO ON...

DO IT

Tanguay's Jersey Store uses a perpetual inventory system and has the following items in its inventory at December 31, 2014:

		Per Unit	
Product	Quantity	Cost	Net Realizable Value
Jerseys	95	$50	$45
Socks	155	5	6

(a) What amount for inventory should Tanguay's Jersey Store report on its balance sheet?
(b) Record any necessary adjustments.

Action Plan
- Calculate the cost of the inventory.
- Calculate the net realizable value of the inventory.
- For each inventory item, determine which number is lower—cost or net realizable value.
- Record a journal entry to adjust the inventory account to net realizable value if required.

SOLUTION

(a)

	Cost		Net Realizable Value		Lower of Cost and Net Realizable Value
Jerseys	(95 × $50)	$4,750	(95 × $45)	$4,275	$4,275
Socks	(155 × $5)	775	(155 × $6)	930	775
Total inventory		$5,525		$5,205	$5,050

(b)

Date	Account	Debit	Credit
Dec. 31	Cost of Goods Sold ($5,525 − $5,050)	475	
	Merchandise Inventory		475
	To record decline in inventory value from its cost of $5,525 to lower of cost and net realizable value of $5,050.		

Related exercise material: BE6–13, BE6–14, and E6–10.

THE NAVIGATOR

REPORTING AND ANALYZING INVENTORY

Presenting Inventory in the Financial Statements

STUDY OBJECTIVE 6
Demonstrate the presentation and analysis of inventory.

How a company classifies its inventory depends on whether the company is a merchandiser or a manufacturer. A merchandiser *buys* its inventory. A manufacturer *produces* its inventory. In a merchandising company, inventory consists of many different items. Textbooks, paper, and pens, for example, are just a few of the inventory items on hand in a bookstore. These items have two common characteristics: (1) they are owned by the company, and (2) they are in a form ready for sale to customers. Only one inventory classification, merchandise inventory, is needed to describe the many different items that make up the total inventory.

In a manufacturing company, some goods may not yet be ready for sale. As a result, inventory is usually classified into three categories: raw materials, work in process, and finished goods. For example, an automobile manufacturer classifies the steel, fibreglass, upholstery material, and other components that are on hand waiting to be used in production as raw materials. Partially completed automobiles on an assembly line are classified as work in process. Automobiles completed and ready for sale are identified as finished goods.

As discussed in the previous section, inventory is reported on the balance sheet at the lower of cost and net realizable value. Inventory is typically recorded as a current asset because management expects to sell it within the next year. But if part of the inventory will not be sold for more than a year, this inventory should be reported as a non-current asset. For example, if inventory is being stockpiled because of concerns about future prices, then it may be appropriate to classify this inventory as a non-current asset.

A company should disclose the following information in its financial statements or the notes to the statements:

1. the total amount of inventory;
2. the cost determination method (specific identification, FIFO, or average);
3. the cost of goods sold;
4. the amount of any writedown to net realizable value; and
5. the amount of any reversals of previous writedowns, including the reason why the writedown was reversed.

Publicly traded and private companies value and report inventory in a similar manner. There are no significant differences in this regard at the introductory accounting level between International Financial Reporting Standards and Accounting Standards for Private Enterprises. The few differences relate to specialized types of inventory and will not be covered in this text.

The inventory and cost of goods sold information reported in the financial statements is also used to analyze how effectively the company is managing its inventory.

Inventory Turnover

Helpful hint Inventory levels can be thought of as a "Goldilocks" issue, in the sense that a merchandiser should maintain a level of inventory that is "just right" as opposed to too high or too low.

A delicate balance must be kept between having too little inventory and too much inventory. On one hand, management wants to have a variety and quantity of merchandise available so that customers will find a wide selection of items in stock. But having too much inventory on hand can cost the company money in storage costs, interest costs (on money tied up in inventory), and costs due to high-tech goods becoming obsolete, or changing fashions. On the other hand, low inventory levels can result in stockouts (item unavailability), lost sales, and unhappy customers.

How quickly a company sells its inventory, or turns it over, is one way to determine whether the company has too much or too little inventory. We can also use this information to evaluate a company's liquidity, or its ability to pay obligations that are expected to come due in the next year. In Chapter 4, we introduced the current and acid-test ratios, which are measures of liquidity. Inventory is a significant component of the current ratio and a high level of inventory will result in a high current ratio. But if the inventory is not turning over very quickly, this may be a problem. In this section, we add another liquidity ratio that is commonly used to evaluate inventory levels: the inventory turnover ratio. We also present a related measure: the average days to sell the inventory.

Inventory Turnover Ratio.

Helpful hint Note that the two components of the inventory turnover formula (cost of goods sold and average inventory) are both based on cost (not sale) price. This ensures that the result is not distorted by the use of different prices (cost and sale).

The **inventory turnover** ratio measures the number of times, on average, inventory is sold (turned over) during the period. It is calculated by dividing the cost of goods sold by average inventory.

Whenever a ratio compares a balance sheet figure (such as inventory) with an income statement figure (such as cost of goods sold), the balance sheet figure must be averaged. Average balance sheet figures are determined by adding beginning and ending balances together and dividing by two. Averages are used to ensure that the balance sheet figures (which represent end-of-period amounts) cover the same period of time as the income statement figures (which represent amounts for the entire period). Illustration 6-18 shows the formula for calculating the inventory turnover ratio for Reitmans (Canada) Limited for fiscal 2012 (dollars in thousands).

ILLUSTRATION 6-18
Inventory turnover

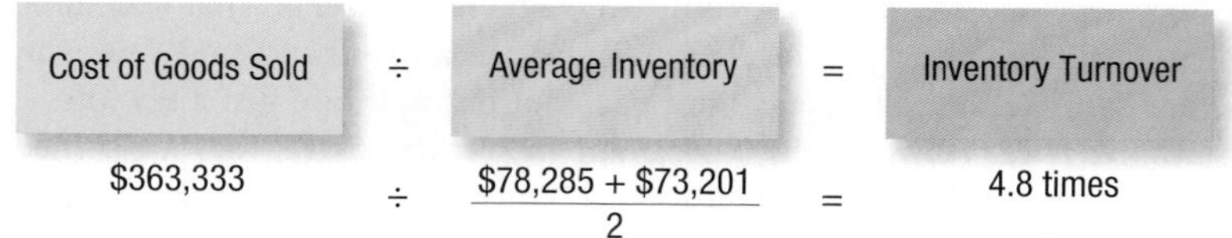

Cost of Goods Sold ÷ Average Inventory = Inventory Turnover
$363,333 ÷ ($78,285 + $73,201) / 2 = 4.8 times

Generally, the more times that inventory turns over each year, the more efficiently sales are being made.

Days Sales in Inventory.

The inventory turnover ratio is complemented by the **days sales in inventory** ratio. It converts the inventory turnover ratio into a measure of the average age of the inventory on hand. This ratio is calculated by dividing 365 days by the inventory turnover ratio, as in Illustration 6-19.

ILLUSTRATION 6-19
Days sales in inventory

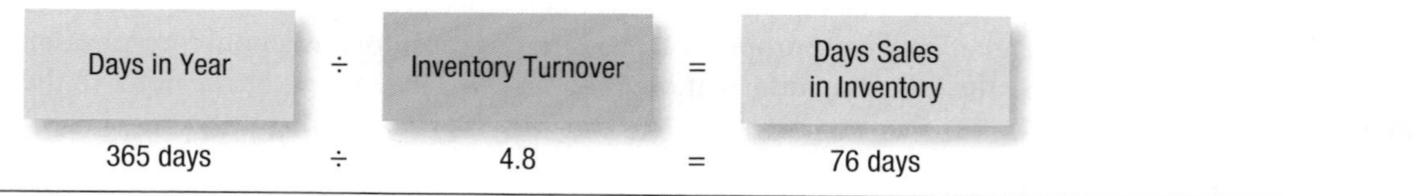

Days in Year ÷ Inventory Turnover = Days Sales in Inventory
365 days ÷ 4.8 = 76 days

Helpful hint Note that inventory turnover and days sales in inventory have an inverse relationship: if one ratio increases, the other one decreases.

This means that Reitmans' inventory, on average, is in stock for 76 days. This ratio must be interpreted carefully: it should be compared with the company's ratio in previous years, and with the industry average. However, you must recognize that this industry average will be different for each type of inventory item (for example, sneakers vs. bicycles). What we see here is a total average only.

BEFORE YOU GO ON...

DO IT

The following information is available for Sanchez Company for three recent years:

	2014	2013	2012
Inventory	$ 40,000	$ 42,000	$ 46,000
Cost of goods sold	123,000	125,000	130,000

Calculate the inventory turnover ratio and days sales in inventory for Sanchez Company for 2014 and 2013 and comment on any trends.

SOLUTION

	2014	2013
Inventory turnover	$3.00 \text{ times} = \dfrac{\$123,000}{[(\$40,000 + 42,000) \div 2]}$	$2.84 \text{ times} = \dfrac{\$125,000}{[(\$42,000 + 46,000) \div 2]}$
Days sales in inventory	122 days = 365 ÷ 3.00	129 days = 365 ÷ 2.84

The inventory turnover ratio has increased in 2014 and decreased the number of days sales in inventory. In general, the higher the inventory turnover and the lower the number of days sales in inventory, the better. Sanchez has improved its inventory management in 2014 compared with 2013.

Related exercise material: BE6–15, BE6–16, E6–11, and E6–12.

Action Plan

- Calculate average inventory using the inventory balance at the beginning and end of the year.
- Divide cost of goods sold by the average inventory for that year to calculate inventory turnover.
- Divide 365 by the inventory turnover to calculate days sales in inventory.
- Recall if it is better for inventory turnover to increase or decrease.

INVENTORY COST FORMULAS IN PERIODIC SYSTEMS

APPENDIX 6A

STUDY OBJECTIVE 7

Calculate ending inventory and cost of goods sold in a periodic inventory system using FIFO and average inventory cost formulas.

Both of the inventory cost formulas described in the chapter for a perpetual inventory system can be used in a periodic inventory system. To show how to use FIFO and average in a periodic system, we will use the data below for Bennett Lighting.

BENNETT LIGHTING
Anti-Bug Lightbulb

Date	Explanation	Units	Unit Cost	Total Cost
Jan. 1	Beginning inventory	100	$10	$ 1,000
Apr. 15	Purchase	200	11	2,200
Aug. 24	Purchase	300	12	3,600
Nov. 27	Purchase	400	13	5,200
Total		1,000		$12,000

These data are the same as those shown earlier in the chapter, except that the sales information has been omitted. In the periodic inventory system, we don't keep track of the number or cost of units sold during the year. Instead we wait until the end of the period to allocate the cost of goods available for sale to ending inventory and cost of goods sold.

Bennett Lighting had a total of 1,000 units available for sale during the year. The total cost of these units was $12,000. A physical inventory count at the end of the year determined that 450 units remained on hand. Using these data, Illustration 6A-1 shows the formula for calculating cost of goods sold that we first learned in Chapter 5.

ILLUSTRATION 6A-1
Formula for cost of goods sold

Helpful hint Under both the perpetual and periodic systems, cost of goods available for sale = cost of goods sold + ending inventory.

If we apply this formula to the unit numbers, we can determine that 550 units must have been sold during the year. The total cost (or "pool of costs") of the 1,000 units available for sale was $12,000. We will demonstrate the allocation of this pool of costs using FIFO and average in the next sections. In a periodic system, *the cost formulas are applied to the ending inventory*, which is then deducted from the cost of goods available for sale to calculate the cost of goods sold.

PERIODIC SYSTEM—FIRST-IN, FIRST-OUT (FIFO)

Similar to perpetual FIFO, the cost of the oldest goods on hand is allocated to the cost of goods sold. This means that the cost of the most recent purchases is assumed to remain in ending inventory. The allocation of the cost of goods available for sale at Bennett Lighting under FIFO is shown in Illustration 6A-2.

ILLUSTRATION 6A-2
Periodic system—FIFO

COST OF GOODS AVAILABLE FOR SALE

Date	Explanation	Units	Unit Cost	Total Cost
Jan. 1	Beginning inventory	100	$10	$ 1,000
Apr. 15	Purchase	200	11	2,200
Aug. 24	Purchase	300	12	3,600
Nov. 27	Purchase	400	13	5,200
	Total	1,000		**$12,000**

Step 1: Ending Inventory

Date	Unit	Unit Cost	Total Cost
Nov. 27	400	$13	$5,200
Aug. 24	50	12	600
Total	450		**$5,800**

Step 2: Cost of Goods Sold

Cost of goods available for sale	$12,000
Less: Ending inventory	5,800
Cost of goods sold	**$ 6,200**

The cost of the ending inventory is determined by taking the unit cost of the most recent purchase and working backward until all units of inventory have been costed. In this example, the 450 units of ending inventory must be costed using the November 27 and August 24 purchase costs. The last purchase was 400 units at $13 on November 27. The remaining 50 units (450 − 400) are costed at the price of the second most recent purchase, $12 on August 24.

Once the cost of the ending inventory is determined, the cost of goods sold is calculated by subtracting the cost of the ending inventory (the cost of the goods not sold) from the cost of the goods available for sale (the pool of costs).

The cost of goods sold can also be separately calculated or proven as shown below. To determine the cost of goods sold using FIFO, simply start at the first item of beginning inventory and count forward until the total number of units sold (550) is reached. Note that, of the 300 units purchased on August 24, only 250 units are assumed to be sold. This agrees with our calculation of ending inventory, where 50 of these units were assumed to be unsold and included in our ending inventory.

Date	Unit	Unit Cost	Cost of Goods Sold
Jan. 1	100	$10	$1,000
Apr. 15	200	11	2,200
Aug. 24	250	12	3,000
Total	550		$6,200

It is also helpful to check that the total of the cost of goods sold and ending inventory is equal to the cost of goods available for sale ($6,200 + $5,800 = $12,000).

PERIODIC SYSTEM—AVERAGE

The weighted average unit cost is calculated in the same manner as we calculated it in a perpetual inventory system: by dividing the cost of the goods available for sale by the units available for sale. The key difference between this calculation in a periodic system and in a perpetual system is that this calculation is done after every purchase in a perpetual system (recall that it is a *moving* average). In a periodic system, it is done only at the end of the period, as shown in Illustration 6A-3.

ILLUSTRATION 6A-3
Calculation of weighted average unit cost

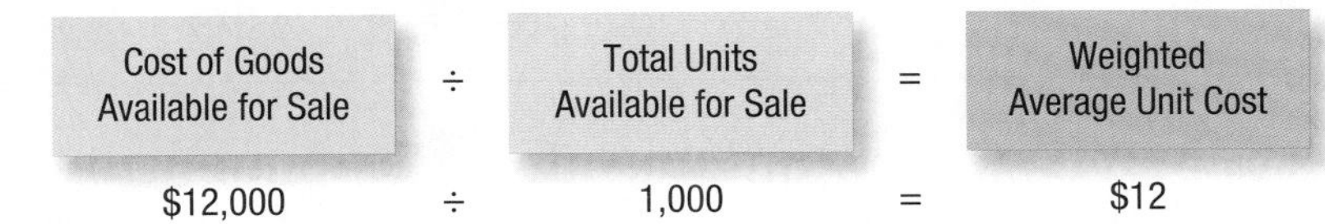

The weighted average unit cost, $12 in this case, is then applied to the units on hand to determine the cost of the ending inventory. The allocation of the cost of goods available for sale at Bennett Lighting using the average cost formula is shown in Illustration 6A-4.

ILLUSTRATION 6A-4
Periodic system—average

COST OF GOODS AVAILABLE FOR SALE

Date	Explanation	Units	Unit Cost	Total Cost
Jan. 1	Beginning inventory	100	$10	$ 1,000
Apr. 15	Purchase	200	11	2,200
Aug. 24	Purchase	300	12	3,600
Nov. 27	Purchase	400	13	5,200
	Total	1,000		**$12,000**

Step 1: Ending Inventory

Calculate unit cost: $12,000 ÷ 1,000 = $12

Units	×	Unit cost	=	Total Cost
450		$12		**$5,400**

Step 2: Cost of Goods Sold

Cost of goods available for sale	$12,000
Less: Ending inventory	5,400
Cost of goods sold	**$ 6,600**

We can prove our calculation of the cost of goods sold under the average cost formula by multiplying the units sold by the weighted average unit cost (550 × $12 = $6,600). And, again, we can prove our calculations by ensuring that the total of the ending inventory and the cost of goods sold equals the cost of goods available for sale ($5,400 + $6,600 = $12,000).

Here is a comparison of FIFO and average in perpetual and periodic inventory systems. *Whether a perpetual or periodic inventory system is used, FIFO will always result in the same cost of goods sold and ending inventory amounts*. For example, a comparison of the results of FIFO perpetual from Illustration 6-7 with results of FIFO periodic from Illustration 6A-2 shows that in both cases, cost of goods sold is $6,200 and ending inventory is $5,800. The results are the same because under both inventory systems, the first costs are the ones assigned to cost of goods sold regardless of when the sales actually happened.

This is not the case under the average cost formula. Notice that under a periodic inventory system in Illustration 6A-4, the ending inventory of $5,400 and the cost of goods sold of $6,600 are **not** the same as the values calculated under a perpetual inventory system in Illustration 6-11, even though the average cost formula was used for both systems. This is because *in a perpetual inventory system, a new (moving) average is calculated with each purchase; in a periodic inventory system, the same weighted average is used to calculate the cost of goods sold for all the units sold during the period*. A summary of these results is shown in Illustration 6A-5. For ease of comparison, the information from Illustration 6-11 has been rounded to the nearest dollar.

ILLUSTRATION 6A-5
Comparison of FIFO and average in perpetual and periodic inventory systems

	FIFO		Average	
	Perpetual	Periodic	Perpetual	Periodic
Cost of goods sold	$ 6,200	$ 6,200	$ 6,222	$ 6,600
Ending inventory balance	5,800	5,800	5,778	5,400
Cost of goods available for sale	$12,000	$12,000	$12,000	$12,000

As you can see, regardless of whether you use the FIFO or average cost formula using either a perpetual or periodic system, adding the cost of goods sold to the ending inventory balance will equal the goods available for sale of $12,000.

BEFORE YOU GO ON...

DO IT

Cookie Cutters Company uses the periodic inventory system. All purchases and sales are on account. The accounting records of Cookie Cutters Company show the following data:

Beginning inventory, June 1	4,000 units at $3
Purchases, June 13	6,000 units at $4
Sales, June 25	$64,000

The physical inventory count at June 30 showed 2,000 units on hand.

(a) Determine the cost of goods available for sale and the number of units sold.
(b) Assume Cookie Cutters uses FIFO. (1) Calculate cost of goods sold and ending inventory. (2) Prepare journal entries to record the June 13 purchase and the June 25 sale.
(c) Assume Cookie Cutters uses average. (1) Calculate cost of goods sold and ending inventory. (2) Prepare journal entries to record the June 13 purchase and the June 25 sale.

SOLUTION

(a) The cost of goods available for sale is $36,000, calculated as follows:

Beginning Inventory, June 1	4,000	units @ $3.00	$12,000
Purchases, June 13	6,000	units @ $4.00	24,000
	10,000		$36,000

Total units available for sale	10,000
Minus: units in ending inventory	2,000
Units sold	8,000

BEFORE YOU GO ON...
continued on next page

(b) FIFO—Periodic

1. Calculations:

Ending inventory:

Date	Units	Unit Cost	Total Cost
June 13	2,000	$4.00	$8,000

Cost of goods sold: $36,000 − $8,000 = $28,000

Check of cost of goods sold:

Date	Units	Unit Cost	Total Cost
June 1	4,000	$3.00	$12,000
13	4,000	4.00	16,000
	8,000		$28,000

Check: $8,000 + $28,000 = $36,000

2. Journal Entries

Date	Account	Debit	Credit
June 13	Purchases	24,000	
	Accounts Payable		24,000
	To record goods purchased on account.		
25	Accounts Receivable	64,000	
	Sales		64,000
	To record credit sale.		

(c) Average—Periodic

1. Calculations:

Weighted average unit cost: $36,000 ÷ 10,000 units = $3.60 per unit
Ending inventory: 2,000 units × $3.60 = $7,200
Cost of goods sold: $36,000 − $7,200 = $28,800
Check of cost of goods sold: 8,000 units × $3.60 = $28,800
Check: $7,200 + $28,800 = $36,000

2. Journal Entries

Date	Account	Debit	Credit
June 13	Purchases	24,000	
	Accounts Payable		24,000
	To record goods purchased on account.		
25	Accounts Receivable	64,000	
	Sales		64,000
	To record credit sale.		

Related exercise material: *BE6–17, *BE6–18, *E6–13, *E6–14, *E6–15, and *E6–16.

BEFORE YOU GO ON...
continued from previous page

Action Plan

- Calculate the cost of goods available for sale.
- Determine the cost of ending inventory first. Then calculate cost of goods sold by subtracting ending inventory from the cost of goods available for sale.
- For FIFO, allocate the most recent costs to the goods on hand (ending inventory). (The first costs will be allocated to the cost of goods sold.)
- For average, determine the weighted average unit cost (cost of goods available for sale ÷ number of units available for sale). Multiply this cost by the number of units on hand.
- Recall that in a periodic inventory system, the cost of goods sold is not recorded at the date of sale. It can only be calculated after the physical inventory count has taken place.

THE NAVIGATOR

ESTIMATING INVENTORIES

APPENDIX 6B

STUDY OBJECTIVE 8
Estimate ending inventory using the gross profit and retail inventory methods.

When a company uses a periodic inventory system, it must be able to do a physical count of its inventory in order to determine the cost of its ending inventory and the cost of goods sold. But what if a company cannot do a physical count? It may be impractical or impossible to count the inventory. Fortunately, it is possible to do an estimate.

There are two reasons for sometimes needing to estimate inventories. First, management may want monthly or quarterly financial statements but does not have the time for, or want the expense of, doing a physical inventory count every month or quarter. Second, a casualty such as a fire or flood may make it impossible to take a physical inventory.

Companies that use a perpetual inventory system are less likely to need inventory estimates since the perpetual inventory system keeps detailed inventory records continuously. *Inventory estimates are usually associated with the periodic system.*

There are two widely used methods of estimating inventories: (1) the gross profit method, and (2) the retail inventory method.

GROSS PROFIT METHOD

The **gross profit method** estimates the cost of ending inventory by applying the gross profit margin to net sales. It is commonly used to prepare interim (for example, monthly) financial statements in a periodic inventory system. This method is relatively simple but effective.

To use this method, a company needs to know its net sales, cost of goods available for sale (beginning inventory + cost of goods purchased), and gross profit margin. Gross profit for the period is estimated by multiplying net sales by the gross profit margin. The estimated gross profit is then used to calculate the estimated cost of goods sold and the estimated ending inventory.

The formulas for using the gross profit method are given in Illustration 6B-1.

ILLUSTRATION 6B-1
Gross profit method formulas

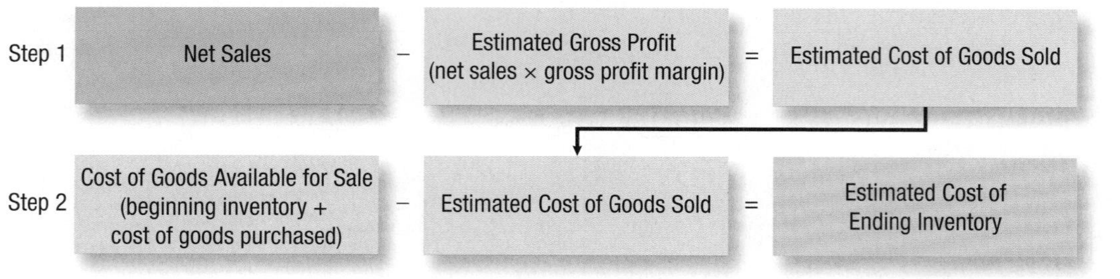

To illustrate, assume that Lalonde Company wants to prepare an income statement for the month of January. Its records show net sales of $200,000, beginning inventory of $40,000, and cost of goods purchased of $120,000. In the preceding year, the company had a 30% gross profit margin. It expects to earn the same margin this year. Given these facts and assumptions, Lalonde can calculate the estimated cost of the ending inventory at January 31 under the gross profit method as follows:

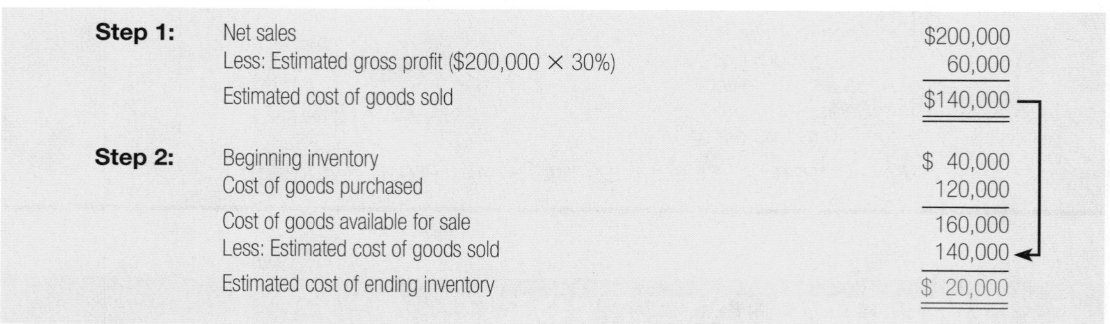

Step 1:	Net sales	$200,000
	Less: Estimated gross profit ($200,000 × 30%)	60,000
	Estimated cost of goods sold	$140,000
Step 2:	Beginning inventory	$ 40,000
	Cost of goods purchased	120,000
	Cost of goods available for sale	160,000
	Less: Estimated cost of goods sold	140,000
	Estimated cost of ending inventory	$ 20,000

The gross profit method *is based on the assumption that the gross profit margin will remain constant from one year to the next.* But it may not remain constant, because of a change in merchandising policies or in market conditions. In such cases, the margin should be adjusted to reflect the current operating conditions. In some cases, a better estimate can be had by applying this method to a department or product line as a whole.

The gross profit method should *not* be used in preparing a company's financial statements at the end of the year. These statements should be based on a physical inventory count, which must be conducted once a year, regardless of whether the merchandiser uses a perpetual or periodic system. Accountants and managers often use the gross profit method to test the reasonableness of the ending inventory amount, however.

RETAIL INVENTORY METHOD

Helpful hint In determining inventory at retail, selling prices on the unit are used. Tracing actual unit costs to invoices is unnecessary.

A retail store, such as Reitmans, has thousands of types of merchandise. In such cases, determining the cost of each type of merchandise can be difficult and time-consuming if the company has used a periodic inventory system. For these retail companies, it can be easier to calculate the selling price, or retail price, of the total inventory than to look at the purchase invoices to find the cost of each individual inventory item. Most retail businesses can establish a relationship between cost and selling price—called the cost-to-retail percentage or ratio. The cost-to-retail percentage is then applied to the ending inventory at retail prices to determine the estimated cost of the inventory. This is called the **retail inventory method** of estimating the cost of inventory.

To use the retail inventory method, a company's records must show both the cost and the retail value of the goods available for sale. The formulas for using the retail inventory method are given in Illustration 6B-2.

ILLUSTRATION 6B-2
Retail inventory method formulas

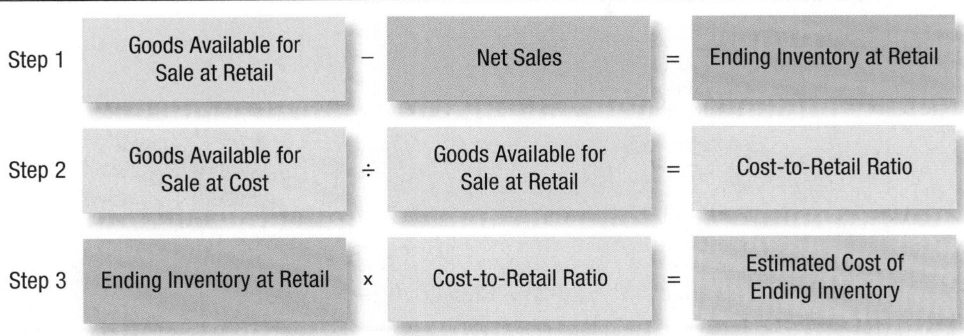

The logic of the retail method can be demonstrated by using unit-cost data. Assume that 10 units purchased at $7 each ($70 in total) are priced to sell for $10 per unit ($100 in total). The cost-to-retail ratio is 70% ($70 ÷ $100). If four units remain unsold, their retail value is $40 and their cost is $28 ($40 × 70%). This amount agrees with the total cost of goods on hand on a per-unit basis (4 × $7).

The following example shows how to apply the retail method, using assumed data for Zboyovsky Co.:

	At Cost	At Retail
Beginning inventory	$14,000	$ 21,500
Goods purchased	61,000	78,500
Goods available for sale	$75,000	100,000
Net sales		70,000
Step 1: Ending inventory at retail		**$ 30,000**
Step 2: Cost-to-retail ratio = $75,000 ÷ $100,000 = **75%**		
Step 3: Estimated cost of ending inventory **$30,000 × 75%** =	$22,500	

Using the retail inventory method also makes it easier to take a physical inventory at the end of the year. The goods on hand can be valued at the prices marked on the merchandise. The cost-to-retail ratio is then applied to the goods on hand at retail to determine the ending inventory at cost. This value can be used for reporting purposes in the year-end financial statements if the results are similar to using cost.

The retail inventory method is also useful for estimating the amount of shrinkage due to breakage, loss, or theft. For example, assume that the retail value of Zboyovsky's physical inventory count is $29,400. When this amount is compared with the estimated retail value of $30,000 that was calculated above, it reveals a $600 estimated inventory shortage at retail. The estimated inventory shortage at cost is $450 ($600 × 75%).

The major disadvantage of the retail method is that it is an averaging technique. It may produce an incorrect inventory valuation if the mix of the ending inventory is not representative of the mix in the goods available for sale. Assume, for example, that the cost-to-retail ratio of 75% in the Zboyovsky Co. illustration consists of equal proportions of inventory items that have cost-to-retail ratios of 70%, 75%, and 80%, respectively. If the ending inventory contains only items with a 70% ratio, an incorrect inventory cost will result. This problem can be lessened by applying the retail method to a department or product line as a whole.

BEFORE YOU GO ON...

DO IT

At May 31, Purcell Company has net sales of $330,000 and cost of goods available for sale of $230,000. Last year, the company had a gross profit margin of 35%. Calculate the estimated cost of the ending inventory.

Action Plan

- Calculate the estimated cost of goods sold.
- Deduct the estimated cost of goods sold from cost of goods available for sale.

SOLUTION

Net sales	$330,000
Less: Estimated gross profit ($330,000 × 35%)	115,500
Estimated cost of goods sold	$214,500
Cost of goods available for sale	$230,000
Less: Estimated cost of goods sold	214,500
Estimated cost of ending inventory	$ 15,500

Related exercise material: *BE6–19, *BE6–20, *E6–17, and *E6–18.

THE NAVIGATOR

Comparing IFRS and ASPE

Key Differences	International Financial Reporting Standards (IFRS)	Accounting Standards for Private Enterprises (ASPE)
No significant differences		

THE NAVIGATOR

DEMONSTRATION PROBLEM 1 (PERPETUAL INVENTORY SYSTEM)

Englehart Company uses a perpetual inventory system. All sales and purchases are on account. The selling price is $9 per unit. The company has the following inventory data for the month of March:

Date	Explanation	Units	Unit Cost	Total Cost	Total Units on Hand
Mar. 1	Beginning inventory	200	$4.30	$ 860	200
10	Purchase	500	4.50	2,250	700
15	Sales	(500)			200
20	Purchase	400	4.75	1,900	600
25	Sales	(400)			200
30	Purchase	300	5.00	1,500	500
		500		$6,510	

Instructions

(a) Determine the cost of ending inventory at March 31 and cost of goods sold for March under (1) FIFO, and (2) average.

(b) Prepare journal entries for the March 25 sale and the March 30 purchase under (1) FIFO, and (2) average.

SOLUTION TO DEMONSTRATION PROBLEM 1

(a) 1. FIFO—Perpetual

	PURCHASES			COST OF GOODS SOLD			BALANCE		
Date	Units	Cost	Total	Units	Cost	Total	Units	Cost	Total
Mar. 1							200	$4.30	$ 860
10	500	$4.50	$2,250				200 500	4.30 4.50	} 3,110
15				200 300	$4.30 4.50	} $2,210	200	4.50	900
20	400	4.75	1,900				200 400	4.50 4.75	} 2,800
25				200 200	4.50 4.75	} 1,850	200	4.75	950
30	300	5.00	1,500				200 300	4.75 5.00	} 2,450
	1,200		$5,650			$4,060			

Check: $860 + $5,650 − $4,060 = $2,450

(a) 2. Average—Perpetual

	PURCHASES			COST OF GOODS SOLD			BALANCE		
Date	Units	Cost	Total	Units	Cost	Total	Units	Cost	Total
Mar. 1							200	$4.30	$ 860
10	500	$4.50	$2,250				700	4.44	3,110
15				500	$4.44	$2,220	200	4.44	890
20	400	4.75	1,900				600	4.65	2,790
25				400	4.65	1,860	200	4.65	930
30	300	5.00	1,500				500	4.86	2,430
	1,200		$5,650	900		$4,080			

Check: $860 + $5,650 − $4,080 = $2,430

(b) 1. & 2. FIFO and average perpetual journal entries

		FIFO—Perpetual		Average—Perpetual	
Mar. 25	Accounts Receivable	3,600		3,600	
	Sales		3,600		3,600
	To record credit sale ($9 × 400).				
	Cost of Goods Sold	1,850		1,860	
	Merchandise Inventory		1,850		1,860
	To record cost of goods.				
30	Merchandise Inventory	1,500		1,500	
	Accounts Payable		1,500		1,500
	To record goods purchased on account.				

Action Plan

- In a perpetual inventory system, cost of goods sold is calculated for each sale and a running balance of the ending inventory on hand is maintained.
- For FIFO, allocate the first costs to the cost of goods sold at the date of each sale. The latest costs will be allocated to the goods on hand (ending inventory).
- For average, determine the weighted average unit cost (cost of goods available for sale ÷ number of units available for sale) after each purchase. Multiply this cost by the number of units sold to determine the cost of goods sold and multiply the weighted average cost per unit by the number of units on hand to determine the cost of the ending inventory.
- Subtract ending inventory from the cost of goods available for sale to determine the cost of goods sold for each cost formula.
- Check your work: do an independent calculation of cost of goods sold and check that cost of goods sold + ending inventory = cost of goods available for sale.
- Recall that there is no difference in recording sales and purchases between the two cost formulas.
- Use the information in the FIFO and average inventory schedules to prepare the cost of goods sold journal entry.

DEMONSTRATION PROBLEM 2 (PERIODIC INVENTORY SYSTEM)

Englehart Company uses a periodic inventory system. All sales and purchases are made on account. The company has the following inventory data for the month of March:

Inventory	March 1	200 units @ $4.30	$ 860
Purchases	March 10	500 units @ $4.50	2,250
	20	400 units @ $4.75	1,900
	30	300 units @ $5.00	1,500
Sales	March 15	500 units @ $9.00	4,500
	25	400 units @ $9.00	3,600

The physical inventory count on March 31 shows 500 units on hand.

Instructions

(a) Determine the cost of ending inventory at March 31 and cost of goods sold for March under (1) FIFO, and (2) average.

(b) Prepare journal entries for the March 25 sale and the March 30 purchase under (1) FIFO, and (2) average.

Action Plan

- In a periodic system, cost of ending inventory and cost of goods sold are determined at the end of the period.
- Calculate cost of goods available for sale, then allocate costs to ending inventory.
- For FIFO, allocate the latest costs (the costs of the newest goods) to the goods on hand. The first costs (the costs of the oldest goods) will be allocated to the cost of goods sold.
- For average, calculate the weighted average unit cost (cost of goods available for sale divided by the total units available for sale). Multiply this cost by the number of units on hand.
- Subtract ending inventory from the cost of goods available for sale to determine the cost of goods sold for each cost formula.
- Check your work: do an independent calculation of cost of goods sold and check that cost of goods sold + ending inventory = cost of goods available for sale.
- Recall that in a periodic inventory system, cost of goods sold is not recorded at the point of sale. Rather, it is calculated at the end of the fiscal period, once the physical inventory count has been taken.

SOLUTION TO DEMONSTRATION PROBLEM 2

The cost of goods available for sale is $6,510, calculated as follows:

Inventory	March 1	200	units @ $4.30	$ 860
Purchases	March 10	500	units @ $4.50	2,250
	20	400	units @ $4.75	1,900
	30	300	units @ $5.00	1,500
		1,400		$6,510

The physical inventory count on March 31 shows 500 units on hand.

The number of units sold is 900 (1,400 units available for sale − 500 units on hand).

(a) 1. FIFO—Periodic

Ending inventory:	Date	Units	Unit Cost	Total Cost
	Mar. 30	300	$5.00	$1,500
	20	200	4.75	950
		500		$2,450

Cost of goods sold: $6,510 − $2,450 = $4,060

Check of cost of goods sold:	Date	Units	Unit Cost	Total Cost
	Mar. 1	200	$4.30	$ 860
	10	500	4.50	2,250
	20	200	4.75	950
		900		$4,060

Check: $4,060 + $2,450 = $6,510

2. Average—Periodic

Weighted average unit cost:	$6,510 ÷ 1,400 units = $4.65 per unit
Ending inventory:	500 units × $4.65 = $2,325
Cost of goods sold:	$6,510 − $2,325 = $4,185
Check of cost of goods sold:	900 units × $4.65 = $4,185
Check:	$4,185 + $2,325 = $6,510

SOLUTION TO DEMONSTRATION PROBLEM 2 continued on next page

SOLUTION TO DEMONSTRATION PROBLEM 2 continued from previous page

(b) 1. & 2. FIFO and average periodic journal entries

		FIFO—Periodic		Average—Periodic	
Mar. 25	Accounts Receivable	3,600		3,600	
	Sales		3,600		3,600
	To record credit sale ($9 × 400).				
30	Purchases	1,500		1,500	
	Accounts Payable		1,500		1,500
	To record goods purchased on account.				

THE NAVIGATOR

Summary of Study Objectives

1. ***Describe the steps in determining inventory quantities.*** The steps in determining inventory quantities are (1) taking a physical inventory of goods on hand, and (2) determining the ownership of goods in transit, on consignment, and in similar situations.

2. ***Calculate cost of goods sold and ending inventory in a perpetual inventory system using the specific identification, FIFO, and average methods of cost determination.*** Costs are allocated to the cost of goods sold account each time a sale occurs in a perpetual inventory system. The cost is determined by specific identification or by one of two cost formulas: FIFO (first-in, first-out) and average.

   Specific identification is used for goods that are not ordinarily interchangeable (that is, they are not identical to one another). This method tracks the actual physical flow of goods, allocating the exact cost of each merchandise item to cost of goods sold and ending inventory.

   The FIFO cost formula assumes a first-in, first-out cost flow for sales. Cost of goods sold consists of the cost of the earliest goods purchased. Ending inventory is determined by allocating the cost of the most recent purchases to the units on hand.

   The average cost formula is used for goods that are homogeneous or non-distinguishable. Under average, a new weighted (moving) average unit cost is calculated after each purchase and is applied to the number of units sold and the number of units remaining in inventory.

3. ***Explain the financial statement effects of inventory cost determination methods.*** Specific identification results in the best match of costs and revenues on the income statement. When prices are rising, average results in a higher cost of goods sold and lower profit than FIFO. Average results in a better match on the income statement of more current costs with current revenues than does FIFO. On the balance sheet, FIFO results in an ending inventory that is closest to the current (replacement) value and the best balance sheet valuation. All three methods result in the same cash flow.

4. ***Determine the financial statement effects of inventory errors.*** An error in beginning inventory will have a reverse effect on profit in the current year. (For example, an overstatement of beginning inventory results in an overstatement of cost of goods sold and an understatement of profit.) An error in the cost of goods purchased will have a reverse effect on profit. (For example, an overstatement of purchases results in an overstatement of cost of goods sold and an understatement of profit.) An error in ending inventory will have a similar effect on profit. (For example, an overstatement of ending inventory results in an understatement of cost of goods sold and an overstatement of profit.) If ending inventory errors are not corrected in the following period, their effect on profit for the second period is reversed and total profit for the two years will be correct. On the balance sheet, ending inventory errors will have the same effects on total assets and total owner's equity, and no effect on liabilities.

5. ***Value inventory at the lower of cost and net realizable value.*** The cost of the ending inventory is compared with its net realizable value. If the cost is lower, no further steps are required. If the net realizable value is lower, a writedown is recorded, which results in an increase in (debit to) cost of goods sold, and a reduction in (credit to) merchandise inventory. The writedown is reversed if the net realizable value of the inventory increases, but the value of the inventory can never be higher than its original cost.

6. ***Demonstrate the presentation and analysis of inventory.*** Ending inventory is reported as a current asset on the balance sheet at the lower of cost and net realizable value. Cost of goods sold is reported as an expense on the income statement. Additional disclosures include the cost determination method.

   The inventory turnover ratio is a measure of liquidity. It is calculated by dividing the cost of goods sold by average inventory. It can be converted to days sales in inventory by dividing 365 days by the inventory turnover ratio. Days sales in inventory tells us, on average, how quickly a merchandiser takes to turn its inventory over once.

7. ***Calculate ending inventory and cost of goods sold in a periodic inventory system using FIFO and average inventory cost formulas (Appendix 6A).*** Under the FIFO cost formula, the cost of the most recent goods purchased is allocated to ending inventory. The cost of the earliest goods on hand is allocated to cost of goods sold. Under the average cost formula, the total cost of goods available for sale is divided by the total units available to calculate a weighted average unit cost. The weighted average unit cost is applied to the number of units on hand at the end of the period to determine ending inventory. Cost of goods sold is calculated by subtracting ending inventory from the cost of goods available for sale.

The main difference between applying cost formulas in a periodic inventory system and applying cost formulas in a perpetual inventory system is the *timing* of the calculations. In a periodic inventory system, the cost formula is applied at the end of the period. In a perpetual inventory system, the cost formula is applied at the date of each sale to determine the cost of goods sold. FIFO will provide the same result under both the perpetual and periodic system, whereas the average formula will yield different results for perpetual and periodic.

8. ***Estimate ending inventory using the gross profit and retail inventory methods (Appendix 6B).*** Two methods of estimating inventories are the gross profit method and the retail inventory method. Under the gross profit method, the gross profit margin is applied to net sales to determine the estimated cost of goods sold. The estimated cost of goods sold is subtracted from the cost of goods available for sale to determine the estimated cost of the ending inventory. Under the retail inventory method, a cost-to-retail ratio is calculated by dividing the cost of goods available for sale by the retail value of the goods available for sale. This ratio is then applied to the ending inventory at retail to determine the estimated cost of the ending inventory.

Glossary

Average cost formula An inventory cost formula that assumes that the goods available for sale are homogeneous or nondistinguishable. The cost of goods sold and the ending inventory are determined using an average cost, calculated by dividing the cost of the goods available for sale by the units available for sale. (p. 264)

Consigned goods Goods held for sale that belong to another party. The party holding the goods is called the consignee, and the party that owns the goods is called the consignor. (p. 259)

Days sales in inventory A liquidity measure of the average number of days that inventory is held prior to being sold. It is calculated as 365 days divided by the inventory turnover ratio. (p. 276)

First-in, first-out (FIFO) cost formula An inventory cost formula that assumes that the costs of the earliest (oldest) goods purchased are the first to be recognized as the cost of goods sold. The costs of the latest goods purchased are assumed to remain in ending inventory. (p. 262)

Full disclosure The requirement that all information that is relevant for decision-making be disclosed. (p. 267)

Gross profit method A method for estimating the cost of the ending inventory by applying the gross profit margin to net sales. (p. 281)

Inventory turnover A liquidity measure of the number of times, on average, that inventory is sold during the period. It is calculated by dividing cost of goods sold by average inventory. Average inventory is calculated by adding beginning inventory and ending inventory balances and dividing the result by two. (p. 276)

Lower of cost and net realizable value (LCNRV) A basis for stating inventory at the lower of its original cost and the net realizable value at the end of the period. (p. 273)

Net realizable value (NRV) The selling price of an inventory item, less any estimated costs required to make the item saleable. (p. 273)

Retail inventory method A method for estimating the cost of the ending inventory by applying a cost-to-retail ratio to the ending inventory at retail prices. (p. 283)

Specific identification An inventory costing method used when goods are distinguishable and not ordinarily interchangeable. It follows the actual physical flow of goods and items are specifically costed to arrive at the cost of goods sold and the cost of the ending inventory. (p. 261)

Weighted average unit cost The average cost of inventory weighted by the number of units purchased at each unit cost. It is calculated by dividing the cost of goods available for sale by the number of units available for sale. (p. 264)

Note: All questions, exercises, and problems below with an asterisk (*) relate to material in Appendices 6A and 6B.

Self-Study Questions

Answers are at the end of the chapter.

(SO 1) K 1. Which of the following should not be included in a company's physical inventory?
(a) Goods held on consignment from another company
(b) Goods shipped on consignment to another company
(c) Goods in transit that were purchased from a supplier and shipped FOB shipping point
(d) Goods in transit that were sold to a customer and shipped FOB destination

(SO 2) C 2. What is the most important factor in determining if specific identification can be used?
(a) Management decides to use it.
(b) The inventory consists of high-priced goods.
(c) The company has a low volume of sales.
(d) The inventory items are not interchangeable.

(SO 2) AP 3. Fine Wine Company uses a perpetual inventory system and has the following beginning inventory, purchases, and sales of inventory in April:

	Units	Unit Cost	Total Cost
Inventory, Apr. 1	8,000	$11	$ 88,000
Purchase, Apr. 9	12,000	12	144,000
Sale, Apr. 12	(15,000)	?	
Purchase, Apr. 18	5,000	13	65,000

What was the average unit cost after the last purchase on April 18?
(a) $11.60 (c) $11.88
(b) $12.00 (d) $12.30

(SO 2) AP 4. Using the data in question 3 above, the cost of goods sold under FIFO is:
(a) $174,000. (c) $185,000.
(b) $172,000. (d) $177,000.

(SO 3) C 5. In periods of rising prices, the average cost formula will produce:
(a) higher profit than FIFO.
(b) the same inventory as FIFO.
(c) lower profit than FIFO.
(d) higher inventory than FIFO.

(SO 4) C 6. In Fran Company, ending inventory is overstated by $4,000. The effects of this error on the current year's cost of goods sold and profit, respectively, are:
(a) understated, overstated.
(b) overstated, understated.
(c) overstated, overstated.
(d) understated, understated.

(SO 4) K 7. Michelle Company made an error that understated ending inventory by $5,000 on December 31, 2013. It did not correct the error in 2013 or 2014. As a result, owner's equity was:
(a) overstated at December 31, 2013, and understated at December 31, 2014.
(b) overstated at December 31, 2013, and properly stated at December 31, 2014.
(c) understated at December 31, 2013, and properly stated at December 31, 2014.
(d) understated at December 31, 2013, and overstated at December 31, 2014.

(SO 5) K 8. Rickety Company purchased 1,000 units of inventory at a cost of $91 each. There are 200 units left in ending inventory. The net realizable value of these units is $80 each. The ending inventory under the lower of cost and net realizable value rule is:
(a) $2,200. (c) $18,200.
(b) $16,000. (d) $80,000.

(SO 6) AP 9. If a company's cost of goods sold is $240,000, its beginning inventory is $50,000, and its ending inventory is $30,000, what are its inventory turnover and days sales in inventory?
(a) 3 times and 122 days.
(b) 6 times and 61 days.
(c) 4.8 times and 76 days.
(d) 8 times and 46 days.

(SO 7) AP*10. Kam Company uses a periodic inventory system and has the following:

	Units	Unit Cost
Inventory, Jan. 1	8,000	$11
Purchase, June 19	13,000	12
Purchase, Nov. 8	5,000	13
	26,000	

If 9,000 units are on hand at December 31, what is the cost of the goods sold under average? Round cost per unit to four decimal places.
(a) $106,962. (c) $180,000.
(b) $108,000. (d) $202,038.

(SO 7) AP*11. Using the data in question 10 above, the ending inventory under FIFO is:
(a) $100,000. (c) $113,000.
(b) $108,000. (d) $117,000.

(SO 8) AP*12. Somers Company has sales of $150,000 and a cost of goods available for sale of $135,000. If the gross profit margin is 30%, the estimated cost of the ending inventory under the gross profit method is:
(a) $15,000. (c) $40,500.
(b) $30,000. (d) $105,000.

(SO 8) AP*13. Deko Company reports the following selected information: cost of goods available for sale at cost, $60,000; at retail, $100,000; and net sales at retail, $70,000. What is the estimated cost of Deko Company's ending inventory under the retail method?
(a) $18,000. (c) $30,000.
(b) $21,000. (d) $42,000.

Questions

(SO 1) C 1. Your friend Tom Wetzel has been hired to help take the physical inventory in Kikujiro's Hardware Store. Explain to Tom what this job will involve.

(SO 1) C 2. Explain to Janine Company whether the buyer or the seller should include goods in transit at year end in their inventory. Also explain when the seller should record the sale.

(SO 1) C 3. What are consigned goods? Which company, the consignee or the consignor, should include consigned goods in its inventory balance? Explain why.

(SO 1) C 4. Your friend, the assistant store manager at Southside Boutique, wants to know if the following items should be included in the store's inventory count: (a) items on hold for customers who promised to return and purchase the items within the next week; (b) items left for alterations by customers; and (c) items taken on approval by customers.

If you need to make any assumptions to answer your friend, include that in your explanation.

(SO 2) C 5. Dave Wier believes that the allocation of the cost of goods available for sale should be based on the actual physical flow of the goods. Explain to Dave why this may be both impractical and inappropriate.

(SO 2) C 6. Explain circumstances in which the specific identification method is used.

(SO 2) C 7. Identify the key differences between the three methods of determining cost for inventories: specific identification, FIFO, and average. Give an example of a type of inventory for which each method might be used.

(SO 2) C 8. Sophie Yue believes that, when the perpetual system is used, the average cost per unit changes with every purchase and every sale. Explain to Sophie why this is not correct.

(SO 3) C 9. Compare the financial statement effects of using the FIFO and average formulas during a period of rising prices on (a) cash, (b) ending inventory, (c) cost of goods sold, and (d) profit.

(SO 3) C 10. Which inventory cost formula—FIFO or average—provides the better income statement valuation? The better balance sheet valuation? Explain.

(SO 3) C 11. What factors should a company consider when it is choosing between the two inventory cost formulas—FIFO and average?

(SO 4) C 12. Mila Company discovers in 2014 that its ending inventory at December 31, 2013, was overstated by $5,000. What effect (understated, overstated, or no effect) will this error have on (a) 2013 profit, (b) 2014 profit, and (c) the combined profit for the two years?

(SO 4) C 13. If an error in ending inventory in one year will have the reverse effect in the following year, does this error need to be corrected when it is discovered?

(SO 5) C 14. Lucy Ritter is studying for the next accounting exam. What should Lucy know about (a) when it is not appropriate to use the cost basis of accounting for inventories, and (b) the meaning of "net realizable value" in the lower of cost and net realizable value method?

(SO 5) K 15. How is net realizable value calculated?

(SO 5) C 16. A company must record a loss (or an increase in cost of goods sold) when net realizable value is lower than cost. Should a company record a gain when net realizable value is higher than cost? Explain.

(SO 6) AN 17. What problems may cause a company's inventory turnover ratio to be too high or too low?

(SO 6) AN 18. If a company's days sales in inventory ratio decreases from one year to the next, would this be viewed as a sign that the company's inventory management has improved or deteriorated? Explain.

(SO 6) K 19. What are the differences, if any, in the valuation and reporting of inventory between companies following IFRS and companies following ASPE?

(SO 7) C *20. Why is it necessary to calculate cost of goods available for sale when applying FIFO or average in a periodic inventory system?

(SO 7) C *21. Vance is studying for his next accounting quiz. He argues that the earliest costs should be used when calculating ending inventory using FIFO in a periodic inventory system because they are the first costs. Is he correct? Why or why not?

(SO 7) C *22. Explain why ending inventory and cost of goods sold under the average cost formula are not the same amounts in a periodic inventory system as they are in a perpetual inventory system.

(SO 8) K *23. When is it necessary to estimate the cost of inventories?

(SO 8) C *24. In order to save the cost of counting inventory at year end, it is acceptable to use the gross profit method to determine ending inventory for the year-end financial statements. Do you agree or disagree? Explain.

(SO 8) C *25. Both the gross profit method and the retail inventory method are based on averages. For each method, describe the average used, how it is determined, and how it is applied.

(SO 8) C *26. Explain the major weakness of the retail method and when it is not appropriate to use it.

Brief Exercises

Identify items in inventory. **(SO 1) K**

BE6–1 Helgeson Company has identified the following items to include or exclude when it takes its physical inventory. Indicate whether each item should be included or excluded.

(a) Goods shipped on consignment by Helgeson to another company
(b) Goods in transit to Helgeson from a supplier, shipped FOB destination
(c) Goods that have already been sold to a customer but are being held for delivery
(d) Goods from another company held on consignment by Helgeson
(e) Goods in transit to a customer, shipped FOB shipping point

BE6–2 The merchandise inventory in Carla's Clothing Store was counted after the close of business on December 31, 2014, the company's year end. It was determined that the total cost of this inventory was $55,500. Carla wants to know if this is the correct amount that should be reported on the company's December 31, 2014, balance sheet or if an adjustment needs to be made for any of the following items:

Calculate inventory balance. **(SO 1) AP**

(a) The count included merchandise "on hold" for customers. These items cost $950 and will be held until noon on January 2, 2015. Carla expects at least one half of the customers will return to purchase the items.
(b) The count also included items costing $1,200 that had been sold but are being held for alterations. The customers have paid in full for these items.
(c) Carla's Clothing Store has $4,250 of merchandise held on consignment for a local designer. These items were included in the inventory count.
(d) A shipment of inventory costing $2,875 was received on January 2, 2015. It had been shipped by the seller on December 30, FOB shipping point. Freight charges are $310. These items were not included in the inventory count.
(e) A second shipment of inventory costing $4,350 was received on January 3, 2015. It had been shipped by the seller on December 31, FOB destination. Freight charges are $390. These items were also not included in the inventory count.

Determine the correct amount of Carla's Clothing Store's merchandise inventory at December 31, 2014.

BE6–3 In October, Claire's Gallery purchased four original paintings for resale for the following amounts: Painting 1, $1,000; Painting 2, $2,000; Painting 3, $3,000; and Painting 4, $4,000. Paintings 3 and 4 were sold during October for $6,500 each. Calculate the cost of goods sold for the month and the ending inventory balance on October 31 using specific identification.

Apply specific identification cost determination method. **(SO 2) AP**

BE6–4 The following are three inventory cost determination methods:

Recommend cost determination method. **(SO 2) AP**

1. Specific identification
2. FIFO
3. Average

Below is a list of different types of companies and their main inventory item. Beside each one, insert the number of the inventory cost determination method above that the company would most likely use.

(a)	________	Grocery store (food)	(e)	________	Car dealership (parts)
(b)	________	Coffee shop (coffee beans)	(f)	________	Gas station (fuel)
(c)	________	Car dealership (automobiles)	(g)	________	Jewellery store (custom-made jewellery)
(d)	________	Clothing store (clothing)	(h)	________	Consignment clothing store (clothing)

BE6–5 First Choice Company uses the FIFO cost formula in a perpetual inventory system. Fill in the missing amounts for items (a) through (k) in the following perpetual inventory schedule:

Apply perpetual FIFO. **(SO 2) AP**

	PURCHASES			COST OF GOODS SOLD			BALANCE		
Date	Units	Cost	Total	Units	Cost	Total	Units	Cost	Total
June 1							200	$25.00	$5,000.00
7	400	$22.00	$8,800.00				(a)	(b)	(c)
18				350	(d)	(e)	(f)	(g)	(h)
26	350	$20.00	7,000.00				(i)	(j)	(k)

BE6–6 Average Joe Company uses the average cost formula in a perpetual inventory system. Fill in the missing amounts for items (a) through (k) in the following perpetual inventory schedule:

Apply perpetual average. **(SO 2) AP**

	PURCHASES			COST OF GOODS SOLD			BALANCE		
Date	Units	Cost	Total	Units	Cost	Total	Units	Cost	Total
June 1							200	$25.00	$5,000.00
7	400	$22.00	$8,800.00				(a)	(b)	(c)
18				350	(d)	(e)	(f)	(g)	(h)
26	350	$20.00	7,000.00				(i)	(j)	(k)

Apply perpetual FIFO and average. **(SO 2) AP**

BE6–7 Yogi & Company uses a perpetual inventory system. The following information is available for November:

		Units	Purchase Price	Sales Price
Nov. 1	Balance	10	$5.00	
4	Purchase	20	$5.50	
7	Purchase	20	$6.00	
10	Sale	(10)		$8.00
12	Sale	(30)		$8.00

Calculate the cost of goods sold and ending inventory under (a) FIFO and (b) average. (*Hint:* Round the average cost per unit to three decimal places.)

Record journal entries using perpetual FIFO and average. **(SO 2) AP**

BE6–8 Refer to the data in BE6–7 for Yogi & Company. Prepare journal entries to record the November 4 purchase and the November 12 sale using (a) FIFO and (b) average. Assume all sales and purchases are on credit.

Identify inventory cost formula. **(SO 3) C**

BE6–9 For each statement that follows, identify the inventory cost formula that best fits the description, assuming a period of rising prices:

(a) It results in a balance sheet inventory amount that is closer to the replacement cost.
(b) It does a better job of matching recent costs against revenue.
(c) It understates the value of the inventory on the balance sheet.
(d) It may overstate gross profit.

Compare impact of inventory cost formulas. **(SO 3) C**

BE6–10 Interactive Tech Company just started business and is trying to decide which inventory cost formula to use. Assuming prices are falling, as they often do in the information technology sector, answer the following questions for Interactive Tech:

(a) Which formula will result in the higher ending inventory? Explain.
(b) Which formula will result in the higher cost of goods sold? Explain.
(c) Which formula will result in the higher cash flow? Explain.
(d) What factors are important for Interactive Tech to consider as it tries to choose the most appropriate inventory cost formula?

Determine effect of beginning inventory error. **(SO 4) AN**

BE6–11 Collie Company incorrectly included $23,000 of goods held on consignment for Retriever Company in Collie's beginning inventory for the year ended December 31, 2013. The ending inventory for 2013 and 2014 was correctly counted. (a) What is the impact on the 2013 financial statements? (b) What is the impact on the 2014 financial statements?

Determine effects of inventory error over two years. **(SO 4) AN**

BE6–12 FirstIn Company reported profit of $90,000 in 2013. When counting its inventory on December 31, 2013, the company forgot to include items stored in a separate room in the warehouse. As a result, ending inventory was understated by $7,000.

(a) What is the correct profit for 2013?
(b) What effect, if any, will this error have on total assets and owner's equity reported on the balance sheet at December 31, 2013?
(c) Assuming the inventory is correctly counted on December 31, 2014, what effect, if any, will this error have on the 2014 financial statements?

Determine LCNRV valuation and prepare adjustment. **(SO 5) AP**

BE6–13 Smart-Tech Office Equipment Company has the following cost and net realizable value data at December 31, 2014:

Inventory Categories	Cost	Net Realizable Value
Computers	$24,000	$21,500
Office Equipment	19,000	19,500
Printers	14,000	10,600

(a) Calculate the lower of cost and net realizable value valuation.
(b) What adjustment should the company record if it uses a perpetual inventory system?

Apply LCNRV. **(SO 5) AP**

BE6–14 Refer to the data in BE6–13 for Smart-Tech Office Equipment Company. Prior to making the adjustment in BE6–13 part (b), Smart-Tech's cost of goods sold for 2014 was $418,500. What is the correct ending inventory and cost of goods sold that should be reported in the financial statements for the year ended December 31, 2014?

BE6–15 Reynold's Company had net sales of $2,500,000, cost of goods sold of $1,150,000, and profit of $500,000 in 2014. The company had a January 1, 2014, inventory balance of $132,000 and a December 31, 2014, inventory balance of $143,000. Calculate the inventory turnover and days sales in inventory ratios for 2014.

Calculate inventory ratios. **(SO 6) AP**

BE6–16 Refer to the data in BE6–15 for Reynold's Company. Assume for 2013 the company had an inventory turnover ratio of 9.1 and 40.1 days sales in inventory. Has the company's inventory management improved or deteriorated in 2014? Explain.

Compare inventory ratios. **(SO 6) C**

***BE6–17** In its first month of operations, Panther Company made three purchases of merchandise in the following sequence: 200 units at $8; 250 units at $7; and 300 units at $6. There are 400 units on hand at the end of the period. Panther uses a periodic inventory system. Calculate the cost of the ending inventory and cost of goods sold under (a) FIFO, and (b) average. (*Hint:* Round to two decimal places for the average cost per unit.)

Apply periodic cost FIFO and average. **(SO 7) AP**

***BE6–18** At the beginning of the year, Seller Company had 700 units with a cost of $3 per unit in its beginning inventory. The following inventory transactions occurred during the month of January:

Record transactions using periodic FIFO and average. **(SO 2, 7) AP**

Jan.	3	Sold 550 units on account for $6 each.
	9	Purchased 1,000 units on account for $4 per unit.
	15	Sold 850 units for cash for $7 each.

Prepare journal entries to record the January transactions assuming that Seller Company uses a periodic inventory system under (a) FIFO and (b) average.

***BE6–19** Jansen Company had beginning inventory of $60,000; net sales of $350,000; and cost of goods purchased of $250,000. In the previous year, the company had a gross profit margin of 40%. Calculate the estimated cost of the ending inventory using the gross profit method.

Apply gross profit method. **(SO 8) AP**

***BE6–20** On July 31, Milna's Fabric Store had the following data related to the retail inventory method: Goods available for sale at cost $25,000; at retail $40,000; and net sales of $30,000. Calculate the estimated cost of the ending inventory using the retail inventory method.

Apply retail inventory method. **(SO 8) AP**

Exercises

E6–1 Shippers Company had the following inventory situations to consider at January 31, its year end:

Identify items in inventory. **(SO 1) K**

1. Goods held on consignment for MailBoxes Etc. since December 22
2. Goods shipped on consignment to Rinehart Holdings on January 5, and still on hand
3. Goods that are still in transit and were shipped to a customer, FOB destination, on January 28
4. Goods that are still in transit and were shipped to a customer, FOB shipping point, on January 27
5. Goods that are still in transit and were purchased from a supplier, FOB destination, on January 25
6. Goods that are still in transit and were purchased from a supplier, FOB shipping point, on January 29
7. Freight costs due on goods in transit from item 6 above
8. Freight costs due on goods in transit from item 3 above
9. Office supplies on hand at January 31

Instructions

Which of the above items should Shipper include in its inventory? Provide an explanation for each.

E6–2 First Bank is considering giving Moghul Company a loan. First, however, it decides that it would be a good idea to have further discussions with Moghul's accountant. One area of particular concern is the inventory account, which has a December 31 balance of $281,000. Discussions with the accountant reveal the following:

Determine correct inventory amount. **(SO 1) AP**

1. The physical count of the inventory did not include goods that cost $95,000 that were shipped to Moghul, FOB shipping point, on December 27 and were still in transit at year end.

2. Moghul sold goods that cost $35,000 to Novotna Company, FOB destination, on December 28. The goods are not expected to arrive at their destination in India until January 12. The goods were not included in the physical inventory because they were not in the warehouse.
3. Moghul sold goods that cost $49,000 to Sterling of Canada, FOB shipping point, on December 30. The goods were received by Sterling on January 8. They were not included in Moghul's physical inventory.
4. On December 31, Board Company had $30,500 of goods held on consignment for Moghul. The goods were not included in Moghul's ending inventory balance.
5. Moghul received goods that cost $28,000 on January 2. The goods were shipped FOB shipping point on December 26 by Cellar Co. The goods were not included in the physical count.
6. On January 2, Moghul received goods that cost $44,000. The goods had been shipped, FOB destination, on December 29. The shipment was a rush order that was supposed to arrive on December 31. This purchase was not included in the ending inventory of $281,000.

Instructions

Determine the correct inventory amount at December 31.

Apply specific identification. **(SO 2) AP**

E6–3 In December, Paul's Paintings purchased the following items:

Date Purchased	Painting	Cost
Dec. 12	1	$1,000
5	2	800
10	3	1,100
19	4	700
20	5	1,200

On December 22, paintings 1 and 5 were sold for $2,500 each.

Instructions

(a) Should Paul's Paintings use specific identification or one of the two cost formulas (FIFO or average) instead? Explain.
(b) Calculate ending inventory and cost of goods sold using specific identification.
(c) Prepare the journal entry to record the December 22 sale.

Apply perpetual FIFO, record journal entries, and calculate gross profit. **(SO 2) AP**

E6–4 On May 1, Black Bear Company had 400 units of inventory on hand, at a cost of $4.00 each. The company uses a perpetual inventory system. All purchases and sales are on account. A record of inventory transactions for the month of May for the company is as follows:

Purchases		Sales	
May 4	1,300 @ $4.10	May 3	300 @ $7.00
14	700 @ $4.40	16	1,000 @ $7.00
29	500 @ $4.75	18	400 @ $7.50

Instructions

(a) Calculate the cost of goods sold and ending inventory using FIFO.
(b) Prepare journal entries to record the May 4 purchase and the May 3 and 16 sales.
(c) Calculate gross profit for May.

Apply perpetual average, record journal entries, and calculate gross profit. **(SO 2) AP**

E6–5 Top Light Company uses a perpetual inventory system. The company began 2014 with 1,000 lamps in inventory at a cost of $12 per unit. During 2014, Top Light had the following purchases and sales of lamps:

February 15	Purchased	2,000 units @ $18 per unit
April 24	Sold	2,500 units @ $30 per unit
June 6	Purchased	3,500 units @ $23 per unit
October 18	Sold	2,000 units @ $33 per unit
December 4	Purchased	1,400 units @ $26 per unit

All purchases and sales are on account.

Instructions

(a) Calculate the cost of goods sold and ending inventory using average. (*Hint:* Round the average cost per unit to three decimal places.)
(b) Prepare journal entries to record the June 6 purchase and the October 18 sale.
(c) Calculate gross profit for the year.

E6–6 Dene Company uses a perpetual inventory system and reports the following inventory transactions for the month of July:

Apply perpetual FIFO and average. Answer questions about results. **(SO 2, 3) AP**

		Units	Unit Cost	Total Cost
July 1	Inventory	150	$5	$ 750
12	Purchases	230	6	1,380
15	Sale	(250)		
16	Purchases	490	7	3,430
23	Purchases	175	8	1,400
27	Sale	(570)		

Instructions

(a) Calculate the cost of goods sold and ending inventory under (1) FIFO and (2) average. (*Hint:* Round the average cost per unit to three decimal places.)
(b) Which cost formula gives the higher ending inventory? Why?
(c) Which cost formula results in the higher cost of goods sold? Why?

E6–7 Sun Care Company uses a perpetual inventory system and reports the following inventory transactions for the month of May:

Apply perpetual FIFO and average. Answer questions about results. **(SO 2, 3) AP**

		Units	Unit Cost
May 1	Inventory	350	$8
4	Purchases	480	7
11	Sale	(510)	
12	Sales return	10	
17	Purchases	150	6
22	Purchases	475	5
29	Sale	(680)	

Instructions

(a) Calculate the cost of goods sold and ending inventory under (1) FIFO and (2) average. (*Hint:* Round the average cost per unit to three decimal places.)
(b) Assuming all units are sold for $15 per unit, calculate gross profit under (1) FIFO and (2) average. Explain why gross profit is not the same under the two methods.
(c) What impact, if any, does the choice of cost formula have on cash flow? Explain.

E6–8 Glacier Fishing Gear reported the following amounts for its cost of goods sold and ending inventory:

Determine effects of inventory errors. **(SO 4) AN**

	2014	2013
Cost of goods sold	$170,000	$175,000
Ending inventory	30,000	30,000

Glacier made two errors: (1) 2013 ending inventory was overstated by $5,500, and (2) 2014 ending inventory was understated by $4,000. (*Hint:* Recall that the ending inventory for 2013 becomes the beginning inventory for 2014.)

Instructions

(a) Calculate the correct cost of goods sold and ending inventory for each year.
(b) Describe the impact of the errors on profit for 2013 and 2014 and on owner's equity at the end of 2013 and 2014.
(c) Explain why it is important that Glacier Fishing Gear correct these errors as soon as they are discovered.

E6–9 Marrakesh Company reported the following income statement data for the years ended December 31:

Correct partial income statements and calculate gross profit margin. **(SO 4) AN**

	2014	2013
Sales	$500,000	$500,000
Cost of goods sold	410,000	410,000
Gross profit	$ 90,000	$ 90,000

The inventories at January 1, 2013, and December 31, 2014, are correct. However, the ending inventory at December 31, 2013, was understated by $20,000.

Instructions

(a) Prepare the correct income statement up to gross profit for the two years.
(b) What is the combined effect of the inventory error on total gross profit for the two years?
(c) Calculate the gross profit margin for each of the two years, before and after the correction.

Determine LCNRV valuation. **(SO 5) AP**

E6–10 Tech Computing Store uses a perpetual inventory system and the FIFO cost formula for valuing inventory. The company is now in the process of comparing the cost of its inventory with its net realizable value. The following data are available at Tech Computing's year end, December 31:

	Units	Unit Cost	Net Realizable Value
Laptop computers	95	$710	$680
Monitors	72	275	210
External hard drives	47	55	80
Tablets	56	300	390

Instructions

(a) Determine the lower of cost and net realizable value of the ending inventory.
(b) Prepare the journal entry required, if any, to record the adjustment from cost to net realizable value.

Determine LCNRV valuation and note disclosures. **(SO 5, 6) AP**

E6–11 Picture Perfect Camera Shop is determining the lower of cost and net realizable value of its inventory. The following data are available at December 31:

		Units	Unit Cost	Net Realizable Value
Cameras:	Nikon	15	$675	$600
	Canon	17	400	425
Lenses:	Sony	22	135	124
	Sigma	20	215	220

Instructions

(a) Determine the lower of cost and net realizable value of the ending inventory.
(b) Prepare the journal entry required, if any, to record the adjustment from cost to net realizable value assuming Picture Perfect Camera Shop uses a perpetual inventory system.
(c) What information regarding its inventory will Picture Perfect Camera Shop need to report in the notes to its financial statements?

Calculate inventory turnover, days sales in inventory, and gross profit margin. **(SO 6) AP**

E6–12 Dartmouth Games reported the following information for a three-year period:

	2014	2013	2012
Ending inventory	$ 20,000	$ 30,000	$ 34,000
Sales	125,000	128,000	115,000
Cost of goods sold	50,000	51,200	46,000
Profit	30,000	42,000	40,000

Instructions

(a) Calculate the inventory turnover, days sales in inventory, and gross profit margin for 2014 and 2013. (*Hint:* In calculating inventory, remember to use the average of the ending inventory balance for the current and the previous year.)
(b) Based on this information, does the company's liquidity appear to be improving or deteriorating?

Apply periodic FIFO and average. **(SO 7) AP**

***E6–13** Lombart Company uses a periodic inventory system. Its records show the following for the month of April, with 25 units on hand at April 30:

		Units	Unit Cost	Total Cost
April 1	Inventory	30	$ 8	$240
12	Purchases	45	11	495
16	Purchases	15	12	180
	Total	90		915

Instructions

(a) Calculate the ending inventory and cost of goods sold at April 30 using the FIFO and average cost formula.
(b) Prove the cost of goods sold calculations.

***E6–14** Dene Company uses a periodic inventory system and its accounting records include the following inventory information for the month of July:

Apply periodic FIFO and average. **(SO 7) AP**

		Units	Unit Cost	Total Cost
July 1	Inventory on hand	150	$5	$ 750
12	Purchase	230	6	1,380
16	Purchase	490	7	3,430
23	Purchase	175	8	1,400

A physical inventory count determined that 225 units were on hand at July 31.

Instructions

(a) Calculate the ending inventory and the cost of goods sold under (1) FIFO and (2) average.
(b) For part 2 of instruction (a), explain why the average unit cost is not $6.50.
(c) How do the results for instruction (a) differ from E6–6, where the same information was used in a perpetual inventory system?

***E6–15** Fish n'Fly sells an ultra-lightweight fishing rod that is considered to be one of the best fishing rods on the market. Information follows for Fish n'Fly's purchases and sales of the ultra-lightweight fishing rod in July:

Apply periodic and perpetual FIFO and average. **(SO 2, 7) AP**

Date	Transaction	Units	Unit Purchase Price	Unit Sales Price
July 1	Beginning inventory	25	$295	
10	Purchase	30	300	
12	Sale	(42)		$450
13	Purchase	35	305	
25	Sale	(45)		460
27	Purchase	20	310	

Instructions

(a) Calculate the cost of goods sold and the ending inventory using FIFO and average, assuming Fish n'Fly uses a perpetual inventory system. (*Hint:* Round the average cost per unit to three decimal places.)
(b) What would be the ending inventory and cost of goods sold if Fish n'Fly used FIFO and average in a periodic inventory system? (*Hint:* Round the average cost per unit to three decimal places.)

***E6–16** Refer to the data for Fish n'Fly in E6–15. Assume that all of Fish n'Fly's sales are for cash and all of its purchases are on account.

Record transactions in perpetual and periodic inventory systems. **(SO 2, 7) AP**

Instructions

(a) Record the purchases and sales for Fish n'Fly in a perpetual inventory system under (1) FIFO and (2) average.
(b) Record the purchases and sales for Fish n'Fly in a periodic inventory system under (1) FIFO and (2) average.

***E6–17** The inventory of Marshall's Merchandise Company was destroyed by fire on June 1. From an examination of the accounting records, the following data for the first five months of the year were obtained: Sales $90,000; Sales Returns and Allowances $1,500; Sales Discounts $700; Freight Out $2,500; Purchases $51,200; Freight In $2,200; Purchase Returns and Allowances $2,400; and Purchase Discounts $1,300.

Estimate inventory loss using gross profit method. **(SO 8) AP**

Instructions

Determine the inventory lost by fire, assuming a beginning inventory of $25,000 and a gross profit margin of 40%.

***E6–18** Zhang Shoe Store uses the retail inventory method for its two departments: men's shoes and women's shoes. The following information is obtained for each department:

Estimate cost of ending inventory using retail method. **(SO 8) AP**

Item	Men's Shoes	Women's Shoes
Beginning inventory at cost	$ 36,000	$ 45,000
Beginning inventory at retail	58,050	95,750
Cost of goods purchased	216,000	315,000
Retail price of goods purchased	348,400	670,200
Net sales	365,000	635,000

Instructions

Calculate the estimated cost of the ending inventory for each shoe department under the retail inventory method.

Problems: Set A

Identify items in inventory. (SO 1) AP

P6–1A Kananaskis Company is trying to determine the value of its ending inventory as at February 28, 2014, the company's year end. The accountant counted everything that was in the warehouse as at February 28, which resulted in an ending inventory valuation of $65,000. However, he was not sure how to treat the following transactions, so he did not include them in inventory:

1. Kananaskis shipped $875 of inventory on consignment to Banff Company on February 20. By February 28, Banff Company had sold $365 of this inventory for Kananaskis.
2. On February 28, Kananaskis was holding merchandise that had been sold to a customer on February 25 but needed some minor alterations. The customer has paid for the goods and will pick them up on March 3 after the alterations are complete. This inventory cost $490 and was sold for $880.
3. In Kananaskis' warehouse on February 28 is $400 of inventory that Craft Producers shipped to Kananaskis on consignment.
4. On February 27, Kananaskis shipped goods costing $950 to a customer and charged the customer $1,300. The goods were shipped FOB destination and the receiving report indicates that the customer received the goods on March 3.
5. On February 26, Seller Company shipped goods to Kananaskis, FOB shipping point. The invoice price was $375 plus $30 for freight. The receiving report indicates that the goods were received by Kananaskis on March 2.
6. Kananaskis had $630 of inventory put aside in the warehouse. The inventory is for a customer who has asked that the goods be shipped on March 10.
7. On February 26, Kananaskis issued a purchase order to acquire goods costing $750. The goods were shipped FOB destination. The receiving report indicates that Kananaskis received the goods on March 2.
8. On February 26, Kananaskis shipped goods to a customer, FOB shipping point. The invoice price was $350 plus $25 for freight. The cost of the items was $280. The receiving report indicates that the goods were received by the customer on March 4.

Instructions

(a) For each of the above transactions, specify whether the item should be included in ending inventory, and if so, at what amount. Explain your reasoning.
(b) What is the revised ending inventory valuation?

TAKING IT FURTHER If the accountant of Kananaskis Company is paid a bonus based on profit, which of these errors might he consider overlooking and not correcting? Explain.

Apply specific identification. (SO 2) AP

P6–2A EastPoint Toyota, a small dealership, has provided you with the following information with respect to its vehicle inventory for the month of November. The company uses the specific identification method.

Date	Explanation	Model	Serial #	Unit Cost	Unit Selling Price
Nov. 1	Inventory	Corolla	C63825	$15,000	
		Corolla	C81362	20,000	
		Camry	G62313	26,000	
		Venza	X3892	27,000	
		Tundra	F1883	22,000	
		Tundra	F1921	25,000	
8	Sales	Corolla	C81362		$22,000
		Camry	G62313		28,000
12	Purchases	Camry	G71811	27,000	
		Camry	G71891	25,000	
		Venza	X4212	28,000	
		Venza	X4214	31,000	
18	Sales	Camry	G71891		27,000
		Venza	X3892		31,000
		Tundra	F1921		29,000
23	Purchases	Tundra	F2182	23,000	
		Camry	G72166	30,000	

Instructions

(a) Determine the cost of goods sold and the ending inventory for the month of November.
(b) Determine the gross profit for the month of November.

TAKING IT FURTHER Should EastPoint Toyota use the specific identification cost determination method or one of the cost formulas? Explain.

P6–3A You are given the following information for Lahti Company for the month ended November 30, 2014:

Apply perpetual FIFO. Record sales and inventory adjustment, calculate gross profit, and answer questions. **(SO 2, 4) AP**

Date	Description	Units	Unit Price
Nov. 1	Beginning inventory	60	$50
9	Purchase	100	46
15	Sale	(120)	
16	Sales return (Nov. 15 sale)	5	
22	Purchase	150	44
29	Sale	(160)	
30	Purchase	45	42

Lahti Company uses a perpetual inventory system. All sales and purchases are on account.

Instructions

(a) Calculate the cost of goods sold and the ending inventory using FIFO.
(b) Assume the sales price was $66 per unit for the goods sold on November 15, and $60 per unit for the sale on November 29. Prepare journal entries to record the November 22 purchase and the November 29 sale.
(c) Calculate gross profit for November.
(d) Assume that at the end of November, the company counted its inventory. There are 78 units on hand. What journal entry, if any, should the company make to record the shortage?
(e) If the company had not discovered this shortage, what would be overstated or understated on the balance sheet and income statement and by what amount?

TAKING IT FURTHER In what respects does FIFO provide more useful information than average?

P6–4A Information for Lahti Company is presented in P6–3A. Assume the same inventory data and that the company uses a perpetual inventory system. Ignore the inventory shortage in P6–3A part (d).

Apply perpetual average and answer questions. **(SO 2, 3) AP**

Instructions

(a) Calculate the cost of goods sold and the ending inventory using average. (*Hint:* Round the average cost per unit to two decimal places.)
(b) Prepare the journal entry to record the November 15 sale and the sales return on November 16.
(c) If the company changes from average to FIFO and prices continue to fall, would you expect the cost of goods sold and ending inventory amounts to be higher or lower?

TAKING IT FURTHER If Lahti Company wishes to change from average to the FIFO cost formula, what factors must it consider before making this change?

P6–5A Fly-Buy Frisbees sells a wide variety of frisbees and uses a perpetual inventory system. On June 1, Fly-Buy Frisbees had five "Fast Flying Frisbees" on hand at a unit cost of $105. During June and July, the company had the following purchases and sales for this frisbee (all for cash):

Apply perpetual FIFO and average. Answer question about financial statement effects. **(SO 2, 3) AP**

	Purchases		Sales	
	Units	Unit Cost	Units	Unit Price
June 4			2	$210
18	5	$115		
30			6	235
July 5	5	120		
12			3	255
25			2	255

Instructions

(a) Determine the cost of goods sold and ending inventory under a perpetual inventory system using (1) FIFO and (2) average. (*Hint:* Round the average cost per unit to two decimal places.)
(b) Calculate gross profit using (1) FIFO and (2) average.
(c) What impact, if any, does the choice of cost formula have on cash flow?

TAKING IT FURTHER What factors should the owner of Fly-Buy Frisbees consider when choosing a cost formula?

Record transactions using perpetual average. Apply LCNRV. (SO 2, 5) AP

P6–6A You are given the following information for Amelia Company. All transactions are settled in cash. Returns are usually not damaged and are restored immediately to inventory for resale. Amelia uses a perpetual inventory system and the average cost formula. Increased competition has reduced the price of the product.

Date	Transaction	Units	Unit Price
July 1	Beginning inventory	25	$10
5	Purchase	55	9
8	Sale	(70)	15
10	Sale returns and allowances	15	15
15	Purchase	50	8
16	Purchase return	(10)	8
20	Sale	(55)	12
25	Purchase	10	7

Instructions

(a) Prepare the required journal entries for the month of July for Amelia Company. (*Hint:* Round the average cost per unit to two decimal places.)
(b) Determine the ending inventory for Amelia.
(c) On July 31, Amelia Company learns that the product has a net realizable value of $8 per unit. Prepare the journal entry, if required, to recognize the decrease in value of this product. If no entry is required, explain why.
(d) What amount should the ending inventory be valued at on the July 31 balance sheet? What amount should the cost of goods sold be valued at on the July income statement?

TAKING IT FURTHER What if Amelia had used FIFO instead of average? How would this affect the July 31 ending inventory on the balance sheet compared with average?

Determine effects of inventory errors. (SO 1, 4) AN

P6–7A The records of Alyssa Company show the following amounts in its December 31 financial statements:

	2014	2013	2012
Total assets	$925,000	$900,000	$850,000
Owner's equity	750,000	700,000	650,000
Cost of goods sold	550,000	550,000	500,000
Profit	90,000	80,000	70,000

Alyssa Company made the following errors in determining its ending inventory:

1. The ending inventory account balance at December 31, 2012, included $20,000 of goods held on consignment for Gillies Company.
2. The ending inventory account balance at December 31, 2013, did not include goods sold and shipped on December 30, 2013, FOB destination. The selling price of these goods was $40,000 and the cost of these goods was $32,000. The goods arrived at the destination on January 4, 2014.

All purchases and sales of inventory were recorded in the correct fiscal year.

Instructions

(a) Calculate the correct amount for each of the following for 2014, 2013, and 2012:
   1. Total assets
   2. Owner's equity
   3. Cost of goods sold
   4. Profit
(b) Indicate the effect of these errors (overstated, understated, or no effect) on cash at the end of 2012, 2013, and 2014.

TAKING IT FURTHER As long as the merchandise inventory balance is correct as at December 31, 2014, is it necessary to correct the errors in the previous years' financial statements? Explain.

Determine effects of inventory errors. Calculate inventory turnover. (SO 4, 6) AN

P6–8A Amanpreet Company has a July 31 fiscal year end and uses a perpetual inventory system. The records of Amanpreet Company show the following data:

	2014	2013	2012
Income statement:			
Sales	$350,000	$330,000	$310,000
Cost of goods sold	245,000	235,000	225,000
Operating expenses	76,000	76,000	76,000
Balance sheet:			
Merchandise inventory	55,000	45,000	35,000

After its July 31, 2014, year end, Amanpreet discovered two errors:

1. At July 31, 2013, Amanpreet had $10,000 of goods held on consignment at another company that were not included in the physical count.
2. In July 2013, Amanpreet recorded a $15,000 inventory purchase on account that should have been recorded in August 2013.

Instructions

(a) Prepare incorrect and corrected income statements for Amanpreet for the years ended July 31, 2012, 2013, and 2014.
(b) What is the impact of these errors on the owner's equity at July 31, 2014?
(c) Calculate the incorrect and correct inventory turnover ratios for 2013 and 2014.

TAKING IT FURTHER Compare the trends in the incorrectly calculated annual profits with the trends in the correctly calculated annual profits. Does it appear that management may have deliberately made these errors, or do they appear to be honest errors? Explain.

P6–9A Copperhead Company has provided you with the following information regarding its inventory of copper for September and October. Copperhead uses a perpetual inventory system.

Apply LCNRV and prepare adjustment. **(SO 5) AP**

	September 30	October 31
Copper inventory (in tonnes)	2,500	2,000
Cost per tonne	$505	$535
NRV per tonne	$540	$520

Instructions

(a) Calculate the cost, the net realizable value, and the amount to be reported on the balance sheet for Copperhead's inventory at (1) September 30 and (2) October 31.
(b) Prepare any journal entries required to record the LCNRV of the copper inventory at (1) September 30 and (2) October 31.
(c) Assume that during the month of November the company did not purchase or sell any copper inventory and that the NRV per tonne was $530 on November 30. Is an adjusting entry required at November 30? Explain. If so, prepare the adjusting entry.
(d) What will have to be disclosed in Copperhead's notes to the financial statements with regard to its copper inventory?

TAKING IT FURTHER Do all companies have to report inventory at the LCNRV on the balance sheet?

P6–10A The following financial information (in US$ millions) is for two major corporations for the three years ended December 31:

Calculate ratios. **(SO 6) AN**

PepsiCo Inc.	2011	2010	2009
Net sales	$66,504	$57,838	$43,232
Cost of sales	31,593	26,575	20,099
Profit	6,462	6,338	5,979
Cash and short-term investments	4,425	6,369	4,135
Accounts receivable	6,912	6,323	4,624
Inventory	3,827	3,372	2,618
Prepaid expenses and other current assets	2,277	1,505	1,194
Current liabilities	18,154	15,892	8,756
Coca-Cola Company			
Net sales	$46,542	$35,119	$30,990
Cost of sales	18,216	12,693	11,088
Profit	8,634	11,859	6,906
Cash and short-term investments	14,035	11,337	9,213
Accounts receivable	4,920	4,430	3,758
Inventory	3,092	2,650	2,354
Prepaid expenses and other current assets	3,450	3,162	2,226
Current liabilities	24,283	18,508	13,721

Instructions

(a) Calculate the inventory turnover, days sales in inventory, current ratio, acid-test ratio, gross profit margin, and profit margin for each company for 2011 and 2010.
(b) Comment on each company's profitability and liquidity.

TAKING IT FURTHER Companies are required to disclose in a significant accounting policies note how they determine the cost of their inventory. Both Pepsi and Coca-Cola state that they use average and FIFO. Under what circumstances would it make sense for a company to use both cost formulas?

Apply periodic FIFO and average. **(SO 7) AP**

***P6–11A** Wolick Company had a beginning inventory on January 1 of 300 units of Product SXL at a cost of $21 per unit. During the year, the following purchases were made:

	Units	Unit Cost
Mar. 15	800	$20
July 20	600	19
Sept. 4	250	18
Dec. 2	100	17

At the end of the year, there were 350 units on hand. Wolick Company uses a periodic inventory system.

Instructions

(a) Determine the cost of goods available for sale.

(b) During the year, Wolick Company sold Product SXL for $33 per unit. Calculate the number of units sold during the year and total sales revenue.

(c) Determine the cost of the ending inventory and the cost of goods sold using (1) FIFO and (2) average. (*Hint:* Round the average cost per unit to two decimal places.)

(d) Calculate gross profit using (1) FIFO and (2) average.

TAKING IT FURTHER The owner of Wolick Company would like to minimize his income taxes. Last year, prices were rising and Wolick Company used the average cost formula. This year, the owner would like to use FIFO. Should the company change? Explain.

Apply periodic and perpetual FIFO. **(SO 2, 7) AP**

***P6–12A** You are given the following information about Meesha Novelty's inventory for the month of July.

Purchases			Sales		
Date	Units	Cost per unit	Date	Units	Price per unit
July 1	400	$3.00	July 2	300	$6.00
10	1,300	3.10	11	1,000	6.00
13	700	3.40	28	400	6.50
27	600	3.75			

Instructions

(a) Calculate the cost of goods available for sale and the number of units of ending inventory.

(b) Assume Meesha uses FIFO periodic. Calculate the cost of ending inventory, cost of the goods sold, and gross profit.

(c) Assume Meesha uses FIFO perpetual. Calculate the cost of ending inventory, cost of the goods sold, and gross profit.

(d) Prepare journal entries to record the July 10 purchase and the July 11 sale using (1) FIFO periodic and (2) FIFO perpetual. Assume both the sale and purchase were for cash.

(e) Compare the results of parts (b) and (c) above and comment.

TAKING IT FURTHER Companies are required to disclose their cost determination method, but not the inventory system (periodic or perpetual). Provide an explanation as to why.

Apply periodic and perpetual average. **(SO 2, 7) AP**

***P6–13A** Aldor Corporation opened a new store on January 1, 2014. During 2014, the first year of operations, the following purchases and sales of inventory were made:

Purchases			Sales		
Date	Units	Cost	Date	Units	Price
Jan. 5	10	$1,000	July 4	15	$2,000
June 11	10	1,200	Dec. 29	35	$2,000
Oct. 18	15	1,300			
Dec. 20	20	1,500			

Instructions

(a) Calculate the cost of goods available for sale and the number of units of ending inventory.

(b) Assume Aldor uses average periodic. Calculate the cost of ending inventory, cost of the goods sold, and gross profit.

(c) Assume Aldor uses average perpetual. Calculate the cost of ending inventory, cost of the goods sold, and gross profit.

(d) Prepare journal entries to record the December 20 purchase and the December 29 sale using (1) average periodic and (2) average perpetual.
(e) Compare the results of parts (b) and (c) above and comment.

TAKING IT FURTHER If a company uses the average cost determination method, are there any benefits to using average perpetual over average periodic? Explain.

***P6–14A** Westor Company lost all of its inventory in a fire on December 28, 2014. The accounting records showed the following gross profit data for November and December:

Determine inventory loss using gross profit method. **(SO 8) AP**

	November	December (to Dec. 28)
Sales	$674,000	$965,390
Sales returns and allowances	14,000	26,600
Purchases	441,190	621,660
Purchase returns and allowances	17,550	22,575
Freight in	6,860	12,300
Beginning inventory	34,050	39,405
Ending inventory	39,405	?

Westor is fully insured for fire losses but must prepare a report for the insurance company.

Instructions

Determine the amount of inventory lost by Westor as a result of the fire using the gross profit method.

TAKING IT FURTHER The insurance adjustor is concerned that this method of calculating the cost of the inventory destroyed might not be accurate. What factors contribute to the accuracy of the ending inventory amount when using the gross profit method?

***P6–15A** Brandon Shoe Store uses the retail inventory method to estimate its monthly ending inventories. The following information is available at November 30, 2014:

Determine ending inventory using retail method. **(SO 8) AP**

	Women's Shoes		Men's Shoes	
	Cost	Retail	Cost	Retail
Beginning inventory	$ 276,000	$ 424,000	$ 191,000	$ 323,000
Purchases	1,181,000	1,801,000	1,046,000	1,772,000
Purchase returns and allowances	24,600	37,000	21,900	36,400
Freight in	6,000		7,200	
Sales		1,826,000		1,651,000
Sales returns and allowances		28,000		25,000

At November 30, Brandon Shoe Store takes a physical inventory count at retail. The actual retail values of the inventories in each department on November 30, 2014, are as follows: Women's Shoes $381,250, and Men's Shoes $426,100.

Instructions

Determine the estimated cost of the ending inventory at November 30, 2014, using the retail inventory method.

TAKING IT FURTHER Calculate the store's loss on November 30, 2014, from theft and other causes, at retail and at cost.

CONTINUING COOKIE CHRONICLE

(*Note:* This is a continuation of the Cookie Chronicle from Chapters 1 through 5.)

Natalie is busy establishing both divisions of her business (cookie classes and mixer sales) and completing her business diploma. Her goals for the next 11 months are to sell one mixer per month and to give two to three classes per week.

The cost of the fine European mixers is expected to increase. Natalie has just negotiated new terms with Kzinski that include shipping costs in the negotiated purchase price. (Mixers will be shipped FOB destination.)

Recall that Natalie has two mixers in inventory: mixer #1 (serial number 12459) and mixer #2 (serial number 23568). Inventory cost for each of these units is $545.

The following mixer purchase and sale transactions occur in February and March, 2014:

Feb. 3 Natalie orders three deluxe mixers on account from Kzinski Supply Co. for $1,650 ($550 each), FOB destination, terms n/30.

	14	Natalie receives mixer #3 (serial number 49295), mixer #4 (serial number 56204), and mixer #5 (serial number 62897).
	19	Natalie sells one deluxe mixer, mixer #4, for $1,050 cash.
March	3	Natalie orders two deluxe mixers on account from Kzinski Supply Co. for $1,142, FOB destination, terms n/30.
	17	Natalie receives mixer #6 (serial number 69896) and mixer #7 (serial number 72531).
	18	Natalie returns mixer #6. It is not the one she ordered.
	27	Natalie sells two deluxe mixers, mixer #2 and mixer #5, for a total of $2,100 cash.

All of the mixers Natalie has purchased and sold are identical. Natalie has accounted for all of these transactions by mixer number to ensure that she does not lose track of mixers on hand and mixers that have been sold. Natalie wonders if she is accounting for the costs of these mixers correctly.

Instructions

(a) Answer Natalie's concerns. Is Natalie accounting for these transactions correctly? Why or why not? What are the alternatives that Natalie could use in accounting for her mixer inventory?

(b) Given that Natalie has accounted for all of these transactions by mixer number, what is the total cost of goods sold for February and March, and the inventory balance at the end of March in Cookie Creations' accounting records?

(c) Using the average cost formula in a perpetual inventory system, prepare a schedule to track the purchases and sales of mixers, and the balance in the mixers inventory account. Use the format from Illustration 6-11.

(d) Prepare a journal entry to correct the March 31 inventory balance from the amount calculated in part (b) to the amount determined in part (c) assuming Natalie decided to use the average cost formula in a perpetual inventory system (instead of recording cost by specific mixer).

(e) Assume instead that Natalie had used the average cost formula to record all of the February and March transactions. Using the information prepared in part (c) above, prepare the journal entries that would be required had Natalie used this cost formula.

CHAPTER 6 BROADENING YOUR PERSPECTIVE

Collaborative Learning Activity

Note to instructor: Additional instructions and material for this group activity can be found on the Instructor Resource Site and in *WileyPLUS*.

BYP6–1 In this group activity, you will work in two different groups to improve your understanding of inventory cost determination methods using a perpetual inventory system. First, you will work in an "expert" group in which you will ensure that each group member thoroughly understands one of the three inventory cost determination methods (specific identification, FIFO, and average). Then you will move to a second group consisting of one student from each of the different expert groups, and take turns teaching the different inventory cost determination methods.

Communication Activity

BYP6–2 You are the controller of Small Toys Inc. Mutahir Kazmi, the president, recently mentioned to you that he found an error in the 2013 financial statements that he believes has now corrected itself. In discussions with the purchasing department, Mutahir determined that the 2013 ending inventory was understated by $1 million. However, the 2014 ending inventory is correct. Mutahir assumes that 2014 profit is correct and comments to you, "What happened has happened—there's no point in worrying about it now."

Instructions

You conclude that Mutahir is wrong. Write a brief, tactful e-mail to him that clarifies the situation.

Ethics Case

BYP6–3 Discount Diamonds carries only one brand and size of diamond—all are therefore identical. Each batch of diamonds that is purchased is carefully coded and marked with its purchase cost. You are given the following data from March:

Mar.	1	Beginning inventory consisted of 140 diamonds at a cost of $500 per diamond.
	3	Purchased 200 diamonds at a cost of $540 each.
	5	Sold 170 diamonds for $800 each.
	10	Purchased 340 diamonds at a cost of $570 each.
	25	Sold 500 diamonds for $850 each.

Instructions

(a) Assuming that the company uses the specific identification cost determination method, do the following:
   1. Show how Discount Diamonds could *maximize* its gross profit for the month by choosing which diamonds to sell on March 5 and March 25.
   2. Show how Discount Diamonds could *minimize* its gross profit for the month by choosing which diamonds to sell on March 5 and March 25.

(b) Assume that Discount Diamonds uses the average cost formula and a perpetual inventory system. How much gross profit would Discount Diamonds report under this cost formula?

(c) Who are the stakeholders in this situation? Is there anything unethical about using the specific identification cost determination and choosing which diamonds to sell?

(d) Should Discount Diamonds choose the average or specific identification method of inventory cost determination?

All About You: Personal Financial Literacy Activity

BYP6–4 In the "All About You" feature, you read about consignment shops and how they provide an alternative to paying full price for quality goods. As a student with a tight budget, you have decided to sell some of your books. You are considering two options: selling the books yourself or taking them to the second-hand bookstore that sells used books on consignment.

Instructions

(a) What is selling on consignment? If you sell your books on consignment, will you be the consignor or the consignee?

(b) What are the advantages and disadvantages of selling your books on consignment?

(c) It is suggested that there should be a written agreement between the consignor and consignee. If you decide to sell your books on consignment, what should be agreed to in writing?

(d) Assume you decide to sell your books on consignment through a second-hand bookstore. What are the risks to you of doing this?

ANSWERS TO CHAPTER QUESTIONS

ANSWERS TO ACCOUNTING IN ACTION INSIGHT QUESTIONS

All About You Insight, p. 260

Q: What is one disadvantage of buying items on consignment?

A: Consignment stores do not typically allow you to return goods, so you need to be very careful when purchasing items.

Business Insight, p. 274

Q: When a company such as Blockbuster is placed in receivership, what would be the impact on how to account for its inventory?

A: As with any company, Blockbuster needs to compare the cost of its inventory with its net realizable value. But when a company is being liquidated, typically its assets will be sold for less than they would have in the normal course of business. We would therefore expect that net realizable value of Blockbuster's inventory would be considerably less than cost and a larger writeoff would be recorded. In the following period when the inventory is sold, assuming the company accurately measured the net realizable value, no further losses will be recorded but the company also won't record any profit on the sales. Thus, companies that are being liquidated must always report that there is a going concern issue.

Remember to go back to the beginning of the chapter to check off your completed work! ←

ANSWERS TO SELF-STUDY QUESTIONS

1. a 2. d 3. d 4. b 5. c 6. a 7. c 8. b 9. b *10. d *11. c *12. b *13. a

CHAPTER 7 INTERNAL CONTROL AND CASH

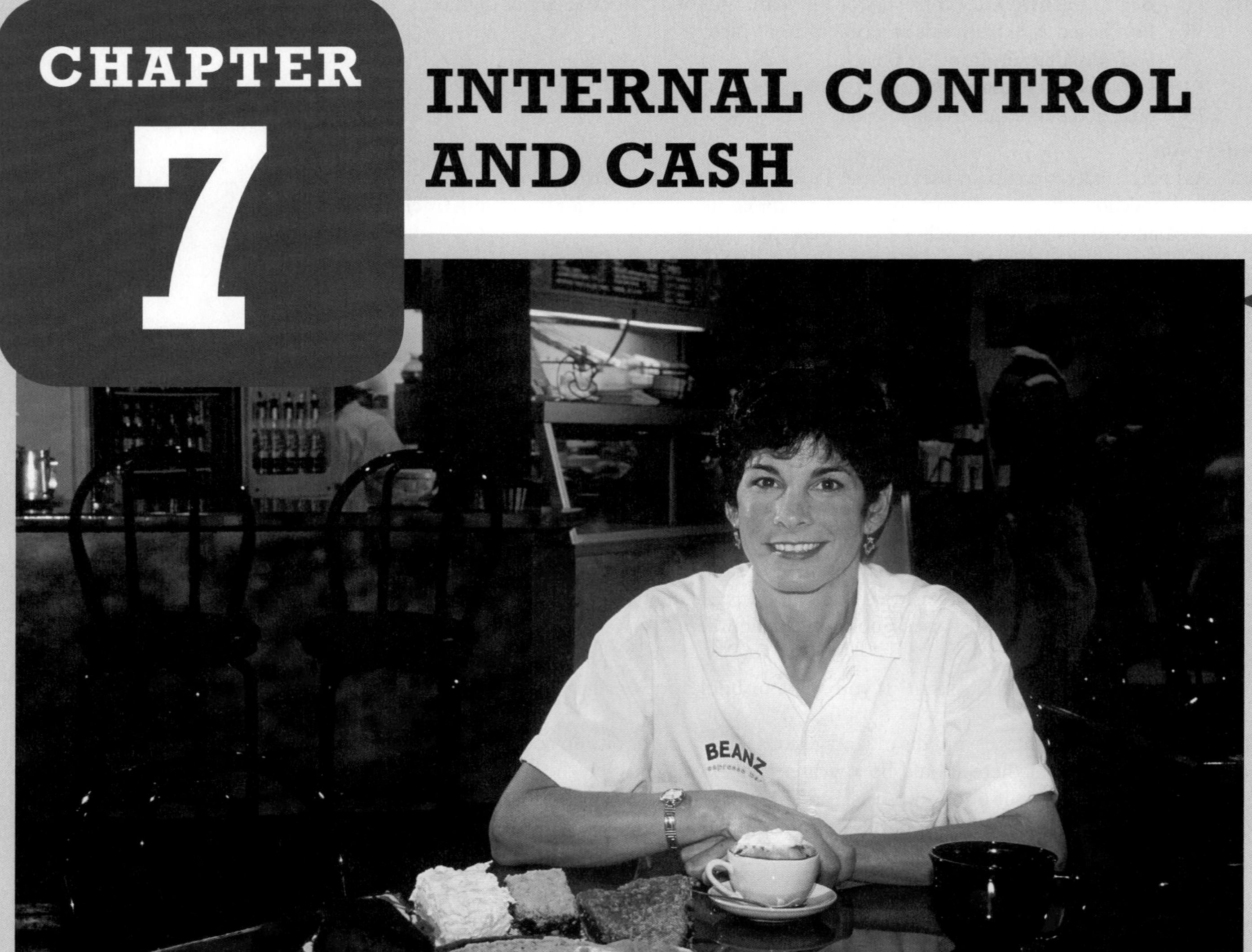

THE NAVIGATOR

- ☐ Understand *Concepts for Review*
- ☐ Read *Feature Story*
- ☐ Scan *Study Objectives*
- ☐ Read *Chapter Preview*
- ☐ Read text and answer *Before You Go On*
- ☐ Review *Comparing IFRS and ASPE*
- ☐ Work *Demonstration Problem*
- ☐ Review *Summary of Study Objectives*
- ☐ Answer *Self-Study Questions*
- ☐ Complete assignments

CONCEPTS FOR REVIEW

Before studying this chapter, you should understand or, if necessary, review:

A. The role of ethics in financial reporting. (Ch. 1, pp. 6–7)

B. How cash transactions are recorded. (Ch. 2, pp. 59–63)

C. How cash is classified on a balance sheet. (Ch. 4, pp. 157–158)

D. What internal control is. (Ch. 6, p. 258)

KEEPING TRACK OF THE CASH

CHARLOTTETOWN, PE—Located right in the heart of downtown Charlottetown, Beanz Espresso Bar is bustling with activity on weekdays. On average, 1,200 customers stop by each day for its selection of specialty coffees, homemade soups, sandwiches, and baked goods.

Lunch is the busiest time for Beanz. The two cash registers are shared by the six staff members working behind the counter on any given shift. "In an ideal situation, one or two people would be designated to ring in orders, but when we get swamped, we all have to work together to keep things running smoothly," says owner Lori Kays, who launched the business with her husband and business partner, Doug Hurry, back in 1995.

The prices of most items are preprogrammed in the machines, which reduces the chances of entry errors. Each register generates a sales report at the end of the day. Ms. Kays checks the day's cash receipts against the report to make sure they match. She also verifies the closing balances for the two floats—$250 for each till. "I tend to allow a few dollars' leeway since we round down amounts here and there when customers are short a few cents."

If the difference is larger, she goes through the register's internal tape to trace the source. "I will backtrack and try to make sure there weren't any payouts for which a receipt should have been turned in—we often make a run to the grocery store for something we need using cash from the till," she explains. For these small items, staff use the Paid Out button on the till and have a receipt/invoice to match the payout. She finds that this is the best way to keep track of these small purchases.

Ms. Kays deposits cash from sales in the bank at the end of the day. She does all of her bookkeeping herself using Simply Accounting software. "I post my sales totals each day and reconcile everything with my bank statements once a month," she says. "At the end of every year, I do everything except the last few adjusting entries before sending things off to the accountants." Careful cash control throughout the year helps ensure that everything adds up every time!

THE NAVIGATOR

STUDY OBJECTIVES

After studying this chapter, you should be able to:

1. Explain the activities that help prevent fraud and achieve internal control.
2. Apply control activities to cash receipts and cash payments.
3. Describe the control features of a bank account.
4. Report cash on the balance sheet.

THE NAVIGATOR

PREVIEW OF CHAPTER SEVEN

As the feature story about Beanz Espresso Bar shows, control of cash is important. Business owners and managers are responsible for safeguarding cash and other assets and for making sure that financial information is reliable. In this chapter, we explain the important features of an internal control system and describe how these controls apply to cash receipts and payments. Then we describe the use of a bank and explain how cash is reported on the balance sheet.

The chapter is organized as follows:

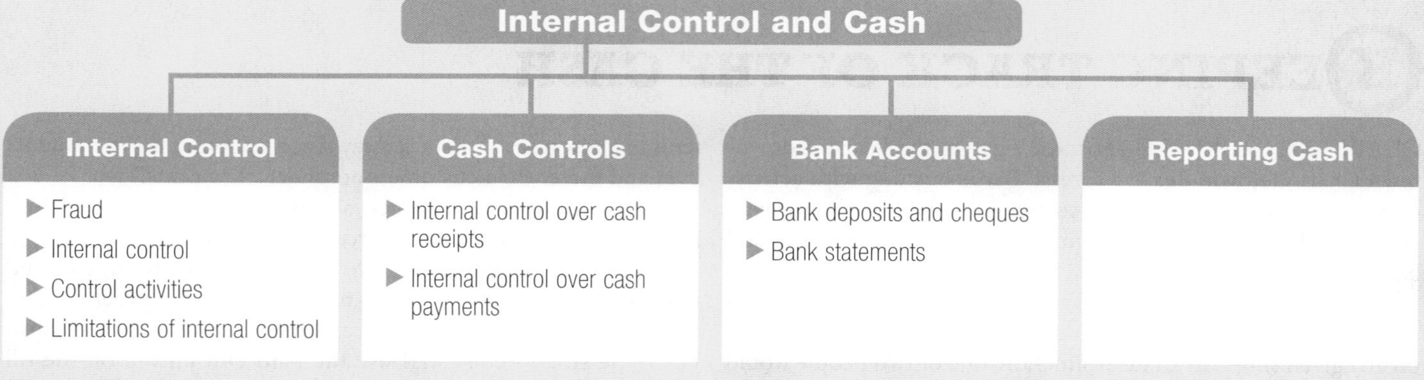

INTERNAL CONTROL

STUDY OBJECTIVE 1
Explain the activities that help prevent fraud and achieve internal control.

Could there be dishonest employees where you work? Unfortunately, the answer is sometimes "yes". In the following sections of this chapter, we will learn about fraud and internal controls that can be put in place to help prevent and detect it.

FRAUD

Fraud is an *intentional* dishonest act that results in personal financial benefit by misappropriating (stealing) assets or misstating financial statements. According to a recent study by KMPG, 80% of frauds in Canada involve people inside an organization. Examples of fraud include the following real occurrences in Canada:

- A trusted bookkeeper stole almost $1 million from 21 non-profit daycare centres.
- The controller of a manufacturing company paid himself $2 million more than his normal pay level by writing unauthorized cheques on the company's payroll account. He got rid of the cancelled cheques when they were returned from the bank and then he altered the books.
- An assistant bank manager stole more than $10 million from a Toronto bank by making loans to fictitious companies.
- A liquor store employee plead guilty to having pocketed $1.6 million. He was the sole order clerk for a program in which foreign diplomats could buy alcohol tax-free but payments had to be made by cash, cheque, or money order. The clerk either kept the cash or remitted only part of the proceeds to his employer.

Why does fraud occur in the workplace? The three main factors that contribute to fraudulent activity in the workplace are shown by the **fraud triangle** in Illustration 7-1.

ILLUSTRATION 7-1
Fraud triangle

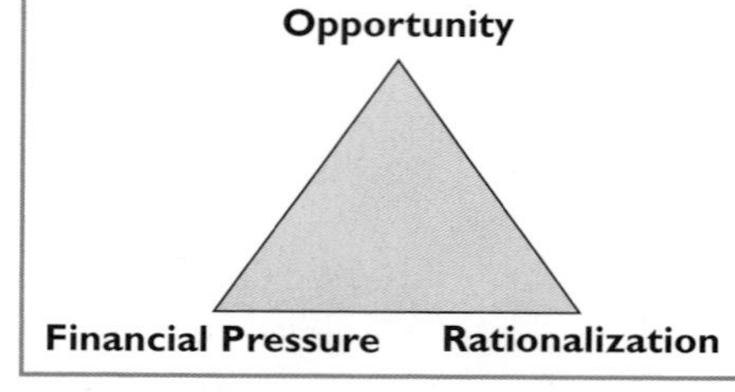

The most important element in the fraud triangle is *opportunity*. For an employee to commit fraud, there must be an opportunity to do so in the workplace. Opportunities occur when the workplace lacks sufficient controls to deter and detect fraud. For example, employees may be more likely to commit a fraud if they are not properly monitored and think they will not be caught.

A second factor that contributes to fraud is *financial pressure*. Employees sometimes commit fraud because of personal financial problems such as too much debt. Excessive lifestyles and drug or gambling addictions may also increase the likelihood that an employee will commit fraud.

The third factor that contributes to fraud is *rationalization*. In order to justify their fraud, employees rationalize their dishonest actions. For example, employees may believe they are underpaid and deserve to be paid more.

INTERNAL CONTROL

The risk of fraud, as well as the possibility of honest errors, emphasizes that a good system of internal control is necessary. **Internal control** consists of all of the related methods and measures that management designs and implements to help an organization achieve the following:

Helpful hint Errors are unintentional mistakes. Irregularities are intentional mistakes and misrepresentations.

1. reliable financial reporting
2. effective and efficient operations
3. compliance with relevant laws and regulations

Internal control has received increased attention in recent years. For example, the *Sarbanes-Oxley Act* governing publicly traded companies was created in the United States to help restore confidence in financial reporting. In Canada, similar legislation requires senior executives, such as CFOs and CEOs, of publicly traded companies to formally certify the effectiveness of their company's internal controls. Effective internal control systems have five basic components:

1. **Control environment:** It is the responsibility of top management to make it clear that the organization values integrity and that unethical behaviour will not be tolerated. Management must lead by example and set the "tone at the top" and expect everyone to stick to the rules. This may include creating a corporate code of conduct, supporting a rigorous internal control program, establishing a hotline for anonymous reporting, ensuring that "whistleblower" protection is put in place and followed, and consistently disciplining employees who break the rules.
2. **Risk assessment:** Companies must identify and analyze the various factors that create risk for the business and must determine how to manage these risks.
3. **Control activities:** To reduce the occurrence of fraud and honest errors, management must design policies and procedures to address the specific risks faced by the company.
4. **Information and communication:** The internal control system must identify, collect, and communicate all relevant information to the appropriate internal and external parties.
5. **Monitoring:** Monitoring involves identifying problems and reporting them to appropriate levels of the organization where action can be taken. To be effective, problems must be communicated to the people who have the authority to act on the information, such as top management or the board of directors.

CONTROL ACTIVITIES

While each component of an internal control system is important, we will focus here on one: control activities. Control activities that apply to most companies include:

- establishment of responsibility
- segregation of duties
- documentation procedures
- physical and IT controls
- independent checks of performance
- human resource controls

Each of these control activities is explained in the following sections.

Establishment of Responsibility

An essential characteristic of internal control is assigning specific responsibilities to specific individuals. **Control and accountability are most effective when only one person is responsible for a task.**

To illustrate, assume that the cash in the cash register at the end of the day at Beanz Espresso Bar in the feature story is $50 less than it should be according to the cash register tape. If only one person at the restaurant has operated the register, that person is probably responsible for the shortage. If two or more individuals have worked the register, however, as happens at Beanz Espresso Bar when the restaurant is busy, it may be impossible to determine who is responsible for the error.

Establishing responsibility is easier when there is a system for proper authorization of an activity. For example, computerized systems often require a passcode that keeps track of who rang up a sale, or who made a journal entry, or who entered an inventory stockroom at a particular time. Using identifying passcodes enables the company to establish responsibility by identifying the particular employee who carried out the activity.

Responsibility for authorizing and approving transactions must also be given to the correct person. For example, the vice-president of finance, not the vice-president of sales—who may be motivated to maximize sales commissions—should establish policies for making credit sales.

Segregation of Duties

Segregation (separation) of duties is essential in a system of internal control. Duties should be divided up so that one person cannot both commit a fraud and cover it up. There are two common ways of applying this control activity:

1. Different individuals should be responsible for related activities.
2. The responsibility for accounting or record keeping for an asset should be separate from the responsibility for physical custody of (direct contact with) that asset.

Related Activities.

When one person is responsible for all related activities, the potential for errors and irregularities increases. For example, companies should assign related purchasing activities to different individuals. Related purchasing activities include ordering merchandise, approving orders, receiving goods, authorizing payment, and paying for the goods or service. Various frauds are possible when one person handles related purchasing activities. For example:

- If the same person is responsible for ordering and for receiving, he can arrange to have an order sent to his home and pretend the goods were received by the company.
- If the same person is responsible for ordering and paying for the merchandise, she can place orders with friends or with suppliers who give kickbacks (a bribe that is paid by a supplier to an employee of the purchaser to ensure that they get the order).
- If a purchasing agent is allowed to order goods without obtaining supervisory approval, the likelihood of the purchasing agent getting kickbacks from suppliers increases.

These abuses are less likely to occur when purchasing tasks are divided.

Similarly, related sales activities should be done by different individuals. Related selling activities include making a sale, shipping (or delivering) the goods to the customer, billing the customer, and receiving payment. Various frauds are possible when one person handles related sales transactions, as the following examples show.

- If a salesperson can make a sale without obtaining supervisory approval, he or she can make sales at unauthorized prices to increase sales commissions.
- A billing clerk who handles billing and receipt could understate the amount that is billed in sales to friends and relatives.
- A shipping clerk who has access to the accounting records could ship goods to himself.

These abuses are less likely to occur when companies divide the sales tasks: salespersons make the sale, shipping department employees ship the goods based on the sales order, and billing department employees prepare the sales invoice after comparing the sales order with the report of goods shipped.

Segregation of selling duties in a small business can be difficult, because there are fewer people. In these situations, the owner must be more involved and adopt more of a "hands-on" role to reduce the risk of fraud.

Custody of Assets.

If the same person has physical custody of an asset and keeps the accounting records for that asset, then errors or theft could be hidden by altering the accounting records. When the employee who keeps the records of an asset is a different person from the employee who keeps the asset itself (the custodian), the employee who keeps the asset is unlikely to use it dishonestly. The separation of accounting responsibility from the custody of assets is especially important for cash and inventories because these assets are vulnerable to unauthorized use or theft.

Documentation Procedures

Documents provide evidence that transactions and events have occurred. At Beanz Espresso Bar, the cash register sales report is the restaurant's documentation for a sale and the amount of cash received. Similarly, a shipping document indicates that goods have been shipped, and a sales invoice indicates that the customer has been billed for the goods. By adding signatures (or initials) to a document, it also becomes possible to identify the individual(s) responsible for the transaction or event.

Control procedures should be established for documents. First, whenever possible, documents should be prenumbered and all documents should be accounted for. Prenumbering helps to prevent a transaction from being recorded more than once, or not at all. Second, source documents (such as original receipts) for accounting entries should be promptly sent to the accounting department to ensure that the transaction be recorded in a timely way. This control helps make the accounting records accurate and reliable.

Documentation as a control procedure also includes ensuring that all controls are written down and kept up to date. Well-maintained documentation procedures ensure that the control activities are not forgotten and can make it easier to train new employees.

Physical and IT Controls

Physical and information technology (IT) controls include mechanical and electronic controls to safeguard (protect) assets and improve the accuracy and reliability of the accounting records. Examples of these controls are shown in Illustration 7-2.

ILLUSTRATION 7-2
Physical and IT controls

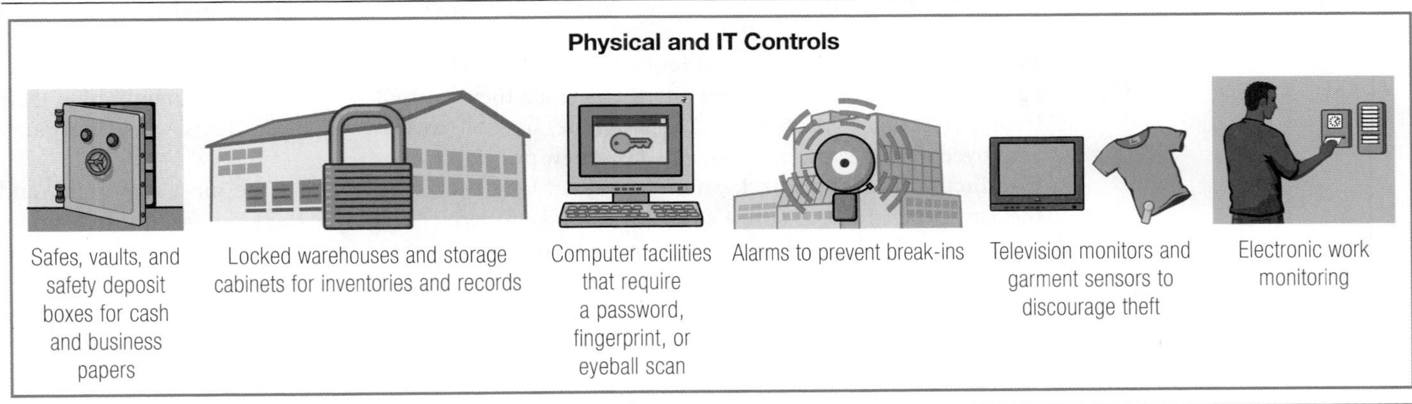
Physical and IT Controls
Safes, vaults, and safety deposit boxes for cash and business papers
Locked warehouses and storage cabinets for inventories and records
Computer facilities that require a password, fingerprint, or eyeball scan
Alarms to prevent break-ins
Television monitors and garment sensors to discourage theft
Electronic work monitoring

Independent Checks of Performance

Most internal control systems include independent internal and/or external reviews of performance and records. This means having an independent person verify that the company's control activities are being correctly followed. To get the most from a performance review:

1. The review should be done periodically or by surprise.
2. The review should be done by someone who is independent of the employee who is responsible for the information.
3. Discrepancies and exceptions should be reported to a management level that can do whatever is necessary to correct the situation.

Internal Review.

Segregating the physical custody of assets from accounting record keeping is not enough to ensure that nothing has been stolen. An independent review still needs to be done. In such a review, the accounting records are compared with existing assets or with external sources of information. The reconciliation of the cash register sales report with the cash in the register by Beanz Espresso Bar owner Lori Kays in the feature story is an example of comparing records with assets. When the person who does the review is the owner or an employee of the organization, we call this an internal review.

Helpful hint Segregating the physical custody of assets from the record-keeping function won't necessarily prevent theft, but it can discourage theft and make it easier to uncover by preventing a dishonest employee from altering the records to "cover up" any theft.

In large companies, control activities, including independent internal reviews, are often monitored by internal auditors. **Internal auditors** are company employees who evaluate the effectiveness of the company's system of internal control. They periodically review the activities of departments and individuals to determine whether the correct control activities are being followed.

In a publicly traded company, a management report addressed to the shareholders is included in the annual report that explains that management is responsible for the system of internal controls. Additionally, the chief executive officer (CEO) and chief financial officer (CFO) must certify that they have evaluated the effectiveness of the company's internal controls over financial reporting.

External Review.

It is useful to contrast independent *internal* reviews with independent *external* reviews. **External auditors** are independent of the company. They are professional accountants hired by a company to report on whether or not the company's financial statements fairly present the company's financial position and results of operations.

All public companies, including Reitmans (Canada) Limited, are required to have an external audit. External auditors plan and perform an audit that will allow them to be reasonably sure that the financial statements do not contain any significant errors.

Human Resource Controls

Human resource control measures include the following:

1. **Bonding of employees who handle cash. Bonding** involves getting insurance protection against the theft of assets by dishonest employees. This measure also helps safeguard cash in two ways: First, the insurance company carefully screens all individuals before adding them to the policy and it may reject risky applicants. Second, bonded employees know that the insurance company will prosecute all offenders.
2. **Rotating employees' duties and requiring employees to take vacations.** These measures discourage employees from attempting any thefts since they will not be able to permanently hide their improper actions. Many banks, for example, have discovered employee thefts when the guilty employee was on vacation or assigned to a new position.
3. **Conducting thorough background checks.** Many people believe that the most important, and the least expensive, measure a company can take to reduce employee theft and fraud is to conduct thorough background checks as part of the hiring process.

LIMITATIONS OF INTERNAL CONTROL

No matter how well it is designed and operated, a company's system of internal control can only give reasonable assurance that assets are properly safeguarded and that accounting records are reliable. The concept of reasonable assurance is based on the belief that the cost of control activities should not be more than their expected benefit.

To illustrate, consider shoplifting losses in retail stores. Such losses could be eliminated by having a security guard stop and search customers as they leave the store. Store managers have concluded, however, that the negative effects of doing this cannot be justified. Instead, stores have tried to control shoplifting losses by using less costly and intrusive procedures such as posting signs that state "We reserve the right to inspect all packages" and "All shoplifters will be prosecuted," using hidden TV cameras and store detectives to watch customer activity, and using sensor equipment at exits.

The human factor is an important limit in every system of internal control. A good system can become ineffective as a result of employee fatigue, carelessness, indifference, or lack of proper training. For example, a receiving clerk may not bother to count goods received, or may alter or "fudge" the counts. Occasionally, two or more individuals may work together to get around controls, which eliminates the protection offered by segregating duties. This is often referred to as **collusion**.

The size of the business may also limit internal control. As mentioned earlier, in small companies employees often "do a little bit of everything," which might make it difficult to segregate duties or have independent checks of performance.

ACCOUNTING IN ACTION
ALL ABOUT YOU INSIGHT

Protect your identity. Personal information, such as your name, date of birth, address, credit card number, and social insurance number (SIN), can be used to steal money from your bank account, make purchases, or even get a job. Are you a victim?

According to a report by the Canadian Anti-Fraud Centre (a joint forces operation of the RCMP, Competition Bureau of Canada, and the Ontario Provincial Police), there were more than 17,000 reported cases of identity fraud in 2011. These victims reported total dollar losses of over $13.2 million. However, it's estimated that far more identity theft occurs than what is reported to police. A 2008 survey of Canadian consumers, conducted by the McMaster eBusiness Research Centre, found that almost 1.7 million Canadian adults had been the victim of some kind of identity fraud in the past year. The victims spent over 20 million hours and more than $150 million to resolve the problems associated with the frauds. More than half of these frauds involved the unauthorized use of credit cards. A key piece of information that identity thieves use to obtain personal data, to receive government benefits and tax refunds, or to get a job, is a person's SIN. To help protect Canadians, the federal government planned by March 2014 to stop issuing SIN cards, instead assigning the numbers via personal letters.

Source: Canadian Anti-Fraud Centre, "Annual Statistical Report 2011: Mass Marketing Fraud & ID Theft Activities"; Carys Mills, "Why Your SIN's Future Is No Longer in the Cards," *The Globe and Mail,* May 15, 2012; Susan Sproule and Norm Archer, "Measuring Identity Theft in Canada: 2008 Consumer Survey," Working Paper 23, McMaster eBusiness Research Centre.

Who is responsible for losses due to unauthorized credit card use?

BEFORE YOU GO ON...

DO IT

In each of the following situations, identify the appropriate control activity and state whether it has been supported or violated.

(a) The purchasing department orders, receives, and pays for merchandise.
(b) All cheques are prenumbered and accounted for.
(c) The internal auditor performs surprise cash account checks.
(d) Extra cash is kept locked in a safe that can only be accessed by the head cashier.
(e) Each cashier has his or her own cash drawer.
(f) The company's controller received a plaque for distinguished service because he had not taken a vacation in five years.

SOLUTION

(a) Violation of segregation of duties
(b) Support of documentation procedures
(c) Support of independent checks of performance
(d) Support of physical and IT controls
(e) Support of establishment of responsibility
(f) Violation of human resource controls (employees should take vacations)

Related exercise material: BE7–1, E7–1, and E7–2.

Action Plan

- Understand each of the control activities: establishment of responsibility, segregation of duties, documentation procedures, physical and IT controls, independent checks of performance, and human resource controls.

THE NAVIGATOR

CASH CONTROLS

STUDY OBJECTIVE 2

Apply control activities to cash receipts and cash payments.

Cash is the one asset that is readily convertible into any other type of asset. It is also easily concealed and transported, lacks owner identification, and is highly desirable. In addition, because of the large volume of cash transactions, errors may easily happen when handling and recording cash. To safeguard cash and ensure the accuracy of the accounting records, effective internal control over cash is essential.

INTERNAL CONTROL OVER CASH RECEIPTS

Cash receipts come from a variety of sources: cash sales; collections on account from customers; the receipt of interest, dividends, and rents; investments by owners; bank loans; and proceeds from the sale of property, plant, and equipment. Generally, internal control over cash receipts is more effective when all cash receipts are deposited intact in the bank account every day. Illustration 7-3 shows examples of how the control activities explained earlier apply to cash receipt transactions.

ILLUSTRATION 7-3
Application of control activities to cash receipts

Control Activities over Cash Receipts

Establishment of Responsibility

Only designated personnel (cashiers) are authorized to handle cash receipts.

Physical and IT Controls

Store cash in safes and bank vaults; limit access to storage areas; use cash registers; deposit all cash in the business bank account daily.

Segregation of Duties

Different individuals receive cash, record cash receipts, and handle cash.

Independent Checks of Performance

Supervisors count cash receipts daily; controller's office compares total receipts with bank deposits daily to ensure that the amounts are equal.

Documentation Procedures

Use remittance advices (mail receipts), cash register tapes, and deposit slips.

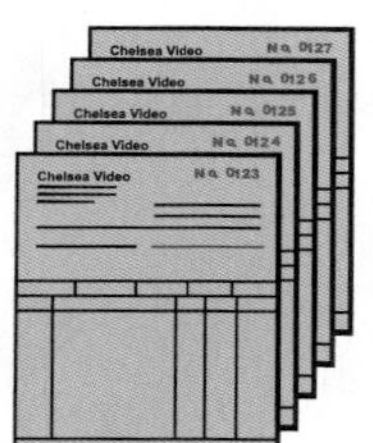

Human Resource Controls

Bond personnel who handle cash; require employees to take vacations; conduct background checks on potential hires.

As might be expected, companies vary considerably in how they apply these principles. To illustrate internal control over cash receipts, we will discuss useful control activities for a retail store with over-the-counter, mail-in, and electronic receipts.

Over-the-Counter Receipts

Control of over-the-counter receipts in retail businesses is centred on cash registers that customers can see. All sales must be entered into the cash register through point-of-sale software that records the sale and updates the inventory records. Scanning bar codes on merchandise reduces the possibility of errors and fraud.

Receipts from cash sales—paid by coins and paper currency—are becoming rarer. Most customers pay by debit or bank credit card. Although banks charge retailers when these cards are used, there are many advantages for retailers that accept these forms of payment. As they are convenient for customers, the business may get more sales. They also improve internal control because employees handle less cash. The point-of-sale cash software separates daily sales according to each type of payment: cash, debit card, credit card, or cheque.

At the end of his or her shift, the cashier should count the cash in the register, record the amount, and turn over the cash and the record of the amount to either a supervisor or the person responsible for making the bank deposit. The procedures will be different in every company, but the basic principles should be the same. The person or persons who handle the cash and make the bank deposit should not be able to make changes to the sales recorded in the point-of-sale system or the accounting records. Employees must also make sure there are receipts on hand for debit or credit card sales and that these match the amounts recorded for each type of payment.

Companies with recurring cash transactions may use a special journal, called a **cash receipts journal**, to record all their receipts of cash. A **special journal** is used to record similar types of transactions. The types of special journals that are used depend largely on the types of transactions that happen frequently.

Debit Card Transactions.

Sales using debit cards are considered cash transactions. Debit cards allow customers to spend only what is in their bank account. When a debit card sale occurs, the bank immediately deducts the cost of the purchase from the customer's bank account. The retailer has a choice about how often the proceeds from debit card transactions are electronically transferred into the retailer's bank account. Some retailers ask the bank to make one deposit at the end of each business day; other retailers wait and have several days of transactions deposited together. Banks usually charge the retailer a transaction fee for each debit card transaction and deduct this fee from the amount deposited in the retailer's bank account.

In many ways, accepting a debit card payment is similar to accepting a personal cheque from a customer. Both are ways for customers to spend the money in their bank accounts. But the major advantage of debit cards is that the retailer knows immediately if the customer has enough money in the bank to pay for the purchase. When a cheque is accepted, it takes several days for the retailer to find out whether the customer had sufficient funds. Most businesses are willing to pay a fee to the bank when customers use debit cards because there is no uncertainty about whether the customer has enough money in their bank account to pay for the purchase.

To illustrate, suppose that on March 21, 10 customers use debit cards to purchase merchandise totalling $800 from Lee Company. Assuming the bank charges Lee Company $0.50 per debit card transaction, the entry made to record these transactions by Lee Company is as follows:

Mar. 21	Debit Card Expense (10 × $0.50)	5	
	Cash ($800 − $5)	795	
	Sales		800
	To record debit card sales.		

A	=	L	+	OE
+795				−5
				+800

↑ Cash flows: +795

In addition to the service charge for each transaction, Lee Company will also pay a monthly rental charge for the point-of-sale equipment that it uses for debit and credit card transactions.

Helpful hint Occasionally you might see a sign at a checkout counter that states that debit cards will only be accepted for payment for transactions that are above a certain minimum amount (for example, $5). Some retailers (especially smaller ones) adopt this policy because the transaction fees they pay on very small sales could cost more than the gross profit that they are making on the sale.

Bank Credit Card Transactions.

Sales using credit cards issued by banks, such as Visa and MasterCard, are considered cash sales by the retailer. A credit card gives customers access to money made available by a bank or other financial institution (essentially a short-term loan that has to be repaid). When a customer uses a bank credit card, the bank transfers the amount of the sale to the retailer's bank, less a service fee.

The rates charged by credit card companies to retailers vary greatly depending on such factors as the type of card used, the method of processing the transaction, as well as the volume of transactions. Retailers with a high number of transactions usually get a lower rate; those with a small number of transactions often pay a higher rate. Similar to debit card transactions, the retailer's bank will wait until the end of the day and make one deposit for the full day's credit card transactions to the retailer's bank account; there is also the option of having one deposit every few days.

The fees for bank credit cards are generally higher than debit card fees. Why? With a debit card, the bank is charging only for transferring the customer's money to the retailer. With a credit card, the bank is taking the risk that the customer may never repay it for the loan. As we will see in Chapter 8, sometimes companies are not able to collect their receivables. Bank credit cards help retailers avoid this problem. Except for the higher bank charges, recording a bank credit card sale is very similar to recording a debit card sale.

Helpful hint Note that while banks generally charge a flat fee for each debit card transaction, the fee that they charge on credit card transactions is a percentage of the amount of the sale.

To illustrate, suppose that on March 21, Lee Company sells $800 of merchandise to customers who use bank credit cards. The banks charge Lee Company a service fee of 3.5% for credit card sales. The entry made to record these transactions by Lee Company is:

Mar. 21	Credit Card Expense ($800 × 3.5%)	28	
	Cash ($800 − $28)	772	
	Sales		800
	To record bank credit card sales.		

A	=	L	+	OE
+772				−28
				+800

↑ Cash flows: +772

In addition to accepting bank credit cards, many large department stores and gasoline companies have their own credit cards. Sales using the retailer's own credit cards are credit sales; they result in accounts receivable, not cash, at the point of sale.

Mail-In Receipts

Helpful hint When billing customers, many companies state "Pay by cheque; do not send cash through the mail." This is done to reduce the risk of cash receipts being misappropriated when they are received.

Although the use of cheques has decreased, many companies still receive payment from their customers via cheques. For high-value purchases in particular, this reduces the service charges paid by the business as compared with credit card sales.

When a cheque is received in the mail, it is usually accompanied by a remittance slip showing the details of payment. All mail-in receipts should be opened in the presence of two mail clerks and the remittance slip compared with the cheque. The remittance slips are sent to the accounting department for recording and the cheques are stamped for deposit only and sent to the person responsible for making the bank deposits. Persons handling the cheques must not be able to alter the accounting records. An independent person should compare the deposit recorded by the bank with the amount recorded in the accounting records. In a small company, where it is not possible to have the necessary segregation of duties, the owner should be responsible for cash receipts.

Electronic Receipts

Electronic funds transfer (EFT) is the electronic exchange or transfer of money from one account to another, either within a single financial institution or across multiple institutions, through computer-based systems. Examples of transactions covered by the term "EFT" include:

- debit and credit card transactions
- pre-authorized debits
- electronic bill payments using on-line banking
- bank machine withdrawals
- prepaid smart cards

EFT transactions have grown dramatically while cheques and cash transactions have decreased. There has also been a rapid growth in the different types of EFTs. Some EFTs are initiated by the customer, such as on-line electronic bill payments. Others are initiated by the company, such as pre-authorized debits. Electronic funds transfers normally result in better internal control since no cash or cheques are handled by company employees. But it is still important to have proper authorization and segregation of duties to ensure an employee cannot divert a customer payment to a personal bank account and then cover it up through fraudulent accounting entries.

ACCOUNTING IN ACTION
BUSINESS INSIGHT

Will that be cash, cheque, or smart phone? Canada recently launched widescale mobile payment—the ability to swipe a mobile phone to pay for everything from a cup of coffee to bus fare. Mobile payment was expected to be a boon to consumers and businesses alike, as it offers unparalleled convenience, especially for purchases of low dollar value. A federal government task force on payment systems estimated that businesses could reduce invoicing costs by up to 80%. Mobile payments also cut down on transaction processing time and reduce cash handling costs.

But many Canadians were sceptical of the technology. One survey found that 4 in 10 Canadians considering using their smart phone to make payments were most concerned about security, and one in three said they would never use the technology. In another survey, roughly 8 in 10 Canadian businesses thought that consumers would worry that hackers could steal their financial or other personal information from their smart phone. The government task force says the reality is quite different, because mobile payments are safer and more secure than the existing payment system.

Sources: Scott Simpson, "Canada Needs Quicker Shift to Mobile Payments, Task Force Says," *Financial Post*, March 27, 2012; Brian Jackson, "Canadians Cautious About Mobile Payment Security," ITBusiness, October 6, 2011; KPMG, "Mobile Payments: Is Canada Ready? Insights from our Global Survey on Mobile Payments," October 2011; "Rogers to Deliver First Mobile Wallet from Canadian Carrier," Rogers Communications news release, November 7, 2013.

How might an organization's marketing department assist in, and benefit from, the implementation of a mobile payments system?

INTERNAL CONTROL OVER CASH PAYMENTS

Cash is disbursed (paid out) for a variety of reasons, such as to pay expenses and liabilities, or to purchase assets. Generally, internal control over cash payments is better when payments are made by cheque or EFT, rather than in cash. Payment by cheque should occur only after specified control procedures have been followed. The paid cheque gives proof of payment. Illustration 7-4 shows examples of how the control activities explained earlier apply to cash payments.

ILLUSTRATION 7-4
Application of control activities over cash payments

Control Activities over Cash Payments

Establishment of Responsibility

Only designated personnel are authorized to sign cheques or approve electronic payments.

Physical and IT Controls

Store cash in safes, limit access to blank cheques and signing machines, and use electronic payments when possible.

Segregation of Duties

Different individuals approve and make payments; cheque signers do not record disbursements in the journal and ledger.

Independent Checks of Performance

Compare cheques with invoices; reconcile bank statement monthly.

Documentation Procedures

Use prenumbered cheques and account for them in sequence; each cheque must have an approved invoice.

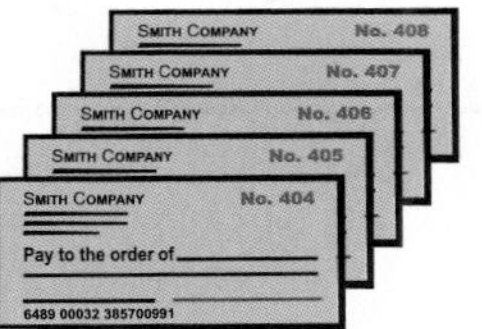

Human Resources

Bond personnel who handle cash, require employees to take vacations, and conduct background checks as part of the hiring process.

Cheques

Good control over cheques includes having them signed by at least two authorized people. The cheque signers should carefully review the supporting documentation for the payment before signing the cheque. There should be a clear segregation of duties between the cheque-signing function and the accounts payable function. Cheques should be prenumbered, and all cheque numbers must be accounted for in the payment and recording process. Cheques should never be pre-signed, and blank (unissued) cheques should be physically controlled.

Many large companies use *purchase orders* to improve their internal control over cash payments. A purchase order documents the details of the purchase and the fact that the purchase has been approved. The purchase order is usually prepared by the purchasing department.

When the good or service is received, the *receiving report* is matched with the purchase order. When the seller's invoice is later received, it is matched to the purchase order and receiving report. An authorized person in the accounts payable department then approves the invoice for payment. A cheque is sent on the due date, and the invoice is stamped "Paid."

The accounting department records the payment of the invoice. Companies that have a lot of cash payments often use a special journal, called a **cash payments journal**, to record all payments of cash.

Electronic Payments

Just as a company may use electronic funds transfer systems to *receive* cash, it can also use those systems to *make payments* to suppliers and employees. For example, when a company pays its employees' salaries using a direct deposit option, the cash is instantly transferred from the company's bank account to each employee's bank account. Electronic pre-authorized payments are often made for things paid on a recurring basis like insurance or loans and interest.

The use of EFT for cash payments will result in better internal control as long as there is proper authorization and segregation of duties. EFT payments also reduce the extra costs of making payments by cheque, such as postage and envelope costs.

Petty Cash Fund

While making payments by EFT and cheques results in better internal control than using cash, it can be both impractical and a nuisance to use cheques or EFT to pay for small amounts. For example, a company may not want to write cheques to pay for postage, couriers, or small purchases of supplies. Beanz in our feature story uses the "Paid Out" button on its cash register to track small cash payments.

Another common way to handle such payments, while maintaining satisfactory control, is to use a **petty cash fund**. Although businesses generally try to keep cash on hand to a minimum to improve their internal control, it is impractical for most businesses to have no cash available. Many businesses establish a Petty Cash Fund for small purchases that might arise. Note that all payments from a petty cash fund must still be authorized and accounted for, no matter how small the dollar amount.

BEFORE YOU GO ON...

DO IT

Prepare journal entries to record the following selected debit and credit card transactions for Bulk Department Store:

July	18	A customer used her debit card to pay for a $650 purchase. Bulk Department Store was charged a $2 service fee.
	22	A customer paid for a $1,200 purchase with her Visa credit card. The bank charges Bulk Department Store a service fee of 3.0%.
	25	A customer paid for a $500 purchase with his Bulk Department Store credit card.

Action Plan

- Debit cards are recorded as cash sales, less the service charge.
- Bank credit cards are recorded as cash sales, less the service charge.
- Nonbank credit cards are recorded as receivables. There is no bank service charge when a customer uses a company credit card.

SOLUTION

July	18	Debit Card Expense	2	
		Cash ($650 − $2)	648	
		Sales		650
		To record debit card sale.		
	22	Credit Card Expense ($1,200 × 3.0%)	36	
		Cash ($1,200 − $36)	1,164	
		Sales		1,200
		To record Visa credit card sale.		
	25	Accounts Receivable	500	
		Sales		500
		To record company credit card sale.		

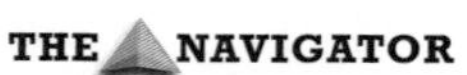

Related exercise material: BE7–2, BE7–3, BE7–4, BE7–5, E7–3, E7-4, and E7–5.

BANK ACCOUNTS

STUDY OBJECTIVE 3

Describe the control features of a bank account.

In the following section, we will learn about the control features of a bank account.

Using a bank makes internal control over cash much stronger. A company can safeguard its cash by using a bank as a depository and reduce the amount of currency that must be kept on hand. In addition, using a bank increases internal control, because it creates a double record of all bank transactions—one by the business and the other by the bank. The asset account Cash, maintained by the company, should have the same balance as the bank's liability account for that company. A **bank reconciliation** compares the bank's balance with the company's balance and explains any differences.

Many companies have more than one bank account. For efficiency of operations and better control, national retailers like Sears may have local bank accounts. Similarly, a company may have a payroll bank account, as well as one or more general bank accounts. A company may also have accounts with different banks in order to have more than one source for short-term loans when needed.

BANK DEPOSITS AND CHEQUES

Bank deposits should be made by an authorized employee, such as the head cashier. Each deposit must be documented by a deposit slip, as shown in Illustration 7-5. Both the company and the bank will need a copy of the deposit slip.

ILLUSTRATION 7-5
Deposit slip (reproduced with permission of BMO Bank of Montreal)

BMO Bank of Montreal

PRESS FIRMLY FOR CLEAR COPIES

BR. TR.	DATE (DAY / MONTH / YEAR)
0 123	april 15,2014

ACCOUNT NUMBER: 1 0 5 0 – 8 0 0

ACCOUNT NAME: Lee Company

Do Not List US$ and CDN$ cheques on same deposit slip

	CHEQUE PARTICULARS	AMOUNT
1.	74-331/724	175.40
2.	19-401/710	425.60
3.	22-815/666	155.56
4.		
5.		
6.		
7.		
8.		
9.		
10.		
11.		
12.		
13.		
14.		
15.		
# OF CHEQUES	TOTAL CHEQUES DEPOSITED $	756.56

Prod. 1045171 - Form. 638 BK (10/02)

MIX Paper from responsible sources FSC FSC® C004212

DEPOSIT SLIP — DEPOSITED BY: S. Gunn

BR. TR.	DATE (DAY / MONTH / YEAR)
0 123	april 15,2014

ACCOUNT NUMBER: 1 0 5 0 – 8 0 0

ACCOUNT NAME: Lee Company

CASH COUNT		
20 X 5	=	100.00
5 X 10	=	50.00
7 X 20	=	140.00
2 X 50	=	100.00
X 100	=	
X	=	
US $ RATE:	=	
TOTAL CASH (NOTES) DEPOSITED	$	390.00
COIN		
50 X $1 coin	=	50.00
X $2 coin	=	
X	=	
X	=	22.00
Loose Coin	=	
TOTAL COIN DEPOSITED	$	72.00
MASTERCARD	$	
# OF CHEQUES — TOTAL CHEQUES DEPOSITED	$	
TOTAL CHEQUES/MASTERCARD DEPOSITED	$	756.56
TOTAL CASH/COIN/CHEQUES DEPOSITED	$	1218.56

While bank deposits increase the bank account balance, cheques decrease it. A cheque is a written order instructing the bank to pay a specific sum of money to a designated recipient. There are three parties to a cheque: (1) the maker (or drawer) who issues the cheque, (2) the bank (or payer) on which the cheque is drawn, and (3) the payee to whom the cheque is payable. A cheque is a negotiable instrument that can be transferred to another party by endorsement.

Each cheque should clearly explain its purpose. The purpose of a cheque can be detailed on the cheque stub, as shown in Illustration 7-6. The purpose of the cheque should also be clear for the payee, either by referencing the invoice directly on the cheque—see the reference to invoice #27622 on the "For" line of the cheque in the illustration—or by attaching a copy of the invoice to the cheque.

ILLUSTRATION 7-6
Cheque (reproduced with permission of BMO Bank of Montreal)

0442
07042014
BALANCE FORWARD 12867 19
TO Watkins Wholesale Supply
RE: Invoice #27662
GST 315 65 2420
GST 105134688
DEPOSITS
DEPOSITS
BALANCE 10447 19

Lee Company
500 Queen Street
Fredericton, NB E3B 5C2
0442
07042014
PAY TO THE ORDER OF Watkins Wholesale Supply $2420.00
Two Thousand Four hundred Twenty XX/100 DOLLARS
FOR Invoice #27662
BMO Bank of Montreal
FREDERICTON MAIN OFFICE
505 KING STREET
FREDERICTON, N. B. E3B 1E7
PER M.S. Lee
PER W.F. Praine
⑈000044⑈ ⑆01234⑉001⑆ 1050⑉800⑈

Automated teller machine cash withdrawals are not allowed on a business bank account where two signatures are required on cheques. There is no way of knowing if both of the authorized individuals are present when the withdrawal is made. The same principle applies to EFT payments on business bank accounts. When two signatures are required, the only way to maintain internal control is to make all payments by cheque or pre-authorized EFT.

How does cash actually flow through the banking system? When cheques, debit cards, and pre-authorized or other payments occur, they may result in one financial institution owing money to another. For example, if a company (the maker) writes a cheque to a supplier (the payee), the payee deposits the cheque in its own bank account.

When the cheque is deposited, it is sent to a regional data centre for processing, usually the same day. When the cheque arrives at the regional data centre, it is "presented" to the payee's financial institution, where it is determined whether the cheque will be honoured or returned (for example, if there are insufficient funds in the account to cover the amount of the cheque, or if a stop payment order has been placed on the cheque by the maker, which stops the money from being paid by the cheque). This process is automated and happens very quickly. In most cases, the cheque will clear the maker's bank account before the next day. **Clearing** is the term used when a cheque or deposit is accepted by the maker's bank. It results in a transfer of funds from the maker's bank to the payee's bank.

BANK STATEMENTS

Each month, the bank sends the company a **bank statement** that shows the company's bank transactions and balance. A typical statement is presented in Illustration 7-7. It shows (1) cheques paid and other debits that reduce the balance in the bank account, (2) deposits and other credits that increase the balance in the bank account, and (3) the account balance after each day's transactions.

Helpful hint Every deposit received by the bank is credited to the customer's account. The reverse happens when the bank "pays" a cheque issued by a company on the company's chequing account balance. Because payment reduces the bank's liability, the amount is debited to the customer's account with the bank.

At first glance, it may appear that the debits and credits reported on the bank statement are backward. How can amounts that decrease the balance, like a cheque, be a debit? And how can amounts that increase the balance, like a deposit, be a credit? Debits and credits are not really backward. To the company, Cash is an asset account. Assets are increased by debits (such as for cash receipts) and decreased by credits (such as for cash payments). To the bank, on the other hand, the bank account is a *liability* account—an amount it must repay to you upon request. Liabilities are increased by credits and decreased by debits. When you deposit money in your bank account, the bank's liability to you increases. That is why the bank shows deposits as credits. When you write a cheque on your account, the bank pays out this amount and decreases (debits) its liability to you.

Note that cheque #442 for $2,420 shown in Illustration 7-6 is the bank statement's April 8 transaction. Although the cheque was written on April 7, it did not clear the bank until April 8. You can also find the deposit slip for $1,218.56 shown in Illustration 7-5 on the bank statement's April 15 transaction. Other deposits and cheques could be found in the same way by examining the supporting documentation kept on file by the company.

Other deductions from the bank account include bank service charges. For example, on April 28, the bank charged Lee Company $30.00 as a monthly charge for operating the bank account.

The bank will include a **debit memorandum** with the bank statement when additional information is needed to explain a charge on the bank statement. The symbol DM (debit memo) is often used on the

ILLUSTRATION 7-7
Bank statement (reproduced with permission of BMO Bank of Montreal)

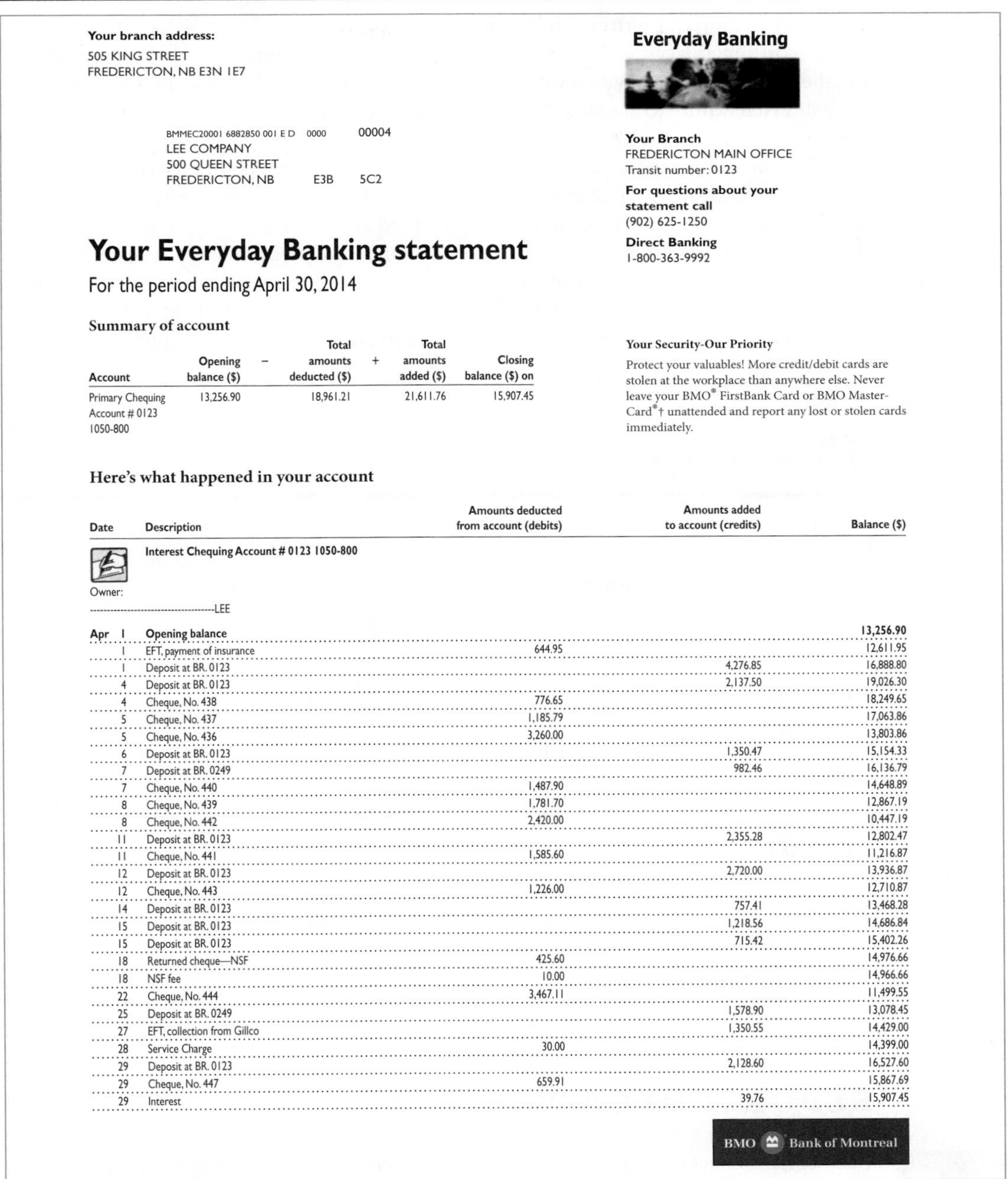

Your branch address:
505 KING STREET
FREDERICTON, NB E3N 1E7

BMMEC20001 6882850 001 E D 0000 00004
LEE COMPANY
500 QUEEN STREET
FREDERICTON, NB E3B 5C2

Everyday Banking

Your Branch
FREDERICTON MAIN OFFICE
Transit number: 0123

For questions about your statement call
(902) 625-1250

Direct Banking
1-800-363-9992

Your Everyday Banking statement

For the period ending April 30, 2014

Summary of account

Account	Opening balance ($)	– Total amounts deducted ($)	+ Total amounts added ($)	Closing balance ($) on
Primary Chequing Account # 0123 1050-800	13,256.90	18,961.21	21,611.76	15,907.45

Your Security-Our Priority

Protect your valuables! More credit/debit cards are stolen at the workplace than anywhere else. Never leave your BMO® FirstBank Card or BMO MasterCard®† unattended and report any lost or stolen cards immediately.

Here's what happened in your account

Interest Chequing Account # 0123 1050-800

Owner:
--------------------------------LEE

Date	Description	Amounts deducted from account (debits)	Amounts added to account (credits)	Balance ($)
Apr 1	**Opening balance**			**13,256.90**
1	EFT, payment of insurance	644.95		12,611.95
1	Deposit at BR. 0123		4,276.85	16,888.80
4	Deposit at BR. 0123		2,137.50	19,026.30
4	Cheque, No. 438	776.65		18,249.65
5	Cheque, No. 437	1,185.79		17,063.86
5	Cheque, No. 436	3,260.00		13,803.86
6	Deposit at BR. 0123		1,350.47	15,154.33
7	Deposit at BR. 0249		982.46	16,136.79
7	Cheque, No. 440	1,487.90		14,648.89
8	Cheque, No. 439	1,781.70		12,867.19
8	Cheque, No. 442	2,420.00		10,447.19
11	Deposit at BR. 0123		2,355.28	12,802.47
11	Cheque, No. 441	1,585.60		11,216.87
12	Deposit at BR. 0123		2,720.00	13,936.87
12	Cheque, No. 443	1,226.00		12,710.87
14	Deposit at BR. 0123		757.41	13,468.28
15	Deposit at BR. 0123		1,218.56	14,686.84
15	Deposit at BR. 0123		715.42	15,402.26
18	Returned cheque—NSF	425.60		14,976.66
18	NSF fee	10.00		14,966.66
22	Cheque, No. 444	3,467.11		11,499.55
25	Deposit at BR. 0249		1,578.90	13,078.45
27	EFT, collection from Gillco		1,350.55	14,429.00
28	Service Charge	30.00		14,399.00
29	Deposit at BR. 0123		2,128.60	16,527.60
29	Cheque, No. 447	659.91		15,867.69
29	Interest		39.76	15,907.45

BMO Bank of Montreal

bank statement for such charges. For example, a debit memorandum is used by the bank when a deposited cheque from a customer does not clear because of insufficient funds in the customer's account. In such a case, the cheque is marked **NSF (not sufficient funds)** or RT (returned item) by the customer's bank, and is returned to the depositor's bank. (NSF cheques are sometimes referred to as "bounced" cheques.) The bank then debits the depositor's account, as shown by the April 18 entry "Returned cheque—NSF" on the bank statement in Illustration 7-7. Note that this cheque for $425.60 was originally included in the deposit made on April 15, detailed in Illustration 7-5. Because the deposit was credited (added) to the bank account on April 15 and the cheque was not honoured, it must be debited (deducted) by the bank on April 18.

The company's bank may also charge the company a service charge of $10 or more for processing the returned cheque. In Illustration 7-7 we can see that BMO writes the entry "NSF fee" on the customer's statement for these charges. The company (depositor) then advises the customer who wrote the NSF cheque that their cheque was returned NSF and that a payment is still owed on the account. The company also usually passes the bank charges on to the customer by adding them to the customer's account balance. In summary, the overall effect of an NSF cheque on the depositor is to create an account receivable, and to reduce cash in the bank account. The customer's own bank will also charge the customer an NSF fee of $40 or more for writing an NSF cheque.

Recording an account receivable assumes that the customer will honour the account due by replacing the bounced cheque with a valid cheque or with cash. This happens in most cases. In the next chapter, we will discuss how to account for uncollectible accounts receivable when customers are unable to pay their accounts.

The bank uses **credit memoranda (CM)** to identify and explain miscellaneous amounts added to the bank account for items such as interest earned on the bank account, and electronic funds transfers into the depositor's account. For example, as explained earlier in the chapter, some retailers accept electronic payments for merchandise sold on account. Funds are electronically transferred from the customer's account to the retailer's account in payment of the bill. In Illustration 7-7, Lee Company collected an electronic payment from a customer for $1,350.55 on April 27, as indicated by the symbol EFT. Also note that in Illustration 7-7, interest of $39.76 has been added to Lee Company's bank balance.

BEFORE YOU GO ON...

DO IT

Bank employees use a system known as the "maker-checker" system. An employee will record an entry in the appropriate journal and then a supervisor will verify and approve the entry. These days as all of a bank's accounts are computerized the employee first enters a batch of entries into the computer and then the entries are posted automatically to the general ledger account after the supervisor approves them on the system.

Access to the computer system is password-protected and task-specific, which means that the computer system will not allow the employee to approve a transaction or the supervisor to record a transaction.

Identify the principles of internal control inherent in the "maker-checker" procedure used by the banks.

Action Plan

- Segregation of duties should be established to ensure that each employee's responsibilities are clearly defined.
- After transactions have been entered by an employee, they should be checked by the employee's manager or supervisor.

SOLUTION

The principles of internal control inherent in the "maker-checker" procedure are:

1. Segregation of duties. The employee records the transactions. The supervisor verifies and approves the transactions.
2. Physical controls. Access to the computer system is password-protected and task-specific.

REPORTING CASH

STUDY OBJECTIVE 4

Report cash on the balance sheet.

Cash consists of coins, currency (paper money), cheques, money orders, travellers' cheques, and money on deposit in a bank or similar depository. Cash does not include cheques that are postdated (payable in the future), staledated (more than six months old), or returned (NSF—not sufficient funds).

Companies report cash in two different statements: the **balance sheet** and the **cash flow statement**. The balance sheet reports the amount of cash available at a point in time (the date of the balance sheet). The cash flow statement shows the sources and uses of cash during a period of time. The cash flow statement was introduced in Chapter 1 and will be discussed in much detail in Chapter 16.

Helpful hint Recall that the balance sheet provides a "snapshot" of a company's financial position at a given point in time. Its cash balance is part of that picture.

When presented on the balance sheet, cash on hand, cash in banks, and petty cash are normally combined and reported simply as Cash. Because it is the most liquid asset owned by a company, Canadian companies have traditionally listed cash first in the current assets section of the balance sheet. As explained and illustrated in Chapter 4, companies following IFRS may choose to list current assets in *increasing* order of liquidity and thus present cash as the last item in current assets. In this textbook, we will continue to follow the rule of listing current assets in *decreasing* order of liquidity as it is expected that this will continue to be the practice of Canadian companies for many years to come.

Many companies combine cash with cash equivalents. **Cash equivalents** are short-term, highly liquid (easily sold) investments that are not subject to significant risk of changes in value, such as term deposits, treasury bills, and guaranteed investment certificates (GICs). To be considered a cash equivalent they typically have maturities of three months or less from the date they are purchased.

A company may have cash that is not available for general use because it is restricted for a special purpose. An example is funds held on deposit until completion of an offer to buy real estate. Cash that has a restricted use—and is in a significant amount—should be reported separately on the balance sheet as **restricted cash**. If the restricted cash is expected to be used within the next year, the amount should be reported as a current asset. When restricted funds will not be used in that time, they should be reported as a non-current asset.

Illustration 7-8 shows how Tim Hortons presents its cash and cash equivalents and restricted cash on its balance sheet.

ILLUSTRATION 7-8
Presentation of cash

TIM HORTONS INC.
Balance Sheet (partial)
January 1, 2012
(in thousands)

Assets	
Current assets	
Cash and cash equivalents	$126,497
Restricted cash and cash equivalents	130,613

In the notes to its financial statements, Tim Hortons states that the company considers short-term investments that are highly liquid and have original maturities of three months or less as cash equivalents. The restricted cash and cash equivalents are related to its Tim Card® quick-pay cash card program. The amount represents the net amount of cash loaded on the cards by customers, less redemptions. The balances are restricted and cannot be used for any purpose other than for settlement of obligations under the cash card program.

Some companies may be in a cash deficit or negative position at year end. This can happen when the company is in an overdraft position at the bank. A **bank overdraft** occurs when withdrawals or payments are more than the amount in the bank account. This becomes a short-term loan from the bank, assuming that the bank does not reject the withdrawal or payment. Most companies have **overdraft protection** up to a certain amount with their banks. In an overdraft situation, the Cash account shows a credit balance in the general ledger and is reported as a current liability called bank indebtedness.

BEFORE YOU GO ON...

DO IT

On December 31, Ranchero Company has the following items: $12,250 in its bank chequing account; $6,400 in its bank savings account; a $250 petty cash fund; $4,300 of postdated cheques from customers; $8,800 in highly liquid short-term investments purchased with maturity dates of less than 90 days; $10,600 of short-term investments with maturity dates of 100 to 365 days; and $5,200 in a bank account restricted for use in settling advance ticket sales. How will each of these items be reported on the balance sheet?

SOLUTION

The following items are reported as current assets on the balance sheet:

1. Cash and cash equivalents		
Bank chequing account	$12,250	
Bank savings account	6,400	
Petty cash fund	250	
Highly liquid investments < 90 days	8,800	
Cash and cash equivalents		$27,700
2. Restricted cash		5,200
3. Short-term investments		10,600

The postdated cheques are not an asset and thus are not included on the balance sheet.

Related exercise material: BE7–6, BE7–7, and E7–6.

Action Plan

- Review which items are included in cash and cash equivalents.
- Determine the difference between cash equivalents and short-term investments.
- Recall that restricted cash balances must be reported separately.

Comparing IFRS and ASPE

Key Differences	International Financial Reporting Standards (IFRS)	Accounting Standards for Private Enterprises (ASPE)
No significant differences		

THE NAVIGATOR

DEMONSTRATION PROBLEM

You are asked to join the board of elders of a local church to help with the control activities for the offerings collection made at weekly services. At a meeting of the board, you learn the following:

1. The board of elders has delegated responsibility for the financial management and audit of the financial records to the finance committee. This group prepares the annual budget and approves major payments but is not involved in collections or record keeping. No audit has been done in recent years, because the same trusted employee has kept church records and served as financial secretary for 15 years. The church does not carry any fidelity insurance.
2. The collection at the weekly service is taken by a team of ushers who volunteer to serve for one month. The ushers take the collection plates to a basement office at the back of the church. They hand their plates to the head usher and return to the church service. After all plates have been turned in, the head usher counts the cash collected in them.

   The head usher then places the cash in the church safe along with a note that includes the amount counted. The safe is unlocked because no one can remember the combination, and after all, it is in a church.
3. The morning after the service, the financial secretary goes to the safe and recounts the collection. The secretary withholds $200 to pay for cash purchases for the week, and deposits the remainder of the collection in the bank. To facilitate the deposit, church members who contribute by cheque are asked to make their cheques payable to "Cash."
4. Each month, the financial secretary reconciles the bank statement and submits a copy of the reconciliation to the board of elders. The reconciliations have rarely revealed any bank errors and have never shown any errors per books.

Instructions

(a) Identify the control weaknesses in the handling of collections.

(b) List the improvements in control activities that should be recommended for (1) the head usher, (2) the ushers, (3) the financial secretary, and (4) the finance committee.

Action Plan

- Review the activities that help prevent fraud and achieve internal control.
- Review the control activities that apply to cash receipts.
- Review the measures to be taken to limit the opportunity to commit fraud.
- Review the importance of segregating duties.
- Review the importance of performing independent checks of performance.

SOLUTION TO DEMONSTRATION PROBLEM

(a) The weaknesses in control activities in the handling of collections include:

- Each usher could take cash from the collection plates en route to the basement office.
- The head usher counts the cash alone so no one would ever know if the head usher stole cash.
- The head usher's notation of the count is left in the safe, with the cash, so no one other than the financial secretary will know if the cash placed in the safe was ever deposited.
- The financial secretary counts the cash alone.
- The financial secretary withholds $200 per week—this is an unapproved payment.
- The cash is vulnerable to robbery when kept in the unlocked safe overnight.
- Cheques are made payable to "Cash" so anyone can cash them.
- The financial secretary has custody of the cash, maintains church records, and prepares the bank reconciliation.
- No annual audits of cash receipts procedures are performed.
- The secretary is not bonded.

SOLUTION TO DEMONSTRATION PROBLEM continued on next page

SOLUTION TO DEMONSTRATION PROBLEM continued from previous page

(b) The improvements should include the following:

1. Head usher
   - The head usher and a finance committee member should take the cash to the office. The cash should be counted by the head usher and the financial secretary in the presence of the finance committee member. The amount counted should be written down on a cash count sheet and copies kept by the secretary and finance committee member.
2. Ushers
   - The ushers should transfer their cash collections to a cash pouch (or bag) held by the head usher. The transfer should be witnessed by a member of the finance committee.
3. Financial secretary
   - Following the count, the financial secretary should prepare a deposit slip in duplicate for the total cash received, and the secretary should immediately deposit the cash in the bank's night deposit vault. A copy of the deposit slip should be given to a finance committee member.
   - A "petty" or small cash fund should be established for the financial secretary to be used for weekly cash expenditures, and requests for replenishment of the fund should be sent to the chairperson of the finance committee for approval. Receipts for items paid from this fund along with the unused cash should be kept in a locked cash box. Periodic counts of the cash box should be performed by a finance committee member to ensure that the cash on hand plus receipts for cash expenditures total the limit (for example, $200) established for the fund.
4. Finance committee
   - A reconciliation of the cash count sheet and the bank deposit slip should be done every time a deposit is made to ensure all cash counted was actually deposited.
   - Members should make their cheques payable to the church, and not to cash.
   - The financial secretary should be bonded.
   - At the end of each month, a member of the finance committee should prepare the bank reconciliation.
   - Annual audits should be performed.

Summary of Study Objectives

1. ***Explain the activities that help prevent fraud and achieve internal control.*** Fraud is an intentional dishonest act that results in a personal financial benefit by misappropriating (stealing) assets or misstating financial statements. The three factors that contribute to fraud (the fraud triangle) are opportunity, financial pressure, and rationalization. Internal control consists of all the related methods and measures that management implements in order to achieve reliable financial reporting, effective and efficient operations, and compliance with relevant laws and regulations. Control activities include establishment of responsibility, segregation of duties, documentation procedures, physical and IT controls, independent checks of performance, and human resource controls.

2. ***Apply control activities to cash receipts and cash payments.*** Internal controls over cash receipts include (a) designating only personnel such as cashiers to handle cash; (b) assigning the duties of handling or receiving cash, and recording cash to different individuals; (c) using remittance advices for mail receipts, cash register tapes (or point-of-sale computerized systems) for over-the-counter receipts, and deposit slips for bank deposits; (d) using company safes and bank vaults to store cash, with only authorized personnel having access, and using cash registers; (e) depositing all cash intact daily; (f) making independent daily counts of register receipts and daily comparisons of total receipts with total deposits; and (g) bonding personnel who handle cash. Debit and credit card transactions increase internal control but have related bank charges. Electronic funds transfer receipts also increase internal control over cash receipts.

   Internal controls over cash payments include (a) authorizing only specified individuals such as the controller to sign cheques and authorize electronic funds transfer payments; (b) assigning the duties of approving items for payment, paying for the items, and recording the payment to different individuals; (c) using prenumbered cheques and accounting for all cheques, with each cheque supported by an approved invoice; (d) storing blank cheques and signing machines in a safe or vault, with access restricted to authorized personnel; (e) comparing each cheque with the approved invoice before issuing the cheque and making monthly reconciliations of bank and book balances; and (f) stamping each approved invoice "Paid" after payment.

3. ***Describe the control features of a bank account.*** A bank account contributes to good internal control by giving physical and IT controls for the storage of cash, reducing the amount of currency that must be kept on hand, and creating a double record of a depositor's bank transactions.

4. ***Report cash on the balance sheet.*** Cash is usually listed first in the current assets section of the balance sheet. Cash may be reported together with highly liquid, very short-term investments called cash equivalents. Cash that is restricted for a special purpose is reported separately as a current asset or a non-current asset, depending on when the cash is expected to be used.

THE NAVIGATOR

Glossary

Bank overdraft What occurs when withdrawals are more than the amount available in the bank account. (p. 323)

Bank reconciliation A comparison of the balance in a company's bank account with the balance in the cash account at a point in time that explains any differences. (p. 318)

Bank statement A statement received monthly from the bank that shows the depositor's bank transactions and balances. (p. 320)

Bonding Obtaining insurance protection against theft by employees. (p. 312)

Cash Resources such as coins, currency (paper money), cheques, money orders, travellers' cheques, and money on deposit in a bank or similar depository. (p. 322)

Cash equivalents Highly liquid, short-term investments with maturities of three months or less that are subject to an insignificant risk of changes in value. (p. 322)

Cash payments journal A special journal used to record all cash paid. (p. 317)

Cash receipts journal A special journal used to record all cash received. (p. 315)

Clearing What occurs when a cheque or deposit is accepted by the maker's bank. Clearing results in a transfer of funds from the maker's bank to the payee's bank. (p. 320)

Credit memoranda (CM) Supporting documentation for increases to a bank account that appear on a bank statement. (p. 322)

Debit memoranda (DM) Supporting documentation for decreases to a bank account that appear on a bank statement. (p. 320)

Electronic funds transfer (EFT) The electronic exchange or transfer of money from one account to another, either within a single financial institution or across multiple institutions, through computer-based systems. (p. 316)

External auditors Auditors who are independent of the organization. They report on whether or not the financial statements fairly present the financial position and performance of an organization. (p. 312)

Fraud An intentional dishonest act that results in a personal financial benefit by misappropriating (stealing) assets or misstating financial statements. (p. 308)

Fraud triangle The three factors that contribute to fraudulent activity by employees: opportunity, financial pressure, and rationalization. (p. 308)

Internal auditors Company employees who evaluate the effectiveness of the company's system of internal control. (p. 312)

Internal control The related methods and measures that management designs and implements to help an organization achieve reliable financial reporting, effective and efficient operations, and compliance with relevant laws and regulations. (p. 309)

NSF (not sufficient funds) cheque A cheque that is not paid by the customer's bank and is returned to the depositor's bank because of insufficient funds in the customer's account. (p. 321)

Petty cash fund A cash fund that is used for paying relatively small amounts. (p. 318)

Restricted cash Cash that is not available for general use, but instead is restricted for a particular purpose. (p. 323)

Special journal A journal that is used to record similar types of transactions, such as all cash receipts or all cash payments. (p. 315)

Self-Study Questions

Answers are at the end of the chapter.

(SO 1) K 1. Which of the following factors does not contribute to the likelihood of fraud?
   (a) Rationalization
   (b) Financial pressure
   (c) Segregation of duties
   (d) Opportunity

(SO 1) K 2. Which of the following factors could limit a company's system of internal control?
   (a) Collusion by two or more employees
   (b) The cost of internal control being greater than the benefit
   (c) Difficulty in segregating duties in small businesses
   (d) All of the above

(SO 2) C 3. Permitting only designated personnel to handle cash receipts is an application of the concept of:
   (a) segregation of duties.
   (b) establishment of responsibility.
   (c) independent checks of performance.
   (d) human resource controls.

(SO 2) AP 4. Franks Jewellers accepted $12,000 of Visa credit card charges for merchandise sold on July 1. Visa charges Franks 5.0% for its credit card use. The entry to record this transaction by Franks Jewellers includes:
(a) a debit to Accounts Receivable of $12,000 and a credit to Sales of $12,000.
(b) a debit to Cash of $11,400 and a credit to Sales of $11,400.
(c) a debit to Accounts Receivable of $11,400, a debit to Credit Card Expense of $600, and a credit to Sales of $12,000.
(d) a debit to Cash of $11,400, a debit to Credit Card Expense of $600, and a credit to Sales of $12,000.

(SO 2) C 5. Authorizing only designated personnel to sign cheques is an application of the principle of:
(a) establishment of responsibility.
(b) segregation of duties.
(c) independent checks of performance.
(d) documentation procedures.

(SO 3) K 6. Bank accounts improve control over cash by:
(a) safeguarding cash by using a bank as a depository.
(b) minimizing the amount of cash that must be kept on hand.
(c) giving a double record of all bank transactions.
(d) all of the above.

(SO 3) AP 7. A company mistakenly recorded a $348 cheque written in payment of an account as $384. The journal entry required to correct this would be:
(a) debit Accounts Payable $36; credit Cash $36.
(b) debit Cash $36; credit Accounts Payable $36.
(c) debit Accounts Payable $348; credit Cash $348.
(d) debit Cash $384; credit Accounts Payable $384.

(SO 4) K 8. Which of the following correctly describes the reporting of cash?
(a) Petty cash is used for major purchases when the seller doesn't accept cheques.
(b) Restricted cash funds are always reported as a current asset.
(c) Cash equivalents may be combined with cash on the balance sheet.
(d) Postdated cheques from customers are included in the Cash account balance.

Questions

(SO 1) K 1. Fraud experts often say there are three primary factors that contribute to employee fraud. Identify the factors and explain what is meant by each.

(SO 1) K 2. Identify and describe the five components of a good internal control system.

(SO 1) C 3. "Internal control can help organizations achieve efficiency of operations." Do you agree? Explain.

(SO 1) K 4. In the ice cream shop, all employees make change out of the same cash register drawer. Is this a violation of internal control? Why or why not?

(SO 1) C 5. Trushi Miyamura is questioning why independent checks of performance are important if the company also segregates duties. Respond to Trushi's question.

(SO 1) C 6. What are documentation procedures? Provide an example and explain how it contributes to good internal control.

(SO 1) C 7. Joan Trainer is trying to design internal control activities so that there is no possibility of errors or theft. Explain to Joan why this may be impractical, and may even be impossible.

(SO 2) C 8. What is the difference between a debit card sale and a bank credit card sale to a retailer? To the customer?

(SO 2) C 9. Over-the-counter cash receipts require special care. Explain the procedures that should be followed at the end of the day (or shift) to ensure proper internal control.

(SO 2) C 10. Best Books has just installed electronic cash registers with scanners in its stores. How do cash registers such as these improve internal control over cash receipts?

(SO 2) C 11. Describe appropriate internal control procedures for handling cheques received by mail.

(SO 2) C 12. Sanjeet argues that no special internal controls are required for electronic funds transfer (EFT) cash receipts because employees are not handling cash or cheques. What is the flaw in Sanjeet's argument? Explain.

(SO 2) C 13. "Use of cash for payments should be avoided. Effective internal control over cash payments can only be achieved by the use of cheques or electronic funds transfer." Is this true? Explain.

(SO 2) C 14. "EFT payments are less expensive for a company because there is a reduced need for internal control as compared with writing cheques." Is this correct? Why or why not?

(SO 2) C 15. Walter's Watches is a small retail store. Walter, the owner of the company, has recently hired a new employee, Wanda, who will be responsible for ordering merchandise, receiving the goods, and authorizing the merchandise invoices for payment. Describe the various ways Wanda could commit a fraud with this arrangement.

(SO 3) K 16. Opening a bank account is a simple procedure. Give four examples of how a bank account improves a company's internal controls.

(SO 4) C 17. "Since cash is an asset, the Cash account must always have a debit balance. If it has a credit balance, that means there is an error in the account." Do you agree? Explain.

(SO 4) C 18. What are cash equivalents? What is restricted cash? How should these be reported on the balance sheet?

Brief Exercises

Identify control activities. **(SO 1) C**

BE7–1 Nathan McPhail is the new owner of Liberty Parking, a parking garage. He has heard about internal control but is not clear about its importance for his business. Explain to Nathan the six types of control activities. Give him an example of how each type of activity might apply to his business.

Identify control activities applicable to cash receipts. **(SO 2) C**

BE7–2 Miramichi Company has the following internal controls over cash receipts. Identify the control activity that is applicable to each of the following:

1. The company conducts thorough background checks on all cashiers prior to making a hiring decision.
2. All sales must be entered into the cash register through a scanner and point-of-sale software.
3. Surprise cash counts are made by the department supervisors.
4. The duties of receiving cash, recording cash, and maintaining custody of cash are assigned to different individuals.
5. At the end his or her shift, the cashier ensures there are receipts on hand for all debit or credit card sales.
6. Each cashier uses a different cash register and uses a separate password.

Record debit and credit card transactions. **(SO 2) AP**

BE7–3 Kopper Kettle Restaurant accepts Visa cards. On April 9, a customer paid for a $175 dinner using his Visa card. The bank charges a 4% fee for each transaction. Prepare the entry that Kopper Kettle must make to record this transaction. Assuming the purchase is made using a Kopper Kettle–issued credit card, would the entry change? Prepare the entry to record the purchase assuming a debit card is used for payment and that the bank charges a $2 fee for each transaction.

Identify control activities applicable to cash payments. **(SO 2) C**

BE7–4 Bujold Company has the following internal controls over cash payments. Identify the control activity that is applicable to each of the following:

1. Company cheques are prenumbered.
2. Blank cheques are stored in a safe in the controller's office.
3. All employees in the accounting department are required to take vacations each year.
4. The bank statement is reconciled monthly by the assistant controller.
5. Both the controller and the treasurer are required to sign cheques or authorize EFT.
6. Cheque signers are not allowed to record cash payments.

Indicate whether control activities are performed by internal or external personnel. **(SO 2) AP**

BE7–5 Place the number corresponding to each of the following characteristics in the appropriate section of the diagram. If a characteristic applies to both internal and external review, place that number in the overlapping section.

1. Conducted by employees of the company itself
2. Conducted by professional accountants hired by the company
3. Designed to improve internal control over company assets
4. Determines whether the company's financial statements fairly represent its financial position and results of operations
5. Involves having an independent person verify that the company's control activities are being correctly followed
6. Required by law for public companies

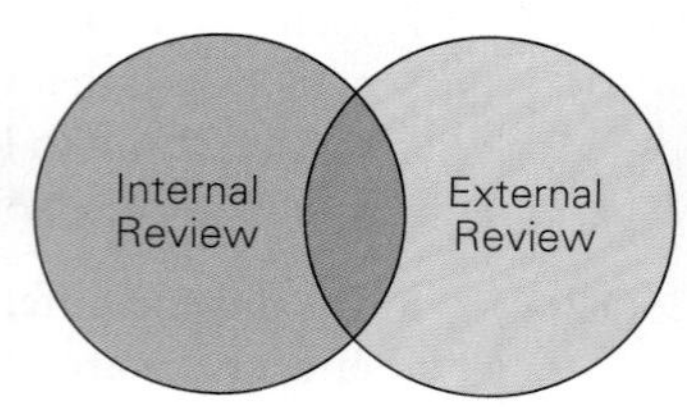

BE7–6 Sirois Company owns the following assets at the balance sheet date:

Calculate cash. (SO 4) AP

Cash in bank—savings account	$ 5,500
Cash on hand	750
Cash refund due from the Canada Revenue Agency	1,000
Cash in bank—chequing account	10,000
Staledated cheques from customers	250
Postdated cheques from customers	500
60-day treasury bill	3,500

What amount should be reported as cash and cash equivalents in the balance sheet?

BE7–7 Dupré Company has the following items: cash in bank $17,500; payroll bank account $6,000; store cash floats $1,500; petty cash fund $250; short-term, highly liquid investments with maturity dates of less than 90 days $15,000; short-term investments with maturity dates of 100 to 365 days $40,000; and Plant Expansion Fund Cash $25,000. The plant expansion will begin in three years. Explain how each item should be reported on the balance sheet.

Explain statement presentation. (SO 4) C

Exercises

E7–1 Discount Toys advertises a customer-friendly return policy. The store allows returns within 30 days for any reason. The store uses a periodic inventory system. When merchandise is returned, store policy instructs employees to:

Identify internal control weaknesses and recommend changes. (SO 1) C

- Complete a prenumbered return form and refund cash from the cash register.
- Provide a copy of the return form to the supervisor for approval.
- Immediately return goods to the shelf.

Instructions

(a) How is it possible for a dishonest store employee to steal from Discount Toys and avoid getting caught?

(b) What changes to the policy would you recommend to the company to reduce the possibility of employee fraud?

E7–2 The following situations suggest either a strength or a weakness in internal control:

Identify internal control strengths and weaknesses and suggest improvements. (SO 1) C

1. At Frederico's, Amanda and Parth work alternate lunch hours. Normally Amanda works the cash register at the checkout counter, but during her lunch hour Parth takes her place. They both use the same cash drawer and count cash together at the end of the day.
2. Sandeep is a very hard-working employee at Stan's Hardware. Sandeep does such a good job that he is responsible for most of the company's office and accounting tasks. The only thing the owner has to do is sign cheques.
3. At Half Pipe Skate, they are very concerned about running an efficient, low-cost business. Consequently, the manager has assigned the same individual to do the purchasing and prepare the receiving reports when the merchandise is delivered.
4. At Traction Tires, most of the tires are stored in a fenced outdoor storage area. One of the employees noticed a place where the fence needed to be repaired and reported this to the manager. The fence was fixed before the close of business that night.
5. The internal auditors at Humber Manufacturing regularly report their findings to senior management, who get the accounting department to investigate and resolve any problems.
6. All employees at Vincent Travel take vacation every year. During that time, with the exception of the controller's position, the employees' duties are assigned to another individual while they are on vacation.

Instructions

(a) State whether each situation above is a strength or a weakness in internal control.

(b) For each weakness, suggest an improvement.

E7–3 The following control procedures are used in Sheridan Company for cash receipts:

Identify weaknesses in internal control over cash receipts and suggest improvements. (SO 1, 2) C

1. To minimize the risk of robbery, cash in excess of $200 is stored in a locked metal box in the office manager's office until it is deposited in the bank. All employees know where the office manager keeps the key to the box.

2. The company has one cash register with a single cash drawer. Any one of three employees may operate the cash register.
3. All employees handling cash receipts are experienced and therefore Sheridan doesn't see the need to ensure that they are bonded.
4. In order to increase efficiency, the assistant controller opens all of the mail, prepares the bank deposit, and prepares the journal entries to record the cash receipts.
5. Due to a lack of storage space, all remittance advices and debit or credit card sales receipts are destroyed each weekend.

Instructions

(a) For each procedure, explain the weaknesses in internal control, and identify the control activity that is violated.
(b) For each weakness, suggest a change in procedure that will result in good internal control.

Prepare entries for debit and credit card sales. **(SO 2) AP**

E7–4 Presented below are three independent situations:

1. On March 15, 44 customers used debit cards to purchase merchandise for a total of $5,814 from Hockey Town. Hockey Town pays a $0.25 debit card fee for each transaction.
2. On June 21, Circle Creations Gallery sells a painting to Constance Furrow for $2,400. Constance uses her Visa bank credit card to pay for the purchase. The bank charges Circle Creations a 2.75% fee for all credit card transactions. On July 17, Constance receives her Visa bill and pays for this purchase.
3. On October 7, A. Ramos uses his store credit card to purchase merchandise from The Bay for $595. On November 10, Ramos receives his credit card bill from The Bay and pays for this purchase.

Instructions

(a) Prepare Hockey Town's journal entries for the transactions in part (1).
(b) Prepare Circle Creations' journal entries for the transactions in part (2).
(c) Prepare The Bay's journal entries for the transactions in part (3).

Identify weaknesses in internal control over cash payments, and suggest improvements. **(SO 1, 2) AP**

E7–5 The following control procedures are used in Centennial Bay General Merchandise for cash payments:

1. Company cheques are not prenumbered and are kept in an unlocked file cabinet in the controller's office.
2. Cheques must be signed by the controller.
3. The purchasing agent verifies that the goods have been received, verifies the accuracy of the invoice, and authorizes the controller to issue a cheque for the purchase.
4. After the controller prepares and signs the cheque, she stamps the invoice "Paid" and files it. She then records the cheque in the journal.
5. Background checks are not conducted on personnel hired for senior positions such as the purchasing agent or controller.
6. The company owner is impressed with how hard the purchasing agent works. He hasn't taken a vacation in two years.
7. Although the controller uses all of her vacation days each year, she uses them to take three-day weekends from May through September. This ensures that she is never out of the office for long.

Instructions

(a) For each procedure, explain the weaknesses in internal control, and identify the control activity that is violated.
(b) For each weakness, suggest a change in procedure that will result in good internal control.

Calculate cash balance and report other items. **(SO 4) AP**

E7–6 A new accountant at Magenta Company is trying to identify which of the following amounts should be reported as the current asset Cash in the year-end balance sheet, as at June 30, 2014:

1. Currency and coins totalling $79 in a locked box used for petty cash transactions
2. A 60-day, $12,000 guaranteed investment certificate, due July 31, 2014
3. June-dated cheques worth $300 that Magenta has received from customers but not yet deposited
4. A $92 cheque received from a customer in payment of her June account, but postdated to July 1
5. A balance of $2,500 in the Royal Bank chequing account
6. A balance of $4,250 in the Royal Bank savings account
7. Prepaid postage of $70 in the postage meter

8. A $100 IOU from the company receptionist
9. Cash register floats of $300
10. Over-the-counter cash receipts for June 30 consisting of $570 of currency and coins, $130 of cheques from customers, $580 of debit card slips, and $750 of bank credit card slips. These amounts were processed by the bank and posted to the bank account on July 1.

Instructions

(a) What amount should Magenta report as its cash and cash equivalents balance at June 30, 2014?
(b) In which financial statement and in which account should the items not included as cash and cash equivalents be reported?

Problems: Set A

Identify internal control activities related to cash receipts. (SO 1, 2) C

P7–1A Strivent Theatre's cashier's booth is located near the entrance to the theatre. Two cashiers are employed. One works from 3:00 p.m. to 7:00 p.m., the other from 7:00 p.m. to 11:00 p.m. Each cashier is bonded. The cashiers receive cash from customers and operate a machine that ejects serially numbered tickets. The rolls of tickets are inserted and locked into the machine by the theatre manager at the beginning of each cashier's shift.

After purchasing a ticket, which is priced according to the customer's age group, the customer takes the ticket to an usher stationed at the entrance of the theatre lobby, about 10 metres from the cashier's booth. The usher tears the ticket in half, admits the customer, and returns the ticket stub to the customer. The other half of the ticket is dropped into a locked box by the usher.

At the end of each cashier's shift, the theatre manager removes the ticket rolls from the machine and makes a cash count. The cash count sheet is initialled by the cashier. At the end of the day, the manager deposits the receipts in total in a bank night deposit vault located in the mall. The manager also sends copies of the deposit slip and the initialled cash count sheets to the theatre company controller for verification, and to the company's accounting department. Receipts from the first shift are stored in a safe located in the manager's office.

Instructions

Identify the internal control activities and how they apply to cash receipts at Strivent Theatre.

TAKING IT FURTHER If the usher and the cashier decide to collaborate to steal cash, how might they do this?

Identify internal control weaknesses for cash receipts and cash payments. (SO 1, 2) C

P7–2A Each of the following independent situations has one or more internal control weaknesses:

1. Board Riders is a small snowboarding club that offers specialized coaching for teenagers who want to improve their skills. Group lessons are offered every day. Members who want a lesson pay a $15 fee directly to the teacher at the start of the lesson that day. Most members pay cash. At the end of the lesson, the teacher reports the number of students and turns over the cash to the office manager.
2. Coloroso Agency offers parenting advice to young single mothers. Most of the agency's revenues are from government grants. The general manager is responsible for all of the accounting work, including approving invoices for payment, preparing and posting all entries into the accounting system, and preparing bank reconciliations.
3. At Nexus Company, each salesperson is responsible for deciding on the correct credit policies for his or her customers. For example, the salesperson decides if Nexus should sell to the customer on credit and how high the credit limit should be. Salespeople receive a commission based on their sales.
4. Algorithm Company is a software company that employs many computer programmers. The company uses accounting software that was created by one of the employees. In order to be more flexible and share the workload, all of the programmers have access to the accounting software program in case changes are needed.
5. The warehouse manager at Orange Wing distributors is well known for running an efficient, cost-saving operation. He has eliminated the requirement for staff to create receiving reports and purchase orders because it was taking staff too long to prepare them.

Instructions

(a) Identify the internal control weaknesses in each situation.
(b) Explain the problems that could occur as a result of these weaknesses.

TAKING IT FURTHER Make recommendations for correcting each situation.

Identify internal control weaknesses over cash receipts and cash payments and suggest improvements. (SO 1, 2) C

P7–3A Cedar Grove Middle School wants to raise money for a new sound system for its auditorium. The main fundraising event is a dance at which the famous disc jockey Attitude Al will play classic and not-so-classic dance tunes. Roger DeMaster, the music teacher, has been given the responsibility for coordinating the fundraising efforts. This is Roger's first experience with fundraising. He asks the Student Representative Council (SRC) to help him with the event.

Roger had 500 unnumbered tickets printed for the dance. He left the tickets in a box on his desk and told the SRC students to take as many tickets as they thought they could sell for $5 each. In order to ensure that no extra tickets would be floating around, he told them to dispose of any unsold tickets. When the students received payment for the tickets, they were to bring the cash back to Roger. He then put it in a locked box in his desk drawer.

Some of the students were responsible for decorating the gymnasium for the dance. Roger gave each of them a key to the cash box. He told them that if they took money out to buy materials, they should put a note in the box saying how much they took and what it was used for. After two weeks, the cash box appeared to be getting full, so Roger asked Freda Stevens to count the money, prepare a deposit slip, and deposit the money in a bank account Roger had opened.

The day of the dance, Roger wrote a cheque from the account to pay Attitude Al. Al said that he accepted only cash and did not give receipts. So Roger took $200 out of the cash box and gave it to Al. At the dance, Roger had Sara Billings working at the entrance to the gymnasium. She collected tickets from students and sold tickets to those who had not prepurchased them. Roger estimated 400 students attended the dance.

The following day, Roger closed out the bank account, which had $250 in it. He gave that amount plus the $180 in the cash box to Principal Skinner. Principal Skinner seemed surprised that, after generating roughly $2,000 in sales, the dance netted only $430 in cash. Roger did not know how to respond.

Instructions

(a) Identify the weaknesses in internal control over cash receipts and cash payments.
(b) What improvements in internal control should the school consider?

TAKING IT FURTHER Often people think internal control activities are too much work and not necessary. Explain how an improved system of internal control could help protect the individuals involved in this situation from being falsely accused of fraud.

Calculate cash balance and report other items. (SO 4) AP

P7–4A A first-year co-op student is trying to determine the amount of cash and cash equivalents that should be reported on a company's balance sheet. The following information was given to the student at year end:

1. The cash float for the cash registers totals $500.
2. The balance in the Petty Cash account is $300.
3. The balance in the company's chequing account is $24,500. The company also has a U.S. bank account, which contained the equivalent of $16,000 Canadian at year end.
4. The company has overdraft protection of $10,000 on its chequing account.
5. The company has a separate bank account with a balance of $4,250. This consists of cash deposits paid by tenants who lease office space from the company. The deposits will be refunded to the tenants at the end of their leases.
6. The company has $14,500 of postdated cheques from customers for payment of accounts receivable.
7. The company has the following short-term investments:
   - $25,000 in treasury bills with a maturity date of less than 90 days
   - $36,000 in shares of Reitmans (Canada) Limited
   - $12,000 in a guaranteed investment certificate that matures in six months.
8. The balance in the company owner's personal bank account is $2,150.
9. The company has NSF cheques from customers totalling $875 that were returned by the bank.

Instructions

(a) Calculate the amount of cash and cash equivalents that should be reported on the year-end balance sheet as a current asset.
(b) Identify where any items that were not reported as cash and cash equivalents in part (a) should be reported.

TAKING IT FURTHER Why are restricted cash balances presented separately from cash?

CONTINUING COOKIE CHRONICLE

(*Note:* This is a continuation of the Cookie Chronicle from Chapters 1 through 6.)

Natalie is struggling to keep up with the recording of her accounting transactions. She is spending a lot of time marketing and selling mixers and giving her cookie classes. Her friend John is an accounting student who runs his own accounting service. He has asked Natalie if she would like to have him do her accounting.

John and Natalie meet and discuss her business. John suggests that he could perform the following procedures for Natalie:

1. Take the deposits to the bank every Friday. All cheques and cash received would be kept in a locked box at Natalie's house.
2. Write and sign all of the cheques. He would review the invoices and send out cheques as soon as the invoices are received.
3. Record all of the deposits in the accounting records.
4. Record all of the cheques in the accounting records.
5. Prepare the monthly bank reconciliation.
6. Transfer Natalie's manual accounting records to his computer accounting program. John maintains the accounting information that he keeps for his clients on his laptop computer.
7. Prepare monthly financial statements for Natalie to review.
8. Write himself a cheque every month for the work he has done for Natalie.

Instructions

(a) Refer to items 1 to 8 above. Identify the procedures that Natalie should perform and explain why.
(b) Identify the procedures that John could perform.
(c) For each procedure that Natalie should perform, identify what could go wrong, in a worst-case scenario, if John were to do it.
(d) Once Natalie decides what procedures she would like John to perform, what are some of the advantages and disadvantages of having John perform these accounting services for Cookie Creations?

BROADENING YOUR PERSPECTIVE — CHAPTER 7

Collaborative Learning Activity

Note to instructor: Additional instructions and material for this group activity can be found on the Instructor Resource Site and in *WileyPLUS*.

BYP7–1 In this group activity, you will identify the strengths and weaknesses of a small coffee shop's processes for sales or purchases and make recommendations for processes that will improve internal control.

Communication Activity

BYP7–2 Tenacity Corporation is a medium-sized private company that sells auto parts. Blake Pike has been with the company from the beginning, ordering the auto parts, taking delivery of the parts, and authorizing payments for them. Blake often signs cheques and prepares the bank reconciliation if the controller is on vacation. The company has grown in size from five employees to 25. Annual sales have increased tenfold. Blake is still performing the same tasks as he was when the company was small and he says that he does not need any help.

Instructions

Write a letter to L. S. Osman, owner of Tenacity Corporation, which outlines a plan to improve internal control within the organization given its recent increase in size. Highlight in your letter any weaknesses you are currently aware of and suggest specific recommendations.

Ethics Case

BYP7–3 Banks charge customers fees of up to $40 per cheque for writing "bounced" cheques; that is, cheques that exceed the balance in the account. It has been estimated that processing bounced cheques costs a bank roughly $5 per cheque. Thus, the profit margin on a bounced cheque is very high. Some banks process cheques from largest amount to smallest. By doing this, they maximize the number of cheques that bounce if a customer overdraws an account.

Instructions

(a) Who are the stakeholders in this situation?

(b) Antonio Freeman had a balance of $1,200 in his chequing account on a day when the bank received the following five cheques for processing against his account:

Cheque Number	Amount	Cheque Number	Amount
3150	$ 35	3165	$550
3158	1,175	3169	180
3162	400		

Assuming a $35 fee per cheque is assessed by the bank, how much fee revenue would the bank generate if it processed cheques (1) from largest to smallest, (2) from smallest to largest, and (3) in the order of the cheque numbers?

(c) Do you think that processing NSF cheques from largest to smallest is an ethical business practice for a bank?

(d) Besides ethical issues, what else should a bank consider when it decides if it should process cheques from largest to smallest?

(e) If you were managing a bank, what would be your policy on bounced cheques?

All About You: Personal Financial Literacy Activity

BYP7–4 In the "All About You" feature, you learned about the dangers of identity theft. To protect yourself from identity theft, you should understand how it can happen and learn what you can do to prevent it. Identity theft occurs when someone steals another person's personal information and uses it to commit a crime by impersonating that person. Thieves can steal things such as social insurance numbers, credit card numbers, and passports. They can do this in any number of ways, including by stealing mail from mailboxes, stealing wallets from cars, getting discarded information from the garbage, tampering with bank machines, and buying information from dishonest employees working in places that store personal information.

There are several signs that you may have been the victim of identity theft. Monthly bills and bank statements may not arrive on time, which could mean a thief has redirected your mail. You may get calls from creditors seeking money for transactions you never authorized, which could mean a thief has opened an account in your name. Your bank account or credit card bill may show charges you never authorized, which could mean a thief stole your credit card and is using it.

The Ontario Ministry of Consumer Services recommends taking steps to protect your identity and reduce the risk of identity theft. Always keep important documents, such as social insurance numbers, passports, and birth certificates, in a safe place. Review statements every month from credit cards and banks to make sure there are no unauthorized charges, and report any errors, no matter how small, right away. If a bill or statement is late, contact the financial institution right away. Always shred old credit card bills and bank statements prior to disposal.

Instructions

Imagine that you and your family fly to Florida to spend spring break in a resort hotel on the beach. Answer the following questions regarding steps you would take to try to prevent identity theft.

(a) What would you do regarding your home mail delivery before you left?

(b) What information would you put on your luggage tags before you left?

(c) What would you do with your passports before you left and after you arrived?

(d) What would you do with your credit cards when you buy souvenirs?

(e) What would you do with your credit card statement when you got home?

ANSWERS TO CHAPTER QUESTIONS

ANSWERS TO ACCOUNTING IN ACTION INSIGHT QUESTIONS

All About You Insight, p. 313

Q: Who is responsible for losses due to unauthorized credit card use?

A: Most major credit card companies offer zero liability for credit card fraud, which protects the cardholder from losses due to fraud. You should find out if your cardholder agreement for any credit cards that you have offers protection from credit card fraud so that you can avoid taking on the identity thief's debts.

Business Insight, p. 316

Q: How might an organization's marketing department assist in, and benefit from, the implementation of a mobile payments system?

A: As you read in the Accounting in Action box, many consumers are worried about security in using their cell phones to make mobile payments. The marketing department could help in creating awareness of the benefits to consumers through social media and other more traditional advertising methods. In doing so, it would also be an opportunity to promote the business.

ANSWERS TO SELF-STUDY QUESTIONS

1. c 2. d 3. b 4. d 5. a 6. d 7. b 8. c

Remember to go back to the beginning of the chapter to check off your completed work!

←

CHAPTER 8 ACCOUNTING FOR RECEIVABLES

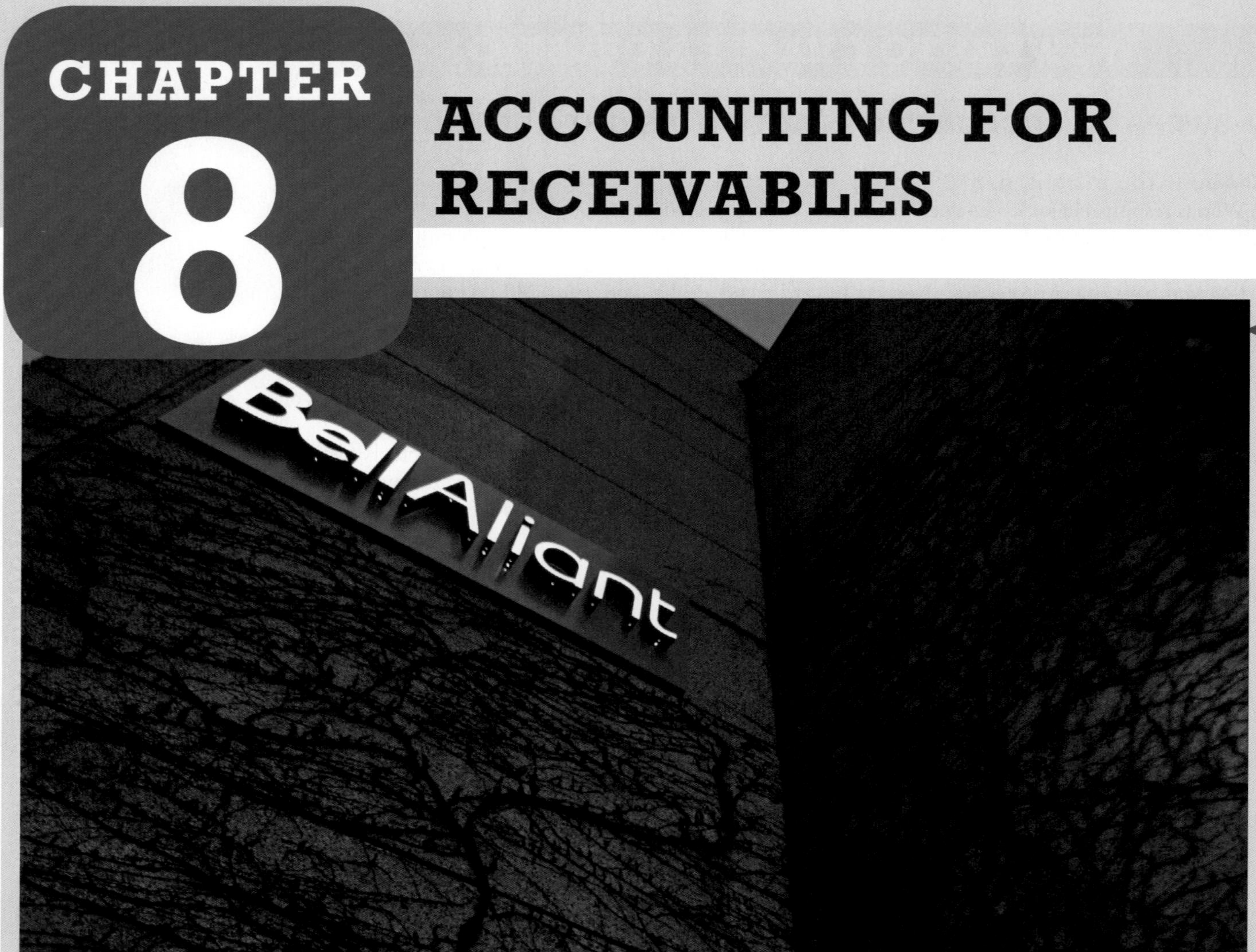

THE NAVIGATOR

- ☐ Understand *Concepts for Review*
- ☐ Read *Feature Story*
- ☐ Scan *Study Objectives*
- ☐ Read *Chapter Preview*
- ☐ Read text and answer *Before You Go On*
- ☐ Review *Comparing IFRS and ASPE*
- ☐ Work *Demonstration Problem*
- ☐ Review *Summary of Study Objectives*
- ☐ Answer *Self-Study Questions*
- ☐ Complete assignments

CONCEPTS FOR REVIEW

Before studying this chapter, you should understand or, if necessary, review:

A. How to record revenue. (ch. 3, pp. 106–107 and ch. 5, pp. 208–211)
B. Why adjusting entries are made. (ch. 3, pp. 99–101)
C. How to calculate interest. (ch. 3, pp. 108–109)
D. What is the difference between permanent and temporary accounts. (ch. 4, p. 146)
E. What is a subsidiary ledger. (ch. 5, pp. 204–205)
F. How to record bank credit card transactions. (ch. 7, pp. 314–316)

TRYING TO COLLECT FROM INCOMMUNICADO CLIENTS

SAINT JOHN, NB—Bell Aliant is the product of the 1999 merger of four Atlantic telephone service providers: New Brunswick Telephone, Maritime Tel, Island Tel, and Newfoundland Tel. The history of these four companies goes back 100 years in providing telephone service to Atlantic Canadians. In 2006, the company expanded westward with the purchase of Bell Canada's rural telephone lines in Ontario and Quebec; at the same time, it sold Bell its wireless business. In 2009, Bell Aliant became the first company in Canada to offer fibre-to-the-home technology to an entire city. Today, Bell Aliant is one of North America's largest regional communications providers, offering voice, data, Internet, and television services to customers across six provinces. With a staff of approximately 7,000, the company earns $2.8 billion a year under the brands Bell Aliant in Atlantic Canada and Bell in Ontario and Quebec, as well as Télébec, Northern Tel, and Kenora Municipal Telephone Services.

Bell Aliant's main sources of revenue are fees for local and long-distance phone services, high-speed Internet services, and television. In most areas, the company's services are bundled with wireless services from Bell Mobility. It also receives revenue from equipment rentals and value-added technology business solutions for large enterprises.

"Our total receivables balance is typically around $370 million at any one month end," says Eleanor Marshall, Vice-President and Treasurer at Bell Aliant.

Certain of Bell Aliant's billing terms are regulated by the Canadian Radio-television and Telecommunications Commission (CRTC). The company bills monthly for services it has provided, and payments are due within 21 days of the billing date. This results in receivables being about 31 to 35 days outstanding, Ms. Marshall explains.

"The vast majority of our consumer customers pay on or slightly before the due date," she says. "We have very few accounts outstanding beyond 30 days." In contrast, businesses take longer to pay, usually 35 to 50 days.

Even though the bills are due within 21 days of the billing date, late payment charges begin to accrue at 30 days from the billing date. "Late payment charges are intended to be punitive. Since we primarily bill monthly recurring charges, we really want customers to pay on time, so they do not get behind," Ms. Marshall explains. "As such, these charges are currently set at 3% per month."

Bell Aliant classifies customers as low risk, high risk, or unknown, and this classification will determine how large and how far in arrears (overdue) the company will allow the bill to get before taking action. It may also require a deposit if a customer has no or poor credit history.

If the bill does not get paid on time, Bell Aliant will start making calls, sending reminder notices and perhaps negotiating new payment terms. If there is still no payment, the company will suspend the account for 21 days, then reconnect for one day, and contact the client again. If the bill still isn't paid, it will permanently disconnect the customer. The company then sends two notices to the client, and finally the bill goes to a collection agency.

"We establish provisions for bad debts long before it gets to this point," Ms. Marshall adds. Receivables are assigned aging categories and certain percentages, which are based on experience, apply to each to estimate the amount of bad debt. The company recognizes bad debt expense, which is typically just under 1% of revenue, each month.

THE NAVIGATOR

STUDY OBJECTIVES

After studying this chapter, you should be able to:

1. Record accounts receivable transactions.
2. Calculate the net realizable value of accounts receivable and account for bad debts.
3. Account for notes receivable.
4. Demonstrate the presentation, analysis, and management of receivables.

THE NAVIGATOR

PREVIEW OF CHAPTER EIGHT

As indicated in our feature story, management of receivables is important for any company that sells on credit, as Bell Aliant does. In this chapter, we will first review the journal entries that companies make when goods and services are sold on account and when cash is collected from those sales. Next, we will learn how companies estimate, record, and then, in some cases, collect their uncollectible accounts. We will also learn about notes receivable, the statement presentation of receivables, and management of receivables.

The chapter is organized as follows:

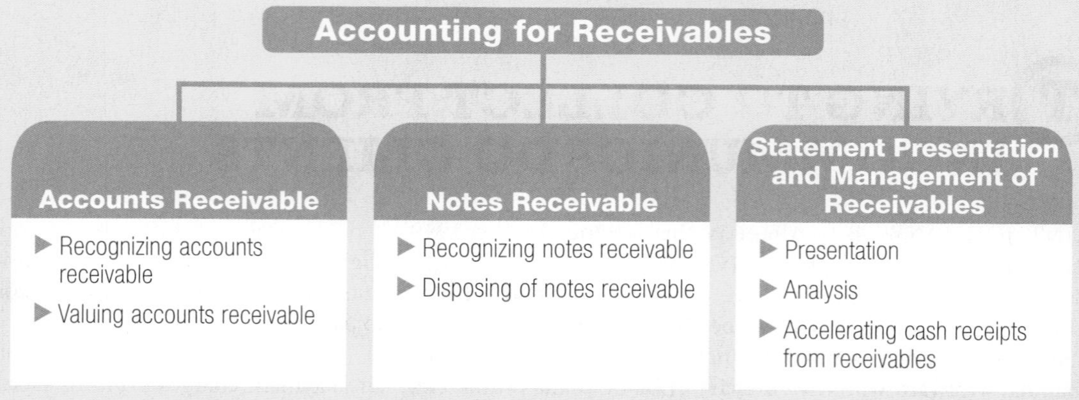

ACCOUNTS RECEIVABLE

The term "receivables" refers to amounts owed to a company by individuals and other companies. They are claims that are expected to be collected in cash. The two most common types of receivables are accounts receivable and notes receivable.

Accounts receivable are amounts owed by customers on account. They result from the sale of goods and services. These receivables are generally expected to be collected within 30 days or so, and are classified as current assets. **Notes receivable** are claims for which formal instruments of credit (a written note) are issued as proof of the debt. A note normally requires the debtor to pay interest and extends for longer than the company's normal credit terms. Accounts and notes receivable that result from sale transactions are often called **trade receivables**. In this section, we will learn about accounts receivable. Notes receivable will be covered later in the chapter.

Accounts receivable are usually the most significant type of claim held by a company. Two important accounting issues—recognizing accounts receivable and valuing accounts receivable—will be discussed in this section. A third issue—accelerating cash receipts from receivables—is discussed later in the chapter.

RECOGNIZING ACCOUNTS RECEIVABLE

STUDY OBJECTIVE 1

Record accounts receivable transactions.

Recognizing accounts receivable is relatively straightforward. Normally, for a service company, an asset, accounts receivable, is recorded when the service is provided on account and the revenue is recognized. The company has an asset because the company is going to receive cash from its customer in the future. For a merchandising company, a receivable is recorded at the point of sale of merchandise on account. Recall that in Chapter 5 we also saw how accounts receivable are reduced by sales returns and allowances and sales discounts. The asset is reduced because the returns and discounts will result in less cash being received from the customer.

To review, assume that Adorable Junior Garment sells merchandise on account to Hudson's Bay on July 1 for $1,000 with payment terms of 2/10, n/30. On July 4, The Bay returns merchandise worth $100 to Adorable Junior Garment. On July 10, Adorable Junior Garment receives payment from The Bay for the balance due. The journal entries to record these transactions on the books of Adorable Junior Garment are as follows:

July 1	Accounts Receivable—The Bay	1,000	
	Sales		1,000
	To record sale of merchandise on account.		
4	Sales Returns and Allowances	100	
	Accounts Receivable—The Bay		100
	To record merchandise returned.		
10	Cash [($1,000 − $100) × 98%]	882	
	Sales Discounts [($1,000 − $100) × 2%]	18	
	Accounts Receivable—The Bay ($1,000 − $100)		900
	To record collection of accounts receivable.		

A	=	L	+	OE
+1,000				+1,000

Cash flows: no effect

A	=	L	+	OE
−100				−100

Cash flows: no effect

A	=	L	+	OE
+882				−18
−900				

↑Cash flows: +882

If Adorable Junior Garment uses a perpetual inventory system, a second journal entry to record the cost of the goods sold (and the cost of the goods returned) would be required for the July 1 and July 4 transactions.

Subsidiary Accounts Receivable Ledger

Adorable Junior Garment does not have only The Bay as a customer. It has hundreds of customers. If it recorded the accounts receivable for each of these customers in only one general ledger account, as we did above in Accounts Receivable, it would be hard to determine the balance owed by a specific customer, such as The Bay, at a specific point in time. It is critical that a company knows what each customer owes so that it can collect the cash owed to it by each customer.

Most companies that sell on account use a subsidiary ledger to keep track of individual customer accounts. As we learned in Chapter 5, a subsidiary ledger gives supporting detail to the general ledger. The company's Accounts Receivable account in the general ledger is the control account that provides the balance in accounts receivable reported on the balance sheet. Illustration 8-1 shows the information

ILLUSTRATION 8-1
Accounts receivable general ledger control account and subsidiary ledger

GENERAL LEDGER

Accounts Receivable is a control account.

Accounts Receivable					No. 112
Date	Explanation	Ref.	Debit	Credit	Balance
2014					
July 4				100	(100)
31			10,000		9,900
31				5,900	**4,000**

ACCOUNTS RECEIVABLE SUBSIDIARY LEDGER

The subsidiary ledger is separate from the general ledger.

Kids Online					No. 112-203
Date	Explanation	Ref.	Debit	Credit	Balance
2014					
July 11	Invoice 1310		6,000		6,000
19	Payment			4,000	**2,000**

Snazzy Kids Co.					No. 112-413
Date	Explanation	Ref.	Debit	Credit	Balance
2014					
July 12	Invoice 1318		3,000		3,000
21	Payment			1,000	**2,000**

The Bay					No. 112-581
Date	Explanation	Ref.	Debit	Credit	Balance
2014					
July 1	Invoice 1215		1,000		1,000
4	Credit Memo 1222			100	900
10	Payment			900	**0**

included in an accounts receivable subsidiary ledger and the general ledger for a simple manual accounting system, using assumed data.

Each entry that affects accounts receivable is basically posted twice: once to the subsidiary ledger and once to the general ledger. Normally, in a manual system, entries to the subsidiary ledger are posted daily, while entries to the general ledger are summarized and posted monthly. For example, the $1,000 sale to The Bay was posted to The Bay's account in the subsidiary ledger on July 1. It was also summarized with other sales entries (Kids Online $6,000 + Snazzy Kids $3,000 + The Bay $1,000 = $10,000) in a special sales journal and posted to the accounts receivable control account in the general ledger at the end of the month, on July 31.

Collections on account (Kids Online $4,000 + Snazzy Kids $1,000 + The Bay $900 = $5,900) were also posted individually to the subsidiary ledger accounts and summarized and posted in total to the general ledger account. Non-recurring entries, such as the sales return of $100, are posted to both the subsidiary and general ledgers individually.

Note that the balance of $4,000 in the control account in the general ledger agrees with the total of the balances in the individual accounts receivable accounts in the subsidiary ledger (Kids Online $2,000 + Snazzy Kids $2,000 + The Bay $0).

Today, most businesses use computerized accounting systems that automatically update the subsidiary ledger and general ledger when a journal entry is recorded. Regardless of whether the accounting system is computerized or manual, the accounting records must provide accurate, up-to-date information for each customer account and the total of the customer account balances must equal the total in the general ledger control account.

Interest Revenue

At the end of each month, the company can use the subsidiary ledger to easily determine the transactions that occurred in each customer's account during the month and then send the customer a statement of transactions for the month. If the customer does not pay in full within a specified period (usually 30 days), most retailers add an interest (financing) charge to the balance due.

When financing charges are added, the seller increases the accounts receivable and recognizes interest revenue. If Kids Online still owes $2,000 at the end of the next month, August 31, and Adorable Junior Garment charges 18% on the balance due, the entry that Adorable Junior Garment will make to record interest revenue of $30 ($2,000 × 18% × 1/12) is as follows:

A	=	L	+	OE
+30				+30

Cash flows: no effect

		Debit	Credit
Aug. 31	Accounts Receivable—Kids Online	30	
	Interest Revenue		30
	To record interest on amount due.		

Bell Aliant in our feature story starts to accrue interest if payment is not received from the customer within 30 days of the billing date. The interest charges are meant to be punitive and the customer charges are 3% per month. As discussed in Chapter 5, interest revenue is included in other revenues in the non-operating section of the income statement.

Nonbank Credit Card Sales

In Chapter 7, we learned that debit and bank credit card sales are typically treated as cash sales. Sales on credit cards that are not directly associated with a bank are reported as credit sales, not cash sales. Nonbank credit card sales result in an account receivable until the credit card company pays the amount owing to the seller.

To illustrate, assume that Kerr Music accepts a nonbank credit card on October 24 for a $500 bill. An asset, accounts receivable, is recorded for the amount of cash that will be received, an expense is recorded for the service fee charged by the credit card company, and revenue is recorded for the amount of the sale. The entry for the sale by Kerr Music (assuming a 4% service fee) is:

A	=	L	+	OE
+480				−20 +500

Cash flows: no effect

		Debit	Credit
Oct. 24	Accounts Receivable—Credit Card Company	480	
	Credit Card Expense ($500 × 4%)	20	
	Sales		500
	To record nonbank credit card sale.		

When Cash is received from the credit card company, the asset Cash is increased and Accounts Receivable is reduced by the amount collected. The entry that Kerr Music will record is as follows:

Nov. 7	Cash	480	
	Accounts Receivable—Credit Card Company		480
	To record nonbank credit card sale.		

A	=	L	+	OE
+480				
−480				

↑Cash flows: +480

Advances in technology have created a rapidly changing credit card industry. Transactions and payments can be processed much more quickly, and often electronically, which reduces the time to collect cash from the credit card company. As collection time becomes shorter, credit card transactions are becoming more like cash transactions to the business.

How does a business know if it should debit Cash or Accounts Receivable when it processes a credit card transaction? Basically, it should consider how long it takes to collect the cash. If it takes longer than a few days to process the transaction and collect the cash, it should be treated as a credit sale, as shown above.

Companies that issue their own credit cards, such as Canadian Tire, always record sales paid by their cards as credit sales. When the credit card transaction results in an account receivable from the customer—as opposed to from the credit card company, as shown above—there is no service fee and the accounting treatment is the same as we have previously seen for accounts receivable.

As discussed in Chapter 7, credit card expenses, along with debit card expenses, are reported as operating expenses in the income statement.

ACCOUNTING IN ACTION
ALL ABOUT YOU INSIGHT

Interest rates on bank credit cards can vary depending on the card's various features; recently, the interest rates on Canadian bank credit cards ranged from 5.99% to 20.5%. Credit cards with lower interest rates usually have annual fees and may only be available to those with an excellent credit rating. Nonbank cards can charge significantly higher interest rates, such as retailer HBC's interest rate of 29.9%. At the same time, the Canadian banks' prime lending rate was 3.0%. The prime lending rate, the rate banks charge their best customers, changes depending on the supply and demand for money. Credit card interest rates, on the other hand, hardly budge at all. Why are credit card rates so much higher than other interest rates?

The higher rate is due to the risk involved. A bank loan, such as a mortgage, is a secured loan because the loan is backed by a tangible asset: a house. Using a credit card is essentially taking out an unsecured loan because nothing physical is used as security for the lender. In addition, credit cards are much more susceptible to fraud, and thus require a consistently high interest rate.

Sources: Credit Cards Canada website; Garry Marr, "Borrowers Will Suffer After Interest Rate Hike," *National Post*, April 17, 2012; "HBC Account Agreement," from the Hudson's Bay Financial Services website.

Should you use credit cards or not? What are the benefits? What are the risks?

BEFORE YOU GO ON...

DO IT

Information for Kinholm Company follows for its first month of operations:

Credit Sales			Cash Collections		
Jan. 5	Sych Co.	$12,000	Jan. 16	Sych Co.	$9,000
9	Downey Inc.	5,000	22	Downey Inc.	3,500
13	Pawlak Co.	6,000	28	Pawlak Co.	6,000

Calculate (a) the balances that appear in the accounts receivable subsidiary ledger for each customer, and (b) the accounts receivable balance that appears in the general ledger at the end of January.

BEFORE YOU GO ON... continued on next page

BEFORE YOU GO ON...
continued from previous page

Action Plan

- Use T accounts as a simple method of calculating account balances.
- Create separate accounts for each customer and post their transactions to their accounts.
- Create one account for the Accounts Receivable general ledger (control) account.
- Post the total credit sales and the total cash collections to the general ledger.

THE NAVIGATOR

SOLUTION

ACCOUNTS RECEIVABLE SUBSIDIARY LEDGER

Sych Co.

Jan. 5	12,000	Jan. 16	9,000
Bal.	3,000		

Downey Inc.

Jan. 9	5,000	Jan. 22	3,500
Bal.	1,500		

Pawlak Co.

Jan. 13	6,000	Jan. 28	6,000
Bal.	0		

GENERAL LEDGER

Accounts Receivable

Jan. 31	23,000[a]	Jan. 31	18,500[b]
Bal.	4,500		

[a] $12,000 + $5,000 + $6,000 = $23,000
[b] $9,000 + $3,500 + $6,000 = $18,500

Related exercise material: BE8–1, BE8–2, BE8–3, BE8–4, E8–1, and E8–2.

VALUING ACCOUNTS RECEIVABLE

STUDY OBJECTIVE 2
Calculate the net realizable value of accounts receivable and account for bad debts.

After receivables are recorded in the accounts, the next question is how these receivables should be reported on the balance sheet. Receivables are assets, but determining the amount to report as an asset is sometimes difficult because some receivables will become *uncollectible*. A receivable can only be reported as an asset if it will give a future benefit. This means that only collectible receivables can be reported as assets in the financial statements. This collectible amount is called the receivables' **net realizable value.** Reporting accounts receivable at net realizable value provides information to investors and creditors on the company's ability to generate cash.

In order to minimize the risk of uncollectible accounts, companies consider the creditworthiness of potential credit customers. But even if a customer satisfies the company's credit requirements before the credit sale was approved, inevitably, some accounts receivable still become uncollectible. For example, a usually reliable customer may suddenly not be able to pay because of an unexpected decrease in its revenues or because it is faced with unexpected bills.

Helpful hint The decision as to whether to grant credit can be thought of as a "Goldilocks" issue. A policy that is too strict will result in lost sales and lost customers, whereas a credit policy that is too easy will result in excessive credit losses.

Why do companies still decide to sell goods or services on credit if there is always a risk of not collecting the receivable? It is because they are expecting that the increase in revenues and profit from selling on credit will be greater than any uncollectible accounts or credit losses. Such losses are considered a normal and necessary risk of doing business on a credit basis.

When receivables are written down to their net realizable value because of expected credit losses, owner's equity must also be reduced so that assets remain equal to liabilities plus owner's equity. As we learned in Chapter 1, a decrease in an asset that results in a decrease in owner's equity (excluding withdrawals by owners) is an expense. The expense for credit losses is called **bad debt expense.**

Alternative terminology Bad debt expense is also sometimes called *uncollectible account expense.*

The key issue in valuing accounts receivable is to estimate the amount of accounts receivable that will not be collected. If the company waits until it knows for sure that a specific account will not be collected, it could end up overstating the asset accounts receivable on the balance sheet and understating expenses.

Consider the following example. Assume that in 2014, Quick Buck Computer Company decides it could increase its revenues by offering computers to students without requiring any money down and with no credit approval process. On campuses across the country, it sells 100,000 computers with a selling price of $400 each. This increases Quick Buck's receivables and revenues by $40 million. The promotion is a huge success! The 2014 balance sheet and income statement look great. Unfortunately, in 2015, nearly 40% of the student customers **default** on (do not pay) their accounts. This makes the 2015 balance sheet and income statement look terrible. Illustration 8-2 shows that the promotion in 2014 was not such a great success after all.

If credit losses are not recorded until they occur, the accounts receivable in the balance sheet are not reported at the amount that is actually *expected* to be collected. Quick Buck Computer's receivables were overstated at the end of 2014, which misrepresented the amount that should have been reported as an asset.

ILLUSTRATION 8-2
Effect of overstating accounts receivable (AR) and understating expenses

Year 2014	Year 2015
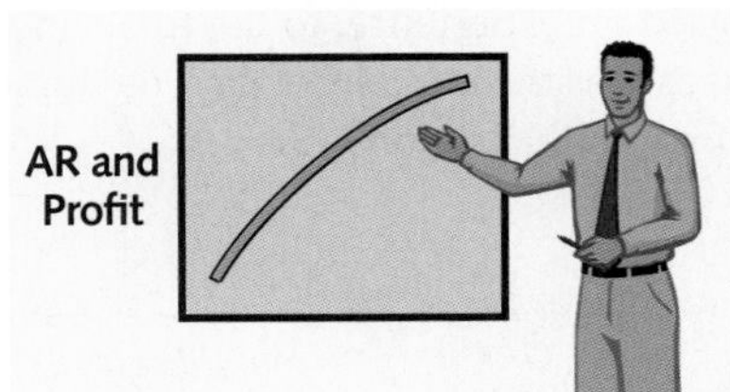	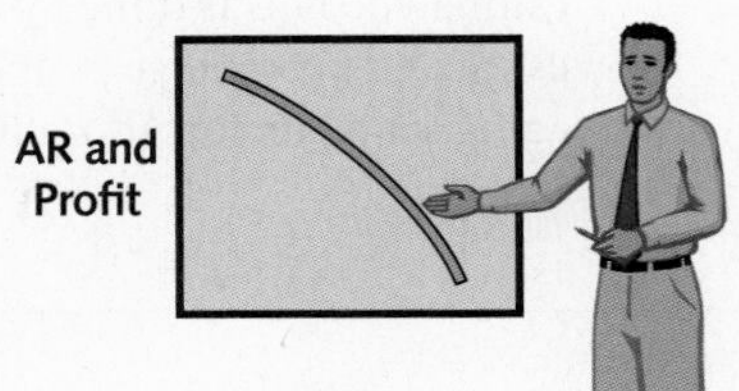
Huge sales promotion. Accounts receivable increase dramatically. Profit increases dramatically.	Customers default on amounts owed. Accounts receivable drop dramatically. Bad debt expense increases and profit decreases dramatically.

In addition, bad debt expense will not be matched to sales revenues in the income statement. Recall from Chapter 3 that expenses that are directly related to revenue must be recorded in the same period as the sales they helped generate. Consequently, Quick Buck Computer Company's profit was overstated in 2014 and understated in 2015 because the revenues were recorded in 2014 and the expenses directly related to the revenue were recorded in 2015.

To avoid overstating assets and profit, we cannot wait until we know *exactly which receivables are uncollectible*. Because we do not know which specific accounts receivable will need to be written off, we use what is known as the **allowance method** in which we estimate uncollectible accounts at the end of each accounting period. In this method, the estimated uncollectible accounts are recorded as a credit balance in a contra asset account, **Allowance for Doubtful Accounts**. The allowance is deducted from Accounts Receivable on the balance sheet to report the *net realizable* value of the receivables.

The allowance method also gives better matching of expenses with revenues on the income statement because credit losses that are expected to result from sales or service revenue in that accounting period are recorded in the same accounting period as when the revenue was earned. The allowance method is required for financial reporting purposes and has three essential features:

1. **Recording estimated uncollectibles:** The amount of uncollectible accounts receivable is estimated at the end of the accounting period. An adjusting journal entry is recorded to adjust the allowance for doubtful accounts to the estimated uncollectible amount and to record bad debt expense.
2. **Writing off uncollectible accounts:** Actual uncollectibles are written off when the specific account is determined to be uncollectible.
3. **Collection of a previously written-off account:** If an account that was previously written off is later collected, the original write off is reversed and the collection is recorded.

We explain these features of the allowance method in the following sections.

1. Recording Estimated Uncollectibles

Estimating the Allowance for Doubtful Accounts.

To illustrate the allowance method, assume that Adorable Junior Garment has accounts receivable of $200,000 at December 31, 2014. Not all of these receivables will be collected. As it is not known at December 31, 2014, which specific accounts are uncollectible, the amount of uncollectibles must be estimated. How is this amount estimated? The most common method used by companies is the percentage of receivables approach.

Under the **percentage of receivables approach**, management uses experience to estimate the percentage of receivables that will become uncollectible accounts. The easiest way to do this is to multiply the total amount of accounts receivable by a percentage based on an overall estimate of the total uncollectible accounts. The problem with this simple approach is that it doesn't take into consideration that the longer a receivable is past due or outstanding, the less likely it is to be collected.

Alternative terminology
The percentage of receivables approach is sometimes referred to as the *balance sheet approach*.

Therefore, the more common practice is to use different percentages depending on how long each of the accounts receivable has been outstanding. This is more sensitive to the actual status of the accounts receivable. Bell Aliant in our feature story uses this approach.

A schedule must be prepared, called an **aging schedule**, which shows the age of each account receivable. After the age of each account receivable is determined, the loss from uncollectible accounts is estimated. This is done by applying percentages, based on experience, to the totals in each category. The estimated percentage of uncollectible accounts increases as the number of days outstanding increases. An aging schedule for Adorable Junior Garment is shown in Illustration 8-3.

ILLUSTRATION 8-3
Aging schedule

		Number of Days Outstanding				
Customer	Total	0–30	31–60	61–90	91–120	Over 120
Bansal Garments	$ 6,000		$ 3,000	$ 3,000		
Bortz Clothing	3,000	$ 3,000				
Kids Online	4,500				$ 2,000	$ 2,500
Snazzy Kids Co.	17,000	2,000	5,000	5,000	5,000	
Tykes n' Tots	26,500	10,000	10,000	6,000	500	
The Bay	42,000	32,000	10,000			
Walmart	61,000	48,000	12,000	1,000		
Others	40,000	5,000	10,000	10,000	5,000	10,000
	$200,000	$100,000	$50,000	$25,000	$12,500	$12,500
Estimated percentage uncollectible		5%	10%	20%	30%	50%
Estimated uncollectible accounts	**$25,000**	$ 5,000	$ 5,000	$ 5,000	$ 3,750	$ 6,250

The $25,000 total for estimated uncollectible accounts is the amount of existing receivables that are expected to become uncollectible in the future. This also means that Adorable Junior Garment expects to collect the remaining accounts receivable of $175,000 ($200,000 of accounts receivable in total less the estimated uncollectible accounts of $25,000). As Adorable Junior Garment expects to collect only $175,000, this is the amount that should be shown in the balance sheet as an asset, not $200,000.

As previously explained, since Adorable Junior Garment doesn't know specifically which accounts receivable it will not collect, we do not know which specific accounts to credit in the subsidiary ledger. We cannot simply credit the Accounts Receivable control account to reduce it from $200,000 to $175,000 because the subsidiary ledger accounts must balance with Accounts Receivable, the control account.

The problem is solved by using the contra asset account, **Allowance for Doubtful Accounts**, instead of crediting Accounts Receivable. Remember that the balance of a contra asset account (a credit) is deducted from the related asset on the balance sheet (a debit). The difference between Adorable Junior Garment's **gross accounts receivable** and its allowance for doubtful accounts is the *net realizable value* (the expected collectible amount) of its accounts receivable. This can be represented by the formula shown in Illustration 8-4.

ILLUSTRATION 8-4
Formula for calculating net realizable value

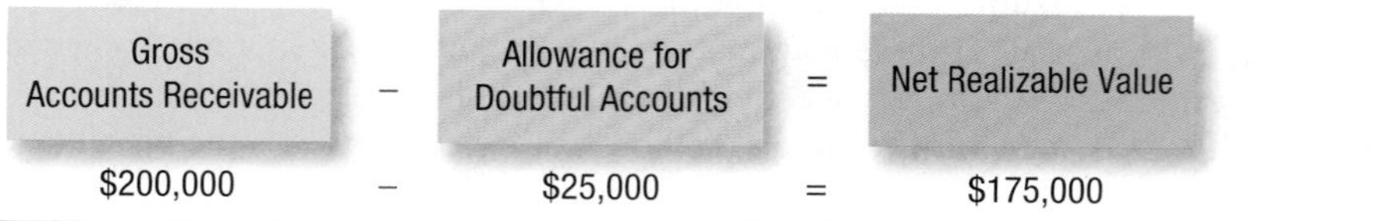

$200,000 − $25,000 = $175,000

In the current assets section of the balance sheet, Accounts Receivable, the Allowance for Doubtful Accounts, and the net realizable value are reported as follows (using assumed data for the other current asset accounts):

ADORABLE JUNIOR GARMENT
Balance Sheet (partial)
December 31, 2014

Current assets		
Cash		$ 14,800
Accounts receivable	$200,000	
Less: Allowance for doubtful accounts	**25,000**	175,000
Merchandise inventory		310,000
Prepaid expenses		25,000
Total current assets		$524,800

Notice that the net realizable value of the accounts receivable—$175,000—is the amount added to cash, merchandise inventory, and prepaid expenses to calculate total current assets, not the total accounts receivable ($14,800 + 175,000 + 310,000 + 25,000).

Determining Bad Debt Expense.

Although the balance in the Allowance for Doubtful Accounts is $25,000, it is important to understand that this is not necessarily equal to the bad debt expense in the income statement. Why? Recall that a contra asset account is a permanent account. That means the balance in a contra asset account is not closed; rather, it is carried forward to the next accounting period. We need to know the unadjusted balance in the Allowance for Doubtful Accounts in order to adjust the account to its required balance of $25,000. This adjusting entry also records the bad debt expense. Since bad debt expense is a temporary account, it is closed at the end of the fiscal year and starts each accounting period with a zero balance. Thus the amount in the adjusting entry will be equal to the bad debt expense reported in the income statement.

Helpful hint The Bad Debts Expense account balance will always be zero at the beginning of the fiscal year; this is not necessarily true for the Allowance for Doubtful Accounts.

To illustrate, let us assume that Adorable Junior Garment has an unadjusted credit balance of $1,000 in its Allowance for Doubtful Accounts. Because the account already has a credit balance, it needs to be adjusted by only the difference between the required balance of $25,000 and the existing balance of $1,000. Thus the amount of the adjusting entry, which is equal to the bad debt expense, is $24,000, as shown in Illustration 8-5.

ILLUSTRATION 8-5
Calculation of bad debt expense—unadjusted credit balance in allowance

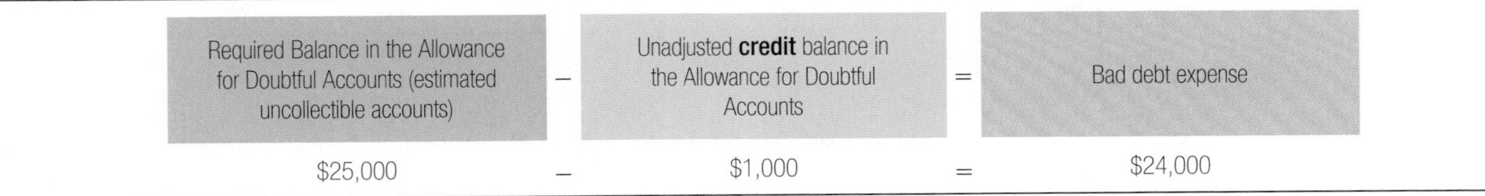

The adjusting entry for $24,000 is as follows:

Dec. 31	Bad Debt Expense	24,000	
	Allowance for Doubtful Accounts		24,000
	To record estimate of uncollectible accounts.		

A	=	L	+	OE
−24,000				−24,000

Cash flows: no effect

After the adjusting entry is posted, the balance in the Allowance for Doubtful Accounts will be equal to the estimated uncollectible accounts calculated in Illustration 8-3. This is shown in Adorable Junior Garment's accounts:

Bad Debt Expense

Dec. 31	Adj.	24,000		

Allowance for Doubtful Accounts

	Dec. 31	Unadj. Bal.	1,000
	31	Adj.	24,000
	Dec. 31	Bal.	**25,000**

Bad debt expense of $24,000 is reported in the income statement in the period when the sales are recognized. Notice this is less than the balance in the Allowance for Doubtful Accounts. This will always be the case when there is a credit amount in the unadjusted balance of the allowance account.

Occasionally, the allowance account will have a debit balance before recording the adjusting entry. This happens when write offs in the year are higher than the previous estimates for bad debts. (We will discuss write offs in the next section.) If there is a debit balance prior to recording the adjusting entry, the debit balance is added to the required balance when the adjusting entry is made. For example, if there had been a $500 debit balance in the Adorable Junior Garment allowance account before adjustment, the adjusting entry would have been for $25,500, to arrive at a credit balance in the allowance account of $25,000. The calculation of the adjusting entry is shown in Illustration 8-6.

ILLUSTRATION 8-6
Calculation of bad debt expense—unadjusted debit balance in the allowance

$25,000 + $500 = $25,500

In this case, the adjusting entry is for $25,500 as follows:

A	=	L	+	OE
−25,500				−25,500

Cash flows: no effect

Dec. 31	Bad Debt Expense	25,500	
	Allowance for Doubtful Accounts		25,500
	To record estimate of uncollectible accounts.		

After the adjusting entry is posted, the balance in the Allowance for Doubtful Accounts is equal to the estimated uncollectible accounts calculated in Illustration 8-3. This is shown in Adorable Junior Garment's accounts:

Bad Debt Expense

Dec. 31 Adj. 25,500	

Allowance for Doubtful Accounts

Debit	Credit
Dec. 31 Unadj. Bal. 500	
	31 Adj. 25,500
	Dec. 31 Bal. **25,000**

Notice that, although the adjusted balance in the Allowance for Doubtful Accounts is the same amount in the two examples shown, the Bad Debt Expense is different. In this case, it is higher than the balance in the allowance in order to compensate for the fact that Adorable Junior Garment underestimated its allowance and bad debts last year.

When preparing annual financial statements, all companies must report accounts receivable at their net realizable value, so companies must estimate the required allowance. However, when preparing monthly financial statements, some companies use a simplified approach in which bad debt expense is calculated by estimating the percent of sales that will not be collected. This approach, called the percentage of sales approach, is covered in post-secondary textbooks.

2. Writing Off Uncollectible Accounts

Companies use various methods for collecting past-due accounts, including letters, calls, and legal actions. Bell Aliant, in our feature story, classifies customers by risk levels, which it uses to determine how large and how far in arrears (overdue) it will allow the bill to get before taking action. Bell Aliant follows up on late accounts with letters and calls, and will cut back or suspend service if the customer does not negotiate new payment terms. If there is still no payment from the customer, service is permanently cut off. The final step involves sending the account to a collection agency.

When all the ways of collecting a past-due account have been tried and collection appears impossible, the account should be written off. To prevent premature write offs, each write off should be approved in writing by management. To keep good internal control, the authorization to write off accounts should not be given to someone who also has responsibilities related to cash or receivables.

To illustrate a receivables write off, assume that the vice-president of finance of Adorable Junior Garment authorizes the write off of a $4,500 balance owed by a delinquent customer, Kids Online, on March 1, 2015. The entry to record the write off is as follows:

Mar. 1	Allowance for Doubtful Accounts	4,500	
	Accounts Receivable—Kids Online		4,500
	Write off of uncollectible account.		

A	=	L	+	OE
+4,500				
−4,500				

Cash flows: no effect

Bad Debt Expense is not increased (debited) when the write off occurs. Under the allowance method, every account write off is debited to the allowance account rather than to Bad Debt Expense. A debit to Bad Debt Expense would be incorrect because the expense was already recognized when the adjusting entry was made for estimated bad debts last year.

Instead, the entry to record the write off of an uncollectible account reduces both Accounts Receivable and Allowance for Doubtful Accounts. After posting, using an assumed balance of $230,000 in Accounts Receivable on February 28, 2015, the general ledger accounts will appear as follows:

Helpful hint The Allowance for Doubtful Accounts is credited (increased) when it is created or adjusted. It is debited (decreased) when an uncollectible account is written off.

Accounts Receivable

Feb. 28	Bal.	230,000	Mar. 1	4,500
Mar. 1	Bal.	225,500		

Allowance for Doubtful Accounts

Mar. 1	4,500	Jan. 1	Bal.	25,000
		Mar. 1	Bal.	20,500

A write off affects only balance sheet accounts. The write off of the account reduces both Accounts Receivable and Allowance for Doubtful Accounts. Net realizable value in the balance sheet remains the same, as shown below:

	Before Write Off	After Write Off
Accounts receivable	$230,000	$225,500
Less: Allowance for doubtful accounts	25,000	20,500
Net realizable value	$205,000	$205,000

As mentioned earlier, the allowance account can sometimes end up in a debit balance position after the write off of an uncollectible account. This can happen if the write offs in the period are more than the opening balance of the allowance. It means the actual credit losses were greater than the estimated credit losses. The balance in Allowance for Doubtful Accounts will be corrected (that is, returned to a credit balance) when the adjusting entry for estimated uncollectible accounts is made at the end of the period.

3. Collection of a Previously Written-Off Uncollectible Account

Occasionally, a company collects cash from a customer after its account has been written off. *Two entries* are required to record the collection of a previously written-off account: (1) the entry previously made when the account was written off is reversed to restore the customer's account; and (2) the collection is recorded in the usual way.

To illustrate, assume that on July 1, 2015, Kids Online pays the $4,500 amount that had been written off on March 1. The entries are as follows:

	(1)		
July 1	Accounts Receivable—Kids Online	4,500	
	Allowance for Doubtful Accounts		4,500
	To reverse write off of Kids Online account.		
	(2)		
July 1	Cash	4,500	
	Accounts Receivable—Kids Online		4,500
	To record collection from Kids Online.		

A	=	L	+	OE
+4,500				
−4,500				

Cash flows: no effect

A	=	L	+	OE
+4,500				
−4,500				

↑ Cash flows: +4,500

Helpful hint If the first entry (to reverse the write off) isn't recorded, the collection of the receivable will cause the balance of the individual account in the Accounts Receivable subsidiary ledger to have a credit (as opposed to a zero) balance. Therefore, the write off must be reversed in the Accounts Receivable subsidiary ledger for Kids Online as shown in the following T account:

Accounts Receivable—Kids Online			
July 1	4,500		
July 1 Bal.	0	July 1	4,500

Note that the collection of a previously written-off account, like the write off of a bad debt, affects only balance sheet accounts. The net effect of the two entries is a debit to Cash and a credit to Allowance for Doubtful Accounts for $4,500. Accounts Receivable is debited and later credited for two reasons. First, the company must reverse the write off. Second, Kids Online did pay, so the Accounts Receivable account in the general ledger and Kids Online's account in the subsidiary ledger, if a subsidiary ledger is used, should show this payment as it will need to be considered in deciding what credit to give to Kids Online in the future.

Summary of Allowance Method

In summary, there are three types of transactions that you may need to record when valuing accounts receivable using the allowance method:

1. The estimated uncollectible accounts is determined by using the percentage of receivables (balance sheet) approach. The estimated uncollectible accounts is the required balance in the Allowance for Doubtful Accounts, which is deducted from Accounts Receivable on the balance sheet to show the net realizable value of the receivables. The estimated uncollectible accounts receivable is recorded by using an adjusting entry at the end of the period in which Bad Debt Expense is debited and the Allowance for Doubtful Accounts is credited. The amount in the adjustment—the bad debt expense—is the difference between the required balance and the unadjusted balance in the allowance account (i.e., it is the amount by which the balance must be increased).
2. Write offs of actual uncollectible accounts are recorded in the *next* accounting period by debiting Allowance for Doubtful Accounts and crediting Accounts Receivable.
3. Later collections of previously written-off accounts, if any, are recorded in *two separate entries*. The first reverses the write off by debiting Accounts Receivable and crediting Allowance for Doubtful Accounts. The second records the normal collection of the account by debiting Cash and crediting Accounts Receivable.

These entries are summarized in the following T accounts:

Accounts Receivable	
Beginning balance	Cash collections
Credit sales	Write offs
Later recoveries	
Ending balance	

Allowance for Doubtful Accounts	
Write offs	Beginning balance
	Reverse write off
	Bad debt adjusting entry
	Ending balance

BEFORE YOU GO ON...

DO IT

The following information for Woo Wholesalers Co. accounts receivable is available at December 31:

Number of Days Outstanding	Accounts Receivable	Estimated Percentage Uncollectible
0–30 days	$ 85,000	5%
31–60 days	25,000	15%
Over 61 days	10,000	25%
Total	$120,000	

(a) Calculate the estimated uncollectible accounts and the net realizable value of Woo's accounts receivable at December 31.
(b) Prepare the adjusting journal entry to record bad debt expense for each of the following independent situations:
 1. The Allowance for Doubtful Accounts has an unadjusted $2,000 credit balance.
 2. The Allowance for Doubtful Accounts has an unadjusted $1,200 debit balance.
(c) Prepare the required journal entry if Woo learns that its $1,500 receivable from Kruger Retailers is not collectible.
(d) Prepare the required journal entries if Woo subsequently collects the $1,500 receivable from Kruger Retailers that was previously written off.

Action Plan

- Apply percentages to the receivables in each age category to determine total estimated uncollectible accounts. This is the ending balance required in the allowance account (not necessarily the amount of the adjustment).
- Net realizable value is equal to the balance in Accounts Receivable minus the required balance in Allowance for Doubtful Accounts.

BEFORE YOU GO ON... continued on next page

SOLUTION

(a) Estimated uncollectible accounts = (\$85,000 × 5%) + (\$25,000 × 15%) + (\$10,000 × 25%)
= \$10,500
Net Realizable Value = \$120,000 − \$10,500
= \$109,500

		Debit	Credit
(b)	1. Bad Debt Expense (\$10,500 − \$2,000)	8,500	
	Allowance for Doubtful Accounts		8,500
	To record estimate of uncollectible accounts.		
	2. Bad Debt Expense (\$10,500 + \$1,200)	11,700	
	Allowance for Doubtful Accounts		11,700
	To record estimate of uncollectible accounts.		
(c)	Allowance for Doubtful Accounts	1,500	
	Accounts Receivable—Kruger Retailers		1,500
	To record write off of account receivable.		
(d)	Accounts Receivable—Kruger Retailers	1,500	
	Allowance for Doubtful Accounts		1,500
	To reverse write off of Kruger Retailers' account receivable.		
	Cash	1,500	
	Accounts Receivable		1,500
	To record collection from Kruger Retailers.		

Related exercise material: BE8–5, BE8–6, BE8–7, BE8–8, BE8–9, BE8–10, E8–4, E8–5, E8–6, and E8–7.

BEFORE YOU GO ON...
continued from previous page

- Use the unadjusted balance in the allowance account to determine the adjusting entry. If the unadjusted balance in the allowance account is a credit, the amount of the adjustment is equal to the required balance minus the unadjusted credit balance. If the unadjusted balance is a debit, the amount of the adjustment is equal to the required balance plus the unadjusted debit balance.
- Record the write offs of accounts and subsequent collection of accounts written off only in the balance sheet accounts, Accounts Receivable and Allowance for Doubtful Accounts.

NOTES RECEIVABLE

STUDY OBJECTIVE 3
Account for notes receivable.

Credit may also be granted in exchange for a formal credit instrument known as a promissory note. A **promissory note** is a written promise to pay a specified amount of money on demand or at a definite time. Promissory notes may be used (1) when individuals and companies lend or borrow money, (2) when the amount of the transaction and the credit period are longer than normal limits, or (3) in the settlement of accounts receivable.

In a promissory note, the party making the promise to pay is called the **maker**. The party to whom payment is to be made is called the **payee**. In the note shown in Illustration 8-7, Higly Inc. is the maker and Wolder Company is the payee. To Wolder Company, the promissory note is a note receivable. To Higly Inc., it is a note payable.

Helpful hint From the *payee's* point of view, a promissory note is a *note receivable*. From the *maker's* point of view, it is a *note payable*.

ILLUSTRATION 8-7
Promissory note

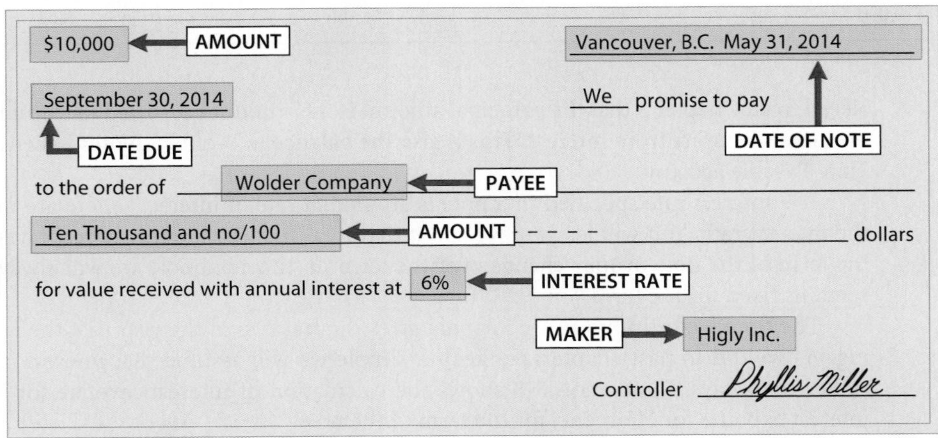

A promissory note might also contain other details such as whether any security is pledged as collateral for the loan and what happens if the maker defaults.

A note receivable is a formal promise to pay an amount that bears interest from the time it is issued until it is due. An account receivable is an informal promise to pay that bears interest only after its due date. Because it is less formal, it does not have as strong a legal claim as a note receivable. Most accounts receivable are due within a short period of time, usually 30 days, while a note can extend over longer periods of time.

There are also similarities between notes and accounts receivable. Both are credit instruments. Both can be sold to another party. Both are valued at their net realizable values. The basic issues in accounting for notes receivable are the same as those for accounts receivable, as follows:

1. Recognizing notes receivable
2. Disposing of notes receivable

RECOGNIZING NOTES RECEIVABLE

Like accounts receivable, a note receivable is an asset, as the company will collect cash in the future. To illustrate the basic entries for notes receivable, we will use the $10,000, four-month, 6% promissory note shown in Illustration 8-7. Assuming that Higly Inc. wrote the note in settlement of an account receivable, Wolder Company makes the following entry for the receipt of the note:

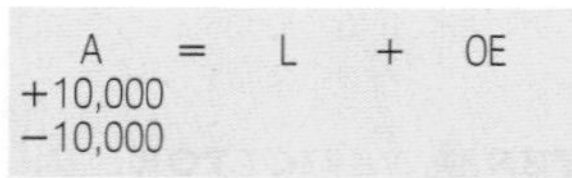

Cash flows: no effect

May 31	Notes Receivable—Higly	10,000	
	Accounts Receivable—Higly		10,000
	To record acceptance of Higly note.		

If a note is exchanged for cash instead of an account receivable, the entry is a debit to Notes Receivable and a credit to Cash for the amount of the loan.

The note receivable is recorded at its principal amount (the value shown on the face of the note). No interest revenue is reported when the note is accepted because, according to the revenue recognition principle, revenue is not recognized until it is earned. Interest is earned (accrued) as time passes.

Recording Interest

As we learned in Chapter 3, the basic formula for calculating interest on an interest-bearing note is the following:

ILLUSTRATION 8-8
Formula for calculating interest

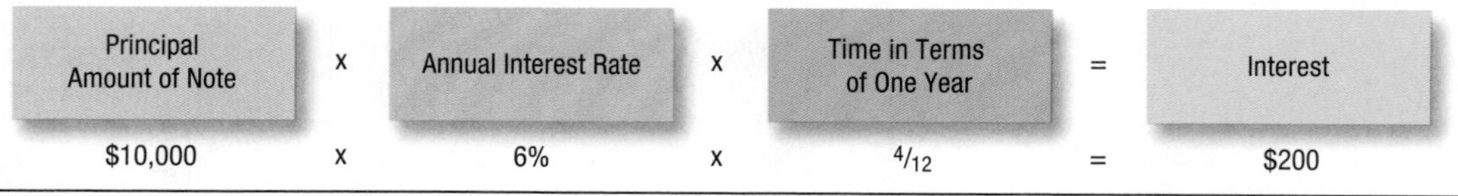

Principal Amount of Note
x
Annual Interest Rate
x
Time in Terms of One Year
=
Interest
$10,000
x
6%
x
4/12
=
$200

Helpful hint At the time the note is accepted, the "time" element of the interest calculation formula is zero. Therefore, the interest is also zero. (Any number multiplied by zero equals zero.)

Recall from Chapter 3 that the principal amount is the amount borrowed, or the amount still outstanding on a loan, separate from interest. This is also the balance in Wolder's Notes Receivable account or Higly's Note Payable account.

The interest rate specified in a note is an *annual* rate of interest. There are many factors that affect the interest rate. You will learn more about that in a finance course. Interest rates may also be fixed for the term of the note or may change over the term. In this textbook, we will always assume that the rate remains fixed for the term.

The time factor in the above formula gives the fraction of the year that the note has been outstanding. As we did in past chapters, to keep it simple we will assume that interest is calculated in months rather than days. Illustration 8-8 shows the calculation of interest revenue for Wolder Company and interest expense for Higly Inc. for the term of the note.

If Wolder Company's year end was June 30, the following adjusting journal entry would be required to accrue interest for the month of June:

A	=	L	+	OE
+50				+50

Cash flows: no effect

June 30	Interest Receivable	50	
	Interest Revenue ($10,000 × 6% × 1/12)		50
	To accrue interest on Higly note receivable.		

Notice that interest on a note receivable is *not* debited to the Notes Receivable account. Instead, a separate asset account for the interest receivable is used. The Note Receivable account balance must be equal to the amount still outstanding on the note, in order to correctly calculate interest.

Valuing Notes Receivable

Like accounts receivable, notes receivable are reported at their *net realizable value*. Each note must be analyzed to determine how likely it is to be collected. If eventual collection is doubtful, bad debt expense and an allowance for doubtful notes must be recorded in the same way as for accounts receivable. Some companies use only one allowance account for both accounts and notes, and call it Allowance for Doubtful Accounts.

DISPOSING OF NOTES RECEIVABLE

Notes are normally held to their maturity date, at which time the principal plus any unpaid interest is collected. This is known as honouring (paying) the note. Sometimes, the maker of the note defaults and an adjustment to the accounts must be made. This is known as dishonouring (not paying) the note.

Honouring of Notes Receivable

A note is honoured when it is paid in full at its maturity date. The amount due at maturity is the principal of the note plus interest for the length of time the note is outstanding (assuming interest is due at maturity rather than monthly). If Higly Inc. honours the note when it is due on September 30—the maturity date—the entry by Wolder Company to record the collection is:

Sept. 30	Cash	10,200	
	Notes Receivable—Higly		10,000
	Interest Revenue		150
	Interest Receivable		50
	To record collection of Higly note.		

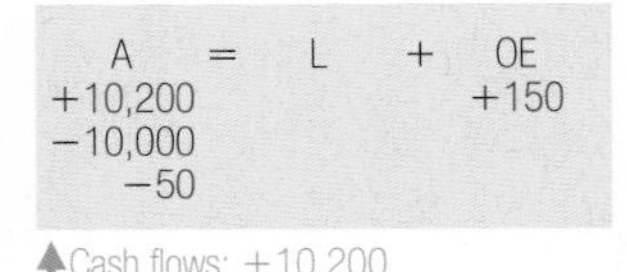

Cash flows: +10,200

This transaction can also be represented in the form of T accounts as follows:

Cash

Sept. 30	10,200	

Notes Receivable—Higly

Beginning Balance	10,000	
Sept. 30		10,000
Ending Balance	0	

Interest Revenue

Sept. 30		150

Interest Receivable

Beginning Balance	50	
Sept. 30		50
Ending Balance	0	

Recall that one month of interest revenue, \$50 (\$10,000 × 6% × 1/12), was accrued on June 30, Wolder's year end. Since that amount was already recorded as revenue *last year, but was not received*, that amount must now be credited to Interest Receivable. Consequently, only three months of interest revenue, \$150 (\$10,000 × 6% × 3/12), is recorded in this period.

Dishonouring of Notes Receivable

A **dishonoured note** is a note that is not paid in full at maturity. Since a dishonoured note receivable is no longer negotiable, the Notes Receivable account must be reduced by the principal of the note. The payee still has a claim against the maker of the note for both the principal and any unpaid interest and will transfer the amount owing to an Accounts Receivable account if there is hope that the amount will eventually be collected.

To illustrate, assume that on September 30, Higly Inc. says that it cannot pay at the present time but Wolder Company expects eventual collection. Wolder would make the following entry at the time the note is dishonoured:

A	=	L	+	OE
+10,200				+150
−10,000				
−50				

Cash flows: no effect

		Debit	Credit
Sept. 30	Accounts Receivable—Higly	10,200	
	Notes Receivable—Higly		10,000
	Interest Revenue		150
	Interest Receivable		50
	To record dishonouring of Higly note where collection is expected.		

Note that the amount recorded in the accounts receivable is the *total amount owed* (interest and principal) by Higly.

Wolder will continue to follow up with Higly. If the amount owing is eventually collected, Wolder will simply debit Cash and credit Accounts Receivable. If Wolder decides at a later date that it will never collect this amount from Higly, Wolder will write off the account receivable in the same way we learned earlier in the chapter—debit Allowance for Doubtful Accounts, and credit Accounts Receivable.

On the other hand, Wolder could directly write the note off on September 30 if it decided there was no hope of collection. Assuming Wolder uses one allowance account for both accounts and notes, it would record the following:

A	=	L	+	OE
+10,050				
−10,000				
−50				

Cash flows: no effect

		Debit	Credit
Sept. 30	Allowance for Doubtful Accounts	10,050	
	Notes Receivable—Higly		10,000
	Interest Receivable		50
	To record dishonouring of Higly note where collection is not expected.		

No interest revenue is recorded, because collection will not occur. The interest receivable that previously had been accrued and recognized as interest revenue in earlier fiscal periods is also written off and the Allowance for Doubtful Accounts is debited for both the principal amount owed and the interest receivable.

BEFORE YOU GO ON...

DO IT

On May 1, Gambit Stores accepts from J. Nyznyk a $3,400, three-month, 5% note in settlement of Nyznyk's overdue account. Interest is due at maturity. Gambit has a June 30 year end.

(a) Prepare the required journal entry to record the issue of the note on May 1, the adjusting journal entry on June 30, and the settlement of the note on August 1 assuming Nyznyk honours the note.

(b) Prepare the required journal entry on August 1 if Nyznyk does not pay the note and collection is not expected in the future.

Action Plan

- Calculate the accrued interest. The formula is: Principal × annual interest rate × time in terms of one year.
- Record the interest accrued on June 30 to follow revenue recognition criteria. Use Interest Receivable, not Notes Receivable, for accrued interest.
- If the note is honoured, calculate the interest accrued after June 30 and the total interest on the note. Record the interest accrued and the collection of the note and the total interest.
- If the note is dishonoured, record the transfer of the note and any interest earned to an accounts receivable account if eventual collection is expected or to an allowance account if collection is not expected. Note that the interest revenue for the current period is only recognized if eventual collection is expected.

SOLUTION

			Debit	Credit
(a)	May 1	Notes Receivable—J. Nyznyk	3,400	
		Accounts Receivable—J. Nyznyk		3,400
		To replace account receivable with 5% note receivable, due August 1.		
	June 30	Interest Receivable	28	
		Interest Revenue ($3,400 × 5% × 2/12)		28
		To record interest earned to June 30.		
	Aug. 1	Cash	3,442	
		Interest Receivable		28
		Notes Receivable—J. Nyznyk		3,400
		Interest Revenue ($3,400 × 5% × 1/12)		14
		To record collection of Nyznyk note plus interest.		
(b)	Aug. 1	Allowance for Doubtful Accounts	3,428	
		Interest Receivable		28
		Notes Receivable—J. Nyznyk		3,400
		To record dishonouring of Nyznyk note as collection is not expected.		

Related exercise material: BE8–11, BE8–12, BE8–13, BE8–14, E8–8, E8–9, and E8–10.

THE NAVIGATOR

STATEMENT PRESENTATION AND MANAGEMENT OF RECEIVABLES

STUDY OBJECTIVE 4
Demonstrate the presentation, analysis, and management of receivables.

The way receivables are presented in the financial statements is important because receivables are directly affected by how a company recognizes its revenue and bad debt expense. In addition, these reported numbers are critical for analyzing a company's liquidity and how well it manages its receivables. In the next sections, we will discuss the presentation, analysis, and management of receivables.

PRESENTATION

Each of the major types of receivables should be identified in the balance sheet or in the notes to the financial statements. Other receivables include interest receivable, loans or advances to employees, and recoverable sales and income taxes. These receivables are generally classified and reported as separate items in the current or noncurrent sections of the balance sheet, according to their due dates. Notes receivable may also be either current assets or long-term assets, depending on their due dates.

In addition to the net realizable value of the receivables shown on the balance sheet, both the gross amount of receivables and the allowance for doubtful accounts must be disclosed in either the balance sheet or the notes to the financial statements.

Bad debt expense is reported in the operating expenses section of the income statement. At the time this textbook was being written, standard setters were proposing that bad debt expense be reported in the revenue section of the income statement as a contra revenue account—a deduction from revenues. If this change is approved, it will decrease both net sales and total operating expenses, but total profit will not change.

Illustration 8-9 shows the presentation of receivables for Shaw Communications Inc., which provides television, Internet, and other media services.

ILLUSTRATION 8-9
Presentation of receivables

SHAW COMMUNICATIONS INC.
Notes to the Financial Statements (partial)
August 31, 2011
(in thousands)

Note 3: Accounts Receivable	2011	2010
Subscriber and trade receivables	$424,451	$209,817
Due from officers and employees	159	148
Due from related parties	1,236	1,689
Miscellaneous receivables	45,768	3,730
	471,614	215,384
Less: Allowance for doubtful accounts	(28,797)	(18,969)
	$442,817	$196,415

Included in operating, general and administrative expenses is a provision for doubtful accounts of $33,686 (2010 – $33,746; 2009 – $19,298).

In Note 3, Shaw discloses the *components* of its receivables. The net realizable value of the accounts receivable of $442 million in 2011 and $196 million in 2010 was reported in the current assets section of Shaw's balance sheet. Note that subscriber and trade receivables increased from $209 million in 2010 to $424 million in 2011. This is because in October 2010, Shaw acquired $296.6 million of receivables when it purchased Canwest Global Communications Corp.

Shaw also reports in its note to the financial statements that its allowance for doubtful accounts is determined by considering the number of days the account is past due, whether or not the customer continues to receive service, the company's collection history, and changes in business circumstances.

ANALYSIS

Management of accounts receivable is critical to a business's success. Accounts receivable are generally the most important source of cash for business. If sales increase, then accounts receivable are also expected to increase. On the other hand, an increase in accounts receivable might signal trouble. Perhaps the company increased its sales by loosening its credit policy, and these receivables may be difficult or impossible to collect. The company could also end up with higher costs because of the increase in sales since it may need more cash to pay for inventory and salaries.

Recall that the ability to pay obligations as they come due is measured by a company's liquidity. How can we tell if a company's management of its receivables is helping or hurting the company's liquidity? One way of doing this is to calculate a ratio called the **receivables turnover ratio**. This ratio measures the number of times, on average, that receivables are collected during the period. It is calculated by dividing net credit sales by average gross receivables during the year.

Unfortunately, companies rarely report the amount of net sales made on credit in their financial statements. As a result, net sales (including both cash and credit sales) is used as a substitute. As long as net sales are used to calculate the ratio for all companies being compared, the comparison is fair.

In Illustration 8-10, the substitute figures of total sales and trade and other receivables were used to calculate Reitmans' 2012 accounts receivable turnover.

ILLUSTRATION 8-10
Receivables turnover

Net Credit Sales	÷	Average Gross Accounts Receivable	=	Receivables Turnover
$1,019,397	÷	$\frac{\$3,033 + \$2,866}{2}$	=	345.6 times

The result indicates an accounts receivable turnover ratio of 345.6 times per year for Reitmans. The higher the turnover ratio, the more liquid the company's receivables are.

A popular variation of the receivables turnover ratio is to convert it into the number of days it takes the company to collect its receivables. This ratio, called the **collection period**, is calculated by dividing 365 days by the receivables turnover, as shown for Reitmans in Illustration 8-11.

ILLUSTRATION 8-11
Collection period

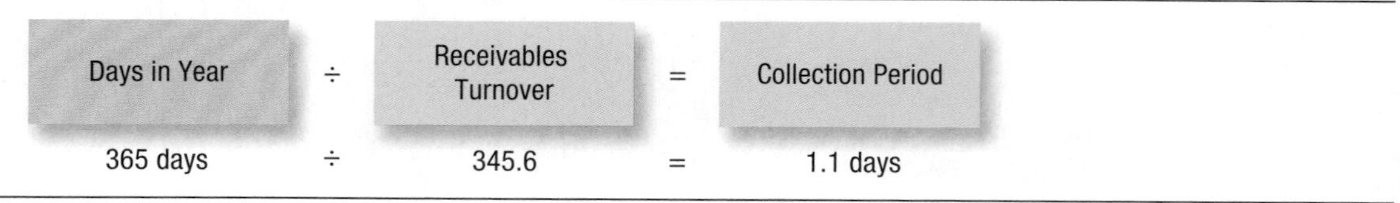

Helpful hint The relationship between receivables turnover and collection period is the same as the relationship between inventory turnover and days sales in inventory (see Chapter 6).

This means that in fiscal 2012, Reitmans collected its receivables, on average, in approximately 1.1 days. Reitmans does not have its own credit card. Its accounts receivable are from customers using credit cards such as MasterCard or Visa where the sales haven't been collected in cash from the credit card company prior to the year end. Reitmans' high turnover ratio and low collection period indicate that the company's receivables are highly liquid and that the company is receiving payment from the credit card companies quickly.

Bell Aliant, in our feature story, states that the vast majority of its consumer customers pay within 30 days but that it takes from 35 to 50 days to collect from businesses. The result is an overall average of between 31 and 35 days.

The collection period is often used to judge how effective a company's credit and collection policies are. The general rule is that the collection period should not be much longer than the credit term period (that is, the time allowed for payment). Accounts receivable are basically an interest-free loan to the customer, so the faster they are collected, the better.

Both the receivables turnover and the collection period are useful for judging how efficiently a company converts its credit sales to cash. Remember that these measures should also be compared with industry averages, and with previous years.

In addition, these measures should be analyzed along with other information about a company's liquidity, including the current ratio and inventory turnover. For example, low receivables may result in a low current ratio, which might make the company look like it has poor liquidity. But the receivables may be low because they are turning over quickly. In general, the faster the turnover, the more reliable the current ratio is for assessing liquidity.

The collection period can also be used to assess the length of a company's operating cycle. Recall from Chapter 4 that the operating cycle is the time it takes to go from cash to cash in producing revenues. In a merchandising company, the operating cycle may be measured by determining the average time that it takes to purchase inventory, sell it on account, and then collect cash from customers. In Chapter 6, we learned how to calculate days sales in inventory, which is the average age of the inventory on hand. The combination of the collection period and days sales in inventory is a useful way to measure the length of a company's operating cycle. Using the number of days sales in inventory calculated in Chapter 6, this calculation is shown in Illustration 8-12 for Reitmans.

ILLUSTRATION 8-12
Operating cycle

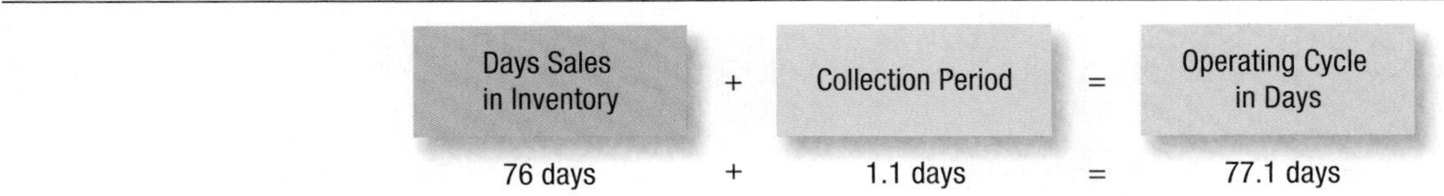

This means that in fiscal 2012, it took 77.1 days on average from the time Reitmans purchased its inventory until it collected the cash from its credit customers.

ACCELERATING CASH RECEIPTS FROM RECEIVABLES

If a company sells on credit, it has to wait until the customer pays the receivable before it has cash available to pay for such items as inventory and operating expenses. As credit sales and receivables increase in size and significance, waiting for receivables to be collected increases costs because the company cannot use the revenue from the sale until cash is collected. If a company can collect cash more quickly from its receivables, it can shorten the cash-to-cash operating cycle discussed in the previous section. One benefit of decreasing the operating cycle is that a company can invest in additional inventory and increase sales and profit.

There are two typical ways to collect cash more quickly from receivables: using the receivables to secure a loan and selling the receivables.

Loans Secured by Receivables

One of the most common ways to speed up cash flow from accounts receivable is to go to a bank and borrow money using accounts receivable as *collateral*. While this does have a cost (interest has to be paid to the bank on the loan), the cash is available for the company to use earlier. The loan can then be repaid as the receivables are collected. Generally, banks are willing to give financing of up to 75% of receivables that are less than 90 days old. Quite often, these arrangements occur through an operating line of credit, which is discussed in Chapter 10.

Sale of Receivables

Companies also frequently sell their receivables to another company because it provides an immediate source of cash. There are two other reasons for the sale of receivables. The first is their size. To be competitive, sellers often give financing to purchasers of their goods to encourage the sale of the product. But the companies may not want to hold large amounts of receivables. As a result, many major companies in the automobile, truck, equipment, computer, and appliance industries have created wholly owned finance companies that accept responsibility for accounts receivable financing. An example is Ford Credit Canada, owned by the Ford Motor Company of Canada.

Another reason for selling receivables is to reduce the costs of monitoring and collecting receivables. For example, it is often more cost-effective for a retailer to sell its receivables to credit card companies, such as Visa and MasterCard, which specialize in billing and collecting accounts receivable.

One way to accelerate receivables collection is by sale to a factor. A **factor** is a finance company or bank that buys receivables from businesses and then collects the cash directly from the customer. If the customer does not pay, the business is usually responsible for reimbursing the factor for the uncollected amounts. This is known as selling receivables on a recourse basis.

ACCOUNTING IN ACTION ACROSS THE ORGANIZATION

U.S. discount department store chain Target Corp. announced in early 2011 that it was going to get out of the credit card business and sell its credit card receivables. The retailer said it wanted to use the money from the sale to buy more inventory, pay down debt, and help pay for its planned expansion into Canada by taking over some Zellers stores from the Hudson's Bay Company. It also wanted to focus on merchandising instead of financial services. A year later, Target said it had not received an acceptable offer for the receivables and would hold off on selling them until late 2012 or early 2013. Some analysts thought that waiting was likely a smart move, because as the economy improves and the number of shoppers defaulting on their credit card payments declines, the value of Target's credit card receivables would increase. Others thought that the delay of the sale meant that the company was overvaluing its receivables. In the third quarter of 2011, Target's bad debts declined by 64% to $40 million, while its profit from its credit card business increased by 10%. In that period, the company's gross credit card receivables totalled $6.1 billion.

Sources: Thomas Lee, "Target Does Things Its Way—For Better or Worse," *Minneapolis StarTribune*, January 25, 2012; James Callan and Matt Townsend, "Target Suspends Efforts to Sell Credit Card Receivables," Bloomberg, January 18, 2012; Karen Talley, "Target Is Entering Canada, Selling Card Receivables," Dow Jones Newswires, January 13, 2011.

What might be the advantages to Target of having its own credit card? What might be the disadvantages?

BEFORE YOU GO ON...

DO IT

The following information is available for Jupiter Company.

	2015	2014	2013
Net credit sales	$1,500,000	$1,300,000	$1,350,000
Gross accounts receivable	127,000	124,000	118,000
Days sales in inventory	44.5 days	43 days	

Calculate the accounts receivable turnover ratio, collection period, and operating cycle in days and comment on any trends.

Action Plan

- Calculate the average gross accounts receivable using the accounts receivable balance at the beginning and end of the year.
- Divide net credit sales by the average accounts receivable for that year to calculate receivables turnover.
- Divide 365 by the receivables turnover to calculate collection period.
- Add the collection period to days sales in inventory to calculate operating cycle in days.

SOLUTION

	2015	2014
Receivables turnover	11.95 times = $\frac{\$1,500,000}{[(127,000 + 124,000) \div 2]}$	10.74 times = $\frac{\$1,300,000}{[(124,000 + 118,000) \div 2]}$
Collection period	30.54 days = $\frac{365 \text{ days}}{11.95 \text{ times}}$	34 days = $\frac{365 \text{ days}}{10.74 \text{ times}}$
Operating cycle in days	75 days = 30.54 + 44.5	77 days = 34 + 43

The accounts receivable turnover has increased and the collection period decreased. In general, it is better to have a higher accounts receivable turnover and a lower collection period. Even though the days sales in inventory had increased, the operating cycle has decreased, which generally is better for the company.

Related exercise material: BE8–15, BE8–16, BE8–17, E8–3, E8–11, E8–12, and E8–13.

THE NAVIGATOR

Comparing IFRS and ASPE

Key Differences	International Financial Reporting Standards (IFRS)	Accounting Standards for Private Enterprises (ASPE)
No significant differences		

THE NAVIGATOR

DEMONSTRATION PROBLEM

On February 28, Dylan Co. had the following balances in select accounts:

Accounts Receivable	$200,000
Allowance for Doubtful Accounts (credit)	12,500

Selected transactions for Dylan Co. follow. Dylan's year end is June 30.

Mar.	1	Sold $20,000 of merchandise to Potter Company, terms n/30.
	1	Accepted Juno Company's $16,500, six-month, 6% note for the balance due on account.
	11	Potter Company returned $600 worth of goods.
	13	Made Dylan Co. credit card sales for $13,200.
	30	Received payment in full from Potter Company.
Apr.	13	Received collections of $8,200 on Dylan Co. credit card sales. Added interest charges of 18% to the remaining balance.
May	10	Wrote off as uncollectible $15,000 of accounts receivable.
June	30	Estimated uncollectible accounts are determined to be $20,000 at June 30.
	30	Recorded the interest accrued on the Juno Company note.
July	16	Received payment in full, $4,000, on an account that was previously written off in May.
Sept.	1	Collected cash from Juno Company in payment of the March 1 note receivable.

Instructions

(a) Prepare the journal entries for the transactions. Ignore cost of goods sold entries for purposes of this question.

(b) Open T accounts for Accounts Receivable and the Allowance for Doubtful Accounts, and post the relevant journal entries to these accounts. Calculate the balance in these accounts at June 30 and at September 1.

(c) Calculate the net realizable value of the accounts receivable at June 30 and September 1.

SOLUTION TO DEMONSTRATION PROBLEM

(a)

Mar.	1	Accounts Receivable—Potter	20,000	
		Sales		20,000
		To record sale on account.		
	1	Notes Receivable—Juno	16,500	
		Accounts Receivable—Juno		16,500
		To record acceptance of Juno Company note.		
	11	Sales Returns and Allowances	600	
		Accounts Receivable—Potter		600
		To record return of goods.		
	13	Accounts Receivable	13,200	
		Sales		13,200
		To record company credit card sales.		
	30	Cash ($20,000 – $600)	19,400	
		Accounts Receivable—Potter		19,400
		To record collection of account receivable.		

Action Plan

- Record receivables at the invoice price.
- Recognize that sales returns and allowances reduce the amount received on accounts receivable.
- Calculate interest by multiplying the principal by the interest rate by the part of the year that has passed.
- Record write offs of accounts and collection of previously written-off accounts only in balance sheet accounts.
- Consider any existing balance in the allowance account when making the adjustment for uncollectible accounts.

SOLUTION TO DEMONSTRATION PROBLEM continued on next page

- Recognize any remaining interest on notes receivable when recording the collection of a note.

SOLUTION TO DEMONSTRATION PROBLEM continued from previous page

Date	Account	Debit	Credit
Apr. 13	Cash	8,200	
	Accounts Receivable		8,200
	To record collection of credit card accounts receivable.		
13	Accounts Receivable [($13,200 – $8,200) × 18% × 1/12]	75	
	Interest Revenue		75
	To record interest on amount due.		
May 10	Allowance for Doubtful Accounts	15,000	
	Accounts Receivable		15,000
	To record write off of accounts receivable.		
June 30	Bad Debt Expense ($20,000 + $2,500)	22,500	
	Allowance for Doubtful Accounts		22,500
	To record estimate of uncollectible accounts.		
30	Interest Receivable ($16,500 × 6% × 4/12)	330	
	Interest Revenue		330
	To record interest earned.		
July 16	Accounts Receivable	4,000	
	Allowance for Doubtful Accounts		4,000
	To reverse write off of account receivable.		
16	Cash	4,000	
	Accounts Receivable		4,000
	To record collection of account receivable.		
Sept. 1	Cash [$16,500 + ($16,500 × 6% × 6/12)]	16,995	
	Interest Revenue ($16,500 × 6% × 2/12)		165
	Interest Receivable		330
	Note Receivable		16,500
	To record collection of note receivable plus interest.		

(b)

Accounts Receivable

		Debit	Credit
Feb. 28	Bal.	200,000	16,500
		20,000	600
		13,200	19,400
		75	8,200
			15,000
June 30	Bal.	173,575	
		4,000	4,000
Sept. 1	Bal.	173,575	

Allowance for Doubtful Accounts

		Debit			Credit
		15,000	Feb. 28	Bal.	12,500
June 30	Bal.	2,500			
			June 30	Adj.	22,500
			June 30	Bal.	20,000
					4,000
			Sept. 1	Bal.	24,000

(c)

	June 30	Sept. 1
Accounts receivable	$173,575	$173,575
Less: Allowance for doubtful accounts	20,000	24,000
Net realizable value	$153,575	$149,575

THE NAVIGATOR

Summary of Study Objectives

1. ***Record accounts receivable transactions.*** Accounts receivable are recorded at the invoice (selling) price. They are reduced by sales returns and allowances, and sales discounts. Accounts receivable subsidiary ledgers are used to keep track of individual account balances. When interest is charged on a past-due receivable, this interest is added to the accounts receivable balance and is recognized as interest revenue. Sales using nonbank credit cards result in a receivable, net of the credit card charges, from the credit card company; sales using company credit cards result in a receivable from the customer.

2. ***Calculate the net realizable value of accounts receivable and account for bad debts.*** Accounts receivable must be reported at their net realizable value on the balance sheet. The allowance method is used to record the estimated uncollectible accounts in the Allowance for Doubtful Accounts. The net realizable value of the receivables is equal to the gross accounts receivable minus the allowance. A percentage of total receivables, or an aging schedule applying different percentages to different categories of receivables, is used to estimate the allowance for doubtful accounts. The allowance method also matches bad debt expense against revenue in the period when the revenue is recognized. Bad debt expense is equal to the difference between the required balance and the unadjusted balance in the allowance for doubtful accounts.

   When a specific account receivable is determined to be uncollectible, the account is written off and the allowance is reduced. When a previously written-off account is collected, two entries are required: the first entry reverses the entry previously made to write off the account, and the second entry records the collection of the receivable.

3. ***Account for notes receivable.*** Notes receivable are recorded at their principal amount. Interest is earned from the date the note is issued until it matures and must be recorded in the correct accounting period when it is earned. Interest receivable is recorded in a separate account from the note. Like accounts receivable, notes receivable are reported at their net realizable value.

   Notes are normally held to maturity. At that time, the principal plus any unpaid interest is due and the note is removed from the accounts. If a note is not paid at maturity, it is said to be dishonoured. If eventual collection is still expected, an account receivable replaces the note receivable and any unpaid interest. Otherwise, the note must be written off.

4. ***Demonstrate the presentation, analysis, and management of receivables.*** Each major type of receivable should be identified in the balance sheet or in the notes to the financial statements. Both the gross amount of receivables and the allowance for doubtful accounts/notes is required to be reported in the balance sheet or the notes to the financial statements. Bad debt expense is reported in the income statement as an operating expense.

   The liquidity of receivables can be evaluated by calculating the receivables turnover and collection period ratios. The receivables turnover is calculated by dividing net credit sales by average gross accounts receivable. This ratio measures how efficiently the company is converting its receivables into sales. The collection period converts the receivables turnover into days, dividing 365 days by the receivables turnover ratio. It shows the number of days, on average, it takes a company to collect its accounts receivable. The combination of the collection period and days sales in inventory is a useful way to measure the length of a company's operating cycle.

   Companies may accelerate the collection of cash by using the receivables to secure a loan or by selling the receivables to a factor.

Glossary

Accounts receivable Amounts owed by customers on account. (p. 338)

Aging schedule A list of accounts receivable organized by the length of time they have been unpaid. (p. 344)

Allowance for Doubtful Accounts A contra asset account that is deducted from gross account receivables to report receivables at their net realizable value. (p. 343)

Allowance method The method of accounting for bad debts that involves estimating uncollectible accounts at the end of each period. (p. 343)

Bad debt expense An expense account to record uncollectible receivables. (p. 342)

Collection period The average number of days that receivables are outstanding. It is calculated by dividing 365 days by the receivables turnover. (p. 354)

Default What happens when the maker of the note does not pay the note in full. Also referred to as dishonouring the note. (p. 342)

Dishonoured note A note that is not paid in full at maturity. (p. 351)

Factor A finance company or bank that buys receivables from businesses and then collects the payments directly from the customers. (p. 356)

Gross accounts receivable The total accounts receivable in the control account in the general ledger; includes both collectible and uncollectible accounts. (p. 344)

Maker The party making the promise to pay a promissory note. (p. 349)

Net realizable value The net amount of receivables expected to be collected; it is the gross amount minus the allowance for doubtful accounts. (p. 342)

Notes receivable Claims for which formal instruments (written instruments) of credit are issued as evidence of the debt. (p. 338)

Payee The party to whom payment on a promissory note is to be made. (p. 349)

Percentage of receivables approach The approach used to estimate uncollectible accounts where the allowance for doubtful accounts is calculated as a percentage of receivables. (p. 343)

Promissory note A written promise to pay a specified amount of money on demand or at a definite time. (p. 349)

Receivables turnover ratio A measure of the liquidity of receivables, calculated by dividing net credit sales by average gross accounts receivable. (p. 354)

Trade receivables Accounts and notes receivable that result from sales transactions. (p. 338)

Self-Study Questions

Answers are at the end of the chapter.

(SO 1) AP 1. On August 10, Pi Company sells merchandise on account to Murray Co. for $2,000, terms 2/10, n/30. On August 15, Murray returns merchandise worth $400 to Pi. On August 20, payment is received from Murray for the balance due. What is the amount of cash received?
(a) $1,560
(b) $1,600
(c) $1,568
(d) $1,960

(SO 1) AP 2. Manery Company accepts a nonbank credit card on September 5 in payment of a $2,000 purchase. The credit card company charges a 2% fee. What is the amount recorded in accounts receivable on September 5?
(a) $2,000
(b) $1,960
(c) $2,040
(d) $0

(SO 2) AP 3. Kartik Company's accounts receivable are $200,000 at the end of the year. The allowance for doubtful accounts has a credit balance of $4,000 before any adjustments have been made. The company estimates that 5% of accounts receivable will not be collected. What is the net realizable value of the accounts receivable at the end of the year?
(a) $196,000
(b) $200,000
(c) $186,000
(d) $190,000

(SO 2) AP 4. Sanderson Company has a credit balance of $6,000 in Allowance for Doubtful Accounts before any adjustments are made. Based on an aging of its accounts receivable at the end of the period, the company estimates that $80,000 of its receivables are uncollectible. What is the amount of bad debt expense that should be reported for this accounting period?
(a) $74,000
(b) $6,000
(c) $86,000
(d) $80,000

(SO 2) AP 5. Use the same information as in question 4, except that Sanderson Company has a debit balance of $6,000 in Allowance for Doubtful Accounts before any adjustments are made. In this situation, what is the amount of bad debt expense that should be reported for this accounting period?
(a) $74,000
(b) $6,000
(c) $86,000
(d) $80,000

(SO 2) AP 6. On January 1, 2014, the Allowance for Doubtful Accounts has a credit balance of $18,000. During 2014, $30,000 of uncollectible accounts receivable were written off. An aging schedule indicates that uncollectible accounts are $20,000 at the end of 2014. What is the required adjustment to the allowance for doubtful accounts at December 31, 2014?
(a) $2,000
(b) $8,000
(c) $20,000
(d) $32,000

(SO 2) AP 7. On January 1, 2014, Allowance for Doubtful Accounts had a credit balance of $40,000. In 2014, $30,000 of uncollectible accounts receivable were written off. On December 31, 2014, the company had accounts receivable of $900,000. Experience indicates that 4% of total receivables will become uncollectible. The adjusting journal entry that would be recorded on December 31, 2014, would be:

(a) Allowance for Doubtful Accounts	26,000	
Accounts Receivable		26,000
(b) Bad Debt Expense	36,000	
Accounts Receivable		36,000
(c) Bad Debt Expense	26,000	
Allowance for Doubtful Accounts		26,000
(d) Bad Debt Expense	36,000	
Allowance for Doubtful Accounts		36,000

(SO 3) AP 8. On June 1, Sorenson Co. accepts a $2,000, four-month, 6% promissory note in settlement of an account with Parton Co. Sorenson has a July 31 fiscal year end. The adjusting entry to record interest on July 31 is:

(a) Interest Receivable	20	
Interest Revenue		20
(b) Interest Receivable	120	
Interest Revenue		120
(c) Notes Receivable	120	
Unearned Interest Revenue		120
(d) Interest Receivable	40	
Interest Revenue		40

(SO 3) AP 9. Schlicht Co. holds Osgrove Inc.'s $10,000, four-month, 9% note. If no interest has been accrued, when the note is collected, the entry made by Schlicht Co. is:

(a) Cash	10,300	
Notes Receivable		10,300
(b) Cash	10,900	
Interest Revenue		900
Notes Receivable		10,000
(c) Accounts Receivable	10,300	
Notes Receivable		10,000
Interest Revenue		300
(d) Cash	10,300	
Notes Receivable		10,000
Interest Revenue		300

(SO 3) AP 10. When a note is dishonoured, an entry is made to:
(a) Reverse the interest revenue previously recognized.
(b) Record bad debt expense.
(c) Record an account receivable for the principal amount of the note and the accrued interest if the company expects to collect the amount owing.
(d) Write off the note whether or not the company expects to collect the amount owing.

(SO 4) C 11. The allowance for doubtful accounts is presented in the financial statements as:
(a) a current liability in the balance sheet.
(b) a deduction from accounts receivable in the balance sheet.
(c) a contra revenue account in the income statement.
(d) an operating expense in the income statement.

(SO 4) AP 12. Moore Company had net credit sales of $800,000 in the year and a cost of goods sold of $500,000. The balance in Accounts Receivable at the beginning of the year was $100,000 and at the end of the year it was $150,000. What were the receivables turnover and collection period ratios, respectively?
(a) 4.0 and 91 days
(b) 5.3 and 69 days
(c) 6.4 and 57 days
(d) 8.0 and 46 days

Questions

(SO 1) C 1. When should a receivable be recorded for a service company? For a merchandising company?

(SO 1) K 2. Why are accounts receivable and notes receivable sometimes called trade receivables?

(SO 1) C 3. (a) What information does a company need to manage its accounts receivable? (b) How is this information tracked in an accounting system?

(SO 1) K 4. Under what circumstances is interest normally recorded for an account receivable?

(SO 1) C 5. Ernie Andrews thinks that a sale on a nonbank credit card should be recorded as a debit to cash, as cash will be received from the credit card company. What is the flaw in Ernie's argument?

(SO 2) C 6. Why can't a company know with certainty whether or not a customer will pay its account receivable?

(SO 2) C 7. ACCT Company has had significant bad debts in previous years. To eliminate the risk of bad debts, the accounting manager of ACCT Company has recommended to the sales manager to make only cash sales. The sales manager does not think this is the best business decision. Do you agree or disagree with the sales manager? What do you recommend the company do to reduce the risk of bad debts?

(SO 2) C 8. What is the net realizable value of accounts receivable? Why is it important that accounts receivable be reported at net realizable value?

(SO 2) K 9. Explain the allowance method of accounting for bad debts. How does this method result in (a) assets not being overstated, and (b) the matching of expenses with revenues?

(SO 2) C 10. (a) What is the purpose of the account Allowance for Doubtful Accounts? (b) Although the normal balance of this account is a credit balance, it sometimes has a debit balance. Explain how this can happen.

(SO 2) C 11. Dimitri doesn't understand why the bad debt expense reported in the income statement is usually not equal to the allowance for doubtful accounts reported in the balance sheet. Explain why this happens.

(SO 2) C 12. Zahra doesn't understand why bad debt expense is not increased when a specific customer account is determined to be uncollectible and written off. Explain.

(SO 2) C 13. What is an aging schedule? How is the aging schedule used to estimate the amount of uncollectibles?

(SO 2) C 14. When an account receivable that was written off is later collected, two journal entries are usually made. Explain why.

(SO 3) K 15. Explain how notes receivable and accounts receivable are the same and how they are different.

(SO 3) C 16. Why will a company take a note receivable from a customer in settlement of a late account receivable?

(SO 3) C 17. Danielle does not understand why a note receivable is not immediately recorded at its maturity value (principal plus interest). After all, you know you are going to collect both the principal amount and the interest and you know how much each will be. Explain to Danielle why notes are recorded at their principal value, rather than at their maturity value.

(SO 3) C 18. What does it mean if a note is dishonoured?

(SO 3) C 19. How would the entries differ if a note receivable is dishonoured and eventual collection is expected versus a note receivable where collection is not expected?

(SO 4) C 20. Mac Leonard is preparing the financial statements and has reported the Allowance for Doubtful Accounts in the current liabilities section of the balance sheet because the normal balance of the allowance is a credit. Do you agree with this treatment? Explain.

(SO 4) C 21. Saucier Company has accounts receivable, notes receivable due in three months, notes receivable due in two years, an allowance for doubtful accounts, sales taxes recoverable, and income tax receivable. How should the receivables be reported on the balance sheet?

(SO 4) C 22. The president of Unlimited Enterprises proudly announces that her company's liquidity has improved. Its current ratio increased substantially this year. Does an increase in the current ratio always indicate improved liquidity? What other ratio(s) might you review to determine whether or not the increase in the current ratio represents an improvement in the company's financial health?

(SO 4) C 23. Canadian Worldwide Communications Co.'s receivables turnover was 6.5 times in 2013 and 5.9 times in 2014. Has the company's receivables management improved or worsened?

(SO 4) C 24. Why might a company not want to have a receivables turnover that is significantly higher than that of its competitors?

(SO 4) K 25. Why do companies sometimes sell their receivables?

Brief Exercises

Identify impact of transaction on receivables, total assets, liabilities, and owner's equity. **(SO 1) K**

BE8–1 Seven transactions follow. For each transaction, indicate if the transaction increases, decreases, or has no effect on (a) accounts receivable, (b) notes receivable, (c) total assets, (d) total liabilities, and (e) owner's equity. (*Hint:* Remember that the accounting equation must always be in balance.) Use the following format, in which the first transaction is given as an example:

Transaction:	(a) Accounts Receivable	(b) Notes Receivable	(c) Total Assets	(d) Total Liabilities	(e) Owner's Equity
1. Performed services on account for a customer.	Increase	No effect	Increase	No effect	Increase
2. A customer paid cash for services to be provided next month.					
3. Performed services for a customer in exchange for a note.					
4. Collected cash from the customer in transaction 1. above.					
5. Performed services for a customer for cash.					
6. Extended a customer's account for three months by accepting a note in exchange for it.					
7. Performed services for a customer who had paid in advance.					

BE8–2 Record the following transactions on the books of Marsh Co:

Record accounts receivable transactions. (SO 1) AP

(a) On September 1, Marsh Co. sold merchandise on account to Pellerin Inc. for $20,000, terms 2/10, n/30. The cost of the merchandise sold was $12,000. Marsh Co. uses a perpetual inventory system.
(b) On September 4, Pellerin Inc. returned merchandise worth $4,000 to Marsh Co. The original cost of the merchandise was $2,400. The merchandise was returned to inventory.
(c) On September 10, Pellerin Inc. paid for the merchandise.

BE8–3 Record the following transactions on the books of Fowler Co.:

Record accounts receivable transactions. (SO 1) AP

(a) On May 1, Fowler Co. sold merchandise on account to Kaneva Inc. for $30,000, terms 2/10, n/30. Ignore any entries that affect inventory and cost of goods sold for purposes of this question.
(b) On May 6, Kaneva Inc. returned merchandise worth $6,000 to Fowler Co.
(c) On June 30, Fowler Co. charged Kaneva Inc. one month's interest for the overdue account. Fowler charges 10% on overdue accounts. (Round the calculation to the nearest dollar.)
(d) On July 5, Kaneva paid the amount owing to Fowler Co.

BE8–4 Imports to You Co. accepted a credit card in payment of a $600 purchase of merchandise on August 7. For each of the following assumptions, prepare the journal entry to record the sale.

Record credit card transactions. (SO 1) AP

(a) The customer used a nonbank card and the company charges a 3% fee.
(b) The customer used a Visa card and Visa charges a 3% fee.
(c) The customer used an Imports to You Co. credit card.

BE8–5 Gourdeau Co. uses an aging schedule to determine its estimated uncollectible accounts at December 31. Complete the following schedule and determine the required balance in the allowance for doubtful accounts and the net realizable value of the accounts receivable.

Complete aging schedule and determine the allowance and net realizable value. (SO 2) AP

Number of Days Outstanding	Accounts Receivable	Estimated % Uncollectible	Estimated Uncollectible Accounts
0–30 days	$265,000	1%	
31–60 days	70,000	4%	
61–90 days	45,000	10%	
Over 90 days	20,000	20%	
Total	$ 400,000		

BE8–6 Refer to the data in BE8–5 for Gourdeau Co.

Determine bad debt expense. (SO 2) AP

(a) Assuming the allowance for doubtful accounts has an unadjusted credit balance of $4,500 at December 31, what is the bad debt expense for the year? (*Hint:* Use a T account to calculate the amount of the adjustment.)
(b) Assume instead that the allowance for doubtful accounts had a debit balance of $2,500. What is the bad debt expense for the year?

BE8–7 Qinshan Ltd. estimates that 4% of total accounts receivable will become uncollectible. Accounts receivable at December 31, 2014, are $250,000.

Determine the allowance and net realizable value and record bad debts. (SO 2) AP

(a) Determine the required balance in the allowance for doubtful accounts and the net realizable value of the accounts receivable.
(b) The allowance for doubtful accounts has an unadjusted debit balance of $1,500 at December 31, 2014. Prepare the adjusting entry to record bad debt expense in 2014. (*Hint:* Use T accounts to calculate the amount of the adjustment.)
(c) Assume instead that the allowance has an unadjusted credit balance of $500 at December 31, 2014. Prepare the adjusting entry to record bad debt expense. (*Hint:* Use T accounts to calculate the amount of the adjustment.)

BE8–8 Stilton Company reported the following in its general ledger. Using your knowledge of receivable transactions, match each of the transactions (a) to (f) with the best description of the economic event.

Analyze accounts receivable transactions. (SO 2) AP

Accounts Receivable

Jan. 1	20,000	(b)	80,000
(a)	120,000	(c)	500
Dec. 31	59,500		
(e)	500	(f)	500

Service Revenue

		120,000	(a)

Allowance for Doubtful Accounts

		Jan. 1	2,000
(c)	500	(d)	900
		Dec. 31	2,400
		(e)	500

Bad Debt Expense

(d)	900		

1. Collect previously written-off account ______
2. Provide service on account ______
3. Write off uncollectible account ______
4. Collect accounts receivable ______
5. Record bad debt expense ______
6. Reverse previously written-off account ______

Record write off and compare net realizable value. **(SO 2) AP**

BE8–9 At the end of 2014, Perry Co. has an allowance for doubtful accounts of $28,000. On January 31, 2015, when it has accounts receivable of $575,000, Perry Co. learns that its $5,500 receivable from Young Inc. is not collectible. Management authorizes a write off.

(a) Record the write off.
(b) What is the net realizable value of the accounts receivable (1) before the write off, and (2) after the write off? Be sure to show your calculations.

Record collection of account previously written off. **(SO 2) AP**

BE8–10 Assume the same information as in BE8–9. Young Inc.'s financial difficulties are over. On June 4, 2014, Perry Co. receives a payment in full of $5,500 from Young Inc. Record this transaction.

Differentiate between accounts receivable and notes receivable. **(SO 1, 3) K**

BE8–11 Place the number corresponding to each of the following characteristics in the appropriate section of the diagram. If a characteristic applies to both Accounts Receivable and Notes Receivable, place that number in the overlapping section.

1. Is shown as an asset on the balance sheet
2. Provides a strong legal claim in the sense that it is a written promise to pay a specific amount at a specific point in time
3. Is considered to be a trade receivable
4. Is usually the most significant type of claim held by a company
5. Can be sold to a third party
6. Its interest accrues from the first day of the receivable
7. Is usually due within 30 days
8. Is shown at its net realizable value

Accounts Receivable
Notes Receivable

Calculate interest on notes receivable. **(SO 3) AP**

BE8–12 Hochelaga Co. has three outstanding notes receivable at its December 31, 2014, fiscal year end. For each note, calculate (a) total interest revenue, (b) interest revenue to be recorded in 2014, and (c) interest revenue to be recorded in 2015.

Issue Date	Term	Principal	Interest Rate
1. August 31, 2014	9 months	$15,000	6%
2. November 1, 2014	6 months	44,000	8%
3. October 1, 2014	15 months	30,000	7%

Record notes receivable transactions. **(SO 3) AP**

BE8–13 Alikhan Co. sold merchandise on account to Emerald Co. for $42,000, terms n/30, on April 1, 2014. Alikhan uses a perpetual inventory system and the merchandise had a cost of $25,200. On June 1, 2014, Emerald gave Alikhan a six-month, 6% promissory note in settlement of the account. Interest is to be paid at maturity. On December 1, Emerald paid the note and accrued interest. Record the above transactions for Alikhan Co. Alikhan Co. has a July 31 fiscal year end and adjusts its accounts annually.

Record notes receivable transactions. **(SO 3) AP**

BE8–14 Lee Company accepts a $27,000, four-month, 6% note receivable in settlement of an account receivable on June 1, 2014. Interest is to be paid at maturity. Lee Company has a December 31 year end and adjusts its accounts annually.

(a) Record (1) the issue of the note on June 1 and (2) the settlement of the note on October 1, assuming the note is honoured.
(b) Assume instead that the note is dishonoured but eventual collection is expected. Record the October 1 journal entry.
(c) Assume instead that the note is dishonoured and eventual collection is not expected. Record the October 1 journal entry.

BE8–15 Chanticlerc Co. lent Sharp Inc. $100,000 cash in exchange for a five-year, 4% note on July 1, 2014. Interest is payable quarterly on January 1, April 1, July 1, and October 1 each year. Chanticlerc Co. has a December 31 year end.

Record notes receivable transactions and indicate statement presentation. **(SO 3, 4) AP**

(a) Record Chanticlerc's entries related to the note up to and including January 1, 2015.
(b) Indicate what amounts will be reported in Chanticlerc's December 31, 2014, balance sheet and where the amounts will be classified.

BE8–16 WAF Company's general ledger included the following accounts at November 30, 2014:

Prepare current assets section. **(SO 4) AP**

Accounts payable	$145,500
Accounts receivable	109,000
Allowance for doubtful accounts	6,950
Bad debt expense	35,970
Cash	74,000
GST recoverable	21,850
Interest receivable	2,500
Interest revenue	10,000
Merchandise inventory	110,800
Note receivable—due April 23, 2015	50,000
Note receivable—due May 21, 2018	150,000
Prepaid expenses	15,300
Short-term investments	80,500

Prepare the current assets section of the balance sheet.

BE8–17 The financial statements of **Maple Leaf Foods Inc.** reported the following for the years ended December 31, 2011, 2010, and 2009.

Prepare current assets section. **(SO 4) AN**

Financial Statement Data (in thousands of dollars)			
	2011	2010	2009
Sales	$4,893,624	$4,968,119	$5,221,602
Accounts receivable	133,504	108,379	372,330

(a) Calculate Maple Leaf's receivables turnover and collection period for 2011 and 2010.
(b) Has the company's liquidity improved or weakened?

Exercises

E8–1 Selected transactions for Theatre Productions follow. Theatre Productions uses a perpetual inventory system.

Identify impact and record accounts receivable transactions. **(SO 1) AP**

May 8	Sold merchandise costing $5,980 to Grande Theatre for $13,000, terms 2/10, n/30.
10	Grande returned $1,000 of the merchandise. This merchandise had originally cost Theatre $460 and was returned to inventory.
May 18	Grande paid Theatre the amount owing.
19	Sold merchandise costing $3,600 to Summer Productions for $6,000, terms 1/10, n/30.
20	Summer Productions returned $500 of the merchandise because it was damaged. The merchandise had originally cost Theatre Productions $300. Theatre Productions scrapped the merchandise.
July 19	Added interest charges for one month to the amount owing by Summer Productions. Theatre charges 15% on outstanding receivables. (*Hint:* Be sure to use the amount of the sale less the return as the principal amount in your interest calculation.)
22	Summer Productions paid the amount owing.

Instructions

(a) For each of these transactions, indicate if the transaction has increased (+) or decreased (−) cash, accounts receivable, inventory, and owner's equity and by how much. If the item is not changed, write NE to indicate there is no effect. Use the following format, in which the first one has been done for you as an example.

Transaction Date	Cash	Accounts Receivable	Inventory	Owner's Equity
May 8	NE	+$13,000	−$5,980	+$7,020

(b) Prepare journal entries to record the above transactions.

Record accounts receivable transactions. Post to subsidiary and general ledgers. **(SO 1) AP**

E8–2 Transactions follow for the Extreme Sports Ltd. store and three of its customers in the company's first month of business:

June 3 Ben Kidd used his Extreme Sports credit card to purchase $1,050 of merchandise.
6 Biljana Pavic used her Extreme Sports credit card to purchase $840 of merchandise.
8 Biljana Pavic returned $210 of merchandise on credit.
9 Nicole Montpetit purchased $421 of merchandise and paid for it with Visa. Visa charges a 2% service fee.
18 Ben Kidd used his Extreme Sports credit card to purchase an additional $348 of merchandise.
19 Bonnie Cutcliffe used her debit card to purchase $230 of merchandise. There is a $0.50 service charge on all debit card transactions.
20 Biljana Pavic made a $315 payment on her credit card account.
23 Nicole Montpetit used her Extreme Sports credit card to purchase $498 of merchandise.
25 Ben Kidd paid the amount owing on his June 3 purchase.
30 Biljana Pavic used her Extreme Sports credit card to purchase $420 of merchandise.

Instructions

(a) Record the above transactions. Ignore any inventory or cost of goods sold entries for purposes of this question.
(b) Set up T accounts for the Accounts Receivable general ledger (control) account and for the Accounts Receivable subsidiary ledger accounts. Post the journal entries to these accounts.
(c) Prepare a list of customers and the balances of their accounts from the subsidiary ledger. Prove that the total of the subsidiary ledger is equal to the control account balance.

Record credit card transactions and indicate statement presentation. **(SO 1, 4) AP**

E8–3 Krazy Hair Salon accepts its own credit card, as well as debit cards and bank and nonbank credit cards. Krazy is charged 3.5% for all bank credit card transactions, 4.25% for all nonbank credit card transactions, and $0.50 per transaction for all debit card transactions. In October and November 2014, the following summary transactions occurred:

Oct. 15 Performed services totalling $15,000 for customers who used Krazy credit cards.
20 Performed services totalling $7,500 for customers who used Visa credit cards.
30 Performed services totalling $2,000 for customers who used nonbank credit cards.
31 Performed services totalling $5,000 for customers who used debit cards (100 transactions).
Nov. 15 Collected $9,000 of payments on Krazy credit cards.
18 Collected the amount owing from the nonbank credit card companies for the October 30 transactions.
30 Added interest charges of 24% to outstanding Krazy credit card balances. Interest is charged after 30 days from date of purchase.

Instructions

(a) Record the above transactions for Krazy Hair Salon.
(b) In addition to these transactions, Krazy Hair Salon had rent expense of $4,000, supplies expense of $500, and salary expense of $5,000 for the months of October and November. Prepare a multi-step income statement for Krazy Hair Salon for the two months ended November 30.

Calculate net realizable value and record bad debts. **(SO 2) AP**

E8–4 Assen Company's general ledger at December 31, 2014, the end of the current year, shows Accounts Receivable $210,000 and Allowance for Doubtful Accounts $1,300 (credit). Uncollectible accounts are estimated to be 10% of accounts receivable.

Instructions

(a) Calculate the net realizable value of the accounts receivable.
(b) Record the adjusting journal entry at December 31, 2014. (*Hint:* Use T accounts to calculate the amount of the adjustment.)
(c) Assume instead that the Allowance for Doubtful Accounts had a debit balance of $2,800 at December 31, 2014. What is the net realizable value of the accounts receivable at December 31, 2014, and what is bad debt expense for 2014? (*Hint:* Use T accounts to calculate the amount of the adjustment.)

Prepare aging schedule and record bad debts. (SO 2) AP

E8–5 Rowen Company has accounts receivable of $241,000 at September 30, 2015. An analysis of the accounts shows the following:

Month of Sale	Balance
September	$170,000
August	35,700
July	20,000
April, May, and June	15,300
	$241,000

Credit terms are 2/10, n/30. On October 1, 2014, the Allowance for Doubtful Accounts had a credit balance of $17,600. During the year, the company wrote off accounts receivable of $19,000 as uncollectible. The company uses an aging schedule to estimate uncollectible accounts. The company's percentage estimates of bad debts are as follows:

Number of Days Outstanding	Estimated % Uncollectible
0–30	1%
31–60	10%
61–90	25%
Over 90	60%

Instructions

(a) Prepare an aging schedule to determine the total estimated uncollectible accounts at September 30, 2015.
(b) What is the net realizable value of the accounts receivable at September 30, 2015?
(c) Prepare the adjusting entry at September 30 to record bad debt expense. (*Hint:* Use T accounts to calculate the amount of the adjustment.)

Determine missing amounts and describe the accounts receivable transactions. (SO 1, 2) AP

E8–6 Chelsea Corporation reported the following information in its general ledger at December 31.

Accounts Receivable

		Debit	Credit
Beg.	bal.	15,000	35,200
		(1)	(2)
End.	bal.	(3)	

Sale

Debit	Credit
	45,000

Allowance for Doubtful Accounts

Debit			Credit
	Beg.	bal.	1,200
800			(4)
	End.	bal.	(5)

Bad Debt Expense

Debit	Credit
(4)	

All sales were on account. At the end of the year, uncollectible accounts were estimated to be 10% of accounts receivable.

Instructions

(a) Using your knowledge of receivables transactions, determine the missing amounts. (*Hint:* You may find it helpful to reconstruct the journal entries.)
(b) Describe each transaction that has been recorded.
(c) What is the amount of cash collected?

Record bad debts, write off, and collection of previously written-off account; calculate net realizable value. (SO 2) AP

E8–7 Accounts receivable transactions are provided below for J Looney Co.

Dec. 31, 2014 The company estimated that 5% of its accounts receivable would become uncollectible. The balances in the accounts receivable account and allowance for doubtful accounts were $650,000 and $2,300 (debit), respectively.

Mar. 5, 2015 The company determined that R. Black's $3,700 account and D. Wight's $6,900 account were uncollectible. The company's accounts receivable were $685,000 before the accounts were written off.

June 6, 2015 Wight paid his account that had been written off on March 5. The company's accounts receivable were $641,000 prior to recording the cash receipt for Wight. (*Hint:* Two entries are required.)

Instructions

(a) Prepare the journal entries on December 31, 2014, March 5, 2015, and June 6, 2015.
(b) Post the journal entries to Allowance for Doubtful Accounts and calculate the new balance after each entry.

(c) Calculate the net realizable value of accounts receivable both before and after writing off the two accounts on March 5, 2015.

(d) Calculate the net realizable value of the accounts receivable both before and after recording the cash receipt from Wight on June 6, 2015.

Calculate interest. (SO 3) AP

E8–8 Data on three promissory notes accepted by Levin Ltd. during 2014 follow.

Date of Note	Term in Months	Principal	Interest Rate	Total Interest	Interest Revenue to Record for Year Ended December 31
Oct. 1	3	$180,000	10%	(c)	(d)
Aug. 1	6	120,000	(b)	$4,800	(e)
Nov. 1	24	(a)	6%	12,000	(f)

Instructions

Determine the missing amounts.

Record notes receivable transactions. (SO 3) AP

E8–9 Passera Supply Co. has the following transactions:

Nov. 1	Lent $60,000 cash to A. Morgan on a one-year, 8% note.
15	Sold goods to H. Giorgi on account for $12,000, terms n/30. The goods cost Passera $7,500. Passera uses the perpetual inventory system.
Dec. 1	Sold goods to Wrightman, Inc., receiving a $21,000, three-month, 6% note. The goods cost Passera $14,000.
15	H. Giorgi was unable to pay her account. Giorgi gave Passera a six-month, 7% note in settlement of her account.
31	Accrued interest revenue on all notes receivable. Interest is due at maturity.
Mar. 1	Collected the amount owing on the Wrightman note.
June 15	H. Giorgi defaults on the note. Future payment is expected.

Instructions

Record the transactions for Passera Supply Co. (Round calculations to the nearest dollar.)

Record notes receivable transactions. (SO 3) AP

E8–10 The following are notes receivable transactions for Rather Co.:

May 1	Received a $15,000, six-month, 6% note from Jioux Company in settlement of an account receivable. Interest is due at maturity.
June 30	Accrued interest on the Jioux note, at Rather's year end. Adjustments are recorded annually.
July 31	Lent $2,000 cash to an employee, Noreen Irvine, receiving a three-month, 5% note. Interest is due at the end of each month.
Aug. 31	Received the interest due from Ms. Irvine.
Sept. 30	Received the interest due from Ms. Irvine.
Oct. 31	Received payment in full for the employee note from Ms. Irvine.
Nov. 1	Jioux Company defaults on its note. Rather does not expect to collect on the note.

Instructions

Record the transactions for Rather Co. (Round calculations to the nearest dollar.)

Record notes receivable transactions and indicate statement presentation. (SO 3, 4) AP

E8–11 Ni Co. has the following notes receivable outstanding at December 31, 2014:

Issue Date	Term	Principal	Interest Rate
1. August 31, 2013	2 years	$15,000	4%
2. October 1, 2013	18 months	46,000	5%
3. February 1, 2014	1 year	32,000	4%
4. May 31, 2014	5 years	22,000	6%
5. October 31, 2014	7 months	9,000	5%

For notes with terms of one year or longer, interest is payable on the first day of each month, for interest earned the previous month. For notes with terms less than one year, interest is payable at maturity.

Instructions

(a) Calculate the interest revenue that Ni Co. will report on its income statement for the year ended December 31, 2014. Indicate where this will be presented on the income statement. (Round calculations to the nearest dollar.)

(b) Calculate the amounts related to these notes that will be reported on Ni Co.'s balance sheet at December 31, 2014. Indicate where they will be presented. Assume all required interest payments have been received on time. (Round calculations to the nearest dollar.)

E8–12 In its first year of operations, AJS Company had sales of $4 million (all on credit) and cost of goods sold of $1,750,000. Sales allowances of $100,000 were given on substandard merchandise. During the year, the company collected $3.2 million cash on account. At year end, December 31, 2014, the credit manager estimates that 4% of the accounts receivable will become uncollectible.

Record bad debts, prepare partial balance sheet, and calculate ratios. **(SO 2, 4) AP**

At December 31, 2014, the balances in selected other accounts were:

Accounts payable	$350,000
Cash	40,000
Interest receivable	1,125
Interest revenue	2,250
Merchandise inventory	325,000
Notes receivable, due April 10, 2017	45,000
Prepaid insurance	8,000
Short-term investments	50,000
Unearned sales revenue	25,000

Instructions

(a) Prepare the journal entry to record the bad debt expense.
(b) Prepare the current assets section of the balance sheet for AJS Company at December 31, 2014.
(c) Calculate the receivables turnover and collection period. (Remember that this is the end of the first year of business.)

E8–13 The following information (in millions) was taken from the December 31 financial statements of **Canadian National Railway Company**:

Calculate ratios and comment. **(SO 4) AN**

	2011	2010	2009
Accounts receivable, gross	$ 836	$ 796	$ 831
Allowance for doubtful accounts	16	21	34
Accounts receivable, net	820	775	797
Revenues	9,028	8,297	7,367
Total current assets	1,848	1,590	1,490
Total current liabilities	1,715	1,906	1,237

Instructions

(a) Calculate the 2011 and 2010 current ratios.
(b) Calculate the receivables turnover and average collection period for 2011 and 2010.
(c) Comment on any improvement or weakening in CN's liquidity and its management of accounts receivable.

Problems: Set A

P8–1A At December 31, 2014, the general ledger and subsidiary ledger for Albert's, a small auto parts store, showed the following:

Record accounts receivable transactions. Post to subsidiary and general ledgers and prepare adjusting entry. **(SO 1, 2) AP**

General Ledger	
Accounts receivable	$75,000
Allowance for doubtful accounts	3,750

Accounts Receivable Subsidiary Ledger	
Best Auto Repair	$ 3,800
Brown's Repair	23,000
Custom Repair	0
Jen's Auto Body	35,000
Luxury Autos	13,200
Total	$75,000

Jan. 3 Brown's Repair paid $18,000 on its account.
4 Custom Repair paid $1,400 on its account that had previously been written off. (*Hint:* Two entries are required.)
8 Jen's Auto Body purchased $3,800 of merchandise on account.
9 Antique Auto Repair paid cash for $1,500 of merchandise.
18 Jen's Auto Body returned $800 of merchandise.

Jan.	19	Luxury Autos paid $13,200 on its account.
	20	Jen's Auto Body paid $25,000 on its account.
	23	Brown's Repair purchased $5,600 on account.
	25	Custom Repair purchased $10,000 of merchandise on Visa.
	26	Luxury Autos purchased $18,000 of merchandise on account.
	31	Albert's determined that the Best Auto Repair account receivable was not collectible.

Instructions

(a) Record the above transactions. Ignore credit card fees and any entries to inventory or cost of goods sold for purposes of this question.
(b) Set up T accounts for the Accounts Receivable general ledger (control) account, the Allowance for Doubtful Accounts general ledger account, and the Accounts Receivable subsidiary ledger accounts. Post the journal entries to these accounts.
(c) Albert's estimated that 10% of accounts receivable is not collectible. Record the required adjustment to the allowance for doubtful accounts.
(d) Prepare a list of customers and the balances of their accounts from the subsidiary ledger. Prove that the total of the subsidiary ledger is equal to the control account balance.

TAKING IT FURTHER What types of errors could result in the total of the account balances in the subsidiary ledger not agreeing with the general ledger control account?

Record accounts receivable and bad debt transactions; show balance sheet presentation. (SO 1, 2, 4) AP

P8–2A Silk Co. reported the following information on its December 31, 2014, balance sheet:

Accounts receivable	$760,000
Less: Allowance for doubtful accounts	76,000

During 2015, the company had the following transactions related to receivables:

1. Sales on account, $2,800,000
2. Sales returns and allowances, $325,000
3. Collections of accounts receivable, $2,410,000
4. Interest added to overdue accounts, $72,000
5. Write offs of accounts considered uncollectible, $58,400
6. Collection of accounts previously written off as uncollectible, $5,200

Instructions

(a) Prepare the summary journal entries to record each of these six transactions.
(b) Enter the December 31, 2014, balances in the Accounts Receivable and Allowance for Doubtful Accounts general ledger accounts, post the entries to the two accounts, and determine the balances.
(c) Calculate the net realizable value of accounts receivable at December 31, 2015. Uncollectible accounts are estimated at 10% of accounts receivable.
(d) Prepare the journal entry to record bad debt expense for 2015.
(e) Show the balance sheet presentation of the receivables as at December 31, 2015.

TAKING IT FURTHER For several years, Silk Co. has estimated uncollectible accounts at 10% of accounts receivable. Discuss whether or not the company should continue to do this at December 31, 2015.

Record accounts receivable and bad debt transactions; show financial statement presentation. (SO 1, 2, 4) AP

P8–3A At the beginning of the current period, Huang Co. had a balance of $100,000 in Accounts Receivable and a $7,000 credit balance in Allowance for Doubtful Accounts. In the period, it had net credit sales of $400,000 and collections of $361,500. It wrote off accounts receivable of $10,500 as uncollectible. After a $1,750 account was written off as uncollectible, it was subsequently collected. This is in addition to the other cash collections. Based on an aging schedule, uncollectible accounts are estimated to be $8,000 at the end of the period.

Instructions

(a) Record sales and collections in the period.
(b) Record the write off of uncollectible accounts in the period.
(c) Record the collection of the account previously written off as uncollectible.
(d) Record the bad debt expense adjusting entry for the period.
(e) Show the balance sheet presentation of the receivables at the end of the period.
(f) What is the amount of bad debt expense on the income statement for the period?

TAKING IT FURTHER Why is bad debt expense not increased when an account receivable is written off because it is determined to be uncollectible?

P8–4A Information on Hohenberger Company for 2014 follows:

Calculate bad debt amounts and answer questions. (SO 2) AP

Total credit sales	$1,000,000
Accounts receivable at December 31	400,000
Uncollectible accounts written off	17,500
Amount collected on accounts previously written off (after write off but before year end)	2,500

Instructions

(a) Assume that Hohenberger Company decides to estimate its uncollectible accounts using the allowance method and an aging schedule. Uncollectible accounts are estimated to be $24,000. What amount of bad debt expense will Hohenberger Company record if Allowance for Doubtful Accounts had an opening balance of $20,000 on January 1, 2014?

(b) Assume the same facts as in part (a) except that the Allowance for Doubtful Accounts had a $12,000 balance on January 1, 2014. What amount of bad debt expense will Hohenberger record on December 31, 2014?

(c) How does the amount of accounts written off during the period affect the amount of bad debt expense recorded at the end of the period?

(d) How does the collection of an account that had previously been written off affect the net realizable value of accounts receivable?

TAKING IT FURTHER Why doesn't a company sell to only those customers it knows for sure it can collect from?

P8–5A Pearson Company uses the allowance method to estimate uncollectible accounts receivable. The company produced the following information from aging its accounts receivable at year end:

Prepare aging schedule and record bad debts and explain method. (SO 2) AP

		Number of Days Outstanding			
	Total	0–30	31–60	61–90	91–120
Accounts receivable	$640,000	$360,000	$140,000	$100,000	$40,000
Estimated % uncollectible		2%	5%	10%	30%
Estimated uncollectible accounts					

The unadjusted balance in Allowance for Doubtful Accounts is a debit of $3,000.

Instructions

(a) Complete the aging schedule and calculate the total estimated uncollectible accounts.

(b) Record the bad debt adjusting entry using the information determined in part (a).

(c) In the following year, $18,000 of the outstanding accounts receivable is determined to be uncollectible. Record the write off of the uncollectible accounts.

(d) The company collects $4,500 of the $18,000 of accounts that was determined to be uncollectible in part (c). The company also expects to collect an additional $1,000. Record the journal entry (or entries) to restore the accounts receivable and the cash collected. Collection of the $1,000 is expected in the near future.

(e) Explain how using the allowance method matches expenses with revenues.

(f) Explain how using the allowance method values Accounts Receivable at net realizable value on the balance sheet.

TAKING IT FURTHER What are the advantages and disadvantages to the company of using an aging schedule to estimate uncollectible accounts, as compared with estimating uncollectible accounts as 10% of total accounts receivable?

P8–6A An aging analysis of Hagiwara Company's accounts receivable at December 31, 2014 and 2015, showed the following:

Prepare aging schedule and record bad debts. (SO 2) AP

Number of Days Outstanding	Estimated % Uncollectible	Accounts Receivable 2015	Accounts Receivable 2014
0–30 days	3%	$115,000	$145,000
31–60 days	6%	35,000	63,000
61–90 days	12%	45,000	38,000
Over 90 days	25%	80,000	24,000
Total		$275,000	$270,000

Additional information:

1. At December 31, 2014, the unadjusted balance in Allowance for Doubtful Accounts was a credit of $6,600.
2. In 2015, $23,500 of accounts was written off as uncollectible and $2,200 of accounts previously written off was collected.

Instructions

(a) Prepare an aging schedule to calculate the estimated uncollectible accounts at December 31, 2014, and at December 31, 2015.

(b) Calculate the net realizable value of Hagiwara's accounts receivable at December 31, 2014, and December 31, 2015.

(c) Record the following:
1. The adjusting entry on December 31, 2014
2. The write off of uncollectible accounts in 2015
3. The collection in 2015 of accounts previously written off
4. The adjusting entry on December 31, 2015

TAKING IT FURTHER What are the implications of the changes in the age of the receivables from 2014 to 2015?

Determine missing amounts. **(SO 2) AN**

P8–7A The following information was reported in Nenshi Company's general ledger at September 30:

Accounts Receivable	
Beg. bal. 845,000	(b)
(a)	(c)
4,200	(f)
End. bal. (d)	

Sales	
	5,370,000

Allowance for Doubtful Accounts	
	Beg. bal. 76,050
50,400	(e)
	(b)
	End. bal. 83,475

Bad Debt Expense	
(e)	

All sales were made on account. Uncollectible accounts are estimated to be 9% of accounts receivable.

Instructions

Determine the missing amounts in Nenshi Company's accounts. State what each of these amounts represents. You will not be able to determine the missing items in alphabetical order. (To solve this problem, it might help if you reconstruct the journal entries.)

TAKING IT FURTHER Explain the differences between bad debt expense and the allowance for doubtful accounts.

Identify impact of accounts receivable and bad debt transactions; determine statement presentation. **(SO 1, 2, 4) AP**

P8–8A Bassano Company prepares monthly financial statements and estimates its uncollectible accounts at the end of each month. Bassano Company has an October 31 fiscal year end, closes temporary accounts annually, and uses a perpetual inventory system.

On August 31, 2014, after completing its month-end adjustments, it had accounts receivable of $74,500, a credit balance of $1,480 in Allowance for Doubtful Accounts, and bad debt expense of $9,860. In September and October, the following occurred:

September

1. Sold $56,300 of merchandise on account; the cost of the merchandise was $25,335.
2. A total of $900 of the merchandise sold on account was returned. These customers were issued credit memos. The cost of the merchandise was $400 and it was returned to inventory.
3. Collected $59,200 cash on account from customers.
4. Interest charges of $800 were charged to outstanding accounts receivable.
5. Recorded the monthly adjustment for bad debts. Uncollectible accounts were estimated to be 4% of accounts receivable.

October

1. Credit sales in the month were $66,300; the cost of the merchandise was $28,700.
2. Received $350 cash from a customer whose account had been written off in July.
3. Collected $58,500 cash, in addition to the cash collected in (2) above, from customers on account.
4. Wrote off $7,500 of accounts receivable as uncollectible.

5. Interest charges of $700 were charged to outstanding accounts receivable.
6. Recorded the year-end adjustment for bad debts. Uncollectible accounts were estimated to be 4% of accounts receivable.

Instructions

(a) For each of these transactions, indicate if the transaction has increased (+) or decreased (−) Cash, Accounts Receivable, Allowance for Doubtful Accounts, Inventory, Total Assets, and Owner's Equity and by how much. If the item is not changed, write NE to indicate there is no effect. Use the following format, in which the first one has been done for you as an example.

Transaction	Cash	Accounts Receivable	Allowance for Doubtful Accounts	Inventory	Total Assets	Owner's Equity
September:						
1.	NE	+$56,300	NE	−$25,335	+$30,965	+$30,965

(b) Show how accounts receivable will appear on the October 31, 2014, balance sheet.

(c) What amount will be reported as bad debt expense on the income statement for the year ended October 31, 2014?

TAKING IT FURTHER If Bassano's credit manager increases the amount of credit checking the company does before granting credit on all of its customers, will that eliminate the bad debts? Explain.

P8–9A Ku Company has an April 30 fiscal year end and adjusts accounts annually. Selected transactions in the year included the following:

Record receivables transactions. (SO 1, 3) AP

Jan. 2	Sold $24,000 of merchandise to Richards Company, terms n/30. The cost of the goods sold was $14,400. Ku uses the perpetual inventory system.
Feb. 1	Accepted a $24,000, four-month, 5% promissory note from Richards Company for the balance due. (See January 2 transaction.) Interest is payable at maturity.
15	Sold $15,000 of merchandise costing $9,000 to Garrison Company and accepted Garrison's three-month, 5% note in payment. Interest is payable at maturity.
Mar. 15	Sold $12,000 of merchandise to Mantha Co., terms n/30. The cost of the merchandise sold was $7,200.
Apr. 30	Accepted a $12,000, two-month, 7% note from Mantha Co. for its balance due. Interest is payable at maturity. (See March 15 transaction.)
30	Accrued interest at year end.
May 15	Collected the Garrison note in full. (See February 15 transaction.)
June 1	Collected the Richards Company note in full. (See February 1 transaction.)
June 30	Mantha Co. dishonours its note of April 30. Mantha Co. is bankrupt and there is no hope of future settlement.
July 13	Sold $6,000 merchandise costing $3,600 to Zorilla Inc. and accepted Zorilla's $6,000, three-month, 7% note for the amount due, with interest payable at maturity.
Oct. 13	The Zorilla Inc. note was dishonoured. (See July 13 transaction.) It is expected that Zorilla will eventually pay the amount owed.

Instructions

Record the above transactions. (Round calculations to the nearest dollar.)

TAKING IT FURTHER What are the advantages and disadvantages of Ku Company accepting notes receivable from its customers?

P8–10A Tardif Company adjusts its books monthly. On September 30, 2014, notes receivable include the following:

Record note receivable transactions; show balance sheet presentation. (SO 3, 4) AP

Issue Date	Maker	Principal	Interest	Term
Aug. 1, 2013	RJF Inc.	$19,000	4.5%	2.5 years
Mar. 31, 2014	Resolute Co.	17,000	5.0%	7 months
May 31, 2014	Imaging Ltd.	17,500	5.5%	18 months
Aug. 31, 2014	Dragon Co.	6,000	8.5%	2 months
Sept. 30, 2014	MGH Corp.	20,500	6.0%	16 months

Interest is payable on the first day of each month for notes with terms of one year or longer. Interest is payable at maturity for notes with terms less than one year. In October, the following transactions were completed:

Oct.	1	Received payment of the interest due from RJF Inc.
	1	Received payment of the interest due from Imaging Ltd.
	31	Received notice that the Dragon Co. note had been dishonoured. (Assume that Dragon is expected to pay in the future.)
	31	Collected the amount owing from Resolute Co.

Instructions

(a) Calculate the balance in the Interest Receivable and Notes Receivable accounts at September 30, 2014.
(b) Record the October transactions and the October 31 adjusting entry for accrued interest receivable.
(c) Enter the balances at October 1 in the receivables accounts, and post the entries to the receivables accounts.
(d) Show the balance sheet presentation of the interest and notes receivable accounts at October 31.
(e) How would the journal entry on October 31 be different if Dragon were not expected to pay in the future?

TAKING IT FURTHER The interest rate for the Dragon note is higher than the other notes. Why might that have been the case?

Prepare assets section of balance sheet; calculate and interpret ratios. **(SO 4) AN**

P8–11A Tocksfor Company's general ledger included the following selected accounts (in thousands) at September 30, 2014:

Accounts payable	$1,077.3
Accounts receivable	590.4
Accumulated depreciation—equipment	858.7
Allowance for doubtful accounts	35.4
Bad debt expense	91.3
Cash	395.6
Cost of goods sold	660.4
Equipment	1,732.8
Interest revenue	19.7
Merchandise inventory	630.9
Notes receivable—due May 15, 2015	96.0
Notes receivable—due in 2018	191.1
Prepaid expenses and deposits	20.1
Sales	4,565.5
Sales discounts	31.3
Short-term investments	194.9
Supplies	21.7
Unearned sales revenue	56.3

Additional information:

1. On September 30, 2013, Accounts Receivable was $611.1 thousand and the Allowance for Doubtful Accounts was $36.6 thousand.
2. The receivables turnover was 8.3 the previous year.

Instructions

(a) Prepare the assets section of the balance sheet.
(b) Calculate the receivables turnover and average collection period. Compare these results with the previous year's results and comment on any trends.

TAKING IT FURTHER What other information should Tocksfor consider when analyzing its receivables turnover and average collection period?

Calculate and interpret ratios. **(SO 4) AN**

P8–12A Presented here is selected financial information (in millions) from the 2011 financial statements of **Rogers Communications Inc.** and **Shaw Communications Inc.**:

	Rogers	**Shaw**
Sales	$12,428	$4,740.9
Allowance for doubtful accounts, beginning of year	138	19.0
Allowance for doubtful accounts, end of year	129	28.8
Accounts receivable balance (net), beginning of year	1,443	196.4
Accounts receivable balance (net), end of year	1,574	442.8

Instructions

(a) Calculate the receivables turnover and average collection period for both companies.
(b) Comment on the difference in their collection experiences.

TAKING IT FURTHER Shaw acquired Canwest Global Communications Corp. in October 2010. As part of the transaction, Shaw acquired $296.6 million of receivables. What impact might this acquisition have on its 2011 receivable turnover ratio? Explain. Note that Shaw's fiscal year end was August 31, 2011.

P8–13A The following ratios are available for Satellite Mechanical:

Evaluate liquidity.
(SO 4) AN

	2015	2014	2013
Current ratio	2.0 to 1	1.6 to 1	1.4 to 1
Acid-test ratio	1.1 to 1	0.8 to 1	0.7 to 1
Receivables turnover	7.3 times	10.1 times	10.3 times
Inventory turnover	6.3 times	6.1 times	6.4 times

Instructions

(a) Calculate the collection period, days sales in inventory, and operating cycle in days for each year.
(b) Has Satellite Mechanical's liquidity improved or weakened over the three-year period? Explain.
(c) Do changes in turnover ratios affect profitability? Explain.
(d) Do changes in turnover ratios affect cash flow? Explain.

TAKING IT FURTHER At the beginning of 2014, the owner of Satellite Mechanical decided to eliminate sales discounts because she thought it was costing the company too much money. The terms of credit sales were changed from 2/10, n/30 to n/30. Evaluate this decision.

CONTINUING COOKIE CHRONICLE

(*Note:* This is a continuation of the Cookie Chronicle from Chapters 1 through 7.)

Natalie has been approached by one of her friends, Curtis Lesperance. Curtis runs a coffee shop where he sells specialty coffees and prepares and sells muffins and cookies. He is very anxious to buy one of Natalie's fine European mixers because he would then be able to prepare larger batches of muffins and cookies. Curtis, however, cannot afford to pay for the mixer for at least 30 days. He has asked Natalie if she would be willing to sell him the mixer on credit.

Natalie comes to you for advice and asks the following questions.

1. Curtis has given me a set of his most recent financial statements. What calculations should I do with the data from these statements? What questions should I ask him after I have analyzed the statements? How will this information help me decide if I should extend credit to Curtis?
2. Is there another alternative to extending credit to Curtis for 30 days?
3. If, instead of extending credit to Curtis for 30 days, I have Curtis sign a promissory note and he is unable to pay at the end of the agreement term, will having that signed promissory note really make any difference?
4. I am thinking seriously about being able to have my customers use credit cards. What are some of the advantages and disadvantages of letting my customers pay by credit card? Are there differences in the types of credit cards that my customers can use?

The following transactions occur in April and May 2014:

April 1	After much thought, Natalie sells a mixer to Curtis for $1,050 (the cost of the mixer was $553). Curtis signs a two-month, 7.5% promissory note. Curtis can repay the note at any time before the due date, with interest accruing to the date of payment.
30	Curtis calls Natalie. He expects to pay the amount outstanding in the next week or so.
May 15	Natalie receives a cheque from Curtis in payment of his balance owing plus interest that has accrued.

Instructions

(a) Answer Natalie's questions.
(b) Prepare journal entries for the transactions that occurred in April and May.

CHAPTER 8 BROADENING YOUR PERSPECTIVE

Collaborative Learning Activity

Note to instructor: Additional instructions and material for this group activity can be found on the Instructor Resource Site and in *WileyPLUS*.

BYP8–1 In this group activity, you will prepare the year-end adjustment for bad debt expense, and finalize the financial statements, using company information given to you by your instructor. You will be required to use professional judgement to determine the amount of the adjustment and explain your rationale. Your instructor will assume the role of the company's external auditor and will judge you on the appropriateness of the amount and your rationale.

Communication Activity

BYP8–2 Toys for Big Boys sells snowmobiles, personal watercraft, ATVs, and other recreational vehicles. Recently, the credit manager of Toys for Big Boys retired. The sales staff threw him a big retirement party—they were glad to see him go because they felt his credit policies restricted their selling ability. The sales staff convinced management that there was no need to replace the credit manager since they could handle this responsibility in addition to their sales positions.

Management was thrilled at year end when sales doubled. However, accounts receivable quadrupled and cash flow was reduced by half. The company's average collection period increased from 30 days to 120 days.

Instructions

In a memo to management, explain the financial impact of allowing the sales staff to manage the credit function. Has the business assumed any additional credit risk? What would you recommend the company do to better manage its increasing accounts receivable?

Ethics Case

BYP8–3 The controller of Proust Company has completed draft financial statements for the year just ended and is reviewing them with the president. As part of the review, he has summarized an aging schedule showing the basis of estimating uncollectible accounts using the following percentages: 0–30 days, 5%; 31–60 days, 10%; 61–90 days, 30%; 91–120 days, 50%; and over 120 days, 80%.

The president of the company, Suzanne Bros, is nervous because the bank expects the company to sustain a growth rate for profit of at least 5% each year over the next two years—the remaining term of its bank loan. The profit growth for the past year was much more than 5% because of certain special orders with high margins, but those orders will not be repeated next year, so it will be very hard to achieve even the same profit next year, and even more difficult to grow it another 5%. It would be easier to show an increase next year if the past year's reported profit had been a little lower. President Bros recalls from an accounting course that bad debt expense is based on certain estimates subject to judgement. She suggests that the controller increase the estimate percentages, which will increase the amount of the required bad debt expense adjustment and therefore lower profit for last year so that it will be easier to show a better growth rate next year.

Instructions

(a) Who are the stakeholders in this case?
(b) Does the president's request create an ethical dilemma for the controller?
(c) Should the controller be concerned with Proust Company's reported profit growth rate in estimating the allowance? Explain your answer.

All About You: Personal Financial Literacy Activity

BYP8–4 In the "All About You" feature, you learned about interest rates charged on credit cards and some of the advantages and disadvantages of credit cards. To get the most from your credit card and to save money, you need to understand the features of your credit card and how interest is charged on credit cards.

The Financial Consumer Agency of Canada provides tips to help you use your credit card wisely. (1) Before applying for a credit card, review its terms and conditions, including things such as interest rates and fees, so you know what you're getting into. (2) Know your spending habits and set a monthly limit on your card accordingly. (3) Limit the number of credit cards you apply for. (4) Don't use your credit card to make impulse purchases. (5) Try to pay off your balance in full every month before the due date. (6) If you can't pay off your balance, make payments as soon as you can, because interest is charged daily. (7) Make regular payments; it's good for your credit rating, which you'll need when you apply for any kind of loan, such as a student loan. (8) If your balance is growing, stop using the card until you can pay it off. (9) Many cards allow you to take a cash advance on it. But interest is charged from the time you get the advance, so avoid using your card for this purpose. (10) When you receive your bill, check to make sure all the charges are correct. (11) Some credit cards have loyalty programs; don't buy things you don't need just to collect points. (12) Don't use your credit card to pay off emergency expenses. Instead, talk to your bank about options that charge less interest, such as a line of credit. (13) Keep your card, your PIN, and password secure.

Instructions

(a) Credit cards provide interest-free loans on the purchase of goods, as long as you pay your bill in full by the end of the grace period, which legally must be at least 21 days from the last date covered by that statement. Assume you used a credit card to purchase books on September 15, and the last date covered by your statement is October 7 and the grace period is 21 days. How many days is the interest-free period?

(b) Suppose you are a university student and you have one month left in the semester and you take a $1,000 cash advance on your credit card on April 1 to cover your living expenses until you get your first paycheque from your summer job on May 15. The interest rate on your credit card is 19%. Assuming that is the only charge on your credit card, calculate the interest you will be charged assuming you pay your bill in full on May 15. (*Hint:* There is no interest-free grace period on cash advances. You will have to pay interest from the date you made the cash advance until the date you repay the whole amount.)

ANSWERS TO CHAPTER QUESTIONS

ANSWERS TO ACCOUNTING IN ACTION INSIGHT QUESTIONS

All About You Insight, p. 341

Q: Should you use credit cards or not?

A: Credit cards can make your life easier, as long as they are used properly. They certainly have advantages: (1) they provide interest-free loans on the purchase of goods, as long as you pay your bill in full by the end of the grace period; (2) monthly credit card statements provide detailed records of all transactions, payments, and returned merchandise; and (3) many transactions, such as Internet purchases, are difficult or impossible to carry out without a credit card.

However, credit cards also have disadvantages: (1) if you do not pay your bill in full every month, expect to pay a very high interest rate on the unpaid balance; (2) they are so easy to use that you might start buying items without thinking about whether you really need them—and can afford them; and (3) credit cards can be stolen, which might damage your credit rating.

Across The Organization, p. 356

Q: What might be the advantages to Target of having its own credit card? What might be the disadvantages?

A: If customers have a Target credit card, they might be more likely to shop at Target rather than at another department store. Target can also earn interest income on any late accounts. The disadvantages might include higher administration costs to operate the credit card division and also the risk of customers defaulting on their credit card payments.

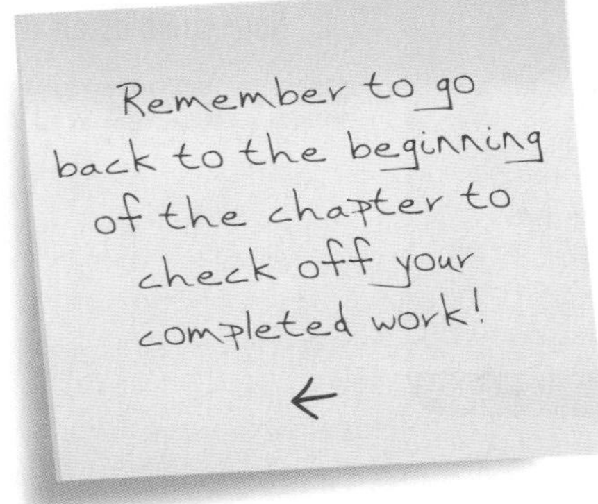
Remember to go back to the beginning of the chapter to check off your completed work!
←

ANSWERS TO SELF-STUDY QUESTIONS

1. c 2. b 3. d 4. a 5. c 6. d 7. c 8. a 9. d 10. c 11. b 12. c

CHAPTER 9

LONG-LIVED ASSETS

THE NAVIGATOR

- ☐ Understand *Concepts for Review*
- ☐ Read *Feature Story*
- ☐ Scan *Study Objectives*
- ☐ Read *Chapter Preview*
- ☐ Read text and answer *Before You Go On*
- ☐ Review *Comparing IFRS and ASPE*
- ☐ Work *Demonstration Problems*
- ☐ Review *Summary of Study Objectives*
- ☐ Answer *Self-Study Questions*
- ☐ Complete assignments

CONCEPTS FOR REVIEW

Before studying this chapter, you should understand or, if necessary, review:

A. Expense recognition criteria (Ch. 3, pp. 98–99).

B. What depreciation is, and how to make adjustments for it. (Ch. 3, pp. 103–104).

C. Non-current assets and the classified balance sheet (Ch. 4, p. 161).

BUILDING FOR LEARNING

TORONTO, ON—When George Brown College in Toronto, one of the oldest colleges in Ontario, was created in 1967, its land and buildings were provided by the provincial government at nominal value. The province launched community colleges to provide vocational training for its burgeoning industries like the automotive sector and forestry. Today, however, colleges have to be much more self-sufficient when adding classrooms, labs, and other facilities.

George Brown's most recent expansion is a brand new, 380,000-square-foot (35,000-square-metre) health sciences building, the first phase of its Waterfront campus overlooking Toronto's harbour, which opened in the fall of 2012. The construction costs were estimated at about $175 million. "Out of that, there's about $92 million roughly that is funding from both the provincial and federal governments," says Controller Ric Ho. "And then we had to put in about $25 million of our own money. And we also are expected to do fundraising, up to $35 million, as part of the capital campaign." The college also expected to receive a capital contribution from Waterfront Toronto, an intergovernmental agency to develop the harbour.

How does the college determine what is a capital versus an operating expenditure and how does it account for these costs? Anything that will be used up within a fiscal year, such as office supplies, is expensed in that year. Anything that has a useful life of more than a year and is worth $5,000 or more is capitalized and depreciated. "There needs to be a threshold because we cannot capitalize every little chair or something that comes around, otherwise your capital asset list is going to be huge and doesn't serve any purpose," says Dominic Noronha, the college's Manager of Financial Services.

The college depreciates the buildings it owns using the straight-line method (partly because it's the simplest) over 40 years. While most buildings last longer than 40 years, "That's the level that's been traditionally used by other colleges," Mr. Noronha says. For space it leases, such as one floor of a building on the nearby Ryerson University campus, George Brown amortizes the leasehold improvements—considered to be assets—over the term of the lease.

Like most colleges, buildings are George Brown's most valuable long-lived assets. Its equipment and buildings have a net book value (or carrying amount) of approximately $328 million. Among its equipment are workshop benches for its programs in the trades, kitchens for its hospitality school, computers for its school of design, and costumes for its animation program. The college depreciates most equipment over five years, although its computer equipment—which can quickly become technologically obsolete—is depreciated over three years. George Brown does not recognize any intangible assets on its books. "We don't have any goodwill or intellectual property, such as patents or copyrights," says Mr. Ho.

THE NAVIGATOR

STUDY OBJECTIVES

After studying this chapter, you should be able to:

1. Determine the cost of property, plant, and equipment.
2. Explain and calculate depreciation.
3. Explain the factors that cause changes in periodic depreciation and calculate revisions.
4. Account for the disposal of property, plant, and equipment.
5. Calculate and record depreciation of natural resources.
6. Identify the basic accounting issues for intangible assets and goodwill.
7. Illustrate the reporting and analysis of long-lived assets.

THE NAVIGATOR

PREVIEW OF CHAPTER NINE

For organizations such as George Brown College, making the right decisions about long-lived assets is critical because these assets represent huge investments. Organizations must make decisions about what assets to acquire, how to account for them, and when to dispose of them.

In this chapter, we address these and other issues surrounding long-lived assets. Our discussions will focus on three types of long-lived assets: (1) property, plant, and equipment; (2) natural resources; and (3) intangible assets.

The chapter is organized as follows:

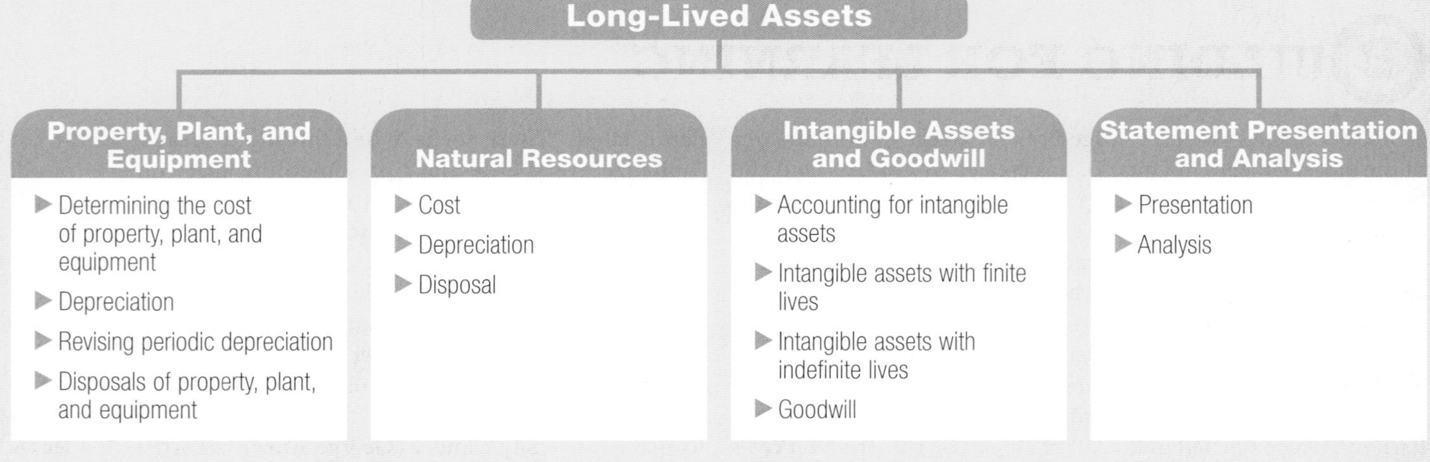

PROPERTY, PLANT, AND EQUIPMENT

Alternative terminology Property, plant, and equipment are also commonly known as *fixed assets*; *land, building, and equipment*; or *capital assets*.

Property, plant, and equipment are long-lived assets that the company owns and uses for the production and sale of goods or services to consumers. They have three characteristics. They (1) have a physical substance (a definite size and shape), (2) are used in the operations of the business, and (3) are not intended for sale to customers. Unlike current assets, these assets are expected to provide services to a company for a number of years.

In the following sections, we will learn more about property, plant, and equipment: determining their cost, their depreciation, and the accounting for their disposal.

DETERMINING THE COST OF PROPERTY, PLANT, AND EQUIPMENT

STUDY OBJECTIVE 1
Determine the cost of property, plant, and equipment.

The cost of an item of property, plant, and equipment includes the following:

1. The purchase price, plus any non-recoverable taxes, less any discounts or rebates
2. The expenditures necessary to bring the asset to the required location and make it ready for its intended use

If there are obligations to dismantle, remove, or restore the asset when it is retired, an initial estimate of these costs is also included in the cost of the long-lived asset. These are known as **asset retirement costs**. Accounting for these costs can be complex and we will leave that discussion to a future accounting course. But you should be aware that the cost of some property, plant, and equipment items includes the cost of retiring the asset. For simplicity, we will assume asset retirement costs are equal to zero in the examples in this text.

Alternative terminology Asset retirement costs are also called *decommissioning costs*.

These costs are **capitalized** (recorded as a debit to property, plant, and equipment), rather than expensed, if it is probable that the company will receive an economic benefit in the future from the asset. Determining which costs to include in a long-lived asset account and which costs to immediately expense instead is very important. Costs that benefit only the current period are expensed. Such costs are called **operating expenditures**. Costs that benefit future periods are included in a long-lived asset account. These costs are called **capital expenditures**.

For example, the cost to purchase equipment is recorded as a capital expenditure, because the equipment will benefit future periods. In addition, the insurance paid on the equipment as it is shipped to the company should also be capitalized because the insurance during transit benefits more than just the current period. It is considered a necessary expenditure to get the equipment to its required location and ready for use.

However, it is also important to note that companies will expense, rather than capitalize, low-cost long-lived assets. For example, George Brown College, in the feature story, capitalizes anything that has a useful life of more than a year and is worth $5,000 or more. This is an application of a concept known as materiality, which you will learn more about in Chapter 11. It allows companies to immediately record immaterial expenditures as an expense.

Subsequent to acquisition, the same distinction exists between capital and operating expenditures. For example, once the asset is in use, having an insurance policy benefits only the current period and is treated as an expense. But major expenditures that are incurred once the asset is in use that increase the life of the asset or its productivity are capitalized. We will discuss expenditures subsequent to acquisition in more depth later in the chapter.

Property, plant, and equipment are often subdivided into four classes:

1. **Land**, such as a building site
2. **Land improvements**, such as driveways, parking lots, fences, and underground sprinkler systems
3. **Buildings**, such as stores, offices, factories, and warehouses
4. **Equipment**, such as store checkout counters, cash registers, office furniture, computer equipment, factory equipment, and delivery equipment and vehicles

Determining the cost of each of the major classes of property, plant, and equipment is explained in the following sections.

Land

The cost of land includes (1) the purchase price, (2) closing costs such as surveying and legal fees, and (3) the costs of preparing the land for its intended use, such as the removal of old buildings, clearing, draining, filling, and grading. All of these costs (less any proceeds from salvaged materials) are debited to the Land account.

To illustrate, assume that the Budovitch Manufacturing Company purchases real estate for $100,000 cash. The property contained an old warehouse that is removed at a net cost of $6,000 ($7,500 to remove it less $1,500 received for materials from the warehouse that were salvaged and later sold). Additional expenditures include the legal fee of $3,000. The cost of the land is $109,000, calculated as follows:

Land	
Cash price of property	$100,000
Net cost of removing warehouse ($7,500 − $1,500)	6,000
Legal fee	3,000
Cost of land	$109,000

When recording the acquisition, Land is debited for $109,000 and Cash is credited for $109,000 (assuming the costs were paid in cash). Land is a unique long-lived asset. Its cost is not depreciated—allocated over its useful life—because land has an unlimited useful life.

Land Improvements

Land improvements are structural additions made to land, such as driveways, sidewalks, fences, and parking lots. Land improvements, unlike land, decline in service potential over time, and require maintenance and replacement. Because of this, land improvements are recorded separately from land and *are* depreciated over their useful lives.

Many students confuse the cost to get land ready for its intended use with land improvements. They think, for example, that removing an old building or grading the land is "improving" the land, and thus incorrectly reason that these costs should be considered land improvements. When classifying costs, it is important to remember that one-time costs required for getting the land ready to use are always charged to the Land account, not the Land Improvement account.

Buildings

All costs that are directly related to the purchase or construction of a building are debited to the Buildings account. When a building is purchased, these costs include the purchase price and closing costs (such as legal fees). The costs of getting a building ready for its intended use can include expenditures for remodelling, and for replacing or repairing the roof, floors, electrical wiring, and plumbing. These costs are also debited to Buildings (that is, capitalized).

When a new building is built, its cost includes the contract price plus payments for architects' fees, building permits, and excavation costs. The interest costs of financing the construction project are also included in the asset's cost when a significant amount of time is needed to get the building ready to be used. In these circumstances, interest costs are considered to be as necessary as materials and labour are. However, only interest costs that occur *during the construction period* are included. After construction is finished, the company records future interest payments on funds borrowed to finance the construction as debits (increases) to Interest Expense, since these costs only benefit the current period.

Equipment

The "equipment" classification is a broad one that can include delivery equipment, office equipment, computers, machinery, vehicles, furniture and fixtures, and other similar assets. The cost of these assets includes the purchase price; freight charges and insurance during transit paid by the purchaser; and the costs of assembling, installing, and testing the equipment. These costs are treated as capital expenditures because they benefit future periods.

Annual costs such as motor vehicle licences and insurance on company trucks and cars are treated as operating expenditures because they are recurring expenditures that are used up in the current year and do not benefit future periods.

To illustrate, assume that 1 Stop Florists purchases a used delivery truck on January 1, 2014, for $24,500 cash. Related expenditures include painting and lettering, $500; a motor vehicle licence, $80; and a one-year insurance policy, $2,600. The cost of the delivery truck is $25,000, calculated as follows:

Delivery Truck	
Cash price	$24,500
Painting and lettering	500
Cost of delivery truck	$25,000

The cost of the motor vehicle licence is recorded as an expense and the cost of the insurance policy is recorded as a prepaid expense (an asset). The entry to record the purchase of the truck and related expenditures, assuming they were all paid for in cash, is as follows:

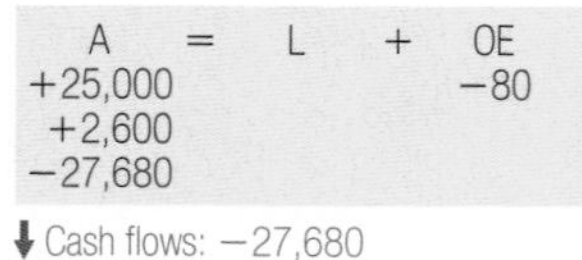

A	=	L	+	OE
+25,000				−80
+2,600				
−27,680				

Cash flows: −27,680

Jan. 1	Vehicles	25,000	
	Licence Expense	80	
	Prepaid Insurance	2,600	
	Cash		27,680
	To record purchase of delivery truck and related expenditures.		

Allocating Cost to Multiple Assets or Significant Components

Multiple Assets.

Alternative terminology A basket purchase is also known as a *lump sum purchase.*

Helpful hint The assets in the basket purchase must be assigned values that add up to the cost of the purchase. This follows the cost principle under GAAP and ensures that the entry to record the purchase is balanced.

Property, plant, and equipment are often purchased together for a single price. This is known as a **basket purchase.** We need to know the cost of each individual asset in order to journalize the purchase, and later calculate the depreciation of each asset. When a basket purchase occurs, we determine individual costs by allocating the total price paid for the group of assets to each individual asset based on its relative fair value.

To illustrate, assume Sega Company purchased land, a building, and some equipment on July 31 for $400,000 cash. The land was appraised at $135,000, the building at $270,000, and the equipment at $45,000. The $400,000 cost should be allocated based on fair values (appraised values), as shown in Illustration 9-1.

Asset	Fair Value	Percent of Total Fair Value			Total Purchase Price		Cost of Each Asset
Land	$135,000	30%	($135,000 ÷ $450,000)	×	$400,000	=	$120,000
Building	270,000	60%	($270,000 ÷ $450,000)	×	$400,000	=	240,000
Equipment	45,000	10%	($ 45,000 ÷ $450,000)	×	$400,000	=	40,000
Totals	$450,000	100%					$400,000

ILLUSTRATION 9-1
Allocating cost in a basket purchase

The journal entry to record this purchase is as follows:

Date	Account	Debit	Credit
July 31	Land	120,000	
	Building	240,000	
	Equipment	40,000	
	Cash		400,000
	To record purchase of land, building, and equipment with costs allocated based on appraised values of $135,000, $270,000, and $45,000, respectively.		

A	=	L	+	OE
+120,000				
+240,000				
+40,000				
−400,000				

Cash flows: −400,000

Significant Components.

When an item of property, plant, and equipment includes individual components that have different useful lives, the cost of the item should be allocated to each of its significant components. This allows each component to be depreciated separately over the different useful lives or possibly by using different depreciation methods. For example, an aircraft and its engine may need to be treated as separate depreciable assets if they have different useful lives.

Separating the cost of the entire asset into its significant components can be accomplished using the same process to allocate cost illustrated above for a basket purchase. The asset's total cost would be allocated to the significant components based on the components' relative fair values. The calculations would be similar to those in Illustration 9-1.

Further discussion of calculating depreciation for the different parts of an asset will be left to a later accounting course. For simplicity, we will assume in this text that all of the components of the depreciable asset have the same useful life, and we will depreciate assets as a whole.

BEFORE YOU GO ON...

DO IT

Assume that factory equipment is purchased on November 6 for $10,000 cash and a $40,000 note payable. Related cash expenditures include insurance during shipping, $500; the annual insurance policy, $750; and installation and testing, $1,000. (a) What is the cost of the equipment? (b) Record these expenditures.

SOLUTION

Factory Equipment	
Purchase price	$50,000
Insurance during shipping	500
Installation and testing	1,000
Cost of equipment	$51,500

The entry to record the purchase and related expenditures is:

Date	Account	Debit	Credit
Nov. 6	Equipment	51,500	
	Prepaid Insurance	750	
	Cash ($10,000 + $500 + $750 + $1,000)		12,250
	Note Payable		40,000
	To record purchase of factory equipment and related expenditures.		

Related exercise material: BE9–1, BE9–2, BE9–3, BE9–4, and E9–1.

Action Plan

- Capitalize expenditures that are made to get the equipment ready for its intended use.
- Expense operating expenditures that benefit only the current period, or are recurring costs.

DEPRECIATION

STUDY OBJECTIVE 2

Explain and calculate depreciation.

Under International Financial Reporting Standards, companies have two models they can choose between to account for their property, plant, and equipment: the cost model or the revaluation model. The cost model is the more commonly used method, and is the only model allowed under ASPE. We will cover the cost model in the following sections of the chapter and refer briefly to the revaluation model in a later section.

The **cost model** records property, plant, and equipment at cost of acquisition. After acquisition, depreciation is recorded each period and the assets are carried at cost less accumulated depreciation. As we learned in Chapter 3, depreciation is the systematic allocation of the cost of a long-lived asset, such as property, plant, and equipment, over the asset's useful life. The cost is allocated to expense over the asset's useful life so that expenses are properly matched with the expected use of the asset.

You will recall that depreciation is recorded through an adjusting journal entry that debits Depreciation Expense and credits Accumulated Depreciation. Depreciation Expense is an operating expense on the income statement. Accumulated Depreciation appears on the balance sheet as a contra account to the related long-lived asset account. The resulting balance, cost less accumulated depreciation, is the carrying amount of the depreciable asset, as defined in Chapter 4.

Alternative terminology An asset's *carrying amount* is also called its *carrying value*, *book value*, or *net book value*.

It is important to understand that **depreciation is a process of cost allocation, not a process of determining an asset's real value.** Illustration 9-2 shows this. Under the cost model, an increase in an asset's fair value is not relevant because property, plant, and equipment are not for resale. (Fair values are only relevant if an impairment loss has occurred, which we will discuss later in the chapter.) As a result, the carrying amount of property, plant, or equipment (cost less accumulated depreciation) may be very different from its fair value.

ILLUSTRATION 9-2
Depreciation as an allocation concept

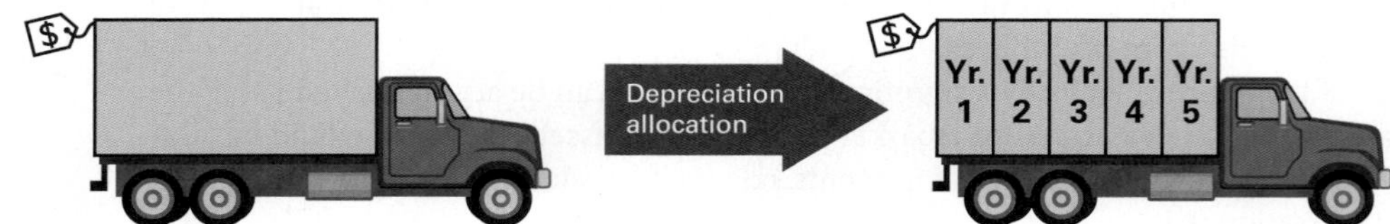

Helpful hint Recall that depreciation is a non-cash item. The standard entry to record depreciation is a debit to Depreciation Expense and a credit to Accumulated Depreciation.

It is also important to understand that **depreciation neither uses up nor provides cash to replace the asset**. The balance in Accumulated Depreciation only represents the total amount of the asset's cost that has been allocated to expense so far. It is not a cash fund. Cash is neither increased nor decreased by the adjusting entry to record depreciation.

During a depreciable asset's useful life, its revenue-producing ability declines because of physical factors such as wear and tear, and economic factors such as obsolescence. For example, a company may replace a truck because it is physically worn out. On the other hand, companies replace computers long before they are physically worn out because improvements in hardware and software have made the old computers obsolete.

Factors in Calculating Depreciation

In Chapter 3, we learned that depreciation expense was calculated by dividing the cost of a depreciable asset by its useful life. At that time, we assumed the asset's residual value was zero. In this chapter, we will now include a residual value when calculating depreciation. Consequently, there are now three factors that affect the calculation of depreciation.

Cost.

The factors that affect the cost of a depreciable asset were explained earlier in this chapter. Remember that the cost of property, plant, and equipment includes the purchase price plus all costs necessary to get the asset ready for use. Cost includes an initial estimate of the retirement costs, if there are any.

Helpful hint Both residual value and useful life are estimates. Although the cost of an asset can be determined with a fair degree of certainty, it might require an estimate of retirement costs.

Useful Life.

Useful life is (a) the period of time over which an asset is expected to be available for use or (b) the number of units of production (such as machine hours) or units of output that are expected to be obtained from an asset. Useful life is an estimate based on such factors as the asset's intended use, its expected need for repair and maintenance, and how vulnerable it is to wearing out or becoming obsolete. The company's past experience with similar assets often helps in estimating the expected useful life. George Brown College, in the feature story, uses a five-year useful life for most of its equipment, but only three years for computers because computer equipment can quickly become technologically obsolete.

Residual Value.

Residual value is the estimated amount that a company would obtain from disposing of the asset at the end of its useful life. Residual value is not depreciated, since the amount is expected to be recovered at the end of the asset's useful life.

Alternative terminology Residual value is sometimes called *salvage value.*

Illustration 9-3 summarizes these three factors in calculating depreciation.

ILLUSTRATION 9-3
Three factors in calculating depreciation

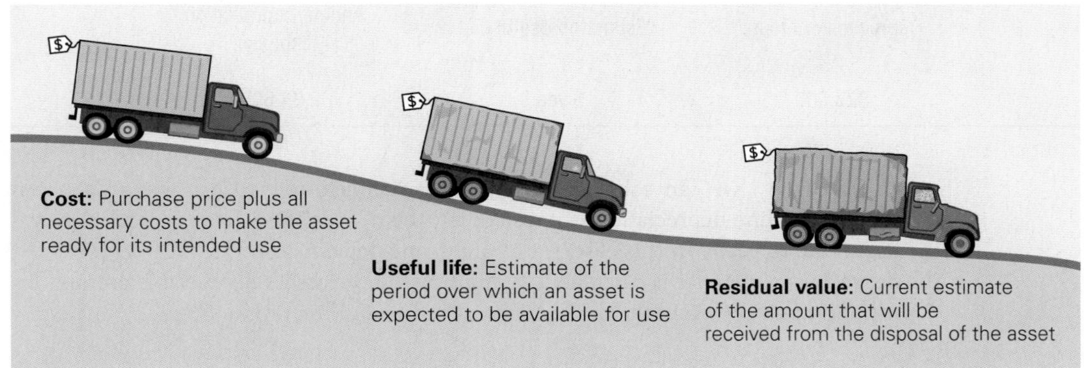

Cost: Purchase price plus all necessary costs to make the asset ready for its intended use
Useful life: Estimate of the period over which an asset is expected to be available for use
Residual value: Current estimate of the amount that will be received from the disposal of the asset

The difference between an asset's cost and its residual value is called the **depreciable amount**, which is the total amount to be depreciated over the useful life. As we learned in Chapter 3, companies reporting under ASPE may use the term "amortization" instead of "depreciation." Because of this, the depreciable amount is often called the amortizable cost.

Depreciation Methods

Depreciation is generally calculated using one of the following methods:

1. Straight-line
2. Diminishing-balance
3. Units-of-production

The straight-line method of depreciation is used by the majority of publicly traded companies. But how do companies decide which of the three depreciation methods to use? Management must choose the method that best matches the estimated pattern in which the asset's future economic benefits are expected to be consumed. The depreciation method must be reviewed at least once a year. If the expected pattern of consumption of the future economic benefits has changed, the depreciation method must be changed, and the change must be disclosed in the notes to the financial statements.

To learn how to calculate the three depreciation methods and to compare them, we will use the following data for the small delivery truck bought by 1 Stop Florists on January 1, 2014:

Cost (as shown earlier in the chapter)	$25,000
Estimated residual value	$2,000
Estimated useful life (in years)	5
Estimated useful life (in kilometres)	200,000

Straight-Line.

The straight-line method was first defined in Chapter 3. We will define it again here, this time including the impact of a residual value on the calculation. The **straight-line method** of calculating depreciation has two steps. First, residual value is deducted from the asset's cost to determine an asset's depreciable amount. Second, the depreciable amount is divided by the asset's useful life to calculate the annual depreciation expense.

The depreciation expense will be the same for each year of the asset's useful life if the cost, the estimated useful life, and the expected residual value do not change. The calculation of depreciation expense in the first year for 1 Stop Florists' delivery truck is shown in Illustration 9-4.

ILLUSTRATION 9-4
Formula for straight-line method

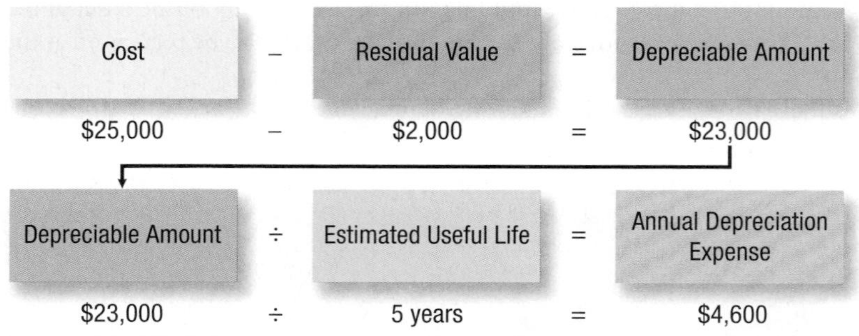

Alternatively, we can calculate an annual percentage rate to use when determining the delivery truck's straight-line depreciation expense. First, the depreciation rate is calculated by dividing 100% by the useful life in years. In this case, the straight-line depreciation rate is 20% (100% ÷ 5 years). Second, the depreciation expense is calculated by multiplying the asset's depreciable amount by the straight-line depreciation rate shown in the depreciation schedule in Illustration 9-5.

ILLUSTRATION 9-5
Straight-line depreciation schedule

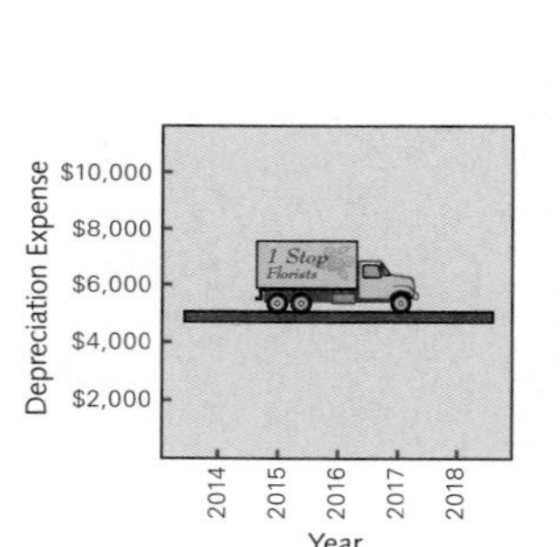

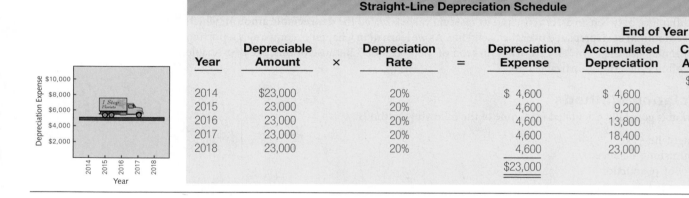

1 STOP FLORISTS
Straight-Line Depreciation Schedule

Year	Depreciable Amount	×	Depreciation Rate	=	Depreciation Expense	End of Year Accumulated Depreciation	End of Year Carrying Amount
							$25,000
2014	$23,000		20%		$ 4,600	$ 4,600	20,400
2015	23,000		20%		4,600	9,200	15,800
2016	23,000		20%		4,600	13,800	11,200
2017	23,000		20%		4,600	18,400	6,600
2018	23,000		20%		4,600	23,000	2,000
					$23,000		

Note that the depreciation expense of $4,600 is the same each year. Also note that the column total for depreciation expense is equal to the asset's depreciable amount, and that the carrying amount at the end of the useful life is equal to the estimated $2,000 residual value.

What happens when an asset is purchased during the year, rather than on January 1 as in our example? In that case, it is necessary to **pro-rate (use a proportional amount of) the annual depreciation for the part of the year that the asset was used.** If 1 Stop Florists' delivery truck was ready to be used on April 1, 2014, the truck would be depreciated for nine months in 2014 (April through December). The depreciation for 2014 would be $3,450 ($23,000 × 20% × $^9/_{12}$). Note that depreciation is normally rounded to the nearest month. Since depreciation is an estimate, calculating it to the nearest day gives a false sense of accuracy.

To keep things simple, some companies establish a policy to calculate partial-period depreciation rather than calculating depreciation monthly. Companies may choose to record a full year's depreciation in the year of acquisition and none in the year of disposal. Others may record a half year's depreciation in the year of acquisition and a half year's depreciation in the year of disposal. Whatever policy is chosen for partial-year depreciation, the impact is not significant in the long run if the policy is used consistently.

Recall that the depreciation method used must be consistent with the pattern in which the economic benefits from owning the asset are expected to be consumed. Therefore, it is appropriate to use the straight-line method when the asset is used quite uniformly throughout its useful life. Examples of assets that deliver their benefit primarily as a function of time include office furniture and fixtures, buildings, warehouses, and garages for motor vehicles. George Brown College, in the feature story, uses straight-line depreciation for its buildings.

Diminishing-Balance.

The **diminishing-balance method** produces a decreasing annual depreciation expense over the asset's useful life. It is called the "diminishing-balance" method because the periodic depreciation is calculated based on the asset's carrying amount, which diminishes each year because accumulated depreciation increases. Annual depreciation expense is calculated by multiplying the carrying amount at the beginning of the year by the depreciation rate. **The depreciation rate remains constant from year to year, but the rate is applied to a carrying amount that declines each year.**

Alternative terminology The diminishing-balance method is also sometimes called the *declining-balance* method.

The carrying amount for the first year is the asset's cost, because the balance in Accumulated Depreciation at the beginning of the asset's useful life is zero. In the following years, the carrying amount is the difference between the cost and the accumulated depreciation at the beginning of the year. Unlike the other depreciation methods, the diminishing-balance method does not use a depreciable amount. **Residual value is not used in determining the amount that the diminishing-balance depreciation rate is applied to.** Residual value does, however, limit the total depreciation that can be taken. Depreciation stops when the asset's carrying amount equals its estimated residual value.

Helpful hint Under the diminishing balance method, depreciation also stops when the accumulated depreciation equals the depreciable amount.

The diminishing-balance method can be applied using different rates, which results in varying speeds of depreciation. You will find rates such as one time (single), two times (double), and even three times (triple) the straight-line rate of depreciation. A depreciation rate that is often used is double the straight-line rate. This method is referred to as the **double diminishing-balance method.**

If 1 Stop Florists uses the double diminishing-balance method, the depreciation rate is 40% (2 × the straight-line rate of 20%). Illustration 9-6 shows the calculation of depreciation on the delivery truck for the first year.

Helpful hint The straight-line rate is determined by dividing 100% by the estimated useful life. In 1 Stop Florists' case, it is 100% ÷ 5 = 20%.

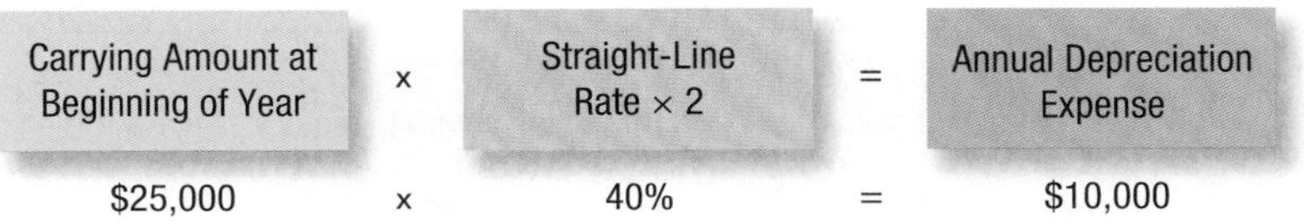

Carrying Amount at Beginning of Year
×
Straight-Line Rate × 2
=
Annual Depreciation Expense

$25,000 × 40% = $10,000

ILLUSTRATION 9-6
Formula for double diminishing-balance method

The depreciation schedule under this method is given in Illustration 9-7.

ILLUSTRATION 9-7
Double diminishing-balance depreciation schedule

1 STOP FLORISTS
Double Diminishing-Balance Depreciation Schedule

						End of Year	
Year	**Carrying Amount Beginning Year**	×	**Depreciation Rate**	=	**Depreciation Expense**	**Accumulated Depreciation**	**Carrying Amount**
							$25,000
2014	$25,000		40%		$10,000	$10,000	15,000
2015	15,000		40%		6,000	16,000	9,000
2016	9,000		40%		3,600	19,600	5,400
2017	5,400		40%		2,160	21,760	3,240
2018	3,240		40%		1,240*	23,000	2,000
					$23,000		

*The calculation of $1,296 ($3,240 × 40%) is adjusted to $1,240 so that the carrying amount will equal the residual value.

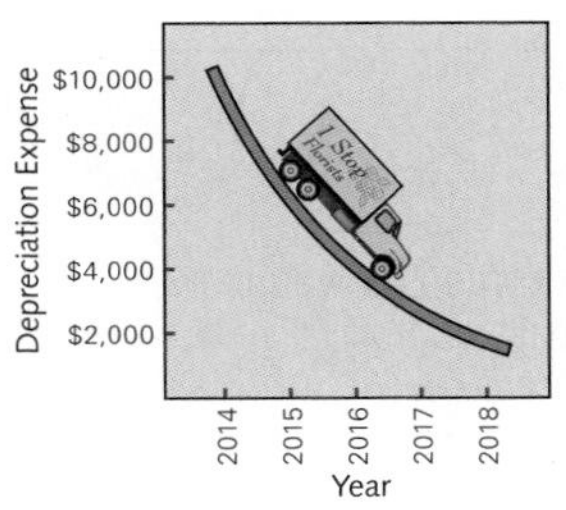

When an asset is purchased during the year, it is necessary to pro-rate the diminishing-balance depreciation in the first year, based on time. For example, if 1 Stop Florists had purchased the delivery truck on April 1, 2014, the depreciation for 2014 would be $7,500 ($25,000 × 40% × 9/12) if depreciation is calculated monthly. The carrying amount for calculating depreciation in 2015 would then become $17,500 ($25,000 − $7,500). The depreciation for 2015 would be $7,000 ($17,500 × 40%). Future calculations would follow from these amounts until the carrying amount equalled the residual value.

Returning to Illustration 9-7, which assumes the asset was bought at the start of the year, you can see that the delivery truck is 70% depreciated ($16,000 ÷ $23,000) at the end of the second year. Under the straight-line method, it would be 40% depreciated ($9,200 ÷ $23,000) at that time. Because the diminishing-balance method produces higher depreciation expense in the early years than in the later years, it is considered an *accelerated* depreciation method. In later years its depreciation expense will be less than the straight-line depreciation expense. Regardless of the method that is used, the total amount of depreciation over the life of the delivery truck is $23,000—the depreciable amount.

Managers must choose the diminishing-balance, or another accelerated method, if the company receives more economic benefit in the early years of the asset's useful life than in the later years. That is, this method is used if the asset, for example, has higher revenue-producing ability in its early years, or if the asset is expected to become less useful over time.

Units-of-Production.

Alternative terminology The units-of-production method is often called the *units-of-activity method* or the *units-of-output method.*

Useful life can be expressed in ways other than time. In the **units-of-production method**, useful life is either the estimated total units of production or total expected use from the asset, *not* the number of years that the asset is expected to be used. The units-of-production method is ideal for equipment whose activity can be measured in units of output, such as kilometres driven or hours in use. The units-of-production method is generally not suitable for buildings or furniture, because depreciation of these assets is more a result of time than of use.

In this method, the total units of production for the entire useful life are estimated. This amount is divided into the depreciable amount (cost − residual value) to determine the depreciable amount per unit. The depreciable amount per unit is then multiplied by the actual units of production during the year to calculate the annual depreciation expense.

To illustrate, assume that the 1 Stop Florists' delivery truck is driven 30,000 km in the first year of a total estimated life of 200,000 km. Illustration 9-8 shows the calculation of depreciation expense in the first year.

ILLUSTRATION 9-8
Formula for units-of-production method

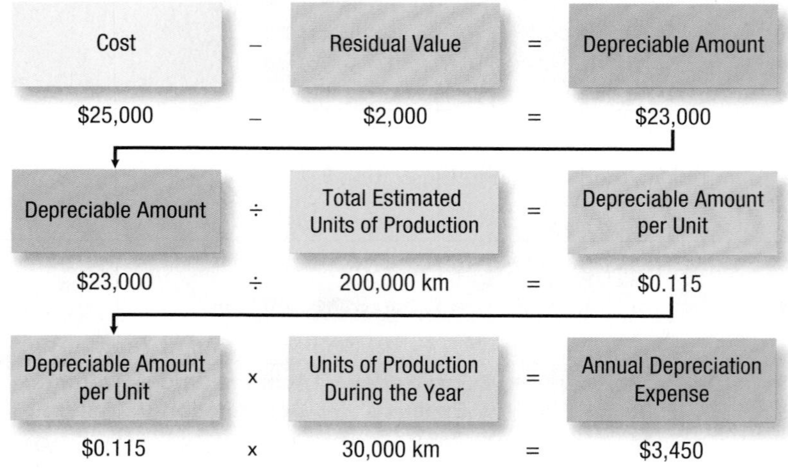

Illustration 9-9 shows the units-of-production depreciation schedule, using assumed units of production (kilometres driven) for the later years.

ILLUSTRATION 9-9
Units-of-production depreciation schedule

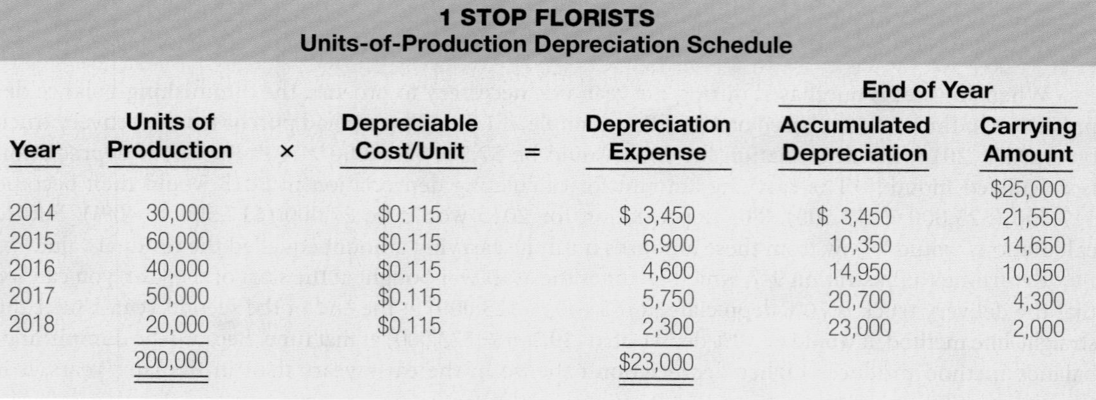

1 STOP FLORISTS
Units-of-Production Depreciation Schedule

Year	Units of Production	×	Depreciable Cost/Unit	=	Depreciation Expense	End of Year Accumulated Depreciation	End of Year Carrying Amount
							$25,000
2014	30,000		$0.115		$ 3,450	$ 3,450	21,550
2015	60,000		$0.115		6,900	10,350	14,650
2016	40,000		$0.115		4,600	14,950	10,050
2017	50,000		$0.115		5,750	20,700	4,300
2018	20,000		$0.115		2,300	23,000	2,000
	200,000				$23,000		

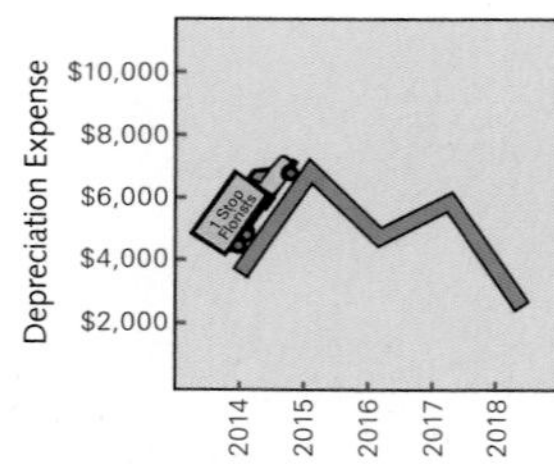

In the example in Illustration 9-9, the total actual units of production equal the original estimated total units of production of 200,000 km. But in most real-life situations, the total actual units of production do not exactly equal the total estimated units of production. This means that the final year's depreciation will have to be adjusted—as we saw in the double diminishing-balance method in Illustration 9-7—so that the ending carrying amount is equal to the estimated residual value.

This method is easy to apply when assets are purchased during the year. The actual units of production already show how much the asset was used during the year. *Therefore, the depreciation calculations do not need to be adjusted for partial periods as is done in the straight-line and diminishing-balance methods.*

The units-of-production method is used for assets whose activity can be measured in units of output. But it can only be used if it is possible to make a reasonable estimate of total activity. Later in this chapter, we will see that this method is widely used to depreciate natural resources. The units-of-production method results in the best matching of expenses with revenues when the asset's productivity varies significantly from one period to another.

Comparison of Depreciation Methods

Illustration 9-10 presents a comparison of annual and total depreciation expense for 1 Stop Florists under each of the three depreciation methods. In addition, if we assume for simplicity that profit before deducting depreciation expense is $50,000 for each of the five years, we can clearly see the impact that the choice of method has on profit.

ILLUSTRATION 9-10
Comparison of depreciation method

	Straight-Line		Double Diminishing-Balance		Units-of-Production	
Year	Depreciation Expense	Profit	Depreciation Expense	Profit	Depreciation Expense	Profit
2014	$ 4,600	$ 45,400	$10,000	$ 40,000	$ 3,450	$ 46,550
2015	4,600	45,400	6,000	44,000	6,900	43,100
2016	4,600	45,400	3,600	46,400	4,600	45,400
2017	4,600	45,400	2,160	47,840	5,750	44,250
2018	4,600	45,400	1,240	48,760	2,300	47,700
	$23,000	$227,000	$23,000	$227,000	$23,000	$227,000

Recall that straight-line depreciation results in the same amount of depreciation expense and therefore profit each year. Diminishing-balance depreciation results in a higher depreciation expense in early years, and therefore lower profit, and a lower depreciation expense and higher profit in later years. Results with the units-of-production method vary, depending on how much the asset is used each year. While the depreciation expense and profit will be different each year for each method, *total* depreciation expense and *total* profit after the five-year period are the same for all three methods.

The balance sheet is also affected by the choice of depreciation method because accumulated depreciation is increased by depreciation expense and owner's equity is increased by profit. There is no impact on cash flow because depreciation does not involve cash.

As explained earlier, management should choose the method that best matches the estimated pattern in which the asset's economic benefits are expected to be consumed. If the economic benefit of owning an asset is fairly consistent over time, the straight-line method is appropriate. The diminishing-balance method is appropriate if the company receives more economic benefit in the early years of the asset's useful life than in the later years. The units-of-production method is appropriate for assets whose usage varies over time. Because companies have more than one type of asset, they often use more than one depreciation method.

Helpful hint Recall that companies that use different depreciation methods for different types of assets are *not* violating the Consistency Principle.

ACCOUNTING IN ACTION
BUSINESS INSIGHT

Why does Morris Formal Wear use the units-of-production method for its tuxedos? The reason is that the Ottawa-based family business wants to track wear and tear on each of its 5,200 tuxedos individually. Each tuxedo has its own bar code. When a tux is rented, a clerk runs its code across an electronic scanner. At year end, the computer adds up the total rentals for each of the tuxedos, then divides this number by expected total use to calculate the rate. For instance, on a two-button black tux, Morris expects a life of 30 rentals. In one year, the tux was rented 13 times. The depreciation rate for that period was 43% (13 ÷ 30) of the depreciable cost.

Is the units-of-production method the best depreciation method for Morris Formal Wear to use for its tuxedos or would you recommend another method? Be sure to provide reasons for your decision.

Depreciation and Income Tax

The Canada Revenue Agency (CRA) allows companies to deduct a specified amount of depreciation expense when they calculate their taxable income. As we have just learned, for accounting purposes, a company must choose the depreciation method that best reflects the pattern in which the asset's future economic benefits are consumed. The CRA does not permit a choice among the three depreciation methods. Instead, it requires taxpayers to use the single diminishing-balance method on the tax return, regardless of what method is used in the financial statements.

Helpful hint Depreciation for accounting purposes is usually different from depreciation for income tax purposes.

In addition, the CRA does not allow taxpayers to estimate the useful lives of assets or depreciation rates. Assets are grouped into various classes and maximum depreciation rates for each class are specified. Depreciation allowed for income tax purposes is calculated on a class (group) basis and is called **capital cost allowance (CCA)**. Capital cost allowance is an optional deduction from taxable income, but depreciation expense is not optional in calculating profit. Consequently, you may see a company deduct depreciation on its income statement, which is required by generally accepted accounting principles, but not deduct CCA for income tax purposes.

Action Plan

- Under straight-line depreciation, annual depreciation expense is equal to the depreciable amount (cost less residual value) divided by the estimated useful life.
- Under double diminishing-balance depreciation, annual depreciation expense is equal to double the straight-line rate of depreciation times the asset's carrying amount at the beginning of the year. Residual values are ignored in this method.
- Under the straight-line and diminishing-balance methods, the annual depreciation expense must be pro-rated (that is, recorded only for the fraction of the year that the asset is in use) if the asset is purchased during the year.
- Under units-of-production depreciation, the depreciable amount per unit is equal to the total depreciable amount divided by the total estimated units of production. The annual depreciation expense is equal to the depreciable amount per unit times the actual number of units it is used for in each year.

BEFORE YOU GO ON...

DO IT

On October 1, 2014, Iron Mountain Ski Company purchases a new snow grooming machine for $52,000. The machine is estimated to have a five-year useful life and a $4,000 residual value. It is also estimated to have a total useful life of 6,000 hours. It is used 1,000 hours in the year ended December 31, 2014, and 1,300 hours in the year ended December 31, 2015. How much depreciation expense should Iron Mountain Ski record in each of 2014 and 2015 under each depreciation method: (a) straight-line, (b) double diminishing-balance, and (c) units-of-production?

SOLUTION

	2014	2015
Straight-line	$2,400	$ 9,600
Double diminishing-balance	5,200	18,720
Units-of-production	8,000	10,400

(a) Straight-line: ($52,000 − $4,000) ÷ 5 years = $9,600 per year
2014: $9,600 × $^3/_{12}$ = $2,400

(b) Double diminishing-balance: 100% ÷ 5 years = 20% straight-line rate
20% × 2 = 40% double diminishing-balance rate
2014: $52,000 × 40% × $^3/_{12}$ = $5,200
2015: ($52,000 − $5,200) × 40% = $18,720

(c) Units-of-production: ($52,000 − $4,000) ÷ 6,000 hours = $8.00 per hour
2014: 1,000 × $8.00 = $8,000
2015: 1,300 × $8.00 = $10,400

Related exercise material: BE9–5, BE9–6, BE9–7, BE9–8, BE9–9, E9–2, E9–3, E9–4, and E9–5.

REVISING PERIODIC DEPRECIATION

STUDY OBJECTIVE 3

Explain the factors that cause changes in periodic depreciation and calculate revisions.

During the useful life of a long-lived asset, the annual depreciation expense needs to be revised if there are changes to one or more of the three factors that affect the calculation of depreciation: the asset's cost, useful life, or residual value. Thus, depreciation needs to be revised if there are (1) capital expenditures during the asset's useful life, (2) impairments in the value of an asset, (3) changes in the asset's fair value when using the revaluation model, and/or (4) changes in the appropriate depreciation method, or in the asset's estimated useful life or residual value. In the following sections, we discuss each of these items and then show how to revise depreciation calculations.

Capital Expenditures During Useful Life

Earlier in the chapter, we learned that companies can have both operating and capital expenditures when a long-lived asset is purchased. Similarly, during the useful life of a long-lived asset, a company may incur costs for ordinary repairs, or for additions or improvements.

Ordinary repairs are costs to *maintain* the asset's operating efficiency and expected productive life. Motor tune-ups and oil changes, repainting a building, or replacing worn-out gears on equipment are examples of ordinary repairs. These costs are frequently fairly small amounts that occur regularly. They may also be larger, infrequent amounts, but if they simply restore an asset to its prior condition, they are considered an ordinary repair. Such repairs are debited to Repair (or Maintenance) Expense as they occur. Ordinary repairs are operating expenditures.

Additions and improvements are costs that are incurred to *increase* the asset's operating efficiency, productive capacity, or expected useful life. These costs are usually large and happen less often than ordinary repairs. Additions and improvements that add to the future cash flows associated with that asset are not expensed as they occur—they are capitalized. As capital expenditures, they are generally debited to the appropriate property, plant, or equipment account, or to the specific component of that asset. The capital expenditure will be depreciated over the remaining life of the original structure or the useful life of the addition. Additions and improvements can also increase the useful life of the original structure. The depreciation calculations need to be revised when a company makes an addition or improvement.

Helpful hint Both ordinary repairs and additions and improvements are ultimately expensed. Ordinary repairs are expensed immediately, whereas additions and improvements are *first capitalized* and *then expensed* through the depreciation process.

Impairments

As noted earlier in the chapter, under the cost model, the carrying amount of property, plant, and equipment is cost less any accumulated depreciation since its acquisition. And, as already discussed, the carrying amount of property, plant, and equipment is rarely the same as its fair value. Remember that the fair value is normally not relevant since property, plant, and equipment are purchased not for resale, but rather for use in the production of goods and services over the long term.

While it is accepted that long-lived assets such as property, plant, and equipment may be *undervalued* on the balance sheet, it is not appropriate if property, plant, and equipment are *overvalued.* Property, plant, and equipment are considered impaired if the asset's carrying amount exceeds its **recoverable amount**. The recoverable amount is the greater of the asset's fair value less costs to sell, or the value in use, which is based on its future cash flows. When an asset is impaired, an **impairment loss** is recorded (as a debit) that is the amount by which the asset's carrying amount exceeds its recoverable amount. The rules for determining if an asset is impaired are somewhat different under ASPE and IFRS. While the details of these differences are left to a later accounting course, it should be noted that under ASPE, impairments are recorded less often.

ASPE

Companies are required to determine on a regular basis if there is any indication of impairment. If there is no such indication, it is not necessary to test the asset for impairment. If there is an indication of possible impairment, then an impairment test must be done. For example, if a machine has become obsolete, or if the market for a product made by a machine has dried up or has become very competitive, there is a strong possibility that an impairment loss exists. Management is then required to do an impairment test, which involves estimating the machine's recoverable amount.

To illustrate an impairment loss on a long-lived asset, assume that on December 31, Piniwa Company reviews its equipment for possible impairment. The equipment has a cost of $800,000 and accumulated depreciation of $200,000. The equipment's recoverable amount is currently $500,000. The amount of the impairment loss is determined by comparing the asset's carrying amount with its recoverable amount as follows:

Carrying amount ($800,000 − $200,000)	$600,000
Recoverable amount	500,000
Impairment loss	$100,000

The journal entry to record the impairment is:

Date	Account	Debit	Credit
Dec. 31	Impairment Loss	100,000	
	Accumulated Depreciation—Equipment		100,000
	To record impairment loss on equipment.		

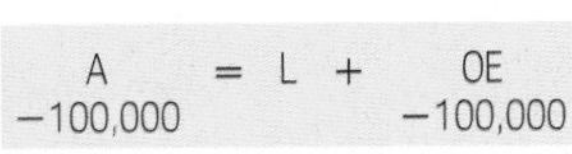

Cash flows: no effect

Assuming that the asset will continue to be used in operations, the impairment loss is reported on the income statement as part of operating profit rather than as "other expense." Often the loss is combined with depreciation expense on the income statement. The Accumulated Depreciation account, not the asset account, is credited for the impairment loss. Recording the loss this way keeps a record of the asset's original cost.

We had previously defined an asset's carrying amount as its cost less accumulated depreciation. This is still the case, but the Accumulated Depreciation account can now include more than just the depreciation recorded on the asset to date. It will also include impairment losses, if there have been any. Future depreciation calculations will need to be revised because of the reduction in the asset's carrying amount.

IFRS allow the reversal of a previously recorded impairment loss. Under IFRS, at each year end, the company must determine whether or not an impairment loss still exists by measuring the asset's recoverable amount. If this recoverable amount exceeds the current carrying amount, then a reversal is recorded. The reversal for an asset is limited to the amount required to increase the asset's carrying amount to what it would have been if the impairment loss had not been recorded. (In other words, it cannot cause an overall increase in the carrying amount of the asset.) When an impairment loss is reversed, we simply credit the impairment loss account and debit the accumulated depreciation account. The reversal will result in additional revisions to depreciation calculations. As previously discussed, although impairment losses are recorded less often under ASPE, once an impairment has been recorded, it cannot be reversed later.

Cost Model Versus Revaluation Model

As previously mentioned, under IFRS, companies can choose to account for their property, plant, and equipment under either the cost model or the revaluation model. We have used the cost model in this chapter because it is used by almost all companies. Only about 3% of companies reporting under IFRS use the revaluation model. The revaluation model is allowed under IFRS mainly because it is particularly useful in countries that experience high rates of inflation or for companies in certain industries, such as investment or real estate companies, where fair values are more relevant than cost. It is not allowed under ASPE.

Under the **revaluation model**, the carrying amount of property, plant, and equipment is its fair value less any accumulated depreciation less any subsequent impairment losses. This model can be applied only to assets whose fair value can be reliably measured, and revaluations must be carried out often enough that the carrying amount is not materially different from the asset's fair value at the balance sheet date. The accounting in the revaluation model is relatively complex and will not be covered in this textbook.

Changes in Depreciation Method, Estimated Useful Life, or Residual Value

As previously explained, the depreciation method used should be consistent with the pattern in which the asset's future economic benefits are expected to be consumed by the company. The appropriateness of the depreciation method should be reviewed at least annually in case there has been a change in the expected pattern. Management must also review its estimates of the useful life and residual value of the company's depreciable assets at least once per year, generally at year end. If wear and tear or obsolescence indicates that the estimates are too low or too high, estimates should be changed. If the depreciation method, estimated useful life, or residual values are changed, this will cause a revision to the depreciation calculations.

Revised Depreciation Calculations

All of the above discussed factors will result in a revision to the depreciation calculation. In each case, *the revision is made for current and future years only*. The revision is not made retroactively for past periods. Thus, when a change in depreciation is made, (1) there is no correction of previously recorded depreciation expense, and (2) depreciation expense for current and future years is revised. The rationale for this treatment is that the original calculation made in the past was based on the best information available at that time. The revision is based on new information that should affect only current and future periods. In addition, if past periods were often restated, users would feel less confident about financial statements.

To calculate the new annual depreciation expense, we must first calculate the asset's carrying amount at the time of the change. This is equal to the asset's original cost minus the accumulated depreciation to date, plus any capital expenditures, minus any impairment in value. We must also determine if the original depreciation method, residual value, and useful life are still appropriate. If not, we must determine which method is now appropriate, and the revised residual value and useful life.

To illustrate how to revise depreciation, assume that 1 Stop Florists decides on December 31, 2017—before recording its depreciation for 2017—to extend the estimated useful life of its truck by one more year (to December 31, 2019) because of its good condition. As a result of using the truck an extra year, the estimated residual value is expected to decline from its original estimate of $2,000 to $700. Assume that the company has been using straight-line depreciation and determines this is still the appropriate method. Recall that the truck was purchased on January 1, 2014, for $25,000 and originally had an estimated useful life of five years, with annual depreciation expense of $4,600.

The carrying amount at December 31, 2017—before recording depreciation for 2017—is $11,200 [$25,000 − (3 × $4,600)]. This is also the amount shown in Illustration 9-5 as the carrying amount at December 31, 2016. The remaining useful life of three years is calculated by taking the original useful life of five years, subtracting the three years where depreciation has already been recorded, and adding the additional estimated years of useful life—in this case one year. The new annual depreciation is $3,500, calculated as in Illustration 9-11.

Helpful hint Carrying amount = Cost − Accumulated depreciation.

ILLUSTRATION 9-11
Formula for revised straight-line depreciation

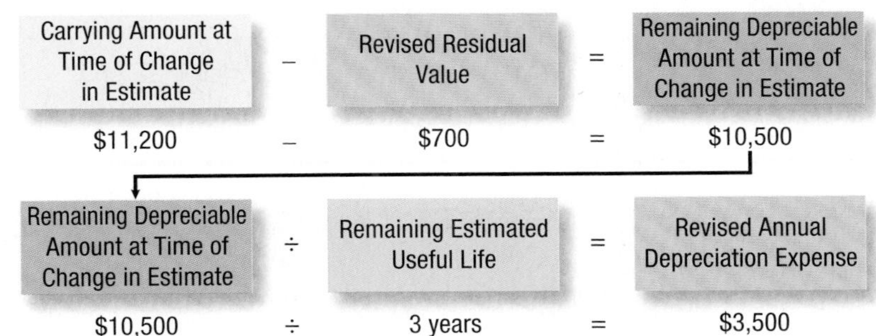

As a result of the revision to the truck's estimated useful life and residual value, 1 Stop Florists will record depreciation expense of $3,500 on December 31 of 2017, 2018, and 2019. The company will not go back and change the depreciation for 2014, 2015, and 2016. Accumulated depreciation will now equal $24,300 [($4,600 × 3) + ($3,500 × 3)] at the end of the six-year useful life instead of the $23,000 that was originally calculated. The $1,300 increase in accumulated depreciation is because the estimated residual value was revised and decreased by $1,300 ($2,000 − $700).

If the units-of-production depreciation method is used, the calculation is the same as we just saw except that the remaining useful life is expressed as units rather than years. If the diminishing-balance method is used, the revised rate would be applied to the carrying amount at the time of the change in estimate. The rate must be revised because the useful life has changed.

Helpful hint If the expected useful life of an asset is extended, the annual depreciation expense will be reduced. This occurs as a result of the depreciable amount being spread over a longer time period.

BEFORE YOU GO ON...

DO IT

On August 1, 1999, just after its year end, Fine Furniture Company purchased a building for $500,000. The company used straight-line depreciation to allocate the cost of this building, estimating a residual value of $50,000 and a useful life of 30 years. After 15 years of use, on August 1, 2014, the company was forced to replace the entire roof at a cost of $25,000 cash. The residual value was expected to remain at $50,000 but the total useful life was now expected to increase to 40 years. Prepare journal entries to record (a) depreciation for the year ended July 31, 2014; (b) the cost of the addition on August 1, 2014; and (c) depreciation for the year ended July 31, 2015.

SOLUTION

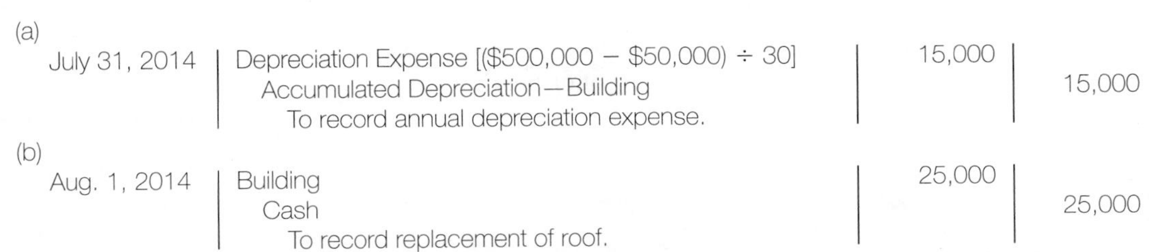

(a)

July 31, 2014	Depreciation Expense [($500,000 − $50,000) ÷ 30]	15,000	
	Accumulated Depreciation—Building		15,000
	To record annual depreciation expense.		

(b)

Aug. 1, 2014	Building	25,000	
	Cash		25,000
	To record replacement of roof.		

Action Plan

- Understand the difference between an operating expenditure (benefits only the current period) and a capital expenditure (benefits future periods).
- To revise annual depreciation, calculate the carrying amount (cost less accumulated depreciation) at the revision date. Note that the cost of any capital expenditure will increase the carrying amount of the asset to be depreciated.

BEFORE YOU GO ON... continued on next page

BEFORE YOU GO ON...
continued from previous page

- Subtract any revised residual value from the carrying amount at the time of the change in estimate (plus the capital expenditure in this case) to determine the remaining depreciable amount.
- Allocate the revised depreciable amount over the remaining (not total) useful life.

(c) Cost:	$500,000
Less: Accumulated depreciation $15,000 per year × 15 years	225,000
Carrying amount before replacement of roof, August 1, 2014	275,000
Add: Capital expenditure (roof)	25,000
Carrying amount after replacement of roof, August 1, 2014	300,000
Less: Revised residual value	50,000
Remaining depreciable amount	250,000
Divide by: Remaining useful life (40 − 15)	÷ 25 years
Revised annual depreciation	$ 10,000

Date	Account	Debit	Credit
July 31, 2015	Depreciation Expense	10,000	
	Accumulated Depreciation—Building		10,000
	To record revised annual depreciation expense.		

Related exercise material: BE9–10, BE9–11, E9–6, E9–7, and E9–8.

STUDY OBJECTIVE 4
Account for the disposal of property, plant, and equipment.

DISPOSALS OF PROPERTY, PLANT, AND EQUIPMENT

Companies dispose of property, plant, or equipment that is no longer useful to them. Illustration 9-12 shows three methods of disposal.

ILLUSTRATION 9-12
Methods of property, plant, and equipment disposal

Retirement
Equipment is scrapped or discarded.

Sale
Equipment is sold.

Exchange
Existing equipment is traded for new equipment.

Steps in Recording Disposals of Property, Plant, and Equipment

Alternative terminology
Derecognition is a term used under IFRS to describe the removal of a long-lived asset from the accounts when it is disposed of or no longer provides any future benefit.

Whatever the disposal method, a company must take the following four steps to record the retirement, sale, or exchange of the property, plant, or equipment:

Step 1: Update Depreciation.
Depreciation must be recorded over the entire period of time an asset is available for use. Therefore, if the disposal occurs in the middle of an accounting period, depreciation must be updated for the fraction of the year since the last time adjusting entries were recorded up to the date of disposal.

Step 2: Calculate the Carrying Amount.
Calculate the carrying amount at the date of disposal after updating the accumulated depreciation for any partial year depreciation calculated in Step 1 above:

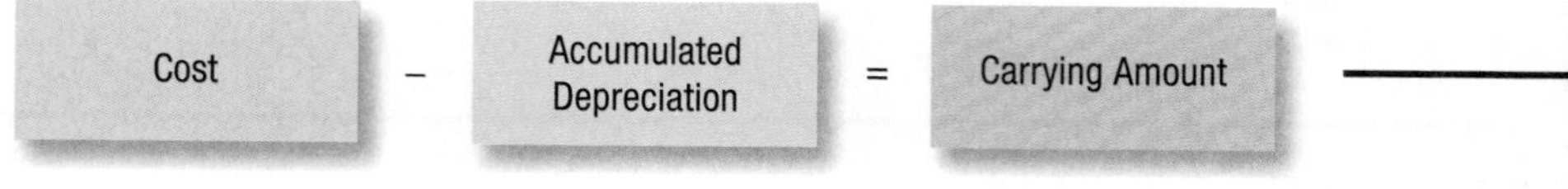

Step 3: Calculate the Gain or Loss.
Determine the amount of the gain or loss on disposal, if any, by comparing the proceeds received from the disposal with the carrying amount at the date of disposal.

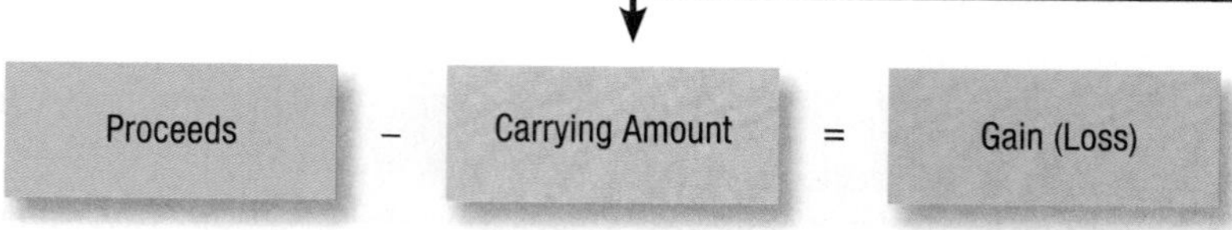

If the proceeds of the sale are more than the carrying amount of the property, plant, or equipment, there is a *gain on disposal*. If the proceeds of the sale are less than the carrying amount of the asset sold, there is a *loss on disposal*.

Step 4: Record the Disposal.

The journal entry to record the disposal always involves removing the asset's cost and the accumulated depreciation from the accounts. These are the same amounts used to calculate the carrying amount in Step 2 above. The journal entry may also include recording the proceeds and the gain or loss on disposal if there are any proceeds and if there is a gain or loss. Gains on disposal are recorded as credits because credits increase owner's equity; losses on disposal are recorded as debits because debits decrease owner's equity.

Helpful hint When a long-lived asset is disposed of, both the asset account and its contra asset account balances must be reduced to zero. The use of T accounts is helpful in preparing entries for disposal.

Dr. Cash (or other account)
Dr. Accumulated Depreciation
Dr. Loss on Disposal OR Cr. Gain on Disposal
  Cr. Property, plant, or equipment account

Gains and losses are reported in the operating section of a multiple-step income statement. Why? Recall that depreciation expense is an estimate. A loss results when the annual depreciation expense has not been high enough so that the carrying amount at the date of disposal is equal to the proceeds. Gains are caused because annual depreciation expense has been too high, so the carrying amount at the date of disposal is less than the proceeds. Thus gains and losses are basically just adjustments to depreciation expense and should be recorded in the same section of the income statement.

Retirement of Property, Plant, and Equipment

Instead of being sold or exchanged, some assets are simply retired at the end of their useful lives. For example, some productive assets used in manufacturing may have highly specialized uses and consequently have no market when the company no longer needs the asset. In this case, the asset is simply retired.

When an asset is retired, there are no proceeds on disposal. The Accumulated Depreciation account is decreased (debited) for the full amount of depreciation taken over the life of the asset. The asset account is reduced (credited) for the asset's original cost. Even if the carrying amount equals zero, a journal entry is still required to remove the asset and its related accumulated depreciation account from the books, as shown in the following example.

To illustrate the retirement of a piece of property, plant, and equipment, assume that on December 31, 2014, Baseyev Enterprises retires equipment, which cost $31,200. At the time of purchase, on January 1, 2011, the equipment was expected to have a four-year useful life and no residual value. Baseyev used straight-line depreciation and the annual depreciation expense was $7,800 per year ($31,200 ÷ 4). The balance in the Accumulated Depreciation account at Baseyev's year end, December 31, 2013, was $23,400 ($7,800 × 3). Before recording the disposal, Baseyev must first record depreciation from the last time it was recorded—December 31, 2013—to the date of disposal—December 31, 2014. As this is one year, the amount to be recorded is $7,800, as shown in the following journal entry:

2014
Dec. 31
	Depreciation Expense
	  Accumulated Depreciation—Equipment
	    To record depreciation expense from last time it was recorded to date of disposal.
		7,800	
			7,800

A	=	L	+	OE
−7,800				−7,800

Cash flows: no effect

After this journal entry is posted, the Equipment and Accumulated Depreciation accounts appear as follows:

Equipment

Jan. 1, 2011	31,200		

Accumulated Depreciation—Equipment

		Dec. 31, 2011	7,800
		Dec. 31, 2012	7,800
		Dec. 31, 2013	7,800
		Balance	23,400
		Dec. 31, 2014	7,800
		Balance	31,200

The equipment is now fully depreciated with a carrying amount of zero (cost of $31,200 − accumulated depreciation of $31,200). As the equipment is being retired, there are zero proceeds, and since the carrying amount is equal to the proceeds and there is no gain or loss on disposal. All that is required is an entry to remove the cost and accumulated depreciation of the equipment, as follows:

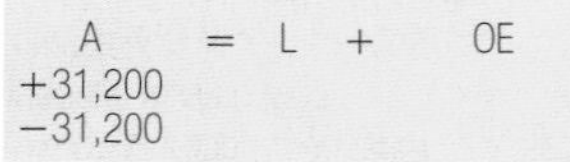

A	=	L	+	OE
+31,200				
−31,200				

Cash flows: no effect

Date	Account	Debit	Credit
2014 Dec. 31	Accumulated Depreciation—Equipment	31,200	
	Equipment		31,200
	To record retirement of fully depreciated equipment.		

After this journal entry is posted, the Equipment and Accumulated Depreciation accounts appear as follows:

Equipment			
Jan. 1, 2011	31,200		
		Dec. 31, 2014	31,200
Balance	0		

Accumulated Depreciation—Equipment			
		Balance	31,200
Dec. 31, 2014	31,200		
		Balance	0

After this entry is posted, the balance in the Equipment and Accumulated Depreciation—Equipment accounts will be zero.

Helpful hint Depreciation spreads the depreciable amount of a long-lived asset over its useful life. The total amount of accumulated depreciation can never be greater than the cost of the asset.

What happens if a company is still using a fully depreciated asset? In this case, the asset and its accumulated depreciation continue to be reported on the balance sheet, without further depreciation, until the asset is retired. Reporting the asset and related depreciation on the balance sheet informs the reader of the financial statements that the asset is still being used by the company. Once an asset is fully depreciated, even if it is still being used, no additional depreciation should be taken. Accumulated depreciation on a piece of property, plant, and equipment can never be more than the asset's cost.

If a piece of property, plant, and equipment is retired before it is fully depreciated and no residual value is received, a loss on disposal occurs. Assume that Baseyev Enterprises retires its equipment on January 1, 2014. The loss on disposal is calculated by subtracting the asset's carrying amount from the proceeds that are received. In this case, there are no proceeds and the carrying amount is $7,800 (cost of $31,200 − accumulated depreciation of $23,400), resulting in a loss of $7,800:

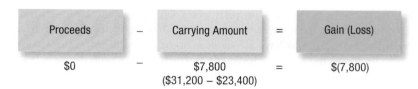

Proceeds	−	Carrying Amount	=	Gain (Loss)
$0	−	$7,800 ($31,200 – $23,400)	=	$(7,800)

The entry to record the retirement of equipment is as follows:

A	=	L	+	OE
+23,400				−7,800
−31,200				

Cash flows: no effect

Date	Account	Debit	Credit
Jan. 1	Accumulated Depreciation—Equipment	23,400	
	Loss on Disposal	7,800	
	Equipment		31,200
	To record retirement of equipment at a loss.		

You should also note that there will never be a gain when an asset is retired. The proceeds are always zero and therefore can never be greater than the carrying amount of the retired asset.

Sale of Property, Plant, and Equipment

In a disposal by sale, there are proceeds that must be recorded. Both gains and losses on disposal are common when an asset is sold. Only by coincidence will the asset's carrying amount and fair value (the proceeds) be the same when the asset is sold. We will illustrate the sale of furniture at both a gain and a loss in the following sections.

Gain on Disposal.

To illustrate a gain, assume that on April 1, 2014, Baseyev Enterprises sells office furniture for $15,000 cash. The office furniture had originally been purchased on January 1, 2010, at a cost of $60,200. At that time, it was estimated that the furniture would have a residual value of $5,000 and a useful life of five years.

The first step is to update any unrecorded depreciation. Annual depreciation using the straight-line method is $11,040 [($60,200 − $5,000) ÷ 5]. The entry to record the depreciation expense and update accumulated depreciation for the first three months of 2014 is as follows:

2014 Apr. 1	Depreciation Expense ($11,040 × 3/12)	2,760	
	Accumulated Depreciation—Furniture		2,760
	To record depreciation expense for the first 3 months of 2014.		

A	=	L	+	OE
−2,760				−2,760

Cash flows: no effect

After this journal entry is posted, the Furniture and Accumulated Depreciation accounts appear as follows:

Furniture

Jan. 1, 2010	60,200		

Accumulated Depreciation—Furniture

		Dec. 31, 2010	11,040
		Dec. 31, 2011	11,040
		Dec. 31, 2012	11,040
		Dec. 31, 2013	11,040
		Apr. 1, 2014	2,760
		Balance	46,920

The second step is to calculate the carrying amount on April 1, 2014. Note that the balance in Accumulated Depreciation of $46,920 is equal to four years (January 1, 2010, to December 31, 2013) at $11,040/year plus $2,760 for 2014.

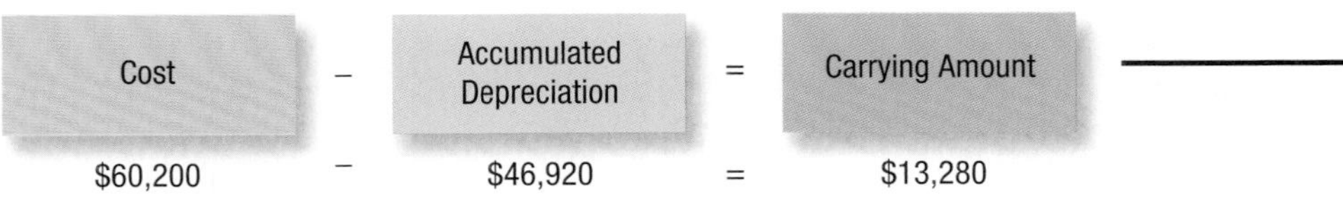

The third step is to calculate the gain or loss on disposal. A $1,720 gain on disposal is determined as follows:

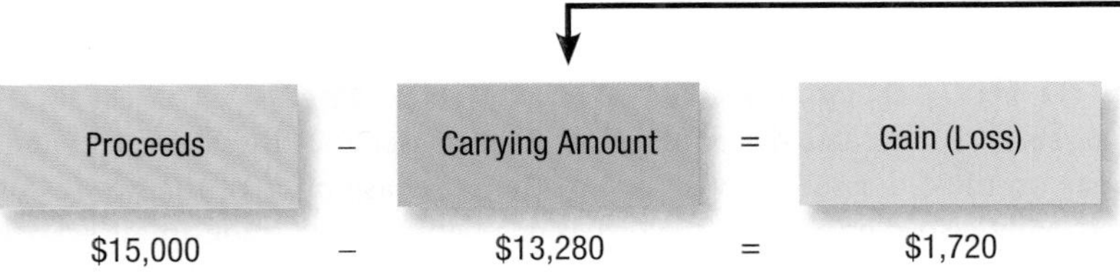

The fourth step is the entry to record the sale of the office furniture as follows:

Apr. 1	Cash	15,000	
	Accumulated Depreciation—Furniture	46,920	
	Gain on Disposal		1,720
	Furniture		60,200
	To record the sale of office furniture at a gain.		

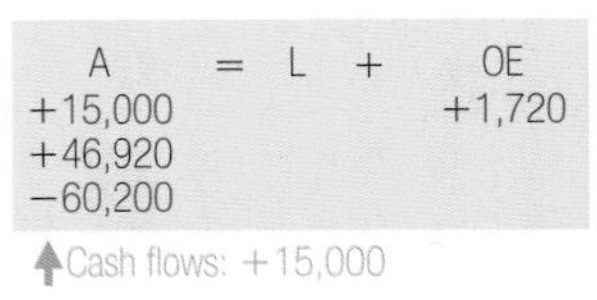

The following T accounts show the above transaction in the form of T accounts.

Cash			
Apr. 1, 2014	15,000		
Balance	15,000		

Accumulated Depreciation—Furniture			
		Balance	46,920
Apr. 1, 2014	46,920		
		Balance	0

Furniture			
Jan. 1, 2010	60,200		
		Apr. 1, 2014	60,200
Balance	0		

Gain on Disposal			
		Apr. 1, 2014 Balance	1,720
		Balance	1,720

Notice that the carrying amount of $13,280 does not appear in the journal entry. Instead, the asset's cost ($60,200) and the total accumulated depreciation ($46,920) are used. **Remember the carrying amount is simply a number calculated to determine the gain or loss.** *It is not an account and cannot be debited or credited.*

Loss on Disposal.

Assume that instead of selling the furniture for $15,000, Baseyev sells it for $9,000. In this case, a loss of $4,280 is calculated as follows:

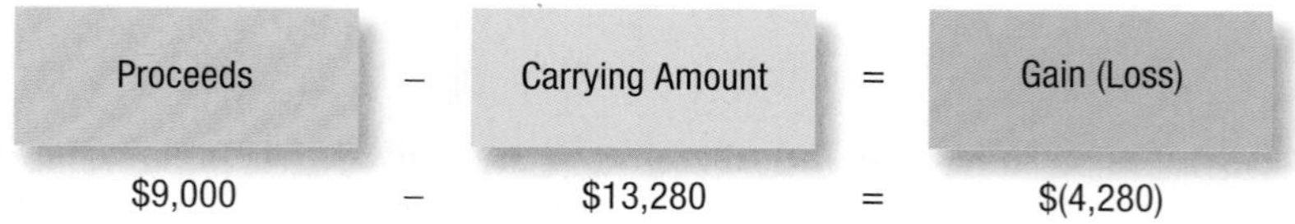

The entry to record the sale of the office furniture is as follows:

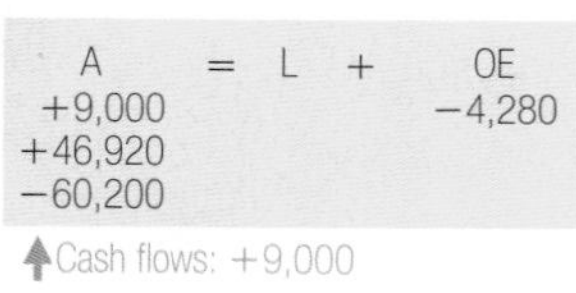

A	= L +	OE
+9,000		−4,280
+46,920		
−60,200		

Cash flows: +9,000

Apr. 1	Cash	9,000	
	Accumulated Depreciation—Furniture	46,920	
	Loss on Disposal	4,280	
	Furniture		60,200
	To record the sale of office furniture at a loss.		

As previously explained, the loss on disposal is the result of not recording enough depreciation expense prior to selling the asset.

Exchanges of Property, Plant, and Equipment

An exchange of assets is recorded as the purchase of a new asset and the sale of an old asset. Typically a **trade-in allowance** on the old asset is given toward the purchase price of the new asset. An additional cash payment is usually also required for the difference between the trade-in allowance and the stated purchase price (list price) of the new asset. The trade-in allowance amount, however, is often affected by price concessions for the new asset and therefore rarely reflects the fair value of the asset that is given up. Consequently, as fair value is what matters, trade-in allowances are ignored for accounting purposes.

Instead of using the stated purchase price, the new asset is recorded at the fair value of the asset given up plus any cash paid (or less any cash received). Instead of using the trade-in allowance, the fair value of the asset given up is used to calculate the gain or loss on the asset being given up. A loss results if the carrying amount of the asset being given up is more than its fair value. A gain results if the carrying amount is less than its fair value.

Thus, the procedure to account for exchanges of assets is as follows:

Step 1: Update any unrecorded depreciation expense on the asset being given up to the date of the exchange.

Step 2: Calculate the carrying amount of the asset being given up (cost − accumulated depreciation).
Step 3: Calculate any gain or loss on disposal [fair value − carrying amount = gain (loss)].
Step 4: Record the exchange as follows:

- Remove the cost and the accumulated depreciation of the asset that is given up.
- Record any gain or loss on disposal.
- Record the new asset at the fair value of the old asset plus any cash paid (or less any cash received).
- Record the cash paid or received.

To illustrate an exchange of long-lived assets, assume that Chilko Company exchanged an old vehicle for a new vehicle on October 1, 2014. The original cost of the old vehicle was $61,000 on January 1, 2009. Depreciation was calculated using the straight-line method, over a six-year useful life, with an estimated residual value of $1,000. The fair value of the old vehicle on October 1, 2014, is $3,000.

The list price of the new vehicle was $51,000. Chilko received an $8,000 trade-in allowance from the vehicle dealership for the old vehicle and paid $43,000 cash ($51,000 − $8,000) for the new vehicle. Chilko's year end is December 31.

The first step is to update the depreciation on the old vehicle for the nine months ended October 1, 2014. Annual depreciation expense is $10,000 [($61,000 − $1,000) ÷ 6], so depreciation for nine months is $7,500 ($10,000 × $^9/_{12}$).

		Debit	Credit
Oct. 1	Depreciation Expense	7,500	
	Accumulated Depreciation—Vehicles		7,500
	To record depreciation expense for the first 9 months of 2014.		

A	=	L	+	OE
−7,500				−7,500

Cash flows: no effect

After this journal entry is posted, the Vehicles and Accumulated Depreciation accounts appear as follows:

Vehicles			
Jan. 1, 2009	61,000		

Accumulated Depreciation—Vehicles			
		Dec. 31, 2009	10,000
		Dec. 31, 2010	10,000
		Dec. 31, 2011	10,000
		Dec. 31, 2012	10,000
		Dec. 31, 2013	10,000
		Oct. 1, 2014	7,500
		Balance	57,500

The next step is to calculate the carrying amount on October 1, 2014. Note that the balance in Accumulated Depreciation of $57,500 is equal to five years (January 1, 2009, to December 31, 2013) at $10,000/year plus $7,500 for 2014.

On October 1, 2014, the carrying amount is $3,500 (cost of $61,000 − accumulated depreciation of $57,500). The loss on disposal on the old vehicle is determined by comparing the carrying amount with the fair value, which represents the proceeds in this situation:

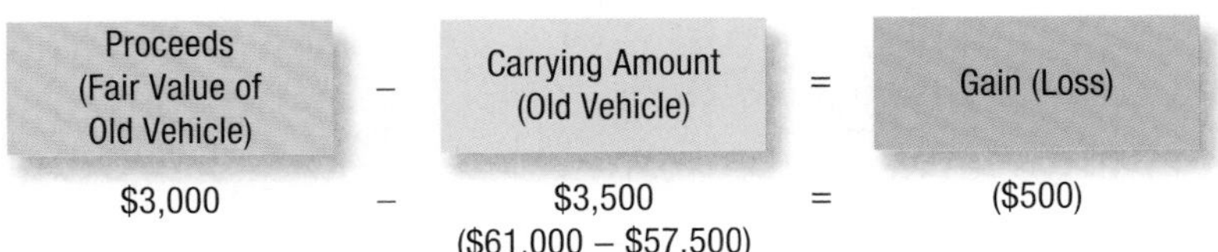

$3,000 − $3,500 ($61,000 – $57,500) = ($500)

The cost of the new vehicle ($46,000) is determined by the fair value of the old vehicle ($3,000) plus the cash paid ($43,000). The entry to record the exchange of vehicles is as follows:

		Debit	Credit
Oct. 1	Vehicles (cost of new vehicle)	46,000	
	Accumulated Depreciation—Vehicles (on the old vehicle)	57,500	
	Loss on Disposal	500	
	Vehicles (cost of old vehicle)		61,000
	Cash		43,000
	To record exchange of vehicles, plus cash.		

A	=	L	+	OE
+46,000				−500
+57,500				
−61,000				
−43,000				

The following T accounts show how the Vehicles and Accumulated Depreciation—Vehicles accounts appear after the old vehicle was exchanged for the new vehicle.

Vehicles			
Jan. 1, 2009	61,000		
Oct. 1, 2014	46,000	Oct. 1, 2014	61,000
Balance	46,000		

Accumulated Depreciation—Vehicles			
		Balance	57,500
Oct. 1, 2014	57,500		
		Balance	0

Note that the exchange of vehicles is not netted. That is, it is shown as a separate increase and decrease to the general ledger account Vehicles. Also note that the list price of $51,000 and the trade-in allowance of $8,000 are ignored in determining the real cost of the new vehicle.

In some situations, the exchange lacks commercial substance or else the fair value of the asset acquired or the asset given up cannot be determined. In such cases, the new long-lived asset is recorded at the carrying amount of the old asset that was given up, plus any cash paid (or less any cash received). Carrying amount is used in these circumstances because the new asset is basically substituted or swapped for the old asset. As the carrying amount of the old asset is used for the carrying amount of the new asset, and the exchange has therefore not changed the operations of the business significantly, no gain or loss is recorded.

BEFORE YOU GO ON...

DO IT

Overland Trucking has a truck that was purchased on January 1, 2010, for $80,000. The truck had been depreciated on a straight-line basis with an estimated residual value of $5,000 and an estimated useful life of five years. Overland has a December 31 year end. Assume each of the following four independent situations:

1. On January 1, 2015, Overland retires the truck.
2. On May 1, 2014, Overland sells the truck for $9,500 cash.
3. On October 1, 2014, Overland sells the truck for $9,500 cash.
4. On November 1, 2014, Overland exchanges the old truck, plus $60,000 cash, for a new truck. The old truck has a fair value of $9,500. The new truck has a list price of $70,000, but the dealer will give Overland a $10,000 trade-in allowance on the old truck.

Prepare the journal entry to record each of these situations.

Action Plan

- Update any unrecorded depreciation for dispositions during the fiscal year.
- Compare the proceeds with the asset's carrying amount to determine if there has been a gain or loss.
- Record any proceeds received and any gain or loss. Remove both the asset and any related accumulated depreciation from the accounts.
- Determine the cash paid in an exchange situation as the difference between the list price and the trade-in allowance.
- Record the cost of the new asset in an exchange situation as the fair value of the asset given up, plus the cash paid.

SOLUTION

$$\frac{\$80{,}000 - \$5{,}000}{5 \text{ years}} = \$15{,}000 \text{ annual depreciation expense}$$

$$\$15{,}000 \div 12 = \$1{,}250 \text{ per month}$$

1. Retirement of truck:

Date	Account	Debit	Credit
Jan. 1, 2015	Accumulated Depreciation—Vehicles ($1,250 × 60 months)	75,000	
	Loss on Disposal [$0 − ($80,000 − $75,000)]	5,000	
	Vehicles		80,000
	To record retirement of truck.		

2. Sale of truck for $9,500 on May 1, 2014:

Date	Account	Debit	Credit
May 1, 2014	Depreciation Expense ($1,250 × 4 months)	5,000	
	Accumulated Depreciation—Vehicles		5,000
	To record depreciation for 4 months.		
	Cash	9,500	
	Accumulated Depreciation—Vehicles ($1,250 × 52 months)	65,000	
	Loss on Disposal [$9,500 − ($80,000 − $65,000)]	5,500	
	Vehicles		80,000
	To record sale of truck at a loss.		

BEFORE YOU GO ON...
continued on next page

BEFORE YOU GO ON...
continued from previous page

3. Sale of truck for $9,500 on Oct. 1, 2014:

Date	Account	Debit	Credit
Oct. 1, 2014	Depreciation Expense ($1,250 × 9 months)	11,250	
	Accumulated Depreciation—Vehicles		11,250
	To record depreciation for 9 months.		
	Cash	9,500	
	Accumulated Depreciation—Vehicles ($1,250 × 57 months)	71,250	
	Gain on Disposal [$9,500 − ($80,000 − $71,250)]		750
	Vehicles		80,000
	To record sale of truck at a gain.		

4. Exchange of truck on Nov. 1, 2014:

Date	Account	Debit	Credit
Nov. 1, 2014	Depreciation Expense ($1,250 × 10 months)	12,500	
	Accumulated Depreciation—Vehicles		12,500
	To record depreciation for 10 months.		
	Vehicles (cost of new) ($9,500 + $60,000)	69,500	
	Accumulated Depreciation—Vehicles ($1,250 × 58 months)	72,500	
	Gain on Disposal [$9,500 − ($80,000 − $72,500)]		2,000
	Vehicles (cost of old)		80,000
	Cash ($70,000 − $10,000)		60,000
	To record exchange of trucks, plus cash.		

Related exercise material: BE9–12, BE9–13, BE9–14, E9–9, and E9–10.

THE NAVIGATOR

NATURAL RESOURCES

STUDY OBJECTIVE 5
Calculate and record depreciation of natural resources.

Natural resources consist of standing timber and underground deposits of oil, gas, and minerals. Canada is rich in natural resources, ranging from the towering rainforests in coastal British Columbia to one of the world's largest nickel deposits in Voisey's Bay, Labrador. These long-lived assets have two characteristics that make them different from other long-lived assets: (1) they are physically extracted in operations such as mining, cutting, or pumping; and (2) only an act of nature can replace them. Because of these characteristics, natural resources are sometimes called *wasting assets.*

Natural resources are tangible assets, similar to property, plant, and equipment. A key distinction between natural resources and property, plant, and equipment is that natural resources physically lose substance, or *deplete*, as they are used. For example, there is less of a tract of timberland (a natural resource) as the timber is cut and sold. When we use equipment, its physical substance remains the same regardless of the product it produces.

COST

The cost of a natural resource is determined in the same way as the cost of property, plant, and equipment and includes all expenditures necessary in acquiring the resource and preparing it for its intended use. These costs are often referred to as acquisition, exploration, and development costs. The cost of a natural resource also includes the estimated future removal and site restoration cleanup costs, which are often large. Restoration costs are usually required in order to return the resource as closely as possible to its natural state at the end of its useful life.

As discussed earlier in the chapter, accounting for asset retirement costs and the allocation of these costs over the useful life of the natural resource is complicated. Further discussion of these concepts is left to an intermediate accounting course. Accounting for exploration and development costs is also very complex. We will, however, look at how the acquisition cost of a natural resource is allocated over its useful life in the next section.

DEPRECIATION

Alternative terminology
Depreciation for natural resources is frequently called *depletion* because the assets physically deplete as the resource is extracted.

The units-of-production method (learned earlier in the chapter) is generally used to calculate the depreciation of wasting assets. Under the units-of-production method, the total cost of the natural resource minus its residual value is divided by the number of units estimated to be in the resource. The result is a depreciable amount per unit of product. The depreciable amount per unit is then multiplied by the number of units extracted, to determine the annual depreciation expense.

To illustrate, assume that Rabbit Lake Company invests $5.5 million in a mine that is estimated to have 10 million tonnes (t) of uranium and a $200,000 residual value. In the first year, 800,000 tonnes of uranium are extracted. Illustration 9-13 shows the formulas and calculations.

ILLUSTRATION 9-13
Formula for units-of-production method for natural resources

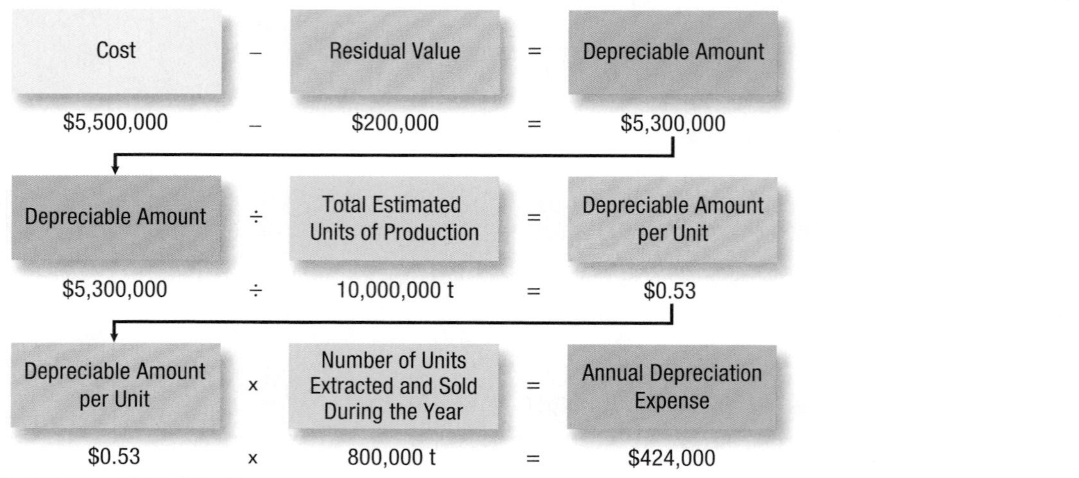

The depreciation expense for the amount of the resource that has been extracted is initially charged (debited) to an inventory account, a current asset. Note that this is not the same as depreciation for property, plant, and equipment, which is recorded as an expense. Depreciation on natural resources is accounted for in this way because the resource extracted is available for sale—similar to merchandise that has been purchased or manufactured for sale, as we learned in Chapter 5.

The entry to record depreciation of the uranium mine for Rabbit Lake Company's first year of operation, ended December 31, 2014, is as follows:

A	= L	+ OE
+424,000		
−424,000		

Cash flows: no effect

Dec. 31	Inventory ($0.53 × 800,000 t)	424,000	
	Accumulated Depreciation—Uranium Mine		424,000
	To record depreciation expense on uranium mine.		

All costs of extracting the natural resource—both current production costs such as labour and depreciation of the natural resource—are recorded as inventory. When sold, the inventory costs are transferred to cost of goods sold and matched with the period's revenue. In other words, the depreciation is charged to the income statement only in the period in which the related goods are *sold*. Depreciation related to goods not yet sold remains in inventory and is reported as a current asset.

For example, assume that Rabbit Lake Company does not sell all of the 800,000 tonnes of uranium extracted in 2014. It sells 700,000 tonnes and stores 100,000 tonnes for later sale. In this situation, Rabbit Lake Company would include $371,000 (700,000 × $0.53) in the cost of the resource sold on its income statement. As mentioned before, the cost of labour and other production costs related to the goods sold would also be included in the cost of the resource sold on the income statement. The remaining depreciation of $53,000 ($424,000 − $371,000) is for the 100,000 tonnes kept for later sale and will be included in inventory in the current assets section of the company's balance sheet.

Like depreciation for property, plant, and equipment, the depreciation of a natural resource needs to be revised if there are capital expenditures during the useful life. Also, the depreciable amount per unit of a natural resource needs to be revised whenever the estimated total units of the resource have changed as a result of new information. Natural resources such as oil and gas deposits and some metals have provided the greatest challenges. Estimates of the total units (also called reserves) of these natural resources are mostly knowledgeable guesses and may be revised whenever more information becomes available.

Natural resources must also be reviewed and tested for impairment annually or more frequently whenever circumstances make this appropriate. For example, Rabbit Lake Company would need to test the uranium mine for impairment if there was a significant and permanent decline in the selling price of uranium. If there is impairment, the uranium mine must be written down to its fair value, an impairment loss must be recorded, and current and future depreciation needs to be revised accordingly.

DISPOSAL

At disposal, just as with property, plant, and equipment, any unrecorded depreciation of natural resources must be updated for the portion of the year up to the date of the disposal. Then proceeds are recorded, the cost and the accumulated depreciation of the natural resource are removed, and a gain or loss, if any, is recorded. As mentioned earlier, there may also be site restoration costs at this time, but we leave the accounting for these costs to a future accounting course.

BEFORE YOU GO ON...

DO IT

High Timber Company invests $14 million in a tract of timber land. It is estimated to have 10 million cunits (1 cunit = 100 cubic feet) of timber and a $500,000 residual value. In the first year, 40,000 cunits of timber are cut, and 30,000 of these cunits are sold. Calculate depreciation for High Timber's first year of operations and allocate it between inventory and cost of goods sold.

SOLUTION

1. Depreciable amount per unit: ($14,000,000 − 500,000) ÷ 10,000,000 cunits = $1.35 per cunit
2. Total depreciation for the year: $1.35 per cunit × 40,000 cunits cut = $54,000
3. Depreciation allocated to inventory: $1.35 per cunit × 10,000 cunits on hand = $13,500
4. Depreciation allocated to expense: $1.35 per cunit × 30,000 cunits sold = $40,500

Related exercise material: BE9–15 and E9–11.

Action Plan

- Use units-of-production depreciation for natural resources.
- Calculate the depreciable amount per unit by dividing the total cost minus the estimated residual value by the total estimated units.
- Multiply the depreciable amount per unit by the number of units cut to determine the total depreciation.
- Allocate the depreciation related to the units that have been cut but not yet sold to inventory.
- Allocate the depreciation related to the units that have been cut and sold to expense.

THE NAVIGATOR

INTANGIBLE ASSETS AND GOODWILL

STUDY OBJECTIVE 6

Identify the basic accounting issues for intangible assets and goodwill.

Similar to property, plant, and equipment, and natural resources, intangible assets provide economic benefits in future periods. They are used to produce products or provide services over these periods and are not intended for sale to customers. However, unlike property, plant, and equipment, and natural resources, which are **tangible assets** because they have a physical substance, **intangible assets** involve rights, privileges, and competitive advantages that have no physical substance. In other words, they are not physical things. Many companies' most valuable assets are intangible. Some widely known intangibles are Alexander Graham Bell's patent on the telephone, the franchises of Tim Hortons, the trade name of President's Choice, and the trademark CBC. On the other hand, some organizations, such as George Brown College in the feature story, do not have intangible assets or goodwill.

An intangible asset must be identifiable, which means it must meet one of the two following criteria: (1) it can be separated from the company and sold, whether or not the company intends to do so, or (2) it is based on contractual or legal rights, regardless of whether or not it can be separated from the company. Since goodwill cannot be separated from a company and sold, there are differences in the accounting for goodwill versus other intangible assets.

ACCOUNTING FOR INTANGIBLE ASSETS

Like tangible assets (property, plant, and equipment, and natural resources), intangible assets are recorded at cost. Cost includes all the costs of acquisition and other costs that are needed to make the intangible asset ready for its intended use—including legal fees and similar charges.

As with tangible assets, companies have a choice of following the cost model or the revaluation model when accounting for intangible assets subsequent to acquisition. The majority of companies use the cost model for all long-lived assets. We will leave further study of the revaluation model, as it applies to intangible assets, for a later accounting course.

Under the cost model, if an intangible asset has a finite (limited) life, its cost must be systematically allocated over its useful life. We called this "depreciation" when discussing tangible assets. With intangible assets, we use the term **amortization**.

For an intangible asset with a finite life, its **amortizable amount** (cost less residual value) should be allocated over the shorter of the (1) estimated useful life and (2) legal life. Intangible assets, by their nature, rarely have any residual value, so the amortizable amount is normally equal to the cost. In addition, the useful life of an intangible asset is usually shorter than its legal life, so useful life is most often used as the amortization period.

When a company estimates the useful life of an intangible asset, it must consider factors such as how long the company expects to use the asset, obsolescence, demand, and other factors that can make the intangible asset ineffective at helping to earn revenue. For example, a patent on a computer chip may have a legal life of 20 years, but with technology changing as rapidly as it does, the chip's useful life may be only four or five years maximum.

Amortization begins as soon as the asset is ready to be used as intended by management. Similar to depreciation, the company must use the amortization method that best matches the pattern with which the asset's future economic benefits are expected to be consumed. If that pattern cannot be determined reliably, the straight-line method should be used.

Just as land is considered to have an indefinite life, there are also intangible assets with an indefinite life. An intangible asset is considered to have an indefinite (unlimited) life when, based on an analysis of all of the relevant factors, there is no foreseeable limit to the period over which the intangible asset is expected to generate net cash inflows for the company. If an intangible has an indefinite life, it is not amortized.

As with tangible assets, companies must determine if there are indicators of impairment on intangible assets' definite lives. If there are indicators, an impairment test is performed. Under IFRS, intangible assets with indefinite lives must be tested for impairment at least once a year even if no indications of impairment are evident. Under ASPE, this annual test is not required unless indicators are present.

Recall from earlier in this chapter that there is impairment if the asset's recoverable amount falls below its carrying amount. If any impairment is evident, the intangible asset is written down to its recoverable amount and an impairment loss recorded. Under IFRS, an impairment loss can be reversed for intangible assets (but not goodwill), similar to property, plant, and equipment. Under ASPE, *losses cannot be reversed.*

Similar to tangible assets, the amortization is revised if there are changes in cost, or useful life, or an impairment loss. The revision is accounted for in the current and future periods; retroactive adjustments are not recorded.

At disposal, just as with tangible assets, the carrying amount of the intangible asset is removed, and a gain or loss, if any, is recorded.

INTANGIBLE ASSETS WITH FINITE LIVES

Examples of intangible assets with finite lives include patents and copyrights. We also include research and development costs in this section because these costs often lead to the creation of patents and copyrights.

Patents

A **patent** is an exclusive right issued by the Canadian Intellectual Property Office of Industry Canada that allows the patent holder to manufacture, sell, or otherwise control an invention for a period of 20 years from the date of the application. A patent cannot be renewed. But the legal life of a patent may be extended if the patent holder obtains new patents for improvements or other changes in the basic design.

The initial cost of a patent is the price paid to acquire it. After it has been acquired, legal costs are often incurred. Legal costs to successfully defend a patent in an infringement suit are considered necessary to prove the patent's validity. They are added to the Patent account and amortized over the patent's remaining life.

The cost of a patent should be amortized over its 20-year legal life or its useful life, whichever is shorter. As mentioned earlier, the useful life should be carefully assessed by considering whether the patent is likely to become ineffective at contributing to revenue before the end of its legal life.

Copyrights

A **copyright** is granted by the Canadian Intellectual Property Office, giving the owner an exclusive right to reproduce and sell an artistic or published work. Copyrights extend for *the life of the creator plus 50 years*. Generally, *a copyright's useful life is significantly shorter than its legal life.*

The cost of a copyright consists of the cost of acquiring and defending it. The cost may only be the fee paid to register the copyright, or it may amount to a great deal more if a copyright infringement suit is involved.

ACCOUNTING IN ACTION
ALL ABOUT YOU INSIGHT

If you copy a song from a CD to your iPod that has a "digital lock" on it to prevent unauthorized copying, you could be liable for a fine ranging from $100 to $5,000 for breaking the digital lock and copying the CD. This is one of the provisions in Canada's new *Copyright Modernization Act*, passed in 2012. The last time the copyright laws were changed was in 1997, before the first MP3 player came on the market. Since that time, the Internet and other new technologies have changed the way we produce and access copyright material. Supporters of the law argue that companies and individuals in the entertainment and creative fields need to have their songs, videos, TV shows, software, electronic books, and other works protected in order to foster creativity and innovation. But the amendments are also intended to give more flexibility to consumers such as officially legalizing the recording of television programs to watch at their convenience.

Sources: Bea Vongdouangchanh, "Parliament Passes New Copyright Law; Geist Says Feds Caved to U.S. on Digital Locks," *The Hill Times*, July 2, 2012; CBC News, "Copyright Bill Finally Clears Commons," CBC website June 19, 2012; Mary Teresa Bitti, "Chambers: Copyright Lawyers Prepare for New Rules," *Financial Post*, March 26, 2012.

Why is it important that the copyrights of artists, writers, musicians, and the entertainment industry be protected?

Research and Development Costs

Research and development (R&D) costs are not intangible assets *by themselves*. But they may lead to patents and copyrights, new processes, and new products. Many companies spend large sums of money on research and development in an ongoing effort to develop new products or processes.

Research and development costs present two accounting problems: (1) it is sometimes difficult to determine the costs related to specific projects and (2) it is also hard to know the extent and timing of future benefits. As a result, accounting distinguishes between research costs and development costs.

Research is original, planned investigation that is done to gain new knowledge and understanding. It is not known at this stage if a future benefit will exist as a result of the research. Therefore, all research costs should be expensed when they are incurred.

Development is the use of research findings and knowledge for a plan or design before the start of commercial production. Development costs with probable future benefits should be capitalized. *All of the following criteria must be met for development costs to be capitalized:*

- The project is technically feasible.
- The company plans to complete the project.
- There are adequate resources to complete the project.
- A market exists for the product.

If any of these conditions are not met, the development costs must be expensed. Illustration 9-14 shows the distinction between research and development. After development is completed, the capitalized development costs are amortized over the useful life of the project developed.

ILLUSTRATION 9-14
Distinction between research and development

Research	Development

Examples • Laboratory research aimed at the discovery of new knowledge • Searching for ways to use new research findings or other knowledge • Forming concepts and designs of possible product or process alternatives	Examples • Testing in search or evaluation of product or process alternatives • Design, construction, and testing of pre-production prototypes and models • Design of tools, moulds, and dies involving new technology

INTANGIBLE ASSETS WITH INDEFINITE LIVES

An intangible asset is considered to have an indefinite life when there is no foreseeable limit to the length of time over which the asset is expected to generate cash. Examples of intangible assets with indefinite lives include trademarks and trade names, franchises, and licences. Intangible assets do not always fit perfectly in a specific category. Sometimes trademarks, trade names, franchises, or licences do have finite lives. In such cases, they would be amortized over the shorter of their legal or useful lives. It is more usual, however, for these intangible assets, along with goodwill, to have indefinite lives.

Trademarks, Trade Names, and Brands

A **trademark** or **trade name** is a word, phrase, jingle, or symbol that identifies a particular enterprise or product. Trade names like President's Choice, KFC, Nike, Tim Hortons, the Blue Jays, and TSN create immediate brand recognition and generally help the sale of a product or service. Each year, Interbrands ranks the world's best brands. In 2012, it ranked Coca-Cola as the most successful brand in the world, followed by Apple, IBM, Google, and Microsoft. In Canada, the most valuable brands in retail included lululemon and Shoppers Drug Mart.

The creator can get an exclusive legal right to the trademark or trade name by registering it with the Canadian Intellectual Property Office. This registration gives continuous protection. It may be renewed every 15 years, as long as the trademark or trade name is in use. In most cases, companies continuously renew their trademarks or trade names. In such cases, as long as the trademark or trade name continues to be marketable, it will have an indefinite useful life.

If the trademark or trade name is purchased, the cost is the purchase price. If the trademark or trade name is developed internally rather than purchased, *it cannot be recognized as an intangible asset on the balance sheet*. The reason is that expenditures on internally developed trademarks or brands

Enerflex provides additional details on the long-lived assets in the notes to its financial statements. For example, in note 10, Enerflex discloses the required information about all of its property, plant, and equipment, which include land, buildings, equipment, assets under construction, assets held for sale, and rental equipment.

Another note, Enerflex's summary of significant accounting policies, discloses that straight-line depreciation is used and provides information on the estimated useful lives of the company's long-lived assets. This note also states that major renewals and improvements in rental equipment and property, plant, and equipment are capitalized. It explains that significant components of property, plant, and equipment that required replacement at regular intervals are accounted for separately. The notes also include information on Enerflex's policies on testing its long-lived assets for impairment. Property, plant, and equipment, rental equipment, and intangible assets are assessed for impairment whenever changes in events or changes in circumstances indicate that the asset's carrying amount may not be recovered. Goodwill is tested for impairment at least annually.

ANALYSIS

Information in the financial statements about long-lived assets allows decision makers to analyze a company's use of its total assets. We will use two ratios to analyze total assets: asset turnover and return on assets.

Asset Turnover

The **asset turnover** ratio indicates how efficiently a company uses its assets; that is, how many dollars of sales are generated by each dollar that is invested in assets. It is calculated by dividing net sales by average total assets. If a company is using its assets efficiently, each dollar of assets will create a high amount of sales. When we compare two companies in the same industry, the one with the higher asset turnover is operating more efficiently. The asset turnover ratio for fiscal 2012 for Reitmans (Canada) Limited (dollars in thousands) is calculated in Illustration 9-16.

ILLUSTRATION 9-16
Asset turnover

Net Sales	÷	Average Total Assets	=	Asset Turnover
$1,019,397	÷	($633,861 + $659,355) ÷ 2	=	1.58 times

The asset turnover ratio shows that each dollar invested in assets produced $1.58 in sales for Reitmans. This ratio varies greatly among different industries—from those that have a large investment in assets (such as utility companies) to those that have much less invested in assets (such as service companies). Asset turnover ratios, therefore, should only be compared for companies that are in the same industry.

Return on Assets

The **return on assets** ratio measures overall profitability. This ratio is calculated by dividing profit by average total assets. The return on assets ratio indicates the amount of profit that is generated by each dollar invested in assets. A high return on assets indicates a profitable company. Illustration 9-17 shows the return on assets for Reitmans (dollars in thousands).

ILLUSTRATION 9-17
Return on assets

Profit	÷	Average Total Assets	=	Return on Assets
$47,539	÷	($633,861 + $659,355) ÷ 2	=	7.4%

Reitmans' return on assets was 7.4% for 2012. As with other ratios, the return on assets should be compared with previous years, with other companies in the same industry, and with industry averages, to determine how well the company has performed.

BEFORE YOU GO ON...

DO IT

The following information is available for Toni's Sporting Goods for three recent years:

	2014	2013	2012
Total assets	$299,650	$259,700	$223,540
Net sales	521,180	487,150	441,280
Profit	26,390	18,210	13,540

Calculate the asset turnover and return on assets ratios for Toni's Sporting Goods for 2014 and 2013 and comment on any trends.

Action Plan

- Calculate average total assets using the total assets at the beginning and end of the year.
- Divide net sales by the average total assets for that year to calculate asset turnover.
- Divide profit by the average total assets for that year to calculate return on assets.
- Recall if it is better for asset turnover and return on assets to increase or decrease.

SOLUTION

	2014	2013
Average total assets	($299,650 + $259,700) ÷ 2 = $279,675	($259,700 + $223,540) ÷ 2 = $241,620
Asset turnover	1.9 times = $\frac{\$521,180}{\$279,675}$	2 times = $\frac{\$487,150}{\$241,620}$
Return on assets	9.4% = $\frac{\$26,390}{\$279,675}$	7.5% = $\frac{\$18,210}{\$241,620}$

In general, it is better to have a higher asset turnover and return on assets. Toni's Sporting Goods' lower asset turnover may indicate it is not using its assets as efficiently in 2014 as compared with 2013. However, the increase in the return on assets indicates improved profitability. Given the decrease in turnover, this is a positive result.

Related exercise material: BE9–17, BE9–18, BE9–19, E9–14, and E9–15.

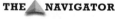

THE NAVIGATOR

Comparing IFRS and ASPE

Key Differences	International Financial Reporting Standards (IFRS)	Accounting Standards for Private Enterprises (ASPE)
Valuing property, plant, and equipment	Choice of cost or revaluation model.	Must use cost model.
Terminology	The term "depreciation" is used for allocating the cost of property, plant, and equipment.	The term "amortization" may be used for allocating the cost of property, plant, and equipment. The term "depreciation" is also accepted.
Impairment of property, plant, and equipment, and finite-life intangible assets	Must look for indicators of impairment annually. If exist, then must test for impairment. Allow for recoveries of previously recorded impairments.	No requirement to look for indicators of impairment annually. Perform tests only if it is apparent they exist. Impairments recorded less often, but cannot later reverse an impairment loss.
Test for impairment of indefinite-life intangible assets	Must perform impairment tests annually. Allows for recoveries of previously recorded impairments.	Same approach as for property, plant, and equipment, and intangible assets with finite lives.
Test for impairment of goodwill	Must be conducted every year.	Conducted only if there is an indication of impairment.
Disclosure	Must provide a reconciliation of the opening and closing carrying amount of each class of assets.	Reconciliation not required.

THE NAVIGATOR

DEMONSTRATION PROBLEM 1

DuPage Company purchases a factory machine at a cost of $17,500 on June 1, 2014. The machine is expected to have a residual value of $1,500 at the end of its four-year useful life on May 31, 2018. DuPage has a December 31 year end.

During its useful life, the machine is expected to be used for 10,000 hours. Actual annual use was as follows: 1,300 hours in 2014; 2,800 hours in 2015; 3,300 hours in 2016; 1,900 hours in 2017; and 700 hours in 2018.

Instructions

Prepare depreciation schedules for the following methods: (a) straight-line, (b) units-of-production, and (c) diminishing-balance using double the straight-line rate.

SOLUTION TO DEMONSTRATION PROBLEM 1

(a) Straight-line method

						End of Year	
Year	Amount	×	Rate	=	Expense	Depreciation	Amount
							$17,500
2014	$16,000[a]		25%[b] × 7/12		$2,333	$ 2,333	15,167
2015	16,000		25%		4,000	6,333	11,167
2016	16,000		25%		4,000	10,333	7,167
2017	16,000		25%		4,000	14,333	3,167
2018	16,000		25% × 5/12		1,667	16,000	1,500

[a] $17,500 − $1,500 = $16,000
[b] 100% ÷ 4 years = 25%

(b) Units-of-production method

						End of Year	
Year	Units of Production	×	Depreciable Amount/Unit	=	Depreciation Expense	Accumulated Depreciation	Carrying Amount
							$17,500
2014	1,300		$1.60[a]		$2,080	$ 2,080	15,420
2015	2,800		1.60		4,480	6,560	10,940
2016	3,300		1.60		5,280	11,840	5,660
2017	1,900		1.60		3,040	14,880	2,620
2018	700		1.60		1,120	16,000	1,500

[a] $17,500 − $1,500 = $16,000 depreciable amount ÷ 10,000 total units = $1.60/unit

(c) Diminishing-balance method

						End of Year	
Year	Carrying Amount Beginning of Year	×	Depreciation Rate (25% × 2)	=	Depreciation Expense	Accumulated Depreciation	Carrying Amounts End of Year
							$17,500
2014	$17,500		50% × 7/12		$5,104	$ 5,104	12,396
2015	12,396		50%		6,198	11,302	6,198
2016	6,198		50%		3,099	14,401	3,099
2017	3,099		50%		1,549	15,950	1,550
2018	1,550		50%		50[a]	16,000	1,500

[a] Adjusted to $50 so that the carrying amount at the end of the year is not less than the residual value.

Action Plan

- Deduct the residual value in the straight-line and units-of-production methods, but not in the diminishing-balance method.
- In the diminishing-balance method, the depreciation rate is applied to the carrying amount (cost − accumulated depreciation). The residual value is not used in the calculations except to make sure the carrying amount is not reduced below the residual value.
- When the asset is purchased during the year, the first year's depreciation for the straight-line and diminishing-balance methods must be adjusted for the part of the year that the asset is owned. No adjustment is required for the units-of-production method. In the straight-line method, the final year must also be adjusted.
- Depreciation should never reduce the asset's carrying amount below its estimated residual value.

DEMONSTRATION PROBLEM 2

On January 1, 2011, Skyline Limousine Co. purchased a specialty limo for $78,000. The vehicle is being amortized by the straight-line method using a four-year service life and a $4,000 residual value. The company's fiscal year ends on December 31.

Instructions

Prepare the journal entry or entries to record the disposal of the limo, assuming that it is:

(a) retired on January 1, 2014.
(b) sold for $15,000 on July 1, 2014.
(c) traded in on a new limousine on January 1, 2014, for a trade-in allowance of $25,000 and cash of $52,000. The fair value of the old vehicle on January 1, 2014, was $20,000.

Action Plan

- Calculate the annual depreciation expense and accumulated depreciation at end of previous year.
- Update the depreciation to the date of the disposal for any partial period.
- Determine the asset's carrying amount at the time of disposal.
- Calculate any gain or loss by comparing proceeds with the carrying amount.
- Remove the asset's carrying amount by debiting accumulated depreciation (for the total depreciation to the date of disposal) and crediting the asset account for the cost of the asset. Record proceeds and any gain or loss.
- Ignore trade-in allowances.
- Record the new asset in an exchange situation at the fair value of the asset given up, plus the cash paid.

THE NAVIGATOR

SOLUTION TO DEMONSTRATION PROBLEM 2

$$\frac{\$78{,}000 - \$4{,}000}{4 \text{ years}} = \$18{,}500 \text{ annual depreciation expense}$$

Accumulated Depreciation at December 31, 2013: $18,500 × 3 years = $55,500

(a)

Date	Account	Debit	Credit
Jan. 1, 2014	Accumulated Depreciation—Vehicles	55,500	
	Loss on Disposal [$0 − ($78,000 − $55,500)]	22,500	
	Vehicles		78,000
	To record retirement of limo.		

(b)

Date	Account	Debit	Credit
July 1, 2014	Depreciation Expense ($18,500 × 6/12)	9,250	
	Accumulated Depreciation—Vehicles		9,250
	To record depreciation for 6 months.		
	Cash	15,000	
	Accumulated Depreciation—Vehicles ($55,500 + $9,250)	64,750	
	Gain on Disposal [$15,000 − ($78,000 − $64,750)]		1,750
	Vehicles		78,000
	To record sale of limo.		

(c)

Date	Account	Debit	Credit
Jan. 1, 2014	Vehicles (cost of new) ($20,000 + $52,000)	72,000	
	Accumulated Depreciation—Vehicles	55,500	
	Loss on Disposal [$20,000 − ($78,000 − $55,500)]	2,500	
	Vehicles (cost of old)		78,000
	Cash		52,000
	To record exchange of limousines, plus cash.		

Summary of Study Objectives

1. ***Determine the cost of property, plant, and equipment.*** The cost of property, plant, and equipment includes all costs that are necessary to acquire the asset and make it ready for its intended use. All costs that benefit future periods (that is, capital expenditures) are included in the cost of the asset. When applicable, cost also includes asset retirement costs. When multiple assets are purchased in one transaction, or when an asset has significant components, the cost is allocated to each individual asset or component using their relative fair values.

2. ***Explain and calculate depreciation.*** After acquisition, assets are accounted for using the cost model or the revaluation model. Depreciation is recorded and assets are carried at cost less accumulated depreciation. Depreciation is the allocation of the cost of a long-lived asset to expense over its useful life (its service life) in a rational and systematic way. Depreciation is not a process of valuation and it does not result in an accumulation of cash. There are three commonly used depreciation methods:

Method	Effect on Annual Depreciation	Calculation
Straight-line	Constant amount	(Cost − residual value) ÷ estimated useful life (in years)
Diminishing-balance	Diminishing amount	Carrying amount at beginning of year × diminishing-balance rate
Units-of-production	Varying amount	(Cost − residual value) ÷ total estimated units of production × actual activity during the year

Each method results in the same amount of depreciation over the asset's useful life. Depreciation expense for income tax purposes is called capital cost allowance (CCA). The single diminishing-balance method is required and depreciation rates are prescribed.

3. ***Explain the factors that cause changes in periodic depreciation and calculate revisions.*** A revision to depreciation will be required if there are (a) capital expenditures during the asset's useful life, (b) impairments in the asset's fair value, (c) changes in the asset's fair value when using the revaluation model, and/or (d) changes in the appropriate depreciation method, estimated useful life, or residual value. An impairment loss must be recorded if the recoverable amount is less than the carrying amount. Only under IFRS can impairment losses be reversed in future periods if the recoverable amount increases. Revisions of periodic depreciation are made in present and future periods, not retroactively. The new annual depreciation is determined by using the depreciable amount (carrying amount less the revised residual value), and the remaining useful life, at the time of the revision.

4. ***Account for the disposal of property, plant, and equipment.*** The accounting for the disposal of a piece of property, plant, or equipment through retirement or sale is as follows:
   (a) Update any unrecorded depreciation for partial periods since depreciation was last recorded.
   (b) Calculate the carrying amount (cost − accumulated depreciation).
   (c) Calculate any gain (proceeds > carrying amount) or loss (proceeds < carrying amount) on disposal.
   (d) Remove the asset and accumulated depreciation accounts at the date of disposal. Record the proceeds received and the gain or loss, if any.

   An exchange of assets is recorded as the purchase of a new asset and the sale of an old asset. The new asset is recorded at the fair value of the asset given up plus any cash paid (or less any cash received). The fair value of the asset given up is compared with its carrying amount to calculate the gain or loss. If the fair value of the new asset or the asset given up cannot be determined, the new long-lived asset is recorded at the carrying amount of the old asset that was given up, plus any cash paid (or less any cash received).

5. ***Calculate and record depreciation of natural resources.*** The units-of-production method of depreciation is generally used for natural resources. The depreciable amount per unit is calculated by dividing the total depreciable amount by the number of units estimated to be in the resource. The depreciable amount per unit is multiplied by the number of units that have been extracted to determine the annual depreciation. The depreciation and any other costs to extract the resource are recorded as inventory until the resource is sold. At that time, the costs are transferred to cost of resource sold on the income statement. Revisions to depreciation will be required for capital expenditures during the asset's useful life, for impairments, and for changes in the total estimated units of the resource.

6. ***Identify the basic accounting issues for intangible assets and goodwill.*** The accounting for tangible and intangible assets is much the same. Intangible assets are reported at cost, which includes all expenditures necessary to prepare the asset for its intended use. An intangible asset with a finite life is amortized over the shorter of its useful life or legal life, usually on a straight-line basis. The extent of the annual impairment tests depends on whether IFRS or ASPE is followed and whether the intangible asset had a finite or indefinite life. Intangible assets with indefinite lives and goodwill are not amortized and are tested at least annually for impairment. Impairment losses on goodwill are never reversed under both IFRS and ASPE. Impairment losses on intangible assets are never reversed under ASPE.

7. ***Illustrate the reporting and analysis of long-lived assets.*** It is common for property, plant, and equipment, and natural resources to be combined in financial statements under the heading "property, plant, and equipment." Intangible assets with finite and indefinite lives are sometimes combined under the heading "intangible assets" or are listed separately. Goodwill must be presented separately. Either on the balance sheet or in the notes, the cost of the major classes of long-lived assets is presented. Accumulated depreciation (if the asset is depreciable) and carrying amount must be disclosed either in the balance sheet or in the notes. The depreciation and amortization methods and rates, as well as the annual depreciation expense, must also be indicated. The company's impairment policy and any impairment losses should be described and reported. Under IFRS, companies must include a reconciliation of the carrying amount at the beginning and end of the period for each class of long-lived assets and state whether the cost or revaluation model is used.

   The asset turnover ratio (net sales ÷ average total assets) is one measure that is used by companies to show how efficiently they are using their assets to generate sales revenue. A second ratio, return on assets (profit ÷ average total assets), calculates how profitable the company is in terms of using its assets to generate profit.

Glossary

Additions and improvements Costs that are incurred to increase the operating efficiency, productive capacity, or expected useful life of property, plant, or equipment. (p. 391)

Amortizable amount The cost minus the residual value of a finite-life intangible asset that is amortized over its useful life. (p. 404)

Amortization The systematic allocation of the amortizable amount of a finite-life intangible asset over its useful life. (p. 404)

Asset retirement costs The cost to dismantle, remove, or restore an asset when it is retired. (p. 380)

Asset turnover A measure of how efficiently a company uses its total assets to generate sales. It is calculated by dividing net sales by average total assets. (p. 409)

Basket purchase The acquisition of a group of assets for a single price. Individual asset costs are determined by allocating relative fair values. (p. 382)

Capital cost allowance (CCA) The depreciation of long-lived assets that is allowed by the Income Tax Act for income tax purposes. It is calculated on a class (group) basis and mainly uses the diminishing-balance method with maximum rates specified for each class of assets. (p. 390)

Capital expenditures Expenditures related to long-lived assets that benefit the company over several accounting periods. (p. 380)

Copyright An exclusive right granted by the federal government allowing the owner to reproduce and sell an artistic or published work. (p. 405)

Cost model A model of accounting for a long-lived asset that carries the asset at its cost less accumulated depreciation or amortization and any impairment losses. (p. 384)

Depreciable amount The cost of a depreciable asset (property, plant, and equipment, or natural resources) less its residual value. (p. 385)

Diminishing-balance method A depreciation method that applies a constant rate to the asset's diminishing carrying amount. This method produces a decreasing annual depreciation expense over the useful life of the asset. (p. 387)

Franchise A contractual arrangement under which the franchisor grants the franchisee the right to sell certain products, offer specific services, or use certain trademarks or trade names, usually inside a specific geographical area. (p. 407)

Goodwill The amount paid to purchase another company that is more than the fair value of the company's net identifiable assets. (p. 407)

Impairment loss The amount by which an asset's carrying amount exceeds its recoverable amount. (p. 391)

Intangible assets Rights, privileges, and competitive advantages that result from owning long-lived assets that have no physical substance. (p. 403)

Land improvements Structural additions to land that have limited useful lives, such as paving, fencing, and lighting. (p. 381)

Licences Operating rights to use public property, granted by a government agency to a company. (p. 407)

Natural resources Long-lived tangible assets, such as standing timber and underground deposits of oil, gas, and minerals, that are physically extracted and are only replaceable by an act of nature. (p. 401)

Operating expenditures Expenditures that benefit only the current period. They are immediately charged against revenues as expenses. (p. 380)

Ordinary repairs Expenditures to maintain the operating efficiency and productive life of the unit. (p. 391)

Patent An exclusive right issued by the federal government that enables the recipient to manufacture, sell, or otherwise control an invention for a period of 20 years from the date of the application. (p. 405)

Property, plant, and equipment Identifiable, long-lived tangible assets, such as land, land improvements, buildings, and equipment, that the company owns and uses for the production and sale of goods or services. (p. 380)

Recoverable amount The higher of the asset's fair value, less costs to sell, and its value in use. (p. 391)

Research and development (R&D) costs Expenditures that may lead to patents, copyrights, new processes, and new products. (p. 405)

Residual value The estimated amount that a company would currently obtain from disposing of the asset if the asset were already as old as it will be, and in the condition it is expected to be in, at the end of its useful life. (p. 385)

Return on assets An overall measure of profitability that indicates the amount of profit that is earned from each dollar invested in assets. It is calculated by dividing profit by average total assets. (p. 409)

Revaluation model A model of accounting for a long-lived asset in which it is carried at its fair value less accumulated depreciation or amortization and any impairment losses. (p. 392)

Royalties Recurring payments that may be required under a franchise agreement and are paid by the franchisee to the franchisor for services provided (for example, advertising, purchasing), and are often proportionate to sales. (p. 407)

Straight-line method A depreciation method in which an asset's depreciable amount is divided by its estimated useful life. This method produces the same periodic depreciation for each year of the asset's useful life. (p. 385)

Tangible assets Long-lived resources that have physical substance, are used in the operations of the business, and are not intended for sale to customers. Tangible assets include property, plant, and equipment, and natural resources. (p. 403)

Trade-in allowance A price reduction offered by the seller when a used asset is exchanged for a new asset as part of the deal. (p. 398)

Trademark (trade name) A word, phrase, jingle, or symbol that distinguishes or identifies a particular enterprise or product. (p. 406)

Units-of-production method A depreciation method in which useful life is expressed in terms of the total estimated units of production or use expected from the asset. Depreciation expense is calculated by multiplying the depreciable amount per unit (cost less residual value divided by total estimated activity) by the actual activity that occurs during the year. (p. 388)

Useful life The period of time over which an asset is expected to be available for use, or the number of units of production (such as machine hours) or units of output that are expected to be obtained from an asset. (p. 384)

Self-Study Questions

Answers are at the end of the chapter.

(SO 1) AP 1. Bulyea Company purchased equipment and incurred the following costs:

Cash price	$36,000
Freight—FOB shipping point	1,000
Insurance during transit	200
Annual licence fee	300
Annual insurance policy	500
Installation and testing	400
Total cost	$38,400

What amount should be recorded as the cost of the equipment?
(a) $36,000 (c) $37,600
(b) $36,200 (d) $38,400

(SO 1) AP 2. Asura Company purchased land, a building, and equipment for a package price of $200,000. The land's fair value at the time of acquisition was $75,000. The building's fair value was $80,000. The equipment's fair value was $50,000. What costs should be debited to the three accounts Land, Building, and Equipment, respectively?
(a) $66,667, $66,667, and $66,666
(b) $73,171, $78,049, and $48,780
(c) $75,000, $80,000, and $50,000
(d) $200,000, $0, and $0

(SO 2) AP 3. Cuso Company purchased equipment on January 1, 2013, at a cost of $40,000. The equipment has an estimated residual value of $10,000 and an estimated useful life of five years. If the straight-line method of depreciation is used, what is the amount of accumulated depreciation at December 31, 2014, the end of the second year of the asset's life?
(a) $6,000 (c) $18,000
(b) $12,000 (d) $24,000

(SO 2) AP 4. Kant Enterprises purchases a truck for $33,000 on July 1, 2014. The truck has an estimated residual value of $3,000, and an estimated useful life of five years, or a total distance of 300,000 km. If 50,000 km are driven in 2014, what amount of depreciation expense would Kant record at December 31, 2014, assuming it uses the units-of-production method?
(a) $2,500 (c) $5,000
(b) $3,000 (d) $5,333

(SO 2) AP 5. Refer to the data for Kant Enterprises in question 4. If Kant uses the double diminishing-balance method of depreciation, what amount of depreciation expense would it record at December 31, 2014?
(a) $6,000 (c) $12,000
(b) $6,600 (d) $13,200

(SO 3) K 6. Which of the following is true regarding revising depreciation calculations?
(a) When the revision is the result of a change in management's estimation of the asset's useful life, past years should be corrected.
(b) Recording an impairment loss will result in an increase in the annual depreciation expense in future years.
(c) Capital expenditures during the asset's useful life do not result in a change in annual depreciation.
(d) Regardless of the reason for the change in depreciation, the revision is made for current and future years only.

(SO 3) AP 7. Rubiat Company has equipment with an original cost of $200,000 and a residual value of $20,000. On December 31, 2014, the accumulated depreciation is $75,000 and the recoverable amount is $100,000. What amount of an impairment loss should the company record?
(a) $0 (c) $25,000
(b) $5,000 (d) $80,000

(SO 4) AP 8. Oviatt Company sold equipment for $10,000. At that time, the equipment had a cost of $45,000 and accumulated depreciation of $30,000. Oviatt should record a:
(a) $5,000 loss on disposal.
(b) $5,000 gain on disposal.
(c) $15,000 loss on disposal.
(d) $15,000 gain on disposal.

(SO 4) AP 9. St. Laurent Company exchanged an old machine with a carrying amount of $10,000 and a fair value of $6,000 for a new machine. The new machine had a list price of $53,000. St. Laurent was offered a trade-in allowance of $11,000, and paid $42,000 cash in the exchange. At what amount should the new machine be recorded on St. Laurent's books?
(a) $42,000 (c) $52,000
(b) $48,000 (d) $53,000

(SO 5) AP 10. On April 1, 2013, Shady Tree Farm Company purchased a Christmas tree farm that has an estimated 100,000 harvestable Christmas trees. The purchase price was $500,000 and the tree farm is expected to have an estimated residual value of $50,000. During the first year of operations, ended January 31, 2014, Shady Tree Farm cut and sold 10,000 trees. What amount of depreciation should be included in cost of goods sold for the year ended January 31?
(a) $37,500 (c) $45,000
(b) $40,500 (d) $50,000

(SO 6) AP 11. Pierce Company incurred $150,000 of research costs in its laboratory to develop a new product in January 2014. On March 31, 2014, Pierce paid $20,000 for legal fees to register the new product. On July 31, 2014, Pierce paid $35,000 for legal fees in a successful defence of the patent. The total amount debited to Patents through July 31, 2014, should be:
(a) $20,000.
(b) $55,000.
(c) $170,000.
(d) $185,000.

(SO 7) AP 12. Cross Continental Rail Services reported net sales of $2,550 million, profit of $178 million, and average total assets of $3,132 million in 2014. What are the company's return on assets and asset turnover?
(a) 0. 81% and 5.7 times
(b) 5.7% and 1.2 times
(c) 7.0% and 5.7 times
(d) 5.7% and 0.81 times

THE NAVIGATOR

Questions

(SO 1) C 1. What are the three characteristics of property, plant, and equipment? In what respect are property, plant, and equipment similar to inventory? How are they different?

(SO 1) C 2. What are the three components of the cost of property, plant, and equipment?

(SO 1) C 3. Blue Hosta Company recently purchased a new vehicle. The company also had to pay for the company's logo to be painted on the vehicle, for a safety inspection, and for an annual insurance policy on the vehicle. Explain how each of these costs should be recorded and why.

(SO 1) C 4. What are land improvements? Should the cost of clearing and grading land be recorded as a land improvement cost or not? Explain.

(SO 1) C 5. Jacques asks why the total cost in a basket purchase has to be allocated to the individual assets. For example, if we purchase land and a building for $250,000, why can we not just debit an account called Land and Building for $250,000? How would you respond to Jacques?

(SO 2) C 6. What is the relationship, if any, between depreciation and (a) cost allocation, (b) asset valuation, and (c) cash?

(SO 2) K 7. Identify and explain the three factors that are used to calculate depreciation. Which, if any, of these factors must be estimated?

(SO 2) C 8. How are annual depreciation and profit different each year over the useful life of an asset, and in total at the end of its useful life, under each of the three depreciation methods?

(SO 2, 3) C 9. What factors should be considered when choosing a depreciation method?

(SO 2) C 10. Kyle has a plan to reduce the amount of income taxes that will have to be paid on his company's profit. He has decided to calculate depreciation expense using very low estimated useful lives on his property, plant, and equipment. Will Kyle's plan work? Why or why not?

(SO 3) C 11. Explain the difference between operating expenditures and capital expenditures during an asset's useful life. Which type of account is debited in each case?

(SO 3) C 12. Under what circumstances will depreciation need to be revised? Should these circumstances also result in the revision of previously recorded depreciation?

(SO 3) C 13. What factors contribute to an impairment loss? In what circumstances, if any, is a company allowed to write up (increase the balance of) its property, plant, and equipment?

(SO 3) C 14. In the fourth year of an asset's five-year useful life, the company decides that the asset will have an eight-year service life. Explain how this will impact the amount of depreciation recorded each year over the asset's useful life.

(SO 4) C 15. If equipment is sold in the middle of a fiscal year, why does depreciation expense have to be recorded for the partial period? Doesn't the subsequent journal entry to record the sale remove the accumulated depreciation from the books anyway?

(SO 4) C 16. Ewing Company owns a machine that is fully depreciated but is still being used. How should Ewing account for this asset and report it on its balance sheet?

(SO 4) K 17. How is a gain or loss on the sale of an item of property, plant, or equipment calculated? Is the calculation the same for an exchange of a piece of property, plant, or equipment?

(SO 4) C 18. How is the carrying amount of an item of property, plant, or equipment calculated? Why does this amount *not* appear in the journal entry to record the disposition of an item of property, plant, or equipment?

(SO 5) K 19. Describe the similarities and differences between natural resources and property, plant, and equipment.

(SO 5) C 20. Why is the units-of-production method used frequently to calculate depreciation for natural resources? Why is the term "depletion" often used instead of "depreciation"?

(SO 6) C 21. Under IFRS and ASPE, what are the differences between the treatment of impairment losses for (a) finite life intangible assets, (b) indefinite life intangible assets, and (c) goodwill?

(SO 6) C 22. What is goodwill? Why can it not be sold to raise cash if a company is planning to expand?

(SO 7) K 23. How should long-lived assets be reported on the balance sheet and income statement? What information should be disclosed in the notes to the financial statements?

(SO 7) C 24. Harpreet understands that inventory turnover refers to the number of times that a company can sell and replace its inventory over the course of the year, but doesn't understand the meaning of asset turnover. Explain the difference between the two ratios to Harpreet.

Brief Exercises

Determine cost of land and land improvements. **(SO 1) AP**

BE9–1 The following costs were incurred by Shumway Company in purchasing land: cash price, \$85,000; legal fees, \$1,500; removal of old building, \$5,000; clearing and grading, \$3,500; installation of a parking lot, \$5,000. (a) What is the cost of the land? (b) What is the cost of the land improvements?

Determine cost of equipment. **(SO 1) AP**

BE9–2 Vroom Company incurs the following costs in purchasing equipment: invoice price, \$40,375; transportation-in, \$625; installation and testing, \$1,000; one-year insurance policy, \$1,750. What is the cost of the equipment?

Identify operating and capital expenditures. **(SO 1) K**

BE9–3 In the space provided, indicate whether each of the following items is an operating expenditure (O) or a capital expenditure (C):

(a) ________ Repaired building roof, \$1,500
(b) ________ Replaced building roof, \$27,500
(c) ________ Purchased building, \$480,000
(d) ________ Paid insurance on equipment in transit, \$550
(e) ________ Purchased supplies, \$350
(f) ________ Purchased truck, \$55,000
(g) ________ Purchased oil and gas for truck, \$125
(h) ________ Rebuilt engine on truck, \$5,000
(i) ________ Replaced tires on truck, \$600
(j) ________ Estimated retirement cost of plant, \$1,000,000
(k) ________ Added new wing to building, \$250,000
(l) ________ Painted interior of building, \$1,500
(m) ________ Replaced an elevator, \$17,500

Record basket purchase. **(SO 1) AP**

BE9–4 Rainbow Company purchased land, a building, and equipment on January 2, 2014, for \$850,000. The company paid \$170,000 cash and signed a mortgage note payable for the remainder. Management's best estimate of the value of the land was \$352,000; of the building, \$396,000; and of the equipment, \$132,000. Record the purchase.

Calculate straight-line depreciation. **(SO 2) AP**

BE9–5 Butters Company acquires equipment at a cost of \$42,000 on January 3, 2014. Management estimates the equipment will have a residual value of \$6,000 at the end of its four-year useful life. Assume the company uses the straight-line method of depreciation. Calculate the depreciation expense (a) for each year of the equipment's life, and (b) in total over the equipment's life. Butters has a December 31 fiscal year end.

Calculate diminishing-balance depreciation. **(SO 2) AP**

BE9–6 Refer to the data given for Butters Company in BE9–5. Assume instead that the company uses the diminishing-balance method and that the diminishing-balance depreciation rate is double the straight-line rate. Calculate the depreciation expense (a) for each year of the equipment's life, and (b) in total over the equipment's life.

Calculate units-of-production depreciation. **(SO 2) AP**

BE9–7 Speedy Taxi Service uses the units-of-production method in calculating depreciation on its taxicabs. Each cab is expected to be driven 550,000 km. Taxi 10 cost \$38,950 and is expected to have a residual value of \$4,300. Taxi 10 is driven 90,000 km in 2013, and 135,000 km in 2014. Calculate (a) the depreciable cost per kilometre (use three decimals), and (b) the depreciation expense for 2013 and 2014.

Calculate partial-year straight-line depreciation. **(SO 2) AP**

BE9–8 Refer to the data given for Butters Company in BE9–5. Assume the equipment was purchased on April 6, 2014, and that the company pro-rates depreciation to the nearest month. Using the straight-line method, calculate the depreciation expense (a) for each year of the equipment's life, and (b) in total over the equipment's life.

Calculate partial-year diminishing-balance depreciation. **(SO 2) AP**

BE9–9 Refer to the data given for Butters Company in BE9–5. Assume the equipment was purchased on April 6, 2014, and that the company has a policy of recording a half year's depreciation in the year of acquisition and a half year's depreciation in the year of disposal. Using the double diminishing-balance method, calculate the depreciation expense (a) for each year of the equipment's life, and (b) in total over the equipment's life.

Determine carrying amount and record impairment loss. **(SO 3) AP**

BE9–10 Cherry Technology purchased equipment on January 4, 2012, for $250,000. The equipment had an estimated useful life of six years and a residual value of $10,000. The company has a December 31 year end and uses straight-line depreciation. On December 31, 2014, the company tests for impairment and determines that the equipment's recoverable amount is $100,000. (a) Calculate the equipment's carrying amount at December 31, 2014 (after recording the annual depreciation). (b) Record the impairment loss.

Calculate revised depreciation. **(SO 3) AP**

BE9–11 Parmar Cleaning Services purchased equipment for $65,000 on January 2, 2011. Management estimated the equipment would have a useful life of seven years and a residual value of $5,500. On January 3, 2014, the equipment was upgraded at a cost of $10,200. After the upgrade, management estimates that the equipment will now have a total useful life of nine years and a residual value of $3,200. The company uses straight-line depreciation and has a December 31 fiscal year end. Calculate annual depreciation expense for 2011 through 2014.

Record disposal by retirement. **(SO 4) AP**

BE9–12 On January 3, 2014, Ruiz Company retires equipment that had an original cost of $25,700. No residual value is received. Prepare journal entries to record the transaction if (a) accumulated depreciation is also $25,700 on this equipment, and (b) the accumulated depreciation is $22,500 instead of $25,700. Ruiz has a December 31 fiscal year end.

Record disposal by sale. **(SO 4) AP**

BE9–13 Mitra Company sells equipment on March 31, 2014, for $15,000 cash. The equipment was purchased on January 5, 2009, at a cost of $86,400, and had an estimated useful life of six years and a residual value of $2,200. Adjusting journal entries are made annually at the company's year end, December 31. Prepare the journal entries to (a) update depreciation to March 31, 2014, (b) record the sale of the equipment, and (c) record the sale of the equipment if Mitra Company received $9,000 cash for it.

Record disposal by exchange of equipment. **(SO 4) AP**

BE9–14 Subramanian Company has equipment with an original cost of $95,000 and, as at December 31, 2013, accumulated depreciation of $78,000. On January 7, 2014, Subramanian exchanges the equipment for new equipment with a list price of $110,000. The dealer gives Subramanian a $20,000 trade-in allowance on the old equipment even though its fair value is only $15,000. Record the January 7, 2014, journal entry for the equipment exchange.

Record depreciation and show balance sheet presentation for natural resources. **(SO 5) AP**

BE9–15 Cuono Mining Co. purchased a mine for $6.5 million that is estimated to have 25 million tonnes of ore and a residual value of $500,000. In the first year, 5 million tonnes of ore are extracted and 3 million tonnes are sold.

(a) Record the depreciation and the cost of the ore extracted for the first year, ended August 31, 2014.
(b) Show how the mine and the ore on hand are reported on the balance sheet on August 31, 2014.

Record acquisition, legal expenditure, and amortization for patent. **(SO 6) AP**

BE9–16 Mabasa Company purchases a patent for $150,000 cash on January 2, 2014. Its legal life is 20 years and its estimated useful life is 8 years. On January 5, 2015, Mabasa paid $30,000 cash to successfully defend the patent in court.

(a) Record the purchase of the patent on January 2, 2014.
(b) Record amortization expense for the year ended December 31, 2014.
(c) Record the legal costs on January 5, 2015.
(d) Calculate amortization expense for 2015.

Identify and classify long-lived assets. **(SO 7) K**

BE9–17 Indicate whether each of the following items is property, plant, and equipment (write "PPE"), a natural resource ("NR"), or an intangible asset ("I"). If the item does not fit any of these categories, write "NA" (not applicable) in the space provided.

(a) ______	Building	(i) ______	Mining equipment
(b) ______	Cost of goods sold	(j) ______	Natural gas deposit
(c) ______	Franchise	(k) ______	Note receivable, due in 3 years
(d) ______	Goodwill	(l) ______	Parking lot
(e) ______	Inventory	(m) ______	Patent
(f) ______	Land	(n) ______	Research costs
(g) ______	Land held for resale	(o) ______	Supplies
(h) ______	Licence right	(p) ______	Trademark

BE9–18 Canadian Tire Corporation, Limited reports the following selected information about long-lived assets at December 31, 2011 (in millions):

Prepare partial balance sheet. **(SO 7) AP**

Accumulated amortization—finite-life intangibles	$ 1.5
Accumulated depreciation—assets under finance lease	138.5
Accumulated depreciation—buildings	1,014.8
Accumulated depreciation—fixtures and equipment	545.6
Accumulated depreciation—leasehold improvements	216.5
Assets under finance lease	267.4
Buildings	2,589.6
Fixtures and equipment	826.0
Construction in progress	137.0
Goodwill	377.6
Land (net of $1.4 of impairments)	748.8
Leasehold improvements	712.5
FGL Sports finite-life intangibles	22.4
FGL Sports indefinite-life intangibles	316.8
Mark's Work Wearhouse indefinite-life intangibles	64.1

FGL Sports and Mark's Work Wearhouse indefinite-life intangibles include legal trademarks such as store brands and banners, as wells as franchise agreements. Finite-life intangibles include certain brands that management has assessed to have a limited life. Prepare a partial balance sheet for Canadian Tire.

BE9–19 Agrium Inc., a global agricultural nutrients producer that is headquartered in Calgary, Alberta, reports the following in its 2011 financial statements (in US$ millions):

Calculate ratios. **(SO 7) AP**

	2011	2010
Net sales	$15,470	$10,743
Profit	1,375	713
Total assets	13,140	12,892

Calculate Agrium's return on assets and asset turnover for 2011.

Exercises

E9–1 The following expenditures related to property, plant, and equipment were made by Pascal Company:

Classify expenditures. **(SO 1) AP**

1. Paid $400,000 for a new plant site.
2. Paid $5,000 in legal fees on the purchase of the plant site.
3. Paid $7,500 for grading the plant site.
4. Paid $4,800 to demolish an old building on the plant site; residual materials were sold for $900.
5. Paid $54,000 for a new delivery truck.
6. Paid $200 freight to have the new delivery truck delivered.
7. Paid $450 to have the company name and advertising slogan painted on the new truck.
8. Paid the $95 motor vehicle licence fee on the new truck.
9. Paid $1,900 for a one-year accident insurance policy on the new delivery truck.
10. Paid $17,500 in architect fees for work on the new plant.
11. Paid $17,500 for paving the parking lots and driveways on the plant site.

Instructions

(a) Explain what types of costs should be included in determining the cost of property, plant, and equipment.

(b) List the numbers of the preceding transactions, and beside each number write the account title that the expenditure should be debited to.

E9–2 Hohenberger Farms purchased real estate for $1,280,000, which included $5,000 in legal fees. It paid $255,000 cash and incurred a mortgage payable for the balance. The real estate included land that was appraised at $476,000, buildings appraised at $748,000, and fences and other land improvements appraised at $136,000. The buildings have an estimated useful life of 60 years and a $50,000 residual value. Land improvements have an estimated 15-year useful life and no residual value.

Record basket purchase and calculate depreciation. **(SO 1, 2) AP**

Instructions

(a) Calculate the cost that should be allocated to each asset purchased.
(b) Record the purchase of the real estate.
(c) Calculate the annual depreciation expense for the buildings and land improvements assuming Hohenberger Farms uses straight-line depreciation.

Calculate cost and depreciation; recommend method. (SO 1, 2) AP

E9–3 Randell Equipment Repair purchased equipment on March 15, 2014, for $75,000. The company also paid the following amounts: $1,000 for delivery charges; $200 for insurance while the machine was in transit; $1,800 for a one-year insurance policy; and $2,800 for testing and installation. The machine was ready for use on April 1, 2014, but the company did not start using it until May 1, 2014.

Randell will depreciate the equipment over 10 years with no residual value. It expects to consume the equipment's future economic benefits evenly over the useful life. The company has a December 31 fiscal year end.

Instructions

(a) Calculate the cost of the equipment.
(b) When should the company begin depreciating the equipment: March 15, April 1, or May 1? Why?
(c) Which depreciation method should the company use? Why?
(d) Calculate the depreciation on the equipment for 2014 and 2015.

Calculate depreciation using three methods; recommend method. (SO 2) AP

E9–4 On June 9, 2013, Dragert Company purchased manufacturing equipment at a cost of $345,000. Dragert estimated that the equipment will produce 600,000 units over its five-year useful life, and have a residual value of $15,000. The company has a December 31 fiscal year end and has a policy of recording a half year's depreciation in the year of acquisition.

Instructions

(a) Calculate depreciation under the straight-line method for 2013 and 2014.
(b) Calculate the depreciation expense under the diminishing-balance method using double the straight-line rate, for 2013 and 2014.
(c) Calculate the depreciation expense under the units-of-production method, assuming the actual number of units produced was 71,000 in 2013 and 118,600 in 2014.
(d) In this situation, what factors should the company consider in determining which depreciation method it should use?

Prepare depreciation schedules and answer questions. (SO 2) AP

E9–5 On April 22, 2013, Sandstone Enterprises purchased equipment for $129,200. The company expects to use the equipment for 12,000 working hours during its four-year life and that it will have a residual value of $14,000. Sandstone has a December 31 year end and pro-rates depreciation to the nearest month. The actual machine usage was: 1,900 hours in 2013, 2,800 hours in 2014, 3,700 hours in 2015, 2,700 hours in 2016, and 1,100 hours in 2017.

Instructions

(a) Prepare a depreciation schedule for the life of the asset under each of the following methods:
    1. straight-line,
    2. diminishing-balance using double the straight-line rate, and
    3. units-of-production.
(b) Which method results in the lowest profit over the life of the asset?
(c) Which method results in the least cash used for depreciation over the life of the asset?

Record depreciation and impairment. (SO 3) AP

E9–6 Hammond Company has a December 31 year end and uses straight-line depreciation for all property, plant, and equipment. On July 1, 2010, the company purchased equipment for $500,000. The equipment had an expected useful life of 10 years and no residual value.

On December 31, 2013, after recording annual depreciation, Hammond reviewed its equipment for possible impairment. Hammond determined that the equipment has a recoverable amount of $225,000. It is not known if the recoverable amount will increase or decrease in the future.

Instructions

(a) Prepare journal entries to record the purchase of the asset on July 1, 2010, and to record depreciation expense on December 31, 2010, and December 31, 2013.
(b) Determine if there is an impairment loss at December 31, 2013, and if there is, prepare a journal entry to record it.

(c) Calculate depreciation expense for 2014 and the carrying amount of the equipment at December 31, 2014.
(d) Assume that the equipment is assessed again for impairment at December 31, 2014, and that the company determines the recoverable amount is $240,000. Should Hammond make an adjustment to reflect the increase in the recoverable amount? Why or why not?

E9–7 Lisa Kim, the new controller of Lafrenière Company, has reviewed the expected useful lives and residual values of selected depreciable assets at December 31, 2014. (Depreciation for 2014 has not been recorded yet.) Her findings are as follows:

Calculate revised depreciation. **(SO 3) AP**

Type of Asset	Date Acquired	Cost	Total Useful Life in Years		Residual Value	
			Current	Proposed	Current	Proposed
Building	Jan. 1, 2002	$800,000	20	30	$40,000	$60,500
Equipment	Jan. 1, 2012	125,000	5	4	5,000	4,000

After discussion, management agrees to accept Lisa's proposed changes. All assets are depreciated by the straight-line method. Lafrenière Company has a December 31 year end.

Instructions

(a) For each asset, calculate the annual depreciation expense using the original estimated useful life and residual value.
(b) Calculate the carrying amount of each asset as at January 1, 2014.
(c) For each asset, calculate the revised annual depreciation expense and the carrying amount at December 31, 2014.
(d) For each asset, calculate the total depreciation expense over the life of the asset assuming the asset is used until the end of its revised useful life.

E9–8 On October 1, 2012, Chignecto Manufacturing Company purchased a piece of high-tech equipment for $90,000 cash. Chignecto estimated the equipment would have a six-year useful life and a residual value of $9,000. The company uses straight-line depreciation and has a September 30 fiscal year end.

Record asset addition and revised depreciation; show balance sheet presentation. **(SO 3) AP**

On October 1, 2014, Chignecto paid $15,000 cash to upgrade the equipment. It is expected that the upgrade will significantly reduce the operating costs of the equipment. Chignecto also reviewed the equipment's expected useful life and estimated that due to changing technology, the equipment's total expected useful life will be four years and its residual value will be $5,000.

Instructions

(a) Calculate the annual depreciation expense for the first two years of the equipment's life.
(b) Calculate the carrying amount of the equipment at September 30, 2014.
(c) Prepare the journal entry to record the expenditure to upgrade the equipment on October 1, 2014.
(d) Record the annual depreciation of the equipment on September 30, 2015.
(e) Show the balance sheet presentation of the equipment on September 30, 2015.

E9–9 The following are some transactions of Surendal Company for 2014. Surendal Company uses straight-line depreciation and has a December 31 year end.

Record disposal of property, plant, and equipment. **(SO 4) AP**

Jan. 2 Scrapped a piece of equipment that originally cost $8,000 and was fully depreciated.
Apr. 1 Retired a piece of equipment that was purchased on January 1, 2005, for $45,000. The equipment had an expected useful life of 10 years with no residual value.
July 30 Sold equipment for $1,100 cash. The equipment was purchased on January 3, 2012, for $12,600 and was depreciated over an expected useful life of three years with no residual value.
Nov. 1 Traded in an old vehicle for a new vehicle, receiving a $10,000 trade-in allowance and paying $36,000 cash. The old vehicle had been purchased on November 1, 2007, at a cost of $35,000. The estimated useful life was eight years and the estimated residual value was $5,000. The fair value of the old vehicle was $7,000 on November 1, 2014.

Instructions

(a) For each of these disposals, prepare a journal entry to record depreciation from January 1, 2014, to the date of disposal, if required.
(b) For each these disposals, indicate if the disposal has increased (+) or decreased (−) Cash, Equipment, Accumulated Depreciation, total property, plant, and equipment (PP&E), and profit, and by how much. If the item is not changed, write "NE" to indicate there is no effect. Use the following format, in which the first one has been done for you as an example.

Transaction	Cash	Equipment	Accumulated Depreciation	Total PP&E	Total Assets	Owner's Equity	Profit
Jan. 2	NE	−$8,000	−$8,000	NE	NE	NE	NE

(c) Record the disposals.

Calculate gain or loss on disposal under different depreciation methods and comment. **(SO 4) AP**

E9–10 On January 3, 2011, Shah Company purchased equipment for $48,000. Shah planned to keep the equipment for four years, and expected the equipment would then be sold for $4,000. On January 5, 2014, Shah sold the computer equipment for $8,000.

Instructions

(a) Calculate the depreciation expense for 2011, 2012, and 2013 under (1) the straight-line method and (2) the double diminishing-balance method.
(b) Calculate the gain or loss on disposal if Shah had used (1) the straight-line method and (2) the double diminishing-balance method.
(c) Explain why the gain or loss on disposal is not the same under the two depreciation methods.
(d) Calculate the total depreciation expense plus the loss or minus the gain under (1) the straight-line method and (2) the double diminishing-balance method. Comment on your findings.

Record depreciation for natural resources; show financial statement presentation; comment on potential impairment. **(SO 5) AP**

E9–11 On July 1, 2014, Phillips Exploration Inc. invests $1.3 million in a mine that is estimated to have 800,000 tonnes of ore. The company estimates that the property will be sold for $100,000 when production at the mine has ended. During the last six months of 2014, 100,000 tonnes of ore are mined and sold. Phillips has a December 31 fiscal year end.

Instructions

(a) Explain why the units-of-production method is often used for depreciating natural resources.
(b) Record the 2014 depreciation.
(c) Show how the mine and any related accounts are reported on the December 31, 2014, income statement and balance sheet.
(d) Assume that the selling price of ore has dropped significantly after December 31, 2014. By June 30, 2015, it is $1.40 per tonne. Does this indicate that the mine may be impaired? Why or why not?

Apply accounting concepts. **(SO 1, 2, 6) AP**

E9–12 An accounting co-op student encountered the following situations at Chin Company:

1. During the year, Chin Company purchased land and paid legal fees on the purchase. The land had an old building, which was demolished. The land was then cleared and graded. Construction of a new building will start next year. All of these costs were included in the cost of land. The student decided that this was incorrect, and prepared a journal entry to put the cost of removing the building and clearing and grading the land in land improvements and the legal fees in legal fee expense.
2. The student learned that Chin is depreciating its buildings and equipment, but not its land. The student could not understand why land was not included, so she prepared journal entries to depreciate all of the company's property, plant, and equipment for the current year end.
3. The student decided that Chin's amortization policy on its intangible assets is wrong. The company is currently amortizing its patents but not its trademarks. The student fixed that for the current year end by adding trademarks to her adjusting entry for amortization. She told a fellow student that she felt she had improved the consistency of the company's accounting policies by making these changes.
4. One of the buildings that Chin uses has a zero carrying amount but a substantial fair value. The co-op student felt that leaving the carrying amount at zero did not benefit the financial information's users—especially the bank—and wrote the building up to its fair value. After all, she reasoned, you write down assets if fair values are lower. She feels that writing them up if their fair value is higher is yet another example of the improved consistency that her employment has brought to the company's accounting practices.

Instructions

Explain whether or not the co-op student's accounting treatment in each of the above situations follows generally accepted accounting principles. If it does not, explain why and what the appropriate accounting treatment should be.

Record acquisition, amortization, and impairment of intangible assets. **(SO 6) AP**

E9–13 Karsch Enterprises, a public company, has a December 31 fiscal year end and uses straight-line amortization for all intangible assets that do not have an unlimited life. The company has provided you with the following information related to its intangible assets and goodwill during 2013 and 2014:

2013

Jan. 9 Purchased a patent with an estimated useful life of five years and a legal life of 20 years for $45,000 cash.

May 15 Purchased another company and recorded goodwill of $450,000 as part of the purchase.

Dec. 31 Recorded adjusting entries as required for amortization.
Dec. 31 Tested assets for impairment and determined the patent and the goodwill's recoverable amounts were $40,000 and $400,000, respectively.

2014

Jan. 2 Incurred legal fees of $30,000 to successfully defend the patent.
Mar. 31 Incurred research costs of $175,000.
Apr. 1 Purchased a copyright for $66,000 cash. The company expects the copyright will benefit the company for 10 years.
July 1 Purchased a trademark with an indefinite expected life for $275,000 cash.
Dec. 31 Recorded adjusting entries as required for amortization.
Dec. 31 Tested assets for impairment and determined the copyright and the trademark's recoverable amounts were in excess of their cost. The patent and the goodwill's recoverable amounts were $45,000 and $425,000, respectively.

Instructions

(a) Record the transactions and adjusting entries as required.
(b) Show the balance sheet presentation of the intangible assets and goodwill at December 31, 2014.

E9–14 Shoppers Drug Mart Corporation reported the following selected information as at December 31, 2011 (in thousands):

Classify long-lived assets; prepare partial balance sheet. **(SO 7) AP**

Accumulated amortization—computer software	$ 136,406
Accumulated amortization—customer relationships	13,691
Accumulated amortization—other intangible assets	6,262
Accumulated amortization—prescription files	64,372
Accumulated depreciation—assets under financing leases	16,411
Accumulated depreciation—buildings	24,325
Accumulated depreciation—equipment, fixtures, and computer equipment	792,644
Accumulated depreciation—leasehold improvements	451,481
Assets under financing leases	127,034
Depreciation and amortization expense	297,682
Buildings	214,043
Computer software	308,478
Customer relationships	50,736
Equipment, fixtures, and computer equipment	1,283,062
Goodwill	2,499,722
Finance expenses	64,038
Investment property	16,372
Land	65,478
Leasehold improvements	1,291,445
Loss on disposal of property, plant, and equipment	1,498
Other non-current assets	39,289
Other intangible assets	9,267
Prescription files	133,987
Properties under development	71,342

Prescription files and customer relationships were acquired in the process of purchasing independent drug stores and are being amortized over their estimated useful lives. Computer software includes the costs of developing the software and is being amortized over its useful life.

Instructions

(a) Identify in which financial statement (balance sheet or income statement) and which section (for example, property, plant, and equipment) each of the above items should be reported.
(b) Prepare the non-current assets section of the balance sheet as at December 31, 2011.

E9–15 Suncor Energy Inc. reported the following information for the fiscal years ended December 31, 2011, and December 31, 2010 (in millions):

Calculate asset turnover and return on assets. **(SO 7) AN**

	Dec. 31, 2011	Dec. 31, 2010
Net revenues	$39,337	$32,003
Profit	4,304	3,829
Total assets, end of year	74,777	68,607
Total assets, beginning of year	68,607	67,799

Instructions

(a) Calculate Suncor's asset turnover and return on assets for the two years.
(b) Comment on what the ratios reveal about Suncor Energy Inc.'s effectiveness in using its assets to generate revenues and produce profit.

Problems: Set A

Record property transactions. (SO 1) AP

P9–1A In 2014, Creasor Company had the following transactions related to the purchase of a property. All transactions were for cash unless otherwise stated.

Jan. 12	Purchased real estate for a future plant site for $420,000, paying $95,000 cash and signing a note payable for the balance. On the site, there was an old building, and the fair values of the land and building were $400,000 and $40,000, respectively. The old building will be demolished and a new one built.
16	Paid $8,500 for legal fees on the real estate purchase.
31	Paid $25,000 to demolish the old building to make room for the new plant.
Feb. 13	Received $10,000 for materials salvaged from the demolished building.
28	Graded and filled the land in preparation for the construction for $9,000.
Mar. 14	Paid $38,000 in architect fees for the building plans.
31	Paid the local municipality $15,000 for building permits.
Apr. 22	Excavation costs for the new building were $17,000.
Sept. 26	The construction of the building was completed. The full cost was $750.000. Paid $150,000 cash and signed a mortgage note payable for the balance.
Sept. 30	Purchased a one-year insurance policy for the building, $4,500.
Oct. 20	Paved the parking lots, driveways, and sidewalks for $45,000.
Nov. 15	Installed a fence for $12,000.

Instructions

(a) Record the above transactions.
(b) Determine the cost of the land, land improvements, and building that will appear on Creasor's December 31, 2014, balance sheet.

TAKING IT FURTHER When should Creasor start to record depreciation and on which assets?

Allocate cost and calculate partial period depreciation. (SO 1, 2) AP

P9–2A In its first year of business, Baumgartner Company purchased land, a building, and equipment on March 5, 2013, for $650,000 in total. The land was valued at $275,000, the building at $343,750, and the equipment at $68,750. Additional information on the depreciable assets follows:

Asset	Residual Value	Useful Life in Years	Depreciation Method
Building	$25,000	60	Straight-line
Equipment	5,000	8	Double diminishing-balance

Instructions

(a) Allocate the purchase cost of the land, building, and equipment to each of the assets.
(b) Baumgartner Company has a December 31 fiscal year end and is trying to decide how to calculate depreciation for assets purchased during the year. Calculate depreciation expense for the building and equipment for 2013 and 2014 assuming:
   1. depreciation is calculated to the nearest whole month.
   2. a half year's depreciation is recorded in the year of acquisition.
(c) Which policy should Baumgartner Company follow in the year of acquisition: recording depreciation to the nearest whole month or recording a half year of depreciation?

TAKING IT FURTHER In the year the asset is purchased should Baumgartner Company record depreciation for the exact number of days the asset is owned? Why or why not?

Determine cost; calculate and compare depreciation under different methods. (SO 1, 2) AP

P9–3A Campagner Company purchased equipment on account on September 3, 2012, at an invoice price of $210,000. On September 4, 2012, it paid $4,400 for delivery of the equipment. A one-year, $1,975 insurance policy on the equipment was purchased on September 6, 2012. On September 20, 2012, Campagner paid $5,600 for installation and testing of the equipment. The equipment was ready for use on October 1, 2012.

Campagner estimates that the equipment's useful life will be four years, with a residual value of $13,000. It also estimates that, in terms of activity, the equipment's useful life will be 75,000 units. Campagner has a September 30 fiscal year end. Assume that actual usage is as follows:

# of Units	Year Ended September 30
15,750	2013
23,900	2014
20,200	2015
15,350	2016

Instructions

(a) Determine the cost of the equipment.
(b) Prepare depreciation schedules for the life of the asset under the following depreciation methods:
  1. straight-line
  2. diminishing-balance at double the straight-line rate
  3. units-of-production
(c) Which method would result in the highest profit for the year ended September 30, 2013? Over the life of the asset?
(d) Which method would result in the least cash used for the year ended September 30, 2013? Over the life of the asset?

TAKING IT FURTHER Assume instead that, when Campagner purchased the equipment, it had a legal obligation to ensure that the equipment was recycled at the end of its useful life. Assume the cost of doing this is significant. Would this have had an impact on the answers to parts (a) and (b) above? Explain.

P9–4A Arnison Company has a December 31 fiscal year end and follows ASPE. The following selected transactions are related to its property, plant, and equipment in 2014:

Account for operating and capital expenditures, and asset impairments.
(SO 1, 3) AP

Jan. 12 All of the company's light bulbs were converted to energy-efficient bulbs for $2,200. Arnison expects that this will save money on its utility bills in the future.
Feb. 6 Paid $5,400 to paint equipment that had started to rust.
Apr. 24 An air conditioning system in the factory was installed for $75,000.
July 19 Windows broken in a labour dispute (not covered by insurance) were replaced for $5,900.
Aug. 21 Paid $26,000 to convert the company's delivery vehicles from gasoline to propane. Arnison expects this will substantially reduce the vehicles' future operating costs, but it will not extend the vehicles' useful lives.
Sept. 20 The exhaust system in a delivery vehicle was repaired for $2,700.
Oct. 25 New parts were added to equipment for $20,000. Arnison expects this will increase the equipment's useful life by four years.
Dec. 31 After recording annual depreciation, Arnison reviewed its property, plant, and equipment for possible impairment. Arnison determined the following:
  1. Land that originally cost $200,000 had previously been written down to $175,000 in 2011 as a result of a decline in the recoverable amount. The current recoverable amount of the land is $220,000.
  2. The recoverable amount of equipment that originally cost $150,000 and has accumulated depreciation of $62,500 is $50,000.

Instructions

(a) For each of these transactions, indicate if the transaction has increased (+) or decreased (−) Land, Buildings, Equipment, Accumulated Depreciation, total property, plant, and equipment (PP&E), and profit, and by how much. If the item is not changed, write "NE" to indicate there is no effect. Use the following format, in which the first one has been done for you as an example.

Transaction	Land	Buildings	Equipment	Accumulated Depreciation	Total PP&E	Profit
Jan. 12	NE	NE	NE	NE	NE	−$2,200

(b) Prepare journal entries to record the above transactions. All transactions are paid in cash.

TAKING IT FURTHER Assume that Arnison also purchases equipment with an expected useful life of 12 years. Assume also that the equipment's engine will need to be replaced every four years. Which useful life should Arnison use when calculating depreciation on the equipment? Explain.

Record impairment and calculate revised depreciation. (SO 3) AP

P9–5A Slope Boss Snowboarding Company, a public company, purchased equipment on January 10, 2010, for $750,000. At that time, management estimated that the equipment would have a useful life of 10 years and a residual value of $50,000. Slope Boss uses the straight-line method of depreciation and has a December 31 year end.

Slope Boss tested the equipment for impairment on December 31, 2014, after recording the annual depreciation expense. It was determined that the equipment's recoverable amount was $320,000, and that the total estimated useful life would be eight years instead of 10, with a residual value of $10,000 instead of $50,000.

Instructions

(a) Calculate the annual depreciation expense for the years 2010 to 2014 and the carrying amount at December 31, 2014.
(b) Record the impairment loss, if any, on December 31, 2014.
(c) What will appear on Slope Boss's 2014 income statement and balance sheet with regard to this equipment?
(d) Assuming no further impairments or recoveries, calculate the annual depreciation expense for the years 2015 to 2017.
(e) Determine the equipment's accumulated depreciation and carrying amount at the end of its useful life.

TAKING IT FURTHER Suggest some possible reasons as to why companies are allowed to record recoveries of previously recorded impairments under IFRS but not under ASPE.

Calculate and compare depreciation and gain or loss on disposal under three methods of depreciation. (SO 2, 4) AP

P9–6A On December 27, 2011, Wolcott Windows purchased a piece of equipment for $107,500. The estimated useful life of the equipment is either three years or 60,000 units, with a residual value of $10,500. The company has a December 31 fiscal year end and normally uses straight-line depreciation. Management is considering the merits of using the units-of-production or diminishing-balance method of depreciation instead of the straight-line method. The actual numbers of units produced by the equipment were 10,000 in 2012, 20,000 in 2013, and 29,000 in 2014. The equipment was sold on January 5, 2015, for $15,000.

Instructions

(a) Calculate the actual cost of owning this equipment.
(b) Calculate the depreciation for the equipment for 2012 to 2014 under (1) the straight-line method; (2) the diminishing-balance method, using a 40% rate; and (3) units-of-production. (*Hint:* Round the depreciable cost per unit to three decimal places.)
(c) Calculate the gain or loss on the sale of the equipment under each of the three methods.
(d) Calculate the total depreciation expense plus the loss on sale (or minus the gain on sale) under each of the three depreciation methods. Compare these totals with your answer in part (a) above. Comment on your results.

TAKING IT FURTHER The owner of Wolcott Windows believes that having a gain or loss on sale indicates the company had made a mistake in calculating depreciation. Do you agree or disagree? Explain.

Record acquisition, depreciation, and disposal of equipment. (SO 2, 4) AP

P9–7A Express Co. purchased equipment on March 1, 2012, for $95,000 on account. The equipment had an estimated useful life of five years, with a residual value of $5,000. The equipment is disposed of on February 1, 2015. Express Co. uses the diminishing-balance method of depreciation with a 20% rate and calculates depreciation for partial periods to the nearest month. The company has an August 31 year end.

Instructions

(a) Record the acquisition of the equipment on March 1, 2012.
(b) Record depreciation at August 31, 2012, 2013, and 2014.
(c) Record the disposal on February 1, 2015, under the following assumptions:
   1. It was scrapped with no residual value.
   2. It was sold for $55,000.
   3. It was sold for $45,000.
   4. It was traded for new equipment with a list price of $97,000. Express was given a trade-in allowance of $52,000 on the old equipment and paid the balance in cash. Express determined the old equipment's fair value to be $47,000 at the date of the exchange.

TAKING IT FURTHER What are the arguments in favour of recording gains and losses on disposals of property, plant, and equipment as part of profit from operations? What are the arguments in favour of recording them as non-operating items?

P9–8A At January 1, 2014, Hammersmith Corporation reported the following property, plant, and equipment accounts:

Record property, plant, and equipment transactions; prepare partial financial statements. (SO 2, 4, 7) AP

Accumulated depreciation—buildings	$31,100,000
Accumulated depreciation—equipment	27,000,000
Buildings	48,700,000
Equipment	75,000,000
Land	10,000,000

Hammersmith uses straight-line depreciation for buildings and equipment and its fiscal year end is December 31. The buildings are estimated to have a 50-year useful life and no residual value; the equipment is estimated to have a 10-year useful life and no residual value. Interest on the notes is payable or collectible annually on the anniversary date of the issue.

During 2014, the following selected transactions occurred:

Apr. 1 Purchased land for $2.2 million. Paid $550,000 cash and issued a three-year, 6% note for the balance.

May 1 Sold equipment for $150,000 cash. The equipment cost $1.4 million when originally purchased on January 1, 2006.

June 1 Sold land for $1.8 million. Received $450,000 cash and accepted a three-year, 5% note for the balance. The land cost $700,000.

July 1 Purchased equipment for $1.1 million cash.

Dec. 31 Retired equipment that cost $500,000 when purchased on December 31, 2004.

Instructions

(a) Record the above transactions.

(b) Record any adjusting entries required at December 31, 2014.

(c) Prepare the property, plant, and equipment section of Hammersmith's balance sheet at December 31, 2014.

TAKING IT FURTHER The owner of Hammersmith suggests the company should start using the revaluation model, not the cost model, for property, plant, and equipment now that it is following IFRS. Comment on this suggestion.

P9–9A The intangible assets reported by Ip Company at December 31, 2013, follow:

Record intangible asset transactions; prepare partial balance sheet. (SO 6, 7) AP

Patent #1	$80,000	
Less: Accumulated amortization	16,000	$ 64,000
Copyright #1	$48,000	
Less: Accumulated amortization	28,800	19,200
Goodwill		220,000
Total		$303,200

Patent #1 was acquired in January 2012 and has an estimated useful life of 10 years. Copyright #1 was acquired in January 2008 and also has an estimated useful life of 10 years. The following cash transactions may have affected intangible assets and goodwill during the year 2014:

Jan. 2 Paid $23,200 of legal costs to successfully defend Patent #1 against infringement by another company.

June 30 Developed a new product, incurring $180,000 in research costs and $60,000 in development costs, which were paid in cash. Patent #2 was granted for the product on July 1. Its estimated useful life is equal to its legal life of 20 years.

Sept. 1 Paid $12,000 to an Olympic athlete to appear in commercials advertising the company's products. The commercials will air in September.

Oct. 1 Acquired a second copyright for $18,000 cash. Copyright #2 has an estimated useful life of six years.

Dec. 31 Determined the recoverable amount of the goodwill to be $240,000. The company had originally paid $250,000 for the goodwill in 2011. In 2012, the company had recorded a $30,000 impairment loss on the goodwill. There is no indication that the patents and copyrights were impaired.

Instructions

(a) Record the above transactions.
(b) Prepare any adjusting journal entries required at December 31, 2014, the company's year end.
(c) Show how the intangible assets and goodwill will be reported on the balance sheet at December 31, 2014.

TAKING IT FURTHER Since intangible assets do not have physical substance, why are they considered to be assets?

Record natural resource transactions; prepare partial financial statements. **(SO 3, 5, 7) AP**

P9–10A Yount Mining Company has a December 31 fiscal year end. The following information relates to its Gough Alexander mine:

1. Yount purchased the Gough Alexander mine on March 31, 2013, for $2.6 million cash. On the same day, modernization of the mine was completed at a cash cost of $260,000. It is estimated that this mine will yield 560,000 tonnes of ore. The mine's estimated residual value is $200,000. Yount expects it will extract all the ore, and then close and sell the mine site in four years.
2. During 2013, Yount extracted and sold 120,000 tonnes of ore from the mine.
3. At the beginning of 2014, Yount reassessed its estimate of the remaining ore in the mine. Yount estimates that there is still 550,000 tonnes of ore in the mine at January 1, 2014. The estimated residual value remains at $200,000.
4. During 2014, Yount extracted and sold 100,000 tonnes of ore from the mine.

Instructions

(a) Prepare the 2013 and 2014 journal entries for the above, including any year-end adjustments.
(b) Show how the Gough Alexander mine will be reported on Yount's December 31, 2014, income statement and balance sheet.

TAKING IT FURTHER If the total estimated amount of units that will be produced (extracted) changes during the life of the natural resource, is it still appropriate to use the units-of-production method? Explain.

Calculate ratios and comment. **(SO 7) AN**

P9–11A Andruski Company and Brar Company both manufacture school science equipment. The following financial information is for three years ended December 31 (in thousands):

Andruski Company	2014	2013	2012
Net sales	$552.0	$515.9	$469.0
Profit	21.4	20.6	18.7
Total assets	702.5	662.8	602.5
Brar Company	**2014**	**2013**	**2012**
Net sales	$1,762.9	$1,588.2	$1,484.3
Profit	96.5	85.4	79.8
Total assets	1,523.5	1,410.7	1,318.4

Instructions

(a) Calculate the asset turnover and return on assets ratios for both companies for 2013 and 2014. Round your answers to two decimal points.
(b) Comment on how effective each of the companies is at using its assets to generate sales and produce profit.

TAKING IT FURTHER After reading the notes to the financial statements, you have determined that Andruski Company uses diminishing-balance depreciation and Brar uses straight-line. Does this affect your ability to compare these two companies?

CONTINUING COOKIE CHRONICLE

(*Note:* This is a continuation of the Cookie Chronicle from Chapters 1 through 8.)

Natalie is thinking of buying a van that will be used only for business. She estimates that she can buy the van for $28,400. Natalie would spend an additional $3,000 to have the van painted. As well, she wants the back seat of the van removed so that she will have lots of room to transport her mixer inventory and baking supplies. The cost of taking out the back seat and installing shelving units is estimated at $1,600. She expects the van to last about five years and to be driven for 200,000 km. The annual cost of vehicle insurance will be $1,440. Natalie estimates that at the end of the five-year useful life, the van will sell for $5,000. Assume that she will buy the van on April 15, 2014, and it will be ready for use on May 1, 2014.

Natalie is concerned about the impact of the van's cost and related depreciation on Cookie Creations' income statement and balance sheet.

Instructions

(a) Determine the cost of the van.
(b) Prepare depreciation schedules for the life of the van under the following depreciation methods:
   1. straight-line.
   2. diminishing-balance at double the straight-line rate.
   3. units-of-production. It is estimated that the van will be driven as follows: 30,000 km in 2014, 37,500 km in 2015, 40,000 km in 2016, 47,500 km in 2017, 35,000 km in 2018, and 10,000 km in 2019.

   Recall that Cookie Creations has a December 31 year end.
(c) Which method of depreciation would result in the highest profit for the year ended December 31, 2014? Over the life of the asset?
(d) Which method would result in the van's highest carrying amount for the year ended December 31, 2014? Over the life of the asset?
(e) Which method would result in the least cash used for the year ended December 31, 2014? Over the life of the asset?
(f) Which method of depreciation would you recommend that Natalie use? Why?

BROADENING YOUR PERSPECTIVE — CHAPTER 9

Collaborative Learning Activity

Note to instructor: Additional instructions and material for this group activity can be found on the Instructor Resource Site and in *WileyPLUS*.

BYP9–1 In this group activity, you will work in two groups to improve your understanding of the different depreciation methods: straight-line, diminishing-value, and units-of-production. First you will work in "expert" groups in which you will ensure that each group member thoroughly understands one method of depreciation. Then you will move to a second group consisting of one student from each of the three expert groups, and take turns teaching each other the different depreciation methods.

Communication Activity

BYP9–2 Kelton Trucking Corporation is a medium-sized publicly owned trucking company with trucks that are driven across North America. The company owns large garages and equipment to repair and maintain the trucks. Ken Bond, the controller, knows that long-lived assets are reviewed annually for impairment. Ken records an impairment loss of $100,000 and the loss appears on the income statement for the current fiscal year. Jim Kelton, the company president, reviews the financial statements and wants more information from Ken about the impairment loss.

Instructions

Write an e-mail to Jim Kelton that explains (a) what might have caused the impairment loss, (b) the journal entry required for the impairment loss, and (c) how this writedown will affect Kelton Trucking's balance sheet and income statement in future years.

Ethics Case

BYP9–3 Finney Container Company has been seeing sales go down for its main product, non-biodegradable plastic cartons. Although some expenses have also reduced in line with the reduced revenues, there has been a decrease in profit because some expenses, such as depreciation, have not declined. The company uses the straight-line depreciation method.

The president, Philip Shapiro, recalling his university accounting classes, instructs his controller to lengthen the estimated asset lives used for depreciation calculations in order to reduce annual depreciation expense and increase profit. The president's compensation includes an annual bonus based on the amount of net profit reported in the income statement.

A processing line of automated plastic-extruding equipment that was purchased for $2.9 million in January 2012 was originally estimated to have a useful life between five and nine years. Therefore, the company used the middle of that estimate, or seven years, as the useful life, and a residual value of $100,000, to calculate the annual straight-line depreciation for the first two years. However, the president now wants to change the equipment's estimated useful life to nine years (total), and to continue using the straight-line method.

The controller is hesitant to make the change, believing it is unethical to increase profit in this way. The president says, "Hey, the useful life is only an estimate. Besides, I've heard that our competition uses a nine-year estimated life on its production equipment. You want the company results to be competitive, don't you? So maybe we were wrong the first time and now we are getting it right. Or you can tell the auditors that we think may be the equipment will last longer now that we are not using it as much."

Instructions

(a) Who are the stakeholders in this situation?
(b) Is the suggested change in asset life unethical, or simply a shrewd business practice by a sharp president?
(c) What would be the impact of the president's proposed change on profit in the year of the change?

All About You: Personal Financial Literacy Activity

BYP9–4 In the "All About You" feature, you learned about actions that have been taken to strengthen Canada's copyright law and the radical changes in technology that are driving the need to update the law. You have recently graduated from a music program and have composed two songs that you believe a recording artist may produce. You are wondering whether you should get copyright protection for your songs.

According to the federal government's Canadian Intellectual Property Office (CIPO), copyright is "the sole right to produce or reproduce a work or a substantial part of it in any form." Copyright protects "literary, artistic, dramatic or musical works (including computer programs) and other subject-matter known as performer's performances, sound recordings and communication signals." You can register copyright for your songs with the CIPO by submitting an application form and a fee. You don't have to register with the CIPO in order for your songs to be protected. However, if you register, you will receive a certificate of registration of copyright to prove you own the copyright.

Instructions

(a) What are the benefits to you of getting copyright registration for your songs?
(b) When you register a copyright you are required to pay a fee for the registration. Should the registration fee for the copyright be recorded as an asset or an expense?
(c) According to the CIPO, copyright infringement is "violation of copyright through the unauthorized use of a work." Provide a specific example of infringement. If you were a professional songwriter, how would copyright infringement of your songs affect your finances?

ANSWERS TO CHAPTER QUESTIONS

ANSWERS TO ACCOUNTING IN ACTION INSIGHT QUESTIONS

Business Insight, p. 389

Q: Is the units-of-production method the best depreciation method for Morris Formal Wear to use for its tuxedos or would you recommend another method?

A: Since Morris Formal Wear wants to track wear and tear on each of its tuxedos, the units-of-production depreciation method is the best choice. Rental tuxedos are the type of long-lived asset that will physically wear out with use much faster than they would become obsolete due to changing tuxedo styles. By keeping track of how many times each tuxedo has been used, instead of just how old they are, the company can make better decisions about when to replace the tuxedos.

All About You Insight, p. 405

Q: Why is it important that the copyrights of artists, writers, musicians, and the entertainment industry be protected?

A: Just as it is important that you as an individual be compensated in your career, it is important that individuals in artistic, music, entertainment, and literary careers be compensated fairly for their creativity. Without fair compensation, Canada's creativity and innovation will be discouraged. Without copyright protection, it may be difficult to ensure that appropriate individuals are fairly compensated and companies may not be willing to invest in creative ventures if the work is not protected.

ANSWERS TO SELF-STUDY QUESTIONS

1. c 2. b 3. b 4. c 5. b 6. d 7. c 8. a 9. b 10. c 11. b 12. d

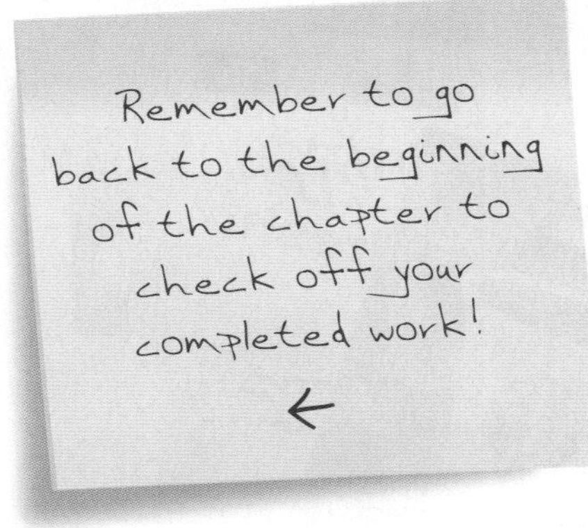
Remember to go
back to the beginning
of the chapter to
check off your
completed work!

CHAPTER 10 CURRENT LIABILITIES

THE NAVIGATOR

- ☐ Understand *Concepts for Review*
- ☐ Read *Feature Story*
- ☐ Scan *Study Objectives*
- ☐ Read *Chapter Preview*
- ☐ Read text and answer *Before You Go On*
- ☐ Review *Comparing IFRS and ASPE*
- ☐ Work *Demonstration Problem*
- ☐ Review *Summary of Study Objectives*
- ☐ Answer *Self-Study Questions*
- ☐ Complete assignments

CONCEPTS FOR REVIEW

Before studying this chapter, you should understand or, if necessary, review:

A. How to make adjusting entries for unearned revenue (Ch. 3, p. 105) and accrued expenses. (Ch. 3, pp. 107–109)

B. The importance of liquidity in evaluating the financial position of a company. (Ch. 4, pp. 165–167)

C. How to account for sales discounts. (Ch. 5, pp. 210–211)

D. Accounting for notes receivable. (Ch. 8, pp. 349–352)

BUSINESSES AND CONSUMERS LOVE GIFT CARDS

OTTAWA, ON—Gift cards are wildly popular in Canada. It's estimated that we spend about $6 billion a year buying cards to give to others to redeem for everything from coffee to televisions. The explosion happened in the mid-2000s, when about 82% of Canada's largest retailers offered gift cards in 2005, compared with just 53% in 2003, according to Statistics Canada. Consumers like the convenience of giving a personalized gift without committing to something the recipient may not like.

Gift cards are popular with businesses because they encourage the recipient to shop at a particular retailer or use a particular service, sometimes spending more money than the value of their card. Companies that are not retailers have recently started offering gift cards to try to develop loyalty to their brand. For example, cards are now available to give the gift of travel for the person who has everything. Air Canada now sells gift cards valued up to $10,000 to try to grab business from competing airlines. In 2012, VIA Rail sold $1.5 million worth of gift cards. The Toronto-based Four Seasons hotel chain sells gift cards valued up to $5,000.

Issuing gift cards creates some accounting issues for a business. A sold gift card is a liability for a business, because there is a good chance that the customer will redeem the card for goods or services that the company has an obligation to provide sometime in the future. Some provinces have passed laws that ban the expiry of gift cards, so companies may have to carry that obligation indefinitely. Businesses do not record revenues from the sales of gift cards until they are redeemed.

Gift cards are good for businesses, but are they good for consumers? The Consumers' Association of Canada estimates that about one quarter of all gift cards are never redeemed, which is bad for consumers. If you don't know what to get someone, the association advises giving cash instead.

If you do give or receive a gift card, there are few rules you should know about. The card must clearly show if there are any limitations on using it. You cannot be charged a fee to reactivate a card, although you may have to pay a fee to replace it if you lose it. If the card was bought in a province that has banned gift card expiry, such as Ontario, the card is valid for as long as the company is in business. Different rules apply to other kinds of transaction cards, such as loyalty program cards where the points you collect may expire after a certain time, and gift certificates issued for specific services, such as sports lessons, which can expire. The rules for gift cards also don't apply to pre-paid phone cards and credit cards.

Sources: Vanessa Lu, "Redeem to Fly: Air Canada Moves into Gift Card Business," *Toronto Star*, May 30, 2013; "Gift Card Rules I Should Know," *The Globe and Mail*, September 21, 2011; "Gift Cards: The Lure of Plastic," CBC News online, December 1, 2008; "Study: Retail Gift Cards," Statistics Canada, The Daily, December 4, 2006.

THE NAVIGATOR

STUDY OBJECTIVES

After studying this chapter, you should be able to:

1. Account for determinable or certain current liabilities.
2. Account for estimated liabilities.
3. Account for contingencies.
4. Prepare the current liabilities section of the balance sheet.

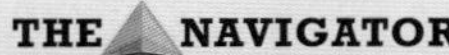

PREVIEW OF CHAPTER TEN

Whether it is a huge company such as one of Canada's chartered banks, or a small business such as your local convenience store, every company has current liabilities. As explained in Chapter 4, current liabilities are obligations that are expected to be settled within one year from the balance sheet date or in the company's normal operating cycle. Obligations that are expected to be paid after one year or longer are classified as non-current liabilities. We explain current liabilities in this chapter and non-current liabilities in Chapter 15.

The chapter is organized as follows:

DETERMINABLE (CERTAIN) CURRENT LIABILITIES

STUDY OBJECTIVE 1
Account for determinable or certain current liabilities.

In Chapter 1, we defined liabilities as present obligations, arising from past events, to make future payments of assets or services. A future commitment is not considered a liability unless an obligation also exists. For example, a company may have made a commitment to purchase an asset in the future, but the obligation normally arises only when the goods are delivered or if the company has entered into an irrevocable agreement. Thus, an essential characteristic of a liability is the existence of a *present* obligation.

Helpful hint Gift cards are an example of an unearned revenue liability where it is necessary to estimate the liability. These are discussed in the next section of this chapter.

Sometimes there is a great deal of uncertainty regarding whether or not a liability exists. Even if it is certain that the liability exists, sometimes we are not certain as to whom we owe, how much we owe, or when we owe. We will discuss this type of liability in the sections on estimated liabilities and contingencies.

In this section of the chapter, we will discuss liabilities where there is no uncertainty about their existence, amount, or timing. Liabilities with a known amount, payee, and due date are often referred to as **determinable liabilities**.

Alternative terminology Determinable liabilities are also referred to as *certain liabilities* or *known liabilities.*

Examples of determinable current liabilities include bank indebtedness from operating lines of credit, and notes payable, accounts payable, sales taxes payable, unearned revenue, and current maturities of long-term debt. This category also includes accrued liabilities such as interest payable.

Accounts payable, or trade accounts payable, are often the largest current liability on a company's balance sheet. For example, as shown on Reitmans' balance sheet in Appendix A, its trade and other payables amount to $63,875 thousand, which is almost 72% of its total current liabilities.

The entries for accounts payable and determinable unearned revenues (that is, revenues that can be calculated) have been explained in previous chapters, and are not included in this section. We will discuss the accounting for other types of current liabilities in this section, including bank indebtedness from an operating line of credit, notes payable, and current maturities of long-term debt. Payroll and employee benefits payable are also examples of determinable liabilities, but these will not be discussed here.

OPERATING LINE OF CREDIT AND BANK OVERDRAFT

Operating Line of Credit

Current assets (such as accounts receivable) do not always turn into cash at the exact time that current liabilities (such as accounts payable) must be paid. Consequently, most companies have an **operating line of credit** at their bank to help them manage temporary cash shortfalls. This means that the company has been pre-authorized by the bank to borrow money when it is needed, up to a pre-set limit.

Security, called **collateral**, is usually required by the bank as protection in case the company is unable to repay the loan. Collateral normally includes some, or all, of the company's current assets (such as accounts receivable or inventories); investments; or property, plant, and equipment.

Money borrowed through a line of credit is normally borrowed on a short-term basis, and is repayable immediately upon request—that is, on demand—by the bank. In reality, repayment is rarely demanded without notice. A line of credit makes it very easy for a company to borrow money. It does not have to make a call or visit its bank to actually arrange the transaction. The bank simply covers any cheques written in excess of the bank account balance, up to the approved credit limit.

Bank Overdraft

Some companies have a negative (credit), or overdrawn, cash balance at year end. This amount is usually called *bank indebtedness, bank overdraft,* or *bank advances.* No special entry or account is required to record the overdrawn amount. The Cash account has a credit balance because the dollar amount of cheques written exceeded the dollar amount of deposits. The credit balance in Cash is reported as a current liability with an appropriate note disclosure.

Interest is usually charged on the overdrawn amount at a floating rate, such as prime plus a specified percentage. The **prime rate** is the interest rate that banks charge their best customers. This rate is usually increased by a specified percentage according to the company's risk profile. The bank will charge a less established borrower a higher rate of interest to compensate for the increased level of risk on the part of the lender.

SHORT-TERM NOTES PAYABLE

The line of credit described above is similar to a **note payable**. Notes payable are obligations in the form of written promissory notes. In Chapter 8, we discussed notes receivable and included an illustration of a promissory note. You will recall that the payee has a note receivable and the maker of the note has a note payable.

Notes payable may be used instead of accounts payable. This gives the lender proof of the obligation in case legal action is needed to collect the debt. Accounts and notes payable that result from purchase transactions (that is, amounts owed to suppliers) are often called **trade payables**. Notes payable are also frequently issued to meet short-term financing needs.

Helpful hint Notes payable are the opposite of notes receivable, and the accounting is similar.

Notes are issued for varying periods. If they are due for payment within one year of the balance sheet date, they are classified as current liabilities. Most notes are interest-bearing, with interest due monthly or at maturity.

To illustrate the accounting for notes payable, assume that Bernier Co. borrows $100,000 from the local caisse populaire (credit union) on March 1 for four months, at an interest rate of 6%. The note matures on July 1 and interest, along with the note's principal amount, is payable at maturity.

Bernier makes the following journal entry when it signs the note and receives the $100,000:

Date	Account	Debit	Credit
Mar. 1	Cash	100,000	
	Notes Payable		100,000
	To record issue of four-month, 6% note to Caisse Populaire Dumoulin.		

A	=	L	+	OE
+100,000		+100,000		

↑Cash flows: +100,000

Interest accrues over the life of the note; therefore, interest expense must be recorded in the period when the borrowed money is used. Also, at year end, all liabilities (all obligations) must be recorded. If Bernier Co. has a March 31 year end, then the interest owing at the end of March must be recorded. An adjusting entry is made to recognize interest expense and interest payable of $500 ($100,000 × 6% × $^1/_{12}$)

Helpful hint Interest is normally calculated using the number of days. In this textbook, we use months in order to simplify the calculations.

Helpful hint Interest rates are always expressed as annual rates, not the rate for the duration of the note.

at March 31. Recall from Chapter 3 that interest is calculated by multiplying the principal amount by the annual interest rate by the fraction of the year in the accrual.

The adjusting entry is:

A	=	L	+	OE
		+500		−500

Cash flows: no effect

Mar. 31	Interest Expense	500	
	Interest Payable		500
	To accrue interest to March 31.		

In the March 31 financial statements, the current liabilities section of the balance sheet will show notes payable of $100,000 and interest payable of $500. In addition, interest expense of $500 will be reported as other expenses in the income statement. **Interest payable is shown separately from the note payable.**

At maturity (July 1), Bernier Co. must pay the face value of the note ($100,000) plus $2,000 interest ($100,000 × 6% × 4/12). One month ($500) of this interest has already been accrued. Interest must also be updated for $1,500 ($100,000 × 6% × 3/12) for the three additional months—April through June—since interest was last recorded. This can be done in one compound entry or in separate journal entries as follows:

A	=	L	+	OE
		+1,500		−1,500

Cash flows: no effect

A	=	L	+	OE
−102,000		−100,000 −2,000		

↓Cash flows: −102,000

July 1	Interest Expense	1,500	
	Interest Payable		1,500
	To accrue interest for April, May, and June.		
1	Notes Payable	100,000	
	Interest Payable ($500 + $1,500)	2,000	
	Cash ($100,000 + $2,000)		102,000
	To record payment of Caisse Populaire Dumoulin note and accrued interest.		

CURRENT MATURITIES OF LONG-TERM DEBT

Companies often have a portion of long-term debt that will be due in the current year. That amount is considered a current liability. Assume that on January 1, 2014, Simonetti Construction issues a $25,000, five-year note payable. Each January 1, starting on January 1, 2015, $5,000 of the note will be repaid. When financial statements are prepared on December 31, 2014, $5,000 should be reported on the balance sheet as a current liability and the remaining $20,000 of the note should be reported as a long-term liability.

It is not necessary to prepare an adjusting entry to recognize the current maturity of long-term debt. The proper statement classification of each liability account is recognized when the balance sheet is prepared. Reitmans reports $1,474 thousand as the "current portion of long-term debt" in the current liabilities section of its balance sheet.

ACCOUNTING IN ACTION
ALL ABOUT YOU INSIGHT

How will you pay for your post-secondary education? Like many Canadian college and university students, you may find yourself applying for a student loan if you don't have enough money from relatives, grants, bursaries, scholarships, and summer jobs to pay for tuition, books, and living expenses. The federal, provincial, and territorial governments offer student loan programs. If you don't qualify for a government student loan, you can apply for a loan from a private financial institution such as banks, trust companies, and credit unions. After you graduate, you must repay the loan by a certain period, usually in smaller amounts at regular intervals. The amount of loan payments you will have to make, to cover the principal and interest, will represent a current determinable liability. This loan will probably be the largest liability you will have incurred in your life, so when applying for a loan, make sure you thoroughly understand the loan process and terms, including how much interest you will have to pay and how long you have to pay back the loan.

Sources: Government of Canada's CanLearn website, "Student Loans & Grants;" Tim Cestnick, "When Student Loans Make Sense…and when They Don't," *The Globe and Mail*, August 21, 2013; May Luong, "The Financial Impact of Student Loans," *Perspectives on Labour and Income*, January 2010, pp. 5–18, Statistics Canada Catalogue No. 75-001-X; "The Graduate's Million-Dollar Promise," *Maclean's* magazine website, January 16, 2013.

A student loan is a current liability, but one that will be worth incurring if it enables you to go to college or university. How could you calculate the return on investment in your future post-secondary education?

BEFORE YOU GO ON...

DO IT

Prepare the journal entry to record the following transaction for DiMaria Enterprises. Round any calculations to the nearest dollar.

Accrue interest on January 31 (the company's year end) for a $10,000, 30-month, 8% note payable issued on December 1. Interest is payable the first of each month, beginning January 1.

SOLUTION

Jan. 31	Interest Expense ($10,000 × 8% × 1/12)	67	
	Interest Payable		67
	To accrue interest on note payable.		

Related exercise material: BE10–1, E10–1, E10–2, and E10–3.

Action Plan

- The formula for interest is as follows: principal (face) value × annual interest rate × time.

THE NAVIGATOR

UNCERTAIN LIABILITIES

In the previous section, we discussed current liabilities where there was a high degree of certainty with regard to whom an amount is owed to, when it is owed, and how much is owed. There was no uncertainty about the liability's existence, amount, or timing. In this section, we will discuss liabilities that have a lower degree of certainty but are still likely to occur. We will then discuss situations where there is an even greater degree of uncertainty if an obligation exists, or where the existence of a liability depends on the outcome of a future event.

ESTIMATED LIABILITIES

STUDY OBJECTIVE 2

Account for estimated liabilities.

An **estimated liability** is a liability that is known to exist but *whose amount and timing are uncertain.* We know we owe someone, but are not necessarily sure how much and when. We may not even know whom we owe. There is a lower degree of certainty than in determinable liabilities, but as long as it is *likely* the company will have to settle the obligation, and the company can reasonably estimate the amount, the liability is recognized. Common estimated liabilities include product warranties, customer loyalty programs, and gift cards. We discuss these three examples in the following sections.

Alternative terminology
Estimated liabilities are also known as *provisions.*

Product Warranties

Product warranties are promises made by the seller to a buyer to repair or replace the product if it is defective or does not perform as intended. Warranties (also known as guarantees) are usually issued by manufacturers. For a specified period of time after the item was sold, a manufacturer may promise to repair the item, replace it, or refund the buyer's money under certain conditions. As a buyer, it is important to read all warranty contracts carefully because the promises they make can be quite different.

Warranties will lead to *future* costs for the manufacturer for the repair or replacement of defective units. At the time of the sale, it is not known which units will become defective, so it is not known in advance whom the company will have to pay, or when it will be paid. But the liability still exists even if the payee, exact amount, and timing are unknown.

There are two possible approaches to accounting for product warranties. Historically, an expense approach has been used to account for the warranty liability. But changes in accounting standards have led some companies to use what is known as a revenue approach. In this chapter, we will illustrate the expense approach. The revenue approach is explained in more advanced accounting textbooks.

Under the expense approach, the warranty liability is measured using the estimated future cost of servicing (honouring) the product's warranty. At the time the product is sold, the costs are not known, but based on their previous experience with a particular product, it is usually not that hard for most companies to estimate it.

This process will also result in the warranty expense being recorded at the same time as the liability. Recognizing both an expense and a liability in the period where the sale occurs also ensures that companies have recognized the full cost of the sale in the period in which the sale occurs. This is known as the **matching principle**, which requires that expenses be matched with revenues and recognized in the same fiscal period. As the actual costs are incurred in subsequent periods, the liability is reduced.

To illustrate the expense approach of accounting for warranty liabilities, assume that Hermann Company sells 10,000 washers and dryers at an average price of $600 in the year ended December 31, 2014. The selling price includes a one-year warranty on parts. Based on past experience, it is expected that 500 units (5%) will be defective, and that warranty repair costs will average $100 per unit.

At December 31, it is necessary to accrue the estimated warranty costs for the 2014 sales. The calculation is as follows:

Number of units sold	10,000
Estimated rate of defective units	× 5%
Total estimated defective units	500
Average warranty repair cost	× $100
Estimated product warranty liability	$50,000

The adjusting entry is:

A	=	L	+	OE
		+50,000		−50,000

Cash flows: no effect

Dec. 31	Warranty Expense	50,000	
	Warranty Liability		50,000
	To accrue estimated warranty costs.		

In 2014, warranty contracts were honoured on 300 units at a total cost of $30,000. These costs are recorded when they are incurred, but for our illustration they are being recorded in one summary journal entry for the year:

A	=	L	+	OE
−30,000		−30,000		

Cash flows: no effect

Dec. 31	Warranty Liability	30,000	
	Repair Parts Inventory (and/or Wages Payable)		30,000
	To record honouring of 300 warranty contracts on 2014 sales.		

In 2014, a warranty expense of $50,000 is reported as an operating expense in the income statement. The estimated warranty liability of $20,000 ($50,000 − $30,000) is classified as a current liability on the balance sheet.

In 2015, all costs incurred to honour warranty contracts on 2014 sales should be debited to the Warranty Liability account, like what was shown above for the 2014 sales. The Warranty Liability account will be carried forward from year to year—increased by the current year's estimated expense and decreased by the actual warranty costs incurred. It is quite likely that the actual expenses will not exactly equal the estimated liability amount. Every year, as is done with accounts receivable and the allowance for doubtful accounts, the warranty liability is reviewed and adjusted if necessary.

Customer Loyalty Programs

Alternative terminology
Customer loyalty programs are also called *promotions* or *incentive programs*.

To attract or keep customers, many companies offer **customer loyalty programs** that result in future savings for the customers on the merchandise or services the company sells. These customer loyalty programs take varying forms. For example, the program may require customers to collect points. A common example of that is airline frequent flyer programs. Or the programs may involve a credit reward that gives a cash discount on future sales. Loyalty programs are designed to increase sales and are important for many businesses.

The most successful loyalty program in Canadian retail history is Canadian Tire "money" (CTM), first introduced in 1958. The "money" resembles real currency (although the bills are considerably smaller than Bank of Canada notes) and is issued with no expiry date. CTM is given out by the cashiers for purchases paid for by cash, debit card, or Canadian Tire Options MasterCard credit card. Customers can use CTM to buy anything at a Canadian Tire store. In fact, some privately owned businesses in Canada also accept CTM as payment since the owners of many of these businesses shop at Canadian Tire.

Customer loyalty programs result in a liability to the business equal to the future savings that customers will receive when they use their points or credit awards. There has been some debate about whether the cost of such programs should be recorded as an expense (similar to the expense approach illustrated earlier in the chapter for warranties) or as a decrease in revenue. While there are a few exceptions, accountants have decided that, when a loyalty program results in a reduced future selling price, it should be accounted for *as a decrease in revenue and not as an expense.*

The liability for customer loyalty programs must be estimated because at the time of the sale, it is not known if or when customers will redeem the reward. But as long as some redemptions are likely, and can be reasonably estimated based on past experience, the decrease in revenue and a related liability should be recorded in the period when the reward was issued to ensure that liabilities are correctly recognized.

To illustrate, assume that Greenville Co-op has a rewards program whereby Greenville Co-op Gas Bar customers get a redemption reward of 3 cents per litre of gasoline that can be used in Greenville Co-op Food Stores on the purchase of groceries. Assume that during January, the gas bar sells 99,000 litres of gasoline. Greenville Co-op estimates that 90% of the rewards issued will be redeemed. At January 31, Greenville will record the following for the redemption rewards issued during January:

Jan. 31	Sales Discount for Redemption Rewards Issued (99,000 × 90% × $0.03)	2,673	
	Redemption Rewards Liability		2,673
	To record the estimated rewards from January sales that will be redeemed.		

A	=	L	+	OE
		+2,673		−2,673

Cash flows: no effect

The account Sales Discount for Redemption Rewards Issued is a *contra sales* account, and is deducted from sales to give net sales in the same way that sales returns and allowances are deducted from sales, as we learned in Chapter 5. The company could debit sales, but instead a contra revenue account is used to allow the company to track the redemption rewards. The Redemption Rewards Liability is reported as a current liability on the balance sheet.

Helpful hint Reductions in revenue are recorded in the period in which the reward is issued, not when it is redeemed.

To illustrate what happens when the rewards are redeemed, assume that on February 1, customers redeem $100 of the rewards in the Greenville Co-op Food Store when purchasing $7,500 of groceries. Greenville Co-op makes the following entry that day (ignoring the cost of sales):

Feb. 1	Rewards Redemption Liability	100	
	Cash ($7,500 − $100)	7,400	
	Grocery Sales Revenue		7,500
	To record grocery sales and the redemption of rewards.		

A	=	L	+	OE
+7,400		−100		+7,500

↑Cash flows: +7,400

Note that when the rewards are redeemed, the amount of cash collected is less than the sales revenue recognized. The liability account is reduced by the difference between the sales revenue and cash collected, which is the amount of the redemption. The liability account should be reviewed periodically and adjusted based on the company's experience with redemption rates.

Gift Cards

Gift cards or gift certificates have become an increasingly popular source of revenue for many companies. They are unearned revenues in that the company receives cash prior to providing the goods or the services. Thus, when gift cards are issued, the Unearned Revenue account (liability) is recorded. When the gift card is redeemed (used), the company will then record the sales or service revenue and reduce or debit the Unearned Revenue account.

Alternative terminology Unearned revenue is sometimes called *deferred revenue.*

As with customer loyalty programs, the difficulty with gift cards, as mentioned in the feature story, is that it is unknown when and even if the card will be redeemed. Typically, the longer a gift card is outstanding, the less likely it is to be redeemed for merchandise. Similarly, gift cards that have been used but have relatively small remaining balances are less likely to be redeemed than newer, high-balance gift cards.

If it is unlikely that the company will have to settle a portion of the liability, then an obligation no longer exists. As with warranties and customer loyalty programs, a company with a gift card program will need to use past experience to estimate the appropriate balance for the liability.

As shown in Reitmans' financial statements in Appendix A, the company has a deferred liability on its balance sheet for both a customer loyalty program as well as gift cards.

BEFORE YOU GO ON...

DO IT

Hockey Gear Company sells hockey skates with a two-year warranty against defects. The company expects that of the units sold each year, 5% will be returned in the first year after they are sold and 2% will be returned in the second year. The average cost to repair or replace a defective unit under warranty is $50. The company reported the following sales and warranty cost information:

	Units Sold	Actual Warranty Costs Incurred
2013	10,000	$20,000
2014	15,000	45,000

Calculate the balance in the Warranty Expense and Warranty Liability accounts at the end of 2014.

Action Plan

- Calculate the warranty expense by multiplying the number of units sold by the percentage that is expected to be returned and by the average warranty cost.
- Record warranty expenses in the period of the sale.
- The warranty liability is increased by the expense in each period and decreased by the actual costs of repairs and replacements.

SOLUTION

2013: Total defective units = 5% + 2% = 7%
10,000 × 7% = 700 × $50 = $35,000

Warranty Expense

35,000	

Warranty Liability

Actual	20,000	Estimate	35,000
		Bal. Dec. 31, 2013	15,000

2014: 15,000 × 7% = 1,050 × $50 = $52,500

Warranty Expense

52,500	

Warranty Liability

Actual	20,000	Estimate	35,000
		Bal. Dec. 31, 2013	15,000
Actual	45,000	Estimate	52,500
		Bal. Dec. 31, 2013	22,500

THE NAVIGATOR

Related exercise material: BE10–2, BE10–3, BE10–4, BE10–5, E10–4, E10–5, and E10–6.

CONTINGENCIES

STUDY OBJECTIVE 3
Account for contingencies.

The current liabilities discussed earlier in this chapter were either definitely determinable or estimable. While it might have been necessary to estimate the timing or amount, in both cases *there was no uncertainty about their existence*. With contingencies there is much more uncertainty about the timing and the amount and even the existence of a liability.

In general, a **contingency** can be defined as an existing condition or situation that is uncertain, where it cannot be known if a loss (and a related liability) will result from the situation until one or more future events happen or do not happen. In some situations, a gain (and a related asset) may arise from the contingency. But assets that are contingent on the outcome of an event are never recorded, and are not discussed in this textbook.

Lawsuits are good examples of contingencies. The existence of a loss and the related liability depend on the outcome of the lawsuit. The settlement of the lawsuit will confirm the existence of the liability, the amount payable, the payee, and/or the date payable. Under ASPE, a liability for a contingent loss is recorded if **both** of the following conditions are met:

1. The contingency is *likely* (the chance of occurrence is high).
2. The amount of the contingency can be *reasonably estimated.*

Therefore, if it is likely that the company will lose a lawsuit, and if the amount can be reliably estimated, then the company must record the loss and the liability. Under IFRS, a liability is recorded if the chance of occurrence is "probable" as opposed to "likely." Probable events are defined as being "more likely than not." Thus IFRS is generally regarded as having a lower threshold for recognizing these liabilities. Under ASPE, only highly likely contingent losses are recognized.

Under ASPE, these liabilities are called **contingent liabilities**, and under IFRS, these liabilities are called **provisions**. Under IFRS, a provision is a liability of uncertain timing or amount. The term "provisions" is often used for other uncertain liabilities, such as warranties, as discussed in the previous section of this chapter.

When a contingent loss is likely, but cannot be reasonably estimated, or if its likelihood of occurrence is not determinable, it is necessary only to disclose the contingency in the notes to the financial statements. In that case, a liability is not recorded.

If a contingency is unlikely—the chance of occurrence is small—it should still be disclosed if the event could have a substantial negative effect on the company's financial position. Otherwise, it does not need to be disclosed. A loan guarantee is an example of a contingency that should be disclosed even if the chance of having to pay is small. General risk contingencies that can affect anyone who is operating a business, such as the possibility of a war, strike, or recession, are not reported in the notes to the financial statements.

ACCOUNTING IN ACTION
BUSINESS INSIGHT

There are many contingencies in the real world. Lawsuits are the most common type of contingency, followed by environmental contingencies. Environmental contingencies generally relate to liabilities that could be incurred in order to clean up environmental problems.

The Canadian National Railway Company discloses the following information in the notes to its consolidated financial statements: "A risk of environmental liability is inherent in railroad and related transportation operations." The company goes on to say, "the magnitude of such... liabilities and the costs of complying with future environmental laws and containing or remediating contamination cannot be reasonably estimated... there can thus be no assurance that liabilities or costs related to environmental matters will not be incurred in the future, or will not have a material adverse effect on the Company's financial position or results of operations in a particular quarter or fiscal year, or that the Company's liquidity will not be adversely impacted by such environmental liabilities or costs."

Source: Canadian National Railway Company, 2011 Annual Information Form.

Environmental contingencies are generally considered to be harder to estimate than contingencies from lawsuits. What might be the reason for this difference?

BEFORE YOU GO ON...

DO IT

A list of possible contingencies follows.

1. A factory risks being damaged by floods. The building is located on a flood plain but has never experienced any damage from flooding in the past.
2. The government may expropriate a company's assets so that a new highway can be built. So far, there have been no discussions about how much the government might pay the company.
3. A public company is being sued for $1 million for unlawful termination of a company executive.
4. A company has guaranteed other companies' loans but the guarantees are unlikely to result in any payments.
5. A private company following ASPE is being sued for negligence and damages by a customer who slipped and broke a leg in the company's store.

Identify whether each of the above should be recorded, disclosed, or not reported.

Action Plan

- Recall that under ASPE, contingent liabilities are recorded if they are likely and can be reasonably estimated.
- Under IFRS, contingent liabilities (called provisions) are accrued when they are probable (more likely than not) and estimable.
- If the amounts cannot be estimated, they are only disclosed. Contingencies are not disclosed if they are unlikely.

SOLUTION

1. No disclosure required.
2. Disclosure required.
3. If it is probable that the company will lose and the amount can be reasonably estimated, then this would be recorded as a provision; otherwise, just disclose.
4. Disclosure required.
5. If it is likely that the company will lose and the amount can be reasonably estimated, then this is recorded as a contingent liability; otherwise, just disclose.

Related exercise material: BE10–6, BE10–7, E10–7, and E10–8.

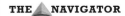

THE NAVIGATOR

FINANCIAL STATEMENT PRESENTATION

STUDY OBJECTIVE 4

Prepare the current liabilities section of the balance sheet.

Current liabilities are generally reported as the first category in the liabilities section of the balance sheet. Each of the main types of current liabilities is listed separately. In addition, the terms of operating lines of credit and notes payable and other information about the individual items are disclosed in the notes to the financial statements.

Similar to current assets, current liabilities are generally listed in order of liquidity (by maturity date). However, this is not always possible, because of the varying maturity dates that may exist for specific obligations such as notes payable. Many companies show bank loans, notes payable, and accounts payable first.

As discussed in Chapter 4, international companies often choose to order their current liabilities in order of reverse liquidity. They also often choose to present their current liabilities following the non-current liabilities.

Illustration 10-1 shows how Shoppers Drug Mart presents its current liabilities in traditional order in its balance sheet.

ILLUSTRATION 10-1
Presentation of current liabilities

SHOPPERS DRUG MART CORPORATION
Balance Sheet (partial)
December 31, 2011
(in thousands)

Current liabilities	
Bank indebtedness	$ 172,262
Accounts payable and accrued liabilities	1,109,444
Income taxes payable	26,538
Dividends payable	53,119
Current portion of long-term debt	249,971
Provisions	12,024
Associate interest	152,880
Total current liabilities	$1,776,238

Income taxes payable and dividends payable are accounts that are used only by corporations and you will learn about these in Chapters 13 and 14. Associate interest is the amount that Shoppers Drug Mart would owe to its associates (owners of the Shoppers Drug Mart stores) if its associate agreements were terminated. Shoppers Drug Mart explains in its notes to its financial statements that it does not expect to pay this amount in the next 12 months. However, because it doesn't have the unconditional right to defer settlement of the liability for at least 12 months, under IFRS, the company must report this amount in current liabilities.

Shoppers Drug Mart also discloses information about its provisions and contingencies in the notes to its financial statements, as shown in Illustration 10-2.

Notice that Shoppers Drug Mart is following the procedures for contingencies discussed earlier in the chapter. For the lawsuits or statements of claim by two of its licensed associate-members [see (a) in Illustration 10-2], the company is unable to reasonably estimate a probable loss. Therefore, it is only disclosed in this note. For the lawsuits or legal claims [see (b) in Illustration 10-2], where it is probable a loss will be incurred, and where the amount can be reasonably measured, the company has recorded a provision in the amounts shown in the note. In addition, Shoppers Drug Mart explains in Note 19 that it has entered into agreements with banks to guarantee a total of $520,000 thousand of its associate-owned stores' bank lines of credit.

Companies must carefully monitor the relationship of current liabilities to current assets. This relationship is critical in evaluating a company's short-term ability to pay debt. There is usually concern when a company has more current liabilities than current assets, because it may not be able to make its payments when they become due.

ILLUSTRATION 10-2
Disclosure of provisions and contingent liabilities

SHOPPERS DRUG MART CORPORATION
Notes to Consolidated Financial Statements (partial)
December 31, 2011

Note 22 PROVISIONS

	2011	2010
Balance, beginning of the financial year	$14,414	$12,071
Provisions made	8,980	12,341
Provisions used	(9,907)	(9,817)
Provisions reversed	(192)	(306)
Unwind of discount	430	125
Balance, end of the financial year	$13,725	$14,414
Balance, end of the financial year, presented as follows:		
Current liabilities	$12,024	$12,562
Long-term liabilities	1,701	1,852
	$13,725	$14,414

(a) The Company has been served with a Statement of Claim in a proposed class proceeding that has been filed in the Ontario Superior Court of Justice by two of its licensed Associate-owners, claiming various declarations and damages of $1,000,000 on behalf of a proposed class comprised of all of its current and former licensed Associate-owners resident in Canada, other than in Québec. The claim alleges, among other things, that Shoppers Drug Mart and two of its affiliates breached contractual and other duties to its Associate-owners by collecting, receiving and/or retaining funds and/or benefits that are in excess of those permitted to be collected, received and/or retained by the applicable agreements. The Company believes that the claim is without merit and will vigorously defend the claim. However, there can be no assurance that the outcome of this claim will be favourable to the Company or that it will not have a material adverse impact on the Company's financial position. The amount payable, if any, is not reasonably determinable at this time.

(b) In addition, the Company is involved in certain legal claims arising in the normal course of business. In the opinion of the Company's management, the eventual settlement of such claims will not have a significant effect on the Company's financial position or results of operations. Management has recorded a provision for these claims based on its best estimate of the final settlements.

Shoppers Drug Mart has current assets of $2,695,647 at December 31, 2011, which results in a positive current ratio. You will recall from Chapter 4 that the current ratio is calculated by dividing current assets by current liabilities. Shoppers Drug Mart's current ratio is 1.52:1 ($2,695,647 ÷ $1,776,238), which indicates that Shoppers Drug Mart has enough current assets to cover its current liabilities.

Recall also that the current ratio should never be interpreted without also looking at the receivables and inventory turnover ratios to ensure that all of the current assets are indeed liquid. It is also important to look at the acid-test ratio. If we wanted to do a more complete analysis of Shoppers Drug Mart's liquidity, we would need additional information.

BEFORE YOU GO ON...

DO IT

The following selected items were included in EastBoat Enterprises' adjusted trial balance at November 30, 2014:

Accounts payable	$ 52,775
Accounts receivable	30,250
Accrued liabilities	18,350
Bank indebtedness	10,400
Merchandise inventory	85,900
Notes payable	100,000
Prepaid expenses	12,000
Unearned revenue	6,500
Warranty liability	8,825

BEFORE YOU GO ON... continued on next page

BEFORE YOU GO ON...
continued from previous page

Additional information:

The $100,000 balance in notes payable consisted of: (1) a six-month, 5%, $25,000 note payable due on March 31, 2015; (2) a two-year, 5.5%, $15,000 note payable due on October 31, 2015; and (3) a three-year, 4.5%, $60,000 note payable due on September 30, 2016.

Prepare the current liabilities section of the balance sheet.

Action Plan
- Determine which items are liabilities.
- Recall that current liabilities are payable within one year of the balance sheet date.

SOLUTION

EASTBOAT ENTERPRISES
Balance Sheet (partial)
November 30, 2014

Current liabilities	
Bank indebtedness	$ 10,400
Accounts payable	52,775
Accrued liabilities	18,350
Unearned revenue	6,500
Warranty liability	8,825
Notes payable	40,000
Total current liabilities	136,850

THE NAVIGATOR

Related exercise material: BE10–8, BE10–9, BE10–10, E10–9, and E10–10.

Comparing IFRS and ASPE

Key Differences	International Financial Reporting Standards (IFRS)	Accounting Standards for Private Enterprises (ASPE)
Conditions necessary to record a liability for a contingent loss.	Chance of occurrence is "probable" or "more likely than not."	Chance of occurrence is "likely."
Terminology	A liability related to a contingent loss is called a "provision."	A liability related to a contingent loss is called a "contingent liability."

THE NAVIGATOR

DEMONSTRATION PROBLEM

Benoit Company has the following selected transactions:

Feb. 1 Signed a $50,000, six-month, 7% note payable to the Central Canadian Bank, receiving $50,000 in cash. Interest is payable at maturity.

10 Cash register receipts totalled $37,565.

The following adjustment data are noted at the end of the month:

1. Interest expense should be accrued on the note.
2. Some sales were made under warranty. Of the units sold under warranty this month, 350 are expected to become defective. Repair costs are estimated to be $40 per defective unit.

Instructions

(a) Record the February transactions. Round your calculations to the nearest dollar.

(b) Record the adjusting entries at February 28.

SOLUTION TO DEMONSTRATION PROBLEM

(a)

Feb.	1	Cash	50,000	
		Notes Payable		50,000
		Issued six-month, 7% note.		
	10	Cash ($37,565 + $4,883)	42,448	
		Sales		42,448

(b)

Feb.	28	Interest Expense ($50,000 × 7% × 1/12)	292	
		Interest Payable		292
		To record accrued interest for February.		
	28	Warranty Expense (350 × $40)	14,000	
		Warranty Liability		14,000
		To record estimated product warranty liability.		

Action Plan

- Remember that interest rates are annual rates and must be adjusted for periods of time less than one year.
- Warranty costs are expensed in the period when the sales occur.

THE NAVIGATOR

Summary of Study Objectives

1. ***Account for determinable or certain current liabilities.*** Liabilities are present obligations arising from past events, to make future payments of assets or services. Determinable liabilities have certainty about their existence, amount, and timing—in other words, they have a known amount, payee, and due date. Examples of determinable current liabilities include operating lines of credit, notes payable, accounts payable, unearned revenue, current maturities of long-term debt, and accrued liabilities such as interest.

2. ***Account for estimated liabilities.*** Estimated liabilities exist, but their amount or timing is uncertain. As long as it is *likely* the company will have to settle the obligation, and the company can reasonably estimate the amount, the liability is recognized. Product warranties, customer loyalty programs, and gift cards result in liabilities that must be estimated. They are recorded either as an expense (or as a decrease in revenue) and a liability in the period when the sales occur. These liabilities are reduced when repairs under warranty or redemptions occur. Gift cards are a type of unearned revenue as they result in a liability until the gift card is redeemed. As some cards are never redeemed, it is necessary to estimate the liability and make adjustments.

3. ***Account for contingencies.*** A contingency is an existing condition or situation that is uncertain, where it cannot be known if a loss (and a related liability) will result until a future event happens, or does not happen. Under ASPE, a liability for a contingent loss is recorded if it is it likely a loss will occur and the amount of the contingency can be reasonably estimated. Under IFRS, the threshold for recording the loss is lower. It is recorded if a loss is probable. Under ASPE, these liabilities are called contingent liabilities, and under IFRS, these liabilities are called provisions. If it is not possible to estimate the amount, these liabilities are only disclosed. They are not disclosed if they are unlikely.

4. ***Prepare the current liabilities section of the balance sheet.*** The nature and amount of each current liability and contingency should be reported in the balance sheet or in the notes accompanying the financial statements. Traditionally, current liabilities are reported first and in order of liquidity. International companies sometimes report current liabilities on the lower section of the balance sheet and in reverse order of liquidity.

THE NAVIGATOR

Glossary

Collateral Property pledged as security for a loan. (p. 435)

Contingency An existing condition or situation that is uncertain, where it cannot be known if a loss (and a related liability) will result from the situation until one or more future events happen or do not happen. (p. 440)

Contingent liability A liability whose existence will be confirmed only by the occurrence or non-occurrence of a future event. (p. 440)

Customer loyalty programs Programs that result in future savings for the customers on the merchandise or services the company sells. (p. 438)

Determinable liability A liability whose existence, amount, and timing are known with certainty. (p. 434)

Estimated liability A liability that is known to exist but whose amount or timing is uncertain. (p. 437)

Notes payable Obligations in the form of written promissory notes. (p. 435)

Operating line of credit Pre-authorized approval to borrow money at a bank when it is needed, up to a pre-set limit. (p. 435)

Prime rate The interest rate banks charge their best customers. (p. 435)

Product warranties Promises made by the seller to a buyer to repair or replace a product if it is defective or does not perform as intended. (p. 437)

Provisions Liabilities of uncertain timing or amount. (p. 440)

Trade payables Accounts and notes payable that result from purchase transactions with suppliers. (p. 435)

Self-Study Questions

Answers are at the end of the chapter.

(SO 1) C 1. Which of the following statements is the best description of a liability?
(a) A liability is a commitment to pay an amount in the future.
(b) A liability arises when an expense is incurred.
(c) A liability is an amount that should have been paid in the past.
(d) A liability is a present obligation, arising from past events, to make future payments of assets or services.

(SO 1) AP 2. Gibraltar Company borrows $55,200 on July 31, 2014, from the East Coast Bank by signing a seven-month, 5% note. Interest is payable at maturity. Assuming Gibraltar has a December 31 fiscal year end, how much interest expense will Gibraltar record in 2014 and in 2015?

	2014	2015
(a)	$ 0	$1,610
(b)	$1,150	$ 460
(c)	$1,380	$ 230
(d)	$1,971	$ 789

(SO 2) AP 3. Big Al's Appliance Store offers a two-year warranty on all appliances sold. The company estimates that 5% of all appliances sold need to be serviced at an average cost of $100 each. At December 31, 2013, the Warranty Liability account had a balance of $20,000. During 2014, the store spends $14,500 repairing 145 appliances. An additional 4,500 appliances are sold in 2014. On the 2014 income statement, warranty expense will be:
(a) $28,000.
(b) $22,500.
(c) $14,500.
(d) $20,000.

(SO 2) K 4. Friendly Department Store has a customer loyalty program in which customers receive points when they make a purchase. The points can be redeemed on future purchases. The value of the points issued should be recorded as:
(a) a contra revenue when the points are issued.
(b) an expense when the points are issued.
(c) a contra revenue when the points are redeemed.
(d) an expense when the points are redeemed.

(SO 3) K 5. Under IFRS, a contingent loss and the related liability should be recorded in the accounts when:
(a) it is probable the contingency will happen, but the amount cannot be reasonably estimated.
(b) it is probable the contingency will happen, and the amount can be reasonably estimated.
(c) it is highly unlikely the contingency will happen, but the amount can be reasonably estimated.
(d) it is unlikely that the users of the financial statements will read the notes.

(SO 4) K 6. On November 1, 2014, SSNL Company borrows $120,000 cash from the bank and issues a two-year, 4% note payable. SSNL must make payments of $5,000 plus interest at the end of each month. On December 31, 2014, what amount will be included in current and in non-current liabilities on the balance sheet?

	Current Liabilities	Non-Current Liabilities
(a)	$60,000	$ 50,000
(b)	$60,000	$ 60,000
(c)	$10,000	$100,000
(d)	$50,000	$ 70,000

THE NAVIGATOR

Questions

(SO 1) K 1. What is a determinable liability? List some examples.

(SO 1) K 2. Why is a present commitment to purchase an asset in the future not recorded as a liability?

(SO 1) K 3. How is interest calculated on a note payable? How is the amount of interest payable at the fiscal year end calculated?

(SO 1) K 4. What is the difference between an operating line of credit and a bank overdraft?

(SO 1) C 5. Laurel Hyatt believes that if a company has a long-term liability, the entire amount should be classified as non-current liabilities. Is Laurel correct? Explain.

(SO 2) C 6. The accountant for Amiable Appliances feels that warranty expense should not be recorded unless an appliance is returned for repair. "Otherwise, how do you know if the appliance will be returned, and if so, how much it will cost to fix?" he says. Do you agree? Explain.

(SO 2) C 7. Why does issuing a customer some form of future savings, when the customer purchases goods or services, result in a liability for the business?

(SO 2) C 8. A restaurant recently started a customer loyalty program. For all bills in excess of $100, the customer receives a 2-for-1 voucher for an appetizer for future meals. How should the restaurant account for the vouchers?

(SO 2) C 9. In what respects are gift cards similar to unearned revenues and why are they classified as a liability? How is a gift card different than an airline's unearned passenger revenue for flights paid in advance?

(SO 1, 2, 3) K 10. What are the differences between determinable, estimated, and contingent liabilities?

(SO 3) C 11. What is a contingency? How is it different from an estimated liability?

(SO 3) C 12. If a company is using ASPE, under what circumstances are a contingent loss and the related liability recorded in the accounts? Under what circumstances are they disclosed only in the notes to the financial statements?

(SO 3) C 13. If a company is using IFRS, under what circumstances are a contingent loss and the related liability recorded in the accounts? How is IFRS different from ASPE in this respect?

(SO 3) C 14. When is it necessary to disclose a contingency even if the chance of occurrence is small?

(SO 4) K 15. In what order are current liabilities generally reported in the balance sheet? Why might this method not always be possible?

(SO 4) K 16. What information about current liabilities should be reported in the notes to the financial statements?

(SO 4) K 17. How can a company determine if its current liabilities are too high?

Brief Exercises

BE10–1 Rabbitt Enterprises borrows $10,500 from LowLand Trust Co. on May 1, 2014, signing a 10-month, 4% note payable. Interest is payable the first of each month, starting June 1. Prepare journal entries for Rabbitt Enterprises to record: (a) the receipt of the proceeds of the note; (b) the first interest payment; (c) an adjusting entry, if required, at Rabbitt's year end, August 31, 2014; and (d) the payment of the note at maturity.

Record note payable. **(SO 1) AP**

BE10–2 In 2014, Song Company introduces a new product that includes a two-year warranty on parts. During 2014, 2,500 units are sold for $400 each. The cost of each unit was $175. The company estimates 5% of the units will be defective and that the average warranty cost will be $85 per unit. The company has a December 31 fiscal year end and prepares adjusting entries on an annual basis. (a) Prepare an adjusting entry at December 31, 2014, to accrue the estimated warranty cost. (b) Assume that the warranty contract was honoured on 25 units during 2014 for a total cost of $2,125 to replace defective parts. Prepare an entry dated December 31 to record honouring these warranties. (c) Calculate the profit earned by the company during 2014 on this new product.

Record warranty. **(SO 2) AP**

BE10–3 One-Stop Department Store has a loyalty program where customers are given One-Stop "Money" for cash or debit card purchases. The amount they receive is equal to 2% of the pre-tax sales total. Customers can use the One-Stop Money to pay for part or all of their next purchase at One-Stop Department Store. On July 3, 2014, Judy Wishloff purchases merchandise for $150. She uses $20 of One-Stop Money that she has from earlier purchases, and pays for the rest of the purchase with cash. What entry or entries will One-Stop Department Store record for this transaction? Ignore taxes.

Record loyalty rewards issued and redeemed. **(SO 2) AP**

BE10–4 Metropolis Books sold 50,000 copies of a best-selling novel in July for $8 each. Included in each book was a $2 mail-in rebate if the customer sends in proof of purchase with a completed rebate form. Metropolis estimates that 10% of the purchasers will claim the rebate. (a) Calculate the net sales revenue Metropolis earned in July on this book. (b) Prepare an adjusting entry at July 31 to accrue the estimated rebate liability. (c) Assume in August that 1,000 rebate forms are received and processed. Prepare one journal entry to record processing the rebate forms.

Record estimated liability for cash rebate program. **(SO 2) AP**

BE10–5 Rikard's Menswear sells $4,750 of gift cards for cash in December 2014. Rikard's has a December 31 fiscal year end and uses a perpetual inventory system. In January 2015, $2,425 of the gift cards are redeemed for merchandise, with a cost of $1,070. Prepare journal entries for Rikard's for December 2014 and January 2015.

Record gift cards issued and redeemed. **(SO 2) AP**

Account for contingencies. (SO 3) C

BE10–6 For each of the following independent situations, indicate whether it should be (1) recorded, (2) disclosed, or (3) neither recorded nor disclosed. Explain your reasoning and indicate if the accounting treatment would be the same or different under IFRS and ASPE.

(a) A customer has sued a company for $1 million. Currently the company is unable to determine if it will win or lose the lawsuit.
(b) A customer has sued a company for $1 million. The company will likely lose the lawsuit.
(c) A competitor has sued a company for $2 million. The lawyers have advised that there is a 55% chance that the company will lose the lawsuit.
(d) A company has guaranteed a $300,000 loan for one of its key suppliers. The supplier has a good credit rating and is not expected to default on the loan.

Discuss contingency. (SO 3) AP

BE10–7 Athabasca Toil & Oil Company, a public company, is a defendant in a lawsuit for improper discharge of pollutants and waste into the Athabasca River. Athabasca's lawyers have advised that it is probable the company will lose this lawsuit and that it could settle out of court for $50,000. Should Athabasca record anything with regard to this lawsuit? Or should it disclose it in the notes to the financial statements? Explain.

Identify current liabilities. (SO 1, 2, 3, 4) K

BE10–8 Identify which of the following items should be classified as a current liability. For those that are not current liabilities, identify where they should be classified.

(a) A product warranty
(b) Cash received in advance for airline tickets
(c) Bank indebtedness
(d) Interest owing on an overdue account payable
(e) Interest due on an overdue account receivable
(f) A lawsuit pending against a company. The company is not sure of the likely outcome.
(g) A $75,000 mortgage payable, of which $5,000 is due in the next year

Calculate current and non-current portion of notes payable. (SO 1, 4) AP

BE10–9 Diamond Dealers has two notes payable outstanding on December 31, 2014, as follows:

(a) A five-year, 5.5%, $60,000 note payable issued on August 31, 2014. Diamond Dealers is required to pay $12,000 plus interest on August 31 each year starting in 2015.
(b) A four-year, 4.5%, $96,000 note payable issued on September 30, 2014. Diamond Dealers is required to pay $2,000 plus interest at the end of each month starting on October 31, 2014. All payments are up to date.

Calculate the amount of each note to be included in current and non-current liabilities on Diamond Dealers' December 31, 2014, balance sheet. Ignore interest.

Prepare current liabilities section and calculate ratios. (SO 4) AP

BE10–10 **Suncor Energy Inc.** reported the following current assets and current liabilities (in millions) at December 31, 2011:

Accounts payable and accrued liabilities	$7,755
Accounts receivable	5,412
Cash and cash equivalents	3,803
Current portion of long-term debt	12
Current portion of provisions	811
Income taxes payable	969
Income taxes receivable	704
Inventories	4,205
Short-term debt	763

(a) Prepare the current liabilities section of the balance sheet.
(b) Calculate the current and acid-test ratios.

Exercises

Record note payable and note receivable; interest paid monthly. (SO 1) AP

E10–1 On June 1, 2014, Novack Company purchases equipment on account from Moleski Manufacturers for $50,000. Novack is unable to pay its account on July 1, 2014, so Moleski agrees to accept a three-month, 7% note payable from Novack. Interest is payable the first of each month, starting August 1, 2014. Novack has an August 31 fiscal year end. Moleski has a December 31 fiscal year end. Both companies adjust their accounts on an annual basis. Novack honours the note at maturity.

Instructions

(a) Record all transactions related to the note for Novack Company.
(b) Record all transactions related to the note for Moleski Manufacturers. Assume the cost of the equipment to Moleski was $30,000.

E10–2 On March 1, 2014, Tundra Trees Company purchased equipment from Edworthy Equipment Dealership in exchange for a seven-month, 8%, $30,000 note payable. Interest is due at maturity. Tundra Trees has a July 31 fiscal year end. Edworthy has a May 31 fiscal year end. Both companies adjust their accounts annually. Tundra honours the note at maturity.

Record note payable and note receivable; interest paid at maturity. **(SO 1) AP**

Instructions

(a) For Tundra Trees, record all transactions related to the note.
(b) For Edworthy Equipment, record all transactions related to the note. Assume the cost of the equipment to Edworthy was $18,000.

E10–3 Charleswood Musical Theatre's season begins in November and ends in April with a different play each month. In October 2014, Charleswood sold 150 season tickets for the 2014–15 season, which sold for $210 each. Charleswood records all season ticket sales as unearned revenue and adjusts its accounts on a monthly basis. The company has a March 31 fiscal year end.

Account for unearned revenue. **(SO 1) AP**

Instructions

(a) Prepare the entry for sale of the season tickets. Date the entry October 31.
(b) Prepare any required adjusting entries on:
  1. November 30, 2014
  2. March 31, 2015
  3. April 30, 2015
(c) Determine the balance (after any required adjustments) in Unearned Revenue on:
  1. November 30, 2014
  2. December 31, 2014
  3. March 31, 2015

E10–4 Castellitto Company began selling blenders on November 1, 2014. The company offers a 75-day warranty for defective merchandise. Based on past experience with other similar products, Castellitto estimates that 2.5% of the units sold will become defective in the warranty period, and that the average cost of replacing or repairing a defective unit is $20. In November, Castellitto sold 30,000 units and 450 defective units were returned. In December, Castellitto sold 32,000 units and 630 defective units were returned. The actual cost of replacing the defective units was $21,600.

Record warranty costs. **(SO 2) AP**

Instructions

(a) Prepare a journal entry to accrue for the estimated warranty costs for the November and December sales at December 31, 2014.
(b) Prepare one summary journal entry at December 31, 2014, to record the cost of replacing the defective blenders returned during November and December.
(c) What amounts will be included in Castellitto's 2014 income statement and balance sheet at December 31, 2014, with regard to the warranty?

E10–5 Silver Cloud Company manufactures and sells computers for $2,000 each, with a two-year parts and labour warranty. Based on prior experience, the company expects, on average, to incur warranty costs equal to 5% of sales. The company reports the following sales and warranty cost information:

Calculate warranty costs for multiple years. **(SO 2) AP**

	Sales (units)	Actual Warranty Costs
2012	500	$30,000
2013	600	46,000
2014	525	53,500

Instructions

(a) Calculate the warranty expense for each year.
(b) Calculate the warranty liability at the end of each year.

E10–6 Steig's Sports Store has a customer loyalty program in which it issues points to customers for every cash purchase that can be applied to future purchases. For every dollar spent, a customer receives three points. Each point is worth one cent. There is no expiry date on the points. Steig's estimates that 35% of the points issued will eventually be redeemed. Steig's has a December 31 year end.

Calculate customer loyalty program liability. **(SO 2) AP**

The program was started in 2014. During 2014, 900,000 points were issued. In 2015, 1.2 million points were issued. Redemptions total 225,000 points in 2014 and 336,000 in 2015.

Instructions

(a) What amount should be recorded as contra revenue (sales discounts for redemption rewards issued) in 2014? In 2015?
(b) What was the value of the points redeemed in 2014? In 2015?
(c) What is the redemption rewards liability that should be reported at December 31, 2014? At December 31, 2015?
(d) When the points are redeemed, how is this accounted for? What is the impact of the point redemptions on profit?

Identify type of liability. **(SO 1, 2, 3) C**

E10–7 A list of possible liabilities follows:

1. An automobile company recalled a particular car model because of a possible problem with the brakes. The company will pay to replace the brakes.
2. A large retail store has a policy of refunding purchases to dissatisfied customers under a widely advertised "money-back, no questions asked" guarantee.
3. A manufacturer offers a three-year warranty at the time of sale.
4. To promote sales, a company offers prizes (such as a chance to win a trip) in return for a specific type of bottle cap.
5. A local community has filed suit against a chemical company, alleging contamination of drinking water. The community is demanding compensation, and the amount is uncertain. The company is vigorously defending itself.

Instructions

(a) State whether you believe each of the above liabilities is determinable, estimable, or contingent, and explain why.
(b) If you identify the liability as contingent in part (a), state what factors should be considered in determining if it should be recorded, disclosed, or neither recorded nor disclosed in the financial statements.

Analyze contingency. **(SO 3) AP**

E10–8 Sleep-a-Bye Baby Company, a public company, is the defendant in a lawsuit alleging that its portable baby cribs are unsafe. The company has offered to replace the cribs free of charge for any concerned parent. Nonetheless, it has been sued for damages and distress amounting to $1.5 million. The company plans to vigorously defend its product safety record in court.

Instructions

(a) What should the company record or report in its financial statements for this situation? Explain why.
(b) What if Sleep-a-Bye Baby Company's lawyers advise that it is likely the company will have to pay damages of $100,000? Does this change what should be recorded or reported in the financial statements? Explain.
(c) How would your answers to parts (a) and (b) change if Sleep-a-Bye Baby Company were a private company that had chosen to follow ASPE?

Calculate current and non-current portion of notes payable, and interest payable. **(SO 1, 4) AP**

E10–9 Emerald Enterprises has three notes payable outstanding on December 31, 2014, as follows:

1. A six-year, 6%, $60,000 note payable issued on March 31, 2014. Emerald Enterprises is required to pay $10,000 plus interest on March 31 each year starting in 2015.
2. A seven-month, 4%, $30,000 note payable issued on July 1, 2014. Interest and principal are payable at maturity.
3. A 30-month, 5%, $120,000 note payable issued on September 1, 2014. Emerald Enterprises is required to pay $4,000 plus interest on the first day of each month starting on October 1, 2014. All payments are up to date.

Instructions

(a) Calculate the current portion of each note payable.
(b) Calculate the non-current portion of each note payable.
(c) Calculate any interest payable at December 31, 2014.

Prepare current liabilities section of balance sheet. Calculate current and acid-test ratios. **(SO 4) AP**

E10–10 The following selected account balances are from LightHouse Distributors' adjusted trial balance at September 30, 2014:

Accounts payable	$ 90,000
Accounts receivable	182,000
Bank overdraft	62,500
Income tax payable	35,000
Interest payable	10,000
Merchandise inventory	275,000
Mortgage payable	150,000
Notes payable	100,000
Prepaid expenses	12,500
Redemption rewards liability	5,000
Unearned gift card revenue	30,000
Warranty liability	22,500

Additional information:

1. On September 30, 2014, the unused operating line of credit is $75,000.
2. Redemption rewards, warranties, and gift cards are expected to be redeemed within one year.
3. Of the mortgage, $10,000 is due each year.
4. Of the note payable, $1,000 is due at the end of each month.

Instructions

(a) Prepare the current liabilities section of the balance sheet.
(b) Calculate LightHouse's current ratio and acid-test ratio.
(c) Explain why the company did not report any cash as part of its current assets.

Problems: Set A

Calculate current and non-current portion of notes payable, and interest payable. **(SO 1, 4) AP**

P10–1A Crab Apple Tree Farm has a December 31 fiscal year end. The company has six notes payable outstanding on December 31, 2014, as follows:

1. A 10-month, 5%, $35,000 note payable issued on August 1, 2014. Interest is payable monthly on the first day of each month starting on September 1.
2. A four-month, 4%, $15,000 note payable issued on September 1, 2014. Interest and principal are payable at maturity.
3. A six-month, 4.5%, $26,000 note payable issued on November 1, 2014. Interest and principal are payable at maturity.
4. A five-year, 3.5%, $60,000 note payable issued on March 31, 2014. Crab Apple Tree Farm is required to pay $12,000 plus interest on March 31 each year starting in 2015.
5. A six-year, 5%, $100,000 note payable issued on October 1, 2014. Crab Apple Tree Farm is required to pay $2,000 plus interest on the first day of each month starting on November 1, 2014. All payments are up to date.
6. A four-year, 5%, $40,000 note payable issued on January 31, 2013. Crab Apple Tree Farm is required to pay $10,000 every January 31 starting in 2014. Interest is payable monthly on the last day of each month, starting on February 28, 2013.

Instructions

(a) Calculate the current portion of each note payable.
(b) Calculate the non-current portion of each note payable.
(c) Calculate any interest payable at December 31, 2014.

TAKING IT FURTHER What are the costs and benefits to the maker and the payee of the note of using a note payable in place of an account payable?

Record note transactions; show financial statement presentation. **(SO 1, 4) AP**

P10–2A The current liabilities section of the December 31, 2013, balance sheet of Learnstream Company included notes payable of $14,000 and interest payable of $490. The note payable was issued to Tanner Company on June 30, 2013. Interest of 7% is payable at maturity, March 31, 2014.

The following selected transactions occurred in the year ended December 31, 2014:

Jan. 12	Purchased merchandise on account from McCoy Company for $20,000, terms n/30. Learnstream uses a perpetual inventory system.
31	Issued a $20,000, three-month, 5% note to McCoy Company in payment of its account. Interest is payable monthly.

Feb. 28	Paid interest on the McCoy note (see January 31 transaction).
Mar. 31	Paid the Tanner note, plus interest.
31	Paid interest on the McCoy note (see January 31 transaction).
Apr. 30	Paid the McCoy note, plus one month's interest (see January 31 transaction).
Aug. 1	Purchased equipment from Drouin Equipment by paying $11,000 cash and signing a $30,000, 10-month, 6% note. Interest is payable at maturity.
Sept. 30	Borrowed $100,000 cash from the First Interprovincial Bank by signing a 10-year, 5% note payable. Interest is payable quarterly on December 31, March 31, June 30, and September 30. Of the principal, $10,000 must be paid each September 30.
Dec. 31	Paid interest on the First Interprovincial Bank note (see September 30 transaction).

Instructions

(a) Record the transactions and any adjustments required at December 31.
(b) Show the balance sheet presentation of notes payable and interest payable at December 31.
(c) Show the income statement presentation of interest expense for the year.

TAKING IT FURTHER Why is it important to correctly classify notes payable as either current or non-current in the balance sheet?

Record current liability transactions; prepare current liabilities section. **(SO 1, 2, 4) AP**

P10–3A On January 1, 2014, Shumway Software Company's general ledger contained these liability accounts:

Accounts payable	$37,900
Redemption rewards liability	4,500
Unearned revenue	15,000

In January, the following selected transactions occurred:

Jan. 2	Issued a $50,000, four-month, 7% note. Interest is payable at maturity.
5	Sold merchandise for $8,800 cash. The cost of this sale was $4,600. Shumway Software uses a perpetual inventory system.
12	Provided services for customers who had paid $8,500 cash in advance.
17	Paid $15,000 to creditors on account.
20	Sold 500 units of a new product on account for $55 per unit. This new product has a one-year warranty. It is estimated that 9% of the units sold will be returned for repair at an average cost of $10 per unit. The cost of this sale was $25 per unit.
29	During the month, provided $2,300 of services for customers who redeemed their customer loyalty rewards.
31	Issued 30,000 loyalty rewards points worth $1 each. Based on past experience, 20% of these points are expected to be redeemed.

Instructions

(a) Record the transactions.
(b) Record adjusting entries for the following:
   1. Interest on the note payable
   2. The estimated warranty liability
(c) Prepare the current liabilities section of the balance sheet at January 31.

TAKING IT FURTHER Do you think that the loyalty rewards points represent a current or long-term liability? Explain the reasons for your choice.

Record warranty transactions. **(SO 2) AP**

P10–4A On January 1, 2012, Hopewell Company began a warranty program to stimulate sales. It is estimated that 5% of the units sold will be returned for repair at an estimated cost of $30 per unit. Sales and warranty figures for the three years ended December 31 are as follows:

	2012	2013	2014
Sales (units)	1,500	1,700	1,800
Sales price per unit	$150	$120	$125
Units returned for repair under warranty	75	90	105
Actual warranty costs	$2,250	$2,400	$2,640

Instructions

(a) Calculate the warranty expense for each year and warranty liability at the end of each year.

(b) Record the warranty transactions for each year. Credit Repair Parts Inventory for the actual warranty costs.
(c) To date, what percentage of the units sold have been returned for repair under warranty? What has been the average actual warranty cost per unit for the three-year period?

TAKING IT FURTHER Assume that at December 31, 2014, management reassesses its original estimates and decides that it is more likely that the company will have to service 7% of the units sold in 2014. Management also determines that the average actual cost per unit incurred to date (as calculated in part [c] above) is more reasonable than its original estimate. What should be the balance in the warranty liability account at December 31, 2014?

Record customer loyalty program and gift card transactions; determine impact on financial statements. **(SO 2) AP**

P10–5A Save-Always Stores started a customer loyalty program at the beginning of 2013 in which customers making cash purchases of gasoline at Save-Always Gas Bars are issued rewards in the form of grocery coupons. For each litre of gasoline purchased, the customer gets a grocery coupon for 3.5 cents that can be redeemed in Save-Always Food Stores. The coupons have no expiry date. Save-Always Stores began selling gift cards in 2014 that do not have expiry dates.

The following are selected transactions in 2013 and 2014:

1. In 2013, the Gas Bars sold 3.5 million litres of gasoline, issuing grocery coupons for these sales.
2. In 2013, customers redeemed $45,000 of the grocery coupons in the Food Stores while purchasing $1.8 million of groceries, paying the balance in cash.
3. In 2014, the Gas Bars sold 4,250,000 litres of gasoline, issuing grocery coupons for these sales.
4. In 2014, customers redeemed $52,500 of the grocery coupons in the Food Stores while purchasing $2,230,000 of groceries, paying for the balance in cash.
5. In 2014, customers purchased $75,000 of gift cards, and $45,400 of the cards were redeemed by the end of the year.

Instructions

(a) Indicate if the following activities will increase, decrease, or have no effect on each of revenues, expenses, and profit:
   1. Issuing grocery coupons
   2. Redeeming grocery coupons
   3. Issuing gift cards
   4. Redeeming gift cards
(b) Record the above transactions.
(c) What balances will be included in current liabilities at December 31, 2013 and 2014, regarding the customer loyalty program and gift cards?

TAKING IT FURTHER What factors should management consider in determining if current liabilities are correctly valued at December 31, 2014?

Discuss reporting of contingencies and record provisions. **(SO 3, 4) AP**

P10–6A Mega Company, a public company, is preparing its financial statements for the year ended December 31, 2014. It is now January 31, 2015, and the following situations are being reviewed to determine the appropriate accounting treatment:

1. Mega Company is being sued for $4 million for a possible malfunction of one of its products. In July 2014, a customer suffered a serious injury while operating the product. The company is vigorously defending itself as it is clear the customer was intoxicated when using the product.
2. In a separate lawsuit, Mega is being sued for $3 million by an employee who was injured on the job in February 2014. It is likely that the company will lose this lawsuit, but a reasonable estimate cannot be made of the amount of the expected settlement.
3. Since June 2012, Mega has guaranteed a $1-million bank loan for one of its main suppliers. In September 2014, the supplier started experiencing financial difficulties, which have continued. On December 16, 2014, the bank called Mega Company to confirm that if the supplier is unable repay the loan in January 2015, the bank will be seeking payment from Mega Company under the guarantee.
4. On December 7, 2014, a potential customer injured himself when he slipped on the floor in the foyer of Mega Company's office building. Mega Company did not have appropriate floor mats in place and melting snow from the customer's boots made the floor very dangerous. Mega has negotiated a potential settlement of $200,000 with the individual's lawyer.

Instructions

For each of the above situations, recommend whether Mega Company should (1) make an accrual in its December 31, 2014, financial statements; (2) disclose the situation in the notes to the financial statements; or (3) not report it. Provide a rationale for your recommendations.

TAKING IT FURTHER What are the potential benefits and costs of making an accrual for a contingency as opposed to only disclosing it in the notes to the financial statements?

Prepare current liabilities section; calculate and comment on ratios.
(SO 4) AP

P10–7A Maple Leaf Foods Inc. reports the following current assets and current liabilities at December 31, 2011 (in thousands):

Accounts payable and accruals	$482,059
Accounts receivable	133,504
Bank indebtedness	36,404
Biological assets	49,265
Current portion of long-term debt	5,618
Income and other taxes recoverable	43,789
Inventories	293,231
Notes receivable	98,545
Other current liabilities	20,409
Prepaid expenses and other assets	24,688
Provisions	44,255

Instructions

(a) Prepare the current liabilities section of the balance sheet.
(b) Calculate the current and acid-test ratios.
(c) At December 31, 2010, Maple Leaf Foods Inc. had current assets of $583,557 thousand, cash, short-term investments plus receivables of $217,751 thousand, and current liabilities of $1,091,960 thousand. Did the current and acid-test ratios improve or weaken in 2011?

TAKING IT FURTHER What other factors should be considered in assessing Maple Leaf Foods' liquidity?

CONTINUING COOKIE CHRONICLE

(*Note:* This is a continuation of the Cookie Chronicle from Chapters 1 through 9.)

Natalie has had much success with her cookie-making lessons over the last number of months. A few parents who have attended have shown interest in purchasing gift certificates from Natalie. Natalie is considering a gift certificate that would include a one-hour cookie-making lesson and all of the supplies needed to create two dozen cookies.

Natalie wants to make sure that she has considered all of the risks and rewards of issuing gift certificates. She has come to you with the following questions:

1. From what I understand, if I sell a gift certificate, I need to be recording the money received as "unearned revenue." I am a little confused. How is the use of this account the same as the money that I received from schools that have paid me a deposit for pre-booked cookie-making lessons?
2. What if I record the sale of gift certificates as revenue instead of unearned revenue? Technically, I have made a sale of a gift certificate and therefore should be recording amounts received as revenue for the sale of a gift certificate. What if a gift certificate is never used? Does this not justify a sale being recorded?
3. How do I make sure that the gift certificates that I have sold are in fact used? How do I make sure that the ones that I have sold have not been duplicated and used again?

Instructions

Answer Natalie's questions.

Cumulative Coverage—Chapters 3 to 10

The unadjusted trial balance of LeBrun Company at its year end, July 31, 2014, is as follows:

LEBRUN COMPANY
Trial Balance
July 31, 2014

	Debit	Credit
Cash	$ 16,750	
Accounts receivable	38,500	
Allowance for doubtful accounts		$ 2,000
Note receivable (due December 31, 2014)	10,000	
Merchandise inventory	45,900	
Prepaid expenses	16,000	
Land	50,000	
Building	155,000	
Accumulated depreciation—building		10,800
Equipment	25,000	
Accumulated depreciation—equipment		12,200
Patent	75,000	
Accumulated amortization—patent		15,000
Accounts payable		78,900
Warranty liability		6,000
Notes payable (due August 1, 2029)		124,200
S. LeBrun, capital		124,700
S. LeBrun, drawings	54,000	
Sales		750,000
Cost of goods sold	450,000	
Operating expenses	188,220	
Interest revenue		400
Interest expense	6,830	
Totals	$1,124,200	$1,124,200

Adjustment information:

1. Estimated uncollectible accounts receivable at July 31 are $3,850.
2. The note receivable bears interest of 8% and was issued on December 31, 2013. Interest is payable the first of each month.
3. A physical count of inventory determined that $39,200 of inventory was actually on hand.
4. Prepaid expenses of $5,500 expired in the year. (Use the account Operating Expenses.)
5. Depreciation is calculated on the long-lived assets using the following methods and useful lives:

   Building: straight-line, 25 years, $15,000 residual value
   Equipment: double diminishing-balance, five years, $2,500 residual value
   Patent: straight-line, five years, no residual value

6. The 6% note payable was issued on August 1, 2004. Interest is paid monthly at the beginning of each month for the previous month's interest. Of the note principal, $1,680 is currently due.
7. Estimated warranty costs for July are $1,975. (Use the account Operating Expenses.)

Instructions

(a) Prepare the adjusting journal entries required at July 31. (Round your calculations to the nearest dollar.)
(b) Prepare an adjusted trial balance at July 31.
(c) Prepare a multiple-step income statement and statement of owner's equity for the year and a balance sheet at July 31.

CHAPTER 10 BROADENING YOUR PERSPECTIVE

Collaborative Learning Activity

Note to instructor: Additional instructions and material for this group activity can be found on the Instructor Resource Site and in *WileyPLUS*.

BYP10–1 In this group activity, your group must decide on the best accounting treatment for a contingency. Your instructor will provide the class with a scenario and each group will be required to decide if an accrual should be made and, if so, for how much. Groups will simultaneously report to the class and will be required to defend their decisions.

Communication Activity

BYP10–2 The Show Time movie theatre sells thousands of gift certificates every year. The certificates can be redeemed at any time since they have no expiry date. Some of them may never be redeemed (because they are lost or forgotten, for example). The owner of the theatre has raised some questions about the accounting for these gift certificates.

Instructions

Write an e-mail to answer the following questions from the owner:

(a) Why is a liability recorded when these certificates are sold? After all, they bring customers into the theatre, where they spend money on snacks and drinks. Why should something that helps generate additional revenue be treated as a liability?

(b) How should the gift certificates that are never redeemed be treated? At some point in the future, can the liability related to them be eliminated? If so, what type of journal entry would be made?

Ethics Case

BYP10–3 Nice Nuke Corporation, which owns and operates a nuclear plant, recently received notice from the provincial government that it has to find a new disposal site for its radioactive waste. The company was also told that it is responsible for the environmental cleanup of the old site. The vice-president of engineering and the vice-president of finance meet to discuss the situation. The engineer says that it could take many years to clean up the site and that the cost could be considerable—a minimum of $50 million and perhaps as much as $100 million.

The vice-president of finance says that there is no way that the company can afford to record this liability. He says he is not even sure that he wants to disclose the potential liability, because of how this could affect the company's share price.

Instructions

(a) Who are the stakeholders in this situation?

(b) What are the alternative reporting options that the company can use?

(c) What is the likely impact of each alternative on the company's financial position?

(d) Is there anything unethical in what the vice-president of finance suggests doing about this potential liability?

(e) What do you recommend the company do?

All About You: Personal Financial Literacy Activity

BYP10–4 As indicated in the "All About You" feature in this chapter, a student loan is a loan that must be repaid. Many post-secondary students get a loan from the federal government's Canada Student Loan program. You may start to repay your loan immediately after completing your studies, but you must start the loan payments no later than six months after finishing. You must pay off the loan in full no later than 10 years after completing your studies.

Assume that when you have completed your post-secondary studies you have a Canada Student Loan of $25,000 with a fixed rate of interest of 9.5%.

Instructions

(a) What is the monthly loan repayment if you do not take advantage of the six-month grace period; that is, you start to repay your loan immediately after the end of your studies? (*Hint:* Under this option, the total number of monthly payments is 120.)

(b) What is the monthly loan repayment if you do take advantage of the six-month grace period and include the grace period interest with your loan balance? (*Hint:* Under this option, the total number of monthly payments is 114.)
(c) What is the monthly loan repayment if you take advantage of the six-month grace period but you pay off the grace period interest with a lump sum payment before you start to repay the loan? (*Hint:* Under this option, the total number of monthly payments is 114.)
(d) Assume that you want to pay off the loan in five years. What would be your monthly payment?

ANSWERS TO CHAPTER QUESTIONS

ANSWERS TO ACCOUNTING IN ACTION INSIGHT QUESTIONS

Business Insight, p. 441

Q: Environmental contingencies are generally considered to be harder to estimate than contingencies from lawsuits. What might be the reason for this difference?

A: The requirement to account for environmental contingencies is relatively new compared with the requirement to account for contingencies from lawsuits. Although it is difficult to predict whether the company will win or lose a lawsuit and what type of settlement may be involved, there is a vast history of case law that can be used to help a company form an opinion. Environmental regulations, in contrast, are still evolving and there is often no system (such as regulatory compliance audits or environmental site assessment data) that would help a company estimate the possible cost, or even the existence, of environmental contingencies for many years.

All About You Insight, p. 436

Q: A student loan is a current liability, but one that will be worth incurring if it enables you to go to college or university. How could you calculate the return on investment in your future post-secondary education?

A: Several organizations, such as Statistics Canada, publish information on-line on how much more college and university graduates earn compared with those without a diploma or degree. Sources such as the Government of Canada's CanLearn website also publish information on-line on the average costs of a college or university education. Divide the total cost of a diploma or degree by the difference in annual earnings of graduates and non-graduates to determine how many years it will take for your post-secondary education to "pay for itself." So, for example, if a four-year bachelor's degree costs roughly $45,000, and bachelor's degree holders earn let's say an average of $15,000 more a year than those without a degree, you would see a return on your university investment after three years.

ANSWERS TO SELF-STUDY QUESTIONS

1. d 2. b 3. b 4. a 5. b 6. a

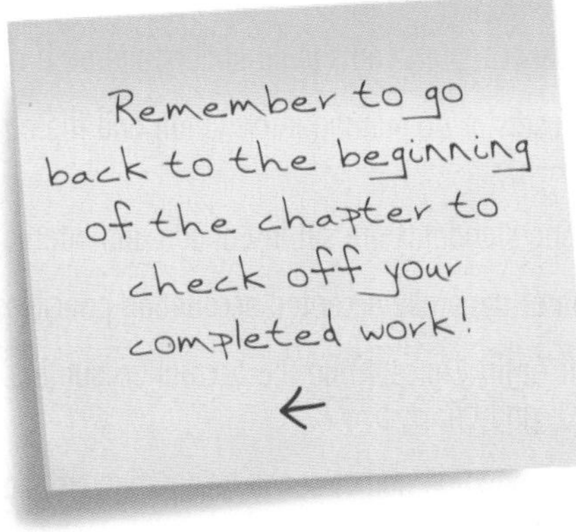
Remember to go
back to the beginning
of the chapter to
check off your
completed work!

CHAPTER 11

FINANCIAL REPORTING CONCEPTS

THE NAVIGATOR

- ❏ Understand *Concepts for Review*
- ❏ Read *Feature Story*
- ❏ Scan *Study Objectives*
- ❏ Read *Chapter Preview*
- ❏ Read text and answer *Before You Go On*
- ❏ Review *Comparing IFRS and ASPE*
- ❏ Work *Demonstration Problem*
- ❏ Review *Summary of Study Objectives*
- ❏ Answer *Self-Study Questions*
- ❏ Complete assignments

CONCEPTS FOR REVIEW

Before studying this chapter, you should understand or, if necessary, review:

A. The external users of accounting information and the objective of financial reporting. (Ch. 1, pp. 5–6)

B. How accounting standards are set in Canada and internationally. (Ch. 1, pp. 9–10)

C. The definition of generally accepted accounting principles (GAAP). (Ch. 1, p. 9)

D. The economic entity concept and the accrual accounting and going concern assumptions. (Ch. 1, p. 10, and Ch. 3, p. 97)

E. The revenue recognition and expense recognition criteria. (Ch. 1, p. 13, and Ch. 3, p. 98)

HIGH STANDARDS FOR CANADIAN ACCOUNTING STANDARDS

TORONTO, ON—By now you're familiar with some of the accounting standards that Canadian companies must follow. But how are these standards set? In Canada, the Accounting Standards Board (AcSB) is responsible for the development of accounting standards for both private and public companies. The AcSB states that it "serves the public interest by establishing standards and guidance for financial reporting by all Canadian entities outside the public sector and by contributing to the development of internationally accepted financial reporting standards."

The AcSB responds to the needs and viewpoints of the entire economic community. The AcSB follows a rigorous process known as "due process" in developing and adopting accounting standards. This can include researching standards in other countries, issuing discussion papers to get preliminary input, and issuing exposure drafts to get feedback on proposed standards. "All of those stages involve a lot of consultation," says Rebecca Villmann, a senior AcSB principal. Before finalizing a standard, "We reach out to stakeholders, from holding one-on-one meetings to group discussions with entities in different industries, lenders, creditors, and investors to get a wide range of views that the board can consider." It can take about a year and half to amend an existing standard, and several years to develop a new one.

How does the AcSB develop or change a standard for private companies reporting under Accounting Standards for Private Enterprises (ASPE)? The AcSB begins the process when areas for improvement are identified. For example, stakeholders have pointed out that there is no standard under ASPE for the agriculture industry to account for "bearer biological assets," like a winery's grapevines. "That is an essential part of what you need to create your product, to grow the grapes, but there isn't specific guidance on how to account for that vine," says Ms. Villmann.

Throughout the process, the AcSB is guided by the financial statement concepts (or conceptual framework) outlined in the *CPA Canada Handbook*. The conceptual framework sets out the objective of financial reporting; the characteristics the financial information needs in order to be useful; the definition of assets, liabilities, revenues, and expenses; and how items could be measured. For example, questions that need to be answered in developing a standard for accounting for agricultural assets such as vines are: Does the proposed standard satisfy the objective of financial reporting by providing useful information? Do the vines meet the definition of an asset? If the vines are reported as an asset, at what amount should they be reported?

How does the AcSB carry out its responsibility to develop standards for public companies reporting under International Financial Reporting Standards (IFRS)? The AcSB contributes to the International Accounting Standards Board's (IASB) standard-setting process, which is similar to the AcSB's process, including being guided by its conceptual framework. The AcSB participates in and monitors the IASB's due process to ensure that Canadians have the opportunity to discuss their views with the IASB and that the IASB considers these views when finalizing standards.

THE NAVIGATOR

STUDY OBJECTIVES

After studying this chapter, you should be able to:

1. Explain the importance of having a conceptual framework of accounting, and list the key components.
2. Identify and apply the objective of financial reporting, as well as the underlying assumption and cost constraint used by accountants.
3. Describe the fundamental and enhancing qualitative characteristics of financial reporting.
4. Identify and apply the basic recognition and measurement concepts of accounting.

THE NAVIGATOR

PREVIEW OF CHAPTER ELEVEN

In the first 10 chapters, you learned the process that leads to the preparation of a company's financial statements. You also learned that users make decisions based on information provided in financial statements, and that to be useful, these statements must communicate financial information to users in an effective way. This means that *generally accepted accounting principles* (GAAP) must be used. Otherwise, we would have to be familiar with each company's particular accounting and reporting practices in order to understand its financial statements. It would be difficult, if not impossible, to compare the financial results of different companies.

This chapter explores the conceptual framework that is used to develop generally accepted accounting principles. The chapter is organized as follows:

Financial Reporting Concepts

The Conceptual Framework of Accounting	The Objective of Financial Reporting, Underlying Assumption, and Constraint	Qualitative Characteristics of Useful Financial Information	Recognition and Measurement Criteria
	▶ The objective of financial reporting ▶ Underlying assumption ▶ Cost constraint ▶ Elements of financial statements	▶ Fundamental characteristics ▶ Enhancing qualitative characteristics ▶ Application of the qualitative characteristics ▶ Differences in qualitative characteristics under IFRS and ASPE ▶ Full disclosure	▶ Revenue recognition criteria ▶ Expense recognition criteria ▶ Measurement of elements ▶ Violation of recognition and measurement concepts: errors and intentional misstatements ▶ Summary of conceptual framework

THE CONCEPTUAL FRAMEWORK OF ACCOUNTING

STUDY OBJECTIVE 1

Explain the importance of having a conceptual framework of accounting, and list the key components.

According to standard setters, the **conceptual framework of accounting** is "a coherent system of interrelated objectives and fundamentals that can lead to consistent standards and that prescribes the nature, function, and limits of financial accounting statements." In other words, the conceptual framework of accounting guides decisions about what to present in financial statements, how to report economic events, and how to communicate such information.

A conceptual framework ensures that we have a coherent set of standards. New standards are easier to understand and are more consistent when they are built on the same foundation as existing standards. As a foundation for accounting, the conceptual framework:

- ensures that existing standards and practices are clear and consistent
- provides guidance in responding to new issues and developing new standards
- assists accountants in the application of accounting standards
- increases financial statement users' understanding of and confidence in the financial statements

Alternative terminology
Recall that, as we saw in Chapter 1, the words "standards" and "principles" mean the same thing in accounting.

It is impossible to create a rule for every situation. Canadian and international standards are therefore based mostly on *general principles* rather than *specific rules*. It is hoped that, with the help of a conceptual framework and their professional judgement, accountants will be able to quickly determine an appropriate accounting treatment for each situation.

Not every country uses the same conceptual framework and/or set of accounting standards. This lack of uniformity has arisen over time because of differences in legal systems, in processes for developing standards, in government requirements, and in economic environments. The International Accounting Standards Board (IASB), the standard-setting body responsible for developing IFRS, was formed to try to reduce these areas of difference and unify global standard setting.

To promote global consistency and comparability, the IASB and its U.S. counterpart, the Financial Accounting Standards Board (FASB), agreed to work together to produce an updated common conceptual framework. At the time of writing, phase one of the project (regarding the objective of financial reporting, qualitative characteristics, and cost constraint) was finalized. The other phases had not yet been completed, so it is expected that there will continue to be changes to the IASB's conceptual framework.

Canada's Accounting Standards Board (AcSB) has committed to update the conceptual framework used in ASPE to be consistent with the IASB's conceptual framework used in IFRS. However, at the time of writing, the AcSB announced that it would defer updating the ASPE conceptual framework as it waited for further progress by IASB on its conceptual framework. This means that, although the conceptual frameworks for IFRS and ASPE are *fundamentally similar*, they are not *identical*. Differences between the two frameworks will be identified in the following sections of this chapter.

We describe the following key components of a conceptual framework in this chapter:

- objective of financial reporting
- underlying assumption
- cost constraint
- elements of financial statements
- qualitative characteristics of useful financial information
- recognition and measurement criteria

Helpful hint Accounting principles are affected by economic and political conditions, which change over time. As a result, accounting principles can and do change.

BEFORE YOU GO ON...

DO IT

Indicate if each of the following statements is true or false.

1. The specific rules for accounting for inventory are a component of the conceptual framework.
2. The use of a common conceptual framework will enhance the consistency and comparability of financial reporting in the global environment.
3. The conceptual framework eliminates the need for financial statement preparers to use professional judgement.
4. The conceptual framework includes recognition and measurement criteria.
5. The conceptual framework provides guidance in developing new standards.

SOLUTION

1. F 2. T 3. F 4. T 5. T

Related exercise material: BE11–1.

Action Plan

- Review the purpose of the conceptual framework.
- Review the components of the conceptual framework.

THE NAVIGATOR

THE OBJECTIVE OF FINANCIAL REPORTING, UNDERLYING ASSUMPTION, AND CONSTRAINT

The first step in establishing accounting standards is to decide on the *purpose* or *objective* of financial reporting. Once this is established, then underlying assumptions and constraints can be determined.

STUDY OBJECTIVE 2

Identify and apply the objective of financial reporting, as well as the underlying assumption and cost constraint used by accountants.

THE OBJECTIVE OF FINANCIAL REPORTING

To decide what the objective of financial reporting should be, some basic questions need to be answered first: Who uses financial statements? Why? What information do the users need? How much do they know about business and accounting? How should financial information be reported to ensure that it is best understood?

The main **objective of financial reporting** is to **provide financial information that is useful to existing and potential investors and creditors in making decisions about a business**. You will recall from earlier chapters that financial statements are prepared for an economic or business unit that is *separate and distinct from its owners*. This is referred to as the **economic entity concept**. An economic (reporting) entity could be one company or a collection of companies consolidated under common ownership.

You will also recall from Chapter 1 that, although a wide variety of users rely on financial reporting, *capital providers* (investors and creditors) are identified as the main users of financial reporting. Capital

Helpful hint The "dragons" on CBC's *Dragons' Den* are capital providers.

providers play a fundamental role in the efficient functioning of the economy by providing capital (cash) to businesses. Businesses require cash to start up, maintain operations, and grow. Cash or capital comes from investors, lenders, and the company's revenue-generating activities.

To make decisions about allocating capital (such as about investing or lending), users look for information in the financial statements about a company's ability to earn a profit and generate future cash flows. To assess this ability, users read the financial statements to determine whether or not management acquired and used the company's resources in the best way possible. Consequently, financial statements must give information about the following:

Helpful hint Recall that assets (economic resources) appear on the left side of the balance sheet, while liabilities and equity (claims on the assets) appear on the right side.

1. Economic resources (assets) and claims on the economic resources (liabilities and equity)
2. Changes in economic resources and in claims on the economic resources
3. Economic performance

UNDERLYING ASSUMPTION

A key assumption, the going concern assumption, creates a foundation for the financial reporting process. You will recall from Chapter 1 that the **going concern assumption** assumes that the company will continue operating for the foreseeable future; that is, long enough to carry out its existing objectives and commitments. Although there will always be business failures, most companies continue operating for a long time.

This assumption has important implications for accounting. If a company is assumed to be a going concern, then financial statement users will find it useful for the company to report assets, such as buildings and equipment, at their cost minus accumulated depreciation (carrying amount). If the company is not a going concern, then the carrying amount will not be relevant. Instead, the financial statement user would want to know what the assets can be sold for or their net realizable value (their market value). Furthermore, if the company is not a going concern, the classification of assets and liabilities as current or non-current would not matter. Labelling anything as non-current would be difficult to justify. The only time the going concern assumption should not be used is when liquidation is likely. If it cannot be assumed that the company is a going concern, this needs to be explicitly stated in the financial statements.

COST CONSTRAINT

The **cost constraint** is a pervasive (overall) constraint that ensures the value of the information provided is greater than the cost of providing it. That is, the benefits of financial reporting information should justify the costs. For example, in the section on the qualitative characteristics of useful financial information, we will recognize that to be useful, the financial information must be complete. To achieve completeness, accountants could record or disclose every financial event that occurs and every uncertainty that exists. However, providing this information increases reporting costs. The costs of providing more information, in some cases, may be greater than the benefits provided.

Helpful hint The cost constraint should not be confused with the cost principle. Recall from Chapter 1 that the cost principle requires items to be reported at their historical cost.

The AcSB applied this constraint when it adopted IFRS for public companies and ASPE for private companies. As discussed in Chapter 1, users of private companies' financial statements generally require less information than users of public companies' financial statements. The board recognized that the cost to private companies of providing financial statements prepared under IFRS was greater than the benefits. Consequently, the board developed ASPE, which is simpler and requires less disclosure than IFRS.

Note that the ASPE conceptual framework refers to this constraint as the *benefit versus cost constraint*.

ELEMENTS OF FINANCIAL STATEMENTS

Elements of financial statements are the basic categories used in the financial statements to meet the objective of financial reporting. These elements include assets, liabilities, equity, revenues, and expenses.

Because these elements are so important, they must be precisely defined and applied in the same way by all reporting entities. Currently the definitions are being reviewed by the IASB and the FASB in their joint project to improve the conceptual framework. You have already been introduced to the definitions of assets, liabilities, equity, revenues, and expenses in earlier chapters. For your review, a summary of the definitions is provided in Illustration 11-1.

ILLUSTRATION 11-1
Elements of financial statements

Element	Definition
Assets	An asset is a resource controlled by a business as a result of a past transaction that is expected to provide future economic benefits to the company.
Liabilities	A liability is a present obligation of the entity arising from an earlier transaction that is expected to result in an outflow from the entity of resources that hold economic benefits.
Equity	Equity is the residual (remaining) interest in the assets of the entity after deducting all its liabilities. (Assets − Liabilities = Equity)
Revenues	Revenue is an increase in assets or a decrease in liabilities that results in an increase in equity, other than those relating to contributions from owners. Under IFRS, revenue also includes gains. Revenue arises in the course of the company's ordinary activities, while gains may or may not arise from ordinary activities.
Expenses	Expenses are decreases in economic benefits during the accounting period in the form of outflows or depletions of assets or incurrences of liabilities that result in decreases in equity, other than those relating to distributions to owners (that is, drawings). Under IFRS, expenses also include losses. Expenses arise from the company's ordinary activities. Losses may or may not arise from the company's ordinary activities.

Under ASPE, gains and losses are listed in separate categories from revenues and expenses, but the basic definitions are similar to those under IFRS.

As indicated in the feature story, one of the questions that will need to be answered when the AcSB develops a standard for accounting biological products such as a winery's grapevines is: Do grapevines fit the definition of an asset? The AcSB will be guided by the key components of the definition of an asset as provided in the conceptual framework. Are the grapevines controlled by the company? Will the grapevines provide a future benefit?

BEFORE YOU GO ON...

DO IT

Presented below are two key concepts in financial reporting:

(a) Going concern
(b) Cost constraint

Identify the concept that applies to the following statements:

1. _______ Private companies may follow ASPE, a simplified version of GAAP.
2. _______ Assets and liabilities are classified as current or non-current.
3. _______ A company expenses inexpensive office supplies when purchased to avoid the cost of tracking the use of supplies and determining the balance on hand at the balance sheet date.
4. _______ Land is recorded at its cost.

Action Plan
- Recall that going concern is an underlying assumption in financial reporting.
- Recall that the cost constraint is a pervasive constraint on financial reporting.

SOLUTION

1. (b) 2. (a) 3. (b) 4. (a)

Related exercise material: BE11–2, BE11–3, BE11–4, E11–1, and E11–2.

THE NAVIGATOR

QUALITATIVE CHARACTERISTICS OF USEFUL FINANCIAL INFORMATION

STUDY OBJECTIVE 3
Describe the fundamental and enhancing qualitative characteristics of financial reporting.

How does a company like Reitmans (Canada) Limited decide how much financial information to disclose? In what format should its financial information be presented? How should assets, liabilities, revenues, and expenses be measured? Remember that the objective of financial reporting is to provide useful information for decision-making. Thus **the main criterion for judging accounting choices is decision usefulness**.

What makes information useful in decision-making? Accounting standard setters have decided that there are two fundamental characteristics that accounting information must have in order to be useful. In addition, there are other characteristics, complementary to the fundamental characteristics, that enhance the usefulness of accounting information. We discuss the *qualitative* characteristics in the following sections.

FUNDAMENTAL CHARACTERISTICS

In order for information to be useful in decision-making, accounting standard setters have agreed that the information should have two fundamental qualitative characteristics: relevance and faithful representation.

Relevance

Accounting information has **relevance** if it makes a difference in coming to a decision. Relevant information has either predictive value or confirmatory value, or both. *Predictive value* helps users forecast future events. For example, the sales and profit reported by Reitmans in its comparative financial statements may be used along with other information to help predict future sales and profit. *Confirmatory value* confirms or corrects prior expectations. The sales and profit reported by Reitmans can also be used to confirm or correct previous predictions made by users.

Materiality is an important component of relevance. An item is material when it is likely to influence the decision of a reasonably careful investor or creditor. It is *immaterial* if including it or leaving it out has no impact on a decision maker. Materiality and relevance are both defined in terms of making a difference to a decision maker. A decision to not disclose certain information may be made because the users do not need that kind of information (it is not relevant) or because the amounts involved are too small to make a difference (they are immaterial). To determine the materiality of an amount, the accountant usually compares it with such items as total assets, total liabilities, gross revenues, cash, and profit.

Materiality is also related to the cost constraint, as illustrated in the following example. Assume that Yanik Co. purchases several inexpensive pieces of office equipment, such as wastepaper baskets. Although it is correct to capitalize these wastepaper baskets and depreciate them over their useful lives, they are usually expensed immediately instead. Immediate expensing is the easiest, and thus the least costly, method of accounting for these items and is justified because these costs are immaterial. Making depreciation schedules for these assets is costly and time-consuming. Expensing the wastepaper baskets will not make a material difference to total assets and profit.

Helpful hint The dollar amount that would be considered "material" depends on the size of the individual organization. An amount of $500 might represent an entire day's sales for a small sole proprietorship, but it would not be significant for BlackBerry or Canadian Tire.

In short, if the item does not make a difference in decision-making, GAAP does not have to be followed.

Faithful Representation

Once it is determined which information is relevant to financial statement users, then how the information is reported must be determined. To be useful, information must be a **faithful representation** of the economic reality of the events that it is reporting and not just the legal form. For example, a company may sign a lease agreement that requires periodic rental payments to be made over the life of the lease. If a company follows the legal form of the transaction, the periodic rental payments will be recorded as rent expense. However, for certain leases, the economic reality is that an asset is purchased and the periodic payments are loan payments. For these leases, it is necessary to record an asset and a liability to show the economic reality.

Faithful representation is achieved when the information is (1) complete, (2) neutral, and (3) free from material error, as explained below.

1. Accounting information is **complete** if it includes all information necessary to show the economic reality of the underlying transactions and events. If information is left out, users will not be able to make appropriate resource allocation decisions. If Reitmans did not disclose when payments are due on its long-term debt, users would not have the necessary information to predict future cash flows. The concept of completeness is discussed further in this chapter in the section on full disclosure.
2. Accounting information is **neutral** if it is free from bias that is intended to attain a predetermined result or to encourage a particular behaviour. For example, accounting information would be biased

if the income statement was prepared so that it resulted in a high enough level of profit that the management team received their bonuses.

3. If an error in accounting information could have an impact on an investor's or creditor's decision, then the error is a **material error**. There will always be some errors in accounting information because estimates, such as estimated useful life and salvage value, are used. If accounting information is to be free from material error, estimates must be based on the best available information and be reasonably accurate. Accountants must use professional judgement and caution when using estimates in financial reporting.

The fundamental qualitative characteristics of accounting information are summarized in Illustration 11-2.

ILLUSTRATION 11-2
Fundamental qualitative characteristics of accounting information

Relevance
1. Provides a basis for forecasts
2. Confirms or corrects prior expectations

Faithful Representation
1. Is complete
2. Is neutral
3. Is free from material error

ENHANCING QUALITATIVE CHARACTERISTICS

Enhancing qualitative characteristics complement the two fundamental qualitative characteristics: relevance and faithful representation. The enhancing characteristics are intended to help users distinguish more useful information from less useful information. Comparability, verifiability, timeliness, and understandability are enhancing characteristics.

Comparability

Accounting information about a company is most useful when it can be compared with accounting information about other companies. There is **comparability** when companies with similar circumstances use the same accounting principles. Comparability enables users to identify the similarities and differences between companies.

Comparability is reduced when companies use different methods of accounting for specific items. For example, there are different methods of determining the cost of goods sold and value assigned to ending inventory, which can result in different amounts of profit. But if each company discloses (states) which cost determination method it uses, the external user can determine whether the financial information for two companies is comparable.

Comparability is easier when accounting policies are used consistently. **Consistency** means that a company uses the same accounting principles and methods *from year to year*. For example, if a company selects FIFO as its inventory cost formula in the first year of operations, it is expected to use FIFO in subsequent years. When financial information has been reported consistently, the financial statements make it possible to do a meaningful analysis of company trends.

This does not mean, however, that a company can never change its accounting policies. Sometimes changes in accounting policies are required by standard setters. For example, when Canadian companies adopted either ASPE or IFRS in 2011, they were required to change some accounting policies. At other times, management may decide that it would be better to change to a new accounting policy, such as a different inventory valuation or amortization method. To do this, management must prove that the new policy will result in more relevant information in the statements.

In the year of a change in an accounting policy, the change and its impact must be disclosed in the notes to the financial statements. This disclosure makes users of the financial statements aware of the lack of consistency. In addition, the financial statements for past years must be *restated* as if the new accounting policy had been used in those years. We will learn more about accounting for, and reporting, changes in accounting policies in Chapter 14.

Verifiability

Verifiability helps assure users that the financial information shows the economic reality of the transaction. Information is verifiable if two knowledgeable and independent people would generally agree that it is faithfully represented. For example, the balance in a bank account can be directly verified by obtaining confirmation of the amount from the bank. Other types of information can be verified by checking inputs to a formula and recalculating the outputs. Information must be verifiable for external professional accountants to audit financial statements and to provide an opinion that the financial statements are presented fairly.

Timeliness

Timeliness means that accounting information is provided when it is still highly useful for decision-making. In other words, it must be available to decision makers *before* it loses its ability to influence decisions. Many people believe that by the time annual financial statements are issued—sometimes up to six months after a company's year end—the information has limited usefulness for decision-making. Timely interim financial reporting is essential to decision-making.

Understandability

For the information in financial statements to be useful, users must be able to understand it. **Understandability** enables reasonably informed users to interpret and comprehend the meaning of the information provided in the financial statements. Users are expected to have a reasonable knowledge of business, economic, and financial activities, and of financial reporting. Users who do not have this level of understanding are expected to rely on professionals who do have an appropriate level of expertise. One of the benefits of using IFRS for Canadian public companies is that their financial statements will now be better understood by global users.

Understandability is greater when the information is classified, characterized, and presented clearly and concisely. In making decisions, users should review and analyze the information carefully.

The enhancing qualitative characteristics of accounting information are summarized in Illustration 11-3.

ILLUSTRATION 11-3
Enhancing qualitative characteristics of useful financial information

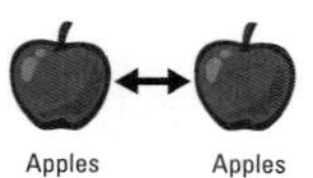

Comparability
1. Different companies use similar accounting principles.
2. A company uses the same accounting policies consistently from year to year.

Verifiability
3. Independent people agree that the economic reality is reported.

Timeliness
4. Information is provided when it is still useful.

Understandability
5. Information is understandable when it is understood by users who have a reasonable knowledge of accounting concepts and procedures.
6. Information is understandable when it is understood by users who have a reasonable knowledge of business and economic conditions.

APPLICATION OF THE QUALITATIVE CHARACTERISTICS

The qualitative characteristics are complementary concepts; that is, *they work together*. It is also important to apply them in the correct order. The qualitative characteristic of relevance should be applied first because it will identify the specific information that would affect the decisions of investors and creditors and that should be included in the financial report.

Once relevance is applied, faithful representation should be applied to ensure that the economic information faithfully represents the economic events being described. Taken together, relevance and faithful representation make financial reporting information decision useful.

Then the enhancing qualitative characteristics—comparability, verifiability, timeliness, and understandability—are applied. They add to the decision usefulness of financial reporting information that is relevant and representationally faithful. They must be applied after the first two characteristics because they cannot, either individually or together, make information useful if it is irrelevant or not faithfully represented. The diagram at right shows the order in which the qualitative characteristics should be applied.

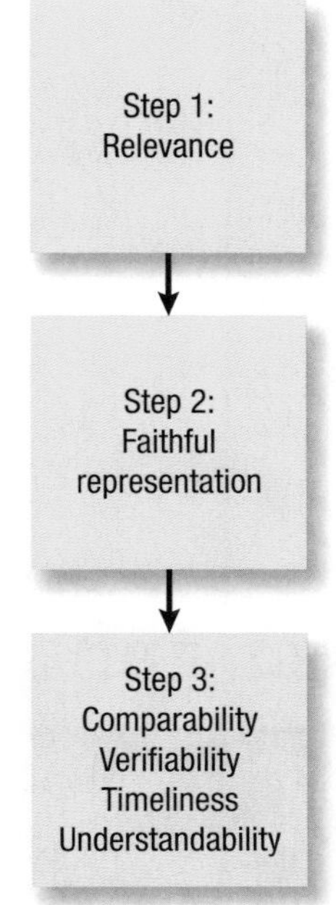

DIFFERENCES IN QUALITATIVE CHARACTERISTICS UNDER IFRS AND ASPE

Earlier in the chapter, we noted that the IFRS and ASPE conceptual frameworks are *fundamentally similar but not identical.* While the conceptual framework for IFRS identifies two fundamental and four enhancing characteristics, the framework for ASPE identifies four principal qualitative characteristics: understandability, relevance, reliability, and comparability.

Note that both conceptual frameworks use relevance as a main characteristic. Faithful representation, identified as a fundamental qualitative characteristic under IFRS, is very similar to reliability, which is identified as a principal qualitative characteristic under ASPE. Under ASPE, information is considered reliable if it is a faithful representation of transactions and events, is verifiable, and is neutral. There is also a difference in how the two standards view understandability and comparability. Under IFRS, they are assigned a lower status because they are identified as enhancing qualitative characteristics, whereas under ASPE, they are considered to be as important as relevance and reliability.

ASPE also recognizes conservatism as a qualitative characteristic of financial information. The concept of conservatism means that, when preparing financial statements, accountants should choose the accounting treatment or estimate that will be the least likely to overstate assets, revenues, and gains and the least likely to understate liabilities, expenses, and losses. However, conservatism does not justify the deliberate understatement of assets, revenues, and gains or the deliberate overstatement of liabilities, expenses, and losses. It should be noted that the IASB eliminated the concept of conservatism when it updated the conceptual framework.

In summary, although at the time the text was written there were some differences between the conceptual frameworks, it is likely these differences will be eliminated because, as mentioned earlier, the AcSB intends to adopt the IASB's conceptual framework and incorporate it into ASPE. The table illustrates the status of qualitative characteristics under IFRS and ASPE.

	IFRS	ASPE
Higher status	Relevance Faithful representation (similar to reliability)	Relevance Reliability (similar to faithful representation) Understandability Comparability Conservatism
Lower status	Understandability Comparability	

FULL DISCLOSURE

Earlier in our discussion of the qualitative characteristic of faithful representation, we recognized that information provided in the financial statements must be complete. This requires that companies fully disclose circumstances and events that make a difference to financial statement users. It is important that investors be made aware of events that can affect a company's financial health.

Full disclosure is followed through two elements in the financial statements: the data they contain and the accompanying notes. For example, one of the notes in the statements summarizes the company's significant accounting policies. The summary includes the methods used by the company when there are alternatives in acceptable accounting principles.

The information that is disclosed in the notes to the financial statements generally falls into three additional categories. The information can:

1. Give supplementary detail or explanation (for example, a schedule of property, plant, and equipment).
2. Explain unrecorded transactions (for example, contingencies, commitments, and subsequent events).
3. Supply new information (for example, information about related-party transactions).

Deciding how much disclosure is enough can be difficult. Accountants must use professional judgement in determining what information is relevant and material to users. Accountants must also consider the cost of providing the information versus the benefits.

ACCOUNTING IN ACTION
ALL ABOUT YOU INSIGHT

You may have used a resumé to find a job. Your resumé is like a company's annual report, describing your recent accomplishments so others can evaluate your performance and try to predict how you will do in the future. Your resumé must be a faithful representation of your background, education, and experience. The temptation to overstate accomplishments is great, however—even at the highest levels of responsibility, as shown in the recent case of a former CEO of Yahoo, Scott Thompson. After just four months at the company's helm, Yahoo announced that Thompson had decided to step down. Although the company did not state the reasons, it was reported that the decision was partly to do with the fact that an activist hedge fund publicized the fact that Thompson had misrepresented his education on his resumé. His biography in the company's annual report stated that he had a degree in accounting and computer science, but his degree is in accounting only. Yahoo's annual report is a legal document filed with the U.S. Securities and Exchange Commission, in which CEOs must swear that all information is truthful. Yahoo said the statement was an "inadvertent error" and hired a lawyer to investigate the statement.

Sources: Michael J. de la Merced and Evelyn M. Rusli, "Yahoo's Chief to Leave as Company Strikes Deal with Loeb," *New York Times*, May 13, 2012; Julianne Pepitone, "Yahoo Confirms CEO Is Out after Resume Scandal," CNNMoney, May 14, 2012; Amir Efrati and Joann S. Lublin, "Yahoo CEO's Downfall," *Wall Street Journal*, May 15, 2012.

What may be the consequences to you if you misrepresent yourself on your resumé?

BEFORE YOU GO ON...

DO IT

Presented below are some of the qualitative characteristics of financial information.

(a) Relevance
(b) Faithful representation
(c) Complete
(d) Neutral
(e) Comparability
(f) Verifiability
(g) Timeliness
(h) Understandability

Match the qualitative characteristics to the following statements:

1. ______ Information is available to decision makers before the information loses its ability to influence decisions.
2. ______ Information is free from bias that is intended to attain a predetermined result.
3. ______ Information makes a difference in a decision.
4. ______ Users are assured that the financial information shows the economic reality of the transaction.
5. ______ All of the information necessary to show the economic reality of transactions is provided.

BEFORE YOU GO ON...
continued on next page

6. ______ Accounting information about one company can be evaluated in relation to accounting information from another company.
7. ______ Accounting information reports the economic reality of a transaction, not its legal form.
8. ______ Accounting information is prepared on the assumption that users have a general understanding of general business and economic conditions and are able to read a financial report.

SOLUTION

1. (g) 2. (d) 3. (a) 4. (f) 5. (c) 6. (e) 7. (b) 8. (h).

Related exercise material: BE11–5, BE11–6, E11–3, and E11–4.

BEFORE YOU GO ON...
continued from previous page

Action Plan

- Review the two fundamental qualitative characteristics.
- Review the enhancing qualitative characteristics.

RECOGNITION AND MEASUREMENT CRITERIA

STUDY OBJECTIVE 4
Identify and apply the basic recognition and measurement concepts of accounting.

You learned in earlier chapters that financial statements are prepared using the accrual basis of accounting. The **accrual basis of accounting** means that transactions affecting a company's financial statements are *recorded in the period in which the events occur, rather than when the company receives cash or pays cash.* Therefore accounting standards are necessary to help accountants answer two questions: (1) when should an event be recorded and (2) at what amount should it be recorded? **Recognition criteria help determine when an event should be recorded** in the financial statements. When an item is recorded in the financial statements, accountants say that it has been recognized. **Measurement criteria provide guidance on what amount should be recorded** for the event.

Generally an item will be included in the financial statements if it meets the definition of an asset, liability, equity, revenue, or expense; if it can be measured; and if a reasonable estimate of the amount can be made. The item is reported in the financial statements in a monetary amount. In Canada, the monetary unit used for financial reporting is generally the Canadian dollar.

There are two important concepts underlying the general criteria. The first concept is that for an asset to be recorded, it must be probable that there will be a future economic benefit, and for a liability to be recognized, it must be probable that economic resources will be given up. For example, a company does not have to be 100% certain that it will collect an account receivable to record the receivable; it just has to be probable that cash will be collected. The second concept is that estimates may be used to record dollar amounts if the precise dollar amount is not known.

Although the general recognition criteria provide guidance for recording events, it is necessary to have more specific criteria for when to recognize revenues and expenses. Should the revenue be recorded when the customer places an order with the company, or when the goods are delivered? How should the transaction be recorded if cash collection is uncertain? The revenue recognition criteria are discussed in the following section. Expense recognition will be discussed later in the chapter.

REVENUE RECOGNITION CRITERIA

In the opinion of many people, the timing of revenue recognition is the most difficult issue in accounting. And it is an issue that has been responsible for many of the accounting scandals of the past decade. For example, when Alexa Life Sciences, the manufacturer of Cold-FX, first started selling its products in the United States in 2006, it failed to recognize that there was considerable risk that a significant amount of the product would be returned by retailers. As a result, the company overstated its 2006 revenues (net sales) by $5.6 million.

Why is revenue recognition such a difficult concept to apply? In some cases, revenue recognition has been intentionally abused in order to overstate profits. However, in most cases, revenue recognition is a difficult concept that requires professional judgement because the activities that generate revenues have become a lot more innovative and complex than in the past. These topics go beyond an introductory accounting course, and include items such as "swap" transactions, "bill and hold" sales arrangements, risk-sharing agreements, complex rights of return, price-protection guarantees, and post-sale maintenance contracts.

Basically, the **revenue recognition criteria** state that revenue is recognized when there has been an increase in an asset or a decrease in a liability due to ordinary profit-generating activities that results in an increase in owners' equity. The question that needs to be answered is, when have assets actually increased or liabilities decreased?

In the following sections, we will discuss revenue recognition criteria for the most common revenue-generating activities:

1. Sale of goods
2. Service contracts and construction contracts

Sale of Goods

Revenue from the sale of goods is recognized when all of the following conditions have been met:

1. The seller has transferred to the buyer the significant risks and rewards of ownership.
2. The seller does not have control over the goods or continuing managerial involvement.
3. The amount of the revenue can be reliably measured.
4. It is probable there will be an increase in economic resources (that is, cash will be collected).
5. Costs relating to the sale of the goods can be reliably measured.

For sales in a retail establishment, these conditions are generally met at the point of sale. Consider a sale by Reitmans for an item that is a final sale and cannot be returned. At the point of sale, the customer pays the cash and takes the merchandise. The company records the sale by debiting Cash and crediting Sales Revenue. In this example, there is no uncertainty about when or how much revenue should be recorded. Cash has been received and the customer has taken ownership of the goods. In the following paragraphs, we discuss common situations where there is more uncertainty as to when or how much revenue should be recognized.

When Goods Are Shipped.

Typically, the risks and rewards of ownership are transferred when legal title passes and the customer is in possession of the goods. For goods that are shipped, the shipping terms determine when the legal title passes. Recall from Chapter 5 that, if the terms of the sale are FOB shipping point, then legal titles passes when the goods are shipped and the seller recognizes revenue on the date the goods are shipped. If the terms of the sale are FOB destination, then legal title passes when the goods arrive at their destination and revenue is recognized on the date the goods are delivered.

When Goods Are Sold on Credit.

When merchandise is sold on credit, revenue is recognized at the point of sale as long as the seller can be reasonably sure that the cash will be collected. If the sale were on credit rather than for cash, the company would record the sale by debiting Accounts Receivable and crediting Sales Revenue. Of course, not all accounts are actually collected. However, as we learned in Chapter 8, revenue can be recognized as long as an estimate can be made of any possible uncollectible accounts. Bad debt expense is recorded for the estimated uncollectible accounts and matched against revenue in the appropriate period.

When Goods May Be Returned for a Refund.

If a company provides refunds to customers for goods that are returned, revenue is recognized at point of sale if the company is able to reliably estimate future returns. The company will report sales net of an allowance for the estimated returns and recognize a liability for the estimated returns in its financial statements. For example, Reitmans' note on significant accounting policy discloses that the sales reported in the income statement are net of returns and estimated possible returns (see Note 3 part I). Note 12 to Reitmans' financial statements discloses that Reitmans recognized a $770,000 liability (provision) for estimated possible sales returns in its January 28, 2012, balance sheet.

When Free Warranty Service Is Provided.

Similarly, if a company provides free warranty service on its merchandise, revenue is recognized at point of sale if the company is able to reliably estimate the future warranty costs. You will recall from Chapter 10 that the estimated warranty expense is recorded and a warranty liability is recognized in its financial statements. If costs relating to the sale cannot be reliably measured, then the revenue cannot be recognized.

When the Sales Transaction Includes the Sale of Goods and a Service Component.

Some sales transactions may include both the sale of goods and a service component. For example, assume a customer pays $3,250 cash for a large screen television and an extended warranty. The extended warranty normally sells for $250 as a separate warranty. The transaction must be recorded in the accounting records to reflect that the customer has paid for two items: the television and the extended warranty. Sales revenue of $3,000 is recorded for the sale of the television and $250 is recorded as unearned warranty revenue to recognize that the store has an obligation (liability) to provide warranty service in the future. Warranty revenue will be recognized when the company satisfies its obligation by providing warranty service.

Service Contracts and Construction Contracts

Generally, in businesses that provide services, revenue is recognized when the service has been provided and it is probable that the cash will be collected. To illustrate, assume your doctor gives you a routine checkup in September, bills the provincial health care plan in October, and receives payment in November. When should your doctor recognize the revenue? The revenue should be recognized in September because that was when the service was performed, the price would have been known, and the receivable was likely to be collected.

Revenue recognition becomes more difficult when the earnings process lasts several years. This happens in the case of long-term service contracts and construction contracts for large projects, such as building bridges, roads, and aircraft. For example, construction on "The Bow"—a large office tower in Calgary that is the second-tallest building in Canada—started in 2007 and was completed in 2012.

Assume that Warrior Construction Co. has a contract to build a dam for the Province of British Columbia for $400 million. Construction is estimated to take three years (starting early in 2012) at a cost of $360 million. If Warrior recognizes revenue only when the construction is complete, it will report no revenues and no profit in the first two years. When completion and sale take place, at the end of 2014, Warrior will report $400 million in revenues, costs of $360 million, and the entire profit of $40 million. Did Warrior really produce no revenues and earn no profit in 2012 and 2013? Obviously not.

In situations like this, if the costs to complete the project can be reasonably estimated, the percentage-of-completion method is typically used to recognize revenue. The **percentage-of-completion method** recognizes revenue on long-term projects as progress is made toward completion based on reasonable estimates of how much of the work has been performed to date. Percentage-of-completion accounting methods are left to more advanced accounting courses.

EXPENSE RECOGNITION CRITERIA

The basic **expense recognition criteria** state that expenses are recognized when there is a decrease in an asset or increase in a liability, excluding transactions with owners that result in a decrease in owners' equity (that is, drawings). This is not necessarily when cash is paid. For example, as supplies are used, the asset Supplies is decreased and an expense is recognized. Alternatively, when a liability for salaries payable is recorded, salaries expense is recognized.

Expense recognition is tied to revenue recognition when there is a direct association between costs incurred and the earning of revenue. For example, there is a direct association between cost of goods sold and sales revenue. As we learned in Chapter 3, this process is commonly referred to as matching. Under matching, revenues and expenses that relate to the same transaction are recorded in the same accounting period. Other examples of expenses that relate directly to revenue are bad debt expense, warranty expense, and salaries paid to sales staff.

Helpful hint Recall from Chapter 9 that depreciation causes an increase to an expense and an increase to a contra asset account (Accumulated Depreciation). Recall also that the contra asset balance is subtracted from the cost of the asset to calculate the asset's carrying value.

Other costs are more difficult to directly associate with revenue. For example, it is difficult to match administrative salary expense or interest expense with the revenue they help to earn. Such costs are therefore expensed in the period when the liability arises.

Sometimes, however, there is no direct relationship between expenses and revenue. When it is hard to find a direct relationship and assets are expected to benefit several accounting periods, a rational and systematic allocation policy can sometimes be developed to allocate the cost of the asset to expense over time. For example, the cost of a long-lived asset can be allocated to depreciation expense over the life of the asset because it can be determined that the asset contributes in some way to revenue generation during its useful life. Allocation requires the accountant to use professional judgement in estimating the benefits that will be received from the asset and how the cost of the asset should be allocated to expense over its productive life.

In other cases, when expenditures are made that do not qualify for the recognition of an asset (that is, they are not capitalized), an expense is recognized immediately. For example, expenditures for research do not qualify for recognition of an asset as it is impossible to determine the future benefits (if any) arising from the research, so the research costs are expensed immediately. Another example is expenditures made for advertising, which are also expensed immediately.

Sometimes a previously recognized asset ceases to have future benefit, and the asset must be expensed for the balance of its remaining value. For example, inventory that is obsolete and cannot be sold is expensed when it becomes apparent it cannot be sold.

In summary, costs need to be analyzed to determine whether it is probable there is a future benefit to the company or not. If there is a direct relationship between the revenues recognized and costs, the costs are recognized as expenses (matched against the revenues) in the period when the revenue is recognized. If it is hard to determine a direct relationship, but the costs are expected to benefit several periods, then it might be appropriate to systematically and rationally allocate (spread) the cost to expense over the periods that are expected to benefit. If there is no future benefit, or if the benefit is uncertain, the costs should simply be expensed in the current period.

MEASUREMENT OF ELEMENTS

So far, we have looked at when items should be recognized or recorded in the accounting records. Now we will look at what dollar amounts should be used to record the items. There are a number of different measurements used in accounting. They include the following:

1. Cost
2. Fair value
3. Amortized cost

Assets are recorded at cost when they are acquired. Cost is used because it is both relevant and provides a faithful representation of the transaction. Cost represents the price paid, the assets sacrificed, or the commitment made at the date of acquisition. Cost is objectively measurable, factual, and verifiable. It is the result of an exchange transaction. Cost is relevant for reporting certain assets in the balance sheet because the assets are intended for use in the business and are not going to be sold.

Alternative terminology
Other common terms for *fair value* are *market value* and *realizable value.*

Most companies use the cost model to report property, plant, and equipment where the carrying value on the balance sheet is cost less accumulated depreciation. However, you will recall from Chapter 9 that, under IFRS, companies can choose to account for their property, plant, and equipment under either the cost model or the revaluation model. Under the revaluation model, the carrying amount of property, plant, and equipment is its fair value less any accumulated depreciation less any subsequent impairment losses.

However, for some assets, it is more relevant to provide the assets' fair value: the amount of cash that is expected to be collected if the asset is sold. Users of financial information are better able to assess the impact of changes in fair value on the company's liquidity and solvency. For example, short-term or trading investments that are purchased for the purpose of resale are reported at their fair value in the financial statements.

Certain assets and liabilities, such as investments in bonds and bonds payable, are measured at amortized cost. We will learn more about amortized cost and investments in bonds and bonds payable in Chapter 15.

Cost is the most common basis used by companies in preparing their financial statements. Cost may be combined with other measurement bases. For example, you will recall from Chapter 6 that inventory is reported at the lower of cost and net realizable value.

VIOLATION OF RECOGNITION AND MEASUREMENT CONCEPTS: ERRORS AND INTENTIONAL MISSTATEMENTS

As we discussed earlier in the chapter, the timing of revenue recognition is considered the most difficult issue in accounting. In some cases, revenue recognition has been intentionally abused. Incorrect application of the expense and measurement criteria can also result in errors or intentional misstatement of the financial statements. In this section, we will discuss what situations might lead management and accountants to behave unethically and abuse accounting principles. We will also examine potential misstatements that can be made in applying the recognition and measurement criteria.

Management may be under pressure to report a certain amount of profit to meet shareholders' (owners') expectations, or management's bonuses may be based on the company achieving a specified profit. In these situations, management may be inclined to overstate profits by overstating revenues or understating expenses. Alternatively, management of some private companies may want to reduce the amount of tax paid and consequently may be inclined to understate profits by understating revenues and overstating expenses. Ways in which revenues or expenses may be misstated in error or intentionally are as follows:

1. **Recognition of revenue or expense in the incorrect accounting period.** For example, the seller might recognize sales revenues for goods that are shipped FOB destination when the goods are shipped and not when the customer receives the goods. This would overstate revenues if the goods were shipped just prior to the company's fiscal year end and received by the customer after the year end. Alternatively, a company might delay recording an expense by recording as an asset an expenditure for which there is no future benefit.
2. **Misstatement of estimates.** Earlier in the chapter, we recognized that companies need to estimate potential returns and record an allowance that reduces net sales. If the allowance is understated, net sales will be overstated. Alternatively, management might understate the estimate for bad debt expense. Estimates cannot be 100% accurate. However, professional judgement needs to be used in arriving at the estimate and the estimates need to be supported and verifiable.
3. **Misstatement of revenue or expense accruals.** In some cases, revenue has been earned or an expense incurred for which the exact amount is not yet known, and thus the accrual must be estimated. Again, professional judgement needs to be used in arriving at the estimate, and the estimate needs to be supported and verifiable. For example, a company may need to estimate the accrual for utilities expense because the bill has not been received. The accountant might use previous utility bills to arrive at a reasonable estimate.
4. **Failure to record a revenue or expense.** Due to poor internal controls and record keeping, the accountant may be unaware that revenue has been earned or an expense incurred.
5. **Failure to apply the correct measurement.** For example, a company may neglect to write down (that is, reduce the value of) inventory to net realizable value. Or alternatively, land might be reported at fair value when the company is following the cost model for property, plant, and equipment.

It is important that accountants analyze transactions carefully to ensure that accounting principles are applied correctly and the financial statements are a faithful representation of the underlying economic events. When adjusting entries are prepared at the end of an accounting period, accountants must give careful attention to determining the appropriate accounting period that revenues and expenses should be recognized in, appropriate measurements and estimates, and if any economic events have occurred that need to be recorded. Accountants need to exercise professional judgement and ethical reasoning to guard against errors or abuse in applying accounting principles.

ACCOUNTING IN ACTION
ETHICS INSIGHT

One of the biggest accounting scandals in Canadian history involved former telecommunications giant Nortel Networks. The company was accused of accruing expenses that did not occur and then reversing these expenses in 2003 in order to turn a profit, after losing money in the 2001 dot-com bust. Nortel allegedly accrued millions of dollars in liabilities related to the company's downsizing, such as lawsuits from suppliers over cancelled contracts and employee severance packages. If the company overestimated the amounts of these liabilities, also known as accruals, reserves, or provisions, it would consider the savings as revenue in the period in which the settlement was reached. Three senior executives were charged with fraud, accused of manipulating earnings in 2003 to trigger millions of dollars in profitability bonuses for themselves. During a six-month trial in 2012, the Crown alleged that the executives ordered extra liabilities to be accrued in 2002, turning a profit into a loss, and then reversed the accruals in 2003, turning a loss into a profit. The Crown argued the accruals should have been reversed earlier. The company restated its financial information several times in the years thereafter, and filed for bankruptcy in 2009. In 2013, the three executives were found not guilty. The judge said the accounting practices were either not fraudulent or were not material for a company as large as Nortel was.

Sources: James Bagnall, "Were Senior Executives Scapegoats for Nortel's Demise?," Postmedia News, January 14, 2012; Jamie Sturgeon, "'Unsupportable' Reserves Remained on Nortel Books, Court Hears," *Financial Post*, March 5, 2012; Janet McFarland, "Nortel Releases $80-million in Accounting Reserves to Reach Profit Threshold: Witness," *Globe and Mail*, April 2, 2012; James Bagnall, "Nortel Witnesses Were 'Accomplices' to Fraud," *Ottawa Citizen*, August 7, 2012; Janet McFarland and Richard Blackwell, "Three Former Nortel Executives Found Not Guilty of Fraud," *Globe and Mail*, January 14, 2013.

Accountants are often required to make estimates when preparing financial statements. What is the difference between what Nortel allegedly did and what we would expect an accountant to do when estimating accruals for adjusting journal entries?

SUMMARY OF CONCEPTUAL FRAMEWORK

As we have seen, the conceptual framework for developing sound reporting practices starts with the objective of financial reporting. It then describes the underlying assumption, the elements of the financial statements, the qualitative (fundamental and enhancing) characteristics of accounting information, and the constraint on financial reporting. Finally, more detailed recognition and measurement criteria are provided. The conceptual framework is summarized in Illustration 11-4.

ILLUSTRATION 11-4
Conceptual framework

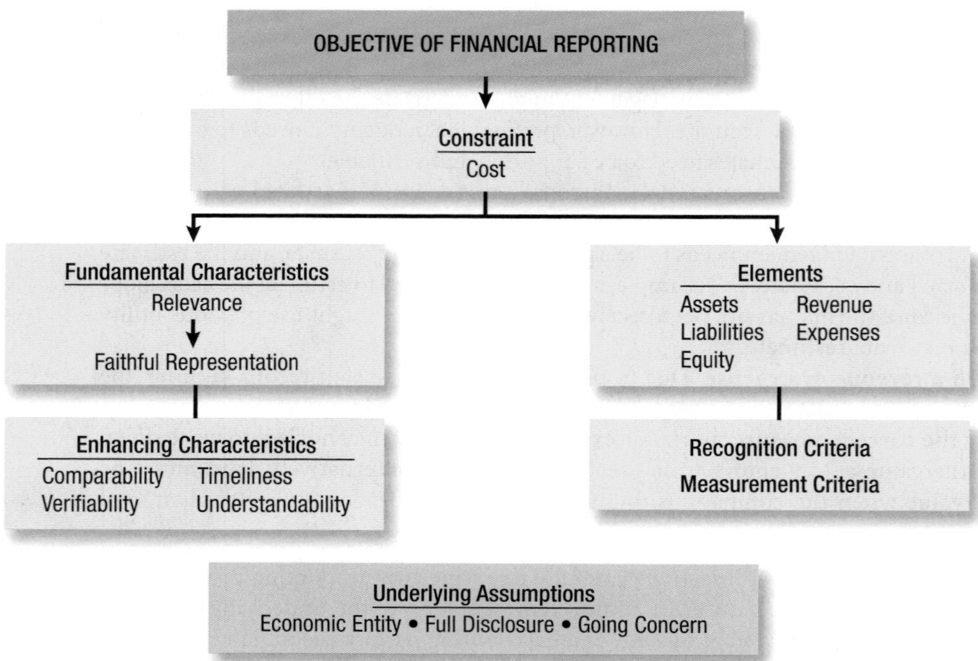

As noted earlier in the chapter, the IASB and FASB continue to work on joint projects to improve the conceptual framework and the revenue recognition criteria. It is anticipated that there will be significant changes to GAAP in the next few years.

BEFORE YOU GO ON...

DO IT

1. For each of the following independent situations, indicate if the revenue should be recognized in 2013 or 2014 and explain why.
   (a) Customer orders widgets on December 15, 2013; widgets are shipped FOB destination on December 24, 2013; customer receives the goods on January 15, 2014.
   (b) Customer orders widgets on December 15, 2013; widgets are shipped FOB shipping point on December 14, 2013; customer receives the goods on January 15, 2014.
   (c) Customer signs a contract, on December 1, 2013, to receive monthly cleaning services. Cleaning services are provided each month from January to December 2014.
   (d) A company ships $100,000 of goods FOB shipping point in the month. The company has a 60-day return policy. Typically, 1% of goods are returned.
2. For each of the following independent situations, indicate if the expense should be recognized in 2013 or 2014 and explain why.
   (a) A company purchases office supplies in December 2013. The supplies are on hand at December 31, 2013, and will be used in 2014.
   (b) A company will pay employees on January 7, 2014, for work performed in December 2013.
   (c) Merchandise inventory with a cost of $50,000 was sold FOB destination on December 28, 2013. Customer received the merchandise on January 10, 2014.
   (d) Equipment with a cost of $75,000 was purchased and installed on December 15, 2013. The equipment has a five-year useful life with no residual value. The company started using the equipment on January 1, 2014.

BEFORE YOU GO ON...
continued on next page

SOLUTION

1. (a) Revenue should be recognized in 2014 as the seller retains ownership until the customer receives the goods.
   (b) Revenue should be recognized in 2013 as ownership of the goods is transferred to the customer when the goods are shipped.
   (c) Revenue should be recognized in 2014 each month as the cleaning service is provided.
   (d) Revenue should be recognized in 2013 as the ownership of the goods has transferred and the company is able to estimate returns. The company would record an allowance for the estimated sales returns and a corresponding liability.
2. (a) Supplies expense should be recognized in 2014 when the supplies are used. At December 31, 2013, the supplies should be reported as an asset because they will provide economic benefit in 2014.
   (b) The salary expense should be recorded in 2013 because the liability Salaries Payable must be recognized in 2013 as the employees provided the service to the company in 2013.
   (c) An expense, cost of goods sold, should be recognized in 2014 when the revenue is recognized. The revenue is recognized in 2014 because ownership transfers when the customer receives the merchandise.
   (d) Depreciation expense will not be recorded in 2013 because the company did not use the equipment during 2013. The economic benefits from the equipment will be realized over five years starting January 1, 2014.

Related exercise material: BE11–7, BE11–8, BE11–9, BE11–10, BE11–11, BE11–12, BE11–13, E11–5, E11–6, E11–7, E11–8, E11–9, and E11–10.

BEFORE YOU GO ON... continued from previous page

Action Plan

- Determine when all the significant risks and rewards of ownership have been transferred to the customer.
- Determine when a service has been provided.
- Determine when an asset has decreased or liability increased that results in a decrease in owners' equity.
- Determine when revenues are recognized for those expenses that should be matched against revenues.
- Determine when the economic benefits are realized for long-lived assets that benefit more than one accounting period.

THE NAVIGATOR

Comparing IFRS and ASPE

Key Differences	International Financial Reporting Standards (IFRS)	Accounting Standards for Private Enterprises (ASPE)
Conceptual framework	Phase one of the IASB and FASB joint project is finalized and adopted (objectives and qualitative characteristics) Remaining phases are still under development	Deferring adoption of the joint project phase one improvements until further progress has been made by the IASB and FASB on the conceptual framework
Constraint	Uses the term "cost constraint"	Uses the term "benefit versus cost constraint"
Definition of elements: gains and losses	Defined as being part of revenues and expenses	Separate definitions for revenues and gains and for expenses and losses
Qualitative characteristics	Identifies two fundamental characteristics: relevance and faithful representation	Identifies four principal characteristics: understandability, relevance, reliability, and comparability Faithful representation is a component of reliability
Conservatism	Not recognized as a qualitative characteristic	Recognized as a qualitative characteristic

THE NAVIGATOR

DEMONSTRATION PROBLEM

Several independent financial reporting situations follow:

1. Young Company recognized sales revenue for a customer order of merchandise inventory that had not yet been shipped.
2. In preparing its financial statements, Casco Company left out information about its depreciation policy.
3. Kenton Company amortized its patent over its legal life of 20 years instead of its estimated economic life of 5 years.
4. Taws Company, a private company reporting under ASPE, reported land that cost $50,000 at its fair value of $100,000.

DEMONSTRATION PROBLEM continued on next page

DEMONSTRATION PROBLEM continued from previous page

5. Aggarwal Company used the cost model in its financial statements that were issued after the company had started liquidation procedures due to bankruptcy. The bankruptcy was not reported in the notes to the financial statements.
6. Yen Yeh Company capitalized the cost and recorded depreciation on its office wastepaper baskets.
7. Mayberry Company used a janitorial service in December to clean its offices. The company recorded the cost of the service when it paid the bill in the following February. Mayberry's year end is December 31.

Instructions

(a) For each of the above situations, indicate the concept (qualitative characteristic, assumption, constraint, recognition criteria, or measurement criteria) in the conceptual framework that has been violated. If there is more than one, list them.

(b) For each situation, provide a brief explanation of how the concept was violated.

Action Plan

- Review the revenue recognition criteria for the sale of goods.
- Review the qualitative characteristics.
- Review the expense recognition criteria.
- Review the measurement criteria.
- Review the underlying assumption of going concern.

SOLUTION TO DEMONSTRATION PROBLEM

(a) Violation	(b) Explanation
1. Revenue recognition criteria	The risks and rewards of ownership have not been transferred to the customer as the goods have not been shipped. Revenue should be recognized when the customer has legal title of the goods.
2. Faithful representation: completeness and comparability	The company should fully disclose information that is relevant to the user. Users would require information on the depreciation policy to enhance comparability with other companies' financial statements. Understanding the depreciation policy may also help users make predictions about the company's future profitability.
3. Expense recognition: matching	The cost of the patent should be allocated to expense over the period for which the company will realize economic benefits.
4. Measurement criteria: cost	The company must use the cost model for financial reporting. The land should be reported at cost.
5. Going concern assumption	If the company is not a going concern, assets should be reported at net realizable value, not cost. There should be a note in the financial statements disclosing that the company is bankrupt.
6. Relevance: materiality	The carrying value of the wastepaper baskets is likely immaterial and therefore is not useful information to the user.
7. Expense recognition	The company has a liability at December 31 for services used during December.

THE NAVIGATOR

Summary of Study Objectives

1. ***Explain the importance of having a conceptual framework of accounting, and list the key components.*** The conceptual framework ensures that there is a consistent and coherent set of accounting standards. Key components of the conceptual framework are the: (1) objective of financial reporting; (2) underlying assumption; (3) cost constraint; (4) elements of financial statements; (5) qualitative characteristics of accounting information; and (6) recognition and measurement criteria.

2. ***Identify and apply the objective of financial reporting, as well as the underlying assumption and cost constraint used by accountants.*** The objective of financial reporting is to provide useful information for investors and creditors in making decisions in their capacity as capital providers. The underlying assumption is that, unless otherwise stated, the financial statements have been prepared using the going concern assumption. The cost constraint exists to ensure the value of the information provided is more than the cost of preparing it.

3. ***Describe the fundamental and enhancing qualitative characteristics of financial reporting.*** The fundamental qualitative characteristics are relevance and faithful representation. Accounting information has relevance if it makes a difference in a decision. Materiality is an important component of relevance. An item is material when it is likely to influence the decision of a reasonably careful investor or creditor. Information

is faithfully represented when it shows the economic reality and is complete, neutral, and free from material error.

The enhancing qualitative characteristics are comparability, verifiability, timeliness, and understandability. Comparability enables users to identify the similarities and differences between companies. The consistent use of accounting policies from year to year is part of the comparability characteristic. Information is verifiable if two knowledgeable and independent people would generally agree that it faithfully represents the economic reality. Timeliness means that accounting information is provided when it is still highly useful for decision-making. Understandability enables reasonably informed users to interpret and comprehend the meaning of the information provided in the financial statements.

4. ***Identify and apply the basic recognition and measurement concepts of accounting.*** The revenue recognition criteria require that revenue be recognized when assets have increased or liabilities have decreased as a result of a transaction with a customer. Expenses are recognized when there is a decrease in an asset or increase in a liability, excluding transactions with owners, which result in a decrease in owners' equity. Three measurements used in accounting are cost, fair value, and amortized cost. Incorrect application of the basic recognition and measurement concepts can lead to material misstatements in the financial statements. Incorrect application can be due to error or intentional misstatement.

THE NAVIGATOR

Glossary

Accrual basis of accounting The method of accounting where revenues are recorded in the period when the transaction occurs and not when cash is received or paid. (p. 469)

Comparability An enhancing qualitative characteristic that accounting information has if it can be compared with the accounting information of other companies because the companies all use the same accounting principles. (p. 465)

Complete The characteristic of accounting information when it provides all information necessary to show the economic reality of the transactions. Completeness is part of the faithful representation fundamental qualitative characteristic of accounting information. (p. 464)

Conceptual framework of accounting A coherent system of interrelated elements that guides the development and application of accounting principles: it includes the objective of financial reporting, assumptions, cost constraint, elements of financial statements, qualitative characteristics of accounting information, and recognition and measurement criteria. (p. 460)

Consistency The use of the same accounting policies from year to year. Consistency is part of the comparability enhancing qualitative characteristic of accounting information. (p. 465)

Cost constraint The constraint that the costs of obtaining and providing information should not be more than the benefits that are gained. (p. 462)

Economic entity concept The concept that the accounting for an economic entity's activities be kept separate and distinct from the accounting for the activities of its owner and all other economic entities. (p. 461)

Elements of financial statements The basic categories in financial statements: assets, liabilities, equity, revenue, and expenses. (p. 462)

Expense recognition criteria The criteria that state that expenses should be recognized when there is a decrease in an asset or increase in a liability, excluding transactions with owners that result in a decrease in owners' equity. (p. 471)

Faithful representation A fundamental qualitative characteristic of accounting information that shows the economic reality of a transaction and not just its legal form. (p. 464)

Full disclosure The accounting concept that recognizes that financial statement information must be complete and requires the disclosure of circumstances and events that make a difference to financial statement users. (p. 467)

Going concern assumption The assumption that the company will continue operating for the foreseeable future; that is, long enough to meet its current objectives and carry out its current commitments. (p. 462)

Material error An error in the accounting information that could impact an investor's or creditor's decision. (p. 465)

Materiality An important component of relevance in which an item is considered material if it is likely to influence the decision of a reasonably careful investor or creditor. (p. 464)

Neutral The characteristic of accounting information when it is free from bias that is intended to attain a predetermined result or to encourage a particular behaviour. Neutrality is part of the faithful representation fundamental qualitative characteristic of accounting information. (p. 464)

Objective of financial reporting The goal of providing useful information for investors and creditors in making decisions in their capacity as capital providers. (p. 461)

Percentage-of-completion method A method of recognizing revenue on a long-term construction or service contract. (p. 471)

Relevance A fundamental qualitative characteristic that accounting information has if it makes a difference in a decision. The information should have predictive and feedback value and be material. (p. 464)

Revenue recognition criteria The criteria that state that revenue should be recognized when there is an increase in assets or decrease in liabilities from profit-generating activities. (p. 469)

Timeliness An enhancing qualitative characteristic that accounting information has if it is provided when it is still highly useful to decision makers. (p. 466)

Understandability An enhancing qualitative characteristic of accounting information that enables reasonably informed users to interpret and comprehend the meaning of the information provided in the financial statements. Understandability is greater when the information is classified, characterized, and presented clearly and concisely. (p. 466)

Verifiability An enhancing qualitative characteristic of accounting information that assures users that the information shows the economic reality of the transaction. (p. 466)

Self-Study Questions

Answers are at the end of the chapter.

(SO 1) K 1. Which of the following is not a reason for having a conceptual framework for financial reporting?
(a) To provide specific rules for every situation in accounting
(b) To ensure that existing standards and practices are clear and consistent
(c) To provide guidance in responding to new issues and developing new standards
(d) To increase financial statement users' understanding of and confidence in the financial statements

(SO 1) K 2. Which of the following is not one of the components of the conceptual framework?
(a) Cost constraint
(b) Specific recommendations for financial statement presentation
(c) Qualitative characteristics
(d) Recognition and measurement concepts

(SO 2) K 3. Which of the following is not information that is required to meet the objective of financial reporting?
(a) Information about the economic resources and claims on the economic resources
(b) Information about the company management's personal economic resources
(c) Information about the changes in economic resources and in claims on the economic resources
(d) Information about the economic performance of the reporting entity

(SO 2) C 4. What is the assumption that financial statements are prepared under that recognizes that the business will continue to operate in the foreseeable future long enough to meet its objectives and carry out its commitments?
(a) Accrual basis of accounting
(b) Economic entity
(c) Going concern
(d) Fair value

(SO 3) K 5. Under IFRS, these qualitative characteristics should be applied in which order?
(a) Relevance, faithful representation, and understandability
(b) Relevance, understandability, and faithful representation
(c) Faithful representation, relevance, and understandability
(d) Understandability, relevance, and faithful representation

(SO 3) K 6. Accounting information faithfully represents an economic event when it is reported
(a) on a timely basis.
(b) on a comparable basis to other companies with the same economic events.
(c) on a consistent basis from year to year.
(d) in a way that portrays the economic reality and not just the legal form of the event.

(SO 3) C 7. An item is considered material when:
(a) it has a value of more than $500.
(b) it affects profits.
(c) not reporting it would influence or change a decision.
(d) it occurs infrequently.

(SO 4) K 8. Which of the following is not a condition that must be met for revenue recognition on the sale of goods?
(a) The seller does not have control over the goods or continuing managerial involvement.
(b) The amount of the revenue can be reliably measured.
(c) Cash is collected.
(d) The seller has transferred to the buyer the significant risks and rewards of ownership.

(SO 4) C 9. Which of the following is not an appropriate time to recognize an expense?
(a) When cash is paid for the purchase of computer equipment
(b) When an expenditure is made that does not qualify for the recognition of an asset
(c) When the cost of computer equipment is allocated over its useful life
(d) When a previously recorded asset no longer has any future benefit

(SO 4) K 10. Which of the following statements about the cost basis of accounting is false?
(a) Cost is relevant for reporting certain assets in the balance sheet because the assets are intended for use in the business and are not going to be sold.
(b) Cost is relevant for reporting all assets on the balance sheet because it is measurable.
(c) Cost is measurable and verifiable.
(d) Cost is not relevant if the business is being liquidated.

THE NAVIGATOR

Questions

(SO 1) C 1. (a) Describe the conceptual framework of accounting and explain how it helps financial reporting. (b) Is the conceptual framework applicable to companies reporting under IFRS, under ASPE, or both?

(SO 2) K 2. (a) What is the main objective of financial reporting? (b) Although there are many users of financial statements, why does this objective identify the *specific users*?

(SO 2) C 3. (a) Briefly describe the going concern assumption. (b) How does the going concern assumption support the use of the cost basis of accounting and the classification of assets and liabilities as current and non-current?

(SO 2) C 4. Describe the cost constraint on financial reporting.

(SO 2) C 5. Jenna believes that the same GAAP should be used by every company, whether large or small and whether public or private. Do you agree? Explain.

(SO 3) K 6. Identify and explain the two fundamental qualitative characteristics of accounting information.

(SO 3) C 7. (a) Briefly describe the concept of materiality. (b) How is materiality related to the qualitative characteristic of relevance?

(SO 3) K 8. Identify and explain the four enhancing qualitative characteristics of accounting information.

(SO 3) K 9. The qualitative characteristics should be applied in a certain order. Identify the order and explain why it matters.

(SO 3) C 10. Identify the differences between the qualitative characteristics identified in the conceptual framework for IFRS and the conceptual framework for ASPE.

(SO 2, 3) C 11. Explain how the cost constraint relates to the quality of completeness.

(SO 3) C 12. The controller of Mustafa Corporation rounded all dollar figures in the company's financial statements to the nearest thousand dollars. "It's not important for our users to know how many pennies we spend," she said. Do you believe rounded financial figures can provide useful information for decision-making? Explain why or why not.

(SO 4) C 13. Why is revenue recognition a difficult concept to apply in practice?

(SO 4) K 14. Describe the general criteria for revenue recognition.

(SO 4) K 15. What are the five conditions that must be met for revenue to be recognized from the sale of goods?

(SO 4) A 16. A customer of JRT Company ordered merchandise inventory on December 15, 2013. The order was packed on December 31 and shipped on January 2, 2014. JRT's year end is December 31. Erin, the accountant, recorded the sales revenue in the December 31, 2013, income statement. She said, "We might as well recognize the revenue at December 31, we know the order was shipped. What difference do a couple of days make?" Do you agree? Explain.

(SO 4) A 17. On March 24, 2014, Greenthumb Landscaping Services received $10,000 for five months of landscaping service to be provided May through September 2014. Greenthumb's year end is April 30. (a) How should the $10,000 received be reported in the April 30, 2014, financial statements? Explain. (b) Assuming Greenthumb prepares monthly financial statements, how should the $10,000 be accounted for from May through September? Explain.

(SO 4) K 18. How is revenue recognized in long-term service and construction contracts?

(SO 4) K 19. Explain how revenue should be recognized if a sales transaction includes both the sale of goods and a service component.

(SO 4) AP 20. A company has a return policy that allows customers to return goods within 30 days of purchase and receive a full refund. Should the company recognize revenue when the goods are sold or when the 30-day return period expires? Explain.

(SO 4) K 21. Describe when expenses should be recognized.

(SO 3, 4) C 22. Explain how the qualitative characteristics of relevance and faithful representation relate to the cost and fair value measurement bases of accounting.

(SO 4) K 23. Identify two situations that might lead management to overstate profits. Identify two ways the profit could be overstated by applying the recognition criteria incorrectly.

Brief Exercises

Identify items included in the conceptual framework. **(SO 1) K**

BE11–1 Indicate which of the following statements are true or false. (Write "T" or "F" beside each item.)

(a) _______ The conceptual framework includes recommendations on how to analyze financial statements.

(b) _______ The conceptual framework identifies the objective of financial reporting.

(c) _______ The conceptual framework is a temporary framework that provides guidance for accountants until standard setters can develop specific rules for every situation.
(d) _______ The conceptual framework defines assets, liabilities, owner's equity, revenue, and expenses.
(e) _______ The conceptual framework provides specific rules for financial statement presentation.
(f) _______ The conceptual framework identifies qualitative characteristics of useful information.
(g) _______ The conceptual framework provides guidance for responding to new issues and developing new standards.

Identify violations of the going concern assumption. (SO 2) C

BE11–2 For each of the following situations, indicate if the going concern assumption has been violated. (Write "Yes" or "No" beside each item.)

(a) _______ A company that is going to continue to operate in the foreseeable future reports all of its assets on the balance sheet at the amount expected to be collected if the assets were sold.
(b) _______ A company that is being liquidated reports current assets, non-current assets, current liabilities, and non-current liabilities on its balance sheet.
(c) _______ A company that is going to operate in the foreseeable future reports its merchandise inventory at cost when the net realizable value is higher than cost.

Identify elements of financial statements. (SO 2) K

BE11–3 Here are the basic elements of financial statements that we learned about in earlier chapters:

1. Assets
2. Liabilities
3. Owner's equity
4. Revenues
5. Expenses

Each statement that follows is an important aspect of an element's definition. Match the elements with the definitions. *Note*: More than one number can be placed in a blank. Each number may be used more than once or not at all.

(a) _______ Increases in assets or decreases in liabilities resulting from the main profit-generating activities of the organization
(b) _______ Existing debts and obligations from past transactions
(c) _______ Resources owned by a business
(d) _______ Goods or services used in the process of earning revenue
(e) _______ A residual claim on total assets after deducting liabilities
(f) _______ The capacity to provide future benefits to the organization

Identify correct application of the cost constraint. (SO 2) AP

BE11–4 For each of the following situations, indicate if it is an example of applying the cost constraint correctly. (Write "Yes" or "No" beside each item.) (*Hint*: Remember that cost constraint and cost represent different concepts.)

(a) _______ The company corrects its financial statements and reissues its annual report after discovering some minor errors in the financial statements.
(b) _______ Inventory is reported at cost when the fair value is higher.
(c) _______ The company expenses small inexpensive office equipment such as pencil sharpeners because of the high cost of tracking the equipment and recording depreciation on it.

Identify qualitative characteristics. (SO 3) K

BE11–5 The following selected items relate to the qualitative characteristics of useful information:

1. Comparability
2. Materiality
3. Neutrality
4. Timeliness
5. Faithful representation
6. Feedback value
7. Predictive value
8. Consistency
9. Understandability
10. Verifiability
11. Complete

Match these qualitative characteristics to the following statements, using numbers 1 to 11.

(a) _______ Accounting information must be available to decision makers before the information loses its ability to influence their decisions.
(b) _______ Accounting information provides a basis to evaluate decisions made in the past.
(c) _______ Accounting information cannot be selected, prepared, or presented to favour one set of interested users over another.
(d) _______ Accounting information reports the economic substance of a transaction, not its legal form.

(e) ________ Accounting information helps reduce uncertainty about the future.
(f) ________ Accounting information must be provided in such a way that knowledgeable and independent people agree that it faithfully represents the economic reality of the transaction or event.
(g) ________ Accounting information about one company can be evaluated in relation to accounting information from another company.
(h) ________ Accounting information is provided in such a way that enables reasonably informed users to interpret and comprehend the meaning of the information provided in the financial statements.
(i) ________ Accounting information in a company is prepared using the same principles and methods year after year.
(j) ________ Accounting information that is insignificant and not likely to influence a decision does not need to be disclosed.
(k) ________ Accounting information includes all information necessary to show the economic reality of the transaction.

BE11–6 Here are some of the accounting concepts relating to the conceptual framework discussed in this chapter:

Identify concepts in the conceptual framework. **(SO 2, 3) C**

1. Going concern assumption
2. Economic entity concept
3. Full disclosure
4. Cost
5. Cost constraint
6. Materiality

Identify by number the accounting assumption, qualitative characteristic, concept, or constraint that describes each situation below. Do not use a number more than once.

(a) ________ is why land is not reported at its liquidation value. (Do not use item 4, cost.)
(b) ________ indicates that personal and business record-keeping should be kept separate.
(c) ________ ensures that all relevant financial information is reported.
(d) ________ requires that GAAP be followed for all significant items.
(e) ________ indicates the value at which an asset is recorded when acquired.

BE11–7 A list of accounting concepts follows:

Identify concepts in the conceptual framework. **(SO 2, 3, 4) C**

1. Revenue recognition
2. Matching
3. Full disclosure
4. Cost
5. Expense recognition
6. Fair value

Match these concepts to the following statements, using numbers 1 to 6.

(a) ________ The Hirjikaka Company reports information about pending lawsuits in the notes to its financial statements.
(b) ________ The Lloyd-Graham Company reduces prepaid insurance to reflect the insurance that has expired.
(c) ________ The Todd Company recognizes revenue at the point of sale, not when the cash is collected.
(d) ________ The Rich Bank reports its short-term investments that are held for resale at market price.
(e) ________ The Hilal Company reports its land at the price it paid for it, not at what it is now worth.
(f) ________ The law firm Thériault, Lévesque, and Picard records an accrual for legal services provided but not yet billed.
(g) ________ The Nickel Company depreciates its mining equipment using the units-of-production method.

BE11–8 Howie, Price, and Liu operate an accounting firm. In March, their staff worked a total of 1,000 hours at an average billing rate of $250 per hour. They sent bills to clients in the month of March that totalled $150,000. They expect to bill the balance of their time in April. The firm's salary costs total $75,000 each month. How much revenue should the firm recognize in the month of March? How much salaries expense?

Determine revenue and expense to be recognized. **(SO 4) AP**

BE11–9 Mullen Manufacturing Ltd. sold $450,000 of merchandise on credit to customers in the month of September. All of the merchandise was sold FOB shipping point. At September 30, $45,000 of the merchandise was in transit. During September, the company collected $250,000 cash from its customers. The company estimates that about 2% of the sales will be returned by customers and that $4,500 of accounts

Determine revenue to be recognized. **(SO 4) AP**

receivable will not be collected. Mullen's allowance for doubtful accounts had a zero balance on September 1. How much revenue should the company recognize for the month of September? Describe how the uncollectible sales and returns by the customers should be accounted for. (*Hint*: Be sure to refer to contra accounts.)

Determine revenue and expenses to be recognized. **(SO 4) AP**

BE11–10 Abbotsford Ltd., a sports equipment wholesaler, sold $350,000 of merchandise to customers during November. The cost of the merchandise shipped was $200,000. All of the merchandise was shipped FOB destination. At November 30, $40,000 of the merchandise was in transit. The cost of the merchandise in transit was $23,000. During November, Abbotsford purchased $90,000 of merchandise inventory and made cash payments for merchandise inventory of $100,000. How much revenue should the company recognize for the month of November? What is the gross profit recognized in November?

Determine revenue to be recognized. **(SO 4) AP**

BE11–11 During December, Willow Appliance Company had sales of $425,000. Included in the sales was $25,000 for extended warranties purchased by customers. No warranty service was provided in December on the appliances sold during December. How much revenue should the company recognize for the month of December? Explain.

Calculate expense. **(SO 4) AP**

BE11–12 Courtney Company reported total operating expenses of $55,000 on its adjusted trial balances for the year ended November 30, 2013. After the preliminary statements were prepared, the accountant became aware of the following situations:

1. The physical inventory count revealed that inventory costing $4,000 was damaged and needed to be scrapped. (*Hint*: Be sure to review the different expense classifications.)
2. Sales staff were owed $2,500 of sales commissions relating to November sales. The sales commissions were paid in December.

Calculate the total operating expenses that should be reported in the November 30, 2013, income statement.

Identify recognition and measurement violations. **(SO 4) AP**

BE11–13 The accountant for Ellery Co., a private company reporting under ASPE, recorded the following journal entries:

1. Land with a cost of $75,000 is reported at its fair value. The following entry was made:

Land	10,000	
Gain on Fair Value Adjustment of Land		10,000

2. Tickets for a musical production were sold in January and the production runs during March. The following entry was recorded in January.

Cash	5,000	
Admission Revenue		5,000

For each journal entry, indicate which recognition or measurement criterion has been violated. Explain.

Exercises

Apply the objective of financial reporting, economic entity concept, and going concern assumption. **(SO 2) AP**

E11–1 The Skate Stop is owned by Marc Bélanger. It sells in-line skates and accessories. It shares rented space with another company, Ride Snowboards. Ride Snowboards is owned by Marc's wife, Dominique Maltais, who was an Olympic bronze medallist in snowboarding. Ride Snowboards sells snowboards and related accessories. The market for in-line skates is growing and Marc wants to expand the amount of inventory The Skate Stop carries. He has asked his bank for a loan to finance the inventory. The bank manager has requested financial statements that are prepared using GAAP.

Instructions

(a) Explain how financial statements will help the bank manager decide whether to lend Marc money for inventory.
(b) Why does the bank manager want the statements to be prepared using GAAP?
(c) Should Marc include Ride Snowboards' financial information in The Skate Stop's financial statements? Explain.
(d) Should Marc report all of the store's assets at cost or what they could be sold for? Explain.

E11–2 Susan began an office cleaning business by investing $5,000 cash and cleaning equipment. Her friend, Voula, recommends that she prepare monthly financial statements.

Discuss financial reporting objective and cost constraint. (**SO 2**) **C**

Instructions

(a) Explain why Voula recommends that she prepare monthly financial statements.
(b) Susan knows that, as a private company, she can choose to follow either ASPE or IFRS. Which one should she choose? Explain.

E11–3 Presented below are selected qualitative characteristics of accounting information.

Identify qualitative characteristics. (**SO 3**) **C**

1. Relevance
2. Neutrality
3. Verifiability
4. Timeliness
5. Faithful representation
6. Comparability
7. Understandability

Instructions

For each of the following situations, indicate which qualitative characteristic was violated.

(a) ________ Allen Ltd. reported its merchandise inventory at a net realizable value of $25,000. The company's auditors disagree with this value and estimated the net realizable value to be $20,000.
(b) ________ Owens Corporation does not issue its annual financial statements for the year ended December 31, 2013, until December 2014.
(c) ________ Silver Mining Ltd. is the only company in the mining industry that uses the straight-line method to depreciate its mining equipment.
(d) ________ Chapman Ltd. switches inventory cost formulas from average to FIFO and back to average in a three-year period.
(e) ________ Enco Ltd. intentionally recorded revenue in 2013 for sales that weren't finalized until 2014 to ensure that management would receive their bonuses, which were based on profits.
(f) ________ World Talk Corporation used terminology in its financial statements and notes to the financial statements that is not commonly used in financial reporting and did not provide explanations of the terminology.
(g) ________ Precise Ltd., a multinational drilling company, reported separately its paper, paper clips, and pens in the balance sheet rather than reporting a single line item for office supplies. Total office supplies were $5,000.
(h) ________ Community Health Foods Ltd. signed a legal agreement to finance the purchase of equipment. The agreement required annual payments of $15,000 for five years. The agreement referred to the payments as rental payments. The company records rent expense when the annual payments are made.

E11–4 Here are some concepts related to the conceptual framework discussed in this chapter:

Identify concepts related to the conceptual framework. (**SO 2, 3**) **C**

1. Going concern assumption
2. Economic entity concept
3. Completeness
4. Cost
5. Cost constraint
6. Materiality

Instructions

Identify by number the concept that describes each situation below. Do not use a number more than once.

(a) ________ Barb Denton runs her accounting practice out of her home. She separates her business records from her household accounts.
(b) ________ The cost to provide financial information should not be more than the benefits.
(c) ________ Significant accounting policies are reported in the notes to the financial statements.
(d) ________ Assets are not stated at their liquidation value. (*Note:* Do not use number 4, Cost.)
(e) ________ Dollar amounts on financial statements are often rounded to the nearest thousand.
(f) ________ Land is recorded at its cost of $100,000 rather than at its market value of $150,000.

E11–5 Several reporting situations follow:

Identify violations of the concepts in the conceptual framework. (**SO 2, 3, 4**) **AP**

1. Thairs Company recognizes revenue during the production cycle. The price of the product and how many items will be sold are not certain.
2. In preparing its financial statements, Sandhu Company left out information about its cost flow assumption for inventories.

3. Martinez Company amortizes patents over their legal life of 20 years instead of their economic (useful) life, which is usually about five years.
4. Ravine Hospital Supply Corporation reports only current assets and current liabilities on its balance sheet. Long-term assets and liabilities are reported as current. The company is unlikely to be liquidated.
5. Barton Company reports inventory on its balance sheet at its current market value of $100,000. The inventory has an original cost of $110,000.
6. Bonilla Company is in its third year of operations and has not yet issued financial statements.
7. Chan Company has inventory on hand that cost $400,000. Chan reports inventory on its balance sheet at its current market value of $425,000.
8. Steph Wolfson, president of the Download Music Company, bought a computer for her personal use. She paid for the computer with company funds and debited the computer account.
9. Sagoo Company decided not to implement a perpetual inventory system that would save $40,000 annually because the cost of the system was $100,000 and it was estimated to have a 10-year life.

Instructions

For each of the above, list what concept in the conceptual framework has been violated, if any.

Identify violation of conceptual framework and correct entries. **(SO 2, 4) AN**

E11–6 Business transactions for Ellis Company and East Air follow:

1. Merchandise inventory worth $50,000 is acquired at a cost of $42,000 from a company going out of business. The following entry is made:

Merchandise Inventory	50,000	
Cash		42,000
Cost of Goods Sold		8,000

2. The president of Ellis Company, Evan Ellis, purchases a computer for personal use and pays for it with his company credit card. The following entry is made:

Office Expense	13,000	
Cash		13,000

3. An asset was recorded for the cost of advertising that appeared on television the previous month. The following entry is made:

Prepaid Advertising	5,000	
Cash		5,000

4. Merchandise inventory with a cost of $280,000 is reported at its fair value of $255,000. The following entry is made:

Cost of Goods Sold	25,000	
Merchandise Inventory		25,000

5. A coffee machine costing $50 is being depreciated over five years. The following adjusting entry is made:

Depreciation Expense	10	
Accumulated Depreciation—Equipment		10

6. East Air sells an airline ticket for $650 in February for a trip scheduled in April. The following entry is made:

Cash	650	
Service Revenue		650

Instructions

In each of the situations above, identify the concept that has been violated, if any. If a journal entry is incorrect, give the correct entry.

Identify point of revenue recognition. **(SO 4) C**

E11–7 The following situations require professional judgement to determine when to recognize revenue from the transactions:

1. Flamingo Airlines sells you a non-refundable airline ticket in September for your flight home at Christmas.
2. Friedman Furniture sells you a home theatre on a no money down, no interest, and no payments for one year promotional deal.

3. The Blue Hawks sell season tickets to their games on-line. Fans can purchase the tickets at any time, although the season doesn't officially begin until April. It runs from April through October.
4. Babineau Company sells merchandise with terms of 2/10, n/30, FOB destination.
5. In September, Confederation College collects tuition revenue for the term from students. The term runs from September through December.
6. The College Bookstore has the following return policy for textbook sales: "Textbooks (new and used) may be returned for seven calendar days from the start of classes. After that time, textbooks (new and used) may be returned within 48 hours of purchase."
7. Computer Company sells computer software. Included in the price of the software is a three-year service contract to update the customer's software.

Instructions
Identify when revenue should be recognized in each of the above situations.

Determine amount of revenue to be recognized. **(SO 4) C**

E11–8 Over the winter months, the Lush Lawns Co. pre-sells fertilizing and weed control lawn services to be performed from May through September, inclusive. If payment is made in full by April 1, a 5% discount is allowed. In March, 350 customers took advantage of the discount and purchased the summer lawn service package for $760 each. In June, 300 customers purchased the package for $800, and in July, 100 purchased it for the same price. For customers who pay after May 1, service starts in the month the customer makes the payment.

Instructions
How much revenue should be recognized by the Lush Lawns Co. in each of the months of March, April, May, June, July, August, and September? Explain.

Determine amount of revenue to be recognized. **(SO 4) AP**

E11–9 Consider the following transactions of the Mitrovica Company, a diversified manufacturing and construction company, for the year ended December 31, 2014:

1. Leased office space to a tenant for a one-year period beginning October 1. Four months of rent at $2,000 per month was received in advance.
2. Received a sales order for merchandise that cost $9,000. It was sold for $16,000 on December 28 to Warfield Company. The goods were shipped FOB shipping point on December 31. Warfield received them on January 3, 2015.
3. Mitrovica introduced a new product into the market. The company shipped new product costing $25,000 to its customers' retail outlets. The customers were billed $50,000 for the product. To promote the product, Mitrovica does not require payment until June 2015 and if Mitrovica's customers do not sell all of the product by June 2015, they can return the unsold product to Mitrovica. The product is new and Mitrovica is uncertain if it will sell.
4. Issued a $5,000, six-month, 4% note receivable on September 1, with interest payable at maturity.
5. Received a sales order from a new customer for $20,000 of merchandise that cost $10,000. The customer was required to prepay the invoice. On December 29, 2014, a cheque for $20,000 was received from the customer. The merchandise was shipped on January 4, 2015.

Instructions
For each item above, indicate the amount of revenue Mitrovica should recognize in 2014. Explain.

Determine amount of expenses to be recognized. **(SO 4) AP**

E11–10 Consider the following events for Reesor Innovations Co. that occurred during 2014.

1. Leased factory space from Whole Properties Company for a one-year period starting November 1, 2014. Six months of rent at $3,000 per month was paid in advance.
2. Incurred $35,000 of research costs for new products. No new products were developed but management believes the research will lead to new products.
3. Used power and water during December for manufacturing. Reesor Innovations Co. will receive the bill in January 2015 and pay it in February 2015. Power and water costs totalling $55,000 have been recorded for the period January 1 to November 30, 2014.
4. New packaging equipment costing $48,000 was installed during November 2014. The equipment was tested in December and will be used for packaging starting in January 2015. The equipment has an estimated useful life of four years and an estimated residual value of $4,000. The company uses straight-line depreciation.

Instructions
For each event, indicate the amount of expense that should be recognized in the 2014 income statement. (*Hint*: Use professional judgement to estimate expense where appropriate.)

Problems: Set A

Comment on the objective of financial reporting and qualitative characteristics. **(SO 2, 3) C**

P11–1A An excerpt from the financial statements of **Reitmans (Canada) Limited** appears in the table below. Note 18, Commitments in the financial statements provides the following information on the future cash payments under lease agreements: "As at January 28, 2012, financial commitments for minimum lease payments under operating leases for retail stores, offices, automobiles and equipment, as well as amounts pertaining to agreements to purchase goods or services that are enforceable and legally binding on the Company, exclusive of additional amounts based on sales, taxes and other costs are payable as follows:"

	Store and Office Operating Leases	Purchase Obligations	Other Operating Leases	Total
Within 1 year	$ 99,202	$102,637	$ 4,498	$206,337
Within 2 years	88,467	326	3,723	92,516
Within 3 years	77,563	117	2,672	80,352
Within 4 years	66,012	—	2,477	68,489
Within 5 years	49,802	—	8	49,810
Subsequent years	89,873	—	—	89,873
Total	$470,919	$103,080	$13,378	$587,377

Instructions

Explain why Reitmans is required to disclose the future cash payments under its commitments. Support your answer with reference to the objective of financial reporting and the qualitative characteristics.

TAKING IT FURTHER In your opinion, which group of creditors would be most interested in this information: short-term or long-term? Explain your reasoning.

Assumptions and concepts—going concern, full disclosure. **(SO 2, 3) AP**

P11–2A During the 2008 and 2009 global economic crisis, several large corporations in both Canada and the United States could not meet their financial commitments and filed for bankruptcy protection. Bankruptcy protection gives companies time to reorganize their operations and financial commitments and to develop a comprehensive restructuring plan, which will allow them to continue to operate. While bankruptcy protection is in place, creditors are prevented from taking any action against the company.

Instructions

(a) What is the potential effect on a company's financial statements if the company files for bankruptcy?
(b) Should companies under bankruptcy protection prepare their statements under the going concern assumption? Explain.

TAKING IT FURTHER Describe the dilemma that a company's management faces in disclosing that a company may not be able to continue as a going concern.

Identify concept or assumption violated and prepare entries. **(SO 2, 3, 4) AN**

P11–3A Czyz and Ng are accountants at Kwick Kopy Printers. Kwick Kopy has not adopted the revaluation model for accounting for its property, plant, and equipment. The accountants are having disagreements over the following transactions during the fiscal year ended December 31, 2014:

1. Kwick Kopy bought equipment on January 1, 2014, for $80,000, including installation costs. The equipment has an estimated useful life of five years. Kwick Kopy depreciates equipment using the double diminishing-balance method. "Since the equipment as installed in our system cannot be removed without considerable damage, it will have no resale value. It should not be depreciated but, instead, expensed immediately," Czyz argues.
2. Depreciation for the year was $43,000. Since the company's profit is expected to be low this year, Czyz suggests deferring depreciation to a year when the profits are higher.
3. Kwick Kopy purchased equipment at a fire sale for $36,000. The equipment would normally have cost $50,000. Czyz believes that the following entry should be made:

Equipment	50,000	
Cash		36,000
Gain on Fair Value Adjustment of Equipment		14,000

4. Czyz says that Kwick Kopy should carry its furnishings on the balance sheet at their liquidation value, which is $30,000 less than cost.
5. Kwick Kopy rented office space for one year, effective September 1, 2014. Six months of rent at $3,000 per month was paid in advance. Czyz believes that the following entry should be made on September 1:

Rent Expense	18,000	
Cash		18,000

6. Land that cost $41,000 was appraised at $60,000. Czyz suggests the following journal entry:

Land	19,000	
Gain on Fair Value Adjustment of Land		19,000

7. On December 15, Kwick Kopy signed a contract with a customer to provide copying services for a six-month period at a rate of $1,500 per month starting January 1, 2015. The customer will pay on a monthly basis. Czyz argues that the contract should be recorded in December because the customer has always paid its bills on time in the past. The customer is legally obligated to pay the monthly amount because a contract has been signed. Czyz believes the following entry should be recorded:

Accounts Receivable	9,000	
Service Revenue		9,000

Ng disagrees with Czyz in each of the situations.

Instructions

(a) For each transaction, indicate why Ng disagrees. Support your answer with reference to the conceptual framework definition of elements, qualitative characteristics, assumption, constraint, recognition, and measurement criteria.
(b) Prepare the correct journal entry to record each transaction.

TAKING IT FURTHER Discuss the circumstances in which it is appropriate to record property, plant, and equipment at its liquidation value.

P11–4A Business transactions for Durkovitch Company from the current year follow. The company has not adopted the revaluation model of accounting for its property, plant, and equipment. The company's year end is December 31.

Identify assumption or concepts and correct entries. **(SO 2, 4) AN**

1. On December 20, an order for $90,000 was received from a customer for products on hand. The customer paid a $10,000 deposit when the order was placed. The order is to be shipped on January 9. The following entry was made on December 20:

Cash	10,000	
Accounts Receivable	80,000	
Sales		90,000

2. Merchandise with a selling price of $78,000 was sold and the customers paid an additional $5,000 for extended warranties. The company has not provided any warranty service on this merchandise yet. The following entry was made:

Cash	83,000	
Sales		83,000

3. The current year had been a very successful one for the company and the company was going to report record high profits. The company recorded $60,000 in additional depreciation expense so that in future years when profits are lower, it can record less depreciation expense. The following entry was made:

Depreciation Expense	60,000	
Accumulated Depreciation		60,000

4. On December 31, merchandise purchased for resale was received. The following entry was made:

Cost of Goods Sold	78,000	
Accounts Payable		78,000

5. Land was purchased on April 30 for $230,000. The company plans to build a warehouse on the land. On December 31, the land would have cost $200,000. The following entry was made:

Loss on Fair Value Adjustment of Land	30,000	
Land		30,000

Instructions

(a) In each of the situations above, identify the assumption or concept that has been violated, if any.
(b) Prepare the journal entry to correct each incorrect transaction identified in part (a), if necessary.

TAKING IT FURTHER Would your answer for item 5. have been different if the Durkovitch Company was a real estate company and the land had been purchased for resale? Explain.

Identify point of revenue recognition. **(SO 4) C**

P11–5A Santa's Christmas Tree Farm, a private company reporting under ASPE, grows pine, fir, and spruce trees. The company cuts and sells the trees for cash during the Christmas season. Most of the trees are exported to the United States. The remaining trees are sold to local tree lot operators.

It normally takes about 12 years for a tree to grow to a good size. The average selling price for a mature tree is $48. The owner of Santa's Christmas Tree Farm believes that the company should recognize revenue at the rate of $4 a year ($48 ÷ 12 years) for each tree that it cuts. The biggest cost of this business is the cost of fertilizing, pruning, and maintaining the trees over the 12-year period. These costs average $40 a tree and the owner believes they should also be spread over the 12-year period.

Instructions

Do you agree with the proposed revenue recognition policy for Santa's Christmas Tree Farm? Explain why or why not. Use the revenue recognition criteria to explain your argument for when the revenue should be recognized for this tree-farming business.

TAKING IT FURTHER Explain how the costs of fertilizing, pruning, and maintaining the trees should be recorded.

Calculate revenue, cost of goods sold, and gross profit. **(SO 4) AP**

P11–6A Mustang Company reported $1.2 million net sales and $635,000 cost of goods sold for the 11 months ended November 30, 2014. Mustang offers a full refund for any merchandise returned within 30 days of sale. Additional information for the month of December is as follows:

1. Refunds paid to customers totalled $20,000. All merchandise was returned to inventory. The cost of the merchandise returned was $10,600.
2. Sales to customers were $125,000 and the cost of the merchandise sold was $66,250.
3. Included in the $125,000 of sales was $12,000 for merchandise shipped FOB destination on December 31, 2014. The customers received the goods on January 5, 2015. The cost of the merchandise shipped on December 31, 2014, was $6,300.
4. The company estimates that during January 2015, it will refund customers $11,000 and that the estimated cost of the inventory returned will be $5,800. These estimated returns relate to the December sales. Normally, returned merchandise is returned to inventory.
5. Mustang's year end is December 31 and the company prepares adjusting journal entries annually.

Instructions

Calculate the net sales, cost of goods sold, and gross profit that Mustang will report in its income statement for the year ended December 31, 2014.

TAKING IT FURTHER How would your response change if the merchandise returned in December and anticipated to be returned in January is not returned to inventory for resale? Explain.

Revenue recognition criteria—sale of goods. **(SO 4) AP**

P11–7A Dave's Deep Discount Furniture Store opened for business on October 1, 2012. To promote the store and develop a loyal customer base, customers could buy furniture with no money down and no payments for 12 months. Customers wishing to take advantage of the special promotion were required to pass a thorough credit check. Of the customers from October 1 to December 31, 2012, most of the customers took advantage of the special promotion; the other customers paid for the furniture in full when it was delivered. Total sales from October 1 to December 31, 2012, were $325,000, of which $250,000 was for customers who chose to delay payment for 12 months. Of the remaining $75,000 of sales, $60,000 worth had been delivered to the customers by December 31, 2012, and the remaining $15,000 would be delivered in January 2013. The accountant for the store made the following entry to record the sales.

Accounts Receivable	15,000	
Cash	60,000	
Sales Revenue		75,000

Dave, the owner, disagreed with the accountant and argued that sales revenue of $325,000 should be recorded in 2012.

Instructions

(a) Identify the revenue recognition criteria that must be met before revenue is recorded for the sale of goods.

(b) Identify the critical factors relating to the Dave's Deep Discount Furniture Store's sales transactions that should be considered in determining how much revenue should be recognized.

(c) Indicate the amount of revenue that should be recognized for the period October 1 to December 31, 2012.

TAKING IT FURTHER Would your response to part (c) be different if the customers were not required to pass a thorough credit check? Explain why or why not.

P11–8A Kamloops Company is a grocery wholesaler and is planning to expand its operations. The company has asked the bank for a loan to finance the expansion. Alphonzo, the company's manager, has prepared the preliminary financial statements. The preliminary financial statements for the year ended December 31, 2014, reported the following:

Identify the objective of financial reporting, identifying elements, and revenue and expense recognition. **(SO 2, 4) AP**

Current assets	$120,000
Current liabilities	80,000
Net sales	560,000
Cost of goods sold	252,000
Total operating expenses	106,000

The bank has requested that Kamloops have an independent professional accountant review the statements. You have been asked to review the statements and during your review you have discovered the following:

1. Kamloops's inventory supplier shipped $15,000 of inventory to Kamloops on December 31, 2014, FOB shipping point. Alphonzo indicated that he did not record the inventory for the year ended December 31, 2014, because it was not received until January 2, 2015.
2. Included in net sales and accounts receivable was $8,400 for merchandise ordered by a customer that was packed and in the warehouse. The customer indicated that they might pick it up on January 10, 2015. The customer will pay for the merchandise within 30 days of pick up. The cost of the merchandise was $4,300 and was included in inventory because the merchandise was still in Kamloops's warehouse.
3. Kamloops offers its customers a full refund for merchandise returned within 15 days of purchase. Sales recorded from December 17 to December 31 were $26,000. Typically, about 5% of sales are returned. The returned goods are scrapped and not returned to inventory. Alphonzo said that "customers had not returned any merchandise from the December 17 to December 31 sales by the company's year end. Any returns from these sales will be recorded in January when the merchandise is returned and the company knows the exact amount of the returns."
4. During the last week of December, the company had run a promotional campaign in the local newspaper. The cost of the campaign was $3,500. Alphonzo recorded it as a prepaid expense because he anticipates that January 2015 sales will be higher as a result of the campaign.

Instructions

(a) Explain how financial statements help the bank with its decision on whether or not to lend money to Kamloops.

(b) Explain why the bank has requested an independent review of the financial statements.

(c) Calculate the correct amounts for current assets, current liabilities, net sales, cost of goods sold, and total operating expenses. Explain each of your corrections.

TAKING IT FURTHER Calculate the current ratio based on (a) the preliminary financial statements and (b) the corrected amounts. Is the current ratio based on the corrected amounts better or worse? Does there appear to be bias in the types of errors that were made? Explain.

CONTINUING COOKIE CHRONICLE

(*Note:* This is a continuation of the Cookie Chronicle from Chapters 1 through 10.)

Natalie's high school friend, Katy Peterson, has been operating a bakery called The Baker's Nook for approximately 10 months. Natalie and Katy usually meet once a month to catch up and discuss problems they have encountered while operating their respective businesses. Katy wishes to borrow from her bank so she can purchase a new state-of-the-art oven. She recognizes that the bank will be evaluating her financial statements.

Katy has recently negotiated a one-year contract with Coffee to Go to provide 1,500 cinnamon buns every week. Coffee to Go, upon receipt of a monthly invoice, will send Katy a cheque by the 15th of the following month. Katy has decided that, because she has signed this contract, she is able to record as revenue in her financial statements the contracted revenue that she is about to earn over the next 12 months.

When Katy negotiated the contract with Coffee to Go, she purchased additional baking supplies to meet the increased demand for cinnamon buns. She has decided that she will not record the purchase of these supplies until the invoice is due, which is in about 30 days. She argues that the amount to be paid for the purchase of baking supplies is relatively small and the amount won't really make much of a difference to the bank when it makes its decision.

Katy assures Natalie that this is the right way to account for this revenue and the purchase of additional baking supplies. She is now sure that the bank will lend her the money that she needs to purchase this new oven.

Natalie is confused and comes to you with the following questions:

1. Is Katy accounting for this revenue correctly?
2. Is Katy accounting for the purchase of the baking supplies correctly?
3. What other information will the bank be considering when deciding whether or not to extend the loan to Katy?
4. Do you think that Katy is being honest when she identifies this revenue as being earned on her income statement?

Instructions

(a) Answer Natalie's questions.
(b) How should Katy be recording this revenue? Why?
(c) How should Katy be recording the purchase of baking supplies? Why?
(d) How could Katy offer the bank proof of this contractual arrangement with Coffee to Go when it reads her financial statements?

Cumulative Coverage—Chapters 6 to 11

Johan Company and Nordlund Company are competing businesses. Both began operations six years ago and they are quite similar. The current balance sheet data for the two companies are as follows:

	Johan Company	Nordlund Company
Cash	$ 70,300	$ 48,400
Accounts receivable	309,700	312,500
Allowance for doubtful accounts	(13,600)	0
Merchandise inventory	463,900	520,200
Property, plant, and equipment	255,300	257,300
Accumulated depreciation	(112,650)	(189,850)
Total assets	$972,950	$948,550
Current liabilities	$440,200	$436,500
Non-current liabilities	78,000	80,000
Total liabilities	518,200	516,500
Owner's equity	454,750	432,050
Total liabilities and owner's equity	$972,950	$948,550

You have been hired as a consultant to do a review of the two companies. Your goal is to determine which one is in a stronger financial position. Your review of their financial statements quickly reveals that the two companies have not followed the same accounting policies. The differences, and your conclusions, are summarized below:

1. Johan Company has had good experience in estimating its uncollectible accounts. A review shows that the amount of its write offs each year has been quite close to the allowances the company provided.

   Nordlund Company has been somewhat slow to recognize its uncollectible accounts. Based on an aging analysis and review of its accounts receivable, it is estimated that $20,000 of its existing accounts will become uncollectible.
2. Johan Company has determined the cost of its merchandise inventory using the average inventory cost formula. The result is that its inventory appears on the balance sheet at an amount that is slightly below its current replacement cost. Based on a detailed physical examination of its merchandise on hand, the current replacement cost of its inventory is estimated at $477,000.

   Nordlund Company has used the FIFO inventory cost formula. The result is that its ending inventory appears on the balance sheet at an amount that is close to its current replacement cost.
3. Johan Company estimated a useful life of 12 years and a residual value of $30,000 for its property, plant, and equipment, and has been depreciating them on a straight-line basis. Nordlund Company has the same type of property, plant, and equipment. However, it estimated a useful life of 10 years and a residual value of $10,000. It has been depreciating its property, plant, and equipment using the double diminishing-balance method.

   Based on engineering studies of these types of property, plant, and equipment, you conclude that Nordlund's estimates and method for calculating depreciation are more appropriate.

Instructions

(a) Where would you find the above information on the two companies' accounting policies? Be specific about what information would be available and where you would find it.

(b) Using similar accounting policies for both companies, revise the balance sheets presented above.

(c) Has preparing the revised statements in part (b) improved the quality of the accounting information for the two companies? If so, how?

BROADENING YOUR PERSPECTIVE — CHAPTER 11

Collaborative Learning Activity

Note to instructor: Additional instructions and material for this group activity can be found on the Instructor Resource Site and in *WileyPLUS*.

BYP11–1 In this group activity, you will be given a set of financial statements and a list of items that might need correcting. You will be required to (a) decide if an adjusting journal entry is required, (b) justify your decision by referring to the conceptual framework (including revenue and expense recognition criteria), and (c) calculate profit. Your decisions may have an impact on the annual bonuses that senior management members hope to receive.

Communication Activity

BYP11–2 Junk Grrlz (Junk) is a wholesale distributor of goods. Junk purchases goods that are not selling from manufacturers and other wholesalers and sells them to discount retail outlets. You are a professional accountant and are preparing Junk's financial statements for the year ended September 30, 2014. The company had $300,000 of real animal fur coats in inventory that were not selling. Junk has not had an order for real fur coats for over a year. The president is reluctant to write off the inventory and consequently signed a sales agreement with Cheap But Good (Cheap). Cheap agreed to buy the coats for $350,000 and could return any coats that it had not sold by December 31, 2014. In addition, Cheap was not required to pay Junk for the coats until December 31, 2014. The coats were shipped to and received by Cheap on September 29, 2014.

Instructions

Write a memo to the president of Junk Grrlz answering the following questions:

(a) When should revenue be recognized on the fur coats sold to Cheap But Good? Explain.
(b) How should the fur coats be reported in Junk's financial statements for the year ended September 30, 2014? Explain.

Ethics Case

BYP11–3 When the IASB and AcSB issue new accounting recommendations, the required implementation date (the date when a company has to start applying the recommendations) is usually 12 months or more after the date of publication. For example, in October 2010, the IASB issued new recommendations for classifying and reporting investments: companies are required to implement the new recommendations for fiscal years starting January 1, 2015. This allows companies some time to change their accounting procedures. Nevertheless, early implementation is usually encouraged for those who are able to do so, because new rules are intended to provide better representation of the company's financial performance and position.

Carol DesChenes, an accountant at Grocery Online, discusses with her vice-president of finance the need for early implementation of a recently issued recommendation. She says it will result in a much more faithful representation of the company's financial position. When the vice-president of finance determines that early implementation will have a negative impact on the profits reported for the year, he strongly discourages Carol from implementing the recommendation until it is required.

Instructions

(a) Who are the stakeholders in this situation?
(b) What, if any, are the ethical considerations in this situation?
(c) What could Carol gain by supporting early implementation? Who might be affected by the decision against early implementation?

All About You: Personal Financial Literacy Activity

BYP11–4 In the "All About You" feature, you learned about the importance of your personal resumé being a faithful representation of your personal background, education, and experience.

To apply this concept further, assume that you are applying for a car loan. The loan application requires that you prepare two reports: (1) a projected cash budget and (2) information about your assets and liabilities. The information in the loan application will be used to determine if the bank manager will approve the loan or not.

Instructions

(a) Why would a bank manager ask you to complete a projected cash budget and provide information about your assets and liabilities in order to decide whether or not to approve your loan? What is the bank manager trying to determine about you?
(b) Describe the qualitative characteristics the information you provide to the bank manager should have for this information to be useful to the bank manager.
(c) The cash budget will primarily be based on future cash inflow and outflows. How might a bank manager verify the reasonableness of the cash budget?
(d) What might be the consequences to you if the bank manager determines the information provided is misleading?

ANSWERS TO CHAPTER QUESTIONS

ANSWERS TO ACCOUNTING IN ACTION INSIGHT QUESTIONS

All About You Insight, p. 468

Q: What may be the consequences to you if you misrepresent yourself on your resumé?

A: If it is determined that you have misrepresented yourself on your resumé, your credibility will be damaged. If your employer determines that you misrepresented yourself, you may lose your job, or at the very least your employer may always question your trustworthiness. You may also find yourself in a job for which you are not qualified and therefore your reputation will be damaged because of your inability to perform to the level required. In addition, it may be difficult for you to get a good reference from your employer when you apply for jobs in the future.

Ethics Insight, p. 473

Q: Accountants are often required to make estimates when preparing financial statements. What is the difference between what Nortel allegedly did and what we would normally expect an accountant to do when estimating accruals for adjusting journal entries?

A: When an accountant makes estimates in the financial statements, these estimates should be made using professional judgement and the best information available at the time to arrive at a reasonable estimate. Differences between these types of estimates and actual amounts are considered to be part of the accounting process. In the case of Nortel, it was accused of not using professional judgement to arrive at the best estimate but intentionally misstating the accruals in the financial statements for the company's benefit. The judge found that the accounting practices were not fraudulent or were not material.

ANSWERS TO SELF-STUDY QUESTIONS

1. a 2. b 3. b 4. c 5. a 6. d 7. c 8. c 9. a 10. b

Remember to go back to the beginning of the chapter to check off your completed work! ←

CHAPTER 12

ACCOUNTING FOR PARTNERSHIPS

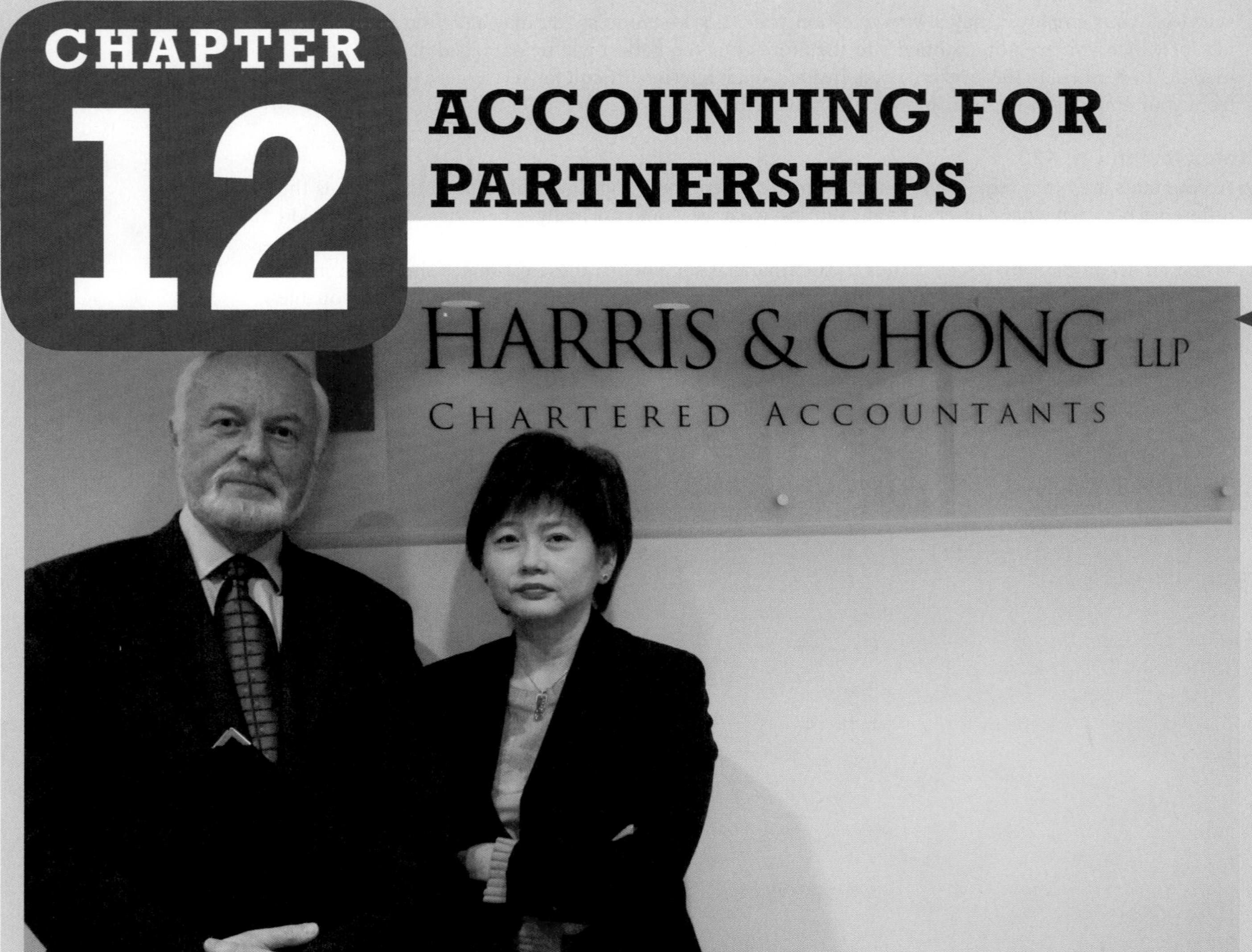

THE NAVIGATOR

- ☐ Understand *Concepts for Review*
- ☐ Read *Feature Story*
- ☐ Scan *Study Objectives*
- ☐ Read *Chapter Preview*
- ☐ Read text and answer *Before You Go On*
- ☐ Review *Comparing IFRS and ASPE*
- ☐ Work *Demonstration Problem*
- ☐ Review *Summary of Study Objectives*
- ☐ Answer *Self-Study Questions*
- ☐ Complete assignments

CONCEPTS FOR REVIEW

Before studying this chapter, you should understand or, if necessary, review:

A. The different forms of business organization. (Ch. 1, pp. 8–9)
B. The cost principle of accounting. (Ch. 1, p. 16)
C. The statement of owner's equity. (Ch. 1, pp. 23–24)
D. How to make closing entries. (Ch. 4, pp. 147–150)
E. The steps in the accounting cycle. (Ch. 4, p. 153)
F. The classified balance sheet. (Ch. 4, pp. 156–164)

JOINING FORCES FOR SUCCESS

TORONTO, ON—The benefit of strength in numbers is what leads some professionals to form partnerships to provide complementary skills to serve the market, and to gain a larger base of clients. A partnership agreement is crucial. It states how the partners, as part owners of the firm, will contribute time, expertise, and money and share in profits and losses. The agreement also states what will happen when a partner leaves the firm or the partnership is wound up.

Harris & Chong LLP is a Toronto-based accounting firm. The "LLP" stands for "limited liability partnership." The partners in a limited liability partnership are not personally liable for the negligent acts of another partner or an employee who is directly supervised by another partner, explains Sonja Chong.

Ms. Chong joined as a junior partner in 1991 when the firm was known as Braithwaite & Harris, after founding partners Bruce Braithwaite and Peter Harris. The firm has ranged from two to four partners, and has consisted of Mr. Harris and Ms. Chong since 2007. Each time a partner leaves or joins, the partnership agreement is amended to adapt to their circumstances. "Partnerships and partners are subject to change from time to time," Ms. Chong says. "You have to be flexible."

Under the firm's partnership agreement, generally a new partner does not have to contribute any equity, but may have to lend money to the partnership to meet operating needs until he or she starts to collect fees from clients. What most partners contribute is their list of clients, so if Harris & Chong admitted another partner, it would likely be a chartered accountant with a strong client base. The firm would also consider admitting junior partners if they had a different or complementary area of expertise the firm could expand upon, or hiring a senior accountant who could be groomed to eventually become a partner.

Peter Harris says that there are many ways of allocating partnership profits. Some partnerships share profits based on a predetermined percentage of the partnership's profit while others may allocate profits proportionately to the revenue each partner generates from their own clients. In the latter situation, costs for things such as rent and staff could be based on a formula that allocates costs in an equitable manner. Of course, formulas can be changed depending on the circumstances.

What happens when a partner leaves? "The most crucial thing that should exist in a partnership agreement is how to divvy things up when you part," Ms. Chong says. Generally, a departing partner would take his or her clients and the balance of his or her capital account represented by accounts receivable and work in progress relating to those clients, less a proportionate share of the firm's liabilities. They could also be required to pay a fair amount to the firm for any office equipment that they may wish to take upon leaving. "In an accounting firm, the most valuable asset is really your clients. Furniture and computers are generally not worth very much," Mr. Harris adds.

THE NAVIGATOR

STUDY OBJECTIVES

After studying this chapter, you should be able to:

1. Describe the characteristics of the partnership form of business organization.
2. Account for the formation of a partnership.
3. Allocate and record profit or loss to partners.
4. Prepare partnership financial statements.
5. Account for the admission of a partner.
6. Account for the withdrawal of a partner.
7. Account for the liquidation of a partnership.

THE NAVIGATOR

PREVIEW OF CHAPTER TWELVE

It is not surprising that Bruce Braithwaite and Peter Harris decided to use the partnership form of organization when they started their accounting practice. They saw an opportunity to combine their expertise and better leverage their resources. In this chapter, we will discuss why the partnership form of organization is often chosen. We will also explain the major issues in accounting for partnerships.

The chapter is organized as follows:

Accounting for Partnerships

Partnership Form of Organization	Basic Partnership Accounting	Admission and Withdrawal of Partners	Liquidation of a Partnership
▶ Characteristics of partnerships ▶ Advantages and disadvantages of partnerships ▶ Partnership agreement	▶ Forming a partnership ▶ Dividing partnership profit or loss ▶ Partnership financial statements	▶ Admission of a partner ▶ Withdrawal of a partner	▶ No capital deficiency ▶ Capital deficiency

PARTNERSHIP FORM OF ORGANIZATION

STUDY OBJECTIVE 1
Describe the characteristics of the partnership form of business organization.

All provinces in Canada have a partnership act that sets out the basic rules for forming and operating partnerships. These acts define a **partnership** as a relationship between people who do business with the intention of making a profit. This does not necessarily mean that there must be a profit—just that profit is the objective. Partnerships are common in professions such as accounting, advertising, law, and medicine. Professional partnerships can vary in size from two partners to thousands.

CHARACTERISTICS OF PARTNERSHIPS

The main characteristics of the partnership form of business organization are shown in Illustration 12-1. They are explained after the illustration.

ILLUSTRATION 12-1
Partnership characteristics

Association of Individuals

Unlimited Liability

Co-Ownership of Property

Mutual Agency

Division of Profit

Limited Life

Association of Individuals

The association of two or more individuals in a partnership can be based on an act as simple as a handshake. However, it is much better to have a legal, written agreement that outlines the rights and obligations of the partners, as in the feature story. Partners who have not put their agreement in writing have found that the absence of a written agreement can sometimes cause later difficulties. In fact, some partnership acts state that if you receive a share of profit from a business, you will be considered a partner in the business unless there is contrary evidence. If there is no formal agreement that says who the partners of a business are, you may be part of a partnership without knowing it!

A partnership is a legal entity for certain purposes. For instance, property (land, buildings, and equipment) can be owned in the name of the partnership. The firm can sue or be sued. A partnership is also an accounting entity for financial reporting purposes. Thus, the personal assets, liabilities, and transactions of the partners are kept separate from the accounting records of the partnership, just as they are in a proprietorship.

However, a partnership is not taxed as a separate entity. It must file an information tax return that reports the partnership's profit and each partner's share of that profit. Each partner must then report his or her share of the partnership profit on their personal income tax returns. The partner's profit is taxed at his or her personal income tax rate, and does *not* depend on how much money the partner withdrew from the partnership during the year.

Helpful hint Partners are taxed on their share of the partnership profits, not their drawings.

Co-Ownership of Property

Partnership assets are owned *jointly* by the partners. If the partnership is dissolved, an asset does not legally return to the partner who originally contributed it. The assets are normally sold and the partners share any gain or loss on disposition according to their profit and loss ratios. After partnership liabilities are paid, each partner then has a claim on any cash that remains: the claim is equal to the balance in the partner's capital account. The specifics of accounting for the liquidation of a partnership are covered later in this chapter.

Similarly, if, in doing business, a partner invests a building in the partnership that is valued at $100,000 and the building is later sold at a gain of $20,000, that partner does not receive the entire gain. The gain becomes part of the partnership profit, which is shared among the partners, as described in the next section.

Division of Profit

Just as property is co-owned, so is partnership profit (or loss). The partners specify how the partnership profit (loss) will be divided when they form the partnership. As explained in the feature story, this can be changed later depending on the circumstances. If the division is not specified, profit (loss) is assumed to be shared equally. We will learn more about dividing partnership profit in a later section of this chapter.

Limited Life

A partnership does not have an unlimited life. Any change in ownership ends the existing partnership. There is a **partnership dissolution** whenever a partner withdraws or a new partner is admitted. When a partnership is dissolved, this does not necessarily mean that the business ends. If the continuing partners agree, operations can continue without any interruption by forming a new partnership.

Mutual Agency

Mutual agency means that each partner acts for the partnership when he or she does partnership business. The action of any partner is binding on all other partners—in other words, the action cannot be cancelled by one of them. This is true even when partners exceed their authority, as long as the act looks appropriate for the partnership. For example, a partner of an accounting firm who purchases a building that is suitable for the business creates a binding contract in the name of the partnership. On the other hand, if a partner in a law firm decides to buy a snowmobile for the partnership, the act would not be binding on the partnership, because the purchase is unrelated to the business.

Unlimited Liability

Each partner is jointly and severally (individually) liable for all partnership liabilities. If one partner incurs a liability, the other partners are also responsible for it. For repayment, creditors first have claims on the partnership assets. If there are not enough assets to pay back the creditors, however, they can then claim the personal assets of any partner, regardless of that partner's equity in the partnership. Because each partner is responsible for all the debts of the partnership, each partner is said to have **unlimited liability**.

Unlimited liability and mutual agency can combine for disastrous results. An unethical or incompetent partner can commit the partnership to a deal that eventually bankrupts the partnership. The creditors may then be able to claim the partners' personal assets—the assets of all the partners, not just those of the partner who made the bad deal. Consequently, an individual must be extremely cautious in choosing a partner.

Because of concerns about unlimited liability, there are now special forms of partnership organization that modify liability. These include limited partnerships and limited liability partnerships, discussed in the next two sections.

Limited Partnerships (LP).

In a **limited partnership**, or "LP," one or more of the partners have unlimited liability. This type of partner is called a *general partner*. A general partner normally contributes work and experience to the partnership and is authorized to manage and represent the partnership. The general partner's liability for the partnership's debts is unlimited.

The other partner(s) have limited liability for the partnership's debts. This type of partner is called a *limited partner*. Limited partners normally give cash or assets to the partnership, but not services. The amount of debt that the limited partner is liable for in the partnership is limited to the amount of capital that he or she contributed to the partnership. In other words, a limited partner's personal assets cannot be sold to repay any partnership debt that is more than the amount that he or she contributed to the partnership.

Helpful hint A limited partner's role is similar to that of an investor as opposed to someone who takes a day-to-day role in the partnership.

A limited partnership is identified in its name with the words "Limited Partnership" or the abbreviation "LP." Limited partnerships are normally used by businesses that offer income tax shelters for investors, such as real estate investment trusts, rental properties, and sports ventures.

Limited Liability Partnerships (LLP).

Most professionals, such as lawyers, doctors, and accountants, form a **limited liability partnership** or "LLP." As noted in the feature story, Harris & Chong operates as a limited liability partnership.

A limited liability partnership is designed to protect innocent partners from the acts of other partners that result in lawsuits against the partnership. That is, partners in an LLP continue to have *unlimited liability for their own negligence* but have *limited liability for other partners' negligence.* In addition to being liable for their own actions, partners are also liable for the actions of employees whom they directly supervise and control.

ADVANTAGES AND DISADVANTAGES OF PARTNERSHIPS

Why do people choose partnerships? Harris & Chong formed a partnership in part to provide complementary skills to serve the market, and to gain a larger base of clients. The two partners can also divide among themselves different areas of responsibility and expertise—assurance, taxation, and business valuation, for example.

A partnership is easily formed and is controlled by fewer government regulations and restrictions than a corporation is. Also, decisions can be made quickly on important matters that affect the firm. This is also true in a proprietorship, but not in a corporation, where some decisions have to be approved by the board of directors.

Partnerships also have some disadvantages: mutual agency, limited life, and unlimited liability in general partnerships. Unlimited liability is the biggest disadvantage. Many individuals fear they may lose not only their initial investment but also their personal assets if those assets are needed to pay partnership creditors. As a result, partnerships often have difficulty getting large amounts of investment capital. That is one reason why the largest businesses in Canada are corporations, not partnerships.

The advantages and disadvantages of the general partnership form of business organization are summarized below.

Advantages	Disadvantages
• Combines skills and resources of two or more individuals	• Mutual agency
• Easily formed	• Limited life
• Fewer government regulations and restrictions than corporations	• Unlimited liability
• Easier decision-making	

PARTNERSHIP AGREEMENT

Ideally, when two or more individuals agree to organize a partnership, their agreement should be expressed as a written contract. Called a **partnership agreement**, this contract contains such basic information as the name and main location of the firm, the purpose of the business, and the date of inception (formation). In addition, relationships among the partners must be specified, such as:

1. The names and capital contributions of partners
2. The rights and duties of partners
3. The basis for sharing profit or loss
4. Provisions for a withdrawal of assets
5. Procedures for submitting disputes to arbitration
6. Procedures for the withdrawal, or addition, of a partner
7. The rights and duties of surviving partners if a partner dies
8. Procedures for the liquidation of the partnership

The importance of a written contract cannot be overemphasized. As discussed in our feature story, for Harris & Chong, a partnership agreement is crucial. If there is no partnership agreement, the provisions of the partnership act will apply, and they may not be what the partners want. For example, as previously discussed, profits and losses are shared equally in the absence of an agreement. The partnership agreement should be written with care so that it considers all possible situations, contingencies, and future disagreements between the partners. In addition, a partnership agreement that is carefully planned reduces ethical conflict among partners. It specifies, in clear language, the process for solving ethical and legal problems, which is especially important when the partnership is in financial distress.

BEFORE YOU GO ON...

DO IT

Answer the following true or false questions:

1. A partnership may be based on a handshake.
2. A partnership is not an accounting entity for financial reporting purposes.
3. A partner pays income tax on the amount of money he or she withdrew from the partnership during the year.
4. Mutual agency means that each partner acts for the partnership when he or she does partnership business.
5. When a partner exceeds his or her authority, and the act looks appropriate for the partnership, the act is not binding on the other partners and the partnership.
6. A partnership has unlimited life.
7. Each partner is jointly and severally liable for all of the partnership liabilities.
8. In a limited partnership, the amount of partnership debt that a limited partner is liable for is limited to the amount of capital that he or she has contributed to the partnership.

SOLUTION

1. T	5. F
2. F	6. F
3. F	7. T
4. T	8. T

Related exercise material: BE12–1, BE12–2, and E12–1.

Action Plan

- Review characteristics of partnerships.

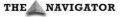

BASIC PARTNERSHIP ACCOUNTING

We now turn to the basic accounting for partnerships. Accounting for a partnership is very similar to accounting for a proprietorship. Just as most proprietorships will choose to use Accounting Standards for Private Enterprises (ASPE), many partnerships are private and will also choose to follow these accounting standards. On the other hand, Limited Partnerships are often public enterprises and these partnerships will follow International Financial Reporting Standards (IFRS). In addition, some large professional partnerships are international and these partnerships must also follow IFRS.

There are three accounting issues where there are some differences between partnerships and proprietorships: formation of a partnership, dividing the partnership profit or loss, and preparing partnership financial statements. There are no significant differences in the accounting for these issues between partnerships following ASPE or IFRS. We will examine each of these in the following sections.

FORMING A PARTNERSHIP

STUDY OBJECTIVE 2
Account for the formation of a partnership.

Each partner's initial investment in a partnership is entered in the partnership records. **These investments should be recorded at the assets' fair value at the date of their transfer to the partnership.** The values used must be agreed to by all of the partners.

To illustrate, assume that M. Gagnon and K. Singh combine their proprietorships on January 2 to start a partnership named Interactive Software. Gagnon and Singh each have the following assets before forming the partnership:

	M. Gagnon		K. Singh	
	Book Value	**Fair Value**	**Book Value**	**Fair Value**
Cash	$ 8,000	$ 8,000	$ 9,000	$ 9,000
Accounts receivable			4,000	4,000
Allowance for doubtful accounts			(700)	(1,000)
Equipment	5,000	4,000		
Accumulated depreciation	(2,000)			
	$11,000	$12,000	$12,300	$12,000

The entries to record the investments in the partnership are:

A	=	L	+	OE
+8,000				+12,000
+4,000				

↑Cash flows: +8,000

A	=	L	+	OE
+9,000				+12,000
+4,000				
−1,000				

↑Cash flows: +9,000

	Investment of M. Gagnon		
Jan. 2	Cash	8,000	
	Equipment	4,000	
	M. Gagnon, Capital		12,000
	To record investment of Gagnon.		
	Investment of K. Singh		
2	Cash	9,000	
	Accounts Receivable	4,000	
	Allowance for Doubtful Accounts		1,000
	K. Singh, Capital		12,000
	To record investment of Singh.		

Helpful hint The fair value of the noncash assets at the date of acquisition becomes the cost of these assets to the partnership. The fair value is what the assets would have cost if they had been purchased at that time. Although the assets aren't new, they are new to the partnership.

Note that neither the original cost of Gagnon's equipment ($5,000) nor its accumulated depreciation ($2,000) is recorded by the partnership. Instead, the equipment is recorded at its fair value of $4,000. Because the equipment has not yet been used by the partnership, and the partnership has not recorded any adjusting entries, there is no accumulated depreciation.

In contrast, Singh's gross claims on customers ($4,000) are carried into the partnership. The allowance for doubtful accounts is adjusted to $1,000 to arrive at a net realizable value of $3,000. A partnership may start with an allowance for doubtful accounts, because it will continue to track and collect existing accounts receivable and some of these are expected to be uncollectible. In addition, this procedure maintains the control and subsidiary relationship between Accounts Receivable and the accounts receivable subsidiary ledger that we learned about in Chapter 8.

After the partnership has been formed, the accounting for transactions is similar to the accounting for any other type of business organization. For example, all transactions with outside parties, such as the performance of services and payment for them, should be recorded in the same way for a partnership as for a proprietorship.

The steps in the accounting cycle that are described in Chapter 4 for a proprietorship are also used for a partnership. For example, a partnership journalizes and posts transactions, prepares a trial balance, journalizes and posts adjusting entries, and prepares an adjusted trial balance. However, there are minor differences in journalizing and posting closing entries and in preparing financial statements, as explained in the following sections. The differences occur because there is more than one owner.

Helpful hint The contra asset account Allowance for Doubtful Accounts is brought into the new business because it represents an estimate of *future* uncollectible receivables. The contra asset Accumulated Depreciation reflects *past* data that *do not* relate to the current partnership.

BEFORE YOU GO ON...

DO IT

On June 1, Eric Brown and Erik Black decide to organize a partnership, E&E Painting. Eric Brown contributes equipment with a cost of $5,000 and $2,000 of accumulated depreciation. Erik Black contributes accounts receivable of $1,200. Eric and Erik agree that the equipment has a fair value of $2,500 and the accounts receivable a net realizable value of $1,000. Erik Black will also contribute the amount of cash required to make his investment equal to Eric Brown's. (a) How much cash must Erik Black contribute? (b) Prepare the journal entries to record their investments in the partnership.

SOLUTION

(a) Fair value of equipment contributed by Eric Brown	$2,500
Less: fair value of accounts receivable contributed by Erik Black	1,000
Cash investment required from Erik Black	$1,500

(b) July 1	Equipment	2,500	
	E. Brown, Capital		2,500
	To record investment of Eric Brown.		
1	Cash	1,500	
	Accounts Receivable	1,200	
	Allowance for Doubtful Accounts		200
	E. Black, Capital		2,500
	To record investment of Erik Black.		

Related exercise material: BE12–3, BE12–4, and E12–2.

Action Plan

- Use fair values for the assets invested in the partnership.
- Each partner's equity is equal to the fair value of the net assets he invested in the partnership.

THE NAVIGATOR

DIVIDING PARTNERSHIP PROFIT OR LOSS

STUDY OBJECTIVE 3

Allocate and record profit or loss to partners.

Partners are not employees of the partnership; *they are its owners*. If a partner works for the partnership, it is to earn profit, not to earn a salary. Thus, as in a proprietorship, when partners withdraw assets from the business, these amounts are called drawings, and are not expenses. In order to track each partner's equity in the business, it is necessary to create a separate drawings account for each partner.

To illustrate, assume that the partners of Interactive Software, M. Gagnon and K. Singh, had cash drawings of $8,000 and $6,000, respectively, for the year ended December 31, 2014. The journal entries (shown in summary format for the year) to record the partners' drawings are:

Dec. 31	M. Gagnon, Drawings	8,000	
	Cash		8,000
	Gagnon's withdrawal of cash for personal use.		
31	K. Singh, Drawings	6,000	
	Cash		6,000
	Singh's withdrawal of cash for personal use.		

A	=	L	+	OE
−8,000				−8,000

↓Cash flows: −8,000

A	=	L	+	OE
−6,000				−6,000

↓Cash flows: −6,000

Alternative terminology The profit and loss ratio is sometimes called the *profit ratio*, or the *income and loss ratio*.

Each partner's share of the partnership's profit or loss is determined according to the partnership's **profit and loss ratio**. This basis for division is usually the same for both profit and losses. As you will see in the following discussion, the profit and loss ratio can be a simple ratio or a more complicated calculation to recognize the different contributions of service and capital by each partner. If the profit and loss ratio is not specified in the partnership agreement, profit and losses are shared equally among the partners.

The partnership's profit or loss is divided between the partners during the process of closing the temporary accounts and updating the capital accounts. In the following sections, we will first review closing entries. We will then illustrate closing entries when profit and loss is shared equally. This is followed by more complex profit and loss ratios and the related closing entries.

Closing Entries

As in a proprietorship, there are four entries to prepare closing entries for a partnership:

Helpful hint Recall that the use of T accounts is recommended to avoid making errors while preparing closing entries.

1. To close revenue accounts: Debit each revenue account for its balance and credit Income Summary for total revenues.
2. To close expense accounts: Debit Income Summary for total expenses and credit each expense account for its balance.
3. To close Income Summary: Debit Income Summary for its balance (which should equal the profit amount) and credit each partner's capital account for his or her share of profit. Conversely, credit Income Summary and debit each partner's capital account for his or her share of a loss.
4. To close drawings: Debit each partner's capital account for the balance in that partner's drawings account, and credit each partner's drawings account for the same amount.

The first two entries are the same as in a proprietorship, as shown in Chapter 4, and are not shown in this chapter. The last two entries are different from those closing entries in a proprietorship because (1) it is necessary to divide profit (or loss) among the partners, and (2) there are two or more owners' capital and drawings accounts (an individual capital and individual drawings account for each partner).

To illustrate the last two closing entries, we will assume that Interactive Software has a profit of $32,000 for the year and that the partners, M. Gagnon and K. Singh, share profit and loss equally. Recall that drawings for the year were $8,000 for Gagnon and $6,000 for Singh. The closing entries on December 31 are as follows:

A	=	L	+	OE
				−32,000
				+16,000
				+16,000

Cash flows: no effect

A	=	L	+	OE
				−8,000
				−6,000
				+8,000
				+6,000

Cash flows: no effect

Date	Account	Debit	Credit
Dec. 31	Income Summary	32,000	
	M. Gagnon, Capital ($32,000 × 50%)		16,000
	K. Singh, Capital ($32,000 × 50%)		16,000
	To close profit to capital accounts.		
31	M. Gagnon, Capital	8,000	
	K. Singh, Capital	6,000	
	M. Gagnon, Drawings		8,000
	K. Singh, Drawings		6,000
	To close drawings accounts to capital accounts.		

Recall from the previous section that both Gagnon and Singh had made investments in the partnership of $12,000 at the beginning of the year. After posting the closing entries, the capital and drawing accounts will appear as shown below:

M. Gagnon, Capital

Date		Debit	Date		Credit
Dec. 31	**Clos.**	**8,000**	Jan. 2		12,000
			Dec. 31	**Clos.**	**16,000**
			Dec. 31	Bal.	20,000

K. Singh, Capital

Date		Debit	Date		Credit
Dec. 31	**Clos.**	**6,000**	Jan. 2		12,000
			Dec. 31	**Clos.**	**16,000**
			Dec. 31	Bal.	22,000

M. Gagnon, Drawings

Date		Debit	Date		Credit
Dec. 31		8,000	Dec. 31	**Clos.**	**8,000**
Dec. 31	Bal.	0			

K. Singh, Drawings

Date		Debit	Date		Credit
Dec. 31		6,000	Dec. 31	**Clos.**	**6,000**
Dec. 31	Bal.	0			

As in a proprietorship, the partners' capital accounts are permanent accounts, and their drawings accounts are temporary accounts.

Profit and Loss Ratios

As Peter Harris noted in our feature story, there are many ways of allocating partnership profits. The partners may share profit and loss equally, or the partnership agreement may specify a more complex basis for sharing profit or loss. The following are typical profit and loss ratios:

1. A fixed ratio, expressed as a proportion (2:1), a percentage (67% and 33%), or a fraction ($^2/_3$ and $^1/_3$)
2. A ratio based either on capital balances at the beginning or end of the year, or on average capital balances during the year
3. Salary allowances to partners and the remainder in a fixed ratio
4. Interest allowances on partners' capital balances and the remainder in a fixed ratio
5. Salary allowances to partners, interest allowances on partners' capital balances, and the remainder in a fixed ratio

Helpful hint It is often easier to work with fractions or percentages (both are equally effective) than proportions when allocating profit or loss. When converting to a fraction, determine the denominator for the fractions by adding the proportions, then use the appropriate proportion to determine each partner's fraction. For example, (2:1) converts to $^2/_3$ and $^1/_3$; (3:5) converts to $^3/_8$ and $^5/_8$; and for three partners using (3:2:1), these proportions convert to $^3/_6$, $^2/_6$, and $^1/_6$.

In each case, the goal is to share profit or loss in a way that fairly reflects each partner's capital investment and service to the partnership.

A fixed ratio is easy to use, and it *may* be a fair basis in some circumstances. Assume, for example, that Hughes and Sami are partners. Each contributes the same amount of capital, but Hughes expects to work full-time in the partnership, while Sami expects to work only half-time. Accordingly, the partners agree to a fixed ratio of two thirds to Hughes and one third to Sami. Note, however, that Hughes would also have to absorb two thirds of any *loss* suffered by the partnership.

A ratio that is based on capital balances may be the right choice when the funds invested in the partnership are the critical factor. Capital balances may also be fair when a manager is hired to run the business and the partners do not plan to take an active role in daily operations. In this case, the partners are essentially investors in the partnership, so the amount of each individual partner's investment is the key consideration in dividing profits fairly.

The three remaining kinds of profit and loss ratios (items 3, 4, and 5 in the list above) recognize specific differences among the partners. These ratios give salary allowances for time worked and interest allowances for capital invested. Any remaining profit or loss is divided using a fixed ratio.

Salary allowances to partners and interest allowances on partners' capital balances are not expenses of the partnership. They are also **not** distributions of cash—partners' drawings are the distributions of cash or other assets. Salary and interest allowances are used only in the calculations that divide profit or loss among partners. In a partnership, as with other companies, salary expense is the cost of services performed by employees. Likewise, interest expense is the cost of borrowing from creditors. As owners, **partners are neither employees nor creditors**.

Helpful hint Note that the Cash account balance is not changed at all during the process of closing the accounts in a proprietorship or a partnership. The purpose of preparing closing entries is to close the temporary accounts and update the capital balances, not distribute any cash.

The only relationship between salary allowances and cash withdrawals is that under some partnership agreements, partners are allowed to make monthly cash withdrawals based on their salary allowance. But in such cases, as with all withdrawals, the withdrawals are debited to each partner's drawings account, *not to salary expense.*

Salaries, Interest, and Remainder in a Fixed Ratio

In three of the profit- and loss-sharing ratios, salary and/or interest allowances must be allocated before the remainder of the profit is divided according to a fixed ratio. This is true even if the salary and/or interest allowances are more than profit. It is also true even if the partnership has suffered a loss for the year. The same basic method of dividing (or allocating) profit or loss is used if there is only a salary allowance, or if there is only an interest allowance, or if both are used. In the illustration that follows, we will use a profit and loss ratio that includes both salary and interest allowances before allocating the remainder (see item 5 from the list of ratios above).

Assume that Sylvie King and Ray Lee are partners in the Kingslee Company. The partnership agreement specifies (1) salary allowances of $8,400 for King and $6,000 for Lee, (2) interest allowances of 5% on capital balances at the beginning of the year, and (3) the remainder to be allocated equally. Capital balances on January 1, 2014, were King $28,000 and Lee $24,000. In 2014, partnership profit is $22,000. The division of profit for the year is shown in Illustration 12-2.

Helpful hint The total of the amounts allocated to each partner must equal the profit or loss. This also ensures that the third closing entry (debiting Income Summary and crediting the capital accounts in a profit situation) is balanced.

ILLUSTRATION 12-2
Division of profit when profit exceeds allowances

KINGSLEE COMPANY Division of Profit Year Ended December 31, 2014			
	S. King	**R. Lee**	**Total**
Profit			$22,000
Salary allowance			
S. King	$ 8,400		
R. Lee		$6,000	
Total			14,400
Profit remaining for allocation			7,600
Interest allowance			
S. King ($28,000 × 5%)	1,400		
R. Lee ($24,000 × 5%)		1,200	
Total			2,600
Profit remaining for allocation			5,000
Fixed ratio (*remainder shared equally*)			
S. King ($5,000 × 50%)	2,500		
R. Lee ($5,000 × 50%)		2,500	
Total			5,000
Profit remaining for allocation			0
Profit allocated to the partners	**$12,300**	**$9,700**	**$22,000**

The entry to record the division of profit is:

A	=	L	+	OE
				−22,000
				+12,300
				+9,700

Cash flows: no effect

Dec. 31	Income Summary	22,000	
	S. King, Capital		12,300
	R. Lee, Capital		9,700
	To transfer profit to partners' capital accounts.		

Let's now look at a situation where the salary and interest allowances are *greater than* profit. Assume that Kingslee Company reports profit of $14,000. In this case, the salary and interest allowances create a deficiency of $3,000 ($14,000 − $14,400 − $2,600). This deficiency is divided equally among the partners as in Illustration 12-3.

ILLUSTRATION 12-3
Division of profit when allowances exceed profit

KINGSLEE COMPANY Division of Profit Year Ended December 31, 2014			
	S. King	**R. Lee**	**Total**
Profit			$14,000
Salary allowance			
S. King	$8,400		
R. Lee		$6,000	
Total			14,400
Profit (deficiency) remaining for allocation			(400)
Interest allowance			
S. King ($28,000 × 5%)	1,400		
R. Lee ($24,000 × 5%)		1,200	
Total			2,600
Profit (deficiency) remaining for allocation			(3,000)

ILLUSTRATION 12-3
(continued)
Division of profit when allowances exceed profit

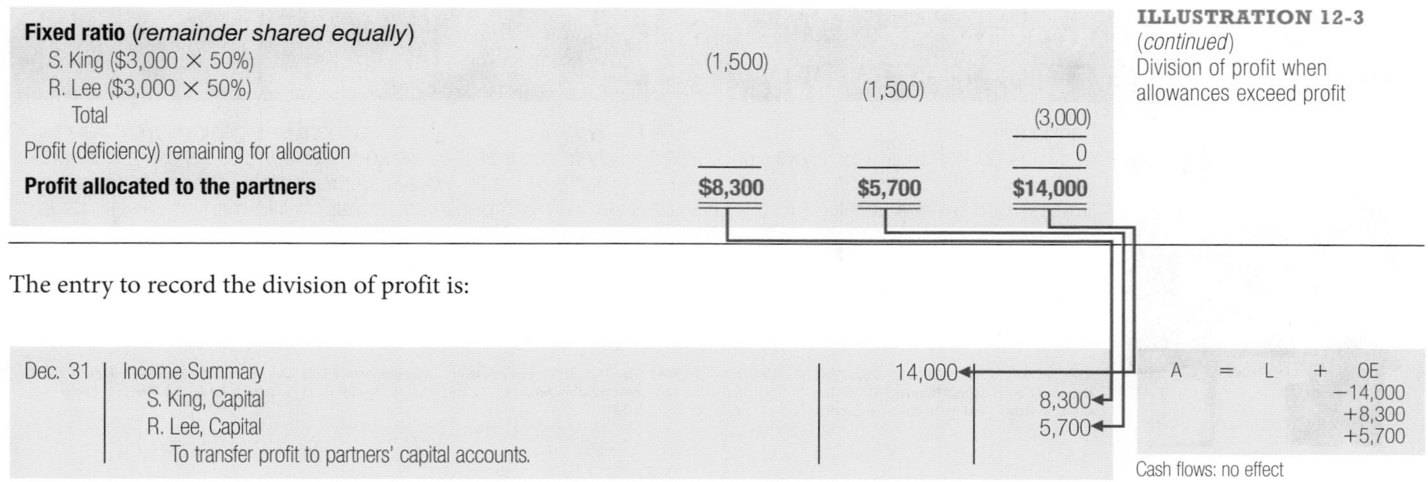

Fixed ratio *(remainder shared equally)*			
S. King ($3,000 × 50%)	(1,500)		
R. Lee ($3,000 × 50%)		(1,500)	
Total			(3,000)
Profit (deficiency) remaining for allocation			0
Profit allocated to the partners	**$8,300**	**$5,700**	**$14,000**

The entry to record the division of profit is:

Date	Account	Debit	Credit
Dec. 31	Income Summary	14,000	
	S. King, Capital		8,300
	R. Lee, Capital		5,700
	To transfer profit to partners' capital accounts.		

A	=	L	+	OE
				−14,000
				+8,300
				+5,700

Cash flows: no effect

Note that in this situation, the partnership *has not suffered a loss*. A profit was earned but it wasn't large enough to cover the salary and interest provisions set out in the partnership agreement. Therefore, the remainder is negative.

Let's now look at a situation where there is a loss. Assume that Kingslee Company reports a loss of $18,000. The salary and interest allowances are still allocated first. After the salary and interest allowances, there is a deficiency of $35,000 ($18,000 + $14,400 + $2,600). The deficiency is then divided equally among the partners as in Illustration 12-4.

ILLUSTRATION 12-4
Division of loss

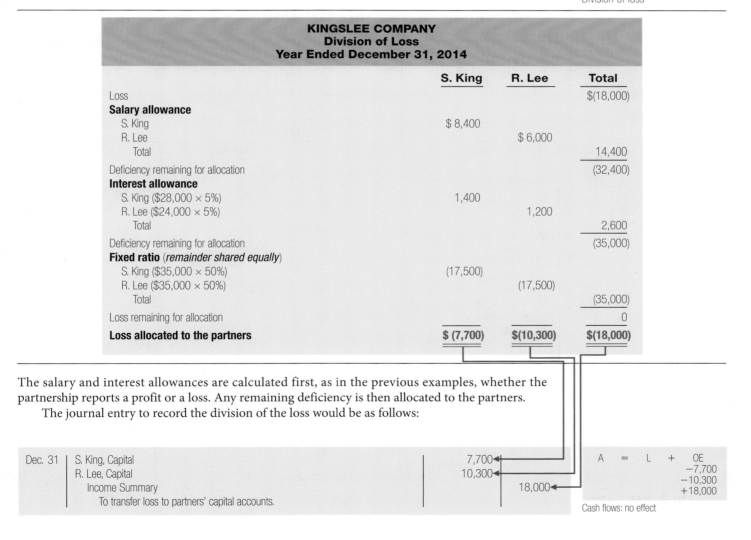

KINGSLEE COMPANY
Division of Loss
Year Ended December 31, 2014

	S. King	**R. Lee**	**Total**
Loss			$(18,000)
Salary allowance			
S. King	$ 8,400		
R. Lee		$ 6,000	
Total			14,400
Deficiency remaining for allocation			(32,400)
Interest allowance			
S. King ($28,000 × 5%)	1,400		
R. Lee ($24,000 × 5%)		1,200	
Total			2,600
Deficiency remaining for allocation			(35,000)
Fixed ratio *(remainder shared equally)*			
S. King ($35,000 × 50%)	(17,500)		
R. Lee ($35,000 × 50%)		(17,500)	
Total			(35,000)
Loss remaining for allocation			0
Loss allocated to the partners	**$ (7,700)**	**$(10,300)**	**$(18,000)**

The salary and interest allowances are calculated first, as in the previous examples, whether the partnership reports a profit or a loss. Any remaining deficiency is then allocated to the partners.

The journal entry to record the division of the loss would be as follows:

Date	Account	Debit	Credit
Dec. 31	S. King, Capital	7,700	
	R. Lee, Capital	10,300	
	Income Summary		18,000
	To transfer loss to partners' capital accounts.		

A	=	L	+	OE
				−7,700
				−10,300
				+18,000

Cash flows: no effect

ACCOUNTING IN ACTION
ACROSS THE ORGANIZATION

Partners in public accounting firms can make big incomes. A few senior partners in large firms may earn as much as $1 million a year. However, a 2013 study found that the average total compensation of partners in Canadian accounting firms of all sizes was around $248,000, while sole proprietors of these accounting firms earned an average total of $133,000 a year. The compensation of partners in many partnerships is similar to the compensation of a proprietor in a proprietorship. Like proprietors, partners are not guaranteed an annual salary—compensation depends entirely on each year's operating results, which could be positive (profit) or negative (loss). Also, a large investment is required of each partner. This capital is at risk for the partner's entire career—often 25 to 30 years—and there is no rate of return on it. Upon leaving, the partner is simply repaid the investment without any adjustment for inflation or increase in value.

Sources: QRI International, "2013 CPA Profession Compensation Study Report," Chartered Professional Accountants Canada, December 2013; Denise Dickins, Thomas G. Noland, and Kenneth M. Washer, "Primer on Partnership-Compensation Models," *The CPA Journal*, August 2005; Michael J. Anderson, "Partner Compensation: Systems Used in Professional Services Firms," Edge International, 2001.

How is the profit earned by a partner in an accounting partnership different from the earnings of a staff accountant in the same partnership?

BEFORE YOU GO ON...

DO IT

LeMay Company reports profit of $72,000 for the year ended May 31, 2014. The partnership agreement specifies (1) salary allowances of $30,000 for L. Leblanc and $24,000 for R. May, (2) an interest allowance of 4% based on average capital account balances, and (3) sharing any remainder on a 60:40 basis (60% to Leblanc, 40% to May). Average capital account balances for the year were $40,000 for Leblanc and $30,000 for May. (a) Prepare a schedule dividing the profit between the two partners. (b) Prepare the closing entry for profit.

SOLUTION

Action Plan

- First allocate the salary allowances and the interest allowances.
- Then apply the partners' fixed ratios to divide the remaining profit or the deficiency.
- In the closing entry, distribute profit or loss among the partners' capital accounts according to the profit and loss ratio.

(a)

LEMAY COMPANY
Division of Profit
Year ended May 31, 2014

	L. Leblanc	R. May	Total
Profit			$72,000
Salary allowance			
L. Leblanc	$30,000		
R. May		$24,000	
Total			54,000
Profit remaining for allocation			18,000
Interest allowance			
L. Leblanc ($40,000 × 4%)	1,600		
R. May ($30,000 × 4%)		1,200	
Total			2,800
Profit remaining for allocation			15,200
Fixed ratio (*remainder shared 60:40*)			
L. Leblanc (60% × $15,200)	9,120		
R. May (40% × $15,200)		6,080	
Total			15,200
Profit remaining for allocation			0
Profit allocated to the partners	$40,720	$31,280	$72,000

(b)

May 31	Income Summary	72,000	
	L. Leblanc, Capital		40,720
	R. May, Capital		31,280
	To close profit to partners' capital accounts.		

THE NAVIGATOR

Related exercise material: BE12–5, BE12–6, BE12–7, BE12–8, BE12–9, E12–3, and E12–4.

PARTNERSHIP FINANCIAL STATEMENTS

STUDY OBJECTIVE 4
Prepare partnership financial statements.

The financial statements of a partnership are very similar to those of a proprietorship. The differences are due to the additional owners involved in a partnership.

The income statement for a partnership is identical to the income statement for a proprietorship. The division of the partnership profit or loss is not an additional financial statement. It is simply a schedule that shows how the profit or loss was allocated to the partners. It is often disclosed as a separate schedule or in a note to the statement.

The statement of equity for a partnership is called the **statement of partners' equity**. Its function is to explain the changes in each partner's individual capital account and in total partnership capital during the year. As in a proprietorship, changes in capital may result from three causes: additional investments by owners, drawings, and each partner's share of the profit or loss.

The statement of partners' equity for Kingslee Company is shown in Illustration 12-5. It is based on the division of $22,000 of profit in Illustration 12-2. The statement includes assumed data for the investments and drawings.

ILLUSTRATION 12-5
Statement of partners' equity

KINGSLEE COMPANY
Statement of Partners' Equity
Year Ended December 31, 2014

	S. King	R. Lee	Total
Capital, January 1	$28,000	$24,000	$52,000
Add: Investments	2,000	0	2,000
Profit	12,300	9,700	22,000
	42,300	33,700	76,000
Less: Drawings	7,000	5,000	12,000
Capital, December 31	**$35,300**	**$28,700**	**$64,000**

The statement of partners' equity is prepared from the income statement and the partners' capital and drawings accounts.

The balance sheet for a partnership is the same as for a proprietorship, except for the equity section. In a proprietorship, the equity section of the balance sheet is called owner's equity. A one-line capital account is reported for the owner. In a partnership, the capital balances of each partner are shown in the balance sheet, in a section called partners' equity. The partners' equity section in Kingslee Company's balance sheet appears in Illustration 12-6.

ILLUSTRATION 12-6
Partners' equity section of a partnership balance sheet

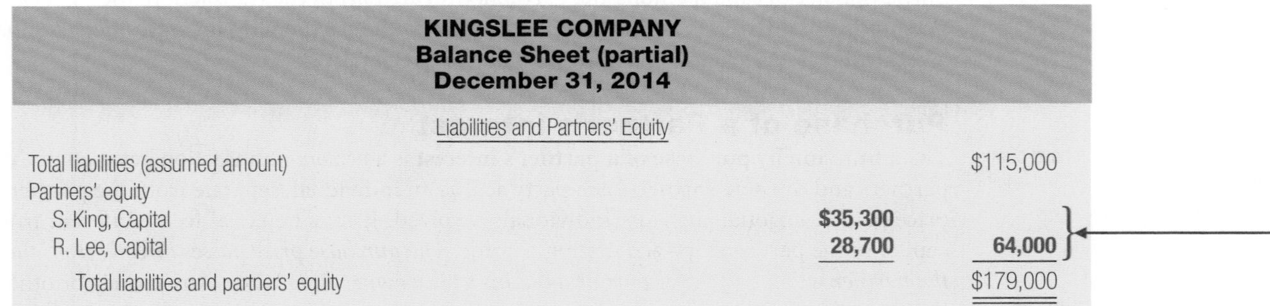

KINGSLEE COMPANY
Balance Sheet (partial)
December 31, 2014

Liabilities and Partners' Equity

Total liabilities (assumed amount)		$115,000
Partners' equity		
S. King, Capital	**$35,300**	
R. Lee, Capital	**28,700**	**64,000**
Total liabilities and partners' equity		$179,000

It is impractical for large partnerships to report each partner's equity separately. For reporting purposes, these amounts are usually aggregated (combined) in the balance sheet.

 **BEFORE YOU GO ON...**

DO IT

The capital accounts of Mindy Dawson and Rania Alam, partners in the Best Skate Company, had balances of $80,000 and $95,000, respectively, on January 1, 2014. During the year, Dawson invested an additional $15,000 and each partner withdrew $50,000. Profit for the year was $150,000 and was shared equally between the partners. Prepare a statement of partners' equity for the year ended December 31, 2014.

Action Plan

- Each partner's capital account is increased by the partner's investments and profit, and decreased by the partner's drawings.
- Allocate profit between the partners according to their profit-sharing agreement.

SOLUTION

BEST SKATE COMPANY
Statement of Partners' Equity
Year Ended December 31, 2014

	M. Dawson	R. Alam	Total
Capital, January 1	$ 80,000	$ 95,000	$175,000
Add: Investments	15,000	0	15,000
Profit	75,000	75,000	150,000
	170,000	170,000	340,000
Less: Drawings	50,000	50,000	100,000
Capital, December 31	$120,000	$120,000	$240,000

THE NAVIGATOR

Related exercise material: BE12–10, E12–5, and E12–6.

ADMISSION AND WITHDRAWAL OF PARTNERS

STUDY OBJECTIVE 5
Account for the admission of a partner.

We have seen how the basic accounting for a partnership works. We now look at how to account for something that happens often in partnerships: the addition or withdrawal of a partner.

ADMISSION OF A PARTNER

The admission of a new partner legally dissolves the existing partnership and begins a new one. From an economic standpoint, the admission of a new partner (or partners) may have only a minor impact on the continuity of the business. For example, in large public accounting or law firms, partners are admitted without any change in operating policies. To recognize the economic effects, it is only necessary to open a capital account for each new partner. In most cases, the accounting records of the old partnership will continue to be used by the new partnership.

A new partner may be admitted by either (1) purchasing all or part of the interest of an existing partner or partners, or (2) investing assets in the partnership. The purchase of a partner's interest involves only a transfer of capital among the partners who are part of the transaction: the total capital of the partnership is not affected. The investment of assets in the partnership increases both the partnership's net assets (total assets less total liabilities) and its total capital.

Purchase of a Partner's Interest

Helpful hint In a purchase of an interest, the total assets and equity in the partnership will not change. No cash is contributed to the partnership.

Helpful hint In this sense, the word "interest" refers to a partner's share in the ownership of the partnership. It does not refer to the interest that would accrue on a note or a loan.

The **admission by purchase of a partner's interest** is a *personal* transaction between one or more existing partners and the new partner. Each party acts as an individual, separate from the partnership entity. The price paid is negotiated by the individuals involved. It may be equal to or different from the partner's capital in the partnership's accounting records. *The purchase price passes directly from the new partner to the partner who is giving up part or all of his or her ownership claims.* Any money or other consideration that is exchanged is the personal property of the participants and not the property of the partnership.

Accounting for the purchase of an interest is straightforward. In the partnership, only the transfer of a partner's capital is recorded. The old partner's capital account is debited for the ownership claims that have been given up. The new partner's capital account is credited with the ownership interest purchased. Total assets, total liabilities, and total capital remain unchanged, as do all individual asset and liability accounts.

To illustrate, assume that on July 1, L. Carson agrees to pay $8,000 each to two partners, D. Arbour and D. Baker, for one third of their interest in the ABC partnership. At the time of Carson's admission, each partner has a $30,000 capital balance. Both partners, therefore, give up $10,000 ($^1/_3 \times$ $30,000) of their capital. The entry to record the admission of Carson is as follows:

July 1	D. Arbour, Capital	10,000	
	D. Baker, Capital	10,000	
	L. Carson, Capital		20,000
	To record admission of Carson by purchase.		

A	=	L	+	OE
				−10,000
				−10,000
				+20,000

Cash flows: no effect

Note that the cash paid by Carson is not recorded by the partnership because it is paid personally to Arbour and Baker. The entry above would be exactly the same regardless of the amount paid by Carson for the one-third interest. If Carson pays $12,000 each to Arbour and Baker for one third of their interest in the partnership, the above entry is still made.

The effect of this transaction on the partners' capital accounts is as follows:

D. Arbour, Capital				D. Baker, Capital				L. Carson, Capital			
		Bal.	30,000			Bal.	30,000				
July 1	**10,000**			July 1	**10,000**					July 1	**20,000**
		Bal.	20,000			Bal.	20,000			Bal.	20,000

Each partner now has a $20,000 ending capital balance and total partnership capital is $60,000 ($20,000 + $20,000 + $20,000). Net assets (assets − liabilities) and total partners' capital remain unchanged. Arbour and Baker continue as partners in the firm, but the capital interest of each has been reduced from $30,000 to $20,000.

Investment of Assets in a Partnership

The admission of a partner by an investment of assets in the partnership is a transaction between the new partner and the partnership. It is sometimes referred to simply as **admission by investment**. *This transaction increases both the net assets and the total capital of the partnership.* Frequently a new partner will contribute cash, but a professional partnership, such as Harris & Chong in the feature story, may be more interested in having a new partner to contribute their clients to the partnership instead of cash. In the second case, there is no change to the assets or equity; although the clients are important to the partnership, they cannot be classified as assets in accounting terms.

To illustrate when cash is invested, assume that instead of purchasing a partner's interest as illustrated in the previous section, Carson invests $30,000 in cash in the ABC partnership for a one-third capital interest. In this case, the entry is:

July 1	Cash	30,000	
	L. Carson, Capital		30,000
	To record admission of Carson by investment.		

A	=	L	+	OE
+30,000				+30,000

↑Cash flows: +30,000

Both net assets and total capital increase by $30,000. The effect of this transaction on the partners' capital accounts is as follows:

D. Arbour, Capital				D. Baker, Capital				L. Carson, Capital			
		Bal.	30,000			Bal.	30,000				
										July 1	**30,000**
		Bal.	30,000			Bal.	30,000			Bal.	30,000

Remember that Carson's one-third capital interest might not result in a one-third profit and loss ratio. Carson's profit and loss ratio should be specified in the new partnership agreement. It may or may not be equal to the one-third capital interest.

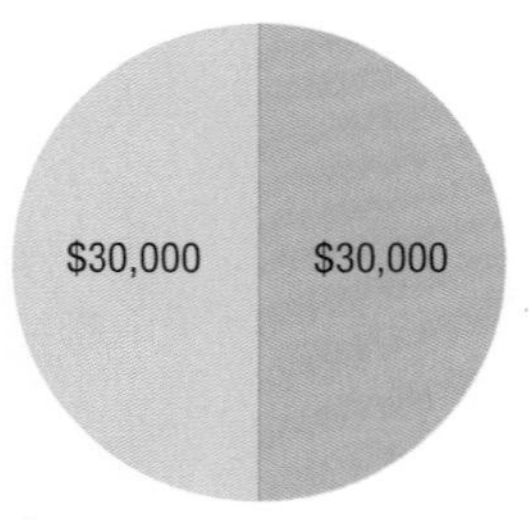

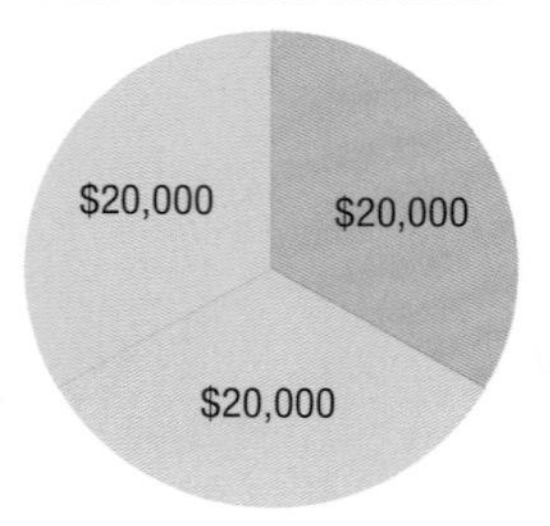

Arbour Baker Carson

The before and after effects of an admission by purchase of an interest or by investment are shown in the following comparison of the net assets and capital balances:

Before Admission of Partner		After Admission of Partner	
		Purchase of a Partner's Interest	Investment of Assets in the Partnership
Net assets	$60,000	$60,000	$90,000
Partners' capital			
D. Arbour	$30,000	$20,000	$30,000
D. Baker	30,000	20,000	30,000
L. Carson		20,000	30,000
Total partners' equity	$60,000	$60,000	$90,000

When an interest is purchased, the partnership's total net assets and total capital do not change. In contrast, when a partner is admitted by investment, both the total net assets and the total capital increase by the amount of cash invested by the new partner.

In an admission by investment, complications occur when the new partner's investment is not the same as the equity in the partnership acquired by the new partner. When those amounts are not the same, the difference is considered a bonus to either (1) the old (existing) partners or (2) the new partner.

Bonus to Old Partners.

The existing partners may want a bonus when admitting a new partner. In an established firm, existing partners may insist on a bonus as compensation for the work they have put into building the partnership over the years. The fair value of some of the partnership's assets (a downtown office in Toronto or Vancouver, for example) may be much higher than their carrying value. If a partnership has been profitable, unrecognized goodwill may exist. Recall from Chapter 9 that goodwill is only recorded when a company is sold. In such cases, the new partner is usually willing to pay a bonus to become a partner. The bonus is allocated to the existing partners based on their profit and loss ratios before the admission of the new partner.

To illustrate, assume that on November 1, the Peart-Huang partnership, owned by Sam Peart and Hal Huang, has total partnership capital of $120,000. Peart has a capital balance of $72,000; Huang has a capital balance of $48,000. The two partners share profits and losses as follows: Peart 60% and Huang 40%.

Peart and Huang agree to admit Lana Trent to a 25% ownership (capital) interest in exchange for a cash investment of $80,000. Trent's capital balance on the new partnership books of $50,000 and the bonus to the old partners are calculated as follows:

Partnership capital before Trent is admitted ($72,000 + $48,000)	$ 120,000
Trent's investment in the partnership	80,000
Partnership capital after Trent is admitted	$200,000
Trent's capital in the partnership ($200,000 × 25%)	$ 50,000
Bonus to the old partners ($80,000 − $50,000)	$ 30,000
The bonus is allocated to the old partners based on their profit and loss ratios:	
To Peart ($30,000 × 60%)	$ 18,000
To Huang ($30,000 × 40%)	12,000
Total bonus allocated to old partners	$ 30,000

The entry to record the admission of Trent on November 1 is:

A	=	L	+	OE
+80,000				+18,000
				+12,000
				+50,000

↑Cash flows: +80,000

Nov. 1	Cash	80,000	
	S. Peart, Capital		18,000
	H. Huang, Capital		12,000
	L. Trent, Capital		50,000
	To record admission of Trent and bonuses to old partners.		

The before and after effects of the admission of a partner who pays a bonus to the old partners are shown in the following comparison of the net assets and capital balances:

Bonus to Old Partners	Before Admission of Partner	After Admission of Partner
Net assets	$120,000	$200,000
Partners' capital		
S. Peart	$ 72,000	$ 90,000
H. Huang	48,000	60,000
L. Trent		50,000
Total capital	$120,000	$200,000

Before Admission of Partner

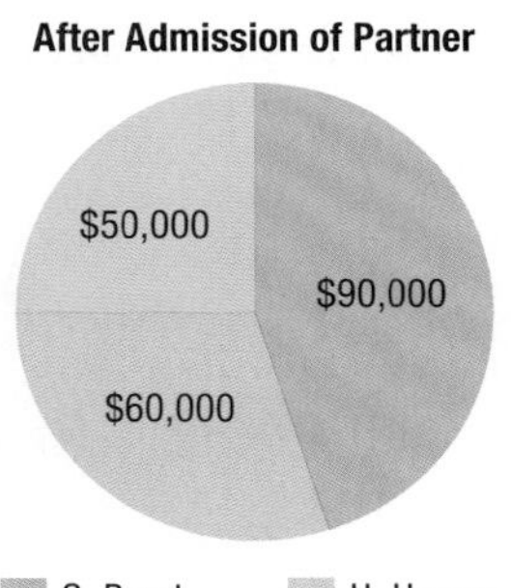

After Admission of Partner

$50,000
$90,000
$60,000

S. Peart H. Huang L. Trent

In summary, Lana Trent invests $80,000 cash in the partnership for a 25% capital interest of $50,000. The difference of $30,000 between these two amounts is a bonus that is allocated to the old partners based on their profit- and loss-sharing ratio as follows: $18,000 to Sam Peart and $12,000 to Hal Huang. The T accounts show the balance in the partners' capital accounts after receipt of the bonus paid by the new partner. This is also shown graphically in the pie charts in the margin.

S. Peart, Capital	
	Nov. 1 72,000 Beginning balance
	Nov. 1 18,000 Share of bonus from Trent
	Nov. 1 90,000 Updated balance

H. Huang, Capital	
	Nov. 1 48,000 Beginning balance
	Nov. 1 12,000 Share of bonus from Trent
	Nov. 1 60,000 Updated balance

L. Trent, Capital	
	Nov. 1 50,000 Investment less bonus paid
	Nov. 1 50,000 Updated balance

Bonus to New Partner.

If a new partner has specific resources or special attributes that the partnership wants, the partnership may be willing to give a bonus to the new partner. For example, the new partner may be able to supply cash that is urgently needed for expansion or to meet maturing debts. Or the new partner may be a recognized expert or authority in a relevant field. Or the new partner may be a celebrity whose name will draw more customers to the business.

A bonus to a new partner decreases the capital balances of the old partners. The amount of the decrease for each partner is based on the profit and loss ratios before the admission of the new partner.

To illustrate, assume instead that on November 1, the Peart-Huang partnership admits Lana Trent to a 25% ownership (capital) interest in exchange for a cash investment of $20,000 (instead of $80,000 as in the previous illustration). Trent's capital balance on the new partnership books of $35,000 and allocation of the bonus from the old partners are calculated as follows:

Partnership capital before Trent is admitted ($72,000 + $48,000)	$120,000
Trent's investment in the partnership	20,000
Partnership capital after Trent is admitted	$140,000
Trent's capital in the partnership ($140,000 × 25%)	$ 35,000
Bonus to the new partner ($35,000 − $20,000)	$ 15,000

The bonus from the old partners is based on their profit and loss ratios:

From Peart ($15,000 × 60%)	$ 9,000
From Huang ($15,000 × 40%)	6,000
Total bonus allocated to the new partner	$ 15,000

The entry to record the admission of Trent on November 1 in this case is:

Date	Account	Debit	Credit
Nov. 1	Cash	20,000	
	S. Peart, Capital	9,000	
	H. Huang, Capital	6,000	
	L. Trent, Capital		35,000
	To record Trent's admission and bonus to new partner.		

A	=	L	+	OE
+20,000				−9,000
				−6,000
				+35,000

↑ Cash flows: +20,000

Before Admission of Partner

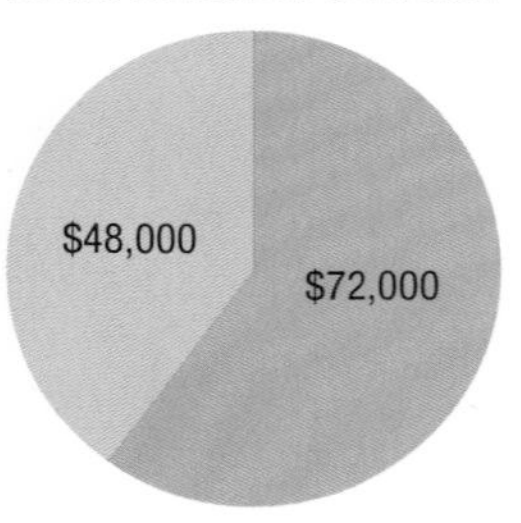

After Admission of Partner

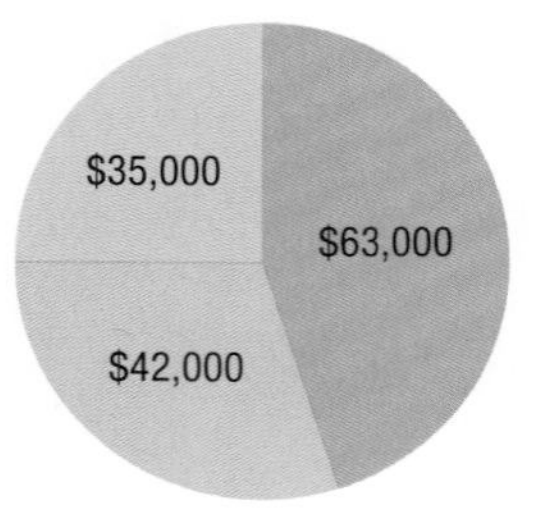

S. Peart H. Huang L. Trent

The before and after effects of the admission of a partner who is paid a bonus by the old partners are shown in the following comparison of the net assets and capital balances:

	Bonus to New Partner	
	Before Admission of Partner	**After Admission of Partner**
Net assets	$120,000	$140,000
Partners' capital		
S. Peart	$ 72,000	$ 63,000
H. Huang	48,000	42,000
L. Trent		35,000
Total capital	$120,000	$140,000

In summary, $20,000 cash was invested in the partnership by Lana Trent for a $35,000 capital credit, and the $15,000 bonus was allocated from the partners' capital accounts as follows: $9,000 from Sam Peart and $6,000 from Hal Huang. The T accounts show the balance in the partners' capital accounts after the bonus is paid to the new partner.

S. Peart, Capital		H. Huang, Capital		L. Trent, Capital	
	Beginning balance 72,000		Beginning balance 48,000		Investment plus bonus 35,000
Share of bonus paid to Trent 9,000		Share of bonus paid to Trent 6,000			
	Updated balance 63,000		Updated balance 42,000		Updated balance 35,000

BEFORE YOU GO ON...

DO IT

I. Shandler and M. Rossetti have a partnership in which they share profit and loss equally. There is a $40,000 balance in each capital account. Record the journal entries on September 1 for each of the independent events below:

(a) Shandler and Rossetti agree to admit A. Rachel as a new one-fourth interest partner. Rachel pays $16,000 in cash directly to each partner.

(b) Shandler and Rossetti agree to admit A. Rachel as a new one-fourth interest partner. Rachel contributes $32,000 to the partnership.

Action Plan

- Recognize that the admission by purchase of a partnership interest is a personal transaction between one or more existing partners and the new partner.
- In an admission by purchase, no cash is received by the partnership and the capital credit for the new partner is not based on the cash paid.
- Recognize that the admission by investment of partnership assets is a transaction between the new partner and the partnership.
- In an admission by investment, determine any bonus to old or new partners by comparing the total capital of the new partnership with the new partner's capital credit. Allocate the bonus based on the old partners' profit and loss ratios.

SOLUTION

(a) Sept. 1	I. Shandler, Capital	10,000	
	M. Rossetti, Capital	10,000	
	A. Rachel, Capital		20,000[1]
	To record admission of Rachel by purchase.		
(b) Sept. 1	Cash	32,000	
	I. Shandler, Capital ($4,000[2] × 50%)		2,000
	M. Rossetti, Capital ($4,000[2] × 50%)		2,000
	A. Rachel, Capital		28,000
	To record admission of Rachel by investment.		

[1]Total capital of partnership: $40,000 + $40,000 = $80,000
Rachel's capital credit: $80,000 × 1/4 = $20,000
[2]Total capital of partnership: $40,000 + $40,000 + $32,000 = $112,000
Rachel's capital credit: $112,000 × 1/4 = $28,000
Bonus to old partners: $32,000 − $28,000 = $4,000 (shared equally)

Related exercise material: BE12–11, BE12–12, E12–7, and E12–8.

WITHDRAWAL OF A PARTNER

STUDY OBJECTIVE 6
Account for the withdrawal of a partner.

Let's now look at the opposite situation, when a partner withdraws. A partner may withdraw from a partnership voluntarily, by selling his or her equity in the firm. He or she may withdraw involuntarily, by reaching mandatory retirement age, by expulsion, or by dying. The withdrawal of a partner, like the admission of a partner, legally dissolves the partnership. However, it is customary to record only the economic effects of the partner's withdrawal, while the partnership reorganizes itself and continues to operate.

As indicated earlier, the partnership agreement should specify the terms of withdrawal. Ms. Chong believes that the most crucial part of a partnership agreement is how to divide things up when a partner leaves. On the other hand, the withdrawal of a partner can also occur outside of the terms of the partnership agreement. For example, when the remaining partners are anxious to remove an uncontrollable partner from the firm, they may agree to pay the departing partner much more than was specified in the original partnership agreement.

Helpful hint The admission and withdrawal of a partner are similar in the sense that they can both be accomplished with personal (non-partnership) assets or partnership assets. In both cases, the use of personal assets leaves the *total* partnership assets and equity unchanged.

The withdrawal of a partner may be done by a payment from partners' personal assets or a payment from partnership assets. Payment from personal assets affects only the remaining partners' capital accounts, not total capital. Payment from partnership assets decreases the total net assets and total capital of the partnership.

After a partner has withdrawn, profit and loss ratios for the remaining partners must be reviewed and specified again. If a new profit and loss ratio is not indicated in the partnership agreement, the remaining partners are assumed to share profit and losses equally.

Payment from Partners' Personal Assets

A **withdrawal by payment from partners' personal assets** is a *personal transaction between the partners.* It is the direct opposite of admitting a new partner who purchases a partner's interest. Payment to the departing partner is made directly from the remaining partners' personal assets. Partnership assets are not involved in any way, and total capital does not change. The effect on the partnership is limited to a transfer and redistribution of the partners' capital balances.

To illustrate, assume that Javad Dargahi, Eddie Kim, and Roberta Viau have capital balances of \$25,000, \$15,000, and \$10,000, respectively. The partnership equity totals \$50,000 (\$25,000 + \$15,000 + \$10,000). Dargahi and Kim agree to buy out Viau's interest. Each agrees to personally pay Viau \$8,000 in exchange for one half of Viau's total interest of \$10,000 on February 1. The entry to record the withdrawal is as follows:

Feb. 1	R. Viau, Capital	10,000	
	J. Dargahi, Capital		5,000
	E. Kim, Capital		5,000
	To record purchase of Viau's interest by other partners..		

A	=	L	+	OE
				−10,000
				+5,000
				+5,000

Cash flows: no effect

The effect of this transaction on the partners' capital accounts is as follows:

J. Dargahi, Capital			E. Kim, Capital			R. Viau, Capital		
	Bal.	25,000		Bal.	15,000		Bal.	10,000
		5,000			5,000	10,000		
	Bal.	30,000		Bal.	20,000		Bal.	0

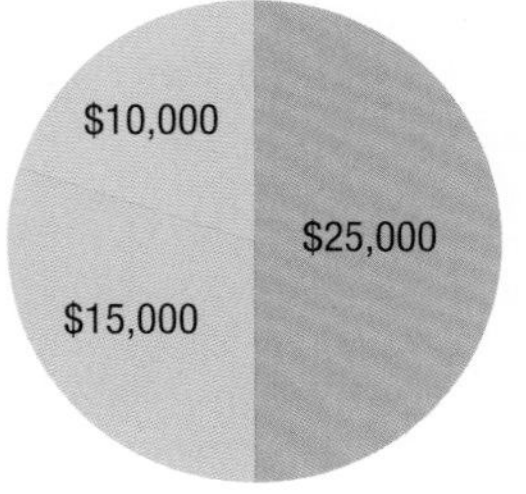

After Viau's Withdrawal

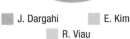

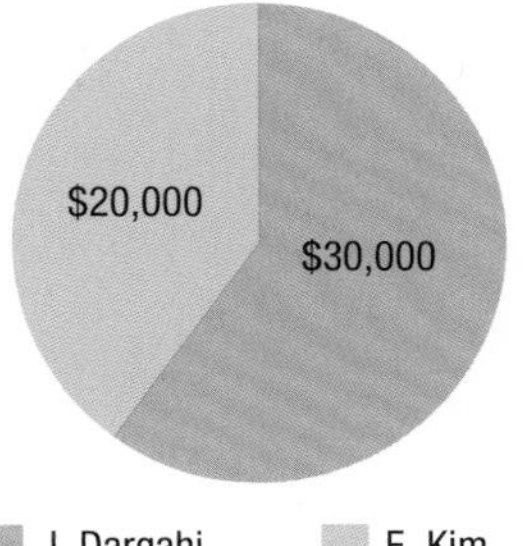

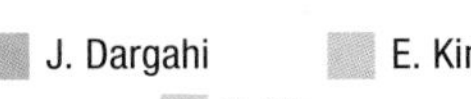

Net assets of \$50,000 remain the same and total partnership capital is also unchanged at \$50,000 (\$30,000 + \$20,000 + \$0). All that has happened is a reallocation of capital amounts. Note also that the \$16,000 paid to Roberta Viau personally is not recorded because this is not partnership cash. Viau's capital is debited for only \$10,000, not the \$16,000 cash that she received. Similarly, both Javad Dargahi and Eddie Kim credit their capital accounts for only \$5,000, not the \$8,000 they each paid. This is because we are showing the accounting for the partnership, not the partners' personal accounting.

Payment from Partnership Assets

A **withdrawal by payment from partnership assets** is a transaction that involves the partnership. Both partnership net assets and total capital are decreased. Using partnership assets to pay for a withdrawing partner's interest is the reverse of admitting a partner through the investment of assets in the partnership.

In accounting for a withdrawal by payment from partnership assets, *asset revaluations should not be made or recorded*. Recording a revaluation to the fair value of the assets at the time of a partner's withdrawal violates the cost principle, which requires assets to be stated at original cost. It would also ignore the going concern assumption, which assumes that the entity will continue indefinitely. The terms of the partnership contract should not dictate the accounting for this event.

To illustrate, assume that instead of Roberta Viau's interest being purchased personally by the other partners, as illustrated in the previous section, her interest is bought out by the partnership. In this case, the entry is:

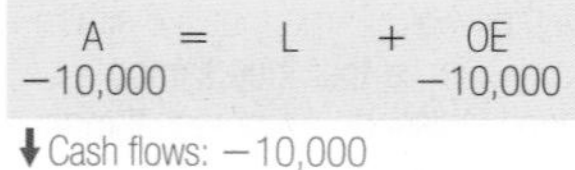

Feb. 1	R. Viau, Capital	10,000	
	Cash		10,000
	To record purchase of Viau's interest by partnership.		

Both net assets and total partnership capital decrease by $10,000. The effect of this transaction on the partners' capital accounts is as follows:

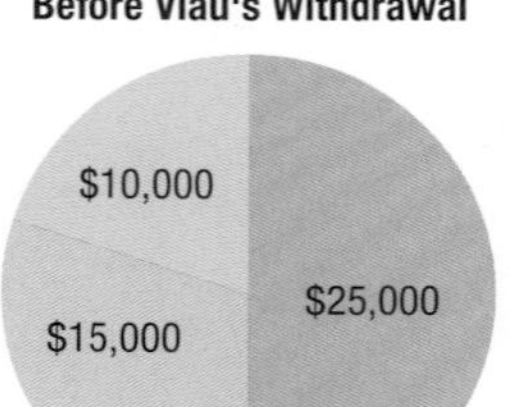

J. Dargahi, Capital			E. Kim, Capital			R. Viau, Capital		
	Bal.	25,000		Bal.	15,000		Bal.	10,000
						10,000		
	Bal.	25,000		Bal.	15,000		Bal.	0

The before and after effects of the withdrawal of a partner when payment is made from personal assets or from partnership assets are shown in the following comparison of the net assets and capital balances:

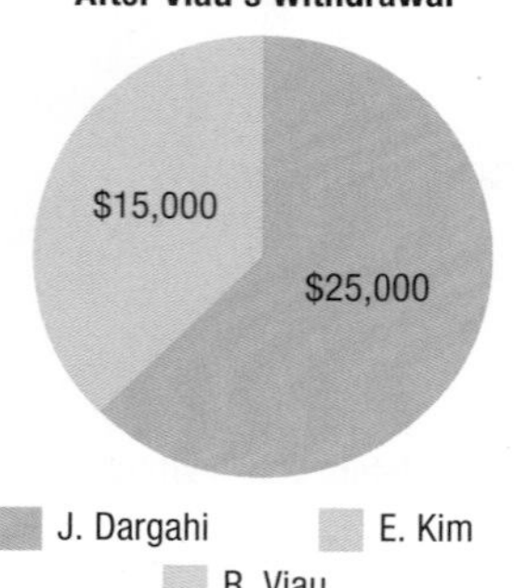

	Before Withdrawal of Partner	After Withdrawal of Partner: Payment from Partners' Personal Assets	After Withdrawal of Partner: Payment from Partnership Assets
Net assets	$50,000	$50,000	$40,000
Partners' capital			
J. Dargahi	$25,000	$30,000	$25,000
E. Kim	15,000	20,000	15,000
R. Viau	10,000	0	0
Total capital	$50,000	$50,000	$40,000

When payment is made from partners' personal assets, *the partnership's total net assets and total capital do not change*. In contrast, when payment is made from the partnership assets, both the total net assets and the total capital decrease.

In a payment from partnership assets, it is rare for the partnership to pay the partner the exact amount of his or her capital account balance, as was assumed above. When the amounts are not the same, the difference between the amount paid and the withdrawing partner's capital balance is considered a bonus to either (1) the departing partner, or (2) the remaining partners.

Bonus to Departing Partner.

A bonus may be paid to a departing partner in any of these situations:

1. The fair value of partnership assets is greater than their carrying amount.
2. There is unrecorded goodwill resulting from the partnership's superior earnings record.
3. The remaining partners are anxious to remove the partner from the firm.

The bonus is deducted from the remaining partners' capital balances based on their profit and loss ratios at the time of the withdrawal.

To illustrate a bonus to a departing partner, assume the following capital balances in the RST Partnership: Fred Roman, $50,000; Dee Sand, $30,000; and Betty Terk, $20,000. The partners share profit in the ratio of 3:2:1, respectively. Terk retires from the partnership on March 1 and receives a cash payment of $25,000 from the firm. The bonus to the departing partner and the allocation of the bonus to the remaining partners is calculated as follows:

Terk's capital balance in the partnership before departing	$20,000
Cash paid from partnership to Terk	25,000
Bonus paid to the departing partner—Terk	$ 5,000
Allocation of bonus from the remaining partners:	
From Roman ($5,000 × 3/5)	$ 3,000
From Sand ($5,000 × 2/5)	2,000
Total bonus to the departing partner—Terk	$ 5,000

Before Terk's Withdrawal

$20,000
$50,000
$30,000

After Terk's Withdrawal

$28,000
$47,000

F. Roman
D. Sand
B. Terk

The entry to record the withdrawal of Terk on March 1 is as follows:

Mar. 1	B. Terk, Capital	20,000	
	F. Roman, Capital	3,000	
	D. Sand, Capital	2,000	
	Cash		25,000
	To record withdrawal of, and bonus to, Terk.		

A	=	L	+	OE
−25,000				−20,000
				−3,000
				−2,000

Cash flows: −25,000

Note that since assets (that is, Cash) decrease by $25,000 with no corresponding change in liabilities, the total capital must also decrease by $25,000 to ensure that the accounting equation is still in balance.

The before and after effects of the withdrawal of a partner when a bonus is paid to the departing partner are shown in the following comparison of the net assets and capital balances:

	Bonus to Departing Partner	
	Before Withdrawal of Partner	**After Withdrawal of Partner**
Net assets	$100,000	$75,000
Partners' capital		
F. Roman	$ 50,000	$47,000
D. Sand	30,000	28,000
B. Terk	20,000	0
Total capital	$100,000	$75,000

In summary, both net assets and capital decreased by $25,000 when $25,000 cash was paid by the partnership to Betty Terk to purchase her $20,000 equity interest. The $5,000 bonus was allocated from the remaining partners' capital accounts according to their profit and loss ratios. Fred Roman and Dee Sand, the remaining partners, will recover the bonus given to Terk as the undervalued assets are used or sold.

Bonus to Remaining Partners.

The departing partner may give a bonus to the remaining partners in the following situations:

1. Recorded assets are overvalued.
2. The partnership has a poor earnings record.
3. The partner is anxious to leave the partnership.

In such cases, the cash paid to the departing partner will be *less than* the departing partner's capital balance. The bonus is allocated (credited) to the capital accounts of the remaining partners based on their profit and loss ratios.

To illustrate, assume, instead of the example above, that Terk is paid only $16,000 for her $20,000 equity when she withdraws from the partnership on March 1. The bonus to the remaining partners is calculated as follows:

Terk's capital balance in the partnership before departing	$20,000
Cash paid from partnership to Terk	16,000
Bonus to the remaining partners	$ 4,000
Allocation of bonus to the remaining partners:	
To Roman ($4,000 × 3/5)	$ 2,400
To Sand ($4,000 × 2/5)	1,600
Total bonus to the remaining partners	$ 4,000

The entry to record the withdrawal on March 1 follows:

A	=	L	+	OE
−16,000				−20,000
				+2,400
				+1,600

Cash flows: −16,000

Mar. 1	B. Terk, Capital	20,000	
	F. Roman, Capital		2,400
	D. Sand, Capital		1,600
	Cash		16,000
	To record withdrawal of Terk and bonus to remaining partners.		

The effect of a partner's withdrawal, when there is a bonus to the remaining partners, is shown in the following comparison of the net assets and capital balances:

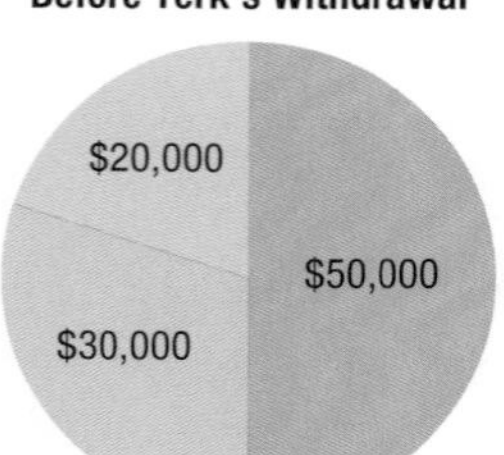

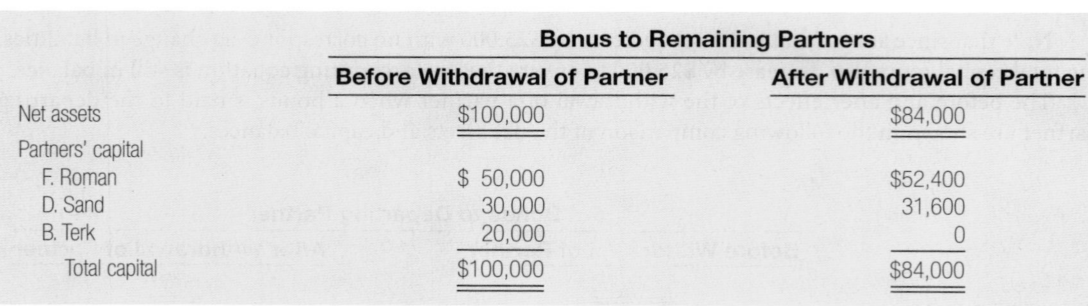

Bonus to Remaining Partners		
	Before Withdrawal of Partner	After Withdrawal of Partner
Net assets	$100,000	$84,000
Partners' capital		
F. Roman	$ 50,000	$52,400
D. Sand	30,000	31,600
B. Terk	20,000	0
Total capital	$100,000	$84,000

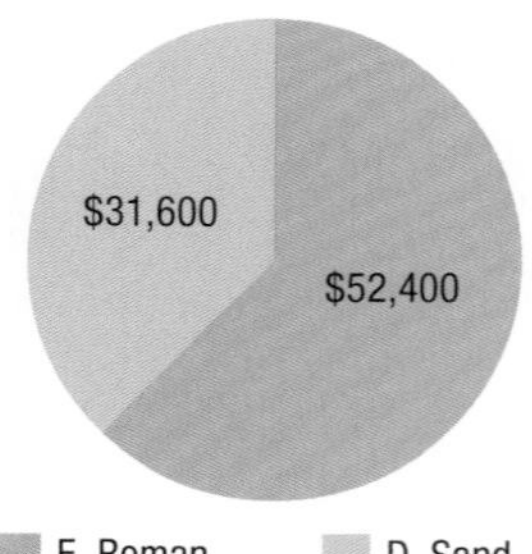

In summary, both net assets and capital decreased by $16,000 when $16,000 cash was paid by the partnership to Betty Terk to purchase her $20,000 equity interest. The $4,000 bonus was allocated to the remaining partners' capital accounts according to their profit and loss ratios and not the remaining partners' capital balances.

Death of a Partner

The death of a partner dissolves the partnership. But there is generally a provision in the partnership agreement for the surviving partners to continue operations. When a partner dies, the partner's equity at the date of death normally has to be determined. This is done by (1) calculating the profit or loss for the year to date, (2) closing the books, and (3) preparing the financial statements.

The death of the partner may be recorded by either of the two methods described earlier in the section for the withdrawal of a partner: (1) payment from the partners' personal assets or (2) payment from the partnership assets. That is, one or more of the surviving partners may agree to use his or her personal assets to purchase the deceased partner's equity. Or, partnership assets may be used to settle with the deceased partner's estate. To make it easier to pay from partnership assets, many partnerships take out life insurance policies on each partner. The partnership is named as the beneficiary. The proceeds from the insurance policy on the deceased partner are then used to settle with the estate.

BEFORE YOU GO ON...

DO IT

S. Hosseinzadeh, M. Bélanger, and C. Laurin have a partnership in which they share profit and loss equally. There is a $40,000 balance in each capital account. Record the journal entries on March 1 for each of the independent events below:

(a) Laurin withdraws from the partnership. Hosseinzadeh and Bélanger each pay Laurin $25,000 out of their personal assets.
(b) Laurin withdraws from the partnership and is paid $30,000 of partnership cash.

Action Plan

- Recognize that the withdrawal by sale of a partnership interest is a personal transaction between one or more remaining partners and the withdrawing partner that does not involve partnership assets.
- Recognize that the withdrawal by payment of partnership assets is a transaction between the withdrawing partner and the partnership.
- In a withdrawal by payment of partnership assets, determine any bonus to the departing or remaining partners by comparing the amount paid with the amount of the withdrawing partner's capital balance. Allocate the bonus based on the remaining partners' profit and loss ratios.

SOLUTION

(a) Mar. 1	C. Laurin, Capital	40,000	
	S. Hosseinzadeh, Capital ($40,000 × ½)		20,000
	M. Bélanger, Capital ($40,000 × ½)		20,000
	To record purchase of Laurin's interest.		
(b) Mar. 1	C. Laurin, Capital	40,000	
	Cash		30,000
	S. Hosseinzadeh, Capital ($10,000[1] × ½)		5,000
	M. Bélanger, Capital ($10,000[1] × ½)		5,000
	To record withdrawal of Laurin by payment of partnership assets and bonus to remaining partners.		

[1]Bonus: $30,000 − $40,000 = $(10,000)

Related exercise material: BE12–13, BE12–14, E12–9, and E12–10.

THE NAVIGATOR

LIQUIDATION OF A PARTNERSHIP

STUDY OBJECTIVE 7

Account for the liquidation of a partnership.

The liquidation of a partnership ends the business. It involves selling the assets of the business, paying liabilities, and distributing any remaining assets to the partners. Liquidation may result from the sale of the business by mutual agreement of the partners or from bankruptcy. A **partnership liquidation** ends *both the legal and the economic life* of the entity.

Before the liquidation process begins, the accounting cycle for the partnership must be completed for the final operating period, even if the liquidation occurs prior to the partnership's year end. This includes preparing adjusting entries, a trial balance, financial statements, closing entries, and a post-closing trial balance (that is, the year-end steps in the accounting cycle). Only permanent accounts (assets, contra assets, liabilities, and each partner's capital) should be open when the liquidation process begins, as the temporary accounts (revenue, expenses, and each partner's drawings) would have been closed to zero.

In liquidation, the sale of noncash assets for cash is called **realization**. Any difference between the carrying amount and the cash proceeds is called the gain or loss on realization. To liquidate a partnership, it is necessary to follow these steps:

1. Sell noncash assets for cash and recognize any gain or loss on realization.
2. Allocate any gain or loss on realization to the partners, based on their profit and loss ratios.
3. Pay partnership liabilities in cash.
4. Distribute the remaining cash to partners, *based on their capital balances.*

Each of the steps must be done in sequence, and creditors must be paid before partners receive any cash distributions.

It sometimes happens, when a partnership is liquidated, that all partners have credit balances in their capital accounts. This situation is called **no capital deficiency**. Alternatively, one or more of the partners' capital accounts may have a debit (negative) balance. This situation is called a **capital deficiency**.

To illustrate each of these situations, assume that Ace Company is liquidated on April 15, 2014, when its post-closing trial balance shows the assets, liabilities, and partners' equity accounts in Illustration 12-7. The profit and loss ratios of the partners are 3:2:1 for R. Aube, P. Chordia, and W. Elliott.

ILLUSTRATION 12-7
Account balances before liquidation

ACE COMPANY
Post-Closing Trial Balance
April 15, 2014

	Debit	Credit
Cash	$ 5,000	
Accounts receivable	33,000	
Equipment	35,000	
Accumulated depreciation—equipment		$ 8,000
Accounts payable		31,000
R. Aube, capital		15,000
P. Chordia, capital		17,800
W. Elliott, capital		1,200
Totals	$73,000	$73,000

NO CAPITAL DEFICIENCY

No capital deficiency means that all partners have credit balances in their capital accounts prior to the final distribution of cash. An example of the steps in the liquidation process with no capital deficiency follows:

1. Assume the noncash assets (accounts receivable and equipment) are sold on April 18 for $75,000. The carrying amount of these assets is $60,000 ($33,000 + $35,000 − $8,000). Thus, a gain of $15,000 is realized on the sale, and the following entry is made:

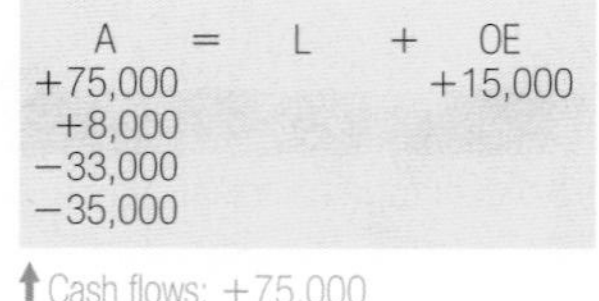

(1)			
Apr. 18	Cash	75,000	
	Accumulated Depreciation—Equipment	8,000	
	Accounts Receivable		33,000
	Equipment		35,000
	Gain on Realization		15,000
	To record realization of noncash assets.		

2. The gain on realization of $15,000 is allocated to the partners based on their profit and loss ratios, which are 3:2:1 (or $^3/_6$, $^2/_6$, and $^1/_6$). The entry is:

A = L + OE
−15,000
+7,500
+5,000
+2,500

Cash flows: no effect

(2)			
Apr. 18	Gain on Realization	15,000	
	R. Aube, Capital ($15,000 × $^3/_6$)		7,500
	P. Chordia, Capital ($15,000 × $^2/_6$)		5,000
	W. Elliott, Capital ($15,000 × $^1/_6$)		2,500
	To allocate gain to partners' capital accounts.		

3. Partnership liabilities consist of accounts payable, $31,000. Creditors are paid in full on April 23 by a cash payment of $31,000. The entry is:

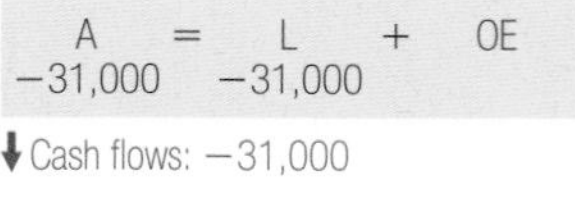

(3)			
Apr. 23	Accounts Payable	31,000	
	Cash		31,000
	To record payment of partnership liabilities.		

Illustration 12-8 shows the account balances after the entries in the first three steps are posted. All of the accounts will have zero balances except for cash and the partners' capital accounts.

ILLUSTRATION 12-8
Partnership liquidation—no capital deficiency

	Assets				= Liabilities +	Partners' Equity		
	Cash	Accounts Receivable	Equipment	Accum. Dep. Equipment	Accounts Payable	R. Aube, Capital	P. Chordia, Capital	W. Elliott, Capital
Account balances prior to liquidation:	$ 5,000	$ 33,000	$ 35,000	$ 8,000	$31,000	$15,000	$ 17,800	$ 1,200
1. & 2. Sale of assets and share of gain	+75,000	−33,000	−35,000	−8,000		+7,500	+5,000	+2,500
Balances	80,000	0	0	0	31,000	22,500	22,800	3,700
3. Payment of accounts payable	−31,000				−31,000			
Balances	49,000	0	0	0	0	22,500	22,800	3,700
4. Distribution of cash to partners	−49,000					−22,500	−22,800	−3,700
Final balances	$ 0	$ 0	$ 0	$ 0	$ 0	$ 0	$ 0	$ 0

4. The remaining cash is distributed to the partners on April 25 based on their capital balances as shown in Illustration 12-8. The entry to record the distribution of cash on April 25 is:

		Debit	Credit
Apr. 25	R. Aube, Capital	22,500	
	P. Chordia, Capital	22,800	
	W. Elliott, Capital	3,700	
	Cash		49,000
	To record distribution of cash to partners.		

A	=	L	+	OE
−49,000				−22,500
				−22,800
				−3,700

Cash flows: −49,000

Cash

	Debit		Credit
Beginning balance	5,000		
(1)	75,000		
		(3)	31,000
		(4)	49,000
Final balance	0		

Accounts Receivable

	Debit		Credit
Beginning balance	33,000	(1)	33,000
Final balance	0		

Equipment

	Debit		Credit
Beginning balance	35,000	(1)	35,000
Final balance	0		

Accumulated Depreciation—Equipment

	Debit		Credit
		Beginning balance	8,000
(1)	8,000		
		Final balance	0

Accounts Payable

	Debit		Credit
		Beginning balance	31,000
(3)	31,000		
		Final balance	0

R. Aube, Capital

	Debit		Credit
		Beginning balance	15,000
		(2)	7,500
(4)	22,500		
		Final balance	0

P. Chordia, Capital

	Debit		Credit
		Beginning balance	17,800
		(2)	5,000
(4)	22,800		
		Final balance	0

W. Elliott, Capital

	Debit		Credit
		Beginning balance	1,200
		(2)	2,500
(4)	3,700		
		Final balance	0

Gain on Realization

	Debit		Credit
		(1)	15,000
(2)	15,000		
		Final balance	0

As shown in Illustration 12-8 and the T accounts accompanying this illustration, after this entry is posted, all of the accounts have zero balances and the liquidation of the partnership is complete.

Two points to remember:

- Gains or losses on sale of assets are allocated to the partners based on the profit and loss ratio.
- **The final cash payment to the partners is based on the balances in the partners' capital accounts, not the profit and loss ratio. The profit and loss ratio is used to divide gains and losses, not cash or other assets.**

CAPITAL DEFICIENCY

Capital deficiency means that at least one partner has a debit (negative) balance in his or her capital account before the final distribution of cash. This may be caused by recurring losses, excessive drawings, or losses from the realization during liquidation.

To illustrate, assume instead that Ace Company (see Illustration 12-7) is almost bankrupt. The partners decide to liquidate by having a going-out-of-business sale on April 18. Many of the accounts receivable cannot be collected, and the equipment is sold at auction at less than its fair value. Cash proceeds from the equipment sale and collections from customers total only $42,000. The loss on liquidation is $18,000 ($60,000 in carrying amount − $42,000 in proceeds). The steps in the liquidation process are as follows:

1. The entry for the realization of noncash assets is recorded on April 18:

A	=	L	+	OE
+42,000				−18,000
+8,000				
−33,000				
−35,000				

↑ Cash flows: +42,000

	(1)		
Apr. 18	Cash	42,000	
	Accumulated Depreciation—Equipment	8,000	
	Loss on Realization	18,000	
	Accounts Receivable		33,000
	Equipment		35,000
	To record realization of noncash assets.		

2. The loss on realization is allocated to the partners based on their profit and loss ratios of 3:2:1 and is recorded as follows:

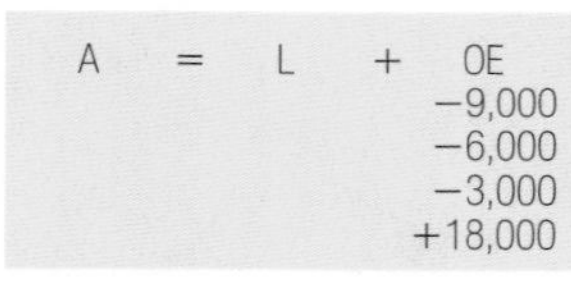

A	=	L	+	OE
				−9,000
				−6,000
				−3,000
				+18,000

Cash flows: no effect

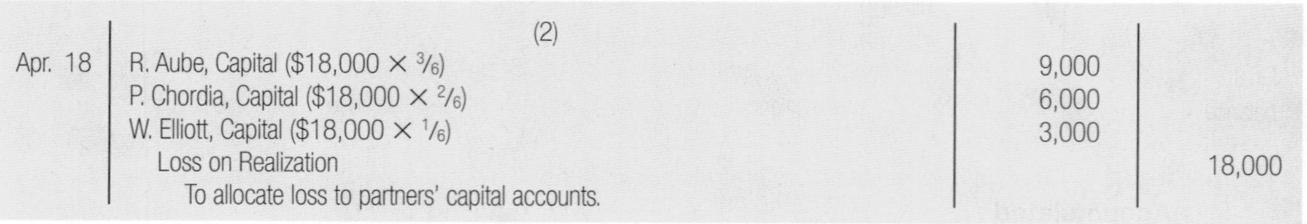

	(2)		
Apr. 18	R. Aube, Capital ($18,000 × 3/6)	9,000	
	P. Chordia, Capital ($18,000 × 2/6)	6,000	
	W. Elliott, Capital ($18,000 × 1/6)	3,000	
	Loss on Realization		18,000
	To allocate loss to partners' capital accounts.		

3. Partnership liabilities are paid on April 23 and recorded:

A	=	L	+	OE
−31,000		−31,000		

↓ Cash flows: −31,000

	(3)		
Apr. 23	Accounts Payable	31,000	
	Cash		31,000
	To record payment of partnership liabilities.		

After posting of the three entries, as shown in Illustration 12-9, there is $16,000 of cash remaining. Two of the partners' capital accounts have credit balances: R. Aube, Capital $6,000; and P. Chordia, Capital $11,800. The illustration shows W. Elliott's capital account as a negative number, which represents a debit balance or capital deficiency of $1,800.

ILLUSTRATION 12-9
Partnership liquidation—capital deficiency

	Assets				= Liabilities +	Partners' Equity		
	Cash	Accounts Receivable	Equipment	Accum. Dep. Equipment	Accounts Payable	R. Aube, Capital	P. Chordia, Capital	W. Elliott, Capital
Account balances prior to liquidation:	$ 5,000	$ 33,000	$ 35,000	$ 8,000	$31,000	$15,000	$17,800	$1,200
1. & 2. Sale of assets and share of loss	+42,000	−33,000	−35,000	−8,000		−9,000	−6,000	−3,000
Balances	47,000	0	0	0	31,000	6,000	11,800	−1,800
3. Payment of accounts payable	−31,000				−31,000			
Balances	16,000	0	0	0	0	6,000	11,800	−1,800

W. Elliott's capital deficiency of $1,800 means that he owes the partnership $1,800. R. Aube and P. Chordia have a legally enforceable claim for that amount against Elliott's personal assets. The final distribution of cash depends on how Elliott's deficiency is settled. Two alternatives for settling are presented next.

Payment of Deficiency

If the partner with the capital deficiency pays the amount owed to the partnership, the deficiency is eliminated. To illustrate, assume that W. Elliott pays $1,800 to the partnership on April 24. The entry to record this payment is as follows:

	(4)		
Apr. 24	Cash	1,800	
	W. Elliott, Capital		1,800
	To record payment of capital deficiency by Elliott.		

A	=	L	+	OE
+1,800				+1,800

↑Cash flows: +1,800

As shown in Illustration 12-10, after posting this entry, the cash balance of $17,800 is now sufficient to pay the two remaining partners with credit balances in the capital accounts ($6,000 + $11,800).

ILLUSTRATION 12-10
Payment of deficiency

	Assets =	Partners' Equity		
	Cash	R. Aube, Capital	P. Chordia, Capital	W. Elliott, Capital
Account balances after selling assets and paying liabilities:	$ 16,000	$ 6,000	$ 11,800	$−1,800
Payment of capital deficiency	+1,800			+1,800
Balances	17,800	6,000	11,800	0
Distribution of cash to partners	−17,800	−6,000	−11,800	
Final balances	$ 0	$ 0	$ 0	$ 0

Cash is distributed based on these balances on April 25. This was step 4 in the list when there was no capital deficiency. The following entry is made:

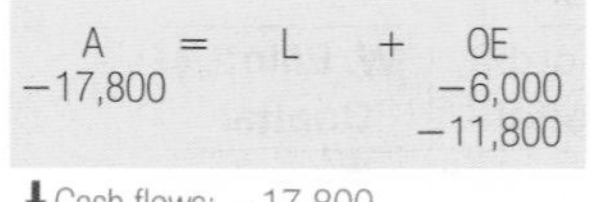

A	=	L	+	OE
−17,800				−6,000
				−11,800

↓Cash flows: −17,800

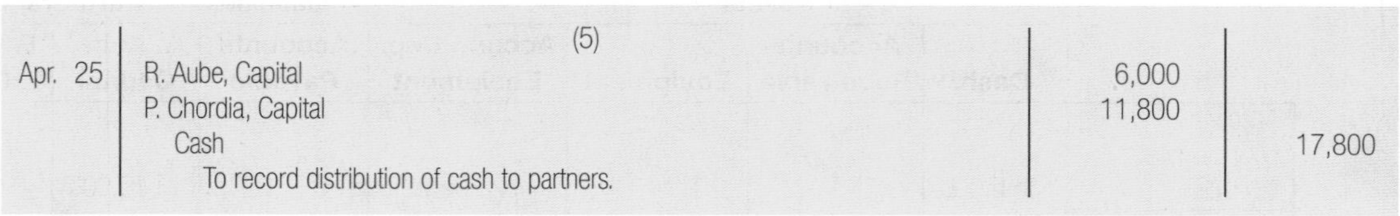

	(5)		
Apr. 25	R. Aube, Capital	6,000	
	P. Chordia, Capital	11,800	
	Cash		17,800
	To record distribution of cash to partners.		

Helpful hint The profit and loss ratio changes when the partner with the capital deficiency is not included. When allocating the loss from the sale of the assets, the profit and loss ratio was divided among the three partners as 3:2:1 or 3/6, 2/6, and 1/6. When Elliott is excluded, the profit and loss ratio is now 3:2 or 3/5 and 2/5.

As shown in Illustration 12-10, and by the T accounts below, after this entry is posted, all accounts will have zero balances and the partnership liquidation is finished.

Cash

Debit		Credit	
Beginning balance	5,000		
(1)	42,000		
		(3)	31,000
(4)	1,800		
		(5)	17,800
Final balance	0		

Accounts Receivable

Debit		Credit	
Beginning balance	33,000		
		(1)	33,000
Final balance	0		

Equipment

Debit		Credit	
Beginning balance	35,000		
		(1)	35,000
Final balance	0		

Accumulated Depreciation—Equipment

Debit		Credit	
		Beginning balance	8,000
(1)	8,000		
		Final balance	0

Accounts Payable

Debit		Credit	
		Beginning balance	31,000
(3)	31,000		
		Final balance	0

R. Aube, Capital

Debit		Credit	
		Beginning balance	15,000
(2)	9,000		
(5)	6,000		
		Final balance	0

P. Chordia, Capital

Debit		Credit	
		Beginning balance	17,800
(2)	6,000		
(5)	11,800		
		Final balance	0

W. Elliott, Capital

Debit		Credit	
		Beginning balance	1,200
(2)	3,000		
		(4)	1,800
		Final balance	0

Loss on Realization

Debit		Credit	
(1)	18,000		
		(2)	18,000
Final balance	0		

Nonpayment of Deficiency

If a partner with a capital deficiency is unable to pay the amount owed to the partnership, the partners with credit balances must absorb the loss. The loss is allocated based on the profit and loss ratios between the partners with credit balances. Recall that the profit and loss ratios of R. Aube and P. Chordia are 3:2 (or 3/5 and 2/5), respectively. The following entry would be made to remove W. Elliott's capital deficiency on April 25:

A	=	L	+	OE
				−1,080
				−720
				+1,800

Cash flows: no effect

	(4)		
Apr. 25	R. Aube, Capital ($1,800 × 3/5)	1,080	
	P. Chordia, Capital ($1,800 × 2/5)	720	
	W. Elliott, Capital		1,800
	To write off Elliott's capital deficiency.		

After posting this entry, the cash balance of $16,000 now equals the sum of the credit balances in the capital accounts ($4,920 + $11,080), as shown in Illustration 12-11:

ILLUSTRATION 12-11
Nonpayment of deficiency

	Assets =		Partners' Equity	
	Cash	**R. Aube, Capital**	**P. Chordia, Capital**	**W. Elliott, Capital**
Account balances after selling assets and paying liabilities:	$ 16,000	$ 6,000	$ 11,800	$−1,800
Write off of capital deficiency	0	−1,080	−720	+1,800
Balances	16,000	4,920	11,080	0
Distribution of cash to partners	−16,000	−4,920	−11,080	
Final balances	$ 0	$ 0	$ 0	$ 0

The entry to record the final distribution of cash is:

	(5)		
Apr. 25	R. Aube, Capital	4,920	
	P. Chordia, Capital	11,080	
	Cash		16,000
	To record distribution of cash to partners.		

A	=	L	+	OE
−16,000				−4,920
				−11,080

↓Cash flows: −16,000

Cash

Debit		Credit	
Beginning balance	5,000		
(1)	42,000		
		(3)	31,000
		(5)	16,000
Final balance	0		

Accounts Receivable

Debit		Credit	
Beginning balance	33,000		
		(1)	33,000
Final balance	0		

Equipment

Debit		Credit	
Beginning balance	35,000		
		(1)	35,000
Final balance	0		

Accumulated Depreciation—Equipment

Debit		Credit	
		Beginning balance	8,000
(1)	8,000		
		Final balance	0

Accounts Payable

Debit		Credit	
		Beginning balance	31,000
(3)	31,000		
		Final balance	0

R. Aube, Capital

Debit		Credit	
		Beginning balance	15,000
(2)	9,000		
(4)	1,080		
(5)	4,920		
		Final balance	0

P. Chordia, Capital

Debit		Credit	
		Beginning balance	17,800
(2)	6,000		
(4)	720		
(5)	11,080		
		Final balance	0

W. Elliott, Capital

Debit		Credit	
		Beginning balance	1,200
(2)	3,000		
		(4)	1,800
		Final balance	0

Loss on Realization

Debit		Credit	
(1)	18,000		
		(2)	18,000
Final balance	0		

After this entry is posted, all accounts will have zero balances, as shown in Illustration 12-11 and the T accounts above, but Aube and Chordia still have a legal claim against Elliott for the deficiency. If Elliott is able to make either a full or a partial payment, it would be split between Aube and Chordia 3:2 in the same way as the deficiency was split.

ACCOUNTING IN ACTION
ALL ABOUT YOU INSIGHT

Many successful businesses start as a simple partnership based on an inspiration, idea, or dream shared by a couple of friends. Bill Hewlett and David Packard became close friends after graduating with degrees in electrical engineering from Stanford University in 1934. Later they began working part-time on a product in a rented garage with $538 in cash and a used drill press. In 1939, the men formalized their partnership, using a coin flip to determine HP's now-iconic name.

In 1968, Bill Gates and Paul Allen met at a computer club meeting at Seattle's private Lakeside School. In Gates's dorm room at Harvard University in 1974, they devised and sold a BASIC platform for the Altair 8800. The university disciplined Gates for running a business in his dorm. A year later, Gates and Allen formed Microsoft, now the world's largest software company.

Larry Page and Sergey Brin met while working on their doctorates in computer science at Stanford in 1995. Working in their dorm rooms, they created a proprietary algorithm for a search engine on the Net that catalogued search results according to the popularity of pages. The result was Google, arguably the world's No. 1 Internet search engine.

Sources: Steve Lohr, "An 'Unvarnished' Peek Into Microsoft's History," *New York Times*, April 17, 2011; "Larry Page and Sergey Brin," *Entrepreneur*, October 16, 2008; Stacy Perman, "Historic Collaborations—Business Partnerships That Changed the World," *Business Week*, November 21, 2008.

If you and a friend wanted to start a partnership, how might you use a partnership agreement to ensure that your partnership becomes successful, instead of ending in an unhappy liquidation?

BEFORE YOU GO ON...

DO IT

S. Anders, J. Haque, and R. Smit, LLP, dissolved their partnership as of August 31. Before liquidation, the three partners shared profit and losses in the ratio of 3:2:4, respectively. After the books were closed on August 31, the following summary accounts remained:

Cash	$ 6,000	S. Anders, Capital	$30,000
Noncash assets	110,000	J. Haque, Capital	20,000
Accounts payable	25,000	R. Smit, Capital	41,000

On September 24, the partnership sold the remaining noncash assets for $74,000 and paid the liabilities. If there is a capital deficiency, none of the partners will be able to pay it. Prepare the journal entries to record (a) the sale of noncash assets, (b) the allocation of any gain or loss on realization, (c) the payment of liabilities, and (d) the distribution of cash to the partners.

Action Plan

- Calculate the gain or loss by comparing cash proceeds with the carrying amount of assets.
- Allocate any gain or loss to each partner's capital account using the profit and loss ratio.
- Allocate the capital deficiency, if there is one, using the profit and loss ratio of the other partners.
- Record the final distribution of cash to each partner to eliminate the balance in each capital account. Do not distribute cash using the profit and loss ratio.

SOLUTION

(a) Sept. 24	Cash	74,000	
	Loss on Realization	36,000	
	Noncash Assets		110,000
	To record realization of noncash assets.		
(b) Sept. 24	S. Anders, Capital ($36,000 × 3/9)	12,000	
	J. Haque, Capital ($36,000 × 2/9)	8,000	
	R. Smit, Capital ($36,000 × 4/9)	16,000	
	Loss on Realization		36,000
	To allocate loss to partners' capital accounts.		
(c) Sept. 24	Accounts Payable	25,000	
	Cash		25,000
	To record payment of liabilities.		
(d) Sept. 24	S. Anders, Capital ($30,000 – $12,000)	18,000	
	J. Haque, Capital ($20,000 – $8,000)	12,000	
	R. Smit, Capital ($41,000 – $16,000)	25,000	
	Cash ($6,000 + $74,000 – $25,000)		55,000
	To record distribution of cash to partners.		

Related exercise material: BE12–15, BE12–16, BE12–17, E12–11, E12–12, E12–13, and E12–14.

THE NAVIGATOR

Comparing IFRS and ASPE

Key Differences	International Financial Reporting Standards (IFRS)	Accounting Standards for Private Enterprises (ASPE)
No significant differences.		

THE NAVIGATOR

DEMONSTRATION PROBLEM

On January 1, 2013, the partners' capital balances in Hollingsworth Company are Lara Holly, $26,000, and Jayden Worth, $24,000. For the year ended December 31, 2013, the partnership reports profit of $32,500. The partnership agreement specifies (1) salary allowances of $12,000 for Holly and $10,000 for Worth, (2) interest allowances on opening capital account balances of 5%, and (3) the remainder to be distributed equally. Neither partner had any drawings in 2013.

In 2014, assume that the following independent transactions occur on January 2:

1. Donna Reichenbacher purchases one half of Lara Holly's capital interest from Holly for $25,000.
2. Marsha Mears is admitted with a 25% capital interest by a cash investment of $37,500.
3. Stan Keewatin is admitted with a 30% capital interest by a cash investment of $32,500.

Instructions

(a) Prepare a schedule that shows the distribution of profit in 2013.
(b) Journalize the division of 2013 profit and its distribution to the partners on December 31.
(c) Journalize each of the independent transactions that occurred on January 2, 2014.

SOLUTION TO DEMONSTRATION PROBLEM

(a)

HOLLINGSWORTH COMPANY
Division of Profit
Year Ended December 31, 2013

	L. Holly	J. Worth	Total
Profit			$32,500
Salary allowance			
L. Holly	$12,000		
J. Worth		$10,000	
Total			22,000
Profit remaining for allocation			10,500
Interest allowance			
L. Holly ($26,000 × 5%)	1,300		
J. Worth ($24,000 × 5%)		1,200	
Total			2,500
Profit remaining for allocation			8,000
Fixed ratio (remainder shared equally)			
L. Holly ($8,000 × 50%)	4,000		
J. Worth ($8,000 × 50%)		4,000	
Total			8,000
Profit remaining for allocation			0
Profit allocated to the partners	$17,300	$15,200	$32,500

Action Plan

- Allocate the partners' salaries and interest allowances, if any, first. Divide the remaining profit among the partners, based on the profit and loss ratio.
- Journalize the division of profit in a closing entry.
- Recognize the admission by purchase of a partnership interest as a personal transaction between an existing partner and the new partner that does not change the assets or total equity of a partnership.
- Recognize the admission by investment of partnership assets as a transaction between the new partner and the partnership that increases both total assets and total equity.
- In an admission by investment, determine any bonus to old or new partners by comparing the total capital of the new partnership with the new partner's capital credit. Allocate the bonus based on the old partners' profit and loss ratios.

SOLUTION TO DEMONSTRATION PROBLEM continued on next page

SOLUTION TO DEMONSTRATION PROBLEM continued from previous page

(b) 2013

Dec. 31	Income Summary	32,500	
	L. Holly, Capital		17,300
	J. Worth, Capital		15,200
	To close profit to partners' capital accounts.		

L. Holly, Capital			J. Worth, Capital		
	Bal.	26,000		Bal.	24,000
		17,300			**15,200**
	Bal.	43,300		Bal.	39,200

(c) 2014

1. Jan. 2	L. Holly, Capital ($43,300 × 50%)	21,650	
	D. Reichenbacher, Capital		21,650
	To record purchase of one half of Holly's interest.		
2. Jan. 2	Cash	37,500	
	L. Holly, Capital ($7,500 × 50%)		3,750
	J. Worth, Capital ($7,500 × 50%)		3,750
	M. Mears, Capital		30,000
	To record admission of Mears by investment and bonus to old partners.		

Total capital after investment: ($43,300 + $39,200 + $37,500)	$120,000
Mears's capital in the partnership: (25% × $120,000)	$30,000
Bonus to old partners: ($37,500 − $30,000)	$7,500

3. Jan. 2	Cash	32,500	
	L. Holly, Capital ($2,000 × 50%)	1,000	
	J. Worth, Capital ($2,000 × 50%)	1,000	
	S. Keewatin, Capital		34,500
	To record admission of Keewatin by investment and bonus to new partner.		

Total capital after investment: ($43,300 + $39,200 + $32,500)	$115,000
Keewatin's capital in the partnership: (30% × $115,000)	$34,500
Bonus to Keewatin: ($34,500 − $32,500)	$2,000

THE NAVIGATOR

Summary of Study Objectives

1. ***Describe the characteristics of the partnership form of business organization.*** The main characteristics of a partnership are (1) the association of individuals, (2) mutual agency, (3) co-ownership of property, (4) limited life, and (5) unlimited liability for a general partnership.

2. ***Account for the formation of a partnership.*** When a partnership is formed, each partner's initial investment should be recorded at the assets' fair value at the date of their transfer to the partnership. If accounts receivable are contributed, both the gross amount and an allowance for doubtful accounts should be recorded. Accumulated depreciation is not carried forward into a partnership.

3. ***Allocate and record profit or loss to partners.*** Profit or loss is divided based on the profit and loss ratio, which may be any of the following: (1) a fixed ratio; (2) a ratio based on beginning, ending, or average capital balances; (3) salaries allocated to partners and the remainder in a fixed ratio; (4) interest on partners' capital balances and the remainder in a fixed ratio; and (5) salaries allocated to partners, interest on partners' capital balances, and the remainder in a fixed ratio.

4. ***Prepare partnership financial statements.*** The financial statements of a partnership are similar to those of a proprietorship. The main differences are that (1) the statement of owners' equity is called the statement of partners' equity, and (2) each partner's capital and drawings account is usually reported on the balance sheet or in a supporting schedule.

5. ***Account for the admission of a partner.*** The entry to record the admission of a new partner by purchase of a partner's interest affects only partners' capital accounts. The entry to record the admission by investment of assets in the partnership (1) increases both net assets and total capital, and (2) may result in the recognition of a bonus to either the old partners or the new partner.

6. ***Account for the withdrawal of a partner.*** The entry to record a withdrawal from the firm when payment is made from partners' personal assets affects only partners' capital accounts.

The entry to record a withdrawal when payment is made from partnership assets (1) decreases net assets and total capital, and (2) may result in recognizing a bonus to either the departing partner or the remaining partners.

7. ***Account for the liquidation of a partnership.*** When a partnership is liquidated, it is necessary to record (1) the sale of noncash assets, (2) the allocation of the gain or loss on realization based on the profit and loss ratio, (3) the payment of partnership liabilities, (4) the removal of any capital deficiency either by repayment or by allocation to the other partners, and (5) the distribution of cash to the partners based on their capital balances.

THE NAVIGATOR

Glossary

Admission by investment Admission of a partner by an investment of assets in the partnership. Both partnership net assets and total capital increase. (p. 509)

Admission by purchase of a partner's interest Admission of a partner through a personal transaction between one or more existing partners and the new partner. It does not change total partnership assets or total capital. (p. 508)

Capital deficiency A debit balance in a partner's capital account after the allocation of a gain or loss on liquidation of a partnership. Capital deficiencies can be repaid or allocated among the remaining partners. (p. 517)

Limited liability partnership (LLP) A partnership in which partners have limited liability for other partners' negligence. (p. 498)

Limited partnership (LP) A partnership in which one or more general partners have unlimited liability, and the other partners, known as limited partners, have limited liability for the obligations of the partnership. (p. 498)

Mutual agency The concept that the action of any partner that applies to the business is binding on all other partners. (p. 497)

No capital deficiency A situation where all partners have credit balances after the allocation of a gain or a loss on liquidation of a partnership. (p. 517)

Partnership An association of individuals who operate a business for profit. (p. 496)

Partnership agreement A written contract that expresses the voluntary agreement of two or more individuals in a partnership. (p. 499)

Partnership dissolution A change in the number of partners that dissolves (ends) the partnership. It does not necessarily end the business. (p. 497)

Partnership liquidation An event that ends both the legal and economic life of a partnership. (p. 517)

Profit and loss ratio The basis for dividing both profit and loss in a partnership. (p. 502)

Realization The sale of noncash assets for cash on the liquidation of a partnership. (p. 517)

Statement of partners' equity The equity statement for a partnership that shows the changes in each partner's capital balance, and in total partnership capital, during the year. (p. 507)

Withdrawal by payment from partners' personal assets Withdrawal of a partner by a personal transaction between partners. It does not change total partnership assets or total capital. (p. 513)

Withdrawal by payment from partnership assets Withdrawal of a partner by a transaction that decreases both partnership net assets and total capital. (p. 513)

Self-Study Questions

Answers are at the end of the chapter.

(SO 1) K 1. Which one of the following is considered to be a disadvantage of the partnership form of organization?
(a) Unlimited life
(b) Limited liability
(c) Mutual agency
(d) Ease of formation

(SO 2) AP 2. Brianne and Stephen are combining their two proprietorships to form a partnership. Brianne's proprietorship has $6,000 of accounts receivable and an allowance for doubtful accounts of $1,000. The partners agree that the fair value of the accounts receivable is $4,800. The entry that the partnership makes to record Brianne's initial contribution includes a
(a) debit to Accounts Receivable for $6,000.
(b) debit to Accounts Receivable for $4,800.
(c) debit to Bad Debts Expense for $200.
(d) credit to Allowance for Doubtful Accounts for $200.

(SO 3) AP 3. The ABC Company reports profit of $60,000. Ahmed, Barrington, and Chang have a salary allowance of $10,000 each and divide any remainder in a fixed ratio of 50%, 30%, and 20%, respectively. What is each partner's share of the profit?

	Ahmed	Barrington	Chang
(a)	$20,000	$20,000	$20,000
(b)	$25,000	$19,000	$16,000
(c)	$30,000	$18,000	$12,000
(d)	$15,000	$ 9,000	$ 6,000

(SO 4) K 4. The purpose of the statement of partners' equity is to explain:
(a) The salary and interest allowances allocated to each partner.
(b) The initial contributions by each partner.
(c) The fair value of each partner's claim on the net assets of the partnership.
(d) The changes in each partner's capital account, and in total partnership capital, during the year.

(SO 5) AP 5. R. Ranken purchases 50% of L. Lars's capital interest in the Kim & Lars partnership for $20,000. The capital balances of Kim and Lars are $40,000 and $30,000, respectively. Ranken's capital balance after the purchase is:
(a) $15,000.
(b) $20,000.
(c) $22,000.
(d) $35,000.

(SO 5) AP 6. Capital balances in the DEA partnership are Delano, Capital $60,000; Egil, Capital $50,000; and Armand, Capital $40,000. The profit and loss ratio is 5:3:2. The DEAR partnership is formed by admitting Ramachandran to the firm with a cash investment of $60,000 for a 25% capital interest. The bonus to be credited to Delano, Capital, in admitting Ramachandran is:
(a) $1,500.
(b) $3,750.
(c) $7,500.
(d) $10,000.

(SO 6) AP 7. Capital balances in the Alouette partnership are Tremblay, Capital $50,000; St-Jean, Capital $40,000; and, Roy, Capital $30,000. The profit and loss ratio is 5:4:3. Roy withdraws from the partnership after being paid $16,000 personally by each of Tremblay and St-Jean. St-Jean's capital balance after recording the withdrawal of Roy is:
(a) $46,000.
(b) $50,000.
(c) $55,000.
(d) $65,000.

(SO 6) AP 8. Capital balances in the TERM partnership are Takako, Capital $50,000; Endo, Capital $40,000; Reiko, Capital $30,000; and Maeda, Capital $20,000. The profit and loss ratio is 4:3:2:1. Maeda withdraws from the firm after receiving $29,000 in cash from the partnership. Endo's capital balance after recording the withdrawal of Maeda is:
(a) $36,000.
(b) $37,000.
(c) $37,300.
(d) $40,000.

(SO 7) AP 9. Fontaine and Tomah were partners in the AFN partnership, sharing profit and losses in a ratio of 3:2. Fontaine's capital account balance was $30,000 and Tomah's was $20,000, immediately before the partnership liquidated on February 19. If noncash assets worth $60,000 were sold for $75,000, what were Fontaine and Tomah's capital account balances after the sale?

	Fontaine	Tomah
(a)	$21,000	$14,000
(b)	$30,000	$20,000
(c)	$39,000	$26,000
(d)	$66,000	$54,000

(SO 7) AP 10. Partners Aikawa, Ito, and Mori shared a profit and loss ratio of 2:1:3 in the AIM Company. After AIM was liquidated, $12,000 cash remained and the balances in the partners' capital accounts were as follows: Aikawa, $9,000 Cr.; Ito, $6,000 Cr.; and Mori, $3,000 Dr. How much cash would be distributed to Aikawa and Ito, respectively, assuming Mori does not repay his capital deficiency?
(a) $7,000 and $5,000
(b) $7,500 and $4,500
(c) $8,000 and $4,000
(d) $9,000 and $6,000

THE NAVIGATOR

Questions

(SO 1) C 1. K. Nasser and T. Yoko are considering a business venture. They ask you to explain the advantages and disadvantages of the partnership form of organization.

(SO 1) C 2. Gurprinder and Harjinder decided to form a partnership and operate a business together. Harjinder is much more cautious and concerned about keeping expenses to a minimum than Gurprinder. Harjinder also has significantly more personal assets than Gurprinder. Should Harjinder have any concerns about using the partnership form of business organization to operate this business? Explain.

(SO 1) K 3. Because of concerns over unlimited liability, there are now special forms of partnership organization that modify that characteristic. Describe these other forms of partnership.

(SO 1) K 4. (a) What items should be specified in a partnership agreement? (b) Why is it important to have this agreement in writing?

(SO 2) K 5. (a) For accounting purposes, when a partner invests assets in a partnership, how is the value of these assets determined? (b) Is this practice consistent with the cost principle? Explain.

(SO 2) K 6. When a partnership is formed, one or more of the partners may contribute equipment as part of their initial investment. How is the accumulated depreciation on this equipment accounted for?

(SO 2) K 7. Franca and Nav are transferring $8,000 of accounts receivable from each of their sole proprietorships into a partnership. They have agreed that $7,000 of Franca's receivables is collectible but it is likely they will collect only $6,000 of the receivables from Nav's proprietorship. How should these receivables be recorded in the partnership? Explain why.

(SO 3) C 8. S. Hark and R. Green are discussing how profit and losses should be divided in a partnership they plan to form. They think they should wait to see who has worked the greater number of hours before agreeing on how to share the profit. What are the advantages and disadvantages of doing this?

(SO 3) C 9. What is the relationship between (a) a salary allowance for allocating profit among partners and (b) partners' cash withdrawals?

(SO 3) C 10. What is the difference between a salary allowance for allocating profit among partners and salary expense? Between an interest allowance and interest expense?

(SO 4) C 11. What is included in a statement of partners' equity? How is it similar to a statement of owner's equity? How is it different?

(SO 4) C 12. The income statement of a partnership includes the details of how the profit or loss is divided among the partners. Do you agree or disagree? Explain.

(SO 5) AP 13. How is the accounting for admission to a partnership by purchase of a partner's interest different from the accounting for admission by an investment of assets in the partnership? In your explanation, also include how the net assets and total capital change after the admission of a partner in each of these two ways.

(SO 5) C 14. R. Minoa decides to invest $25,000 in a partnership for a one-sixth capital interest. Will Minoa's capital balance automatically be $25,000? Does Minoa necessarily also acquire a one-sixth profit and loss ratio through this investment?

(SO 5) C 15. What are some reasons why the existing partners may be willing to give a new partner a bonus for joining a partnership?

(SO 6) C 16. What is the impact on a partnership's balance sheet when (a) a partner withdraws by payment from partners' personal assets, and (b) a partner withdraws by payment from partnership assets?

(SO 6) C 17. Under what circumstances will a partner who is leaving a partnership give the remaining partners a bonus?

(SO 6) C 18. What is the purpose of a partnership's obtaining life insurance policies on each of the partners?

(SO 7) C 19. How is the liquidation of a partnership different from the dissolution of a partnership?

(SO 7) K 20. Identify the five potential steps in liquidating a partnership.

(SO 7) C 21. What basis is used for making the final distribution of cash to the partners when there is a capital deficiency and the deficiency is paid by the partner with the deficiency? And when it is not paid?

(SO 7) C 22. Joe and Rajiv are discussing the liquidation of a partnership. Joe argues that all cash should be distributed to partners based on their profit and loss ratios. Is he correct? Explain.

Brief Exercises

BE12–1 The following terms were introduced in this chapter:

Identify partnership terminology. (SO 1) K

1. Profit and loss ratio
2. Admission by investment
3. Partnership liquidation
4. Mutual agency
5. Salary allowance
6. Withdrawal by payment from partners' personal assets
7. Capital deficiency
8. Limited liability partnership
9. General partnership
10. Partnership dissolution

Match the terms with the following descriptions:

(a) ______ Partners have limited liability.
(b) ______ Partners have unlimited liability.
(c) ______ It is the basis for dividing profit and loss.
(d) ______ Partnership assets and capital increase with the change in partners.

(e) ______ Partnership assets and capital stay the same with the change in partners.
(f) ______ Actions of partners are binding on all other partners.
(g) ______ It is a compensation for differences in personal effort put into the partnership.
(h) ______ Partnership is changed by the addition or withdrawal of a partner.
(i) ______ There is a debit balance in a partner's capital account.
(j) ______ Partnership is ended.

Identify partnership characteristics. (SO 1) K

BE12–2 Place the number corresponding to each of the following characteristics in the appropriate section of the diagram. If a characteristic applies to both proprietorships and partnerships, place that number in the overlapping section.

1. Creditors have the first claim to the assets of the business
2. An association of individuals
3. Relatively easy to form
4. The simplest form of business organization
5. Relatively free from government regulation
6. Unlimited liability
7. Income taxes are paid at a personal level rather than at a business level.

Proprietorship | Partnership

Record formation of partnership. (SO 2) AP

BE12–3 R. Black and B. Rivers decide to organize the Black River Partnership. Black contributes $10,000 cash and equipment that originally cost $7,000. The accumulated depreciation on the equipment is $2,500 and the fair value is $4,000. Rivers contributes $2,400 of accounts receivable, of which the partners agree that $2,000 is collectible. Rivers will also contribute the amount of cash required so both partners have the same amount in their capital accounts. Prepare the entry to record each partner's investment in the partnership on July 1, 2014.

Prepare opening balance sheet. (SO 2) AP

BE12–4 Data for Black River Partnership are presented in BE12–3. (a) Prepare the assets section of the partnership's balance sheet at July 1, 2014. (b) What is the total amount of partners' equity on July 1, 2014?

Convert proportions into fractions and percentages. (SO 3) AP

BE12–5 Fixed profit and loss ratios can be expressed as proportions, fractions, or percentages. For each of the following proportions, determine the equivalent fractions or percentages:

	Proportions	Fractions	Percentages
(a)	2:1		
(b)	6:4		
(c)	3:8		
(d)	4:3:2		
(e)	1:2:1		

Calculate division of profit and record closing entries. (SO 3) AP

BE12–6 During the fiscal year ended November 30, 2014, the profit for Scrivens & Bernier Partnership was $84,000. The partners, A. Scrivens and D. Bernier, share profits and losses in a 3:5 ratio, respectively. (a) Calculate the division of profit to each partner. (b) Prepare entries to close the income summary and drawings accounts assuming the partners withdrew $35,000 each during the year.

Calculate division of profit. (SO 3) AP

BE12–7 MET Co. reports profit of $70,000 for the current year. Partner salary allowances are J. Moses $24,000; T. Eaton $30,000; and M. Tung-Ching $5,000. The profit and loss ratio is 5:3:2. Calculate the division of profit to each partner.

Calculate division of profit. (SO 3) AP

BE12–8 The MillStone Partnership reported profit of $60,000 for the year ended February 28, 2014. Salary allowances are $45,000 for H. Mills and $25,000 for S. Stone. Interest allowances of 5% are calculated on each partner's opening capital account balance. Capital account balances at March 1, 2013, were as follows: H. Mills $72,000 (Cr.) and S. Stone $47,000 (Cr.). Any remainder is shared equally. Calculate the division of profit to each partner.

Calculate and record division of loss. (SO 3) AP

BE12–9 Tognazzini Company had a $15,000 loss for the year ended October 31, 2014. The company is a partnership owned by Lilia and Terry Tognazzini. Salary allowances for the partners are Lilia $25,000 and Terry $16,000. Interest allowances are Lilia $5,000 and Terry $9,000. The remainder is shared 75% by Lilia and 25% by Terry. (a) Calculate the loss to be allocated to each partner. (b) Prepare a journal entry to close the income summary account.

Prepare financial statements. (SO 4) AP

BE12–10 The medical practice of Dr. W. Jarratt and Dr. M. Bramstrup had the following general ledger account balances at April 30, 2014, its fiscal year end:

Accounts payable	$25,000	M. Bramstrup, drawings	$120,000
Accumulated depreciation—equipment	15,000	Operating expenses	145,000
Cash	35,000	Service revenue	375,000
Equipment	75,000	W. Jarratt, capital	35,000
M. Bramstrup, capital	50,000	W. Jarratt, drawings	125,000

(a) Calculate the profit or loss for the year.
(b) Prepare the statement of partners' equity and the balance sheet, assuming the doctors share profit or loss equally. (*Hint:* Since the closing entries have not been recorded, the capital balances do not include either partner's share of the profit or loss for the fiscal year.)

BE12–11 In ABC Co., the capital balances of the partners are A. Ali $30,000; S. Babson $25,000; and K. Carter $36,000. The partners share profit equally. On June 9 of the current year, D. Dutton is admitted to the partnership by purchasing one half of K. Carter's interest for $20,000. (a) Journalize the admission of Dutton on June 9. (b) How would the entry change if Dutton had paid $20,000 to purchase one half of A. Ali's interest instead of K. Carter's interest?

Record admission of partner. **(SO 5) AP**

BE12–12 In the EZ Co., the capital balances of the partners are J. Edie $48,000 and K. Zane $32,000. The partners share profit in a 5:3 ratio, respectively. On October 1 of the current year, when she invests $40,000 cash in the partnership, J. Kerns is admitted to the partnership with a 40% interest. (a) Journalize the admission of Kerns on October 1. (b) What would the journal entry be if Kerns had paid $60,000 for a 40% interest in the partnership?

Record admission of partner. **(SO 5) AP**

BE12–13 On December 31, 2014, capital balances of the partners in Manitoba Maple Co. are R. Neepawa $45,000; S. Altona $35,000; and T. Morden $25,000. The partners share profit in a 5:3:2 ratio, respectively. Morden decides that she is going to leave the partnership. Journalize the withdrawal of Morden assuming:

Record withdrawal of partner. **(SO 6) AP**

(a) Neepawa and Altona both pay Morden $17,000 from their personal assets to each receive 50% of Morden's equity.
(b) Neepawa and Altona both pay Morden $12,000 from their personal assets to each receive 50% of Morden's equity.
(c) Neepawa pays Morden $30,000 from her personal assets to receive 100% of Morden's equity.

BE12–14 Data for Manitoba Maple Co. are presented in BE12–13. Instead of a payment from personal assets, assume that Morden receives cash from the partnership when she withdraws from the partnership. Journalize the withdrawal of Morden if she receives (a) $35,000 cash, and (b) $20,000 cash.

Record withdrawal of partner. **(SO 6) AP**

BE12–15 On November 15 of the current year, the account balances in Greenscape Partnership were Cash $8,000; Other Assets $17,000; D. Dupuis, Capital $12,000; V. Dueck, Capital $10,000; and B. Veitch, Capital $3,000. The three partners share profit and losses equally. The other assets are sold for $20,000 cash. Prepare journal entries to (a) record the sale of the other assets, (b) distribute any resulting gain or loss to the capital accounts, and (c) record the final distribution of cash to the partners.

Record partnership liquidation. **(SO 7) AP**

BE12–16 Data for Greenscape Partnership are presented in BE12–15. Assume that the other assets were sold for $14,000 cash instead of $20,000. Prepare journal entries to (a) record the sale of the other assets, (b) distribute any resulting gain or loss to the capital accounts, and (c) record the final distribution of cash to the partners.

Record partnership liquidation. **(SO 7) AP**

BE12–17 Before the distribution of cash to the partners on April 30 of the current year, the accounts in LMN Enterprises are as follows:

Record partnership liquidation. **(SO 7) AP**

	Debit	Credit
Cash	$40,000	
G. Lodge, Capital	4,000	
L. McDonald, Capital		$20,000
A. Norin, Capital		24,000

The profit and loss ratio is 4:3:2. (a) Assuming Lodge repays her capital deficiency, prepare the entry on April 30 to record (1) Lodge's payment of $4,000 in cash to the partnership, and (2) the distribution of cash to the partners. (b) Assuming Lodge is not able to repay her capital deficiency, prepare the entry on April 30 to record (1) the absorption of Lodge's capital deficiency by the other partners, and (2) the distribution of cash to the partners.

Exercises

Determine form of organization. (SO 1) AN

E12–1 Presented below are three independent situations:

1. Angelique Gloss and David Deutsch, two students looking for summer employment, decide to open a home meal replacement business. Each day, they prepare nutritious, ready-to-bake meals, which they sell to people on their way home from work.
2. Joe Daigle and Cathy Goodfellow own a ski repair business and a ski shop, respectively. They have decided to combine their businesses. They expect that in the coming year they will need a large amount of money to expand their operations.
3. Three business professors have formed a business to offer income tax preparation services to the community. They expect to hire students during the busy season.
4. Myles Anawak would like to organize a company that buys and leases commercial real estate. Myles will need to raise a large amount of capital so that he can buy commercial property for lease.

Instructions

In each of the above situations, explain whether the partnership form of organization is the best choice for the business. Explain your reasoning.

Record formation of partnership and prepare partial balance sheet. (SO 2) AP

E12–2 Hollis Sourman and Heidi Sweetgrass have each operated a proprietorship for several years. On January 1, 2014, they decide to form the Sour and Sweet Partnership and transfer the assets from their proprietorships to the partnership. The following information is available:

	Hollis Sourman		Heidi Sweetgrass	
	Book Value	Fair Value	Book Value	Fair Value
Cash	$10,000	$10,000	$7,000	$7,000
Accounts receivable			6,500	6,500
Allowance for doubtful accounts			(500)	(1,500)
Equipment	12,000	6,000		
Accumulated depreciation	(4,000)			

Instructions

(a) Prepare entries to record the partners' investment in the Sour and Sweet Partnership.
(b) Prepare the assets section of the balance sheet at January 1, 2014.

Calculate and record division of profit. (SO 3) AP

E12–3 R. Huma and W. Howe have capital balances on July 1, 2014, of $60,000 and $55,000, respectively. The partnership profit-sharing agreement specifies (1) salary allowances of $30,000 for Huma and $22,000 for Howe, (2) interest at 5% on beginning capital balances, and (3) for the remaining profit or loss to be shared 60% by Huma and 40% by Howe.

Instructions

(a) Prepare a schedule showing the division of profit for the year ended June 30, 2015, assuming profit is (1) $70,000, and (2) $55,000.
(b) Journalize the allocation of profit in each of the situations in part (a).

Calculate and record division of loss. (SO 3) AP

E12–4 Daisey Brodsky and Jim Leigh began a partnership on February 1, 2014, by investing $62,000 and $88,000, respectively. They agree to share profit and losses by allocating yearly salary allowances of $60,000 to Daisey and $40,000 to Jim, an interest allowance of 8% on their investments, and to split the remainder 55:45. During the year, Daisey withdrew $30,000 and Jim withdrew $22,000. The partnership recorded a loss of $15,000 in its first fiscal year.

Instructions

(a) Prepare a schedule showing the division of the loss for the year.
(b) Prepare the journal entry to close the income summary account at the end of the year.
(c) How much of the loss should be allocated to each partner if Daisey and Jim failed to agree on the method of sharing profit or loss?

Prepare partial financial statements and closing entries. (SO 3, 4) AP

E12–5 Copperfield Developments is a partnership owned by Alvaro Rodriguez and Elisabetta Carrieri. On December 31, 2013, the partners' capital balances are Alvaro $61,000 and Elisabetta $79,000. During 2014, Elisabetta invested $4,000 cash into the partnership; drawings were $32,000 by Alvaro and $55,000 by Elisabetta, and profit was $77,000. Alvaro and Elizabetta share profit based on a 3:4 ratio.

Instructions

(a) Prepare the statement of partners' equity for the year.
(b) Prepare the partners' equity section of the balance sheet at year end.
(c) Prepare entries to close the income summary and drawings accounts.

E12–6 Dr. J. Kovacik and Dr. S. Donovan have been operating a dental practice as a partnership for several years. The fixed profit and loss ratio is 60% for Dr. Kovacik and 40% for Dr. Donovan. The dental practice had the following general ledger account balances at November 30, 2014, its fiscal year end:

Prepare financial statements and closing entries. **(SO 3, 4) AP**

Cash	$ 32,000
Supplies	15,750
Equipment	175,500
Accumulated depreciation—equipment	41,250
Accounts payable	15,000
Note payable, due 2018	50,000
J. Kovacik, capital	58,000
J. Kovacik, drawings	140,000
S. Donovan, capital	32,000
S. Donovan, drawings	90,000
Fees earned	422,000
Salaries expense	78,500
Office expense	81,500
Interest expense	5,000

Instructions

(a) Prepare financial statements for the partnership.
(b) Prepare closing entries.

E12–7 A. Veveris and J. Rubenis share profit on a 2:1 basis, respectively. They have capital balances of $42,000 and $33,000, respectively, when S. Weiss is admitted to the partnership on September 1, 2014.

Record admission of partner. **(SO 5) AP**

Instructions

(a) Prepare the journal entry to record the admission of Weiss under each of the following independent assumptions:
  1. Weiss purchases 50% of Ververis's equity for $25,000.
  2. Weiss purchases 25% of Ververis's and Rubenis's equity for $15,000 and $10,000, respectively.
  3. Weiss invests $25,000 cash in the partnership for a 25% interest in the partnership.
(b) For each of these alternatives, indicate the balance in each partner's capital account and total partners' equity after Weiss is admitted to the partnership.

E12–8 Olive Oil Imports is a partnership owned by Magda Stavros and Nick Hatzimalis. The partners share profit on a 3:2 basis, respectively. On January 1, 2014, they have capital balances of $95,000 and $65,000, respectively. On that day, Magda and Nick agree to admit Iona Xanthos to the partnership in exchange for an investment of cash into the partnership.

Record admission of partner. **(SO 5) AP**

Instructions

(a) Prepare the journal entry to record the admission of Iona on January 1 under each of the following independent assumptions:
  1. Iona invests $65,000 cash for a 33⅓% ownership interest.
  2. Iona invests $95,000 cash for a 33⅓% ownership interest.
(b) For each of these alternatives, indicate the balance in each partner's capital account and total partners' equity after Iona is admitted to the partnership.
(c) Calculate the amount Iona would have to pay for a 33⅓% ownership interest where there would be no bonus to the old partners or to Iona.

E12–9 Julie Lane, Sara Miles, and Amber Noll have capital balances of $50,000, $40,000, and $30,000, respectively. The profit and loss ratio is 5:3:2. Assume Noll withdraws from the partnership on December 31 of the current year under each of the following independent conditions:

Record withdrawal of partner. **(SO 6) AP**

1. Lane and Miles agree to purchase Noll's equity by paying $17,500 each from their personal assets. Each purchaser receives 50% of Noll's equity.
2. Miles agrees to purchase all of Noll's equity by paying $35,000 cash from her personal assets.
3. Noll withdraws $30,000 cash from the partnership.
4. Noll withdraws $35,000 cash from the partnership.

Instructions

(a) Journalize the withdrawal of Noll under each of the above assumptions.
(b) Determine the balances in the partners' capital accounts and in total partners' equity after Noll has withdrawn, for conditions 1 and 4 above.

Record withdrawal of partner. (SO 6) AP

E12–10 Dale Nagel, Keith White, and Issa Mbango have capital balances of $95,000, $73,000, and $65,000, respectively. They share profit or loss on a 4:3:2 basis. White withdraws from the partnership on September 30 of the current year.

Instructions

(a) Journalize the withdrawal of White under each of the following assumptions.
    1. White is paid $85,000 cash from partnership assets.
    2. White is paid $68,000 cash from partnership assets.
    3. White sells his interest in the partnership to Emily Wolstenholme for $68,000 cash.
(b) Determine the balances in the partners' capital accounts and in total partners' equity after White has withdrawn from the partnership for conditions 2 and 3 above.

Calculate amounts paid on liquidation of partnership. (SO 7) AP

E12–11 Windl, Houghton, and Pesowski decided to liquidate their partnership on October 1. Before the noncash assets were sold, the capital account balances were Windl, $86,250; Houghton, $34,500; and Pesowski, $51,750. The partners divide profits and losses equally. After the noncash assets are sold and the liabilities are paid, the partnership has $172,500 of cash.

Instructions

(a) How much cash will each partner receive in the final liquidation?
(b) Assume instead that there is $139,500 of cash after the noncash assets are sold and the liabilities are paid. How much cash will each partner receive?

Calculate amounts paid on liquidation of partnership. (SO 7) AP

E12–12 At December 31, Baylee Company has cash of $40,000, equipment of $130,000, accumulated depreciation of $40,000, liabilities of $55,000, and the following partners' capital balances: H. Bayer $45,000 and J. Leech $30,000. The partnership is liquidated on December 31 of the current year and $100,000 cash is received for the equipment. Bayer and Leech share profits and losses equally.

Instructions

(a) How much is the gain or loss on the disposal of the noncash assets?
(b) How much of that gain or loss is allocated to each partner?
(c) How much cash will be paid to each of the partners when the company is liquidated on December 31?

Record partnership liquidation. (SO 7) AP

E12–13 Data for the Baylee Company partnership are presented in E12–12.

Instructions

Prepare the entries to record (a) the sale of the equipment, (b) the allocation to the partners of the gain or loss on liquidation, (c) the payment of creditors, and (d) the distribution of cash to the partners.

Record partnership liquidation. (SO 7) AP

E12–14 Ole Lundquist, Arnt Olson, and Stig Lindholm decided to liquidate the LOL partnership on December 31 of the current year, and go their separate ways. The partners share profit and losses equally. As at December 31, the partnership had cash of $15,000, noncash assets of $120,000, and liabilities of $20,000. Before selling their noncash assets, the partners had capital balances of $45,000, $60,000, and $10,000, respectively. The noncash assets were sold for $84,000 and the creditors were paid.

Instructions

(a) Calculate the loss on the sale of the noncash assets and the amount of cash remaining after paying the liabilities.
(b) Calculate the balance in each of the partners' capital accounts after allocating the loss from the sale of the noncash assets and paying the liabilities.

(c) Assume that all of the partners have the personal resources to cover a deficit in their capital accounts. Prepare journal entries to record any cash receipts from the partners to cover any existing deficit and to record the final distribution of cash.
(d) Now assume that the partners do not have the personal resources to cover a deficit in their capital accounts. Prepare journal entries to allocate any deficit to the remaining partners and to record the final distribution of cash.

Problems: Set A

P12–1A Patricia Derbyshire and Ann Oleksiw are interested in starting a marketing company that will focus on branding for performers and musicians in the entertainment industry. Patricia is very creative and understands how the entertainment industry operates. Ann has exceptional administrative and customer relations skills.

Discuss advantages and disadvantages of partnerships and partnership agreements. **(SO 1) C**

Instructions

(a) What are the advantages and disadvantages for these two individuals of forming a partnership as opposed to setting up a corporation?
(b) Assuming they decide to form a partnership, what should be included in their partnership agreement? Be specific given the nature of their business and the two partners.

TAKING IT FURTHER How can a partnership agreement help reduce the effects of mutual agency?

P12–2A The trial balances of two proprietorships on January 1, 2014, follow:

Record formation of partnership and prepare balance sheet. **(SO 2, 4) AP**

	Domic Company		Dasilva Company	
	Dr.	Cr.	Dr.	Cr.
Cash	$ 9,000		$10,000	
Accounts receivable	13,500		24,000	
Allowance for doubtful accounts		$ 3,000		$ 5,500
Merchandise inventory	11,500		15,500	
Equipment	40,000		31,000	
Accumulated depreciation—equipment		24,000		13,000
Accounts payable		11,000		34,000
I. Domic, capital		36,000		
P. Dasilva, capital				28,000
	$74,000	$74,000	$80,500	$80,500

Domic and Dasilva decide to form a partnership on January 1 and agree on the following valuations for the noncash assets that they are each contributing:

	Domic	Dasilva
Accounts receivable—net realizable value	$ 9,000	$21,000
Merchandise inventory	14,000	13,000
Equipment	18,000	15,000

All of the assets in each of the proprietorships will be transferred to the partnership. The partnership will also assume all the liabilities of the two proprietorships. Domic and Dasilva are also agreed that Dasilva will invest the amount of cash required so their investments in the partnership are equal.

Instructions

(a) Prepare separate journal entries to record the transfer of each proprietorship's assets and liabilities to the partnership on January 1.
(b) Journalize the additional cash investment.
(c) Prepare a balance sheet for the partnership at January 1.

TAKING IT FURTHER What are some of the advantages of two individuals such as Domic and Dasilva operating as a partnership instead of as two separate proprietorships?

Calculate and record division of profit. Prepare statement of partners' equity. (SO 3, 4) AP

P12–3A At the end of its first year of operations, on December 31, 2014, CDW Company's accounts show the following:

Partner	Drawings	Capital
J. Chapman-Brown	$10,000	$30,000
C. Duperé	8,000	40,000
H. Weir	6,000	50,000

The capital balance represents each partner's initial capital investment. No closing entries for profit (loss) or drawings have been recorded as yet.

Instructions

(a) Journalize the entry to record the division of profit for the year ended December 31, 2014, under each of the following independent assumptions:
  1. Profit is $40,000. Duperé and Weir are given salary allowances of $8,000 and $12,000, respectively. The remainder is shared equally.
  2. Profit is $40,000. Each partner is allowed interest of 5% on beginning capital balances. Chapman-Brown, Duperé, and Weir are given salary allowances of $15,000, $20,000, and $18,000, respectively. The remainder is shared in a ratio of 5:3:2.

(b) Journalize the entry to close each partner's drawings account.

(c) Prepare a statement of partners' equity for the year under assumption (2) in part (a) above.

TAKING IT FURTHER Explain why partnerships such as CDW Company include an interest allowance in their profit- and loss-sharing arrangements.

Calculate division of profit or loss. Prepare income statement, statement of partners' equity, and closing entries. (SO 3, 4) AP

P12–4A Veda Storey and Gordon Rogers have a partnership agreement with the following provisions for sharing profit or loss:

1. A salary allowance of $30,000 to Storey and $40,000 to Rogers
2. An interest allowance of 4% on capital balances at the beginning of the year
3. The remainder to be divided between Storey and Rogers on a 2:3 basis

The capital balances on January 1, 2014, for Storey and Rogers were $80,000 and $100,000, respectively. For the year ended December 31, 2014, the Storey Rogers Partnership had sales of $340,000; cost of goods sold of $250,000; operating expenses of $130,000; V. Storey drawings of $24,000; and G. Rogers drawings of $32,000.

Instructions

(a) Prepare an income statement for Storey Rogers Partnership for the year.

(b) Prepare a schedule to show how the profit or loss will be allocated to the two partners.

(c) Prepare a statement of partners' equity for the year.

(d) Prepare closing entries at December 31.

TAKING IT FURTHER Assume that gross profit was lower than expected for 2014 because Rogers sold a significant amount of inventory to friends at substantially reduced prices. These arrangements were made without Storey's approval. She therefore argues that she should be allocated her salary allowance and the remaining loss should be allocated to Rogers. Is this reasonable?

Prepare financial statements and closing entries. (SO 3, 4) AP

P12–5A Below is an alphabetical listing of the accounts in the general ledger of the Kant-Adder accounting firm at the partnership's fiscal year end, March 31, 2014. Adjusting entries for the year have been posted and included in these balances.

Accounts payable	$ 12,500	Note payable	$ 50,000
Accounts receivable	61,000	Rent expense	36,000
Accumulated depreciation—equipment	12,000	Salaries expense	80,000
Cash	14,000	Salaries payable	8,000
Depreciation expense	8,000	Supplies	1,500
Equipment	42,000	Supplies expense	5,000
Fees earned	255,000	U. Adder, capital	30,000
I. Kant, capital	30,000	U. Adder, drawings	60,000
I. Kant, drawings	90,000	Unearned revenue	5,000
Interest expense	5,000		

Additional information:

1. The balance in Kant's capital account includes an additional $5,000 investment during the year.
2. $1,500 of the note payable is due within the next year.
3. Kant and Adder share profit in the ratio of 2:1, respectively.

Instructions

(a) Prepare an income statement, statement of partners' equity, and balance sheet.
(b) Journalize the closing entries.

TAKING IT FURTHER Each partner's drawings are larger than their respective capital account balances. Is this a problem?

P12–6A Tyler Gilligan and Matt Melnyk, two college friends, decided to set up a snow removal business called Ty & Matt Snow Removal Services. On January 1, 2014, they put their resources together, shook hands, and started their business. They each contributed the following to the business:

Prepare entries to form a partnership, allocate profit, and close temporary accounts; prepare financial statements. **(SO 1, 2, 3, 4) AP**

	Tyler Gilligan		Matt Melnyk	
	Original Cost	Fair Value	Original Cost	Fair Value
Cash	$ 2,000	$ 2,000	$ 1,000	$ 1,000
Equipment	3,000	2,000		
Vehicle			25,000	10,000

At the end of the first year of business, Tyler, who was studying accounting, provided the following information:

TY & MATT SNOW REMOVAL SERVICES Income Statement Year ended December 31, 2014		
Service revenue		$50,000
Expenses		
Supplies expense	$ 6,000	
Depreciation expense	2,400	
Salaries expense	30,000	38,400
Profit		$11,600

Additional information:

1. Salaries expense is $20,000 and $10,000 cash paid to Tyler and Matt, respectively, during the year.
2. All revenues were collected in cash.
3. All supplies were paid for in cash. At the end of the year, there were no supplies on hand.
4. Tyler estimates that the equipment and vehicle have five-year useful lives, with no residual value. He used the straight-line method to calculate depreciation expense.
5. There is $17,000 in the bank account at December 31, 2014.

Instructions

(a) Prepare the entries to record each partner's investment in the partnership on January 2, 2014.
(b) Prepare journal entries to correct the errors, if any, on the income statement.
(c) Calculate the correct profit and the amount to be allocated to each partner.
(d) Prepare a statement of partners' equity for the year ended December 31, 2014.
(e) Prepare a balance sheet at December 31, 2014.
(f) Prepare closing entries for 2014.

TAKING IT FURTHER Tyler is not happy about how the profit was allocated. He says that he works twice as hard as Matt. Matt argues that he made a larger contribution to start the partnership. What should Tyler and Matt do to deal with their concerns?

P12–7A At April 30 of the current year, partners' capital balances and the profit- and loss-sharing ratio in SOS Enterprises are as follows:

Record admission of partner. **(SO 5) AP**

Partner	Capital Balance	Profit and Loss Ratio
R. Sanga	$40,000	3
K. Osborne	$20,000	2
W. Sanga	$60,000	4

On May 1, the SOSO Company is formed by admitting N. Okongwu to the firm as a partner.

Instructions

Journalize the admission of Okongwu under each of the following independent assumptions:

(a) Okongwu purchases 50% of W. Sanga's ownership interest by paying W. Sanga $32,000 cash.
(b) Okongwu purchases 50% of Osborne's ownership interest by paying Osborne $13,000 cash.
(c) Okongwu invests $70,000 cash in the partnership for a 40% ownership interest.
(d) Okongwu invests $40,000 in the partnership for a 20% ownership interest.
(e) Okongwu invests $30,000 in the partnership for a 20% ownership interest.

TAKING IT FURTHER Why would a new partner be willing to pay a bonus to the existing partners in order to join a partnership? Give an example of a situation where this might happen.

Record withdrawal of partner. **(SO 6) AP**

P12–8A On December 31, the capital balances and profit and loss ratios in the EVA Company are as follows:

Partner	Capital Balance	Profit and Loss Ratio
R. Edmondson	$140,000	60%
P. Velianoski	$ 60,000	30%
R. Antoni	$ 49,000	10%

Antoni is withdrawing from the partnership.

Instructions

Journalize the withdrawal of Antoni under each of the following independent assumptions:

(a) Each of the remaining partners agrees to pay $29,000 cash from personal funds to purchase Antoni's ownership equity. Each partner receives 50% of Antoni's equity.
(b) Velianoski agrees to purchase Antoni's ownership interest for $58,000 cash.
(c) Antoni is paid $58,000 from partnership assets.
(d) Antoni is paid $38,200 from partnership assets.

TAKING IT FURTHER What factors are important in deciding whether the withdrawing partner should be paid from the remaining partners' personal assets or from the partnership's assets?

Record withdrawal and admission of partners; allocate profit. **(SO 3, 5, 6) AP**

P12–9A Triple A Accountants is a partnership with three partners. On February 28, 2014, the three partners, M. Kumar, H. Deol, and A. Kassam, have capital balances of $85,000, $72,000, and $43,000, respectively. The profit and loss ratio is 4:3:1. On March 1, 2014, Deol withdraws from the partnership and they agree to pay him $90,000 cash from the partnership assets.

After Deol leaves, Kumar and Kassam agree to a 4:2 profit ratio. During the year ended February 28, 2015, the partnership earns a profit of $24,000. Neither Kumar nor Kassam makes any withdrawals because the partnership is short of cash after paying Deol. On March 1, 2015, Kumar and Kassam agree to admit C. Mawani to the partnership with a 45% interest for $75,000 cash. After Mawani is admitted, the new profit ratio will be 4:2:5 for Kumar, Kassam, and Mawani, respectively.

Instructions

(a) Journalize the withdrawal of Deol from the partnership.
(b) What are the balances in Kumar's and Kassam's capital accounts after Deol leaves the partnership?
(c) Prepare the journal entry to close the income summary account on February 28, 2015.
(d) What is the total partnership capital on March 1, 2015, prior to admitting Mawani?
(e) Prepare the journal entry to record the admission of Mawani into the partnership.
(f) What is the balance in each of the partners' capital accounts after Mawani is admitted to the partnership?

TAKING IT FURTHER Why would the remaining partners agree to pay a bonus to a partner who is withdrawing from the partnership?

P12–10A The partners in Cottage Country Company decided to liquidate the company on April 30, 2014, when balances in the company's accounts were as follows:

Prepare and post entries for partnership liquidation. **(SO 7) AP**

Cash	$11,700	Accumulated depreciation	$16,800
Accounts receivable	23,500	Accounts payable	30,200
Allowance for doubtful accounts	1,700	K. Bogue, capital	42,100
Inventory	47,100	T. O'Connor, capital	18,800
Equipment	28,600	D. Pasic, capital	1,300

The partners share profit and loss 5:3:2 for Bogue, O'Connor, and Pasic, respectively. During the process of liquidation, the transactions below were completed in the sequence shown:

1. A total of $18,000 was collected from the accounts receivable on May 4.
2. The inventory and equipment were sold for $50,000 cash on May 6.
3. Liabilities were paid in full on May 7.
4. Pasic paid his capital deficiency on May 9.
5. Cash was paid to the partners with credit balances on May 12.

Instructions

(a) Prepare the entries to record the transactions.
(b) Post the transactions to the cash and capital accounts.
(c) Assume instead that Pasic is unable to repay his capital deficiency. Prepare the entry to record (1) the reallocation of his deficiency, and (2) the final distribution of cash.

TAKING IT FURTHER When determining how the cash is distributed to partners in a liquidation, the profit and loss ratio should be used. Is this correct or incorrect? Why?

P12–11A The three partners of Hawkdale Veterinary Clinic agree to liquidate their partnership on August 8, 2014. At that point, the accounting records show the following balances:

Record liquidation of partnership. **(SO 7) AP**

Cash	$150,000	R. Coolsaet, capital	$230,000
Supplies	400,000	E. Gillis, capital	170,000
Bank loan payable	125,000	D. Wykes, capital	25,000

The three partners share profit and loss equally.

Instructions

(a) Journalize the liquidation of the partnership on August 8 under each of the following independent assumptions:
   1. The supplies are sold for $430,000 cash, the bank loan payable is paid, and the remaining cash is paid to the partners.
   2. The supplies are sold for $310,000 cash and the bank loan payable is paid. Assume that any partners with a debit capital balance pay the amount owed to the partnership.
(b) Refer to item 2 above. Assume instead that any partners with a debit capital balance are unable to pay the amount owed to the partnership. Journalize the reallocation of the deficiency and final distribution of cash to the remaining partners.

TAKING IT FURTHER What can partners do when a partnership is first created to reduce the possibility that one of the partners will have a deficit (debit balance) when the partnership is liquidated?

P12–12A On March 2, 2013, Zoe Moreau, Karen Krneta, and Veronica Visentin start a partnership to operate a personal coaching and lifestyle consulting practice for professional women. Zoe will focus on work-life balance issues, Karen on matters of style, and Veronica on health and fitness. They sign a partnership agreement to split profits in a 3:2:3 ratio for Zoe, Karen, and Veronica, respectively. The following are the transactions for MKV Personal Coaching:

Account for formation of a partnership, allocation of profits, and withdrawal and admission of partners; prepare partial balance sheet. **(SO 2, 3, 4, 5, 6) AP**

2013

Mar. 2 The partners contribute assets to the partnership at the following agreed amounts:

	Z. Moreau	K. Krneta	V. Visentin
Cash	$15,000	$10,000	$20,000
Furniture		17,000	
Equipment	18,000		13,000
Total	$33,000	$27,000	$33,000

They also agree that the partnership will assume responsibility for Karen's note payable of $5,000.

Dec. 20 Zoe, Karen, and Veronica each withdraw $30,000 cash as a "year-end bonus." No other withdrawals were made during the year.

31 Total profit for 2013 was $110,000.

2014

Jan. 5 Zoe and Veronica approve Karen's request to withdraw from the partnership for personal reasons. They agree to pay Karen $15,000 cash from the partnership.

6 Zoe and Veronica agree to change their profit-sharing ratio to 4:5, respectively.

Dec. 20 Zoe and Veronica withdraw $42,750 and $45,000 cash, respectively, from the partnership.

31 Total profit for 2014 was $123,750.

2015

Jan. 4 Zoe and Veronica agree to admit Dela Hirjikaka to the partnership. Dela will focus on providing training in organizational skills to clients. Dela invests $31,000 cash for a 25% ownership in the partnership.

Instructions

(a) Record the above transactions. For the profit earned each year, calculate how it is to be allocated and record the closing of the income summary account.

(b) Prepare the partners' equity section of the balance sheet after Dela is admitted to the partnership.

TAKING IT FURTHER Every time a new partner is admitted to a partnership or a partner withdraws from a partnership, it is necessary to completely close the accounting records of the existing partnership and start new accounting records for the new partnership. Do you agree or disagree? Explain.

CONTINUING COOKIE CHRONICLE

(*Note:* This is a continuation of the Cookie Chronicle from Chapters 1 through 11.)

Because Natalie has been so successful operating Cookie Creations, Katy would like to have Natalie become her partner. Katy believes that together they will create a thriving cookie-making business. Recall that Katy is Natalie's high school friend and has been operating her bakery for approximately 10 months.

Natalie is quite happy with her current business set-up. Up until now, she had not considered joining forces with anyone. From past meetings with Katy, however, Natalie has gathered the following information about Katy's business and compared it with her own results.

- The current fair values of the assets and liabilities of both businesses are as follows:

	The Baker's Nook	Cookie Creations
Cash	$ 1,500	$8,050
Accounts receivable	5,250	800
Merchandise inventory	500	1,200
Supplies	350	450
Equipment	7,500	1,500
Bank loan payable	10,000	0

All assets would be transferred into the partnership. The partnership would assume all of the liabilities of the two proprietorships. The Baker's Nook bank loan is due on October 31, 2015.

- Katy operates her business from leased premises. She has just signed a lease for 12 months. Monthly rent will be $1,000; Katy's landlord has agreed to draw up a new lease agreement that would be signed by both partners.
- Katy has no assets and has a lot of student loans and credit card debt. Natalie's assets consist of investments in Canada Savings Bonds. Natalie has no personal liabilities.
- Katy is reluctant to have a partnership agreement drawn up. She thinks it's a waste of both time and money. As Katy and Natalie have been friends for a long time, Katy is confident that all problems can be easily resolved over a nice meal.

Natalie believes that it may be a good idea to establish a partnership with Katy. She comes to you with the following questions:

1. Do I really need a formalized partnership agreement drawn up? What would be the point of having one if Katy and I agree on all major decisions? What type of information should the partnership agreement contain?
2. I would like to have Katy contribute the same amount of capital as I am contributing. How much additional cash, in addition to the amount in Katy's proprietorship, would Katy have to borrow to invest in the partnership so that she and I have the same capital balances?
3. Katy has a lot of personal debt. Should this affect my decision about whether or not to go forward with this business venture? Why or why not?
4. What other issues should I consider before I say yes or no to Katy?

Instructions

(a) Answer Natalie's questions.

(b) Assume that Natalie and Katy go ahead and form a partnership called Cookie Creations and More on August 1, 2014, and that Katy is able to borrow the additional cash she needs to contribute to the partnership. Prepare a balance sheet for the partnership at August 1.

BROADENING YOUR PERSPECTIVE — CHAPTER 12

Collaborative Learning Activity

Note to instructor: Additional instructions and handout material for this group activity can be found on the Instructor Resource Site and in *WileyPLUS*.

BYP12–1 In this group activity, you will be given two independent scenarios: one involving the admission of a partner, and one involving the withdrawal of a partner. You will be required to determine the balance in the cash account and in each partner's capital account after the change in ownership.

Communication Activity

BYP12–2 You are an expert in forming partnerships. Dr. Konu Chatterjie and Dr. Sheila Unger want to establish a partnership to practise medicine. They will meet with you to discuss their plans. However, you will first send them a letter that outlines the issues they need to consider beforehand.

Instructions

Write a letter, in good form, discussing the different types of partnership organizations and the advantages and disadvantages of each type so that the doctors can start thinking about their needs.

Ethics Case

BYP12–3 Susan and Erin operate a spa as partners and share profits and losses equally. Their business has been more successful than they expected and is operating profitably. Erin works hard to maximize profits. She schedules appointments from 8 a.m. to 6 p.m. daily and she even works weekends. Susan schedules her appointments from 9 a.m. to 5 p.m. and does not work weekends. Susan regularly makes much larger withdrawals of cash than Erin does, but tells Erin not to worry. "I never make a withdrawal without you knowing about it," she says to Erin, "so it's properly recorded in my drawings account and charged against my capital at the end of the year." To date, Susan's withdrawals are twice as much as Erin's.

Instructions

(a) Who are the stakeholders in this situation?
(b) Identify the problems with Susan's actions. In what ways are they unethical?
(c) What provisions could be put in the partnership agreement so that the differences in Susan's and Erin's work and withdrawal habits are no longer unfair to Erin?

All About You: Personal Financial Literacy Activity

BYP12–4 In the "All About You" feature, we learned about some famous partnerships. The Beatles and the Rolling Stones were popular music bands that started in the early 1960s. However, the Beatles broke up in 1970 after disagreements, including a disagreement on who should be their financial advisor. In contrast, the Rolling Stones have continued to play together and even went on tour to celebrate 50 years together as a band.

You and a couple of friends have decided to form an "indie" band. An indie band records and publishes its music independently from commercial record labels, thus maintaining control over its music and career. You play the guitar and sing; your friends are a bass player and a keyboard player. You have written the lyrics to a couple of songs and the music for the lyrics was composed by the band. After the songs are recorded, the band intends to register the recordings with SOCAN. SOCAN sells access to music registered with it by collecting licence fees from anyone playing or broadcasting live or recorded music. SOCAN then pays the musicians a royalty.

The three of you have decided to get together and discuss some of the issues that may arise and what should be addressed in the band's agreement.

Instructions

(a) Is the band a partnership even if a partnership agreement is never created?
(b) Identify the different types of revenues that the band may earn.
(c) Identify the costs that the band will incur to earn these revenues.
(d) Identify issues that may arise when the band is determining how the revenues and costs should be shared by the members.
(e) Identify issues that may arise if one of the band members wants to leave the band. How might this be addressed in the agreement?
(f) Identify issues that may arise if a new member joins the band after the band has already successfully recorded music and is receiving royalties.
(g) Identify issues that may arise if one of the band members does a solo recording or performance.
(h) Identify issues that may arise if the band decides to split up.

ANSWERS TO CHAPTER QUESTIONS

Answers to Accounting in Action Insight Questions

Across the Organization, p. 506

Q: How is the profit earned by a partner in an accounting partnership different from the earnings of a staff accountant in the same partnership?

A: The earnings paid to a staff accountant is recorded as salaries expense, which reduces profit. This amount is fixed in advance. The profit earned by a partner varies depending on the partnership's earnings during the year and the profit-sharing arrangements among all the partners. A partner can receive cash payments in the form of withdrawals during the year, but these are recorded as reductions of capital and not as salary expense.

All About You Insight, p. 524

Q: If you and a friend wanted to start a partnership, how might you use a partnership agreement to ensure that your partnership becomes successful, instead of ending in an unhappy liquidation?

A: A partnership agreement should include: Who are the partners? What is each partner contributing? What are each partner's duties? How is profit (loss) shared? How will disputes be resolved? Addressing these items in advance may assist in resolving issues that might arise as the partnership evolves.

ANSWERS TO SELF-STUDY QUESTIONS

1. c 2. a 3. b 4. d 5. a 6. b 7. c 8. b 9. c 10. a

Remember to go back to the beginning of the chapter to check off your completed work!

←

CHAPTER 13

INTRODUCTION TO CORPORATIONS

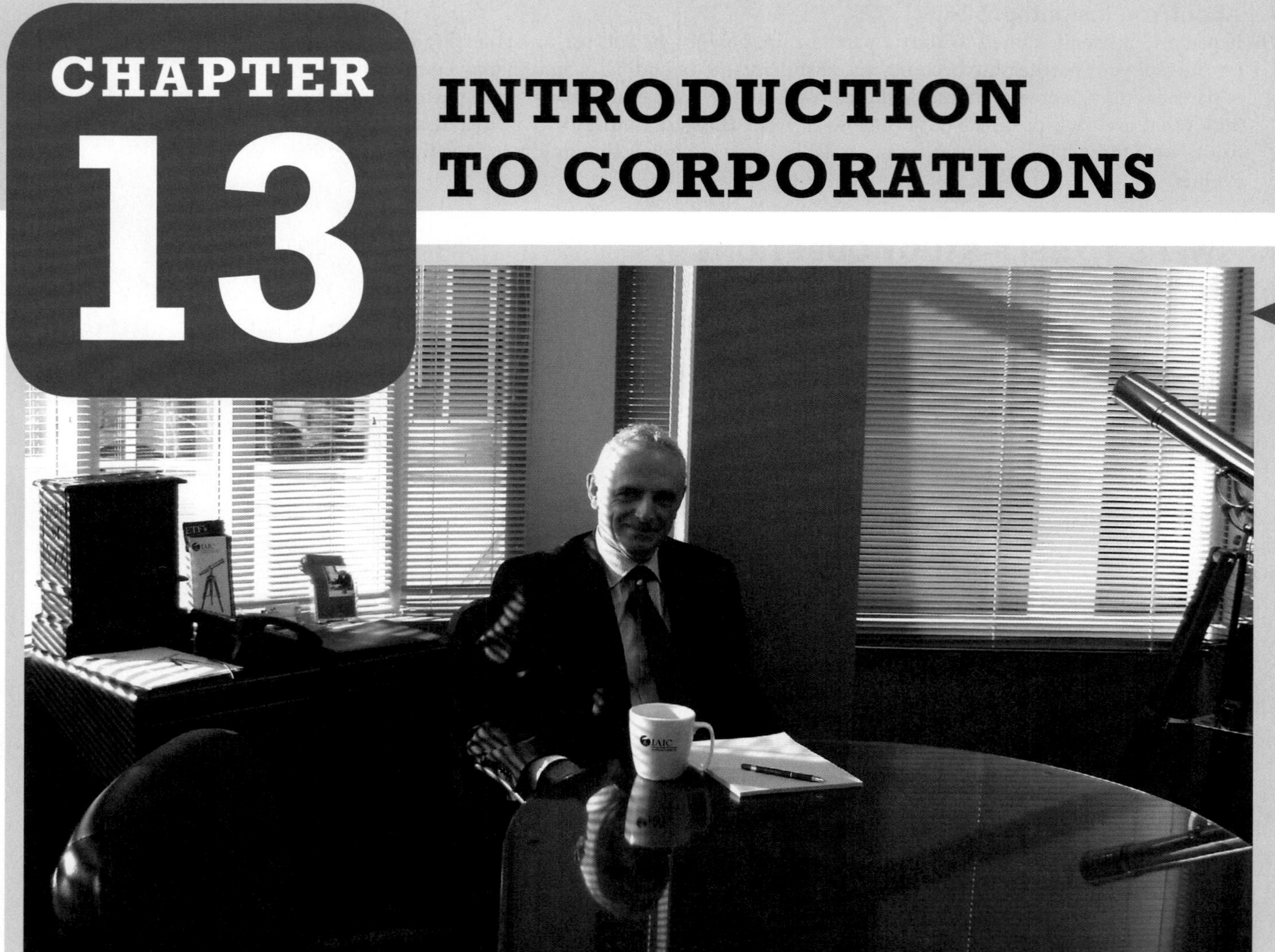

THE NAVIGATOR

- ☐ Understand *Concepts for Review*
- ☐ Read *Feature Story*
- ☐ Scan *Study Objectives*
- ☐ Read *Chapter Preview*
- ☐ Read text and answer *Before You Go On*
- ☐ Review *Comparing IFRS and ASPE*
- ☐ Work *Demonstration Problem*
- ☐ Review *Summary of Study Objectives*
- ☐ Answer *Self-Study Questions*
- ☐ Complete assignments

CONCEPTS FOR REVIEW

Before studying this chapter, you should understand or, if necessary, review:

A. The differences between the forms of business organization. (Ch. 1, pp. 8 and 14)

B. The content of the equity section of the balance sheet for the different forms of organization. (Ch. 1, p. 23)

C. How to prepare closing entries for a proprietorship (Ch. 4, pp. 147–150) and for a partnership. (Ch. 12, p. 502)

WHEN INCORPORATING MAKES GOOD BUSINESS SENSE

MISSISSAUGA, ON—When you think of a Canadian corporation, companies such as Canadian Tire, Scotiabank, or Tim Hortons might come to mind. Most of the largest corporations are public—they issue shares to the public to raise money to grow the business. But in fact, in Canada there are also many private corporations, whose shares are owned by just a few people. Most of these private corporations are small and medium-sized enterprises.

The decision to incorporate is based on business, legal, and tax reasons, says Keith Doxsee, President of Doxsee & Co., a chartered accounting firm that among other things provides advice and help to businesses looking to incorporate. The business owners need to consider if they will earn enough money to justify the expense of incorporation, and how many people are going to be involved in running and profiting from the business.

One of the first things to consider is whether the business is a financial and legal liability risk. "If you do something, are you likely to be sued if anything goes wrong? If you are, then you need to consider incorporation," Mr. Doxsee says. That's because, in a corporation, the shareholders are usually only liable for any financial obligations such as lawsuits or debts up to the amount they invested in the business but directors have responsibility for other liabilities such as taxes and unpaid wages. "A corporation provides you with a shield against most liabilities that would arise," he says. With a sole proprietorship or partnership, all the owners are liable for all the business's obligations, and their personal assets could be at stake.

There can be big tax advantages to incorporating, which allows corporations to defer paying income taxes so they can put more income toward growing the business. So any business that might be starting small but has a business plan for fast growth, such as one in the high-tech industry, could incorporate at the start in order to generate working capital. Corporations pay an average of 15% income tax on the first $500,000 in corporate profits (depending on the province), whereas individuals earning more than $133,000 pay about 47%, Mr. Doxsee says.

Corporations are also good structures for some family-run businesses. For example, with a husband and wife ownership team, one spouse could be a shareholder and director and one only a shareholder, limiting their personal liability to just the director. Or the spouse in the lower personal income tax bracket could own more shares than the other and earn higher dividends but pay lower taxes.

However, Mr. Doxsee advises against forming a corporation for sole proprietors who do not intend on leaving income in the business to grow. That's because "once you take money out of the company, you have to pay personal tax on that as a dividend or salary." In that case, there is no financial advantage to being incorporated, and the costs and administrative burden of incorporating and filing annual corporate income tax returns are not worth it, he says.

THE NAVIGATOR

STUDY OBJECTIVES

After studying this chapter, you should be able to:

1. Identify and discuss characteristics of the corporate form of organization.
2. Account for the issuance of common and preferred shares.
3. Prepare a corporate income statement.
4. Account for cash dividends.
5. Prepare a statement of retained earnings and closing entries for a corporation.
6. Prepare the shareholders' equity section of the balance sheet and calculate return on equity.

THE NAVIGATOR

PREVIEW OF CHAPTER THIRTEEN

Many incorporated companies start out as unincorporated proprietorships or partnerships and later incorporate. Because of its advantages, the corporation dominates as the most common form of business organization. In this chapter, we will explain the essential features of a corporation, issuing share capital, corporate income tax, cash dividends, and retained earnings. Financial statements for a corporation reporting under ASPE, including an income statement, statement of retained earnings, and the shareholders' equity section of a balance sheet, are also shown. In Chapter 14, we will look at additional topics for corporations and the different corporate financial statements required under IFRS.

The chapter is organized as follows:

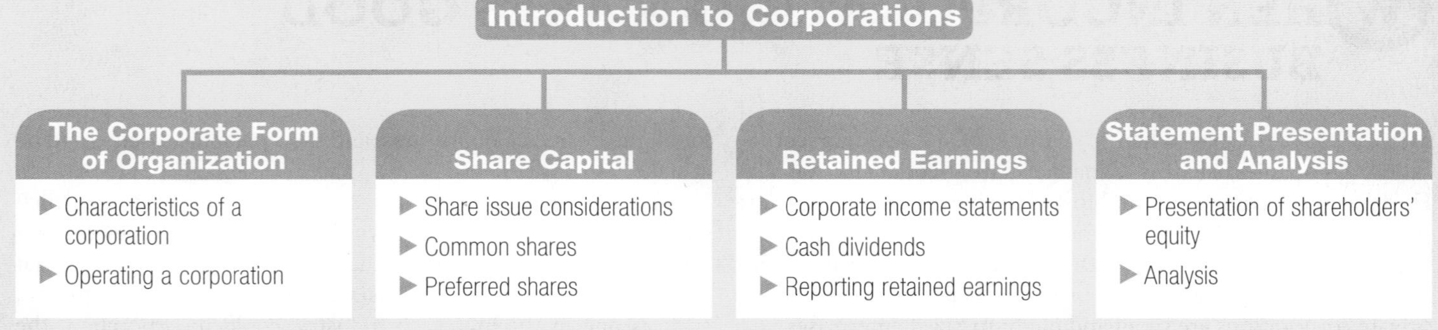

THE CORPORATE FORM OF ORGANIZATION

STUDY OBJECTIVE 1

Identify and discuss characteristics of the corporate form of organization.

A **corporation** is a legal entity that is separate from its owners, who are known as **shareholders**. Corporations can be classified in a variety of ways. Two common classifications are *by purpose* and *by ownership*. For example, a corporation may be organized for the purpose of making a profit (such as Canadian Tire) or it may be **not-for-profit** (such as the Canadian Cancer Society).

In classification by ownership, there is a difference between public and private corporations. A **public corporation** is a corporation whose shares are available for purchase by the general public in an organized securities market, such as the Toronto Stock Exchange; it may have thousands of shareholders. All public corporations are "publicly accountable enterprises" and, as such, must follow International Financial Reporting Standards (IFRS). Most of the largest Canadian corporations are publicly held. Examples of publicly held corporations are Royal Bank of Canada, Magna International Inc., and, of course, Reitmans (Canada) Limited, as featured in Appendix A.

In contrast, a **private corporation**—often called a privately or closely held corporation—is a corporation whose shares are held by a few shareholders and are not available for the general public to purchase. Private companies are generally much smaller than publicly held companies, although there are notable exceptions, such as McCain Foods, The Jim Pattison Group, and the Irving companies. A private company has the choice of following IFRS or Accounting Standards for Private Enterprises (ASPE) unless it is considered a publicly accountable enterprise because, for example, it has bonds that are publicly held.

CHARACTERISTICS OF A CORPORATION

Regardless of the purpose or ownership of a corporation, there are many characteristics that make corporations different from proprietorships and partnerships. The most important ones are explained below.

Separate Legal Existence

As an entity that is separate from its owners, the corporation acts under its own name rather than in the name of its shareholders. A corporation may buy, own, and sell property. It may borrow money and enter into legally binding contracts in its own name. It may also sue or be sued, and it pays income tax as a separate legal entity.

Remember that in a proprietorship or partnership, the acts of the owners (partners) bind the proprietorship or partnership. In contrast, the acts of owners (shareholders) do not bind a corporation unless these individuals are also official agents of the corporation. For example, if you owned shares of Reitmans (Canada) Limited, you would not have the right to purchase or lease a new building on behalf of the corporation unless you were an official agent of the corporation.

Limited Liability of Shareholders

Since a corporation is a separate legal entity, creditors have access to corporate assets only to have their claims repaid to them. The liability of each shareholder is limited to the amount that he or she invested in the shares of the corporation. This means that shareholders cannot be made to pay for the company's liabilities out of their personal assets, which can be done in the case of a proprietorship and a general partnership.

Limited liability is a significant advantage for the corporate form of organization, just as it is for a limited, or limited liability, partnership. However, in private corporations, creditors may demand a personal guarantee from a controlling shareholder. This makes the controlling shareholder's personal assets available, if required, for satisfying the creditor's claim—which eliminates or reduces the limited liability advantage. Also, as Keith Doxsee explains in our feature story, if a shareholder is also a director of the corporation, they are personally responsible for certain liabilities such as unpaid wages.

Transferable Ownership Rights

Shares of capital represent ownership of a corporation. These are transferable units. Shareholders may dispose of part or all of their interest in a corporation simply by selling their shares. In a public corporation, the transfer of shares is entirely decided by the shareholder. It does not require the approval of either the corporation or other shareholders. However, in some private corporations, there may be a shareholders' agreement that limits how, and to whom, a shareholder can sell his or her shares.

The transfer of ownership rights between shareholders has no effect on the corporation's operating activities and it doesn't affect the corporation's assets, liabilities, and total equity. The transfer of these ownership rights is a transaction between individual shareholders. The company is only involved in the original issue or sale of the share capital. Therefore, whenever a shareholder sells his or her shares to another investor, the company does not record a journal entry.

Ability to Acquire Capital

Corporations may issue shares in order to obtain capital (cash) for operations or new investments. Buying shares in a corporation is often attractive to an investor because a shareholder has limited liability and, in a public company, shares are easily transferable. Also, because only small amounts of money need to be invested, many individuals can become shareholders. For these reasons, a successful corporation's ability to obtain capital is almost unlimited.

Note that the "almost unlimited" ability of a corporation to acquire capital by issuing shares is only true for large, public corporations. Private corporations can have as much difficulty getting capital as any proprietorship or partnership.

Continuous Life

Corporations have an unlimited life. Since a corporation is a separate legal entity, its continuance as a going concern is not affected by the withdrawal, death, or incapacity of a shareholder, employee, or officer. As a result, a successful corporation can have a continuous and indefinite life. For example, the Hudson's Bay Company, the oldest commercial corporation in North America, was founded in 1670 and is still going strong. Its shareholders have changed over the years, but the corporation itself continues. In contrast, proprietorships end if anything happens to the proprietor and partnerships must reorganize if anything happens to one of the partners.

Government Regulations

Canadian companies may be incorporated federally, under the terms of the *Canada Business Corporations Act*, or provincially, under the terms of a provincial business corporations act. Federal and provincial laws specify the requirements for issuing shares, distributing income to shareholders, and reacquiring shares. Similarly, provincial securities commissions' regulations control the sale of share capital to the general public. When a corporation's shares are listed and traded on foreign securities markets, the corporation must also respect the reporting requirements of these exchanges. Respecting international, federal, provincial, and securities regulations increases costs and complexity for corporations.

Income Tax

Proprietorships and partnerships do not pay income tax as separate entities. Instead, each owner's (or partner's) share of profit from these organizations is reported on his or her personal income tax return. Income tax is then paid by the individual on this amount. In terms of income tax, it does not matter how much cash a proprietor or partner withdraws from the business. The owner is taxed on the profit, not on the cash withdrawals (their drawings).

Corporations, on the other hand, must pay federal and provincial income tax as separate legal entities. Income tax rates vary based on the type of income and by province. In general, as Keith Doxsee explains in the feature story, corporate income tax rates are lower than the rate an individual would pay on the same amount of profit, especially in the case of small businesses.

In addition to the potential for reduced income tax, another advantage of incorporation is being able to delay personal income tax. The shareholders do not pay income tax on the profit, instead they pay income tax if they receive dividends or a salary from the corporation. Thus, some people argue that corporate income is taxed twice: once at the corporate level and again at the individual level when the dividend is received. This is not exactly true, however, as individuals receive a dividend tax credit to offset most of the tax paid at the corporate level.

Helpful hint Note that income tax considerations can be an advantage or a disadvantage of incorporating, depending on the individual situation.

To determine whether incorporating will result in more or less income tax for a proprietorship or partnership, it is wise to get expert advice. Income tax laws are complex, and careful tax planning is essential for any business venture.

The following list summarizes the advantages and disadvantages of the corporate form of business organization:

Advantages	Disadvantages
• Separate legal existence • Limited liability of shareholders • Potential for deferred or reduced income tax • Transferable ownership rights • Greater ability to acquire capital • Continuous life	• Increased cost and complexity to follow government regulations • Potential for additional income tax

OPERATING A CORPORATION

There are a few differences between operating a business using the corporate form of organization and using a partnership or proprietorship.

Forming a Corporation

Proprietorships and partnerships can be formed and begin operations without any formalities. On the other hand, the process of creating a corporation requires that the organizers submit articles of incorporation to the federal or provincial government for approval.

Articles of incorporation form the company's "constitution." They include information such as (1) the name and purpose of the corporation, (2) the number of shares and the kinds of shares to be authorized, and (3) the location of the corporation's head office. Anyone can apply to incorporate a company, as long as he or she is over the age of 18, of sound mind, and not bankrupt.

After receiving its articles of incorporation, the corporation sets its bylaws. The bylaws are the internal rules and procedures for operations. Corporations that operate interprovincially must also get a licence from each province they do business in. The licence ensures that the corporation's operating activities respect the laws of the province.

The costs of forming a corporation are called **organization costs**. These costs include legal fees, accounting fees, and registration costs. Under both ASPE and IFRS, these costs are recorded as expenses in the period when they are incurred.

Ownership Rights of Shareholders

Shareholders purchase ownership rights in the form of shares. Depending on the company's articles of incorporation, it may be authorized to issue different classes of shares, such as Class A, Class B, and so on. The rights and privileges for each class of shares are stated in the articles of incorporation. The different classes are often identified by the generic terms *common shares* and *preferred shares*. When a corporation has only one class of shares, this class has the rights and privileges of **common shares**. Each common share gives the shareholder the following ownership rights:

Helpful hint All corporations have common shares, while some have both common and preferred shares.

Vote: Shareholders have the right to vote on the election of the board of directors and appointment of external auditors. Each shareholder normally has one vote for each common share owned.

Dividends: Shareholders share in the distribution of the corporate profit through dividends, proportionate to the number of shares owned, if the board of directors declares a dividend.

Liquidation: Shareholders share in any assets that remain after liquidation, in proportion to the number of shares owned. This is known as a residual claim because shareholders are paid only if any cash remains after all the assets have been sold and the liabilities paid.

Corporation Management

Shareholders legally own the corporation. But as just explained, they have limited rights. They manage the corporation indirectly through the board of directors that they elect. The board, in turn, decides on the company's operating policies and selects officers—such as a chief executive officer (CEO) and other executive officers—to execute policy and to perform daily management functions. This structure is shown in Illustration 13-1.

ILLUSTRATION 13-1
Authority structure in corporations

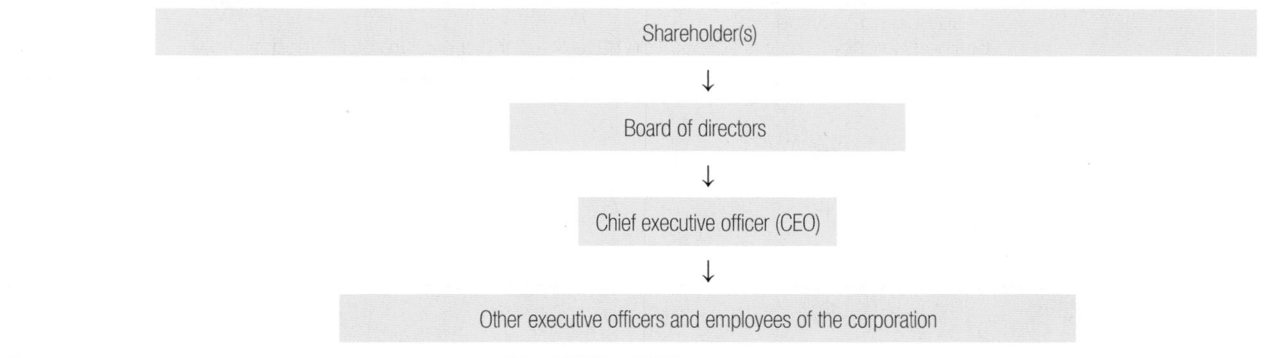

In a small private company, it is possible to have only one shareholder, who elects him- or herself to be the only person on the board of directors. In that capacity, he or she can appoint him- or herself as the CEO. On the other hand, the authority structure of a corporation makes it possible for it to hire professional managers to run the business, which is generally the case in public corporations.

Distribution of Profit—Dividends

Profits can be either reinvested by a company or distributed to its shareholders as dividends. A **dividend** is a pro rata distribution of a portion of a corporation's profits to its shareholders. "Pro rata" means that if you own, say, 10% of a corporation's shares, you will receive 10% of the total dividend paid to all shareholders. Dividends in corporations are somewhat similar to drawings in proprietorships or partnerships.

Helpful hint In all businesses, profits can be reinvested or paid out to the owners (it is usually a combination of the two). These payments are in the form of drawings for proprietorships and partnerships and dividends for corporations.

ACCOUNTING IN ACTION
ALL ABOUT YOU INSIGHT

If you are starting a business, you need to ask if it is better to use a proprietorship or to incorporate. The best form of organization for a business start-up may not be the best as the business's profits increase. When you start your business, a proprietorship is generally more advantageous because it involves relatively low start-up costs and low regulatory costs. Also, if your proprietorship suffers losses in its early years, these losses may be deducted against your other personal income, thus reducing your personal tax. As your business becomes profitable, there may be advantages if it is incorporated, especially in terms of tax savings. For example, some Canadian private corporations are eligible for a small business deduction that reduces the federal tax rate to 11% on the first $500,000 of taxable income. In comparison, your personal federal tax rate may be as high as 29% on taxable income over $132,406. Most owners of a corporation will need to take some income out of the business and must decide if it should be a salary or dividends. If the owner is paid a salary, it will reduce corporate income taxes, but the owner will pay personal income taxes on employment income. Personal income taxes paid on dividends are less than those on employment income. But if an individual only has dividend income, he or she cannot contribute to the Canada Pension Plan (CPP) or a Registered Retirement Savings Plan (RRSP). As you can see, deciding whether to incorporate or not is a complex matter.

Given the complexity of tax planning, and the impact that taxes could have on the advantages of incorporating, what should you do before deciding to incorporate your business?

BEFORE YOU GO ON...

DO IT

Indicate if each of the following sentences is true or false:

_______ 1. Shareholders of a corporation have unlimited liability.
_______ 2. A corporation does not journalize the transfer of shares from one shareholder to another.
_______ 3. A corporation does not pay income tax on its profits.
_______ 4. Corporations are separate legal entities and continue to exist after the death of a shareholder.
_______ 5. The articles of incorporation contain information about the kinds of shares a corporation is authorized to issue.
_______ 6. The shareholders of a corporation have the right to declare a dividend.

SOLUTION

1. False
2. True
3. False
4. True
5. True
6. False

Related exercise material: BE13–1 and E13–2.

Action Plan

- Review the characteristics and operation of a corporation.

THE NAVIGATOR

SHARE CAPITAL

STUDY OBJECTIVE 2

Account for the issuance of common and preferred shares.

You may recall from Chapters 1 and 4 that the shareholders' equity section of a balance sheet includes (1) share capital (contributed capital), and (2) retained earnings (earned capital). **Share capital** is increased by amounts paid or contributed to the corporation by shareholders in exchange for shares of ownership. In the following section, we will look at issuing shares and the two main classes of shares—common shares and preferred shares. We will learn about retained earnings later in the chapter.

SHARE ISSUE CONSIDERATIONS

A corporation must determine how many different classes of shares it will issue, the specific rights and privileges of each class of shares, and how many of each class of shares can be sold to shareholders. It also has to decide how many to sell and at what price.

Authorized Share Capital

A corporation's **authorized shares**—the total number of each class of shares a corporation is allowed to sell—is indicated in its articles of incorporation. It may be specified as an unlimited number or a certain number (such as 500,000 shares authorized). Most corporations in Canada have an unlimited number of authorized shares. If a number is specified, the number of authorized shares normally reflects the company's initial need for capital and what it expects to need in the future. The authorization of share capital does not result in a formal accounting entry, because the event has no immediate effect on either assets or shareholders' equity.

Helpful hint The authorized shares represents the number of shares that a corporation *is allowed to issue*, not the number that it actually has issued.

Issue of Shares

Issued shares are the authorized shares that have been sold. If a corporation has issued all of its authorized shares, it must get approval to change its articles of incorporation before it can issue additional shares. To find out how many shares can still be issued without changing the articles of incorporation, the total shares issued are subtracted from the total authorized.

A corporation can issue common shares in two ways: either directly to investors or indirectly through an investment dealer (brokerage house) that specializes in making potential investors aware of securities. Direct issue is typical in private corporations; indirect issue is typical for public corporations. The first time a corporation's shares are offered to the public, the offer is called an **initial public offering (IPO)**.

Once shares have been issued, investors can buy and sell them to each other, rather than buying them from the company. In public companies, the shares are traded on a **secondary market**, or stock exchange. When a company's shares are sold among investors, there is no impact on the company's financial position. The only change in the company records is the name of the shareholder, not the number of shares issued.

Market Value of Shares

The market value of a public company's shares changes according to the interaction between buyers and sellers on the secondary market. To some extent, the price follows the trend of a company's profit and dividends. The price also depends to some extent on how well the company is expected to perform in the future. Factors that a company cannot control (such as an embargo on oil, changes in interest rates, the outcome of an election, terrorism, and war) can also influence market prices.

For each listed security, the financial press reports the highest and lowest prices of the shares for the year; the annual dividend rate; the highest, lowest, and closing prices for the day; and the net change from the previous day. The total volume of shares traded on a particular day is also reported. Shares that are regularly bought and sold on the secondary market are considered to be actively traded. When shares are actively traded, the quoted market value of the share is considered to be a very good indication of the fair value of the shares.

Helpful hint The market price for a company's shares is determined in the same way that prices in all free markets are determined: based on the forces of supply and demand.

Legal Capital

The distinction between share capital and retained earnings is important for both legal and financial reasons. Retained earnings can be distributed to shareholders as dividends or retained in the company for operating needs. On the other hand, share capital is **legal capital** that cannot be distributed to shareholders. Because shareholders have limited liability, legal capital must remain invested in the company for the protection of corporate creditors. In a proprietorship or a partnership, there is no such thing as legal capital. Proprietors or partners may withdraw whatever amount they choose because a company's creditor can access the owner's personal assets if the creditor suffers a loss.

Some countries, notably the United States, assign a par or stated value to shares to determine the amount of legal capital. The use of par value shares is rare in Canada, with fewer than 1% of publicly traded companies issuing par value shares. In fact, companies that are incorporated federally, as well as companies that incorporate in most Canadian provinces, are not allowed to issue shares with par values.

In Canada, **no par value shares**—shares that have not been assigned any specific value—are normally issued. When no par value shares are issued, all of the proceeds received from the sale of the shares are considered to be legal capital. In this text, we will assume that all of the shares in the examples and end of chapter material have no par value.

COMMON SHARES

All corporations must issue common shares. Some corporations also issue preferred shares, which have different rights and privileges than common shares. We will look at common shares in this section, and preferred shares in the next.

Issuing Shares for Cash

As discussed earlier, when no par value common shares are issued, the entire proceeds from the issue become legal capital. That means that the proceeds of the share issue are credited to the Common Share account. Most of the time, shares are issued in exchange for cash, particularly in large corporations.

To illustrate the issue of common shares for cash, assume that Hydroslide Inc., a private company, is authorized to issue an unlimited number of common shares. It issues 20,000 of these shares for $1 cash per share on January 2. The entry to record this transaction is as follows:

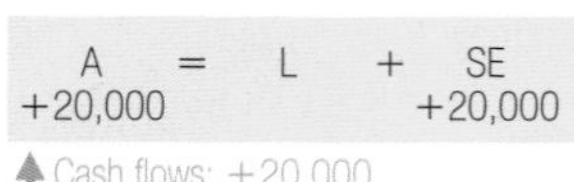

Cash flows: +20,000

Jan. 2	Cash	20,000	
	Common Shares		20,000
	To record issue of 20,000 common shares.		

Issuing Shares for Services or Noncash Assets

Helpful hint Fair value is the amount that would be agreed upon in an arm's-length transaction between knowledgeable, willing parties, or as the result of a bargaining process over the value of the good or service.

Although it is more usual to issue common shares for cash, shares are sometimes issued in exchange for services (such as compensation to lawyers or consultants) or for noncash assets (land, buildings, and equipment). When this happens, should the transaction be recorded at the fair value of the goods or services received, or at the fair value of the shares given up?

Under IFRS, the fair value of the goods or services received should be used, and it is presumed that this value can be determined except in rare cases. If the fair value of the goods or services received cannot be reliably determined, then the transaction is recorded at the fair value of the shares given in exchange. Under ASPE, the rules are more flexible; the transaction should be valued at whichever amount can be more reliably measured—the fair value of the goods or services received or the fair value of the shares issued. As a private company's shares are not widely traded, it can be very difficult to measure the fair value of the shares. Thus it is more likely that the value of the goods or services received will be used in recording the transaction.

To illustrate, assume that on February 25, the lawyer who helped Hydroslide incorporate billed the company $3,900 for her services. If Hydroslide has limited cash available, it may offer to issue common shares to the lawyer instead of cash. If the lawyer agrees, the challenge is to determine how many shares to offer in exchange for the legal services. As Hydroslide is a private company, its shares are not actively traded in a stock market. Therefore, it is difficult to determine the fair value per share, which in turn makes it difficult to know how many shares to issue.

Recall from the previous example that Hydroslide issued shares for $1 cash each at the beginning of the year. Therefore, it may offer the lawyer 3,900 shares in exchange for the legal services. On the other hand, the lawyer may argue that she wants 4,000 shares because she is not getting paid in cash. The actual number of shares issued will be the result of a negotiation between the company and the lawyer. Regardless of the number of shares issued, the transaction is recorded at the fair value of the lawyer's services received, not at the value of the shares given up, because the fair value of the lawyer's services can be more reliably determined based on his or her hourly billing rate. For purposes of this example, we will assume that 4,000 shares are issued. Accordingly, the entry is recorded at $3,900 as follows:

A	=	L	+	SE
				−3,900
				+3,900

Cash flows: no effect

Feb. 25	Legal Fees Expense	3,900	
	Common Shares		3,900
	To record issue of 4,000 common shares for legal services.		

If shares are issued in exchange for land, buildings, or equipment, it is often necessary to use an appraiser to determine the fair value of the asset. Appraised values are often used as a reasonable estimate of the fair value of the asset, assuming the appraiser has the appropriate independence and expertise.

Helpful hint The asking or list price of land, buildings, or equipment is rarely the fair value of the asset. Asking or list prices are typically used only to start the bargaining process.

To illustrate, assume that FlexIt Ltd., a public company, issues 10,000 shares on October 1 to acquire refurbished bottling equipment. Assuming that an appraisal valued the equipment at $72,000, the following entry is made:

Oct. 1	Equipment	72,000	
	Common Shares		72,000
	To record issue of 10,000 common shares for equipment.		

A	=	L	+	SE
+72,000				+72,000

Cash flows: no effect

If the fair value of the equipment could not be determined, and if FlexIt's shares are actively traded with a market value of $7 per share, the equipment would be recorded at the fair value of the shares given up, $70,000 (10,000 × $7).

PREFERRED SHARES

A corporation may issue preferred shares in addition to common shares. **Preferred shares** have a preference, or priority, over common shares in certain areas. Typically, preferred shareholders have priority over (1) dividends (distributions of profit) and (2) assets if the company is liquidated. They generally do not have voting rights.

Like common shares, preferred shares may be issued for cash or for noncash assets or services. When a company has more than one class of shares, the transactions for each class should be recorded in separate accounts (for example, Preferred Shares, Common Shares).

Unlike common shares, the annual dividend rate that the preferred shareholder may receive is specified in the articles of incorporation. The rate may be expressed as a percentage of the issue price or as a specific dollar amount. For example, if the annual dividend rate on the preferred shares is specified as $5 per share, these shares would be referred to as "$5 preferred shares." The dividend rate is always stated as an annual rate.

Helpful hint Note that the dollar amount preceding Preferred Shares (for example, $10 Preferred Shares) represents the annual dividend for the shares, not the share price.

To illustrate, assume that Hydroslide Inc. issues 500, $5 preferred shares for $100 per share on July 7. The entry to record this transaction is as follows:

July 7	Cash (500 × $100)	50,000	
	Preferred Shares		50,000
	To record issue of 500, $5 preferred shares.		

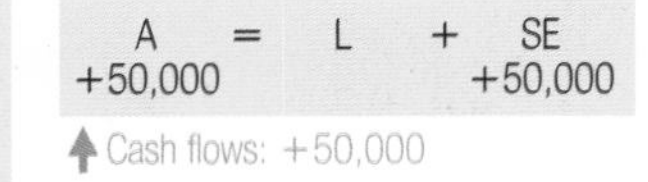

A	=	L	+	SE
+50,000				+50,000

Cash flows: +50,000

Some typical features of preferred shares, including dividend and liquidation preferences, are discussed next.

Dividend Preference

Preferred shareholders have the right to share in the distribution of dividends before common shareholders. For example, using the example of Hydroslide's $5 preferred shares explained above, the common shareholders will not receive any dividends in the current year until preferred shareholders have first received $5 for every share they own.

The first claim to dividends does not, however, guarantee that dividends will be paid. Dividends depend on many factors, such as having enough retained earnings and available cash. In addition, all dividends must be formally approved and declared by the board of directors.

Preferred shares may have a **cumulative** dividend feature. This means that preferred shareholders must be paid dividends from the current year as well as any unpaid dividends from past years before common shareholders receive any dividends. When preferred shares are cumulative, preferred dividends that are not declared in a period are called **dividends in arrears**. Preferred shares without this feature are called **noncumulative**. A dividend on a noncumulative preferred share that is not paid in any particular year is lost forever. If a company has both cumulative and noncumulative preferred shares, the cumulative preferred shares will have priority over the noncumulative shares when dividends are declared.

To illustrate the cumulative dividend feature, assume that Hydroslide Inc.'s $5 preferred shares are cumulative. Hydroslide's annual total preferred dividend is $2,500 (500 × $5 per share). If dividends are two years in arrears, Hydroslide's preferred shareholders are entitled to receive the following dividends:

Dividends in arrears ($2,500 × 2)	$5,000
Current year dividends	2,500
Total preferred dividends	$7,500

No distribution can be made to common shareholders until this entire preferred dividend is paid. In other words, dividends cannot be paid on common shares while any preferred shares are in arrears.

Dividends in arrears *are not considered a liability*. There is no obligation to pay a dividend until one is declared by the board of directors. However, the amount of dividends in arrears should be disclosed in the notes to the financial statements. This allows investors to assess the potential impact of a future dividend declaration on the corporation's financial position.

Even though there is no requirement to pay an annual dividend, companies that do not meet their dividend obligations—whether cumulative or noncumulative—are not looked upon favourably by the investment community. When discussing one company's failure to pay its preferred dividend, a financial officer noted, "Not meeting your obligations on something like that is a major black mark on your record." The accounting entries for dividends are explained later in this chapter.

Liquidation Preference

In addition to having a priority claim on the distribution of income over common shares, preferred shares also have a priority claim on corporate assets if the corporation fails. This means that if the company is bankrupt, preferred shareholders will get money back before common shareholders do. The preference to assets can be for the legal capital of the shares or for a specified liquidating value. So, while creditors still rank above all shareholders in terms of preference, preferred shareholders rank above the common shareholders, and this is important as the money usually runs out before everyone gets paid.

Because of these two preferential rights—the right to dividends and assets—preferred shareholders generally do not mind that they do not have the voting right that common shareholders have.

Convertible Preferred

As an investment, preferred shares are even more attractive when there is a conversion privilege. Nearly half of the companies in Canada that report having preferred shares also have a conversion feature. **Convertible preferred shares** give preferred shareholders the option of exchanging their preferred shares for common shares at a specified ratio. They are purchased by investors who want the greater security of preferred shares but who also want the option of converting their preferred shares to common shares if the fair value (market price) of the common shares increases significantly.

To illustrate, assume that Ross Industries Inc. issues 1,000 convertible preferred shares at $100 per share. One preferred share is convertible into 10 common shares. The current fair value of the common shares is $9 per share. At this point, holders of the preferred shares would not want to convert, because they would exchange preferred shares worth $100,000 (1,000 × $100) for common shares worth only $90,000 (10,000 × $9). However, if the fair value of the common shares were to increase to $10.50 per share, it would be profitable for shareholders to convert their preferred shares to common shares.

When the shares are converted, the *cost* of the preferred shares is transferred to the Common Shares account and no gain or loss is recorded. As it is seldom possible to determine the original cost of the preferred shares that are involved in the conversion, the average cost per share of the preferred shares is used instead. This is calculated by dividing the balance in the Preferred Shares account by the number of preferred shares issued immediately prior to the conversion.

To illustrate, assume that the 1,000 preferred shares of Ross Industries Ltd. with an average cost of $100 per share are converted into 10,000 common shares when the fair values of the two classes of shares are $101 and $12 per share, respectively, on June 10. The entry to record the conversion is:

June 10	Preferred Shares	100,000	
	Common Shares		100,000
	To record conversion of 1,000 preferred shares into 10,000 common shares.		

A	=	L	+	SE
				−100,000
				+100,000

Cash flows: no effect

Note that the fair value of the shares is *not* used by the corporation in recording the transaction because the total amount of share capital has not changed. But fair values are used by the preferred shareholders in their *decision* to convert.

Redeemable and Retractable Preferred

Many preferred shares are issued with a redemption or call feature. **Redeemable** (or **callable**) **preferred shares** give the issuing corporation the right to purchase the shares from shareholders at specified future dates and prices. The redemption feature gives a corporation some flexibility: it allows the corporation to eliminate the preferred shares in situations where doing this will benefit it.

Often, shares that are redeemable are also convertible. Sometimes, companies will redeem or call their preferred shares to force investors to convert those preferred shares into common shares.

Retractable preferred shares are similar to redeemable preferred shares except that the shareholders can redeem shares at their option instead of the corporation redeeming the shares at its option. The retraction usually occurs at an arranged price and date.

Helpful hint The two features benefit different parties. Redeemable shares are at the option of the corporation. Retractable shares are at the option of the shareholder.

When preferred shares are redeemable or retractable, the distinction between equity and debt is not clear. Redeemable and retractable preferred shares are similar in some ways to debt. They both offer a rate of return to the investor, and with the redemption or retraction of the shares, they both offer a repayment of the principal investment.

Recall from Chapter 11 that in order for accounting information to be useful, it must be presented in accordance with its economic substance rather than its form. Therefore, redeemable and retractable preferred shares may be presented in the *liabilities* section of the balance sheet rather than in the shareholders' equity section if, depending on the exact terms of the redemption or retraction, they have more of the features of debt than of equity. Accounting for these types of shares is left to more advanced accounting courses.

ACCOUNTING IN ACTION
ACROSS THE ORGANIZATION

There are many reasons why some companies issue preferred shares to raise cash instead of borrowing or issuing common shares. Normally, companies pay a fixed dividend on preferred shares, but they aren't legally required to, so they can skip issuing dividends during tough times—something they can't do with interest payments on debt. Debt also has to be repaid at a certain time, whereas preferred shares do not normally have a maturity date. Preferred shares are considered equity and so do not show up on a company's books as a liability, which can help its credit rating. Since the fixed dividend is an attractive feature to some investors, issuing preferred shares can be a "win-win" arrangement.

While these are some financial reasons for companies to issue preferred shares, there is also an important strategic reason, particularly for private companies. Unlike common shareholders, preferred shareholders generally do not have voting rights, such as the right to elect members to the board of directors, so the common shareholders will not lose or reduce their voting control over business matters.

Sources: Nick Louth, "Preference Shares Boast Yields of 7–10%," *Financial Times*, May 18, 2012; Mark Koba, "Preferred Stock: CNBC Explains," CNBC, January 5, 2012; David Aston, "Are Preferred Shares a Good Buy?", *MoneySense* magazine, November 2011; Alex Kocic, "Why Issue Preferred Shares?," eHow.

Why might the "no maturity date" feature of preferred shares be useful to an organization?

BEFORE YOU GO ON...

DO IT

Turin Corporation, a private company, was incorporated on March 1. The following are selected transactions over the next several months:

Mar. 15	Issued 120,000 common shares for cash at $8 per share.
Apr. 2	Issued 3,200 common shares to its lawyers in settlement of their bill for $25,000. Turin's president and the law firm agreed that the shares had a fair value of $8 each.
May 22	Issued 10,000 preferred shares for $90 each. Each share was convertible into 10 common shares.
Oct. 5	Preferred shareholders converted 2,000 of the preferred shares into common. At that point, it was estimated that the fair values of the common and preferred shares were $10 and $92, respectively.

Record the share transactions.

Action Plan

- Credit the Common Shares account for the entire proceeds.
- When shares are issued for services, use the fair value of what is received to determine the dollar amount of the transaction. If this amount cannot be determined, use the fair value of what is given up.
- Credit the Preferred Shares account for the entire proceeds of the share issue.
- Use the cost to record the conversion. Fair values are irrelevant.

SOLUTION

Mar. 5	Cash	960,000	
	Common Shares (120,000 × $8)		960,000
	To record issue of 120,000 shares at $8 per share.		
Apr. 2	Legal Fees Expense	25,000	
	Common Shares		25,000
	To record issue of 3,200 shares for $25,000 of lawyers' fees.		
May 22	Cash	900,000	
	Preferred Shares (10,000 × $90)		900,000
	To record issue of 10,000 preferred shares at $90.		
Oct. 5	Preferred Shares (2,000 × $90)	180,000	
	Common Shares		180,000
	To record conversion of 2,000 preferred shares into 20,000 (2,000 × 10) common shares at an average cost of $90 per preferred share.		

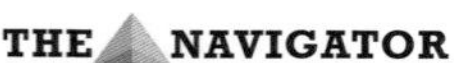

Related exercise material: BE13–2, BE13–3, BE13–4, BE13–5, BE13–6, BE13–7, E13–1, E13–3, E13–4, E13–5, and E13–6.

RETAINED EARNINGS

STUDY OBJECTIVE 3

Prepare a corporate income statement.

Retained earnings are earned capital (cumulative profit or loss since incorporation) that has been retained in the company for future use. In other words, it is the cumulative profit that has not been distributed to shareholders. In the following sections, we will learn about two major components of retained earnings: (1) profit, and how it is reported on a corporation's income statement; and (2) cash distributions to owners (dividends) that reduce retained earnings. We will also learn how retained earnings are reported in the financial statements for companies following ASPE, and examine closing entries for a corporation.

Helpful hint In all businesses, equity increases in two key ways: through investment and through profit. In proprietorships and partnerships, both of these increases are credited to capital. In a corporation, contributed capital represents investment and retained earnings represents profit that has been kept in the business.

CORPORATE INCOME STATEMENTS

In a corporation, unlike a proprietorship or partnership, income tax expense must be deducted when determining profit. Income tax expense is based on profit before income tax, which is calculated by subtracting all of the other expenses from total revenue. Although there are many complexities in corporate income tax, in this text we will keep it straightforward by simply multiplying profit before income tax by the income tax rate to determine income tax expense.

To illustrate, we will assume that Media General Limited had profit before income tax of $281,250 and a 20% income tax rate, which results in $56,250 ($281,250 × 20%) of income tax expense. Because income tax expense is based on profit before income tax, both of these amounts are shown on the income statement. Using assumed data for revenues and expenses, the condensed, multiple-step income statement for Media General Limited is shown in Illustration 13-2.

ILLUSTRATION 13-2
Corporate income statement

MEDIA GENERAL LIMITED **Income Statement** **Year Ended December 31, 2014**	
Sales	$800,000
Cost of goods sold	420,000
Gross profit	380,000
Operating expenses	94,000
Profit from operations	286,000
Interest expense	4,750
Profit before income tax	**281,250**
Income tax expense	**56,250**
Profit	$225,000

Income taxes affect not only the income statement (through the Income Tax Expense account) but also the balance sheet (through a liability account called Income Tax Payable). Companies prepare a corporate income tax return (called a T2) annually to determine their taxable income and income tax payable. However, the Canada Revenue Agency requires income tax to be estimated in advance and paid (remitted to taxing authorities) in monthly instalments, rather than waiting until the end of the company's fiscal year.

After a company determines its total income tax payable at year end, it compares this amount with the total income tax instalments paid during the year. The difference between the income tax paid and income tax payable results in either an additional amount payable or a refund. Companies have six months after their fiscal year end to submit their corporate income tax return, or else they will incur late filing penalties on any balance due.

Once the additional liability (or receivable) has been determined, an adjusting entry is required. Assume Media General Limited had originally estimated that its taxable income would be $210,000. It has a 20% income tax rate, so its income tax was anticipated to be $42,000 ($210,000 × 20%). Media General remitted monthly instalments in the amount of $3,500 per month ($42,000 ÷ 12). At year end, Media General actually reports taxable income (profit before income tax) of $281,250. Its total income tax liability is $56,250 ($281,250 × 20%), and not $42,000 as estimated. Assuming it has already recorded and remitted $42,000 of income tax, the required adjusting entry is for $14,250 ($56,250 − $42,000) and is recorded as follows:

Dec. 31	Income Tax Expense	14,250	
	Income Tax Payable		14,250
	To adjust estimated income tax expense to actual.		

A	=	L	+	SE
		+14,250		−14,250

Cash flows: no effect

Media General's income statement reports income tax expense of $56,250. The balance sheet reports a current liability of $14,250.

The Media General Limited example is typical of a private company following ASPE. In Chapter 14, we will learn about additional complexities that affect corporate income statements, including information required under IFRS.

BEFORE YOU GO ON...

DO IT

For the year ended June 30, 2014, Viceron Inc. had service revenue of $350,000; operating expenses of $195,000; and interest expense of $14,000. The company has a 25% income tax rate. (a) Determine income tax expense. (b) Prepare an income statement. (c) Prepare the entry to record income tax, assuming that $30,000 had been previously accrued.

SOLUTION

Action Plan

- Determine profit before income tax by deducting expenses from revenues.
- Calculate income tax expense by multiplying profit before income tax by the tax rate.
- Prepare the income statement, deducting income tax expense from profit before income tax.
- Deduct the income tax previously accrued from income tax expense to prepare the entry to record income tax.

(a) Profit before income tax = $350,000 − $195,000 − $14,000 = $141,000
Income tax expense = $141,000 × 25% = $35,250

(b)

VICERON INC.
Income Statement
Year Ended June 30, 2014

Service revenue	$350,000
Operating expenses	195,000
Profit from operations	155,000
Interest expense	14,000
Profit before income tax	141,000
Income tax expense	35,250
Profit	$105,750

(c)

Date	Account	Debit	Credit
June 30	Income Tax Expense ($35,250 − $30,000)	5,250	
	Income Tax Payable		5,250
	To adjust estimated income tax expense to actual.		

THE NAVIGATOR

Related exercise material: BE13–8 and E13–7.

CASH DIVIDENDS

STUDY OBJECTIVE 4
Account for cash dividends.

A **cash dividend** is a distribution of cash, on a pro rata (per share) basis, to shareholders. Cash dividends are the most common type of dividend in practice but stock dividends are also declared on occasion. We will learn about stock dividends in Chapter 14.

Necessary Conditions to Pay Cash Dividends

For a corporation to pay a cash dividend, it must have *all three of the following*:

1. **Enough cash.** A company must keep enough cash on hand to pay for its ongoing operations and to pay its bills as they come due. Under the *Canada Business Corporations Act*, a corporation cannot pay a dividend if it would then become unable to pay its liabilities. Therefore, a company must consider its ongoing cash needs before paying shareholders a cash dividend.
2. **The maintenance of legal capital.** As discussed earlier, in order to protect creditors, a company must maintain its legal capital. Under the *Canada Business Corporations Act*, a company must ensure that the dividend does not reduce the realizable value of its assets below the total of its liabilities and legal capital. Under some provincial legislation, a company must also have enough retained earnings before it can pay a dividend. In those cases, a corporation is not allowed to create or increase a deficit (negative retained earnings) by declaring the dividend.

   In addition to maintaining legal capital, there may be specific **retained earnings restrictions** that make a portion of the Retained Earnings balance unavailable for dividends. For example, a company may have long-term debt contracts that restrict retained earnings as a condition of the loan. These restrictions are known as **debt covenants**, which, among other things, can limit the payment of dividends in order to make it more likely that the corporation will be able to meet required loan payments.

3. **A declaration of dividends by the board of directors.** A company cannot pay dividends unless its board of directors decides to do so, at which point the board "declares" the dividend to be payable. The board of directors has full authority to determine the amount of retained earnings to be distributed as a dividend and the amount to keep in the business. Dividends do not accrue like interest on a note payable. Even if the preferred shares are cumulative, dividends in arrears are not a liability until they are declared.

Helpful hint Recall that shareholders' equity consists of contributed capital and retained earnings. Therefore, if a company tried to declare a dividend that caused a deficit in the Retained Earnings account, it would essentially be returning part of the contributed capital to the shareholders.

Entries for Cash Dividends

There are three important dates for dividends: (1) the declaration date, (2) the record date, and (3) the payment date. Normally, there are several weeks between each date and the next one. Accounting entries are required on two of the dates: the declaration date and the payment date.

On the **declaration date**, a company's board of directors formally declares (authorizes) the cash dividend and announces it to shareholders. Declaring a cash dividend commits the corporation to a legal obligation. The obligation is binding and cannot be rescinded (reversed). An entry is required to recognize the increase in Cash Dividends (which results in a decrease in Retained Earnings) and the increase in a current liability account, Dividends Payable. Cash dividends can be paid to preferred and common shareholders. If dividends are paid to the common shareholders, remember that preferred shareholders have to be paid first.

To illustrate a cash dividend, assume that on December 1, the directors of Media General Limited declare a $0.50-per-share quarterly cash dividend on the company's 100,000 common shares. Media does not have any preferred shares and thus does not need to pay them as well. The dividend totals $50,000 ($0.50 × 100,000) and is payable on January 23 to shareholders on December 30. The entry to record the declaration is as follows:

	Declaration Date		
Dec. 1	Cash Dividends—Common	50,000	
	Dividends Payable		50,000
	To record declaration of cash dividend.		

A	=	L	+	SE
		+50,000		−50,000

Cash flows: no effect

Note that the balance in Dividends Payable is a current liability. It will normally be paid within the next month or so. In the case of Media General, it will be paid on January 23. Also note that the Cash Dividends—Common account is similar to the owner's drawings accounts in proprietorships and partnerships.

Instead of debiting a Cash Dividends account, it is also acceptable to debit Retained Earnings when the dividends are declared because dividends reduce retained earnings. The only difference is that, if a Cash Dividends account is debited, then it will have to be closed at the end of the accounting period. While that is an extra step, the advantage of debiting a Cash Dividends account, instead of Retained Earnings, is that it is easier to keep track of the dividends declared during the period.

On the **record date**, ownership of the shares is determined so that the corporation knows who to pay the dividend to. These shareholders are known as the shareholders of record on that date. This date is particularly important for public corporations whose share ownership constantly changes as shares are bought and sold on the secondary market. For Media General, the record date is December 30. No entry is required on this date because the corporation's liability was recognized on the declaration date and is unchanged.

Helpful hint Between the declaration date and the record date, the number of shares remains the same. The purpose of the record date is to identify the persons or entities that will receive the dividend, not to determine the total amount of the dividend liability.

On the **payment date**, dividend cheques are mailed to shareholders and the payment of the dividend is recorded. The entry on January 23, the payment date, is as follows:

	Payment Date		
Jan. 23	Dividends Payable	50,000	
	Cash		50,000
	To record payment of cash dividend.		

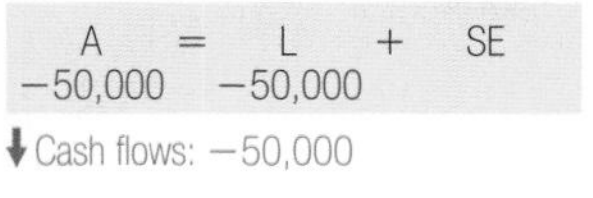

A	=	L	+	SE
−50,000		−50,000		

Cash flows: −50,000

Note that the declaration of a cash dividend increases liabilities and reduces shareholders' equity. The payment of the dividend reduces both assets and liabilities, but has no effect on shareholders' equity. The cumulative effect of the declaration and payment of a cash dividend is to decrease both shareholders' equity (through the Retained Earnings account) and total assets (through the Cash account).

The key dates for dividends are shown in Illustration 13-3.

ILLUSTRATION 13-3
Key dividend dates

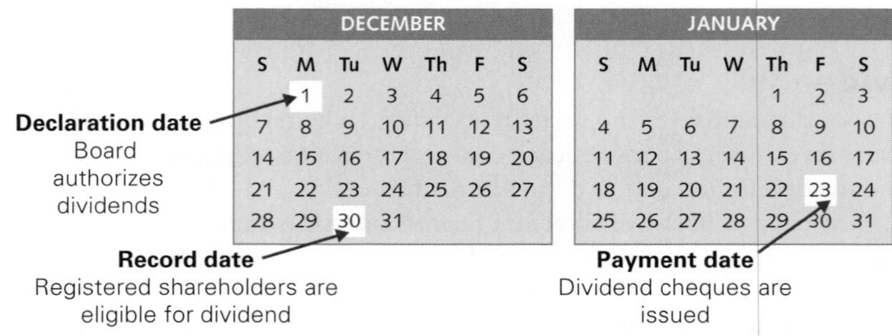

Dividends in a corporation are the equivalent of drawings in a proprietorship or a partnership. Dividends reduce shareholders' equity, just as drawings reduce owner's equity in a proprietorship and partners' equity in a partnership.

BEFORE YOU GO ON...

DO IT

The board of directors of the Blue Heron Corporation met on December 22 and voted in favour of declaring both the annual preferred share dividend and a $1 common share dividend to shareholders of record on January 1. The dividend will be paid on January 15. The company has 30,000, $4 noncumulative preferred shares and 150,000 common shares. Prepare the entries required on each of these dates.

Action Plan

- Remember that as soon as a dividend is declared, the liability account Dividends Payable is credited and the company has an obligation to pay it on the payment date.
- The date of record is used to determine who will receive the dividend.
- On the payment date, there is no impact on shareholders' equity but assets and liabilities are reduced.

SOLUTION

Dec. 22	Cash Dividends—Preferred (30,000 × $4)	120,000	
	Cash Dividends—Common (150,000 × $1)	150,000	
	Dividends Payable ($120,000 + $150,000)		270,000
	To record declaration of cash dividend.		
Jan. 1	No journal entry		
Jan. 15	Dividends Payable	270,000	
	Cash		270,000
	To record payment of cash dividend.		

Related exercise material: BE13–9 and E13–8.

THE NAVIGATOR

STUDY OBJECTIVE 5
Prepare a statement of retained earnings and closing entries for a corporation.

REPORTING RETAINED EARNINGS

Statement of Retained Earnings (ASPE)

All corporations are required to provide information on each of the transactions and events that changed retained earnings during the period and to show how ending retained earnings has been calculated. For companies following ASPE, this information is reported in a **statement of retained earnings**. In Chapter 14, you will learn how companies following IFRS include this information in a statement of changes in shareholders' equity.

A statement of retained earnings is similar to the statement of owner's equity prepared for a proprietorship. The income statement must be prepared before the statement of retained earnings in order to determine the profit that will be added to (or loss that will be deducted from) beginning retained earnings. As in the statement of owner's equity, the statement of retained earnings starts with the beginning balance, and then shows all of the changes in order to calculate the ending balance.

As cash dividends declared reduce retained earnings, this amount is shown as a deduction in the statement of retained earnings. This is similar to deducting drawings in a statement of owner's equity. However, it should be noted that **the statement of retained earnings reports the amount of dividends declared, not the amount of dividends paid.** Frequently these are the same amounts. But as we saw in the previous section, dividends can be declared in one year and paid in the next; thus dividends declared and dividends paid during the year are not always the same amounts.

To illustrate, assume that Media General Limited had $928,000 of retained earnings at January 1, 2014, and declared total cash dividends of $200,000 in 2014. Recall from Illustration 13-2 that the company had profit of $225,000 in 2014. Its statement of retained earnings for the year ended December 31, 2014, is shown in Illustration 13-4.

ILLUSTRATION 13-4
Statement of retained earnings

MEDIA GENERAL LIMITED Statement of Retained Earnings Year Ended December 31, 2014	
Retained earnings, January 1	$ 928,000
Add: Profit	225,000
	1,153,000
Less: Cash dividends	200,000
Retained earnings, December 31	$ 953,000

Closing Entries for a Corporation

As in a proprietorship or partnership, it is necessary to close all of a corporation's temporary accounts to a zero balance at the end of the accounting period to get the accounts in the general ledger ready for the next period. It is also necessary to update the balance in the Retained Earnings account to its year-end balance.

Recall that journalizing and posting closing entries and preparing a post-closing trial balance are the final steps in the accounting cycle. Also recall that in a proprietorship or partnership, each revenue and expense account (which combine to produce profit or loss) is closed to Income Summary, which is then closed to the owner's capital account, and drawings are also closed to the owner's capital account.

In a corporation, the process is the same, except that the income summary and the dividend accounts are closed to Retained Earnings. The closing process for a corporation is shown in Illustration 13-5.

ILLUSTRATION 13-5
Closing process for a corporation

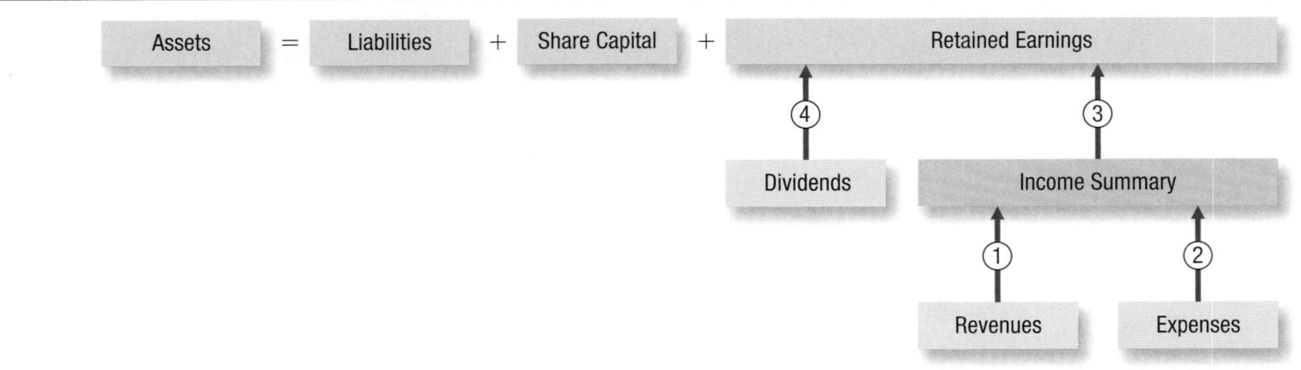

Notice that the closing process does not affect assets, liabilities, or share capital accounts.

To illustrate the closing journal entries, use the income statement accounts shown for Media General Limited in Illustration 13-2. Also recall from Illustration 13-4 that it declared dividends of $200,000 in 2014. The Cash Dividends account will also need to be closed. The closing entries follow:

A	=	L	+	SE
				−800,000
				+800,000

Cash flows: no effect

A	=	L	+	SE
				−575,000
				+575,000

Cash flows: no effect

A	=	L	+	SE
				−225,000
				+225,000

Cash flows: no effect

A	=	L	+	SE
				−200,000
				+200,000

Cash flows: no effect

Date	Account	Debit	Credit
Dec. 31	Sales	800,000	
	Income Summary		800,000
	To close revenue to income summary.		
31	Income Summary	575,000	
	Cost of Goods Sold		420,000
	Operating Expenses		94,000
	Interest Expense		4,750
	Income Tax Expense		56,250
	To close expenses to income summary.		
31	Income Summary ($800,000 − $575,000)	225,000	
	Retained Earnings		225,000
	To close income summary to retained earnings.		
31	Retained Earnings	200,000	
	Cash Dividends—Common		200,000
	To close dividends to retained earnings.		

Posting the closing entries to the Income Summary and Retained Earnings accounts follows:

Income Summary

	Debit		Credit
Clos.	575,000	Clos.	800,000
		Bal.	225,000
Clos.	225,000		
		Bal.	0

Retained Earnings

	Debit		Credit
		Bal.	928,000
Clos.	200,000	Clos.	225,000
		Bal.	953,000

Although not shown, after posting the closing entries, all of the revenue, expense, and dividend accounts will have a zero balance.

After these entries are posted, the Retained Earnings account (a permanent account) is updated in the general ledger to the December 31, 2014, balance of $953,000, previously shown in the statement of retained earnings. This ending balance is reported in the shareholders' equity section of the balance sheet. The normal balance of the Retained Earnings account is a credit. If total losses and dividends to date are greater than total profit to date, the Retained Earnings account will have a debit balance, which is called a **deficit**. The ending Retained Earnings balance becomes the opening balance for the next period.

BEFORE YOU GO ON...

DO IT

On January 1, 2014, SlopeBack Ltd. had a balance of $326,700 in its retained earnings account. During the year, it declared $100,000 cash dividends and paid $75,000. Its profit in 2014 was $115,000, calculated as follows:

Sales		$425,000
Cost of goods sold	$202,500	
Selling expenses	75,000	
Income tax expense	32,500	310,000
Profit		$115,000

(a) Prepare a statement of retained earnings.
(b) Prepare closing entries.
(c) Post closing entries to the income summary and retained earnings accounts.

BEFORE YOU GO ON...
continued on next page

SOLUTION

(a)

SLOPEBACK LTD.
Statement of Retained Earnings
Year Ended December 31, 2014

Retained earnings, January 1, 2014	$326,700
Add: Profit	115,000
	441,700
Less: Cash dividends	100,000
Retained earnings, December 31, 2014	$341,700

(b)

Date	Account	Debit	Credit
Dec. 31	Sales	425,000	
	Income Summary		425,000
	To close revenue to income summary.		
31	Income Summary	310,000	
	Cost of Goods Sold		202,500
	Selling Expenses		75,000
	Income Tax Expense		32,500
	To close expenses to income summary.		
31	Income Summary	115,000	
	Retained Earnings		115,000
	To close income summary ($425,000 – $310,000) to retained earnings.		
31	Retained Earnings	100,000	
	Cash Dividends—Common		100,000
	To close dividends to retained earnings.		

(c)

Income Summary

Clos.	310,000	Clos.	425,000
		Bal.	115,000
Clos.	115,000		
		Bal.	0

Retained Earnings

		Bal.	326,700
Clos.	100,000	Clos.	115,000
		Bal.	341,700

Related exercise material: BE13–10, BE13–11, E13–9, and E13–10.

BEFORE YOU GO ON...
continued from previous page

Action Plan

- A statement of retained earnings shows the changes in the company's retained earnings. It starts with the previous year's retained earnings. Then profit is added and dividends declared are deducted to determine the ending balance.
- Dividends declared are shown on the statement of retained earnings.
- Closing entries are similar to proprietorships and partnerships except that the Income Summary and Cash Dividends accounts are closed to Retained Earnings.

THE NAVIGATOR

STATEMENT PRESENTATION AND ANALYSIS

STUDY OBJECTIVE 6
Prepare the shareholders' equity section of the balance sheet and calculate return on equity.

In this section, we explain the preparation and presentation of the shareholders' equity section of the balance sheet and then learn how to use this information to calculate an important profitability measure—the return on equity ratio.

PRESENTATION OF SHAREHOLDERS' EQUITY

As explained earlier in the chapter, shareholders' equity always includes two parts: (1) share capital and (2) retained earnings. On the balance sheet, share capital may be shown as part of contributed capital, as explained below. Corporations following IFRS will also have a third section called accumulated other comprehensive income, illustrated in Chapter 14. Companies following ASPE do not have accumulated other comprehensive income.

Contributed Capital

Contributed capital is the total amount contributed by, or accruing to, the shareholders. Within contributed capital, there are two classifications shown on the balance sheet:

1. **Share capital.** This category consists of preferred and common shares. Because of the additional rights they possess, preferred shares are shown before common shares. The number of shares authorized, number of shares issued, and any particular share features (such as convertible) are reported for each class of shares either on the balance sheet or in a note to the financial statements.

   Private companies following ASPE are not required to disclose the number of shares authorized, only the number issued and their related rights and privileges.

2. **Contributed surplus.** This category includes other amounts contributed by shareholders (in addition to contributions for share capital), or amounts that accrue to shareholders from transactions such as reacquiring and retiring shares. Other situations not discussed in this textbook can also result in contributed surplus. If a company has a variety of sources of contributed surplus, it is important to distinguish each one. For many companies, there is no contributed surplus. In those situations, it is more common to use the category "share capital" instead of "contributed capital" on the balance sheet.

Alternative terminology
Contributed surplus is also known as *additional contributed capital.*

Retained Earnings

Recall that retained earnings are the cumulative profit (or loss) since incorporation that has been retained (that is, not distributed to shareholders). The statement of retained earnings provides information on how the account changed during the year. On the balance sheet, the year-end balance in retained earnings is shown in shareholders' equity. A deficit is reported as a deduction from shareholders' equity, rather than as an addition.

Sample Shareholders' Equity Section

The shareholders' equity section of Jagoe Inc. is shown in Illustration 13-6. Jagoe's preferred shares dividend rate is $6 per year; 50,000 noncumulative preferred shares have been authorized; and 6,000 shares are issued for $770,000.

The company has authorized an unlimited number of common shares; at December 31, 2014, 400,000 shares are issued for $2.8 million. Jagoe's ending retained earnings is $1,050,000.

ILLUSTRATION 13-6
Shareholders' equity section

JAGOE INC.
Balance Sheet (partial)
December 31, 2014

Shareholders' equity		
Share capital		
$6 noncumulative preferred shares, 50,000 shares authorized, 6,000 shares issued	$ 770,000	
Common shares, unlimited shares authorized, 400,000 shares issued	2,800,000	
Total share capital		$3,570,000
Retained earnings		1,050,000
Total shareholders' equity		$4,620,000

ANALYSIS

There are many ratios determined from the shareholders' equity section of the balance sheet. We will learn about return on equity here. In the next chapter, we will learn about earnings per share and the price-earnings and dividend payout ratios.

Return on Equity

Return on equity, also known as return on investment, is considered by many to be *the* most important measure of a company's profitability. This ratio is used by management and investors to evaluate how many dollars are earned for each dollar invested by the shareholders. It is expressed as a percentage and can be used to compare investment opportunities in the marketplace. *The higher the ratio, the better.*

Return on equity is a widely published figure. Illustration 13-7 calculates the return on equity ratio for Reitmans (Canada) Limited ($ in thousands).

ILLUSTRATION 13-7
Return on equity

Profit	÷	Average Shareholders' Equity	=	Return on Equity
$47,539	÷	($492,852 + $512,800) ÷ 2	=	9.5%

Reitmans' return on equity, at 9.5%, is below the industry average, which was reported as 20.2% by Reuters. Return on equity can vary significantly by company and by industry.

Calculations can be done to produce a return on equity for common shareholders only. This is done by dividing profit available to common shareholders by the average common shareholders' equity. Profit available to common shareholders is profit less any preferred dividends. Common shareholders' equity is total shareholders' equity less the legal capital of any preferred shares. Recall that everything else belongs to the common, or residual, shareholders.

BEFORE YOU GO ON...

DO IT

The following information is available for Tanim's Sewing Goods for three recent years:

	2014	2013	2012
Total shareholders' equity	$659,200	$599,822	$558,850
Profit	79,170	54,630	40,620

Calculate return on equity for Tanim's Sewing Goods for 2014 and 2013 and comment on any trends.

SOLUTION

	2014	2013
Average shareholders' equity	($659,200 + $599,822) ÷ 2 = $629,511	($599,822 + $558,850) ÷ 2 = $579,336
Return on equity	12.6% = $79,170 / $629,511	9.4% = $54,630 / $579,336

The increase in the return on equity indicates improved profitability over the two years.

Related exercise material: BE13–12, BE13–13, E13–11, and E13–12.

Action Plan

- Calculate average shareholders' equity using the total shareholders' equity at the beginning and end of the year.
- Divide profit by the average shareholders' equity for that year to calculate return on equity.
- Recall if it is better for return on equity to increase or decrease.

THE NAVIGATOR

Comparing IFRS and ASPE

Key Differences	International Financial Reporting Standards (IFRS)	Accounting Standards for Private Enterprises (ASPE)
Issue of shares for noncash goods or services	Record the transaction at the fair value of the goods or services received. If this value cannot be reliably determined, then the fair value of the shares given up is used.	Record the transaction at the most reliable of the two values—the fair value of the goods or services received or the fair value of the shares. As private company shares are not traded, it is often difficult to measure their fair value. Thus, in practice, the fair value of the goods or services received is used more often.
Changes in retained earnings	Presented in a statement of changes in shareholders' equity.	Presented in a statement of retained earnings.
Accumulated other comprehensive income	Reported in shareholders' equity on the balance sheet.	Not required under ASPE.
Authorized share capital	Must present the number of shares authorized for each class of shares.	Not required under ASPE.

THE NAVIGATOR

DEMONSTRATION PROBLEM

On January 2, 2014, Rolman Corporation began operations. Its articles of incorporation authorize it to issue an unlimited number of common shares and 500,000, $3 noncumulative preferred shares. In its first year, 2014, the company had the following selected transactions:

Jan. 2	Issued 50,000 common shares to Rowena Rolman for $10 cash per share.
Jan. 10	Issued 1,500 common shares to Rowena's brother in exchange for a used vehicle. The vehicle was appraised at $15,000.
June 30	Declared a $0.25 dividend to the common shareholders of record on July 1, payable July 5.
July 5	Paid the common share dividend.
Oct. 1	Issued 1,000 preferred shares to Rowena's grandmother for $60 cash per share.
Dec. 30	Declared the $0.75 quarterly preferred share dividend, and a $0.25 common share dividend. Both dividends are payable on January 5 to the shareholders of record on January 1.

During 2014, the company had Service Revenue of $240,000, and Operating Expenses of $180,000. The company has a 15% income tax rate and did not make any instalments during the year. Rowena has decided the company will use ASPE.

Instructions

(a) Journalize the transactions (ignore the revenues and expenses).
(b) Prepare an income statement and record the journal entry to record income tax expense.
(c) Prepare a statement of retained earnings and the shareholders' equity section of the balance sheet.
(d) Prepare closing entries.

Action Plan

- Credit the Common Shares and Preferred Shares accounts for the entire proceeds.
- When shares are issued for noncash assets, use the fair value of what is received to establish the amount of the transaction.
- Determine profit before income tax by deducting expenses from revenues.
- Calculate income tax expense by multiplying profit before income tax by the tax rate.
- Prepare the income statement, deducting income tax expense from profit before income tax.
- A statement of retained earnings shows all of the changes in the company's retained earnings, which includes profit and dividends declared (not dividends paid).
- Closing entries are similar to proprietorships and partnerships

SOLUTION TO DEMONSTRATION PROBLEM

(a)

Date	Account Titles and Explanation	Debit	Credit
Jan. 2	Cash	500,000	
	Common Shares (50,000 × $10)		500,000
	To record issue of 50,000 common shares at $10.		
Jan. 10	Vehicles	15,000	
	Common Shares		15,000
	To record issue of 1,500 common shares for a vehicle.		
June 30	Cash Dividends—Common ($0.25 × 51,500)	12,875	
	Dividends Payable		12,875
	To record declaration of a $0.25 common share dividend.		
July 5	Dividends Payable	12,875	
	Cash		12,875
	To record payment of cash dividend.		
Oct. 1	Cash ($60 × 1,000)	60,000	
	Preferred Shares		60,000
	To record issue of 1,000 preferred shares at $60 per share.		
Dec. 30	Cash Dividends—Common ($0.25 × 51,500)	12,875	
	Cash Dividends—Preferred ($0.75 × 1,000)	750	
	Dividends Payable ($12,875 + $750)		13,625
	To record declaration of $0.75 quarterly preferred share dividend and $0.25 common share dividend.		

SOLUTION TO DEMONSTRATION PROBLEM continued on next page

SOLUTION TO DEMONSTRATION PROBLEM continued from previous page

except that the Income Summary and Cash Dividends accounts are closed to Retained Earnings rather than Capital.

- On the balance sheet, separate shareholders' equity into share capital and retained earnings.

(b)

ROLMAN CORPORATION
Income Statement
Year Ended December 31, 2014

Service revenue	$240,000
Operating expenses	180,000
Profit before income tax	60,000
Income tax expense	9,000
Profit	$ 51,000

Date	Account	Debit	Credit
Dec. 31	Income Tax Expense ($60,000 × 15%)	9,000	
	Income Tax Payable		9,000
	To record 15% income taxes for 2014.		

(c)

ROLMAN CORPORATION
Statement of Retained Earnings
Year Ended December 31, 2014

Retained earnings, January 1		$ 0
Add: Profit for the year		51,000
		51,000
Less: Common share dividends	$25,750	
Preferred share dividends	750	26,500
Retained earnings, December 31		$24,500

ROLMAN CORPORATION
Balance Sheet (partial)
December 31, 2014

Shareholders' equity		
Share capital		
Preferred shares, $3 noncumulative, 1,000 issued	$ 60,000	
Common shares, 51,500 issued	515,000[1]	
Total share capital		$575,000
Retained earnings		24,500
Total shareholders' equity		$599,500

[1]500,000 + 15,000 = 515,000

(d)

Date	Account	Debit	Credit
Dec. 31	Service Revenue	240,000	
	Income Summary		240,000
	To close revenue to income summary.		
31	Income Summary	189,000	
	Operating Expenses		180,000
	Income Tax Expense		9,000
	To close expenses to income summary.		
31	Income Summary ($240,000 − $189,000)	51,000	
	Retained Earnings		51,000
	To close income summary to Retained Earnings.		
31	Retained Earnings	26,500	
	Cash Dividends—Common		25,750
	Cash Dividends—Preferred		750
	To close dividends to Retained Earnings.		

THE NAVIGATOR

Summary of Study Objectives

1. ***Identify and discuss characteristics of the corporate form of organization.*** The major characteristics of a corporation are as follows: separate legal existence, limited liability of shareholders, transferable ownership rights, ability to acquire capital, continuous life, government regulations, and corporate income tax. Corporations must be incorporated federally or provincially, and may have shareholders of different classes. Each class of shares carries different rights and privileges. The rights of common share owners are restricted to the right to elect the board of directors, to receive a proportionate share of dividends, if declared, and to receive the remaining assets if the corporation is liquidated. Corporations are managed by the board of directors.

2. ***Account for the issuance of common and preferred shares.*** When shares are issued, the entire proceeds from the issue become legal capital and are credited to the Common Shares account. When shares are issued for noncash assets or services, the fair value of the consideration received is used if it can be determined. If not, the fair value of the consideration given up is used. The accounting for preferred shares is similar to the accounting for common shares.

   Preferred shares typically do not have voting rights but do have priority over common shares to receive (1) dividends, and (2) assets, if the company is liquidated. The dividend is specified and may be cumulative or noncumulative. Cumulative preferred shares must be paid dividends for the current year as well as any unpaid dividends from previous years before the common shares receive any dividends. Noncumulative preferred shares lose the right to unpaid dividends from prior years. In addition, preferred shares may be convertible, redeemable, and/or retractable. Convertible preferred shares allow their holder to convert them into common shares at a specified ratio. Redeemable preferred shares give the corporation the right to redeem the shares for cash, whereas retractable preferred shares give the shareholder the right to convert the shares to cash.

3. ***Prepare a corporate income statement.*** Corporate income statements are similar to the income statements for proprietorships and partnerships, with one exception. Income tax expense must be reported in a separate section before profit in the corporation's income statement.

4. ***Account for cash dividends.*** Dividends are similar to drawings in that they are a distribution of profit to the owners (shareholders). Entries for cash dividends are required at the declaration date and the payment date. Cash dividends reduce assets and shareholders' equity (retained earnings).

5. ***Prepare a statement of retained earnings and closing entries for a corporation.*** Retained earnings are increased by profit, and decreased by losses and dividends. Companies reporting under ASPE are required to prepare a statement of retained earnings showing the beginning balance, changes during the year, and ending balance of retained earnings. In a corporation, the income summary account and dividends accounts are closed to retained earnings.

6. ***Prepare the shareholders' equity section of the balance sheet and calculate return on equity.*** Within the shareholders' equity section of the balance sheet, all corporations will report contributed capital and retained earnings. Within contributed capital, two classifications may be shown if applicable: share capital and additional contributed surplus. Corporations reporting under IFRS will also have another component in shareholders' equity, which will be introduced in Chapter 14.

   Return on equity is calculated by dividing profit by average shareholders' equity. It is an important measure of a company's profitability.

THE NAVIGATOR

Glossary

Authorized shares The total number of each class of shares a corporation is allowed to sell, as indicated in its articles of incorporation. This amount may be specified or unlimited. (p. 551)

Cash dividend A pro rata (equal) distribution of cash on a per share basis to shareholders. (p. 558)

Common shares Shares where the owners have the right to (1) vote on the election of the board of directors, (2) share in the distribution of profit through dividends, and (3) share any assets that remain after all debts and shares with priority rights have been paid. If the corporation has only one class of shares, these are the common shares. (p. 549)

Contributed capital The total amount contributed by, or accruing to, the shareholders. Consists of share capital and contributed surplus. (p. 564)

Convertible preferred shares Preferred shares that the shareholder can convert into common shares at a specified ratio. (p. 554)

Corporation A business organized as a separate legal entity, with most of the rights and privileges of a person. Shares are evidence of ownership. (p. 546)

Cumulative A feature of preferred shares that entitles the shareholder to receive current dividends and unpaid prior-year dividends before common shareholders receive any dividends. (p. 553)

Debt covenant A restriction in a loan agreement that, among other things, may limit the use of corporate assets for the payment of dividends. (p. 559)

Declaration date The date when the board of directors formally declares a dividend and announces it to shareholders. (p. 559)

Deficit A debit balance in the Retained Earnings account created when total losses and dividends to date are greater than total profit to date; it is reported as a deduction from shareholders' equity. (p. 562)

Dividend A distribution of profit by a corporation to its shareholders on a pro rata basis. (p. 549)

Dividends in arrears Dividends on cumulative preferred shares that were not declared. (p. 553)

Initial public offering (IPO) The initial offering of a corporation's shares to the public. (p. 551)

Issued shares The authorized shares that have been sold. (p. 551)

Legal capital The share capital that must be retained in the business for the protection of corporate creditors. (p. 551)

No par value shares Share capital that has not been given a specific value. All the proceeds from the sale of no par value shares are treated as legal capital. (p. 551)

Noncumulative Preferred shares that are entitled to the current dividend, but not to any unpaid amounts from previous years. (p. 554)

Organization costs Costs incurred in the formation of a corporation that are expensed in the fiscal period during which they are incurred. (p. 549)

Payment date The date when cash dividends are paid to shareholders. (p. 559)

Preferred shares Shares that have contractual preferences over common shares. (p. 553)

Private corporation A corporation that has only a few shareholders. Its shares are not available for sale to the general public. (p. 546)

Public corporation A corporation that may have thousands of shareholders. Its shares are usually traded on an organized securities market. (p. 546)

Record date The date when ownership of shares is determined for dividend purposes. (p. 559)

Redeemable (callable) preferred shares Preferred shares that give the issuer the right to purchase the shares from shareholders at specified future dates and prices. (p. 555)

Retained earnings Earned capital (cumulative profit less losses and amounts distributed to shareholders since incorporation) that has been retained for future use. If negative (that is, a debit balance), it is called a *deficit*. (p. 556)

Retained earnings restrictions Circumstances that make a portion of retained earnings currently unavailable for dividends. (p. 558)

Retractable preferred shares Preferred shares that give the shareholder the right to sell the shares to the issuer at specified future dates and prices. (p. 555)

Return on equity A measure of profitability from the shareholders' point of view. It is calculated by dividing profit by average common shareholders' equity. (p. 564)

Secondary market A market where investors buy and sell shares of public companies from each other, rather than from the company. (p. 551)

Share capital The amount paid, or contributed, to the corporation by shareholders in exchange for shares of ownership. It can consist of preferred and common shares. (p. 550)

Statement of retained earnings A financial statement that shows the changes in retained earnings during the year, used only under ASPE. (p. 560)

Self-Study Questions

Answers are at the end of the chapter.

(SO 1) K 1. An important characteristic unique to a corporation is that:
(a) it is separate and distinct from its owners.
(b) owner liability is unlimited.
(c) owners personally manage the company.
(d) ownership rights are not transferable.

(SO 1) AP 2. Ilona Schiller purchased 100 common shares of Tim Hortons Inc. on the Toronto Stock Exchange for $50 per share. Tim Hortons Inc. had originally issued these shares at $33. This transaction will have what impact on Tim Hortons Inc.'s Common Shares account?
(a) Increase of $1,700 (c) Increase of $5,000
(b) Increase of $3,300 (d) No effect

(SO 2) AP 3. ABC Corporation issues 1,000 common shares at $12 per share. In recording the transaction, a credit is made to:
(a) Gain on Sale of Shares for $12,000.
(b) Common Shares for $12,000.
(c) Investment in ABC Common Shares for $12,000.
(d) Cash for $12,000.

(SO 2) K 4. Which of the following is *not* true? Preferred shares:
(a) have priority over common shareholder dividends.
(b) have priority over common shareholders for assets in the event of liquidation.
(c) generally have voting rights.
(d) can be reacquired.

(SO 3) AP 5. In 2014, Westney Corp. had $420,000 of revenue and $206,000 of operating expenses. The company has a 15% income tax rate. What is the company's profit for the year?
(a) $32,100. (c) $214,000.
(b) $181,900. (d) $246,100.

(SO 4) K 6. The necessary conditions to pay a cash dividend include:
(a) approval from the shareholders, and enough cash to pay all current liabilities.
(b) total profit for the year must be in excess of the dividend.
(c) a declaration from the board, and enough cash to pay for its ongoing operations and pay its bills as they come due.
(d) all authorized shares have been issued.

(SO 4) K 7. The dates on which a corporation will record a journal entry with regard to a cash dividend are the:
(a) record date and payment date.
(b) declaration date and record date.
(c) declaration date, record date, and payment date.
(d) declaration date and payment date.

(SO 5) AP 8. Ajax Netscape Ltd. began operations on January 1, 2013, when common shares were issued for $285,000 cash. In 2013, the company had a loss of $57,000. In 2014, the company had a profit of $123,000. On December 31, 2014, the company declared a $30,000 cash dividend payable on

January 8, 2015. The statement of retained earnings for 2014 will show which of the following amounts?

	Beginning retained earnings	Ending retained earnings
(a)	$ (57,000)	$ 36,000
(b)	228,000	321,000
(c)	(57,000)	66,000
(d)	0	93,000

(SO 6) C 9. The shareholders' equity section of a balance sheet for a company reporting under ASPE will never report:
(a) the total number of shares issued.
(b) accumulated other comprehensive income.
(c) a deficit (debit balance in Retained Earnings).
(d) cumulative preferred shares.

(SO 6) AP 10. If a company's profit is $50,000, its total assets $1 million, its average common shareholders' equity $500,000, and its net sales $800,000, its return on equity is:
(a) 3.3%.
(b) 5%.
(c) 6.25%.
(d) 10%.

THE NAVIGATOR

Questions

(SO 1) C 1. Corporations can be classified in different ways. For example, they may be classified by purpose (such as profit or not-for-profit) or by ownership (such as public or private). Explain the difference between each of these types of classifications.

(SO 1) C 2. Natalie Gerster, a student, asks for your help in understanding the following characteristics of a corporation: (a) limited liability of shareholders, (b) transferable ownership rights, and (c) ability to acquire capital. Explain to Natalie how these characteristics work together to create a significant advantage for the corporate form of organization.

(SO 1) C 3. What are the advantages and disadvantages of a corporation compared with a proprietorship or partnership? Explain why some of the advantages of the corporate form of organization may not apply to small, privately held corporations.

(SO 1) C 4. Explain the ownership rights of shareholders and the authority structure in a corporation.

(SO 2) C 5. Explain the difference between authorized and issued shares. For a corporation, why is the number of authorized shares important? Of issued shares?

(SO 2) C 6. Paul Joyce purchases 100 common shares of TechTop Ltd. for $12 per share from the company's initial public offering. Later, Paul purchases 200 more TechTop Ltd. common shares for $20 each on the Toronto Stock Exchange, using his own online brokerage account. Explain the impact of each of these transactions on TechTop's assets, liabilities, and shareholders' equity. (*Hint:* Refer to secondary markets in your response.)

(SO 2) C 7. Equipment with an estimated fair value of $25,000 is acquired by issuing 1,000 common shares. How should this transaction be recorded? Include in your explanation how this might be different for a company following IFRS or ASPE.

(SO 2) AP 8. Compare the rights of preferred shareholders with the rights of common shareholders. Include in your answer the areas in which preferred shares are given priority over common shares.

(SO 2) C 9. What is the difference between noncumulative and cumulative preferred shares? What are the differences among convertible, redeemable, and retractable preferred shares?

(SO 2) AP 10. Following two years of no dividend payments to either their cumulative preferred or common shareholders, management decides to declare a dividend for all shareholders. (a) Is the company required to pay either (or both) groups of shareholders for the previous two years of missed dividends? (b) Should the company report a liability for the years of missed dividends or are there any other reporting requirements?

(SO 2) AP 11. A preferred shareholder converts her convertible preferred shares into common shares. What effect does this have on the corporation's (a) total assets, (b) total liabilities, and (c) total shareholders' equity? (*Hint:* Consider what journal entry would be made to record the conversion.)

(SO 3) C 12. What is the main difference between income statements for corporations and income statements for proprietorships and partnerships? Why does this difference exist?

(SO 4) K 13. A dividend is a "pro rata" distribution of retained earnings. Explain what "pro rata" means.

(SO 4) K 14. At what point does a cash dividend become a liability of a company? What entries are made for cash dividends on the declaration date, the record date, and the payment date?

(SO 4) C 15. Why is having enough retained earnings a requirement for paying a cash dividend, even if the company has sufficient cash to make the payment?

(SO 5) C 16. Explain what information is included in a statement of retained earnings. In what ways is it similar to a statement of owner's equity and in what ways is it different?

(SO 5) C 17. Explain how temporary accounts are closed in a corporation. In what ways are closing entries similar to those of a proprietorship and in what ways are they different?

(SO 6) K 18. The shareholders' equity is divided into major components. Identify and explain what each component represents.

(SO 6) C 19. Parker Inc. and Shaughnessy Inc. have the same annual earnings ($100,000); however, the companies have different amounts of shareholders' equity. Average shareholders' equity for Parker is $300,000 and for Shaughnessy is $350,000. Which company would you consider a better investment and why?

Brief Exercises

BE13–1 For each characteristic listed, identify which type of business organization best fits the description. There may be more than one answer in some cases. The first one has been done for you as an example.

Distinguish between characteristics of different business organizations. **(SO 1) C**

Characteristic	Proprietorship	Partnership	Corporation
1. Continuous life			X
2. Unlimited liability			
3. Ease of formation			
4. Separate legal existence			
5. Ability to acquire capital			
6. Shared skills and resources			
7. Fewer government regulations			
8. Separation of ownership and management			
9. Owners' acts are binding			
10. Easy transfer of ownership rights			

BE13–2 On August 5, Hansen Corporation issued 2,000 common shares for $12 per share. On September 10, Hansen issued an additional 500 shares for $13 per share. (a) Record the share transactions. (b) What is the average cost per share of the common shares following the last transaction?

Record issue of common shares. **(SO 2) AP**

BE13–3 Juke Joint Ltd., a private company, began operations on March 12 by issuing 5,000 common shares for $20 cash per share. On September 10, the company issued 500 common shares in exchange for equipment with an appraised value of $9,500. (a) Assuming the company uses ASPE, prepare a journal entry to record the September 10 transaction and provide a rationale for the value. (b) How might your answer change if Juke Joint was a public company?

Record issue of common shares in noncash transaction and provide rationale. **(SO 2) AP**

BE13-4 Place the number corresponding to each of the following characteristics in the appropriate section of the diagram. If a characteristic applies to both common and preferred shares, place that number in the overlapping section.

Distinguish between characteristics of preferred shares and common shares. **(SO 2) C**

1. Receive a lower priority than creditors in terms of their claim to the assets of the business in the event of liquidation.
2. The shares may have cumulative dividends.
3. The shares carry voting rights.
4. Every corporation has this type of share.
5. The shares may be convertible.
6. They are part of a corporation's share capital.

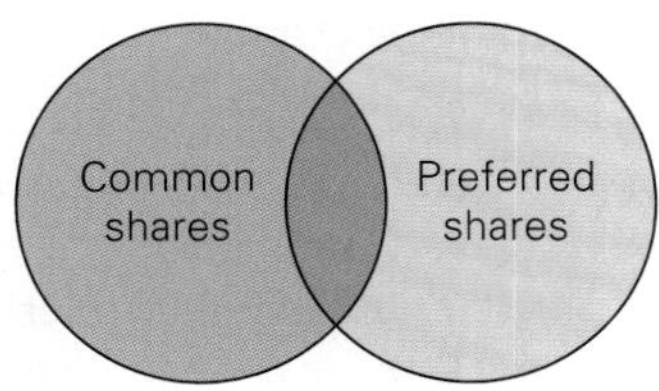

Record issue of preferred shares. **(SO 2) AP**

BE13–5 StarLight Ltd. is authorized to issue 10,000, $4 noncumulative preferred shares. On January 13, it issued 3,000 preferred shares for $90 cash per share. (a) Prepare a journal entry to record the transaction. (b) Determine the total amount of dividends that must be paid to the preferred shareholders prior to paying a dividend to common shareholders.

Determine dividends in arrears. **(SO 2) AP**

BE13–6 Gosselin Incorporated had 45,000, $2.50 preferred shares issued. It did not pay a dividend to the preferred shareholders in 2013 and 2014. (a) What are the dividends in arrears, if any, at December 31, 2014, if the shares are cumulative and if they are noncumulative? (b) How are dividends in arrears reported in the financial statements?

Record conversion of preferred shares. **(SO 2) AP**

BE13–7 Progressive Parts Corporation issued 25,000 preferred shares on May 10 for $35 each. Each share is convertible into two common shares. On November 21, the preferred shares had a fair value of $37 each, and the common shares $19 each. On this day, 5,000 of the preferred shares are converted into common shares. (a) Journalize the issue of the preferred shares on May 10. (b) Journalize the conversion of the preferred shares on November 21.

Record income tax and prepare corporate income statement. **(SO 3) AP**

BE13–8 For the year ended June 30, 2014, Viceron Inc. had Service Revenue of $800,000 and Operating Expenses of $575,000. The company has a 15% income tax rate. It has not paid any income tax instalments or accrued for income tax expense. Prepare (a) the journal entry to record income tax, and (b) the income statement.

Record cash dividend. **(SO 4) AP**

BE13–9 On October 14, the board of directors of Celery Cede Corp. voted to declare the annual preferred share dividend to shareholders of record on November 1, payable on November 21. The company is authorized to issue 100,000, $5.25 noncumulative preferred shares; 25,000 have been issued. Prepare the required entries on each of these dates.

Prepare a statement of retained earnings. **(SO 5) AP**

BE13–10 For the year ending December 31, 2014, Grayfair Inc. reports profit of $175,000. During the year, the company declared a total of $120,000 cash dividends and paid $85,000 of these dividends. Prepare a statement of retained earnings for the year, assuming the balance in Retained Earnings on December 31, 2013, was $248,000.

Record closing entries and post to retained earnings. **(SO 5) AP**

BE13–11 For the year ended December 31, 2014, Huron Lake Enterprises Ltd. had the following revenues and expenses: Sales, $745,000; Cost of Goods Sold, $450,000; Operating Expenses, $135,000; and Income Tax Expense, $35,000. The company also declared $25,000 of dividends to the common shareholders on each of June 30 and December 31. The dividend declared on December 31 will be paid on January 10, 2015. (a) Prepare closing entries. (b) Post the entries to the Retained Earnings account assuming the balance in that account on December 31, 2013, was $382,000.

Prepare shareholders' equity section. **(SO 6) AP**

BE13–12 True Green Nurseries Ltd. is a private company that follows ASPE. It is authorized to issue an unlimited number of both common and $6.50 cumulative preferred shares. On December 31, 2014, there were 15,000 common and 1,000 preferred shares issued with the following balances: Common Shares, $150,000; and Preferred Shares, $100,000. The statement of retained earnings showed retained earnings of $285,000 at December 31, 2014. The dividend on the preferred shares was two years in arrears. Prepare the shareholders' equity section of the balance sheet on December 31, 2014.

Calculate return on equity. **(SO 6) AP**

BE13–13 For the year ended December 31, 2011, **Canada Bread Company, Limited** reported (in thousands) net revenue $1,595,456; profit $51,951; beginning shareholders' equity $638,995; and ending shareholders' equity $663,602. (a) Calculate the return on equity. (b) Canada Bread has no preferred shares. Would its return on *common shareholders' equity* be the same as, or different from, its *return on equity*? Why?

Exercises

Identify terminology. **(SO 1, 2) K**

E13–1 Here are some of the terms discussed in the chapter:

1. Retained earnings
2. Issued shares
3. Legal capital
4. Liquidation preference
5. Authorized shares
6. Public corporation
7. Convertible
8. Retractable preferred shares
9. Cumulative
10. Initial public offering
11. Redeemable preferred shares
12. Secondary market

Instructions
For each description, write the number of the term it best matches.

(a) ________ Preferred shares that give the shareholder the right to redeem shares at their option
(b) ________ The type of corporation whose shares are traded in an organized security market, such as the Toronto Stock Exchange
(c) ________ Preferred shares that give the issuing corporation the right to repurchase the shares at a specified price and date
(d) ________ The maximum number of shares a corporation is allowed to sell
(e) ________ The number of shares a corporation has actually sold
(f) ________ The first time a corporation's shares are offered for sale to the public
(g) ________ Where investors buy and sell shares from each other, rather than from the company
(h) ________ The element of shareholders' equity that is increased by profit and decreased by losses
(i) ________ A preference to get money back before common shareholders if the company is bankrupt
(j) ________ The share capital that must be retained in the business for the protection of corporate creditors
(k) ________ A feature that allows preferred shareholders to exchange their shares for common shares
(l) ________ A preference to collect unpaid dividends on preferred shares before common shareholders can receive a dividend

E13–2 As an accountant for the consulting firm Insite, you are asked by a client to provide advice on the form of organization her new business in the medical industry should take. After a brief conversation, you have learned the following about your client's needs:

Identify the characteristics of a corporation. **(SO 1) C**

1. The client has several children whom she expects to become involved in the business, and to whom she will want to transfer ownership in the future.
2. Companies in this industry tend to be sued frequently.
3. Profit (and taxable income) are expected to be significant in the early years.
4. The company is expected to grow significantly, and your client expects to need substantial funding in the next few years to manage this growth.

Instructions
Write a brief report to advise your client on why organizing as a corporation may, or may not, be the appropriate choice.

E13–3 Santiago Corp., a private corporation, received its articles of incorporation on January 3, 2014. It is authorized to issue an unlimited number of common shares and $1 preferred shares. It had the following share transactions during the year:

Record issue of shares in cash and noncash transactions. **(SO 2) AP**

Jan. 12	Issued 50,000 common shares for $5 per share.
24	Issued 950 common shares in payment of a $4,500 bill for legal services.
July 11	Issued 1,000 preferred shares for $25 per share.
Oct. 1	Issued 10,000 common shares in exchange for land. The land's fair value was estimated to be $55,000. Santiago's accountant estimated that the fair value of the shares issued might be as high as $6 per share.

Instructions
(a) Journalize the share transactions.
(b) Calculate the average cost for the common shares.
(c) Assume instead that Santiago's shares trade on the TSX Venture Exchange. How might this affect the value assigned to the shares issued on October 1?

E13–4 Southwest Corporation is authorized to issue an unlimited amount of common shares, and as at December 31, 2013, has 9,000 shares issued. Manji and MacDonald each own 4,500 of these shares. On December 31, 2013, the balances in Southwest's shareholders' equity are as follows:

Record issue of shares in cash and noncash transactions. **(SO 2) AP**

Common Shares	$18,000
Retained Earnings	35,000

On January 1, 2014, Mah bills Southwest Corporation $5,000 for legal services. As Southwest Corporation has a limited amount of cash, Manji and MacDonald suggest to Mah that the corporation issue shares in exchange for the legal services instead of paying the bill in cash. After a series of negotiations, Mah agrees but wants a 10% ownership interest in the corporation.

Instructions

(a) How many shares would Southwest Corporation need to issue to Mah in order for Mah to have a 10% ownership interest?
(b) Assuming Southwest uses ASPE, prepare the journal entry to record the issue of shares. Include an explanation for the value used in the journal entry.
(c) Why might Manji and MacDonald not want to issue shares to Mah?

Determine conversion date and record conversion of preferred shares. (SO 2) AP

E13–5 New Wave Pool Corporation is authorized to issue common and $3 convertible preferred shares. Each preferred share is convertible into four common shares. On July 2, the company issued 100,000 preferred shares for $110 per share. The common shares were trading at $25 on September 7, $27.50 on September 19, and $29 on September 28.

Instructions

(a) On which date or dates would the preferred shareholders consider converting their shares to common? Why?
(b) Journalize the conversion of the preferred shares using the date chosen in part (a).
(c) Assume also that the preferred shares are redeemable at $115 per share at the option of the company. How, if at all, will this affect the preferred shareholders' decision to convert?

Determine dividends in arrears. (SO 2) AP

E13–6 Windswept Power Corporation issued 150,000, $4.50 cumulative preferred shares to fund its first investment in wind generators. In its first year of operations, it paid $450,000 of dividends to its preferred shareholders. In its second year, the company paid dividends of $900,000 to its preferred shareholders.

Instructions

(a) What is the total annual preferred dividend supposed to be for the preferred shareholders?
(b) Calculate any dividends in arrears in years 1 and 2.
(c) Explain how dividends in arrears should be reported in the financial statements.
(d) If the preferred shares were noncumulative rather than cumulative, how much dividend would the company likely have paid its preferred shareholders in year 2?

Prepare income statement and entry to record income tax. (SO 3) AP

E13–7 Shrunk Inc. has recorded all necessary adjusting entries, except for income tax expense, at its fiscal year end, July 31, 2014. The following information has been taken from the adjusted trial balance:

Accounts payable	$ 25,500	Interest expense	$ 5,000
Cash dividends—common	60,000	Notes payable	100,000
Common shares	200,000	Retained earnings (Aug. 1, 2013)	352,000
Cost of goods sold	310,000	Salaries expense	140,000
Dividends payable	15,000	Sales	665,000
Income tax expense	30,000	Supplies expense	10,000
Income tax payable	3,000	Unearned revenue	12,000

All accounts have normal balances and total assets equal $817,500. Shrunk has a 20% income tax rate.

Instructions

Prepare a multiple-step income statement and the required journal entry to adjust income tax expense.

Determine split between preferred and common shares and record cash dividend transactions. (SO 2, 4) AP

E13–8 Accentrics Limited has the following information available regarding its share capital at December 31, 2013:

Preferred shares, $3.50 cumulative, 20,000 shares issued	$1,000,000
Preferred shares, $4.50 noncumulative, 10,000 shares issued	500,000
Common shares, 300,000 shares issued	1,500,000

The shares were issued when the corporation began operations on January 1, 2012. No dividends were declared during 2012 and 2013. On October 30, 2014, the board of directors declares the required preferred share dividends and a $0.50 dividend for each of the common shares. The dividends are payable on December 1, 2014, to the shareholders of record on November 16, 2014.

Instructions

(a) How much will be paid to each class of shares?
(b) Prepare journal entries on the appropriate dates for the 2014 dividends.
(c) Assume instead that the maximum cash dividend the company can pay in 2014 is $200,000. Determine the dividends in arrears, if any, at December 31, 2014.

E13–9 Refer to the data given in E13–7 for Shrunk Inc.

Prepare a statement of retained earnings and closing entries. (SO 5) AP

Instructions

(a) Prepare a statement of retained earnings.
(b) Prepare closing entries and post to the Income Summary and Retained Earnings accounts.

E13–10 Didsbury Digital Ltd. has a September 30 fiscal year end and a 15% income tax rate. The following information is available for its 2014 year end:

Record income tax; prepare an income statement and statement of retained earnings. (SO 3, 4, 5) AP

1. Earned $529,000 service revenue and incurred $442,000 operating expenses. Interest expense was $2,500.
2. Recorded and remitted $10,000 of income tax (related to the 2014 fiscal year) during the year.
3. On October 5, 2013, paid $50,000 of dividends that had been declared on September 25, 2013.
4. On September 28, 2014, declared $40,000 of dividends payable on October 8, 2014.
5. Retained earnings on September 30, 2013, were $237,500.
6. Issued common shares for $25,000 cash on July 2, 2014.

Instructions

(a) Prepare an income statement and record the adjustment to income tax.
(b) Prepare a statement of retained earnings.

E13–11 Raiders Limited is a private company that follows ASPE. It is authorized to issue an unlimited number of both common and $5 cumulative preferred shares. On December 31, 2014, there were 35,000 common and 1,000 preferred shares issued. The common shares had been issued at an average cost of $10 per share; the preferred shares at $105. The balance in the Retained Earnings account on January 1, 2014, was $287,000. During 2014, the company had profit of $125,000 and declared a total of $75,000 of dividends, of which $56,250 was paid during the year.

Prepare shareholders' equity section and calculate return on equity. (SO 6) AP

Instructions

(a) Prepare the shareholders' equity section of the balance sheet on December 31, 2014.
(b) Calculate return on equity for 2014. Assume there were no changes in the Common Shares account during the year.

E13–12 Ozabal Inc., a private company, is authorized to issue an unlimited number of common shares and 100,000 noncumulative $4 preferred shares. It began operations on January 1, 2014, and the following are selected transactions during 2014:

Record share issue, dividends, and income tax; prepare partial income statement and balance sheet and statement of retained earnings. (SO 2, 3, 4, 5, 6) AP

Jan.	1	Issued 300,000 common shares for $150,000 cash.
	2	Issued 30,000 preferred shares for $40 cash per share.
Dec.	1	Declared a total of $225,000 in dividends, payable on January 5, to shareholders of record on December 13.
	31	Determined that it had total revenues of $915,000 and operating expenses of $610,000.

Ozabal elected to report under ASPE. It has a 15% income tax rate and did not pay income tax instalments during the year.

Instructions

(a) Record the share issue and dividend transactions.
(b) Prepare a partial income statement starting with profit before income taxes and record an adjusting entry for income tax.
(c) Prepare a statement of retained earnings and the shareholders' equity section of the balance sheet.

Problems: Set A

P13–1A Presented below are five independent situations:

Determine form of business organization. (SO 1) AN

1. After passing their final accounting exam, four students put together plans to offer bookkeeping services to small companies. The students have signed an agreement that details how the profits of this new business will be shared.

2. Darien Enns has had so many people ask about the new solar and wind equipment he recently added to his home, he has decided to start a company that will offer planning, design, and installation of alternative power technology. To launch the business, Darien will need substantial funding to purchase a service truck, a special crane, and the solar- and wind-generating equipment. He expects the business to grow quickly and that he will have to hire additional employees and triple the number of trucks and cranes owned by the business. Darien has no way to provide funding for the start of the business, and he also understands that the expected growth will require large additional cash investments.
3. Joanna Hirsh lives 12 months a year on Look About Bay, where most of her neighbours have summer cottages. To generate income in her retirement, Joanna has decided to offer cottage inspection services for residents while they are away. Joanna will need a snowmobile to access the buildings in the winter. She also hopes to expand her service to surrounding areas. Expansion will require hiring more inspectors and purchasing additional snowmobiles.
4. After working in the construction industry for several years, Joel Pahlson has decided to offer his own roofing services to homeowners.
5. Frank Holton owns a small two-seater airplane to fly hunters and hikers to remote areas in northern Ontario. Demand for Frank's services has grown so much that he plans to hire additional pilots and purchase four larger planes. Frank will also purchase liability insurance in case of accidents, and plans to maintain control of the company.

Instructions

In each case, explain what form of organization the business is likely to take: proprietorship, partnership, or corporation. Give reasons for your choice.

TAKING IT FURTHER Since a corporation is a separate legal entity, what gives employees the authority to complete a transaction on behalf of the company?

Record and post share transactions. Determine balances and answer questions. (SO 2) AP

P13–2A Wetland Corporation, a private corporation, was organized on February 1, 2013. It is authorized to issue 100,000, $6 noncumulative preferred shares, and an unlimited number of common shares. The following transactions were completed during the first year:

Feb. 10	Issued 80,000 common shares at $4 per share.
Mar. 1	Issued 5,000 preferred shares at $115 per share.
Apr. 1	Issued 22,500 common shares for land. The asking price of the land was $100,000 and its appraised value was $90,000.
June 20	Issued 78,000 common shares at $4.50 per share.
July 7	Issued 10,000 common shares to lawyers to pay for their bill of $45,000 for services they performed in helping the company organize.
Sept. 1	Issued 10,000 common shares at $5 per share.
Nov. 1	Issued 1,000 preferred shares at $117 per share.

Instructions

(a) Journalize the transactions.
(b) Open general ledger accounts and post to the shareholders' equity accounts.
(c) Determine the number of shares issued and the average cost per share for both common and preferred shares.
(d) How many more shares is the company authorized to issue for each class of shares?
(e) If the preferred shares were cumulative instead of noncumulative, would this have changed the amount investors were willing to pay for the shares? Explain.

TAKING IT FURTHER If Wetland was a public corporation, how might that affect the journal entry recorded for the April 1 and July 7 issues of common shares?

Allocate dividends between preferred and common shares. (SO 2) AP

P13–3A At the beginning of its first year of operations, Northwoods Limited has 5,000, $4 preferred shares and 50,000 common shares.

Instructions

Using the format shown below, allocate the total dividend paid in each year to the preferred and common shareholders, assuming that the preferred shares are (a) noncumulative, and (b) cumulative.

Year	Dividend Paid	(a) Noncumulative Preferred	(a) Common	(b) Cumulative Preferred	(b) Common
1	$20,000				
2	15,000				
3	30,000				
4	35,000				

TAKING IT FURTHER Why would an investor choose to invest in common shares if preferred share dividends have a higher priority?

P13–4A Pro Com Ltd. issues 8,000, $5 cumulative preferred shares (convertible into two common shares apiece) at $66, and 15,000 common shares (at $30 each) at the beginning of 2012. During the years 2013 and 2014, the following transactions affected Pro Com's shareholders' equity accounts:

Allocate dividends between preferred and common shares and record conversion. **(SO 2, 4) AP**

2013	
Jan. 10	Paid $12,000 of annual dividends to preferred shareholders.

2014	
Jan. 10	Paid annual dividend to preferred shareholders and a $4,000 dividend to common shareholders.
Mar. 1	The preferred shares were converted into common shares.

Instructions

(a) Journalize each of the transactions.
(b) Are there any additional reporting requirements regarding preferred share dividends in either 2013 or 2014?
(c) What factors affect preferred shareholders' decision to convert their shares into common shares?

TAKING IT FURTHER Why might investors be willing to pay more for preferred shares that have a conversion option?

P13–5A Zurich Limited is a private corporation reporting under ASPE. At December 31, 2014, its general ledger contained the following summary data:

Record dividends; prepare income statement and statement of retained earnings. **(SO 3, 4, 5) AP**

Cost of goods sold	$1,225,000
Interest expense	35,000
Interest revenue	12,500
Operating expenses	210,000
Retained earnings, January 1	550,000
Sales	1,650,000

Additional information:

1. In 2014, common share dividends of $25,000 were declared on June 30 and December 31. The dividends were paid on July 8, 2014, and January 8, 2015, respectively.
2. The company's income tax rate is 20%.

Instructions

(a) Record the dividend transactions in 2014.
(b) Determine income tax expense and prepare a multiple-step income statement for 2014.
(c) Prepare a statement of retained earnings for 2014.

TAKING IT FURTHER Compare a statement of retained earnings with a statement of owner's equity.

P13–6A Memphis Ltd. is a private corporation reporting under ASPE. It has recorded all necessary adjusting entries, except for income tax expense, at its fiscal year end October 31, 2014. The following information has been taken from the adjusted trial balance:

Adjust income tax; prepare income statement, statement of retained earnings, and closing entries. **(SO 3, 4, 5) AP**

Accounts payable	$ 15,800	Interest expense	$ 4,500
Cash dividends—common	80,000	Notes payable	75,000
Common shares	100,000	Rent expense	28,800
Depreciation expense	34,375	Retained earnings (Nov. 1, 2013)	430,000
Dividends payable	20,000	Salaries expense	195,000
Income tax expense	25,000	Service revenue	445,000
Income tax payable	2,500	Unearned revenue	22,300
Insurance expense	6,900		

All accounts have normal balances and total assets equal $736,025. Memphis has a 20% income tax rate.

Instructions

(a) Record the entry to adjust income tax expense and prepare a multiple-step income statement for the year.
(b) Prepare a statement of retained earnings for the year.
(c) Prepare closing entries.
(d) Post the closing entries to the Income Summary and Retained Earnings accounts and compare with the financial statements.

TAKING IT FURTHER Why is the entry to adjust income tax expense usually the last adjusting entry prepared each year?

Record and post transactions; prepare shareholders' equity section. **(SO 2, 4, 6) AP**

P13–7A On January 1, 2014, Schipper Ltd. had the following shareholders' equity accounts:

Common shares (1,000,000 issued)	$1,500,000
Retained earnings	1,800,000

The company was also authorized to issue an unlimited number of $4 noncumulative preferred shares. As at January 1, 2014, none had been issued. During 2014, the corporation had the following transactions and events related to its shareholders' equity:

Jan. 2	Issued 100,000 preferred shares for $50 per share.
Apr. 1	Paid quarterly dividend to preferred shareholders.
July 1	Paid quarterly dividend to preferred shareholders.
Aug. 12	Issued 100,000 common shares for $1.70 per share.
Oct. 1	Paid quarterly dividend to preferred shareholders and a $0.25 per share dividend to the common shareholders.
Dec. 31	Loss for the year was $100,000.

Instructions

(a) Journalize the transactions and the entries to close dividends and the Income Summary account.
(b) Open general ledger accounts for the shareholders' equity accounts and post entries from part (a).
(c) Prepare the shareholders' equity section of the balance sheet at December 31, 2014, including any required disclosures. Assume Schipper is reporting under ASPE.

TAKING IT FURTHER Schipper incurred a loss in 2014. Are companies allowed to declare and pay dividends during a year when they have a loss? Explain your reasoning.

Record and post transactions; prepare shareholders' equity section. **(SO 2, 4, 6) AP**

P13–8A Cattrall Corporation is authorized to issue an unlimited number of $5 cumulative preferred shares and an unlimited number of common shares. On February 1, 2014, the general ledger contained the following shareholders' equity accounts:

Preferred shares (10,000 shares issued)	$ 475,000
Common shares (70,000 shares issued)	1,050,000
Retained earnings	700,000

The following equity transactions occurred during the year ended January 31, 2015:

Feb. 28	Issued 5,000 preferred shares for $275,000.
Apr. 12	Issued 200,000 common shares for $3.2 million.
May 25	Issued 5,000 common shares in exchange for land. At the time of the exchange, the land was valued at $75,000.
Jan. 1	Paid dividend of $2.50 per share to preferred shareholders.
31	A loss of $50,000 was incurred for the year.

Instructions

(a) Journalize the transactions and the entries to close dividends and the Income Summary account.
(b) Open general ledger accounts for the shareholders' equity accounts and post entries from part (a).
(c) Prepare the shareholders' equity section of the balance sheet at January 31, 2015, including any required disclosures. Assume Cattrall is reporting under ASPE.

TAKING IT FURTHER What are the difficulties in determining how many shares to issue in exchange for noncash assets as well as how to value the transaction?

P13–9A Choke Cherry Ltd. is a private company reporting under ASPE. Its adjusted trial balance at its fiscal year end, December 31, 2014, is shown below:

Prepare financial statements and closing entries. **(SO 3, 5, 6) AP**

CHOKE CHERRY LTD.
Adjusted Trial Balance
December 31, 2014

	Debit	Credit
Cash	$ 28,000	
Inventory	26,500	
Supplies	5,000	
Equipment	300,000	
Accumulated depreciation—equipment		$ 65,000
Accounts payable		34,000
Income tax payable		8,985
Unearned revenue		21,000
Note payable ($12,000 is due in 2015)		30,000
Preferred shares ($4 noncumulative, 1,000 issued)		40,000
Common shares (120,000 issued)		60,000
Retained earnings		73,000
Cash dividends—preferred	4,000	
Cash dividends—common	50,000	
Sales revenue		515,000
Cost of goods sold	159,000	
Depreciation expense	20,000	
Income tax expense	14,385	
Insurance expense	8,200	
Interest expense	1,800	
Rent expense	32,600	
Salaries expense	185,000	
Supplies expense	12,500	
	$846,985	$846,985

Instructions

(a) Prepare an income statement, statement of retained earnings, and balance sheet.
(b) Journalize the closing entries.

TAKING IT FURTHER What are the differences between dividends paid to owners of corporations and withdrawals by owners of proprietorships or partnerships?

P13–10A Northwood Architects Ltd. is a private company reporting under ASPE. It is authorized to issue an unlimited number of common and $3 cumulative preferred shares. The following is an alphabetical list of its adjusted accounts at March 31, 2014, its fiscal year end. All accounts have normal balances.

Prepare financial statements and calculate return on equity. **(SO 3, 5, 6) AP**

Accounts payable	$ 21,350	Income tax expense	$ 16,535
Accounts receivable	38,700	Insurance expense	6,550
Accumulated depreciation—equipment	23,650	Interest expense	3,000
Cash	54,600	Note payable	50,000
Cash dividends—common	40,000	Preferred shares	56,250
Cash dividends—preferred	4,500	Prepaid expenses	6,150
Common shares	75,000	Rent expense	35,800
Consulting revenue	404,500	Retained earnings	64,800
Depreciation expense	11,825	Salaries expense	245,400
Dividends payable	15,000	Salaries payable	2,310
Equipment	224,000	Supplies expense	25,800

The note payable is due in 2016. There are 1,500 preferred and 75,000 common shares issued.

Instructions

(a) Prepare an income statement, statement of retained earnings, and balance sheet.
(b) Calculate return on equity. *Note:* No shares were issued during the year.

TAKING IT FURTHER Why is it important that retained earnings be tracked and presented separately from share capital in the balance sheet?

Calculate return on assets and equity and comment. **(SO 6) AP**

P13–11A The following financial information (in millions) is for two major corporations for the three fiscal years ended December 31 as follows:

	2011	2010	2009
Canadian Pacific Railway Limited			
Profit	$ 570	$ 651	$ 550
Shareholders' equity	4,649	4,824	4,658
Total assets	14,110	13,676	14,155
Canadian National Railway Company			
Profit	$ 2,457	$ 2,104	$ 1,854
Shareholders' equity	10,680	11,284	11,233
Total assets	26,026	25,206	25,176

Instructions

(a) Calculate return on assets and return on equity for each company for 2011 and 2010. Comment on whether their ratios have improved or deteriorated.
(b) Compare Canadian Pacific's ratios with Canadian National's.
(c) The industry average for return on equity in 2011 was 5.33%. Compare the two companies' performance with the industry average.

TAKING IT FURTHER Using your findings in this question to illustrate, explain why it is important to use comparisons in evaluating ratios.

Record transactions and adjustments; prepare financial statements. **(SO 2, 3, 4, 5, 6) AP**

P13–12A Maple Corporation, a private company, is authorized to issue an unlimited number of common shares and 500,000, $2.50 cumulative preferred shares. It began operations on January 1, 2014, and the following transactions occurred in 2014:

Jan.	1	Issued 5,000 common shares for $50,000 cash.
	2	Issued 1,000 preferred shares for $35 cash per share.
Dec.	1	Declared a total of $12,500 in dividends, payable on January 5, to shareholders of record on December 13.

The following information is also available with respect to the company's operations during the year:

1. Collected $349,000 cash for consulting revenue earned.
2. Paid $184,200 salaries expense; $48,000 rent expense; and $15,000 office expense.
3. Purchased equipment for $150,000 cash.
4. At December 31, determined that the following adjustments were required:
   - Depreciation on the equipment, $15,000
   - Consulting revenue earned but not yet collected in cash, $16,000
   - Accrued salaries expense, $5,800
   - Income tax rate, 15%. No instalments were made during the year.

Maple elected to report under ASPE.

Instructions

(a) Record the share issue and dividend transactions.
(b) Record summary journal entries for transactions (1) to (3) and adjusting entries for items in (4).
(c) Open an account for Cash and post transactions.
(d) Prepare an income statement, statement of retained earnings, and balance sheet.

TAKING IT FURTHER Why are common shareholders sometimes referred to as "residual owners" when a corporation has both common and preferred shareholders?

CONTINUING COOKIE CHRONICLE

(*Note:* This is a continuation of the Cookie Chronicle from Chapters 1 through 12.)

Recall (from Chapter 12) that Natalie had been considering forming a partnership with Katy, a high school friend. Natalie has concluded that she and Katy are not compatible to operate a business together and Natalie has continued on her own.

Natalie's parents, Janet and Brian Koebel, have been operating Koebel's Family Bakery Ltd., a private corporation, for a number of years. They are very proud of Natalie and the success of Cookie Creations and have decided that it may be time to get Natalie involved with the operation of the family business.

In anticipation of Natalie graduating, and in hopes of spending a little more time away from the bakery, they have discussed with Natalie the possibility of her becoming one of the shareholders of Koebel's Family Bakery Ltd. In addition, once Natalie has graduated, Natalie would assume the full-time position of administrator. Natalie could continue to provide cookie-making lessons and sell mixers; however, that would now be done by Koebel's Family Bakery rather than by Natalie's Cookie Creations.

The share capital and the retained earnings of Koebel's Family Bakery Ltd. at August 1, 2013, are as follows:

$6 cumulative preferred shares, 10,000 shares authorized, none issued	
Common shares, unlimited number of shares authorized, 200 shares issued	$ 200
Retained earnings	116,251

Profit before income tax for the year ended July 31, 2014, was $255,823. The company has an 18% income tax rate. A cash dividend of $85,000 was declared on July 15, 2014, to common shareholders of record on July 20, 2014, and was paid on July 30, 2014.

Based on the bakery's success, the Koebels would like to issue 10 shares to Natalie for $1,200 per share. Natalie would contribute the fair value of Cookie Creations' assets in exchange for the shares of Koebel's Family Bakery as follows:

	Cookie Creations
Cash	$8,050
Accounts receivable	800
Merchandise inventory	1,200
Supplies	450
Equipment	1,500

The sale of shares by Koebel's Family Bakery to Natalie is expected to take place on August 1, 2014. Currently, Janet and Brian each own 100 shares. Assume Koebel's Family Bakery reports using ASPE.

Instructions

(a) Prepare the journal entries required for the cash dividend declared on July 15 and paid on July 30, 2014. Who received the cash dividend, and for what amount?

(b) Prepare the statement of retained earnings for the year ended July 31, 2014.

(c) Prepare the shareholders' equity section of the balance sheet at July 31, 2014.

(d) Assume that Natalie purchases the shares of Koebel's Family Bakery Ltd. on August 1, 2014, in exchange for the fair value of assets held by Cookie Creations. Prepare the journal entries required by Koebel's Family Bakery Ltd.

(e) Determine the number of shares issued and the average cost per common share before and after Natalie purchases the shares of Koebel's Family Bakery. Why is there a significant change in value?

(f) How do you think a value of $1,200 per share was determined when Janet and Brian were attempting to come up with the number of shares to be sold to Natalie? Do you think that the number of shares Natalie received in exchange for the assets of Cookie Creations is fair? Why or why not?

CHAPTER 13 BROADENING YOUR PERSPECTIVE

Collaborative Learning Activity

Note to instructor: Additional instructions and material for this group activity can be found on the Instructor Resource Site and in *WileyPLUS*.

BYP13–1 In this group activity, you will be forming a new corporation and making decisions about the number of shares to be issued to the founding shareholders as well as to an individual who becomes a shareholder at a later date. You will also prepare a corporate income statement and balance sheet for this corporation.

Communication Activity

BYP13–2 Your cousin owns 100% of the common shares of a corporation, Ghost River Back Country Limited, a retail company specializing in outdoor clothing and equipment. The company has the opportunity to purchase land and a building in a desirable location that would be used to operate a second store. Your cousin is very excited about this opportunity but is wondering about the best way to finance this purchase as the company currently does not have excess cash. She and the seller are currently considering the possibility of issuing new shares of Ghost River Back Country Limited to the seller to pay for the land and buildings.

Instructions

Write a memo to your cousin explaining some of the advantages and disadvantages to issuing either common or preferred shares, compared with borrowing money, to purchase the land and buildings. Also include in your discussion any issues in terms of recording the transaction if shares are issued.

Ethics Case

BYP13–3 The R&D division of Simplex Chemical Corp. has just developed a chemical to sterilize the voracious mountain pine beetles that are invading Western Canada's forests. The president of Simplex is anxious to get the new chemical to market and has already named it PinebeetleX101. Simplex's profits need a boost and the president's job is in jeopardy because of decreasing sales and profits. Simplex has an opportunity to sell this chemical in several Central American countries, where the laws about proving a product's safety before beginning to use it or sell it are much more relaxed than in Canada.

The director of Simplex's R&D division strongly recommends more laboratory testing for side effects of this chemical on other insects, birds, animals, plants, and even humans. He cautions the president, "We could be sued from all sides if the chemical has tragic side effects that we didn't even test for in the labs." The president answers, "We can't wait an additional year for your lab tests. We can avoid losses from such lawsuits by creating a new separate corporation called Simplex Central America Inc., which will be 100% owned by Simplex Chemical Corp., to operate our business in those countries. We will invest just the patent covering this chemical in Simplex Central America Inc. That corporation will have limited liability so we can't lose any more than the assets that we put into it. Since we will own 100% of the shares of Simplex Central America Inc., we can put ourselves on its board of directors, and then we can make it pay dividends to Simplex Chemical Corp. when it makes a profit. We'll reap the benefits if the chemical works and is safe, and avoid the losses from lawsuits if it's a disaster."

The following week, Simplex Chemical Corp. creates the new 100%-owned corporation Simplex Central America Inc., sells it the chemical patent for PinebeetleX101 for $10, delivers a shipload of the chemicals, and watches the spraying begin.

Instructions

(a) Who are the stakeholders in this situation?
(b) Are the president's motives and actions ethical?
(c) Can Simplex Chemical Corp. be certain that it is protected against all losses related to the activities of Simplex Central America Inc.?

All About You: Personal Financial Literacy Activity

BYP13–4 As you learned in the "All About You" feature, the decision to incorporate or not is complex. After you have completed your post-secondary education, you may be an entrepreneur and may need to decide if and when to incorporate your business. And if you decide to incorporate, you will also need to know more about how. You will also have to decide whether to incorporate with the provincial or federal government. Benefits to incorporating federally include the right to use your company name across the country (a status almost as heightened as trademark protection), the right to carry on business anywhere in Canada, global recognition as an incorporated company, and bilingual service from federal government employees who provide services to corporations. If your company starts out doing business in one province but intends to expand into other provinces, you may want to incorporate federally to make that transition easier later on.

Almost any kind and size of business can incorporate federally under the *Canada Business Corporations Act.* However, some types of organizations, such as financial institutions, cooperatives, Chambers of Commerce, and non-profit organizations, must incorporate under different legislation. Anyone who is 18 years old or older, is not of unsound mind, and who has never been bankrupt, along with any company or corporate body, may incorporate under the *Canada Business Corporations Act.*

Instructions

For the following scenarios, state whether you should incorporate federally under the *Canada Business Corporations Act.* If not, state the form of business you should choose or whether you should incorporate provincially. Provide explanations for your answers. (*Hint:* Review the forms of business organization in Chapter 1.)

(a) You are 17 and live in Ottawa. You want to open a lawn-mowing business in Ottawa and across the river in Gatineau, Quebec, employing several students as a summer job.
(b) After you graduate from post-secondary education, you and two friends have a hard time finding a job and decide to start a non-profit organization to help youths find work.
(c) In college, you decide to start a mail-order business making jam, selling it across Canada.
(d) After graduating with an accounting degree, you start a chain of national bookkeeping and accounting franchises called Account on Us. You expect to expand quickly because you think the name is catchy and people will remember it and spread it by word of mouth and social media.

ANSWERS TO CHAPTER QUESTIONS

ANSWERS TO ACCOUNTING IN ACTION INSIGHT QUESTIONS

All About You Insight, p. 550

Q: Given the complexity of tax planning, and the impact that taxes could have on the advantages of incorporating, what should you do before deciding to incorporate your business?
A: The business owner should seek expert tax advice to ensure the benefits of incorporating are greater than the costs.

Across the Organization, p. 555

Q: Why might the "no maturity date" feature of preferred shares be useful to an organization?
A: The "no maturity date" feature can provide management with flexibility in terms of the timing of redeeming the preferred shares. With debt, a company cannot predict with certainty if it will have cash to repay the debt on the maturity date, which makes debt riskier to the company. With preferred shares, a company can include a redemption feature, which it is not required to act on if it doesn't have the cash.

ANSWERS TO SELF-STUDY QUESTIONS

1. a 2. d 3. b 4. c 5. b 6. c 7. d 8. a 9. b 10. d

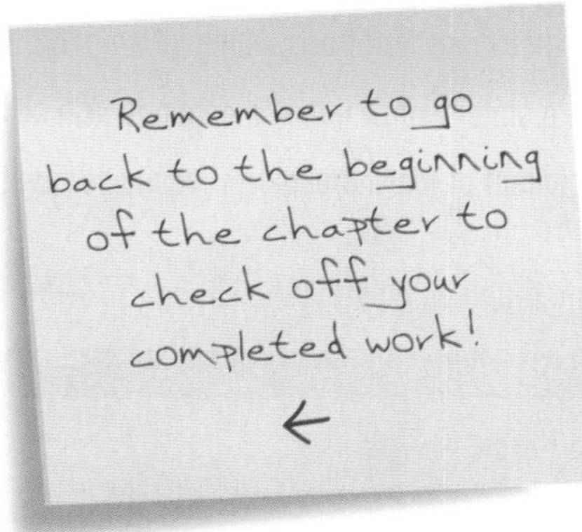
Remember to go
back to the beginning
of the chapter to
check off your
completed work!
←

CHAPTER 14

CORPORATIONS: ADDITIONAL TOPICS AND IFRS

THE NAVIGATOR

- ☐ Understand *Concepts for Review*
- ☐ Read *Feature Story*
- ☐ Scan *Study Objectives*
- ☐ Read *Chapter Preview*
- ☐ Read text and answer *Before You Go On*
- ☐ Review *Comparing IFRS and ASPE*
- ☐ Work *Demonstration Problem*
- ☐ Review *Summary of Study Objectives*
- ☐ Answer *Self-Study Questions*
- ☐ Complete assignments

CONCEPTS FOR REVIEW

Before studying this chapter, you should understand or, if necessary, review:

A. How to record cash dividends. (Ch. 13, pp. 559–560)

B. How to account for share transactions. (Ch. 13, pp. 552–555)

C. The qualitative characteristics of accounting information. (Ch. 11, pp. 463–466)

D. How to prepare a statement of retained earnings. (Ch. 13, pp. 560–561)

E. The form and content of the shareholders' equity section of the balance sheet. (Ch. 13, pp. 563–564)

F. How to calculate return on equity. (Ch. 13, pp. 564–565)

BREWING SHAREHOLDER RETURN

OAKVILLE, ON—Public corporations issue shares, but they can buy some of their shares back, as well. One reason why companies sometimes do this is that they may be sitting on a large amount of cash. For example, at the end of its 2011 fiscal year, Tim Hortons Inc., the iconic quick service restaurant franchise chain, had cash and cash equivalents of nearly $127 million.

With consistently healthy cash flows, a priority for Tim Hortons is to invest in the business. "We turn around and reinvest quite a bit of our free cash flow in capital expenditures, such as building new restaurants, renovating existing restaurants, and building new manufacturing facilities or distribution centres," says Diana Fife, Vice President, Financial Reporting.

If there is still money left over after making all its desired capital expenditures, then the company may want to make sure it has a solid balance sheet so it can weather any economic storms, like the 2008 global financial crisis, when Tim Hortons did not need to rely on banks for funding. Once the company is assured its balance sheet is strong, it really needs to return the rest to shareholders because to sit on cash idly is not a good investment decision. It doesn't earn you very much today with interest rates the way they are, and if the cash coffer is built up too significantly, you could be subject to a takeover.

To return money to shareholders, Tim Hortons has considered the right balance between issuing dividends to existing shareholders and buying back some of its shares. As of 2012, the company had undergone six consecutive major share repurchase programs since it went public in 2006. For example, in early 2012, the company announced plans to start a new share repurchase program to buy up to $200 million in common shares.

Tim Hortons has a dividend policy whereby it commits to paying out a certain percentage of its profit to shareholders every year. Since becoming a public company, it increased its quarterly dividend six times, ranging from an 11% increase to a 31% increase.

The company also sets a target that it communicates to shareholders each year to achieve a certain earnings per share for the upcoming year. For 2012, that target was earnings per share of $2.65 to $2.75. If it achieves same-store sales growth and if it delivers the targeted number of new restaurants for the year, then that translates to earnings. It is a real partnership with the restaurant owners. If the restaurant owners are growing their businesses, then Tim Hortons is too.

THE NAVIGATOR

STUDY OBJECTIVES

After studying this chapter, you should be able to:

1. Account for stock dividends and stock splits and compare their financial impact.
2. Account for the reacquisition of shares.
3. Prepare an income statement showing continuing and discontinued operations, and prepare a statement of comprehensive income.
4. Explain the accounting for different types of accounting changes and account for corrections of prior period errors.
5. Prepare a statement of changes in shareholders' equity.
6. Evaluate earnings and dividend performance.

THE NAVIGATOR

PREVIEW OF CHAPTER FOURTEEN

This chapter builds on the introduction to corporations in Chapter 13 and discusses issues that are either more complex or more likely to be encountered only by public companies. Financial statements required for a corporation reporting under IFRS—the statements of comprehensive income and changes in shareholders' equity—are also shown. The chapter is organized as follows:

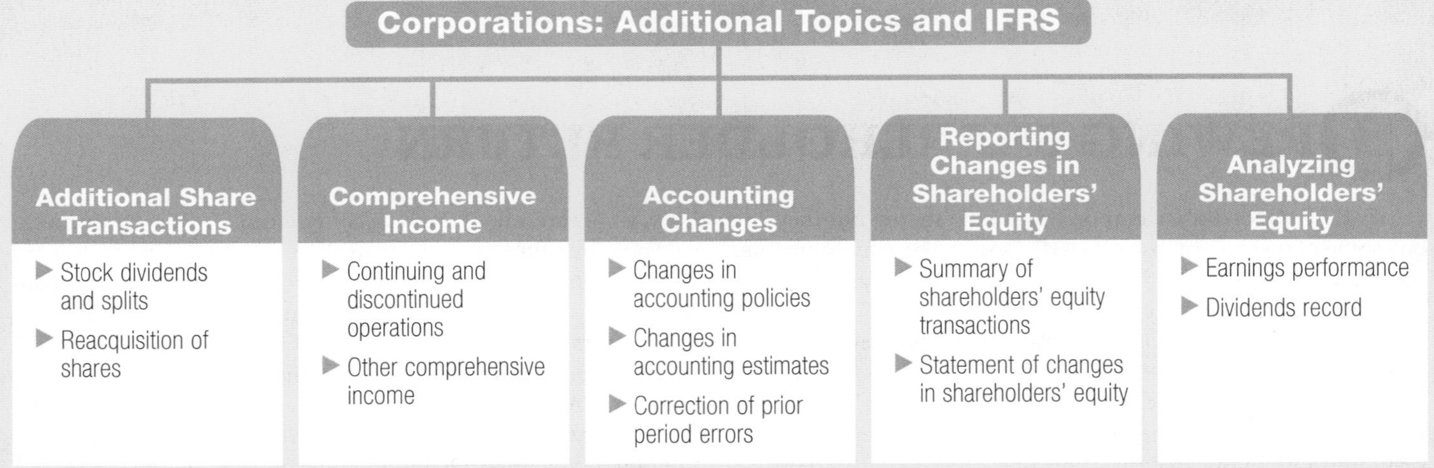

ADDITIONAL SHARE TRANSACTIONS

Recall from Chapter 13 that shares can be issued for cash and for noncash assets or services, and that they can be issued when preferred shares are converted into common shares. Shares can also be issued as the result of stock dividends, stock splits, and stock options. Companies may also decide to reacquire previously issued shares.

STOCK DIVIDENDS AND STOCK SPLITS

STUDY OBJECTIVE 1
Account for stock dividends and stock splits and compare their financial impact.

Recall from Chapter 13 that a dividend is a pro rata distribution of a portion of a corporation's retained earnings to its shareholders. Cash dividends, covered in Chapter 13, are the most common type of dividend and are used in both private and public corporations.

Stock dividends are another type of dividend rarely used in private corporations; they are more common in public corporations. Stock splits are not dividends, but have some similarities with stock dividends and also are typically used only in public corporations.

Stock Dividends

A **stock dividend** is a distribution of the corporation's own shares to shareholders. Whereas a cash dividend is paid in cash, a stock dividend is distributed (issued) in shares. And while a cash dividend decreases assets and shareholders' equity, a stock dividend does not change either assets or shareholders' equity. A stock dividend results in a decrease in retained earnings and an increase in share capital, but there is no change in *total* shareholders' equity.

From the company's point of view, no cash has been paid, and no liabilities have been assumed. What are the purposes and benefits of a stock dividend? A corporation generally issues stock dividends for one or more of the following reasons:

1. To satisfy shareholders' dividend expectations without spending cash.
2. To increase the marketability of the corporation's shares. When the number of shares increases, the market price per share tends to decrease. Decreasing the market price makes it easier for investors to purchase the shares.
3. To emphasize that a portion of shareholders' equity has been permanently retained in the business and is unavailable for cash dividends.

The size of the stock dividend and the value to be assigned to each share are determined by the board of directors when the dividend is declared. It is common for companies to assign the fair value per share for stock dividends at the declaration date.

To illustrate the accounting for stock dividends, assume that on June 30, IBR Inc. declares a 10% stock dividend on its 50,000 common shares, to be distributed on August 5 to shareholders of record on July 20. This means 5,000 (10% × 50,000) shares will be issued. In recording the transaction, **the fair value at the declaration date is used**, not the fair value on the record or distribution dates.

Assuming the fair value (the current trading price) of its shares on June 30 is $15 per share, the amount debited to Stock Dividends is $75,000 (5,000 × $15). The entry to record the declaration of the stock dividend is as follows:

	Declaration Date		
June 30	Stock Dividends	75,000	
	Stock Dividends Distributable		75,000
	To record declaration of 10% stock dividend.		

A	=	L	+	SE
				+75,000
				−75,000

Cash flows: no effect

At the declaration date, the Stock Dividends account is increased by the fair value of the shares to be issued. This will result in a decrease in Retained Earnings, similar to cash dividends, when the Stock Dividends account is closed. **Stock Dividends Distributable**, a shareholders' equity account, is increased by the same amount. Stock Dividends Distributable *is not a liability*, because assets will not be used to pay the dividend. Instead, it will be "paid" with common shares. If a balance sheet is prepared before the dividend shares are issued, the Stock Dividends Distributable account is reported as share capital in the shareholders' equity section of the balance sheet.

Helpful hint As with cash dividends, it is also acceptable to directly debit Retained Earnings. This eliminates the need to close the stock dividends account at the end of the year but might make it more difficult to track the amount of each type of dividend declared.

As with cash dividends, no entry is required at the record date. When the dividend shares are issued on August 5, the **distribution date**, the account Stock Dividends Distributable is debited and the account Common Shares is credited:

Helpful hint Note that stock dividends have a "distribution date" whereas cash dividends have a "payment date."

	Distribution Date		
Aug. 5	Stock Dividends Distributable	75,000	
	Common Shares		75,000
	To record issue of 5,000 common shares in a stock dividend.		

A	=	L	+	SE
				+75,000
				−75,000

Cash flows: no effect

Note that neither of the above entries changes shareholders' equity in total. However, the composition of shareholders' equity changes because a portion of Retained Earnings is transferred to the Common Shares account. The number of shares issued has also increased. These effects are shown below for IBR Inc. using assumed data for Retained Earnings and Common Shares prior to the stock dividend:

	Before Stock Dividend	After Stock Dividend
Shareholders' equity		
Common shares	$500,000	$575,000
Retained earnings	300,000	225,000
Total shareholders' equity	**$800,000**	**$800,000**
Total number of common shares issued	50,000	55,000

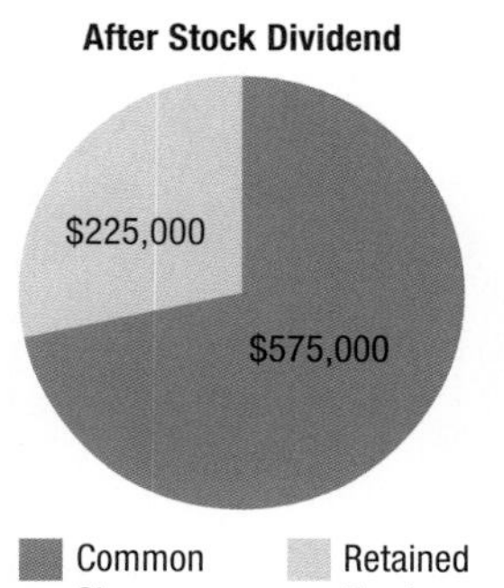

In this example, the account Common Shares is increased (credited) by $75,000 and Retained Earnings is decreased (debited) by the same amount. Total shareholders' equity remains unchanged at $800,000, the total before and after the stock dividend. The pie charts in the margin show the effects of issuing the stock dividend on both Common Shares and Retained Earnings.

Stock Splits

A **stock split**, like a stock dividend, involves the issue of additional shares to shareholders according to their percentage ownership. However, a stock split is usually much larger than a stock dividend.

The purpose of a stock split is to increase the shares' marketability by lowering the fair value per share. A lower fair value attracts more investors and makes it easier for the corporation to issue additional shares. On the other hand, sometimes companies will decrease the number of shares outstanding by doing a **reverse stock split**. Instead of issuing two stocks for one, they issue one stock for two, to increase the fair value per share.

The effect of a split on fair value is generally inversely proportional to the size of the split. For example, in a 2-for-1 stock split, since there are twice as many shares, the fair value will normally decrease by half. Sometimes, due to increased investor interest, the share price will quickly rise beyond its split value.

In a stock split, the number of shares is increased by a specified proportion. For example, in a 2-for-1 split, one share is exchanged for two shares. A stock split does not have any effect on share capital, retained earnings, or shareholders' equity. Only the number of shares increases.

A stock split is illustrated below for IBR Inc.'s common shares. For the illustration, we assume that, instead of a 10% stock dividend, IBR splits its 50,000 common shares on a 2-for-1 basis.

	Before Stock Split	After Stock Split
Shareholders' equity		
Common shares	$500,000	$500,000
Retained earnings	300,000	300,000
Total shareholders' equity	**$800,000**	**$800,000**
Total number of common shares issued	50,000	100,000

Because a stock split does not affect the balances in any shareholders' equity accounts, it is not necessary to prepare a formal journal entry to record it. Only a memo entry explaining the details of the split is needed.

Either common or preferred shares can be split. If preferred shares that have a stated dividend rate are split, then the dividend must also be adjusted for the effects of the split. For example, if 10,000, $6 preferred shares are split 3 for 1, then after the split there will be 30,000 preferred shares with a $2 annual dividend. The total dividend before and after the split remains unchanged at $60,000 (10,000 × $6 before and 30,000 × $2 after). After all, it is the same shareholders who held 10,000 shares before the split who now hold 30,000 shares.

Comparison of Effects

Significant differences among stock splits, stock dividends, and cash dividends (after payment) are shown below.

		Shareholders' Equity	
	Assets	Share Capital	Retained Earnings
Cash dividend	Decrease	No effect	Decrease
Stock dividend	No effect	Increase	Decrease
Stock split	No effect	No effect	No effect

Cash dividends reduce assets and shareholders' equity. Stock dividends increase share capital (the Common Shares or Preferred Shares account) and decrease retained earnings by the same amount, so they don't change *total* shareholders' equity. Stock splits do not affect any account balances. However, both a stock dividend and a stock split increase the number of shares issued.

Note that since stock dividends and splits neither increase nor decrease the assets in the company, investors are not receiving anything they did not already own. In a sense, it is like having a piece of pie and cutting it into smaller pieces. They are no better or worse off, as they have the same amount of pie.

To illustrate a stock dividend or stock split for the common shareholders, assume that a shareholder owns 1,000 of IBR Inc.'s 50,000 common shares. If IBR declares a 10% stock dividend, the shareholder will receive 100 shares (10% × 1,000). On the other hand, if IBR splits its shares on a 2-for-1 basis, the shareholder will receive 1,000 shares. Will the shareholder's ownership interest change? As shown in Illustration 14-1, there is no change.

ILLUSTRATION 14-1
Effect of stock dividend and stock split for shareholders

	Stock Dividend			Stock Split		
	Company	Shareholder		Company	Shareholder	
	Total Shares issued	# Shares	Ownership Interest	Total Shares issued	# Shares	Ownership Interest
Before	50,000	1,000	2%	50,000	1,000	2%
New shares issued	5,000	100		50,000	1,000	
After	55,000	1,100	2%	100,000	2,000	2%

ACCOUNTING IN ACTION
ACROSS THE ORGANIZATION

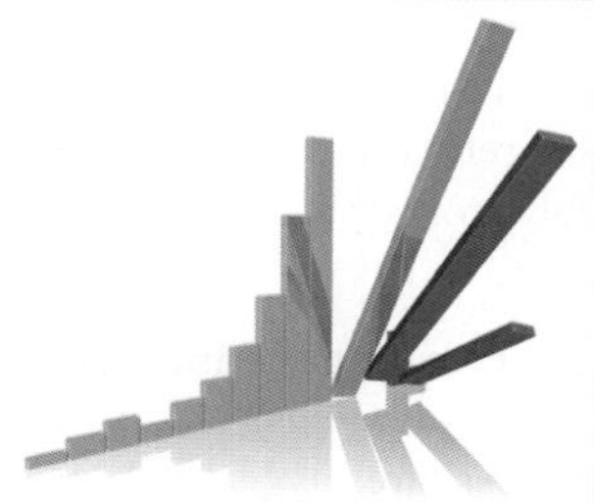

Stock exchanges usually require publicly traded stocks to maintain a minimum value or they will be delisted, meaning a company's shares will no longer be traded. The New York Stock Exchange (NYSE), for example, requires shares to be worth a daily average of at least US$1 over a consecutive 30-day trading period. The shares of Toronto-based Kingsway Financial Services Inc., an insurance holding company, recently were at risk of dipping below that minimum. To avoid being delisted on the NYSE, it implemented a reverse stock split. As approved by shareholders at an annual meeting, Kingsway offered shareholders one share for every four that they owned, as at July 3, 2012. The consolidation reduced the number of common shares from approximately 52 million to about 13 million. By increasing the fair value per share, Kingsway could continue to trade on the NYSE, along with the Toronto Stock Exchange. In the months immediately after the 1-for-4 split, Kingsway's shares were consistently trading above $1.75.

There were other advantages, too. "The Company's Board believes a reverse stock split would have the additional benefit of attracting a broader range of institutional and other investors. The Board also believes that a higher share price will reduce per share transaction fees and certain administrative costs," Kingsway stated.

Sources: "Kingsway Implements Previously Announced Share Consolidation," company news release, July 3, 2012; Rick Aristotle Munarriz, "Reverse Splits Aren't All Bad," Motley Fool newsletter, March 20, 2012; "Kingsway Announces Reverse Stock Split," company news release, January 27, 2012; "Detailed Quote for Kingsway Financial Services Inc. (KFS)," QuoteMedia

If a company announces a reverse stock split, is this considered a positive or negative sign about the future of the company?

BEFORE YOU GO ON...

DO IT

Sing CD Corporation has had five years of high profits. Due to this success, the market price of its 500,000 common shares tripled from $15 to $45 per share. During this period, the Common Shares account remained the same at $2 million. Retained earnings increased from $1.5 million to $10 million. President Bill Edmondson is considering either (a) a 10% stock dividend, or (b) a 2-for-1 stock split. He asks you to show the before-and-after effects of each option on the Common Shares and Retained Earnings accounts and on the number of shares.

SOLUTION

(a) With a 10% stock dividend, 50,000 new shares will be issued (500,000 × 10%). The stock dividend amount is $2,250,000 (50,000 × $45). The new balance in Common Shares is $4,250,000 ($2,000,000 + $2,250,000). In Retained Earnings, it is $7,750,000 ($10,000,000 − $2,250,000).

(b) With a 2-for-1 stock split, 500,000 new shares will be issued. The account balances in Common Shares and Retained Earnings after the stock split are the same as they were before: $2 million and $10 million, respectively.

Action Plan

- Calculate the stock dividend effect on Retained Earnings by multiplying the stock dividend percentage by the number of existing shares to determine the number of new shares to be issued. Multiply the number of new shares by the shares' market price.
- A stock dividend increases the number of shares and affects both Common Shares and Retained Earnings.
- A stock split increases the number of shares but does not affect Common Shares and Retained Earnings.

BEFORE YOU GO ON...
continued on next page

BEFORE YOU GO ON...
continued from previous page

The effects in the shareholders' equity accounts of each option are as follows:

	Original Balances	After Stock Dividend	After Stock Split
Common shares	$ 2,000,000	$ 4,250,000	$ 2,000,000
Retained earnings	10,000,000	7,750,000	10,000,000
Total shareholders' equity	$12,000,000	$12,000,000	$12,000,000
Total number of common shares issued	500,000	550,000	1,000,000

Related exercise material: BE14–1, BE14–2, BE14–3, E14–1, and E14–2.

REACQUISITION OF SHARES

STUDY OBJECTIVE 2
Account for the reacquisition of shares.

Companies can "buy back" or reacquire their own shares from shareholders. Typically, the reasons for doing this will be different for a private company as opposed to a public company. Private companies reacquire shares when there is a change in business circumstances or a change in the needs of the shareholders. For example, a private corporation may have an agreement in which it must reacquire the shares owned by an employee if the employee leaves the company.

A public corporation may acquire its own shares for any number of reasons. For example, as explained in our feature story, Tim Hortons repurchases its shares as a way of returning cash to shareholders when the cash is not needed to grow the business. Other reasons a public corporation may reacquire shares include the following:

1. To increase trading of the company's shares in the securities market in the hope of increasing the company's fair value.
2. To reduce the number of shares issued, which will increase earnings per share.
3. To eliminate hostile shareholders by buying them out.
4. To have additional shares available so that they can be reissued to officers and employees through bonus and stock compensation plans, or can be used to acquire other companies.

For federally incorporated companies, and most provincially incorporated companies, the repurchased shares must be retired and cancelled. This restores the shares to the status of authorized but unissued shares. In some Canadian provinces, in the United States, and internationally, reacquired shares can also be held for subsequent reissue. If the shares are not retired and cancelled, they are referred to as **treasury shares.**

Whether the company is private or public, the following steps are required to record a reacquisition of common (or preferred) shares:

1. **Remove the cost of the shares from the share capital account:** Recall that, when a long-lived asset is retired, the cost of the asset must be deleted (credited) from the appropriate asset account. Similarly, the cost of the common shares that are reacquired and retired must be determined and this amount is then deleted (debited) from the Common Shares account.

   In order to determine the cost of the common shares reacquired, it is necessary to calculate an **average cost per share**. It is impractical, and often impossible, to determine the cost of each individual common share that is reacquired. An average cost per common share is therefore calculated by dividing the balance in the Common Shares account by the number of shares issued at the transaction date.
2. **Record the cash paid:** The Cash account is credited for the amount paid to reacquire the shares. Note that a public company has little choice in what it has to pay to reacquire the shares (it can only decide when to make the reacquisition). It must purchase the shares on the secondary market by paying the current market price on the date of purchase.
3. **Record the "gain" or "loss" on reacquisition:** The difference between the cash paid to reacquire the shares and their average cost is basically a "gain" or "loss" on reacquisition. However, because companies cannot realize a gain or suffer a loss from share transactions with their own shareholders, these amounts are not reported on the income statement. They are seen instead as an excess or deficiency that belongs to the shareholders. As a result, the amount is reported as an increase or decrease in the shareholders' equity section of the balance sheet.

The accounting for the reacquisition of shares differs depending on whether the shares are reacquired by paying less than the average cost or more than the average cost. We will examine each situation in the next two sections.

Reacquisition below Average Cost

When a company reacquires its shares for less than what the shareholder originally paid, the company has a "gain" on reacquisition. This "gain" is part of the contributed capital of the company because it represents an additional investment by the shareholders. It is recorded in the account Contributed Surplus—Reacquisition of Shares and is shown in the contributed capital section of the shareholders' equity section on the balance sheet, along with the share capital, to indicate the total capital contributed by the shareholders.

To illustrate the reacquisition of common shares at a price less than average cost, assume that Campagner Inc. has an unlimited number of common shares authorized, and a total of 75,000 common shares issued. It has a balance in its Common Shares account of $150,000. The average cost of Campagner's common shares is therefore $2 per share ($150,000 ÷ 75,000).

On September 23, Campagner reacquired 5,000 of its common shares at a price of $1.50 per share. Since the average cost of the shares is $0.50 ($2.00 − $1.50) more than the price paid to reacquire them, there is an additional contribution to shareholders' equity. The entry is recorded as follows:

Sept. 23	Common Shares (5,000 × $2)	10,000	
	Contributed Surplus—Reacquisition of Shares		2,500
	Cash (5,000 × $1.50)		7,500
	To record reacquisition and retirement of 5,000 common shares.		

A	=	L	+	SE
−7,500				−10,000
				+2,500

↓ Cash flows: −7,500

After this entry, Campagner still has an unlimited number of shares authorized, but only 70,000 (75,000 − 5,000) shares issued, and a balance of $140,000 ($150,000 − $10,000) in its Common Shares account. The average cost is still $2 per share ($140,000 ÷ 70,000).

Reacquisition above Average Cost

If shares are reacquired at a price greater than average cost, then the company has a "loss" on reacquisition and shareholders' equity will need to be reduced by the difference between these two amounts. If there is any balance in the contributed surplus account from previous reacquisitions, this amount would first be reduced (debited). However, contributed surplus cannot be reduced below zero. In other words, contributed surplus can never have a negative, or debit, balance. Instead, if the debit amount is greater than the balance in contributed surplus, the difference is recorded in Retained Earnings, which can go into a deficit (debit) position. The following two examples show how to record the reacquisition of shares with and without a balance in a contributed surplus account.

Balance in the Contributed Surplus Account.

To illustrate, we will continue with the Campagner Inc. example. Assume that on December 5, Campagner Inc. reacquires an additional 10,000 shares, this time for $2.75 per share. Assuming no additional shares have been issued since September 23, the average cost of the shares is still $2.00, as previously shown. The result is a loss of $0.75 ($2.00 − $2.75) per share. The total loss is $7,500 (10,000 × $0.75). As there is only $2,500 in the Contributed Surplus account, the rest of the loss is recorded as a reduction of retained earnings as follows:

Dec. 5	Common Shares (10,000 × $2)	20,000	
	Contributed Surplus—Reacquisition of Shares	2,500	
	Retained Earnings ($7,500 − $2,500)	5,000	
	Cash (10,000 × $2.75)		27,500
	To record reacquisition and retirement of 10,000 common shares.		

A	=	L	+	SE
−27,500				−20,000
				−2,500
				−5,000

↓ Cash flows: −27,500

After this entry, Campagner still has an unlimited number of shares authorized, but only 60,000 (70,000 − 10,000) shares issued, and a balance of $120,000 ($140,000 − $20,000) in its Common Shares account. The average cost is still $2 per share ($120,000 ÷ 60,000).

No Balance in the Contributed Surplus Account.

To illustrate, we will continue with the Campagner Inc. example. Assume that on December 27, Campagner Inc. reacquires an additional 2,000 shares, this time for $2.25 per share. Assuming no additional shares have been issued since the previous transaction on December 5, the average cost of the shares is still $2.00, as previously shown. The result is a loss of $0.25 ($2.00 − $2.25) per share. The total loss is $500 (2,000 × $0.25). As there is no balance in the Contributed Surplus account, the full amount of the loss is recorded as a reduction of retained earnings, as follows:

A	=	L	+	SE
−4,500				−4,000
				−500

Cash flows: −4,500

Dec. 27	Common Shares (2,000 × $2)	4,000	
	Retained Earnings	500	
	Cash (2,000 × $2.25)		4,500
	To record reacquisition and retirement of 2,000 common shares.		

Note that the reductions to retained earnings on December 5 and 27 will never be reversed, even if the company later reacquires shares below cost.

In summary, the only difference in the accounting for a reacquisition at prices below or above the average cost has to do with recording the difference between the average cost of the shares and the amount of cash paid to reacquire them. If the shares are reacquired at a price below the average cost, the difference is always credited to a contributed surplus account. If the shares are reacquired at a price above their average cost, the difference is debited first to the contributed surplus account from any previous reacquisition below cost of the same class of shares, and then to the Retained Earnings account if there is no credit balance left in the contributed surplus account.

Action Plan

- Determine the average cost of the shares by dividing the balance in the Common Shares account by the number of shares issued.
- Reduce the Common Shares account by the number of shares reacquired times the average cost per share.
- Compare the cost of the shares reacquired with the cash paid to reacquire the shares.
- If the cost is less than the cash paid, the company has a "gain" and records it as contributed surplus.
- If the reacquisition price is above the average cost, debit the difference to Retained Earnings unless there is already a balance in a contributed surplus account from previous reacquisitions and retirements.

THE NAVIGATOR

BEFORE YOU GO ON...

DO IT

Jimmo Corporation reported having 25,000 common shares issued for a total share capital of $100,000 on its December 31, 2013, balance sheet. On February 15, 2014, it reacquired 4,000 of these shares. This is the first time Jimmo has reacquired any of its shares. Record the reacquisition of the shares assuming the company paid (a) $14,000, and (b) $18,000, to reacquire the shares.

SOLUTION

(a)

Feb. 15	Common Shares (4,000 × $4.00)	16,000	
	Contributed Surplus—Reacquisition of Shares ($16,000 − $14,000)		2,000
	Cash		14,000
	To record reacquisition and retirement of 4,000 common shares at an average cost of $4.00 ($100,000 ÷ 25,000).		

(b)

Feb. 15	Common Shares (4,000 × $4.00)	16,000	
	Retained Earnings ($18,000 − $16,000)	2,000	
	Cash		18,000
	To record reacquisition and retirement of 4,000 common shares at an average cost of $4.00 ($100,000 ÷ 25,000).		

Related exercise material: BE14–4, BE14–5, and E14–3.

COMPREHENSIVE INCOME

In Chapter 13, we introduced corporate income tax and how to prepare an income statement for a corporation. In the following section, we will build on those concepts and show how to prepare an income statement when a company has gains or losses from discontinued operations. We also introduce the concept of other comprehensive income for companies following IFRS and show how it is combined with profit to determine comprehensive income.

STUDY OBJECTIVE 3

Prepare an income statement showing continuing and discontinued operations, and prepare a statement of comprehensive income.

CONTINUING AND DISCONTINUED OPERATIONS

Recall from Chapter 11 that investors need accounting information that is relevant in making decisions about such things as whether or not they should buy (or sell) shares of a company. Creditors need to know if they should lend to a company or not. Thus both investors and creditors use the income statement to evaluate a company's profitability and performance in the previous accounting period. But they are often even more interested in being able to predict or forecast how much profit the company may earn the following year. In order to provide this information, it is necessary to divide the company's profit or loss between its continuing and discontinued operations.

Continuing operations are the revenues, expenses, and profit or loss generated from the company's ongoing activities. **Discontinued operations** refer to the disposal or reclassification to "held for sale" of a component of an entity. A **component of an entity** is a separate major line of business or geographic area of operations. It must be possible to clearly separate operations and cash flows from the rest of the entity in order to be considered a component of an entity.

Many large corporations have multiple separate major lines of business. For example, Canadian Tire reports that it operates principally in two business segments: retail and financial services. Reitmans, as it operates only in the women's apparel retail sector, does not have separate business segments.

When a component of an entity is disposed of, the disposal is reported separately on the income statement as a nonrecurring item called discontinued operations. In order to fully separate profit earned (or losses incurred) in a company's continuing operations from its discontinued operations, it is necessary to also allocate income tax expense or savings to the two categories. This is known as **intraperiod tax allocation.** In intraperiod tax allocation, the income tax expense or saving is associated with certain items or categories, and the items are reported net of applicable income tax. The general concept is "let the tax follow the profit or loss."

The profit (or loss) reported in the discontinued operations section consists of two parts: the profit (loss) from these operations and the gain (loss) on disposal of the segment. Both items are presented net of applicable income tax.

To illustrate, assume Leads Inc. has a 30% income tax rate and that in 2014 it sold its unprofitable kayak manufacturing division. The following information is available:

1. Profit before income tax on its continuing operations is $156,000. (Details are shown in the income statement in Illustration 14-2.)
2. The loss from operating the kayak manufacturing division during 2014 (prior to selling it) is $70,000.
3. The loss from selling the assets in the kayak manufacturing division is $50,000.

Note that the losses in the kayak manufacturing division will result in income tax savings, as opposed to income tax expense. Income tax expense (or savings) is allocated to each of these items and is calculated as follows:

1. Income tax expense on continuing operations is $46,800 ($156,000 × 30%).
2. The income tax savings on the loss from operating the kayak manufacturing prior to its sale is $21,000 ($70,000 × 30%).
3. The income savings on the loss on disposal of the assets in this division is $15,000 ($50,000 × 30%).

On the income statement, the losses of $70,000 and $50,000 from the two components of the discontinued operations are not shown. Instead, the losses are shown minus the income tax savings, and the income tax savings are shown as part of the description of the discontinued item. Deducting the income tax is referred to as "net of tax" and is calculated as follows: loss from the kayak manufacturing division operations is $49,000 ($70,000 − $21,000) and the loss on disposal of the kayak manufacturing division is $35,000 ($50,000 − $15,000).

Illustration 14-2 shows how the continuing and discontinued operations are reported in Leads' income statement.

ILLUSTRATION 14-2
Income statement presentation with discontinued operations

LEADS INC. **Income Statement** **Year Ended December 31, 2014**			
Sales		$800,000	Continuing operations
Cost of goods sold		600,000	
Gross profit		200,000	
Operating expenses		40,000	
Profit from operations		160,000	
Other expenses		4,000	
Profit before income tax		156,000	
Income tax expense		46,800	
Profit from continuing operations		109,200	
Discontinued operations			Discontinued operations
Loss from kayak manufacturing operations, net of $21,000 income tax savings	**$49,000**		
Loss on disposal of kayak manufacturing division, net of $15,000 income tax savings	**35,000**	**84,000**	
Profit		$ 25,200	

Note that the captions "Profit from continuing operations" and "Discontinued operations" are used. This presentation clearly indicates the separate effects of continuing operations and discontinued operations on profit. This allows us to separate the effects of operations that are not relevant to the company's ongoing performance.

Companies reporting under IFRS and ASPE must both report discontinued operations separately from continuing operations.

OTHER COMPREHENSIVE INCOME

Under IFRS, there are certain gains (and losses) that do not affect and are not included in profit but are still added to (or deducted from) shareholders' equity. These gains and losses that are not included in profit are referred to as **other comprehensive income (loss)**. The total of profit plus other comprehensive income is referred to as comprehensive income. Thus **comprehensive income** includes all changes in shareholders' equity during a period except for changes that result from the sale or repurchase of shares or from the payment of dividends. Companies following ASPE do not report other comprehensive income or comprehensive income. There are several types of gains or losses that are considered other comprehensive income. In this chapter we will tell you how to classify these gains and losses.

Other comprehensive income is reported separately from profit for two important reasons: (1) it protects profit from sudden changes that could simply be caused by fluctuations in fair value, and (2) it informs the financial statement user of the cash that would have been received if the investment had actually been sold at year end because the investment is reported at its fair value.

Statement of Comprehensive Income

Companies reporting under IFRS must prepare a **statement of comprehensive income** that shows all of the items included in comprehensive income. There are two possible formats for this statement:

1. **All-inclusive format.** A statement of comprehensive income can include all components of profit or loss and other comprehensive income in a single statement. In this case, the traditional profit

or loss is shown as a subtotal in arriving at comprehensive income. By showing all of the revenues and expenses and resulting profit or loss found in the traditional income statement, in combination with other sources of income, the statement of comprehensive income makes it easier to evaluate a company's profitability on an "all-inclusive" basis. If using this format, the company would not prepare a traditional income statement.

2. **Separate statement.** The other option is to present the traditional income statement, followed by a separate statement of comprehensive income. In this case, the statement of comprehensive income starts with the profit or loss that was reported on the income statement. Then the other comprehensive income gains or losses are added to, or deducted from, profit to calculate comprehensive income. Reitmans, as shown in Appendix A, has used this format.

Similar to discontinued operations, other comprehensive income must be reported net of income tax. Each other comprehensive income item can be shown net of income tax, or if a company has several items in other comprehensive income, it can show the total income tax on the other comprehensive items as one number. In this textbook, we will show each other comprehensive income item net of income tax.

To illustrate a comprehensive income statement, we will continue our example with Leads Inc. Recall that Leads Inc. has prepared a separate traditional income statement, with profit of $25,200, as shown in Illustration 14-2. Assume that Leads Inc. also has equity investments where the gains and losses are recognized as other comprehensive income and that in 2014 Leads had a loss on these equity investments of $5,000. This will be shown in the statement of comprehensive income net of $1,500 ($5,000 × 30%) of income tax at $3,500 ($5,000 − $1,500). This information is presented in Illustration 14-3 in a statement of comprehensive income for Leads Inc.

ILLUSTRATION 14-3
Statement of comprehensive income

LEADS INC. Statement of Comprehensive Income Year Ended December 31, 2014	
Profit	$25,200
Other comprehensive income (loss)	
Loss on equity investments, net of $1,500 of income tax savings	(3,500)
Comprehensive income	$21,700

Accumulated Other Comprehensive Income

The cumulative amount of other comprehensive income and losses over the life of the company is reported as a separate component in shareholders' equity on the balance sheet, called **accumulated other comprehensive income**. Thus, every year, the other comprehensive income or loss is either added to, or deducted from, beginning Accumulated Other Comprehensive Income to determine ending Accumulated Other Comprehensive Income. Later in the chapter, we will illustrate how this is reported on the statement of changes in shareholders' equity.

However, profit is always added to (losses deducted from) retained earnings. This is still the case even if a company reports other comprehensive income. Thus it is always necessary to divide comprehensive income into profit (or loss) and other comprehensive income (or loss).

Using assumed data for beginning retained earnings and accumulated other comprehensive income, and assuming no dividends or other changes to retained earnings, the following diagram shows how Leads Inc.'s comprehensive income is allocated to these two shareholders' equity accounts.

Balance Sheet Account	Balance January 1, 2014	Allocation of Comprehensive Income		Balance December 31, 2014
Retained earnings	$338,500	Profit	$25,200	$363,700
Accumulated other comprehensive income	31,400	Other comprehensive income (loss)	(3,500)	27,900

BEFORE YOU GO ON...

DO IT

Quinn Ltd. reports comprehensive income in a single statement of comprehensive income. In 2014, the company reported profit before income tax of $400,000; a pre-tax loss on discontinued operations of $75,000; a pre-tax gain on the disposal of the assets from the discontinued operations of $30,000; and other comprehensive income from a gain on an unrealized foreign currency translation adjustment of $14,000 before tax. The company has a 25% income tax rate. Prepare a statement of comprehensive income, beginning with profit before income tax.

Action Plan

- Allocate income tax between income from continuing operations, income from discontinued operations, and other comprehensive income items.
- Separately disclose (1) the results of operations of the discontinued division, and (2) the disposal of the discontinued operation.
- A statement of comprehensive income presents other comprehensive income amounts, net of income tax, following the profit for the year.

SOLUTION

QUINN LTD.
Statement of Comprehensive Income (partial)
Year Ended December 31, 2014

Profit before income tax		$400,000
Income tax expense		100,000[1]
Profit from continuing operations		300,000
Discontinued operations		
Loss from operations, net of $18,750[2] income tax savings	$56,250[3]	
Gain on disposal of assets, net of $7,500[4] income tax expense	22,500[5]	33,750
Profit		266,250
Other comprehensive income		
Unrealized gain on foreign currency translation adjustment, net of $3,500[6] income tax expense		10,500[7]
Comprehensive income		$276,750

[1] $400,000 × 25% = $100,000
[2] $75,000 × 25% = $18,750
[3] $75,000 − $18,750 = $56,250
[4] $30,000 × 25% = $7,500
[5] $30,000 − $7,500 = $22,500
[6] $14,000 × 25% = $3,500
[7] $14,000 − $3,500 = $10,500

THE NAVIGATOR

Related exercise material: BE14–6, BE14–7, BE14–8, E14–4, and E14–5.

ACCOUNTING CHANGES

STUDY OBJECTIVE 4

Explain the accounting for different types of accounting changes and account for corrections of prior period errors.

In order to increase comparability between companies, there are specific accounting and reporting requirements that companies must follow when they have a change in accounting policies, a change in an estimate, or they need to correct an error made in a previous accounting period.

CHANGES IN ACCOUNTING POLICIES

To make comparisons from one year to the next easier, financial statements for the current period are prepared using the same accounting policies that were used for the preceding period. This improves comparability, an important characteristic of accounting information that we learned about in Chapter 11. An accounting policy used in the current year can be different from the one used in the previous year only if the change (1) is required by generally accepted accounting principles or (2) results in the financial statements providing more reliable and relevant information. This is called a **change in accounting policy**.

The change that all Canadian companies had to make in 2011 to either IFRS or ASPE is an example of a change in accounting policy because of a change in generally accepted accounting principles. **When there is a change in accounting policy, companies are required to retroactively apply the new standards** except if it is impractical to do so. That means the company must recalculate and restate all of the related accounts as if it had always followed the new policy. But, if significant estimates are required, or if the required information is not available, then it is not possible for prior financial statements to be restated for comparative purposes. Whether or not the prior periods are restated, companies must disclose the details of the change to the new policy in their notes to the financial statements.

If the company starts using a new accounting method because of a change in circumstances, this is *not* considered a change in accounting policy, and the company does not retroactively change prior periods as in the case of a change in accounting policy. For example, in Chapter 9, we explained that companies must review their choice of depreciation methods each year. If a change in circumstances indicates the depreciation method must be changed, then the company will simply start using the new method in the current and future periods.

CHANGES IN ACCOUNTING ESTIMATES

In accounting, estimates of future conditions and events are often made. For example, in order to calculate depreciation, it is necessary to estimate the useful life of the depreciable asset. Recording bad debt expense also requires estimates to be made. As time passes, it is very possible that there may be a change in circumstances or new information about the estimate is available that indicates the need for a **change in an accounting estimate**.

A change in an accounting estimate does not mean an error was made in the prior period. Since it is not an error, we do not go back and correct the prior periods. Instead, we use the new estimate to change our calculations in the current and future periods. In Chapter 9, an example of how to account for a change in an estimate was shown—the revision of depreciation when there was a change in the estimated useful life or residual value of the long-lived asset.

CORRECTION OF PRIOR PERIOD ERRORS

Suppose that a corporation's temporary accounts have been closed and the financial statements have been issued. The corporation then discovers that a material (significant) error has been made in a revenue or expense account in a prior year that misstated that year's profit. This also means that the Retained Earnings account is incorrect because the incorrect amount of revenue or expense was transferred to retained earnings in the closing entries. Thus the **correction of a prior period error** is made directly to Retained Earnings since the effect of the error is now in this account.

Alternative terminology
Corrections of prior period errors are frequently called *prior period adjustments*.

Entries to Correct Prior Period Errors

The entry to correct a prior period error includes a debit or credit to Retained Earnings, net of income tax, a debit or credit to income tax payable for the change in income tax, and a debit or a credit to the related asset or liability account. To illustrate, assume that Baumgartner Inc. discovers in 2014 that it overstated its cost of goods sold in 2013 by $10,000 as a result of errors in counting inventory. Because cost of goods sold (an expense account) was overstated, profit before income tax was understated by the same amount, $10,000. If we assume an income tax rate of 30%, income tax expense would also be understated by $3,000 ($10,000 × 30%). The overall effect on profit is to understate it by $7,000 ($10,000 − $3,000).

If profit is understated, then retained earnings at the end of 2013 would also be understated by the same amount, $7,000, which is referred to as the "after-tax difference" or the "error net of income tax."

The following table details the effect of this error on the prior year's income statement, using assumed data for revenues and expenses:

	Incorrect	**Correct**	**Difference**
Revenues	$900,000	$900,000	$ 0
Expenses	**550,000**	**540,000**	**10,000**
Profit before income tax	350,000	360,000	10,000
Income tax expense (30%)	**105,000**	**108,000**	**3,000**
Profit	$245,000	$252,000	$ 7,000

In addition to overstating cost of goods sold by $10,000, the error will result in merchandise inventory being understated by the same amount. You will recall that we learned about the pervasive impact of inventory errors in Chapter 6.

The entry for the correction of this error, discovered on February 12, 2014, is as follows:

A	=	L	+	SE
+10,000		+3,000		+7,000

Cash flows: no effect

Feb. 12	Merchandise Inventory	10,000	
	Income Tax Payable		3,000
	Retained Earnings		7,000
	To adjust for overstatement of cost of goods sold in a prior period.		

A credit to an income statement account, in this case Cost of Goods Sold, instead of Retained Earnings, would be incorrect because the error is for a prior year and the temporary accounts would already have been closed at the end of that fiscal period.

Presentation of Corrections of Prior Period Errors

Corrections of prior period errors must also be reported in the financial statements. They are added to (or deducted from, depending on the direction of the adjustment) the beginning Retained Earnings balance. They are also reported net of the related income tax in the same way that the correcting entry to retained earnings was net of tax. The method of reporting is similar to reporting gains or losses from discontinued operations or other comprehensive income, as shown earlier in the chapter.

To illustrate, using the adjustment we journalized above—the correction for the overstatement of cost of goods sold—assume that Baumgartner had previously reported $750,000 of retained earnings at December 31, 2013, which is also the beginning balance in Retained Earnings on January 1, 2014. It is still necessary to show this as the beginning balance, even though we now know it is incorrect. The phrase "as previously reported" is added so users know this amount was reported as the ending balance in the previous year.

As the error was found in 2014, it is reported as a correction to beginning retained earnings in the 2014 financial statements. Also shown is the correct, or adjusted, beginning retained earnings balance. Illustration 14-4 shows how the correction of Baumgartner's prior period error will be presented in its 2014 financial statements:

ILLUSTRATION 14-4
Presentation of a correction of a prior period error

Retained earnings, January 1, 2014, as previously reported	$750,000
Add: Correction for overstatement of cost of goods sold in 2013, net of $3,000 income tax expense	**7,000**
Retained earnings, January 1, 2014, as adjusted	$757,000

This is shown on the statement of retained earnings if the company is following ASPE. If the company is following IFRS, as we will see later in the chapter, it is shown in the retained earnings section of the statement of changes in shareholders' equity. The effects of the change should also be detailed and disclosed in a note to the statements. The prior year's financial statements are also corrected if they are shown for comparative purposes with the current year's statements.

The accounting for a change in accounting policy is similar to the correction of prior period errors. Opening retained earnings is adjusted for the cumulative effect of the change, net of the applicable income tax.

BEFORE YOU GO ON...

DO IT

Tran Corporation reported retained earnings of $5,130,000 at December 31, 2013. In 2014, the company earns $2 million of profit and declares and pays a $275,000 cash dividend. On March 7, 2014, Tran found an error made in 2013 when it purchased land; the $275,000 cost of the land was debited to Legal Expense in error. Tran's income tax rate is 30%. (a) Prepare the journal entry to correct the error. (b) Prepare a statement of retained earnings for the year ended December 31, 2014.

Action Plan

- Calculate the tax effect of the error by multiplying the error by the tax rate.
- If expenses were overstated in a prior year, that means income tax expense was understated. It also means that profit and retained earnings were understated by the difference between the error and the related tax.

SOLUTION

(a)

Mar. 7	Land	275,000	
	Income tax payable ($275,000 × 30%)		82,500
	Retained Earnings ($275,000 − $82,500)		192,500
	To correct for overstatement of legal expenses in a prior period.		

BEFORE YOU GO ON...
continued on next page

(b)

TRAN CORPORATION Statement of Retained Earnings Year Ended December 31, 2014	
Balance, January 1, 2014, as previously reported	$5,130,000
Add: Correction for overstatement of legal expenses in 2013, net of $82,500 income tax	192,500
Balance, January 1, 2014, as adjusted	5,322,500
Add: Profit	2,000,000
	7,322,500
Less: Cash dividend	275,000
Balance, December 31, 2014	$7,047,500

Related exercise material: BE14–9, BE14–10, E14–6, and E14–7.

BEFORE YOU GO ON...
continued from previous page

- When reporting the correction of the error, begin with retained earnings as reported at the end of the previous year.
- Add or subtract corrections of prior period errors, net of applicable income tax, to arrive at the adjusted opening retained earnings balance.
- Add profit to and subtract dividends declared from the adjusted opening retained earnings balance to arrive at the ending balance in retained earnings.

THE NAVIGATOR

REPORTING CHANGES IN SHAREHOLDERS' EQUITY

STUDY OBJECTIVE 5
Prepare a statement of changes in shareholders' equity.

Companies reporting under IFRS are required to disclose all changes affecting shareholders' equity in a **statement of changes in shareholders' equity**. This statement shows the changes in total shareholders' equity during the year, as well as changes in each shareholders' equity account, including contributed capital, retained earnings, and accumulated other comprehensive income. Under ASPE, companies do not prepare a statement of changes in shareholders' equity. Instead they prepare a statement of retained earnings, with details about changes in other equity accounts disclosed in the notes to the statements.

In the following sections, we will first review the transactions that affect shareholders' equity and then show how to prepare a statement of changes in shareholders' equity.

Alternative terminology
The statement of changes in shareholders' equity is also called the *statement of shareholders' equity* or *statement of changes in equity*.

SUMMARY OF SHAREHOLDERS' EQUITY TRANSACTIONS

In Chapter 13, and earlier in this chapter, you have learned several transactions and events that affect shareholders' equity accounts. These are summarized in Illustration 14-5.

It is important to review this summary and make sure you understand each of these transactions and their impact on the shareholders' equity accounts. This is the information that is included in the statement of changes in shareholders' equity.

ILLUSTRATION 14-5
Summary of transactions affecting shareholders' equity

Transaction	Impact on Shareholders' Equity Accounts
1. Issuance of share capital	1. Common or Preferred Shares is increased.
2. Reacquisition of share capital	2. Common or Preferred Shares is decreased. Contributed Surplus may be increased or decreased. Retained Earnings may be decreased.
3. Correction of a prior period error that affected the prior year's ending retained earnings	3. Opening Retained Earnings is either increased or decreased as required to make the correction.
4. Cumulative effect of a change in accounting policy on the prior year's ending retained earnings	4. Opening Retained Earnings is either increased or decreased as required to make the adjustment.
5. Profit (or loss)	5. Retained Earnings is increased (or decreased).
6. Other comprehensive income (or loss)	6. Accumulated Other Comprehensive Income is increased (decreased).
7. Cash dividends are declared	7. Retained Earnings is decreased.
8. Stock dividends are declared	8. Retained Earnings is decreased and Stock Dividends Distributable is increased.
9. Stock dividends are distributed	9. Stock Dividends Distributable is decreased and Common Shares is increased.
10. Stock split	10. Number of shares issued increases; there is no effect on account balances.

STATEMENT OF CHANGES IN SHAREHOLDERS' EQUITY

To explain and illustrate the preparation of a statement of changes in shareholders' equity, we will use financial information from Tech International Inc. Illustration 14-6 presents Tech International's prior year shareholders' equity section of the balance sheet and its current year statement of comprehensive income.

ILLUSTRATION 14-6
Tech International's financial information

TECH INTERNATIONAL INC.
Balance Sheet (partial)
December 31, 2013

Shareholders' equity	
Share capital	
Common shares, unlimited number authorized, 1,000,000 shares issued	$2,980,000
Contributed surplus—reacquired shares	20,000
	3,000,000
Retained earnings	190,000
Accumulated other comprehensive income	385,700
Total shareholders' equity	$3,575,700

TECH INTERNATIONAL INC.
Statement of Comprehensive Income
Year Ended December 31, 2014

Profit	$349,800
Other comprehensive income	
Gain on equity investments, net of $132,000 of income tax expense	198,000
Comprehensive income	$547,800

During 2014, Tech International entered into a number of transactions that affected its shareholders' equity accounts, as follows:

1. On January 21, Tech International reacquired 25,000 common shares for $115,000. As you learned previously in this chapter, Common Shares is decreased by $74,500 [($2,980,000 ÷ 1,000,000) × 25,000]. Contributed Surplus—Reacquired Shares is decreased by its balance of $20,000. Retained Earnings is decreased by $20,500 ($115,000 − $74,500 − $20,000).
2. On March 4, Tech International declared a 4% stock dividend to be distributed on April 10 to shareholders of record on March 20. The fair value of its shares on March 4 was $4.75. As the total shares issued at that point amounted to 975,000 (1,000,000 − 25,000), 39,000 shares are distributed (975,000 × 4%) at $185,250 (39,000 × $4.75).
3. On September 22, Tech International sold 50,000 common shares at $5 per share for a total of $250,000 cash.
4. On November 9, Tech International declared cash dividends of $100,000 to be paid on January 2, 2015, to shareholders of record on December 7, 2014.

It was also determined that cost of goods sold had been overstated by $70,000 in 2013. Tech International has an income tax rate of 40%. The income tax impact of the overstatement was $28,000 ($70,000 × 40%). The net impact of the error on opening retained earnings was $42,000 ($70,000 − $28,000).

In the statement of changes in shareholders' equity, this information is organized by shareholders' equity account. For each account, the beginning balance from the prior-year balance sheet is shown, followed by the increases and decreases during the year. The ending balance is calculated for each shareholders' equity account and then the overall total of shareholders' equity is determined.

Remember that comprehensive income is divided into profit and other comprehensive income in terms of its impact on shareholders' equity. Profit is added to Retained Earnings, and Other Comprehensive Income is added to Accumulated Other Comprehensive Income.

In Illustration 14-7, Tech International's statement of changes in equity for 2014 has been prepared using the above information.

ILLUSTRATION 14-7
Statement of changes in shareholders' equity

TECH INTERNATIONAL INC.
Statement of Changes in Shareholders' Equity
Year Ended December 31, 2014

Share capital, common shares	
Balance, January 1, 1,000,000 shares issued	$2,980,000
Reacquired 25,000 shares	(74,500)
Stock dividend issued, 39,000 shares	185,250
Issued for cash, 50,000 shares	250,000
Balance, December 31, 1,064,000 shares issued	3,340,750
Stock dividends distributable	
Balance, January 1	0
Stock dividend declared	185,250
Stock dividend distributed	(185,250)
Balance, December 31	0
Contributed surplus—reacquired shares	
Balance, January 1	20,000
Reacquired common shares	(20,000)
Balance, December 31	0
Retained earnings	
Balance, January 1, as previously reported	190,000
Correction for overstatement of cost of goods sold in 2013, net of $28,000 of income tax expense	42,000
Balance, January 1, as adjusted	232,000
Profit	349,800
Reacquired common shares	(20,500)
Stock dividends	(185,250)
Cash dividends	(100,000)
Balance, December 31	276,050
Accumulated other comprehensive income	
Balance, January 1	385,700
Other comprehensive income	198,000
Balance, December 31	583,700
Shareholders' equity, December 31	$4,200,500

Note that the end-of-year balances shown in the statement of changes in shareholders' equity are the amounts that are reported on the shareholders' equity section of the December 31, 2014, balance sheet.

BEFORE YOU GO ON...

DO IT

Balsam Lake Corporation had the following shareholders' equity balances at January 1, 2014:

Common shares, unlimited number authorized, 500,000 issued	$1,000,000
Retained earnings	600,000
Accumulated other comprehensive income	100,000

The following selected information is available for the year ended December 31, 2014:

1. Issued 100,000 common shares for $300,000 cash.
2. Declared dividends of $50,000.
3. Reported profit of $360,000.
4. Reported a loss after tax on equity investments of $25,000 as other comprehensive loss.

BEFORE YOU GO ON... continued on next page

BEFORE YOU GO ON...
continued from previous page

Action Plan

- The statement of shareholders' equity covers a specific period of time, starting with the opening balances and ending with the ending balances for the period.
- Include all of the changes in each shareholders' equity account, as well as total shareholders' equity.
- Recall that comprehensive income consists of both profit and other comprehensive income.

SOLUTION

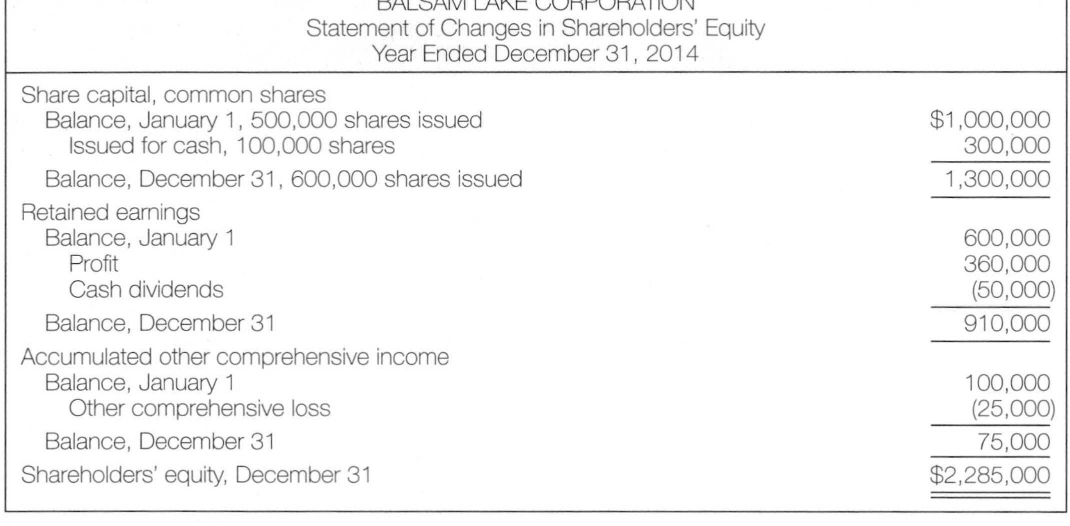

BALSAM LAKE CORPORATION
Statement of Changes in Shareholders' Equity
Year Ended December 31, 2014

Share capital, common shares	
Balance, January 1, 500,000 shares issued	$1,000,000
Issued for cash, 100,000 shares	300,000
Balance, December 31, 600,000 shares issued	1,300,000
Retained earnings	
Balance, January 1	600,000
Profit	360,000
Cash dividends	(50,000)
Balance, December 31	910,000
Accumulated other comprehensive income	
Balance, January 1	100,000
Other comprehensive loss	(25,000)
Balance, December 31	75,000
Shareholders' equity, December 31	$2,285,000

THE NAVIGATOR

Related exercise material: BE14–11, BE14–12, E14–8, E14–9, and E14–10.

ANALYZING SHAREHOLDERS' EQUITY

STUDY OBJECTIVE 6
Evaluate earnings and dividend performance.

Shares are generally purchased by investors for potential capital gains (increases in the shares' market price) or for potential income (dividends). Consequently, investors are interested in both a company's earnings performance and its dividend record.

EARNINGS PERFORMANCE

When shareholders want to analyze their investment in a company, they can measure the company's earnings performance, or profitability, in several different ways. We learned about one measure in Chapter 13: the return on equity ratio. Two other ratios are widely used by existing shareholders and potential investors: earnings per share and the price-earnings ratio.

Earnings per share is useful because shareholders usually think in terms of the number of shares they own—or plan to buy or sell—so determining profit per share makes it easier for the shareholder to understand the return on his or her investment. Some companies, such as Tim Hortons in our feature story, even communicate to their shareholders their targeted earnings per share for the upcoming year.

Investors and others also link earnings per share to the market price per share. This relationship produces the second ratio: the price-earnings ratio.

Earnings per Share

Earnings per share (EPS) indicates the profit earned by each common share. Thus, earnings per share is reported only for common shares. When a company has both preferred and common shares, the current year's dividend declared on preferred shares is subtracted from profit to determine the income available to common shareholders. Illustration 14-8 shows the formula for calculating EPS.

ILLUSTRATION 14-8
Earnings per share formula

Profit Minus Preferred Dividends	÷	Weighted Average Number of Common Shares	=	Earnings per Share
($47,539 − $0)	÷	66,101	=	$0.72

To show the calculation of earnings per share, the illustration uses data (in thousands) from Reitmans' 2012 financial statements. Reitmans' profit, or net earnings as Reitmans calls it, of $47,539,000 is divided by the weighted average number of common shares, 66,101,000, to determine its earnings per share of $0.72.

In determining the numerator of the earnings per share calculation ($47,539,000), note that Reitmans had no preferred dividends to subtract from profit. If it did, any preferred dividends declared for the current year would be subtracted from profit to determine the income available for the common shareholders. In addition, note that if preferred shares are cumulative, the dividend is deducted whether or not it is declared.

For the denominator of the earnings per share calculation (66,101), the **weighted average number of shares** is used instead of the ending balance, or a straight average. If there is no change in the number of common shares issued during the year, the weighted average number of shares will be the same as the ending balance. If new shares are issued in the year, these shares are adjusted for the fraction of the year they are outstanding to determine the weighted average number of shares. This is done because the issue of shares during the period changes the amount of net assets that income can be earned on.

To illustrate the calculation of the weighted average number of common shares, assume that a company had 100,000 common shares on January 1. It reacquired and retired 7,500 shares on May 1, and issued an additional 10,000 shares on October 1. The weighted average number of shares for the year would be calculated as follows:

Date	Actual Number	Fraction of Year	Weighted Average
Jan. 1	100,000	$\times$ 12/12 =	100,000
May 1	(7,500)	$\times$ 8/12 =	(5,000)
Oct. 1	10,000	$\times$ 3/12 =	2,500
	102,500		97,500

As illustrated, 102,500 shares were actually issued by the end of the year. Of these, 100,000 were outstanding at the beginning of the year and are allocated a full weight, 12 months out of 12. The 7,500 reacquired shares were only issued for four months (January 1 to April 30) and should be included for 4/12 of the year. Consequently, a weighted average of 5,000 shares must be deducted for the portion of the year when they were no longer issued, May 1 to December 31, or 8/12 of the year. As 10,000 of the shares have only been outstanding for three months (from October 1 to December 31), they are weighted for 3/12 of the year, resulting in 2,500 weighted shares. In total, the company's weighted average number of shares is 97,500 for the year. In the next calendar year, the 102,500 shares would receive a full weight (unless some of these shares are repurchased) because all 102,500 shares would be outstanding for the entire year.

Helpful hint Recall that a weighted (as opposed to a simple) average was also used in the average method of calculating inventory and cost of goods sold in Chapter 6.

The disclosure of earnings per share is required for companies reporting under IFRS. This disclosure is so important that EPS must be reported directly on the statement of comprehensive income or income statement if presented separately, and it also has to be explained in the notes to the financial statements. It is the only ratio that is reported in this way. Companies using ASPE are not required to report EPS.

Complex Capital Structure.

When a corporation has securities that may be converted into common shares, it has what is called a complex capital structure. One example of a convertible security is convertible preferred shares. When the preferred shares are converted into common shares, the additional common shares will result in a reduced, or diluted, earnings per share figure.

Two earnings per share figures are calculated when a corporation has a complex capital structure. The first earnings per share figure is called **basic earnings per share**. The earnings per share amount we calculated in Illustration 14-8, $0.72, is known as basic earnings per share, which is what Reitmans reported on its income statement for fiscal 2012.

The second earnings per share figure is called **fully diluted earnings per share**. This figure calculates *hypothetical* earnings per share as though *all* securities that can be converted into, or exchanged for, common shares have been (even though they really have not). Reitmans, which has other securities that can be converted into common shares (stock options, in this case), is considered to have a complex capital structure. It reports fully diluted earnings per share of $0.72 for fiscal 2012, which is identical to its basic earnings per share, because its stock options are *anti-dilutive*. That means if the stock options had been exercised, it would have increased earnings per share. As companies are not allowed to report fully diluted earnings per share higher than basic earnings per share, Reitmans reports the same amount for both figures.

The calculation of fully diluted earnings per share is complex. In addition, the determination of the weighted average number of shares for both basic and fully diluted earnings per share becomes more complicated when there are stock dividends and stock splits during the year. Further discussion of these and other earnings per share complexities is left to a later accounting course.

Price-Earnings Ratio

Comparing the earnings per share amounts of different companies is not very helpful, because there are big differences in the numbers of shares in companies and in the share prices. In order to compare earnings across companies, we instead calculate the **price-earnings (PE) ratio**. The price-earnings ratio is a frequently quoted statistic that gives the ratio of the market price of each common share to its earnings per share.

To illustrate, we will calculate the price-earnings ratio for Reitmans (Canada) Limited. Reitmans' earnings per share for the year ended January 28, 2012, was $0.72, as shown in Illustration 14-8. Its market price per share for its Class A shares at year end was $14.64. Illustration 14-9 shows Reitmans' price-earnings ratio.

ILLUSTRATION 14-9
Price-earnings ratio formula

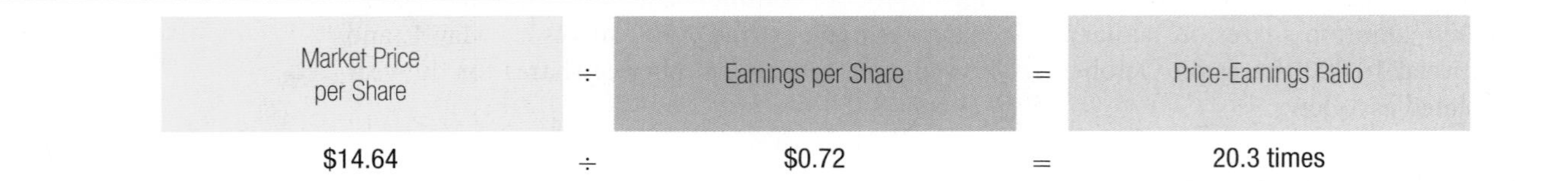

Market Price per Share
÷
Earnings per Share
=
Price-Earnings Ratio
$14.64
÷
$0.72
=
20.3 times

This ratio indicates that Reitmans' shares are trading at more than 20 times their earnings. The PE ratio reflects investors' assessment of a company's future earnings. The ratio of price to earnings will be higher if investors think that current income levels will continue or increase. It will be lower if investors think that income will decrease.

Helpful hint Since earnings per share (EPS) is used in calculating the price-earnings ratio, it must be calculated first.

The price-earnings ratio is not relevant for private companies. Private companies will not have a readily available market price per share, and, as discussed above, if they follow ASPE, they also do not report earnings per share in their financial statements.

DIVIDENDS RECORD

In order to remain in business, companies must honour their interest payments to creditors, bankers, and debt holders. But the payment of dividends to shareholders is another matter. Many companies can survive, and even thrive, without such payouts. For example, high-growth companies generally do not pay dividends. Their policy is to retain all of their earnings to finance their growth.

On the other hand, some companies, such as Tim Hortons in our feature story, have a dividend policy where they commit to paying out a portion of their profit to shareholders every year. Presumably, investors who feel that regular dividends are important will buy shares in companies that pay periodic dividends, and those who feel that the share price and the potential for capital gains are more important will buy shares in companies that retain earnings.

One way of assessing a company's dividend-paying policy is to calculate the **payout ratio**, which tells you what percentage of profit the company is distributing to its shareholders. The payout ratio is calculated by dividing cash dividends by profit. This ratio can also be expressed on a per-share basis by dividing dividends per share by earnings per share. The payout ratio can be calculated for total dividends, for common dividends, or for preferred dividends. The formula to calculate the payout ratio is shown in Illustration 14-10.

ILLUSTRATION 14-10
Payout ratio

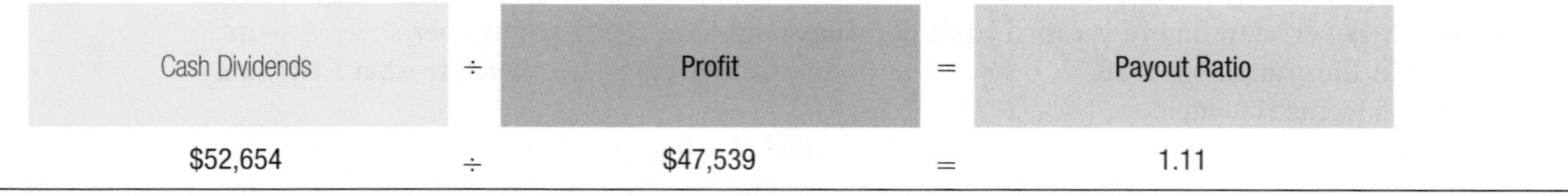

Reitmans' payout ratio is 1.11. This indicates that, for every dollar of profit earned during the fiscal year, the company has paid approximately $1.11 to the owners. As the company paid out more dividends than its profit, Reitmans' retained earnings are lower at the end of the year than at the beginning of the year.

Reitmans' payout ratio, at 1.11, is well above the industry average, which was reported as 0.38 by Reuters. A high payout ratio such as Reitmans' could be a warning signal—it could mean the company is failing to reinvest enough of its profit in its operations. On the other hand, it can also be caused when profits have dropped but the dividend payment has been left at a level that is fairly consistent from one year to the next. This is a common practice for public companies such as Reitmans. It provides a signal that management expects profits to recover the following year. It appears that this might be the case for Reitmans, as its dividends in 2012 were very close to its dividends in 2011, but its profit was approximately 45% lower in 2012 than 2011.

Like most ratios, the payout ratio varies with the industry. For example, utility companies have high payout ratios. But companies that have high growth rates generally tend to have low payout ratios because they reinvest their profit in the company.

ACCOUNTING IN ACTION
ALL ABOUT YOU INSIGHT

Suppose you have some extra cash. Should you invest it in some shares of a public company or put it in a savings account and earn interest? Buying shares in a company is a greater risk than putting the cash in a savings account. Investing in a company's shares carries neither a promise that your investment will be returned to you nor a guarantee that your investment will earn income. However, investing in shares can often provide higher income than a savings account. Shareholders can earn income by receiving dividends or by selling the shares at a price higher than what they paid for them. Share prices are determined by the interaction of the buyers and the sellers in the market. Share prices can be influenced by both objective factors, such as a company's profits, and subjective factors, such as future share price expectations, including unverified rumours. Nevertheless, if a company prospers, the price of its common shares will typically rise in the long run. If the company doesn't prosper, or if external factors such as the economy are negative, the share price will likely decline.

If you were thinking about investing in a company, where might you find information about the company's dividend policy, its profitability, and its share price?

BEFORE YOU GO ON...

DO IT

Stewart Limited, a publicly traded company, reported profit of $249,750 on its October 31 year-end income statement. The shareholders' equity section of its balance sheet reported 3,000, $2 noncumulative preferred shares and 50,000 common shares. Of the common shares, 40,000 had been issued since the beginning of the year, 15,000 were issued on March 1, and 5,000 were repurchased on August 1. The preferred dividend was declared and paid during the year. The market price per share on October 31 was $40.

(a) Calculate Stewart's earnings per share. (b) Calculate Stewart's price-earnings ratio.

SOLUTION

(a) Preferred dividends: 3,000 preferred shares × $2 dividend per share = $6,000
Income available to common shareholders: $249,750 − $6,000 = $243,750
Weighted average number of common shares:

Date	Actual Number	Fraction of Year	Weighted Average
Nov. 1	40,000	× 12/12 =	40,000
Mar. 1	15,000	× 8/12 =	10,000
Aug. 1	(5,000)	× 3/12 =	(1,250)
	50,000		48,750

Earnings per share: $\frac{\$243,750}{48,750} = \$5$

(b) Price-earnings ratio: $40 ÷ $5 = 8

Related exercise material: BE14–13, BE14–14, BE14–15, E14–11, E14–12, and E14–13.

Action Plan

- Subtract the preferred dividends from profit to determine the income available for common shareholders.
- Adjust the shares for the fraction of the year they were outstanding to determine the weighted average number of shares.
- Divide the income available for common shareholders by the weighted average number of shares to calculate the earnings per share.

THE NAVIGATOR

Comparing IFRS and ASPE

Key Differences	International Financial Reporting Standards (IFRS)	Accounting Standards for Private Enterprises (ASPE)
Other comprehensive income and statement of comprehensive income	Required	Not required
Statement of changes in shareholders' equity	Required	Changes in retained earnings presented in the statement of retained earnings. Changes to other shareholders' equity accounts presented in the notes.
EPS	Required	Not required

THE NAVIGATOR

DEMONSTRATION PROBLEM

On January 1, 2014, Bacola Corporation, a public company, had the following shareholders' equity accounts:

Common shares, unlimited number authorized, 260,000 issued	$3,120,000
Retained earnings	3,200,000
Accumulated other comprehensive income	75,000

During the year, the following transactions occurred:

Jan. 18 Reacquired 10,000 common shares for $13 per share.
Apr. 10 Discovered that it had understated its cost of goods sold in 2013 by $50,000.
June 1 Announced a 2-for-1 stock split of the common shares. Immediately before the split, the share price was $13.50 per share.
June 30 Declared a $0.40 cash dividend to common shareholders of record on July 16, payable August 1.
Aug. 1 Paid the dividend declared on June 30.
Nov. 30 Reacquired 40,000 common shares for $5.50 per share.
Dec. 30 Declared a 5% stock dividend to common shareholders of record on January 15, distributable January 31. On December 30, the share price was $5 per share. On January 15, it was $5.50 per share, and on January 31, it was $6 per share.

In addition, Bacola Corporation reported profit of $590,000 and a pre-tax loss on equity investments of $60,000, which is other comprehensive income (loss).

The company has a 30% income tax rate.

Instructions

(a) Record the transactions.
(b) Prepare a statement of comprehensive income.
(c) Prepare a statement of changes in shareholders' equity.
(d) Prepare the shareholders' equity section of the balance sheet.

SOLUTION TO DEMONSTRATION PROBLEM

(a)

Date	Account	Debit	Credit
Jan. 18	Common Shares [($3,120,000 ÷ 260,000) × 10,000]	120,000	
	Retained Earnings ($130,000 − $120,000)	10,000	
	Cash ($13 × 10,000)		130,000
	Reacquired 10,000 common shares.		
Apr. 10	Retained Earnings ($50,000 − $15,000)	35,000	
	Income Tax Payable ($50,000 × 30%)	15,000	
	Merchandise Inventory		50,000
	To adjust for understatement of cost of goods sold in 2013.		

SOLUTION TO DEMONSTRATION PROBLEM continued on next page

SOLUTION TO DEMONSTRATION PROBLEM continued from previous page

Date	Account	Debit	Credit
June 1	Memo entry only about 2-for-1 stock split.		
	Now 500,000 [(260,000 − 10,000) × 2] common shares.		
30	Cash Dividend—Common	200,000	
	Dividend Payable		200,000
	To record cash dividend ($0.40 × 500,000).		
Aug. 1	Dividend Payable	200,000	
	Cash		200,000
	To record payment of cash dividend.		
Nov. 30	Common Shares [($3,000,000 ÷ 500,000) × 40,000]	240,000	
	Contributed Surplus—Reacquisition of Common Shares		20,000
	Cash ($5.50 × 40,000)		220,000
	Reacquired 40,000 common shares for $20,000 ($240,000 − $220,000) less than cost.		

Common Shares	Number	Cost
Jan. 1, Balance	260,000	$3,120,000
Jan. 18 reacquisition	(10,000)	(120,000)
June 1 2-for-1 split	250,000	0
Balance Nov. 30	500,000	$3,000,000

Date	Account	Debit	Credit
Dec. 30	Stock Dividend (23,000 × $5)	115,000	
	Stock Dividend Distributable		115,000
	To record stock dividend to common shareholders (460,000 × 5% = 23,000).		

Common Shares	Number	Cost
Balance Nov. 30	500,000	$3,000,000
Nov. 30 reacquisition	(40,000)	(240,000)
Balance Dec. 30	460,000	$2,760,000

(b)

BACOLA CORPORATION
Statement of Comprehensive Income
Year ended December 31, 2014

Profit	$590,000
Other comprehensive income (loss)	
Loss on equity investments, net of $18,000[1] of income tax savings	(42,000)[2]
Comprehensive income	$548,000

[1]$18,000 = $60,000 × 30% [2]$42,000 = $60,000 − $18,000

(c)

BACOLA CORPORATION
Statement of Changes in Shareholders' Equity
Year ended December 31, 2014

Common shares	
Balance, January 1, 260,000 common shares issued	$3,120,000
Reacquired 10,000 common shares	(120,000)
Issued 250,000 common shares in a 2-for-1 split	0
Reacquired 40,000 common shares	(240,000)
Balance, December 31, 460,000 common shares issued	2,760,000
Stock dividends distributable	
Balance, January 1	0
Common stock dividend declared, 23,000 shares	115,000
Balance, December 31, 23,000 shares	115,000
Contributed Surplus—Reacquisition of Common Shares	
Balance, January 1	0
Reacquired common shares	20,000
Balance, December 31	20,000

SOLUTION TO DEMONSTRATION PROBLEM continued on next page

Action Plan

- Keep a running total of the number of shares issued and total cost of shares.
- When shares are reacquired, reduce Common Shares by the cost of the shares. If reacquiring for less than cost, the gain is credited to a contributed surplus account. If reacquiring for more than cost, the loss is first debited to any previous contributed surplus, then to retained earnings.
- Errors from prior periods are corrected, net of income tax, to the retained earnings account.
- Adjust the number of shares for the stock split, but make no journal entry.
- Make journal entries for dividends on the declaration and payment dates, but not on the record date.
- Apply the stock dividend percentage to the number of shares issued. Multiply the new shares to be issued by the shares' fair value at the date of declaration.
- If not prepared on an all-inclusive basis, the statement of comprehensive income starts with profit. Other comprehensive income (loss) is added to (deducted from) profit on a net-of-tax basis.
- Recall that the statement of changes in shareholders' equity explains the changes for the period in the beginning and ending balances of each shareholders' equity account.
- The balance sheet reports shareholders' equity at the end of the period. These numbers are the ending balances on the statement of changes in shareholders' equity.

SOLUTION TO DEMONSTRATION PROBLEM continued from previous page

Retained earnings	
Balance, January 1, as previously reported	3,200,000
Less: Correction for understatement of cost of goods sold in 2013, net of $15,000 of income tax	(35,000)
Balance, January 1, as adjusted	3,165,000
Profit	590,000
Reacquired common shares	(10,000)
Cash dividends	(200,000)
Stock dividends	(115,000)
Balance, December 31	3,430,000
Accumulated other comprehensive income	
Balance, January 1	75,000
Other comprehensive income (loss)	(42,000)
Balance, December 31	33,000
Shareholders' equity, December 31	$6,358,000

(d)

BACOLA CORPORATION
Balance Sheet (partial)
December 31, 2014

Shareholders' equity	
Contributed capital	
Common shares, unlimited number authorized, 460,000 issued	$2,760,000
Contributed surplus—reacquisition of common shares	20,000
Common stock dividend distributable, 23,000 shares	115,000
Total contributed capital	2,895,000
Retained earnings	3,430,000
Accumulated other comprehensive income	33,000
Total shareholders' equity	$6,358,000

THE NAVIGATOR

Summary of Study Objectives

1. ***Account for stock dividends and stock splits and compare their financial impact.*** Entries for stock dividends are required at the declaration and distribution dates but not at the record date. There is no entry for a stock split. Stock dividends reduce retained earnings and increase common shares, but have no impact on total shareholders' equity. Both stock dividends and stock splits increase the number of shares issued. Stock dividends and splits reduce the fair value of the shares, but have no impact on the company's financial position.

2. ***Account for the reacquisition of shares.*** When shares are reacquired, the average cost is debited to the Common Shares account. If the shares are reacquired at a price below the average cost, the difference is credited to a contributed surplus account. If the shares are reacquired at a price above the average cost, the difference is debited first to a contributed surplus account if a balance exists, and then to the Retained Earnings account.

3. ***Prepare an income statement showing continuing and discontinued operations, and prepare a statement of comprehensive income.*** Gains or losses on discontinued operations must be presented net of income tax after profit (or loss) from continuing operations. Companies following IFRS must prepare a statement of comprehensive income that reports all increases and decreases to shareholders' equity during a period except changes resulting from the sale or repurchase of shares and from the payment of dividends. The statement of comprehensive income can be prepared on an all-inclusive basis, or can start with profit or loss as shown on a separate income statement.

4. ***Explain the accounting for different types of accounting changes and account for corrections of prior period errors.*** A change in accounting policy, from the method used in the previous year, is allowed only when there is a change in GAAP or if it results in the financial statements providing more reliable and relevant information. These changes are applied retroactively when possible. A change in an accounting estimate is not an error and only the current and future periods are revised. If an error in a prior year's profit and retained earnings is found after the temporary accounts have been closed and the statements have been issued, then beginning retained earnings is adjusted. This is shown in the financial statements as a correction to beginning retained earnings net of the related income tax impact.

5. ***Prepare a statement of changes in shareholders' equity.*** A statement of changes in shareholders' equity explains all of the changes in each of the shareholders' equity accounts, and in total, for the reporting period. This includes changes in contributed capital (common shares, preferred shares, and any other contributed surplus accounts), retained earnings, and accumulated other comprehensive income. The statement is required for companies reporting under IFRS.

6. ***Evaluate earnings and dividend performance.*** Profitability measures that are used to analyze shareholders' equity include return on equity (discussed in Chapter 13), earnings per share, the price-earnings ratio, and the payout ratio. Earnings (loss) per share is calculated by dividing profit (loss) available to the common shareholders by the weighted average number of common shares and is reported only under IFRS. The price-earnings ratio is calculated by dividing the market price per share by the earnings per share. The payout ratio is calculated by dividing cash dividends by profit.

Glossary

Accumulated other comprehensive income The cumulative amount of other comprehensive income and losses over the life of the company reported as a separate amount in shareholders' equity. (p. 595)

Basic earnings per share The profit (or loss) earned by each common share. It is calculated by subtracting any preferred dividends declared from profit and dividing the result by the weighted average number of common shares. (p. 603)

Change in accounting estimate A change in an accounting estimate because of a change in circumstances or because new information about the estimate is available that indicates that the estimate needs to be changed. (p. 597)

Change in accounting policy The use of a generally accepted accounting policy in the current year that is different from the one used in the preceding year. (p. 596)

Component of an entity A separate major product line, line of business, or geographic area of operations. (p. 593)

Comprehensive income All changes in shareholders' equity during a period except for changes resulting from the sale or repurchase of shares, or from the payment of dividends. (p. 594)

Continuing operations The revenues, expenses, and profit or loss generated from a company's ongoing activities. (p. 593)

Correction of a prior period error The correction of an error in previously issued financial statements. (p. 597)

Discontinued operations A component of an enterprise that has been disposed of or is reclassified as "held for sale." (p. 593)

Distribution date The date when stock dividends are distributed to shareholders. (p. 587)

Earnings per share (EPS) The profit (or loss) earned by each common share. (p. 602)

Fully diluted earnings per share Earnings per share adjusted for the maximum possible dilution that would occur if securities were converted, or changed, into common shares. (p. 603)

Intraperiod tax allocation The procedure of associating income tax expense with the specific item that directly affects the income tax for the period. (p. 593)

Other comprehensive income (loss) Gains and losses that are not included in profit but affect shareholders' equity. (p. 594)

Payout ratio A ratio that measures the percentage of income distributed as cash dividends. It is calculated by dividing cash dividends by profit. (p. 604)

Price-earnings (PE) ratio The ratio of the price of a common share to earnings per common share. (p. 604)

Reverse stock split A decrease in the number of shares outstanding. A 1-for-3 reverse stock split would reduce the amount of shares owned by a shareholder to one for every three shares owned before the split. (p. 588)

Statement of changes in shareholders' equity A statement that reports all increases and decreases to shareholders' equity during a period. (p. 599)

Statement of comprehensive income A statement that reports all items included in comprehensive income during a period. (p. 594)

Stock dividend A pro rata distribution of the corporation's own shares to shareholders. (p. 586)

Stock split The issue of additional shares to shareholders in a multiple, such as 2 for 1. A 2-for-1 stock split means that two new shares are issued in exchange for one old share. (p. 587)

Treasury shares A corporation's own shares that have been reacquired and not yet retired or cancelled. They are held in "treasury" for later reissue or cancellation. (p. 590)

Weighted average number of shares The number of common shares outstanding during the year, with any shares purchased or issued during the year weighted by the fraction of the year that they have been outstanding. (p. 603)

Self-Study Questions

Answers are at the end of the chapter.

(SO 1) K 1. Which of the following statements about stock dividends and stock splits is correct?
   (a) A stock dividend decreases total shareholders' equity; a stock split increases total shareholders' equity.
   (b) Both result in an increased percentage ownership for shareholders.
   (c) Both are recorded at the fair value of the shares on the declaration date.
   (d) Both result in no change in total shareholders' equity.

(SO 2) C 2. A company will buy back its own shares to:
   (a) increase the share price.
   (b) decrease the share price.
   (c) increase the number of shares available for dividends.
   (d) save cash.

(SO 2) AP 3. Common shares are repurchased for $150,000 by a company with Contributed Surplus—Reacquisition of Shares $75,000; and Retained Earnings $750,000. The repurchased shares have an average cost of $125,000. The journal entry to record the repurchase would include a:
(a) debit to Retained Earnings of $25,000.
(b) credit to Contributed Surplus—Reacquisition of Shares of $25,000.
(c) debit to Contributed Surplus—Reacquisition of Shares of $25,000.
(d) debit to Common Shares of $150,000.

(SO 3) K 4. Discontinued operations:
(a) are reported as part of operating expenses on the income statement.
(b) are reported separately on the income statement as a nonrecurring item.
(c) are never presented net of applicable income tax.
(d) result in an entry to retained earnings directly.

(SO 3) K 5. A statement of comprehensive income:
(a) must include all components of profit and loss and other comprehensive income.
(b) does not include profit or loss from the traditional income statement.
(c) is required for companies reporting under IFRS and ASPE.
(d) is required for companies reporting under IFRS only.

(SO 4) K 6. Which of the following statements about changes in accounting policies is incorrect?
(a) Changing an accounting policy from the one used in the preceding period is allowed only if it is required by GAAP or results in more relevant information.
(b) When a change in an accounting policy is required, it must be applied on a retroactive basis, except if it is impractical to do so.
(c) If the company is able to make the change on a retroactive basis, it is not necessary to disclose the details of the change in the notes.
(d) A change in circumstances is not considered a change in accounting policy.

(SO 4) K 7. A correction of a prior period error is reported:
(a) in the income statement.
(b) directly in the shareholders' equity section of the balance sheet.
(c) in either the statement of retained earnings or the statement of changes in shareholders' equity as an adjustment to the beginning balance of retained earnings.
(d) in either the statement of retained earnings or the statement of changes in shareholders' equity as an adjustment to the ending balance of retained earnings.

(SO 5) AP 8. Which of the following is not included in a statement of changes in shareholders' equity?
(a) A reacquisition of share capital
(b) Accumulated other comprehensive income
(c) Stock dividends
(d) Fair value of common shares

(SO 6) AP 9. For the year ended May 31, 2014, Sonic Corporation reported profit of $42,000. At the beginning of the year, it had 10,000 common shares issued. On February 28, 2014, it had issued 8,000 common shares for cash. The market price per share was $66.50 on May 31, 2014. It had no preferred shares. What were its earnings per share and price-earnings ratios?
(a) $2.33 and 28 times
(b) $3.00 and 22 times
(c) $3.50 and 19 times
(d) $4.20 and 16 times

(SO 6) C 10. Bernard Dupuis is nearing retirement and would like to invest in shares that will give him a steady income. Bernard should choose shares with a high:
(a) earnings per share.
(b) price-earnings ratio.
(c) payout ratio.
(d) return on equity.

THE NAVIGATOR

Questions

(SO 1) K 1. What entries (if any) are made for stock dividends on common shares on (a) the declaration date, (b) the record date, and (c) the distribution date?

(SO 1) C 2. Freddy Investor says, "The shares I recently bought just declared a 2-for-1 stock split. Now I've doubled my investment!" Is Freddy correct—is he any better off after the stock split?

(SO 1) C 3. Contrast the effects of a cash dividend, stock dividend, and stock split on a company's (a) assets, (b) liabilities, (c) share capital, (d) retained earnings, and (e) number of shares.

(SO 2) C 4. Why would a company repurchase some of its shares? Give some reasons.

(SO 2) C 5. Wilmor, Inc. repurchases 1,000 of its own common shares. What effect does this transaction have on (a) total assets, (b) total liabilities, and (c) total shareholders' equity?

(SO 2) C 6. Explain how the accounting for the reacquisition of shares changes depending on whether the reacquisition price is greater or lower than average cost.

(SO 2) C 7. Ciana Chiasson is confused. She says, "I don't understand why sometimes, when the price paid to reacquire shares is greater than their average cost, the 'loss on reacquisition' is debited to a contributed surplus account. But at other times, it is debited to the Retained Earnings account. And sometimes it is even debited to both!" Help Ciana understand.

(SO 3) C 8. Explain intraperiod income tax allocation and why it is important.

(SO 3) C 9. What are discontinued operations? Why is it important to report discontinued operations separately from profit or loss from continuing operations?

(SO 3) C 10. Explain the terms "comprehensive income," "other comprehensive income," and "accumulated other comprehensive income." Include in your explanation how and where they are reported in the financial statements.

(SO 3) C 11. Explain the two methods of preparing a statement of comprehensive income.

(SO 4) C 12. When is a company allowed to change an accounting policy? How should it be accounted for in the financial statements?

(SO 4) C 13. Under what circumstances will a company change an accounting estimate? How is it accounted for, and why is it not considered an error?

(SO 4) C 14. If there was an error in a revenue or expense in a prior period, why isn't that account adjusted when the error is corrected? Instead, how is that error corrected in the accounting records and how is it reported in the financial statements?

(SO 5) K 15. How is comprehensive income reported in the statement of changes in shareholders' equity?

(SO 6) C 16. Distinguish between basic earnings per share and fully diluted earnings per share.

(SO 6) C 17. When calculating EPS: (a) Why is profit available to the common shareholders not always the same as profit? (b) Why is the weighted average number of shares used instead of the number of shares issued at the end of the year?

(SO 6) AP 18. Bowmile Company has a price-earnings ratio of 9 times and a payout ratio of 40%. Van Kampen has a price-earnings ratio of 22 times and a payout ratio of 5%. Which company's shares would be better for an investor interested in large capital gains versus steady income? Why?

(SO 6) C 19. If all other factors stay the same, indicate whether each of the following is generally considered favourable or unfavourable by a potential investor: (a) a decrease in return on equity, (b) an increase in earnings per share, (c) a decrease in the price-earnings ratio, and (d) an increase in the payout ratio.

Brief Exercises

Record stock dividend and determine percentage ownership. **(SO 1) AP**

BE14–1 On March 1, Houseboat Ltd. had 400,000 common shares issued and the balance in its Common Share account was $600,000. The company declared a 5% stock dividend to shareholders of record on March 14, to be distributed on March 31. The fair value per share was $5 on March 1, $4.85 on March 14, and $5.35 on March 31. (a) Prepare the entries on the appropriate dates to record the stock dividend. (b) Assume that Wei Tse owned 2,000 shares prior to the stock dividend. Determine Wei's percentage ownership of the company before and after the stock dividend.

Analyze impact of stock dividend. **(SO 1) AP**

BE14–2 The shareholders' equity section of Ferndale Corporation's balance sheet consists of 225,000 common shares for $2 million, and retained earnings of $600,000. A 10% stock dividend is declared when the fair value per share is $12. Show the before-and-after effects of the dividend on (a) share capital, (b) retained earnings, (c) total shareholders' equity, and (d) the number of shares.

Compare cash dividend, stock dividend, and stock split. **(SO 1) AP**

BE14–3 Indicate whether each of the following transactions would increase (+), decrease (−), or have no effect (NE) on total assets, total liabilities, total shareholders' equity, and the number of shares:

Transaction	Assets	Liabilities	Shareholders' Equity	Number of Shares
(a) Declared a cash dividend.				
(b) Paid the cash dividend declared in part (a).				
(c) Declared a stock dividend.				
(d) Distributed the stock dividend declared in part (c).				
(e) Split stock 2 for 1.				

Record reacquisition of shares. **(SO 2) AP**

BE14–4 On December 31, 2013, Liquorice Treats Limited reported 40,000 common shares issued for a total cost of $250,000. On April 5, 2014, it reacquired 8,000 of these shares. This is the first time Liquorice Treats has reacquired any of its shares. Record the reacquisition of the shares assuming the company paid (a) $45,000 and (b) $60,000 to reacquire the shares.

Calculate average cost per share; record reacquisition. **(SO 2) AP**

BE14–5 On February 7, 2014, Estabrooks Corp. had a balance of $315,000 in its common share account. These shares had been issued as follows:

Date	# of Shares Issued	Cost
March 1, 2012	10,000	$ 50,000
November 8, 2013	15,000	265,000

On February 8, 2014, Estabrooks paid $10,000 to reacquire 1,000 shares. On December 22, 2014, it paid $28,000 to reacquire 2,000 shares. (a) Determine the average cost per share on February 7, 2014. (b) Record the two transactions in which Estabrooks reacquired its shares.

Calculate income tax on continuing and discontinued operations. **(SO 3) AP**

BE14–6 St. Gelais Corporation reported the following pre-tax amounts for the year ended August 31, 2014: profit before income tax (on the company's continuing operations), $320,000; loss from operations of discontinued operations, $85,000; and gain on disposal of assets of discontinued operations, $60,000. St. Gelais is subject to a 20% income tax rate. Calculate (a) the income tax expense on continuing operations, (b) any income tax expense or savings on each item of discontinued operations, and (c) profit.

Prepare an income statement with discontinued operations. **(SO 3) AP**

BE14–7 Refer to the data given for St. Gelais Corporation in BE14–6. Assume that the profit before income tax of $320,000 is from $500,000 of revenue and $180,000 of operating expenses. Prepare an income statement.

Prepare statement of comprehensive income. **(SO 3) AP**

BE14–8 For the year ended December 31, 2014, Jet Set Airlines reported profit of $920,000 and a gain on an equity investment of $66,000, before income tax. This gain is other comprehensive income. Jet Set has a tax rate of 30%. (a) Prepare a statement of comprehensive income. (b) Jet Set had an accumulated other comprehensive loss of $31,550 at January 1, 2014. What amount would it report in the shareholders' equity section of its balance sheet on December 31, 2014?

Record correction of prior period error. **(SO 4) AP**

BE14–9 On March 1, 2014, Broadfoot Bakeries, Inc. discovered an error in its inventory count on December 31, 2013. The error had caused the prior year's cost of goods sold to be overstated by $110,000. The income tax rate is 25%. Prepare the journal entry to correct this error.

Prepare a statement of retained earnings with correction of prior period error. **(SO 4) AP**

BE14–10 Broadfoot Bakeries, Inc. reported retained earnings of $394,000 on December 31, 2013. For the year ended December 31, 2014, the company had profit of $128,000, and it declared and paid dividends of $44,000. Assuming the company reports under ASPE, and referring to the data for Broadfoot Bakeries in BE14–9, prepare a statement of retained earnings.

Complete a statement of changes in shareholders' equity. **(SO 5) AP**

BE14–11 Peninsula Supply Corporation reported the following statement of changes in shareholders' equity for the years ended December 31, 2013 and 2014. Determine the missing amounts.

PENINSULA SUPPLY CORPORATION
Statement of Changes in Shareholders' Equity
Year Ended December 31

	2014		2013	
	Number of Shares	Amount	Number of Shares	Amount
Common shares, unlimited authorized				
Balance, January 1	500,000	$ (b)	500,000	$600,000
Issued shares for cash	50,000	32,500		0
Reacquired shares	(25,000)	(c)		0
Balance, December 31	(a)	603,750	500,000	600,000
Contributed surplus—reacquisition of common shares				
Balance, January 1		15,000		15,000
Reacquired common shares		8,000		0
Balance, December 31		(d)		15,000
Retained earnings				
Balance, January 1		179,500		190,000
Profit (loss)		22,500		(h)
Common dividends—Cash		(e)		(30,000)
Balance, December 31		181,000		179,500
Accumulated other comprehensive income				
Balance, January 1		51,000		(i)
Other comprehensive income (loss)		(f)		(3,000)
Balance, December 31		68,000		51,000
Shareholders' equity, December 31		$ (g)		$ (j)

BE14–12 Refer to the data for Peninsula Supply Corporation presented in BE14–11. (a) Prepare the comprehensive income statement for 2014. (b) Prepare the shareholders' equity section of the balance sheet at December 31, 2014.

Prepare a comprehensive income statement and shareholders' equity section of a balance sheet. **(SO 3, 5) AP**

BE14–13 Monk Corporation had 20,000 common shares on January 1, 2014. On March 1, 5,000 shares were repurchased. On June 1 and September 30, 6,000 and 10,000 shares were issued, respectively. Calculate (a) the number of shares issued at December 31, 2014, and (b) the weighted average number of shares.

Calculate weighted average number of shares. **(SO 6) AP**

BE14–14 Northlake Limited reports profit of $454,000 and its weighted average number of common shares is 220,000. Northlake also has 22,000, $2.50 preferred shares. Calculate earnings per share under each of the following independent assumptions:

(a) preferred shares are cumulative and the dividend was paid.
(b) preferred shares are cumulative and the dividend was not paid.
(c) preferred shares are noncumulative and the dividend was paid.
(d) preferred shares are noncumulative and the dividend was not paid.

Calculate earnings per share. **(SO 6) AP**

BE14–15 Highlink, Inc. reported earnings per share of $4. Its common shares were selling at $24 per share. During the same year, the company paid an $0.80 per share cash dividend. Calculate the price-earnings ratio and the payout ratio.

Calculate price-earnings and payout ratios. **(SO 6) AP**

Exercises

E14–1 Smart Mart Inc. is considering one of three options: (1) paying a $0.40 cash dividend, (2) distributing a 5% stock dividend, or (3) effecting (implementing) a 2-for-1 stock split. The current fair value is $14 per share.

Compare cash dividend, stock dividend, and stock split. **(SO 1) AP**

Instructions

Help Smart Mart decide what to do by completing the following chart (treat each possibility independently):

	Before Action	After Cash Dividend	After Stock Dividend	After Stock Split
Total assets	$1,875,000			
Total liabilities	$ 75,000			
Common shares	1,200,000			
Retained earnings	600,000			
Total shareholders' equity	1,800,000			
Total liabilities and shareholders' equity	$1,875,000			
Number of common shares	60,000			

E14–2 Before preparing financial statements for the current year, the chief accountant for Patel Ltd. discovered the following errors in the accounts:

Prepare correcting entries for dividends and stock split. **(SO 1) AP**

1. Patel has 20,000, $4 noncumulative preferred shares issued. It paid the preferred shareholders the quarterly dividend, and recorded it as a debit to Dividends Expense and a credit to Cash.
2. A 5% stock dividend (1,000 shares) was declared on the common shares when the fair value per share was $12. To record the declaration, Retained Earnings was debited and Dividends Payable was credited. The shares have not been issued yet.
3. The company declared a 2-for-1 stock split on its 20,000, $4 noncumulative preferred shares. The average cost of the preferred shares before the split was $70. The split was recorded as a debit to Retained Earnings of $1.4 million and a credit to Preferred Shares of $1.4 million.
4. After the stock split described in (3) above, the declaration of the quarterly dividend was recorded as a debit to Cash Dividends—Preferred for $40,000 and a credit to Dividends Payable for $40,000.

Instructions

Prepare any correcting entries that are needed.

E14–3 Moosonee Co. Ltd. had the following share transactions during its first year of operations:

Record issue and reacquisition of shares. **(SO 2) AP**

Jan. 6 Issued 200,000 common shares for $1.50 per share.
12 Issued 50,000 common shares for $1.75 per share.

Mar. 17	Issued 1,000 preferred shares for $105 per share.
July 18	Issued 1 million common shares for $2 per share.
Nov. 17	Reacquired 200,000 common shares for $1.95 per share.
Dec. 30	Reacquired 150,000 common shares for $1.80 per share.

Instructions

(a) Journalize the transactions.
(b) How many common shares remain at the end of the year and what is their average cost?

Prepare income statement with discontinued items and statement of comprehensive income. **(SO 3) AP**

E14–4 Top Brands Limited reported the following selected information for the year ended March 31, 2014:

Advertising expense	$ 7,000	Interest expense	$ 5,500
Cash dividends	5,000	Loss on discontinued operations	18,000
Depreciation expense	3,000	Loss on equity investments	3,000
Fees earned	62,000	Rent revenue	34,000
Gain on disposal of equipment	1,500	Retained earnings, April 1, 2013	19,000
Income tax payable	6,600	Training programs expense	8,000

The company's income tax rate is 30%. The company reports gains and losses on its equity investments as other comprehensive income.

Instructions

Prepare income statement and a separate statement of comprehensive income for Top Brands Limited.

Prepare statement of comprehensive income, all-inclusive format, with discontinued operations. **(SO 3) AP**

E14–5 Cherkas Ltd. has profit from continuing operations of $320,000 for the year ended December 31, 2014. It also has the following items (before considering income tax):

1. A net gain of $60,000 from the discontinuance of a component of the entity, which includes a $90,000 profit from the operation of the segment and a $30,000 loss on its disposal
2. Other comprehensive income of a gain on equity investments of $20,000

Assume that the income tax rate on all items is 30%.

Instructions

Prepare a partial statement of comprehensive income, beginning with profit from continuing operations, using the all-inclusive format.

Record correction of prior period error and prepare statement of retained earnings. **(SO 4) AP**

E14–6 On July 9, 2014, Silver Fox Enterprises Inc. discovered it had recorded the $75,000 purchase of land as legal expense on November 8, 2013. The company had reported retained earnings of $573,500 at its previous year end, December 31, 2013.

During 2014, Silver Fox had profit of $193,000 and it declared and paid cash dividends of $216,000. Silver Fox has a 25% income tax rate.

Instructions

(a) Prepare the journal entry to correct the error.
(b) Assuming the company reports under ASPE, prepare a statement of retained earnings.
(c) If Silver Fox uses IFRS, what are the differences in how it would present this information?

Prepare a statement of retained earnings with correction of prior period error. **(SO 1, 2, 3, 4) AP**

E14–7 On January 1, 2014, Fyre Lite Corporation had retained earnings of $650,000. During the year, Fyre Lite had the following selected transactions:

1. Declared and paid cash dividends, $245,000.
2. Earned profit before income tax, $750,000.
3. Corrected a prior period error of $85,000, before income tax, which resulted in an understatement of profit in 2013.
4. Reacquired 25,000 common shares for $50,000 more than the original issue price. This was the first time the company had ever reacquired its own shares.
5. Completed a 3-for-1 stock split of the common shares.

Fyre Lite has a 25% income tax rate and reports under ASPE.

Instructions

(a) Prepare a statement of retained earnings for the year ended December 31, 2014.
(b) If any of the above items are not included in this statement, indicate their presentation.

Indicate effects of transactions on shareholders' equity. **(SO 1, 4, 5) AP**

E14–8 Kettle Creek Corporation had the following transactions and events:

1. Declared a cash dividend.
2. Paid the cash dividend declared in (1).

3. Issued common shares for cash.
4. Completed a 2-for-1 stock split of the common shares.
5. Declared a stock dividend on the common shares.
6. Distributed the stock dividend declared in (5).
7. Made a correction of a prior period error for an understatement of profit.
8. Adopted a new accounting policy that resulted in the recording of a gain on a long-lived asset revaluation.
9. Repurchased common shares for less than their initial issue price.
10. Comprehensive income included profit and a gain on equity investments reported as other comprehensive income.

Instructions

Indicate the effect(s) of each of the above items on the subdivisions of shareholders' equity. Present your answer in tabular form with the following columns. Use "I" for increase, "D" for decrease, and "NE" for no effect. Item 1 is given as an example.

	Contributed Capital		Retained	Accumulated Other	
Item	Share Capital	Additional	Earnings	Comprehensive Income	Total Shareholders' Equity
1.	NE	NE	D	NE	D

E14–9 On January 1, 2014, Hewitt Corporation had an unlimited number of common shares authorized, and 120,000 of them issued for $1.2 million. It also had retained earnings of $750,000 and accumulated other comprehensive income of $17,000. During the year, the following occurred:

Prepare statement of comprehensive income and statement of changes in shareholders' equity. **(SO 1, 3, 5) AP**

1. Issued 60,000 common shares at $15 per share on July 1.
2. Declared a 3-for-2 stock split on September 30 when the fair value was $19 per share.
3. Declared a 5% stock dividend on December 9 to common shareholders of record at December 30, distributable on January 16, 2015. At the declaration date, the fair value of the common shares was $22 per share.
4. Earned profit of $390,000 for the year.
5. Loss on equity investments reported as other comprehensive income was $48,000 before income tax. The company's income tax rate is 35%.

Instructions

(a) Prepare a statement of comprehensive income starting with profit.
(b) Prepare a statement of changes in shareholders' equity.

E14–10 Ruby Red Rental Corporation had the following balances in its shareholders' equity accounts at January 1, 2014:

Prepare statement of changes in shareholders' equity. **(SO 2, 3, 5) AP**

Accumulated other comprehensive income (loss)	$ (25,000)
Contributed Surplus—Reacquisition of Common Shares	540,000
Retained earnings	1,500,000
Common shares (32,000 shares)	800,000

Ruby Red had the following transactions and events during 2014:

Feb. 2	Repurchased 1,000 shares for $44,500.
Apr. 17	Declared and paid cash dividends of $70,000.
Oct. 29	Issued 2,000 shares for $104,000.
Dec. 31	Reported comprehensive income of $425,000, which included other comprehensive income of $40,000.

Instructions

Prepare a statement of changes in shareholders' equity at December 31, 2014.

E14–11 Schmidt Limited reported profit of $465,325 for its November 30, 2014, year end. Cash dividends of $90,000 on the common shares and of $65,000 on the noncumulative preferred shares were declared and paid during the year. The following information is available regarding Schmidt's common shares:

Calculate earnings per share. **(SO 6) AP**

Dec. 1, 2013	The opening number of common shares was 60,000.
Feb. 28, 2014	Sold 10,000 common shares for $200,000 cash.
May 31, 2014	Reacquired 5,000 common shares for $90,000 cash.
Nov. 1, 2014	Issued 15,000 common shares in exchange for land with a fair value of $310,000.

Instructions

(a) Calculate the profit available for the common shareholders.
(b) Calculate the weighted average number of common shares for the year.
(c) Calculate earnings per share for the year.
(d) Calculate earnings per share if no dividends had been declared and paid during the year.

Calculate earnings per share. **(SO 6) AP**

E14–12 On December 31, 2013, Shankman Corporation has 3,000, $4 preferred shares and 100,000 common shares. During the year, the company had the following share transactions:

Jan. 1	Sold 1,000 preferred shares for cash.
Mar. 31	Sold 12,000 common shares for cash.
June 1	Reacquired 14,000 common shares for cash.
Dec. 1	Sold 24,000 common shares for cash.

Shankman's profit in 2014 is $478,000.

Instructions

(a) Calculate the weighted average number of common shares for the year.
(b) Calculate earnings per share under each of the following four independent assumptions:
   1. Assume that the preferred shares are cumulative and that the dividend to the preferred shareholders was (i) declared, and (ii) not declared.
   2. Assume that the preferred shares are noncumulative and that the dividend to the preferred shareholders was (i) declared, and (ii) not declared.

Calculate ratios and comment. **(SO 6) AP**

E14–13 The following financial information is available for First Interprovincial Bank as at October 31 (in thousands, except for per share amounts):

	2014	2013	2012
Profit	$1,978	$2,131	$2,663
Preferred share dividends (total)	$73	$43	$30
Weighted average number of common shares	502	500	501
Dividends per common share	$2.50	$2.25	$2.10
Market price per common share	$43.00	$49.75	$56.25

Instructions

(a) Calculate the earnings per share, price-earnings ratio, and payout ratio for the common shareholders for each of the three years.
(b) Using the information in part (a), comment on First Interprovincial Bank's earnings performance and dividend record.

Problems: Set A

Compare impact of cash dividend, stock dividend, and stock split. **(SO 1) AP**

P14–1A The condensed balance sheet of Laporte Corporation reports the following:

LAPORTE CORPORATION
Balance Sheet (partial)
June 30, 2014

Total assets		$12,000,000
Liabilities and shareholders' equity		
Total liabilities		$ 4,000,000
Shareholders' equity		
Common shares, unlimited number authorized, 400,000 issued	2,000,000	
Retained earnings	6,000,000	
Total shareholders' equity		8,000,000
Total liabilities and shareholders' equity		$12,000,000

The market price of the common shares is currently $30 per share. Laporte wants to assess the impact of three possible alternatives on the corporation and its shareholders. The alternatives are:

1. Payment of a $1.50 per share cash dividend
2. Distribution of a 5% stock dividend
3. A 3-for-2 stock split

Instructions

(a) For each alternative, determine the impact on (1) assets, (2) liabilities, (3) common shares, (4) retained earnings, (5) total shareholders' equity, and (6) the number of shares.

(b) Assume a Laporte shareholder currently owns 1,000 common shares at a cost of $28,000. What is the impact of each alternative for the shareholder, assuming that the shares' market price changes proportionately with each of them?

TAKING IT FURTHER What are the advantages and disadvantages to the company of a stock split?

P14–2A On December 31, 2013, LeBlanc Corporation had the following shareholders' equity accounts:

Record and post transactions; prepare shareholders' equity section. **(SO 1, 2) AP**

LEBLANC CORPORATION Balance Sheet (partial) December 31, 2013	
Shareholders' equity	
Common shares (unlimited number of shares authorized, 90,000 issued)	$1,100,000
Retained earnings	540,000
Total shareholders' equity	$1,640,000

During the year, the following transactions occurred:

Jan. 15	Declared a $1 per share cash dividend to shareholders of record on January 31, payable February 15.
July 1	Announced a 3-for-2 stock split. The market price per share on the date of the announcement was $15.
Dec. 15	Declared a 10% stock dividend to shareholders of record on December 30, distributable on January 15. On December 15, the market price of each share was $10; on December 30, $12; and on January 15, $11.
31	Determined that profit before income tax for the year was $450,000. The company has a 30% income tax rate.

Instructions

(a) Journalize the transactions and closing entries.

(b) Enter the beginning balances and post the entries in part (a) to the shareholders' equity accounts. (*Note*: Open additional shareholders' equity accounts as needed.)

(c) Prepare the shareholders' equity section of the balance sheet at December 31, 2014.

TAKING IT FURTHER Stock splits and stock dividends do not change the company's total assets. Given that, why does share price change after a stock split or stock dividend?

P14–3A Advanced Technologies Inc. reported the following information related to its shareholders' equity on January 1:

Determine impact of reacquired shares. **(SO 2) AP**

Common shares, 1,000,000 authorized, 500,000 shares issued	$1,500,000
Contributed surplus—reacquisition of common shares	15,000
Retained earnings	720,000

During the year, the following transactions related to common shares occurred in the order listed:

1. Issued 35,000 shares at $4.20 per share.
2. Reacquired 10,000 shares at $3.00 per share.
3. Issued 5,000 shares at $4.50 per share.
4. Reacquired 18,000 shares at $4 per share.
5. Reacquired 75,000 shares at $3 per share.

Instructions

(a) Calculate the number of shares authorized and issued at the end of the year.
(b) Determine the ending balances in each of the following accounts: Common Shares; Contributed Surplus—Reacquisition of Common Shares; and Retained Earnings.

TAKING IT FURTHER Why is it important to report the number of shares issued? The number authorized?

Record stock dividends, splits, and reacquisition of shares. Show impact of transactions on accounts. **(SO 1, 2) AP**

P14–4A The following shareholders' equity accounts are reported by Branch Inc. on January 1:

Common shares (unlimited authorized, 150,000 issued)	$2,400,000
Preferred shares ($4 cumulative, convertible, 100,000 authorized, 5,000 issued)	375,000
Contributed surplus—reacquisition of common shares	30,000
Retained earnings	1,275,000

The following selected transactions occurred during the year:

Feb. 11	Issued 50,000 common shares at $20 per share.
Mar. 2	Reacquired 20,000 common shares at $22 per share.
May 3	Shareholders converted 1,000 preferred shares into 4,000 common shares. The fair value per preferred share was $80; per common share, $24.
June 14	Split the common shares 2-for-1 when the common shares were trading at $30 per share.
July 25	Reacquired 500 preferred shares at $70 per share.
Sept. 16	Reacquired 50,000 common shares for $17 per share.
Oct. 27	Declared a 5% common stock dividend distributable on December 13 to shareholders of record on November 24. The fair value of the common shares on October 27 was $19 per share.
Dec. 13	Distributed the stock dividend declared on October 27. The fair value of the common shares on December 13 was $21 per share.

Instructions

(a) Prepare a chart that shows for each class of shares (1) number of shares issued, (2) total cost, and (3) average cost per share. Enter the January 1 data into the chart.
(b) Prepare journal entries for the transactions. Update the chart in part (a) as required for the transactions. After each transaction, determine the number issued, total cost, and average cost per share.
(c) Show how each class of shares will be presented in the shareholders' equity section of the balance sheet at December 31.

TAKING IT FURTHER Provide possible reasons why Branch Inc. split the common shares and issued a stock dividend.

Prepare income statement with EPS and statement of comprehensive income. **(SO 3, 6) AP**

P14–5A The ledger of Port Hope Corporation at November 30, 2014, contains the following summary data:

Cash dividends—common	$ 65,000
Cash dividends—preferred	25,000
Common shares	325,000
Cost of goods sold	7,280,000
Depreciation expense	355,000
Net sales	9,124,000
Operating expenses	1,120,000
Other comprehensive loss (before income tax)	83,000
Other revenues	48,000
Preferred shares ($5 noncumulative)	400,000
Retained earnings, December 1, 2013	755,000

Your analysis reveals the following additional information:

1. The company has a 25% income tax rate.
2. The communications devices division was discontinued on August 31. The profit from operations for the division up to that day was $20,000 before income tax. The division was sold at a loss of $75,000 before income tax.
3. There were 200,000 common and 5,000 preferred shares issued on December 1, 2013, with no changes during the year.

Instructions

(a) Prepare a multiple-step income statement for the year including EPS.
(b) Prepare a statement of comprehensive income as a separate statement.

TAKING IT FURTHER Why are gains and losses from discontinued operations reported separately from continuing operations?

P14–6A The ledger of Hammond Limited at October 31, 2014, contains the following summary data:

Correct error from prior period; prepare statement of comprehensive income—all-inclusive format; show presentation of retained earnings. **(SO 2, 3, 4) AP**

Cash dividends—common	$ 120,000
Common shares	650,000
Depreciation expense	87,000
Fees earned	1,476,000
Operating expenses	929,000
Other comprehensive gain (before income tax)	48,000
Interest expense	54,000
Retained earnings, November 1, 2013	575,000

Your analysis reveals the following additional information:

1. The company has a 25% income tax rate.
2. On March 19, 2014, Hammond discovered an error made in the previous fiscal year. A $57,000 payment of a note payable had been recorded as interest expense.
3. On April 10, 2014, common shares costing $75,000 were reacquired for $97,500. This is the first time the company has reacquired common shares.

Instructions

(a) Prepare a journal entry to correct the prior period error.
(b) Prepare a comprehensive income statement on an all-inclusive basis.
(c) Illustrate how the changes in retained earnings will be shown in the financial statements.

TAKING IT FURTHER If an error from a previous period is found and corrected, why is it also important to restate the prior years' data shown for comparative purposes?

P14–7A The post-closing trial balance of Jeyakumar Corporation at December 31, 2014, contains the following shareholders' equity accounts:

Record and post transactions; prepare a statement of changes in shareholders' equity. **(SO 2, 4, 5) AP**

$5 noncumulative preferred shares (10,000 issued)	$1,100,000
Common shares (400,000 issued)	2,000,000
Retained earnings	3,146,000

A review of the accounting records reveals the following:

1. The January 1, 2014, balance in Common Shares was $1,280,000 (320,000 shares), the balance in Contributed Surplus—Reacquisition of Common Shares was $30,000, and the balance in Retained Earnings was $2,443,500.
2. One of the company's shareholders needed cash for a personal expenditure. On January 15, the company agreed to reacquire 20,000 shares from this shareholder for $7 per share.
3. On July 1, the company corrected a prior period error that resulted in an increase to the Long-Term Investments account, as well as to the prior year's profit of $250,000 before income tax.
4. On October 1, 100,000 common shares were sold for $8 per share.
5. The preferred shareholders' dividend was declared and paid in 2014 for two quarters. Due to a cash shortage, the last two quarters' dividends were not paid.
6. Profit for the year before income tax was $760,000. The company has a 25% income tax rate.

Instructions

(a) Open general ledger accounts for the shareholders' equity accounts listed in (1) above and enter opening balances.
(b) Prepare journal entries to record transactions (2) to (5) and post to general ledger accounts.
(c) Prepare entries to close dividends and the Income Summary account and post.

(d) Prepare a statement of changes in shareholders' equity for the year.
(e) Compare the balances in the general ledger accounts with the closing balances on the statement of changes in shareholders' equity.

TAKING IT FURTHER Why is the prior period adjustment for the error in a prior year's profit recorded in the Retained Earnings account instead of being a correction to profit in the 2014 financial statements?

Record and post transactions; prepare financial statements. **(SO 1, 2, 3, 4, 5) AP**

P14–8A The shareholders' equity accounts of Cedeno Inc. at December 31, 2013, are as follows:

Common shares (unlimited number of shares authorized, 1,000,000 issued)	$3,000,000
Stock dividends distributable	400,000
Contributed surplus—reacquired common shares	5,000
Retained earnings	1,200,000

Cedeno has a 30% income tax rate. During 2014, the following transactions and events occurred:

Jan. 20 Issued 100,000 common shares as a result of a 10% stock dividend declared on December 15, 2013. The shares' fair value was $4 on December 15 and $5 on January 20.
Feb. 12 Issued 50,000 common shares for $5 per share.
Mar. 31 Corrected an error in the December 31, 2013, inventory that had overstated the cost of goods sold for 2013 by $60,000.
Nov. 2 Reacquired 25,000 shares for $2.50 each.
Dec. 31 Declared a cash dividend to the common shareholders of $0.50 per share to shareholders of record at January 15, payable January 31.
31 Determined that profit was $280,000.
31 Determined that other comprehensive loss was $28,000 before income tax.

Instructions
(a) Journalize the transactions and summary closing entries.
(b) Enter the beginning balances and post the entries in part (a) to the shareholders' equity accounts. (*Note*: Open additional shareholders' equity accounts as needed.)
(c) Prepare a statement of comprehensive income beginning with profit.
(d) Prepare a statement of changes in shareholders' equity.
(e) Prepare the shareholders' equity section of the balance sheet at December 31, 2014.

TAKING IT FURTHER Explain the two methods of preparing a statement of comprehensive income. Is one method better than the other?

Prepare a statement of changes in shareholders' equity. **(SO 5) AP**

P14–9A The shareholders' equity accounts of Tsui, Inc. at December 31, 2013, are as follows:

Preferred shares, $3 noncumulative, unlimited number authorized, 4,000 issued	$400,000
Common shares, unlimited number authorized, 160,000 issued	800,000
Retained earnings	450,000
Accumulated other comprehensive loss	(50,000)

Tsui has a 35% income tax rate. During the following fiscal year, ended December 31, 2014, the company had the following transactions and events:

Feb. 1 Discovered a $70,000 understatement of 2013 cost of goods sold.
July 12 Announced a 2-for-1 preferred stock split. The market price of the preferred shares at the date of announcement was $150.
Oct. 1 Adopted a new accounting policy that resulted in a cumulative decrease to prior years' profit of $30,000 before income tax.
Dec. 1 Declared a 10% stock dividend to common shareholders of record at December 20, distributable on January 12. The fair value of the common shares was $12 per share.
18 Declared the annual cash dividend ($1.50 post-split) to the preferred shareholders of record on January 10, 2015, payable on January 31, 2015.
31 Determined that for 2014, profit before income tax was $350,000 and other comprehensive income, net of income tax expense of $35,000, was $65,000.

Instructions

Prepare a statement of changes in shareholders' equity for the year ended December 31, 2014.

TAKING IT FURTHER How does comprehensive income impact the shareholders' equity in the balance sheet? Is this the same for companies following ASPE?

P14–10A The shareholders' equity accounts of Blue Bay Logistics Ltd. on April 1, 2013, the beginning of the fiscal year, are as follows:

Calculate earnings per share. **(SO 6) AP**

$6 preferred shares (20,000 issued)	$1,800,000
Common shares (500,000 issued)	3,750,000
Retained earnings	1,550,000
Total shareholders' equity	$7,100,000

During the year, the following transactions occurred:

2013	
June 1	Reacquired 12,000 common shares for $9 per share.
July 1	Issued 50,000 common shares for $10 per share.
Sept. 30	Reacquired 8,000 common shares for $9.50 per share.

2014	
Jan. 31	Issued 60,000 common shares in exchange for land. The land's fair value was $600,000.
Mar. 31	Profit for the year ended March 31, 2014, was $973,600.

Instructions

(a) Calculate the weighted average number of common shares for the year.

(b) Assuming the preferred shares are cumulative and one year in arrears:
  1. Calculate the earnings per share if no preferred dividends are declared during the year.
  2. Calculate the earnings per share if the preferred share dividends for the current and prior year are declared during the year.

(c) Assuming the preferred shares are noncumulative:
  1. Calculate the earnings per share if no preferred share dividends are declared during the year.
  2. Calculate the earnings per share if the company declares a preferred share dividend of $80,000.

TAKING IT FURTHER Why is earnings per share an important measure for common shareholders but not for preferred shareholders?

P14–11A The following financial information (in millions except for market price per share) is for two major corporations for the three fiscal years ended December 31 as follows:

Calculate ratios and comment. **(SO 6) AN**

Canadian Pacific Railway Limited	2011	2010	2009
Weighted average number of common shares	169.5	168.8	166.3
Profit	$ 570	$ 651	$ 550
Dividends	$ 198	$ 179	$ 166
Market price per share (December 31)	$67.67	$64.81	$54.00
Canadian National Railway Company	2011	2010	2009
Weighted average number of common shares	451.1	466.3	469.2
Profit	$2,457	$2,104	$1,854
Dividends	$ 585	$ 503	$ 474
Market price per share (December 31)	$78.56	$66.47	$54.36

Neither company has preferred shares issued.

Instructions

(a) Calculate earnings per share and the price-earnings and dividend payout ratios for each company for 2011, 2010, and 2009. Comment on whether their ratios have improved or deteriorated.

(b) Compare Canadian Pacific's ratios with Canadian National's.

TAKING IT FURTHER Why is the presentation of fully diluted earnings per share required under IFRS, given that it is a *hypothetical* number?

Calculate and evaluate ratios with discontinued operations. **(SO 4, 6) AP**

P14–12A Highlander Inc. reported the following selected information for the last three years (in millions, except for per share amounts):

	2014	2013	2012
Net sales	$4,000	$3,100	$2,600
Average shareholders' equity	3,400	2,400	1,800
Preferred dividends	20	20	15
Profit from continuing operations	$1,160	$ 810	$ 570
Loss on disposal of discontinued operations	340		
Loss from discontinued operations	110	80	70
Profit	$ 710	$ 730	$ 500
Weighted average number of common shares	300	290	280
Market price per share	$45.50	$33.65	$44.80

Instructions

(a) Calculate Highlander's return on equity, earnings per share, and price-earnings ratios before and after discontinued operations for 2014, 2013, and 2012.

(b) Evaluate Highlander's performance over the last three years before and after discontinued operations.

(c) Explain how reporting discontinued operations separately would affect your analysis of Highlander's performance.

TAKING IT FURTHER Why is it important that discontinued operations be reported separately only if the operations qualify as a *component of an entity*?

CONTINUING COOKIE CHRONICLE

(*Note:* This is a continuation of the Cookie Chronicle from Chapters 1 through 13.)

Natalie is planning on completing college in April 2015. In the meantime, she tries to spend approximately 20 hours a week at Koebel's Family Bakery. She is developing an understanding of all of the business operations so she can step into her new position as administrator on May 1, 2015. There are challenges every day when operating a business and she is thrilled to be a part of the process. Janet and Brian are also thrilled to have Natalie on board and believe that Natalie's input has been instrumental in helping make some of their critical business decisions.

To ensure that Natalie does not consider other business opportunities and leave the bakery, Janet and Brian would like to provide Natalie with a greater ownership interest in Koebel's Family Bakery Ltd. An alternative that is being discussed is the buyback of shares by Koebel's Family Bakery from Janet and Brian to enable Natalie to hold a one-third ownership interest in the bakery without having to purchase additional shares.

Recall that on August 1, 2014, Natalie purchased 10 shares of Koebel's Family Bakery Ltd. for $1,200 per share and that Brian and Janet each own 100 of the remaining 200 shares.

The shareholders' equity accounts of Koebel's Family Bakery Ltd. are as follows:

Common shares	$ 12,200
Retained earnings	241,026

Janet and Brian are thinking that it might be best for all three of them to each own 10 shares of Koebel's Family Bakery Ltd. They are confused, however, about the process of shares being reacquired and have come to you with the following questions:

1. If Koebel's Family Bakery Ltd. reacquires the common shares we hold, how will a fair value for each common share reacquired be determined?
2. Natalie has recently purchased shares in Koebel's Family Bakery Ltd. for $1,200 per share. Is this amount a fair value to use as a purchase price for reacquisition of the shares? Why or why not?
3. How much cash will Koebel's Family Bakery Ltd. need to reacquire the shares that we hold if we assume a price of $1,200 per share?
4. Last year the bakery paid total dividends of $85,000. If our shares are reacquired, will Koebel's Family Bakery Ltd. be able to pay a dividend next year? Do you think there will be enough in retained earnings to pay a dividend? Will the amount of the dividend we each receive change once Natalie owns a one-third interest in the company?
5. If we choose not to have the company reacquire our shares, then how can we ensure that Natalie stays on with us?

Instructions

(a) Answer Janet and Brian's questions.
(b) Prepare the journal entry to record the reacquisition of shares by Koebel's Family Bakery Ltd. from Janet and Brian assuming that $1,200 per share is a fair value.
(c) Calculate the amount of share capital after the shares have been reacquired from Janet and Brian and the average cost per share.

BROADENING YOUR PERSPECTIVE CHAPTER 14

Collaborative Learning Activity

Note to instructor: Additional instructions and material for this group activity can be found on the Instructor Resource Site and in *WileyPLUS*.

BYP14–1 In this group activity, you will complete a statement of changes in shareholders' equity and recreate the journal entries underlying those changes through your analysis of the incomplete information given.

Communication Activity

BYP14–2 Earnings per share is the most commonly cited financial ratio. Indeed, share prices rise and fall in reaction to a company's earnings per share. The price-earnings ratio is also published in many newspapers' stock market listings.

Instructions

Write a memo explaining why earnings per share and the price-earnings ratio are so important to investors. Explain how both ratios are calculated and how they relate to each other. Include in your memo an explanation of how to interpret a high or low price-earnings ratio. Also comment on why you think earnings per share is not required to be reported under ASPE.

Ethics Case

BYP14–3 Flambeau Corporation has paid 40 consecutive quarterly cash dividends (10 years' worth). Increasing competition over the last six months has greatly squeezed profit margins. With only enough cash to meet day-to-day operating needs, the president, Vince Ramsey, has decided that a stock dividend instead of a cash dividend should be declared. He tells Flambeau's Vice-President of Finance, Janice Rahn, to issue a press release stating that the company is extending its consecutive dividend record with the issue of a 5% stock dividend. "Write the press release to convince the shareholders that the stock dividend is just as good as a cash dividend," Ramsey orders. "Just watch our share price rise when we announce the stock dividend. It must be a good thing if that happens."

Instructions

(a) Who are the stakeholders in this situation?
(b) Is there anything unethical about Ramsey's intentions or actions?
(c) As a shareholder, would you rather receive a cash dividend or a stock dividend? Why?

All About You: Personal Financial Literacy Activity

BYP14–4 In the "All About You" feature, we learned about investing in shares of a company. You have recently inherited $10,000 and you are considering investing in **Canadian Tire Corporation, Limited's** common shares and you want to learn more about the company. You get a copy of the company's 2011 annual report. In it, you see that Canadian Tire has four main business lines: Canadian Tire retail (its retail stores and gas bars), Financial Services (which offers its branded credit cards), Mark's (the clothing chain), and FGL Sports (which sells sporting goods through stores such as Sport Chek and Sports Experts).

Instructions

(a) How might information on Canadian Tire Corporation's four main business lines help you with your decision in whether to buy shares in the company?
(b) The company declared cash dividends per share of $1.125 in 2011 and $0.905 in 2010. How might this information be helpful with your investment decision?
(c) Canadian Tire's basic earnings per share at December 31, 2011, was $5.73. Its share price was $65.90 on December 30, 2011. Calculate Canadian Tire's price-earnings ratio at December 31, 2011. Can you compare Canadian Tire's PE ratio with that of similar Canadian companies you might want to invest in? Explain your answer.

ANSWERS TO CHAPTER QUESTIONS

ANSWERS TO ACCOUNTING IN ACTION INSIGHT QUESTIONS

Across the Organization, p. 589

Q: If a company announces a reverse stock split, is this considered a positive or negative sign about the future of the company?

A: Although a company declares a reverse stock split because its share price is unacceptably low—and that happens when a company is not doing well—the reverse split doesn't change whether or not the company can improve its performance in the future. A reverse stock split, similar to a normal stock split, doesn't change anything about the company, because the total value of the company remains the same. Therefore, it can be argued that a reverse split shouldn't be considered either positive or negative.

All About You Insight, p. 605

Q: If you were thinking of investing in a company, where might you find information about the company's dividend policy, its profitability, and its share price?

A: The company website will usually provide the company's annual report, which includes information about the company's performance and future plans in the Management Discussion and Analysis. As well, the annual report will include the financial statements, which provide information about the company's profitability and dividend policy. Some company websites also provide information on the share price. Another source is System for Electronic Document Analysis and Retrieval (SEDAR), an official repository of public company reports that are filed with the Canadian Securities Administrators. Investors can also subscribe to services to obtain financial research reports on companies.

ANSWERS TO SELF-STUDY QUESTIONS

1. d 2. a 3. c 4. b 5. d 6. c 7. c 8. d 9. c 10. c

Remember to go back to the beginning of the chapter to check off your completed work!

←

CHAPTER 15 NON-CURRENT LIABILITIES

THE NAVIGATOR

- ☐ Understand *Concepts for Review*
- ☐ Read *Feature Story*
- ☐ Scan *Study Objectives*
- ☐ Read *Chapter Preview*
- ☐ Read text and answer *Before You Go On*
- ☐ Compare *IFRS and ASPE*
- ☐ Work *Demonstration Problems*
- ☐ Review *Summary of Study Objectives*
- ☐ Answer *Self-Study Questions*
- ☐ Complete assignments

CONCEPTS FOR REVIEW

Before studying this chapter, you should understand or, if necessary, review:

A. How to record adjusting entries for interest expense. (Ch. 3, pp. 108–109)

B. What a current liability is, and what a non-current liability is. (Ch. 4, pp. 188–189 and Ch. 10, pp. 434–436)

C. How to record entries for the issue of notes payable and related interest expense. (Ch. 10, pp. 435–436)

D. The fundamental qualitative characteristic of faithful representation. (Ch. 11, pp. 464–465)

E. How to calculate return on equity and earnings per share. (Ch. 13, pp. 564–565 and Ch. 14, pp. 602–603)

DEBT ISSUE INJECTS POWER INTO ELECTRIC COMPANY

MONTREAL, QC—Hydro-Québec generates, transmits, and distributes electricity for residents and businesses throughout the province of Quebec. This requires developing hydroelectric power to meet growing demand. The company conducts energy-related research and develops new generation, transmission, and distribution technologies. Its projects may include building hydroelectric facilities, refurbishing generating stations, adding transmission capacity, connecting communities to the grid, expanding energy interchanges with Ontario, the Atlantic Provinces, and the U.S. Northeast, or purchasing wind power from independent producers.

This type of development obviously requires a significant amount of capital. As Hydro-Québec's sole shareholder, the Quebec government guarantees most of its borrowings, which can be quite substantial.

The company raises funds by issuing bonds. For example, one issue was launched in July 2012 for $500 million. This debenture, which will mature on February 15, 2050, was issued at a premium price; that is, a price that is above its face value. The coupon rate was 5%, but the yield rate was 3.444%. Having a yield rate that is less than the coupon rate reduces the cost of borrowing for the company since the net proceeds will be slightly more than $500 million for each issue.

Hydro-Québec's decision to take on this long-term debt is simply "a question of cost," says Jean-Hugues Lafleur, Vice President, Financing, Treasury and Pension Fund. "[To have a rate] below 4% is a good opportunity to finance the company . . . Considering that inflation on a long-term basis is around 2% and being able to finance the company at below 4%, the real cost of the interest rate is something like 2%."

The funds will be used for Hydro-Québec's investment program and the refinancing of debt. "Our company has very long-term assets, so it just makes sense in terms of asset-liability management to issue long-term paper," Mr. Lafleur continues. "Most of our investment program is to build long-term facilities such as dams or generating stations. The depreciation periods for these assets can go up to 100 years."

For the last decade, Hydro-Québec's annual financing needs have been approximately $2.5 billion on average and have been met mainly on the Canadian market. Part of the company's financing and debt management strategy is to stagger debt maturities to maintain the stability of the annual financing program. Recent bond issues are added to others issued in previous years, all maturing on different dates. They are reported on the financial statements as liabilities and will be amortized over the duration of the debt at the yield to maturity rate, not the coupon rate.

The electricity company's investment and financing strategy has been effective. Credit rating agencies such as Moody's and Standard & Poor's all give Hydro-Québec an A rating or better.

The lead manager for Hydro-Québec's bond issue was National Bank Financial Inc., with RBC Dominion Securities Inc. and Scotia Capital Inc. acting as co-lead managers, and BMO Nesbitt Burns Inc., Casgrain & Company Limited, CIBC World Markets Inc., Desjardins Securities Inc., Laurentian Bank Securities Inc., and the Toronto Dominion Bank acting as other managers. With that type of backing, coupled with its success in debt management and research and investment, the Quebec utility will no doubt be able to continue to finance itself easily on the bond markets.

THE NAVIGATOR

STUDY OBJECTIVES

After studying this chapter, you should be able to:

1. Compare the impact of issuing debt instead of equity.
2. Account for bonds payable.
3. Account for instalment notes payable.
4. Explain and illustrate the methods for the presentation and analysis of non-current liabilities.

THE NAVIGATOR

PREVIEW OF CHAPTER FIFTEEN

As you can see from the feature story, Hydro-Québec borrowed $500 million in July 2012 by issuing bonds. The bonds will mature on February 15, 2050, and the funds borrowed will be used to finance non-current assets such as dams or generating stations. The bonds are classified as non-current liabilities because they are obligations that are not due within the next year. In this chapter, we will explain the accounting for the major types of non-current liabilities reported on the balance sheet. These liabilities include bonds and instalment notes.

The chapter is organized as follows:

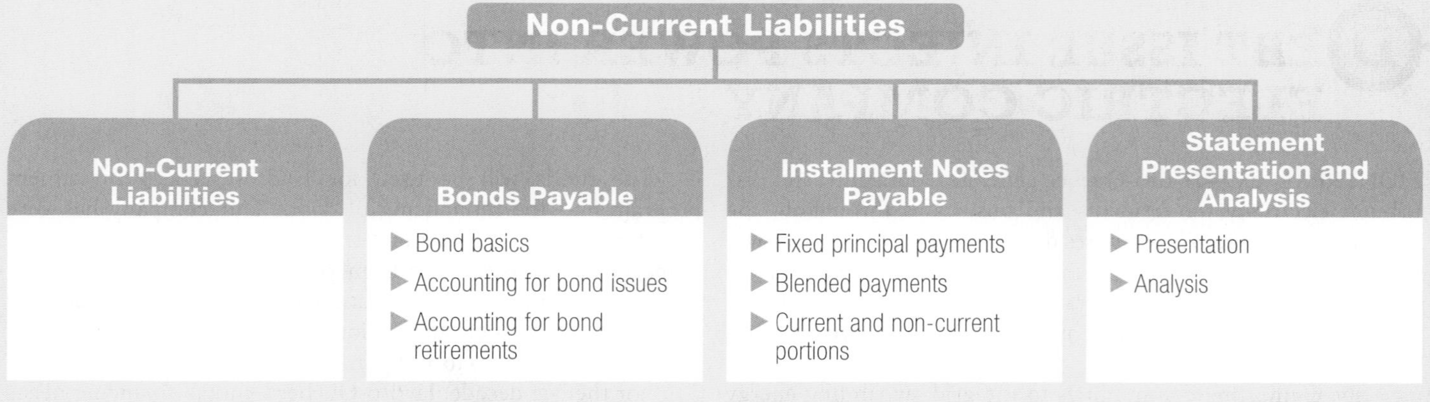

THE NAVIGATOR

NON-CURRENT LIABILITIES

STUDY OBJECTIVE 1
Compare the impact of issuing debt instead of equity.

You will recall from Chapter 10 that a current liability is an obligation (debt) that is expected to be settled (paid) within one year from the balance sheet date or during the company's normal operating cycle, whichever is longer. Debt that is not current is a **non-current liability**. Common examples of non-current liabilities include bonds payable and instalment notes payable. More specifically, non-current liabilities such as these are examples of financial instruments and are referred to as *financial liabilities* because there is a contract between two or more parties to pay cash in the future.

Alternative terminology
Non-current liabilities are also referred to as *long-term liabilities.*

Just as people need money for long periods of time, so do companies. Sometimes, large corporations need much more money than the average bank can lend for certain types of projects, such as purchasing another company or constructing dams and generating stations as Hydro-Québec does. The solution is to raise money by issuing debt securities (such as bonds payable) or equity securities (such as common shares) to the investing public. In this way, thousands of investors each lend part of the capital that is needed. By issuing bonds, Hydro-Québec was able to raise $500 million in July 2012.

Whenever a company decides that it needs long-term financing, it must first decide if it should issue debt or equity. For a corporation that wants long-term financing, debt offers some advantages over equity, as shown in Illustration 15-1.

ILLUSTRATION 15-1
Advantages of debt over equity financing

	1. Shareholder control is not affected. Debt holders (lenders) do not have voting rights, so the existing common shareholders keep full control of the company.
	2. Income tax savings result. Interest expense is deductible for income tax purposes. Dividends are not.
	3. Earnings per share may be higher. Although interest expense reduces profit, earnings per share is often higher under debt financing because no additional common shares are issued.
	4. Return on equity may be higher. Although profit is lower, return on equity is often higher under debt financing because shareholders' equity is proportionately lower than profit.

To show the potential effect on earnings per share and return on equity, assume that Microsystems Inc. has 100,000 common shares and shareholders' equity of $2.5 million and is considering two plans for financing the construction of a new $5-million plant. Plan A is to use equity by issuing 200,000 common shares for $25 per share. Plan B is to use debt by issuing $5 million of 4% bonds payable. Once the new plant is built, Microsystems expects to earn an additional $1.5 million of profit before interest and income tax. The income tax rate is expected to be 30%.

The effects on earnings per share and return on equity for each plan are shown in Illustration 15-2.

ILLUSTRATION 15-2
Comparison of effects of issuing equity versus debt

	Plan A: Issue Equity	Plan B: Issue Debt
Profit before interest and income tax	$1,500,000	$1,500,000
Interest expense	0	200,000[6]
Profit before income tax	1,500,000	1,300,000
Income tax expense	450,000[1]	390,000[7]
Profit	$1,050,000	$ 910,000
Number of shares	300,000[2]	100,000
Earnings per share	**$3.50[3]**	**$9.10[8]**
Shareholders' equity	$8,550,000[4]	$3,410,000[9]
Return on equity	**12%[5]**	**27%[10]**

Calculations:

[1] 30% × $1,500,000 = $450,000
[2] 100,000 + 200,000 = 300,000
[3] $1,050,000 ÷ 300,000 = $3.50
[4] $2,500,000 + ($25 × 200,000) + $1,050,000 = $8,550,000
[5] $1,050,000 ÷ $8,550,000 = 12%

[6] $5,000,000 × 4% = $200,000
[7] 30% × $1,300,000 = $390,000
[8] $910,000 ÷ 100,000 = $9.10
[9] $2,500,000 + $910,000 = $3,410,000
[10] $910,000 ÷ $3,410,000 = 27%

Profit is $140,000 ($1,050,000 − $910,000) lower with long-term debt financing. However, when this profit is spread over 200,000 fewer shares, earnings per share jumps from $3.50 per share to $9.10 per share. We learned about earnings per share in Chapter 14. Earnings per share is calculated by dividing the profit available for the common shareholders by the weighted average number of shares. For this illustration, we have assumed that the shares were issued for the entire period.

After seeing the effect of debt on earnings per share, one might ask why companies do not rely exclusively on debt financing rather than equity financing. The answer is that debt is riskier than equity because interest must be paid regularly each period and the principal of the debt must be paid at maturity. If a company is unable to pay its interest or principal, creditors could force the company to sell its assets to repay its liabilities. In contrast, if equity is issued, a company is not required to pay dividends or repay the shareholders' investment.

Helpful hint Recall from Chapter 13 that dividends on preferred and common shares are only paid when three necessary conditions are present, including having enough cash to pay for ongoing operations. However, interest on bonds must be paid even if the corporation fails to turn a profit.

Even if it is riskier, most companies still choose to issue debt. They do this because money that is borrowed increases earnings per share and it also produces a higher return on equity for the shareholders. You may have heard the saying about "using other people's money to make money." In general, debt can increase the return on equity if the company can borrow at one rate and invest the borrowed money in company operations that earn a higher rate. Borrowing at one rate and investing at a different rate is known as **financial leverage**. Financial leverage is said to be "positive" if the rate of return is higher than the rate of borrowing. It is said to be "negative" if the rate of return is lower than the rate of borrowing.

As we can see in Illustration 15-2, Microsystems' return on equity increases from 12% in Plan A, where equity financing is used, to 27% in Plan B, where debt financing is used. Even though profit is lower under debt financing, there is much less equity to spread the profit across. If equity financing is used, shareholders' equity is $8,550,000. If debt financing is used, shareholders' equity is only $3,410,000. In Chapter 13, we learned that the return on equity ratio is calculated by dividing profit by average shareholders' equity. For this illustration, we have assumed that the shareholders' equity is the average amount.

Each company must decide what *the right mix of debt and equity* is for its particular circumstances. There is a risk with debt financing, and the risk increases with the amount of debt a company has. The risk that goes with debt must be compared with the superior return that may be generated by using debt. As we have just seen, earnings per share and return on equity can improve with the use of debt. Later in this chapter, we will introduce some ratios that will help us evaluate whether a company has too much debt or if the debt is reasonable.

ACCOUNTING IN ACTION
ALL ABOUT YOU INSIGHT

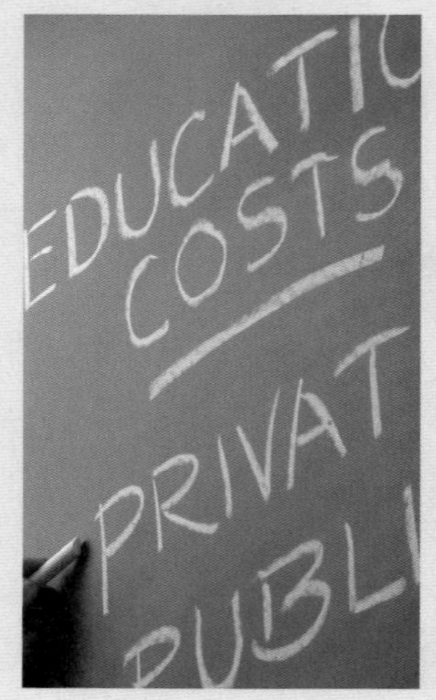

Having enough cash to pay for education and living expenses while going to college or university is often a problem for students. One option is to use student loans. The federal, provincial, and territorial governments as well as private financial institutions all offer student loan programs.

Just like a business, a student can benefit from financial leverage, by borrowing for an education that will result in higher future earnings. Research shows that post-secondary graduates are more likely to be employed, and they earn more than those who do not continue their studies past high school. Over their working life, a college graduate will earn $394,000 more than a high school graduate, while a bachelor's degree holder will earn $745,800 more, according to the former Canada Millennium Scholarship Foundation. Meanwhile, the Association of Universities and Colleges of Canada estimates that university graduates earn an average of $1.3 million more than high school graduates over their career.

While student loan programs offer interest-free financing while the student is in school, eventually they have to be paid. Just as with businesses, too much leverage can result in graduates struggling to make their loan payments.

Sources: Joseph Berger and Andrew Parkin, "The Value of a Degree: Education and Earnings in Canada," *The Price of Knowledge: Access and Student Finance in Canada*, vol. 4, chapter 1, 2009; Association of Universities and Colleges of Canada, "The Value of a University Degree," September 2010.

What should you consider in your decision about how much is appropriate to borrow for your education?

BEFORE YOU GO ON...

DO IT

Nunez Ltd. is considering two alternatives to finance the purchase of new manufacturing equipment at the beginning of the year. The new equipment will increase profit before interest and tax by $3 million annually. The alternatives are:

(a) issue 100,000 shares at a market price of $20 per share, or
(b) issue $2 million of 3% bonds at face value.

Nunez has 400,000 common shares outstanding and $4 million of shareholders' equity. The tax rate is 30%.

Calculate the effects of each of the alternatives on earnings per share.

Action Plan

Alternative (a): Issue 100,000 common shares at a market price of $20 per share.

- Apply the tax rate to the increase in profit to determine the income tax expense.
- Deduct the income tax expense calculated from the increase in profit before interest and tax to determine the profit.
- Add the additional shares issued to the shares outstanding to determine the weighted average number of shares.
- Divide profit by the weighted average number of shares.

Alternative (b): Issue $2 million of 3% bonds at face value.

- Apply the interest rate on the bonds to the amount of bonds issued to determine the interest expense.
- Deduct the interest expense from the increase in profit before interest and tax to determine the profit before tax.
- Apply the tax rate to the profit before tax to determine income tax expense.
- Deduct the income tax expense calculated from the increase in profit before tax to determine the profit.
- Divide the profit by the number of shares outstanding.

SOLUTION

	Alternative (a) Issue shares	Alternative (b) Issue bonds
Profit before interest and tax	$3,000,000	$3,000,000
Interest expense ($2,000,000 × 3%)	0	60,000
Profit before income tax	3,000,000	2,940,000
Income tax expense	900,000	882,000
Profit	$2,100,000	$2,058,000
Number of shares	500,000	400,000
Earnings per share	$ 4.20	$ 5.15

Related exercise material: BE15–1, BE15–2, and E15–1.

THE NAVIGATOR

BONDS PAYABLE

STUDY OBJECTIVE 2
Account for bonds payable.

Like other kinds of non-current debt, **bonds** represent a promise to repay a principal amount at a specific maturity date. In addition, periodic interest is paid (normally semi-annually) at a specified rate on the principal amount. Bonds are also similar to shares: they are sold to, and purchased by, investors on organized securities exchanges. Bonds are usually sold in small denominations ($1,000 or multiples of $1,000). As a result, bonds attract many investors.

Bond credit-rating agencies help investors assess the risk level or creditworthiness of bonds. The highest-quality bonds are graded as AAA bonds, superior quality as AA, and good quality as A. Credit rating agencies all give Hydro-Québec an A rating or higher. The credit-rating scale goes down to C, and finally to the D or default category. Generally, bonds rated below BBB (or its equivalent) are called *junk bonds*. Junk bonds are considered speculative and have a higher risk of default (of not being repaid).

The Standard & Poor's credit rating agency also adds a plus or a minus to each grade category from A to C to distinguish credit risk even more. Hydro-Québec's bonds were rated A+ by Standard & Poor's, which indicates that the bonds are of good quality and have a low credit risk.

Interest rates are linked to credit ratings. Normally, the higher the credit rating, the lower the interest rate. For example, banks might pay 1% or 2% on a term deposit, because there is almost no risk. On the other hand, a corporate bond rated AAA might pay 3% or 4%. A corporate bond rated BBB will likely have to pay a higher rate because the risk is higher. Interest rates vary with risk, but they also vary with duration, the type of bond, the general state of the economy, and many other factors. So, although some interest rates have been given here as examples, they may be quite different right now in practice. Hydro-Québec took advantage of low interest rates in July 2012 and issued bonds at interest rates below 4%.

Helpful hint Bonds, like other forms of investment, are subject to the risk-return relationship, which states that riskier investments must offer higher potential rates of return to compensate the investors for their risk.

There are many different kinds of bonds. Most bonds are **term bonds**, which mature at a single specified future date. Large corporations like Hydro Quebec issue **debentures**, which are unsecured bonds that are issued against the company's general credit. Some companies issue **redeemable bonds** that can be retired (redeemed) at a stated dollar amount at the option of the company before they mature.

BOND BASICS

In the next few sections, we will look at some basic questions about bonds, including how they are issued and traded. We will also show you how to calculate the price the bonds will trade at. This is referred to as the **market value of the bonds**.

Issuing Procedures

In a corporation, approval by the board of directors is required before bonds can be issued. In authorizing the bond issue, the board of directors must state the number of bonds to be authorized (the total number of bonds the company is allowed to sell), the total face value, the contractual interest rate, and the maturity date. As happens with issues of share capital, the total number of bonds authorized is often more than the number of bonds the company plans to issue immediately. This is done intentionally to help ensure that the company will have the flexibility it needs to meet future cash requirements by selling more bonds.

The **face value** of the bonds is the amount that the company (known as the *issuer*) must pay at the maturity date. The **contractual interest rate** is the rate that is used to determine the amount of interest the borrower pays and the investor receives. Usually, the contractual rate is stated as an annual rate and interest is paid semi-annually. For example, the contractual interest rate on Hydro-Québec's bonds is 5% a year, but interest is paid semi-annually at a rate of 2.5% (5% × $^6/_{12}$). The **maturity date** is the date when the final payment is due to the investor from the company. The maturity date for Hydro-Québec's bonds is February 15, 2050. All of these details are included in a **bond certificate**, which is issued to investors to provide evidence of an investor's credit claim against the company.

Alternative terminology Face value is also called *par value* and *maturity value*. The contractual interest rate is commonly known as the *coupon interest rate* or *stated interest rate*.

Bond Trading

Corporate bonds, like shares of public corporations, are traded on organized securities exchanges. Thus, bondholders have the opportunity to convert their bonds into cash at any time by selling the bonds at the current market price. Illustration 15-3 shows one example of bond prices and yields, which are published daily in the financial press:

ILLUSTRATION 15-3
Bond price and yield

Issuer	Coupon	Coupon Frequency	Maturity Date	Price	Yield
Bell CDA	6.100	S	2035-Mar-16	115.44	4.95

This bond listing for Bell Canada (Bell CDA) bonds indicates that these bonds have a contractual (coupon) interest rate of 6.1% per year and a semi-annual (S) interest payment (coupon frequency). This means Bell will pay each $1,000 bondholder interest of $30.50 ($1,000 × 6.1% × 6/12) twice a year. The bonds mature on March 16, 2035.

Bond prices are quoted as a percentage of the bonds' face value, which is usually $1,000. In this particular case, the price of 115.44 means $1,154.40 ($1,000 × 115.44%) was the selling price, or market value, of each $1,000 bond on the date of the above listing. The yield, or market interest rate, on the bonds is 4.95% on the date of the above listing. The **market interest rate** is the rate that investors demand for lending their money. Note that the reason these bonds are currently selling at a premium is because the contractual interest rate is higher than the market interest rate, thereby making them more desirable for investors. We will learn more about market interest rates and bond premiums in the next section.

Alternative terminology Market interest rate or yield is also referred to as the *effective rate*.

As is the case with share transactions, transactions between a bondholder and other investors (that is, those conducted on secondary markets) are *not journalized by the issuing corporation*. For example, if Vinod Thakkar sells his Bell Canada bonds to Julie Tarrel, the transaction is between Vinod and Julie. There is no impact on the issuer's—Bell Canada's—financial position. Bell Canada (or its trustee) will change the name of the bondholder in its records. But the issuer—Bell Canada—only makes journal entries when it issues or buys back bonds and pays interest.

Determining the Market Value of Bonds

If you were an investor wanting to purchase a bond, how would you determine how much to pay? To be more specific, assume that Candlestick Inc. issues a zero-interest bond (pays no interest) with a face value of $1 million due in five years. For this bond, the only cash you receive is $1 million at the end of five years. Would you pay $1 million for this bond? We hope not! One million dollars received five years from now is not nearly as valuable as $1 million received today.

The reason you should not pay $1 million relates to the *time value of money*. If you had $1 million today, you could invest it. From that investment, you would earn interest. At the end of five years, your investment would be worth much more than $1 million. If someone were to pay you $1 million five years from now, you would want to find out its equivalent today. In other words, you would want to determine how much must be invested today at current interest rates to have $1 million in five years. That amount—what must be invested today at a specific rate of interest over a specific amount of time—is called the **present value**.

Helpful hint "A dollar today is better than a dollar tomorrow" is a simple way to think of the time value of money.

The present value of a bond is the price or market value at which it should sell in the marketplace (what it is worth in today's dollars). Market value (present value), therefore, depends on the three factors: (1) the dollar amounts to be received in the future, (2) the length of time until the amounts are received, and (3) the market interest rate. The process of finding the present value is called *discounting the future amounts.*

To illustrate, assume that on January 1, 2014, Candlestick issues $1 million of 5% bonds due in five years, with interest payable semi-annually. The purchaser of the bonds would receive two cash inflows: (1) the principal of $1 million to be paid at maturity, and (2) 10 interest payments of $25,000 ($1,000,000 × 5% × 6/12) received semi-annually over the term of the bonds. Illustration 15-4 shows the time diagram for both cash flows.

ILLUSTRATION 15-4
Time diagram of bond cash flows

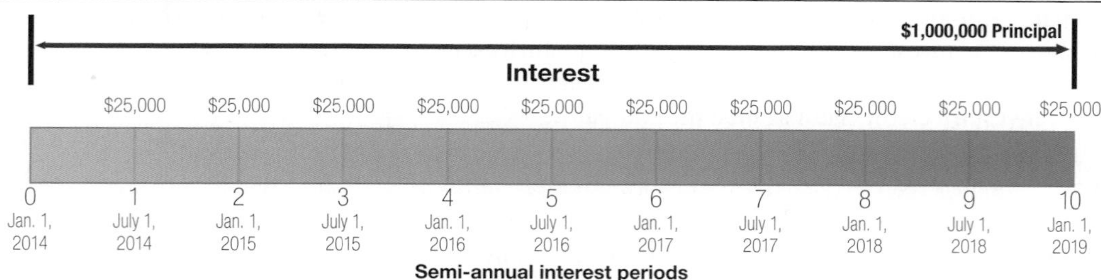

Note that there is no interest payment on January 1, 2014—time period 0—because the bonds have not been outstanding for any period of time, so no interest has been incurred. In the formula for calculating simple interest (I = P × R × T), if any of the three variables to the right of the equal sign is zero, the interest will also be zero.

The current market value of a bond is equal to *the present value of all the future cash flows promised by the bond.* A bond's future cash flows are the face value to be repaid at maturity and the periodic interest payments. The present value calculation of Candlestick's bonds is shown below. We will identify the variables and go through the procedures used to calculate the present value. As you read through these procedures, you should refer to this calculation.

Present value of \$1 million (face value) received in 10 periods \$1,000,000 × 0.78120 (n = 10, i = 2.5%)[1]	\$ 781,200
Present value of \$25,000 (interest payments) received for each of 10 periods \$25,000 × 8.75206 (n = 10, i = 2.5%)	218,800
Present value (current market price) of bonds	**\$1,000,000**

[1] When n = number of interest periods and i = interest rate.

There are standard tables available to determine the present value factors that are used (for example, 0.78120 and 8.75206). We have reproduced these tables in Appendix PV—Present Value Concepts at the end of this book and you should look at them as you read the following procedures for calculating the present value of a bond.

1. **Calculating the present value of the face value of the bond:** Use Table PV-1 (the present value of 1) to determine the correct factor to use to calculate the present value of the face value, which is a single payment, paid at maturity. The appropriate factor is found at the intersection of the number of periods (n) and the interest rate (i).

   When interest is paid semi-annually, the number of periods, (n), will be double the number of years to maturity and the interest rate, (i), will be half of the annual market interest rate. In the Candlestick example, the five years to maturity means that there are 10 semi-annual interest periods [n = 10 or (5 × 2)]. The 5% annual market interest rate means that there is a 2.5% semi-annual market rate [i = 2.5% or (5% × 6/12)]. In the Candlestick example, the present value factor to be used for n = 10 and i = 2.5% is 0.78120.
2. **Calculating the present value of the interest payments:** Use Table PV-2 (the present value of an annuity of 1) to calculate the present value of the interest, which is paid every six months. In Candlestick's case, interest of \$25,000 (\$1,000,000 × 5% × 6/12) is paid every six months. The present value factor is found using the same number of periods (n) and interest rate (i) as is used to calculate the present value of the principal. In Candlestick's case, the present value factor to be used to calculate the present value of the interest payments for n = 10 and i = 2.5% is 8.75206.

Note that the bonds' face value and contractual interest rate are always used to calculate the interest payment. *While the contractual interest rate is used to determine the interest payment, the market interest rate is always used to determine the present value.* In the Candlestick example, the contractual rate and the market rate are the same. When these two rates are the same, the present value (market value) of the bonds equals the face value.

Helpful hint The market rate, rather than the contractual rate, is always used to calculate the present value of bonds because investors will always compare various investment opportunities before they decide where they want to put their money.

The present value can also be determined mathematically using a financial calculator or spreadsheet program. The same variables as described above are used. The present value of the bond can be calculated in one calculation, rather than calculating the present value of the face value and the interest separately. The inputs (variables) required to calculate present value are the **future value** (*FV*), which is the face amount to be paid at maturity; the market rate of interest per interest period (i); the number of interest periods (n); and the interest payment (*PMT*). In the Candlestick example, the future value (*FV*) is \$1 million, the interest rate (i) is 2.5%, the number of interest periods (n) is 10, and the payment (*PMT*) is \$25,000.

The specific methodology and required settings differ for different financial calculators, so it is important to read the manual before using it to calculate present values. However, the inputs and the concepts are the same for all calculators. You should be aware that the present value amounts will most likely differ by a few dollars from those calculated using present value tables. This is because the factors in the present value tables are rounded to five decimal places.

There is further discussion of present value concepts in Appendix PV at the end of this book.

Discount or Premium on Bonds

The present value illustration above assumed that the market interest rate and the contractual interest rate paid on the bonds were the same. However, this is rarely the case because market interest rates change daily. They are influenced by the type of bond issued, the state of the economy, current industry conditions, and the company's performance. The market and contractual interest rates are often quite different. As a result, bonds will generally sell either below or above face value.

To illustrate, suppose that investors have one of two options: (1) purchase bonds that have just been issued with a contractual interest rate of 6%, or (2) purchase bonds issued at an earlier date with a lower contractual interest rate of 5%. If the bonds are of equal risk, investors will choose the 6% investment. To make the investments equal, investors will therefore demand a rate of interest higher than the 5% contractual interest rate provided in option 2. But investors cannot change the contractual interest rate. What they can do, instead, is pay less than the face value for the bonds. By paying less for the bonds, investors can effectively get the market interest rate of 6%. In these cases, bonds sell at a **discount**.

On the other hand, the market interest rate may be lower than the contractual interest rate. In that case, investors will have to pay more than face value for the bonds. That is, if the market interest rate is 4% and the contractual interest rate is 5%, the issuer will require more funds from the investors. In these cases, bonds sell at a **premium**. You will recall from the feature story that Hydro-Québec issued bonds with a contractual interest rate of 5% at a market rate of interest of 3.444%. Hydro-Québec sold these bonds at a premium because the market interest rate was lower than the contractual interest rate. The relationship between bond contractual interest rates and market interest rates, and the resultant selling price, is shown in Illustration 15-5.

ILLUSTRATION 15-5
Interest rates and bond prices

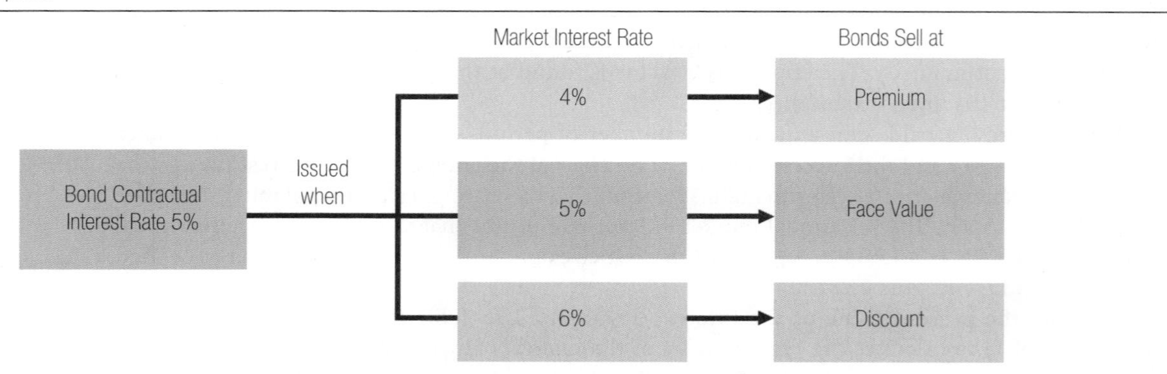

As was the case with Hydro-Québec's bond issue described in the feature story, issuing bonds at an amount different from face value is quite common. You recall that the board of directors is required to authorize a bond issue and that this authorization includes establishing the contractual interest rate. As mentioned earlier, the board may authorize more than they intend to issue immediately so that the company has flexibility to issue more bonds at later date. The board will establish a contractual interest rate based on the market rate when the bonds are authorized. However, by the time a company decides to issue the bonds, prints the bond certificates, and markets the bonds, it will be a coincidence if the market rate and the contractual rate are the same. Thus, the sale of bonds at a discount does not mean that the issuer's financial strength is questionable. Nor does the sale of bonds at a premium indicate superior financial strength. After the bonds are issued, the difference between the contractual rate and the market interest rate will change as the market interest rate fluctuates. However, the fluctuations in the market interest rate after the bonds are issued do not have an impact on the accounting for the bond issue.

ACCOUNTING FOR BOND ISSUES

Bonds can be issued at face value, below face value (at a discount), or above face value (at a premium).

Issuing Bonds at Face Value

To illustrate the accounting for bonds, let's continue the example discussed in the last section, where Candlestick Inc. issues five-year, 5%, $1-million bonds on January 1, 2014, to yield a market interest rate of 5%. These bonds are issued at 100 (100% of face value). The bonds' market value is equal to the face value.

The entry to record the sale is as follows:

Jan. 1.	Cash	1,000,000	
	Bonds Payable		1,000,000
	To record sale of bonds at face value.		

A	=	L	+	SE
+1,000,000		+1,000,000		

↑ Cash flows: +1,000,000

These bonds payable are reported at **amortized cost** in the non-current liabilities section of the balance sheet because the maturity date (January 1, 2019) is more than one year away. Amortized cost is the face value of the bonds minus any unamortized discount or plus any unamortized premium. In this example, because the bonds were issued at face value, the amortized cost is $1 million, the face value of the bonds.

Over the term (life) of the bonds, entries are required for bond interest. Interest is payable semi-annually on January 1 and July 1 on the bonds described above. As shown earlier, the semi-annual **interest payment** is determined using the face value of the bonds and the contractual interest rate. In the Candlestick bond example, the interest payment is $25,000 ($1,000,000 [face value] × 5% [contractual rate] × 6/12).

The **effective-interest method** is used to calculate **interest expense** so that the expense reflects the *actual cost of borrowing*. The effective-interest method uses the market interest rate, at the date the bonds were issued, applied to the amortized cost of the bonds payable to determine interest expense. On July 1, 2014, the first interest payment date, Candlestick will record interest expense of $25,000 ($1,000,000 [amortized cost] × 5% [market rate] × 6/12). In this example, the contractual interest rate is equal to the market rate, so the interest expense is equal to the interest payment. The entry for the interest payment, assuming no previous accrual of interest, is:

July 1	Interest Expense	25,000	
	Cash		25,000
	To record payment of bond interest.		

A	=	L	+	SE
−25,000				−25,000

↓ Cash flows: −25,000

At December 31, Candlestick's year end, an adjusting entry is needed to recognize the $25,000 of interest expense incurred since July 1. The entry is as follows:

Dec. 31	Interest Expense	25,000	
	Interest Payable		25,000
	To accrue bond interest.		

A	=	L	+	SE
		+25,000		−25,000

Cash flows: no effect

Interest payable is classified as a current liability because it is scheduled for payment within the next year (in fact, it is due the next day in this case). When the interest is paid on January 1, 2015, Interest Payable is debited and Cash is credited for $25,000.

Issuing Bonds at a Discount

To illustrate the issue of bonds at a discount (below face value), assume that on January 1, 2014, the Candlestick bonds are issued to yield a market interest rate of 6% rather than 5%, as we assumed in the previous section.

Whether using the present value tables, a financial calculator, or a spreadsheet program, the following variables are used to determine the selling price of the bonds:

Future value (FV) = $1,000,000
Number of semi-annual interest periods (n) = 10 (5 years × 2)
Semi-annual market interest rate (i) = 3% (6% annual market rate × ½)
Interest payments (PMT) = $25,000 ($1,000,000 × 5% [contractual rate] × ½)

Remember to always use the market interest rate to determine the present value factor (*i*) and the contractual interest rate to determine the interest payment. Using the present value tables in Appendix PV, we can determine that the bonds will sell for $957,345 (95.7345% of face value):

Present value of $1 million received in 10 periods $1,000,000 × 0.74409 ($n = 10, i = 3\%$)	$744,090
Present value of $25,000 received for each of 10 periods $25,000 × 8.53020 ($n = 10, i = 3\%$)	213,255
Present value (market price) of bonds	$957,345

The issue price of $957,345 results in a bond discount of $42,655 ($1,000,000 − $957,345). The entry to record the bond issue is as follows:

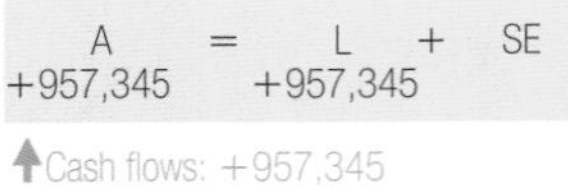

Jan. 1	Cash	957,345	
	Bonds Payable		957,345
	To record sale of bonds at a discount.		

You will recall that bonds payable are reported at amortized cost. At the date the bonds are issued, the issue price is equal to amortized cost. In this example, the issue cost of $957,345 is equal to the face value of $1 million less the unamortized discount of $42,655, which, by definition, is the amortized cost.

The issue of bonds at a discount (below face value) will result in a total cost of borrowing that is higher than the bond interest paid. That is, the issuing corporation must pay not only the contractual interest rate over the term of the bonds, but it must also repay the face value (rather than the issue price) at maturity. Candlestick must repay $1 million at maturity even though it only received $957,345 from the sale of the bonds. Therefore, the difference between the issue price ($957,345) and the face value ($1,000,000) of the bonds—the discount ($42,655)—is an additional cost of borrowing.

Amortizing the Discount.

The total cost of borrowing—the interest payments and bond discount—must be allocated to interest expense over the life of the bonds. The allocation of the bond discount over the life of the bonds is called **amortizing the discount**. The amortization of the discount increases the amount of interest expense that is reported each period. The higher interest expense reflects the actual cost of borrowing. Amortizing the discount over the life of the bonds is an example of ensuring that accounting information faithfully represents the economic reality of the events—an accounting concept we learned about in Chapter 11.

Recall that the effective-interest method is used to calculate the interest expense on all financial liabilities, such as bonds payable. This method is also used to calculate the amortization of the bond discount (and premiums, which will be discussed in the next section) each period. There are three steps required to calculate the amortization amount using the effective-interest method:

1. **Interest expense:** Calculate interest expense by multiplying the amortized cost of the bonds at the beginning of the interest period by the market (effective) interest rate.
2. **Interest paid (or accrued):** Calculate the bond interest paid by multiplying the face value of the bonds by the contractual interest rate.
3. **Amortization amount:** The amortization amount is the difference between the amounts calculated in steps (1) and (2).

These steps are shown in Illustration 15-6.

ILLUSTRATION 15-6
Calculation of amortization using the effective-interest method

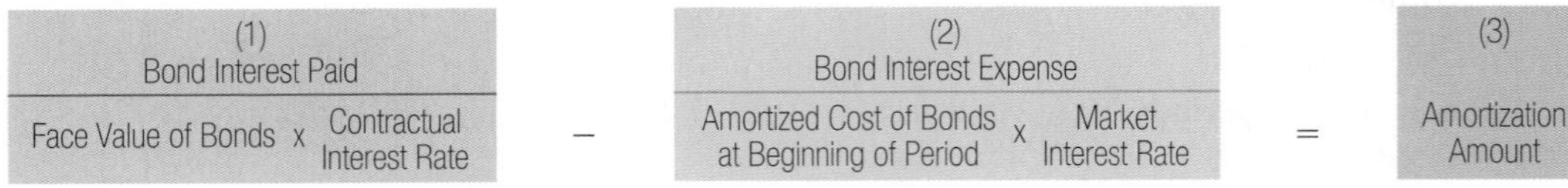

For Candlestick, interest expense for the first period is $28,720, calculated by multiplying the amortized cost of the bonds at the beginning of the period by the market interest rate ($957,345 × 6% × 6/12). The interest payment, $25,000, is calculated by multiplying the bonds' face value by the contractual interest rate ($1,000,000 × 5% × 6/12). The discount amortization is $3,720, the difference between the interest expense and the interest paid ($28,720 − $25,000).

We record the interest expense, amortization of the discount, and payment of interest on the first interest payment date as follows:

July 1	Interest Expense ($957,345 × 6% × 6/12)	28,720	
	Cash ($1,000,000 × 5% × 6/12)		25,000
	Bonds Payable ($28,720 − $25,000)		3,720
	To record payment of bond interest and amortization of bond discount.		

A	=	L	+	SE
−25,000		+3,720		−28,720

↓Cash flows: −25,000

Note that the amortization of the bond discount is recorded as an increase (credit) in the Bonds Payable account, which reduces the bond discount. Also note that, as previously explained, the interest expense includes both the interest payment ($25,000) and the bond discount amortization ($3,720). Remember that issuing a bond at a discount increases the cost of borrowing above the contractual interest rate.

At the second interest period, the bond's amortized cost is now $961,065 ($957,345 + $3,720). The amortized cost will continue to increase by the amount of the discount amortization until at the maturity date the bonds' amortized cost equals their face value—the amount the company is required to pay the bondholders.

To calculate the interest expense for the second interest period, we multiply the amortized cost of the bonds by the market interest rate to arrive at $28,832 ($961,065 × 6% × 6/12). The interest payment is unchanged at $25,000. The amortization is $3,832, the difference between the interest expense and the interest paid ($28,832 − $25,000).

At Candlestick's year end, the following adjusting entry is made for the second interest period:

Dec. 31	Interest Expense ($961,065 × 6% × 6/12)	28,832	
	Interest Payable ($1,000,000 × 5% × 6/12)		25,000
	Bonds Payable ($28,832 − $25,000)		3,832
	To record accrual of bond interest and amortization of bond discount.		

A	=	L	+	SE
		+3,832		−28,832
		+25,000		

Cash flows: no effect

Note that Interest Payable is credited rather than Cash because the next interest payment date is January 1. On January 1, the Interest Payable account will be debited and the Cash account credited.

To make it easier to calculate the interest expense and the discount amortization, a bond discount amortization schedule can be prepared first. Then the journal entries to record interest expense can be recorded using the information in the schedule. The bond discount amortization schedule for Candlestick is shown in Illustration 15-7. For simplicity, amounts have been rounded to the nearest dollar in this schedule.

ILLUSTRATION 15-7
Bond discount amortization schedule—effective-interest method

Semi-Annual Interest Period	(A) Interest Payment ($1,000,000 × 5% × 6/12)	(B) Interest Expense (D × 6% × 6/12)	(C) Discount Amortization (B − A)	(D) Bond Amortized Cost (D + C)
Issue date (Jan. 1, 2014)				$ 957,345
1 (July 1)	$ 25,000	$ 28,720	$ 3,720	961,065
2 (Jan. 1, 2015)	25,000	28,832	3,832	964,897
3 (July 1)	25,000	28,947	3,947	968,844
4 (Jan. 1, 2016)	25,000	29,065	4,065	972,909
5 (July 1)	25,000	29,187	4,187	977,096
6 (Jan. 1, 2017)	25,000	29,313	4,313	981,409
7 (July 1)	25,000	29,442	4,442	985,851
8 (Jan. 1, 2018)	25,000	29,576	4,576	990,427
9 (July 1)	25,000	29,713	4,713	995,140
10 (Jan. 1, 2019)	25,000	29,860[1]	4,860	1,000,000
	$250,000	$292,655	$42,655	

[1] $6 difference due to rounding.

We have highlighted periods 1 and 2 in columns A, B, and C in the amortization schedule shown in Illustration 15-7 because these three columns give the numbers for each period's journal entries. You should compare the information in the schedule for periods 1 and 2, highlighted in red, with the July 1 and December 31, 2014, journal entries previously recorded.

- Column A gives the amount of the credit to Cash (or Interest Payable). Note that the amounts in this column stay the same because the face value of the bonds ($1,000,000) and the semi-annual contractual interest rate (2.5%) are the same each period.
- Column B shows the debit to Interest Expense. It is calculated by multiplying the bond's amortized cost at the beginning of the period by the semi-annual market interest rate. Note that while the semi-annual market interest rate (3%) stays constant each interest period, the interest expense increases because the bond's amortized cost increases.
- Column C is the credit to Bonds Payable. It is the amortization of the bond discount, which is the difference between the interest expense and the interest payment. The amounts in this column increase throughout the amortization period because the interest expense increases. Notice that the total of this column—$42,655—is equal to the discount when the bond was issued on January 1, 2014.
- Column D is the bond's amortized cost. Note that the amortized cost of the bonds increases by the discount amortization amount each period until it reaches the face value of $1 million at the end of period 10 (January 1, 2019), when the discount is fully amortized. This is because Candlestick must repay $1 million at maturity even though it received only $957,345 from the sale of the bonds on January 1, 2014.

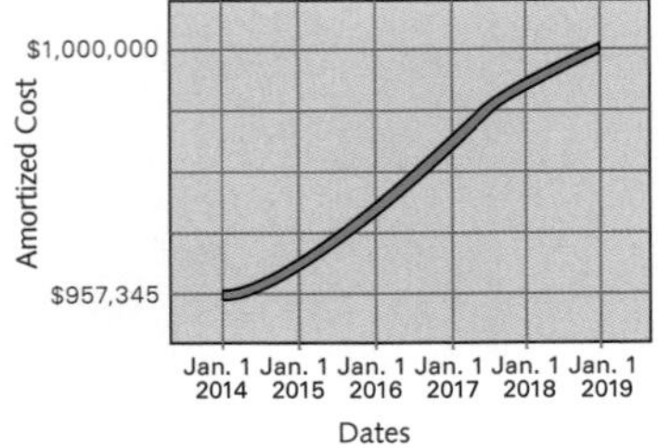

Issuing Bonds at a Premium

To illustrate the issue of bonds at a premium (above face value), assume instead that on January 1, 2014, Candlestick's five-year, 5% bonds are issued to yield a market interest rate of 4%. When the market interest rate is lower than the contractual interest rate, investors will pay a premium for the bonds. Receiving a premium will result in a cost of borrowing of 4%.

The variables used to determine the issue price of the bonds are:

Future value (FV) = $1,000,000
Number of semi-annual interest periods (n) = 10 (5 years × 2)
Semi-annual market interest rate (i) = 2% (4% annual market interest rate × 6/12)
Semi-annual interest payments (PMT) = $25,000 ($1,000,000 × 5% [contractual rate] × 6/12)

Note that the only variable that has changed from the previous example is the market interest rate. Using the present value tables in Appendix PV, we determine that the bonds will sell for $1,044,915 as follows:

Present value of $1 million received in 10 periods $1,000,000 × 0.82035 ($n$ = 10, i = 2)	$ 820,350
Present value of $25,000 received for each of 10 periods $25,000 × 8.98259 ($n$ = 10, i = 2)	224,565
Present value (market price) of bonds (104.4915% of face value)	$1,044,915

This issue price results in a premium of $44,915 ($1,044,915 − $1,000,000). The entry to record the sale would be as follows:

A	=	L	+	SE
+1,044,915		+1,044,915		

↑Cash flows: +1,044,915

Jan. 1	Cash	1,044,915	
	Bonds Payable		1,044,915
	To record sale of bonds at a premium.		

As previously stated, bonds are reported at amortized cost, which is equal to the issue price at the date the bonds are issued. In this example, the bonds' amortized cost is $1,044,915: the face value of the bonds of $1 million plus the unamortized premium of $44,915.

The issue of bonds above face value causes the total cost of borrowing to be less than the bond interest paid. The bond premium is considered a reduction in the cost of borrowing. Candlestick will repay only $1 million at maturity, even though it received $1,044,915 from the sale of the bonds.

Amortizing the Premium.

The total cost of borrowing—the interest payments less the bond premium—must be allocated to interest expense over the life of the bonds. The allocation of the bond premium over the life of the bonds is called **amortizing the premium**. The amortization of the premium reduces the amount of interest expense that is recorded each period.

The same method—the effective-interest method—used to allocate bond discounts is also used to allocate bond premiums to interest expense. For the first interest period, the interest expense is $20,898, calculated by multiplying the bonds' carrying amount by the market interest rate ($1,044,915 × 4% × 6/12). The interest payment, $25,000, is the same as for the bonds issued at discount as it is calculated by multiplying the bonds' face value by the contractual interest rate ($1,000,000 × 5% × 6/12). The premium amortization is then calculated as the difference between the interest paid and the interest expense ($25,000 − $20,898 = $4,102).

The entry on the first interest payment date is as follows:

July 1	Interest Expense ($1,044,915 × 4% × 6/12)	20,898	
	Bonds Payable ($25,000 − $20,898)	4,102	
	Cash ($1,000,000 × 5% × 6/12)		25,000
	To record payment of bond interest and amortization of bond premium.		

A	=	L	+	SE
−25,000		−4,120		−20,898

↓Cash flows: −25,000

Note that the amortization of the bond premium is recorded as a decrease (debit) in the Bonds Payable account, which reduces the bond premium, and that the interest expense is less than the interest payment. This reflects the reduced cost of borrowing.

For the second interest period, the bonds' amortized cost is now $1,040,813 ($1,044,915 − $4,102). The amortized cost will continue to decrease by the amount of the premium amortization until at the maturity date, the bonds' amortized cost equals their face value—the amount the company is required to pay the bondholders.

To calculate the interest expense for the second interest period, we multiply the amortized cost of the bonds by the market interest rate to arrive at $20,816 ($1,040,813 × 4% × 6/12). The interest payment is unchanged at $25,000. As before, the amortization is the difference between the interest paid and the interest expense ($25,000 − $20,816 = $4,184).

For the second interest period, at Candlestick's year end, the following adjusting entry is made:

Dec. 31	Interest Expense ($1,040,813 × 4% × 6/12)	20,816	
	Bonds Payable ($25,000 − $20,816)	4,184	
	Interest Payable ($1,000,000 × 5% × 6/12)		25,000
	To record accrual of bond interest and amortization of bond premium.		

A	=	L	+	SE
		−4,184		−20,816
		+25,000		

Cash flows: no effect

As in the case where bonds are issued at a discount, a bond premium amortization schedule can be prepared to make it easier to calculate interest expense and amortization of the premium. The bond premium amortization schedule is shown in Illustration 15-8. Figures have been rounded to the nearest dollar for simplicity.

ILLUSTRATION 15-8
Bond premium amortization schedule—effective-interest method

Semi-Annual Interest Period	(A) Interest Payment ($1,000,000 × 5% × 6/12)	(B) Interest Expense (D × 4% × 6/12)	(C) Discount Amortization (A − B)	(D) Bond Amortized Cost (D − C)
Issue date (Jan. 1, 2014)				$1,044,915
1 (July 1)	$ 25,000	$ 20,898	$ 4,102	1,040,813
2 (Jan. 1, 2015)	25,000	20,816	4,184	1,036,629
3 (July 1)	25,000	20,733	4,267	1,032,362
4 (Jan. 1, 2016)	25,000	20,647	4,353	1,028,009
5 (July 1)	25,000	20,560	4,440	1,023,569
6 (Jan. 1, 2017)	25,000	20,471	4,529	1,019,040
7 (July 1)	25,000	20,381	4,619	1,014,421
8 (Jan. 1, 2018)	25,000	20,288	4,712	1,009,709
9 (July 1)	25,000	20,194	4,806	1,004,903
10 (Jan. 1, 2019)	25,000	20,097[1]	4,903	1,000,000
	$250,000	$205,085	$44,915	

[1] $1 difference due to rounding.

Recall from Illustration 15-7 that columns A, B, and C in the amortization schedule give the numbers for each period's journal entries. You should compare the information, highlighted in red, in the schedule for periods 1 and 2 with the July 1 and December 31, 2014, journal entries previously recorded.

- Column A gives the amount of the credit to Cash (or Interest Payable). The amounts in this column stay the same because the face value of the bonds and the semi-annual contractual interest rate are the same each period.
- Column B shows the debit to Interest Expense. It is calculated by multiplying the bonds' amortized cost at the beginning of the period by the semi-annual market interest rate. Note that while the semi-annual market interest rate (2%) stays constant each interest period, the interest expense decreases because the bond's amortized cost decreases.
- Column C is the debit to Bonds Payable. It is the difference between the interest payment and the interest expense. The amounts in this column increase throughout the amortization period because the interest expense decreases as the amortized cost of the bonds decreases. Notice that the total of this column—$44,915—is equal to the premium when the bond was issued on January 1, 2014.
- Column D is the bond's amortized cost. Note that the amortized cost of the bonds decreases by the premium amortization amount each period until it reaches the face value of $1 million at the end of period 10 (January 1, 2019). Note that even though Candlestick received $1,044,915 from the sale of the bonds on January 1, 2014, it is only required to pay $1 million at maturity.

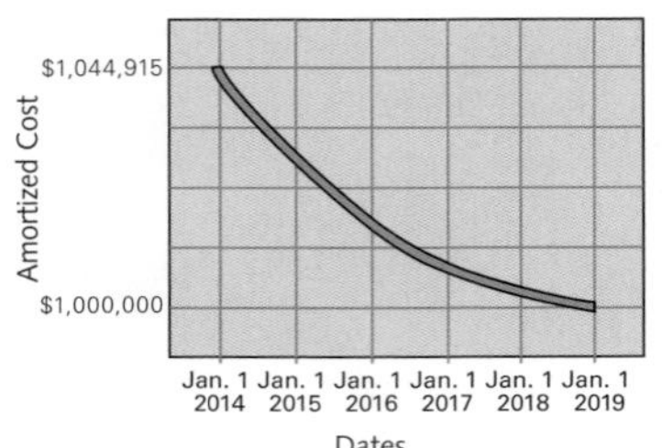

Comparison of Issuing Bonds at a Discount Versus at a Premium

Illustration 15-9 summarizes some of the differences between issuing a bond at a discount and a premium under the effective-interest method of amortization.

ILLUSTRATION 15-9
Comparison of the effects of issuing bonds at a discount or a premium

	Bond Issued at a Discount	Bond Issued at a Premium
Market interest rate	Greater than the contractual interest rate	Less than the contractual interest rate
Periodic interest payment	Same each period	Same each period
Periodic interest expense	Greater than the interest payment Increases each period	Less than the interest payment Decreases each period
Bond's amortized cost	Increases to face value at maturity	Decreases to face value at maturity

The effective-interest method is required for companies reporting under IFRS. Private companies reporting under ASPE can choose to use either the effective-interest method or other methods if they do not materially differ from the effective-interest method. Because the use of the effective-interest method is prevalent, we focus on this method in this text.

ACCOUNTING FOR BOND RETIREMENTS

Bonds may be retired either (1) when they mature, or (2) when the issuing corporation purchases them from the bondholders on the open market before they mature. Some bonds have special redemption provisions that allow them to be retired before they mature. As we learned earlier in this chapter, redeemable bonds can be retired at a stated dollar amount at the option of the company.

The retirement of bonds at and before maturity are explained in the following sections.

Redeeming Bonds at Maturity

Regardless of the issue price of bonds, the amortized cost of the bonds at maturity will equal their face value. By the time the bonds mature, any discount or premium will be fully amortized.

Assuming that the interest for the last interest period has been paid and recorded, the entry to record the redemption of the Candlestick bonds at maturity, January 1, 2019, is as follows:

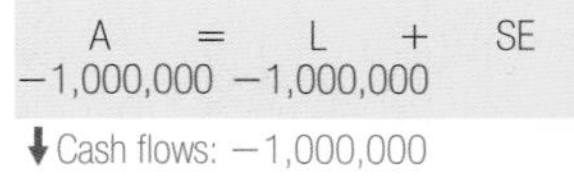

Jan. 1	Bonds Payable	1,000,000	
	Cash		1,000,000
	To record redemption of bonds at maturity.		

Because the amortized cost of the bonds equals the face value at maturity, there is no gain or loss.

Redeeming Bonds before Maturity

Why would a company want to have the option to retire its bonds early? If interest rates drop, it can be a good idea financially to retire the bond issue and replace it with a new bond issue at a lower interest rate. Or, a company may become financially able to repay its debt earlier than expected. When a company purchases non-redeemable bonds on the open market, it pays the going market price. If the bonds are redeemable, the company will pay the bondholders an amount that was specified at the time of issue, known as the **redemption price**. To make the bonds more attractive to investors, the redemption price is usually a few percentage points above the face value.

Alternative terminology
Redemption price is also referred to as the *call price*.

If the bonds are redeemed between semi-annual interest payment dates, it will be necessary to pay the required interest and record the related amortization of any premiums or discounts. To record the redemption of bonds, it is necessary to (1) eliminate the amortized cost of the bonds (balance in Bonds Payable account), (2) record the cash paid, and (3) recognize the gain or loss on redemption.

A loss on redemption is recorded if the cash paid is more than the amortized cost of the bonds. There is a gain on redemption when the cash paid is less than the amortized cost of the bonds. This is shown in Illustration 15-10.

ILLUSTRATION 15-10
Loss and gain on redemption of bonds

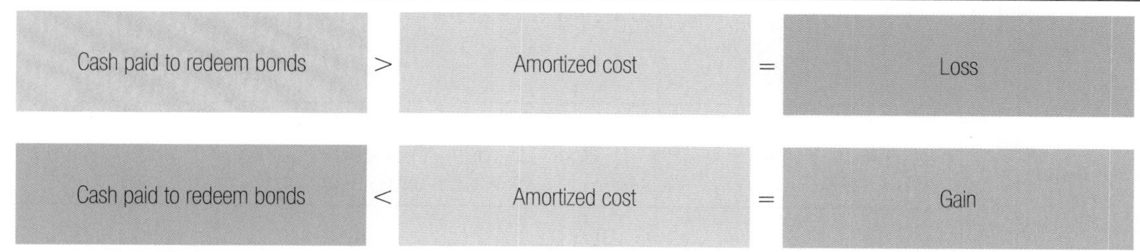

To illustrate, assume that Candlestick sells its bonds that were issued at a premium as described in the last section. It retires its bonds at 101 at the end of the fourth year (eighth period) after paying the semi-annual interest. The premium amortization schedule in Illustration 15-8 shows that the bonds' amortized cost at the redemption date (January 1, 2018) is $1,009,709. The entry to record the redemption on January 1, 2018 (end of the eighth interest period) is:

Jan. 1	Bonds Payable	1,009,709	
	Loss on Bond Redemption	291	
	Cash ($1,000,000 × 101%)		1,010,000
	To record redemption of bonds at 101.		

A	=	L	+	SE
−1,010,000		−1,009,709		−291

↓Cash flows: −1,010,000

There is a loss on the bond redemption because Candlestick paid $1,010,000—$291 more to redeem the bonds than the amortized cost of the bonds of $1,009,709.

Losses and gains on bond redemption are reported separately in the income statement as other expenses or other revenues similar to interest expense.

BEFORE YOU GO ON...

DO IT

On January 1, 2013, R & B Inc. issues $500,000 of 10-year, 4% bonds to yield a market interest rate of 5%, which resulted in an issue price of 92.21. Interest is paid semi-annually on January 1 and July 1. On January 1, 2015, the company redeems the bonds at 97 after making and recording the semi-annual interest payment.

(a) Use present value factors to prove the issue price of the bonds of 92.21. Round all calculations to the nearest dollar.
(b) Prepare the entry to record the issue of the bonds on January 1, 2013.
(c) Prepare an amortization schedule for the first four interest periods. Round all calculations to the nearest dollar.
(d) Prepare the entries to record the accrual of interest and amortization of any bond discount or premium on December 31, 2014.
(e) Prepare the entry to record the payment of interest on January 1, 2015.
(f) Prepare the entry to record the redemption of the bonds on January 1, 2015.

Action Plan

- Identify the key inputs required to determine present value, whether using tables or a financial calculator. Remember to double the number of periods and halve the annual interest rate when the interest is paid semi-annually.

BEFORE YOU GO ON... continued on next page

BEFORE YOU GO ON...
continued from previous page

SOLUTION

(a) Key inputs: Future value (*FV*) = $500,000
Semi-annual market interest rate (*i*) = 2.5% (5% × 6/12)
Interest payment (*PMT*) = $10,000 ($500,000 × 4% × 6/12)
Number of semi-annual periods (*n*) = 20 (10 × 2)

Present value of $500,000 received in 20 periods 500,000 × 0.61027 (*n* = 20, *i* = 2.5)	$305,135
Present value of $10,000 received for each of 20 periods $10,000 × 15.58916 (*n* = 20, *i* = 2.5)	155,892
Present value (issue price)	$461,027

Proof: Issue price = $461,027 ÷ $500,000 = 92.21%

- To calculate the present value (issue price), use the semi-annual market interest rate for (*i*). Use the face value of the bonds and the contractual interest rate to calculate the semi-annual interest payments (*PMT*). The interest payments, which recur periodically, are an annuity. The face value of the bonds is the (*FV*), which is a single sum.
- Debit cash and credit bonds payable for the amount the bonds were issued at.
- Calculate the interest expense by multiplying the semi-annual market rate (half of the market or yield rate) by the amortized cost of the bonds payable.
- The amount of the discount (premium) amortization is the difference between the interest payment and the interest expense.
- The amortized cost of the bonds issued at a discount increases by the amount of the discount amortization each interest period. The amortized cost of the bonds issued at a premium decreases by the amount of the premium amortization each interest period.
- To record the redemption, eliminate the amortized cost of the bonds, record the cash paid, and calculate and record the gain or loss (the difference between the cash paid and the amortized cost).

(b)

	Date	Account	Debit	Credit
(1)	Jan. 1, 2013	Cash	461,050	
		Bonds Payable		461,050
		To record issue of bonds at 92.21.		

(c)

R & B INC.
Bond Discount Amortization Schedule
Effective-Interest Method

Semi-Annual Interest Period	(A) Interest Payment ($500,000 × 4% × 6/12)	(B) Interest Expense (D × 5% × 6/12)	(C) Discount Amortization (B − A)	(D) Bond Amortized Cost (D + C)
Issue date (Jan. 1, 2013)				$461,050
1 (July 1)	$10,000	$11,526	$1,526	462,576
2 (Jan. 1, 2014)	10,000	11,564	1,564	464,140
3 (July 1)	10,000	11,603	1,603	465,743
4 (Jan. 1, 2015)	10,000	11,643	1,643	467,386

	Date	Account	Debit	Credit
(d)	Dec. 31, 2014	Interest Expense	11,643	
		Bonds Payable		1,643
		Interest Payable		10,000
		To record accrual of interest and amortization of discount.		
(e)	Jan. 1, 2015	Interest Payable	10,000	
		Cash		10,000
		To record payment of bond interest.		
(f)	Jan. 1, 2015	Bonds Payable	467,386	
		Loss on Bond Redemption ($485,000 − $467,386)	17,614	
		Cash ($500,000 × 97%)		485,000
		To record redemption of bonds at 97.		

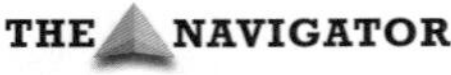

Related exercise material: BE15–3, BE15–4, BE15–5, BE15–6, BE15–7, BE15–8, BE15–9, BE15–10, E15–2, E15–3, E15–4, E15–5, E15–6, E15–7, and E15–8.

INSTALMENT NOTES PAYABLE

STUDY OBJECTIVE 3
Account for instalment notes payable.

You will recall that we first learned about notes payable in Chapter 10, where they were included as an example of a current liability. Non-current notes payable are similar to short-term notes payable except that the terms of the notes are normally for more than one year. While short-term notes are normally repayable in full at maturity, most non-current notes are repayable in a series of periodic payments and are referred to as **instalment notes**. These payments are known as **instalments** and are paid monthly, quarterly, semi-annually, or at another defined period.

Notes and bonds are also quite similar. Both have a fixed maturity date and pay interest. However, whereas bonds have a contractual or fixed interest rate, notes may have either a fixed interest rate or a floating interest rate. A **fixed interest rate** is constant for the entire term of the note. A **floating** (or **variable) interest rate** changes as market rates change. A floating interest rate is often based on the prime borrowing rate. Prime is the interest rate that banks charge their most creditworthy customers. This rate is usually increased by a specified percentage that matches the company's risk profile—in other words, it depends on how risky the company is judged to be.

Similar to bonds, a non-current note may be unsecured or secured. A secured note pledges title to specific assets as security for the loan, often known as **collateral**. Secured notes are commonly known as *mortgages*. A **mortgage note payable** is widely used by individuals to purchase homes. It is also used by many companies to acquire property, plant, and equipment. Unsecured notes are issued against the general credit of the borrower. There are no assets used as collateral.

As explained earlier, most non-current notes payable are paid in instalments. Each instalment payment consists of (1) interest on the unpaid balance of the loan, and (2) a reduction of loan principal. Payments generally take one of two forms: (1) fixed principal payments plus interest, or (2) blended principal and interest payments. Let's look at each of these payment patterns in more detail.

FIXED PRINCIPAL PAYMENTS

Instalment notes with fixed principal payments are repayable in **equal periodic amounts, plus interest.** To illustrate, assume that on January 1, 2014, Bélanger Ltée issues a $120,000, five-year, 7% note payable to finance a new research laboratory. The entry to record the issue of the note payable is as follows:

Alternative terminology
Ltée is the French term for Ltd.

Jan. 1	Cash	120,000	
	Notes Payable		120,000
	To record five-year, 7% note payable.		

A	=	L	+	SE
+1,20,000		+1,20,000		

↑Cash flows: +1,20,000

The terms of the note provide for equal monthly instalment payments of $2,000 ($120,000 ÷ 60 monthly periods) on the first of each month, plus interest, based on an annual rate of 7%, on the outstanding principal balance. Monthly interest expense is calculated by multiplying the outstanding principal balance by the interest rate. The calculation of interest expense for notes payable is similar to that of bonds payable—both use the effective-interest method.

For the first payment date—February 1—interest expense is $700 ($120,000 × 7% × 1/12). Since 7% is an annual interest rate, it must be adjusted for the monthly time period. The cash payment of $2,700 for the month of February is the sum of the instalment payment, $2,000, which is applied against the principal, plus the interest, $700.

The entry to record the first instalment payment on February 1 is as follows:

Feb. 1	Interest Expense ($120,000 × 7% × 1/12)	700	
	Notes Payable	2,000	
	Cash ($2,000 + $700)		2,700
	To record monthly payment on note.		

A	=	L	+	SE
−2,700		−2,000		−700

↓Cash flows: −2,700

An instalment payment schedule is a useful tool to help organize this information and prepare journal entries. The instalment payment schedule for the first few months for Bélanger Ltée, rounded to the nearest dollar, is shown in Illustration 15-11.

ILLUSTRATION 15-11
Instalment payment schedule—fixed principal payments

BÉLANGER LTÉE
Instalment Payment Schedule—Fixed Principal Payments

Interest Period	(A) Cash Payment (B + C)	(B) Interest Expense (D × 7% × 1/12)	(C) Reduction of Principal ($120,000 ÷ 60)	(D) Principal Balance (D − C)
Jan. 1				$120,000
Feb. 1	$2,700	$700	$2,000	118,000
Mar. 1	2,688	688	2,000	116,000
Apr. 1	2,677	677	2,000	114,000

Column A, the cash payment, is the total of the instalment payment, $2,000 (Column C), plus the interest (Column B). The cash payment changes each period because the interest amount changes. Column B determines the interest expense, which decreases each period because the principal balance, on which interest is calculated, decreases. Column C is the portion of the payment that is applied against the principal. The monthly reduction of principal of $2,000 per month is constant each period in a "fixed principal payment" pattern. Column D is the principal balance, which decreases each period by the amount of the instalment payment (Column C).

In summary, with fixed principal payments, the interest decreases each period (as the principal decreases). The portion applied to the reduction of loan principal stays constant, but because of the decreasing interest, the total cash payment decreases.

BLENDED PAYMENTS

Instalment notes with blended payments are repayable in **equal periodic amounts that include the principal and the interest**. With blended payments, the amounts of interest and principal that are applied to the loan change with each payment. Specifically, as happens with fixed principal payments, the interest decreases each period (as the principal decreases). In contrast to fixed principal payments, however, the portion that is applied to the loan principal increases each period.

To illustrate, assume that instead of fixed principal payments, Bélanger Ltée repays its $120,000 note payable in blended payments of $2,376 each month. The blended payment is calculated using present value calculations as shown in Appendix PV. As with the fixed principal payments illustrated in the previous section, monthly interest expense is calculated by multiplying the outstanding principal balance by the interest rate. For the first payment date—February 1—interest expense is $700 ($120,000 × 7% × $^1/_{12}$ months). The payment of $2,376 is fixed for each month, and includes interest and principal amounts, which will vary. In February, the principal balance will be reduced by $1,676, which is the difference between the payment of $2,376 and the interest amount of $700.

The entry to record the issue of the note payable is the same as in the previous section. The amounts in the journal entry to record the payment on February 1 change as follows:

A	=	L	+	SE
−2,376		−1,676		−700

Cash flows: −2,376

Feb. 1	Interest Expense ($120,000 × 7% × $^1/_{12}$)	700	
	Notes Payable ($2,376 − $700)	1,676	
	Cash		2,376
	To record monthly payment on note.		

An instalment payment schedule can also be prepared for blended principal and interest payments. Illustration 15-12 shows the instalment payment schedule for the first few months for Bélanger Ltée, rounded to the nearest dollar.

ILLUSTRATION 15-12
Instalment payment schedule—blended payments

BÉLANGER LTÉE
Instalment Payment Schedule—Blended Payments

Interest Period	(A) Cash Payment	(B) Interest Expense (D × 7% × $^1/_{12}$)	(C) Reduction of Principal (A − B)	(D) Principal Balance (D − C)
Jan. 1				$120,000
Feb. 1	$2,376	$700	$1,676	118,324
Mar. 1	2,376	690	1,686	116,638
Apr. 1	2,376	680	1,696	114,942

Column A, the cash payment, is specified and is the same for each period. The amount of this cash payment can be calculated using present value techniques discussed earlier in the chapter and in Appendix PV to this textbook. Column B determines the interest expense, which decreases each period because the principal balance on which interest is calculated also decreases. Column C is the amount by which the principal is reduced. This is the difference between the cash payment of $2,376 (Column A) and the interest for the period (Column B). Consequently, this amount will increase each period. Column D is the principal balance, which decreases each period by an increasing amount; that is, by the reduction of the principal amount from Column C.

In summary, with blended payments, the interest decreases each period as the principal decreases. The cash payment stays constant, but because of the decreasing interest, the reduction of principal increases.

Illustration 15-13 summarizes the differences between instalment notes payable with fixed principal payments and blended principal payments.

ILLUSTRATION 15-13
Difference between instalment notes with fixed principal payments and blended principal payments

Instalment Payment Pattern	Principal	Interest	Total Cash Payments
Fixed principal plus interest	Constant: Reduction of principal equal each period	Decreases: Interest expense decreases each period	Decreases: Total cash payment decreases each period
Blended principal and interest	Increases: Reduction of principal increases each period	Decreases: Interest expense decreases each period	Constant: Total cash payment equal each period

CURRENT AND NON-CURRENT PORTIONS

With both types of instalment notes payable, the reduction in principal for the next year must be reported as a current liability, and is normally called "Current portion of note payable." The remaining unpaid principal is classified as a non-current liability. No journal entry is necessary; it is simply a reclassification of amounts for the balance sheet. For example, consider the following fixed principal annual instalment payment schedule shown in Illustration 15-14.

ILLUSTRATION 15-14
Current and non-current portion of note payable

Interest Period	Cash Payment	Interest Expense	Reduction of Principal	Principal Balance
Issue Date				$50,000
2013	$13,500	$3,500	$10,000	40,000
2014	12,800	2,800	10,000	**30,000**
2015	12,100	2,100	**10,000**	20,000
2016	11,400	1,400	10,000	10,000
2017	10,700	700	10,000	0

If financial statements were being prepared at the end of 2014, the company would report $30,000 as its total liability for the bank loan, shown in red in the principal balance column. Of this, $10,000 ($30,000 − $20,000)—the amount to be repaid within the next year (2015), which is also highlighted above in red—would be reported as a current liability. The company would report $20,000—the amount to be repaid beyond next year (2016 and 2017)—as a non-current liability. This amount is highlighted in blue in Illustration 15-14. Note that when the current portion ($10,000) and the non-current portion ($20,000) are added together, the amount should agree with the total amount owing at the end of 2014 ($30,000).

ACCOUNTING IN ACTION
BUSINESS INSIGHT

Canadians are racking up record levels of debt. Statistics Canada reported in 2012 that Canadian households owed an average amount equivalent to 152% of their incomes. The federal finance minister and governor of the Bank of Canada repeatedly warned Canadians to tighten their spending and save more for retirement. Many blamed record-low interest rates for enticing Canadians to borrow beyond their means, which is one reason why housing prices and mortgage debt were increasing. While banks were criticized for slashing mortgage rates in wars to lure customers, they were asking the federal government to reduce the maximum period for government-insured mortgages instead of hiking interest rates. The government did so in mid-2012, lowering the amortization period from 30 years to 25 years and limiting homeowners with government-insured mortgages to spending no more than 44% of income on housing and other debt. The government hoped the moves would curb mortgage debt, since it would be harder to get a mortgage in the first place, and the mortgages would have to be paid off faster.

Sources: Grant Robertson, "BMO Kicks Off New Mortgage Fight," *Globe and Mail*, March 7, 2012; Jason Fekete, "Ottawa Tightens Mortgage Rules to Avert Household Debt Crisis," *Financial Post*, June 21, 2012; Andy Johnson, "Canadian Consumer Debt Level Hits Record High," CTV News, August 23, 2012.

What impact will the decrease in the amortization period from 30 to 25 years have on homebuyers?

BEFORE YOU GO ON...

DO IT

On December 31, 2013, Tian Inc. issued a $500,000, 15-year, 8% mortgage note payable. The terms provide for semi-annual blended payments of $28,915 on June 30 and December 31. (a) Prepare an instalment payment schedule for the first two years of the note (through to December 31, 2015). (b) Prepare the journal entries required to record the issue of the note on December 31, 2013, and the first two instalment payments. (c) Show the presentation of the liability on the balance sheet at December 31, 2014.

Action Plan

- For the instalment payment schedule, multiply the interest rate by the principal balance at the beginning of the period to determine the interest expense. Remember to adjust the interest rate to the semi-annual rate. The reduction of principal is the difference between the cash payment and the interest expense.
- Use the amortization table to record the semi-annual mortgage payments.
- Remember to separate the current and non-current portions of the note in the balance sheet. The current portion is the amount of principal that will be repaid in the next year (2015). The total of the current and non-current portions should equal the outstanding principal balance in the amortization table at December 31, 2014.

SOLUTION

(a)

Interest Period	Cash Payment	Interest Expense	Reduction of Principal	Principal Balance
Dec. 31, 2013				$500,000
June 30, 2014	$28,915	$20,000	$ 8,915	491,085
Dec. 31, 2014	28,915	19,643	9,272	481,813
June 30, 2015	28,915	19,273	9,642	472,171
Dec. 31, 2015	28,915	18,887	10,028	462,143

(b)

Date	Account	Debit	Credit
Dec. 31, 2013	Cash	500,000	
	Mortgage Note Payable		500,000
	To record issue of 15-year, 8% mortgage note payable.		
June 30, 2014	Interest Expense ($500,000 × 8% × 6/12)	20,000	
	Mortgage Note Payable ($28,915 − $20,000)	8,915	
	Cash		28,915
	To record semi-annual payment on note.		
Dec. 31, 2014	Interest Expense ($491,085 × 8% × 6/12)	19,643	
	Mortgage Note Payable ($28,915 − $19,643)	9,272	
	Cash		28,915
	To record semi-annual payment on note.		

(c)

TIAN INC.
December 31, 2014
Balance Sheet (Partial)

Current liabilities	
Current portion of mortgage note payable ($9,642 + $10,028)	$ 19,670
Non-current liabilities	
Mortgage note payable	462,143
Total liabilities	$481,813

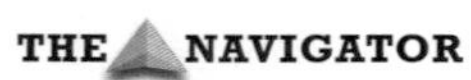

Related exercise material: BE15–11, BE15–12, BE15–13, BE15–14, E15–9, E15–10, E15–11, E15–12, and E15–13.

STATEMENT PRESENTATION AND ANALYSIS

STUDY OBJECTIVE 4

Explain and illustrate the methods for the presentation and analysis of non-current liabilities.

Liabilities are a significant amount on the financial statements and they have to be disclosed in detail so they can be properly understood by investors and creditors. These and other users are very interested in assessing a company's solvency (its ability to pay) with regard to its non-current liabilities. We will look at the presentation and analysis of liabilities in the next sections.

PRESENTATION

The liabilities section of the balance sheet for Wick Company Ltd. is presented in Illustration 15-15.

ILLUSTRATION 15-15
Liabilities section of a balance sheet

WICK COMPANY LTD. Balance Sheet (partial) December 31, 2014	
Current Liabilities	
Accounts payable	$ 70,000
Interest payable	18,400
Current portion of mortgage note payable	55,520
Total current liabilities	143,920
Non-current liabilities	
Bonds payable, 4%, due in 2018	920,000
Mortgage notes payable, 8%, due in 2021	444,480
Total non-current liabilities	1,364,480
Total liabilities	$1,508,400

You will recall that the principal payments for the next year on notes payable are reported in current liabilities and the remaining unpaid principal is classified in non-current liabilities. In the Wick example, the company has a mortgage note payable of $500,000 ($55,520 + $444,480); $55,520 will be paid in 2015 and the remaining amount of $444,480 classified in non-current liabilities will be paid off in instalments from 2016 to 2021.

Note that Wick is reporting bond interest payable of $18,400 in current liabilities as the interest will be paid in 2015 and bonds payable of $920,000 in non-current liabilities because the bonds mature in 2018. Note that there is no current portion of bonds payable as the bonds are paid off in one lump sum at maturity.

Full disclosure of debt is very important. Summary data are usually presented in the balance sheet, and detailed data (interest rate, maturity date, redemption price, convertibility, and any assets pledged as collateral) are shown in a supporting schedule or in the notes to the financial statements. The amount of debt maturing within 12 months of the balance sheet date should be reported under current liabilities.

ANALYSIS

A company's investors and creditors are interested in analyzing its liquidity and solvency. Short-term creditors are interested in liquidity ratios, which measure a company's ability to repay its short-term debt and to meet unexpected needs for cash. We learned about liquidity ratios such as the current ratio, inventory turnover, and receivables turnover in earlier chapters.

Long-term creditors and investors are more interested in solvency ratios, which measure a company's ability to repay its non-current liabilities and survive over a long period of time. They are particularly interested in a company's ability to pay interest when it is due and to repay its debt at maturity. Two examples of solvency ratios are debt to total assets and the interest coverage ratio. They are explained next.

Debt to Total Assets

Debt to total assets measures the percentage of the total assets that is financed by creditors rather than by shareholders. Financing provided by creditors is riskier than financing provided by shareholders, because debt must be repaid at specific points in time whether the company is doing well or not.

Illustration 15-16 shows how the debt to total assets ratio is calculated. Using data from Reitmans' financial statements (in thousands), the ratio is calculated by dividing total liabilities (both current and long-term) by total assets ($ in thousands).

Helpful hint Some users compare the proportion of the total assets that is financed by creditors with the proportion that is financed by shareholders. This ratio is called the *debt to equity ratio.*

ILLUSTRATION 15-16
Debt to total assets

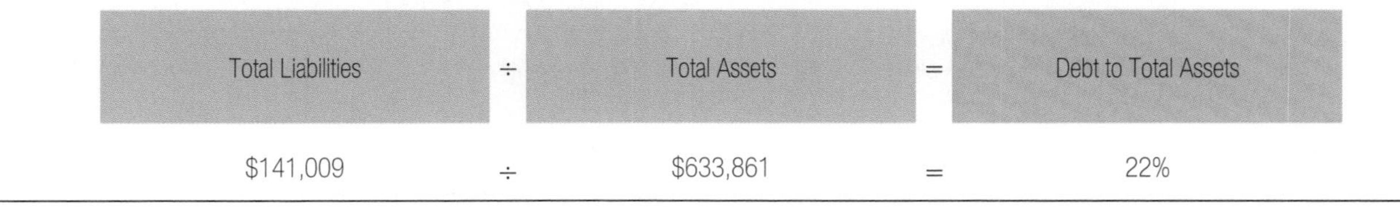

Total Liabilities	÷	Total Assets	=	Debt to Total Assets
$141,009	÷	$633,861	=	22%

This means that 22% of Reitmans' assets are financed by creditors. The remainder, 78% (100% − 22%), has been financed by shareholders. In general, the higher the percentage of debt to total assets, the greater the risk that the company may be unable to meet its maturing obligations.

While you may assume that having no, or a low, debt to total assets ratio is ideal, recall that we learned at the beginning of this chapter that some debt may be good for a company. As previously shown, in some circumstances, a company can increase its earnings per share and return on equity by increasing how much debt financing it relies on.

Interest Coverage

The debt to total assets ratio must be interpreted in light of the company's ability to handle its debt. That is, a company might have a high debt to total assets ratio but still be able to easily pay its interest payments. Alternatively, a company may have a low debt to total assets ratio and struggle to cover its interest payments.

Alternative terminology
The interest coverage ratio is also commonly known as the *times interest earned ratio*.

The **interest coverage ratio** indicates the company's ability to meet interest payments as they come due. It is calculated by dividing profit before interest expense and income tax expense by interest expense. The numerator is often abbreviated and called **EBIT**, which stands for "earnings before interest and tax." EBIT can be calculated by adding back interest expense and income tax expense to profit. Because these amounts were originally deducted to determine profit, adding them back has the effect of cancelling them.

ILLUSTRATION 15-17
Interest coverage

Illustration 15-17 calculates interest coverage for Reitmans ($ in thousands).

Profit + Interest Expense + Income Tax Expense (EBIT)	÷	Interest Expense	=	Interest Coverage
$47,539 + $1,509 + $18,333	÷	$1,509	=	45 times

With an interest coverage ratio (EBIT) of 45 times, Reitmans appears well equipped to handle its interest payments.

BEFORE YOU GO ON...

DO IT

Gleason Ltd. reported the following selected data at December 31, 2013, and 2012.

	2013	2012
Total assets	$515,000	$529,000
Total liabilities	309,000	302,000
Interest expense	13,000	12,000
Income tax expense	25,500	22,500
Profit	85,000	75,000

Calculate Gleason Ltd.'s (a) debt to total assets, and (b) interest coverage ratios for each of the years 2013 and 2012 and comment on any trends.

Action Plan

- Divide the total liabilities by the total assets to calculate the debt to total assets ratio.
- Add the interest expense and income tax expense to profit to calculate earnings before interest and income tax.
- Divide the earnings before interest and income tax expense by the interest expense to calculate the interest coverage ratio.

SOLUTION

	2013	2012
(a) Debt to total assets	$309,000 ÷ $515,000 = 60%	$302,000 ÷ $529,000 = 57%
(b) Interest coverage	($85,000 + $25,500 + $13,000) ÷ $13,000 = $9.5 times	($75,000 + $22,500 + $12,000) ÷ $12,000 = 9.1 times

Gleason's debt to total assets increased in 2013 over 2012. In general, the higher the debt to total assets, the greater the risk that the company may be unable to meet its maturing obligations. The company's interest coverage ratio increased to 9.5 times. In general it is better to have a higher interest coverage ratio. Even though Gleason's debt to total assets increased, given the increase in interest coverage, the company seems well equipped to meet its interest payments.

THE NAVIGATOR

Related exercise material: BE15–15, BE15–16, BE15–17, E15–15, E15–16, and E15–17.

Comparing IFRS and ASPE

Key Differences	International Financial Reporting Standards (IFRS)	Accounting Standards for Private Enterprises (ASPE)
Bond discount and premium amortization	Must use the effective-interest method to amortize any bond discount or premium.	Normally will use the effective-interest method to amortize any bond discount or premium but permitted to use alternative methods if the results do not differ materially from the effective-interest method.

THE NAVIGATOR

DEMONSTRATION PROBLEM 1

Demonstration Problems

On January 1, 2011, Feng Inc. issued $500,000 of 10-year, 7% bonds at 93.205 because the market interest rate was 8%. Interest is payable semi-annually on January 1 and July 1. Feng's year end is June 30. On January 1, 2014, Feng redeemed all of these bonds at 90 after making the semi-annual interest payment.

Instructions

(a) Using present value factors, prove the issue price of the bonds of 93.205. Round all calculations to the nearest dollar.
(b) Prepare the journal entry to record the issue of the bonds on January 1, 2011.
(c) Prepare a bond discount amortization schedule for the first six interest periods.
(d) Prepare the journal entry to accrue the first interest payment on June 30.
(e) Show the presentation of the interest payable and the bonds payable on Feng's balance sheet on June 30, 2011.
(f) Prepare the journal entry to record the payment of the interest on January 1, 2014, and the redemption of the bonds on January 1, 2014.

SOLUTION TO DEMONSTRATION PROBLEM 1

(a)

1. $500,000 × 93.205%	$466,025
2. Key inputs:	
Future value (*FV*) = $500,000	
Market interest rate (*i*) = 4% (8% × 6/12)	
Interest payment (*PMT*) = $17,500 ($500,000 × 7% × 6/12)	
Number of semi-annual periods (*n*) = 20 (10 × 2)	
Present value of $500,000 received in 20 periods	
$500,000 × 0.45639 (*n* = 20, *i* = 4%)	$228,195
Present value of $17,500 received for each of 20 periods	
$17,500 × 13.59033 (*n* = 20, *i* = 4%)	237,830
Present value (market price) of bonds	$466,025

(b)

Date	Account	Debit	Credit
Jan. 1, 2011	Cash	466,025	
	Bonds Payable		466,025
	To record issue of 10-year, 7% bonds.		

Action Plan

- Calculate the proceeds using the stated percentage rate; multiply the face value by the issue price expressed as a percentage (for example, 93.205%).
- Identify the key inputs required to determine present value, whether using tables or a financial calculator.
- Calculate the present value (issue price) using the semi-annual market interest rate for (*i*). Use the face value of the bonds and the contractual interest rate to calculate the semi-annual interest payments. The face value of the bonds is the (*FV*), which is a single sum. The interest payments, which recur periodically, are an annuity. Don't forget to double the number of interest periods and halve the interest rate for semi-annual interest.

SOLUTION TO DEMONSTRATION PROBLEM continued on next page

SOLUTION TO DEMONSTRATION PROBLEM continued from previous page

- If the proceeds are greater than the face value, the difference is a premium. If the proceeds are less than the face value, the difference is a discount.
- Debit cash and credit bonds payable for the amount the bonds were issued at.
- Calculate the interest expense by multiplying the semi-annual market rate by the amortized cost of the bonds payable.
- The amount of the discount (premium) amortization is the difference between the interest payment and the interest expense.
- Amortization of a bond discount increases interest expense; amortization of a bond premium decreases interest expense.
- To record the redemption: update any partial period interest and amortization if required, (2) eliminate the amortized cost of the bonds by removing the balance from the Bonds Payable account, (3) record the cash paid, and (4) calculate and record the gain or loss (the difference between the cash paid and the amortized cost).

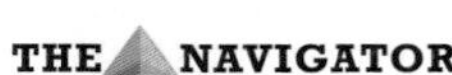

(c)

FENG INC.
Bond Discount Amortization Schedule
Effective-Interest Method

Semi-Annual Interest Period	(A) Interest Payment ($500,000 × 7% × 6/12)	(B) Interest Expense (D × 8% × 6/12)	(C) Discount Amortization (B − A)	(D) Bond Amortized Cost (D + C)
Issue date (Jan. 1, 2011)				$466,025
1 (July 1)	$17,500	$18,641	$1,141	467,166
2 (Jan. 1, 2012)	17,500	18,687	1,187	468,353
3 (July 1)	17,500	18,734	1,234	469,587
4 (Jan. 1, 2013)	17,500	18,783	1,283	470,870
5 (July 1)	17,500	18,835	1,335	472,205
6 (Jan. 1, 2014)	17,500	18,888	1,388	473,593

(d)

Date	Account	Debit	Credit
June 30, 2011	Bond Interest Expense	18,641	
	Bonds Payable		1,141
	Interest Payable		17,500
	To record accrual of semi-annual interest.		

(e)

FENG INC.
Balance Sheet (partial)
June 30, 2011

Current liabilities	
Interest payable	17,500
Non-current liabilities	
Bonds payable	$467,166

(f)

Date	Account	Debit	Credit
Jan. 1, 2014	Interest Expense	18,888	
	Bonds Payable		1,388
	Cash		17,500
	To record accrual of semi-annual interest.		
Jan. 1, 2014	Bonds Payable	473, 593	
	Cash ($500,000 × 90%)		450,000
	Gain on Redemption of Bonds ($473,593 − 450,000)		23,593
	To record redemption of bonds.		

DEMONSTRATION PROBLEM 2

Note: This demonstration problem uses the same facts as those shown in the "Do It" problem at the end of the Instalment Notes Payable section, but the nature and amount of the payment are changed.

On December 31, 2013, Tian Inc. issued a $500,000, 15-year, 8% mortgage note payable. The terms provide for semi-annual fixed principal payments of $16,667 on June 30 and December 31. Tian's year end is December 31.

Instructions

Round your answers to the nearest dollar.

(a) Prepare an instalment payment schedule for the first two years of the note (through to December 31, 2015).

(b) Prepare the journal entries to record the issue of the note on December 31, 2013, and the first two instalment payments.
(c) Indicate the current and non-current amounts for the mortgage note payable at December 31, 2014.
(d) What is the difference between your results here using a fixed principal payment and the results shown using a blended payment for the same situation illustrated in the "Do It" problem at the end of the Instalment Notes Payable section?

SOLUTION TO DEMONSTRATION PROBLEM 2

(a)

Semi-Annual Interest Period	Cash Payment	Interest Expense	Reduction of Principal	Principal Balance
Issue Date (Dec. 31, 2013)				$500,000
1 (June 30, 2014)	$36,667[1]	$20,000[2]	$16,667[3]	483,333[4]
2 (Dec. 31)	36,000	19,333	16,667	466,666
3 (June 30, 2015)	35,334	18,667	16,667	449,999
4 (Dec. 31)	34,667	18,000	16,667	433,332

[1] $20,000 + $16,667 = $36,667
[2] $500,000 × 8% × 6/12 = $20,000
[3] $500,000 ÷ 30 periods = $16,667
[4] $500,000 − $16,667 = $483,333

(b)

Date	Account	Debit	Credit
Dec. 31, 2013	Cash	500,000	
	Mortgage Note Payable		500,000
	To record issue of 15-year, 8% mortgage note payable.		
June 30, 2014	Interest Expense	20,000	
	Mortgage Note Payable	16,667	
	Cash		36,667
	To record semi-annual payment on note.		
Dec. 31, 2014	Interest Expense	19,333	
	Mortgage Note Payable	16,667	
	Cash		36,000
	To record semi-annual payment on note.		

(c) The current liability is $33,334 ($16,667 + $16,667).
The non-current liability is $433,332.
The total liability is $466,666, the balance at the end of the second period, December 31, 2014.

(d) In a blended payment situation, the cash payment stays constant. In a fixed principal payment situation, the reduction of the principal stays constant. In both situations, the same amount of principal is repaid over the same period of time—just in a different payment pattern.

Action Plan

- Determine the amount of the fixed principal payment by dividing the principal borrowed ($500,000) by the number of periods (15 years × 2).
- Determine the interest expense for the mortgage by multiplying the semi-annual interest rate by the principal balance at the beginning of the period. The cash payment is the total of the principal payment and interest expense.
- Use the payment schedule to record the reduction of principal, the interest expense, and the cash payment.
- The current portion of the mortgage note payable is the amount of principal that will be repaid in the next year. The non-current portion is the remaining balance.

THE NAVIGATOR

Summary of Study Objectives

1. ***Compare the impact of issuing debt instead of equity.*** Debt offers the following advantages over equity: (1) shareholder control is not affected, (2) income tax savings result, (3) earnings per share may be higher, and (4) return on equity may be higher.
2. ***Account for bonds payable.*** The market value of bonds is determined using present value factors to determine the present value of the interest and principal cash flows generated by the bond relative to the current market interest rate. When bonds are issued, the Bonds Payable account is credited for the bonds' market value (present value). Bonds are issued at a discount if the market interest rate is higher than the contractual interest rate. Bonds are issued at a premium if the market interest rate is lower than the contractual interest rate.

   Bond discounts and bond premiums are amortized to interest expense over the life of the bond using the effective-interest method of amortization. Amortization of the bond discount or premium is the difference between the interest paid and the interest expense. Interest paid is calculated by multiplying the face value of the bonds by the contractual interest rate. Interest expense is calculated by multiplying the amortized cost of the bonds at the beginning of the interest period by the market interest rate. The amortization of a bond discount increases interest expense. The amortization of a bond premium decreases interest expense.

When bonds are retired at maturity, Bonds Payable is debited and Cash is credited. There is no gain or loss at retirement. When bonds are redeemed before maturity, it is necessary to (1) pay and record any unrecorded interest, (2) eliminate the amortized cost of the bonds at the redemption date, (3) record the cash paid, and (4) recognize any gain or loss on redemption.

3. ***Account for instalment notes payable.*** Instalment notes payable are repayable in a series of instalments. Each payment consists of (1) interest on the unpaid balance of the note, and (2) a reduction of the principal balance. These payments can be either (1) fixed principal plus interest payments or (2) blended principal and interest payments. With fixed principal payments, the reduction in principal is constant but the cash payment and interest decrease each period (as the principal decreases). With blended payments, the cash payment is constant but the interest decreases and the principal reduction increases each period.

4. ***Explain and illustrate the methods for the presentation and analysis of non-current liabilities.*** The current portion of debt is the amount of the principal that must be paid within one year of the balance sheet date. This amount is reported as a current liability in the balance sheet, and the remaining portion of the principal is reported as a non-current liability. The nature of each liability should be described in the notes accompanying the financial statements. A company's long-term solvency may be analyzed by calculating two ratios. Debt to total assets indicates the proportion of company assets that is financed by debt. Interest coverage measures a company's ability to meet its interest payments as they come due.

THE NAVIGATOR

Glossary

Amortized cost The face value (principal amount) of the bonds less any unamortized discount or plus any unamortized premium. (p. 635)

Amortizing the discount The allocation of the bond discount to interest expense over the life of the bonds. (p. 636)

Amortizing the premium The allocation of the bond premium to interest expense over the life of the bonds. (p. 638)

Bond A debt security that is traded on an organized securities exchange, is issued to investors, and has these properties: the principal amount will be repaid at a designated maturity date and periodic interest is paid (normally semi-annually) at a specified rate on the principal amount. (p. 631)

Bond certificate A legal document indicating the name of the issuer, the face value of the bond, and other data such as the contractual interest rate and maturity date of the bond. (p. 631)

Collateral Assets pledged as security on a loan. (p. 643)

Contractual interest rate The rate that determines the amount of interest the borrower pays and the investor receives. (p. 631)

Debentures Bonds issued against the general credit of the borrower. Also called *unsecured bonds*. (p. 631)

Debt to total assets The ratio of total liabilities to total assets. Indicates the proportion of assets that is financed by debt. (p. 647)

Discount (on bonds payable) The difference that results when bonds' selling price is less than their face value. This occurs when the market interest rate is greater than the contractual interest rate. (p. 634)

EBIT Earnings before interest and tax, calculated as profit + interest expense + income tax expense. (p. 648)

Effective-interest method of amortization A method of calculating interest expense and of amortizing a bond discount or bond premium that results in periodic interest expense equal to a constant percentage of the amortized cost of the bonds. (p. 635)

Face value The amount of principal that the issuer must pay at the bond's maturity date. (p. 631)

Financial leverage Borrowing at one rate and investing at a different rate. (p. 629)

Fixed interest rate An interest rate that is constant (unchanged) over the term of the debt. (p. 643)

Floating (or variable) interest rate An interest rate that changes over the term of the debt with fluctuating market rates. (p. 643)

Future value An amount that will be paid in the future. In the case of bonds payable, it is the face amount of the bonds. (p. 633)

Instalment note Normally a long-term note that is payable in series of periodic payments. (p. 642)

Instalments A series of periodic payments made to repay a note payable. (p. 642)

Interest coverage ratio A measure of a company's ability to meet its interest obligations. It is calculated by dividing profit (earnings) before interest expense and income tax expense (EBIT) by interest expense. (p. 648)

Market (effective) interest rate The rate that investors require for lending money to a company. (p. 632)

Market value of the bond The price that the bond trades at. (p. 631)

Maturity date The date on which the final payment on a debt security is due to be repaid by the issuer to the investor. (p. 631)

Mortgage note payable An instalment note payable that pledges title to specific assets as security for a loan. (p. 643)

Non-current liability Obligations that are expected to be paid after one year or longer. (p. 628)

Premium (on bonds payable) The difference that results when bonds' selling price is greater than their face value. This occurs when the market interest rate is less than the contractual interest rate. (p. 634)

Present value The amount that must be invested today at a specified interest rate to have a certain amount in the future. (p. 632)

Redeemable bonds Bonds that the issuer can retire at a stated dollar amount before maturity. Also known as *callable bonds*. (p. 631)

Redemption price An amount that a company pays to buy back bonds that is specified at the time the bonds are issued. (p. 641)

Term bonds Bonds that mature at a single specified future date. (p. 631)

Self-Study Questions

Answers are at the end of the chapter.

(SO 1) K 1. The best description of positive financial leverage is:
(a) a company borrows at a rate that is lower than the return it earns on its investment.
(b) a company does not have to pay dividends.
(c) a company borrows at a rate that is higher than the return it earns on its investment.
(d) a company's income tax is reduced because of the interest paid on its debt.

(SO 2) K 2. If bonds are issued at a discount, it indicates that:
(a) the contractual interest rate is higher than the market interest rate.
(b) the market interest rate is higher than the contractual interest rate.
(c) the contractual interest rate and the market interest rate are the same.
(d) the bonds are junk bonds.

(SO 2) K 3. Communications Inc. issues $1 million of 10-year, 4% bonds when the market rate of interest is 5%. Interest is paid semi-annually. Investors will:
(a) not buy the bonds because the market rate of interest is higher than the contractual rate of interest.
(b) buy the bonds for $1 million.
(c) buy the bonds for more than $1 million.
(d) buy the bonds for less than $1 million.

(SO 2) AP 4. On January 1, Shears Corp. issues $400,000 of five-year, 4% bonds at 101. The entry to record the issue of the bonds is:
(a) debit to Cash for $400,000 and credit to Bonds Payable for $400,000.
(b) credit to Cash for $400,000 and debit to Bonds Payable for $400,000.
(c) credit to Cash for $404,000 and debit to Bonds Payable for $404,000.
(d) debit to Cash for $404,000 and credit to Bonds Payable for $404,000.

(SO 2) K 5. When bonds are issued at a discount, the discount is amortized over the life of the bonds. The best reason for amortizing the bond discount is to:
(a) reflect that the bond discount is considered an increase in the cost of borrowing.
(b) decrease the carrying value of the bond to its face value at maturity.
(c) reflect that the bond discount is considered a reduction in the cost of borrowing.
(d) ensure the bond payable is recorded at its fair value over the life of the bond.

(SO 2) AP 6. On January 1, Diaz Corporation issued $2 million of five-year, 7% bonds with interest payable on July 1 and January 1. The bonds sold for $1,918,880. The market rate of interest for these bonds was 8%. On the first interest date, the entry to record the payment of semi-annual interest would be:
(a) a debit to Interest Expense of $67,161, a credit to Cash of $70,000, and a debit to Bonds Payable of $2,839.
(b) a debit to Interest Expense of $70,000 and a credit to Cash of $70,000.
(c) a debit to Interest Expense of $80,000, a credit to Cash of $70,000, and a credit to Bonds Payable of $10,000.
(d) a debit to Interest Expense of $76,755, a credit to Cash of $70,000, and a credit to Bonds Payable of $6,755.

(SO 2) AP 7. Schissler Corporation redeems its $100,000 face value bonds at 105 on January 1, after the payment of semi-annual interest. The amortized cost of the bonds at the redemption date is $103,745. The entry to record the redemption will be:
(a) a debit to Bonds Payable of $103,745 and a credit to Cash of $103,745.
(b) a debit to Bonds Payable of $100,000, a debit to Loss on Bond Redemption of $3,745, and a credit to Cash of $103,745.
(c) a debit to Bonds Payable of $103,745, a debit to Loss on Bond Redemption of $1,255, and a credit to Cash of $105,000.
(d) a debit to Bonds Payable of $105,000 and a credit to Cash of $105,000.

(SO 3) AP 8. Zhang Inc. issues a $497,000, three-year, 7% instalment note payable on January 1. The note will be paid in three annual blended payments of $189,383 each. What is the amount of interest expense that should be recognized by Zhang in the second year?
(a) $21,533
(b) $23,193
(c) $23,968
(d) $34,790

(SO 3) AP 9. Assume that the note issued by Zhang Inc. in question 8 above will be paid with fixed principal payments of $165,667 each. What is the amount

of interest expense that should be recognized by Zhang in the second year?
(a) $25,628
(b) $23,193
(c) $11,596
(d) $34,790

(SO 3) AP 10. Manufacturing Inc. issued a $100,000, five-year, 5% note payable on January 1, 2014. The terms provide for annual blended payments of $23,098. The entry to record the first payment on December 31, 2014, is:
(a) a debit to Interest Expense of $5,000, a debit to Notes Payable of $18,098, and a credit to Cash of $23,098.
(b) a debit to Notes Payable of $23,098 and a credit to Cash of $23,098.
(c) a debit to Interest Expense of $5,000, a debit to Notes Payable of $23,098, and a credit to Cash of $28,098.
(d) a debit to Notes Payable of $20,000, a debit to Interest Expense of $3,098, and a credit to Cash of $23,098.

(SO 5) AN 11. Which of the following situations would most likely indicate that a company's solvency has deteriorated?
(a) Increasing debt to total assets and increasing interest coverage ratios
(b) Decreasing debt to total assets and decreasing interest coverage ratios
(c) Increasing debt to total assets and decreasing interest coverage ratios
(d) Decreasing debt to total assets and increasing interest coverage ratios

Questions

(SO 1) C 1. What is the difference between a current liability and a non-current liability? Give two examples of each type of liability.

(SO 1) C 2. As a source of long-term financing, what are the major advantages of using debt over equity? What are the disadvantages?

(SO 1) C 3. Amanda knows that interest expense reduces profit. So she doesn't understand how earnings per share and return on equity can be *higher* when a company finances with debt than if the company issues equity. Explain this to Amanda.

(SO 2) C 4. (a) Explain the difference between a contractual interest rate and market interest rate. (b) Explain why one rate changes over the term of the bonds and the other stays the same.

(SO 2) C 5. Eduardo wants to know why a board of directors doesn't set the contractual interest rate at the market interest rate on the date of issue when it authorizes a bond issue. He argues that if the contractual interest rate was set at the market rate, then companies would not have to issue bonds at a premium or discount. Explain the reasons for premiums and discounts to Eduardo.

(SO 2) C 6. Assume that Stoney Inc. sold bonds with a face value of $100,000 for $102,000. Was the market interest rate equal to, less than, or greater than the bonds' contractual interest rate? Explain.

(SO 2) C 7. How will the total cost of borrowing be affected if a bond is sold (a) at a discount and (b) at a premium?

(SO 2) C 8. Geoff doesn't understand why the interest expense recorded is higher than the cash paid for interest when bonds are issued at a discount and why the interest expense is lower than the cash paid when bonds are issued at premium. Explain this to Geoff.

(SO 2) K 9. Explain how the bond discount amortization is calculated using the effective-interest method when bonds are issued at a discount.

(SO 2) C 10. Why is there no gain or loss when bonds are redeemed at maturity, but there usually is a gain or loss when bonds are redeemed before maturity?

(SO 3) C 11. The Canada Student Loans Program charges interest at prime plus an added percentage, such as 2.5%, on its loans to students. Is this a fixed or floating rate? Explain.

(SO 3) C 12. What is the difference between instalment notes payable with fixed principal payments and those with blended payments?

(SO 3) AP 13. Magda borrowed $15,000 from the bank and signed a three-year, 6% instalment note payable with fixed principal payments. She wants to know how to calculate what the annual fixed principal payment will be. Explain.

(SO 3) AP 14. Bob Holowachuk, a friend of yours, recently purchased a home for $300,000. He paid $30,000 as a cash down payment and financed the remainder with a 20-year, 6% mortgage, payable in blended payments of $1,934 per month. At the end of the first month, Bob received a statement from the bank indicating that only $584 of the principal was paid during the month. At this rate, he calculated that it will take over 38 years to pay off the mortgage. Do you agree? Explain.

(SO 5) K 15. In addition to what is reported in the balance sheet for non-current liabilities, what information is provided in the notes to the financial statements?

(SO 5) K 16. How are the current and non-current portions of a mortgage note payable determined for presenting them in the liabilities section of the balance sheet?

(SO 5) K 17. Distinguish between liquidity and solvency. Mention two ratios that are used to measure each.

(SO 5) C 18. Abira is wondering why the debt to total assets and interest coverage ratios are calculated. Answer her question and explain why the debt to total assets ratio should never be interpreted without also referring to the interest coverage ratio.

(SO 5) C 19. Ling Wei doesn't understand how the interest coverage ratio can decrease when the debt to total assets increased. Explain this to Ling.

Brief Exercises

BE15–1 Place the number corresponding to each of the following characteristics in the appropriate section of the diagram. If a characteristic applies to both bonds payable and common shares, place that number in the overlapping section.

Compare debt and equity financing alternatives. **(SO 1) C**

1. Shown on the right side of the balance sheet
2. A form of equity financing
3. A form of debt financing
4. Represents ownership in a corporation
5. Can be bought or sold on a secondary market
6. Prices will tend to fluctuate
7. By law, the corporation must pay the investor a return on their investment.

BE15–2 Monk Inc. is considering two alternatives to finance its construction of a new $4-million plant at the beginning of the year: (a) issue 200,000 common shares at a market price of $20 per share, or (b) issue $4 million of 6% bonds at face value. Once the new plant is built, Monk expects to earn an additional $1 million of profit before interest and income tax. It has 500,000 common shares and $10 million of shareholders' equity before the new financing. Complete the following table for the year.

Compare debt and equity financing alternatives. **(SO 1) AP**

	(a) Issue Equity	(b) Issue Debt
Profit before interest and income tax	$1,000,000	$1,000,000
Interest expense		
Profit before income tax		
Income tax expense (25%)		
Profit		
Number of shares		
Earnings per share		

BE15-3 Estabrooks Corp. issued $500,000 of 10-year, 5% bonds with interest payable semi-annually. How much did Estabrooks receive from the sale of these bonds if the market interest rate was (a) 4%, (b) 5%, and (c) 6%?

Calculate present value of bond. **(SO 2) AP**

BE15–4 Rockwell Corporation issued $2 million of five-year, 3% bonds dated January 1, 2014, at 100. Interest is payable semi-annually on January 1 and July 1. Rockwell has a December 31 year end.

Record bond transactions. **(SO 2) AP**

(a) Prepare the journal entry to record the sale of these bonds on January 1, 2014.
(b) Prepare the journal entry to record the first interest payment on July 1, 2014.
(c) Prepare the adjusting journal entry on December 31, 2014, to accrue the interest expense.

BE15–5 The Town of Moosawaw issued $1 million of five-year, 5% bonds dated January 1, 2014. Interest is payable semi-annually on July 1 and January 1.

Record issue of bonds; show balance sheet presentation. **(SO 2) AP**

(a) Record the sale of these bonds on January 1, 2014, and the first interest payment on July 1, 2014, assuming that the bonds were issued at 98 and that the semi-annual amortization amount for the first interest period is $1,766.
(b) Record the sale of these bonds on January 1, 2014, and the first interest payment on July 1, 2014, assuming that the bonds were issued at 100.

(c) Record the sale of these bonds on January 1, 2014, and the first interest payment on July 1, 2014, assuming that the bonds were issued at 102 and that the semi-annual amortization amount for the first interest period is $1,804.
(d) What will be the amortized cost at maturity, January 1, 2019, under each of the three different issue prices?

Record bond transactions using effective-interest amortization. (SO 2) AP

BE15–6 On May 1, 2014, Jianhua Corporation issued $120,000 of 10-year, 6% bonds, with interest payable semi-annually on November 1 and May 1. The bonds were issued to yield a market interest rate of 5%.

(a) Calculate the proceeds from the bonds' issue.
(b) Record the issue of the bonds on May 1, 2014.
(c) Record the payment of interest on November 1, 2014.

Complete amortization schedule and answer questions. (SO 2) AP

BE15–7 A partial bond amortization schedule for $2-million, 5-year bonds is presented below:

Semi-Annual Interest Period	Interest [2]	Interest [3]	[1] Amortization	Bond Amortized Cost
Issue Date				$1,912,479
1 (Apr. 30)	$40,000	[4]	$7,812	1,920,291
2 (Oct. 31)	40,000	$48,007	[5]	[6]

(a) Fill in the missing words or amounts for items [1] through [6].
(b) What is the bonds' face value?
(c) What is the bonds' contractual interest rate? The market interest rate?
(d) Explain why interest expense differs from the amount of interest paid.

Prepare amortization schedule. (SO 2) AP

BE15–8 Turpin Ltd. issued $1 million of five-year, 4% bonds dated May 1, 2014, for $1,046,110 when the market interest rate was 3%. Interest is paid semi-annually on May 1 and November 1. Prepare an amortization schedule for the first three interest payments.

Record bond interest using amortization schedule. (SO 2) AP

BE15–9 Chiasson Corp. issued $300,000, 5-year bonds with interest paid semi-annually. A partial bond amortization schedule for Chiasson Corp. is provided below. Chiasson has a December 31 year end.

Semi-Annual Interest Period	Interest Payment	Interest Expense	Amortization	Bond Amortized Cost
Jan. 1, 2014				$286,872
July 1, 2014	$6,000	$7,172	$1,172	288,044
Jan. 1, 2015	6,000	7,201	1,201	289,245
July 1, 2015	6,000	7,231	1,231	290,476

(a) Was the bond issued at a premium or discount? Explain your reasoning.
(b) Record the interest payment on July 1, 2014.
(c) Record the adjusting entry on December 31, 2014.
(d) Record the interest payment on January 1, 2015.

Record redemption of bonds using amortization schedule. (SO 2) AP

BE15–10 Refer to the amortization schedule presented in BE15–9 for Chiasson Corp.

(a) Assuming Chiasson redeems these bonds at 100 on January 1, 2015, after the interest has been paid, prepare the journal entry to record the redemption.
(b) Assuming Chiasson redeems these bonds at 101 on January 1, 2015, after the interest has been paid, prepare the journal entry to record the redemption.
(c) Assuming Chiasson redeems these bonds at 95 on January 1, 2015, after the interest has been paid, prepare the journal entry to record the redemption.

Prepare instalment payment schedule. (SO 3) AP

BE15–11 You qualify for a $10,000 loan from the Canada Student Loans Program to help finance your post-secondary education. Once you graduate, you start repaying this note payable at an interest rate of 4.8%. The monthly cash payment is $105.09, principal and interest, for 120 payments (10 years). Prepare an instalment payment schedule for the first four payments.

BE15–12 Eaton Inc. issues a $360,000, 10-year, 6% mortgage note payable on November 30, 2013, to obtain financing for a new building. The terms provide for monthly instalment payments. Prepare the journal entries to record the mortgage loan on November 30, 2013, and the first two payments on December 31, 2013, and January 31, 2014, assuming the payment is:

Record note transactions. **(SO 3) AP**

(a) a fixed principal payment of $3,000.
(b) a blended payment of $3,997.

BE15–13 The following instalment payment schedule is for an instalment note payable:

Calculate current and non-current portion of notes payable. **(SO 3) AP**

Interest Period	Cash Payment	Interest Expense	Reduction of Principal	Principal Balance
Jan. 1, 2013				$40,000
Jan. 1, 2014	12,000	2,000	10,000	30,000
Jan. 1, 2015	11,500	1,500	10,000	20,000
Jan. 1, 2016	11,000	1,000	10,000	10,000
Jan. 1, 2017	10,500	500	10,000	0

(a) What are the non-current and current portions of the note at December 31, 2013?
(b) What are the non-current and current portions of the note at December 31, 2016?

BE15–14 Elbow Lake Corp. issues a $600,000, four-year, 4% note payable on March 31, 2013. The terms provide for fixed principal payments annually of $150,000.

Record note transaction; show balance sheet presentation. **(SO 3) AP**

(a) Prepare the journal entries to record the note on March 31, 2013, and the first payment on March 31, 2014.
(b) Show the balance sheet presentation of the current and non-current liability related to the note as at March 31, 2014.

BE15–15 Cooke Inc. issued a $240,000, 10-year, 8% note payable on October 1, 2013. The terms provide for blended payments of $8,773 payable in quarterly instalments on January 1, April 1, July 1, and October 1. Below is a partial instalment schedule for the note payable.

Show balance sheet presentation. **(SO 5) AP**

Interest Period	Cash Payment	Interest Expense	Reduction of Principal	Principal Balance
Oct. 1, 2013				$240,000
Jan. 1, 2014	$8,773	$4,800	$3,973	236,027
Apr. 1, 2014	8,773	4,721	4,052	231,975
July 1, 2014	8,773	4,639	4,134	227,841
Oct. 1, 2014	8,773	4,557	4,216	223,625
Jan. 1, 2015	8,773	4,472	4,301	219,324

Show the balance sheet presentation of the current and non-current liability related to the note as at December 31, 2013.

BE15–16 Selected liability items for Waugh Corporation at December 31, 2014, follow. Prepare the liabilities section of Waugh's balance sheet.

Prepare liabilities section of balance sheet. **(SO 5) AP**

Accounts payable	$ 48,000	Income tax payable	$ 8,000
Bonds payable, due 2028	1,035,000	Notes payable, (net of current portion)	145,000
Current portion of notes payable	25,000	Interest payable	26,000

BE15–17 **Molson Coors Brewing Company** reported the following selected data at December 31, 2011 (in US$ millions):

Calculate solvency ratios. **(SO 5) AP**

Total assets	$12,423.8
Total liabilities	4,733.6
Interest expense	118.7
Income tax expense	99.4
Profit	677.1

Calculate the company's (a) debt to total assets, and (b) interest coverage ratios.

Exercises

Compare debt and equity financing alternatives. (SO 1) AP

E15–1 East-West Airlines is considering two alternatives to finance the purchase of a fleet of airplanes. These alternatives are (1) to issue 120,000 common shares at $45 per share, and (2) to issue 10-year, 5% bonds for $5.4 million. It is estimated that the company will earn an additional $1.2 million before interest and income tax as a result of this purchase. The company has an income tax rate of 30%. It has 200,000 common shares issued and average shareholders' equity of $12 million before the new financing.

Instructions

(a) Calculate the profit for each financing alternative.
(b) Calculate the earnings per share and return on equity for each alternative.
(c) Which financing alternative would you recommend for East-West Airlines? Why?

Calculate present value of bonds. (SO 2) AP

E15–2 Central College is about to issue $1 million of 10-year bonds that pay a 6% annual interest rate, with interest payable semi-annually.

Instructions

(a) Calculate the issue price of these bonds if the market interest rate is (1) 5%, (2) 6%, and (3) 7%.
(b) Calculate the interest expense for the first interest period if the market interest rate is (1) 5%, (2) 6%, and (3) 7%.
(c) Calculate the interest payment if the market interest rate is (1) 5%, (2) 6%, and (3) 7%.

Record bond transactions; show balance sheet presentation. (SO 2) AP

E15–3 On September 1, 2013, Priora Corporation issued $600,000 of 10-year, 3% bonds at 96. Interest is payable semi-annually on September 1 and March 1. Priora's fiscal year end is February 28.

Instructions

(a) Is the market rate of interest higher or lower than 3%? Explain.
(b) Record the issue of the bonds on September 1, 2013.
(c) Record the accrual of interest on February 28, 2014, assuming the semi-annual amortization amount for this interest period is $1,014.
(d) Identify what amounts, if any, would be reported as a current liability and non-current liability with respect to the bonds and bond interest accounts on February 28, 2014.
(e) Record the payment of interest on March 1, 2014.

Record bond transactions; show balance sheet presentation. (SO 2) AP

E15–4 On July 31, 2013, Mooney Inc. issued $500,000 of five-year, 4% bonds at 102. Interest is payable semi-annually on July 31 and January 31. Mooney's fiscal year end is January 31.

Instructions

(a) Is the market rate of interest higher or lower than 4%? Explain.
(b) Record the issue of the bonds on July 31, 2013.
(c) Record the payment of interest on January 31, 2014, assuming the semi-annual amortization amount for this interest period is $923.
(d) Identify what amounts, if any, would be reported as a current liability and non-current liability with respect to the bonds and bond interest accounts on January 31, 2014.

Answer questions about amortization schedule. (SO 2) AP

E15–5 Mertsis Corporation issued $400,000 five-year bonds on April 1, 2011. Interest is paid semi-annually on April 1 and October 1 and the company's year end is March 31. Below is a partial amortization schedule for the first few years of the bond issue.

Semi-Annual Interest Period	Interest Payment	Interest Expense	Amortization	Bond Amortized Cost
April 1, 2011				$418,444
October 1, 2011	$8,000	$6,277	$1,723	416,721
April 1, 2012	8,000	6,251	1,749	414,972
October 1, 2012	8,000	6,225	1,775	413,197
April 1, 2013	8,000	6,198	1,802	411,395
October 1, 2013	8,000	6,171	1,829	409,566
April 1, 2014	8,000	6,143	1,857	407,709

Instructions

(a) Were the bonds issued at a discount or at a premium?
(b) What is the bonds' face value?
(c) What will the bonds' amortized cost be at the maturity date?
(d) What is the bonds' contractual interest rate? The market interest rate?
(e) Identify what amounts, if any, would be reported as a current liability and non-current liability with respect to the bonds and bond interest accounts on March 31, 2013.
(f) What will be the total interest payment over the five-year life of the bonds? Total interest expense?
(g) Would your answers in part (f) change if the bonds had been issued at a discount instead of a premium or at a premium instead of a discount? Explain.

E15–6 On January 1, 2012, Chilton Ltd. issued $500,000, 5%, five-year bonds. The bonds were issued to yield a market interest rate of 6%. Chilton's year end is December 31. On January 1, 2014, immediately after making and recording the semi-annual interest payment, Chilton redeemed the bonds. A partial bond amortization schedule is presented below.

Record interest and redemption of bonds. **(SO 2) AP**

Semi-Annual Interest Period	Interest Payment	Interest Expense	Amortization	Bond Amortized Cost
January 1, 2012				$478,674
July 1, 2012	$12,500	$14,360	$1,860	480,534
January 1, 2013	12,500	14,416	1,916	482,450
July 1, 2013	12,500	14,474	1,974	484,424
January 1, 2014	12,500	14,533	2,033	486,457
July 1, 2014	12,500	14,594	2,094	488,551
January 1, 2015	12,500	14,657	2,157	490,708

Instructions

(a) Prepare the journal entry to record the payment of interest on July 1, 2013.
(b) Prepare the journal entry to accrue the interest expense on December 31, 2013.
(c) Prepare the journal entry to record the payment of interest on January 1, 2014.
(d) Prepare the journal entry to record the redemption of the bonds assuming they were redeemed at 100.
(e) Prepare the journal entry to record the redemption of the bonds assuming they were redeemed at 96.

E15–7 Ontario Inc. issued $800,000 of 10-year, 4% bonds on January 1, 2013, when the market interest rate was 5%. Interest is payable semi-annually on July 1 and January 1. Ontario has a December 31 year end.

Record interest and redemption of bonds. **(SO 2) AP**

Instructions

(a) Calculate the bonds' issue price.
(b) Record the issue of the bonds.
(c) Prepare an amortization schedule through to December 31, 2014 (four interest periods).
(d) Record the accrual of the interest on December 31, 2014.
(e) Identify what amounts, if any, would be reported as a current liability and a non-current liability with respect to the bonds and bond interest accounts on December 31, 2014.
(f) Record the payment of interest on January 1, 2015.

E15–8 Frauts Corporation issued $600,000 of 10-year, 8% bonds on January 1, 2014, for $642,637. This price resulted in a market interest rate of 7% on the bonds. Interest is payable semi-annually on July 1 and January 1. Frauts has a December 31 year end. On January 1, 2015, immediately after making and recording the semi-annual interest payment, the bonds were redeemed at 104.

Record bond transactions. **(SO 2, 6) AP**

Instructions

(a) Record the issue of the bonds on January 1, 2014.
(b) Prepare an amortization schedule through to December 31, 2015 (four interest periods).
(c) Record the payment of interest on July 1, 2014.
(d) Record the accrual of interest on December 31, 2014.
(e) Record the redemption of the bonds on January 1, 2015.

E15–9 Cove Resort Corp. issued a 20-year, 5%, $300,000 mortgage note payable to finance the construction of a new building on December 31, 2014. The terms provide for semi-annual instalment payments on June 30 and December 31.

Record mortgage note payable. **(SO 3) AP**

Instructions

Prepare the journal entries to record the mortgage note payable and the first two instalment payments assuming the payment is:

(a) a fixed principal payment of $7,500.
(b) a blended payment of $11,951.

Analyze instalment payment schedule and identify current and non-current portions. (SO 3) AP

E15–10 The following instalment payment schedule is for an instalment note payable:

Interest Period	Cash Payment	Interest Expense	Reduction of Principal	Principal Balance
Jan. 1, 2013				100,000
Jan. 1, 2014	23,097	5,000	18,097	81,903
Jan. 1, 2015	23,097	4,095	19,002	62,901
Jan. 1, 2016	23,097	3,145	19,952	42,949
Jan. 1, 2017	23,097	2,147	20,950	21,999
Jan. 1, 2018	23,097	1,100	21,999	0

Instructions

(a) Is this a fixed principal or blended payment schedule?
(b) What is the interest rate on the note?
(c) Prepare the journal entry to record the first instalment payment.
(d) What are the non-current and current portions of the note at the end of period 2?

Analyze instalment payment schedule and identify current and non-current portions. (SO 3) AP

E15–11 The following instalment payment schedule is for an instalment note payable:

Interest Period	Cash Payment	Interest Expense	Reduction of Principal	Principal Balance
Jan. 1, 2013				$150,000
July 1, 2013	24,750	6,000	18,750	131,250
Jan. 1, 2014	24,000	5,250	18,750	112,500
July 1, 2014	23,250	4,500	18,750	93,750
Jan. 1, 2015	22,500	3,750	18,750	75,000

Instructions

(a) Is this a fixed principal or blended payment schedule? Explain your choice.
(b) What is the interest rate on the note?
(c) What is the maturity date on the note?
(d) Prepare the journal entry to record the first instalment payment.
(e) What are the non-current and current portions of the note at the end of period 2?

Prepare instalment payment schedule and record note payable. Identify balance sheet presentation. (SO 3) AP

E15–12 On January 1, 2014, Wolstenholme Corp. borrows $15,000 by signing a three-year, 6% note payable. The note is repayable in three annual blended payments of $5,612 on December 31 of each year.

Instructions

(a) Prepare an instalment payment schedule for the note.
(b) Prepare journal entries to record the note and the first instalment payment.
(c) What amounts would be reported as current and non-current in the liabilities section of Wolstenholme's balance sheet on December 31, 2014?

Prepare instalment payment schedule and record note payable. Identify balance sheet presentation. (SO 3) AP

E15–13 Referring to the data presented in E15–12 for Wolstenholme Corp., assume the payments are annual fixed principal payments instead of blended payments.

Instructions

(a) Calculate the annual principal payment.
(b) Prepare an instalment payment schedule for the note.
(c) Prepare journal entries to record the note and the first instalment payment.
(d) What amounts would be reported as current and non-current in the liabilities section of Wolstenholme's balance sheet on December 31, 2014?

E15–14 Shoppers Drug Mart Corporation reported the following selected data (in millions):

Analyze solvency. (SO 4) AP

	2011	2010
Total assets	$7,300.3	$7,044.2
Total liabilities	3,032.5	2,941.6
Profit	613.9	591.9
Income tax expense	232.9	244.8
Interest expense	64.0	60.6

Instructions

(a) Calculate the debt to total assets and interest coverage ratios for 2011 and 2010. Did Shoppers' solvency improve, worsen, or remain unchanged in 2011?

E15–15 The Utopia Paper Company requires $5 million of financing to upgrade its production facilities. It has a choice to finance the upgrade with a 6% non-current loan or to issue additional shares. The company currently has total assets of $12 million, total liabilities of $8 million, shareholders' equity of $4 million, and profit of $2 million. It projects that profit will be $315,000 higher if debt is issued and $525,000 higher if shares are issued. Assume the project is invested in at the beginning of the year.

Calculate ratios under financing alternatives. (SO 1, 5) AP

Instructions

(a) Calculate the debt to total assets and return on equity ratios under each financing alternative.
(b) Which financing alternative would you recommend for Utopia Paper? Why?

E15–16 The adjusted trial balance for Ray Corporation at July 31, 2014, the corporation's fiscal year end, contained the following:

Prepare non-current liabilities section of balance sheet. (SO 5) AP

Accounts payable	$ 96,000	Note payable	$140,000
Accounts receivable	112,000	Note receivable, due December 2014	35,000
Bonds payable, due 2018	205,000	Unearned revenue	10,000
Interest payable	5,000		

Total payments on the note payable in the fiscal year 2015 will be $27,000: $7,000 is for interest and $20,000 for principal repayments.

Instructions

(a) Prepare the non-current liabilities section of the balance sheet as at July 31, 2014.
(b) Some of the accounts above belong in the balance sheet but not in its non-current liabilities section. What is the correct classification for them?

Problems: Set A

P15–1A The following is from Creasor Corp.'s balance sheet:

Record bond transactions. (SO 2) AP

CREASOR CORP. Balance Sheet (partial) December 31, 2013	
Current liabilities	
Interest payable	$ 50,000
Non-current liabilities	
Bonds payable, due January 1, 2017	2,500,000

Interest is payable semi-annually on January 1 and July 1. The bonds were issued at par.

Instructions

(a) What is the contractual rate of interest on the bonds?
(b) Record the payment of the bond interest on January 1, 2014.
(c) Assume that on January 1, 2014, after paying interest, Creasor redeems $625,000 of the bonds at 102. Record the redemption of the bonds.
(d) Record the payment of the bond interest on July 1, 2014, on the remaining bonds.
(e) Prepare the adjusting entry on December 31, 2014, to accrue the interest on the remaining bonds.
(f) Prepare the entry to record the repayment of the remaining bonds on January 1, 2017.

TAKING IT FURTHER Was the market rate of interest higher or lower than the contractual rate of interest on January 1, 2014, when the bonds were redeemed? Explain.

Record bond transactions; show balance sheet presentation. (SO 2) AP

P15–2A On May 1, 2013, MEM Corp. issued $900,000 of five-year, 7% bonds at 103. The bonds pay interest annually on May 1. MEM's year end is April 30.

Instructions

(a) Record the issue of the bonds on May 1, 2013.
(b) Record the accrual of interest on April 30, 2014, assuming the amortization amount is $4,763.
(c) What amounts related to the bonds would be reported as current and non-current in the liabilities section of MEM's April 30, 2014, balance sheet?
(d) Record the payment of interest on May 1, 2014.
(e) Assume that on May 1, 2014, after payment of the interest, MEM redeems all of the bonds at 104. Record the redemption of the bonds.

TAKING IT FURTHER What was the market rate of interest on May 1, 2013, when MEM issued the bonds?

Record bond transactions and answer questions. (SO 2) AP

P15–3A On July 1, 2013, Webhancer Corp. issued $4 million of 10-year, 5% bonds at $4,327,029. This price resulted in a 4% market interest rate on the bonds. The bonds pay semi-annual interest on July 1 and January 1, and Webhancer has a December 31 year end.

Instructions

(a) Record the following transactions:
   1. The issue of the bonds on July 1, 2013
   2. The accrual of interest on December 31, 2013
   3. The payment of interest on January 1, 2014
   4. The payment of interest on July 1, 2014
(b) Answer the following questions:
   1. What amount of interest expense is reported for 2013?
   2. Would the bond interest expense reported in 2013 be the same as, greater than, or less than the amount that would be reported if the bonds had been issued at a discount rather than at a premium? Explain.
   3. Determine the total cost of borrowing over the life of the bonds.
   4. Would the total bond interest expense be greater than, the same as, or less than the total interest expense that would be reported if the bonds had been issued at a discount rather than at a premium? Explain.
   5. Assuming that the bonds were issued at a market interest rate of 6%, calculate the issue price of the bonds. Determine the total cost of borrowing over the life of the bonds.

TAKING IT FURTHER Explain what the impact would be on interest expense if the market rate of interest changed to 4.5% in December 2013 after the bonds were issued.

Fill in missing amounts in amortization schedule, record bond transactions, and show balance sheet presentation. (SO 2, 5) AP

P15–4A On January 1, 2013, Global Satellites issued $1.4-million, 10-year bonds. The bonds pay semi-annual interest on July 1 and January 1, and Global has a December 31 year end. A partial bond amortization schedule is presented below:

Semi-Annual Interest Period	Interest Payment	Interest Expense	Amortization	Bond Amortized Cost
January 1, 2013				$1,300,514
July 1, 2013	$[1]	$[2]	$3,518	1,304,032
January 1, 2014	42,000	45,641	3,641	1,307,673
July 1, 2014	42,000	45,769	[3]	1,311,442
January 1, 2015	42,000	45,900	[4]	[5]
July 1, 2015	42,000	46,037	4,037	1,319,379
January 1, 2016	42,000	46,178	4,178	1,323,557

Instructions

(a) Were the bonds issued at a premium or a discount?
(b) Fill in the missing amounts for [1] through [5].
(c) What is the face value of the bonds?
(d) What is the contractual rate of interest?

(e) What was the market interest rate when the bonds were issued?
(f) Record the issue of the bonds on January 1, 2013.
(g) Record the interest payment on July 1, 2014.
(h) Record the accrual of interest on December 31, 2014.
(i) What amounts would be reported as current and non-current in the liabilities section of Global's December 31, 2014, balance sheet?
(j) Record the interest payment on January 1, 2015.
(k) Assuming, immediately after the interest payment the bonds were redeemed on January 1, 2015, when the market interest rate was 5%, calculate the amount Global paid to redeem the bonds. (*Hint*: Use the number of interest periods remaining to calculate the amount paid to redeem the bonds.)
(l) Record the redemption of the bonds on January 1, 2015.

TAKING IT FURTHER Why would Global's board of directors not have set the contractual interest rate at the market interest rate on the date of issue when it authorized the bond issue?

P15–5A On January 1, 2013, Alberta Hydro Ltd. issued bonds with a maturity value of $8 million when the market rate of interest was 4%. The bonds have a coupon (contractual) interest rate of 5% and mature on January 1, 2023. Interest on the bonds is payable semi-annually on July 1 and January 1 of each year. The company's year end is December 31.

Record bond transactions; show balance sheet presentation. **(SO 2, 5) AP**

Instructions

(a) Calculate the issue price of the bonds.
(b) Prepare a bond amortization schedule from date of issue up to and including January 1, 2015.
(c) Prepare all of the required journal entries related to the bonds that Alberta Hydro will record during 2013, including any adjusting journal entries at December 31, 2013.
(d) What amounts would be reported as current and non-current in the liabilities section of Alberta Hydro's December 31, 2013, balance sheet?
(e) Record the payment of interest on January 1, 2014.
(f) The bonds were redeemed on January 1, 2015 (after the interest had been paid and recorded) at 102. Prepare the journal entry for the redemption of the bonds.
(g) Assume instead the bonds were not redeemed on January 1, 2015. Record the entry for the repayment of the bonds on January 1, 2023.
(h) What will be the total interest payment over the 10-year life of the bonds? What will be the total interest expense over the 10-year life of the bonds?

TAKING IT FURTHER Explain why the total interest payment over the 10-year life of the bonds is equal to or different than the total interest expense over the 10-year life of the bonds.

P15–6A A local company has just approached a venture capitalist for financing to develop a ski hill. On April 1, 2013, the venture capitalist loaned the company $1 million at an interest rate of 5%. The loan is repayable over four years in fixed principal payments. The first payment is due March 31, 2014. The ski hill operator's year end will be December 31.

Prepare instalment payment schedule, record note transactions, and show balance sheet presentation. **(SO 3, 5) AP**

Instructions

(a) Record the issue of the note payable on April 1, 2013.
(b) Calculate the amount of the fixed principal payment.
(c) Prepare an instalment payment schedule.
(d) Record the accrual of interest on December 31, 2013, and the instalment payment on March 31, 2014.
(e) What amounts would be reported as current and non-current in the liabilities section of the company's December 31, 2013, balance sheet?
(f) Record the accrual of interest on December 31, 2014, and the instalment payment on March 31, 2015.

TAKING IT FURTHER Explain how the interest expense and reduction of the note payable would change in parts (b) and (c) if the note had been repayable in blended payments of $282,012, rather than in fixed principal payments.

P15–7A Olsen Well Services Ltd. purchased equipment for $900,000 on September 30, 2013. The equipment was purchased with a $150,000 cash down payment and through the issue of a $750,000, five-year, 3.6% mortgage note payable for the balance. The terms provide for the mortgage to be repaid in monthly blended payments of $13,677 starting on October 31.

Record note transactions. **(SO 3) AP**

Instructions

(a) Record the issue of the note payable on September 30.
(b) Record the first two instalment payments on October 31 and November 30.
(c) Repeat part (b) assuming that the terms provided for monthly fixed principal payments of $12,500, rather than blended payments of $13,677.

TAKING IT FURTHER If the instalments are fixed principal payments of $12,500, will the interest expense over the life of the note be greater than, the same as, or less than if the instalments are a blended payment of $13,677? Explain.

Prepare instalment payment schedule and record note transactions. Show balance sheet presentation.
(SO 3) AP

P15–8A Kinyae Electronics issues a $700,000, 10-year, 7% mortgage note payable on December 31, 2013, to help finance a plant expansion. The terms of the note provide for semi-annual blended payments of $49,253. Payments are due on June 30 and December 31.

Instructions

(a) Prepare an instalment payment schedule for the first two years. Round all calculations to the nearest dollar.
(b) Record the issue of the mortgage note payable on December 31, 2013.
(c) Show how the mortgage liability should be reported on the balance sheet at December 31, 2013. (*Hint*: Remember to report any current portion separately from the non-current liability.)
(d) Record the first two instalment payments on June 30, 2014, and December 31, 2014.
(e) If Kinyae made instalments of fixed principal payments on a semi-annual basis, what would the fixed principal payment be?
(f) Assuming Kinyae made fixed principal payments, record the first two instalments.

TAKING IT FURTHER Indicate the advantages and disadvantages of making fixed principal payments versus blended payments.

Calculate and analyze solvency ratios.
(SO 4) AN

P15–9A Loblaw Companies Limited reported the following selected information (in millions):

	2011	2010
Total assets	$17,428	$16,841
Total liabilities	11,421	11,238
Interest expense	327	353
Income tax expense	288	319
Profit	769	675

Instructions

(a) Calculate Loblaw's debt to total assets and interest coverage ratios for each year.
(b) Based on the ratios calculated in part (a), what conclusions can you make about Loblaw's solvency?

TAKING IT FURTHER Businesses try to keep their expenses low in order to maximize profits. Is income tax expense controllable in the same way that some other expenses are? Is a high income tax expense necessarily a problem?

Prepare liabilities section of balance sheet and analyze leverage.
(SO 5) AP

P15–10A The adjusted trial balance for Sykes Ltd. at October 31, 2014, contained the following:

Accounts payable	$ 57,000	Income tax expense	$ 11,800
Accounts receivable	98,000	Income tax payable	5,900
Allowance for doubtful accounts	4,900	Note payable	230,211
Bonds payable, due 2020	500,000	Interest expense	53,330
Interest payable	15,000	Note receivable, due 2015	35,000
Common shares	350,000	Retained earnings, November 1, 2013	824,793
Dividends	25,000	Unearned revenue	10,000

Total payments on the note payable in the next 12 months will be $20,800, of which $11,125 is for interest. Sykes reported profit for the year ended October 31, 2014, of $36,000. No common shares were issued during the year.

Instructions

(a) Prepare the liabilities and shareholders' equity section of the balance sheet.
(b) Calculate Sykes's debt to assets and interest coverage ratios for the year ended October 31, 2014.
(c) Based on the ratios calculated in part (b), what conclusions can you make about Sykes's solvency?

TAKING IT FURTHER What other information would help in the analysis of the company's solvency?

CONTINUING COOKIE CHRONICLE

(*Note:* This is a continuation of the Cookie Chronicle from Chapters 1 through 14.)

Janet, Brian, and Natalie have recently negotiated a contract to provide cupcakes on a weekly basis to a number of coffee shops in their area. As a result of the anticipated demand for cupcakes, they are making plans to purchase an additional commercial oven. The cost of this oven is estimated at $25,000, and the company already has $4,000 set aside for the purchase. Janet, Brian, and Natalie have met with their bank manager. She is willing to lend Koebel's Family Bakery Ltd. $21,000 on September 1, 2014, for a period of three years at a 4% interest rate.

The bank manager has set out the following two payment alternatives:

Alternative 1: The terms provide for fixed principal payments of $3,500 on September 1 and March 1 of each year.

Alternative 2: The terms provide for blended payments of $3,749 on September 1 and March 1 of each year.

Janet, Brian, and Natalie ask you to help them decide which alternative is better for them.

Instructions

(a) Prepare instalment payment schedules for each of the alternatives for the full term of the loan.
(b) Prepare the journal entry for the purchase of the oven and the issue of the note payable on September 1, 2014.
(c) Prepare the journal entries for the first two instalment payments under each alternative.
(d) Determine the current portion of the note payable and the non-current portion of the note payable as at July 31, 2015, the company's year end, under each alternative.
(e) Prepare the adjusting journal entries required at July 31, 2015, the company's year end, under each alternative.
(f) Which payment alternative do you recommend? Why?

Cumulative Coverage—Chapters 13 to 15

Plankton Corporation's trial balance at December 31, 2015, is presented below:

PLANKTON CORPORATION
Trial Balance
December 31, 2015

	Debit	Credit
Cash	$ 48,000	
Accounts receivable	51,000	
Allowance for doubtful accounts		$ 2,500
Merchandise inventory	22,700	
Land	190,000	
Building	215,000	
Accumulated depreciation—building		40,000
Equipment	40,000	
Accumulated depreciation—equipment		15,000
Accounts payable		18,775
Income tax payable		4,500
Bonds payable (6%, due January 1, 2019)		126,025
Common shares, unlimited number of no par value shares authorized, 100,000 issued		100,000
Retained earnings		110,775
Accumulated other comprehensive income		5,000
Sales		750,000
Cost of goods sold	370,000	
Operating expenses	180,000	
Interest revenue		375
Interest expense	6,250	
Income tax expense	50,000	
Total	$1,172,950	$1,172,950

All transactions and adjustments for 2015 have been recorded and reported in the trial balance except for the items described below.

Jan. 7 Issued 1,000 preferred shares for $25,000. In total, 100,000, $2, non-cumulative, convertible, preferred shares are authorized. Each preferred share is convertible into five common shares.

Sept. 25 Five hundred of the preferred shares issued on January 7 were converted into common shares.

Nov. 30 Obtained a $50,000 bank loan by issuing a three-year, 6% note payable. Plankton is required to make equal blended payments of $1,521 at the end of each month. The first payment was made on December 31. Note that at December 31, $15,757 of the note payable is due within the next year.

Dec. 1 Declared the annual dividend on the preferred shares on December 1 to shareholders of record on December 23, payable on January 15.

31 The annual interest is due on the bonds payable on January 1, 2016. The par value of the bonds is $130,000 and the bonds were issued when the market interest rate was 7%.

Instructions

(a) Record the transactions.
(b) Prepare an updated trial balance at December 31, 2015, that includes these transactions.
(c) Using the income statement accounts in the trial balance, calculate income before income tax. Assuming Plankton has a 28% income tax rate, prepare the journal entry to adjust income taxes for the year. Note that Plankton has recorded $50,000 of income tax expense for the year to date. Update the trial balance for this additional entry.
(d) Prepare the following financial statements for Plankton: (1) income statement, (2) statement of changes in shareholders' equity, and (3) balance sheet.

CHAPTER 15 BROADENING YOUR PERSPECTIVE

Collaborative Learning Activity

Note to instructor: Additional instructions and material for this group activity can be found on the Instructor Resource Site and in *WileyPLUS*.

BYP15–1 In this group activity, you will analyze and compare three financing alternatives for the purchase of a new vehicle. Your instructor will evaluate your group on your analysis as well as your rationale for selecting one of the alternatives.

Communication Activity

BYP15–2 Financial statement users are interested in the obligations that a company has from past transactions. It is important to determine which liabilities are current and which are non-current. Some company obligations are not recorded on the balance sheet itself, however; instead they are disclosed in the notes to the financial statements.

Instructions

Write a memorandum to a friend of yours who has inherited some money and would like to invest in some companies. Your friend plans to get professional advice before investing but would like you to review some basics with her. For instance, she is trying to determine the amount of cash that a company will have to pay within the next five years. She knows she should start with the liabilities that are on the balance sheet, but she is wondering if any of those can be settled without the company having to write a cheque. (*Hint:* A review of Reitmans' financial statements in Appendix A will help you.)

Ethics Case

BYP15–3 Lehman Brothers, a giant investment company in the United States, announced in September 2008 that it would file for bankruptcy protection after suffering huge losses in the mortgage market. In 2010, the bankruptcy examiner's report stated that Lehman's accounting had misled investors. One of the tricks that Lehman used was to temporarily transfer investment assets to a related company in exchange for cash. The company then used the cash to temporarily reduce its liabilities by paying off debt, thus making its balance sheet look better than it was. After the company's financial statements were published, it borrowed the cash again and took back the assets.

Instructions

(a) Who are the stakeholders in this situation?
(b) Explain what the impact of paying debt off will be on the debt to total assets ratio.
(c) Explain how paying debt off and then immediately borrowing again, right after the financial statements are published, could mislead investors. (*Hint*: Consider the fundamental qualitative characteristics, discussed in Chapter 11, that accounting information should have to be useful to investors and creditors.)

All About You: Personal Financial Literacy Activity

BYP15–4 As indicated in the "All About You" feature in this chapter, a student can benefit from financial leverage by borrowing to pay for an education. However, too much leverage can result in graduates struggling to make their loan payments. With most government student loan programs, you have at least six months' grace after your post-secondary education before you have to start paying back your loan. If you take advantage of the grace period, the maximum number of monthly payments is 114, which represents a period of 10 years (120 months) minus the six-month grace period, as mentioned in the Personal Financial Literacy Activity in Chapter 10. However, you may request an extended amortization period of up to 174 months by revising the terms of your loan agreement.

Assume that when you graduate from post-secondary education, you owe $30,000 on a government student loan that you must pay back.

(a) Assume that you take advantage of the grace period and the grace period interest is included in your loan balance. Also assume a fixed interest rate of 9.5% and 174 months of repayment.
   1. What is the amount of each monthly payment?
   2. How much interest is payable over the 174 months?
(b) Assume that you accept a position when you graduate that pays you an annual salary of $48,000. After the required deductions for income tax, CPP, EI, and health benefits, your monthly paycheque is $2,800. You rent an apartment for $750 a month, have monthly payments on a car loan of $300, and your other costs for groceries, cable, Internet, insurance, gas, and phone total $1,100. How much will you have left at the end of the month to make payments on your student loan and other expenditures, such as clothes and entertainment? Can you afford to repay a $30,000 student loan over 174 months?

ANSWERS TO CHAPTER QUESTIONS

ANSWERS TO ACCOUNTING IN ACTION INSIGHT QUESTIONS

All About You Insight, p. 630

Q: What should you consider in your decision about how much is appropriate to borrow for your education?

A: You should consider the cost of tuition and books; living expenses; other sources of cash, such as parents, part-time job, and scholarships and grants; expected income upon graduation; living expenses and other financial commitments after graduation; and expected interest rates and payment schedule on the student loan.

Business Insight, p. 645

Q: What impact will the decrease in the amortization period from 30 to 25 years have on homebuyers?

A: The amortization period is the period over which the principal will be paid. Reducing the amortization period will result in homebuyers making higher monthly payments. With the government also limiting homeowners with government-insured mortgages to spending no more than 44% of their incomes on housing and other debt, many homebuyers will be forced to purchase less expensive homes.

Remember to go back to the beginning of the chapter to check off your completed work! ←

ANSWERS TO SELF-STUDY QUESTIONS

1. a 2. b 3. d 4. d 5. a 6. d 7. c 8. c 9. b 10. a 11. c

CHAPTER 16 THE CASH FLOW STATEMENT

THE NAVIGATOR

- ☐ Understand *Concepts for Review*
- ☐ Read *Feature Story*
- ☐ Scan *Study Objectives*
- ☐ Read *Chapter Preview*
- ☐ Read text and answer *Before You Go On*
- ☐ Review *Comparing IFRS and ASPE*
- ☐ Work *Demonstration Problem*
- ☐ Review *Summary of Study Objectives*
- ☐ Answer *Self-Study Questions*
- ☐ Complete assignments

CONCEPTS FOR REVIEW

Before studying this chapter, you should understand or, if necessary, review:

A. The difference between the accrual basis and the cash basis of accounting. (Ch. 3, p. 97)

B. The definition of cash and cash equivalents. (Ch. 7 pp. 322–323)

C. The major items included in a corporation's balance sheet. (Ch. 4, pp. 156–161 and Ch. 13, pp. 563–565)

D. The major items included in a corporation's income statement. (Ch. 13, pp. 556–558)

E. The declaration and payment of dividends. (Ch. 13, pp. 558–560)

F. The accounting for reacquisition of shares. (Ch. 14, pp. 590–592)

G. The amortization of premiums and discounts on bonds payable. (Ch. 15, pp. 634–640)

CASH MANAGEMENT KEEPS CLEARWATER SAILING

BEDFORD, NS—Clearwater Seafoods is a leader in the global seafood industry, recognized for its consistent quality, wide diversity, and commitment to preserving the environment. Operating for more than 30 years, Clearwater manages a large fleet of vessels in Canada and Argentina, as well as several processing plants throughout Eastern Canada, and exports its products throughout the world, with a focus on the United States, Asia, and Western Europe.

After experiencing challenging conditions in 2008 and 2009, due in part to the global liquidity crisis, Clearwater had strong operating results in 2010 and 2011. "On the back of these strong results, we refinanced our debt facilities several times during this period, each time increasing our flexibility and reducing our cost," says Tyrone Cotie, Treasurer at Clearwater.

Over the past several years Clearwater has formalized a number of its policies and goals to promote strong liquidity and continued access to capital to fund its growth plan.

To maintain adequate liquidity, Clearwater uses cash balances, together with available credit, when funding seasonal working capital demands, capital expenditures, and other commitments. Due to the seasonality of Clearwater's business, sales and gross profit are typically higher in the second half of the calendar year and capital expenditures are typically higher in the first half of the year. This usually results in Clearwater using up some of its liquidity in the first half of the year.

Clearwater's short-term goal is to generate cash flows from operations to fund interest, scheduled loan payments, and capital expenditures and to use free cash flow to reduce debt and invest in growth securities. Clearwater's goal is to grow free cash flows such that it can reduce debt and pay a sustainable dividend to its shareholders.

Clearwater is focused on managing its free cash flows by managing working capital and capital spending. It manages its investment in trade receivables through having tight collection terms and manages its investment in inventories through regular forecasting and close review of any slow-moving items.

To manage its capital spending, Clearwater grades investments in property, plant, equipment and harvesting licences as either return on investment (ROI) or maintenance capital. Significant expenditures that are expected to have a return in excess of the cost of capital are classified as ROI, while expenditures that have less than the average cost of capital are classified as maintenance, as are all refits of its vessels. In addition, Clearwater regularly reviews and liquidates underperforming and non-core assets.

Cash flows generated from operations are a key indicator of the company's health. "The sustainability of a business is ultimately linked to its ability to generate cash," Mr. Cotie says.

THE NAVIGATOR

STUDY OBJECTIVES

After studying this chapter, you should be able to:

1. Describe the purpose and content of the cash flow statement.
2. Prepare a cash flow statement using either the indirect or the direct method.
3. Analyze the cash flow statement.

THE NAVIGATOR

PREVIEW OF CHAPTER SIXTEEN

As Tyrone Cotie in our feature story states, the sustainability of a business is ultimately linked to its ability to generate cash. So how do companies generate cash? How do they use cash? How is this information presented in the financial statements so users can assess a company's ability to generate cash? This chapter, which presents the cash flow statement, will answer these and similar questions.

The chapter is organized as follows:

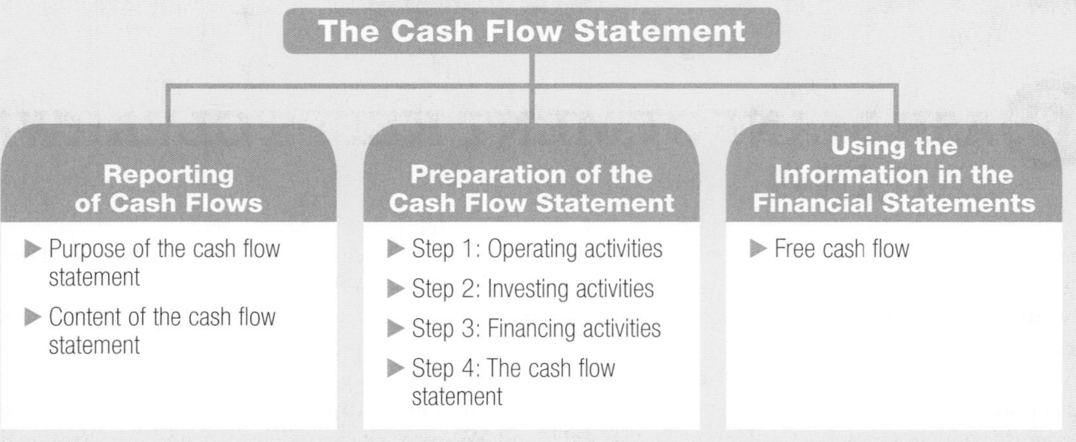

REPORTING OF CASH FLOWS

STUDY OBJECTIVE 1
Describe the purpose and content of the cash flow statement.

The financial statements we have studied so far present only partial information about a company's cash flows (cash receipts and cash payments). For example, comparative balance sheets show the increase in property, plant, and equipment during the year, but they do not show how the additions were financed or paid for. The income statement shows profit, but it does not indicate the amount of cash that was generated by operations. The statement of comprehensive income reports changes in fair values of certain equity investments, but not the cash generated from the sale of these investments. Similarly, the statement of retained earnings or the statement of changes in shareholders' equity shows the amount of cash dividends that was *declared*, but not the amount of cash dividends that was actually *paid* during the year.

PURPOSE OF THE CASH FLOW STATEMENT

Alternative terminology
Under IFRS, the cash flow statement is commonly referred to as the *statement of cash flows*.

The **cash flow statement** gives information about the cash receipts, cash payments, and net change in cash that result from **operating**, **investing**, and **financing** activities during a period. In other words, the statement provides information about *where the cash came from, what the cash was used for*, and *how much it changed*. Reporting the causes of changes in cash helps investors, creditors, and other interested parties understand what is happening to a company's most liquid resource—its cash.

The information in a cash flow statement should help investors, creditors, and others evaluate the following aspects of the company's financial position.

1. **Ability to generate future cash flows:** Investors, creditors, and other stakeholders are interested in how much cash the company will generate in the future. By examining the cash flow statement, and seeing where cash came from and what it was used for, users can predict the amounts, timing, and uncertainty of future cash flows better than they can from examining just the balance sheet and income statement.
2. **Ability to pay dividends and meet obligations:** If a company does not have enough cash, employees cannot be paid, debts settled, or dividends paid. Employees, creditors, and shareholders are particularly interested in this statement because it is the only one that shows the flow of cash in a company.
3. **Investing and financing transactions during the period:** By examining where the cash came from and what it was used for, users can better understand why non-current assets and liabilities changed during the period.

4. **Difference between profit and cash provided (used) by operating activities:** Profit gives information about the success or failure of a business. However, some people are critical of accrual-based profit because it requires many estimates, allocations, and assumptions. As a result, the reliability of the profit amount is often challenged. This is not true of cash. If readers of the cash flow statement understand the reasons for the difference between profit and net cash provided by operating activities, they can then decide for themselves how reliable the profit amount is.

CONTENT OF THE CASH FLOW STATEMENT

Before we can start preparing the cash flow statement, we must first understand what it includes and why. We will begin by reviewing the definition of cash used in the cash flow statement and then we will discuss how cash receipts and payments are classified within the statement.

Definition of Cash

The cash flow statement is often prepared using "cash and cash equivalents" as its basis. You will recall from Chapter 7 that cash consists of cash on hand (coins, paper currency, cheques) and money on deposit at a bank less any bank overdrafts, and that cash equivalents are short-term, highly liquid debt investments that are readily convertible to known amounts of cash. Generally, only debt investments that are due within three months can be considered cash equivalents. Because of the varying definitions of "cash" that can be used in this statement, companies must clearly define cash as it is used in their particular statement.

Classification of Cash Flows

The cash flow statement classifies cash receipts and cash payments into three types of activities: (1) operating, (2) investing, and (3) financing activities. The transactions and other events for each kind of activity are as follows:

1. **Operating activities** include the cash effects of transactions that create revenues and expenses. They affect profit and generally relate to changes in noncash current assets and liabilities.
2. **Investing activities** include (a) purchasing and disposing of non-trading investments (including non-trading short-term investments) and long-lived assets, and (b) lending money and collecting the loans. They generally affect non-current asset accounts. Note that generally accepted accounting principles require the purchase and sale of trading investments to be included in operating activities and not investing activities.
3. **Financing activities** include (a) obtaining cash from issuing debt and repaying the amounts borrowed, and (b) obtaining cash from shareholders and paying them dividends. Financing activities generally affect non-current liability and shareholders' equity accounts.

Helpful hint Trading investments are debt or equity securities that are held for sale in the near-term, mainly to generate earnings from short-term price differences. Trading investments, also called held-for-trading investments or trading securities, are covered in detail in Appendix B.

Illustration 16-1 lists typical cash receipts (inflows) and cash payments (outflows) in each of the three classifications.

ILLUSTRATION 16-1
Cash receipts and payments classified by activity

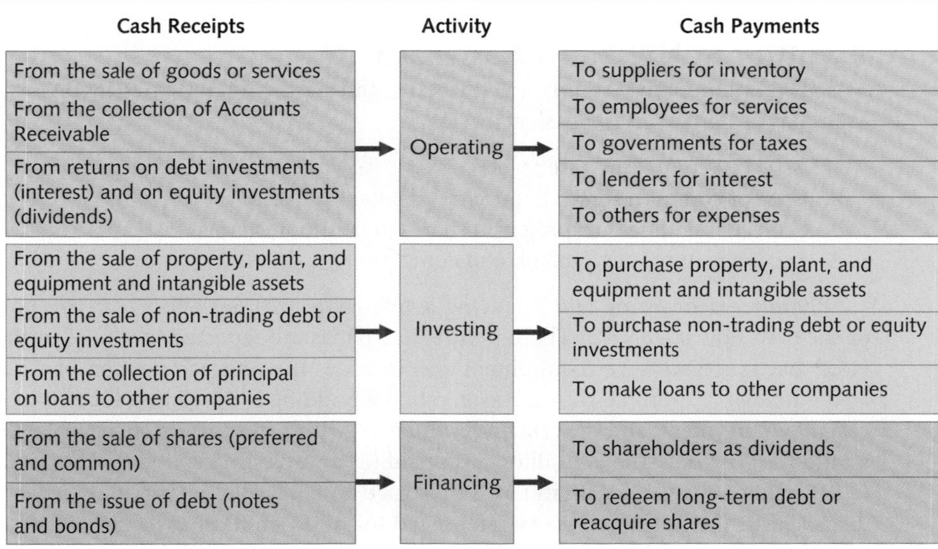

As you can see, some cash flows that are related to investing or financing activities are classified as operating activities. For example, receipts of investment revenue (interest and dividends) earned from debt or equity securities are classified as operating activities. So are payments of interest to lenders of debt. Why are these considered operating activities? It is because these items are reported in the income statement where results of operations are shown.

Illustration 16-2 shows general guidelines that can be followed in the classification of cash flows.

ILLUSTRATION 16-2
Operating, investing, and financing activities

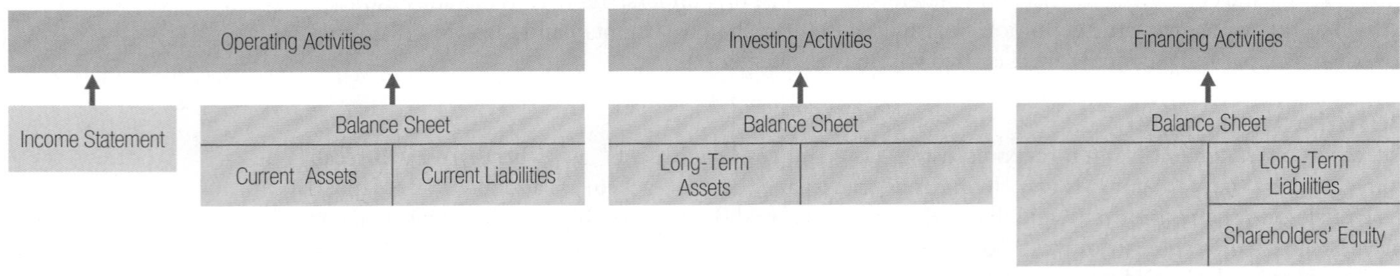

Note that these are general guidelines and that there are some exceptions to these guidelines. There are situations when current asset and current liability accounts do not result from operating activities. One such example is notes receivable that have been issued for lending purposes rather than for trade. The issue and repayment of notes receivable such as these are reported in the investing section. Similarly, short-term notes payable that do not relate to purchase transactions are an example of a current liability that does not relate to operating activities. These are shown in the financing activities section of the cash flow statement. Another example is short-term investments purchased to earn interest. These investments are reported in the investing activities section.

Companies reporting under IFRS have a choice as to where to classify interest and dividends. Interest and dividends received may be classified as either an operating or investing activity; interest and dividends paid may be classified as either an operating or financing activity. Once the choice is made, it must be applied consistently.

Private companies reporting under ASPE must classify interest (received and paid) and dividends received as operating activities. Under ASPE, dividends paid are classified as financing activities. Although public companies have a choice under IFRS as to how to classify interest and dividends, most public companies follow the classification required under ASPE. Because the classification required under ASPE is the most common practice, we have illustrated this classification in Illustration 16-2 and follow it in this textbook.

Significant Noncash Activities

Not all of a company's significant investing and financing activities involve cash. The following are examples of significant noncash activities:

1. Issue of debt to purchase assets
2. Issue of common shares to purchase assets
3. Conversion of debt or preferred shares to common shares
4. Exchange of property, plant, and equipment

Significant investing and financing activities that do not affect cash are not reported in the body of the cash flow statement. These noncash activities are reported in a note to the financial statements. Note that this disclosure requirement also includes the noncash portion of a partial cash transaction, as the following example shows. Assume that a building is purchased for \$10 million with a \$1-million cash down payment, and the remainder financed with a mortgage note payable. The cash flow statement would disclose only the \$1 million cash paid (as an investing activity). The acquisition of the building (a \$10-million investing activity) by a mortgage note payable (a \$9-million financing activity) would be disclosed in the notes and cross-referenced to the \$1-million cash outflow reported in the investing activities section of the cash flow statement.

ACCOUNTING IN ACTION
ALL ABOUT YOU INSIGHT

Similar to a business, you need to consider your cash situation. How much can you afford to spend, and what are your sources of cash? For many Canadians, using a credit card to easily access cash means they spend more than they can afford. In 2011, the average Canadian's debt load, excluding mortgages, reached a record high of $25,960, although the amount of credit card debt declined by 3.4% as Canadians moved more of their credit card balances to lines of credit, which charge lower interest rates. Observers say that while consumers are getting smarter about credit, they're still spending too much. "It's about attacking lifestyle issues—fundamental buying and spending," said Keith Emery, operations director of Credit Canada, a non-profit credit counselling agency that helps consumers get out of debt.

Sources: Tracy Sherlock, "Canadians Trimming Credit Card Debts: Study," *Vancouver Sun*, July 20, 2012; Roma Luciw, "Average Canadian's Consumer Debt Hits $25,960," *Globe and Mail*, February 23, 2012; "Credit Card Debt Falls in 2011," The Canadian Press, January 10, 2012; Marlene Habib, "Credit Card Debt Eases but Still Dogs Canadians," CBC News, October 26, 2011.

Is it appropriate to use your credit card to pay for your operating activities such as your groceries, clothes, and entertainment? Is it appropriate to use your credit card to finance your investment activities such as tuition or, if you have a large enough limit, a car?

BEFORE YOU GO ON...

DO IT

Carrier Moulding Ltd. had the following transactions:

1. Issued common shares for cash.
2. Sold a long-term equity investment.
3. Purchased a tractor-trailer truck. Made a cash down payment and financed the remainder with a mortgage note payable.
4. Paid for inventory purchases.
5. Collected cash for services provided.
6. Paid the blended monthly mortgage payment (interest and principal) on the note payable.

Classify each of these transactions by type of cash flow activity. Indicate whether the transaction would be reported as a cash inflow or cash outflow.

SOLUTION

1. Financing activity; cash inflow
2. Investing activity; cash inflow
3. Investing activity; cash outflow for down payment. The remainder is a noncash investing (tractor-trailer truck) and financing (mortgage note payable) activity.
4. Operating activity; cash outflow
5. Operating activity; cash inflow
6. Operating activity; cash outflow for the interest portion of the payment. Financing activity; cash outflow for the principal portion of the payment.

Related exercise material: BE16–1, BE16–2, and E16–1.

Action Plan

- Identify the three types of activities that are used to report all cash inflows and outflows.
- Report as operating activities the cash effects of transactions that create revenues and expenses, and that are included when profit is determined.
- Report as investing activities transactions to (a) acquire and dispose of non-trading investments and long-lived assets, and (b) lend money and collect loans.
- Report as financing activities transactions to (a) obtain cash by issuing debt and repaying the amounts borrowed, and (b) obtain cash from shareholders and pay them dividends.

THE NAVIGATOR

PREPARATION OF THE CASH FLOW STATEMENT

STUDY OBJECTIVE 2

Prepare a cash flow statement using either the indirect or the direct method.

In Chapter 1, we showed the cash flow statement for Softbyte in Illustration 1-11, which has been reproduced here in Illustration 16-3.

The cash flow statement covers the same period of time as the income statement and statements of comprehensive income, retained earnings, and changes in shareholders' equity (for example, for the year ended). As explained earlier in the chapter, note that the cash inflows and outflows are classified into the

ILLUSTRATION 16-3
Cash flow statement

SOFTBYTE Cash Flow Statement Month Ended September 30, 2014		
Operating activities		
Cash receipts from customers	$ 3,300	
Cash payments for operating expenses	(1,950)	
Net cash provided by operating activities		$ 1,350
Investing activities		
Purchase of equipment	$ (7,000)	
Net cash used by investing activities		(7,000)
Financing activities		
Investments by owner	$15,000	
Drawings by owner	(1,300)	
Net cash provided by financing activities		13,700
Net increase in cash		8,050
Cash, September 1, 2011		0
Cash, September 30, 2011		$ 8,050

three types of activities (operating, investing, and financing) that we discussed in the preceding section. The operating activities section is always presented first. We will learn there are two methods to prepare the operating activities section: the indirect method and the direct method. In Illustration 16-3, Softbyte's operating activities section has been prepared using the direct method.

The operating activities section is followed by the investing activities and financing activities sections. Any significant noncash investing and financing activities are reported in a note to the financial statements.

Helpful hint When cash is "provided," the cash balance increases. When cash is "used," the cash balance decreases.

A subtotal is calculated for each of the sections (operating, investing, and financing) to determine the net increase or decrease in cash from each activity. If there is a net increase in cash, we say that cash was "provided by" that activity. If there is a net decrease in cash, we say that cash was "used by" that activity. Illustration 16-3 shows that Softbyte's operating and financing activities provided cash and its investing activities used cash.

The subtotals for the three activities are totalled to determine the net increase or decrease in cash for the period. This amount is then added to (if a net increase) or subtracted from (if a net decrease) the beginning-of-period cash balance to obtain the end-of-period cash balance. The end-of-period cash balance must agree with the cash balance reported on the balance sheet. Illustration 16-3 shows a net increase in Softbyte's cash of $8,050. As the company was started on September 1, 2014, with a zero cash balance, this increase resulted in a $8,050 cash balance at September 30, 2014, the amount reported on both the cash flow statement in Illustration 16-3 and on the balance sheet in Illustration 1-11.

Now that we understand the content and format of a cash flow statement, where do we find the information to prepare it? We could examine the cash account in the general ledger and sort each cash receipt and payment into the different types of operating activities, investing activities, or financing activities shown in Illustration 16-1. But this is not practical or necessary. Instead, we prepare the cash flow *by examining the changes in all of the other accounts.*

The information to prepare this statement usually comes from three sources:

1. The **comparative balance sheet** shows the balances at the beginning and end of the period for each asset, liability, and shareholders' equity item. This information is used to determine the changes in each asset, liability, and shareholders' equity item during that period.
2. The **income statement** helps us determine the amount of cash provided or used by operating activities during the period.
3. **Additional information** includes transaction data that are needed to determine how cash was provided or used during the period. The statement of comprehensive income and the statements of retained earnings or changes in shareholders' equity (or the statement of owner's equity in a proprietorship) also provide information about cash receipts and payments.

The four steps to prepare the cash flow statement from these data sources are shown in Illustration 16-4.

ILLUSTRATION 16-4
Steps in preparing the cash flow statement

Step 1: Prepare operating activities section.
Determine the net cash provided (used) by operating activities by converting net income from an accrual basis to a cash basis. To do this, analyze the current year's income statement, relevant current asset and current liability accounts from the comparative balance sheets, and selected information.

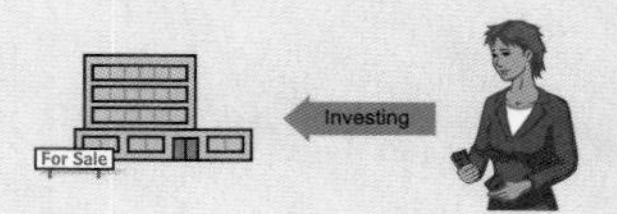

Step 2: Prepare investing activities section.
Determine the net cash provided (used) by investing activities by analyzing changes in non-current asset accounts from the comparative balance sheets, and selected information.

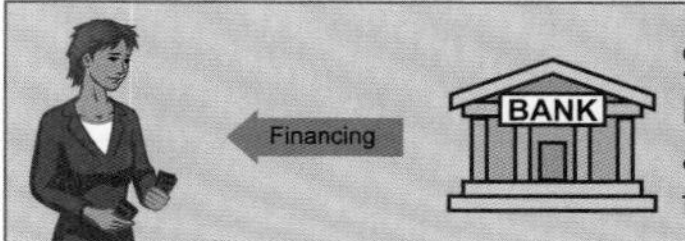

Step 3: Prepare financing activities section.
Determine the net cash provided (used) by financing activities by analyzing changes in non-current liability and equity accounts from the comparative balance sheets, and selected information.

Step 4: Complete the cash flow statement.
Determine the net increase (decrease) in cash. Compare the net change in cash reported on the statement of cash flows with the change in cash reported on the statement of financial position to make sure the amounts agree.

To explain and illustrate the preparation of a cash flow statement, we will use financial information from Computer Services Corporation. Illustration 16-5 presents Computer Services' current- and prior-year balance sheets, its current-year income statement, and related financial information.

ILLUSTRATION 16-5
Computer Services' financial information

COMPUTER SERVICES CORPORATION
Balance Sheets
December 31

Assets	**2014**	**2013**	**Increase (Decrease)**
Current assets			
Cash	$ 55,000	$ 33,000	$ 22,000
Accounts receivable	20,000	30,000	(10,000)
Inventory	15,000	10,000	5,000
Prepaid expenses	5,000	1,000	4,000
Property, plant, and equipment			
Land	130,000	20,000	110,000
Building	160,000	40,000	120,000
Accumulated depreciation—building	(11,000)	(5,000)	6,000
Equipment	27,000	10,000	17,000
Accumulated depreciation—equipment	(3,000)	(1,000)	2,000
Total assets	$398,000	$138,000	
Liabilities and Shareholders' Equity			
Current liabilities			
Accounts payable	$ 28,000	$ 12,000	$ 16,000
Income tax payable	6,000	8,000	(2,000)
Non-current liabilities			
Bonds payable	130,000	20,000	110,000
Shareholders' equity			
Common shares	70,000	50,000	20,000
Retained earnings	164,000	48,000	116,000
Total liabilities and shareholders' equity	$398,000	$138,000	

ILLUSTRATION 16-5
Computer Services' financial information (*continued*)

COMPUTER SERVICES CORPORATION Income Statement Year Ended December 31, 2014		
Sales revenue		$507,000
Cost of goods sold		150,000
Gross profit		357,000
Operating expenses	$111,000	
Depreciation expense	9,000	
Loss on sale of equipment	3,000	123,000
Profit from operations		234,000
Other expenses		
Interest expense		42,000
Profit before income tax		192,000
Income tax expense		47,000
Profit		$145,000

Additional information for 2014:

1. A $29,000 cash dividend was paid.
2. Land was acquired by issuing $110,000 of long-term bonds.
3. Equipment costing $25,000 was purchased for cash.
4. Equipment with a carrying amount of $7,000 (cost of $8,000, less accumulated depreciation of $1,000) was sold for $4,000 cash.
5. Depreciation expense consists of $6,000 for the building and $3,000 for equipment.

We will now apply the four steps using the above information for Computer Services Corporation. In the following sections, we will review the journal entries to record transactions and analyze T accounts for balance sheet accounts in order to help you understand the preparation of the cash flow statement.

STEP 1: OPERATING ACTIVITIES

Determine the Net Cash Provided (Used) by Operating Activities by Converting Profit from an Accrual Basis to a Cash Basis

In order to perform this step and determine the cash provided (used) by operating activities, profit must be converted from an accrual basis to a cash basis. Why is this necessary? Under generally accepted accounting principles, companies use the accrual basis of accounting. For example, sales revenues are recorded for both cash sales and sales on account. Similarly, many expenses are recorded that have not yet been paid in cash and some expenses incurred, such as depreciation, are never paid in cash. Thus, under the accrual basis of accounting, profit is not the same as net cash provided by operating activities.

Profit can be converted to net cash provided (used) by operating activities by one of two methods: (1) the indirect method or (2) the direct method. Illustration 16-6 shows an example, using assumed data for a service company, of cash flow from operating activities prepared under both methods.

Note that both methods arrive at the same total amount for "Net cash provided (used) by operating activities" of $101,000. The difference is which items they disclose. The **indirect method** converts total profit from an accrual basis to a cash basis by starting with profit of $100,000 and adjusting it for items that do not affect cash. The **direct method** converts each individual revenue and expense account from an accrual basis to a cash basis, to report cash receipts and payments for major classes of operating activities.

The two methods are explained in two independent sections. Section 1 explains the indirect method and section 2 explains the direct method. Your teacher may ask you to learn only one of the methods. If so, when you have finished the section assigned by your teacher, turn to "Step 2: Investing Activities."

ILLUSTRATION 16-6
Cash flow from operating activities under the indirect method and direct method

SAMPLE
Cash Flow Statement (partial)
Year ended December 31, XXXX

Indirect Method			Direct Method		
Operating activities			Operating activities		
Profit		$100,000	Cash receipts from customers		$185,000
Adjustments to reconcile profit to net cash provided (used) by operating activities:			Cash payments		
Depreciation expense	$ 6,000		For operating expenses	$(54,000)	
Gain on sale of equipment	(4,000)		For interest	(5,000)	
Decrease in accounts receivable	2,000		For income tax	(25,000)	(84,00)
Decrease in accounts payable	(3,000)	1,000			
Net cash provided by operating activities		101,000	Net cash provided by operating activities		101,000

SECTION 1: INDIRECT METHOD

While the direct method is preferred by standard setters, most companies use the indirect method. They prefer this method for three reasons: (1) it is easier to prepare, (2) it focuses on the differences between profit and net cash flow from operating activities, and (3) it reveals less detail to competitors.

Illustration 16-7 shows three types of adjustments that are made to adjust profit for items that affect accrual-based profit but do not affect cash. The first two types of adjustments are found on the income statement. The last type of adjustment—changes to current asset and current liability accounts—is found on the balance sheet.

ILLUSTRATION 16-7
Adjustments to convert profit to net cash provided (used) by operating activities

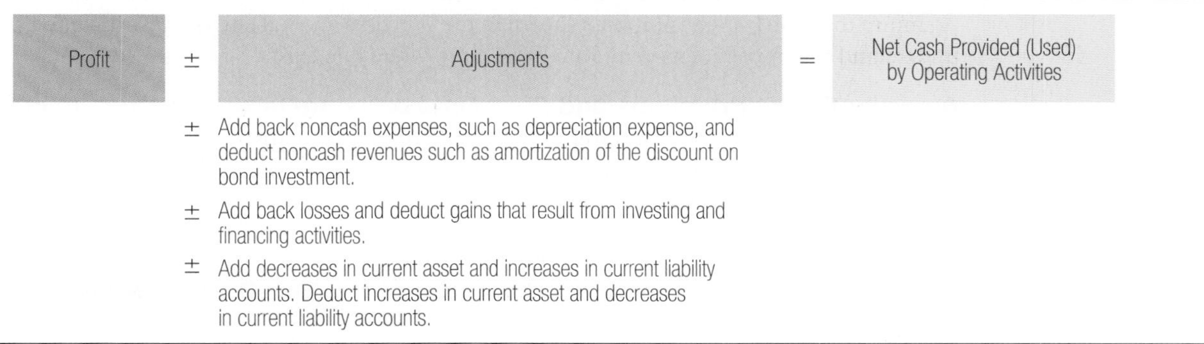

Profit
±
Adjustments
=
Net Cash Provided (Used) by Operating Activities
± Add back noncash expenses, such as depreciation expense, and deduct noncash revenues such as amortization of the discount on bond investment.
± Add back losses and deduct gains that result from investing and financing activities.
± Add decreases in current asset and increases in current liability accounts. Deduct increases in current asset and decreases in current liability accounts.

The next three subsections explain each type of adjustment.

Noncash Expenses and Revenues

Depreciation Expense.

The income statement includes expenses that do not use cash, such as depreciation expense. For example, Computer Services' income statement reports a depreciation expense of $9,000, which was recorded as follows:

Helpful hint In the indirect method, expenses with no cash outflows are added back to profit. Revenues with no cash inflows are deducted from profit.

Depreciation Expense	9,000	
Accumulated Depreciation—Building		6,000
Accumulated Depreciation—Equipment		3,000

A	=	L	+	SE
−6,000				−9,000
−3,000				

Cash flows: no effect

As shown in the journal entry, depreciation does not use cash, so depreciation expense is added back to profit in order to arrive at net cash provided (used) by operating activities. It is important to understand that depreciation expense is not added to operating activities as if it were a source of cash. **It is added to cancel the deduction that was created by the depreciation expense when profit was determined.**

A partial operating activities section of the cash flow statement for Computer Services is shown below, with the addition of the noncash expense to profit highlighted in red.

Operating activities	
Profit	$145,000
Adjustments to reconcile profit to net cash provided (used) by operating activities:	
Depreciation expense	9,000

Amortization of Bonds Payable Premiums and Discounts.

Another example of a noncash expense is the amortization of the discounts and premiums on bonds payable when bonds are not issued at par. Recall from Chapter 15 that the journal entries to record interest expense and amortize bonds payable discounts and premiums, using assumed data, are as follows.

A	=	L	+	SE
−25,000		+1,000		−26,000

↓Cash flows: −25,000

A	=	L	+	SE
−25,000		−1,500		−23,500

↓Cash flows: −25,000

Bonds Payable Issued at a Discount			Bonds Payable Issued at a Premium		
Interest Expense	26,000		Interest Expense	23,500	
Bonds Payable		1,000	Bonds Payable	1,500	
Cash		25,000	Cash		25,000

The amortization of a bond discount results in interest expense being higher than the cash paid to the bond investors. So the amortization of a bond discount, the amount credited to bonds payable, must be added back to profit to determine the net cash provided (used) by operating activities.

The amortization of a bond premium for the issuer results in interest expense being lower than the cash payment to the bond investors. So the amortization of a bond premium, the amount debited to bonds payable, must be deducted from profit to determine the net cash provided (used) by operating activities.

Note that the Computer Services bonds payable were issued at par and thus there was no discount or premium to amortize. The amounts shown in the previous journal entries were included only to help you understand the impact of a premium or discount, when one exists.

Amortization of Premiums and Discounts on Long-Term Investments in Bonds.

Profit must also be adjusted for the effects of the amortization of discounts and premiums for investments in bonds. The journal entries to amortize discounts and premiums on long-term investments in bonds using assumed data are as follows:

A	=	L	+	SE
+25,000				+26,000
+1,000				

↑Cash flows: +25,000

A	=	L	+	SE
+25,000				+23,500
−1,500				

↑Cash flows: +25,000

Long-Term Bond Investment at a Discount			Long-Term Bond Investment at a Premium		
Cash	25,000		Cash	25,000	
Long-Term Investment—Bonds	1,000		Long-Term Investment—Bonds		1,500
Interest Revenue		26,000	Interest Revenue		23,500

The amortization of a bond discount for an investor results in interest revenue being greater than the cash receipts. Thus the amortization of the discount must be deducted from profit. Conversely, the amortization of a bond premium for an investor results in interest revenue being less than the cash receipts, so the amortization of the premium must be added to profit.

Gains and Losses

Cash received from the sale of long-lived assets should be reported in the investing activities section of the cash flow statement. Consequently, all gains and losses from investing activities must be eliminated from profit to arrive at net cash from operating activities.

Why is this necessary? Perhaps it will help if we review the accounting for the sale of a long-lived asset. The sale of a long-lived asset is recorded by (1) recognizing the cash that is received, (2) removing the asset and accumulated depreciation account, and (3) recognizing any gain or loss on the sale.

To illustrate, recall that Computer Services' income statement reported a $3,000 loss on the sale of equipment. With the additional information provided in Illustration 16-5, we can reconstruct the journal entry to record the sale of equipment:

Helpful hint Gains are deducted from, and losses are added to, profit in the indirect method.

Cash	4,000	
Accumulated Depreciation—Equipment	1,000	
Loss on Sale of Equipment	3,000	
Equipment		8,000

A	=	L	+	SE
+4,000				−3,000
+1,000				
−8,000				

↑ Cash flows: +4,000

The $4,000 of cash that is received is not considered part of operating activities; rather it is part of investing activities. Selling long-lived assets is not part of a company's primary activities. **There is therefore no cash inflow (or outflow) from operating activities.** Logically, then, to calculate the net cash provided (used) by operating activities, we have to eliminate the gain or loss on the sale of an asset from profit.

To eliminate the $3,000 loss on the sale of equipment, we have to add it back to profit to arrive at net cash provided (used) by operating activities. Adding back the loss cancels the original deduction. This is illustrated in the following partial cash flow statement for Computer Services:

Operating activities	
Profit	$145,000
Adjustments to reconcile profit to net cash provided (used) by operating activities:	
Depreciation expense	9,000
Loss on sale of equipment	3,000

If a gain on sale occurs, the gain is deducted from profit in order to determine net cash provided (used) by operating activities. For both a gain and a loss, the actual amount of cash received from the sale of the asset is reported as a source of cash in the investing activities section of the cash flow statement.

Gains and losses are also possible in other circumstances, such as when debt is retired. The same adjustment guidelines apply to debt as described for gains and losses on the sale of assets, except that the cash paid to retire the debt is reported in financing activities, rather than investing activities.

Changes in Noncash Current Asset and Current Liability Accounts

In addition to the noncash expenses and revenues and gains and losses discussed in the previous two sections, there are other reasons why profit is not the same amount as cash from operations. We know that revenues and expenses are recorded using accrual basis accounting, not cash basis accounting. When revenues and expenses are recorded using accrual basis accounting, it is necessary to adjust profit for the changes in the related noncash current assets and current liabilities to determine the amount of cash provided from operations. In this section, we will illustrate why these adjustments are necessary and how the adjustments are determined.

Changes in Noncash Current Assets.

The adjustments to profit that are required for changes in noncash current asset accounts to arrive at net cash provided (used) by operating activities are shown in Illustration 16-8.

ILLUSTRATION 16-8 Adjustments to profit for changes in noncash current asset accounts

Increase in noncash current assets	Deduct
Decrease in noncash current assets	Add

We will illustrate these adjustments by analyzing the changes in Computer Services' current asset accounts and related journal entries.

Changes in Accounts Receivable. Illustration 16-5 indicated that Computer Services had $507,000 in sales revenue reported on its income statement. Assuming all sales are on account, the entry to record sales is (in summary for the year):

A	=	L	+	SE
+507,000				+507,000

Cash flows: no effect

Accounts Receivable	507,000	
Sales Revenue		507,000

Sales increased profit by $507,000, but did cash also increase by the same amount? To answer this question, we need to analyze Computer Services' accounts receivable because accounts receivable is increased when a sale is made and decreased when cash is collected. Illustration 16-5 indicates that Computer Services started the year with a balance of $30,000 in accounts receivable and ended with $20,000. Using these amounts and the sales recorded in the above journal entry, we analyze the Accounts Receivable account to determine the amount of cash collected from customers as follows:

$10,000 net decrease

Accounts Receivable				
Jan. 1	Balance	30,000		
	Sales revenue	507,000	Receipts from customers	517,000
Dec. 31	Balance	20,000		

Note that cash receipts from customers are $517,000, which is $10,000 ($517,000 − $507,000) larger than sales revenue. Also note that Computer Services' accounts receivable decreased by $10,000 (from $30,000 to $20,000) during the year. When accounts receivable decrease during the year, revenues on an accrual basis are lower than revenues on a cash basis. In other words, more cash was collected during the period than was recorded as revenue.

Thus, in order to adjust profit to cash provided (used) by operating activities, we have to add $10,000 for the decrease in accounts receivable. This is illustrated in the following partial cash flow statement for Computer Services:

Operating activities	
Profit	$145,000
Adjustments to reconcile profit to net cash provided (used) by operating activities:	
Depreciation expense	9,000
Loss on sale of equipment	3,000
Decrease in accounts receivable	10,000

Using the same logic, this means that when the accounts receivable balance increases during the year, revenues on an accrual basis are higher than cash receipts. Therefore, the amount of the increase in accounts receivable is deducted from profit to arrive at net cash provided (used) by operating activities.

You should also note that the adjustment to profit, for the decrease in accounts receivable, is the same regardless of the actual amount of sales on account during the year. For example, we could have assumed all of the $507,000 sales were for cash. Since accounts receivable still decreased by $10,000, it means that $10,000 of cash was collected from customers, over and above the cash sales during the year.

Changes in Inventory. Computer Services reported $150,000 of cost of goods sold expense in its income statement. Assuming a perpetual inventory system is being used, the summary journal entry to record Computer Services' cost of goods sold is as follows:

A	=	L	+	SE
−150,000				−150,000

Cash flows: no effect

Cost of Goods Sold	150,000	
Inventory		150,000

Cost of goods sold decreased profit by $150,000, but how much cash was used to pay for inventory during the period? To answer this question, we need to first determine the cost of goods purchased for the period by analyzing the Inventory account. Recall from Chapter 5 that the Inventory account decreases when inventory is sold and increases when inventory is purchased. Illustration 16-5 indicates that Computer Services started the year with a balance of $10,000 in inventory and ended with $15,000. Using these amounts and the cost of goods sold recorded in the above journal entry, we analyze the Inventory account to determine the cost of goods purchased as follows:

		Inventory			
Jan. 1	Balance	10,000			
	Purchases	155,000	Cost of goods sold	150,000	$5,000 net increase
Dec. 31	Balance	15,000			

The cost of goods purchased during the period is $155,000, which is $5,000 ($155,000 − $150,000) greater than the cost of goods sold expense reported in the income statement. Note that this difference is equal to the increase in inventory during the period ($15,000 − $10,000). When the inventory account increases, more inventory was purchased during the period than was recorded as cost of goods sold. Since the cost of goods sold of $150,000 has already been deducted from Sales on the income statement, we simply deduct the $5,000 increase in inventory on the cash flow statement. This deduction is illustrated in the partial cash flow statement for Computer Services (Illustration 16-10) presented at the end of this section.

Following the same logic, if inventory had decreased, this would mean that the cost of goods purchased was less than the cost of goods sold and we would add the decrease back to profit.

This adjustment does not completely convert cost of goods sold to cash paid for inventory. It just converts the cost of goods sold to the cost of goods purchased during the year. The analysis of accounts payable—shown later—completes the calculation of payments made to suppliers by converting the cost of goods purchased from an accrual basis to a cash basis.

Changes in Prepaid Expenses. Computer Services reported $111,000 of operating expenses in its income statement. This means that profit decreased by $111,000, but what was the amount of cash paid for operating expenses? To answer this question, we analyze the Prepaid Expenses account because the account is increased when a prepayment is made and decreased when an expense is recorded in the income statement. To help us determine the cash paid for operating expenses, we can assume the following summary journal entry was made to record the operating expenses:

Operating Expenses	111,000	
Prepaid Expenses		111,000

A	=	L	+	SE
−111,000				−111,000

Cash flows: no effect

Computer Services started the year with a balance of $1,000 in the Prepaid Expense account and ended with $5,000. Using these amounts and the operating expenses recorded in the above journal entry, we analyze the Prepaid Expenses account to determine the cash paid for operating expenses as follows:

		Prepaid Expenses			
Jan. 1	Balance	1,000			
	Payments for expenses	115,000	Operating expenses	111,000	$4,000 net increase
Dec. 31	Balance	5,000			

The cash paid for operating expenses is $115,000, which is $4,000 ($115,000 − $111,000) greater than the operating expenses reported in the income statement. Note that this difference is equal to the increase in prepaid expenses during the period ($5,000 − $1,000). When prepaid expenses increase, cash paid for expenses is higher than the expenses reported in the income statement on an accrual basis. In other words, cash payments were made in the current period, but the expenses will not be recorded in the income statement until future periods. Since operating expenses of $111,000 have already been deducted on the income statement, we simply deduct the $4,000 increase in prepaid expenses on the cash flow statement to convert profit to net cash provided (used) by operating activities. This deduction is illustrated in the partial cash flow statement for Computer Services (Illustration 16-10) presented at the end of this section.

If prepaid expenses decreased during the period, this would mean that the cash paid for expenses was less than the operating expenses recorded in the income statement and we would add the decrease back to profit when calculating cash provided (used) by operating activities.

If Computer Services had any accrued expenses payable, such as Salaries Payable, these would also have to be considered before we could completely determine the amount of cash paid for operating expenses. We will look at changes in current liability accounts in the next section.

Changes in Current Liabilities.

The adjustments to profit that are required for changes in noncash current liability accounts to arrive at net cash provided (used) by operating activities are shown in Illustration 16-9.

ILLUSTRATION 16-9
Adjustments to profit for changes in noncash current liability accounts

Increase in noncash current liabilities	Add
Decrease in noncash current liabilities	Deduct

We will illustrate these adjustments by analyzing the changes in Computer Services' current liability accounts: Accounts Payable and Income Tax Payable.

Changes in Accounts Payable. In some companies, the Accounts Payable account is used to record only purchases of inventory on account and an accrued expense payable account is used to record other credit purchases. For simplicity, in this chapter we have made this assumption.

You will recall that we determined, in the analysis of Computer Services' Inventory account earlier, that the cost of goods purchased was $155,000. Assuming all of the purchases were on account, the entry to record the purchases is (in summary):

A	=	L	+	SE
+155,000		+155,000		

Cash flows: no effect

	Debit	Credit
Inventory	155,000	
Accounts Payable		155,000

The amount of inventory purchased was $155,000, but what amount of cash was paid to suppliers for goods purchased? We can answer this question by analyzing the Accounts Payable account, because it is increased by the cost of goods purchased and decreased by cash paid to suppliers. Illustration 16-5 indicates that Computer Services started the year with a balance of $12,000 in accounts payable and ended with $28,000. Using these amounts and the accounts payable recorded in the above journal entry, we analyze the Accounts Payable account to determine the cash paid for inventory as follows:

Accounts Payable

			Jan. 1	Balance	12,000
$16,000 net increase	Payments to suppliers	139,000		Purchases	155,000
			Dec. 31	Balance	28,000

The cash paid to suppliers for inventory is $139,000, which is $16,000 ($155,000 − $139,000) less than the cost of goods purchased. Note that this difference is equal to the increase in accounts payable during the period ($28,000 − $12,000). When the balance in the Accounts Payable account increases, it means that the cash paid to suppliers was less than the purchases made during the period. Since cost of goods sold of $150,000 has already been deducted on the income statement and we have also deducted the $5,000 increase in inventory to adjust for the cost of goods purchased, we simply add the $16,000 increase in accounts payable on the cash flow statement to convert profit to net cash provided (used) by operating activities. This deduction is illustrated in the partial cash flow statement for Computer Services (Illustration 16-10) presented at the end of this section.

Note that if the Accounts Payable account decreased, it would mean that the cash paid to suppliers was more than the cost of goods purchased. Therefore the decrease is deducted from profit.

In summary, the conversion of the cost of goods sold on the income statement to the cash paid for goods purchased involves two steps: (1) The change in the Inventory account adjusts the cost of goods sold to the cost of goods purchased. (2) The change in the Accounts Payable account adjusts the cost of goods purchased to the payments to suppliers. These changes for Computer Services are summarized as follows:

Cost of goods sold	$150,000
Add: Increase in inventory	5,000
Cost of goods purchased	155,000
Less: Increase in accounts payable	16,000
Cash payments to suppliers	$139,000

Changes in Income Tax Payable. Computer Services reported $47,000 in income tax expense on the income statement. The journal entry to record the income tax expense is as follows:

Income Tax Expense	47,000	
Income Tax Payable		47,000

A	=	L	+	SE
		+47,000		−47,000

Cash flows: no effect

This means that profit decreased by $47,000, but how much cash was paid for income tax? To answer this question, we need to analyze Computer Services' Income Tax Payable account because it increases when income tax expense is recorded and decreases when income tax is paid. Computer Services started the year with a balance of $8,000 in Income Tax Payable and ended with $6,000. Using these amounts and the income tax payable recorded in the above journal entry, we analyze the Income Tax Payable account to determine the cash paid for income tax as follows:

Income Tax Payable

		Jan. 1	Balance	8,000
Payments for income tax	49,000		Income tax expense	47,000
		Dec. 31	Balance	6,000

$2,000 net decrease

The cash paid for income tax is $49,000, which is $2,000 ($49,000 − $47,000) more than the income tax expense. Note that this difference is equal to the decrease in income tax payable during the period ($8,000 − $6,000). When the Income Tax Payable account decreases, it means that more income tax was paid than recorded as expense in the income statement. Since income tax expense of $47,000 has already been deducted on the income statement, we simply deduct the $2,000 decrease in income tax payable on the cash flow statement to convert profit to net cash provided (used) by operating activities. This deduction is illustrated in the partial cash flow statement for Computer Services (Illustration 16-10) presented at the end of this section.

If Computer Services had other accrued expenses payable, they would be analyzed similarly to the Income Tax Payable account.

The partial cash flow statement that follows in Illustration 16-10 shows the impact on operating activities of the changes in current asset and current liability accounts. (The changes are highlighted in red.) It also shows the adjustments that were described earlier for noncash expenses and gains and losses. The operating activities section of the cash flow statement is now complete.

Helpful hint Whether the indirect or direct method (described in Section 2 below) is used, net cash provided (used) by operating activities will be the same.

ILLUSTRATION 16-10
Net cash provided by operating activities—indirect method

COMPUTER SERVICES CORPORATION Cash Flow Statement (partial) Year Ended December 31, 2014		
Operating activities		
Profit		$145,000
Adjustments to reconcile profit to net cash provided (used) by operating activities:		
Depreciation expense	$ 9,000	
Loss on sale of equipment	3,000	
Decrease in accounts receivable	10,000	
Increase in inventory	(5,000)	
Increase in prepaid expenses	(4,000)	
Increase in accounts payable	16,000	
Decrease in income tax payable	(2,000)	27,000
Net cash provided by operating activities		172,000

Note that the increase or decrease for each noncash current asset and current liability has been either added or deducted as originally shown in Illustrations 16-8 and 16-9. In summary, Computer Services earned a profit of $145,000 and the profit-generating activities generated cash of $172,000 during the year.

Summary of Conversion to Net Cash Provided (Used) by Operating Activities—Indirect Method

As shown in Illustration 16-10, the cash flow statement prepared by the indirect method starts with profit. Profit is then adjusted to arrive at net cash provided (used) by operating activities. Adjustments to profit that are typically required are summarized as follows:

Noncash expenses	Depreciation expense	Add
	Amortization expense (intangible assets)	Add
	Amortization of discount on bond payable	Add
	Amortization of premium on bond payable	Deduct
Noncash revenues	Amortization of discount on bond investment	Deduct
	Amortization of premium on bond investment	Add
Gains and losses	Gain on sale of asset	Deduct
	Loss on sale of asset	Add
Changes in noncash current asset and current liability accounts	Increase in current asset account	Deduct
	Decrease in current asset account	Add
	Increase in current liability account	Add
	Decrease in current liability account	Deduct

BEFORE YOU GO ON...

DO IT

Selected financial information follows for Reynolds Ltd. at December 31. Prepare the operating activities section of the cash flow statement using the indirect method.

	2014	2013	Increase (Decrease)
Current assets			
Cash	$54,000	$37,000	$17,000
Accounts receivable	68,000	26,000	42,000
Inventories	54,000	10,000	44,000
Prepaid expenses	4,000	6,000	(2,000)
Current liabilities			
Accounts payable	23,000	50,000	(27,000)
Accrued expenses payable	10,000	0	10,000

BEFORE YOU GO ON...
continued on next page

BEFORE YOU GO ON...
continued from previous page

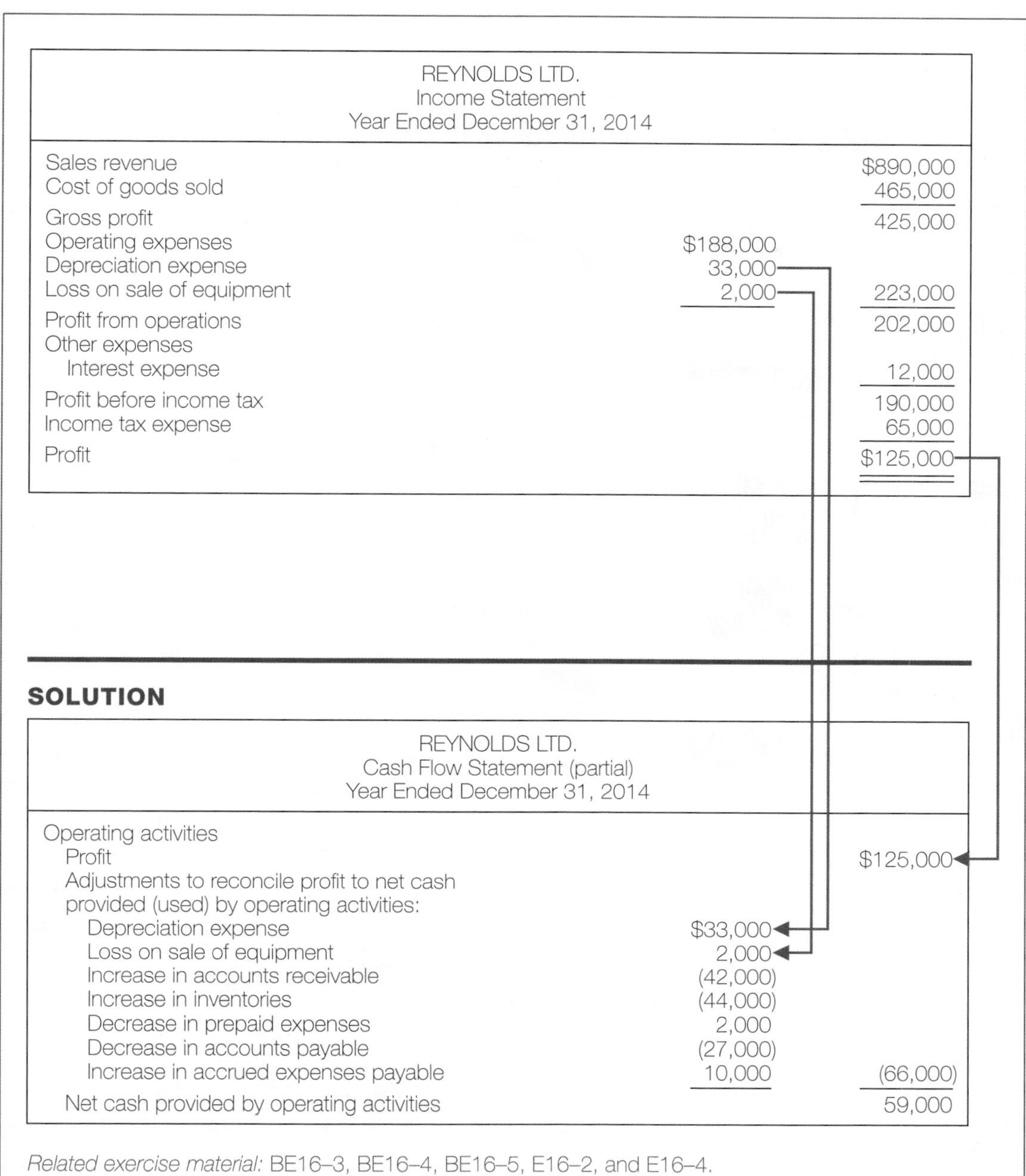

REYNOLDS LTD. Income Statement Year Ended December 31, 2014		
Sales revenue		$890,000
Cost of goods sold		465,000
Gross profit		425,000
Operating expenses	$188,000	
Depreciation expense	33,000	
Loss on sale of equipment	2,000	223,000
Profit from operations		202,000
Other expenses		
Interest expense		12,000
Profit before income tax		190,000
Income tax expense		65,000
Profit		$125,000

SOLUTION

REYNOLDS LTD. Cash Flow Statement (partial) Year Ended December 31, 2014		
Operating activities		
Profit		$125,000
Adjustments to reconcile profit to net cash provided (used) by operating activities:		
Depreciation expense	$33,000	
Loss on sale of equipment	2,000	
Increase in accounts receivable	(42,000)	
Increase in inventories	(44,000)	
Decrease in prepaid expenses	2,000	
Decrease in accounts payable	(27,000)	
Increase in accrued expenses payable	10,000	(66,000)
Net cash provided by operating activities		59,000

Related exercise material: BE16–3, BE16–4, BE16–5, E16–2, and E16–4.

Action Plan

- Start with profit reported on the income statement to determine the net cash provided (used) by operating activities.
- Examine the income statement: Add noncash expenses and deduct noncash revenues. Add losses and deduct gains.
- Analyze the current assets and current liabilities in the balance sheet. Add decreases in related noncash current asset accounts and increases in related noncash liability accounts. Deduct increases in related noncash current asset and decreases in related noncash liability accounts.

THE NAVIGATOR

SECTION 2: DIRECT METHOD

As mentioned earlier in the chapter, although both the indirect and direct methods of determining cash provided (used) by operating activities are acceptable choices under IFRS and ASPE, the direct method is preferred by the standard setters. As presented in Illustration 16-6, a cash flow statement prepared under the direct method reports cash receipts and cash payments for major classes of operating activities. By reporting cash receipts and payments, the direct method provides information that is useful to investors and creditors in predicting future cash flows that is not available under the indirect method. The difference between the cash receipts and cash payments is the net cash provided (used) by operating activities. These relationships are shown in Illustration 16-11.

Under the direct method, net cash provided (used) by operating activities is calculated by adjusting each individual revenue and expense item in the income statement from the accrual basis to the cash basis. The adjustments that are required to convert the related revenues and expenses from an accrual system to a cash system are summarized in Illustration 16-12.

Helpful hint In the indirect method, profit is adjusted to determine cash provided (used) in operating activities. In the direct method, each revenue and expense is adjusted to determine cash receipts and cash payments for operating activities.

ILLUSTRATION 16-11
Major classes of operating cash receipts and payments

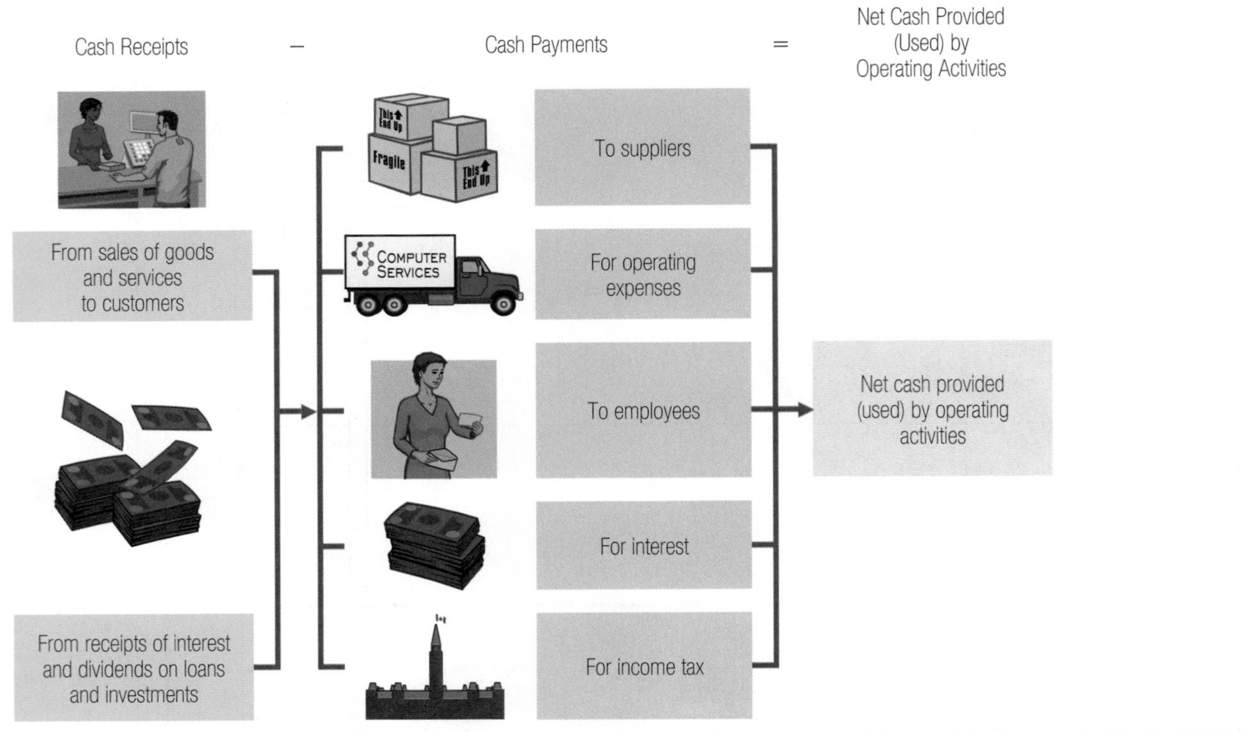

ILLUSTRATION 16-12
Summary of adjustments required to convert revenues and expenses from accrual to cash

	Revenues	Expenses
Current assets		
Increase in account balance	Deduct	Add
Decrease in account balance	Add	Deduct
Current liabilities		
Increase in account balance	Add	Deduct
Decrease in account balance	Deduct	Add

We will explain the reasoning behind these adjustments for Computer Services Corporation, first for cash receipts and then for cash payments, in the following subsections.

Cash Receipts

Computer Services has only one source of cash receipts: its customers.

Cash Receipts from Customers.

The income statement for Computer Services reported sales revenue from customers of $507,000. But how much was received in cash from customers? To answer this question, we need to analyze Computer Services' accounts receivable because Accounts Receivable is increased when a sale is made and decreased when cash is collected.

Assuming all the sales are on account, Computer Services' journal entry to record sales is (in summary for the year):

A	=	L	+	SE
+507,000				+507,000

Cash flows: no effect

Account	Debit	Credit
Accounts Receivable	507,000	
Sales Revenue		507,000

Illustration 16-5 indicates that Computer Services started the year with a balance of $30,000 in Accounts Receivable and ended with $20,000. Using these amounts and the sales recorded in the above journal entry, we analyze the Accounts Receivable account to determine the amount of cash collected from customers as follows:

Accounts Receivable

Jan. 1	Balance	30,000		
	Sales revenue	507,000	Receipts from customers	517,000
Dec. 31	Balance	20,000		

} $10,000 net decrease

The analysis of the accounts receivable shows that cash receipts from customers that are reported in the cash flow statement are $517,000. Note that cash receipts from customers are $10,000 ($517,000 − $507,000) greater than sales revenue. Note also that this is equal to the $10,000 decrease in accounts receivable during the year ($30,000 − $20,000). When the Accounts Receivable account decreases during the year, revenues on an accrual basis are lower than revenues on a cash basis. In other words, more cash was collected during the period than was recorded as revenue.

Note that this is basically the same analysis that we illustrated in the previous section on the indirect method. The difference between the two methods is in the presentation of the information on the cash flow statement.

To summarize, cash receipts from customers ($517,000) can be calculated by adding the decrease in accounts receivable ($10,000) to sales revenues ($507,000). This calculation is shown in Illustration 16-13.

ILLUSTRATION 16-13
Formula to calculate cash receipts from customers—direct method

Cash receipts from customers	=	Revenue		+ Decrease in accounts receivable or − Increase in accounts receivable
$517,000	=	$507,000	+	$10,000

When the Accounts Receivable account balance increases during the year, revenues on an accrual basis are higher than cash receipts. In other words, revenues have increased, but not all of these revenues resulted in cash receipts. Therefore, the amount of the increase in accounts receivable is deducted from sales revenues to arrive at cash receipts from customers.

Cash Receipts from Interest and Dividends.

Computer Services does not have cash receipts from any source other than customers. If an income statement reports other revenues, such as interest and/or dividend revenue, these amounts must be adjusted for any accrued amounts receivable to determine the actual cash receipts. As in Illustration 16-13, increases in accrued receivables would be deducted from accrual-based revenues. Decreases in accrued receivable accounts would be added to accrual-based revenues.

In addition, interest revenue from a long-term investment in bonds must be adjusted for the amortization of any discount or premium on the investment. The journal entries to amortize bond discounts and premiums on investments using assumed data are as follows:

Long-Term Bond Investment at a Discount			Long-Term Bond Investment at a Premium		
Cash	25,000		Cash	25,000	
Long-Term Investment—Bonds	1,000		Long-Term Investment—Bonds		1,500
Interest Revenue		26,000	Interest Revenue		23,500

A	=	L	+	SE
+25,000				+26,000
+1,000				

↑Cash flows: +25,000

A	=	L	+	SE
+25,000				+23,500
−1,500				

↑Cash flows: +25,000

The amortization of a bond discount for an investor results in interest revenue being greater than the cash receipts. Thus the amortization of the discount must be deducted from interest revenue to calculate cash receipts from interest. Conversely, the amortization of a bond premium for an investor results in interest revenue being less than the cash receipts and so the amortization of the premium must be added to interest revenue to calculate cash receipts from interest.

Cash Payments

Computer Services has many sources of cash payments: to suppliers and for operating expenses, interest, and income taxes. We will analyze each of these in the next sections.

Cash Payments to Suppliers.

Computer Services reported cost of goods sold of $150,000 on its income statement. But how much cash was paid to suppliers? To answer that, two steps are required:

1. Determine the cost of goods purchased for the year.
2. Then determine cash payments to suppliers.

The two steps in adjusting cost of goods sold to cash payments to suppliers can be performed by an analysis of the Inventory and Accounts Payable accounts.

Step 1: Cost of Goods Purchased. Computer Services reported $150,000 in cost of goods sold expense in its income statement. Assuming a perpetual inventory system is being used, the summary journal entry to record the cost of goods sold is as follows:

A	=	L	+	SE
−150,000				−150,000

Cash flows: no effect

Account	Debit	Credit
Cost of Goods Sold	150,000	
Inventory		150,000

By analyzing the inventory account, we can determine the cost of goods purchased. The Inventory account increases when inventory purchases are made and decreases when inventory is sold. Computer Services started the year with a balance of $10,000 in inventory and ended with $15,000. Using these amounts and the cost of goods sold recorded in the above journal entry, we analyze the Inventory account to determine the cost of goods purchased as follows:

Inventory

Jan. 1	Balance	10,000			
	Purchases	155,000		Cost of goods sold	150,000
Dec. 31	Balance	15,000			

$5,000 net increase

The cost of goods purchased during the period is $155,000, which is $5,000 ($155,000 − $150,000) greater than the cost of goods sold expense reported in the income statement. Note that this difference is equal to the $5,000 increase in the Inventory account during the period ($15,000 − $10,000). When the Inventory account increases, more goods were purchased during the period than was recorded in cost of goods sold. Thus, cost of goods purchased ($155,000) can be calculated by simply adding the increase in inventory ($5,000) to cost of goods sold ($150,000).

Following the same logic, if the Inventory account decreased, this would mean that the cost of goods purchased was less than the cost of goods sold and the decrease in inventory can be deducted from cost of goods sold to arrive at cost of goods purchased.

Step 2: Cash Payments to Suppliers. Assuming all of the purchases were on account, the journal entry to record the purchases is (in summary):

A	=	L	+	SE
+155,000		+155,000		

Cash flows: no effect

Account	Debit	Credit
Inventory	155,000	
Accounts Payable		155,000

By analyzing the Accounts Payable account, we can determine the cash payments to suppliers because the account is increased by the cost of goods purchased and decreased by cash paid to suppliers. Computer Services started the year with a balance of $12,000 in accounts payable and ended with $28,000. Using these amounts and the purchases of inventory in the previous journal entry, we analyze the Accounts Payable account to determine the cash paid to suppliers as follows:

Accounts Payable

			Jan. 1	Balance	12,000
	Payments to suppliers	139,000		Purchases	155,000
			Dec. 31	Balance	28,000

$16,000 net increase

The cash payments to suppliers are $139,000, which is $16,000 ($155,000 − $139,000) less than the cost of goods purchased. Note that this difference is equal to the $16,000 increase in the Accounts Payable account during the period ($28,000 − $12,000). When the Accounts Payable account increases, it means that the cash paid to suppliers was less than the purchases made during the period. Thus cash payments to suppliers ($139,000) can be calculated by deducting the increase in accounts payable ($16,000) from cost of goods purchased ($155,000).

Note that, if accounts payable decreased, it would mean that the cash paid to suppliers was more than the cost of goods purchased. Thus the decrease in accounts payable is added to the cost of goods purchased to arrive at cash payments to suppliers.

To summarize, the calculation of cash payments to suppliers is calculated as shown in Illustration 16-14.

ILLUSTRATION 16-14
Formula to calculate cash payments to suppliers—direct method

Cash payments to suppliers	=	Cost of goods sold	{ + Increase in inventory or − Decrease in inventory	{ + Decrease in accounts payable or − Increase in accounts payable
$139,000	=	$150,000 +	$5,000	− $16,000

In this analysis, we have assumed that the Accounts Payable account is used only to record purchases of inventory on account. An accrued expenses payable account is used to record other credit purchases.

Cash Payments for Operating Expenses.

Computer Services reported $111,000 of operating expenses in its income statement. This means that profit decreased by $111,000, but what was the amount of cash paid for operating expenses? To answer this question, we need to analyze the Prepaid Expenses account because it is increased when a prepayment is made and decreased when an expense is recorded in the income statement. Assume the following summary journal entry was made to record the operating expenses:

	Debit	Credit
Operating Expenses	111,000	
Prepaid Expenses		111,000

A	=	L	+	SE
−111,000				−111,000

Cash flows: no effect

Computer Services started the year with a balance of $1,000 in the Prepaid Expenses account and ended with $5,000. Using these amounts and the operating expenses recorded in the previous journal entry, we analyze the Prepaid Expenses account to determine the cash paid for operating expenses as follows:

Prepaid Expenses

Jan. 1	Balance	1,000		
	Payments for expenses	115,000	Operating expenses	111,000
Dec. 31	Balance	5,000		

} $4,000 net increase

The cash paid for operating expenses is $115,000, which is $4,000 ($115,000 − $111,000) greater than the operating expenses reported in the income statement. Note that this difference is equal to the $4,000 increase in the Prepaid Expenses account during the period ($5,000 − $1,000). When the balance in the Prepaid Expenses account increases, this means cash paid for expenses is higher than the expenses reported in the income statement. In other words, cash payments were made in the current period, but the expenses will not be recorded in the income statement until future periods. Thus cash payments for operating expenses ($115,000) is calculated by adding the increase ($4,000) in prepaid expenses to the operating expenses ($111,000) reported in the income statement. If prepaid expenses decrease, the decrease is deducted from operating expenses.

Operating expenses must also be adjusted for changes in accrued liability accounts (also called accrued expenses payable). Computer Services does not have any accrued expenses payable related to its operating expenses. If it did, any changes in the Accrued Expenses Payable account would affect operating expenses as follows: When accrued expenses payable increase during the year, operating expenses reported are higher than they are on a cash basis. To determine cash payments for operating expenses, an increase in accrued expenses payable is deducted from operating expenses. On the other hand, a decrease in accrued expenses payable is added to operating expenses because the cash payments are greater than the operating expenses.

To summarize, Computer Services' cash payments for operating expenses were $115,000, calculated as in Illustration 16-15.

ILLUSTRATION 16-15
Formula to calculate cash payments for operating expenses—direct method

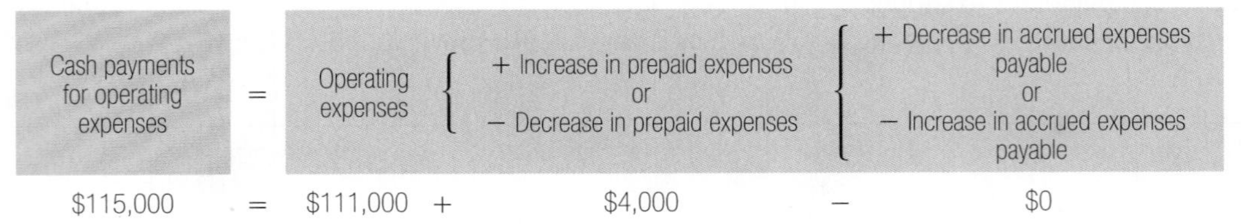

Cash Payments to Employees.

Companies may report payments to employees separately from operating expenses. To determine payments to employees, you would have to know the salary expense amount on the income statement and any salaries payable on the comparative balance sheets. Cash payments to employees, reported on the cash flow statement, would equal the salary expense, plus any decrease (or less any increase) during the period in salaries payable.

Cash Payments for Interest.

Computer Services reports $42,000 of interest expense on its income statement in Illustration 16-5. This amount equals the cash paid, since the comparative balance sheets indicated no interest payable at the beginning or end of the year. If the comparative balance sheets reported interest payable, cash payments for interest would be calculated by adding a decrease in interest payable to interest expense and deducting an increase in interest payable to interest expense.

If a company has bonds payable sold at a premium or discount, interest expense will include the amortization of bond discounts and premiums. That means interest expense will not equal the cash payments for interest. Recall from Chapter 15 that the journal entries, using assumed data, to record interest expense and amortize bond discounts and premiums are recorded as follows:

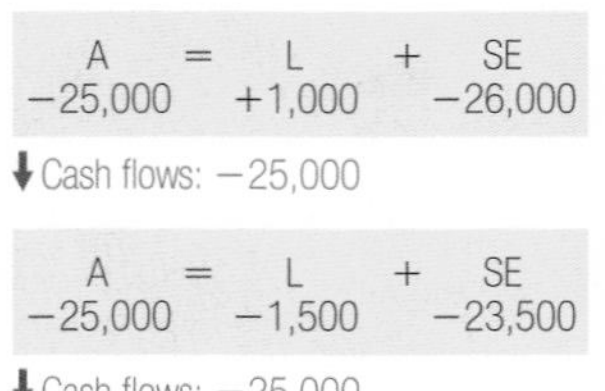

Bonds Payable Issued at a Discount			**Bonds Payable Issued at a Premium**		
Interest Expense	26,000		Interest Expense	23,500	
Bonds Payable		1,000	Bonds Payable	1,500	
Cash		25,000	Cash		25,000

The amortization of a bonds payable discount results in interest expense being higher than the cash payment to the bond investors. So the amortization of a bond discount, the amount credited to bonds payable, must be deducted from interest expense to determine cash payments for interest.

The amortization of a bonds payable premium results in interest expense being lower than the cash payment to the bond investors. So the amortization of a bond premium, the amount debited to bonds payable, must be added to interest expense to determine cash payments for interest.

To summarize, the relationship among cash payments for interest, interest expense, changes in interest payable (if any), and amortization of premiums or discounts (if any) is shown in Illustration 16-16.

ILLUSTRATION 16-16
Formula to calculate cash payments for interest—direct method

Cash payments for interest	=	Interest expense	+ Decrease in interest payable or − Increase in interest payable		+ Amortization of bond premium or − Amortization of bond discount
$42,000	=	$42,000 +	$0	+	$0

Note that the Computer Services bonds payable were issued at par and thus there was no discount or premium to amortize. The amounts shown in the previous journal entries were included only to help you understand the impact of a premium or discount, when one exists.

Cash Payments for Income Tax.

Computer Services reported $47,000 in income tax expense on the income statement. The journal entry to record the income tax expense is as follows:

Income Tax Expense	47,000	
Income Tax Payable		47,000

A	=	L	+	SE
		+47,000		−47,000

Cash flows: no effect

This means that profit decreased by $47,000, but how much cash was paid for income tax? To answer this question, we need to analyze Computer Services' Income Tax Payable account because it increases when income tax expense is recorded and decreases when income tax is paid. Computer Services started the year with a balance of $8,000 in income tax payable and ended with $6,000. Using these amounts and the income tax payable recorded in the above journal entry, we analyze the Income Tax Payable account to determine the cash paid for income tax as follows:

Income Tax Payable					
		Jan. 1	Balance	8,000	
Payments for income tax	49,000		Income tax expense	47,000	$2,000 net decrease
		Dec. 31	Balance	6,000	

The cash paid for income tax is $49,000, which is $2,000 ($49,000 − $47,000) more than the income tax expense. Note that this difference is equal to the $2,000 decrease in income tax payable during the period ($8,000 − $6,000). When income tax payable decreases, it means that more income tax was paid than recorded as expense in the income statement. Thus the payments for income tax ($49,000) are calculated by adding the decrease in income tax payable ($2,000) to income tax expense ($47,000). An increase in income tax payable is deducted from income tax expense.

The relationship among cash payments for income tax, income tax expense, and changes in income tax payable is shown in Illustration 16-17.

ILLUSTRATION 16-17
Formula to calculate cash payments for income tax—direct method

Cash payments for income tax	=	Income tax expense		+ Decrease in income tax payable or − Increase in income tax payable
$49,000	=	$47,000	+	$2,000

Cash Payments (Receipts) for Trading Investments.

You will recall that trading investments are classified as an operating activity. Thus any cash payments made to purchase trading investments and any cash receipts for the sale of trading investments will be reported in the operating activities section of the cash flow statement. Typically, the payments and receipts for trading investments are reported as a net amount. For example, if cash paid to purchase trading investments is greater than cash received for the sale of trading investments, a net cash payment is reported.

All of the revenues and expenses in the Computer Services income statement have now been adjusted to a cash basis. This information is put together in Illustration 16-18, which shows the operating activities section of the cash flow statement using the direct method.

Helpful hint Note that in the operating activities section, positive numbers indicate cash inflows (receipts) and negative numbers indicate cash outflows (payments). As well, whether the direct or indirect method is used, net cash provided (used) by operating activities will be the same.

ILLUSTRATION 16-18
Net cash provided by operating activities—direct method

COMPUTER SERVICES CORPORATION
Cash Flow Statement (partial)
Year Ended December 31, 2014

Operating activities		
Cash receipts from customers		$517,000
Cash payments		
To suppliers	$(139,000)	
For operating expenses	(115,000)	
For interest	(42,000)	
For income tax	(49,000)	(345,000)
Net cash provided by operating activities		172,000

BEFORE YOU GO ON...

DO IT

Selected financial information follows for Reynolds Ltd. at December 31. Prepare the operating activities section of the cash flow statement using the direct method.

	2014	2013	Increase (Decrease)
Current assets			
Cash	$54,000	$37,000	$17,000
Accounts receivable	68,000	26,000	42,000
Inventories	54,000	10,000	44,000
Prepaid expenses	4,000	6,000	(2,000)
Current liabilities			
Accounts payable	23,000	50,000	(27,000)
Accrued expenses payable	10,000	0	10,000

REYNOLDS LTD.
Income Statement
Year Ended December 31, 2014

Sales revenue		$890,000
Cost of goods sold		465,000
Gross profit		425,000
Operating expenses	$188,000	
Depreciation expense	33,000	
Loss on sale of equipment	2,000	223,000
Profit from operations		202,000
Other expenses		
Interest expense		12,000
Profit before income tax		190,000
Income tax expense		65,000
Profit		$125,000

Action Plan

- Determine the net cash provided (used) by operating activities by adjusting each revenue and expense item for changes in the related current asset and current liability account.
- To adjust revenues for changes in related current asset and current liability accounts, add decreases in current asset accounts and increases in current liability accounts. Deduct increases in current asset accounts and decreases in current liability accounts.
- To adjust expenses for changes in related current asset and current liability accounts, add increases in current asset accounts and decreases in current liability accounts. Deduct decreases in current asset accounts and increases in current liability accounts.
- Assume that the accounts payable relate to suppliers and that the accrued expenses payable relate to operating expenses.
- Report cash receipts and cash payments by major sources and uses: cash receipts from customers and cash payments to suppliers, for operating expenses, to employees, for interest, and for income taxes.

SOLUTION

REYNOLDS LTD.
Cash Flow Statement (partial)
Year Ended December 31, 2014

Operating activities		
Cash receipts from customers		$848,000[1]
Cash payments		
To suppliers	$(536,000)[2]	
For operating expenses	(176,000)[3]	
For interest	(12,000)	
For income tax	(65,000)	(789,000)
Net cash provided by operating activities		59,000

Calculations:
[1] Cash receipts from customers: $890,000 − $42,000 = $848,000
[2] Payments to suppliers: $465,000 + $44,000 + $27,000 = $536,000
[3] Payments for operating expenses: $188,000 − $2,000 − $10,000 = $176,000

THE NAVIGATOR

Related exercise material: BE16–6, BE16–7, BE16–8, BE16–9, BE16–10, BE16–11, BE16–12, BE16–13, E16–3, E16–5, E16–6, and E16–7.

STEP 2: INVESTING ACTIVITIES

Determine the Net Cash Provided (Used) by Investing Activities by Analyzing Changes in Long-Term Asset Accounts

Regardless of whether the indirect or direct method is used to calculate operating activities, investing and financing activities are measured and reported in the same way. Investing activities affect long-term asset accounts, such as long-term investments; property, plant, and equipment; and intangible assets. There are exceptions. For example, short-term debt instruments purchased to earn interest and short-term notes receivable issued for loans rather than for trade transactions are reported as investing activities.

To determine the investing activities, the balance sheet and additional information in Illustration 16-5 must be examined. The change in each long-term asset account is analyzed to determine what effect, if any, it had on cash. Computer Services has no short-term investments or notes receivable but does have three long-term asset accounts that must be analyzed: Land, Building, and Equipment.

LAND

Land increased by $110,000 during the year, as reported in Computer Services' balance sheet. The additional information in Illustration 16-5 states that this land was purchased by issuing long-term bonds. The journal entry to record the purchase of the land is as follows:

Land	110,000	
Bonds Payable		110,000

A	=	L	+	SE
+110,000		+110,000		

Cash flows: no effect

As shown in the journal entry, issuing bonds for land has no effect on cash and is not reported in the cash flow statement. It is, however, a significant noncash investing and financing activity that must be disclosed in a note to the statement.

BUILDING

The Building account increased by $120,000 during the year. What caused this increase? No additional information has been given for this change. Whenever unexplained differences in accounts occur, we assume the transaction was for cash. That is, we would assume the entry to record the acquisition or expansion of the building is as follows:

Building	120,000	
Cash		120,000

A	=	L	+	SE
+120,000				
−120,000				

↓Cash flows: −120,000

The cash outflow for the purchase of the building is reported as an investing activity in the cash flow statement.

Accumulated Depreciation—Building

The Accumulated Depreciation—Building account increased by $6,000 during the year:

Accumulated Depreciation—Building

	Jan. 1	Balance	5,000
		Depreciation expense	6,000
	Dec. 31	Balance	11,000

} $6,000 net increase

As explained in the additional information in Illustration 16-5, this increase resulted from the depreciation expense reported on the income statement for the building. The journal entry to record the depreciation expense is as follows:

Depreciation Expense	6,000	
Accumulated Depreciation—Building		6,000

A	=	L	+	SE
−6,000				−6,000

Cash flows: no effect

As the journal entry shows, depreciation expense is a noncash charge and does not affect the cash flow statement.

EQUIPMENT

Computer Services' Equipment account increased by $17,000. The additional information for Illustration 16-5 explains that this was a net increase resulting from two different transactions: (1) a purchase of equipment for $25,000 cash, and (2) a sale of equipment with a carrying amount of $7,000 (cost of $8,000, less accumulated depreciation of $1,000) for $4,000 cash. The journal entry to record the purchase of equipment is as follows:

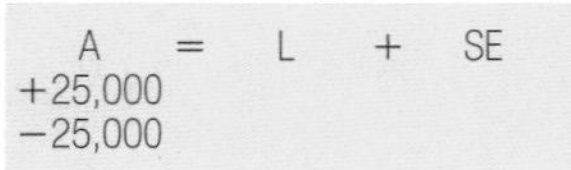

↓Cash flows: −25,000

Account	Debit	Credit
Equipment	25,000	
Cash		25,000

The purchase of the equipment is reported as a $25,000 cash outflow in the investing section of the cash flow statement.

The journal entry to record the sale of the equipment is as follows:

A	=	L	+	SE
+4,000				−3,000
+1,000				
−8,000				

↑Cash flows: +4,000

Account	Debit	Credit
Cash	4,000	
Accumulated Depreciation—Equipment	1,000	
Loss on Sale of Equipment	3,000	
Equipment		8,000

The $4,000 cash proceeds from the sale of the equipment is reported as a cash inflow in the investing section of the cash flow statement.

The T account below summarizes the changes in the Equipment account during the year:

$17,000 net increase

		Equipment		
Jan. 1	Balance	10,000		
	Purchases of equipment	25,000	Cost of equipment sold	8,000
Dec. 31	Balance	27,000		

Note that, for the sale of the equipment, it is the cash proceeds that are reported on the cash flow statement, not the cost of the equipment sold, that is credited to the Equipment account.

Also note that each transaction, both the purchase and the sale, must be reported separately on the cash flow statement. It is not correct to report the net change in a long-term balance sheet account as simply an increase or decrease in that account.

In the above example, you were given additional information about both the purchase and the sale of equipment. Often, in analyzing accounts, you will be given just one piece of information and are expected to deduce the information that is missing. For example, if you knew the beginning and ending balances of the Equipment account as well as the fact that the cost of the equipment sold was $8,000, you could determine that the cost of the equipment purchased must have been $25,000.

Accumulated Depreciation—Equipment

The accumulated depreciation for equipment increased by $2,000. This change does not represent the depreciation expense for the year. In fact, the information in Illustration 16-5 told us that there was $3,000 of depreciation expense for the equipment and that the equipment sold had $1,000 of accumulated depreciation.

The journal entry to record the depreciation expense is as follows:

A	=	L	+	SE
−3,000				−3,000

Cash flows: no effect

Account	Debit	Credit
Depreciation Expense	3,000	
Accumulated Depreciation—Equipment		3,000

This journal entry, combined with the journal entry shown earlier for the sale of the equipment, helps us understand the changes to the accumulated depreciation account. The T account below for Accumulated Depreciation—Equipment shows that these two items explain the overall net increase of $2,000.

Accumulated Depreciation—Equipment

		Jan. 1	Balance	1,000	
Sale of equipment	1,000		Depreciation expense	3,000	$2,000 net increase
		Dec. 31	Balance	3,000	

As we have seen, the sale of the equipment affects one account on Computer Services' income statement (Loss on Sale of Equipment) and three accounts on its balance sheet (Cash, Equipment, and Accumulated Depreciation). In the cash flow statement, it is important to report the effects of this sale in one place: the investing activities section. The overall result is that the sale of the equipment ends up having no impact on the operating activities section of the cash flow statement. Instead, the cash proceeds received from the sale of the equipment are shown fully in the investing activities section.

Helpful hint Note that in the investing activities section, positive numbers indicate cash inflows (receipts) and negative numbers indicate cash outflows (payments).

The investing activities section of Computer Services' cash flow statement is shown in Illustration 16-19 and reports the changes in the three accounts: Land, Building, and Equipment.

ILLUSTRATION 16-19
Net cash used by investing activities

COMPUTER SERVICES CORPORATION
Cash Flow Statement (partial)
Year Ended December 31, 2014

Investing activities		
Purchase of building	$(120,000)	
Purchase of equipment	(25,000)	
Sale of equipment	4,000	
Net cash used by investing activities		$(141,000)
Note x: Significant noncash investing and financing activities		
Issue of bonds to purchase land		$ 110,000

 **BEFORE YOU GO ON...**

DO IT

Kamal Corporation reported an opening balance of $146,000 and an ending balance of $135,000 in its Equipment account and an opening balance of $47,000 and an ending balance of $62,000 in its Accumulated Depreciation—Equipment account. During the year, it sold equipment with a cost of $21,000 for cash at a gain on the sale of $1,000. It also purchased equipment for cash. It recorded depreciation expense of $31,000. Calculate (a) the cash received from the sale of the equipment, and (b) the cash paid for equipment.

Action Plan

- Prepare a T account for Accumulated Depreciation—Equipment and record the beginning and ending balances and the depreciation expense. Recall that depreciation expense increases accumulated depreciation. Use this information to calculate the accumulated depreciation of the equipment sold during the year.
- Prepare a T account for Equipment and record the beginning and ending balances and the cost of the equipment sold. Use this information to calculate the cost of the equipment purchased.

SOLUTION

(a) Cash received from sale of equipment = $6,000

Accumulated Depreciation—Equipment

		Opening balance	47,000
Sale of equipment	16,000*	Depreciation expense	31,000
		Ending balance	62,000

* $16,000 = $47,000 + $31,000 − $62,000

BEFORE YOU GO ON... continued on next page

BEFORE YOU GO ON...
continued from previous page

- Prepare journal entries to help you determine the impact of the transactions on cash.
- Calculate the carrying amount of the equipment sold. Remember that the carrying amount is equal to the cost of the equipment sold less the accumulated depreciation on the equipment sold.
- Calculate the cash proceeds on the sale of the equipment. Since there is a gain on sale, the equipment sold for more than its carrying amount. Therefore, add the gain on sale to the carrying amount to determine the cash proceeds.

Carrying amount of equipment sold: $21,000 − $16,000 = $5,000
Carrying amount of the equipment sold plus the gain on sale = $5,000 + $1,000 = $6,000

The journal entries to record the depreciation expense and the sale of the equipment are as follows:

Depreciation Expense	31,000	
Accumulated Depreciation—Equipment		31,000
Cash	6,000	
Accumulated Depreciation—Equipment	16,000	
Gain on Sale of Equipment		1,000
Equipment		21,000

(b) Cash paid for equipment = $10,000

Equipment			
Opening bal.	146,000		
Purchase of Equipment	10,000**	Sale of Equipment	21,000
Ending bal.	135,000		

** $10,000 = $135,000 + $21,000 − $146,000

The journal entry to record the purchase of equipment is as follows:

Equipment	10,000	
Cash		10,000

Related exercise material: BE16–14 and BE16–15.

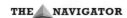

THE NAVIGATOR

STEP 3: FINANCING ACTIVITIES

Determine the Net Cash Provided (Used) by Financing Activities by Analyzing Changes in Long-Term Liability and Equity Accounts

The third step in preparing a cash flow statement is to analyze the changes in long-term liability and equity accounts. If short-term notes payable are issued for lending purposes rather than for trade, they should also be reported in the financing activities section. Computer Services has no notes payable but has one long-term liability account, Bonds Payable, and two shareholders' equity accounts, Common Shares and Retained Earnings.

BONDS PAYABLE

Bonds Payable increased by $110,000. As indicated earlier, land was acquired from the issue of these bonds. This noncash transaction is reported as a note to the cash flow statement because it is a significant financing activity.

COMMON SHARES

Computer Services' Common Shares account increased by $20,000. Since there is no additional information about any reacquisition of shares, we assume that this change is due entirely to the issue of additional common shares for cash. The entry to record the issue of common shares is as follows:

Cash	20,000	
Common Shares		20,000

A	=	L	+	SE
+20,000				+20,000

↑Cash flows: +20,000

This cash inflow is reported in the financing activities section of the cash flow statement. If the company had also reacquired shares, the amount of cash paid to reacquire the common shares would be reported as a cash outflow in the financing section.

RETAINED EARNINGS

Retained earnings increased by $116,000 during the year, but what caused this increase? Were there any non-operating cash transactions that changed retained earnings? We know that profit increases retained earnings and that Computer Services reported profit of $145,000 for the year. The journal entry to record profit in the Retained Earnings account is as follows:

Income Summary	145,000	
Retained Earnings		145,000

A	=	L	+	SE
				−145,000 +145,000

Cash flows: no effect

Computer Services started the year with $48,000 in its Retained Earnings account and ended the year with $164,000. Using these amounts and the profit recorded in the above journal entry, we analyze the Retained Earnings account to determine the dividends declared as follows:

Retained Earnings

		Jan. 1	Balance	48,000
Cash dividend	29,000		Profit	145,000
		Dec. 31	Balance	164,000

} $116,000 net increase

Note that the Retained Earnings account above only reports the dividend declared. This amount must be adjusted to determine the dividend paid, if there is any change in the balance of the Dividends Payable account reported in the current liabilities section of the balance sheet. The relationship among cash payments for dividends, dividends declared, and changes in dividends payable is shown in Illustration 16-20.

ILLUSTRATION 16-20
Formula to calculate dividends paid in cash

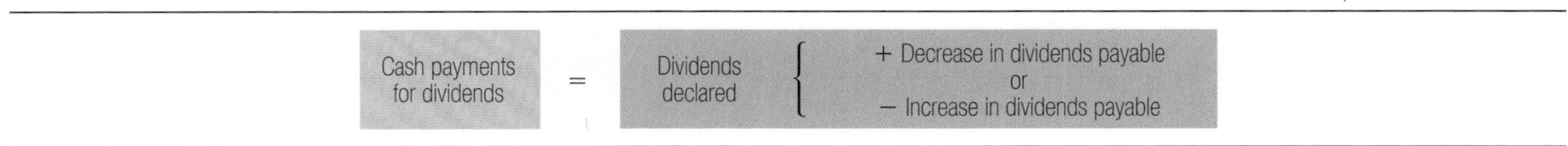

Cash payments for dividends
=
Dividends declared
+ Decrease in dividends payable
or
− Increase in dividends payable

The additional information for Illustration 16-5 indicates that Computer Services paid a cash dividend of $29,000. In this example, the dividends declared are equal to the dividends paid. The cash dividend paid is reported as a cash outflow in the financing activities section of the cash flow statement.

Helpful hint Note that in the financing activities section, positive numbers indicate cash inflows (receipts) and negative numbers indicate cash outflows (payments).

The financing activities section of Computer Services' cash flow statement is in Illustration 16-21 and reports the issue of common shares and payment of a dividend. The information on the significant noncash financing activity of bonds being issued to purchase land has already been illustrated and is not included here.

ILLUSTRATION 16-21
Net cash used by financing activities

COMPUTER SERVICES CORPORATION Cash Flow Statement (partial) Year Ended December 31, 2014		
Financing activities		
Issue of common shares	$20,000	
Payment of cash dividend	(29,000)	
Net cash used by financing activities		$(9,000)

BEFORE YOU GO ON...

DO IT

La Tuque Corporation reported an opening balance of $80,000 and an ending balance of $95,000 in its Common Shares account and an opening balance of $15,000 and an ending balance of $20,000 in its Contributed Surplus—Reacquisition of Common Shares account. During the year, it issued $50,000 of common shares for cash and reacquired common shares for cash. Calculate the cash paid to reacquire the shares.

Action Plan

- Prepare a T account for Common Shares and record the beginning and ending balances and the cost of the new shares issued. Use this information to determine the cost of the shares reacquired.
- Prepare a T account for Contributed Surplus—Reacquisition of Common Shares and record the beginning and ending balances. Use this information to determine the change in the account as a result of the reacquisition of the shares.
- Prepare journal entries to help you record the transactions in the Common Shares and Contributed Surplus—Reacquisition of Common Shares accounts, and to determine the impact on cash.
- An increase in contributed surplus indicates that the company paid less than the cost of the common shares to reacquire them. Deduct this increase from the cost of the shares to determine the cash paid.

SOLUTION

Cash paid to reacquire shares = $30,000

The journal entry to record the issue of shares is as follows:

Cash	50,000	
Common Shares		50,000

Common Shares

		Opening balance	80,000
Reacquisition of shares	35,000*	Issue of shares	50,000
		Ending balance	95,000

* $35,000 = $80,000 + $50,000 − $95,000

Contributed Surplus—Reacquisition of Common Shares

		Opening balance	15,000
		Reacquisition of shares	5,000**
		Ending balance	20,000

** $5,000 = $20,000 − $15,000

The journal entry to record the reacquisition of common shares is as follows:

Common Shares	35,000	
Contributed Surplus—Reacquisition of Common Shares		5,000
Cash***		30,000

***Cash paid for reacquisition of shares: $35,000 − $5,000 = $30,000

Related exercise material: BE16–16, BE16–17, and E16–9.

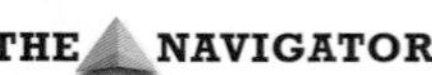

STEP 4: THE CASH FLOW STATEMENT

Prepare the Cash Flow Statement and Determine the Net Increase (Decrease) in Cash

The final step is to calculate the overall net increase or decrease in cash for the year by adding cash provided or used in each of the three sections of the cash flow statement. Computer Services' net increase in cash of $22,000 is calculated as follows:

Net cash provided by operating activities	$172,000
Net cash used by investing activities	(141,000)
Net cash used by financing activities	(9,000)
Net increase in cash	$ 22,000

The $22,000 net increase in cash is then added to cash at the beginning of the year of $33,000 to equal $55,000 of cash at the end of the year. This number is compared with the cash account balance in the end-of-the-year balance sheet, which also shows that cash is $55,000 at the end of the year. This is known as proving the cash balance. If cash at the end of the year on the cash flow statement is not equal to cash on the balance sheet, there is an error in the cash flow statement, which will need to be found and corrected.

Using this information and the partial cash flow statements shown in Illustrations 16-10, 16-18, 16-19, and 16-21, we can now present a complete cash flow statement for Computer Services Corporation. Illustration 16-22 presents the statement using the indirect method of preparing the operating activities section from Illustration 16-10. Illustration 16-23 presents the statement using the direct method of preparing the operating activities section from Illustration 16-18. Notice that, while the operating activities sections differ in the indirect and direct methods, the investing and financing activities sections are exactly the same in the two statements.

ILLUSTRATION 16-22
Cash flow statement—indirect method

COMPUTER SERVICES CORPORATION
Cash Flow Statement
Year Ended December 31, 2014

Operating activities		
Profit		$145,000
Adjustments to reconcile profit to net cash provided (used) by operating activities:		
Depreciation expense	$ 9,000	
Loss on sale of equipment	3,000	
Decrease in accounts receivable	10,000	
Increase in inventory	(5,000)	
Increase in prepaid expenses	(4,000)	
Increase in accounts payable	16,000	
Decrease in income tax payable	(2,000)	27,000
Net cash provided by operating activities		172,000
Investing activities		
Purchase of building	$(120,000)	
Purchase of equipment	(25,000)	
Sale of equipment	4,000	
Net cash used by investing activities		(141,000)
Financing activities		
Issue of common shares	$ 20,000	
Payment of cash dividend	(29,000)	
Net cash used by financing activities		(9,000)
Net increase in cash		22,000
Cash, January 1		33,000
Cash, December 31		$ 55,000
Note x: Significant noncash investing and financing activities; Issue of bonds to purchase land		$110,000

ILLUSTRATION 16-23
Cash flow statement—direct method

COMPUTER SERVICES CORPORATION
Cash Flow Statement
Year Ended December 31, 2014

Operating activities		
Cash receipts from customers		$517,000
Cash payments		
To suppliers	$(139,000)	
For operating expenses	(115,000)	
For interest	(42,000)	
For income tax	(49,000)	(345,000)
Net cash provided by operating activities		172,000
Investing activities		
Purchase of building	$(120,000)	
Purchase of equipment	(25,000)	
Sale of equipment	4,000	
Net cash used by investing activities		(141,000)
Financing activities		
Issue of common shares	20,000	
Payment of cash dividend	(29,000)	
Net cash used by financing activities		(9,000)
Net increase in cash		22,000
Cash, January 1		33,000
Cash, December 31		$ 55,000

Note x: Significant noncash investing and financing activities;
Issue of bonds to purchase land $110,000

BEFORE YOU GO ON...

DO IT

Selected information follows for Reynolds Ltd. at December 31. Prepare a cash flow statement.

	2014	2013	Increase (Decrease)
Cash	$ 54,000	$ 37,000	$ 17,000
Property, plant, and equipment			
Land	45,000	70,000	(25,000)
Buildings	200,000	200,000	0
Accumulated depreciation—buildings	(21,000)	(11,000)	10,000
Equipment	193,000	68,000	125,000
Accumulated depreciation—equipment	(28,000)	(10,000)	18,000
Long-term liabilities and shareholders' equity			
Bonds payable	110,000	150,000	(40,000)
Common shares	220,000	60,000	160,000
Retained earnings	206,000	136,000	70,000

Additional information:

1. Cash provided from operating activities was $59,000 as shown in the Before You Go On at the end of the section "Step 1: Operating Activities."
2. Equipment was bought for cash. Equipment with a cost of $41,000 and a carrying amount of $36,000 was sold at a loss of $2,000.
3. Bonds of $40,000 were redeemed at their face value for cash.
4. Profit was $125,000 and a cash dividend was paid.

BEFORE YOU GO ON...
continued on next page

SOLUTION

REYNOLDS LTD. Cash Flow Statement Year Ended December 31, 2014		
Operating activities		
Net cash provided by operating activities		$ 59,000
Investing activities		
Sale of land	$ 25,000	
Sale of equipment	34,000[1]	
Purchase of equipment	(166,000)[2]	
Net cash used by investing activities		(107,000)
Financing activities		
Redemption of bonds	$ (40,000)	
Issue of common shares	160,000	
Payment of dividends	(55,000)[3]	
Net cash provided by financing activities		65,000
Net increase in cash		17,000
Cash, January 1		37,000
Cash, December 31		$ 54,000

[1]Sale of equipment: $36,000 (carrying amount) − $2,000 (loss) = $34,000
[2]Purchase of equipment: $68,000 (opening Equipment balance) − $41,000 (cost of equipment sold) − $193,000 (ending Equipment balance) = $166,000 (purchase of equipment)
[3]Payment of dividends: $136,000 (opening Retained Earnings) + $125,000 (profit) − $206,000 (ending Retained Earnings) = $55,000 (Dividends)

Related exercise material: BE16–18, E16–10, E16–11, and E16–12.

BEFORE YOU GO ON...
continued from previous page

Action Plan

- Determine the net cash provided (used) by investing activities. Investing activities generally relate to changes in long-term asset accounts.
- Determine the net cash provided (used) by financing activities. Financing activities generally relate to changes in long-term liability and shareholders' equity accounts.
- Determine the net increase (decrease) in cash and add it to the beginning-of-period cash. Verify that this amount agrees with the end-of-period cash balance reported on the balance sheet.

THE NAVIGATOR

USING THE INFORMATION IN THE FINANCIAL STATEMENTS

STUDY OBJECTIVE 3
Analyze the cash flow statement.

The cash flow statement gives information about a company's financial health that cannot be found in the other financial statements. None of the other financial statements give enough information for decision-making by themselves. The income statement; statements of comprehensive income, retained earnings, and changes in shareholders' equity; and the balance sheet must be read along with the cash flow statement in order to fully understand a company's financial situation.

For example, the income statement might show a profitable company. However, a rapidly growing company might also find it difficult to pay its current liabilities because its cash is being used to finance its growth. Both successful and unsuccessful companies can have problems with cash flow. According to Clearwater Seafoods in our feature story, the sustainability of a business is linked to its ability to generate cash. Clearwater considers cash flows generated from operations as a key indicator of the company's health.

Consider the condensed income and cash flow data shown below for three different companies, each operating in the same industry.

	Atzemis Company	Barber Company	Collins Company
Profit (loss)	$ 75,000	$ 25,000	$(50,000)
Cash provided (used) by operating activities	$100,000	$(25,000)	$(25,000)
Cash provided (used) by investing activities	(50,000)	(25,000)	35,000
Cash provided (used) by financing activities	(25,000)	75,000	15,000
Net increase in cash	$ 25,000	$ 25,000	$ 25,000

In this example, we have assumed that each company has the same change in cash, an increase of $25,000. However, this increase in cash is generated quite differently by each company. Atzemis reports profit of $75,000 and a positive cash flow from operating activities of $100,000. How can Atzemis's cash provided by operating activities be higher than its profit? This could occur in any of these three situations: if it has (1) noncash expenses such as depreciation, (2) reduced current assets such as receivables or inventory, or (3) increased current liabilities such as accounts payable. Depending on which of the situations created Atzemis's higher cash flow from operating activities, there could be different implications. For example, if receivables are lower, this could be because the company is collecting them faster. If so, this is a good thing. Alternatively, receivables could have decreased because sales decreased. This is not good, and has implications for future profitability.

For now, we know that Atzemis's operating activities produced a positive cash flow of $100,000, which allowed it to invest $50,000 in its long-lived assets and repay $25,000 of its debt and/or pay dividends. Based only on this information, Atzemis appears to be in a strong financial position. As explained in the feature story about Clearwater, cash flows generated from operations are a key indicator of a company's health.

Barber Company, which also produced a positive profit, used $25,000 in its operating activities. How could Barber's profit result in a negative operating cash flow? Barber may be in the early start-up stages of its development. It may have quickly increasing receivables and inventories, with lower amounts of noncash expenses. It was able to end up with the same cash balance as Atzemis only because it borrowed money. If Barber is indeed a new and rapidly growing company, this is fine. If not, this type of cash flow pattern would not be sustainable in the long run.

Assuming Barber is a start-up company, its cash flow figures appear to be reasonable. For example, early in its operations, during its growth stage, one would expect a company to generate a small amount of profit (or a loss) and negative cash from its operating activities. It will likely also be spending large amounts to purchase productive assets, and will finance these purchases by issuing debt or equity securities. Thus, during its early years, cash from operating and investing activities will likely be negative, while cash from financing activities will be positive.

Collins Company, which reported both a loss and a negative cash flow from operating activities, is able to produce a positive change in cash only by selling long-lived assets and borrowing additional debt. A company that generates cash mainly from investing activities is usually in a downsizing or restructuring situation. This is fine if the assets being disposed of are unnecessary or unprofitable. However, if the company is in a position where it must sell off income-producing assets to generate cash, then this will affect future revenue and profitability.

As you can see from the above example, analyzing cash flows from different activities along with the information in the other financial statements can provide significant information about a company's overall financial health and activities.

FREE CASH FLOW

Another way of evaluating cash flows is to determine how much discretionary cash flow a company has—in other words, how much cash it has available to expand, repay debt, pay dividends, or do whatever it best determines. This discretionary cash flow is a measure of solvency known as "free cash flow." As indicated in the feature story, Clearwater's goal is to grow free cash flows so it can reduce debt and pay a sustainable dividend to its shareholders.

Free cash flow describes the cash remaining from operating activities after making cash outlays for capital expenditures. Using net cash provided by operating activities as a proxy for free cash flow is not enough as it does not take into account the fact that a company must invest in productive assets, such as property, plant, and equipment, just to maintain its current level of operations. However, the cash flow statement rarely separates investing activities into those required for maintenance and those used for expansion. So we are often forced to use the net cash used by investing activities rather than capital expenditures incurred to maintain productive capacity when calculating free cash flow.

To calculate free cash flow, the net cash used for investing activities is deducted from the net cash provided by operating activities. Illustration 16-24 uses data from Reitmans' cash flow statement (in $ thousands) to illustrate the calculation of free cash flow.

ILLUSTRATION 16-24
Free cash flow

Cash Provided (Used) by Operating Activities	−	Cash Used (Provided) by Investing Activities	=	Free Cash Flow
$96,937	−	$59,574	=	$37,363

Reitmans had a positive free cash flow of $37,363 thousand. The cash Reitmans produced from operating activities was more than sufficient to cover its current year's investing activities. We are not able to determine whether these investing activities were incurred by Reitmans to maintain its existing productive capacity, to expand, or for both purposes. However, we do know from the cash flow statement that Reitmans used all of its free cash flow, as well as cash and cash equivalents on hand from the previous year, to repurchase shares and pay long-term debt and dividends. This resulted in an overall reduction in cash and cash equivalents.

ACCOUNTING IN ACTION
ETHICS INSIGHT

While investors tend to view the cash flow statement as a true picture of a company's financial situation, some advisors say it can be manipulated to make things look better. Among other things, management can misclassify cash into operating, investing, and financing activities. That is what allegedly happened with Sino-Forest Corp., a Chinese-based forestry company with an office in Canada. When the company acquired timber in China, it recorded the purchases on the cash flow statement as cash used in investing activities. After selling the timber, Sino-Forest treated the sales revenue as cash provided by operating activities. As a result, the cash flow statement showed cash inflow from the sale of timber in its operating activities and cash outflow for the purchase of the timber in its investing activities—allegedly overstating cash from operations by excluding the cost of timber sold. Most companies record such purchases as an outflow of cash from operating activities. In 2012, Sino-Forest sought bankruptcy protection and put itself up for sale. Investors who lost billions of dollars after allegations that the company exaggerated its assets were considering launching a class action lawsuit. At the time of writing, Sino-Forest was being investigated by Canadian authorities for fraud, which the company denied.

Sources: Jeff Gray and Andy Hoffman, "Report Alleges Possibility Sino-Forest 'An Accounting Fiction,'" *Globe and Mail,* July 18, 2012; Charmaine Noronha, "Timber Company Sino-Forest Files for Bankruptcy in Ontario Court," Associated Press, *The China Post,* April 1, 2012; Al Rosen and Mark Rosen, "Don't Be Suckered by Cash Flow Statements," *Advisor,* August 1, 2011.

Why would management of a company want to overstate cash flow from operating activities?

BEFORE YOU GO ON...

DO IT

Artindale Inc. reported the following information:

	2015	2014
Profit (loss)	$50,000	$ (5,000)
Cash provided (used) by operating activities	25,000	(10,000)
Cash provided (used) by investing activities	(10,000)	(70,000)
Cash provided (used) by financing activities	(8,000)	100,000

Calculate free cash flow for each of the years and comment on Artindale's stage of development in 2014 and 2015.

SOLUTION

	2015	2014
Free cash flow	$15,000 = $25,000 − $10,000	$(80,000) = $(10,000) + $(70,000)

Artindale had negative free cash flow in 2014 and its cash was provided through its financing activities, indicating the company may have been in the start-up phase of its development. In 2015, the company had positive free cash flow and was profitable, indicating that the company was able to start generating profit and cash from its operations, continue to invest, and have cash available to reduce financing or pay dividends.

Related exercise material: BE16–19, E16–13, and E16–14.

Action Plan

- Calculate the free cash flow by deducting cash provided (used) by investing activities from cash provided (used) by operating activities.

THE NAVIGATOR

Comparing IFRS and ASPE

Key Differences	International Financial Reporting Standards (IFRS)	Accounting Standards for Private Enterprises (ASPE)
Classification of interest and dividends	Interest and dividends received may be classified as operating or investing activities. Interest and dividends paid may be classified as operating or financing activities. Once the choice is made, it must be applied consistently.	Interest and dividends received are classified as operating activities. Interest paid is classified as an operating activity. Dividends paid are classified as a financing activity.

THE NAVIGATOR

DEMONSTRATION PROBLEM

The income statement for the year ended December 31, 2014, for Kiriakou Manufacturing Ltd. contains the following condensed information:

KIRIAKOU MANUFACTURING LTD.
Income Statement
Year Ended December 31, 2014

Sales		$6,583,000
Cost of goods sold		3,572,000
Gross profit		3,011,000
Operating expenses	$2,289,000	
Gain on sale of equipment	(24,000)	2,265,000
Profit from operations		746,000
Other expenses		
Interest expense		85,000
Profit before income tax		661,000
Income tax expense		298,000
Profit		$ 363,000

Kiriakou's comparative balance sheet at December 31 contained the following account balances:

	2014	2013
Cash	$ 204,500	$ 180,000
Accounts receivable	775,000	610,000
Inventories	834,000	917,000
Prepaid expenses	29,000	25,000
Equipment	6,906,000	7,065,000
Accumulated depreciation—equipment	(2,497,000)	(2,355,000)
Total assets	$6,251,500	$6,442,000
Accounts payable	$ 517,000	$ 601,000
Interest payable	6,000	0
Income taxes payable	24,500	20,000
Dividends payable	5,000	10,000
Long-term notes payable	1,500,000	2,000,000
Common shares	3,075,000	3,000,000
Retained earnings	1,124,000	811,000
Total liabilities and shareholders' equity	$6,251,500	$6,442,000

DEMONSTRATION PROBLEM continued on next page

DEMONSTRATION PROBLEM continued from previous page

Additional information:

1. Operating expenses include depreciation expense of $880,000.
2. Accounts payable relate to the purchase of inventory.
3. Equipment that cost $984,000 was sold at a gain of $24,000.
4. New equipment was purchased during the year for $825,000.
5. Dividends declared in 2014 totalled $50,000.
6. Common shares were sold for $75,000 cash.

Instructions

Prepare the cash flow statement using (a) the indirect method or (b) the direct method, as assigned by your teacher.

Action Plan

- Determine the net cash provided (used) by operating activities. Operating activities generally relate to revenues and expenses shown on the income statement, which are affected by changes in related noncash current assets and current liabilities in the balance sheet, and noncash items in the income statement. In the indirect method, convert profit from an accrual basis to a cash basis. In the direct method, convert each revenue and expense from an accrual basis to a cash basis.
- Determine the net cash provided (used) by investing activities. Investing activities generally relate to changes in long-term assets.
- Determine the proceeds on sale of equipment by analyzing the accumulated depreciation account to determine the accumulated depreciation on the asset sold. Then calculate the carrying amount, which is then added to the gain to determine proceeds.
- Determine the net cash provided (used) by financing activities. Financing activities generally relate to changes in long-term liability and shareholders' equity accounts.
- Dividends paid are equal to dividends declared plus a decrease in dividends payable or minus an increase in dividends payable.
- Determine the net increase (decrease) in cash and add it to the beginning-of-period cash balance. Verify that this amount agrees with the end-of-period cash balance reported on the balance sheet.
- Note the similarities and differences between the indirect and direct methods: both methods report the same total amount of cash provided (used) by operating activities but report different detail in this section. The information in the investing and financing sections is the same in both methods.

SOLUTION TO DEMONSTRATION PROBLEM

(a) Indirect method

KIRIAKOU MANUFACTURING LTD.
Cash Flow Statement
Year Ended December 31, 2014

Operating activities		
Profit		$ 363,000
Adjustments to reconcile profit to net cash provided by operating activities:		
Depreciation expense	$ 880,000	
Gain on sale of equipment	(24,000)	
Increase in accounts receivable	(165,000)	
Decrease in inventories	83,000	
Increase in prepaid expenses	(4,000)	
Decrease in accounts payable	(84,000)	
Increase in interest payable	6,000	
Increase in income taxes payable	4,500	696,500
Net cash provided by operating activities		1,059,500
Investing activities		
Sale of equipment	$ 270,000	
Purchase of equipment	(825,000)	
Net cash used by investing activities		(555,000)
Financing activities		
Repayment of notes payable ($2,000,000 − $1,500,000)	$(500,000)	
Issue of common shares	75,000	
Payment of cash dividends ($50,000 + $10,000 − $5,000)	(55,000)	
Net cash used by financing activities		(480,000)
Net increase in cash		24,500
Cash, January 1		180,000
Cash, December 31		$ 204,500

Calculations:

Accumulated depreciation on machinery sold: $2,355,000 (accumulated depreciation beginning) + $880,000 (depreciation expense) − $2,497,000 (accumulated depreciation ending) = $738,000

Carrying amount of machinery sold: $984,000 (cost of equipment sold) − $738,000 (accumulated depreciation) = $246,000

Proceeds on sale: $246,000 (carrying amount) + $24,000 (gain) = $270,000

SOLUTION TO DEMONSTRATION PROBLEM continued on next page

SOLUTION TO DEMONSTRATION PROBLEM continued from previous page

(b) Direct method

KIRIAKOU MANUFACTURING LTD.
Cash Flow Statement
Year Ended December 31, 2014

Operating activities		
Cash receipts from customers		$6,418,000[1]
Cash payments		
To suppliers	$(3,573,000)[2]	
For operating expenses	(1,413,000)[3]	
For interest	(79,000)[4]	
For income tax	(293,500)[5]	(5,358,500)
Net cash provided by operating activities		1,059,500
Investing activities		
Sale of machinery	$ 270,000	
Purchase of machinery	(825,000)	
Net cash used by investing activities		(555,000)
Financing activities		
Repayment of note payable	$ (500,000)	
Issue of common shares	75,000	
Payment of cash dividends	(55,000)	
Net cash used by financing activities		(480,000)
Net increase in cash		24,500
Cash, January		180,000
Cash, December 31		$ 204,500

Calculations:
[1] Cash receipts from customers: $6,583,000 (sales) − $165,000 = $6,418,000
[2] $3,572,000 − $83,000 + $84,000 = $3,573,000
[3] $2,289,000 − $880,000 + $4,000 = $1,413,000
[4] $85,000 − $6,000 = $79,000
[5] $298,000 − $4,500 = $293,500

THE NAVIGATOR

Summary of Study Objectives

1. ***Describe the purpose and content of the cash flow statement.*** The cash flow statement gives information about the cash receipts and cash payments resulting from a company's operating, investing, and financing activities during the period.

   In general, operating activities include the cash effects of transactions that affect profit. Investing activities generally include cash flows resulting from changes in long-term asset items. Financing activities generally include cash flows resulting from changes in long-term liability and shareholders' equity items.

2. ***Prepare a cash flow statement using either the indirect or the direct method.*** There are four steps to prepare a cash flow statement: (1) Determine the net cash provided (used) by operating activities. In the indirect method, this is done by converting profit from an accrual basis to a cash basis. In the direct method, this is done by converting each revenue and expense from an accrual basis to a cash basis. (2) Analyze the changes in long-term asset accounts and record them as investing activities, or as significant noncash transactions. (3) Analyze the changes in long-term liability and equity accounts and record them as financing activities, or as significant noncash transactions. (4) Prepare the cash flow statement and determine the net increase or decrease in cash.

3. ***Analyze the cash flow statement.*** The cash flow statement must be read along with the other financial statements in order to adequately assess a company's financial position. In addition, it is important to understand how the net change in cash is affected by each type of activity—operating, investing, and financing—especially when different companies are being compared. Free cash flow is a measure of solvency: it indicates how much of the cash that was generated from operating activities during the current year is available after making necessary payments for capital expenditures. It is calculated by subtracting the cash used by investing activities from the cash provided by operating activities.

THE NAVIGATOR

Glossary

Cash flow statement A financial statement that gives information about a company's cash receipts and cash payments during a period and classifies them as operating, investing, and financing activities. (p. 670)

Direct method A method of determining the net cash provided (used) by operating activities by adjusting each item in the income statement from the accrual basis to the cash basis. (p. 676)

Financing activities Cash flow activities from long-term liability and equity accounts. These include (a) obtaining cash by issuing debt and repaying the amounts borrowed, and (b) obtaining cash from shareholders and providing them with a return on their investment. (p. 671)

Free cash flow Cash provided by operating activities less cash used by investing activities. (p. 702)

Indirect method A method of preparing a cash flow statement in which profit is adjusted for items that did not affect cash, to determine net cash provided (used) by operating activities. (p. 676)

Investing activities Cash flow activities from long-term asset accounts. These include (a) acquiring and disposing of investments and long-lived assets, and (b) lending money and collecting on those loans. (p. 671)

Operating activities Cash flow activities that include the cash effects of transactions that create revenues and expenses, and thus affect profit. (p. 671)

Self-Study Questions

Answers are at the end of the chapter.

(SO 1) C 1. Which of the following is an example of a cash flow from an operating activity?
(a) A payment of cash for income tax
(b) A receipt of cash from the sale of common shares
(c) A payment of cash for the purchase of equipment used in operations
(d) A receipt of cash from the issue of a mortgage payable

(SO 1) C 2. Which of the following is an example of a cash flow from an investing activity?
(a) A receipt of cash from the issue of bonds
(b) A payment of cash to purchase common shares
(c) A receipt of cash from the sale of equipment
(d) The acquisition of land by issuing bonds

(SO 1) C 3. For a company reporting under ASPE, which of the following is an example of a cash flow from a financing activity?
(a) A receipt of cash from the sale of land
(b) An issue of debt for land
(c) A payment of dividends
(d) A cash purchase of inventory

(SO 2) AP 4. A company had profit of $215,000. Depreciation expense is $27,000. During the year, Accounts Receivable and Inventory increased by $25,000 and $18,000, respectively. Prepaid Expenses and Accounts Payable decreased by $2,000 and $8,000, respectively. There was also a loss on the sale of equipment of $3,000. Net cash provided by operating activities is:
(a) $196,000.
(b) $245,000.
(c) $193,000.
(d) $234,000.

(SO 2) C 5. It is necessary to make an adjustment for the gain or loss on a sale of a long-lived asset to determine cash provided (used) by operating activities under the indirect method because
(a) the sale of a long-lived asset is a financing activity, not an operating activity.
(b) the gain or loss is generally not recorded in the same period that cash is received from the sale of the long-lived asset.
(c) the gain or loss on the sale of a long-lived asset is the result of incorrectly recording depreciation expense over the life of the asset.
(d) the gain or loss is not equal to the cash proceeds received on the sale.

(SO 2) AP 6. The beginning balance in Accounts Receivable is $44,000. The ending balance is $42,000. Sales during the period are $149,000. Cash receipts from customers are:
(a) $151,000.
(b) $149,000.
(c) $147,000.
(d) $107,000.

(SO 2) AP 7. Retained earnings were $197,000 at the beginning of the year and $386,500 at the end of the year. Profit was $200,000. Dividends payable were $2,000 at the beginning of the year and $2,500 at the end of the year. What amount should be reported in the financing activities section of the cash flow statement for dividend payments?
(a) $500
(b) $10,000
(c) $10,500
(d) $11,000

(SO 2) AP 8. The acquisition of land by issuing common shares is
(a) reported in the cash flow statement as both an investing and a financing transaction.
(b) a noncash transaction and would be reported in the cash flow statement only if using the indirect method.
(c) reported in the cash flow statement only if the statement is prepared using the direct method.
(d) an investing and financing transaction that is not reported in the cash flow statement because it is a noncash transaction.

(SO 3) C 9. If a company is in its first year of business and is rapidly growing, it would be normal to see:
(a) negative cash from operating and investing activities, and positive cash from financing activities.
(b) negative cash from operating activities, and positive cash from investing and financing activities.
(c) positive cash from operating activities, and negative cash from investing and financing activities.
(d) positive cash from operating and financing activities, and negative cash from investing activities.

(SO 3) K 10. Free cash flow gives an indication of a company's ability to generate:
(a) sales.
(b) profit.
(c) cash for discretionary uses.
(d) cash for investments.

THE NAVIGATOR

Questions

(SO 1) C 1. What is a cash flow statement and how is it useful to investors and creditors?

(SO 1) K 2. How is cash generally defined for purposes of the cash flow statement?

(SO 1) C 3. What are "cash equivalents"? Why might a company include cash equivalents with cash when preparing its cash flow statement?

(SO 1) C 4. Identify, and describe the differences among, the three types of activities reported in the cash flow statement. Give an example of each.

(SO 1) K 5. What are the general guidelines in terms of the classification of income statement and balance sheet items to operating, investing, and financing activities? Give an example of an exception to these guidelines.

(SO 1) C 6. Mandeep, the president of Cool Air Inc., a public company, asked the controller to reclassify $1 million of cash payments for interest from the operating activities section to the financing section of the cash flow statement. "We can change it back next year and report it in operating activities next year if we want to." Explain why Mandeep may want to reclassify the interest payments. Is Mandeep correct about changing the classification the following year? Why or why not?

(SO 1) K 7. During the year, Wind and Solar Power Ltd. issued $1 million of common shares in exchange for windmill equipment. Cam, the chief financial officer, argues that the acquisition of equipment is an investing activity and the issue of common shares is a financing activity and therefore should be reported in the cash flow statement. Is Cam correct? Explain why or why not.

(SO 2) C 8. What information is used in preparing the cash flow statement?

(SO 2) C 9. Explain why the increase or decrease in cash is not equal to the profit or loss reported in the income statement. How can a company's cash balance decrease when the company has earned profit? Conversely, how can cash increase when a company has incurred a loss?

(SO 2) C 10. Explain why increases in noncash current asset account balances are deducted from profit and increases in noncash current liability account balances are added to profit when determining cash provided (used) by operating activities using the indirect method.

(SO 2) C 11. Fresh Foods Inc. uses the indirect method to report cash provided from operating activities. Vijay, the company president, argues, "Depreciation should not be reported as a cash inflow in the operating section of the cash flow statement, because it is not a cash flow." Is Vijay correct? Explain why or why not.

(SO 2) C 12. Gail doesn't understand why losses are added and gains are deducted from profit when calculating cash provided (used) by operating activities in the indirect method. She argues that losses must be deducted and gains added as they are on the income statement. Explain to Gail why this is not correct.

(SO 2) C 13. For bonds payable, explain why the amortization of a bond discount is added and the amortization of a bond premium is deducted when calculating cash provided (used) by operating activities in the indirect method.

(SO 2) C 14. Environmental Equipment Ltd. reported $500,000 of sales on its income statement and $475,000 of cash collected from customers on its cash flow statement. Provide reasons why cash collected from customers is not equal to the sales reported in the income statement.

(SO 2) C 15. Under the direct method, why is depreciation expense not reported in the operating activities section?

(SO 2) A 16. During the year, Financial Services Inc. purchased $1 million of 10-year bonds for $980,000 to earn interest. Financial Services reported interest revenue of $27,300 on its investment in the bonds in its income statement and cash receipts for interest of $25,000 in its cash flow statement. Terry, the VP finance, argued, "The cash receipts for interest must be understated; the company has received all the interest owed to it. Therefore, the cash collected should equal the interest revenue reported." Is Terry correct? Explain why or why not.

(SO 2) C 17. Contrast the advantages and disadvantages of the direct and indirect methods of preparing the cash flow statement. Are both methods acceptable? Which method is preferred by standard setters? Which method is more popular? Why?

(SO 2) C 18. Goh Corporation changed its method of reporting operating activities from the indirect method to the direct method in order to make its cash flow statement more informative to its readers. Will this change increase, decrease, or not affect the net cash provided (used) by operating activities? Explain.

(SO 2) C 19. Explain how the sale of equipment at a gain is reported on a cash flow statement. Do the same for the sale of equipment at a loss.

(SO 2) C 20. If a company reported cash dividends of $80,000 in its statement of changes in shareholders' equity, would this amount also be reported as a cash outflow in the cash flow statement? Explain why or why not.

(SO 2) C 21. When should short-term notes receivable be reported in the operating activities section and when should they be reported in the investing activities section of the cash flow statement?

(SO 3) C 22. In general, should a financially healthy, growing company be providing or using cash in each of the three activities in the cash flow statement? Explain why this would normally be expected.

(SO 3) C 23. A company reported a small profit on the income statement and negative cash flow from operating and investing activities on the cash flow statement. The company reported positive cash flow from its financing activities. What might this indicate about the company's stage of development? Explain.

(SO 3) C 24. How is it possible for a company to report positive net cash from operating activities but have a negative free cash flow?

Brief Exercises

Indicate impact of transactions on cash. **(SO 1) AP**

BE16–1 For each of the following transactions, indicate whether it will increase (+), decrease (−), or have no effect (NE) on a company's cash flows:

(a) ______ Repayment of a mortgage payable
(b) ______ Sale of land for cash at a loss
(c) ______ Reacquisition of common shares
(d) ______ Acquisition of equipment by an issue of common shares
(e) ______ Issuing preferred shares for cash
(f) ______ Collection of accounts receivable
(g) ______ Recording depreciation expense
(h) ______ Declaring cash dividends

Classify transactions by activity. **(SO 1) C**

BE16–2 Assuming the company is reporting under ASPE, classify each of the transactions listed in BE16–1 as an operating (O), investing (I), financing (F), or significant noncash investing and financing activity (NC). If a transaction does not belong in any of these classifications, explain why.

Indicate impact on cash from operating activities—indirect method. **(SO 2) AP**

BE16–3 Indicate whether each of the following transactions would be added to (+) or subtracted from (−) profit in determining the cash provided (used) by operating activities using the indirect method:

(a) ______ Depreciation expense
(b) ______ Decrease in accounts receivable
(c) ______ Increase in inventory
(d) ______ Decrease in accounts payable
(e) ______ Increase in income tax payable
(f) ______ Loss on sale of equipment
(g) ______ Impairment loss for goodwill
(h) ______ Decrease in prepaid insurance

Calculate cash from operating activities—indirect method. **(SO 2) AP**

BE16–4 Diamond Ltd. reported profit of $850,000 for the year ended November 30, 2014. Depreciation expense for the year was $175,000, accounts receivable decreased by $80,000, prepaid expenses increased by $35,000, accounts payable decreased by $170,000, and the company incurred a loss on sale of equipment of $25,000. Calculate the net cash provided (used) by operating activities using the indirect method.

Calculate cash from operating activities—indirect method. (SO 2) AP

BE16–5 Manoharan Ltd. reported the following information in its balance sheet and income statement for the year ended March 31, 2014:

	2014	2013
Accounts receivable	60,000	40,000
Inventory	63,000	70,000
Prepaid expenses	4,000	6,000
Accounts payable	35,000	40,000
Income tax payable	16,000	10,000
Depreciation expense	50,000	
Gain on sale of equipment	45,200	
Profit	330,000	

Calculate the net cash provided (used) by operating activities using the indirect method.

Calculate cash receipts from customers—direct method. (SO 2) AP

BE16–6 Westcoast Corporation reported the following in its December 31, 2014, financial statements.

	2014	2013
Accounts receivable balance, December 31	$123,850	$137,500
Sales revenue	640,000	

Calculate the cash receipts from customers.

Calculate cash payments to suppliers—direct method. (SO 2) AP

BE16–7 Winter Sportswear Inc. reported the following in its December 31, 2014, financial statements.

	2014	2013
Inventory	$55,600	$50,000
Accounts payable	62,200	55,000
Cost of goods sold	89,500	

Calculate (a) the cost of goods purchased, and (b) cash payments to suppliers.

Calculate cash payments for operating expenses—direct method. (SO 2) AP

BE16–8 Linus Corporation reported the following in its March 31, 2014, financial statements.

	2014	2013
Prepaid expenses	$ 23,400	$12,500
Accrued expenses payable	14,900	8,500
Operating expenses	100,000	

Calculate the cash payments for operating expenses.

Calculate cash payments to employees—direct method. (SO 2) AP

BE16–9 ICE Inc. reported the following in its December 31, 2014, financial statements.

	2014	2013
Salaries payable	$ 2,500	$4,000
Salaries expense	188,000	

Calculate the cash payments to employees.

Calculate cash payments for interest—direct method. (SO 2) AP

BE16–10 RES Inc. reported the following with respect to its bonds payable in the 2014 financial statements.

	2014	2013
Interest payable	$ 10,000	$ 10,000
Bonds payable	455,000	460,000
Interest expense	25,000	

(a) Were the bonds sold at a premium or a discount?
(b) Calculate the cash payments for interest.

Calculate cash payments for operating expenses—direct method. (SO 2) AP

BE16–11 Excellence Corporation reports operating expenses of $100,000, including depreciation expense of $15,000, amortization expense of $2,500, and a gain of $500 on the disposal of equipment during the current year. During this same period, prepaid expenses increased by $6,600 and accrued expenses payable decreased by $2,400. Calculate the cash payments for operating expenses.

BE16–12 Home Grocery Corporation reported the following in its 2014 financial statements.

Calculate cash payments for income tax—direct method. (SO 2) AP

	2014	2013
Income tax payable	$17,000	$8,000
Income tax expense	90,000	

Calculate the cash payments for income tax.

BE16–13 Angus Meat Corporation reported the following information for the year ended December 31:

Calculate cash from operating activities—direct method. (SO 2) AP

Balance sheet accounts:	2014	2013	Income statement accounts:	2014
Accounts receivable	$85,000	$60,000	Sales	$375,000
Inventory	62,000	55,000	Gain on sale of land	15,000
Prepaid expenses	5,000	9,000	Cost of goods sold	150,000
Accounts payable	35,000	42,000	Operating expenses	75,000
Income tax payable	14,000	9,000	Depreciation expense	20,000
			Income tax expense	50,000

Calculate the net cash provided (used) by operating activities using the direct method.

BE16–14 The T accounts for equipment and the related accumulated depreciation for Trevis Corporation are as follows:

Calculate cash received from sale of equipment. (SO 2) AP

Equipment			
Beg. bal.	80,000		
Purchases	41,600	Disposals	24,000
End. bal.	97,600		

Accumulated Depreciation—Equipment			
		Beg. bal.	44,500
Disposals	5,500	Depreciation	12,000
		End. bal.	51,000

In addition, Trevis's income statement reported a loss on the sale of equipment of $1,500. (a) What will be reported on the cash flow statement with regard to the sale of equipment if Trevis uses the indirect method? (b) If Trevis uses the direct method?

BE16–15 Selected information follows for Cathrea Select Corporation at December 31:

Prepare the investing activities section of the cash flow statement. (SO 2) AP

	2014	2013
Land	$ 95,000	$180,000
Buildings	250,000	250,000
Accumulated depreciation—buildings	(55,000)	(45,000)
Equipment	237,000	148,000
Accumulated depreciation—equipment	(86,000)	(78,000)

Additional information:

1. Land was sold for cash at a gain of $35,000.
2. Equipment was bought for cash.
3. Equipment with a cost of $58,000 and a carrying amount of $18,000 was sold at a gain of $5,000.

Prepare the investing activities section of the cash flow statement.

BE16–16 The following was reported in Shania Ltd.'s 2014 financial statements.

Calculate cash paid for dividends. (SO 2) AP

	2014	2013
Dividends payable	$ 24,000	$ 20,000
Retained earnings	261,000	114,000
Profit	197,000	

Calculate cash payments for dividends.

BE16–17 Selected information follows for Cathrea Select Corporation at December 31:

Prepare the financing activities section of the cash flow statement. (SO 2) AP

	2014	2013
Dividends payable	$ 20,000	$ 15,000
Bonds payable	995,000	990,000
Mortgage notes payable	475,000	200,000
Common shares	55,000	45,000
Retained earnings	165,000	85,000

Additional information:

1. Interest expense on the bonds payable was $55,000, which included $5,000 of amortization of the bond discount.
2. Principal payments on the mortgage payable were $25,000.
3. A building was purchased for $500,000 by paying $200,000 cash and signing a mortgage note payable for the balance.
4. Profit for the year was $145,000.

Assuming the company reports under ASPE, prepare the financing activities section of the cash flow statement.

Prepare cash flow statement. **(SO 2) AP**

BE16–18 The following information is available for Baker Corporation for the year ended April 30, 2014:

Cash, May 1, 2013	$ 8,500
Cash provided by operating activities	49,000
Other cash receipts	
Sale of equipment at a loss of $1,200	6,000
Issue of non-trade note payable	20,000
Other cash payments	
Dividends	25,000
Reacquisition of common shares	19,000
Purchase of land for $100,000, partially financed by issuing a $75,000 mortgage note payable	25,000
Additional information	
Issued a $75,000 mortgage note payable to partially finance purchase of land for $100,000.	

Prepare a cash flow statement for the year, including any required note disclosure.

Use cash flows to identify new company. **(SO 3) AN**

BE16–19 Two companies reported the following information.

	Company A	Company B
Profit (loss)	$ (5,000)	$100,000
Cash provided (used) by operating activities	(10,000)	50,000
Cash provided (used) by investing activities	(70,000)	30,000
Cash provided (used) by financing activities	120,000	(100,000)

(a) Calculate free cash flow for each company.
(b) Which company is more likely to be in the early stages of its development? Explain.

Exercises

Classify transactions. **(SO 1) AP**

E16–1 Eng Corporation, a private corporation reporting under ASPE, had the following transactions:

Transaction	(a) Classification	(b) Cash Inflow or Outflow
1. Sold inventory for $1,000 cash.	O	+$1,000
2. Purchased a machine for $30,000. Made a $5,000 down payment and issued a long-term note for the remainder.	______	______
3. Issued common shares for $50,000.	______	______
4. Collected $16,000 of accounts receivable.	______	______
5. Paid a $25,000 cash dividend.	______	______
6. Redeemed bonds having an amortized cost of $200,000 for $175,000.	______	______
7. Paid $18,000 on accounts payable.	______	______
8. Purchased inventory for $28,000 on account.	______	______
9. Purchased a long-term investment in bonds for $100,000.	______	______
10. Sold equipment with a carrying amount of $16,000 for $13,000.	______	______
11. Paid $12,000 interest expense on long-term notes payable.	______	______

Instructions

Complete the above table for each of the following requirements. The first one has been done for you as an example.

(a) Classify each transaction as an operating activity (O), investing activity (I), financing activity (F), or noncash transaction (NC).
(b) Specify whether the transaction represents a cash inflow (+), cash outflow (−), or has no effect (NE) on cash, and in what amount.

E16–2 Pesci Ltd. is a private company reporting under ASPE. Its income statement and changes in current assets and current liabilities for the year are reported below:

Prepare operating activities section—indirect method. **(SO 2) AP**

PESCI LTD.
Income Statement
Year Ended November 30, 2014

Sales		$948,000
Cost of goods sold		490,000
Gross profit		458,000
Operating expenses	$310,000	
Depreciation expense	50,000	
Gain on sale of equipment	(10,000)	350,000
Profit before income tax		108,000
Income tax expense		30,000
Profit		$ 78,000

Changes in current assets and current liabilities were as follows:		
Accounts receivable	$36,000	decrease
Inventory	19,000	increase
Prepaid expenses	2,000	increase
Accounts payable	12,000	decrease
Dividends payable	5,000	decrease
Income taxes payable	4,000	decrease

Instructions

Prepare the operating activities section of the cash flow statement using the indirect method.

E16–3 Using the data presented for Pesci Ltd. in E16–2, prepare the operating activities section of the cash flow statement using the direct method.

Prepare operating activities section—direct method. **(SO 2) AP**

E16–4 The current assets and liabilities sections of the comparative balance sheets of Charron Inc., a private company reporting under ASPE, at October 31 are presented below:

Prepare operating activities section—indirect method. **(SO 2) AP**

CHARTRAND INC.
Comparative Balance Sheet Accounts

	2014	2013
Cash	$99,000	$105,000
Accounts receivable	52,000	41,000
Inventory	32,500	46,000
Prepaid expenses	7,500	5,800
Accounts payable	43,000	36,000
Accrued expenses payable	5,000	8,000
Dividends payable	24,000	17,000
Income taxes payable	6,800	11,800

CHARTRAND INC. Income Statement Year Ended October 31, 2014		
Sales		$625,000
Cost of goods sold		390,000
Gross profit		235,000
Operating expenses	$88,000	
Depreciation expense	23,000	
Loss on sale of equipment	10,000	121,000
Profit before income taxes		114,000
Income taxes		29,000
Profit		$ 85,000

Instructions

Prepare the operating activities section of the cash flow statement using the indirect method.

Calculate operating cash flows—direct method. **(SO 2) AP**

E16–5 The following information is taken from the general ledger of Robinson Limited:

1. Sales revenue	$275,000
Accounts receivable, January 1	22,900
Accounts receivable, December 31	37,000
2. Cost of goods sold	$110,000
Inventory, January 1	9,200
Inventory, December 31	5,900
Accounts payable, January 1	8,600
Accounts payable, December 31	6,900
3. Operating expenses	$ 70,000
Depreciation expense (included in operating expenses)	20,000
Prepaid expenses, January 1	3,000
Prepaid expenses, December 31	5,500
Accrued expenses payable, January 1	6,500
Accrued expenses payable, December 31	4,500
4. Interest expense	$ 18,000
Interest payable, January 1	4,000
Interest payable, December 31	4,000
Bonds payable, January 1	395,000
Bonds payable, December 31	397,000

Instructions

Using the direct method, calculate:

(a) cash receipts from customers
(b) cash payments to suppliers
(c) cash payments for operating expenses
(d) cash payments for interest expense

Prepare operating activities section—direct method. **(SO 2) AP**

E16–6 Hammond Ltd. completed its first year of operations on September 30, 2014. Hammond reported the following information at September 30, 2014:

HAMMOND LTD. Selected balance sheet account balances at September 30, 2014	
Accounts receivable	$23,000
Prepaid expenses	3,100
Accrued expenses payable	10,500
Interest payable	500
Dividends payable	3,800
Income taxes payable	9,800

HAMMOND LTD. Income Statement Year Ended September 30, 2014		
Service revenue		$285,000
Operating expenses	$122,000	
Depreciation expense	12,300	
Gain on sale of equipment	(5,750)	128,550
Profit from operations		156,450
Interest expense		4,000
Profit before income tax		152,450
Income tax expense		38,500
Profit		$113,950

Instructions
Assuming that Hammond reports under ASPE, prepare the operating section of a cash flow statement using the direct method.

Prepare operating activities section—direct method. **(SO 2) AP**

E16–7 The income statement and account balances for Chartrand Inc. are presented in E16–4.

Instructions
Prepare the operating section of a cash flow statement using the direct method.

Determine investing and financing activities. **(SO 2) AP**

E16–8 Dupré Corp. is a private company reporting under ASPE. The following selected accounts are from the general ledger for the year ended December 31, 2014:

Equipment			
Jan. 1	260,000		
July 31	65,000	Nov. 10	46,000
Sept. 2	53,000		
Dec. 31	332,000		

Accumulated Depreciation—Equipment			
		Jan. 1	117,000
Nov. 10	38,000		
		Dec. 31	33,000
		Dec. 31	112,000

Notes Payable			
		Jan. 1	0
Dec. 2	10,000	Sept. 2	50,000
		Dec. 31	40,000

Retained Earnings			
		Jan. 1	130,000
Aug. 23	8,000	Dec. 31	84,000
		Dec. 31	206,000

Additional information:

July 31 Equipment was purchased for cash.
Sept. 2 Equipment was purchased and partially financed through the issue of a note.
Aug. 23 A cash dividend was paid.
Nov. 10 A loss of $3,000 was incurred on the sale of equipment.
Dec. 2 A partial payment on the note payable was made plus $375 of interest.
Dec. 31 Depreciation expense was recorded for the year.
Dec. 31 Closing entries were recorded.

Instructions

From the postings in the above accounts and additional information provided, indicate what information would be reported in the investing and/or financing activities sections of the cash flow statement, including any required note disclosure.

Determine investing and financing activities. **(SO 2) AP**

E16–9 Preferred Homes Ltd., a private company reporting under ASPE, reported the following for the year ended September 30, 2014:

	2014	2013
Land	$300,000	$200,000
Building	350,000	350,000
Equipment	139,000	125,000
Accumulated depreciation	65,000	55,000
Dividends payable	10,000	20,000
Mortgage note payable	110,000	50,000
Common shares	225,000	150,000
Contributed surplus—reacquisition of common shares	10,000	0
Retained earnings	220,000	80,000
Depreciation expense	15,000	
Gain on equipment sold	2,000	
Profit	210,000	

Additional information:

1. Equipment was purchased for $20,000.
2. Land was purchased for $35,000 cash and a mortgage note payable was issued.
3. Common shares were issued for $100,000 cash.
4. During the year, Preferred Homes Ltd. redeemed some common shares.

Instructions

Prepare the investing and financing activities sections of the cash flow statement and any required note disclosure. (*Hint:* Use T accounts to help you calculate the cash flows.)

Prepare cash flow statement—indirect method. **(SO 2) AP**

E16–10 Shankman Limited is a private company reporting under ASPE. Its comparative balance sheet at December 31 is as follows:

SHANKMAN LIMITED
Balance Sheet
December 31

Assets	2014	2013
Cash	$ 114,000	$ 85,000
Accounts receivable	750,000	600,000
Inventory	500,000	330,000
Prepaid insurance	18,000	25,000
Equipment and vehicles	1,250,000	1,000,000
Accumulated depreciation	(350,000)	(280,000)
Total assets	$2,282,000	$ 1,760,000
Liabilities and Shareholders' Equity		
Accounts payable	$ 226,000	$ 200,000
Salaries payable	30,000	40,000
Interest payable	26,000	20,000
Notes payable (non-trade)	500,000	350,000
Preferred shares	200,000	0
Common shares	400,000	400,000
Retained earnings	900,000	750,000
Total liabilities and shareholders' equity	$2,282,000	$1,760,000

Additional information:

1. Profit for 2014 was $200,000.

2. Equipment was purchased during the year. No equipment was sold.
3. Cash dividends were paid to the preferred shareholders during the year.

Instructions

Prepare the cash flow statement using the indirect method.

E16–11 The accounting records of Flypaper Airlines Inc. reveal the following transactions and events for the year ended March 31, 2014:

Prepare cash flow statement—direct method. **(SO 2) AP**

Payment of interest	$ 8,000	Common shares issued in exchange for land	$ 35,000
Cash sales	53,000	Payment of salaries	51,000
Receipt of dividend revenue	14,000	Depreciation expense	16,000
Payment of income tax	7,500	Proceeds from sale of aircraft	212,000
Profit	38,000	Purchase of equipment for cash	22,000
Payment of accounts payable	110,000	Loss on sale of aircraft	3,000
Payment for land	174,000	Payment of dividends	14,000
Collection of accounts receivable	201,000	Payment of operating expenses	28,000

Additional information:

Flypaper Airlines' cash on April 1, 2013, was $35,000.

Instructions

Assuming Flypaper reports under ASPE, prepare a cash flow statement using the direct method.

E16–12 The comparative balance sheet for Storm Adventures Ltd., a private company reporting under ASPE, follows:

Prepare cash flow statement—indirect and direct methods. **(SO 2) AP**

STORM ADVENTURES LTD.
Balance Sheet
December 31

Assets	2014	2013
Cash	$ 43,000	$ 12,600
Accounts receivable	76,000	85,000
Inventories	160,000	172,000
Prepaid expenses	12,000	5,000
Land	50,000	75,000
Equipment	270,000	190,000
Accumulated depreciation	(90,000)	(40,000)
Total assets	$521,000	$499,600
Liabilities and Shareholders' Equity		
Accounts payable	$ 43,000	$ 38,000
Dividends payable	7,500	5,000
Income taxes payable	2,500	6,000
Bonds payable	120,000	180,000
Common shares	207,000	167,000
Retained earnings	141,000	103,600
Total liabilities and shareholders' equity	$521,000	$499,600

Additional information:

1. Profit for 2014 was $69,900.
2. Bonds payable of $60,000 were retired at maturity.
3. Common shares were issued for $40,000.
4. Land was sold at a loss of $10,000.
5. No equipment was sold during 2014.
6. Net sales for the year were $678,000.
7. Cost of goods sold for the year was $439,800.
8. Operating expenses (not including depreciation expense) were $80,000.
9. Interest expense was $5,000.
10. Income tax expense was $23,300.

Instructions

Prepare a cash flow statement using (a) the indirect method or (b) the direct method, as assigned by your teacher.

Compare cash flows for two companies. **(SO 3) AN**

E16–13 Condensed cash flow statements are as follows for two companies operating in the same industry:

	Company A	Company B
Cash provided (used) by operating activities	$200,000	$(180,000)
Cash provided (used) by investing activities	(20,000)	(20,000)
Cash provided (used) by financing activities	(60,000)	320,000
Increase in cash	120,000	120,000
Cash, beginning of period	30,000	30,000
Cash, end of period	$150,000	$ 150,000

Instructions

Which company is in a better financial position? Explain why.

Calculate and discuss free cash flow. **(SO 3) AN**

E16–14 Selected information for a recent year follows for **Bank of Montreal** and **Scotiabank** (in millions):

	Bank of Montreal	Scotiabank
Profit	$ 3,266	$ 5,268
Cash provided (used) by operating activities	572	1,063
Cash provided (used) by investing activities	(12,768)	(33,778)
Cash provided (used) by financing activities	13,757	33,338

Instructions

(a) Calculate the increase or decrease in cash for each company.
(b) Calculate the free cash flow for each company.
(c) Which company appears to be in a stronger financial position? Explain.
(d) In what way might a bank's free cash flow be different from the free cash flow of a manufacturing company?

Problems: Set A

Classify transactions by activity. Indicate impact on cash and profit. **(SO 1) AP**

P16–1A You are provided with the following transactions that took place during a recent fiscal year:

Transaction	(a) Classification	(b) Cash	(c) Profit
1. Paid telephone bill for the month.	O	–	–
2. Sold equipment for cash, at a loss.	______	______	______
3. Acquired a building by paying 10% in cash and signing a mortgage payable for the balance.	______	______	______
4. Made principal repayments on the mortgage.	______	______	______
5. Paid interest on the mortgage.	______	______	______
6. Sold inventory on account, at a price greater than cost.	______	______	______
7. Paid wages owing (previously accrued) to employees.	______	______	______
8. Declared and distributed a stock dividend to common shareholders.	______	______	______
9. Paid rent in advance.	______	______	______
10. Sold inventory for cash, at a price greater than cost.	______	______	______
11. Wrote down the value of inventory to net realizable value, which was lower than cost.	______	______	______
12. Received semi-annual bond interest.	______	______	______
13. Received dividends on an investment in associate.	______	______	______
14. Issued common shares.	______	______	______
15. Paid a cash dividend to common shareholders.	______	______	______
16. Collected cash from customers on account.	______	______	______
17. Collected service revenue in advance.	______	______	______

Instructions

Assuming the company is reporting under IFRS, complete the above table for each of the following requirements. The first one has been done for you as an example.

(a) Classify each transaction as an operating activity (O), an investing activity (I), a financing activity (F), or a noncash transaction (NC) on the cash flow statement. If there is a choice of how a transaction is classified, indicate the alternative classifications.

(b) Specify whether the transaction will increase (+), decrease (−), or have no effect (NE) on cash reported on the balance sheet.

(c) Specify whether the transaction will increase (+), decrease (−), or have no effect (NE) on profit reported on the income statement.

TAKING IT FURTHER Explain how an operating activity can increase cash but not increase profit.

P16–2A Molloy Ltd. reported the following for the fiscal year 2014:

Prepare operating activities section—indirect and direct methods. **(SO 2) AP**

MOLLOY LTD. Income Statement Year Ended September 30, 2014		
Sales		$580,000
Cost of goods sold		340,000
Gross profit		240,000
Operating expenses	$ 96,000	
Depreciation expense	25,000	
Gain on sale of land	(35,000)	86,000
Profit before income tax		154,000
Income tax expense		38,000
Profit		$116,000

Additional information:

1. Accounts receivable decreased by $15,000 during the year.
2. Inventory increased by $7,000 during the year.
3. Prepaid expenses decreased by $5,000 during the year.
4. Accounts payable to suppliers increased by $10,000 during the year.
5. Accrued expenses payable increased by $4,000 during the year.
6. Income tax payable decreased by $6,000 during the year.

Instructions

Prepare the operating activities section of the cash flow statement using (a) the indirect method or (b) the direct method, as assigned by your teacher.

TAKING IT FURTHER In what circumstances will the direct method result in a different amount of cash provided (used) by operations than the indirect method.

P16–3A The income statement of Hanalei International Inc. contained the following condensed information:

Prepare operating activities section—indirect and direct methods. **(SO 2) AP**

HANALEI INTERNATIONAL INC. Income Statement Year Ended December 31, 2014		
Service revenue		$480,000
Operating expenses	$245,000	
Depreciation expense	35,000	
Loss on sale of equipment	25,000	305,000
Profit from operations		175,000
Other revenues and expenses		
Interest expense		10,000
Profit before income taxes		165,000
Income tax expense		41,250
Profit		$123,750

Hanalei's balance sheet contained the following comparative data at December 31:

	2014	2013
Accounts receivable	$52,000	$40,000
Prepaid insurance	5,000	8,000
Accounts payable	30,000	41,000
Interest payable	2,000	1,250
Income tax payable	3,000	4,500
Unearned revenue	12,000	8,000

Additional information: Accounts payable relate to operating expenses.

Instructions

Assuming Hanalei reports under ASPE, prepare the operating activities section of the cash flow statement using (a) the indirect method or (b) the direct method, as assigned by your teacher.

TAKING IT FURTHER What are the advantages and disadvantages of the direct method of determining cash provided (used) by operating activities?

Calculate cash flows for investing and financing activities. (SO 2) AP

P16–4A The following selected account balances were reported in the financial statements of Trudeau Inc., a private company reporting under ASPE, at year end:

	2014	2013
Cash	$ 22,125	$ 10,000
Buildings	850,000	750,000
Equipment	393,000	340,000
Land	100,000	60,000
Accumulated depreciation—buildings	307,500	300,000
Accumulated depreciation—equipment	124,000	94,000
Dividends payable	6,250	2,500
Bonds payable	590,000	585,000
Mortgage notes payable	340,000	310,000
Preferred shares: 2,250 shares in 2014; 2,750 in 2013	225,000	275,000
Common shares: 54,000 shares in 2014; 40,000 in 2013	540,000	410,000
Contributed surplus—reacquisition of common shares	2,000	0
Retained earnings	200,000	100,000
Cash dividends declared	25,000	10,000
Depreciation expense—buildings	25,000	42,500
Depreciation expense—equipment	49,125	27,000
Gain on sale of equipment	1,000	0
Loss on sale of building	10,000	0
Interest expense	48,250	44,750

Additional information:

1. Purchased $75,000 of equipment for $10,000 cash and a mortgage note payable for the remainder.
2. Equipment was also sold during the year.
3. Sold a building that originally cost $50,000.
4. Used cash to purchase land and a building.
5. Included in interest expense is amortization of the bond payable discount, $5,000.
6. Mortgage payments included interest and principal amounts.
7. Converted 500 preferred shares to 5,000 common shares.
8. Common shares were issued for cash.
9. Reacquired 1,000 common shares with an average cost of $10/share for cash during the year.

Instructions

(a) Determine the amount of any cash inflows or outflows related to investing activities in 2014. (*Hint:* Use T accounts to calculate the cash flows.)

(b) What was the amount of profit reported by Trudeau Inc. in 2014?

(c) Determine the amount of any cash inflows or outflows related to financing activities in 2014. (*Hint:* Use T accounts to calculate the cash flows.)
(d) Identify and determine the amount of any noncash financing activities in 2014.
(e) Calculate the cash from net cash provided (used) by operating activities. (*Hint:* Using the cash balances provided, calculate increase or decrease in cash first.)

TAKING IT FURTHER Is it unfavourable for a company to have a net cash outflow from investing activities?

P16–5A Coyote Ltd., a private company reporting under ASPE, reported the following for the years ended May 31, 2014, and 2013.

Prepare a cash flow statement—indirect method. (**SO 2) AP**

COYOTE LTD.
Balance Sheet
May 31

Assets	2014	2013
Cash	$ 12,600	$ 43,000
Accounts receivable	85,000	76,000
Inventories	172,000	160,000
Prepaid expenses	5,000	7,500
Land	125,000	75,000
Equipment	325,000	190,000
Accumulated depreciation	(68,250)	(40,000)
Total assets	$656,350	$511,500
Liabilities and Shareholders' Equity		
Accounts payable	$ 43,000	$ 38,000
Dividends payable	7,500	5,000
Income taxes payable	2,500	6,000
Mortgage note payable	125,000	80,000
Common shares	217,000	167,000
Retained earnings	261,350	215,500
Total liabilities and shareholders' equity	$656,350	$511,500

Additional information:

1. Profit for 2014 was $108,000.
2. Common shares were issued for $50,000.
3. Land with a cost of $50,000 was sold at a loss of $20,000.
4. Purchased land with a cost of $100,000 with a $55,000 down payment and financed the remainder with a mortgage note payable.
5. No equipment was sold during 2014.

Instructions
Prepare a cash flow statement for the year using the indirect method.

TAKING IT FURTHER Is it always unfavourable for a company to have a net cash outflow from financing activities?

P16–6A Refer to the information presented for Coyote Ltd. in P16–5A.

Prepare cash flow statement—direct method. (**SO 2) AP**

Additional information:

1. Net sales for the year were $673,250.
2. Cost of goods sold for the year was $403,950.
3. Operating expenses, including depreciation expense, were $100,300.
4. Interest expense was $5,000.
5. Income tax expense was $36,000.
6. Accounts payable is used for merchandise purchases.

Instructions
Prepare a cash flow statement for the year using the direct method.

TAKING IT FURTHER Indicate what transactions might be classified differently if the company was reporting under IFRS instead of ASPE.

Prepare cash flow statement—indirect method. **(SO 2) AP**

P16–7A Condensed financial data follow for Lancer Ltd.

LANCER LTD.
Balance Sheet
December 31

Assets	2014	2013
Cash	$ 97,800	$ 48,400
Accounts receivable	75,800	43,000
Inventory	122,500	92,850
Prepaid expenses	38,400	26,000
Property, plant, and equipment	398,000	356,500
Accumulated depreciation	(50,000)	(52,000)
Total assets	$682,500	$514,750
Liabilities and Shareholders' Equity		
Accounts payable	$107,000	$ 77,300
Accrued expenses payable	11,500	7,000
Notes payable (non-trade)	110,000	150,000
Common shares	220,000	175,000
Retained earnings	234,000	105,450
Total liabilities and shareholders' equity	$682,500	$514,750

LANCER LTD.
Income Statement
Year Ended December 31, 2014

Sales		$492,780
Cost of goods sold		185,460
Gross profit		307,320
Operating expenses	$62,410	
Depreciation expense	46,500	
Loss on sale of equipment	7,500	116,410
Profit from operations		190,910
Other expenses		
Interest expense		4,730
Profit before income tax		186,180
Income tax expense		45,000
Profit		$141,180

Additional information:

1. New equipment costing $99,000 was purchased for $39,000 cash and a $60,000 note payable.
2. Equipment with an original cost of $57,500 was sold at a loss of $7,500.
3. Notes payable matured during the year and were repaid.

Instructions

Prepare a cash flow statement for the year using the indirect method.

TAKING IT FURTHER If a company has a loss, does that also mean that there has been a net reduction in cash from operating activities? Explain.

P16–8A Refer to the information presented for Lancer Ltd. in P16–7A.

Prepare cash flow statement—direct method. (SO 2) AP

Additional information:

1. Accounts payable relate only to merchandise creditors.
2. Accrued expenses payable and prepaid expenses relate to operating expenses.

Instructions

Prepare a cash flow statement for the year using the direct method.

TAKING IT FURTHER Lancer Ltd.'s cash balance more than doubled in 2014. Briefly explain what caused this, using the cash flow statement.

P16–9A The financial statements of Wetaskiwin Ltd., a private company reporting under ASPE, follow:

Prepare cash flow statement—indirect method. (SO 2) AP

WETASKIWIN LTD.
Balance Sheet
December 31

Assets	2014	2013
Cash	$ 9,000	$ 10,000
Short-term notes receivable	14,000	23,000
Accounts receivable	28,000	14,000
Inventory	29,000	25,000
Property, plant, and equipment	73,000	78,000
Accumulated depreciation	(30,000)	(24,000)
Total assets	$123,000	$126,000
Liabilities and Shareholders' Equity		
Accounts payable	$ 25,000	$ 43,000
Income tax payable	3,000	20,000
Notes payable	15,000	10,000
Common shares	25,000	25,000
Retained earnings	55,000	28,000
Total liabilities and shareholders' equity	$123,000	$126,000

WETASKIWIN LTD.
Income Statement
Year Ended December 31, 2014

Sales		$286,000
Cost of goods sold		194,000
Gross profit		92,000
Operating expenses	$38,000	
Loss on sale of equipment	2,000	40,000
Profit from operations		52,000
Other revenues and expenses		
Interest revenue	$(1,000)	
Interest expense	2,000	1,000
Profit before income tax		51,000
Income tax expense		15,000
Profit		$ 36,000

Additional information:

1. Short-term notes receivable are from loans to other companies. During the year, the company collected the outstanding balance at December 31, 2013, and made new loans in the amount of $14,000.
2. Equipment was sold during the year. This equipment cost $15,000 originally and had a carrying amount of $10,000 at the time of sale.
3. Equipment costing $10,000 was purchased in exchange for a $10,000 note payable.
4. Depreciation expense is included in operating expenses.

Instructions
Prepare a cash flow statement for the year using the indirect method.

TAKING IT FURTHER Wetaskiwin Ltd. had a relatively small change in its cash balance in 2014; cash decreased by only $1,000. Is it still necessary or important to prepare a cash flow statement? Explain.

Prepare cash flow statement—direct method. (SO 2) AP

P16–10A Refer to the information presented for Wetaskiwin Ltd. in P16–9A.

Additional information:

1. Accounts receivable are from the sale of merchandise on credit.
2. Accounts payable relate to the purchase of merchandise on credit.

Instructions
Prepare a cash flow statement for the year using the direct method.

TAKING IT FURTHER Wetaskiwin Ltd. had a positive cash balance at the beginning and end of 2014. Given that, is it possible that the company could have had a negative cash balance at one or more points during the year? Explain.

Prepare cash flow statement—indirect method. (SO 2) AP

P16–11A Presented below is the comparative balance sheet for Diatessaron Inc., a private company reporting under ASPE, at December 31, 2014, and 2013:

DIATESSARON INC.
Balance Sheet
December 31

Assets	2014	2013
Cash	$ 67,000	$ 98,000
Accounts receivable	101,000	75,000
Inventory	205,000	155,500
Property, plant, and equipment	636,500	460,000
Less: Accumulated depreciation	(162,500)	(140,000)
	$847,000	$648,500
Liabilities and Shareholders' Equity		
Accounts payable	$ 57,500	$ 47,000
Dividends payable	6,000	0
Income tax payable	14,000	15,000
Long-term notes payable	25,000	0
Common shares	630,000	525,000
Retained earnings	114,500	61,500
	$847,000	$648,500

DIATESSARON INC. Income Statement Year Ended December 31, 2014		
Sales		$663,000
Cost of goods sold		432,000
Gross profit		231,000
Operating expenses	$147,500	
Loss on sale of equipment	3,000	150,500
Profit from operations		80,500
Interest expense	3,000	
Interest revenue	(4,500)	(1,500)
Profit before income tax		82,000
Income tax expense		14,000
Profit		$ 68,000

Additional information:

1. Cash dividends of $15,000 were declared.
2. Depreciation expense is included in the operating expenses.
3. The company issued 10,500 common shares for cash on March 2, 2014. The fair value of the shares was $10 per share. The proceeds were used to purchase additional equipment during the year for $101,500 cash.
4. Equipment that originally cost $30,000 was sold during the year for cash. The equipment had a carrying value of $9,000 at the time of sale.
5. The company issued a note payable for $28,000 and repaid $3,000 by year end.

Instructions

Prepare a cash flow statement for the year using the indirect method.

TAKING IT FURTHER Is it necessary to show both the proceeds from issuing a new note payable and the partial repayment of notes payable? Or is it sufficient to simply show the net increase or decrease in notes payable, as is done with accounts payable? Explain.

P16–12A Refer to the information presented for Diatessaron Inc. in P16–11A.

Prepare cash flow statement—direct method. **(SO 2) AP**

Additional information:

1. All purchases of inventory are on credit.
2. Accounts payable is used only to record purchases of inventory.

Instructions

Prepare a cash flow statement for the year using the direct method.

TAKING IT FURTHER Why is it necessary to know that Accounts Payable is used for purchases of inventory when using the direct method, but not the indirect method?

P16–13A Selected information (in US$ millions) for two close competitors, **Potash Corporation of Saskatchewan Inc.** and **Agrium Inc.**, follows for the year ended December 31, 2011:

Calculate free cash flow and evaluate cash. **(SO 3) AN**

	Potash	Agrium
Profit	$3,081	$1,508
Cash provided by operating activities	3,485	1,350
Cash used by investing activities	(2,251)	(151)
Cash used by financing activities	(1,216)	(423)
Cash and cash equivalents, end of period	430	635
Dividends paid	(208)	(18)

Instructions

(a) Calculate the free cash flow for each company.
(b) Which company appears to be in the stronger financial position?

TAKING IT FURTHER By comparing the companies' cash flows, can you tell which company is likely in a growth stage? Explain.

CONTINUING COOKIE CHRONICLE

(*Note:* This is a continuation of the Cookie Chronicle from Chapters 1 through 15.)

Koebel's Family Bakery Ltd. has been providing cupcakes to Coffee Beans Ltd., a private company, on a weekly basis over the last two years. Coffee Beans, thrilled with the quality of goods and service it is receiving from Koebel's, has approached the Koebels to join its team. Coffee Beans is expanding and hopes that the Koebels would consider the sale of Koebel's Family Bakery Ltd. shares to Coffee Beans. In exchange, Janet, Brian, and Natalie would then become both shareholders and employees of Coffee Beans Ltd.

Janet, Brian, and Natalie have worked hard to achieve the success that Koebel's Family Bakery has achieved. They are reluctant to join another team unless they can be reasonably assured that there will be future growth in the business they are investing in.

Selected information for Koebel's Family Bakery and Coffee Beans follows:

	Koebel's Family Bakery Ltd. Year Ended July 31, 2015	Coffee Beans Ltd. Year Ended November 30, 2014	Coffee Beans Ltd. Year Ended November 30, 2013
Profit	$ 199,629	$ 1,465,466	$ 1,259,966
Net cash provided by operating activities	$ 235,279	$ 1,137,650	$ 2,324,547
Net cash used by investing activities	(157,833)	(4,545,728)	(3,036,676)
Net cash (used) provided by financing activities	(37,071)	7,406,647	955,201
Cash, end of year	199,443	4,469,552	470,983
Current liabilities	31,121	5,190,005	5,046,240
Total liabilities	81,551	10,398,638	7,076,968
Dividends paid	120,000	0	0

Instructions

(a) Calculate the net increase in cash and the amount of cash at the beginning of the year that would have been included on the cash flow statement for each company.
(b) Calculate free cash flow for each company.
(c) Compare the provision and use of cash in each of the three activities—operating, investing, and financing—by each company.
(d) Based on information provided in parts (a) and (b), identify why Coffee Beans is pursuing an investment in Koebel's Family Bakery Ltd.
(e) Based on information provided in parts (a) and (b), identify for the Koebels some of the issues they should consider and additional information they would require before making the decision to sell their shares and/or be employed by Coffee Beans Ltd.

BROADENING YOUR PERSPECTIVE

CHAPTER 16

Collaborative Learning Activity

Note to instructor: Additional instructions and handout material for this group activity can be found on the Instructor Resource Site and in *WileyPLUS*.

BYP16–1 In this group activity, you will be given a balance sheet at the beginning of the year, the income statement and cash flow statement for the year, and additional data. Using that information, you will prepare the year-end balance sheet.

Communication Activity

BYP16–2 Many investors today prefer the cash flow statement over the income statement. They believe that cash-based data are a better measure of performance than accrual-based data because the estimates and judgements that are required for accrual accounting allow management too much discretion to manipulate the results.

Instructions

Write a brief memo explaining whether or not it is harder for management to manipulate income using cash-based data than accrual-based data. In your answer, say which financial statement, in your opinion, is the best measure of a company's performance, and explain why.

Ethics Case

BYP16–3 Paradis Corporation has paid cash dividends for eight years in a row. The board of directors' policy requires that, in order to declare a dividend, cash provided by operating activities as reported in Paradis' cash flow statement must exceed $1 million. President and CEO Phil Monat's job is secure as long as he produces annual operating cash flows to support the usual dividend.

At the end of the current year, controller Rick Kwan informs president Monat of some disappointing news. The net cash provided by operating activities is only $970,000. The president says to Rick, "We must get that amount above $1 million. Isn't there some way to increase this amount?" Rick answers, "These figures were prepared by my assistant. I'll go back to my office and see what I can do." The president replies, "I know you won't let me down, Rick."

After examining the cash flow statement carefully, Rick concludes that he can get the operating cash flows above $1 million by reclassifying interest paid from the operating activities section, where it has been classified in the past, to the financing activities section. The company is a publicly traded company reporting under IFRS. He returns to the president, saying, "You can tell the board to declare its usual dividend. Our net cash flow provided by operating activities is $1.03 million." "Good man, Rick! I knew I could count on you," exclaims the president.

Instructions

(a) Should any other factors, besides cash provided by operating activities, be considered by the board in setting the dividend policy?
(b) Who are the stakeholders in this situation?
(c) Was there anything unethical about the president's actions? Was there anything unethical about the controller's actions?
(d) Are the board members or anyone else likely to discover the reclassification?
(e) Would your answers to parts (b) and (c) change if Paradis were a private company reporting under ASPE?

All About You: Personal Financial Literacy Activity

BYP16–4 In the "All About You" feature, you read that many Canadians have big debt loads and negative cash flows. Assume you are a student enrolled in your second year of university and have just learned about the importance of managing cash flows and how to prepare a cash flow statement. You want to use your knowledge to prepare a cash budget for the upcoming year, September 1, 2013, to August 31, 2014. To help you prepare next year's cash budget, you have prepared a cash flow statement for the past year, September 1, 2012, to August 31, 2013.

MY CASH FLOW STATEMENT Year Ended August 31, 2013	
Operating Activities	
Cash received from summer job	$ 8,000
Cash contribution from parents	3,600
Cash paid for rent, utilities, cable, Internet	(4,000)
Cash paid for groceries	(3,200)
Cash paid for clothes	(3,000)
Cash paid for gas, insurance, parking	(4,420)
Cash paid for miscellaneous	(500)
Cash paid for interest on credit card	(180)
Cash used in operating activities	(3,700)
Investing Activities	
Tuition and books	(7,000)
Laptop and printer	(1,200)
Cash used in investing activities	(8,200)
Financing Activities	
Student loan	7,500
Loan from parents	1,500
Purchases on credit card	1,000
Cash provided from financing activities	10,000
Decrease in cash	(1,900)
Cash, September 1, 2012	4,000
Cash, August 31, 2013	$ 2,100

Instructions

(a) Comment on your cash position on August 31, 2013, compared with September 1, 2012.

(b) Prepare a cash flow forecast for September 1, 2013, to August 31, 2014, based on the following estimates and assumptions:

1. Tuition and books $7,500
2. Student loan $7,500
3. Your parents will contribute $4,000 toward your rent, utilities, cable, and Internet. You will not have to pay your parents back for this contribution.
4. Rent, utilities, cable, and Internet $4,000
5. Groceries $3,600
6. Gas, insurance, and parking $4,600
7. Clothes $3,000
8. Miscellaneous $500
9. You plan to pay off the amount owed on your credit card right away.
10. Your parents will lend you an additional $1,500 if you need it.
11. You are pretty sure that you will be rehired by the same company next summer; however, you do not think you will get a raise in pay.

(c) What is the amount of cash you forecast you will have at August 31, 2014?

(d) Will you need to borrow the additional $1,500 from your parents?

(e) Will you be able to pay off the $1,000 owed on your credit card? Should you try to do so?

(f) What actions may you be able to take to improve your cash flow?

ANSWERS TO CHAPTER QUESTIONS

ANSWERS TO ACCOUNTING IN ACTION INSIGHT QUESTIONS

All About You Insight, p. 673

Q: Is it appropriate to use your credit card to pay for your operating activities such as your groceries, clothes, and entertainment? Is it appropriate to use your credit card to finance your investment activities such as tuition or, if you have a large enough limit, a car?

A: Credit cards should never be used for a long-term financing activity because of the high interest rates charged by credit card companies. They can be effectively used for short-term operating activities such as paying for your groceries, clothes, and entertainment, provided that you are able to pay off the full amount of your credit card balance when the payment is due and avoid any interest charges. And credit cards should only be used for long-term investing activities if you will have enough cash to pay off the credit card bill before its due date and avoid interest charges. Long-term investment activities should be financed with long-term financing, if you do not have the cash to pay off the credit card bill before its due date. If you are buying a car or financing your education, you need either a long-term bank loan or a student loan where your payment schedule will match your long-term use of that car or education.

Ethics Insight, p. 703

Q: Why would management of a company want to overstate cash flow from operating activities?

A: The ability to generate cash flows from operating activities is critical to a company's ability to survive and expand. A company must generate cash flows from its operations to pay off debt, pay dividends, and invest in new assets that will allow the company grow. Generally, investors and creditors will be more willing to invest or lend to companies that report higher cash flows from operating activities.

ANSWERS TO SELF-STUDY QUESTIONS

1. a 2. c 3. c 4. a 5. d 6. a 7. b 8. d 9. a 10. c

Remember to go back to the beginning of the chapter to check off your completed work!

←

CHAPTER 17 FINANCIAL STATEMENT ANALYSIS

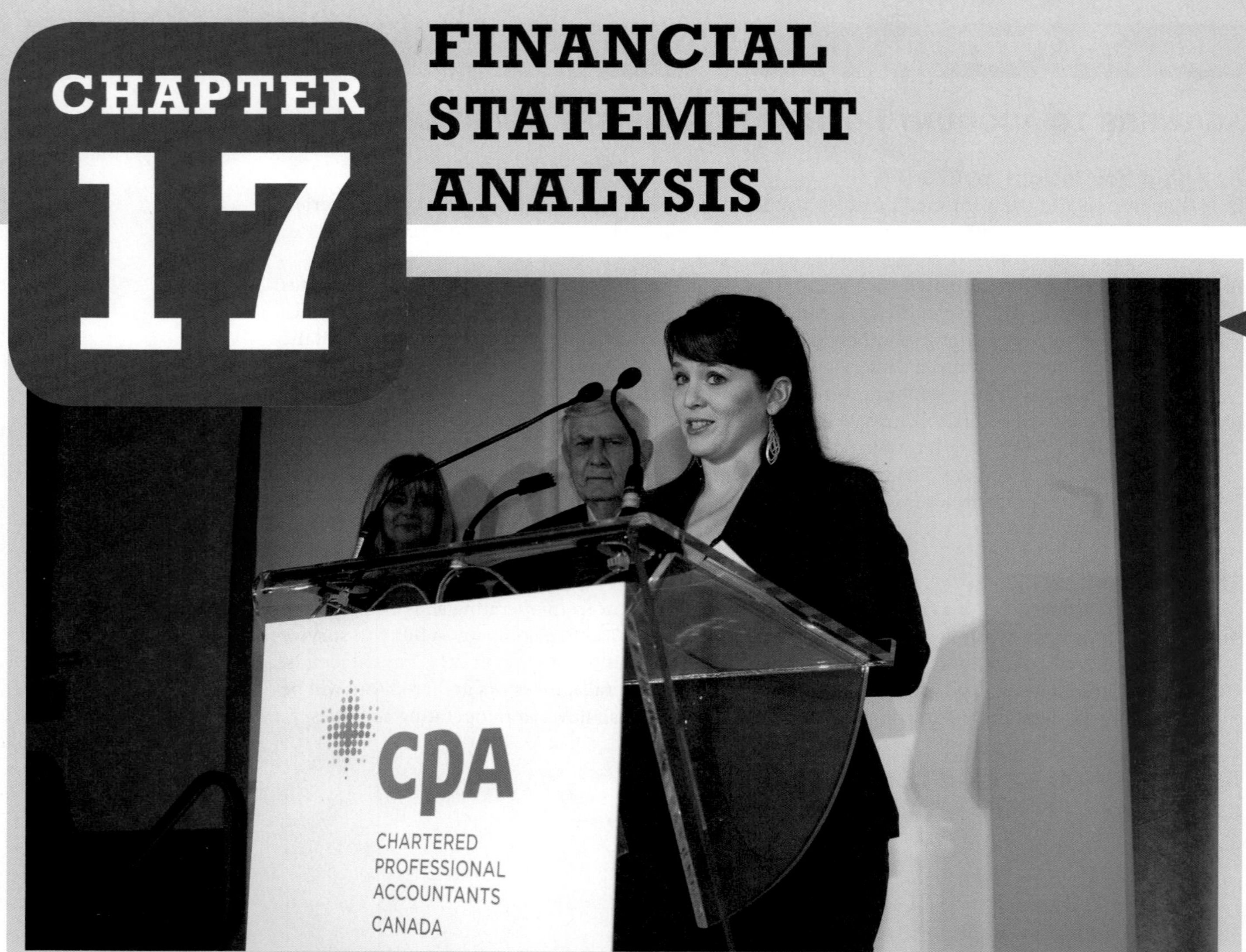

THE NAVIGATOR

- ☐ Understand *Concepts for Review*
- ☐ Read *Feature Story*
- ☐ Scan *Study Objectives*
- ☐ Read *Chapter Preview*
- ☐ Read text and answer *Before You Go On*
- ☐ Review *Comparing IFRS and ASPE*
- ☐ Work *Demonstration Problem*
- ☐ Review *Summary of Study Objectives*
- ☐ Answer *Self-Study Questions*
- ☐ Complete assignments

CONCEPTS FOR REVIEW

Before studying this chapter, you should understand or, if necessary, review:

A. The content and classification of a balance sheet. (Ch. 4, pp. 156–161, and Ch. 13, pp. 563–564)

B. The content and classification of a multiple-step income statement. (Ch. 5, pp. 217–219)

C. The content of a statement of comprehensive income. (Ch. 14, pp. 594–596)

D. The ratios introduced in previous chapters: current ratio, acid-test (Ch. 4, pp. 165–166); gross profit margin, profit margin (Ch. 5, pp. 220–221); inventory turnover, days sales in inventory (Ch. 6, pp. 276–277); receivables turnover, collection period, operating cycle (Ch. 8, pp. 354–355); asset turnover, return on assets (Ch. 9, pp. 409–410); return on equity (Ch. 13, pp. 584–585); earnings per share, price-earnings, payout (Ch. 14, pp. 602–605); debt to total assets, interest coverage (Ch. 15, pp. 647–649); and free cash flow (Ch. 16, pp. 702–703).

PRESENTING THE WHOLE PICTURE

TORONTO, ON—In the high-stakes world of investing and lending, it's not who you know that counts, but what you know. Effective communication enables investors, creditors, and others to know whether a company is doing well, what its past performance has been, and what its future prospects are. The annual report plays a significant role in keeping a company's stakeholders informed.

While most annual reports follow the same basic format, they can vary in their presentation, content, and most importantly, the quality of the information they provide. That's where the annual Corporate Reporting Awards from the Chartered Professional Accountants of Canada (formerly the Canadian Institute of Chartered Accountants) come in. "Successful companies understand it is good business to get their story out in a useful, understandable, relevant, and reliable way," said CPA Canada's president and CEO, Kevin Dancey. "The awards program goes beyond identifying and honouring the best reporting practices; it aims to spread the best to the rest." One such company honoured recently is the Potash Corporation of Saskatchewan, whose official Carmen Manderscheid is shown accepting a CPA Canada Corporate Reporting Award on its behalf.

Canadian Tire Corporation, Limited has been one of the winners of the CPA Canada's Corporate Reporting Awards for five of the past seven years in its category: consumer products. Its annual report starts by identifying reasons to invest in Canadian Tire, including its positive financial highlights and key financial measures. It clearly identifies who and what Canadian Tire is, and has been, over its 90-year history in Canada.

Canadian Tire's annual report, similar to other corporate annual reports, features messages from its chairperson and its CEO, information about the company's products and services, financial statements accompanied by a management discussion and analysis (MD&A), and information about its leadership team and board of directors. Its MD&A includes an in-depth presentation of its strategic goals, including what has been accomplished as well as what has not, and its plans for the future. This year's corporate reporting awards judges said it was noteworthy that "the messaging to shareholders emphasizes the organization's strategies to manage the economy and competitiveness of the industry."

The company's annual report clearly communicates meaningful and transparent information to its stakeholders. "Canadian Tire strives to maintain a high standard of disclosure and investor communication" and is committed to "full and transparent disclosure," the company's 2011 annual report states.

THE NAVIGATOR

STUDY OBJECTIVES

After studying this chapter, you should be able to:

1. Identify the need for, and tools of, financial statement analysis.
2. Explain and apply horizontal analysis.
3. Explain and apply vertical analysis.
4. Identify and use ratios to analyze liquidity.
5. Identify and use ratios to analyze solvency.
6. Identify and use ratios to analyze profitability.
7. Recognize the limitations of financial statement analysis.

THE NAVIGATOR

PREVIEW OF CHAPTER SEVENTEEN

An important lesson can be learned from Canadian Tire's annual report described in our feature story. Effective communication is the key to decision-making. The purpose of this chapter is to introduce the tools used in financial statement analysis to help users evaluate, and make decisions about, a company's financial performance and position.

We will use three common tools of analysis—horizontal, vertical, and ratio—to analyze the financial statements of a hypothetical publicly traded, regional chain of stores called Hometown Tires and More. We will then compare this analysis with Canadian Tire, a publicly traded national chain of stores and one of Hometown Tires and More's competitors. We will conclude our discussion with some of the limiting factors users should be aware of in their analysis of financial information.

The chapter is organized as follows:

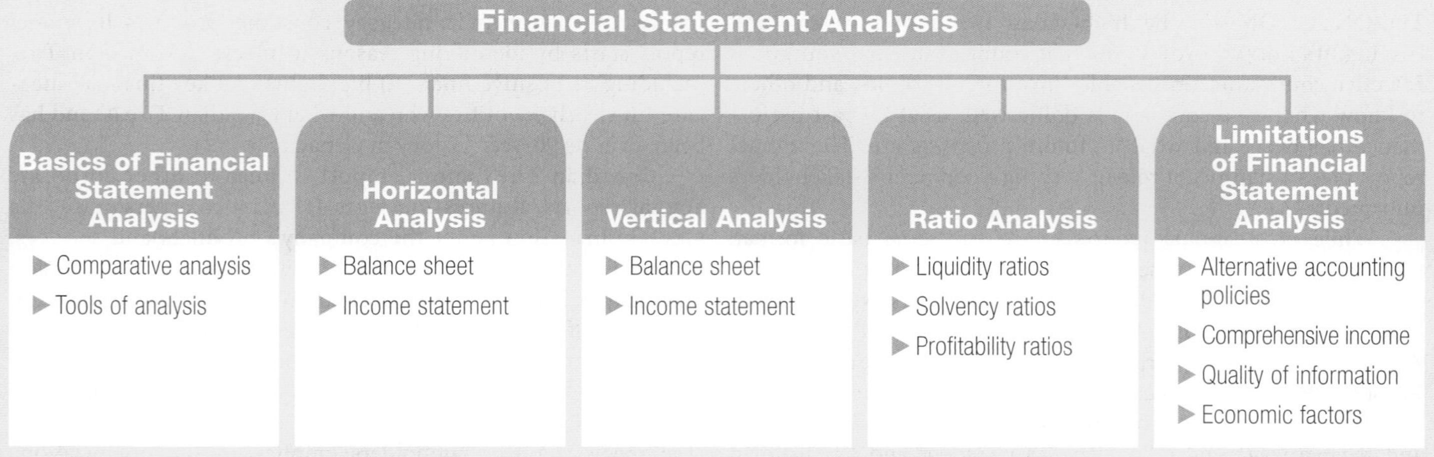

BASICS OF FINANCIAL STATEMENT ANALYSIS

STUDY OBJECTIVE 1

Identify the need for, and tools of, financial statement analysis.

Financial statement analysis involves evaluating three characteristics of a company: its liquidity, solvency, and profitability. We learned in Chapters 1 and 11 that the objective of financial reporting is to give capital providers (investors and creditors) information useful for decision-making. Each of these primary users—investors and creditors—is interested in a company's liquidity, solvency, and/or profitability depending on its decision needs.

For example, short-term creditors, such as suppliers or bankers, are primarily interested in liquidity—the ability of a borrower to pay its obligations when they come due. The borrower's liquidity is extremely important in evaluating the safety of a short-term loan. A long-term creditor, such as a bondholder, is most interested in solvency measures to determine the company's ability to survive over a long period of time. Long-term creditors consider such measures as the amount of debt in the company's capital structure and its ability to meet interest payments. Investors (both current and potential shareholders) are interested in a company's profitability. They want to assess the probability of receiving dividend income and the growth potential of the share price. Creditors are also often interested in profitability, because a company's profit, or lack of it, can affect its ability to obtain financing.

COMPARATIVE ANALYSIS

In analyzing financial statements, the users of financial information must make comparisons in order to evaluate a company's past and current performance and position, and to use this information to help determine future expectations. Comparisons are needed because, although every item reported in a financial statement has significance, it has limited value on its own. When Canadian Tire reported trade and other receivables of $829.3 million on its balance sheet dated December 31, 2011, we know that the company had that amount of receivables on that date. However, we do not know if that amount is an increase or decrease compared with past years, or if Canadian Tire is collecting its receivables on a timely basis. To get this information, the amount of receivables must be compared with other financial statement data.

When you compare any one financial statement item with a related financial statement item or items, the value and usefulness of the information increases for analysis purposes. Comparisons can be made on several different bases, including the following:

1. **Intracompany basis.** This basis compares an item or financial relationship inside or within a company in the current year with one or more prior years. Intracompany comparisons are useful for identifying changes in financial relationships and discovering trends.
2. **Intercompany basis.** This basis compares an item or financial relationship of one company with the same item or relationship in one or more competing companies. Intercompany comparisons are useful for understanding a company's competitive position.

In some circumstances, a third basis of comparison, an industry basis, is also performed. This basis compares an item or financial relationship of a company with industry averages. However, for a company like Canadian Tire, determining which industry it is actually in can be problematic as it sells much more than tires. Canadian Tire sells a wide range of home, tools, leisure, and automotive products in its retail stores, in addition to apparel, sporting goods, gasoline, and financial services in some of its other businesses. Consequently, comparison with industry averages for diversified companies such as Canadian Tire has less relevance than intra- and intercompany comparisons.

TOOLS OF ANALYSIS

We use various tools to evaluate the significance of financial statement data for decision-making. Three commonly used tools are:

1. **Horizontal analysis.** This tool compares data, such as line items in a company's financial statements, by expressing them as percentage increases and decreases over two or more years (periods).
2. **Vertical analysis.** This tool compares data by expressing line items in a company's financial statement as a percentage of a total amount within the same financial statement and year (period).
3. **Ratio analysis.** This tool expresses the relationship between selected items of financial statement data within the same year (period).

Horizontal analysis helps identify changes and trends *over time*. For example, Canadian Tire could compare its trade and other receivables balance over the last five years to determine whether it has increased or decreased over that period of time. Horizontal analysis is used mainly in intracompany comparisons. As we learned above, an intracompany analysis involves financial data *within* a company.

Vertical analysis focuses on the relationships between items on the same financial statement. For example, Canadian Tire could compare its trade and other receivables with its total assets to determine the relative proportion of its receivables in an intracompany comparison. Or it could compare this percentage relationship with that of one of its competitors in an intercompany comparison. Vertical analysis is used in both intracompany and intercompany comparisons. It is helpful to compare the relative contribution made by each financial statement item both *within* a company (intracompany) and *between* two or more companies (intercompany).

Vertical percentages can also be compared across time. Canadian Tire can compare its trade and other receivables as a percentage of its total assets for the current year with that of prior years (intracompany), and can compare this percentage with that of its competitors (intercompany).

Ratio analysis helps us understand the relationship among selected items presented in one or more financial statements. For example, horizontal analysis can determine whether Canadian Tire's receivables have increased or decreased over time and vertical analysis can determine the proportion that Canadian Tire's receivables constitute of its total assets. However, only ratio analysis can relate receivables to revenues by calculating the receivables turnover ratio to determine how effectively the company is collecting its receivables. Ratio analysis is also used in both intracompany and intercompany comparisons. Canadian Tire can compare its receivables turnover ratio for the current year with that of prior years (intracompany), and can compare this ratio with that of its competitors (intercompany).

While horizontal and vertical analysis are being introduced in this chapter, you should already have some familiarity with ratio analysis, which was introduced in past chapters. In the following sections, we will explain and illustrate each of the three types of analysis: horizontal, vertical, and ratio.

BEFORE YOU GO ON...

DO IT

Identify the appropriate basis of comparison and tool of analysis for each of the following financial situations.

	Basis of Comparison	Tool of Analysis
1. Analysis of a company's operating expenses over a 10-year period		
2. Comparison of a company's cost of goods sold with its net sales for the current period		
3. Comparison of a company's profit versus its net sales (profit margin) for the current period with that of a competitor		

Action Plan

- Recall that the two bases of comparison are intracompany and intercompany. "Intra" means within and "inter" means between.
- Recall that there are three tools of analysis: horizontal, vertical, and ratio.

SOLUTION

Basis of Comparison	Tool of Analysis
1. Intracompany	Horizontal
2. Intracompany	Vertical
3. Intercompany	Ratio

Related exercise material: BE17–1 and BE17–2.

HORIZONTAL ANALYSIS

STUDY OBJECTIVE 2
Explain and apply horizontal analysis.

Horizontal analysis, also called **trend analysis**, is a technique for comparing a series of data, such as line items in a company's financial statements, over a period of time. The term "horizontal analysis" means that we view financial statement data from left to right (or right to left) across time.

The purpose of horizontal analysis is to determine the percentage increase or decrease that has taken place over time. This change may be expressed as a percentage of a base period or as a percentage change between periods. For example, total revenue figures and horizontal analysis percentages for Canadian Tire for the most recent five-year period are shown in Illustration 17-1.

ILLUSTRATION 17-1
Horizontal analysis for Canadian Tire's revenue

CANADIAN TIRE CORPORATION, LIMITED
Year Ended December 31
(in millions)

	2011	2010	2009	2008	2007
Revenue	$10,387.1	$9,213.1	$8,686.5	$9,121.3	$8,606.1
% of base-year (2007) amount	120.7%	107.1%	100.9%	106.0%	100.0%
% change between years	12.7%	6.1%	(4.8)%	6.0%	—

If we assume that 2007 is the base year, we can express revenue as a percentage of the base-year amount. We call this a **horizontal percentage of base-period amount**. It is calculated by dividing the amount for the specific year (or period) we are analyzing by the base-year (or period) amount, as shown in Illustration 17-2.

ILLUSTRATION 17-2
Horizontal percentage of base-period amount formula

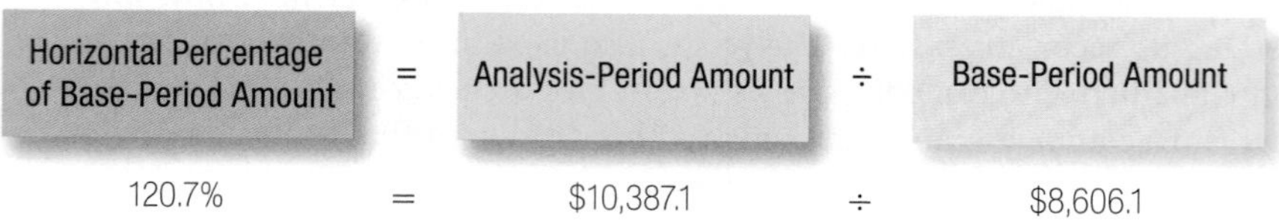

We can determine that Canadian Tire's total revenue in 2011 is 120.7% of the total revenue in 2007 by dividing $10,387.1 million by $8,606.1 million and multiplying the resulting decimal amount by 100 to convert it to a percentage. In other words, revenue in 2011 is 20.7% greater than revenue four years earlier, in 2007. From this horizontal analysis of a base-year amount, shown in the second row of Illustration 17-1, we can easily see Canadian Tire's revenue trend. Revenue has increased each year except in 2009.

We can also use horizontal analysis to measure the percentage change between any two periods of time. This is known as a **horizontal percentage change for period**. It is calculated by dividing the dollar amount of the change between the specific year (or period) under analysis and the prior year (or period) by the prior-year (or period) amount, as shown in Illustration 17-3.

ILLUSTRATION 17-3
Horizontal percentage change for period formula

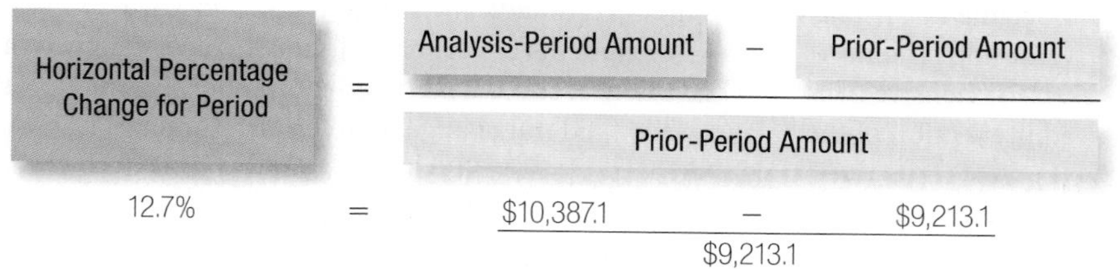

$$12.7\% = \frac{\$10,387.1 - \$9,213.1}{\$9,213.1}$$

For example, we can determine that Canadian Tire's revenue increased by $1,174 million ($10,387.1 million − $9,213.1 million) between 2010 and 2011. This increase can then be expressed as a percentage, 12.7%, by dividing the amount of the change between the two years, $1,174 million, by the amount in the prior year, $9,213.1 million, and multiplying by 100. That is, in 2011, revenue increased by 12.7% compared with 2010. The horizontal percentage change for the period in Canadian Tire's revenue between each of the last five years (between 2011 and 2010, 2010 and 2009, 2009 and 2008, and 2008 and 2007) is presented in the last row of Illustration 17-1. No percentage change can be calculated for 2007 since 2006 data are not included.

BALANCE SHEET

To further illustrate horizontal analysis, we will use the hypothetical financial statements of Hometown Tires and More Inc. Its two-year condensed balance sheet, which shows dollar amount and percentage changes, is presented in Illustration 17-4.

ILLUSTRATION 17-4
Horizontal analysis of balance sheet—percentage change for a period

HOMETOWN TIRES AND MORE INC.
Balance Sheet
December 31

			Increase (Decrease)	
Assets	2011	2010	Amount	Percentage
Current assets				
Cash	$ 50,000	$ 55,000	$ (5,000)	(9.1)%
Trading investments	20,000	35,000	(15,000)	(42.9)%
Accounts receivable	72,500	50,000	22,500	45.0%
Inventory	372,500	340,000	32,500	9.6%
Prepaid expenses	30,000	20,000	10,000	50.0%
Total current assets	545,000	500,000	45,000	9.0%
Property, plant, and equipment	400,000	450,000	(50,000)	(11.1)%
Intangible assets	55,000	65,000	(10,000)	(15.4)%
Total assets	$1,000,000	$1,015,000	$(15,000)	(1.5)%
Liabilities and Shareholders' Equity				
Liabilities				
Current liabilities	$ 337,700	$ 333,500	$ 4,200	1.3%
Non-current liabilities	400,000	475,000	(75,000)	(15.8)%
Total liabilities	737,700	808,500	(70,800)	(8.8)%
Shareholders' equity				
Common shares (300,000 shares issued)	90,000	90,000	0	0.0%
Retained earnings	152,300	96,500	55,800	57.8%
Accumulated other comprehensive income	20,000	20,000	0	0.0%
Total shareholders' equity	262,300	206,500	55,800	27.0%
Total liabilities and shareholders' equity	$1,000,000	$1,015,000	$(15,000)	(1.5)%

The horizontal percentages in Illustration 17-4 are an example of a percentage change for a period, and not a percentage of a base-period amount. It makes sense to calculate the percentage change for a period in this illustration since only two periods are under analysis. In a horizontal analysis, while the amount column of the increase or decrease is additive (for example, the decrease in total liabilities of $70,800 is equal to +$4,200 − $75,000), the percentage column is not additive (8.8% is not equal to +1.3% − 15.8%).

The horizontal analysis of Hometown Tires and More's comparative balance sheet shows that several changes have occurred between 2010 and 2011. In the current assets section, trading investments decreased by $15,000, or 42.9%. We will learn when we look at the income statement later that this change was due to a decline in the fair value of the investments and not to the sale of any of these investments. Losses on fair value adjustments of trading investments are reported in the income statement and not in the statement of comprehensive income. This is why accumulated other comprehensive income, shown in the shareholders' equity section of the balance sheet, did not change between 2010 and 2011.

Accounts receivable increased by $22,500, or 45%. We will look at the income statement in the next section to determine whether sales increased by the same proportion as receivables. If not, this may indicate that the receivables are slow-moving.

Inventory increased by a larger dollar amount, $32,500, than did accounts receivable but not by as large a percentage: 9.6% for inventory compared with 45% for accounts receivable. Inventory may have changed because of increased sales; we will investigate this further when we analyze the income statement. Prepaid expenses also increased by 50% in 2011. One has to be careful in interpreting percentage changes like this. Because it is a proportionately large change ($10,000) on a small base amount ($20,000), the percentage change is not as meaningful as it first appears.

The carrying amounts of both property, plant, and equipment and intangible assets decreased in 2011. This means that the company is disposing of more long-lived assets than it is acquiring (or that its depreciation and amortization exceeds the acquisition of new assets). Overall, total assets decreased by $15,000, or 1.5%, from 2010 to 2011.

Current liabilities increased by 1.3%. Changes in current assets and current liabilities usually move in the same direction; that is, normally both will increase or both will decrease. In this case, both have risen, although current assets have increased more than current liabilities. This is better than the inverse: current liabilities increasing more than current assets.

Non-current liabilities decreased by $75,000, or 15.8%, in 2011. Retained earnings in the shareholders' equity section of the balance sheet increased significantly in 2011, by 57.8%. This suggests that Hometown Tires and More is financing its business by retaining and reinvesting profit, rather than by adding to its debt.

INCOME STATEMENT

ILLUSTRATION 17-5
Horizontal analysis of income statement—percentage change for period

Illustration 17-5 presents a horizontal analysis of Hometown Tires and More's condensed income statement for the years 2010 and 2011.

HOMETOWN TIRES AND MORE INC.
Income Statement
Years Ended December 31

			Increase (Decrease)	
	2011	**2010**	**Amount**	**Percentage**
Sales	$2,095,000	$1,960,000	$135,000	6.9%
Sales returns and allowances	98,000	123,000	(25,000)	(20.3)%
Net sales	1,997,000	1,837,000	160,000	8.7%
Cost of goods sold	1,381,000	1,240,000	141,000	11.4%
Gross profit	616,000	597,000	19,000	3.2%
Operating expenses	457,000	440,000	17,000	3.9%
Profit from operations	159,000	157,000	2,000	1.3%
Other expenses				
Interest expense	27,000	29,500	(2,500)	(8.5)%
Loss on fair value adjustment of trading investments	15,000	0	15,000	n/a
Profit before income tax	117,000	127,500	(10,500)	(8.2)%
Income tax expense	23,400	25,500	(2,100)	(8.2)%
Profit	$ 93,600	$ 102,000	$ (8,400)	(8.2)%

Horizontal analysis of the income statement, illustrating dollar amounts and percentage changes for the period, shows that net sales increased by 8.7%. Sales do not appear to have increased at the same rate as receivables, though. Recall from Illustration 17-4 that receivables increased by 45%. Later in the chapter, we will look at the receivables turnover ratio in the ratio analysis section to determine whether receivables are being collected more slowly or not. However, we must be cautious in over-interpreting this increase. This type of business relies a lot on cash sales, not credit sales.

To continue with our horizontal analysis of the income statement, we can observe that similar to net sales, cost of goods sold also increased. However, it is interesting to note that while cost of goods sold increased by 11.4%, net sales only increased by 8.7%. This is not a sustainable situation over the long run and the relationship between pricing and costs will need to be carefully monitored. Recall also that in Illustration 17-4 we observed that inventory increased by 9.6%. The cost of goods sold increased not only at a faster rate than sales, but also at a faster rate than inventory. We will look at the inventory turnover ratio later in the chapter to determine whether these increases are reasonable.

The net result of the changes in net sales and cost of goods sold is an increase in gross profit of 3.2%. Operating expenses outpaced this percentage increase at 3.9%. Normally, management tries to control operating expenses wherever possible, so we would hope to see operating expenses decrease or at least increase at a lower rate than gross profit.

Other expenses increased, primarily because of the loss on fair value adjustment related to the trading investments that was mentioned in the last section. Note that profit declined by the same amount as profit before income tax, 8.2%. This indicates that although income tax expense declined in 2011, its decline was proportionate to profit before income tax in each year. (That is, income tax expense is unchanged at 20% of profit before income tax in each year.)

A horizontal analysis of the changes between periods is pretty straightforward and is quite useful. But complications can occur in making the calculations. If an item has a small value in a base or prior year and a large value in the next year, the percentage change could be disproportionately large and may not be meaningful. In addition, if a negative amount appears in the base or prior year and there is a positive amount the following year, or vice versa, no percentage change can be calculated. Or, if an item has no value (that is, zero) in a base or prior year and a value in the next year, no percentage change can be calculated. That was the case with the loss on fair value adjustment of trading investments reported in 2011. Because there was no loss reported in 2010, no percentage change could be calculated.

We have not included a horizontal analysis of Hometown Tires and More's statement of changes in shareholders' equity or cash flow statement. An analysis of these statements is not as useful as the horizontal analyses performed on the balance sheet and income statement. The amounts presented in the statement of changes in shareholders' equity and cash flow statement give details about the changes between two periods. The value of these statements comes from the analysis of the changes during the year, and not from percentage comparisons of these changes against a base amount.

Hometown Tires and More did not have any other comprehensive income in 2011, so it did not present a separate statement of comprehensive income. However, if it had, it might have been useful to analyze the changes in its sources of other comprehensive income. You should note, however, that these changes can vary widely from year to year, which can result in a horizontal analysis of other comprehensive income having limited value.

BEFORE YOU GO ON...

DO IT

Selected, condensed information (in thousands) from Bonora Ltd.'s income statements follows:

	2014	2013	2012	2011
Net sales	$8,646	$9,468	$6,294	$5,035
Cost of goods sold	6,746	7,322	5,217	4,099
Gross profit	1,900	2,146	1,077	936
Operating expenses	1,396	1,504	948	641
Profit from operations	504	642	129	295
Income tax expense	76	96	19	44
Profit	$ 428	$ 546	$ 110	$ 251

BEFORE YOU GO ON...
continued on next page

BEFORE YOU GO ON...
continued from previous page

(a) Using horizontal analysis, calculate the percentage of the base-year amount for 2011 to 2014, assuming that 2011 is the base year.
(b) Using horizontal analysis, calculate the percentage change between each of the following sets of years: 2014 and 2013; 2013 and 2012; and 2012 and 2011.

Action Plan

- Horizontal percentage of base-year amount: Set the base-year (2011) dollar amounts at 100%. Express each subsequent year's amount as a percentage of the base-year amount by dividing the dollar amount for the year under analysis by the base-year amount and multiplying the resulting decimal by 100 to convert it to percentage form.
- Horizontal percentage change for year: Find the percentage change between two years by dividing the dollar amount of the change between the current year and the prior year by the prior-year amount.

SOLUTION

(a) Horizontal percentage of base-year amount

	2014	2013	2012	2011
Net sales	171.7%	188.0%	125.0%	100.0%
Cost of goods sold	164.6%	178.6%	127.3%	100.0%
Gross profit	203.0%	229.3%	115.1%	100.0%
Operating expenses	217.8%	234.6%	147.9%	100.0%
Profit from operations	170.8%	217.6%	43.7%	100.0%
Income tax expense	172.7%	218.2%	43.2%	100.0%
Profit	170.5%	217.5%	43.8%	100.0%

(b) Horizontal percentage change for year

	2013 to 2014	2012 to 2013	2011 to 2012
Net sales	(8.7)%	50.4%	25.0%
Cost of goods sold	(7.9)%	40.3%	27.3%
Gross profit	(11.5)%	99.3%	15.1%
Operating expenses	(7.2)%	58.6%	47.9%
Profit from operations	(21.5)%	397.7%	(56.3)%
Income tax expense	(20.8)%	405.3%	(56.8)%
Profit	(21.6)%	396.4%	(56.2)%

Related exercise material: BE17–3, BE17–4, E17–1, and E17–2.

THE NAVIGATOR

VERTICAL ANALYSIS

STUDY OBJECTIVE 3
Explain and apply vertical analysis.

Vertical analysis, also called **common size analysis**, is a technique for comparing an amount in a company's financial statements with a total (base) amount within the same financial statement. The term "vertical analysis" means that we view financial statement data from up to down (or down to up) within the same period of time.

Note that while horizontal analysis compares data across more than one year, vertical analysis compares data within the same year. These data are expressed as a percentage, known as the **vertical percentage of base amount**. It is calculated by dividing the financial statement amount under analysis by the relevant total or base amount for that particular financial statement, as shown in Illustration 17-6.

ILLUSTRATION 17-6
Vertical percentage of base amount formula

Vertical Percentage of Base Amount = Analysis Amount ÷ Base Amount

The base amount commonly used for the balance sheet is *total assets*. The base amount for the income statement is usually *revenues* for a service company and *net sales* for a merchandising company. The base amounts in vertical analysis are always equal to 100%.

BALANCE SHEET

We will illustrate vertical analysis using Hometown Tires and More's balance sheet by first calculating a vertical percentage of a base amount for two years in an intracompany comparison. Then we will vertically compare Hometown Tires and More's balance sheet with a competitor's balance sheet in an intercompany comparison.

Intracompany Comparison

Illustration 17-7 shows a vertical analysis of Hometown Tires and More's comparative balance sheet. As was mentioned above, this analysis uses *total assets* as the base amount. Note that, based on the accounting equation (A = L + OE), *total liabilities and shareholders' equity* equals total assets so the same base amount (for example, total assets) can be used for both assets as well as liabilities and shareholders' equity items.

ILLUSTRATION 17-7
Vertical analysis of balance sheet—percentage of base amount

HOMETOWN TIRES AND MORE INC.
Balance Sheet
December 31

	2011		2010	
Assets	Amount	Percentage	Amount	Percentage
Current assets				
Cash	$ 50,000	5.0%	$ 55,000	5.4%
Trading investments	20,000	2.0%	35,000	3.5%
Accounts receivable	72,500	7.2%	50,000	4.9%
Inventory	372,500	37.3%	340,000	33.5%
Prepaid expenses	30,000	3.0%	20,000	2.0%
Total current assets	545,000	54.5%	500,000	49.3%
Property, plant, and equipment	400,000	40.0%	450,000	44.3%
Intangible assets	55,000	5.5%	65,000	6.4%
Total assets	$1,000,000	100.0%	$1,015,000	100.0%
Liabilities and Shareholders' Equity				
Liabilities				
Current liabilities	$ 337,700	33.8%	$ 333,500	32.9%
Non-current liabilities	400,000	40.0%	475,000	46.8%
Total liabilities	737,700	73.8%	808,500	79.7%
Shareholders' equity				
Common shares (300,000 shares issued)	90,000	9.0%	90,000	8.8%
Retained earnings	152,300	15.2%	96,500	9.5%
Accumulated other comprehensive income	20,000	2.0%	20,000	2.0%
Total shareholders' equity	262,300	26.2%	206,500	20.3%
Total liabilities and shareholders' equity	$1,000,000	100.0%	$1,015,000	100.0%

Vertical analysis shows the size of each item in the balance sheet compared with a base amount for each of 2011 and 2010. In addition to reviewing the respective proportion of each item in the balance sheet within a specific year, vertical analysis can also be used to compare changes in the individual asset, liability, and shareholders' equity items between years.

For example, we can see that current assets increased from 49.3% of total assets in 2010 to 54.5% of total assets in 2011. We can also see that the biggest change was in inventory, which increased from 33.5% of total assets in 2010 to 37.3% in 2011. This is contrary to what we first observed in Illustration 17-4, where it appeared that prepaid expenses had the greatest percentage increase in the current assets category. In Illustration 17-7, prepaid expenses increased by only one percentage point of total assets, from 2% in 2010 to 3% in 2011. You will recall our earlier words of caution about interpreting such a large percentage change (the 50% horizontal percentage change for period) as was presented for prepaid expenses in Illustration 17-4.

Helpful hint When comparing one percentage with another percentage, the difference is expressed in "percentage points."

The carrying amounts of property, plant, and equipment and intangible assets decreased in absolute dollar amounts, as we saw in Illustration 17-4, and also decreased as relative percentages of total assets, as shown in Illustration 17-7. Property, plant, and equipment decreased from 44.3% in 2010 to 40% in 2011 and intangible assets decreased from 6.4% in 2010 to 5.5% in 2011.

Non-current liabilities decreased from 46.8% to 40%, while retained earnings increased from 9.5% to 15.2% of total liabilities and shareholders' equity between 2010 and 2011. These results reinforce the earlier observation that Hometown Tires and More is financing its growth by retaining profit, rather than by taking on additional debt.

Note that Hometown Tires and More has only one class of share capital—common shares—issued. Its common shares didn't actually change between 2010 and 2011, yet common shares represent a different percentage of total assets in each year (8.8% in 2010 and 9.0% in 2011). This is because the base (total assets) has changed in each year while the amount of common shares has not.

Intercompany Comparison

Helpful hint Because it uses percentages, vertical analysis can serve to "level the playing field" and allow for meaningful comparisons between companies of different sizes.

The above vertical analysis illustrated an intracompany comparison—we compared changes in Hometown Tires and More's balance sheet between 2010 and 2011. We can also use vertical analysis to compare companies in an intercompany comparison. This is a particularly helpful technique when companies are of different sizes.

For example, Hometown Tires and More's main competitor is Canadian Tire. Using vertical analysis, the condensed balance sheet (or the income statement) of the small retail company Hometown Tires and More can be more meaningfully compared with the balance sheet (or income statement) of the giant retailer Canadian Tire, as shown in Illustration 17-8.

ILLUSTRATION 17-8
Intercompany balance sheet comparison—vertical analysis

BALANCE SHEETS
December 31, 2011
(in thousands)

	Hometown Tires and More		Canadian Tire	
Assets	Amount (in thousands)	Percentage	Amount (in millions)	Percentage
Current assets	$ 545.0	54.5%	$ 6,956.6	56.4%
Long-term receivables and other assets	0.0	0.0%	778.1	6.3%
Long-term investments	0.0	0.0%	128.2	1.0%
Property, plant, and equipment	400.0	40.0%	3,365.9	27.3%
Intangible assets	55.0	5.5%	1,110.0	9.0%
Total assets	$1,000.0	100.0%	$12,338.8	100.0%
Liabilities and Shareholders' Equity				
Liabilities				
Current liabilities	$ 337.7	33.8%	$ 4,153.0	33.7%
Non-current liabilities	400.0	40.0%	3,776.8	30.6%
Total liabilities	737.7	73.8%	7,929.8	64.3%
Shareholders' equity				
Share capital	90.0	9.0%	711.6	5.8%
Retained earnings	152.3	15.2%	3,686.4	29.9%
Accumulated other comprehensive income	20.0	2.0%	11.0	0.0%
Total shareholders' equity	262.3	26.2%	4,409.0	35.7%
Total liabilities and shareholders' equity	$1,000.0	100.0%	$12,338.8	100.0%

Helpful hint Long-term investments are securities that are held in order to (a) generate an ongoing source of income from interest or dividends or (b) generate capital gains by selling the securities for more than was paid for them.

Canadian Tire's total assets are 12,339 times greater than the total assets of the much smaller Hometown Tires and More. Vertical analysis helps eliminate this difference in size. For example, although Hometown Tires and More has fewer dollars of property, plant, and equipment compared with Canadian Tire ($400,000 compared with $3,365.9 million), using percentages, its proportion of property, plant, and equipment is much larger (40% compared with 27.3%).

Although Hometown Tires and More has fewer dollars of debt than Canadian Tire ($737,700 compared with $7,929.8 million), it has a higher debt percentage than does Canadian Tire (73.8% compared with 64.3%). This is not surprising given that Hometown Tires and More, as a much smaller company, may not have the same access to equity financing as does Canadian Tire. Alternatively, it may have deliberately chosen to finance its operations with more debt than equity proportionately than Canadian Tire. Regardless of the rationale, the company does have a lower equity base than Canadian Tire (26.2% compared with 35.7%).

INCOME STATEMENT

We would like to now illustrate an intracompany comparison using vertical analysis of Hometown Tires and More's income statement. A vertical analysis of the percentage of the base amount for each of 2010 and 2011 is shown in Illustration 17-9, with *net sales* used as the base amount.

ILLUSTRATION 17-9
Vertical analysis of income statement—percentage of base amount

HOMETOWN TIRES AND MORE INC.
Income Statement
Year Ended December 31

	2011		2010	
	Amount	**Percentage**	**Amount**	**Percentage**
Sales	$2,095,000	104.9%	$1,960,000	106.7%
Sales returns and allowances	98,000	4.9%	123,000	6.7%
Net sales	1,997,000	100.0%	1,837,000	100.0%
Cost of goods sold	1,381,000	69.2%	1,240,000	67.5%
Gross profit	616,000	30.8%	597,000	32.5%
Operating expenses	457,000	22.9%	440,000	24.0%
Profit from operations	159,000	7.9%	157,000	8.5%
Other expenses				
Interest expense	27,000	1.3%	29,500	1.6%
Loss on fair value adjustment of trading investments	15,000	0.7%	0	0.0%
Profit before income tax	117,000	5.9%	127,500	6.9%
Income tax expense	23,400	1.2%	25,500	1.4%
Profit	$ 93,600	4.7%	$ 102,000	5.5%

We can see that the cost of goods sold as a percentage of net sales increased by 1.7 percentage points (from 67.5% to 69.2%) between 2010 and 2011. Operating expenses declined as a percentage of net sales by 1.1 percentage points (from 24.0% to 22.9%). As a result, profit from operations did not change substantially between 2010 and 2011: it declined by 0.6 percentage points (from 8.5% to 7.9%). Profit before income tax declined between 2010 and 2011 from 6.9% to 5.9%. Profit declined as well as a percentage of net sales from 2010 to 2011: it decreased by 0.8 percentage points. Although we saw Hometown Tires and More's profit decrease by 8.2% between 2010 and 2011 in Illustration 17-5, its profitability is relatively unchanged (less than 1%) in comparison with net sales.

A vertical analysis can also be performed on the statement of comprehensive income, statement of changes in shareholders' equity, and cash flow statement. However, this is rarely done as there is no logical base amount.

Vertical analysis can also be applied to intercompany comparisons of the income statement, similar to our comparison of Hometown Tires and More and Canadian Tire in the balance sheet section above although we have not chosen to do so here.

 **BEFORE YOU GO ON...**

DO IT

Selected, condensed information (in thousands) from Bonora Ltd.'s income statements follows:

	2014	2013	2012	2011
Net sales	$8,646	$9,468	$6,294	$5,035
Cost of goods sold	6,746	7,322	5,217	4,099
Gross profit	1,900	2,146	1,077	936
Operating expenses	1,396	1,504	948	641
Profit from operations	504	642	129	295
Income tax expense	76	96	19	44
Profit	$ 428	$ 546	$ 110	$ 251

Using vertical analysis, calculate the percentage of the base amount for each year.

Action Plan

- Vertical percentage of base amount: Find the relative percentage by dividing the specific income statement amount by the base amount (net sales) for each year.

SOLUTION

	2014	2013	2012	2011
Net sales	100%	100%	100%	100%
Cost of goods sold	78%	77%	83%	81%
Gross profit	22%	23%	17%	19%
Operating expenses	16%	16%	15%	13%
Profit from operations	6%	7%	2%	6%
Income tax expense	1%	1%	0%	1%
Profit	5%	6%	2%	5%

Related exercise material: BE17–5, BE17–6, E17–3, E17–4, and E17–5.

RATIO ANALYSIS

Ratio analysis expresses the relationships between selected financial statement items and is the most widely used tool of financial analysis. Ratios are generally classified into three types:

1. **Liquidity ratios.** These measure a company's short-term ability to pay its maturing obligations and to meet unexpected needs for cash.
2. **Solvency ratios.** These measure a company's ability to survive over a long period of time.
3. **Profitability ratios.** These measure a company's operating success for a specific period of time.

In earlier chapters, we presented liquidity, solvency, and profitability ratios for evaluating a company's financial condition. In this section, we provide an example of a comprehensive financial analysis using these ratios. This analysis uses two bases for comparisons: (1) intracompany, comparing two years of data (2010 and 2011) for Hometown Tires and More, and (2) intercompany, comparing Hometown Tires and More with Canadian Tire, its main competitor, for the year ended December 31, 2011.

You will recall that earlier in the chapter Hometown Tires and More's balance sheet was presented in Illustration 17-4 and its income statement in Illustration 17-5. We will use the information in these two financial statements, plus additional data that will be introduced as required, to calculate Hometown Tires and More's ratios in the next three sections. You can use these data to review the calculations for each 2011 ratio calculated for Hometown Tires and More to make sure you understand where the numbers came from. Detailed calculations are not shown for the ratios presented for Hometown Tires and More for 2010 or for Canadian Tire for 2011.

LIQUIDITY RATIOS

STUDY OBJECTIVE 4

Identify and use ratios to analyze liquidity.

Liquidity ratios measure a company's short-term ability to pay its maturing obligations and to meet unexpected needs for cash. Short-term creditors, such as suppliers and bankers, are particularly interested in assessing liquidity. Liquidity ratios include the current ratio, the acid-test ratio, receivables turnover, collection period, inventory turnover, days sales in inventory, and the operating cycle.

Current Ratio

The current ratio is a widely used measure of a company's liquidity and short-term debt-paying ability. The ratio is calculated by dividing current assets by current liabilities. The 2011 and 2010 current ratios for Hometown Tires and More (intracompany basis of comparison) and 2011 current ratio for Canadian Tire (intercompany basis of comparison) are shown below.

$$\text{Current ratio} = \frac{\text{Current assets}}{\text{Current liabilities}}$$

Hometown Tires and More **2011**	Hometown Tires and More **2010** = 1.5:1	Intracompany
$\frac{\$545,000}{\$337,700} = 1.6:1$	Canadian Tire **2011** = 1.7:1	Intercompany

What does the ratio actually mean? The 2011 ratio of 1.6:1 means that for every dollar of current liabilities, Hometown Tires and More has $1.60 of current assets. Hometown Tires and More's current ratio increased slightly between 2010 and 2011. Although its 2011 ratio is marginally lower than Canadian Tire's current ratio of 1.7:1, Hometown Tires and More appears to have more than enough current assets to pay its current liabilities.

Acid-Test Ratio

The current ratio is only one measure of liquidity. It does not consider what the current assets are composed of. For example, a satisfactory current ratio does not disclose the fact that a portion of the current assets may be tied up in inventory or prepayments. The acid-test ratio differs from the current ratio by excluding assets that are less liquid, such as inventory, which takes longer to be converted to cash. For merchandising companies, inventory must be sold before any accounts receivable or cash can be created.

The acid-test ratio is calculated by dividing the sum of cash, short-term investments, and receivables by current liabilities. Short-term investments include trading investments, such as reported by Hometown Tires and More, and short-term debt instruments purchased to earn interest.

The 2011 and 2010 acid-test ratios for Hometown Tires and More and 2011 acid-test ratio for Canadian Tire are shown below.

$$\text{Acid-test ratio} = \frac{\text{Cash} + \text{Short-term investments} + \text{Receivables}}{\text{Current liabilities}}$$

Hometown Tires and More **2011**	Hometown Tires and More **2010** = 0.4:1	Intracompany
$\frac{\$50,000 + \$20,000 + \$72,500}{\$337,700} = 0.4:1$	Canadian Tire **2011** = 0.3:1	Intercompany

What does the ratio actually mean? The 2011 ratio of 0.4:1 means that for every dollar of current liabilities, Hometown Tires and More has $0.40 of highly liquid current assets. The company's acid-test ratio is unchanged from 2010. However, it is much lower than its current ratio of 1.6:1. This likely means that Hometown Tires and More has a large balance in its inventory and/or prepaid accounts. In addition, given that the current ratio increased while the acid-test ratio did not change in 2011, inventory and/or prepaid expenses likely increased. We will investigate the liquidity of both companies' inventory shortly, as this is the more significant account of the two.

Hometown Tires and More's acid-test ratio is marginally higher than that of Canadian Tire. This is interesting given that its current ratio was lower. Hometown Tires and More has a higher proportion of liquid assets (cash, short-term investments, and receivables) compared with its current liabilities than does Canadian Tire.

Receivables Turnover

Helpful hint To calculate an average balance sheet amount such as accounts receivable, add together the balance at the beginning of the year (which is the same as the balance at the end of the prior year) and the balance at the end of the year and divide the sum by 2.

The acid-test ratio does not consider the impact of uncollectible receivables on liquidity. A dollar of cash is more available to pay bills than a dollar of an overdue account receivable. The receivables turnover ratio is used to assess the liquidity of the receivables. It measures the number of times, on average, that receivables are collected during the period. The receivables turnover is calculated by dividing net credit sales (net sales less cash sales) by the average gross accounts receivable.

You will recall from earlier chapters that when a figure from the income statement is compared with a figure from the balance sheet in a ratio, the balance sheet figure is averaged by adding together the beginning and ending balances and dividing them by 2. That is because income statement figures cover a period of time (that is, a year) and balance sheet figures are at a point in time—in this case, the beginning and the end of the year. That is why average receivables are used in the calculation of the receivables turnover ratio shown below. Comparisons of end-of-period figures with end-of-period figures, or period figures with period figures, do not require averaging, as we saw in the current ratio and acid-test ratios calculated above.

Assuming that all sales are credit sales and that there is no allowance for doubtful accounts, the 2011 and 2010 receivables turnover figures for Hometown Tires and More and 2011 receivables turnover ratio for Canadian Tire are shown below.

$\text{Receivables turnover} = \dfrac{\text{Net credit sales}}{\text{Average gross accounts receivable}}$		
Hometown Tires and More **2011** $\dfrac{\$1,997,000}{(\$72,500 + \$50,000) \div 2} = 32.6$ times	Hometown Tires and More **2010** = 38.7 times	Intracompany
	Canadian Tire **2011** = 13.8 times	Intercompany

Hometown Tires and More's receivables turn over (are collected) 32.6 times a year. In general, the faster the receivables turnover, the better and more reliable the current ratio is for assessing liquidity.

Although Hometown Tires and More's receivables turnover declined (worsened) from 38.7 times in 2010 to 32.6 times in 2011, it is still much higher than Canadian Tire's receivables turnover of 13.8 times a year. Why is Hometown Tires and More's receivables turnover so much higher than that of Canadian Tire? Hometown Tires and More likely has fewer sales on account and therefore fewer receivables. More of its sales are for cash. Canadian Tire, on the other hand, has receivables from its franchise stores and company credit card, which may take longer to collect.

It is important to be careful in interpreting this ratio. We assumed that all sales were credit sales, when in fact, this is not a reasonable assumption. Companies do not disclose their credit and cash sales separately. However, intracompany and intercompany comparisons can still be made, since the same assumption—all sales were credit sales—was applied to Canadian Tire's data.

Collection Period.

A popular variation of the receivables turnover is to convert it into a collection period stated in days. This is calculated by dividing the receivables turnover into the number of days in a year (365 days). Hometown Tires and More's collection period for 2011 and 2010 and Canadian Tire's collection period for 2011 are shown below.

$\text{Collection period} = \dfrac{\text{Days in year}}{\text{Receivables turnover}}$		
Hometown Tires and More **2011** $\dfrac{365 \text{ days}}{32.6} = 11$ days	Hometown Tires and More **2010** = 9 days	Intracompany
	Canadian Tire **2011** = 26 days	Intercompany

The effectiveness of a company's credit and collection policies is much easier to interpret using the collection period, rather than the receivables turnover ratio. Hometown Tires and More's receivables were collected every 11 days in 2011. Although weaker than in 2010, they are still being collected faster than those of Canadian Tire. In addition, this collection period is well under the normal 30-day payment period. The general rule is that the collection period should not be more than the credit-term period (the time allowed for payment). Even Canadian Tire's higher collection period of 26 days is still a reasonable one. So, despite earlier concerns, receivables management appears to be in good shape for both companies.

ACCOUNTING IN ACTION
ACROSS THE ORGANIZATION

It is during economic downturns that a company's receivables turnover and average collection period ratios need to be closely watched. During difficult times, management may face pressure to loosen the company's credit policy in order to boost sales. If credit is extended to risky customers who pay late, or who do not pay at all, then the average collection period will increase and the receivables turnover will decrease. That's why it is important to interpret a company's ability to manage its receivables in the context of its current credit policy, economic conditions, and industry averages, as well as prior receivables ratios.

What other liquidity ratios should be monitored, and by what department(s), across the organization?

Inventory Turnover

Inventory turnover measures the average number of times that the inventory is sold during the period. Its purpose is to measure the liquidity of the inventory. The inventory turnover is calculated by dividing the cost of goods sold by the average inventory.

Hometown Tires and More's 2011 and 2010 inventory turnover figures and the 2011 inventory turnover ratio for Canadian Tire are shown below.

$\text{Inventory turnover} = \frac{\text{Cost of goods sold}}{\text{Average inventory}}$		
Hometown Tires and More **2011** $\frac{\$1,381,000}{(\$372,500 + \$340,000) \div 2} = 3.9 \text{ times}$	Hometown Tires and More **2010** = 3.9 times	Intracompany
	Canadian Tire **2011** = 6.2 times	Intercompany

Hometown Tires and More turns over (sells) its entire inventory 3.9 times a year. Its inventory turnover was unchanged between 2010 and 2011. Hometown Tires and More's turnover ratio of 3.9 times is low compared with that of Canadian Tire's turnover of 6.2 times.

Generally, the faster inventory is sold, the less cash there is tied up in inventory and the less chance there is of inventory becoming obsolete. In addition, the higher the inventory turnover, the more reliable the current ratio is for assessing liquidity. We made this same statement earlier in this chapter with respect to the receivables turnover ratio. That is, if the receivables and inventory turnover ratios are declining, the current ratio may increase simply because of higher balances of receivables and inventory included in current assets. In such cases, the turnover ratios are more relevant than the current ratio as measures of liquidity.

Days Sales in Inventory.

A variant of inventory turnover is the days sales in inventory. This is calculated by dividing the inventory turnover into the number of days in a year (365 days). Hometown Tires and More's days sales in inventory for 2011 and 2010 and the 2011 days sales in inventory for Canadian Tire are shown below.

Days sales in inventory = $\frac{\text{Days in year}}{\text{Inventory turnover}}$		
Hometown Tires and More **2011** $\frac{365\text{ days}}{3.9}$ = 94 days	Hometown Tires and More **2010** = 94 days	Intracompany
	Canadian Tire **2011** = 59 days	Intercompany

Hometown Tires and More's inventory turnover of 3.9 times divided into 365 days is approximately 94 days. In other words, Hometown Tires and More has 94 days' (more than three months') worth of inventory on hand. This is relatively slow compared with Canadian Tire's 59 days.

It is important to use judgement in interpreting both the inventory turnover and days sales in inventory ratios. Remember that Hometown Tires and More is composed of a few stores throughout the region, while Canadian Tire has more than 1,700 stores across the nation. Canadian Tire is large enough to take advantage of just-in-time and other computerized inventory management techniques, whereas Hometown Tires and More likely does not have such sophisticated inventory options.

Nonetheless, Hometown Tires and More must keep a close eye on its inventory. It runs the risk of being left with unsaleable inventory, not to mention the additional costs of financing and carrying this inventory over a longer period of time.

Operating Cycle

Alternative terminology
The *operating cycle* is also known as the *cash conversion cycle*.

The operating cycle measures the average time it takes to purchase inventory, sell it on account, and collect the cash from customers. It is calculated by adding the days sales in inventory and the collection period together. The 2011 and 2010 operating cycle figures for Hometown Tires and More and 2011 operating cycle for Canadian Tire are shown below.

Operating cycle = Days sales in inventory + Collection period		
Hometown Tires and More **2011** 94 days + 11 days = 105 days	Hometown Tires and More **2010** = 103 days	Intracompany
	Canadian Tire **2011** = 85 days	Intercompany

In 2011, it took Hometown Tires and More an average of 105 days (more than three months) from the time it purchased its inventory to sell it on account and collect the cash. This was two days slower than its operating cycle in 2010. Canadian Tire's operating cycle was much faster (shorter) than Hometown Tires and More's in 2011.

Liquidity Conclusion

In an intracompany comparison for the years 2011 and 2010, as shown in Illustration 17-10, Hometown Tires and More's current ratio increased slightly while its acid-test and inventory turnover ratios remained unchanged from 2010 to 2011. Although its receivables turnover ratio declined, it is still a strong

ILLUSTRATION 17-10
Intracompany comparison of liquidity ratios

HOMETOWN TIRES AND MORE INC.			
Liquidity Ratio	**2011**	**2010**	**Comparison**
Current ratio	1.6:1	1.5:1	Better
Acid-test ratio	0.4:1	0.4:1	No change
Receivables turnover	32.6 times	38.7 times	Worse
Collection period	11 days	9 days	Worse
Inventory turnover	3.9 times	3.9 times	No change
Days sales in inventory	94 days	94 days	No change
Operating cycle	105 days	103 days	Worse

result, and well within the normal collection period. And while its inventory turnover ratio did not change between 2010 and 2011, it is taking a long time to sell its inventory, which could be problematic in future. Because Hometown Tires and More's receivables turnover ratio declined, its operating cycle—composed of both receivables and inventory—also declined in 2011.

In an intercompany comparison for 2011, as shown in Illustration 17-11, Hometown Tires and More's overall liquidity is worse than that of Canadian Tire. While its acid-test ratio, receivables turnover, and collection period are better than that of Canadian Tire, this is not as significant a factor in assessing its liquidity as is the management of its inventory. Hometown Tires and More's inventory turnover, days sales in inventory, and resulting operating cycle are worse than that of Canadian Tire.

ILLUSTRATION 17-11
Intercompany comparison of liquidity ratios

Liquidity Ratio	Hometown Tires and More	Canadian Tire	Comparison
Current ratio	1.6:1	1.7:1	Worse
Acid-test ratio	0.4:1	0.3:1	Better
Receivables turnover	32.6 times	13.8 times	Better
Collection period	11 days	26 days	Better
Inventory turnover	3.9 times	6.2 times	Worse
Days sales in inventory	94 days	59 days	Worse
Operating cycle	105 days	85 days	Worse

Summary of Liquidity Ratios

Illustration 17-12 summarizes the liquidity ratios we have used in this chapter, and throughout the textbook. In addition to the ratio formula and purpose, the desired direction (higher or lower) of the result is included.

ILLUSTRATION 17-12
Liquidity ratios

Liquidity Ratio	Formula	Purpose	Desired Result
Current ratio	$\frac{\text{Current assets}}{\text{Current liabilities}}$	Measures short-term debt-paying ability.	Higher
Acid-test	$\frac{\text{Cash + Short-term investments + Accounts receivable}}{\text{Current liabilities}}$	Measures immediate short-term debt-paying ability.	Higher
Receivables turnover	$\frac{\text{Net credit sales}}{\text{Average gross accounts receivable}}$	Measures liquidity of receivables.	Higher
Collection period	$\frac{\text{Days in year}}{\text{Receivables turnover}}$	Measures number of days receivables are outstanding.	Lower
Inventory turnover	$\frac{\text{Cost of goods sold}}{\text{Average inventory}}$	Measures liquidity of inventory.	Higher
Days sales in inventory	$\frac{\text{Days in year}}{\text{Inventory turnover}}$	Measures number of days inventory is on hand.	Lower
Operating cycle	Days sales in inventory + Collection period	Measures number of days to purchase inventory, sell it on account, and collect the cash.	Lower

To summarize, a higher result is generally considered to be better for the current, acid-test, receivables turnover, and inventory turnover ratios. For those ratios that use turnover ratios in their denominators—the collection period and days sales in inventory—as well as the operating cycle, which is the combination of both of these, a lower result is better. That is, you want to take fewer days to collect receivables and have fewer days of inventory on hand—a lower operating cycle—than the opposite situation.

Of course, there are exceptions. A current ratio can be artificially high at times because of higher balances of receivables and inventory included in current assets that are the result of slow-moving inventory or uncollectible receivables. This is why it is important never to conclude an assessment of liquidity based only on one ratio. In the case of the current ratio, it should always be interpreted along with the acid-test, receivables turnover, and inventory turnover ratios. Likewise, the acid-test ratio should always be interpreted along with the receivables turnover ratio.

BEFORE YOU GO ON...

DO IT

The following liquidity ratios are available for two fast food companies:

	Henny Penny	Chicken Licken
Current ratio	1.3:1	1.5:1
Acid-test ratio	1.0:1	0.8:1
Receivables turnover	52 times	73 times
Inventory turnover	40 times	26 times

(a) Calculate the collection period, days sales in inventory, and operating cycle for each company.
(b) Indicate which company—Henny Penny or Chicken Licken—has the better result for each of the ratios provided above, in addition to the ratios you calculated in part (a).
(c) Overall, which of the two companies is more liquid? Explain.

Action Plan

- Review the formula for each ratio so you understand how it is calculated and how to interpret it.
- Remember that for liquidity ratios, a higher result is usually better except for the collection period, days sales in inventory, and operating cycle ratios.
- Review the impact of the receivables and inventory turnover ratios on the current ratio before concluding your analysis.
- Consider any industry factors that may affect your analysis.

SOLUTION

(a)

	Henny Penny	Chicken Licken
Collection period	365 ÷ 52 = 7 days	365 ÷ 73 = 5 days
Days sales in inventory	365 ÷ 40 times = 9 days	365 ÷ 26 = 14 days
Operating cycle	7 + 9 = 16 days	5 + 14 = 19 days

(b)

	Henny Penny	Chicken Licken	Comparison
Current ratio	1.3:1	1.5:1	Chicken Licken
Acid-test ratio	1.0:1	0.8:1	Henny Penny
Receivables turnover	52 times	73 times	Chicken Licken
Inventory turnover	40 times	26 times	Henny Penny
Collection period	7 days	5 days	Chicken Licken
Days sales in inventory	9 days	14 days	Henny Penny
Operating cycle	16 days	19 days	Henny Penny

(c) Henny Penny is the more liquid of the two companies. Although its receivables turnover is not as strong as that of Chicken Licken (52 times compared with 73 times), the collection period is still only 7 days, which is an excellent collection period by any standard. Of course, you wouldn't expect a fast food business to have many receivables anyway.

Henny Penny's inventory turnover, which is more important for a fast food business, is stronger than that of Chicken Licken. This slower inventory turnover may be artificially making Chicken Licken's current ratio look better than that of Henny Penny. This hunch is proven by the fact that although Chicken Licken has the (apparently) better current ratio, Henny Penny has the better acid-test ratio, which excludes the effect of inventory. In addition, Henny Penny has the better operating cycle of the two companies.

THE NAVIGATOR

Related exercise material: BE17–7, BE17–8, BE17–9, E17–6, and E17–7.

SOLVENCY RATIOS

STUDY OBJECTIVE 5

Identify and use ratios to analyze solvency.

Solvency ratios measure a company's ability to survive over a long period of time. Long-term creditors are interested in a company's long-term solvency, particularly its ability to pay interest as it comes due and to repay the face value of debt at maturity. Solvency ratios include debt to total assets, interest coverage, and free cash flow.

Debt to Total Assets

Debt to total assets measures the percentage of the total assets that is provided by creditors. It is calculated by dividing total liabilities (both current and long-term) by total assets. The higher the percentage of total debt to total assets, the greater the risk that the company may be unable to meet its maturing obligations. The lower the debt to total assets ratio, the more net assets there are to repay creditors if the company becomes insolvent. So, from a lender's point of view, a low ratio of debt to total assets is desirable.

Hometown Tires and More's 2011 and 2010 debt to total assets ratios and the 2011 debt to total assets ratio for Canadian Tire are shown below.

$\text{Debt to total assets} = \frac{\text{Total liabilities}}{\text{Total assets}}$		
Hometown Tires and More **2011** $\frac{\$737,700}{\$1,000,000} = 73.8\%$	Hometown Tires and More **2010** = 79.7%	Intracompany
	Canadian Tire **2011** = 64.3%	Intercompany

A ratio of 73.8% means that creditors have provided 73.8% of Hometown Tires and More's total assets. Although its ratio declined (improved) in 2011, Hometown Tires and More's debt to total assets ratio is higher (worse) than Canadian Tire's ratio of 64.3%.

Although Hometown Tires and More has a high debt position, a more relevant calculation is whether or not it can afford this level of debt. The debt to total assets ratio should never be interpreted without also looking at the interest coverage ratio, discussed in the next section. A company may have a low debt to total assets ratio but be unable to cover its interest obligations. Alternatively, a company may have a high debt to total assets ratio but be easily able to cover its interest.

Interest Coverage

The interest coverage ratio gives an indication of the company's ability to make its interest payments as they come due. It is calculated by dividing profit before interest expense and income tax expense by interest expense. Note that the interest coverage ratio uses profit before interest expense and income tax expense. This is often abbreviated as EBIT, which stands for earnings before interest and tax. The term "earnings" is used instead of "profit" in this phrase—both are commonly used and mean the same thing. EBIT represents the amount that is considered to be available to cover interest.

The 2011 and 2010 interest coverage ratios for Hometown Tires and More and 2011 interest coverage ratio for Canadian Tire are shown below.

$\text{Interest coverage} = \frac{\text{Profit + Interest expense + Income tax expense}}{\text{Interest expense}}$		
Hometown Tires and More **2011** $\frac{\$93,600 + \$27,000 + \$23,400}{\$27,000} = 5.3 \text{ times}$	Hometown Tires and More **2010** = 5.3 times	Intracompany
	Canadian Tire **2011** = 5.1 times	Intercompany

Despite Hometown Tires and More's high debt to total assets ratio, it is able to cover its interest payments. Its profit before interest and income tax was 5.3 times the amount needed for interest expense in 2011 and 2010. Hometown Tires and More's interest coverage remained unchanged in 2011, despite the improvement in its debt to total assets ratio. It is interesting to note that, although Hometown Tires and More's debt to total assets ratio was worse than that of Canadian Tire, its interest coverage ratio is slightly better than Canadian Tire's coverage ratio of 5.1 times. Nonetheless, both companies are well equipped to handle their interest payments, with coverage ratios in excess of 5 times.

Free Cash Flow

One indication of a company's solvency, as well as of its ability to expand operations, repay debt, or pay dividends, is the amount of excess cash it generates after paying to maintain its current productive capacity. This amount is referred to as free cash flow.

Hometown Tires and More's cash flow statement was not included in the illustrations shown earlier in the chapter. For your information and for the purpose of the calculation below, its cash provided by operating activities for the year ended December 31, 2011, was $122,800 and its cash used by investing activities was $40,000 for the same period.

The 2011 and 2010 free cash flow amounts for Hometown Tires and More and 2011 free cash flow for Canadian Tire are shown below.

Free cash flow = Cash provided (used) by operating activities − Cash used (provided) by investing activities		
Hometown Tires and More **2011** $122,800 − $40,000 = $82,800	Hometown Tires and More **2010** = $100,000	Intracompany
	Canadian Tire **2011** = $244.1 million	Intercompany

Hometown Tires and More has $82,800 of "free" cash to invest in additional property, plant, and equipment; repay debt; and/or pay dividends. This is less than the $100,000 it had available in 2010. Canadian Tire reported a larger amount of free cash in 2011. It generated $244.1 million more from its operating activities than it spent on investing activities. However, as noted earlier, it is hard to make a meaningful comparison of absolute dollar amounts for two companies of such different sizes.

Solvency Conclusion

In an intracompany comparison for the years 2011 and 2010, as shown in Illustration 17-13, Hometown Tires and More's solvency generally improved in 2011, as its debt to total assets ratio improved and its interest coverage ratio remained unchanged. Its free cash flow declined.

ILLUSTRATION 17-13
Intracompany comparison of solvency ratios

HOMETOWN TIRES AND MORE			
Solvency Ratio	**2011**	**2010**	**Comparison**
Debt to total assets	73.8%	79.7%	Better
Interest coverage	5.3 times	5.3 times	No change
Free cash flow	$82,800	$100,000	Worse

Despite an improvement in solvency within Hometown Tires and More, in an intercompany comparison shown in Illustration 17-14, its solvency was found to be generally worse than that of Canadian Tire in 2011. Despite having a slightly higher interest coverage ratio, it has a much larger proportion of debt to assets and lower free cash flow.

ILLUSTRATION 17-14
Intercompany comparison of solvency ratios

Solvency Ratio	Hometown Tires and More	Canadian Tire	Comparison
Debt to total assets	73.8%	64.3%	Worse
Interest coverage	5.3 times	5.1 times	Better
Free cash flow	$82,800	$244,100,000	Worse

It is important to distinguish between Hometown Tires and More and Canadian Tire in this analysis, as they are very different types of companies. Hometown Tires and More, as a small regional company, relies mainly on debt for its financing and has to generate enough profit to cover its interest payments. In contrast, Canadian Tire, a large national company, relies more on equity for its financing needs.

Summary of Solvency Ratios

Illustration 17-15 summarizes the solvency ratios we have used in this chapter, and throughout the textbook.

ILLUSTRATION 17-15
Solvency ratios

Solvency Ratio	Formula	Purpose	Desired Result
Debt to total assets	$\frac{\text{Total liabilities}}{\text{Total assets}}$	Measures percentage of total assets provided by creditors.	Lower
Interest coverage	$\frac{\text{Profit + Interest expense + Income tax expense (EBIT)}}{\text{Interest expense}}$	Measures ability to meet interest payments.	Higher
Free cash flow	Cash provided (used) by operating activities − Cash used (provided) by investing activities	Measures cash generated from operating activities that management can use after paying capital expenditures.	Higher

For the debt to total assets ratio, a lower result is generally considered to be better. Having less debt reduces a company's dependence on debt financing and offers more flexibility for future financing alternatives. For the interest coverage ratio and free cash flow measure, a higher result is better.

It is important to interpret the debt to total assets and interest coverage ratios together. For example, a company may have a high debt to total assets ratio and a high interest coverage ratio, which indicates that it is able to handle a high level of debt. Or, it may have a low debt to total assets ratio and a low interest coverage ratio, indicating it has difficulty in paying its interest even for a low amount of debt. Consequently, you should always interpret a company's solvency after considering the interrelationship of these two ratios.

BEFORE YOU GO ON...

DO IT

Selected information from the financial statements of the Home Affairs Corporation follows:

	2014	2013
Total assets	$1,000,000	$1,015,000
Total liabilities	737,000	809,000
Interest expense	32,000	32,500
Income tax expense	48,400	50,500
Profit	193,600	202,000

(a) Calculate the debt to total assets and interest coverage ratios for each year.
(b) Indicate whether each of the ratios you calculated in part (a) has improved or deteriorated in 2014, compared with 2013.
(c) Overall, has Home Affairs' solvency improved or deteriorated in 2014?

SOLUTION

(a) and (b)

	(a) 2014	(a) 2013	(b) Comparison
Debt to total assets	$\frac{\$737,700}{\$1,000,000} = 73.7\%$	$\frac{\$809,000}{\$1,015,000} = 79.7\%$	Better
Interest coverage	$\frac{\$193,600 + \$32,000 + \$48,400}{\$32,000}$ = 8.6 times	$\frac{\$202,000 + \$32,500 + \$50,500}{\$32,500}$ = 8.8 times	Worse

(c) Overall, Home Affairs' solvency has improved in 2012. The debt to total assets ratio has declined (improved) in 2012. While the interest coverage ratio declined (deteriorated) marginally between 2011 and 2012, the company still has a strong coverage ratio at 8.6 times. Taken together, this leads us to conclude that overall solvency has improved.

Related exercise material: BE17–10, BE17–11, BE17–12, E17–8, and E17–9.

Action Plan

- Review the formula for each ratio so you understand how it is calculated and how to interpret it.
- The debt to total assets ratio should always be interpreted together with the interest coverage ratio.
- Remember that for debt to total assets, a lower result is better. For other solvency ratios, a higher result is better.

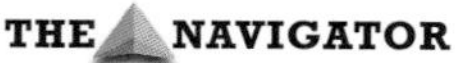

PROFITABILITY RATIOS

STUDY OBJECTIVE 6

Identify and use ratios to analyze profitability.

Profitability ratios measure a company's operating success for a specific period of time. A company's profit, or lack of it, affects its ability to obtain debt and equity financing, its liquidity position, and its growth. Investors and creditors are therefore interested in evaluating profitability. Profitability ratios include the gross profit margin, profit margin, asset turnover, return on assets, return on equity, earnings per share, price-earnings, and payout ratios.

Gross Profit Margin

The gross profit margin is determined by dividing gross profit (net sales less cost of goods sold) by net sales. This ratio indicates the relative relationship between net sales and cost of goods sold. Gross profit margins should be watched closely over time. If the gross profit margin is too high, the company may lose sales if its pricing is not competitive. If the gross profit margin is too low, the company may not have enough margin to cover its expenses.

Hometown Tires and More's gross profit margin figures for 2011 and 2010 and Canadian Tire's gross profit margin for 2011 are shown below.

$$\text{Gross profit margin} = \frac{\text{Gross profit}}{\text{Net sales}}$$

Hometown Tires and More **2011**		
$\frac{\$616,000}{\$1,997,000} = 30.8\%$	Hometown Tires and More **2010** = 32.5%	Intracompany
	Canadian Tire **2011** = 29.5%	Intercompany

Hometown Tires and More's gross profit margin for 2011 means that 30.8 cents of each dollar of its sales that year went to cover operating and other expenses and generate a profit. Hometown Tires and More's gross profit margin declined slightly, from 32.5% in 2010 to 30.8% in 2011.

Hometown Tires and More's gross profit margin is slightly higher than Canadian Tire's. This could be the result of several factors. It may be that Hometown Tires and More sells a different mix of merchandise than does Canadian Tire. In addition, Hometown Tires and More's prices may be higher in general not only because of increased costs, but also because the company offers a higher level of personal service.

Profit Margin

Profit margin is a measure of the percentage of each dollar of sales that results in profit. It is calculated by dividing profit by net sales. Hometown Tires and More's 2011 and 2010 profit margin figures and Canadian Tire's 2011 profit margin are shown below.

$$\text{Profit margin} = \frac{\text{Profit}}{\text{Net sales}}$$

Hometown Tires and More **2011**		
$\frac{\$93,600}{\$1,997,000} = 4.7\%$	Hometown Tires and More **2010** = 5.6%	Intracompany
	Canadian Tire **2011** = 4.5%	Intercompany

Hometown Tires and More's profit margin declined between 2010 and 2011, at 4.7% of net sales, primarily because of the loss due to the fair value adjustment of trading investments. The profit margin, although declining, is still above that of Canadian Tire.

Asset Turnover

Asset turnover measures how efficiently a company uses its assets to generate sales. It is determined by dividing net sales by average total assets. The resulting number shows the dollars of sales produced by each dollar of assets.

The 2011 and 2010 asset turnover ratios for Hometown Tires and More and 2011 asset turnover ratio for Canadian Tire are shown below.

$\text{Asset turnover} = \frac{\text{Net sales}}{\text{Average total assets}}$		
Hometown Tires and More **2011** $\frac{\$1,997,000}{(\$1,000,000 + \$1,015,000) \div 2} = 2.0$ times	Hometown Tires and More **2010** = 1.7 times	Intracompany
	Canadian Tire **2011** = 0.9 times	Intercompany

In 2011, Hometown Tires and More generated $2 of sales for each dollar it had invested in assets. This ratio improved from 2010, when its asset turnover was 1.7 times, or $1.70 of sales for each dollar of assets. Its 2011 asset turnover is also much higher than that of Canadian Tire. Its assets may be newer and more efficient than Canadian Tire's.

Return on Assets

An overall measure of profitability is return on assets. This ratio is calculated by dividing profit by average total assets. Hometown Tires and More's return on assets figures for 2011 and 2010 and Canadian Tire's return on assets for 2011 are shown below.

$\text{Return on assets} = \frac{\text{Profit}}{\text{Average total assets}}$		
Hometown Tires and More **2011** $\frac{\$93,600}{(\$1,000,000 + \$1,015,000) \div 2} = 9.3\%$	Hometown Tires and More **2010** = 9.7%	Intracompany
	Canadian Tire **2011** = 4.0%	Intercompany

Hometown Tires and More's return on assets declined (worsened) from 2010 to 2011. Still, its 2011 return of 9.3% is more than double that of Canadian Tire. Although the percentage is high, it must be analyzed in perspective. Hometown Tires and More's assets have been decreasing and profit is being compared with a relatively small asset base. Consequently, it results in a higher percentage proportionately.

Return on Equity

A popular measure of profitability is the return on equity ratio. This ratio shows how many dollars of profit were earned for each dollar invested by the shareholders. It is calculated by dividing profit by average total shareholders' equity.

Alternative terminology *Return on equity* is also known as *return on investment.*

Although we calculate this ratio using total shareholders' equity below, it can also be calculated using only the common shareholders' equity if there is more than one class of shares. In such cases, the numerator, profit, is reduced by any preferred dividends to determine the profit available for common shareholders. The denominator, average total shareholders' equity, is reduced by any share capital belonging to the preferred shareholders to determine average common shareholders' equity. You will recall that Hometown Tires and More has only one class of share capital—common shares—so it has no preferred shares or preferred dividends.

The return on equity figures for Hometown Tires and More for 2011 and 2010 and return on equity for Canadian Tire for 2011 are shown below.

$\text{Return on equity} = \frac{\text{Profit}}{\text{Average shareholders' equity}}$		
Hometown Tires and More **2011** $\frac{\$93,600}{(\$262,300 + \$206,500) \div 2} = 39.9\%$	Hometown Tires and More **2010** = 50.9%	Intracompany
	Canadian Tire **2011** = 11.1%	Intercompany

Although it declined (worsened) in 2011, Hometown Tires and More's return on equity is unusually high at 39.9%. The return on equity figure for Canadian Tire is much lower at 11.1%.

Note that Hometown Tires and More's 2011 return on equity of 39.9% is much higher than its return on assets of 9.3%. The reason is that Hometown Tires and More has made effective use of financial leverage. You will recall that we first learned about financial leverage in Chapter 15. Financial leverage is said to be positive if a company is able to earn a higher return on equity by using borrowed money in its operations than it has to pay on the borrowed money. Use of financial leverage has enabled Hometown Tires and More to use money supplied by creditors to increase its return to the shareholders. Recall that Hometown Tires and More has proportionately more debt than Canadian Tire. Given that it is able to create positive financial leverage on its borrowings, it is not surprising that Hometown Tires and More's return on equity is higher than Canadian Tire's.

Earnings per Share (EPS)

Earnings per share is a measure of the profit earned on each common share. Shareholders usually think in terms of the number of shares they own or plan to buy or sell. Reducing profit to a per-share basis gives a useful measure of profitability. This measure is widely used and reported. Because of the importance of the earnings per share ratio, publicly traded companies are required to present it directly on the income statement. As we mentioned earlier in this textbook, private companies using ASPE are not required to report earnings per share.

Earnings per share is calculated by dividing the profit available to common shareholders (profit less preferred dividends) by the weighted average number of common shares. Hometown Tires and More's profit was reported in Illustration 17-5 and its number of common shares was reported in Illustration 17-4. You will recall that Hometown Tires and More does not have any preferred shares, so there are no preferred dividends to consider in this calculation. There has been no change in the number of common shares over the past three years; consequently, the weighted average number of shares is the same as the issued number—300,000.

The earnings per share figures for Hometown Tires and More for 2011 and 2010 and earnings per share for Canadian Tire for 2011 are shown below.

$\text{Earnings per share} = \frac{\text{Profit} - \text{Preferred dividends}}{\text{Weighted average number of common shares}}$		
Hometown Tires and More **2011** $\frac{\$93,600 - \$0}{300,000} = \$0.31$	Hometown Tires and More **2010** = $0.34	Intracompany
	Canadian Tire **2011** = $5.73	Intercompany

Hometown Tires and More's earnings per share declined by $0.03 per share ($0.34 − $0.31) in 2011. Comparisons with Canadian Tire are not meaningful, because of the large differences in the number of shares issued by companies for different purposes. The only meaningful EPS comparison is an intra-company one.

Price-Earnings (PE) Ratio

The price-earnings (PE) ratio is an often-quoted measure of the ratio of the market price of each common share to the earnings per share. The price-earnings ratio reflects investors' assessments of a company's future profitability. It is calculated by dividing the market price per share by earnings per share. The current market price of Hometown Tires and More's shares is $1.40/share. Earnings per share were calculated above.

The price-earnings ratios for Hometown Tires and More for 2011 and 2010 and the price-earnings ratio for Canadian Tire for 2011 are shown below.

$\text{Price-earnings ratio} = \frac{\text{Market price per share}}{\text{Earnings per share}}$		
Hometown Tires and More **2011** $\frac{\$1.40}{\$0.31} = 4.5$ times	Hometown Tires and More **2010** = 3.5 times	Intracompany
	Canadian Tire **2011** = 12.7 times	Intercompany

In 2011, Hometown Tires and More's shares were valued at 4.5 times its earnings. The earnings per share, although declining, are still strong and the price of the shares has increased, indicating investors believe the company has expectations of future increases in profitability. Canadian Tire's 2011 price-earnings ratio is 12.7 times, which is much higher than Hometown Tires and More's ratio of 4.5 times.

In general, a higher price-earnings ratio means that investors favour the company. They are willing to pay more for the shares because they believe the company has good prospects for long-term growth and profit in the future.

Payout Ratio

The payout ratio measures the percentage of profit distributed as cash dividends. It is calculated by dividing cash dividends by profit. Hometown Tires and More paid $37,800 in dividends in 2011. Its profit was reported earlier in Illustration 17-5.

The 2011 and 2010 payout ratios for Hometown Tires and More and 2011 payout ratio for Canadian Tire are shown below.

$$\text{Payout ratio} = \frac{\text{Cash dividends}}{\text{Profit}}$$

Hometown Tires and More **2011**		
$\frac{\$37,800}{\$93,600} = 40.4\%$	Hometown Tires and More **2010** = 35.3%	Intracompany
	Canadian Tire **2011** = 19.6%	Intercompany

Hometown Tires and More's 2011 payout ratio of 40.4% increased over its 2010 payout ratio and is more than double the payout ratio of Canadian Tire. Many companies with stable earnings have high payout ratios. For example, BCE Inc. recently had a payout ratio in excess of 70%. Companies that are expanding rapidly normally have low, or no, payout ratios. BlackBerry, for example, had a zero payout ratio.

Profitability Conclusion

In an intracompany comparison, as shown in Illustration 17-16, Hometown Tires and More's overall profitability declined between 2010 and 2011. All of its profitability measures declined except for its asset turnover, price-earnings, and payout ratios.

ILLUSTRATION 17-16
Intracompany comparison of profitability ratios

HOMETOWN TIRES AND MORE			
Profitability Ratio	**2011**	**2010**	**Comparison**
Gross profit margin	30.8%	32.5%	Worse
Profit margin	4.7%	5.6%	Worse
Asset turnover	2.0 times	1.7 times	Better
Return on assets	9.3%	9.7%	Worse
Return on equity	39.9%	50.9%	Worse
Earnings per share	$0.31	$0.34	Worse
Price-earnings ratio	4.5 times	3.5 times	Better
Payout ratio	40.4%	35.3%	Better

In an intercompany comparison, as shown in Illustration 17-17, Hometown Tires and More's overall profitability is better than that of Canadian Tire on all but one measure. Despite its lower profitability performance, investors are favouring Canadian Tire rather than Hometown Tires and More, as evidenced by the price-earnings ratio.

ILLUSTRATION 17-17
Intercompany comparison of profitability ratios

Profitability Ratio	Hometown Tires and More	Canadian Tire	Comparison
Gross profit margin	30.8%	29.5%	Better
Profit margin	4.7%	4.5%	Better
Asset turnover	2.0 times	0.9 times	Better
Return on assets	9.3%	4.0%	Better
Return on equity	39.9%	11.1%	Better
Earnings per share	$0.31	$5.73	n/a
Price-earnings ratio	4.5 times	12.7 times	Worse
Payout ratio	40.4%	19.6%	Better

Summary of Profitability Ratios

Illustration 17-18 summarizes the profitability ratios we have used in this chapter, and throughout the textbook.

ILLUSTRATION 17-18
Profitability ratios

Profitability Ratio	Formula	Purpose	Desired Result
Gross profit margin	$\frac{\text{Gross profit}}{\text{Net sales}}$	Measures margin between selling price and cost of goods sold.	Higher
Profit margin	$\frac{\text{Profit}}{\text{Net sales}}$	Measures amount of profit generated by each dollar of sales.	Higher
Asset turnover	$\frac{\text{Net sales}}{\text{Average total assets}}$	Measures how efficiently assets are used to generate sales.	Higher
Return on assets	$\frac{\text{Profit}}{\text{Average total assets}}$	Measures overall profitability of assets.	Higher
Return on equity	$\frac{\text{Profit}}{\text{Average shareholders' equity}}$	Measures profitability of shareholders' investment.	Higher
Earnings per share	$\frac{\text{Profit} - \text{Preferred dividends}}{\text{Weighted average number of common shares}}$	Measures amount of profit earned on each common share.	Higher
Price-earnings ratio	$\frac{\text{Market price per share}}{\text{Earnings per share}}$	Measures relationship between market price per share and earnings per share.	Higher
Payout ratio	$\frac{\text{Cash dividends}}{\text{Profit}}$	Measures percentage of profit distributed as cash dividends.	Higher

For the profitability ratios shown in Illustration 17-18, a higher result is generally considered to be better. However, there are some user-related considerations with respect to the price-earnings and payout ratios that must be understood. A higher price-earnings ratio generally means that investors favour that company and have high expectations of future profitability. However, some investors avoid shares with high PE ratios in the belief that they are overpriced, so not everyone prefers a high PE ratio.

Investors interested in purchasing a company's shares for income purposes (in the form of a dividend) are interested in companies with a high payout ratio. Investors more interested in purchasing a company's shares for growth purposes (for the share price's appreciation) are interested in a low payout ratio. They would prefer to see the company retain its profit rather than pay it out.

We have shown liquidity, solvency, and profitability ratios in separate sections in this chapter. However, it is important to recognize that financial statement analysis should not focus on one section in isolation from the others. Liquidity, solvency, and profitability are closely interrelated in most companies. For example, a company's profitability is affected by the availability of financing and short-term liquidity. Similarly, a company's solvency not only requires satisfactory liquidity but is also affected by its profitability.

It is also important to recognize that the ratios shown in Illustrations 17-12, 17-15, and 17-18 are only examples of commonly used ratios. You will find more examples as you learn more about financial analysis.

ACCOUNTING IN ACTION
ALL ABOUT YOU INSIGHT

More Canadians are investing in the stock market largely because of the ease of trading stocks on-line. Traders range from students like you tracking their investments to seniors making adjustments to their retirement savings. Everybody wants to buy and sell stocks just at the right time. How do investors predict what stock prices will do and when to buy and sell stock?

Two early pioneers in providing investment advice to the masses were Tom and David Gardner, brothers who created an on-line investor service called The Motley Fool. Tom and David view themselves as twenty-first-century "fools," revealing the "truths" of the stock markets to small investors. Its website offers Fool followers stock quotes, company research reports, personal finance information, news, on-line seminars, and message boards. The Motley Fool has grown substantially since its inception in 1993, offering even the most inexperienced investor the basic advice needed to master his or her own financial affairs.

Critics of on-line investor services, and in particular message boards, contend that they can exacerbate the rumour mill. They suggest that, because of the excitement created by some message board postings, share prices can get bid up to unreasonable levels. One potentially troubling aspect of message boards is that participants on a board rarely give their real identities—instead using aliases. Consequently, there is little to stop people from putting misinformation on the board to influence a share's price in the direction they desire.

Sources: Motley Fool website; Don E. Giacomino and Michael D. Akers, "Examining an Online Investment Research Service: The Motley Fool," *Journal of Business and Economics Research*, volume 9, number 1, January 2011; Stacy Forster, "Motley Fool to 'Educate, Amuse, Enrich' . . . and Advise Investors," *The Wall Street Journal Online*, September 6, 2001.

Suppose you are thinking about investing in shares of Tim Hortons. You scanned a variety of investor websites and found messages posted by two different investors. One says it's time to buy Tim Hortons shares; the other says it isn't. How should you decide whether to buy the shares or not?

BEFORE YOU GO ON...

DO IT

Selected information from the financial statements of two competitor companies follows:

	Marauder Corporation	Maverick Limited
Total assets, beginning of year	$388,000	$372,000
Total assets, end of year	434,000	536,000
Total shareholders' equity, beginning of year	269,000	296,000
Total shareholders' equity, end of year	294,000	344,000
Net sales	660,000	780,000
Gross profit	175,000	248,000
Profit	68,000	105,000

(a) For each company, calculate the following ratios: gross profit margin, profit margin, asset turnover, return on assets, and return on equity.

(b) Indicate which company—Marauder or Maverick—has the better result for each of the ratios you calculated in part (a).

(c) Overall, which of the two companies is more profitable? Explain.

SOLUTION

(a)

	Marauder	Maverick
Gross profit margin	$\frac{\$175,000}{\$660,000} = 26.5\%$	$\frac{\$248,000}{\$780,000} = 31.8\%$
Profit margin	$\frac{\$68,000}{\$660,000} = 10.3\%$	$\frac{\$105,000}{\$780,000} = 13.5\%$
Asset turnover	$\frac{\$660,000}{(\$388,000 + \$434,000) \div 2} = 1.6 \text{ times}$	$\frac{\$780,000}{(\$372,000 + \$536,000) \div 2} = 1.7 \text{ times}$
Return on assets	$\frac{\$68,000}{(\$388,000 + \$434,000) \div 2} = 16.5\%$	$\frac{\$105,000}{(\$372,000 + \$536,000) \div 2} = 23.1\%$
Return on equity	$\frac{\$68,000}{(\$269,000 + \$294,000) \div 2} = 24.2\%$	$\frac{\$105,000}{(\$296,000 + \$344,000) \div 2} = 32.8\%$

Action Plan

- Review the formula for each ratio so you understand how it is calculated and how to interpret it.
- Don't forget to average the balance sheet figures [(beginning of period + end of period) ÷ 2] when comparing them with a period figure (for example, net sales and profit).
- Remember that for profitability ratios, a higher result is usually better.

BEFORE YOU GO ON... continued on next page

BEFORE YOU GO ON...
continued from previous page

(b)

	Marauder	Maverick	Stronger Result
Gross profit margin	26.5%	31.8%	Maverick
Profit margin	10.3%	13.5%	Maverick
Asset turnover	1.6 times	1.7 times	Maverick
Return on assets	16.5%	23.1%	Maverick
Return on equity	24.2%	32.8%	Maverick

(c) Maverick Limited is more profitable than Marauder Corporation on all profitability ratios.

THE NAVIGATOR

Related exercise material: BE17–13, BE17–14, BE17–15, BE17–16, BE17–17, E17–10, E17–11, E17–12, E17–13, E17–14, and E17–15.

LIMITATIONS OF FINANCIAL STATEMENT ANALYSIS

STUDY OBJECTIVE 7

Recognize the limitations of financial statement analysis.

Business decisions are frequently made by using one or more of the analytical tools illustrated in this chapter. But you should be aware of the limitations of these tools and of the financial statements they are based on.

ALTERNATIVE ACCOUNTING POLICIES

There are a wide variety of different accounting policies and practices that companies can use. For example, companies may use different inventory cost determination methods (specific identification, FIFO, or average) or different depreciation methods (straight-line, diminishing-balance, or units-of-production) depending on the pattern of the revenues (economic benefits) their assets produce. Different methods can result in differing financial positions and performance, which will reduce comparability.

For example, Canadian Tire uses the diminishing-balance method of depreciation for much of its property, plant, and equipment. Hometown Tires and More uses the straight-line method of depreciation. Consequently, profit and total assets could be different—depending on the amount of property, plant, and equipment and at what point in its useful life it is—simply because of the use of different depreciation methods. This would affect a number of solvency and profitability ratios.

Recall, however, that although depreciation expense and the carrying amount of property, plant, and equipment may be different in one or more periods because of the choice of depreciation methods, in total, over the life of the assets, there is no difference. We call differences created from alternative accounting policies "artificial" or timing differences. Although it is possible to detect differences in accounting policies by reading the notes to the financial statements, adjusting the financial data to compensate for the use of different policies can be difficult for the average user. In real life, analysts spend a great deal of time adjusting financial statement data for these types of differences in order to improve the comparability of the ratios.

Intercompany comparability may also be hindered by differing accounting policy options available for private companies. While Hometown Tires and More is a publicly traded company using IFRS, it may have competitors that are private companies. You will recall that private companies have the choice of adopting IFRS or Accounting Standards for Private Enterprises. If a private company has chosen not to adopt IFRS, which is the most likely scenario, further complications can arise in trying to compare a private company with a public company for certain accounting policies.

Intracompany comparability can be affected by the use of different accounting policies over different periods of time. As has been discussed throughout this text, publicly traded companies such as Canadian Tire adopted IFRS effective January 1, 2011. Although results for the 2010 fiscal year were required to be restated using IFRS for comparability purposes, prior years may not have been converted from Canadian generally accepted accounting principles into IFRS. In fact, Canadian Tire notes in the 10-year summary of financial information included in its annual report that results for the years 2002 through 2009 have *not* been converted to IFRS. Consequently, comparing ratios based on IFRS figures with those based on pre-changeover Canadian GAAP may result in misleading trends.

COMPREHENSIVE INCOME

Most financial analysis ratios exclude other comprehensive income. For example, profitability ratios generally use data from the income statement and not the statement of comprehensive income, which includes both profit and other comprehensive income. In fact, there are no standard ratio formulas incorporating comprehensive income.

Nonetheless, it is important to review the amount and source of other comprehensive income in any financial analysis. For example, Canadian Tire reported a profit of $467 million for the year ended December 31, 2011. During the same year, it reported other comprehensive income of $29.1 million, which resulted in total comprehensive income of $496.1 million ($467.0 + $29.1). Canadian Tire's profit margin, illustrated earlier in this chapter, was 4.5%. However, if a profit margin was calculated using total comprehensive income rather than just profit, it would have been 4.8% instead of 4.5%.

This difference is not significant enough to affect decision-making. However, in cases where other comprehensive income is significant, and depending on the source of the income, some analysts will adjust profitability ratios to incorporate the effect of total comprehensive income. Of course you will recall from past chapters that private companies following ASPE do not report comprehensive income, so this limitation would apply only to public and private companies following IFRS.

QUALITY OF INFORMATION

In evaluating a company's financial performance, the quality of the information provided is extremely important. A company that has a high quality index includes full and transparent information that will not confuse or mislead users of the financial statements. As we discussed in our feature story, financial statements for companies like Canadian Tire, with full and transparent disclosure practices, have a high quality of information value. Other companies may limit the information they disclose. In such cases, the quality of the information will decrease.

Fortunately, the chief executive officer and chief financial officer of a publicly traded company must ensure, and personally declare, that the reported financial information is accurate, relevant, and understandable. In addition, audit committees are held responsible for reviewing the quality of the underlying estimates, accounting policies, and judgements involved in the preparation of the financial statements.

A strong corporate governance process, including an active board of directors and audit committee, is essential to ensuring the quality of information. Canadian Tire has received commendations from the judges in the annual Corporate Reporting Awards program mentioned in our chapter-opening feature story for its corporate governance disclosure. According to the judges, "The expectations and responsibilities of directors are clearly outlined, well organized and easy-to-read in the corporate governance disclosures."

ECONOMIC FACTORS

You cannot properly interpret a financial analysis without also considering the economic circumstances in which a company operates. Economic measures such as the rate of interest, unemployment, and changes in demand and supply can have a significant impact on a company's performance.

For example, in 2011 we saw many companies restructure or downsize their operations. Others closed or were bought by other companies; and still others were evaluating their options to operate effectively during what has been termed an "economic slump." During times like these, horizontal analyses and ratios compared across years can lose much of their relevance. When losses result in negative numbers, it is difficult to calculate percentages and ratios, much less interpret them. Vertical analyses become more useful in such times. If a company has losses, they must be assessed based on the factors driving the loss in the current period. Less attention should be paid to comparing the losses with results from prior periods.

One must use this information, along with non-financial information, to try to assess what changes relate to the economic situation and what changes relate to factors that management can, or should be able to, control. For example, have operating expenses increased faster than revenues? Why? Are consumers not spending? Are prices too high? Have expenses not been adequately controlled or adjusted for the current marketplace? Particular attention must be paid to the company's results compared with those of its competitors.

BEFORE YOU GO ON...

DO IT

HSBC Bank Canada reported the following selected information (in millions) for the year ended December 31, 2011:

Total revenue	$3,250
Profit	704
Other comprehensive income	203
Total comprehensive income	907

Action Plan

- Recall the formula for profit margin: Profit ÷ Net sales (or Revenue). Substitute total comprehensive income instead of profit to determine the impact of other comprehensive income on profitability.

BEFORE YOU GO ON... continued on next page

BEFORE YOU GO ON...
continued from previous page

- To determine the significance of other comprehensive income, compare the ratios with and without other comprehensive income and assess whether the change in the ratio is significant enough to affect decision-making.

(a) Calculate the profit margin using (1) profit as the numerator, and (2) total comprehensive income as the numerator.
(b) Should other comprehensive income be considered a significant factor in the analysis of HSBC Bank's profitability?

SOLUTION

(a)

($ in millions)	(1)	(2)
Profit margin	$\frac{\$704}{\$3,250} = 21.7\ \%$	$\frac{\$907}{\$3,250} = 27.9\ \%$

(b) The two ratios differ by 28.6% [(27.9% − 21.7%) ÷ 21.7%]. The inclusion of other comprehensive income in the calculation of the profitability ratios is likely significant enough to make a difference in a user's decision-making.

Related exercise material: BE17–18 and E17–16.

Comparing IFRS and ASPE

Key Differences	International Financial Reporting Standards (IFRS)	Accounting Standards for Private Enterprises (ASPE)
Earnings per share	Must be calculated and reported on the face of the income statement or statement of comprehensive income.	Earnings per share are not required to be reported.
Differences in accounting policy	Depending on the extent and significance of differences in accounting policies, comparisons may be difficult if a publicly traded company is compared with a private company using ASPE.	Depending on the extent and significance of differences in accounting policies, comparisons may be difficult if a private company using ASPE is compared with a public or private company using IFRS.
Comprehensive income	If other comprehensive income is significant, selected profitability ratios should be recalculated using total comprehensive income rather than profit.	Comprehensive income is not reported.

THE NAVIGATOR

DEMONSTRATION PROBLEM

Selected liquidity, solvency, and profitability ratios follow for two companies for a recent year:

	Kicking Horse	La Biche
Liquidity		
Current ratio	2.2:1	1.8:1
Collection period	28 days	20 days
Days sales in inventory	66 days	58 days
Solvency		
Debt to total assets	44.2%	44.4%
Interest coverage	9.1 times	10.2 times
Profitability		
Gross profit margin	37.1%	39.5%
Profit margin	8.8%	16.3%
Asset turnover	0.1 times	0.1 times
Return on assets	0.9%	1.6%
Return on equity	1.6%	2.9%

Action Plan

- Remember that for liquidity ratios, a higher result is usually better unless a ratio is the inverse of an original ratio (for example, collection period that uses the receivables turnover ratio in the denominator), in which case a lower result is better.

Instructions

(a) For each of the above ratios, identify which company, Kicking Horse (KH) or La Biche (LB), has the stronger result.
(b) Which company is more liquid? Explain.
(c) Which company is more solvent? Explain.
(d) Which company is more profitable? Explain.

DEMONSTRATION PROBLEM continued on next page

DEMONSTRATION PROBLEM continued from previous page

SOLUTION TO DEMONSTRATION PROBLEM

(a)

	Stronger Result		Stronger Result
Current ratio	KH	Gross profit margin	LB
Collection period	LB	Profit margin	LB
Days sales in inventory	LB	Asset turnover	No difference
Debt to total assets	KH	Return on assets	LB
Interest coverage	LB	Return on equity	LB

(b) La Biche is more liquid than Kicking Horse. Although Kicking Horse appears to have a stronger current ratio than La Biche, it is slower at collecting its receivables and selling its inventory. Regardless, it should be noted that both companies still have good collection periods (less than 30 days). Still, La Biche's operating cycle is only 78 days (20 + 58) compared with Kicking Horse's 94 days (28 + 66).

(c) La Biche is more solvent than Kicking Horse. Although its debt to total assets ratio is marginally higher (worse) than that of Kicking Horse, its interest coverage ratio is also higher (better), indicating its ability to handle its debt.

(d) La Biche is more profitable than Kicking Horse on all profitability measures except for asset turnover, which is the same for both companies.

- The current ratio should always be interpreted together with the receivables turnover/collection period and inventory turnover/days sales in inventory ratios to ensure that the current ratio has not been artificially inflated by slow-moving receivables or inventory.
- The debt to total assets ratio, for which a lower result is usually better, should always be interpreted together with the interest coverage ratio, for which a higher result is usually better.
- Remember that for profitability ratios, a higher result is usually better.

THE NAVIGATOR

Summary of Study Objectives

1. ***Identify the need for, and tools of, financial statement analysis.*** Users of financial statements make comparisons in order to evaluate a company's past, current, and future performance and position. There are two commonly used bases of comparison: intracompany (within a company) and intercompany (between companies). The tools of financial analysis include horizontal, vertical, and ratio analysis.

2. ***Explain and apply horizontal analysis.*** Horizontal analysis is a technique for evaluating a series of data, such as line items in a company's financial statements, by expressing them as percentage increases or decreases over two or more periods of time. The horizontal percentage of a base-period amount is calculated by dividing the amount for the specific period under analysis by a base-period amount. This percentage calculation normally covers multiple periods. The horizontal percentage change for a period is calculated by dividing the dollar amount of the change between the specific period under analysis and the prior period by the prior-period amount. This percentage calculation normally covers two periods only.

3. ***Explain and apply vertical analysis.*** Vertical analysis is a technique for evaluating data within one period by expressing each item in a financial statement as a percentage of a relevant total (base amount) in the same financial statement. The vertical percentage of a base-period amount is calculated by dividing the financial statement amount under analysis by the base amount for that particular financial statement, which is usually total assets for the balance sheet and revenues or net sales for the income statement.

4. ***Identify and use ratios to analyze liquidity.*** Liquidity ratios include the current ratio, acid-test ratio, receivables turnover, collection period, inventory turnover, days sales in inventory, and operating cycle. The formula, purpose, and desired result for each liquidity ratio are presented in Illustration 17-12.

5. ***Identify and use ratios to analyze solvency.*** Solvency ratios include debt to total assets, interest coverage, and free cash flow. The formula, purpose, and desired result for each solvency ratio are presented in Illustration 17-15.

6. ***Identify and use ratios to analyze profitability.*** Profitability ratios include the gross profit margin, profit margin, asset turnover, return on assets, return on equity, earnings per share, price-earnings, and payout ratios. The formula, purpose, and desired result for each profitability ratio are presented in Illustration 17-18.

7. ***Recognize the limitations of financial statement analysis.*** The usefulness of analytical tools can be limited by (1) the use of alternative accounting policies, (2) significant amounts of other comprehensive income, (3) the quality of the information provided, and (4) economic factors.

THE NAVIGATOR

Glossary

Horizontal analysis A technique for evaluating a series of financial statement data over multiple periods of time to determine the percentage increase or decrease that has taken place. Also known as trend analysis. (p. 734)

Horizontal percentage change for period A percentage measuring the change from one period to the next period. It is calculated by dividing the dollar amount of the change between the specific period under analysis and the prior period by the prior-period amount. (p. 735)

Horizontal percentage of base-period amount A percentage measuring the change since a base period. It is calculated by dividing the amount for the specific period under analysis by the base-period amount. (p. 734)

Liquidity ratios Measures of a company's short-term ability to pay its maturing obligations and to meet unexpected needs for cash. (p. 743)

Profitability ratios Measures of a company's operating success for a specific period of time. (p. 752)

Ratio analysis A technique for evaluating financial statements that expresses the relationship between selected financial statement data. (p. 742)

Solvency ratios Measures of a company's ability to survive over a long period of time. (p. 748)

Vertical analysis A technique for evaluating financial statement data within a period. Each item in a financial statement is expressed as a percentage of a total or base amount. Total assets is usually the base amount used in the balance sheet; total revenues or net sales in the income statement. Also known as common size analysis. (p. 738)

Vertical percentage of base amount A percentage measuring the proportion of an amount in a financial statement within a period. It is calculated by dividing the financial statement amount under analysis by the base amount for that particular financial statement and period of time. (p. 738)

THE NAVIGATOR

Self-Study Questions

Answers are at the end of the chapter.

(SO 1) K 1. A comparison of operating expenses for a company over a five-year period is an example of which of the following comparative bases and analysis tools?
(a) Intracompany, horizontal analysis
(b) Intracompany, vertical analysis
(c) Intercompany, horizontal analysis
(d) Intercompany, vertical analysis

(SO 2) AP 2. Rankin Corporation reported net sales of $300,000, $330,000, and $360,000 in the years 2012, 2013, and 2014, respectively. If 2012 is the base year, what is the horizontal percentage of the base-year amount for 2014?
(a) 83%
(c) 110%
(b) 92%
(d) 120%

(SO 2) AP 3. As indicated in Question 2 above, Rankin Corporation reported net sales of $300,000, $330,000, and $360,000 in the years 2012, 2013, and 2014, respectively. What is the horizontal percentage change for each year?
(a) 110% from 2012 to 2013 and 109% from 2013 to 2014
(b) 110% from 2012 to 2013 and 120% from 2013 to 2014
(c) 10% from 2012 to 2013 and 9% from 2013 to 2014
(d) 10% from 2012 to 2013 and 20% from 2013 to 2014

(SO 3) C 4. The following schedule shows what type of analysis?

	2014		2013	
	Amount	Percentage	Amount	Percentage
Current assets	$200,000	25%	$175,000	21%
Property, plant, and equipment	600,000	75%	650,000	79%
Total assets	$800,000	100%	$825,000	100%

(a) Horizontal analysis
(b) Ratio analysis
(c) Vertical analysis
(d) Intercompany comparison

(SO 3) K 5. In a vertical analysis, the base amount for depreciation expense is generally:
(a) net sales.
(b) depreciation expense in a previous year.
(c) total assets.
(d) total property, plant, and equipment.

Use the following selected financial data to answer items 6 to 8. Round all ratios to one decimal spot. Calculations involving days should be rounded to the nearest day.

	2014	2013
Accounts receivable	$ 45,000	$ 41,000
Inventory	34,000	28,000
Total shareholders' equity	572,000	438,000
Net credit sales	684,000	597,000
Cost of goods sold	450,000	398,000
Interest expense	14,000	12,000
Income tax expense	22,000	18,000
Profit	134,000	90,000

(SO 4) AP 6. What is the operating cycle for 2014?
(a) 20 days (c) 101 days
(b) 48 days (d) 124 days

(SO 5) AP 7. What is the interest coverage ratio for 2014?
(a) 7.3 times (c) 11.2 times
(b) 10.6 times (d) 12.1 times

(SO 6) AP 8. What is the return on equity for 2014?
(a) 22.2% (c) 26.5%
(b) 23.4% (d) 135.4%

(SO 4, 5, 6) AN 9. Which of the following changes in ratios are *both* indicative of an improvement rather than a deterioration in a company's financial situation?
(a) Increasing debt to total assets and interest coverage ratios

(b) Increasing current ratio and increasing days sales in inventory
(c) Decreasing asset turnover and return on equity ratios
(d) Decreasing collection period and increasing gross profit margin

(SO 7) C 10. Which of the following situations most likely indicates that a financial analysis should be interpreted with caution?
(a) Different inventory cost formulas are being used by competing companies with similar inventory.
(b) A company had no other comprehensive income.
(c) The economy is stable.
(d) The quality of information is high.

THE NAVIGATOR

Questions

(SO 1) C 1. What are the differences between the two bases of comparison: (a) intracompany and (b) intercompany?

(SO 1) C 2. (a) Identify the three commonly used tools of analysis. (b) Explain whether each is normally used in an intracompany and/or intercompany comparison.

(SO 2) K 3. Explain how the percentage of a base-period amount and the percentage change for a period are calculated in horizontal analysis.

(SO 2) C 4. Explain how a horizontal analysis is affected if an account (a) has no value in a base year and a value in the next year, or (b) has a negative value in the base year and a positive value in the next year.

(SO 2, 3) C 5. Horizontal analysis and vertical analysis are two different tools used in financial statement analysis. Explain how they are similar, and how they differ.

(SO 2, 3) C 6. **Facebook** became a public corporation in May 2012. Can a meaningful horizontal and vertical analysis be prepared for its first full year of operations as a public company, the year ended December 31, 2012? Explain.

(SO 3) K 7. What base amount is usually assigned a 100% value in a vertical analysis of (a) the balance sheet and (b) the income statement?

(SO 3) C 8. Can vertical analysis be used to compare two companies of different sizes, such as **Walmart**, the world's largest retailer, and **Costco**, the eighth-largest retailer in the world? Explain.

(SO 4) K 9. (a) What do liquidity ratios measure? (b) What types of users would be most interested in liquidity ratios?

(SO 4) AN 10. A high current ratio does not always indicate that a company has a strong liquidity position. Describe two situations that might result in the current ratio appearing to be "artificially" high.

(SO 4) AN 11. Aubut Corporation, a large national retail store, has an operating cycle of 30 days. Its nearest competitor, Benoit Corporation, has an operating cycle of 10 days. Does Aubut have a liquidity problem?

(SO 4) C 12. Identify for which liquidity ratios a lower result might be better, and explain why.

(SO 5) K 13. (a) What do solvency ratios measure? (b) What types of users would be most interested in solvency ratios?

(SO 5) C 14. Wong Ltd. reported a debt to total assets of 37% and an interest coverage ratio of 3 times in the current year. Its nearest competitor, Shin Ltd., has a debt to total assets ratio of 39% and an interest coverage ratio of 2.5 times. Is Wong's solvency better or worse than that of Shin?

(SO 5) C 15. Identify for which solvency ratios a lower result might be better, and explain why.

(SO 6) K 16. (a) What do profitability ratios measure? (b) What types of users would be most interested in profitability ratios?

(SO 6) AN 17. The return on assets for **McDonald's** is 16.9%. During the same period, it reported a return on equity of 37.9%. Has McDonald's made effective use of leverage? Explain.

(SO 6) AN 18. If you were an investor interested in buying the shares of a company with growth potential, would you look for a company that had high or low price-earnings and payout ratios? If you were interested in buying the shares of a company with income potential, would your answer change? Explain.

(SO 4, 5, 6) C 19. Name the ratio(s) that should be used to help answer each of the following questions.
(a) How efficient is a company at using its assets to produce sales?
(b) What is the company's ability to pay its obligations immediately without selling inventory?
(c) How long does it take to purchase inventory, sell it on account, and collect the cash?
(d) How many dollars of profit were earned for each dollar invested by the shareholders?
(e) How able is a company to pay interest charges as they come due?

(SO 7) C 20. Identify and briefly explain the limitations of financial statement analysis.

(SO 7) AN 21. **McCain Foods** and **Cavendish Farms** are both private companies in the food-processing industry. McCain Foods uses IFRS and Cavendish Farms uses ASPE. What impact might these differing standards have when comparing ratios of these two companies?

(SO 7) C 22. Explain what other comprehensive income is and when it should be considered in comparing ratios from one company to another.

Brief Exercises

Match terms with descriptions. **(SO 1) K**

BE17–1 Match each of the following terms with the most appropriate description.

	Terms	Description
______	1. Intracompany	(a) An analysis tool that expresses relationships among selected items of financial statement data
______	2. Intercompany	(b) An analysis tool that evaluates data by expressing an item in a financial statement as a percentage of a total or base amount within the same financial statement
______	3. Horizontal analysis	(c) Comparisons made between companies
______	4. Vertical analysis	(d) An analysis tool that evaluates data by calculating and comparing the percentage increase or decrease of an item in a financial statement over multiple periods of time
______	5. Ratio analysis	(e) Comparisons made within a company

Identify comparisons and tools. **(SO 1) C**

BE17–2 Identify the appropriate basis of comparison—intracompany or intercompany—and better tool of analysis—horizontal or vertical—to use for each of the following financial situations.

	Basis of Comparison	Tool of Analysis
1. Analysis of a company's dividend history		
2. Comparison of different-sized companies		
3. Comparison of gross profit to net sales among competitors		
4. Calculation of a company's sales growth over time		

Prepare horizontal analysis. **(SO 2) AP**

BE17–3 Comparative data (in thousands) from the balance sheet of Winisk Ltd. are shown below. Using horizontal analysis, calculate the percentage of the base-year amount, assuming 2012 is the base year.

	2014	2013	2012
Cash	$ 24	$ 45	$ 30
Accounts receivable	268	227	197
Inventory	499	481	395
Prepaid expenses	22	0	10
Total current assets	$813	$753	$632

Prepare horizontal analysis. **(SO 2) AP**

BE17–4 Refer to BE17–3. Using horizontal analysis, calculate the percentage change for each year.

Prepare horizontal and vertical analyses. **(SO 2, 3) AP**

BE17–5 Comparative data from the balance sheet of Rioux Ltd. are shown below. (a) Using horizontal analysis, calculate the percentage of the base-year amount, using 2012 as the base year. (b) Using vertical analysis, calculate the percentage of the base amount for each year.

	2014	2013	2012
Current assets	$1,530,000	$1,175,000	$1,225,000
Property, plant, and equipment	3,130,000	2,800,000	2,850,000
Goodwill	90,000	100,000	0
Total assets	$4,750,000	$4,075,000	$4,075,000

BE17–6 Selected data (in thousands) from the income statement of JTI Inc. are shown below. Using vertical analysis, calculate the percentage of the base amount for the current year.

Prepare vertical analysis. **(SO 3) AP**

Net sales	$1,934
Cost of goods sold	1,612
Gross profit	322
Operating expenses	218
Profit before income tax	104
Income tax expense	31
Profit	$ 73

BE17–7 For each of the following liquidity ratios, indicate whether the change would be viewed as an improvement or deterioration:

Compare liquidity ratios. **(SO 4) C**

(a) A decrease in the receivables turnover
(b) A decrease in the collection period
(c) An increase in the days sales in inventory
(d) An increase in the inventory turnover
(e) A decrease in the acid-test ratio
(f) An increase in the operating cycle

BE17–8 Selected financial data for Shumway Ltd. are shown below. (a) Calculate for each of 2013 and 2014, the following ratios: (1) receivables turnover, (2) collection period, (3) inventory turnover. (4) days sales in inventory, and (5) operating cycle. (b) Based on the ratios calculated in part (a), what conclusion(s) can be drawn about the management of the receivables and inventory?

Calculate and evaluate liquidity ratios. **(SO 4) AN**

	2014	2013	2012
Net sales	$6,420,000	$6,240,000	$5,430,000
Cost of goods sold	4,540,000	4,550,000	3,950,000
Accounts receivable (gross)	850,000	750,000	650,000
Inventory	1,020,000	980,000	840,000

BE17–9 Holysh Inc. reported a current ratio of 1.5:1 in the current year, which is higher than last year's current ratio of 1.3:1. It also reported an acid-test ratio of 1:1, which is higher than last year's acid-test ratio of 0.6:1; receivables turnover of 8 times, which is less than last year's receivables turnover of 9 times; and an inventory turnover of 6 times, which is less than last year's inventory turnover of 7 times. Is Holysh's liquidity improving or deteriorating? Explain.

Evaluate liquidity. **(SO 4) AN**

BE17–10 For each of the following solvency ratios, indicate whether the change would be viewed as an improvement or deterioration:

Compare solvency ratios. **(SO 5) C**

(a) A decrease in debt to total assets
(b) A decrease in interest coverage
(c) An increase in free cash flow
(d) A decrease in debt to total assets combined with an increase in interest coverage

BE17–11 **Shoppers Drug Mart** reported the following selected financial data (in thousands) for a recent year:

Calculate solvency ratios. **(SO 5) AP**

Interest expense	$ 64,038
Income tax expense	232,933
Profit	613,934
Total assets	7,300,310
Total liabilities	3,032,480
Cash provided by operating activities	973,838
Cash used by investing activities	349,172

Calculate the following ratios: (a) debt to total assets, (b) interest coverage, and (c) free cash flow.

Evaluate solvency. (SO 5) AN

BE17–12 The Culleye Corporation reported the following solvency ratios:

	2014	2013
Debt to total assets	56.0%	52.8%
Interest coverage	5.1 times	3.3 times

(a) Identify whether each of the above solvency ratios is better or worse in 2014, compared with 2013.
(b) Has Culleye's overall solvency position improved or deteriorated in 2014? Explain.

Compare profitability ratios. (SO 6) C

BE17–13 For each of the following profitability ratios, indicate whether the change would be viewed as an improvement or deterioration:

(a) An increase in the gross profit margin
(b) A decrease in asset turnover
(c) An increase in return on equity
(d) A decrease in earnings per share
(e) A decrease in the profit margin

Calculate profitability ratios. (SO 6) AP

BE17–14 Loblaw reported sales of $31,250 million, cost of goods sold of $23,894 million, and profit of $769 million for a recent year. Its total assets were $16,841 million at the beginning of the year and $17,428 million at the end of the year. Calculate the (a) gross profit margin, (b) profit margin, (c) asset turnover, and (d) return on assets ratios.

Evaluate investor ratios. (SO 6) AN

BE17–15 Recently, the price-earnings ratio of **Apple** was 17 times and the price-earnings ratio of the **Bank of Montreal** was 11 times. The payout ratio of each company was 0% and 53%, respectively. Which company's shares would you purchase for growth? For income? Explain.

Classify ratios. (SO 4, 5, 6) K

BE17–16 (a) Indicate whether each of the following ratios is a liquidity (L) ratio, a solvency (S) ratio, or a profitability (P) ratio. (b) Indicate whether a higher or lower result is normally desirable.

(a)	(b)	
_____	_______	Acid-test
_____	_______	Asset turnover
_____	_______	Collection period
_____	_______	Debt to total assets
_____	_______	Gross profit margin
_____	_______	Interest coverage
_____	_______	Inventory turnover
_____	_______	Operating cycle
_____	_______	Profit margin
_____	_______	Return on equity

Calculate averages. (SO 4, 6) AP

BE17–17 Selected comparative information (in thousands) is available for the Halpenny Corporation.

	2014	2013	2012
Accounts receivable	$ 1,090	$ 965	$ 880
Total assets	27,510	26,760	23,815
Total shareholders' equity	12,830	12,575	10,930

Halpenny wishes to calculate ratios for 2014 and 2013. (a) Calculate the average amounts to be used for accounts receivable, total assets, and total shareholders' equity in a ratio calculation in (1) 2014 and (2) 2013. (b) Identify for which ratio each of the above average amounts would be used. (c) Why are averages used in certain ratio calculations and not in others?

Evaluate impact of alternative cost formulas on inventory turnover. (SO 4, 7) AN

BE17–18 Stirling Corporation and Bute Inc. have similar types of inventory. At the end of the current year, Stirling reported an average inventory amount of $10,000, calculated using the FIFO cost formula. Bute reported an average inventory amount of $12,000, calculated using the average cost formula. Stirling reported cost of goods sold of $200,000, while Bute reported cost of goods sold of $180,000. Inventory prices have been falling during the current year. (a) Calculate the inventory turnover ratio for each company. (b) How might the fact that Stirling and Bute use different inventory cost formulas affect your comparison of the inventory turnover ratio between the two companies?

Exercises

E17–1 Comparative data from the balance sheet of Dressaire Inc. are shown below.

Prepare horizontal analysis. (SO 2) AP

	2014	2013	2012
Current assets	$120,000	$ 80,000	$100,000
Non-current assets	400,000	350,000	300,000
Current liabilities	90,000	70,000	65,000
Non-current liabilities	145,000	125,000	150,000
Common shares	150,000	115,000	100,000
Retained earnings	135,000	120,000	85,000

Instructions

(a) Using horizontal analysis, calculate the percentage of the base-year amount, using 2012 as the base year.
(b) Using horizontal analysis, calculate the percentage change for each year.

E17–2 Selected horizontal percentages of the base-year amount from Coastal Ltd.'s horizontally analyzed income statement are shown below.

Determine change in profit. (SO 2) AN

	2014	2013	2012
Net sales	101%	110%	100%
Cost of goods sold	100%	111%	100%
Operating expenses	99%	112%	100%
Income tax expense	106%	105%	100%

Instructions

Based on the above horizontal percentages, did Coastal's profit increase, decrease, or remain unchanged over the three-year period? Explain.

E17–3 Comparative data from the income statement of Fleetwood Corporation are shown below.

Prepare vertical analysis. (SO 3) AP

	2014	2013
Net sales	$800,000	$600,000
Cost of goods sold	550,000	375,000
Gross profit	250,000	225,000
Operating expenses	175,000	125,000
Profit before income tax	75,000	100,000
Income tax expense	18,750	25,000
Profit	$ 56,250	$ 75,000

Instructions

Using vertical analysis, calculate the percentage of the base amount for each year.

E17–4 Comparative data from the balance sheet of **lululemon athletica** are shown below.

Prepare horizontal and vertical analyses and identify changes. (SO 2, 3) AN

LULULEMON ATHLETICA INC.
Balance Sheet
January 29, 2012, and January 30, 2011
(in U.S. thousands)

Assets	2012	2011
Current assets	$527,093	$389,279
Non-current assets	207,541	110,023
Total assets	$734,634	$499,302
Liabilities and Shareholders' Equity		
Current liabilities	$103,439	$ 85,364
Non-current liabilities	25,014	19,645
Total liabilities	128,453	105,009
Shareholders' equity	606,181	394,293
Total liabilities and shareholders' equity	$734,634	$499,302

Instructions

(a) Using horizontal analysis, calculate the percentage change for 2012.
(b) Using vertical analysis, calculate the percentage of the base amount for each year.
(c) Based on your calculations in parts (a) and (b), identify any significant changes from 2011 to 2012.

Determine change in profit. (SO 3) AN

E17–5 Selected vertical percentages of the base amount from Waubon Corp.'s vertically analyzed income statement are shown below.

	2012	2011	2010
Net sales	100.0%	100.0%	100.0%
Cost of goods sold	59.4%	60.5%	60.0%
Operating expenses	19.6%	20.4%	20.0%
Income tax expense	4.2%	3.8%	4.0%

Instructions

Based on the above vertical percentages, did Waubon's profit as a percentage of sales increase, decrease, or remain unchanged over the three-year period? Explain.

Calculate and compare liquidity ratios. (SO 4) AP

E17–6 Nordstar, Inc. operates hardware stores in several provinces. Selected comparative financial statement data are shown below.

NORDSTAR, INC.
Balance Sheet (partial)
December 31 (in millions)

	2014	2013	2012
Current assets			
Cash	$ 30	$ 91	$ 60
Short-term investments	55	60	40
Accounts receivable	676	586	496
Inventory	628	525	575
Prepaid expenses	41	52	29
Total current assets	$1,430	$1,314	$1,200
Total current liabilities	$ 890	$ 825	$ 750

Additional information:

(in millions)	2014	2013
Net credit sales	$4,190	$3,940
Cost of goods sold	2,900	2,650

Instructions

(a) Calculate all possible liquidity ratios for 2014 and 2013.
(b) Indicate whether each of the liquidity ratios calculated in part (a) is better or worse in 2014.

Evaluate liquidity. (SO 4) AN

E17–7 The following selected ratios are available for Pampered Pets Inc.:

	2014	2013	2012
Current ratio	2.6:1	1.4:1	2.1:1
Acid-test	0.8:1	0.6:1	0.7:1
Receivables turnover	6.7 times	7.4 times	8.2 times
Inventory turnover	7.5 times	8.7 times	9.9 times
Operating cycle	103 days	91 days	81 days

Instructions

(a) Has the company's collection of its receivables improved or weakened over the last three years?
(b) Is the company selling its inventory faster or slower than in past years?
(c) Overall, has the company's liquidity improved or weakened over the last three years? Explain.

E17–8 The following selected information (in thousands) is available for Osborne Inc.:

Calculate and compare solvency ratios. **(SO 5) AP**

	2014	2013
Total assets	$3,886	$3,708
Total liabilities	2,177	1,959
Interest expense	14	27
Income tax expense	174	152
Profit	406	375
Cash provided by operating activities	850	580
Cash used by investing activities	400	300

Instructions

(a) Calculate all possible solvency ratios for 2014 and 2013.
(b) Indicate whether each of the solvency ratios calculated in part (a) is better or worse in 2014.

E17–9 The following selected ratios are available for Ice Inc.:

Evaluate solvency. **(SO 5) AN**

	2014	2013	2012
Debt to total assets	50%	45%	40%
Interest coverage	2.0 times	1.5 times	1.0 times

Instructions

(a) Has the debt to total assets improved or weakened over the last three years?
(b) Has the interest coverage improved or weakened over the last three years?
(c) Overall, has the company's solvency improved or weakened over the last three years?

E17–10 The following selected information is for Xtreme Corporation:

Calculate and compare profitability ratios. **(SO 6) AP**

	2014	2013	2012
Total assets	$350,000	$275,000	$274,467
Total shareholders' equity	133,500	100,000	50,000
Net sales	500,000	400,000	300,000
Cost of goods sold	375,000	290,000	180,000
Profit	33,500	30,000	20,000

Instructions

(a) Calculate the gross profit margin, profit margin, asset turnover, return on assets, and return on equity ratios for 2014 and 2013.
(b) Indicate whether each of the profitability ratios calculated in part (a) is better or worse in 2014.

E17–11 Talisman Energy and **Suncor Energy** reported the following investor-related information recently:

Evaluate profitability. **(SO 6) AN**

	Talisman Energy	Suncor Energy
Earnings per share	$1.35	$3.02
Payout ratio	19.9%	14.3%
Price-earnings ratio	11.6 times	9.6 times
Profit margin	16.6%	11.7%
Return on equity	14.6%	12.4%

Instructions

(a) Based on the above information, can you tell which company is more profitable?
(b) Which company do investors favour?
(c) Which company would investors most likely purchase shares in for growth purposes? For dividend income?

E17–12 The following is a selected list of ratios comparing Long Inc. and Circular Corporation for a recent year:

Classify and compare ratios. **(SO 1, 4, 5, 6) C**

	Long	Circular	(a)	(b)
Acid-test	1.1:1	0.8:1		
Asset turnover	1.7 times	1.6 times		
Current ratio	1.3:1	1.6:1		
Debt to total assets	30.1%	40.6%		
Gross profit margin	38.7%	38.6%		
Interest coverage	5.6 times	2.3 times		
Inventory turnover	5.8 times	5.1 times		
Operating cycle	119 days	134 days		
Profit margin	10.4%	8.5%		
Receivables turnover	6.5 times	5.9 times		
Return on assets	17.2%	13.7%		
Return on equity	24.8%	28.2%		

Instructions

(a) Classify each of the above ratios as a liquidity (L), solvency (S), or profitability (P) ratio.

(b) For each of the above ratios, indicate whether Long's ratio is better (B) or worse (W) than that reported by Circular.

(c) Identify whether the comparison done in part (b) is an intracompany comparison or an intercompany comparison.

Calculate and classify ratios. **(SO 4, 5, 6) AP**

E17–13 Selected comparative financial data (in thousands, except for share price) for **Indigo Books & Music** are shown below.

	2011	2010
Revenue	$1,017,325	$968,927
Interest expense	212	214
Income tax expense	2,682	12,537
Profit	11,346	34,923
Total current assets	342,373	351,044
Total assets	516,180	519,842
Total current liabilities	238,434	244,665
Total liabilities	246,713	254,042
Total shareholders' equity	263,120	258,969
Cash provided by operating activities	18,441	62,245
Cash used by investing activities	43,201	48,947
Market price per share	12.29	16.73
Weighted average number of common shares	24,874	24,550

Instructions

(a) Calculate the following ratios for 2011:

1. Asset turnover
2. Current ratio
3. Debt to total assets
4. Earnings per share
5. Free cash flow
6. Interest coverage
7. Price-earnings ratio
8. Profit margin
9. Return on assets
10. Return on equity

(b) Indicate whether each of the above ratios is a measure of liquidity (L), solvency (S), or profitability (P).

Calculate missing information. **(SO 4, 5, 6) AN**

E17–14 Presented below is an incomplete income statement for Riverdance Limited.

RIVERDANCE LIMITED
Income Statement
Year Ended December 31, 2014

Net sales	(a)
Cost of goods sold	(b)
Gross profit	(c)
Operating expenses	(d)
Profit before income taxes	(e)
Income tax expense	(f)
Profit	(g)

Additional information:

1. The asset turnover is 3 times and average total assets are $100,000.
2. The gross profit margin is 40%.
3. The income tax rate is 25%.
4. The profit margin is 15%.

Instructions

Calculate the missing information using the ratios. (*Hint:* Start with one ratio and get as much information as possible from it before trying another ratio. You may not be able to calculate the missing amounts in the same sequence as they are presented above.)

E17–15 Presented below is an incomplete balance sheet for the Main River Corp.

Calculate missing information. **(SO 4, 5, 6) AN**

MAIN RIVER CORP.
Balance Sheet
December 31, 2014

Assets	
Current assets	
Cash	$20,000
Accounts receivable	(a)
Inventory	(b)
Total current assets	365,000
Non-current assets	435,000
Total assets	$ (c)
Liabilities and Shareholders' Equity	
Current liabilities	$ (d)
Non-current liabilities	(e)
Total liabilities	(f)
Shareholders' equity	(g)
Total liabilities and shareholders' equity	$ (h)

Additional information:

1. Assume average balances equal ending balances for the purpose of this exercise.
2. The receivables turnover ratio is 13 times and net credit sales are $1,950,000.
3. The inventory turnover ratio is 6.5 times and cost of goods sold is $1,267,500.
4. The current ratio is 2:1.
5. The debt to total assets ratio is 70%.

Instructions

Calculate the missing information using the ratios. (*Hint:* Start with one ratio and get as much information as possible from it before trying another ratio. You may not be able to calculate the missing amounts in the same sequence as they are presented above.)

E17–16 A company reported the following selected information (in thousands):

Determine impact of other comprehensive income on profitability. **(SO 6, 7) AN**

	2014	2013	2012
Profit	$933	$ 867	$1,321
Other comprehensive income (loss)	(117)	793	(2,658)
Total comprehensive income (loss)	816	1,660	(1,337)

Instructions

Explain whether other comprehensive income would affect your analysis of this company's profitability, and if so, how.

Problems: Set A

Prepare horizontal analysis and identify changes.
(SO 2, 7) AN

P17–1A The following condensed financial information is available for **WestJet Airlines**:

WESTJET AIRLINES LTD.
Income Statement
Year Ended December 31 (in millions)

	2011	2010	2009	2008
Revenue	$3,072	$2,607	$2,281	$2,550
Operating expenses	2,815	2,416	2,070	2,257
Profit from operations	257	191	211	293
Other expenses	49	58	74	38
Profit before income taxes	208	133	137	255
Income tax expense	59	43	39	77
Profit	$ 149	$ 90	$ 98	$ 178

WESTJET AIRLINES LTD.
Balance Sheet
December 31 (in thousands)

Assets	2011	2010	2009	2008
Current assets	$1,425	$1,285	$1,129	$ 926
Non-current assets	2,049	2,099	2,221	2,353
Total assets	$3,474	$3,384	$3,350	$3,279
Liabilities and Shareholders' Equity				
Current liabilities	$ 942	$ 840	$ 756	$ 740
Non-current liabilities	1,162	1,240	1,362	1,453
Total liabilities	2,104	2,080	2,118	2,193
Shareholders' equity	1,370	1,304	1,232	1,086
Total liabilities and shareholders' equity	$3,474	$3,384	$3,350	$3,279

Instructions

(a) Using horizontal analysis, calculate the percentage of the base-year amount for the income statement and balance sheet, assuming 2008 is the base year.

(b) Using the horizontal analyses you prepared in part (a), identify any significant changes between 2008 and 2011.

(c) Which do you think would be more useful—calculating the percentage of the base-year amount or calculating the percentage change between periods—to analyze WestJet between 2008 and 2011? Explain.

TAKING IT FURTHER WestJet's financial information for 2010 and 2011 was prepared using IFRS. The financial information for 2008 and 2009 was prepared using the pre-changeover Canadian GAAP. How might these differing standards affect your interpretation of the horizontal analysis?

P17–2A A horizontal and vertical analysis of the income statement for a retail company selling a wide variety of general merchandise is shown below.

Interpret horizontal and vertical analysis.
(SO 2, 3, 7) AN

RETAIL CORPORATION
Horizontal Income Statement
Year Ended January 31

	2014	2013	2012	2011
Net sales	140.0%	111.0%	114.0%	100.0%
Cost of goods sold	148.3%	113.3%	116.7%	100.0%
Gross profit	127.5%	107.5%	110.0%	100.0%
Operating expenses	171.4%	133.1%	126.9%	100.0%
Profit from operations	93.3%	87.6%	96.9%	100.0%
Other revenues and expenses				
Interest expense	40.0%	60.0%	80.0%	100.0%
Other revenue	240.0%	140.0%	200.0%	100.0%
Profit before income tax	140.0%	110.8%	113.8%	100.0%
Income tax expense	160.0%	116.0%	124.0%	100.0%
Profit	135.2%	109.5%	111.4%	100.0%

RETAIL CORPORATION
Vertical Income Statement
Year Ended January 31

	2014	2013	2012	2011
Net sales	100.0%	100.0%	100.0%	100.0%
Cost of goods sold	63.6%	61.2%	61.4%	60.0%
Gross profit	36.4%	38.8%	38.6%	40.0%
Operating expenses	21.4%	21.0%	19.5%	17.5%
Profit from operations	15.0%	17.8%	19.1%	22.5%
Other revenues and expenses				
Interest expense	(2.9)%	(5.4)%	(7.0)%	(10.0)%
Other revenue	0.9%	0.6%	0.9%	0.5%
Profit before income tax	13.0%	13.0%	13.0%	13.0%
Income tax expense	2.9%	2.6%	2.7%	2.5%
Profit	10.1%	10.4%	10.3%	10.5%

Instructions

(a) How effectively has the company controlled its cost of goods sold and operating expenses over the four-year period?
(b) Identify any other income statement components that have significantly changed over the four-year period for the company.
(c) Identify any additional information that might be helpful to you in your analysis of this company over the four-year period.

TAKING IT FURTHER In a vertical analysis, the company's profit before income tax has remained unchanged at 13% of revenue over the four-year period. Yet, in a horizontal analysis, profit before income tax has grown 40% over that period of time. Explain how this is possible.

Prepare vertical analysis, calculate profitability ratios, and compare.
(SO 1, 3, 6) AN

P17–3A Comparative income statement data for Chen Inc. and Chuan Ltd., two competitors, are shown below for the year ended December 31, 2014.

	Chen	Chuan
Net sales	$1,849,035	$539,038
Cost of goods sold	1,060,490	338,006
Gross profit	788,545	201,032
Operating expenses	502,275	89,000
Profit from operations	286,270	112,032
Interest expense	6,800	1,252
Profit before income tax	279,470	110,780
Income tax expense	83,841	27,695
Profit	$ 195,629	$ 83,085
Additional information:		
Average total assets	$ 894,750	$251,313
Average total shareholders' equity	724,430	186,238

Instructions

(a) Using vertical analysis, calculate the percentage of the base amount for each year of the income statement for each company.
(b) Calculate the gross profit margin, profit margin, asset turnover, return on assets, and return on equity ratios for 2014 for each company.
(c) Using the information calculated in parts (a) and (b), compare the profitability of each company.
(d) Is your comparison in part (c) an intracompany comparison or an intercompany comparison? Explain.

TAKING IT FURTHER How is your assessment of profitability affected by the differing sizes of the two companies, if at all? Explain.

Calculate ratios.
(SO 4, 5, 6) AP

P17–4A Comparative financial statements for The Cable Company Ltd. are shown below.

THE CABLE COMPANY LTD.
Income Statement
Year Ended December 31

	2014	2013
Net sales	$1,948,500	$1,700,500
Cost of goods sold	1,025,500	946,000
Gross profit	923,000	754,500
Operating expenses	516,000	449,000
Profit from operations	407,000	305,500
Interest expense	28,000	19,000
Profit before income tax	379,000	286,500
Income tax expense	113,700	86,000
Profit	$ 265,300	$ 200,500

THE CABLE COMPANY LTD.
Balance Sheet
December 31

Assets	2014	2013
Current assets		
Cash	$ 68,100	$ 64,200
Accounts receivable	107,800	102,800
Inventory	143,000	115,500
Total current assets	318,900	282,500
Property, plant, and equipment	679,300	570,300
Total assets	$998,200	$852,800
Liabilities and Shareholders' Equity		
Current liabilities		
Accounts payable	$155,000	$125,400
Income tax payable	43,500	42,000
Current portion of mortgage payable	10,000	20,000
Total current liabilities	208,500	187,400
Mortgage payable	104,000	200,000
Total liabilities	312,500	387,400
Shareholders' equity		
Common shares (56,000 issued in 2014; 60,000 in 2013)	168,000	180,000
Retained earnings	517,700	285,400
Total shareholders' equity	685,700	465,400
Total liabilities and shareholders' equity	$998,200	$852,800

Additional information:

1. All sales were on account.
2. The allowance for doubtful accounts was $5,400 in 2014 and $5,100 in 2013.
3. On July 1, 2014, 4,000 shares were reacquired for $10 per share and cancelled.
4. In 2014, $5,000 of dividends were paid to the common shareholders.
5. Cash provided by operating activities was $316,200.
6. Cash used by investing activities was $161,300.

Instructions

Calculate all possible liquidity, solvency, and profitability ratios for 2014.

TAKING IT FURTHER Based on the ratios you have calculated for 2014, can you determine whether The Cable Company's liquidity, solvency, and profitability are strong or weak? If not, what additional information would you require?

Calculate and evaluate ratios. **(SO 1, 4, 5, 6) AN**

P17–5A Comparative financial statements for Click and Clack Ltd. are shown below.

CLICK AND CLACK LTD.
Income Statement
Year Ended December 31

	2014	2013
Net sales	$900,000	$840,000
Cost of goods sold	620,000	575,000
Gross profit	280,000	265,000
Operating expenses	164,000	160,000
Profit from operations	116,000	105,000
Other expenses		
Interest expense	30,000	20,000
Profit before income tax	86,000	85,000
Income tax expense	22,000	20,000
Profit	$ 64,000	$ 65,000

CLICK AND CLACK LTD.
Balance Sheet
December 31

Assets	2014	2013	2012
Cash	$ 70,000	$ 65,000	$ 10,000
Accounts receivable	139,000	130,000	108,000
Inventories	130,000	125,000	97,000
Prepaid expenses	25,000	23,000	115,000
Land, buildings, and equipment	390,000	305,000	300,000
Total assets	$754,000	$648,000	$630,000
Liabilities and Shareholders' Equity			
Liabilities			
Notes payable	$110,000	$100,000	$100,000
Accounts payable	45,000	42,000	60,000
Accrued liabilities	32,000	40,000	30,000
Bonds payable, due 2018	190,000	150,000	181,000
Total liabilities	377,000	332,000	371,000
Shareholders' equity			
Common shares (20,000 issued)	200,000	200,000	200,000
Retained earnings	177,000	116,000	59,000
Total shareholders' equity	377,000	316,000	259,000
Total liabilities and shareholders' equity	$754,000	$648,000	$630,000

Additional information:

1. Seventy-five percent of the sales were on account.
2. The allowance for doubtful accounts was $4,000 in 2014, $5,000 in 2013, and $3,000 in 2012.
3. In 2014 and 2013, dividends of $3,000 and $8,000, respectively, were paid to the common shareholders.
4. Cash provided by operating activities was $73,500 in 2014 and $129,000 in 2013.
5. Cash used by investing activities was $115,500 in 2014 and $35,000 in 2013.

Instructions

(a) Calculate all possible liquidity, solvency, and profitability ratios for 2014 and 2013.

(b) Identify whether the change in each ratio from 2013 to 2014 calculated in part (a) was favourable (F), unfavourable (U), or no change (NC).

(c) Explain whether overall (1) liquidity, (2) solvency, and (3) profitability improved, deteriorated, or remained the same between 2013 and 2014.

TAKING IT FURTHER Does this problem employ an intracompany comparison or an intercompany comparison? Which do you think is more useful?

P17–6A Selected financial data for **Tim Hortons** and **Starbucks** are presented below for a recent year.

Calculate and evaluate ratios. **(SO 4, 5, 6, 7) AN**

	Tim Hortons (in CAD$ millions)	Starbucks (in US$ millions)
Statement of Comprehensive Income (Loss)		
Total revenue	$2,536.5	$11,700.4
Cost of sales	1,527.4	4,949.3
Gross profit	1,009.1	6,751.1
Operating expenses	136.9	5,022.6
Profit from operations	872.2	1,728.5
Interest expense	26.6	33.3
Other non-operating income	(2.4)	(115.9)
Profit before income tax	848.0	1,811.1
Income tax expense	200.9	563.1
Profit	647.1	1,248.0
Other comprehensive loss	(46.7)	(10.9)
Total comprehensive income	$ 600.4	$ 1,237.1
Balance Sheet		
Current assets	$1,009.1	$ 3,794.9
Non-current assets	1,472.4	3,565.5
Total assets	$2,481.5	$ 7,360.4
Current liabilities	$ 491.5	$ 2,075.8
Non-current liabilities	547.6	897.3
Total liabilities	1,039.1	2,973.1
Shareholders' equity	1,442.4	4,387.3
Total liabilities and shareholders' equity	$2,481.5	$ 7,360.4
Additional information:		
Average accounts receivable	$ 181.0	$ 344.6
Average inventories	90.6	754.6
Average total assets	2,287.9	6,873.2
Average total shareholders' equity	1,349.1	4,034.8

Instructions

(a) For each company, calculate the following ratios:

1. Current ratio
2. Receivables turnover
3. Inventory turnover
4. Operating cycle
5. Debt to total assets
6. Interest coverage
7. Gross profit margin
8. Profit margin
9. Asset turnover
10. Return on assets
11. Return on equity

(b) Compare the liquidity, solvency, and profitability of the two companies.

TAKING IT FURTHER How should other comprehensive loss be factored into your analysis above?

Evaluate ratios.
(SO 4, 5, 6) AN

P17–7A Selected ratios for two companies operating in the office supply industry follow.

Ratio	Fournitures Ltée	Supplies Unlimited
Acid-test	1.0:1	0.8:1
Asset turnover	2.6 times	2.2 times
Current ratio	1.7:1	2.8:1
Debt to total assets	35.0%	30.3%
Gross profit margin	23.9%	35.4%
Interest coverage	4.2 times	6.6 times
Inventory turnover	6.0 times	3.1 times
Operating cycle	92 days	158 days
Price-earnings ratio	19.0 times	15.2 times
Profit margin	5.6%	4.1%
Receivables turnover	11.8 times	9.1 times
Return on assets	14.6%	9.0%
Return on equity	19.8%	12.5%

Instructions

(a) Both companies offer their customers credit terms of net 30 days. Indicate the ratio(s) that should be used to assess how well the accounts receivable are managed. Which company appears to be managing its accounts receivable better?
(b) Indicate the ratio(s) that should be used to assess inventory management. Which company appears to be managing its inventory better?
(c) Supplies Unlimited's current ratio is higher than Fourniture's. Identify two possible reasons for this.
(d) Which company is more solvent? Identify the ratio(s) that should be used to determine this and defend your choice.
(e) You notice that Fourniture's gross profit margin is significantly less than Supplies Unlimited's but its profit margin is higher. Identify two possible reasons for this.
(f) Which company do investors appear to believe has greater prospects for future profitability? Indicate the ratio(s) you used to reach this conclusion and explain your reasoning.

TAKING IT FURTHER Which company is using leverage more effectively? Explain.

Evaluate ratios.
(SO 4, 5, 6) AN

P17–8A The following ratios are available for agricultural chemicals competitors **Potash Corporation of Sas katchewan (PotashCorp)** and **Agrium** for a recent year:

	PotashCorp	Agrium
Liquidity		
Current ratio	1.1:1	2.1:1
Acid-test	0.8:1	1.2:1
Receivables turnover	10.7 times	8.3 times
Inventory turnover	6.8 times	4.1 times
Operating cycle	88 days	133 days
Solvency		
Debt to total assets	36.6%	26.9%
Interest coverage	18.3 times	63.1 times
Profitability		
Gross profit margin	49.2%	28.0%
Profit margin	35.4%	9.8%
Asset turnover	0.6 times	1.2 times
Return on assets	19.4%	11.6%
Return on equity	42.4%	25.9%

Instructions

(a) Which company is more liquid? Explain.
(b) Which company is more solvent? Explain.
(c) Which company is more profitable? Explain.

TAKING IT FURTHER The price-earnings ratio for Potash Corp is 12.3 times, compared with Agrium's PE ratio of 9 times. Which company do investors favour? Is your answer consistent with your analysis of the two companies' profitability in part (c)?

P17–9A Presented here are an incomplete income statement and balance sheet for Schwenke Corporation.

Calculate missing information. **(SO 4, 5, 6) AN**

SCHWENKE CORPORATION
Income Statement
Year Ended December 31, 2014

Net sales	$ (a)
Cost of goods sold	(b)
Gross profit	(c)
Operating expenses	333,750
Profit from operations	(d)
Interest expense	10,500
Profit before income taxes	(e)
Income tax expense	(f)
Profit	$124,600

SCHWENKE CORPORATION
Balance Sheet
December 31, 2014

Assets	
Current assets	
Cash	$ 7,500
Accounts receivable	(g)
Inventory	(h)
Total current assets	(i)
Property, plant, and equipment	(j)
Total assets	$ (k)
Liabilities	
Current liabilities	$ (l)
Non-current liabilities	120,000
Total liabilities	(m)
Shareholders' Equity	
Common shares	250,000
Retained earnings	400,000
Total shareholders' equity	650,000
Total liabilities and shareholders' equity	$ (n)

Additional information:

1. The gross profit margin is 40%.
2. The income tax rate is 20%.
3. The inventory turnover is 8 times.
4. The current ratio is 3:1.
5. The asset turnover is 1.5 times.

Instructions

Calculate the missing information using the ratios. Use ending balances instead of average balances, where averages are required for ratio calculations. Show your calculations.

TAKING IT FURTHER Why is it not possible to calculate the missing amounts in the same sequence (a, b, c, and so on) that they are presented above?

CONTINUING COOKIE CHRONICLE

(*Note:* This is a continuation of the Cookie Chronicle from Chapters 1 through 16.)

The Koebels have considered the offer extended by Coffee Beans Ltd. (see Chapter 16) and have turned it down. Instead, Brian, Janet, and Natalie have decided to continue operating Koebel's Family Bakery Ltd. and to expand the business.

Koebel's Family Bakery Ltd. has excess cash for the expansion but needs time to organize it. In the meantime, the cash could be invested. The Koebels have been approached by a family friend who works in the investment industry. This family friend has made a strong recommendation to buy shares in Cookies and Cream Ltd., a public company. Because Janet, Brian, and Natalie are familiar with the bakery business, they believe that investing in a public company that operates a bakery could be a good investment. The investment in Cookies and Cream Ltd. could provide a significant return on a short-term basis while the Koebels organize for the expansion.

In order to assess this investment, Natalie has calculated several ratios for both Cookies and Cream Ltd. and Koebel's Family Bakery as follows:

Ratio	Cookies and Cream Ltd. Year End 2014	Cookies and Cream Ltd. Year End 2013	Koebel's Family Bakery Ltd. Year End 2014
Current ratio	1.0:1.0	1.1:1.0	8.4:1:0
Receivables turnover	15.6 times	18.5 times	47.8 times
Inventory turnover	21.4 times	22.6 times	7.6 times
Debt to total assets	31%	30%	13%
Times interest earned	61 times	31 times	65 times
Return on common shareholders' equity	7.8%	8.1%	36.9%
Return on total assets	5.4%	5.7%	32%
Gross profit margin	19.5%	21%	75.3%
Profit margin	3.3%	3.9%	22.1%
Dividend payout	32%	9.8%	60%
Price-earnings ratio	24 times	19 times	n/a

Instructions

(a) Which company is more liquid? Explain.
(b) Which company is more solvent? Explain.
(c) Which company is more profitable? Explain.
(d) Are Cookies and Cream Ltd.'s ratios improving? Explain.
(e) Overall, why do you think that the ratios of Koebel's are stronger than those of Cookies and Cream Ltd.?
(f) What other considerations must the Koebels keep in mind before making an investment in any public company?

CHAPTER 17 BROADENING YOUR PERSPECTIVE

Communication Activity

BYP17–1 You are a new member of the audit committee and board of directors of EasyMix Cement Inc. EasyMix was a private company using ASPE until last year, when it became a publicly traded company using IFRS. You are about to attend your first meeting of the audit committee, at which the year-end financial results, including key ratios, will be presented.

Instructions

Identify any of the limitations of financial statement analysis that you believe may apply to EasyMix. Prioritize your list and prepare questions that you should raise at the audit committee meeting to help you better understand the financial results and ratios presented.

Ethics Case

BYP17–2 Sabra Surkis, president of Surkis Industries, wants to issue a press release to improve her company's image and boost its share price, which has been gradually falling. As controller, you have been asked to provide a list of financial ratios along with some other operating statistics from Surkis Industries' first-quarter operations for the current year.

Two days after you provide the ratios and data requested, Carol Dunn, the public relations director of Surkis, asks you to review the financial and operating data contained in the press release written by the president and edited by Carol. In the news release, the president highlights the sales increase of 5.2% over last year's first quarter and the positive change in the current ratio from 1.1:1 last year to 1.5:1 this year. She also emphasizes that production was up 10.1% over the prior year's first quarter.

You note that the release contains only positive or improved ratios, and none of the negative or weakened ratios. For instance, there is no mention that the debt to total assets ratio has increased from 35.1% to 44.9%. Nor is it mentioned that the operating cycle has increased by 19%. There is also no indication that the reported profit for the quarter would have been a loss if the estimated lives of Surkis's machinery had not been increased by 20%.

Helpful hint Companies use different terminology in their annual reports., e.g., if you look up the annual report for Canadian Tire you will see that it uses the words 'Net Income' instead of 'Profit' and 'Inventory cost of sales' for 'Cost of goods sold'. These are some subtle differences that you should be aware of when you compare the annual reports of various companies.

Instructions

(a) Who are the stakeholders in this situation?
(b) Is there anything unethical in president Surkis's actions?
(c) Should you as controller remain silent? Does Carol have any responsibility?

All About You: Personal Financial Literacy Activity

BYP17–3 In the "All About You" feature, you learned that there are on-line investment services that provide advice to investors. These services offer stock quotes, company research reports, personal finance information, news, on-line seminars, and message boards. However, it is also important that as an investor you differentiate good information from bad information. Reading the financial statements and preparing a ratio analysis is one step in evaluating an investment. You have recently inherited $10,000 cash and you are considering investing in **Canadian Tire Corporation, Limited's** shares.

You obtain a copy of Canadian Tire's 2012 annual report and see the following information (in $ millions, except per share amounts) in the financial statements.

Current assets	$ 7,748.6	Interest expense	144.3
Current liabilities	4,624.1	Income tax expense	178.0
Cost of goods sold	7,545.3	Gross profit	3,497.9
Total liabilities	8,417.8	Net sales	11,427.2
Total assets	13,181.4	Cash Dividends	101.7
Profit	499.2	Earnings per share	6.13

Instructions

(a) Calculate the following ratios for the 2012 fiscal year. Compare these to the 2011 ratios shown in the Ratio Analysis section of the chapter for Canadian Tire and reproduced in parentheses after each ratio below. For each ratio, has it improved or deteriorated from 2011?
 1. Current ratio (1.7:1)
 2. Inventory turnover (6.2 times)
 3. Debt to total assets (64.3%)
 4. Interest coverage (5.1 times)
 5. Gross profit margin (29.5%)
 6. Profit margin (4.5%)
 7. Return on assets (4.0%)
 8. Return on equity (11.1%)
 9. Price-earnings ratio (12.7 times)
 10. Payout ratio (19.6%)
(b) Based on your brief analysis of Canadian Tire's ratios, do you think buying Canadian Tire's shares is a good investment for you? Explain.
(c) If you are investing in the stock market, will you rely solely on your analysis of the financial statements? The history of Canadian Tire's stock price? Or do you think you might rely on both your financial statement analysis and the history of the stock price? Explain.
(d) In the "All About You" feature, we learned that critics of message boards on investment services' sites say that message boards can intensify the rumour mill. Do you think that you should ignore message boards when making investment decisions? Explain.

ANSWERS TO CHAPTER QUESTIONS

ANSWERS TO ACCOUNTING IN ACTION INSIGHT QUESTIONS

Across the Organization, p. 745

Q: What other liquidity ratios should be monitored, and by what department(s), across the organization?

A: The inventory turnover and days sales in inventory ratios would be monitored closely by both the purchasing and sales departments to make sure that the inventory is saleable. The finance department will also monitor these ratios to ensure that the cost of carrying the inventory is not unreasonable. The finance department would also watch the acid-test ratio in order to assess its cash flow requirements.

All About You Insight, p. 757

Q: Suppose you are thinking about investing in shares of Tim Hortons. You scanned a variety of investor websites and found messages posted by two different investors. One says it's time to buy Tim Hortons shares; the other says it isn't. How should you decide whether to buy the shares or not?

A: Before purchasing any shares, you must ensure that you can differentiate the good information from the bad and don't get carried away by rumours. You should read the company's financial statements and calculate and review any relevant ratios (such as liquidity, solvency, and profitability). You should also consider non-financial factors (such as the economy) in your decision.

ANSWERS TO SELF-STUDY QUESTIONS

1. a 2. d 3. c 4. c 5. a 6. b 7. d 8. c 9. d 10. a

Remember to go back to the beginning of the chapter to check off your completed work! ←

APPENDIX A SPECIMEN FINANCIAL STATEMENTS

REITMANS (CANADA) LIMITED

In this appendix, we illustrate current financial reporting with a sample set of corporate financial statements that are prepared in accordance with International Financial Reporting Standards (IFRS).

Reitmans' financial statement package features a statement of earnings, statement of comprehensive income, balance sheets, statement of changes in shareholders' equity, and statement of cash flows, which are reproduced in this appendix. The financial statement package also includes notes to the financial statements and two reports: a statement of management's responsibilities for financial reporting and the independent auditors' report.

We encourage students to use these financial statements in conjunction with the relevant material in the textbook.

Annual reports, including the financial statements, are reviewed in detail in *WileyPLUS*.

REITMANS (CANADA) LIMITED
STATEMENTS OF EARNINGS
(in thousands of Canadian dollars except per share amounts)

	For the years ended	
	January 28, 2012	**January 29, 2011**
Sales	**$ 1,019,397**	$ 1,059,000
Cost of goods sold (note 7)	**363,333**	350,671
Gross profit	**656,064**	708,329
Selling and distribution expenses	**547,367**	528,676
Administrative expenses	**46,878**	55,511
Results from operating activities	**61,819**	124,142
Finance income (note 19)	**5,562**	4,505
Finance costs (note 19)	**1,509**	845
Earnings before income taxes	**65,872**	127,802
Income taxes (note 11)	**18,333**	38,817
Net earnings	**$ 47,539**	$ 88,985
Earnings per share (note 20):		
Basic	**$ 0.72**	$ 1.33
Diluted	**0.72**	1.32

REITMANS (CANADA) LIMITED
STATEMENTS OF COMPREHENSIVE INCOME
(in thousands of Canadian dollars)

	For the years ended	
	January 28, 2012	**January 29, 2011**
Net earnings	**$ 47,539**	$ 88,985
Other comprehensive income:		
Net change in fair value of available-for-sale financial assets (net of tax of $79; 2011 - $427) (note 19)	**530**	2,866
Reclassification of realized gains on available-for-sale financial assets to net earnings (net of tax of $22) (note 19)	**—**	(145)
Reclassification of impairment loss on available-for-sale financial assets to net earnings (net of tax of $9; 2011 - $11) (note 19)	**64**	67
Defined benefit actuarial losses (net of tax of $1,041; 2011 - $272) (note 15)	**(2,965)**	(777)
Total comprehensive income	**$ 45,168**	$ 90,996

REITMANS (CANADA) LIMITED
BALANCE SHEETS
(in thousands of Canadian dollars)

	January 28, 2012	January 29, 2011	January 31, 2010
ASSETS			
CURRENT ASSETS			
Cash and cash equivalents (note 5)	$ 196,835	$ 230,034	$ 228,577
Marketable securities	71,442	70,413	48,026
Trade and other receivables	3,033	2,866	2,926
Derivative financial asset (note 6)	751	—	—
Income taxes recoverable	4,735	—	—
Inventories (note 7)	78,285	73,201	63,127
Prepaid expenses	11,902	12,491	11,010
Total Current Assets	366,983	389,005	353,666
NON-CURRENT ASSETS			
Property and equipment (note 8)	184,221	193,064	208,362
Intangible assets (note 9)	17,057	13,841	9,964
Goodwill (note 10)	42,426	42,426	42,426
Deferred income taxes (note 11)	23,174	21,021	18,313
Total Non-Current Assets	266,878	270,352	279,065
TOTAL ASSETS	$ 633,861	$ 659,357	$ 632,731
LIABILITIES AND SHAREHOLDERS' EQUITY			
CURRENT LIABILITIES			
Trade and other payables (note 12)	$ 63,875	$ 64,093	$ 54,684
Derivative financial liability (note 6)	1,505	—	—
Deferred revenue (note 13)	22,278	19,834	18,122
Income taxes payable	—	5,998	4,677
Current portion of long-term debt (note 14)	1,474	1,384	1,300
Total Current Liabilities	89,132	91,309	78,783
NON-CURRENT LIABILITIES			
Other payables (note 12)	11,110	10,180	9,105
Deferred revenue (note 13)	—	2,384	2,686
Deferred lease credits	17,317	19,011	20,609
Long-term debt (note 14)	8,573	10,047	11,431
Pension liability (note 15)	14,877	13,626	11,865
Total Non-Current Liabilities	51,877	55,248	55,696
SHAREHOLDERS' EQUITY			
Share capital (note 16)	39,890	29,614	25,888
Contributed surplus	5,158	6,266	5,164
Retained earnings	439,067	468,777	461,845
Accumulated other comprehensive income (note 16)	8,737	8,143	5,355
Total Shareholders' Equity	492,852	512,800	498,252
TOTAL LIABILITIES AND SHAREHOLDERS' EQUITY	$ 633,861	$ 659,357	$ 632,731
Commitments (note 18)			

REITMANS (CANADA) LIMITED
STATEMENTS OF CHANGES IN SHAREHOLDERS' EQUITY
(in thousands of Canadian dollars)

	For the years ended	
	January 28, 2012	**January 29, 2011**
SHARE CAPITAL		
Balance, beginning of the year	**$ 29,614**	$ 25,888
Cash consideration on exercise of share options (note 16)	**8,828**	3,569
Ascribed value credited to share capital from exercise of share options (note 16)	**2,228**	888
Cancellation of shares pursuant to share repurchase program (note 16)	**(780)**	(731)
Balance, end of the year	**39,890**	29,614
CONTRIBUTED SURPLUS		
Balance, beginning of the year	**6,266**	5,164
Share-based compensation costs (note 17)	**1,120**	1,990
Ascribed value credited to share capital from exercise of share options (note 16)	**(2,228)**	(888)
Balance, end of the year	**5,158**	6,266
RETAINED EARNINGS		
Balance, beginning of the year	**468,777**	461,845
Net earnings	**47,539**	88,985
Dividends (note 16)	**(52,654)**	(51,895)
Premium on repurchase of Class A non-voting shares (note 16)	**(21,630)**	(29,381)
Defined benefit actuarial losses (net of tax of $1,041; 2011 - $272) (note 15)	**(2,965)**	(777)
Balance, end of the year	**439,067**	468,777
ACCUMULATED OTHER COMPREHENSIVE INCOME		
Balance, beginning of the year	**8,143**	5,355
Net change in fair value of available-for-sale financial assets (net of tax of $79; 2011 - $427) (note 19)	**530**	2,866
Reclassification of realized gains on available-for-sale financial assets to net earnings (net of tax of $22) (note 19)	**—**	(145)
Reclassification of impairment loss on available-for-sale financial assets to net earnings (net of tax of $9; 2011 - $11) (note 19)	**64**	67
Balance, end of the year (note 16)	**8,737**	8,143
Total Shareholders' Equity	**$ 492,852**	$ 512,800

REITMANS (CANADA) LIMITED
STATEMENTS OF CASH FLOWS
(in thousands of Canadian dollars)

	For the years ended	
	January 28, 2012	**January 29, 2011**
CASH FLOWS FROM (USED IN) OPERATING ACTIVITIES		
Net earnings	**$ 47,539**	$ 88,985
Adjustments for:		
Depreciation, amortization and impairment losses	**64,990**	59,754
Share-based compensation costs	**1,120**	1,990
Amortization of deferred lease credits	**(4,635)**	(4,956)
Deferred lease credits	**2,941**	3,358
Pension contribution	**(4,245)**	(629)
Pension expense	**1,490**	1,341
Realized gain on sale of marketable securities	**—**	(167)
Impairment loss on available-for-sale financial assets	**73**	78
Net change in fair value of derivatives	**754**	—
Foreign exchange loss (gain)	**2,942**	(31)
Interest and dividend income, net	**(4,147)**	(3,068)
Interest paid	**(682)**	(797)
Interest received	**1,316**	1,273
Dividends received	**3,460**	2,546
Income taxes	**18,333**	38,817
	131,249	188,494
Changes in:		
Trade and other receivables	**(114)**	106
Inventories	**(5,084)**	(10,074)
Prepaid expenses	**589**	(1,481)
Trade and other payables	**504**	9,073
Deferred revenue	**60**	1,410
Cash generated from operating activities	**127,204**	187,528
Income taxes received	**793**	6,040
Income taxes paid	**(31,060)**	(46,388)
Net cash flows from operating activities	**96,937**	147,180
CASH FLOWS (USED IN) FROM INVESTING ACTIVITIES		
Purchases of marketable securities	**(420)**	(20,803)
Proceeds on sale of marketable securities	**—**	1,709
Additions to property and equipment and intangible assets	**(59,154)**	(46,922)
Cash flows used in investing activities	**(59,574)**	(66,016)
CASH FLOWS (USED IN) FROM FINANCING ACTIVITIES		
Dividends paid	**(52,654)**	(51,895)
Purchase of Class A non-voting shares for cancellation	**(22,410)**	(30,112)
Repayment of long-term debt	**(1,384)**	(1,300)
Proceeds from exercise of share options	**8,828**	3,569
Cash flows used in financing activities	**(67,620)**	(79,738)
FOREIGN EXCHANGE (LOSS) GAIN ON CASH HELD IN FOREIGN CURRENCY	**(2,942)**	31
NET (DECREASE) INCREASE IN CASH AND CASH EQUIVALENTS	**(33,199)**	1,457
CASH AND CASH EQUIVALENTS, BEGINNING OF THE YEAR	**230,034**	228,577
CASH AND CASH EQUIVALENTS, END OF THE YEAR	**$ 196,835**	$ 230,034

Supplementary cash flow information (note 25)

APPENDIX B INVESTMENTS

Investments can include debt and equity, and can be made by individuals or corporations. Investments can be made to generate investment income or for strategic purposes. They can be held for a short or long period of time. The way in which a company accounts for its investments is determined by the nature and purpose of the investment.

CLASSIFYING INVESTMENTS

STUDY OBJECTIVE 1

Identify reasons to invest and classify instruments.

Corporations generally purchase **debt instruments** and **equity instruments** for one of two reasons: (1) as a non-strategic investment to generate investment income or (2) as a strategic investment to maintain a long-term operating relationship with another company by influencing or controlling the company in some way.

Companies use **non-strategic investments** for various reasons:

1. A company may have cash that it does not immediately need. A company may experience seasonal fluctuations in sales that would lead to idle cash.
2. When investing excess cash for short periods of time, corporations invest in debt securities, usually money-market instruments, which are low risk and highly liquid.
3. Excess cash may also be invested for a longer term in debt securities for the purpose of earning interest income (for example, bonds) or to earn dividend income (for example, equities).
4. Companies also invest in debt and equity instruments for the purpose of selling in the short term at a gain. This includes investments in common or preferred shares and debt instruments such as bonds. These investments are referred to as **trading investments** or trading securities. They are reported at fair value on the balance sheet.

Generally, non-strategic investments are classified and reported based on the purpose of the investment and on whether it is debt or equity, as shown in Illustration B-1.

ILLUSTRATION B-1
Classification and reporting of non-strategic investments under IFRS

Type of Instrument	Purpose	Balance Sheet Classification and Valuation	
Short-term debt instruments	Held to earn interest income	Current assets	Amortized cost
Long-term debt instruments	Held to earn interest income	Non-current assets	Amortized cost
Short- or long-term debt instruments	Trading	Current assets	Fair value
Equity instruments	Trading	Current assets	Fair value

BEFORE YOU GO ON...

DO IT

ABC Corp., a public company reporting under IFRS, made the following investments during the year.

1. Purchased bonds to earn interest income.
2. Purchased common shares of a company, to be sold if the share price increases.
3. Purchased bonds with the intent to trade at a gain.

For each investment, indicate if it should be reported at amortized cost or fair value.

SOLUTION

1. amortized cost 2. fair value 3. fair value

Related exercise material: BEB–1.

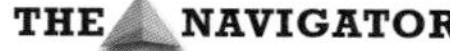

ACCOUNTING FOR DEBT INVESTMENTS REPORTED AT AMORTIZED COST

STUDY OBJECTIVE 2

Account for debt investments that are reported at amortized cost.

As mentioned in the previous section, under IFRS, debt instruments purchased to earn interest income are reported at amortized cost. Under ASPE, all investments in debt instruments are reported at amortized cost, whether they are purchased to trade or to earn interest. You will recall from Chapter 15 that amortized cost is the maturity value or principal less any unamortized discount, or plus any unamortized premium, and that the effective-interest method is used to amortize any discount or premium and record interest expense on long-term debt. This method is also used to record interest revenue and amortize any premiums or discounts on debt investments reported at amortized cost. By using the effective-interest method, interest revenue reflects the actual interest earned on the investment.

Debt instruments that are valued at amortized cost can include both short-term and long-term debt instruments. **Short-term debt instruments** are instruments that will mature within 12 months of the balance sheet date. **Long-term debt instruments** are instruments with a maturity of longer than 12 months after the balance sheet date. Regardless of the term of the debt, the accounting for all debt instruments reported at amortized cost has some basic similarities. Entries are required to record the following.

1. **The acquisition:** Debt instruments are recorded at the purchase price paid for the investment.
2. **Interest revenue and amortization of any discount or premium:** Interest revenue is recognized as it accrues and any discount or premium is amortized using the effective-interest method. The investment is reported at amortized cost on the balance sheet.
3. **The sale or disposition at maturity:** When the instrument matures or is sold, the cash received is recorded, and its carrying amount (amortized cost) is eliminated. If the instrument is sold before maturity, a gain is recorded if the cash received is greater than the amortized cost of the investment and a loss is recorded if the cash received is less than the amortized cost. This is shown in illustration B-2.

ILLUSTRATION B-2
Gain and loss on sale of investment in debt instrument valued at amortized cost

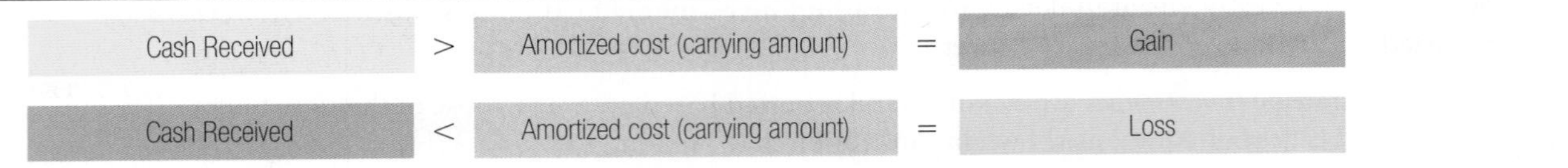

You will recall that debt instruments include money-market instruments as well as bonds, and a large variety of other debt securities. The following sections illustrate accounting for debt investments at amortized cost for bonds.

BONDS

Bonds were discussed in Chapter 15 from the liability side; that is, from the issuer's perspective. Corporations, governments, and universities issue bonds that are then purchased by investors. The issuer of the bonds is known as the **investee**. The purchaser of the bonds, or the bondholder, is known as the **investor**. The investor's accounting for bonds reported at amortized cost is illustrated below. To illustrate the investor's accounting, we will use the Candlestick Inc. bond example in Chapter 15. Recall that Candlestick, the investee, issued $1 million of five-year, 5% bonds on January 1, 2014, and that interest is paid semi-annually on January 1 and July 1.

Recording Acquisition of Bonds

At acquisition, the investment in bonds is recorded at the purchase price. Recall from Chapter 15 that bonds will sell at a premium (purchase price is above face value) if the market interest rate is lower than the contract rate of 5%. Bonds are sold at a discount (purchase price is below face value) if the market interest rate is higher than the contract rate of 5%.

Assume that Candlestick issues the bonds, at a premium, to yield a market interest rate of 4% and that Kadir Inc., the investor, purchases $100,000 (10%) of these bonds. The market price of the bonds is 104.4915. Kadir will pay $104,491 ($100,000 × 1.044915) and records the purchase as follows:

Jan. 1	Long-Term Investment—Candlestick Bonds	104,491	
	Cash		104,491
	To record purchase of Candlestick bonds.		

A = L + SE
+104,491
−104,491
Cash flows: −104,491

Given that the bonds are being held to earn interest revenue and not to trade, and the term of the bonds is five years, the bonds will be reported in non-current assets on the balance sheet.

As you go through this illustration of accounting for bonds at amortized cost from the investor's perspective, you may want to refer to the section on "Issuing Bonds at a Premium" in Chapter 15 to see the similarities and differences in the accounting for bonds between the investor and investee. Note that the amount Kadir Inc. paid for the Candlestick bonds is 10% ($1,044,915 × 10%) of the amount that Candlestick recorded in Bonds Payable when it issued the bonds.

Recording Interest Revenue and Amortizing the Discount or Premium

When bonds are reported at amortized cost, any premium or discount recorded in the investment account is amortized to interest revenue over the remaining term of the bonds. If there is a bond premium, interest revenue is reduced by the amortization amount. If there is a bond discount, interest revenue is increased by the amortization amount. Recall from earlier in the appendix that, like the issuer of the bonds, the investor uses the effective-interest method of amortization.

To continue the Kadir example, recall that Candlestick makes semi-annual interest payments on July 1 and January 1. The interest received, $2,500, is calculated by multiplying the bonds' face value by the contractual interest rate ($100,000 × 5% × 6⁄12). Interest revenue is calculated by multiplying the amortized cost (carrying value) of the long-term investment by the market interest rate. On July 1, 2014, Kadir will record $2,090 interest revenue ($104,491 × 4% × 6⁄12). The amortization of the premium or discount is the difference between the interest received and the interest revenue or $410 ($2,500 − $2,090). The premium amortization is credited to the investment account, which reduces the amortized cost (carrying amount) of the investment.

The entry to record the receipt of the interest and amortization of the premium on July 1, 2014, is as follows:

July 1	Cash	2,500	
	Long-Term Investment—Candlestick Bonds		410
	Interest Revenue		2,090
	To record receipt of interest on Candlestick bonds.		

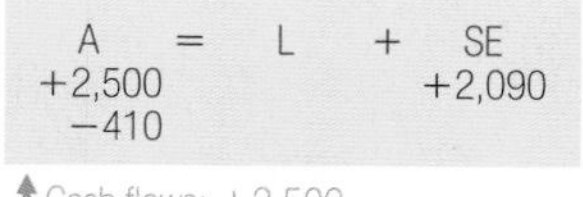

Cash flows: +2,500

The interest revenue is less than the cash received. The purchase of the bonds at a premium causes the total interest earned to be less than the total interest received. If Kadir holds the bonds until maturity, the long-term investment's amortized cost (carrying value) will be $100,000, the face value of the bonds.

Normally, investors prepare an amortization schedule to make it easier to calculate the interest revenue and the premium or discount amortization. The amortization schedule is very similar to the one shown in Chapter 15's Illustration 15-8 for the investee, Candlestick Inc. For Kadir, the investor, the amortization schedule shows interest received instead of interest paid in column A and interest revenue instead of interest expense in column B.

Illustration B-3 compares the recording of the bonds as an investment for Kadir Inc. (the investor) and as a liability for Candlestick (the investee) for the bond issue and first interest payment date.

ILLUSTRATION B-3
Comparison of bond investment and liability

KADIR INC. (INVESTOR)

Jan. 1	Long-Term Investment—Candlestick Bonds	104,491	
	Cash		104,491
July 1	Cash	2,500	
	Long-Term Investment—Candlestick Bonds		410
	Interest Revenue		2,090

CANDLESTICK INC. (INVESTEE)

Jan. 1	Cash	1,044,915	
	Bonds Payable		1,044,915
July 1	Interest Expense	20,898	
	Bonds Payable	4,102	
	Cash		25,000

Note that on January 1, 2014, Kadir recorded a non-current asset, and Candlestick recorded a non-current liability. On July 1, 2014, Kadir recorded interest revenue and Candlestick recorded interest expense.

In this example, because Kadir (the investor) purchased 10% of the Candlestick bonds, the interest that Kadir receives semi-annually ($2,500) is 10% of the interest paid ($25,000) by Candlestick. Also note that, because Kadir purchased the bonds directly from Candlestick, the interest revenue ($2,090) and premium amortization ($410) are 10% of the interest expense ($20,898) and premium amortization ($4,102) that are recorded by Candlestick.

Recording the Maturity of Bonds

Regardless of the bonds' purchase price, their amortized cost at maturity will equal their face value. By the time the bonds mature, any discount or premium will be fully amortized. Assuming that the interest for the last interest period has been received and recorded, the entry to record the receipt of cash for the Candlestick Bonds at maturity, January 1, 2019, is as follows:

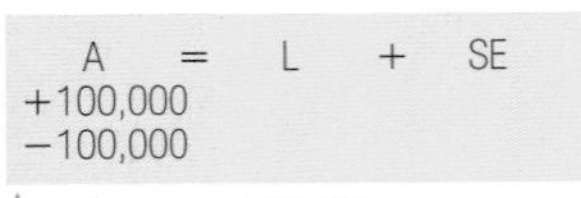

↑Cash flows: +100,000

Date	Account	Debit	Credit
Jan. 1	Cash	100,000	
	Long-Term Investment—Candlestick Bonds		100,000
	To record maturity of Candlestick bonds.		

Because the amortized cost of the bonds equals the face value at maturity, there is no gain or loss.

Sale of Bonds Before Maturity

Although a company may purchase bonds to earn interest revenue, it may be necessary to sell the bonds before maturity if the company needs the cash, or the company may choose to sell the bonds because interest rates have increased and it can earn a higher return.

To record the sale of bonds, it is necessary to first update any unrecorded interest and the amortization of the discount or premium. Then an entry is prepared to (1) record the cash received, (2) remove the amortized cost of the bonds, and (3) recognize the gain or loss on sale. Interest must be updated if the bonds are sold between semi-annual interest payment dates.

To illustrate, assume Kadir sells its investment in Candlestick Bonds on January 1, 2017, for $99,500. The amortized cost of the bonds on January 1, 2017, is $101,904. Assuming that the interest for the interest date of January 1, 2017, has been received and recorded, the entry to record the sale of the bonds is as follows:

A	=	L	+	SE
+99,500				−2,404
−101,904				

↑Cash flows: +99,500

Date	Account	Debit	Credit
Jan. 1	Cash	99,500	
	Loss on Sale of Candlestick Bonds	2,404	
	Long-Term Investment—Candlestick Bonds		101,904
	To record sale of Candlestick bonds.		

As shown in Illustration B-3, a loss is recognized on the sale of the bonds as the bonds were sold at a price ($99,500) that was less than the amortized cost ($101,904). Conversely, a gain on sale is recognized if the bonds are sold at a price that is greater than the amortized cost of the bonds. Losses and gains on sale are reported in other expenses or other revenues, respectively.

Action Plan

- To create the amortization table, calculate the cash interest received by multiplying the face value of the bonds by the semi-annual contractual interest rate. Calculate the interest revenue by multiplying the amortized cost of the bonds by the semi-annual market interest rate.

BEFORE YOU GO ON...

DO IT

During 2014, Wang Corporation had the following transactions for debt investments purchased to earn interest:

Jan. 1 Purchased 10-year, 5% Hillary Corp. bonds with a face value of $30,000 for $27,768. The market interest rate is 6%. Interest is payable semi-annually on July 1 and January 1.

July 1 Received semi-annual interest on investment in Hillary bonds.

(a) Prepare a bond amortization schedule for the first three interest periods for Wang's investment in the Hillary bonds.
(b) Record the above transactions for Wang Corporation.
(c) Prepare the adjusting entry for the accrual of interest on December 31, Wang's year end.

BEFORE YOU GO ON... continued on next page

SOLUTION

(a)

Bond Discount Amortization Schedule—Investee Effective-Interest Method				
	(A)	(B)	(C)	(D)
Interest Period	Interest Received ($30,000 × 5% × 6/12)	Interest Revenue (D × 6% × 6/12)	Discount Amortization (A − B)	Bond Amortized Cost (D + C)
Purchase Jan. 1, 2014				$27,768
(1) July 1, 2014	$750	$833	$83	27,851
(2) Jan. 1, 2015	750	836	86	27,937
(3) July 1, 2015	750	838	88	28,025
(4) Jan. 1, 2016	750	841	91	28,116

(b)

Date	Account	Debit	Credit
Jan. 1	Long-Term Investment—Hillary Bonds	27,768	
	Cash		27,768
	To record purchase of Hillary bonds.		
July 1	Cash	750	
	Long-Term Investment—Hillary Bonds	83	
	Interest Revenue		833
	To record interest received on bonds.		

(c)

Date	Account	Debit	Credit
Dec. 31	Interest Receivable	750	
	Long-Term Investment—Hillary Bonds	86	
	Interest Revenue		836
	To accrue semi-annual interest on Hillary bonds.		

Related exercise material: BEB–2, BEB–3, EB–1, and EB–3.

BEFORE YOU GO ON...
continued from previous page

- In the amortization table, the amount of the discount (premium) amortization is the difference between the interest received and the interest revenue. The amortized cost of the bonds purchased increases by the amount of the discount amortization and decreases by the amount of the premium amortization.
- When investments are purchased, they are recorded at their purchase price.
- Interest revenue is recorded as it accrues.
- The investments are reported at amortized cost on the balance sheet; therefore, premiums and discounts on these investments are amortized when interest revenue is recognized. Use the amortization schedule to record the interest revenue on the bonds.
- When the investments mature, the cash received is recorded and the investment account is eliminated.

ACCOUNTING FOR TRADING INVESTMENTS

STUDY OBJECTIVE 3
Account for trading investments.

Illustration B-1 showed that debt and equity instruments purchased principally for trading are reported at fair value on the balance sheet. Under IFRS, trading investments reported at fair value may include investments in common or preferred shares and debt instruments such as bonds that are purchased with the intent of selling the instrument at a gain. Under ASPE, only trading investments in equity securities will be reported at fair value.

You will recall from Chapter 1 that **fair value** is generally the amount an asset could be sold for in the market. Debt and equity instruments purchased for trading are typically traded on public markets, so the fair value of the instrument is typically the quoted market price. The advantage of using fair value is that it allows users to better predict the future cash flows and assess the company's liquidity and solvency.

Alternative terminology Another common term for fair value is *market value.*

In accounting for trading investments reported at fair value, entries are required to record the following.

1. **The acquisition:** Trading investments are recorded at their fair value on the date of purchase.
2. **Interest and dividend revenue:** Interest revenue is recognized as it accrues and dividend revenue is recognized when the company receives the cash dividend or becomes entitled to the cash dividend. You will recall from Chapter 13 that an investor will be entitled to receive a dividend from the company paying dividends (investee) if the investor holds the shares on the date of record.
3. **Fair value adjustments:** Because trading investments are reported at fair value on the balance sheet, accounting entries are required to adjust the investment's carrying value for any increases or decreases in its fair value. This is referred to as a **fair value adjustment**. A gain is recorded if the fair value is higher than the carrying value and a loss is recorded if the fair value is less than the carrying value. This is shown in Illustration B-4.

ILLUSTRATION B-4
Gains and losses on fair value adjustments

Fair Value versus Carrying Value	Change to Carrying Value of Asset	Income Statement Account
Fair value higher than carrying value	Increase carrying value of investment to fair value	Record a gain on fair value adjustment
Fair value less than carrying value	Decrease carrying value of investment to fair value	Record a loss on fair value adjustment

Gains and losses on fair value adjustments for trading investments are reported in the income statement.

4. **The sale of the investment:** When the investment is sold, the cash received is recorded, the investment account is eliminated, and a gain or loss is recorded. Like investments reported at amortized cost, the gain or loss is equal to the difference between the cash received and the carrying value of the investment.

EQUITY INVESTMENTS—COMMON SHARES

Recording Acquisitions of Shares

Helpful hint The entries for investments in common shares are also used for investments in preferred shares.

When an equity instrument is purchased for trading, the investment is recorded at fair value, which is equal to the price the shares are trading at on the date of purchase. Assume, for example, that on July 1, 2014, Leonard Corporation purchases 500 common shares of Gleason Ltd. at $30 per share. Leonard Corporation purchased the shares to trade.

The entry to record the equity investment is as follows:

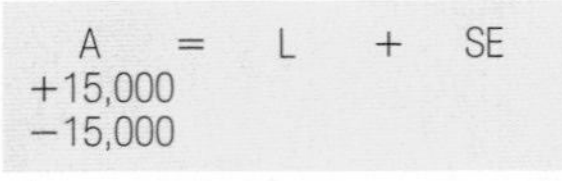

Cash flows: −15,000

July 1	Trading Investments—Gleason Common Shares	15,000	
	Cash (500 × $30)		15,000
	To record purchase of 500 Gleason common shares.		

Since this investment was made with the intent of selling it at a profit, the investment is reported as a current asset on the balance sheet.

Recording Dividend Revenue

During the time the shares are held, entries are required for any cash dividends that are received. If a $2 per share dividend is received by Leonard on December 1, the entry is as follows:

Cash flows: +1,000

Dec. 1	Cash (500 × $2)	1,000	
	Dividend Revenue		1,000
	To record receipt of cash dividend.		

Dividend revenue is reported under other revenues in the income statement.

Recording Fair Value Adjustments at the Balance Sheet Date

On December 31, 2014, Leonard's fiscal year end, Gleason Ltd.'s shares are trading on the stock exchange at $33. This is an increase of $3 ($33 − $30) per share and, as explained earlier, results in a gain. The entry to record the adjustment to fair value is as follows:

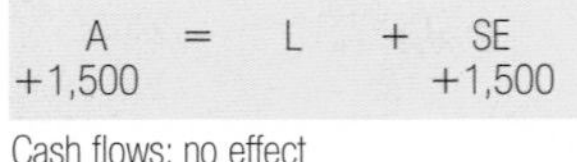

Cash flows: no effect

Dec. 31	Trading Investments—Gleason Common Shares (500 × $3)	1,500	
	Gain on Fair Value Adjustment of Trading Investments		1,500
	To record adjustment of Gleason shares to fair value.		

The investment in Gleason shares will be reported on the balance sheet at its fair value of $16,500 ($15,000 + $1,500), which is the new carrying value of the investment. The gain on fair value adjustment is reported under other revenues in the income statement.

Recording Sales of Shares

When shares are sold, the difference between the proceeds from the sale and the carrying value of the shares is recognized as a gain or loss. Assume that Leonard receives proceeds of $17,000 on the sale of its Gleason common shares on October 10, 2015. Because the shares' carrying value is $16,500, there is a gain of $500 ($17,000 − $16,500). The entry to record the sale is as follows:

		Debit	Credit
Oct. 10	Cash	17,000	
	Trading Investments—Gleason Common Shares		16,500
	Gain on Sale of Trading Investments ($17,000 − $16,500)		500
	To record sale of Gleason common shares.		

A	=	L	+	SE
+17,000				+500
−16,500				

↑Cash flows: +17,000

This gain is reported under other revenue in the income statement.

DEBT INVESTMENTS—BONDS

Recording Acquisitions of Bonds

The following example illustrates the accounting for bonds purchased to trade. Remember that the reporting of bonds at fair value will only apply to companies following IFRS, as companies reporting under ASPE report all debt investments at amortized cost. At acquisition, an investment in bonds for trading purposes is recorded at its fair value, which is equal to the price the bonds are trading at on the date of purchase. Assume Kuhl Corporation acquires $50,000 face value of Doan Inc. 10-year, 6% bonds on January 1, 2014, at a discount for $49,000. Kuhl Corporation purchased the bonds to trade. The entry to record the investment is as follows:

		Debit	Credit
Jan. 1	Trading Investments—Doan Bonds	49,000	
	Cash		49,000
	To record purchase of Doan bonds.		

A	=	L	+	SE
+49,000				
−49,000				

↓Cash flows: −49,000

Recording Interest Revenue

The bonds pay interest of $1,500 ($50,000 × 6% × 6⁄12) semi-annually on July 1 and January 1. The following entry records the receipt of interest on July 1, 2014.

		Debit	Credit
July 1	Cash	1,500	
	Interest Revenue		1,500
	To record receipt of interest on Doan bonds.		

A	=	L	+	SE
+1,500				+1,500

↑Cash flows: +1,500

Note that interest revenue is equal to the cash received. The $1,000 discount, the difference between the face value ($50,000) and the purchase price ($49,000) on the bonds, is not amortized to interest revenue. The bonds are purchased to trade and are held for a short period of time; therefore, any misstatement of interest revenue from not amortizing the premium or discount is considered insignificant.

Assuming Kuhl's financial year end is December 31, an entry is required to accrue interest revenue for the interest earned. The following entry records the accrual of interest on December 31:

		Debit	Credit
Dec. 31	Interest Receivable	1,500	
	Interest Revenue		1,500
	To record accrual of interest on Doan bonds.		

A	=	L	+	SE
+1,500				+1,500

Cash flows: no effect

Note that on January 1, 2015, when the interest payment is received from Doan, interest receivable will be credited.

Recording Fair Value Adjustments at the Balance Sheet Date

You will recall from Chapter 15 that bonds trade on the public market at prices that reflect the current market interest rate. If the market interest rate changes after a company purchases bonds, the bonds' fair value will be different from their purchase price. If the market interest rate increases, the bonds' fair value will decrease, and if the market interest rate decreases, the bonds' fair value will increase. Assume that on December 31, 2014, Kuhl's financial year end, the market interest rate increased and the bonds are trading at $48,000. The entry to record the adjustment to fair value is as follows:

A	=	L	+	SE
−1,000				−1,000

Cash flows: no effect

Date	Account	Debit	Credit
Dec. 31	Loss on Fair Value Adjustment of Trading Investments ($49,000 − $48,000)	1,000	
	Trading Investments—Doan Bonds		1,000
	To record adjustment to fair value.		

The investment in Doan bonds will be reported on the balance sheet in current assets at its fair value of $48,000, which is the new carrying value of the bonds. The loss on fair value adjustment is reported under other expenses in the income statement.

Recording Sales of Bonds

When the bonds are sold, it is necessary to first update any unrecorded interest up to the date of sale. Then (1) debit Cash for the proceeds received, (2) credit the investment account for the bonds' carrying value, and (3) record any gain or loss on sale. Any difference between the proceeds from the sale of the bonds and the carrying value is recorded as a gain or loss.

Assume, for example, that Kuhl receives $47,500 on the sale of the Doan bonds on July 1, 2015, after receiving (and recording) the interest due. Since the bonds' carrying value is $48,000, a loss of $500 is recorded. The entry to record the sale is as follows:

A	=	L	+	SE
+47,500				−500
−48,000				

↑Cash flows: +47,500

Date	Account	Debit	Credit
July 1	Cash	47,500	
	Loss on Sale of Trading Investments ($48,000 − $47,500)	500	
	Trading Investments—Doan Bonds		48,000
	To record sale of Doan bonds.		

The loss on the sale of the bonds is reported as other expenses in the income statement.

Recording Bonds for Investor and Investee

Using the Kuhl Corporation example, Illustration B-5 compares the recording of the bonds as a trading investment reported at fair value for Kuhl (the investor) and the recording of the bonds as a long-term liability for Doan (the investee). For the purpose of this illustration, we have assumed that the discount amortization is $150 for the first interest period, $140 for the second interest period, and $130 for the third interest period.

ILLUSTRATION B-5
Comparison of debt trading investment and long-term liability

KUHL CORPORATION (INVESTOR)

Date	Account	Debit	Credit
Jan. 1	Trading Investments—Doan Bonds	49,000	
	Cash		49,000
July 1	Cash	1,500	
	Interest Revenue		1,500
Dec. 31	Interest Receivable	1,500	
	Interest Revenue		1,500
31	Loss on Fair Value Adjustment of Trading Investments	1,000	
	Trading Investments—Doan Bonds		1,000
Jan. 1	Cash	1,500	
	Interest Receivable		1,500
July 1	Cash	1,500	
	Interest Revenue		1,500
1	Cash	47,500	
	Loss on Sale of Trading Investments	500	
	Trading Investments—Doan Bonds		48,000

DOAN INC. (INVESTEE)

Date	Account	Debit	Credit
Jan. 1	Cash	49,000	
	Bonds Payable		49,000
July 1	Interest Expense	1,650	
	Bonds Payable		150
	Cash		1,500
Dec. 31	Interest Expense	1,640	
	Bonds Payable		140
	Interest Payable		1,500
Jan. 1	Interest Payable	1,500	
	Cash		1,500
July 1	Interest Expense	1,630	
	Bonds Payable		130
	Cash		1,500

Note that accounting for a trading investment in bonds (an asset) for an investor differs from the accounting for bonds payable (a liability) for an investee in several ways. First, the investor does not amortize any premium or discount. Second, the investee does not record a fair value adjustment. Last, assuming that Kuhl, the investor, sold its bonds on the open market, the investee or issuer, Doan Inc., is not affected by this transaction. It would only be affected if the bonds were redeemed before maturity or repaid at maturity.

BEFORE YOU GO ON...

DO IT

During 2014, Lang Corporation had the following transactions:

Jan. 2	Purchased an investment in Utility Corp. $20,000, five-year, 4% bonds for $20,455 to trade. The market interest rate is 3.5%.
July 1	Received semi-annual interest on the Utility Corp. bonds.
2	Sold half of the Utility Corp. bonds for $10,500.
Sept. 1	Purchased 1,000 common shares of Electric Ltd. for $15 per share to trade.
Nov. 1	Received a $2 dividend on the Electric Ltd. shares.
Dec. 31	The Utility Corp. bonds' fair value was $9,750. The Electric Ltd. shares were trading at $14 per share.

(a) Record the above transactions.
(b) Prepare the required adjusting journal entries at December 31, Lang's financial year end.
(c) Identify where the investments would be reported in the balance sheet.
(d) Identify where the interest revenue, dividend revenue, and gains and losses will be reported.
(e) Assume that on January 15, 2015, Lang sells the Electric Ltd. shares for $13.50 per share. Record the sale of the shares.

SOLUTION

(a)

Jan. 2	Trading Investments—Utility Corp. Bonds	20,455	
	Cash		20,455
	To record purchase of Utility Corp. bonds.		
July 1	Cash	400	
	Interest Revenue		400
	To record receipt of interest.		
2	Cash	10,500	
	Trading Investments—Utility Corp. Bonds		10,228
	Gain on Sale of Trading Investments		272
	To record sale of half of Utility Corp. bonds.		
Sept. 1	Trading Investments—Electric Ltd. Common Shares	15,000	
	Cash		15,000
	To record purchase of Electric Ltd. common shares.		
Nov. 1	Cash	2,000	
	Dividend Revenue		2,000
	To record dividends received (1,000 × $2).		

(b)

Dec. 31	Interest Receivable ($10,000 × 4% × 6⁄12)	200	
	Interest Revenue		200
	To accrue semi-annual interest on Utility Corp. bonds.		
31	Loss on Fair Value Adjustment on Trading Investments	477	
	Trading Investments—Utility Corp. Bonds		477
	To record fair value adjustment on bonds ($10,227 − $9,750).		
31	Loss on Fair Value Adjustment on Trading Investments	1,000	
	Trading Investments—Electric Ltd. Common Shares		1,000
	To record fair value adjustment on Electric Ltd. common shares [1,000 × ($15 − $14)].		

(c) The investments will be reported in current assets on the balance sheet.

Action Plan

- Record the interest received as the amount of interest revenue.
- When the bonds are sold, the difference between the bonds' carrying value and the proceeds is reported as a gain or loss.
- Record the interest accrued on the bonds held for the period July 2 to December 31.
- Fair value adjustments are the difference between the investments' carrying value and fair value.
- When the shares are sold, the difference between the shares' carrying value and the proceeds is reported as a gain or loss

BEFORE YOU GO ON... continued on next page

BEFORE YOU GO ON...
continued from previous page

(d) Interest revenue, dividend revenue, and gain on sale will be reported in other revenues in the income statement. The losses from the fair value adjustments will be reported in other expenses in the income statement.

(e)

Jan. 15	Cash (1,000 × $13.50)	13,500	
	Loss on Sale of Trading Investments ($14,000 − $13,500)	500	
	Trading Investments—Electric Ltd. Common Shares		14,000
	To record sale of Electric Ltd. common shares.		

THE NAVIGATOR

Related exercise material: BEB–4, BEB–5, BEB–6, BEB–7, BEB–8, EB–2, EB–4, EB–5, EB–6, and EB–7.

CONCLUSION

Companies purchase debt and equity securities of other companies for two main reasons: (1) for non-strategic reasons as a source of investment income, and (2) for strategic reasons, such as gaining control of a competitor, influencing strategic alliances, or moving into a new line of business.

Non-strategic investments are debt and equity securities that are purchased for purposes of earning interest or dividend revenue or for the purpose of selling them in the short term at a gain. Investments purchased for selling in the short term are referred to as trading investments and are reported at fair value. Debt investments reported at amortized cost may be short-term or long-term. Strategic investments are always investments in equity securities and are classified as long-term investments.

Companies reporting under IFRS report debt investments purchased for the purposes of earning interest income at amortized cost. Companies reporting under ASPE report all investments in debt instruments at amortized cost. Debt investments include money-market instruments, bonds, and similar items. Entries are required to record the (1) acquisition, (2) interest revenue, and (3) maturity or sale. Interest revenue is recognized as it accrues and any discount or premium is amortized using the effective-interest method.

Trading investments are reported at fair value. Under IFRS, these investments can be either debt or equity securities that are purchased for the purpose of selling in the short term at a gain. Under ASPE, only investments in equity securities will be reported at fair value. An equity investment may be in either preferred or common shares of another corporation. Entries are required to record the (1) acquisition, (2) investment revenue, (3) fair value adjustments, and (4) sale. The gains and losses resulting from fair value adjustments are reported in profit.

Glossary

Debt instruments Debt obligations such as money-market instruments, bonds, or similar items that can be bought and sold. Also called *debt securities*. (p. B1)

Equity instruments An ownership interest in a corporation such as preferred and common shares. Also called *equity securities*. (p. B1)

Fair value The amount the investment can be sold for in the market. Typically this will be the quoted market price in a public market. (p. B5)

Fair value adjustment An accounting entry to adjust the carrying value of the investment for any increases or decreases in its fair value. (p. B5)

Investee The corporation that issues (sells) the debt or equity securities that investors purchase. (p. B2)

Investor The corporation that buys (owns) the debt or equity securities issued by another company. (p. B2)

Long-term debt instruments Debt instruments with a maturity of longer than 12 months after the balance sheet date. (p. B2)

Non-strategic investment An investment that is purchased mainly to generate investment income. (p. B1)

Short-term debt instruments Debt instruments that mature within 12 months of the balance sheet date. (p. B2)

Trading investments Debt or equity securities that are bought and held for sale in the near term, mainly to generate earnings from short-term price differences. Also referred to as *trading securities* and *held-for-trading investments*. (p. B1)

Brief Exercises

BEB–1 On January 1, 2014, Chan Ltd. purchased $600,000 of five-year, 4% bonds at par from Pullen Corporation. Interest is received semi-annually on July 1 and January 1. Chan purchased the bonds to earn interest. At December 31, 2014, the bonds were trading at 101. Prepare the journal entries to record (a) the purchase of the bonds on January 1, (b) the receipt of interest on July 1, and (c) any adjusting entries required at December 31.

Account for debt investment reported at amortized cost. **(SO 2) AP**

BEB–2 Strand Corp. purchased $300,000 of five-year, 4% Hydrocor bonds at 99 on June 30, 2014. Strand Corp. purchased the bonds to earn interest. Interest is paid semi-annually each June 30 and December 31. The semi-annual amortization amount for the first interest period is $273. At December 31, 2014, the bonds were trading at 98. Prepare the required journal entries on June 30 and December 31, 2014.

Account for debt investment reported at amortized cost. **(SO 2) AP**

BEB–3 Using the data presented in BEB–2, assume Strand Corp. is a public company and that it purchased Hydrocor's bonds to trade. Prepare the journal entries to record (a) the purchase of the bonds on June 30, 2014; (b) the receipt of the first interest payment on December 31, 2014; and (c) any required adjusting journal entries on December 31, 2014.

Account for trading investment. **(SO 3) AP**

BEB–4 Using the data presented in BEB–2 and BEB–3, assume Strand Corp. sells the bonds on January 1, 2015, at 98. Prepare the journal entry to record the sale of the bonds under each set of assumptions.

Account for sale of trading investment. **(SO 3) AP**

BEB–5 On August 1, McLain Finance Inc. buys 3,000 Datawave common shares as a trading investment for $114,000 cash. On October 15, McLain receives a cash dividend of $2.75 per share from Datawave. On December 1, McLain sells the shares for $120,000 cash. Prepare the journal entries to record the (a) purchase of the shares, (b) receipt of the dividend, and (c) sale of the shares.

Account for trading investment. **(SO 3) AP**

BEB–6 Nakagama Limited owns 10,000 common shares of Deal Inc. purchased for selling in the near term. The carrying value of Deal Inc.'s common shares at November 30, 2014, is $46,000. The fair value of the investment at November 30 and December 31, 2014, is $44,000 and $47,000, respectively. The company prepares adjusting journal entries monthly. Prepare the required adjusting entries to record the securities at fair value at November 30 and December 31.

Account for trading investment. **(SO 3) AP**

BEB–7 Using the data presented in BEB–6, assume that the investment in Deal Inc.'s common shares is sold on January 15, 2015, for $49,000. Prepare the journal entry to record the sale of the investment.

Account for trading investment. **(SO 3) AP**

Exercises

EB–1 On July 1, 2014, Imperial Inc., a public company, purchased $500,000 of Acme Corp. 10-year, 4% bonds for $461,000 to earn interest. The bonds had a market interest rate of 5%. The bonds pay interest semi-annually on January 1 and July 1. Imperial Inc. has a December 31 year end. At December 31, 2014, the bonds are trading at 96.

Record debt investment reported at amortized cost and bond liability. **(SO 2) AP**

Instructions

(a) Assuming Imperial Inc. purchased the bonds from Acme Corp., record the purchase of the bonds on July 1 for (1) Imperial Inc., and (2) Acme Corp.
(b) Record any adjusting journal entries that are required at December 31 for (1) Imperial Inc., and (2) Acme Corp.
(c) Record the receipt of the first interest payment on January 1, 2015, for (1) Imperial Inc., and (2) Acme Corp.
(d) Compare the accounting for the bond investment with that of the bond liability.

EB–2 Using the data presented in EB–1, assume that Imperial Inc. purchased the bonds to trade.

Record debt investment for trading purposes. **(SO 3) AP**

Instructions

(a) Record the purchase of the bonds on July 1, 2014.
(b) Record any adjusting journal entries that are required at December 31, 2014.

(c) Indicate how the investment is presented on Imperial Inc.'s December 31, 2014, balance sheet.
(d) Record the receipt of the first interest payment on January 1, 2015.
(e) Assume the bonds are sold on the market at 97 on July 1, 2015, after the semi-annual interest payment has been received and recorded. Record the sale of the bonds.
(f) Explain why Acme Corp. will not record an entry for the bonds sold by Imperial on July 1, 2015.

Use a bond amortization schedule to record debt investment transactions at amortized cost. (SO 2) AP

EB–3 On April 1, 2013, Bight Corporation issued $400,000, five-year bonds. On this date, Shoreline Corporation purchased the bonds from Bight to earn interest. Interest is received semi-annually on April 1 and October 1 and Shoreline's year end is March 31. Below is a partial amortization schedule for the first few years of the bond issue.

Semi-Annual Interest Period	Interest Received	Interest Revenue	Amortization	Bond Amortized Cost
April 1, 2013				$418,444
October 1, 2013	$8,000	$6,277	$1,723	416,721
April 1, 2014	8,000	6,251	1,749	414,972
October 1, 2014	8,000	6,225	1,775	413,197

Instructions
(a) Were the bonds purchased at a discount or at a premium?
(b) What is the face value of the bonds?
(c) What will the bonds' amortized cost be at the maturity date?
(d) What is the bonds' contractual interest rate? The market interest rate?
(e) Prepare the journal entries to record the purchase of the bonds, the receipt of interest on October 1, 2013, the accrual of interest on March 31, 2014, and the receipt of interest on April 1, 2014.
(f) If Shoreline holds the investment until maturity, what will be the total interest received over the 10-year life of the bonds? Total interest revenue?

Record debt trading investment transactions. (SO 3) AP

EB–4 Piper Corporation, a public company, had the following transactions with trading investments:

Jan.	1	Purchased $120,000 of Harris Corp. 6% bonds at 101, to yield a market interest rate of 5.8%. Interest is payable semi-annually on July 1 and January 1.
July	1	Received semi-annual interest on Harris bonds.
	1	Sold half of the Harris bonds for $64,000.
Dec.	31	Accrued interest at Piper's year end.
	31	Piper's bonds were trading at 100.

Instructions
(a) Record the above transactions.
(b) How would your entry on July 1 change if the bonds were purchased to earn interest?

Record debt and equity trading investments. (SO 3) AP

EB–5 Following is information for Marcel Ltée's trading investments. Marcel is a public company and has a December 31 year end.

2014

Sept.	28	Purchased 3,500 shares of Cygman Limited for $40 per share.
Oct.	1	Purchased $300,000 of Rauk Inc. 4% bonds at face value. The bonds pay interest semi-annually on April 1 and October 1.
Nov.	12	Sold 1,900 Cygman shares for $42 per share.
Dec.	1	Received $1.50 per share dividend from Cygman.
	31	Cygman shares were trading at $38 per share and the Rauk bonds were trading at 101.

2015

Mar.	31	Sold the remaining Cygman shares for $40 per share.
Apr.	1	Received interest on the Rauk bonds.
Oct.	1	Received interest on the Rauk bonds.
Dec.	31	Rauk bonds were trading at 100.

Instructions
Record the above transactions, including any required adjusting entries, for 2014 and 2015.

EB–6 At December 31, 2014, the trading investments for Yanik, Inc., are as follows:

Record adjusting entry for trading investments, show statement presentation, and record sale. **(SO 3) AP**

Security	Carrying Value	Fair Value
Co. A common shares	$18,500	$16,000
Co. B preferred shares	12,500	14,000
Co. C five-year, 4% bonds	23,000	19,000
Totals	$54,000	$49,000

Instructions

(a) Prepare the adjusting entries required at December 31 to report the investment portfolio at fair value.

(b) Show the financial statement presentation of the trading investments and the gains and losses on fair value adjustments at December 31, 2014.

(c) Assuming that on March 20, 2015, Yanik sold Co. B preferred shares for $13,500, prepare the journal entry to record this transaction.

EB–7 The following was reported by Church Financial in its December 31, 2014, financial statements:

Determine equity trading investment transactions. **(SO 3) AP**

Trading investments, December 31, 2013	$11,000
Trading investments, December 31, 2014	15,000
Gain on fair value adjustment	2,500
Loss on sale of trading investment	3,000

The carrying value of the investments sold was $4,000.

Instructions

(a) What is the cash amount received on the sale of the investment?

(b) Prepare the journal entries that were recorded by Church to record the sale of the investment and the gain on fair value adjustment at December 31, 2014.

(c) Post the journal entries to the Trading Investments T account.

(d) Calculate the amount of trading investments purchased in 2014. Prepare the entry to record the purchase.

Problems: Set A

PB–1A On January 1, 2014, Morrison Inc., a public company, purchased $600,000 of Pearl Corporation's five-year, 4% bonds for $627,660, when the market interest rate was 3%. Interest is received semi-annually on July 1 and January 1. Morrison's year end is December 31. Morrison intends to hold Pearl's bonds until January 1, 2019, the date the bonds mature. The bonds' fair value on December 31, 2014, was $620,000.

Record debt investment; show statement presentation. **(SO 2, 3) AP**

Instructions

(a) Record the purchase of the bonds on January 1, 2014.

(b) Prepare the entry to record the receipt of interest on July 1, 2014.

(c) Prepare the adjusting entries required at December 31, 2014.

(d) Prepare the entry to record the receipt of interest on January 1, 2015.

(e) Prepare the entry to record the repayment of the bonds on January 1, 2019. Assume the entry to record the last interest payment has been recorded.

(f) How would your answers to parts (b) through (e) change if the bonds were purchased for the purpose of trading?

TAKING IT FURTHER What was the market interest rate on December 31, 2014, when the bonds' fair value was $631,500? (*Hint:* How many interest periods are left after January 1, 2015?)

PB–2A On January 1, 2014, Power Ltd. issued bonds with a maturity value of $5 million for $4,797,000, when the market rate of interest was 8%. The bonds have a coupon (contractual) interest rate of 7% and mature on January 1, 2019. Interest on the bonds is payable semi-annually on July 1 and January 1 of each year. On January 1, 2014, Finance Company purchased Power Ltd. bonds with a maturity value of $1 million to earn interest. On December 31, 2014, the bonds were trading at 98. Both companies' year end is December 31.

Record debt investment at amortized cost and fair value, prepare bond amortization schedule, and record liability; show statement presentation. **(SO 2, 3) AP**

Instructions

(a) What amount did Finance Company pay for Power Ltd.'s bonds?
(b) Prepare the journal entry for Finance Company (investor) on January 1, 2014.
(c) Prepare a bond amortization schedule for Finance Company for the first four interest periods.
(d) Prepare the journal entries for Finance Company to record (1) the receipt of interest on July 1, 2014; (2) the accrual of interest on December 31, 2014; and (3) the receipt of interest on January 1, 2015.
(e) Prepare the journal entry for Power Ltd. (investee) on January 1, 2014.
(f) Using the bond amortization schedule prepared in part (c) to calculate the interest expense and interest payments, prepare the journal entries for Power Ltd. to record (1) the payment of interest on July 1, 2014; (2) the accrual of interest on December 31, 2014; and (3) the payment of interest on January 1, 2015.

TAKING IT FURTHER Assume that Finance Company needed cash and sold the bonds on the open market on January 1, 2015, for 99.5 after receiving and recording the semi-annual interest payment. Indicate the amount of gain or loss that Finance Company would record if the bonds were purchased to (1) earn interest, and (2) trade.

Record equity and debt trading investments; show statement presentation.
(SO 3) AP

PB–3A During the year ended December 31, 2014, Rakai Corporation, a public company, had the following transactions in trading investments:

Feb. 1 Purchased 575 IBF common shares for $25,300.
Mar. 1 Purchased 1,500 Raimundo common shares for $48,000.
Apr. 1 Purchased $200,000 of CRT 3% bonds for $210,000. Interest is payable semi-annually on April 1 and October 1.
July 1 Received a cash dividend of $1.50 per share on the IBF common shares.
Aug. 1 Sold 250 IBF common shares at $48 per share.
Oct. 1 Received the semi-annual interest on the CRT bonds.
1 Sold the CRT bonds for $215,000.
Dec. 31 The fair values of the IBF and Raimundo common shares were $50 and $28 per share, respectively.

Instructions

Record the transactions and any required year-end adjusting entries.

TAKING IT FURTHER If Rakai Corporation anticipated that it would need the cash that was used to invest in the trading investments in the near future, should the company have invested in equity securities?

Remember to go
back to the beginning
of the appendix to
check off your
completed work!
←

APPENDIX PV PRESENT VALUE CONCEPTS

Present value concepts are widely used by accountants in the preparation of financial statements. Under IFRS, these concepts are more widely applied than under ASPE. This appendix will explain the basics that you must be aware of to understand related topics in this text.

INTEREST AND CALCULATING PRESENT VALUES

STUDY OBJECTIVE 1
Calculate simple and compound interest, and the present value of a single future amount.

Interest is payment for the use of money. It is the difference between the amount borrowed or invested (the principal) and the amount repaid or collected. The amount of interest to be paid or collected is usually stated as a percentage rate over a specific period of time. The rate of interest is generally stated as an annual rate to allow for easier comparison between loan alternatives with different terms.

The amount of interest involved in any financing transaction is based on three elements:

1. **Principal** (p): The original amount borrowed or invested
2. **Interest rate** (i): An annual percentage of the principal
3. **Number of periods** (n): The time period that the principal is borrowed or invested

SIMPLE AND COMPOUND INTEREST

When calculating interest, it is important to know when and how to use simple or compound interest.

Simple Interest

Simple interest is calculated on the principal amount only. In accounting, simple interest is used in accrual accounting to record the amount of interest revenue earned or expense incurred on a loan. Accruals for interest can be easily calculated at the end of each accounting period and prorated for partial periods where appropriate.

Simple interest is usually expressed as shown in Illustration PV-1.

ILLUSTRATION PV-1
Simple interest formula

Interest	=	Principal (p)	×	Interest Rate (i)	×	Number of Periods (n)

For example, if you borrowed $1,000 for three years at a simple interest rate of 9% annually, you would pay $270 in total interest, calculated as follows:

Interest $= p \times i \times n$	Year 1		Year 2		Year 3		
$= \$1{,}000 \times 9\% \times 3$	$90	+	$90	+	$90	=	$270
$= \$270$							

Compound Interest

Compound interest is the return on (or growth of) the principal for two or more time periods. Compounding calculates interest not only on the principal but also on the interest earned to date on that principal, assuming the interest is left on deposit (that is, it is added to the original principal amount).

To illustrate the difference between simple and compound interest, assume that you deposit $1,000 in the Last Canadian Bank, where it will earn simple interest of 9% per year, and you deposit another $1,000 in the First Canadian Bank, where it will earn interest of 9% per year compounded annually. Also assume that in both cases you will not withdraw any interest until three years from the date of deposit. The calculations of interest to be received and the accumulated year-end balances are given in Illustration PV-2.

ILLUSTRATION PV-2
Simple versus compound interest

LAST CANADIAN BANK		
Simple Interest Calculation	Simple Interest	Accumulated Year-End Balance
Year 1 $1,000.00 × 9%	$ 90.00	$1,090.00
Year 2 $1,000.00 × 9%	90.00	$1,180.00
Year 3 $1,000.00 × 9%	90.00	$1,270.00
	$270.00	

$25.03 Difference

FIRST CANADIAN BANK		
Compound Interest Calculation	Compound Interest	Accumulated Year-End Balance
Year 1 $1,000.00 × 9%	$ 90.00	$1,090.00
Year 2 $1,090.00 × 9%	98.10	$1,188.10
Year 3 $1,188.10 × 9%	106.93	$1,295.03
	$295.03	

Note in Illustration PV-2 that simple interest uses the initial principal of $1,000 to calculate the interest in all three years. Compound interest uses the accumulated balance (principal plus interest to date) at each year end to calculate interest in the following year. This explains why your compound interest account is larger: you are earning interest on interest. For practical purposes, compounding assumes that unpaid interest earned becomes a part of the principal. The accumulated balance at the end of each year becomes the new principal on which interest is earned during the next year. Assuming all else is equal (especially risk), if you had a choice between investing your money at simple interest or at compound interest, you would choose compound interest. In the example, compounding provides $25.03 of additional interest income.

When borrowing or lending money, the lending agreement should always state whether interest will be calculated using the simple or compound method. If the compound method is used, the frequency of compounding must also be stated. The shorter the amount of time between compounding calculations (that is, the more frequent the compounding), the more interest will be earned.

Compound interest is used in most business transactions. Simple interest is generally applicable only to short-term loans of one year or less. The shorter the term of the loan, the smaller the difference between simple and compound interest and therefore the parties will agree to use simple interest. Present value concepts use compound interest.

PRESENT VALUE OF A SINGLE FUTURE AMOUNT

In the previous example on compound and simple interest, the initial principal was given. It was used to calculate the interest earned and the value of the investment at the end of three years. **The initial principal, invested at the beginning of year one, is the present value (PV)** of the investment. **The value of the investment at the end of three years is the future value (FV)** of the investment.

You are probably more accustomed to being given the present value and then calculating the future value. But in business, there are many situations in which the future value (the cash flows that will occur in the future) is known, and it is necessary to calculate the present value (the value of those future cash flows at the beginning). For example, we determine the market price of a bond by calculating the present value of the future principal and interest payments. Calculating the amount to be reported for fixed and intangible assets, notes payable, pensions, and finance lease liabilities can also involve present value calculations.

Present value calculations are always based on three variables:

1. The *dollar amount* to be received (the future amount or future value)
2. The *length of time* until the amount is received (the number of periods)
3. The *interest rate* (the discount rate) per period

Alternative terminology The discount rate is also referred to as the *effective rate*, or the *imputed rate*.

The process of determining the present value is often referred to as **discounting the future cash flows**. The word "discount" has many meanings in accounting, each of which varies with the context in which it is being used. Be careful not to confuse the use of this term.

In the following section, we will show four methods of calculating the present value of a single future amount: present value formula, present value tables, financial calculators, and Excel.

Present Value Formula

To illustrate present value concepts, assume that you want to invest a sum of money at 5% in order to have \$1,000 at the end of one year. The amount that you would need to invest today is called the present value of \$1,000 discounted for one year at 5%.

The variables in this example are shown in the time diagram in Illustration PV-3.

ILLUSTRATION PV-3
Time diagram for the present value of \$1,000 discounted for one period at 5%

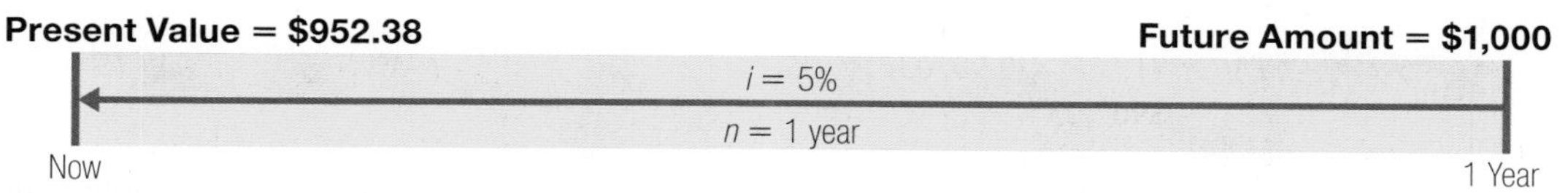

The formula used to determine the present value for any interest (discount) rate (i), number of periods (n), and future amount (FV) is shown in Illustration PV-4.

ILLUSTRATION PV-4
Present value of a single future amount formula

$$\text{Present value } (PV) = \frac{\text{Future value } (FV)}{(1 + i)^n}$$
$$= FV \div (1 + i)^n$$

In applying this formula to calculate the present value (PV) for the above example, the future value (FV) of \$1,000, the interest (discount) rate (i) of 5%, and the number of periods (n) of 1 are used as follows:

Alternative terminology The present value of a single future amount formula is also called the *present value of 1 formula.*

$$\begin{aligned} PV &= \$1{,}000 \div (1 + 5\%)^1 \\ &= \$1{,}000 \div 1.05 \\ &= \$952.38 \end{aligned}$$

If the single future cash flow of \$1,000 is to be received in two years and discounted at 5%, its present value is calculated as follows:

$$\begin{aligned} PV &= \$1{,}000 \div (1 + 5\%)^2 \\ &= \$1{,}000 \div 1.05^2 \text{ or } [(\$1{,}000 \div 1.05) \div 1.05] \\ &= \$907.03 \end{aligned}$$

The time diagram in Illustration PV-5 shows the variables used to calculate the present value when cash is received in two years.

ILLUSTRATION PV-5
Time diagram for present value of \$1,000 discounted for two periods at 5%

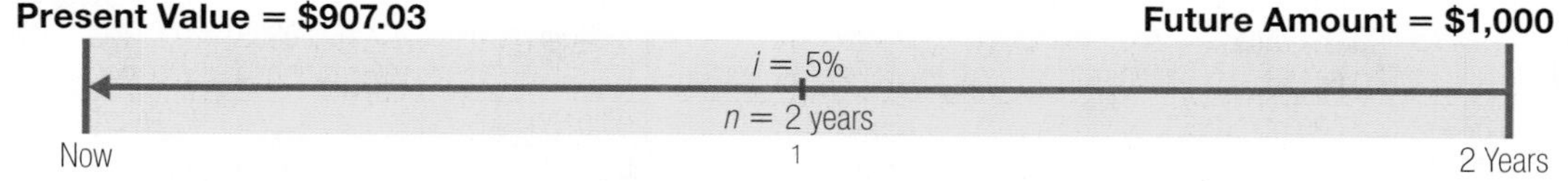

Present Value Tables

The present value may also be determined through tables that show the present value of 1 for n periods for different periodic interest rates or discount rates. In Table PV-1, the rows represent the number of discounting periods and the columns represent the periodic interest or discount rates. The five-digit decimal numbers in the respective rows and columns are the factors for the present value of 1.

When present value tables are used, the present value is calculated by multiplying the future cash amount by the present value factor specified at the intersection of the number of periods and the discount rate. For example, if the discount rate is 5% and the number of periods is 1, Table PV-1 shows that the present value factor is 0.95238. Then the present value of $1,000 discounted at 5% for one period is calculated as follows:

$$\begin{aligned} PV &= \$1{,}000 \times 0.95238 \\ &= \$952.38 \end{aligned}$$

For two periods at a discount rate of 5%, the present value factor is 0.90703. The present value of $1,000 discounted at 5% for two periods is calculated as follows:

$$\begin{aligned} PV &= \$1{,}000 \times 0.90703 \\ &= \$907.03 \end{aligned}$$

Note that the present values in these two examples are identical to the amounts determined previously when using the present value formula. This is because the factors in a present value table have been calculated using the present value formula. The benefit of using a present value table is that it can be quicker than using the formula. If you are using a simple calculator (not a financial calculator) or doing the calculations by hand, there are more calculations involved as the number of periods increases, making it more tedious than using the present value tables.

Table PV-1 can also be used if you know the present value and wish to determine the future cash flow. The present value amount is divided by the present value factor specified at the intersection of the number of periods and the discount rate in Table PV-1. For example, it can easily be determined that an initial investment of $907.03 will grow to yield a future amount of $1,000 in two periods, at an annual discount rate of 5% ($1,000 = $907.03 ÷ 0.90703).

TABLE PV-1
PRESENT VALUE OF 1

$$PV = \frac{1}{(1 + i)^n}$$

(n) Periods	2%	2½%	3%	4%	5%	6%	7%	8%	9%	10%	11%	12%	15%
1	0.98039	0.97561	0.97087	0.96154	0.95238	0.94340	0.93458	0.92593	0.91743	0.90909	0.90090	0.89286	0.86957
2	0.96117	0.95181	0.94260	0.92456	0.90703	0.89000	0.87344	0.85734	0.84168	0.82645	0.81162	0.79719	0.75614
3	0.94232	0.92860	0.91514	0.88900	0.86384	0.83962	0.81630	0.79383	0.77218	0.75131	0.73119	0.71178	0.65752
4	0.92385	0.90595	0.88849	0.85480	0.82270	0.79209	0.76290	0.73503	0.70843	0.68301	0.65873	0.63552	0.57175
5	0.90573	0.88385	0.86261	0.82193	0.78353	0.74726	0.71299	0.68058	0.64993	0.62092	0.59345	0.56743	0.49718
6	0.88797	0.86230	0.83748	0.79031	0.74622	0.70496	0.66634	0.63017	0.59627	0.56447	0.53464	0.50663	0.43233
7	0.87056	0.84127	0.81309	0.75992	0.71068	0.66506	0.62275	0.58349	0.54703	0.51316	0.48166	0.45235	0.37594
8	0.85349	0.82075	0.78941	0.73069	0.67684	0.62741	0.58201	0.54027	0.50187	0.46651	0.43393	0.40388	0.32690
9	0.83676	0.80073	0.76642	0.70259	0.64461	0.59190	0.54393	0.50025	0.46043	0.42410	0.39092	0.36061	0.28426
10	0.82035	0.78120	0.74409	0.67556	0.61391	0.55839	0.50835	0.46319	0.42241	0.38554	0.35218	0.32197	0.24718
11	0.80426	0.76214	0.72242	0.64958	0.58468	0.52679	0.47509	0.42888	0.38753	0.35049	0.31728	0.28748	0.21494
12	0.78849	0.74356	0.70138	0.62460	0.55684	0.49697	0.44401	0.39711	0.35553	0.31863	0.28584	0.25668	0.18691
13	0.77303	0.72542	0.68095	0.60057	0.53032	0.46884	0.41496	0.36770	0.32618	0.28966	0.25751	0.22917	0.16253
14	0.75788	0.70773	0.66112	0.57748	0.50507	0.44230	0.38782	0.34046	0.29925	0.26333	0.23199	0.20462	0.14133
15	0.74301	0.69047	0.64186	0.55526	0.48102	0.41727	0.36245	0.31524	0.27454	0.23939	0.20900	0.18270	0.12289
16	0.72845	0.67362	0.62317	0.53391	0.45811	0.39365	0.33873	0.29189	0.25187	0.21763	0.18829	0.16312	0.10686
17	0.71416	0.65720	0.60502	0.51337	0.43630	0.37136	0.31657	0.27027	0.23107	0.19784	0.16963	0.14564	0.09293
18	0.70016	0.64117	0.58739	0.49363	0.41552	0.35034	0.29586	0.25025	0.21199	0.17986	0.15282	0.13004	0.08081
19	0.68643	0.62553	0.57029	0.47464	0.39573	0.33051	0.27651	0.23171	0.19449	0.16351	0.13768	0.11611	0.07027
20	0.67297	0.61027	0.55368	0.45639	0.37689	0.31180	0.25842	0.21455	0.17843	0.14864	0.12403	0.10367	0.06110

Financial Calculators

Present values can also be calculated using financial calculators. Financial calculators have five distinctive keys on the numeric pad, usually in a row and in a different colour than other keys on the pad. The five keys correspond to the five possible variables that could be used in a present value calculation, as shown in Illustration PV-6.

ILLUSTRATION PV-6
Financial calculator keys

Present Value Variable	Financial Calculator Key
Present value	PV
Interest rate (or discount rate)	I/Y
Number of periods for compounding	N
Annuity payment amount	PMT
Future value	FV

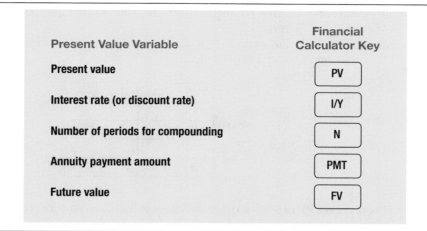

To calculate the present value, **enter each of the other variable amounts followed by pressing the corresponding key for that variable amount**. If an amount represents an outflow of cash, a negative value for the amount must be entered. Once the four known variables are entered, in any order, press the CPT (compute or equivalent key) and the PV variable key and the answer will appear on screen. When calculating the present value of a single future amount, enter zero for the annuity payment amount, followed by the PMT key. We will learn about annuity payments in the next section of the appendix.

Helpful hint Always begin by clearing the calculator.

For example, if you are calculating the present value of a single future cash flow of $1,000 to be received in two years and discounted at 5%, the data are entered into the financial calculator as follows:

Enter:	5	2	0	1000			Result
Press:	I/Y	N	PMT	FV	CPT	PV	**$(907.03)**

Note that the result is the same as with the present value formula and tables except the calculator shows $907.03 as a negative number. The reason the present value is a negative number is to demonstrate that an outflow (negative) of cash today of $907.03 will provide a future inflow (positive) of cash of $1,000.00 in two years using an annual interest rate of 5%.

Helpful hint The interest rate is entered as a whole number, not as a percentage. In this example, the 5% interest rate is entered as "5" and not ".05" or "5%".

The present value amounts calculated with a financial calculator can be slightly different than those calculated with present value tables. That is because the numbers in a present value table are rounded. For example, in Table PV-1 the factors are rounded to five digits. In a financial calculator, only the final answer is rounded to the number of digits you have specified in the viewing screen.

Computer Spreadsheets

Present value calculations can also be prepared very easily using a computer spreadsheet. For example, in Excel, use the insert function (*fx*) icon (commonly found at the top of the screen or near the cell content bar). Click on this icon and a pop-up screen will appear, allowing you to select a function. Select the category Financial then select the PV function. Another pop-up box will appear, allowing you to enter the necessary information. The terms are very similar to a financial calculator. A comparison is shown in the table below.

Present value variable	Excel variable	Financial calculator key
Present value	PV	PV
Interest rate (or discount rate)	RATE	I/Y
Number of periods	NPER	N
Annuity payment amount	PMT	PMT
Future value	FV	FV

Excel will also ask for the type of annuity. For all of the calculations in this textbook, you should enter "0," which indicates that the payment is at the end of the period. You will learn about annuities with payments at the beginning of the period in other courses.

One difference between Excel and financial calculators is how the interest rate is entered. With Excel, a 5% interest rate is entered as either .05 or 5%. Similar to financial calculators, cash outflows should be entered as negative numbers. The PV formula can also be typed directly into a cell as follows: =PV(rate,nper,pmt,fv,type).

Continuing with the example shown previously, the following data should be used in the =PV(rate,nper,pmt,fv,type) formula in Excel:

RATE	.05
NPER	2
PMT	$0.00
FV	$1,000.00
Type	0

The result is a PV of $(907.03), which is the same as the result obtained using the financial calculator.

Summary of Methods

A major benefit of using a financial calculator or a spreadsheet is that you are not restricted to the interest rates or numbers of periods on a present value table. In Table PV-1, present value factors have been calculated for 13 interest rates (there are 13 columns in that table) and the maximum number of periods is 20. With a financial calculator, you could, for example, calculate the present value of a future amount to be received in 25 periods using any discount rate not in a present value table, such as 5.75%.

Regardless of the method used in calculating present values, **a higher discount rate produces a smaller present value**. For example, using an 8% discount rate, the present value of $1,000 due one year from now is $925.93 versus $952.38 at 5%. You should also realize that **the further away from the present the future cash flow is, the smaller the present value**. For example, using the discount rate of 5%, the present value of $1,000 due in five years is 783.53 compared with $952.38 in one year.

BEFORE YOU GO ON...

DO IT

Suppose you have a winning lottery ticket and the lottery commission gives you the option of taking $10,000 three years from now, or taking the present value of $10,000 now. If an 8% discount rate is used, what is the present value of your winnings of $10,000 three years from now? Show the calculation using one of: (a) the present value formula; (b) Table PV-1; (c) a financial calculator; or (d) Excel functions.

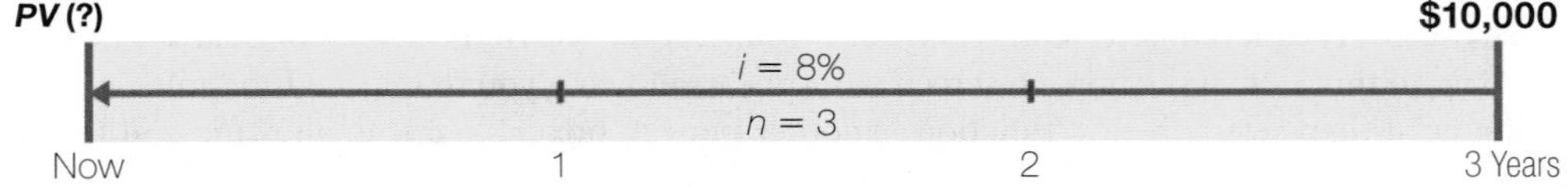

Action Plan (Do It)

- Note that $10,000 is the future value, the number of periods is 3, and the discount rate is 8%.

SOLUTION

(a) Using the present value formula:

$$PV = \$10{,}000 \div (1 + 8\%)^3$$
$$= \$10{,}000 \div 1.08^3 \text{ or } \{[(\$10{,}000 \div 1.08) \div 1.08] \div 1.08\}$$
$$= \$7{,}938.32$$

(b) Using the present value factor from Table PV-1:
The present value factor for three periods at 8% is

$$PV = \$10{,}000 \times 0.79383$$
$$= \$7{,}938.30$$

BEFORE YOU GO ON...
continued on next page

(c) Using a financial calculator:

Enter:	8	3	0	10000			Result
Press:	I/Y	N	PMT	FV	CPT	PV	$(7,938.32)

(d) Using the Excel PV function, the data used in the =PV(rate,nper,pmt,fv,type) formula are:

RATE	.08
NPER	3
PMT	$0.00
FV	$10,000.00
Type	0

PV = $ (7,938.32)

DO IT AGAIN

Determine the amount you must deposit now in your savings account, paying 3% interest, in order to accumulate $5,000 for a down payment on a hybrid electric car four years from now. Show the calculation using one of (a) present value formula, (b) Table PV-1, (c) financial calculator, or (d) Excel functions.

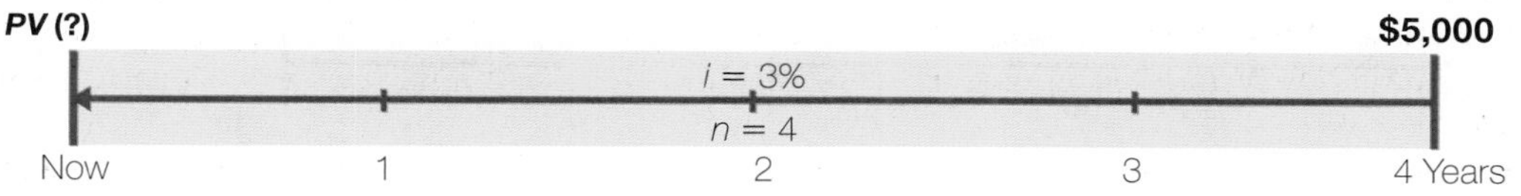

SOLUTION

The amount you must deposit now in your savings account is the present value calculated as follows:

(a) Using the present value formula:

$$\begin{aligned} PV &= \$5{,}000 \div (1 + 3\%)^4 \\ &= \$5{,}000 \div 1.03^4 \text{ or } (\{[(\$5{,}000 \div 1.03) \div 1.03] \div 1.03\} \div 1.03) \\ &= \$4{,}442.44 \end{aligned}$$

(b) Using the present value factor from Table PV-1:
The present value factor for four periods at 3% is 0.88849.

$$PV = \$5{,}000 \times 0.88849$$
$$PV = \$4{,}442.45$$

(c) Using a financial calculator:

Enter:	3	4	0	5000			Result
Press:	I/Y	N	PMT	FV	CPT	PV	$(4,442.44)

(d) Using the Excel PV function, the data used in the =PV(rate,nper,pmt,fv,type) formula are:

RATE	.03
NPER	4
PMT	$0.00
FV	$5,000.00
Type	0

PV = $(4,442.44)

Related exercise material: BEPV–1, BEPV–2, BEPV–3, BEPV–4, and BEPV–5.

BEFORE YOU GO ON...
continued from previous page

- Recall that the present value of $10,000 to be received in three years is less than $10,000 because interest can be earned on an amount invested today (that is, the present value) over the next three years.
- Understand that the discount rate used to calculate the present value is the compound interest rate that would be used to earn $10,000 in three years if the present value is invested today.
- Remember that the answer obtained from the different methods will be slightly different due to rounding of the PV factors.
- Draw a time diagram showing when the future value will be received, the discount rate, and the number of periods.

Action Plan (Do It Again)

- Note that $5,000 is the future value, $n = 4$, and $i = 3\%$.

THE NAVIGATOR

PRESENT VALUE OF A SERIES OF FUTURE CASH FLOWS (ANNUITIES)

STUDY OBJECTIVE 2
Calculate the present value of a series of future cash flows (annuities).

The preceding discussion was for the discounting of only a single future amount. Businesses and individuals frequently engage in transactions in which a series of equal dollar amounts are to be received or paid periodically. Examples of a series of periodic receipts or payments are loan agreements, instalment sales, mortgage notes, lease (rental) contracts, and pension obligations. These series of periodic receipts or payments are called **annuities**. In calculating the present value of an annuity, it is necessary to know (1) the discount rate (i), (2) the number of discount periods (n), and (3) the amount of the periodic receipts or payments (PMT).

CALCULATING THE PRESENT VALUE OF AN ANNUITY

To illustrate the calculation of the present value of an annuity, assume that you will receive $1,000 cash annually for three years, and that the discount rate is 4%. This situation is shown in the time diagram in Illustration PV-7.

ILLUSTRATION PV-7
Time diagram for a three-year annuity

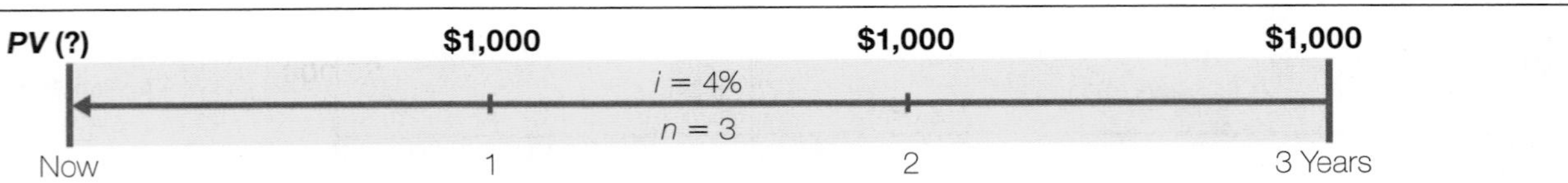

One method of calculating the present value of this annuity is to use the present value formula to determine the present value of each of the three $1,000 payments and then add those amounts as follows:

$$\begin{aligned} PV &= [\$1,000 \div (1 + 4\%)^1] + [\$1,000 \div (1 + 4\%)^2] + [\$1,000 \div (1 + 4\%)^3] \\ &= \$961.54 + \$924.56 + \$889.00 \\ &= \$2,775.10 \end{aligned}$$

The same result is achieved by using present value factors from Table PV-1, as shown in Illustration PV-8.

ILLUSTRATION PV-8
Present value of a series of cash flows

Future Value	×	Present Value of 1 Factor at 4%	=	Present Value
$1,000 (one year away)		0.96154		$ 961.54
1,000 (two years away)		0.92456		924.56
1,000 (three years away)		0.88900		889.00
		2.77510		$2,775.10

Determining the present value of each single future cash flow, and then adding the present values, is required when the periodic cash flows are not the same in each period. But when the future receipts are the same in each period, there are other ways to calculate present value.

Present Value of an Annuity Formula

One way to calculate present value of a series of periodic payments is to use the present value of an ordinary annuity formula, as shown in Illustration PV-9.

ILLUSTRATION PV-9
Present value of an ordinary annuity of 1 formula

$$\text{Present value } (PV) = \text{Future value } (FV) \times \frac{1 - \frac{1}{(1+i)^n}}{i}$$

$$= \$1{,}000 \times [(1 - (1 \div (1 + 4\%)^3)) \div 4\%]$$
$$= \$1{,}000 \times [(1 - (1 \div (1.04)^3)) \div 0.04]$$
$$= \$1{,}000 \times [(1 - (1 \div 1.124864)) \div 0.04]$$
$$= \$1{,}000 \times [(1 - 0.888996359) \div 0.04]$$
$$= \$1{,}000 \times 2.77509$$
$$= \$2{,}775.09$$

Present Value Tables

The second way to calculate the present value of a series of periodic payments is to use a present value of an annuity table. Table PV-2 shows the present value of 1 to be received periodically for a given number of periods at different discount rates. You can see in Table PV-2 that the present value factor of an annuity of 1 for three periods at 4% is 2.77509. This present value factor is the total of the three individual present value factors, as shown in Illustration PV-8.[1] Applying this present value factor to the annual cash flow of $1,000 produces a present value of $2,775.09 ($1,000 × 2.77509).

TABLE PV-2
PRESENT VALUE OF AN ANNUITY OF 1

$$PV = \frac{1 - \frac{1}{(1+i)^n}}{i}$$

(n) Periods	2%	2½%	3%	4%	5%	6%	7%	8%	9%	10%	11%	12%	15%
1	0.98039	0.97561	0.97087	0.96154	0.95238	0.94340	0.93458	0.92593	0.91743	0.90909	0.90090	0.89286	0.86957
2	1.94156	1.92742	1.91347	1.88609	1.85941	1.83339	1.80802	1.78326	1.75911	1.73554	1.71252	1.69005	1.62571
3	2.88388	2.85602	2.82861	2.77509	2.72325	2.67301	2.62432	2.57710	2.53129	2.48685	2.44371	2.40183	2.28323
4	3.80773	3.76197	3.71710	3.62990	3.54595	3.46511	3.38721	3.31213	3.23972	3.16987	3.10245	3.03735	2.85498
5	4.71346	4.64583	4.57971	4.45182	4.32948	4.21236	4.10020	3.99271	3.88965	3.79079	3.69590	3.60478	3.35216
6	5.60143	5.50813	5.41719	5.24214	5.07569	4.91732	4.76654	4.62288	4.48592	4.35526	4.23054	4.11141	3.78448
7	6.47199	6.34939	6.23028	6.00205	5.78637	5.58238	5.38929	5.20637	5.03295	4.86842	4.71220	4.56376	4.16042
8	7.32548	7.17014	7.01969	6.73274	6.46321	6.20979	5.97130	5.74664	5.53482	5.33493	5.14612	4.96764	4.48732
9	8.16224	7.97087	7.78611	7.43533	7.10782	6.80169	6.51523	6.24689	5.99525	5.75902	5.53705	5.32825	4.77158
10	8.98259	8.75206	8.53020	8.11090	7.72173	7.36009	7.02358	6.71008	6.41766	6.14457	5.88923	5.65022	5.01877
11	9.78685	9.51421	9.25262	8.76048	8.30641	7.88687	7.49867	7.13896	6.80519	6.49506	6.20652	5.93770	5.23371
12	10.57534	10.25776	9.95400	9.38507	8.86325	8.38384	7.94269	7.53608	7.16073	6.81369	6.49236	6.19437	5.42062
13	11.34837	10.98319	10.63496	9.98565	9.39357	8.85268	8.35765	7.90378	7.48690	7.10336	6.74987	6.42355	5.58315
14	12.10625	11.69091	11.29607	10.56312	9.89864	9.29498	8.74547	8.24424	7.78615	7.36669	6.98187	6.62817	5.72448
15	12.84926	12.38138	11.93794	11.11839	10.37966	9.71225	9.10791	8.55948	8.06069	7.60608	7.19087	6.81086	5.84737
16	13.57771	13.05500	12.56110	11.65230	10.83777	10.10590	9.44665	8.85137	8.31256	7.82371	7.37916	6.97399	5.95423
17	14.29187	13.71220	13.16612	12.16567	11.27407	10.47726	9.76322	9.12164	8.54363	8.02155	7.54879	7.11963	6.04716
18	14.99203	14.35336	13.75351	12.65930	11.68959	10.82760	10.05909	9.37189	8.75563	8.20141	7.70162	7.24967	6.12797
19	15.67846	14.97889	14.32380	13.13394	12.08532	11.15812	10.33560	9.60360	8.95011	8.36492	7.83929	7.36578	6.19823
20	16.35143	15.58916	14.87747	13.59033	12.46221	11.46992	10.59401	9.81815	9.12855	8.51356	7.96333	7.46944	6.25933

Financial Calculators

The third method of calculating present value of a series of periodic payments is to use a financial calculator and input the variables as follows:

Enter:	4	3	1000	0		Result
Press:	I/Y	N	PMT	FV	CPT PV	$(2,775.09)

[1]The difference of 0.00001 between 2.77509 and 2.77510 is due to rounding.

When using a financial calculator to calculate the present value of an annuity, it is also necessary to specify if the annual cash flow is at the end of each period or the beginning. In **an ordinary annuity, the payments are at the end of each period**, as in our example. In **an annuity in arrears, the first payment starts immediately, at the beginning of the first period**. In this appendix and textbook, all of the annuity examples are ordinary annuities with the payments at the end of each period. Generally this is also the default setting on new calculators. But you should learn how to set your calculator for the two types of annuities. This will be slightly different for different calculators so you may need to check your calculator's user manual to learn how to switch between the two types of annuities.

Computer Spreadsheets

Using the Excel PV function, the data used in the =PV(rate,nper,pmt,fv,type) formula and the result for this example are:

RATE	.04
NPER	3
PMT	$1,000.00
FV	$0.00
Type	0

The result is a PV of $(2,775.09).

INTEREST RATES AND TIME PERIODS

In the preceding calculations, the discounting has been done on an annual basis using an annual interest rate. There are situations where adjustments may be required to the interest rate, the time period, or both.

Using Time Periods of Less Than One Year

Discounting, or compounding, may be done over shorter periods of time than one year, such as monthly, quarterly, or semi-annually. When the time frame is less than one year, it is necessary to convert the annual interest rate to the applicable time frame. Assume, for example, that the investor in Illustration PV-7 received $500 semi-annually for three years instead of $1,000 annually. In this case, the number of periods (n) becomes six (three annual periods × 2), and the discount rate (i) is 2% (4% × 6/12 months).

If present value tables are used to determine the present value, the appropriate present value factor from Table PV-2 is 5.60143. The present value of the future cash flows is $2,800.72 (5.60143 × $500). This amount is slightly higher than the $2,775.09 calculated in Illustration PV-9 because interest is calculated twice during the same year. Thus, interest is compounded on the first half-year's interest.

Limitations of Present Value Tables

As previously discussed, one of the limitations of the present value tables is that the tables contain a limited number of interest rates. This is particularly a problem when time periods of less than one year are used. For example, if the annual interest rate was 7% and the payments were semi-annual, you would need to use the present value factor for 3.5%, which has not been included in Tables PV-1 or PV-2 in this textbook due to space limitations. If the payments were quarterly, you would need to use 1.75%, which is also not in the PV tables.

You will likely find PV tables to be of very limited value in other courses or in your own life. Consequently, we highly recommend you learn how to use either a financial calculator or a computer spreadsheet to perform these calculations.

BEFORE YOU GO ON...

DO IT

Corkum Company has just signed a capital lease contract for equipment that requires rental payments of $6,000 each, to be paid at the end of each of the next five years. The appropriate discount rate is 6%. What is the present value of the rental payments; that is, the amount used to capitalize the leased equipment? Show the calculation using one of (a) the present value of an annuity formula; (b) Table PV-2; (c) a financial calculator; or (d) Excel functions.

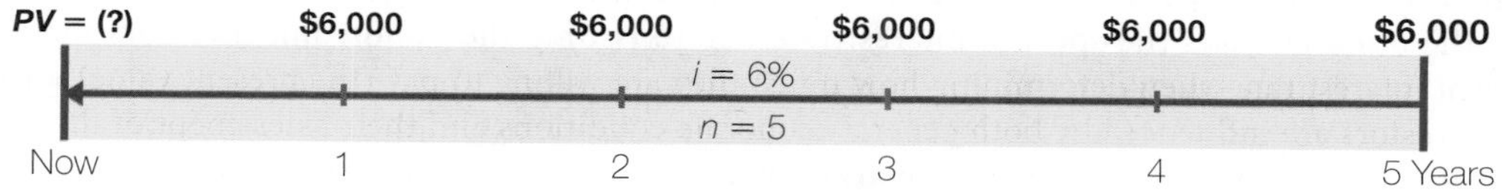

SOLUTION

The present value of lease rental payments of $6,000 paid at the end of each year for five years, discounted at 6%, is calculated as follows:

(a) Using the present value of an annuity formula:

$$\begin{aligned} PV &= \$6,000 \times [(1 - (1 \div (1 + 6\%)^5)) \div 6\%] \\ &= \$6,000 \times [(1 - (1 \div (1.06)^5)) \div 0.06] \\ &= \$6,000 \times [(1 - (1 \div 1.33823)) \div 0.06] \\ &= \$6,000 \times [(1 - .747258) \div 0.06] \\ &= \$6,000 \times 4.21236 \\ &= \$25,274.16 \end{aligned}$$

(b) Using the present value factor from Table PV-2:
The present value factor from Table PV-2 is 4.21236 (five periods at 6%).

$$PV = \$6,000 \times 4.21236$$
$$PV = \$25,274.16$$

(c) Using a financial calculator:

Enter:	6	5	6000	0			Result
Press:	I/Y	N	PMT	FV	CPT	PV	$(25,274.18)

(d) Using Excel functions and the PV formula =PV(rate,nper,pmt,fv,type):

RATE	.06
NPER	5
PMT	$6,000.00
FV	$0.00
Type	0

PV = $ (25,274.18)

Related exercise material: BEPV–6 and BEPV–7.

Action Plan

- Draw a time diagram showing when the future value will be received, the discount rate, and the number of periods.
- Note that each of the future payments is the same amount paid at even intervals; therefore, use present value of an annuity calculations to determine the present value (i = 6% and n = 5).

THE NAVIGATOR

APPLYING PRESENT VALUE CONCEPTS

CALCULATING THE MARKET PRICE OR PRESENT VALUE OF A BOND

STUDY OBJECTIVE 3
Calculate the present value of a bond.

The present value (or market price) of a bond is a function of three variables: (1) the payment amounts, (2) the length of time until the amounts are paid, and (3) the market interest rate, also known as the discount rate.

The first variable (dollars to be paid) is made up of two elements: (1) the principal amount (a single sum), and (2) a series of interest payments (an annuity). To calculate the present value of the bond, both the principal amount and the interest payments must be discounted, which requires two different calculations. The present value of a bond can be calculated using present value formulas, factors from the two present value tables, a financial calculator, or Excel.

It is important to note that **the interest rate used to determine the annual or semi-annual interest payments is fixed over the life of a bond**. This is the **bond's contractual interest rate**. The company issuing the bond chooses the specific interest rate before issuing the bonds. But investors may use a different interest rate when determining how much they are willing to pay (the present value) for the bonds. Investors are influenced by both general economic conditions and their assessment of the company issuing the bonds. **Investors use the market interest rate to determine the present value of the bonds**. In the following sections, we will illustrate how to calculate the present value of the bonds using a market interest rate that is equal to, greater than, or less than the contractual interest rate.

Market Interest Rate Equals the Contractual Interest Rate

When the investor's market interest rate is equal to the bond's contractual interest rate, the bonds' present value will equal their face value. To illustrate, assume there is a bond issue of five-year, 6% bonds with a face value of $100,000. Interest is payable **semi-annually** on January 1 and July 1. In this case, the investor will receive (1) $100,000 at maturity, and (2) a series of 10 $3,000 interest payments [($100,000 × 6%) × 6⁄12 months] over the term of the bonds. The length of time (n) is the total number of interest periods (10 periods = 5 years × 2 payments per year), and the discount rate (i) is the rate per semi-annual interest period (3% = 6% × 6⁄12 months). The time diagram in Illustration PV-10 shows the variables involved in this discounting situation.

ILLUSTRATION PV-10
Time diagram for the present value of a five-year, 6% bond paying interest semi-annually

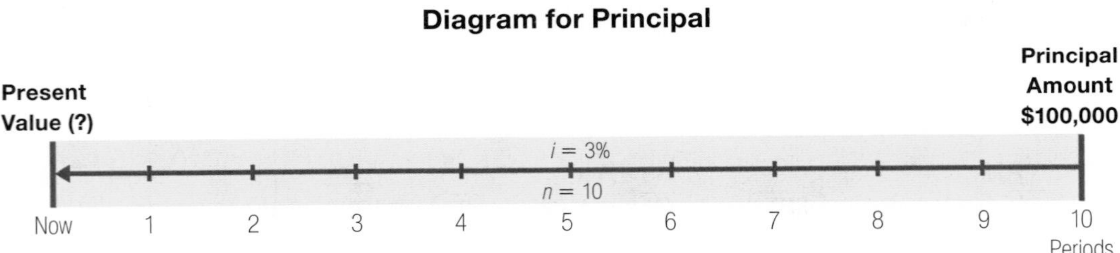

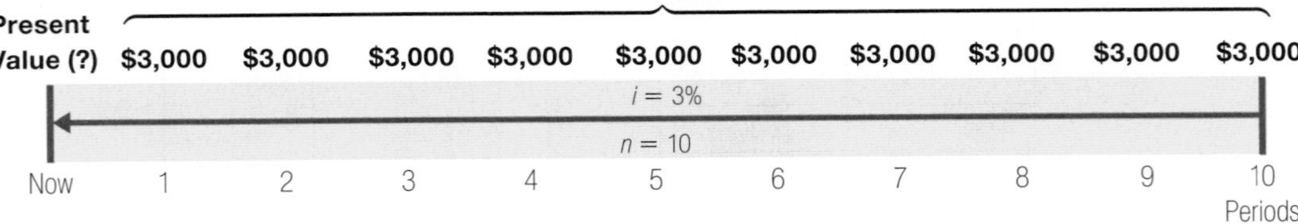

The calculation of the present value of these bonds using factors from the appropriate present value tables is shown in Illustration PV-11.

ILLUSTRATION PV-11
Present value of bonds (market rate equals contractual rate)

6% Contractual Rate and 6% Market Rate	
Present value of principal to be received at maturity	
$100,000 × PV of 1 due in 10 periods (*n*) at 3% (*i*)	
$100,000 × 0.74409 (Table PV-1)	$ 74,409
Present value of interest to be received periodically over the term of the bonds	
$3,000 × PV of 1 due periodically for 10 periods (*n*) at 3% (*i*)	
$3,000 × 8.53020 (Table PV-2)	25,591*
Present value of bonds	$100,000
*Rounded	

Using a financial calculator or Excel functions would yield the same result. Thus, when the market rate is the same as the contractual rate, the bonds will sell at face value.

Market Interest Rate Is Greater Than the Contractual Interest Rate

Now assume that the investor's market rate of return is 8%, not 6%. The future cash flows are again $100,000 and $3,000, respectively. **These cash flows are based on the bond contract and do not vary with the investor's rate of return.** But the investor's rate of return can vary, depending on available rates in the marketplace. If the market interest rate is 8%, then the present value is calculated using this rate. In this case, 4% (8% × 6⁄12 months) will be used because the bonds pay interest semi-annually. The present value of the bonds is $91,889, as calculated in Illustration PV-12.

ILLUSTRATION PV-12
Present value of bonds (market rate greater than contractual rate)

6% Contractual Rate and 8% Market Rate	
Present value of principal to be received at maturity	
$100,000 × PV of 1 due in 10 periods (*n*) at 4% (*i*)	
$100,000 × 0.67556 (Table PV-1)	$67,556
Present value of interest to be received periodically over the term of the bonds	
$3,000 × PV of 1 due periodically for 10 periods (*n*) at 4% (*i*)	
$3,000 × 8.11090 (Table PV-2)	24,333*
Present value of bonds	$91,889
*Rounded	

While it was necessary to use both PV tables (one for the semi-annual interest payment and one for the final payment of the bond principal) in the previous calculation, the financial calculator and Excel can both handle the two sources of cash flows in a single calculation. This is another major benefit of using a financial calculator or Excel compared with using present value tables or formulas.

If using a financial calculator, the interest payments and future repayment of principal should both be entered as negative numbers because they represent cash outflows. The result shown for the present value will then be a positive number, which is consistent with the fact that the company will receive cash when it issues a bond. The data entered for this example and the result are as follows:

Enter:	4	10	−3000	−100000		Result
Press:	I/Y	N	PMT	FV	CPT PV	$91,889.10

Similarly, if using Excel functions, the interest payments and future repayment of principal are entered as negative numbers in the PV formula =PV(rate,nper,pmt,fv,type). The data entered and the result are as follows:

RATE	.04
NPER	10
PMT	$(3,000.00)
FV	$(100,000.00)
Type	0

Result: PV = $ 91,889.10

In this situation, the bonds will sell for $91,889, at a discount of $8,111. **If the market interest rate is greater than the contract interest rate, the bonds will always sell at a discount.** If investors determine that the bond's contract interest rate is too low, they will compensate by paying less for the bonds. Note that they will still collect the full $100,000 at the maturity date.

Market Interest Rate Is Less Than the Contractual Interest Rate

On the other hand, the market rate might be lower than the contractual interest rate. In this case, the interest paid on the bonds is higher than what investors expected to earn. As a result, they will compensate by paying more for the bonds. If the market interest rate is 5%, the present value will be calculated using 2.5% (5% × 6⁄12 months) as the discount rate. The cash payments and number of periods remain the same. In this case, the present value of the bonds is $104,376, calculated as in Illustration PV-13.

ILLUSTRATION PV-13
Present value of bonds (market rate less than contractual rate)

6% Contractual Rate and 5% Market Rate	
Present value of principal to be received at maturity	
$100,000 × PV of 1 due in 10 periods (*n*) at 2.5% (*i*)	
$100,000 × 0.78120 (Table PV-1)	$ 78,120
Present value of interest to be received periodically over the term of the bonds	
$3,000 × PV of 1 due periodically for 10 periods (*n*) at 2.5% (*i*)	
$3,000 × 8.75206 (Table PV-2)	26,256*
Present value of bonds	$104,376
*Rounded	

If using a financial calculator, the data entered and the result are as follows:

Enter:	2.5	10	−3000	−100000		Result
Press:	I/Y	N	PMT	FV	CPT PV	$104,376.03

If using Excel functions and the PV formula =PV(rate,nper,pmt,fv,type), the data entered and the result are as follows:

RATE	.025
NPER	10
PMT	$(3,000.00)
FV	$(100,000.00)
Type	0

Result: PV = $104,376.03

These bonds will sell for $104,376, at a premium of $4,376. **If the market interest rate is less than the contractual interest rate, the bonds will always sell at a premium.**

 BEFORE YOU GO ON...

DO IT

Forest Lake Enterprises issued $1 million of six-year, 4.5% bonds that pay interest semi-annually. The market rate of interest for the bonds at the issue date is 4%. What cash proceeds did Forest Lake Enterprises receive from the issue of the bonds?

SOLUTION

1. Amount to be received at maturity is the face value of the bonds, $1,000,000
2. Semi-annual interest payment = $22,500 ($1,000,000 × 4.5% × 6⁄12 months)
3. Number of periods n = 12 (6 years × 2 payments a year)
4. Discount rate i = 2% (4% ÷ 2 payments a year)

The cash proceeds that Forest Lake will receive from issuing the bonds is the present value of principal to be received at maturity plus the present value of the interest received periodically, calculated as follows:

Present value of principal to be received at maturity:	
$1,000,000 × 0.78849 (PV of $1 due in 12 periods at 2% from Table PV-1)	$ 788,490
Present value of interest to be received periodically over the term of the bonds:	
$22,500 × 10.57534 (PV of $1 due each period for 12 periods at 2% from Table PV-2)	237,945
Present value of bonds	$1,026,435[2]

If using a financial calculator, the data entered and the result are as follows:

						Result
Enter:	2	12	−22500	−1000000		
Press:	I/Y	N	PMT	FV	CPT PV	$1,026,438.35

If using Excel functions and the PV formula =PV(rate,nper,pmt,fv,type), the data entered and the result are as follows:

RATE	.02
NPER	12
PMT	$(22,500.00)
FV	$(1,000,000.00)
Type	0

Result: PV = $1,026,438.35

[2]Note the financial calculator and Excel results are the same amount but they are slightly different than the PV table calculation because the factors in the PV tables are rounded.

Related exercise material: BEPV–8 and BEPV–9.

Action Plan

- Note that Forest Lake will be able to sell these bonds at a premium because the bonds pay higher interest (4.5%) than the current market interest rate (4%).
- Recall that the contractual interest rate is used to determine the interest payment; the market rate is used to determine the present value.
- Adjust the interest rates and number of periods for the effect of the semi-annual periods.
- Use Table PV-1 to determine the present value of the principal and Table PV-2 to determine the present value of the interest payments.
- You can instead use a financial calculator, remembering to enter the interest and principal payments as negative numbers.
- You can instead use Excel functions, entering the interest and principal payments as negative numbers.

THE NAVIGATOR

USING PRESENT VALUE CONCEPTS WITH NOTES PAYABLE

STUDY OBJECTIVE 4

Apply present value concepts to notes payable to calculate the periodic payments, the interest rate, or the number of periods.

Long-term notes payable are normally repayable in a series of periodic payments. Examples of long-term notes payable include unsecured notes, mortgages (which are secured notes on real property, such as a house), and loans (for example, student or car).

The present value of the note payable is the amount borrowed and thus typically doesn't need to be calculated as in the case of a bond payable. The future value of a note payable is zero because the note will be paid in full through the periodic payments, which include both interest and principal. Instead, present value concepts are often used with notes payable to determine one of the following three variables: (1) the payment amount, (2) the length of time until the amounts are paid (time to maturity date), or (3) the market interest rate.

Calculating the Periodic Payment for a Note Payable

Payments for a long-term note payable may be fixed principal payments plus interest, or blended principal and interest payments. To illustrate these two types of payments, we will assume that Heathcote Company obtains a five-year note payable, with an 8% interest rate, to purchase a piece of equipment costing $25,000.

Fixed Principal Payments Plus Interest.

If we first assume that repayment is to be in fixed principal payments plus interest, paid annually, then the payment amount would be $5,000 ($25,000 ÷ 5 years) for principal plus 8% interest on the outstanding balance. Illustration PV-14 shows how the interest and periodic cash payment are determined for this note.

ILLUSTRATION PV-14
Note payable amortization table with fixed principal payments plus interest

	(A)	(B)	(C)	(D)
Interest Period	Cash Payment (B) + (C)	Interest Expense (D) × 8%	Fixed Reduction of Principal $25,000 ÷ 5	Principal Balance (D) − (C)
Start of Year 1				$25,000
End of Year 1	$ 7,000	$2,000	$ 5,000	20,000
End of Year 2	6,600	1,600	5,000	15,000
End of Year 3	6,200	1,200	5,000	10,000
End of Year 4	5,800	800	5,000	5,000
End of Year 5	5,400	400	5,000	0
Totals	$31,000	$6,000	$25,000	

Note that the periodic cash payment is a different amount each period because the interest is a different amount each month. Recall that an annuity, by definition, is an equal payment each period. That means we cannot use present value concepts, as they have been introduced in this appendix, to analyze the note. Instead we will focus on notes payable with blended payments, which are the same amount each period, in the following section of this appendix.

Blended Principal Plus Interest Payments.

In the case of blended principal and interest payments, the periodic payment is an annuity and thus present value concepts can be used to calculate the amount of the annual payment. As long as four of the five present value amounts (present value, interest rate, number of periods, payments, and future value) are known, they can be used to calculate the one unknown.

Present Value Tables. If we divide the total loan amount of $25,000 by the present value factor for an annuity from Table PV-2 for $i = 8\%$ and $n = 5$, then we can determine that the annual payment is $6,261.41 ($25,000 ÷ 3.99271). Illustration PV-15 shows the note payable amortization table using the annuity of $6,262.41 as the annual cash payment.

ILLUSTRATION PV-15
Note payable amortization table with blended principal plus interest payments

	(A)	(B)	(C)	(D)
Interest Period	Cash Payment	Interest Expense (D) × 8%	Reduction of Principal (A) − (B)	Principal Balance (D) − (C)
Start of Year 1				$25,000.00
End of Year 1	$ 6,261.41	$2,000.00	$ 4,261.41	20,738.59
End of Year 2	6,261.41	1,659.09	4,602.32	16,136.27
End of Year 3	6,261.41	1,290.90	4,970.51	11,165.76
End of Year 4	6,261.41	893.26	5,368.15	5,797.61
End of Year 5	6,261.41	463.80	5,797.61	0
Totals	$31,307.05	$6,307.05	$25,000.00	

We can see from this illustration that the periodic blended payment of $6,261.41 is exactly the amount needed to pay the required interest plus the note in full by the end of year 5. Recall that the balance of zero at the end of year 5 is also the future value of the note payable.

Financial Calculators. If using a financial calculator to determine the periodic payment, the data entered and the result are as follows:

Enter:	8	5	25000	0			Result
Press:	I/Y	N	PV	FV	CPT	PMT	$(6,261.41)

Excel Functions. If using the Excel PMT formula =PMT(rate,nper,pv,fv,type), the data entered and the result are as follows:

RATE	.08
NPER	5
PV	$25,000.00
FV	$0.00
Type	0

Result: PMT = $(6,261.41)

While the above three methods all provided the same periodic payment, the financial calculator and Excel functions are more useful as they can be used for any interest rate and any number of periods, not just those included in the PV table.

Calculating the Interest Rate for a Note Payable

There are several situations in which it may be necessary to calculate the effective interest rate. For example, sometimes businesses offer financing with stated interest rates below market interest rates to stimulate sales. Examples of notes with stated interest rates below market are seen in advertisements offering no payment for two years. As we have seen in the case of bonds, if the contractual or stated interest rate is less than the market or effective interest rate, then the present value of the loan will be less than the face value. With a zero-interest-rate note, the market or effective interest rate in the transaction must be imputed using present value calculations.

As an example, assume that a furniture retailer is offering "No payment for two years, or $150 off on items with a sticker price of $2,000." The implicit interest cost over the two years is $150, and the present value of the asset is then $1,850 ($2,000 − $150). From Table PV-1, the effective interest rate can be determined as follows:

$$\text{PV} \div \text{FV} = \text{discount factor} \qquad \$1,850 \div \$2,000 = 0.925$$

Looking at the $n = 2$ row, this would represent an interest rate of approximately 4%. Most notes have an interest cost, whether explicitly stated or not.

Using a financial calculator will result in a more precise interest rate calculation. In this example, the data entered and the result are as follows:

Enter:	2	1850	0	−2000			Result
Press:	N	PV	PMT	FV	CPT	I/Y	3.975%

In the Excel RATE formula =RATE(nper,pmt,pv,fv,type), the data entered and the result are as follows:

Helpful hint Remember to correctly enter cash inflows as positive numbers and cash outflows as negative numbers or the financial calculator will give an error message when calculating the interest rate.

NPER	2
PMT	$0.00
PV	$1,850.00
FV	$(2,000.00)
Type	0

Result: RATE = 3.975%

Also note that the purchaser should record the furniture at a cost of $1,850 even if the purchaser chose the option of no payment for two years. In this case, the purchaser will recognize interest expense of $73.54 ($1,850 × 3.975%) in the first year and $76.46 [($1,850 + $73.54) × 3.975%] in the second year.

Canada Student Loans: Calculation of Time to Pay

The Canadian federal government, in an effort to encourage post-secondary education, offers loans to eligible students with no interest accruing while they maintain their full-time student status. When schooling is complete, the entire Canada Student Loan must be repaid within 10 years. Repayment of the loan can be at a fixed rate of prime plus 5%, or a floating rate of prime plus 2.5%. One calculation you might be interested in is how long it will take to repay your Canada Student Loan if you have a certain amount of money available to make monthly payments.

Let's assume that you attend school for four years and borrow $2,500 per year. Upon graduation, because there was no interest while you were a student, you have a total debt of $10,000. Also assume you have opted for a fixed rate of interest of 8% while repaying the loan. If you can pay $150 a month, will you be able to repay the loan within the 120 months (10 years × 12 months per year) allowed? To determine the answer to this question, you need to know in how many months the loan will be repaid.

Using a financial calculator, the data entered and the result are as follows:

Enter:	8 ÷ 12 or 0.6667	10,000	−150	0		Result
Press:	I/Y	PV	PMT	FV	CPT N	88.46

Note that, because you are making monthly payments, the annual interest rate of 8% must be adjusted to a monthly rate of 0.6667%. Also note that the payments are a negative number because they are a cash outflow. The present value is a positive number because it is equal to the amount borrowed, which was a cash inflow. The future value is zero because the loan will be fully paid at maturity.

The result of 88.46 means that you would need to make 89 monthly payments: the first 88 months at $150 per month, and the last month at a lesser amount for the remaining balance. This is less than 120 months, which means that you will be able to pay your student loan in the allowed period.

The same result can be obtained using the Excel NPER formula =NPER(rate,pmt,pv,fv,type). The data entered and the result are as follows:

RATE	.08/12 = .006667
PMT	$(150.00)
PV	$10,000.00
FV	$0.00
Type	0

Result: NPER = 88.46 periods

This particular example could not be done with the PV tables in this textbook because of the interest rate. Since we are making monthly payments, we must also use a monthly interest rate. The monthly interest rate of 0.6667% is less than the lowest percentage on the table and thus the table cannot be used.

BEFORE YOU GO ON...

DO IT

You are about to purchase your first car for $25,000. You pay $1,000 cash and finance the remaining amount at an annual interest rate of 7% over a period of 48 months. How much is your monthly payment, assuming you make equal blended principal and interest payments each month?

BEFORE YOU GO ON...
continued on next page

BEFORE YOU GO ON...

continued from previous page

SOLUTION

1. The monthly payment is equal to the present value divided by the PV factor: $24,000 ÷ 41.76019 = $574.71
2. Using a financial calculator, the data entered and the result are as follows:

Enter:	7 ÷ 12 or 0.5833	48	24000	0		Result
Press:	I/Y	N	PV	FV	CPT PMT	$(574.71)

3. Using Excel functions, the formula is: =PMT(rate,nper,pv,fv,type).

RATE	.07 ÷ 12 = .005833
NPER	48
PV	$24,000.00
FV	$0.00
Type	0

Result: PMT = $(574.71)

Related exercise material: BEPV–10, BEPV–11, BEPV–12, BEPV–13, BEPV–14, BEPV–15, BEPV–16, BEPV–17, and BEPV–18.

Action Plan

- Use $n = 48$ and $i = 0.5833\%$ (7% ÷ 12 months), PV = $24,000, and FV = $0.
- If using present value factors, this number is 41.76019.
- Alternatively, you may use a financial calculator or Excel functions to calculate the payment.

THE NAVIGATOR

ASSETS: ESTIMATING VALUE IN USE USING FUTURE CASH FLOWS

STUDY OBJECTIVE 5

Estimate the value of an asset using future cash flows.

As we have learned in a previous section, a bond can be valued based on future cash flows. So too can an asset. In Chapter 9, you learned that companies are required to regularly determine whether the value of property, plant, and equipment has been impaired. Recall that an asset is impaired if the carrying amount reported on the balance sheet is greater than its recoverable amount. The recoverable amount is either the asset's fair value or its *value in use*. Determining the value in use requires the application of present value concepts. The calculation of value in use is a two-step process: (1) estimate future cash flows, and (2) calculate the present value of these cash flows.

For example, assume JB Company owns a specialized piece of equipment used in its manufacturing process. JB needs to determine the asset's value in use to test for impairment. As the first step in determining value in use, JB's management estimates that the equipment will last for another five years and that it will generate the following future cash flows at the end of each year:

Year 1	Year 2	Year 3	Year 4	Year 5
$9,000	$10,000	$13,000	$10,000	$7,000

In the second step of determining value in use, JB calculates the present value of each of these future cash flows. Using a discount rate of 8%, the present value of each future cash flow is shown in Illustration PV-16.

ILLUSTRATION PV-16
Present value of estimated future cash flows of specialized equipment

	Year 1	Year 2	Year 3	Year 4	Year 5
Future cash flows	$9,000	$10,000	$13,000	$10,000	$7,000
Present value factor[3]	0.92593	0.85734	0.79383	0.73503	0.68058
Present value amount	$8,333	$ 8,573	$10,320	$ 7,350	$4,764

[3]The appropriate interest rate to be used is based on current market rates; however, adjustments for uncertainties related to the specific asset may be made. Further discussion on this topic is covered in more advanced texts.

The value in use of JB's specialized equipment is the sum of the present value of each year's cash flow, $39,340 ($8,333 + $8,573 + $10,320 + $7,350 + $4,764). A financial calculator or Excel functions could also be used in this calculation, although there would have to be five different calculations made because of the irregular amounts for the annual future cash flows. If this amount is less than the asset's carrying amount, JB will be required to record an impairment, as shown in Chapter 9.

The present value method of estimating the value in use of an asset can also be used for intangible assets. For example, assume JB purchases a licence from Redo Industries for the right to manufacture and sell products using Redo's processes and technologies. JB estimates it will earn $6,000 per year from this licence over the next 10 years. What is the value in use to JB of this licence?

Since JB expects to earn the same amount each year, Table PV-2 is used to find the present value factor of the annuity after determining the appropriate discount rate. As pointed out in the previous example, JB should choose a rate based on current market rates; however, adjustments for uncertainties related to the specific asset may be required. Assuming JB uses 8% as the discount rate, the present value factor from Table PV-2 for 10 periods is 6.71008. The value in use of the licence is $40,260 ($6,000 × 6.71008).

If using a financial calculator, the data entered and the result are as follows:

Enter:	8	10	6000	0			Result
Press:	I/Y	N	PMT	FV	CPT	PV	$(40,260.49)

If using Excel functions and the PV formula =PV(rate,nper,pmt,fv,type), the data entered and the result are as follows:

RATE	.08
NPER	10
PMT	$6,000.00
FV	$0.00
Type	0

Result: PV = $(40,260.49)

The results using the financial calculator and Excel functions are negative as they represent the amount you should be willing to pay today to receive $6,000 per year for 10 years if the discount rate is 8%.

BEFORE YOU GO ON...

DO IT

You are attempting to estimate the value in use of your company's production equipment, which you estimate will be used in operations for another eight years. You estimate that the equipment will generate annual cash flows of $16,000, at the end of each year, for the remainder of its productive life, and that 9% is the appropriate discount rate. What is the value in use of this equipment?

Action Plan

- Identify future cash flows.
- Use Table PV-2 to determine the present value of an annuity factor for $n = 8$ and $i = 9\%$ and calculate the present value.
- Alternatively, use a financial calculator or Excel functions to solve.

SOLUTION

The value in use is equal to the present value of the estimated annual future cash flows for the remaining life of the asset discounted at an appropriate discount rate.

Future annual cash flows:	$16,000
Number of periods:	8
Discount rate:	9%
Present value annuity factor (n = 8, i = 9%):	5.53482
Present value:	$88,557 = $16,000 × 5.53482

If using a financial calculator, the data entered and the result are as follows:

Enter:	9	8	16000	0			Result
Press:	I/Y	N	PMT	FV	CPT	PV	$(88,557.11)

BEFORE YOU GO ON...
continued on next page

BEFORE YOU GO ON...
continued from previous page

If using Excel functions and the PV formula =PV(rate,nper,pmt,fv,type), the data entered and the result are as follows:

RATE	.09
NPER	8
PMT	$16,000.00
FV	$0.00
Type	0

Result PV = $(88,557.11)

Related exercise material: BEPV–19, BEPV–20, and BEPV–21.

THE NAVIGATOR

Brief Exercises

BEPV–1 Determine the amount of interest that will be earned on each of the following investments:

Calculate simple and compound interest. **(SO 1)**

	Investment	(i) Interest Rate	(n) Number of Periods	Type of Interest
(a)	$1,000	5%	1	Simple
(b)	$500	4%	2	Simple
(c)	$500	4%	2	Compound

BEPV–2 Wong Ltd. is considering an investment that will return a lump sum of $600,000 five years from now. What amount should Wong Ltd. pay for this investment in order to earn a 4% return?

Calculate present value of a single-sum investment. **(SO 1)**

BEPV–3 Mohammed's parents invest $8,000 in a 10-year guaranteed investment certificate (GIC) in his name. The investment pays 4% annually. How much will the GIC yield when it matures? Compare the interest earned in the first and second five-year periods, and provide an explanation for the difference.

Calculate future value of a single-sum investment and demonstrate the effect of compounding. **(SO 1)**

BEPV–4 Xin Su has been offered the opportunity to invest $44,401 now. The investment will earn 7% per year, and at the end of that time will return Xin $100,000. How many years must Xin wait to receive $100,000?

Calculate number of periods of a single investment sum. **(SO 1)**

BEPV–5 If Jin Fei invests $3,152 now, she will receive $10,000 at the end of 15 years. What annual rate of interest will Jin earn on her investment? Round your answer to the nearest whole number.

Calculate interest rate on single sum. **(SO 1)**

BEPV–6 Tarzwell Ltd. is considering investing in an annuity contract that will return $25,000 at the end of each year for 15 years. What amount should Tarzwell Ltd. pay for this investment if it earns a 6% return?

Calculate present value of an annuity investment. **(SO 2)**

BEPV–7 For each of the following cases, indicate in the chart below the appropriate discount rate (i) and the appropriate number of periods (n) to be used in present value calculations. Show calculations. The first one has been completed as an example.

Determine number of periods and discount rate. **(SO 2)**

	Annual Interest Rate	Number of Years	Frequency of Payments	(n) Number of periods	(i) Discount Rate
1.	6%	2	Quarterly	$2 \times 4 = 8$	$6\% \div 4 = 1.5\%$
2.	5%	8	Semi-annually		
3.	7%	5	Annually		
4.	4%	3	Quarterly		
5.	2%	6	Semi-annually		
6.	6%	9	Monthly		

Calculate present value of bonds. (SO 3)

BEPV–8 New Line Railroad Co. is about to issue $100,000 of 10-year bonds that pay a 5.5% annual interest rate, with interest payable semi-annually. The market interest rate is 5%. How much can New Line expect to receive for the sale of these bonds?

Calculate present value of bonds. (SO 3)

BEPV–9 Assume the same information as in BEPV–8, except that the market interest rate is 6% instead of 5%. In this case, how much can New Line expect to receive from the sale of these bonds?

Calculate payment on note. (SO 4)

BEPV–10 Marsdon Company receives a six-year, $50,000 note that bears interest at 8% from a customer. The customer will make annual blended principal plus interest payments at the end of each year. What is the annual payment that Marsdon will receive from its customer?

Calculate payment on note. (SO 4)

BEPV–11 Assume the same information as BEPV–10, except that the interest rate is 9% instead of 8%. What is the annual payment that Marsdon will receive from its customer?

Calculate effective interest rate on note. (SO 4)

BEPV–12 Phang Ltd. issues a six-year, $1,058,871 mortgage note on January 1, 2014, to obtain financing for new equipment. The terms provide for semi-annual instalment payments of $112,825. What is the effective interest rate on the mortgage note payable?

Calculate quarterly payments on note payable. (SO 4)

BEPV–13 The municipality of Lansdown issued a three-year, 5% mortgage note payable for $185,000 to finance the purchase of three salt trucks. The terms provide for equal quarterly blended principal plus interest payments. What are the quarterly payments on the note?

Determine how long to repay note. (SO 4)

BEPV–14 You have borrowed $18,000. If the annual rate of interest is 4%, how long will it take you to repay the note if you are making semi-annual blended principal plus interest payments of $1,702?

Calculate annual payments. (SO 4)

BEPV–15 You would like to purchase a car that costs $32,000, and the dealer offers financing over a five-year period at 3%. If repayments are to be made annually, what would your annual payments be?

Calculate trade-in value of car. (SO 4)

BEPV–16 Assume the same information as in BEPV–15, except that you can only afford to make annual payments of $6,500. If you decide to trade in your present car to help reduce the amount of financing required, what trade-in value would you need to negotiate to ensure your annual payment is $6,500?

Compare financing options. (SO 4)

BEPV–17 As CFO of a small manufacturing firm, you have been asked to determine the best financing for the purchase of a new piece of equipment. If the vendor is offering repayment options of $10,000 per year for five years, or only one payment of $46,000 at the end of two years, which option would you recommend? The current market rate of interest is 8%.

Compare financing options. (SO 4)

BEPV–18 If the market rate of interest in BEPV–17 was 10%, would you choose the same option?

Calculate value of machine for purchase decision. (SO 5)

BEPV–19 Sam Waterston owns a garage and is contemplating purchasing a tire retreading machine for $16,100. After estimating costs and revenues, Sam projects a net cash flow from the retreading machine of $2,690 annually for eight years. Sam hopes to earn a return of 11% on such investments. What is the present value of the retreading operation? Should Sam Waterston purchase the retreading machine?

Calculate value in use for a machine. (SO 5)

BEPV–20 Lee Company must perform an impairment test on its equipment. The equipment will produce the following cash flows: Year 1, $35,000; Year 2, $45,000; Year 3, $55,000. Lee requires a minimum rate of return of 10%. What is the value in use for this equipment?

Calculate value in use of a patent. (SO 5)

BEPV–21 Tsung Company signs a contract to sell the use of its patented manufacturing technology to Herlitz Corp. for 12 years. The contract for this transaction stipulates that Herlitz Corp. pays Tsung $21,000 at the end of each year for the use of this technology. Using a discount rate of 4%, what is the value in use of the patented manufacturing technology?

Name Index

Note: page references followed by an *f* indicates an illustration or a figure; page references followed by an *n* indicates a note.

Subject Index

Note: page references followed by an *f* indicates an illustration or figure.

Photo Credits

Chapter 1 Opener: The Canadian Press Images-Mario Beauregard; Page 5: © iStockphoto/Andreas Rodriguez; Page 25: © iStockphoto/Jacob Wackerhausen. **Chapter 2** Opener: Courtesy Prestige Dance Academy; Page 55: © iStockphoto/NevinGiesbrecht; Page 68: © iStockphoto/mihalec. **Chapter 3** Opener: © iStockphoto/peterspiro; Page 99: © iStockphoto/Ashwin82; Page 105: © iStockphoto/spxChrome. **Chapter 4** Opener: Courtesy Laurel Hyatt; Page 164: © iStockphoto/WillSelarep. **Chapter 5** Opener: Courtesy Moulé; Page 212: © iStockphoto/Leah-Anne Thompson. **Chapter 6** Opener: Courtesy Gravitypope/Louise Dirks; Page 260: © iStockphoto/SimplyCreativePhotography; Page 274: © iStockphoto/Lewis Wright. **Chapter 7** Opener: © Barrett & MacKay Photo; Page 313: © iStockphoto/Peter Garbet; Page 316: © iStockphoto/ARICAN. **Chapter 8** Opener: Cindy Wilson/Telegraph-Journal; Page 341: © iStockphoto/Marcus Clackson; Page 356: AP/Charles Krupa/The Canadian Press. **Chapter 9** Opener: THE CANADIAN PRESS/Colin Perkel; Page 389: © iStockphoto/DNY59; Page 405: © iStockphoto/Chris Reed. **Chapter 10** Opener: © iStockphoto/skodonnell; Page 436: © iStockphoto/YinYang. Page 441: The Canadian Press/Marcos Townsend. **Chapter 11** Opener: Photo shows Rebecca Villmann, Principal, Accounting Standards Board. Photo courtesy of Accounting Standards Board, 2012; Page 468: © iStockphoto/DNY59; Page 473: Frank Gunn/The Canadian Press. **Chapter 12** Opener: Courtesy Harris & Chong LLP; Page 506: © iStockphoto/Aldo Murillo; Page 524: The Canadian Press/Ben Margot. **Chapter 13** Opener: Courtesy Doxsee & Co.; Page 550: © iStockphoto/George Paul; Page 555: iStockphoto/Björn Meyer. **Chapter 14** Opener: © iStockphoto/Diane Labombarbe; Page 589: © iStockphoto/Aaliya Landholt; Page 605: © Sheriar Hirjikaka, 2012. **Chapter 15** Opener: The Canadian Press Images-Mario Beauregard; Page 630: © iStockphoto/DNY59; Page 645: © iStockphoto/ozlemonal. **Chapter 16** Opener: Courtesy Clearwater Seafoods; Page 673: © iStockphoto/Pawel Gaul; Page 703: © iStockphoto/wsfurlan. **Chapter 17** Opener: Courtesy of CPA Canada; Page 745: © iStockphoto/Kyu Oh; Page 757: CD1 WENN Photos/Newscom.